Handbook of Moral Development

Edited by

Melanie Killen
University of Maryland

Judith G. Smetana
University of Rochester

Psychology Press
Taylor & Francis Group

New York   London

First Published by Lawrence Erlbaum Associates, Inc., Publishers
10 Industrial Avenue
Mahwah, New Jersey 07430

Reprinted 2010 by Psychology Press

Library of Congress Cataloging-in-Publication Data

Handbook of moral development / edited by Melanie Killen, Judith Smetana.
    p. cm.
   Includes bibliographical references and index.
   ISBN 0-8058-4751-0 (case : alk. paper)
  1. Moral development.   I. Killen, Melanie.   II. Smetana, Judith G., 1951–

BF723.M54H354   2005
155.2′5—dc22

                            2005010881

Handbook of Moral Development

For Rob, Sasha, and Jacob (M.K.) and Ron, Joshua, and Jeremy (J.G.S.), with love and gratitude

CONTENTS

PREFACE

Research on moral development, whether examined in terms of affect, cognition, emotions, behavior, or neuroscience, as well as its applications for education or clinical settings, has greatly expanded over the past 20 years. At present, however, there is no single volume that brings together the diverse research and scholarship on morality in its multiple forms. Yet, scholars, researchers, and educators remain occupied with understanding how morality develops through childhood, adolescence, and adulthood. This Handbook fills this gap by bringing together the theorizing and research of 44 scholars in 26 chapters on diverse aspects of moral development.

We, as the editors of this Handbook, were approached by Bill Webber, the senior editor at Lawrence Erlbaum Associates, Inc., a little over two years ago, at the *Jean Piaget Society: The Society for the Study of Knowledge and Development,* to undertake this project. Bill's enthusiasm for this project was contagious, and we saw this as a great and much-needed opportunity to pull together the current research and scholarship on morality. The authors of these chapters cross-referenced other chapters within the volume, thus, demonstrating integrations across areas. We are delighted with the results. This Handbook includes a diverse array of chapters, covering the areas of culture, emotions, empathy, conscience, socialization, intergroup relationships, education, rights, values, nature, altruism, aggression, gender, delinquency, biology, primatology, reciprocity, character education, community service, and youth development.

This Handbook is intended as a resource for scholars, professionals, and graduate and undergraduate students. In our view, one cannot understand morality in all its diversity without understanding its roots in childhood and adolescence. Thus, we anticipate that scholars and students from different fields of psychology (developmental, cognitive, clinical, community, educational, comparative), education (human development, curriculum), anthropology (cultural), sociology, philosophy (ethics), and political science (social justice, ethics) will find this Handbook useful and informative.

The last *Handbook of Moral Development,* edited by W. Kurtines and J. Gewirtz, was published in 1991 and reflected the leading edge of the work of the late 1980s. Thus, it has been almost 20 years since a Handbook on moral development was published. The current

Handbook has been designed to be an updated, comprehensive, edited volume written by international experts in the field of moral development and representing foundational theories, conceptual frameworks, and cutting edge research from a wide cross-section of perspectives.

—Melanie Killen and Judith G. Smetana
Editors

Contributors List

Erin Adams
Ferkauf Graduate School
  of Psychology
Yeshiva University
1300 Morris Park Avenue
Bronx, NY 10461

William F. Arsenio
Ferkauf Graduate School
  of Psychology
Yeshiva University
1300 Morris Park Avenue
Bronx, NY 10461

Robert Atkins
Rutgers, The State University
  of New Jersey
College of Nursing
Conklin Hall, Rm. 212
180 University Avenue
Newark, New Jersey 07102-1897

Victor Battistich
University of Missouri-St. Louis
402 Marillac Hall
One University Blvd.
St. Louis, MO 63121-4499

Marvin W. Berkowitz
University of Missouri-St. Louis
College of Education
Marillac Hall 402
8001 Natural Bridge Road
St. Louis, MO 63121-4499

Melinda Bier
University of Missouri-St. Louis
402 Marillac Hall
One University Blvd.
St. Louis, MO 63121-4499

Gustavo Carlo
Department of Psychology
University of Nebraska-Lincoln
320 Burnett Hall
Lincoln, NE 68588-0308

Thomas M. Donnelly
Camden College of Arts and
  Sciences
Rutgers, The State University
  of NJ
311 North Fifth Street
Camden, NJ 08102

Judy Dunn
Social Genetic & Developmental
   Psychiatry Research Centre
Institute of Psychiatry
111 Denmark Hill London
SE5 8AF
United Kingdom

Nancy Eisenberg
Department of Psychology
Arizona State University
Box 871104
Tempe, AZ 85287-1104

Douglas P. Fry
Laakarinkatu 4 A 14
Ovi Koodi 1305
FIN-00250 Helsinki
FINLAND

Jason Gold
Ferkauf Graduate School
   of Psychology
Yeshiva University
1300 Morris Park Avenue
Bronx, NY 10461

Sara E. Goldstein
Department of Psychology
University of New Orleans
New Orleans, LA 70148

Joan E. Grusec
Department of Psychology
Sidney Smith Hall Rm 4028
University of Toronto
Toronto, ON M5S 3G3
CANADA

Daniel Hart
Department of Psychology
Rutgers University, The State University
   of New Jersey
Camden, NJ 08102

Paul D. Hastings
Department of Psychology, PY 170-10
Concordia University
7141 Sherbrooke Street West
Montreal Quebec H4B 1R6
CANADA

Charles C. Helwig
Department of Psychology
University of Toronto
Toronto, ON M5S 3G3
CANADA

Peter H. Kahn, Jr.
Department of Psychology
University of Washington
BOX 351525
Seattle, WA 98195-1525

Melanie Killen
Department of Human Development
3304 Benjamin Building
University of Maryland
College Park, MD 20742-1131

Leon Kuczynski
Department of Family Relations
& Applied Nutrition
University of Guelph
Guelph, ON NIG 2W1
CANADA

Daniel K. Lapsley
Department of Educational Psychology
Teachers College 526
Ball State University
Muncie, IN 47306

Nancy Geyelin Margie
Department of Human Development
University of Maryland
3304 Benjamin Building
College Park, MD 20742-1131

Meredith McGinley
Department of Psychology
University of Nebraska
279 Burnett Hall
Lincoln, NE 68588-0308

Kelly McShane
Centre for Research in Human
    Development
Department of Psychology
Concordia University
7141 Sherbrooke Street West
Montreal Quebec H4B 1R6
CANADA

Sara Meyer
Department of Psychology
University of California, Davis
One Shields Ave.
Davis, CA 95616-8686

Joan G. Miller
Department of Psychology
New School for Social Research
65 Fifth Avenue
New York, NY 10003

Darcia Narvaez
Department of Psychology
University of Notre Dame
118 Haggar Hall
Notre Dame, IN 46556

Geoffrey S. Navara
Department of Family Relations and
    Applied Nutrition
University of Guelph
Guelph, Ontario
N1G 2W1
CANADA

Larry Nucci
College of Education MC 147
University of Illinois at Chicago
1040 W. Harrison Street
Chicago, IL 60607-7133

Adrienne Sadovsky
Department of Psychology
Arizona State University
Tempe, AZ 85287

Stephen Sherblom
University of Missouri-St. Louis
College of Education
467 Marillac Hall
One University Blvd.
St. Louis, MO 63121-4499

Stefanie Sinno
Department of Human Development
3304 Benjamin building
University of Maryland
College Park, MD 20742-1131

Judith G. Smetana
Department of Clinical & Social Sciences
    in Psychology
Meliora Hall, RC 270266
University of Rochester
Rochester, NY 14627

Tracy Spinrad
Department of Family and Human
    Development
Arizona State University
Tempe, AZ 85287

Mark B. Tappan
Education Program
Colby College
Waterville, ME 04901

Stephen J. Thoma
University of Alabama
Department of Human Development
106 East Annex, Box 870158
Tuscaloosa, AL 35487-0158

Ross A. Thompson
Department of Psychology
University of California, Davis
One Shields Ave.
Davis, CA 95616-8686

John Tisak
Department of Psychology
Bowling Green State University
Bowling Green, OH 43403

Marie S. Tisak
Psychology Department
Bowling Green State University
Bowling Green, OH 43403

Elliot Turiel
Graduate School of Education
University of California, Berkeley
Berkeley, CA 94720

Peter Verbeek
Miyazaki International College
1405 Kano, Kiyotake-cho
Miyazaki 889-1605
JAPAN

Cecilia Wainryb
Department of Psychology
University of Utah
Salt Lake City, UT 84112

Lawrence J. Walker
Department of Psychology
University of British Columbia
Vancouver, B.C. V6T 1Z4
CANADA

Carolyn Zahn-Waxler
Department of Psychology
University of Wisconsin
1202 West Johnson St.
Madison, WI 53706-1696

HANDBOOK OF MORAL DEVELOPMENT

I

Introduction

The psychological study of moral development has undergone a major transformation over the past several decades. The field has expanded greatly, both in terms of the diversity of theoretical perspectives represented, as well as in the range of topics studied. Theories have expanded to consider current developments in other areas of psychology, including social psychology, cognitive psychology, and the neurosciences, as well as scholarship in other social science disciplines, including anthropology, sociology, political science, ethics, and philosophy. For instance, recent work in biology has contributed to thinking about the biological basis of morality; philosophical writings have informed current definitions of morality; scholarship in sociology has provided new ways of thinking about the role of social groups and juvenile delinquency; anthropological writing has contributed to debates about the role and definition of culture; new research in social psychology has led to renewed interest in morality as it pertains to intergroup relationships, racism, and prejudice; and educational research on teaching and effective classrooms has enriched developmental research on moral education. Moreover, research on moral development now includes a diverse range of topics, including civil liberties, culture, intergroup relationships, gender hierarchies, family relationships, parenting, conscience, values, community service, aggression, nature, children's rights, victimization, and educational programs designed to implement developmental and character education programs. Although multiple forces have led to these changes in the field, the expansiveness of the theoretical formulations has generated new research directions with implications for research and scholarship in multiple fields. *Handbook of Moral Development* represents the diversity and multidisciplinary influences on current theorizing about the psychological study of moral development and the range and broad scope of topics being considered. To highlight the diversity of the topics, we organized the 26 chapters into six parts that represent the conceptual themes of these different theoretical perspectives and topics: Part II, Structuralism and Moral Development Stages; Part III, Social Domain Theory and Social Justice; Part IV, Conscience, Socialization, and Internalization; Part V, Social Interactional, Sociocultural, and Comparative Approaches; Part VI, Empathy, Emotions, and Aggression; and Part VII, Moral Education, Character Development, and Community Service.

THE ORIGINS AND GLOBALITY OF THE FIELD

The history of psychological theorizing and research on the moral growth of the child started with the notions of conscience, first elaborated by Sigmund Freud, and moral autonomy, as characterized by Jean Piaget. These theorists, who were influenced by many other early developmentalists at the time, including George Herbert Mead and James Baldwin, charted distinct lines of work. Freud focused on parent–child relationships, emotions, and guilt, whereas Piaget focused on peer relationships, cognition, justice, and reflection. The focus at the time was much more on broad theorizing, with much less attention to operationalization of constructs and systematic reporting of the methodologies of the research.

DIFFERENTIATION

To employ Heinz Werner's (1957) developmental metaphor, by the 1960s, the psychological study of children's morality became highly differentiated. Behaviorists such as B. F. Skinner and other learning theorists contested Freud's notions of conscience and values by conducting experiments designed to assess moral behavior. Furthermore, Piaget's work was greatly expanded by Kohlberg (1969), in his six-stage sequence of moral judgment development.

To a large extent, these different lines of work represented the "grand theories" of developmental psychology (psychoanalysis, learning theory, and cognitive–developmental theory), and to the extent that they represented different paradigms, or world views, there was also little overlap among theories. The moral theories generated from these models were highly differentiated and represented competing interpretations of the origins, nature of change, sequence, acquisition, and end state of morality in the individual. For example, Freudian theories emphasize identification with parental values as the mechanism by which morality became internalized. In contrast, learning theories chart the reinforcement contingencies that serve to explain the acquisition of moral values. Cognitive–developmental theories focus on the construction of moral knowledge (reflection and abstraction), which serve as a counterposition to both Freudian notions of internalized guilt and Skinnerian theories of conditioning. Freud's psychosexual stage theory views morality as formed by age 5, whereas Kohlberg's structural–developmental stage theory views principled morality as emerging relatively late in development, when individuals reach the highest stage of his 6-stage sequence. In contrast, learning theory rejects the stage notion entirely and defines mature morality in terms of the child's successful internalization of the norms and values of their culture. Thus, each theory has clearly identified answers to the basic developmental questions of the origins and acquisition of morality and the nature of change.

HIERARCHIC INTEGRATION AND COMMON GROUND

To borrow from Werner again, and as represented in the contributions to this volume, the field is currently at a stage of hierarchical integration. Some of the theoretical positions represented in this volume were clearly influenced by the grand theories and have drawn from these different approaches in exciting and novel directions. Social learning theory has been transformed into a much more interactive and transactional perspective, one that embraces the role of cognition and internal mental states. Cognitive–developmental theory has progressed along multiple trajectories that range from stage notions to domain specificity views. For example, included in various cognitive–developmental research programs are detailed analyses of parental influences on moral development, the role of social interaction and experience, and the role of culture. Similarly, researchers influenced by the Freudian accounts of internalized guilt also study moral cognition and peer relationships, once the hallmark of the structural–developmental approach.

At the same time, it is also evident from the contributions to this volume that a variety of other theoretical perspectives have become part of the current discourse about moral development. For instance, evolutionary, comparative, and sociocultural approaches all have flourished in recent years and have provided competing theoretical viewpoints. In fact, the pluralism that characterizes the current state of the field has resulted in lines of theorizing and research that are integrative, nuanced, complex, and multifaceted.

Hybrid theories do not make the intellectual debates any less visible or pervasive; there remain clear differences in current-day accounts of the developmental acquisition of morality in the child, adolescent, and adult. What has changed is the complexity of the theories and the degree of overlap in the description of the account of morality in the individual. To a large extent, most current theories acknowledge that morality encompasses cognition and judgment, emotions and biology. Furthermore, most theories examine the contribution of diverse social relationships on the acquisition of morality, including the family (parents and siblings), peer relationships (including the wide range of friends, nonfriends, acquaintances), and nonfamilial adults. And, most theories view morality as developing from early childhood through adolescence or young adulthood, rather than as occurring either in early childhood or in late adolescence.

DIFFERENTIATION AND CURRENT DEBATES

Although there has been greater integration and consideration of other points of view in recent years, many of the same issues that have been debated over past decades remain unresolved and highly contentious to this day. For instance, the different perspectives in this volume contain some sharp disagreements regarding the relative weights given to biology and culture; the extent to which morality can be universalized or is culturally relative; the role of the family, including how much and in what ways parents and other nonparental adults influence the acquisition of moral values; the relative emphasis that should be given to cognition versus emotions; the characterization of conscience; the extent to which boys and girls differ in their moral orientation or in the extent of their moral growth; the role that cultural ideologies play on the formation of morality in societies; whether schools should advocate for character education or focus on enhancing moral reflection and discussion; and whether nonhuman primates, nature, and the environment should count in the moral equation. In our view, these debates are an important indication of the vitality of the field, and are likely to lead to new theoretical advances, novel empirical questions, and new programmatic lines of research.

Debates about morality also pervade most aspects of current social life. Issues of school segregation, poverty, educational achievement gaps, child labor, sexual abuses, housing and job discrimination, prejudice, immigrants' rights, territorial wars, distribution of resources, and civil liberties all reflect moral issues that are hotly contested because they involve competing views of justice, fairness, others' welfare, care, empathy, and altruism. Thus, an understanding of children's morality has implications that extend far beyond polite academic debate; indeed, how we view morality could have far-reaching implications for our vision of a fair and just society and how to achieve it. Most current policy discussions and political debates that bear on moral development rarely draw on moral development theory and research. Although topics such as child poverty, educational achievement gaps, and school segregation clearly fall within the moral domain, there are few outlets for bridging the gap between research and application. Yet, solutions to the vast array of problems that fall within the moral domain involve understanding children's social experiences, adult attitudes about children's experiences, and cultural expectations about how these issues should be addressed. We hope that in a few small ways, the research described in this volume may help to provide solutions to the often vexing dilemmas that we confront when making attempts to improve the lives of children, which in turn, advances the course of society towards justice, fairness, and equality.

This *Handbook of Moral Development* contains a wealth of information about how morality has been defined, studied, and examined in children, adolescents, and adults. The scholars who have contributed to this volume are experts in these areas of moral life, and their chapters provide detailed summaries of current theory and research in the field of moral development, which we anticipate will be of interest to scholars, policy makers, educators, and professionals who work with children. The expansiveness of the field of moral development is well reflected; collectively and individually, the chapters chart our current theoretical and empirical knowledge of children's and adolescents' moral development. At the same time, we have asked each author to summarize the unanswered research questions and needed research directions in their area of study, and the chapters indicate that our knowledge is not complete and that much work remains to be done. We anticipate that this volume will contribute to the continued liveliness of the scholarly discourse about moral development and to new advances in theorizing and research.

ACKNOWLEDGMENTS

We are grateful to Lori Stone, Senior Editor at LEA, for her support and encouragement of this project, and Rebecca Larsen at LEA, who provided helpful assistance. Alexandra (Sasha) Henning served as our editorial assistant, and we appreciate her organized updates on the progress of the volume. We thank the wonderful contributors to this volume, who responded to the challenges of writing these chapters with unusual timeliness and enthusiasm and replied to our editorial feedback so gracefully. We greatly enjoyed reading each chapter, and learning about exciting new research areas in the field of moral development.

II

STRUCTURALISM AND MORAL DEVELOPMENT STAGES

This part introduces readers to the theory and research on moral development conducted from the structural–developmental approach. This theoretical perspective was initially formulated by Jean Piaget and extended by Lawrence Kohlberg and more contemporary colleagues, who charted a generation of research on moral judgment, moral reasoning, and social interactional approaches to moral development. Although Piaget published his highly influential book, *The Moral Judgment of the Child,* in 1932, Piaget's theory was not widely known to American psychologists until the 1960s; during the 1970s and 1980s, Kohlberg's stage theory became the dominant paradigm for research on moral development. Piaget's and Kohlberg's groundbreaking work moved the moral development field from a focus on behavioral approaches to morality to a consideration of qualitative shifts with age in moral judgment. As is widely known, Kohlberg used responses to hypothetical dilemmas that opposed conflicting concerns with law, life, interpersonal obligations, trust, and authority to propose that moral judgments develop through a series of six universal, sequential, and hierarchical stages of progressively more differentiated and integrated concepts of justice. Kohlberg's theory focused on the underlying structure of individuals' moral judgments rather than on the content or particular decisions that individuals made.

In Chapter 1, Elliot Turiel places structural–developmental theories, including both the approaches discussed in this and in the following section of the volume, in a broad historical and theoretical context. Turiel's chapter argues for studying the development of morality through analyses of reasoning. His assertions draw on recent scholarship from moral philosophy, political science, and cultural anthropology; he also compares the structural–developmental focus on reasoning and rationality to approaches to morality that prioritize emotions. He considers Piaget's and Kohlberg's contributions to the understanding of children's moral judgments and then describes how research from the social domain perspective (which is the focus of Part III) developed to address limitations and inconsistencies in Piaget's and Kohlberg's approaches. Turiel concludes with a structural–developmental analysis of morality and social justice that integrates the findings from psychological, philosophical, anthropological, and sociological perspectives.

In Chapter 2, Daniel Lapsley describes the development of moral stage theory as it emerged within the cognitive–developmental tradition. Lapsley provides a deeply theoretical and insightful overview of the basic tenets of structural–developmental theory and their instantiation in Piaget's and Kohlberg's theories, as well as in the work of Damon, Selman, Rest, Turiel, and Eisenberg-Berg. His chapter reviews the foundational assumptions of the structural–developmental approach and provides readers with details about the controversies and empirical findings of the model. Chapter 3, by Stephen Thoma, discusses theory and research on the Defining Issues Test, which was initially developed by James Rest in the early 1970s as a paper-and-pencil alternative to Kohlberg's semistructured interview measure of moral judgment development. Although heavily influenced by Kohlberg's theoretical model, Rest's program of research has become a distinct branch of research, and in his chapter Thoma provides a comprehensive evolution of this research program.

Chapter 3, by Lawrence Walker, reviews and evaluates the ongoing controversies regarding gender and morality. As Walker describes, the issues in this debate stem from Carol Gilligan's controversial claims regarding gender differences in moral orientations, which rocked the field in the mid-1980s following the publication of her book, *In a Different Voice*. She claimed that boys and men are characterized by an ethic of justice, whereas girls women are characterized by an ethic of care and that Kohlberg's theory is biased against women's distinctive moral voice. Walker's chapter evaluates the controversy based on the evidence accumulated over the past 20 years and provides an up-to-date, thorough, and systematic analysis of the controversy. Moreover, Walker provides a number of insightful suggestions for avenues of research that take into account both care and justice in analyses of moral development. Although the debates have largely subsided, Walker's chapter reminds us how much these debates have enriched and enlivened the field.

1

Thought, Emotions, and Social Interactional Processes in Moral Development

Elliot Turiel
University of California, Berkeley

Scholars, researchers, scientists, and theorists spend much of their time, obtain their liveli-hood, and define themselves professionally by, to put it colloquially, trying to figure things out. They examine particular sets of phenomena and attempt to provide the most coherent, tight, and logical explanations they can. In doing so, they gather data and other forms of information to help them understand the phenomena. In turn, they examine data with at least two principles in mind: to provide support for their explanations and to alter their explanations when not supported by data. Those who engage in these activities are hu-man beings who, in the field of psychology, study human beings and attempt to explain how human beings (and in many cases, other animals) function. When those human be-ings are psychologists engaged in study and explanations of morality, they, of course, are attempting to explain how humans (and nonhumans) function in a realm we label *moral-ity*. Furthermore, such psychologists often attempt to define the realm of morality and to characterize its features (they might do so themselves or rely on moral philosophers).

In many psychological analyses there is asynchrony between the ways psychologists engage in their scholarship and research and their characterizations of human beings. The source of the asynchrony is that whereas they "try to figure things out," and all that goes along with it in the enterprise of conducting research and formulating theories, the psychologists' theories have humans operating in fundamentally different ways that do not entail thought, explanation, or the weighing of data and evidence. One obvious and perhaps unambiguous example is that of B. F. Skinner, who was for much of the twentieth century a prominent and highly regarded experimental psychologist for his seemingly powerful explanations of human behavior. The type of thought he used to formulate his theoretical framework and the ways he used evidence were excluded from the psychological processes, based on principles of operant conditioning that he attributed to all human activity (Skinner, 1971). The illustrative example that comes from Skinner (and, incidentally, most other behaviorists) is unambiguous because he maintained that human functioning in thought, language, and action is due to the ways people display conditioned behaviors that are by definition mechanistic and not purposeful, nor intentional, nor based on thought and deliberation.

The extent of the asynchrony between the activities of psychological theorists and their explanations of human functioning can vary. For instance, it might be maintained that humans are capable of scholarly and scientific thinking but usually do not engage in it (or that it comes only with special training and education). Matters become more complicated when it comes to explanations of morality. Whereas Skinner and other behaviorists do not distinguish between the principles of behavior that account for morality and any other realm, others maintain that morality is a realm that is very (radically?) different from some other realms, such as the scientific realm. For instance, it might be maintained that humans do try to figure things out in certain realms of life, but that morality involves nonrational adherence to behaviors. Even in these views there is some asynchrony because the psychologists do engage in analyses of morality. The claim would be that psychological (or for that matter philosophical) analysis of morality is a different enterprise from the lived morality (presumably, this applies to the analyst as well). In these views, a disconnect is presumed between human behaviors in different realms (e.g., the scientific and moral). Taking this line of thought further, some maintain that reasoning about moral matters, insofar as it is observed, is illusory because it largely involves rationalizations that are discrepant from the true, nonrational causes of behaviors in the moral realm.

In a tradition of developmental research on morality and other realms that can be traced to the work of Piaget (1932), there is synchrony between the mental activities obviously available to scholars, researchers, scientists, and theorists and the mental activities seen as part of the ways human beings function in the realm of morality. The main focus of this chapter is these approaches, which are sometimes labeled "structural–developmental" or "cognitive–developmental." Since the time of Piaget's early work on the development of moral judgments, many have undertaken research that is, in a general way, in line with his approach and that is based on the presumption that people "try to figure things out." An extension of Piaget's early work on moral development was provided by Kohlberg (1969, 1971), who did a great deal to promote the structural–developmental approach. Kohlberg's work has, in turn, influenced many researchers (including research discussed in this volume by Lapsley [chap. 2], Thoma [chap. 3], and Walker [chap. 4]). A variant of the structural–developmental approach is also taken in "social domain" theory, which is the approach of this author (Turiel, 1983b, 2002) and of the authors of a number of chapters in this volume.

The aims of this chapter are to discuss some of the general parameters of the structural–developmental approach through a focus on several interrelated issues addressed not only by psychologists, but also by philosophers, political scientists, and anthropologists. This chapter includes discussion of issues that may be applicable across structural–developmental approaches and issues that stem directly from social domain theory. Much of the evidence in support of propositions put forth here is presented in other chapters. Accordingly, the reader will be directed to those chapters when relevant. First, propositions put forth by some contemporary philosophers, political theorists, and anthropologists are considered as a means of outlining the broad parameters on definitions of morality and the role of thought that are at the heart of the structural–developmental approach to the development of morality. Then, the role of emotions in relation to judgment is considered. This is followed by discussions of how moral judgments are applied in different contexts, and whether and how individuals accept and oppose societal arrangements and cultural practices, as well as the connections of social opposition and resistance to social justice.

THOUGHT AND MORALITY

Kohlberg (1968), entitled one of his essays, "The Child as a Moral Philosopher." In asserting that children are moral philosophers, Kohlberg did not mean that they attempt to formulate philosophical principles to explicate the nature of morality, as do professional philosophers. Rather, he used the phrase to convey two fundamental sets of ideas. One is that human moral functioning involves thinking, along with emotions, of a systematic kind about matters of right and wrong in social relationships. Central to moral functioning are the ways people conceptualize issues of right and wrong based on their understandings of rights, justice, fairness, and the welfare of people. The second set of ideas conveyed is that moral understandings begin to be formed in systematic ways in childhood and that there are developmental transformations in those ways of thinking from childhood to adulthood.

The assumption that thought is centrally involved in human moral functioning has far-reaching implications for how morality has been conceptualized by social scientists. First, it means that the psychological study of morality requires a good deal of work in ways of defining the realm and ways of distinguishing it from other social realms. To use terms common in Piaget's theory, epistemological analyses provide necessary guidelines for psychological analyses of human thought (also see Kohlberg, 1971, and Turiel, 1983a). Just as we cannot study thinking about, as examples, mathematics, physics, or esthetics, without knowing about the parameters of those domains, we cannot study morality without definitional bases. Furthermore, if morality does involve figuring things out, then it is not explicable through fixed biological dispositions, nonrational dispositions, such as notions of conscience or character, as mainly emotionally driven, through the acquisition of social norms, or adherence to cultural practices or orientations.

Definitions and conceptualizations of morality are connected to a conception of what is fundamental to human beings. As put by Nussbaum, a philosopher and political theorist, "human beings are above all reasoning beings." Nussbaum was referring to a core assumption of the "tradition of liberalism" (1999, p. 71), which is not meant to refer to a political ideology, but rather a philosophical perspective "in the tradition of Kantian liberalism represented today in the political thought of John Rawls, and also the classical Utilitarian liberal tradition of John Stuart Mill" (Nussbaum, 1999, p. 57). The core features of the tradition, as agreed upon by philosophers like Kant, Mill, and Rawls (as well as Dworkin, 1977; Gewirth, 1982; and Habermas, 1993), are the following:

> At he heart of this tradition is a twofold intuition about human beings: namely, that all, just by being human, are of equal dignity and worth, no matter where they are situated in society, and that the primary source of this worth is a power of moral choice within them, a power that consists in the ability to plan a life in accordance with one's own evaluations of ends. To these two intuitions—which link liberalism at its core to the thought of the Greek and Roman Stoics—the liberal tradition adds one more, which the stoics did not emphasize: that the moral equality of persons gives them a fair claim to certain types of treatment at the hands of society and politics. What this treatment is will be a subject of debate within the tradition,

but the shared starting point is that this treatment must do two closely related things. It must respect and promote the liberty of choice, and it must respect and promote the equal worth of persons as choosers. (Nussbaum, 1999, p. 54)

Nussbaum adds that a basic moral premise in these approaches is that each person be treated as an end and not as a means to other goals. Within these views morality entails substantive considerations of welfare, justice, and rights and is not defined by traditions or the common practices of a group or collectivity (society, culture). As reasoning beings, humans have the power of moral choice and plan their lives with autonomy and agency. In turn, people's moral choices entail the recognition that humans are of equal dignity and worth and should be accorded freedoms and fair treatment by each other and by society.

Psychological research on children's social and moral development has yielded a wealth of evidence in support of the propositions that humans are reasoning beings and that they reason within a realm that we can label moral about welfare, justice, and rights in ways that involve concerns with dignity, worth, freedom, and treatment of persons. One strong indication of this is that starting at a young age children begin to form judgments entailing distinctions among different domains of social interactions (Turiel, 1983b, 1998, 2002). The research has shown that children discriminate issues pertaining to harm, benefits to persons, justice, and rights from issues pertaining to the customary and conventional practices of social systems. In turn, the moral and conventional domains are discriminated from arenas of personal choices and jurisdiction, which pertain to realms of activities judged part of individual autonomy. Personal choices are not subject to legitimate conventional–societal regulation and are seen as distinct from welfare and justice considerations. The force and relevance of distinctions that people draw among moral, conventional, and personal matters is exemplified by research showing that those judgments play out in a variety of aspects of social relationships. These include social interactions in the family and schools (Smetana, chap. 5, this volume; Nucci, chap. 24, this volume), matters pertaining to cultural practices (Wainryb, chap. 8), the environment (Kahn, chap. 7), social exclusion and intergroup relationships (Killen, Margie, & Sinno, chap. 6), aggressiveness (Tisak, Tisak, & Goldstein, chap. 22), and rights (Helwig, chap. 7).

Another strong indication that humans are reasoning beings is that they apply their moral concepts in flexible ways in particular situations or contexts. People typically weigh and balance different considerations when making decisions and drawing conclusions within the parameters of situations. The clearest example of findings in this regard comes from research on rights (see Helwig, chap. 7, this volume). The evidence is clear that people in the different cultures endorse individual rights in some situations and not others. The parameters of the situation play a role in how judgments are made as to whether rights should be upheld. Other moral and social considerations are considered in relation to rights, and priorities are made as to which should take precedence. These issues are discussed further in a subsequent section, but for now the salient point is that neither fixed attitudes nor the force of situations determine decisions. People recognize the different moral and social components and evaluate their relative merits.

To say that humans are reasoning beings with flexibility of thought does not mean that emotions do not play a role. It does mean, however, that morality is not primarily driven by emotions. It also means that it is not mainly emotions that guide the formation of judgments about right and wrong. Rather, emotions are embedded in reasoning, with emotions involving evaluative appraisals, so that "the entire distinction between reason and emotions begins to be called into question, and one can no longer assume that a thinker who focuses on reason is excluding emotion" (Nussbaum, 1999, p. 72). Moreover, in this perspective emotions are subject to reflection and critical evaluation. Emotional experiences can inform the development of thought and, reciprocally, thinking can inform the development and maintenance of emotion. Consequently, it is important to draw distinctions among emotions with regard to the development of morality. Often, it is aversive emotions like fear, anxiety, shame, embarrassment, guilt, and disgust that have been regarded as central to moral functioning. The avoidance of aversive emotions is seen as the source of moral regulation and control over acts of transgression. The alternative view, consistent with the idea that emotions involve evaluative appraisals, is that emotions like sympathy, empathy, love, affection, and respect are central in the developmental process and in the types of moral judgments that people hold (Okin, 1989; Rawls, 1971). For Piaget (1932), for instance, respect for persons, either in an earlier developmental form of "unilateral respect" or a later form of "mutual respect," was key to judgments about welfare and justice. These questions are addressed in later sections, particularly in light of the often mistaken assumption that structural–developmental explanations exclude emotions by virtue of the idea that humans are reasoning beings.

In discussing the types of reasoning and emotional evaluative appraisals that go into morality, Nussbaum (1999) stated (as already quoted) "all, just by being human, are of equal dignity and worth, no matter where they are situated in society," that people have "a fair claim to certain types of treatment at the hands of society," and that the treatment by society "must respect and promote the liberty of choice." An immediate reaction to these assertions might well be that they are Western moral conceptions and that they do not apply to morality that is structured by social hierarchy. Indeed, Nussbaum and others (e.g., Okin, 1989) contrast the emphasis of the "liberal tradition" on the equality of human beings with philosophical traditions that revolve around beliefs in natural or tradition-based hierarchies. Furthermore, it is evident that people who are situated in different places on the social hierarchy often are not treated with equal dignity and worth and are not necessarily given fair claims to certain types of treatment. Societies are structured with relationships of dominance and subordination with regard to, as examples, social caste, social class, ethnicity, and gender. Many cultural practices are consistent with hierarchical distinctions in that they involve favorable treatment of groups with greater power or in dominant positions.

Does all this mean that the types of propositions Nussbaum identified as part of the liberal tradition represent one kind of morality stemming from Western cultures? Perhaps so if it were the case that (a) societies or cultures are homogeneous, harmonious groupings speaking with one moral voice, having shared understandings about social relationships and what constitutes the good life or fair treatment, and (b) development involves acceptance of the group's orientations and practices.

Contemporary philosophers and political theorists working within the liberal tradition are led to the conclusions that the position applies across cultures, that cultures are neither harmonious nor homogeneous, and that there are fundamental disagreements rather than shared understandings among people, especially people in different positions on the social hierarchy. Nussbaum has argued that "cultures are not monoliths; people are not stamped out like coins by the power machine of social convention" (1999, p. 32). Although these views follow from her presumptions about reasoning and emotions, they are also informed by her work in several South East Asian nations on the quality of the lives of women in developing nations (see Nussbaum, 1995). Implicit in the view that cultures are not monoliths is that they are not formed or defined by shared understandings or shared commitments to tradition, public ideology, or societal norms. It may seem that the nonrelativistic proposition that morality is based on reasoning about welfare, justice, and rights would imply that there are shared or common understandings on the grounds that everyone maintains these concepts. Moral judgments, however, stand alongside other social or personal concepts in the context of societies that are not necessarily structured by fair treatment and reciprocity. If people do maintain similar moral judgments, then the expectation would be that those who are not treated equally or fairly (e.g., those in subordinate positions) will contest the ways moral prescriptions are applied (or are not adequately applied) in existing societal arrangements and cultural practices. Focusing on issues of gender inequality and oppression, Okin has maintained that understandings are not shared: "oppressors and oppressed—when the voice of the latter can be heard at all— often disagree fundamentally" (1989, p. 67). Fundamental disagreements go well beyond those that exist between groups like oppressors and those they oppress. There can be disagreements and conflicts within those groups and even within seemingly close social units like the family.

The propositions put forth by philosophers regarding cultures and shared understandings are paralleled in analyses by cultural anthropologists and supported by ethnographic evidence (Abu-Lughod, 1991, 1993; Spiro, 1993; Wikan, 1991, 1996, 2002). A clear parallel is seen in propositions put forth by both Abu-Lughod and Wikan, based on extensive studies in non-Western cultures. Abu-Lughod stated that "by focusing closely on particular individuals and their changing relationships, one would necessarily subvert the most problematic connotations of culture: homogeneity, coherence, and timelessness" (1991, p. 154). According to Abu-Lughod, this is because people make "choices, struggle with others, make conflicting statements, argue about points of view on the same events." Wikan also criticized approaches that provide a "concept of culture as a seamless whole and society as a bounded group manifesting inherently valued order...(that) effectively masked human misery and quenched dissenting voices" (1991, p. 290). Furthermore, she has claimed that the term *culture* all too often "covers up the complexity of human existence, the fact that we are both children of 'our culture' and unique individuals" (Wikan, 2002, p. 88).

These views of philosophers and anthropologists have far-reaching methodological implications in that it is claimed that large groups of people are not sufficiently heard or studied—namely, those in subordinate positions, the oppressed, and dissenting voices. Deep and commonly existing disagreements and conflicts are masked by a tendency to concentrate on those in positions of power and of higher status. Moreover, the philosophers have claimed, and the anthropologists have documented empirically, that people commonly oppose, resist, and attempt to subvert certain societal arrangements and cultural practices (see also Turiel, 2002, 2003a; Turiel & Perkins, 2004; Wainryb, chap. 8, this volume). Heterogeneity, lack of shared understandings, and social opposition have significant implications for explanations of social and moral development. Simply put for now, they are inconsistent with the proposition that development entails acceptance of, or identification with, a group's moral or cultural orientation and its practices. The study of the perspectives of those in lower positions in social hierarchies and analyses of how morality pertains to social inequalities, power, and oppression as embedded in societal arrangements and cultural practices are central to an understanding of the dynamics of social interactions and the development of morality. In all cultures people in subordinate positions combat inequalities and injustices through opposition, resistance, and acts of subversion in their daily lives. Moreover, the existence of such pervasive activities leads to the view that morality involves judgments that are constructed in development through the individual's interactions in a multifaceted social world.

CONSCIENCE, CHARACTER, FEAR, ANXIETY, AND GUILT

One of the generally agreed upon features of morality is that it involves actions perceived to be binding on people. This is the *ought* or *should* quality of morality that is the subject of a variety of types of philosophical analyses (Brandt, 1959; Frankena, 1963). Many moral philosophers have been concerned with ways of characterizing procedures, judgments, and reasoning that lead to a sense of obligation. In that case, judgments about obligations can be compatible with opposition and resistance to cultural practices and to the ways individuals are treated by society. By contrast, in much of the field of psychology the sense of ought or obligation, not surprisingly, has been psychologized in the sense that there is a search for psychological mechanisms that produce changes involving accommodations to the values, norms, and practices of society. Morality, then, is basically a form of compliance that becomes part of the individual through the formation of, as examples, habits, conscience, or traits of character. In that context, opposition and resistance would be viewed as that which comes from the assertion of nonmoral or immoral individual drives, needs, interests, and desires.

In those views, which were prominent throughout the first half of the twentieth century, a duality is drawn between the natural inclinations of individuals and social relationships, and by extension with society. It takes a good deal of psychological work to effect a change in natural inclinations and to maintain those changes. Much of that psychological work is borne by experiences of aversive emotions. It makes sense that aversive emotions were seen as necessary to affect change in the young toward sociability; it is their natural inclinations toward fulfilling needs and desires that must be shaped to fit social values, norms, and standards. A clear example is Freud's (1923, 1930) explanation of moral development, where the idea of conscience (in the superego) embodies the internalized dual nature of instincts or drives in clash with a sense of obligation to control those drives by adhering to societal standards. Freud's theory is both atypical and typical in its approach to these matters. It is atypical in the propositions that (a) very strong, biologically based instincts around sexuality and aggression motivate behavior, (b) the strength of those instincts are maintained to produce intense inner conflicts, and (c) the fears and anxieties in an intense set of conflicts (in the Oedipal crisis) at a particular age period produce a shift by which social standards are internalized. In turn, standards are maintained by intense feelings of guilt, defined as introjected and inner-directed aggression. Freud's theory is typical with regard to the propositions that fears and anxieties are a source of the acquisition of social behaviors (often referred to as *conscience* or *character*) entailing an internalization of societal standards, which serve to replace the young child's natural tendencies toward fulfillment of needs and desires.

It is not only aversive emotions that are seen as contributing to the formation of morality. In Freudian theory, the child's attachments to parents serve to intensify the conflicts experienced due to fear and anxiety. In behaviorist explanations, both positive and negative reinforcements contribute to learning—to the formation of socially based habits of behavior that displace behaviors driven by needs of self-interest (especially in Skinner, 1971). Nevertheless, the main emphasis in research on supposedly moral acquisition was on aversive emotions. The best example to illustrate that approach is the types of experiments conducted in the 1960s to examine the formation of control over behavior and learning to act in honest ways. A large number of so-called forbidden toy experiments were conducted with children to assess if they would or would not learn to resist the temptation to act in ways prohibited by an adult in the absence of adult supervision.

In a typical experiment a child is brought into an experimental room with toys that are more or less desirable. The child is instructed to avoid playing with some of the toys, but not told which ones. As the child attempts to play with certain toys (the forbidden/more desirable ones) he or she is administered punishments (e.g., a reprimand from the experimenter) that are timed differently. Some punishments are timed early (they come just as the child is about to pick up the toy) or late (they come after the child has started to play with the toy). At some point the child is left alone in the room, having been led to believe that he or she is not under adult supervision—all the while being surreptitiously observed by the experimenters. The measures of learning or acquisition of moral behaviors are based on the extent to which the children played with the forbidden toys when left alone. A consistent finding was that early punishment was more effective than late punishment. These experiments, of course, were meant to simulate natural conditions, such as in the family, to pinpoint the mechanisms at work in children's learning of the control of behavior or the formation of conscience. The main explicit standard embedded in the experiments seems to be an action designated by the adult as prohibited and its acquisition by the child through the administration of punishments. Moral acquisition comes about through the pairing of the aversive emotions of fear and anxiety with actions. The findings on early punishment were interpreted as due to a greater effectiveness for internalization of the association of anxiety to the onset of an act.

The broad conception of morality in this approach was that conscience is largely formed through and regulated by strong emotions. As put by Aronfreed, "Conscience is the term that has been used traditionally to refer to the cognitive and affective processes which constitute an internalized moral governor over an individual's conduct" (1968, p. 2). Aronfreed contrasted the idea of both cognitive and affective processes that involve internalized governing forces with rational processes. He went on to say that the classical Greek conceptions of morality as an "essentially rational phenomenon," contrasts with "the powerful affective components which we are now inclined to regard as indispensable to internalized control over social conduct," and with the historical trend "toward increasing emphasis on the affective, inarticulate, and impelling features of conscience" (Aronfreed, 1968, p. 2).

Although Aronfreed and others included cognitive processes in governing moral conduct, much of it was through the lens of powerful affective, aversive components that follow transgressions of learned behaviors. He identified three kinds of "cognitive structures" that "determine the child's qualitative experience of the aversive changes of affective state" (p. 242) attached to their transgressions: fear, guilt, and shame. The anxiety associated with social actions internalized through the learning process can result in one of the three aversive states or a combination of them. Shame is connected to the reactions of others, whereas guilt is connected to the actor's moral evaluations. As put by Aronfreed, *shame* refers to "the extent that its qualitative experience is determined by a cognitive orientation toward the visibility of a transgression" (p. 249) and *guilt* refers to the "extent that the quality of the transgressor's affective experience is determined by moral evaluation of the transgression" (p. 245).

There have been several shifts in orientation since the time emphasis was placed on aversive emotions as examined in experimental paradigms like the forbidden toy experiments. One shift has been to the study of the influences of child-rearing practices on the internalization of parental standards (Hoffman, 1970). That research has led to a de-emphasis of fear and anxiety due to punishment as causes of learning since physical punishment was shown to be less effective than parental approval and disapproval (often labeled *love withdrawal*), which in turn is less effective than communications from parents about moral matters (the labeling of such communications as *induction* reflects the view that they are forms of discipline). Another shift has been toward greater consideration of nonaversive emotions—especially sympathy and empathy (e.g., Eisenberg & Fabes, 1998; Hoffman, 1984, 2000). In Hoffman's (2000) approach, for instance, emotions stemming from evolution and appearing early in life are combined with an internalization of societal norms and values.

Another set of shifts in emphasis on the part of those who place emotions at the forefront has been to connect morality to evolutionary processes, the brain, neurology, and culture. An interesting treatise that includes discussion of morality is Damasio's (1994, 2003) analyses of the connections among biological processes, rationality, emotions, and feelings. Damasio argued for examining the mind as embodied: "I suggested that feelings are a powerful influence on reason, that the brain systems required by the former are enmeshed in those needed by the latter, and that such specific systems are interwoven with those that regulate the body" (2003, p. 245).

Damasio is careful to not give the impression that rationality or reasoning are less important than feelings or that thought is driven by emotions. He maintained that his formulations should not be taken as a case for "tolerance for relaxed standards of intellectual performance" (p. 246) because he allows a role for emotions and feelings. However, he does want to avoid the dualist notion, traced to Descartes (hence his title, *Descartes' Error: Emotion, Reason, and the Human Brain*), that splits the mind from brain and body. Descartes' error was, to quote, "the abysmal separation of body and mind, between the sizable, dimensioned, mechanically operated, infinitely divisible body stuff, on the one hand, and the unsizable, unidimensioned, un-pushupullable, nondivisible mind stuff" (p. 250). For Damasio, Descartes' wide influence (as seen in studies of the mind and medical treatment or disease, for example) through his error was to lead scholars to separate operations of the mind from the operations of the biological organism. Reasoning and moral judgments cannot be separated from emotions and feelings that involve physical pain and other emotional upheavals.

This is all well and good. Neurophysiologic and neuropsychological investigations of the type undertaken by Damasio and others are important to understanding connections of the brain to emotions, feelings, and morality. However, valid and meaningful connections can only be made if one works with valid and meaningful conceptions of reasoning and morality. Damasio seems much less concerned with questions about meaningful definitions, conceptions, and assessments of reasoning and morality than is evident in his concerns with neurology, emotions, and feelings. He approached reasoning in general ways, without discriminating among the different theoretical formulations about it. Surely, to understand connections among brain, thought, and emotions it is important to assess reasoning appropriately. As an example, someone who does not accept the validity of assessments of intellectual performance through tests of IQ would hardly be satisfied with studies supporting the hypotheses based on such assessments. Damasio also treats morality in general ways, without clear or detailed definitional analyses.

DAMASIO'S (AND OTHERS') ERRORS

As Nussbaum (1999) stated, the central issue is not whether emotion is excluded from analyses of human thought. Rather, the important issues are which emotions, and how, are involved in what—that is, what types of conceptions and analyses of morality are utilized? Damasio lists a range of aversive and positive social emotions that may be connected to morality, including sympathy, embarrassment, shame, guilt, pride, jealousy, envy, gratitude, admiration, indignation, and contempt. How these emotions are linked to morality is ambiguous, as is the conception of morality. In one effort at specifying the nature of social and moral behaviors, Damasio stated, " The picture I am drawing for humans is that of an organism that comes to life designed with an automatic survival mechanism, and to which education and acculturation add a set of socially permissible decision-making strategies that, in turn, remarkably improve the quality of that survival, and serve as the basis for constructing a person" (1994, p. 126). Beyond these statements, which seem to rely on an interaction of a biological organism with educational and cultural experiences embodying the socially permissible, Damasio repeatedly refers to "social conventions and ethical rules" to encompass morality. He also at times makes general statements about cultural instruments of religious beliefs, law, and justice. The meaning of social conventions and ethical rules are largely left unspecified, except that they are circularly regarded as manifestations of homeostatic and cooperative relationships regulated by culture.

Damasio's first error is that he assumes he can draw connections among brain, emotions, feelings, and morality without specifying what is meant by social conventions and ethical rules (or law and justice, for that matter). Left unsaid is what constitutes social conventions and cultural rules, how they are acquired in the process of development, and how they are represented in the thoughts and feelings of individuals: Are they internalized habits of behavior reflecting societal standards? Do they involve manifestations of participation in cultural networks? Do they involve complex judgments and understandings about matters like welfare, justice, and rights? Analyses of how and which emotions and feelings are connected to morality may very well depend on which of these conceptions is valid. As examples, certain feelings (the aversive ones) may be more in line with a conception of moral behavior as learned habits than as stemming from judgments about welfare, justice, and rights, which may be more aligned with emotions like sympathy, empathy, and respect. In turn, Damasio leaves unsaid whether there are important differences between social conventions and ethical rules (and ethical principles). If judgments and behaviors around social conventions differ from those around moral rules and principles, it may well be that emotions and feelings differ by each type (as evidenced by research described by Arsenio, Gold, & Adams, chap. 21, this volume).

The vagueness in Damasio's treatment of the realm of morality leads to a questionable assumption about homeostasis and social cooperation. Basically, he places the burden of morality on the social system and, thereby, fails to consider how moral reasoning can entail autonomy and concerns with equal worth of human beings and fair treatment by society. Invoking social conventions and ethical rules again, he maintains that they become mechanisms for exerting homeostasis at the level of the social group in the context of social hierarchies and inequalities: "It is not difficult to imagine the emergence of justice and honor out of practices of cooperation. Yet another layer of social emotions, expressed in the form of dominant or submissive behaviors within the group, would have played an important role in the give and take that define cooperation" (Damasio, 2003, p. 162).

It is within groups (family, tribe, city, and nation) that positive emotions (what Damasio refers to as "nice" emotions and adaptive altruism) take hold, whereas negative emotions ("nasty and brutish") are directed to those outside the group: "The result is anger, resentment, and violence, all of which we can recognize as a possible embryo of tribal hatreds, racism, and war" (Damasio, 2003, p. 163).

There is no doubt that anger, resentment, and violence have been and are often directed to groups other than one's own (although humans also strive for cooperation with other groups). There is, however, much doubt to be cast on the ideas that primarily positive emotions and corresponding actions are directed toward people in the family, tribe, city, or nation, and on the idea that dominance and subordination make for unchallenged relationships of cooperation (homeostasis). Within tribes, cities, nations, and cultures there is a good deal of anger, resentment, and even violence between groups, especially groups in different positions in the social hierarchy and in positions of dominance and subordination. The most obvious examples pertain to groups of different races, social classes, and gender. The conflicts around relationships between men and women—including the family—most clearly show that cooperation often does not always hold sway within groups. Conflicts, anger, aggressiveness, resentment, and sometimes violence occur between parents and children and between husbands and wives (Nussbaum, 2000; Okin, 1989; Shantz & Hartup, 1992; Turiel, 2002). Conflicts among family members result in deception, at the expense of openness and cooperation (Turiel & Perkins, 2004). The maltreatment of women by family members and others is well documented. Maltreatment extends to beatings, as well as culturally sanctioned honor killings and "bride burnings" in several societies (Wikan, 2002). Nussbaum has stated the matter in stark terms: "Women in much of the world lack support for fundamental functions of life. They are less well nourished than men, less healthy, and more vulnerable to physical violence and sexual abuse" (2000, p. 1).

Damasio is aware of the phenomena of opposition and resistance. Spinoza is another philosopher who looms large in his writings—the title of another book is *Looking for Spinoza: Joy, Sorrow, and the Feeling Brain* (2003). Damasio writes persuasively about how Spinoza had to combat the Church and State because they prohibited his writings, designating them as dangerous books. Apparently, the Church considered Spinoza's writings to be an "all out assault on organized religion and the political power structure" (Damasio, 2003, p. 20). Spinoza took his writings underground, publishing under the name of a fictitious printer, listing an incorrect city, and leaving the author's page blank. Spinoza resorted to deception to subvert a system with which he disagreed. It appears that Descartes did too; the inscription he prepared for his own tombstone read, "He who hid well, lived well" (see Damasio, 2003, p. 21).

People's judgments about inadequacies in existing societal arrangements are important to explanations of moral functioning and development. If the root of morality is the attainment of homeostasis or equilibrium that stems from cooperation achieved through a societal system, then people can exist in harmonious relationships of inequalities, including acceptance of domination and subordination. In some cultural analyses, inequalities are seen as acceptable to members of the group because of *asymmetrical reciprocity*; that is, the subordinate accepts his or her status and is compensated by the advantages of the care given by those in dominant positions, and because of an upbringing that shapes the individual to participate in a collective system of interdependence and duties (see Markus & Kitayama, 1991; Shweder, Much, Mahapatra, & Park, 1997). By contrast, if social relationships are evaluated and judged by standards that can differ from those embedded in societal arrangements and cultural practices, then it is likely that people will critique, oppose, and resist inequalities and conditions that allow for injustices in domination and subordination.

Intuitions and Emotions: Does Reasoning Have to Be Slow?

As stated, Damasio was careful not to make the claim that reasoning is driven by emotions and to avoid reductionistic positions. He proposed an interactional view involving biology, emotions, feelings, and processes of reasoning. Some others deliberately relegate reasoning to, at best, a secondary status in moral reactions. As one example, Haidt (2001) privileges what he labels "intuitions," which are intertwined with emotional reactions. It is immediate, reflexive reactions such as revulsion, disgust, and sympathy that trigger the response that an act is wrong. The judgment that an act is wrong is more akin to perception; it involves an immediate gut reaction without reasoning. Moral intuitions cause moral judgments (by which it appears he means evaluations of acts as wrong). One of the key defining features of moral intuitions is quantitative; they occur rapidly, without effort, and automatically. They also occur without intentionality. Haidt proposes that intuitions are due to evolutionary adaptations shaped by culture. Built-in moral intuitions must be given expression; it is culture that provides a context for their expression (referred to as externalization). In the process, the outcome in children and among adults is a morality that is unique to their culture or group and often includes asymmetrical reciprocity with acceptance of dominance and subordination (see Haidt, 2001, p. 826). Immersion in a culture, its customs, and social relationships produce an influence on individuals. (Is this a moral universalism due to evolution or a moral relativism due to culture? It is hard to say.)

In this view, humans are reasoning beings only in secondary ways. What is reasoning in Haidt's perspective? Its features contrast with intuitions in that it is slow, requires effort, and makes use of evidence. Moral reasoning is used mainly after the fact to justify to self and others why an act is intuitively grasped as wrong: "when faced with a social demand for a verbal justification one becomes a lawyer building a case rather than a judge searching for the truth" (Haidt, 2001, p. 814). Moral reasoning is also used to persuade and rationalize. This position is in dramatic contrast with Nussbaum's ideas as to what is fundamental to morality. Human beings do not have the power of moral choice nor the ability to plan a life in accord with one's evaluations of ends.

Clearly, in writing about his position on morality, Haidt is searching for the truth. He engaged in a detailed, effortful argument using reasoning and tried to muster evidence in support of the proposition that people are not moral reasoners. This represents the type of asynchrony between the cognitive activities of psychologists and the activities they attribute to humans in their theories that I discussed previously. In this case, Haidt makes explicit a distinction between what scholars do and what most everyone else does. Whereas Haidt can deal with evidence, the majority cannot. As he put it, it has been "found that most people have difficulty understanding what evidence is, and when pressed to give evidence in support of their theories they generally give anecdotes or illustrative examples instead" (Haidt, 2001, p. 821), and that "by going through all the steps of hypothesis testing, even though every step can be biased by self-serving motivations, people can maintain an illusion of objectivity about the way they think" (p. 823). Most people are not concerned with reflection on moral matters. It is philosophers and those with a "high need" for cognition who engage in private or personal reflection.

Just as Haidt raises questions about the ways evidence is used by lay persons (and other psychologists), we can raise questions about how he uses evidence (and illustrative examples). Without getting into a great deal of detail here, it is striking that his use of evidence is rather selective. By his admission, most of the evidence cited is from nonmoral realms. He refers to a number of studies from social psychology that appear to support the idea that people are biased, emotive, intuitive, and unconcerned with evidence. However, he omits mention of large bodies of research from developmental and cognitive psychology in realms like number, mathematical reasoning, classification, understandings of space and physics more generally, causality, intentionality, and theories of mind. Those studies show that people make judgments that are not necessarily immediate, rapid, and categorical, and that can be intentional, deliberative, and reflective. People do reason and are not intuitive in many realms of knowledge. The research also shows that such reasoning can become immediate and rapid. Conceptualizations of, for example, number and arithmetic may be acquired laboriously over time but, once acquired, are applied in rapid fashion. As another example, a large body of research shows that a good deal of cognitive work occurs from ages 3 to 5 years in the formation of understandings of others' minds. Once those understandings are formed, however, children use them in an immediate, rapid fashion. That a concept is used rapidly does not mean that it does not involve complex processes of reasoning. It is circular to distinguish intuitions from reasoning on the basis of a quantitative dimension of speed. Independent criteria as to the nature or quality of the process are necessary.

Insofar as Haidt discusses research on morality, it is on moral reasoning. For the most part, he proclaims that research on moral reasoning only reveals what people do in the way of justification to convince others or to rationalize in a post hoc way positions they hold for other reasons. However, he does not provide evidence as to how the moral reasoning investigated in so many studies fails to account for moral evaluations or how it is that such reasoning is mainly used for purposes of persuasion and rationalization. It is simply asserted to be so.

Haidt does attempt to provide a definition of morality. But it is minimal and, he states, broad so as to allow a large area of marginally moral judgments. *Morality* is defined as evaluations as good and bad of the "actions or character of a person that are made with respect to a set of virtues held to be obligatory by a culture or subculture" (Haidt, 2001, p. 817). The broadness of the definition also serves to avoid the difficult parts in providing a definition that allows us to know the distinguishing features of the realm. It serves the dubious purposes of placing the source of all morality in the group (culture or subculture) and classifying any act deemed by a group obligatory as moral (relativism?). The definition also raises questions as to how to locate actions held by a group (by whom, where, extent of agreement). The definition certainly implies that meanings are shared within cultures.

Like lay persons, Haidt uses illustrative examples to support his argument. An example that he seems to regard as prototypical is that of incest—an example that could be viewed as shared within cultures, yet applicable across cultures, and an evolutionary adaptation. Incest is illustrative of the position because it is one of those acts, even when it is specified that it is consensual and there is no risk of pregnancy occurring, to which people react immediately with a gut reaction that it is wrong and are unable to explain why. The example, conveyed at the very start of Haidt's essay, is of a brother and sister who go on vacation and, with all precautions, decide to make love. The act is intuitively grasped as wrong because most people say "something like, 'I don't' know, I can't explain it. I just know it's wrong'" (Haidt, 2001, p. 814).

A key question is the generality of an example like this one (or examples like people judging it wrong to eat dogs, etc.). Does it apply to people's moral lives more generally and meaningfully? Suppose we consider other examples that some people might also respond to immediately and emotionally, such as ones set in a U.S. southern state (perhaps Mississippi, perhaps Alabama) anywhere between the 1920s and 1950s: A Black man and a White woman decide to make love; a Black woman and a White man decide to get married; a Black person wants to eat in a restaurant reserved for Whites; a Black boy who is 15 years old drinks from a water fountain designated "for Whites only."

There is little doubt that large numbers of White people would have had strong, gut reactions, in an immediate way that all these acts are wrong. They would have maintained that they know they are just wrong. When pressed, would have they said that they know it is just wrong (they cannot explain it) or would they have invoked reasons pertaining to the sanctity of the White race or the maintenance of the fabric of society? In Haidt's view, however, it is emotionally based intuitions that are at work and if reasons had been given, they would merely be post hoc rationalizations. Moreover, are we wiling to say that such responses to many examples reflect evolutionary adaptations also reflecting intuitions shared within cultures and yet applicable across cultures (as is seen to apply to incest)? What about the perspectives of those (such as those of Blacks or others who believe racial discrimination is wrong) who judged that such practices are wrong and should be changed? How does that relate to judgments about incest, if at all?

As discussed below, these types of examples reveal that moral judgments are often more than intuitions; they involve concepts about different groups, social relationships, perspectives on society, and distinctions between when rights should be applied and when they should be denied. This is so, even though many, especially Black people, would have reacted in a seemingly rapid and unreflective way to these examples by claiming that it is not wrong for consenting adults to engage in sex or get married. Similarly, an immediate reaction might be that it is wrong to reserve certain restaurants or water fountains for White people. Again, those reactions are complex and involve reasoning about rights, fairness, and welfare, as well as about the injustices of the dominance and power exerted by one group on another.

Therefore, there is a reductionism in the use of an example like incest to illustrate all manner of moral decisions. The position is also reductionistic in its treatment of moral decisions as mainly intuitive. We can consider another example of a type of act that might appear on the surface to fit the idea that moral judgments involve unreflective and immediate evaluations of acts as wrong. I am referring to acts of physical harm (e.g., one child hits another). Often, people do rapidly respond to such acts as wrong. This would seem to be a clear example of social intuition as the source of judgments of right and wrong. It is not! For children, and even adults, reactions to acts of physical harm are not straightforward. Although children do judge many acts of physical harm as wrong, they are also readily able to articulate reasons, especially that it is not good to inflict pain, that people do not like to feel the experience of pain. Moreover, they express sympathy and empathy, in evaluative appraisals, for those who experience the physical harm (see Arsenio, Gold, & Adams, chap. 21, this volume; Nucci & Nucci, 1982a, 1982b; Nucci & Turiel, 1978). In addition, children distinguish between acts of physical harm that are wrong in some circumstances (e.g., unprovoked acts of hitting) and acts of harm that are justified in other circumstances (e.g., in retaliation for provocations; see Astor, 1994; Tisak, Tisak, & Goldstein, chap. 22, this volume). Among adults, there are instances in which people subordinate the judgment that it is wrong to inflict harm to other social considerations (Milgram, 1974).

As a related example, let us consider the following act: a large, muscular man hits a 5-year-old child. Is this not the type of act that epitomizes that most people respond with a strong emotional reaction and the reflexive judgment that it is wrong? Not necessarily, because judgments of various kinds are made about the act. In the first place, people consider the reasons or intentions behind the act. If the adult hitting the child is his or her father, and doing it after the child's misdeed (we call that *spanking*), then many people do not respond to the act as wrong. Research has shown that people distinguish between spanking (which does involve hitting and inflicting pain) and hitting for other reasons (Wainryb, 1991). Whereas the latter is judged to be categorically wrong (because it harms the child), the former is judged acceptable (because it is intended to further the welfare of the child). Judgments about these issues include a variety of emotional and cognitive features (dismissed out of hand by Haidt) that go into the moral decision-making process. In the example of spanking (as well as for issues like abortion, homosexuality, and pornography; see Smetana, 1982; Turiel, Hildebrandt, & Wainryb, 1991), what can be referred to as *informational assumptions* are involved in judgments about the act (with regard to spanking, it is psychological assumptions about the effects of punishment on learning). Many moral decisions include a coordination of different moral and/or nonmoral features (how this applies to issues of rights, and honesty is discussed next).

MULTIPLE SOCIAL INTERACTIONS AND RECIPROCITY

In the shift from behaviorism to the propositions seen in the approach put forth by Damasio (2003), as well as in the biological cultural views regarding moral intuitions, we do see a greater recognition that morality is not the straightforward learning of behaviors through their association with aversive emotions. Nevertheless, significant commonalities exist between behaviorist and intuitionist propositions. Each reduces moral evaluations and actions to nonintentional, noncontrolled reactions to stimuli or events. In each, there is a denial of flexibility of people's thought in dealing with the parameters of situations or events. From the perspective of structural–developmental approaches, therefore, a great deal of significance is left out, particularly reciprocity, obligation, consideration of the nature of social relationships, and the requirements in social interactions for the attainment of moral aims and ends. In addition, the possibility of transformations in reciprocity and obligation are also omitted.

As is well known, Piaget (1932) conducted a series of studies on children's moral judgments and actions very early in his career (a topic he did not research again). Piaget's ideas regarding moral development centered on reciprocity, obligation, social interactions, and transformations that occur with age. In fact, Piaget was quite aware back in 1932 of propositions, not dissimilar to ones put forth by Haidt (2001) and others, that were aimed at explaining morality through biological/intuitionist reactions. Piaget quoted Antipoff (1928), who had proposed that a sense of justice involved "an innate and instinctive moral manifestation, which in order to develop really requires neither preliminary experience nor socialization amongst other children. . . . We have an inclusive affective perception, an elementary moral 'structure' which the child seems to possess very easily and which enables him to grasp simultaneously evil and its cause, innocence and guilt. We may say that what we have here is an *affective perception of justice*" (quoted in Piaget, 1932, p. 228).

Piaget pointed out that Antipoff's research did not demonstrate innateness because she observed children who were between the ages of 3 and 9 years. By the age of 3, children would have experienced social interactions, including influences from adults. According to Piaget, however, adults do not simply transmit morality to children and they constitute only one aspect of children's social experiences:

> Socialization in no way constitutes the result of a unidirectional cause such as the pressure of the adult community upon the child through such means as education in the family and subsequently in the school. Rather, . . . it involves the intervention of a multiplicity of interactions of different types and sometimes with opposed effects. In contrast with the somewhat academic sociology of the Durkheim school which reduces society to a single whole, collective consciousness, and its action to a unidirectional process of physical and spiritual constraint, the concrete sociology which the personal and social development of the child obliges us to construct must be wary of sweeping generalities if it is to make sense of the systems of relations and interdependencies actually involved. (1951/1995, p. 276)

Piaget maintained that society is not a "simple whole" and that it does not produce in its members an adherence to presumed norms of the social system. At the heart of Piaget's perspective on moral development are the ideas that socialization does not involve a unidirectional cause, that there are multiple social interactions, and that there are systems of relations and interdependencies. These propositions, which are shared in most subsequent structural–developmental approaches, differ not only from Durkheim's early twentieth-century academic sociology, but also from the types of interactions proposed by Damasio between "a biological organism with educational and cultural experiences embodying the socially permissible" (1994, p. 126). In particular, Piaget proposed that development does not involve an accommodation to the socially permissible, that the multiplicity of experiences influencing development includes relations with adults and peers, and that educational and cultural experiences, insofar as they are mainly with adults, can impede the development of morality.

The types of systems of relations and interdependencies considered by Piaget included children's reciprocal social interactions, and relations among thought, emotion, and actions. As is well known, Piaget proposed that there are two major phases of the development of moral judgments corresponding with two major types of social interactions. Following a premoral period based on regularities, children's moral judgments are heteronomous and are mainly associated with children's relationships with adults (parents and others in authority). Heteronomy is chiefly characterized by one-way or unilateral respect for adults and their rules. As such, heteronomous thinking entails a sense of sacredness of rules and the judgment that they are unalterable. The origins of morality, therefore, are in the sense of obligation stemming from respect for adults and their rules. Heteronomy is an unequilibrated form of morality that can shift with the influences of relationships of greater equality than those between children and adults. Relationships with peers allow for reciprocity and provide the conditions for a shift to autonomous thinking, involving mutual respect and concerns with fairness, justice, and cooperation.

For an understanding of the type of structural–developmental approach to morality initiated by Piaget, it is important to consider the ways he viewed evaluative emotional appraisals to be connected to moral reasoning and its development, because emotions were very much a part of the formulation. The emotions identified by Piaget were not, for the most part, the aversive ones often linked to moral learning. Instead, central to the formulation are the emotions of affection, sympathy, compassion, and, most importantly, respect. What may be regarded as aversive emotions of fear, vindictiveness, and jealousy were a smaller part of the equation. In Piaget's view, combinations of in-born or very early emerging emotions of fear, affection, and sympathy, as well as vindictiveness and compassion, help form the basis for the development of morality. However, he regarded instinctive tendencies "a necessary but not a sufficient condition for the formation of morality" (p. 344), and he maintained that "the child's behavior towards persons shows signs from the first of those sympathetic tendencies and affective reactions in which one can easily see the raw material of all subsequent moral behavior. But an intelligent act can only be called logical and a good-hearted impulse moral from the moment that certain norms impress a given structure and rules of equilibrium upon this material" (p. 405). It is especially the combination of fear, affection, and sympathy in relation to adults that is intertwined with social interactions and processes of reasoning that make for the emergence of heteronomy.

In Piaget's view, the emotions experienced by very young children (and the appreciation of regularities) do not represent morality which requires a sense of obligation. Fear, affection, and sympathy in young children are mainly directed toward adults and become coordinated and transformed into strong feelings of respect for others. Initially, however, strong feelings of respect are unilateral; they are experienced as one-way feelings toward adults. It is such feelings of respect that produce a sense of obligation, which is necessary for morality. Feelings of respect combine with conceptions about rules and directives from authorities for a morality based on the ideas that rules are sacred and unalterable, that they must be followed, and that the good involves adherence to adult commands. As put by Piaget, "this respect is the source of moral obligation and of the sense of duty: every command coming from a respected person is the starting point of an obligatory rule. . . . Right is to obey the will of the adult. Wrong is to have a will of one's own" (1932, p. 193).

The child's entry into morality that comes with obligations based on unilateral respect is insufficient for an adequate morality, which must involve autonomy and cooperation. Again, an intertwining of emotions of respect and concepts about social relationships makes for transformations in children's morality. The next level of autonomy requires a shift from unilateral to mutual respect. Mutual respect, which emerges from peer relationships involving greater equality than in children's relationships with adults, is connected to sympathy and compassion, and goes hand in hand with conceptions of justice in cooperative activities. It is at the level of autonomy that children construct their understandings of the nature of rules and laws and reciprocal norms: "Autonomy therefore appears only with reciprocity, when mutual respect is strong enough to make the individual feel from within the desire to treat others as he himself would wish to be treated" (Piaget, 1932, p. 194).

By *autonomy*, Piaget did not mean freedom from social or moral requirements. Rather, he meant that the individual "participates in elaboration of norms instead of receiving them ready-made as happens in the case of the norms of unilateral respect that lie behind heteronomous morality" (Piaget, 1960/1995, p. 315). The idea that children participate in the elaboration of norms is a central part of one of Piaget's major contributions to explanations of social, moral, and cognitive development. It captures the essence of mental development as a constructive process through the individual's interaction with the environment and is in opposition to explanations of development as determined either by biologic-genetic traits, intuitions, or by what is ready made in the environment (e.g., society, culture, ideology, religious precepts). In Piaget's later and extensive research on nonsocial aspects of mental development, he applied processes of construction to development from infancy to adolescence. In his early work, as reflected in the idea that young children receive norms ready made, he essentially distinguished between older children's constructions, whose moral judgments are based on elaboration of norms, and younger children's nonconstruction of norms.

In the process, Piaget put forth an interesting but flawed proposition regarding moral development: The development of moral judgments involves a process of differentiating judgments about reciprocity and justice from acceptance of the ready made (i.e., rules and authority of adults). In the minds of young children, the two are confounded so that moral obligation is judged to be "respect for age—respect for older children, and, above all, respect for adults" (1932, p. 98), in conjunction with the beliefs that rules are sacred and unalterable and that the "right is to obey the will of the adult" (p. 193).

In the undifferentiated state of heteronomous thinking, justice is subordinated to obeying rules and authority: "If distributive justice is brought into conflict with adult authority, the youngest subjects will believe authority right and justice wrong" (Piaget, 1932, p. 304). The shift to autonomy, with a transformation of emotions of unilateral respect into mutual respect, brings new conceptualizations of reciprocity, justice, and cooperation; for further details of Piaget's descriptions of the levels of heteronomy and autonomy, see Kohlberg (1963), Piaget (1932, 1960/1995), Turiel (1983a, 1983b), and Turiel and Smetana (1998).

The proposition that young children subordinate justice to authority, rules, and customs is important to consider with regard to subsequent structural–developmental formulations. A number of years after Piaget's research on moral development, Kohlberg (1963, 1969, 1971, 1984) extended Piaget's general propositions regarding thought and development while maintaining the idea of differentiations in the process of development in a 6-stage sequence of moral judgments. In Kohlberg's formulation (discussed by Lapsley, chap. 2, this volume), the start of moral judgments entails a lack of differentiation between moral values from material values and concerns with punishment (the stage 1 punishment and obedience orientation) and from the interests and needs of persons (the stage 2 orientation to individualism, instrumental purpose). As a consequence, Kohlberg maintained that in early and middle childhood, moral judgments are not based on respect for authority, sacredness of rules, or judgments that rules must always be followed (the features of heteronomy). It is not until adolescence that morality is based on the need to maintain rules, authority, and the conventional social system (the stage 4 rule and authority maintaining orientation). Moral judgments are then part of emerging conceptions of social systems and respect for the institutionalized laws and authority. It is not until late adolescence and adulthood that moral judgments of welfare, justice, and rights become differentiated from the rules and conventions of the social system (stages 5 and 6 of principled morality).

A large body of research has, on the one hand, provided very strong evidence that the types of differentiations proposed by both Piaget and Kohlberg do not adequately characterize the development of moral judgments, and, on the other hand, strongly supported fundamental propositions put forth by Piaget and Kohlberg regarding the construction of moral judgments of welfare, justice, and rights through reciprocal interactions with multifaceted aspects of the social environment. The findings have been summarized elsewhere (Smetana, 1995; Tisak, 1995; Turiel, 1983b, 1998). The research shows that young children make distinctively moral judgments (first mainly about welfare and then about justice and rights), which are differentiated from judgments about the realms of social conventions (societal-based uniformities) and personal jurisdiction. We have delineated the characteristics of these three domains, which constitute three distinct pathways of development associated with different types of social interactions and emotional reactions (Arsenio, Gold, & Adams, chap. 21, this volume; Nucci & Turiel, 1978).

The origins of this line of research was in efforts (Turiel, 1975) undertaken to explain how moral issues become distinguished from issues of social conventions and conceptions of fixed rules in the transition from stage 4 to stage 5—as outlined in Kohlberg's formulations. Unexpectedly, it turned out that children of about 9 to 11 years of age did not confuse conventions with moral prescriptions and, instead, conceptualized each in different terms (Turiel, 1975). Subsequent research showed that even younger children made similar differentiations (Turiel, 1978, 1979). Sustained programs of research since that time have consistently shown that these different types of judgments constitute different domains. A variety of research procedures have been used, including observations of social interactions, assessments of judgments about hypothetical situations, and assessments of judgments about events in which children and adolescents had participated. In one study (Turiel, 2002) the social interactions of elementary and middle school children were observed in a variety of settings (classroom, play, lunch). A substantial number of observed events could readily be classified in accord with the criteria for the moral and conventional domains. Judgments about these events elicited shortly after they occurred differed by domain and closely corresponded to the judgments made by the same (and other) children about comparable hypothetical situations. Another aspect of the results of the study was consistent with findings with younger children in a number of observational studies (Nucci & Nucci, 1982a, 1982b; Nucci & Turiel, 1978; Nucci, Turiel, & Encarnacion-Gawrych, 1983; Nucci & Weber, 1995). The emotions associated with moral events focused on expressions of hurt, anger at victimization, feelings of obligation, and feelings of concern for others' welfare (note that feelings are about something, not just feelings). Emotions associated with conventional events tend to be neutral, and do not focus on the experiences of, or concerns for others (for more fine-grained analyses, see Arsenio, Gold, & Adams, chap. 21, this volume, and Nucci, 2001).

Several chapters in this volume represent different but interrelated programs of research within the domain framework, and the ways moral, conventional, and personal judgments are relevant to development and social interactions. In the remainder of this chapter, two types of issues are discussed that strongly support a structural–developmental perspective on social development. One pertains to the ways moral and social concepts are applied and coordinated in situational contexts. Research on trust or deception and on rights is considered for these purposes. The second pertains to whether and how individuals oppose and resist cultural practices and societal norms at variance with moral judgments about welfare, justice, and rights. For these purposes, research on the perspectives of those in lower or subordinate positions in social hierarchies is discussed.

HONESTY AND RIGHTS: ABSOLUTISM AND RELATIVISM

Honesty and rights can be and have been viewed as moral obligations, though each in different ways. Honesty is often treated as a trait or virtue or responsibility that from a moral point of view must be followed. In that case, it would be wrong to lie or deceive others and good to tell the truth. Honesty is seen as a moral imperative from various theoretical perspectives. People should tell the truth because it is a virtue, or because it reflects a trait of character, or because it is necessary for society to function, or because it is a readily grasped moral intuition, or because it is necessary to maintain trust in social relationships. There is a sense in which honesty is treated as an absolute and there is virtually no discussion of honesty as relative to a society or culture. Discussions of rights have the quality of being treated as absolute, but there are discussions of rights as culturally specific. On the one side, it is said by some that rights are central to some cultures but not others. Western cultures are supposedly based on a morality of personal rights and individual autonomy, whereas in non-Western cultures the concept of rights is not central because of a moral orientation to the group and interdependence (a sort of relativism). However, within a culture oriented to rights, the concept is said to imply that rights must always be upheld (a sort of absolutism).

Findings from research on honesty and rights fail to support these various propositions. Although people in most places believe in the value of honesty, there are many situations in which most people subordinate honesty to other moral and social considerations. Rights, too, are treated seriously in most places and are not culturally specific, but there are many situations in which people subordinate rights to other moral and social considerations. In other words, the endorsement of honesty or rights varies by situation or context. Those findings do not simply reflect the pull or force of situations. Rather, they show systematic patterns of coordination, with flexibility of thought, of different types of judgments that take into account perceived aspects of situations.

Several recent studies on honesty and deception demonstrate that people systematically evaluate the consequences of telling the truth or engaging in deception to further the welfare of persons, achieve justice, and promote individual autonomy when it is perceived to be unfairly restricted. In one study, physicians were presented with hypothetical stories that depicted doctors who consider deceiving insurance companies as the only means of obtaining approval for a treatment or diagnostic procedure for a patient (Freeman, Rathore, Weinfurt, Schulman, & Sulmasy, 1999). The stories depicted medical conditions of different degrees of severity. In the two most severe conditions (life-threatening ones), the majority thought that the doctor was justified in engaging in deception. In other conditions the percentages accepting deception were considerably lower, with the fewest (3%) judging that deception was legitimate for purposes of cosmetic surgery. Moreover, there is evidence that physicians actually do engage in deception of insurance companies (Wynia, Cummins, VanGeest, & Wilson, 2000).

No doubt, the physicians participating in the study would judge honesty to be good and dishonesty wrong. However, at the same time they judge deception acceptable in some situations as a means of promoting the welfare of their patients. Other research has shown a corresponding pattern in judgments about deception in close relationships—between husbands and wives (Turiel, Perkins, & Mensing, in preparation). The study was designed to include situations depicting a husband only who works outside the home, with a wife engaging in deception, and the reverse, where only a wife works and a husband engages in deception. One situation depicted a spouse who tightly controls the family finances and the other maintains a secret bank account. Other situations involved secretly seeing a friend disliked by the spouse, shopping for clothes, and attending meetings of a support group for a drinking problem (the meetings are kept secret because a spouse does not want the other to attend).

The majority of the college undergraduates and adults in the study judged it acceptable for the wife to maintain a secret bank account. However, fewer judged it acceptable for a husband to engage in such deception even though it is the wife who works and controls the finances. It seems that the more general structure of power in society is taken into account in making these decisions. Men are accorded greater power and control over women, and family relationships are frequently based on the type of injustice that grants greater privileges and entitlements to men over women (Hochschild, 1989; Nussbaum, 1999, 2000; Okin, 1989). Similar patterns were found for situations that involved friendships and shopping, but the differences between judgments about the activities of husbands and wives were not statistically significant. In turn, almost all judged deception by a husband or wife as legitimate in the situation involving deception to attend meetings of a support group for a drinking problem.

Concerns with welfare, as well as fairness in relationships entailing power and control, are also involved in adolescents' judgments about deception of parents or friends. In another study (Perkins, 2003), judgments were assessed about three types of situations depicting an adolescent who deceives either parents or friends. One involved parents or peers telling an adolescent to act in ways that might be considered morally wrong (i.e., not to befriend another of a different race; to physically confront another who is teasing him or her); a second involved directives about issues of personal choice (not to date someone the parents or peers do not like and not to join a club because they think it is a waste of time); and the third type involved directives about personal issues with prudential or pragmatic considerations (completing homework and not riding a motorcycle).

Most of the adolescents judged that it is acceptable to deceive parents about the demands considered morally wrong (on the grounds of preventing injustice or harm). The majority also thought that deception was justified when parents interfered with personal choices. However, the majority thought that deception was not justified with regard to the prudential matters on the grounds that it is legitimate for parents to concern themselves with the welfare of their children (most thought the restrictions were not legitimate in the case of the moral and personal matters). Fewer adolescents judged deception of peers acceptable than deception of parents for the morally relevant and personal issues. Deception of peers regarding prudential issues was judged in about the same way as the personal issues, but as more acceptable in this realm than deception of parents. Although the adolescents thought that the restrictions directed by peers were not legitimate, they were less likely to accept deception of peers than of parents. It was thought that friends, who are in relationships of equality and mutuality, could confront each other about these matters without resorting to deception.

For these adolescents, honesty in social relationships is not a straightforward matter of believing that deception is wrong. However, they do not devalue honesty. Most said, in response to a general question, that lying is wrong; the large majority also thought that it is not justifiable to lie to parents or peers to cover up damage to property. As with the physicians, however, there are situations in which they believe that honesty needs to be subordinated to other considerations. Because of power differences, most of the adolescents believed it is necessary to deceive parents when they dictate actions that are unjust or when parents attempt to impose restrictions on what are regarded as activities that should be under personal jurisdiction.

Common patterns are, therefore, evident in the studies on deception. Judgments about deception vary by context among physicians in relation to insurance companies, among adolescents in relationships with parents or peers, and within marital relationships. Clearly, in some circumstances dishonesty is judged to be wrong by all these groups. Just as clearly, deception is judged right in some circumstances.

The findings from research on deception, therefore, show that people make flexible judgments about matters that they regard as morally important. Acting honestly is important to them because maintaining trust is judged a necessary moral goal. However, maintaining and promoting people's physical or emotional welfare and combating injustices are also important moral goals. The findings show that people do not, in mechanistic or emotionally blind ways, pursue any of these goals. They clearly recognize that conflicts between moral goals need to be addressed and somehow reconciled by creating priorities. The issue of honesty is not treated in an absolutistic fashion. Honesty is neither treated arbitrarily nor in a relativistic fashion. It is judged morally important, but in the context of other considerations.

A similar story can be told about research on concepts of rights. Maintaining personal rights is not an idea restricted to Western societies (see Helwig, chap. 7, this volume; Turiel, 2002; Turiel & Wainryb, 1998). Furthermore, in neither Western nor non-Western cultures is the concept of rights applied in an absolutistic way. Whereas rights are endorsed in the abstract and in some situations, in other situations they are subordinated to competing moral and social considerations (such as the welfare of persons and community interests). The evidence for these propositions regarding rights is even more extensive than for honesty; throughout the twentieth century a number of large-scale studies were conducted on attitudes toward rights (Hyman & Sheatsley, 1953; McClosky, 1964; McClosky & Brill, 1983; Stouffer, 1955). The surveys consistently found that most Americans endorse rights (e.g., to freedom of speech, religion, assembly, dissent, privacy) and that they also endorse the subordination of the same rights under some circumstances (e.g., to prevent physical and emotional harm, to promote fairness, and to maintain community standards). The details of much of this research are discussed by Helwig (chap. 7, this volume), who also discusses research on children's and adolescents' judgments about rights (see also

Turiel, Killen, & Helwig, 1987). The main purpose in raising this issue here is to show that strongly held moral goals, as with honesty, are judged flexibly and with recognition of contexts that embed other moral and social considerations. Again, the issues are not treated in absolute ways, rigidly, mechanistically; nor are they driven by emotions and unreflective intuitions.

CULTURE AND THOUGHT: IT IS NOT ALL HARMONIOUS

The issues of honesty and rights bear on another aspect of the structural–developmental approach: that people actively make judgments about welfare, justice, and rights that they apply to existing societal arrangements and cultural practices. As stressed, development is a constructive process stemming from children's interactions with multiple aspects of the social environment. Moral development does not involve accommodation to social expectations, rules, or norms, and moral functioning does not entail compliance with authority dictates, societal arrangements, or cultural practices. It would follow, therefore, that insofar as people perceive societal arrangements and cultural practices to foster injustices or unequally restrict the rights of certain groups, there would be opposition. That is, the approach outlined implies that individuals scrutinize and critique existing practices, which may well result in opposition and resistance (Turiel, 2003a; Turiel & Perkins, 2004). Conversely, widespread opposition and resistance to cultural practices indicate that moral development is a process of construction of judgments about what ought to exist rather than an acceptance of what exists socially or culturally.

The research on deception provides evidence for the idea that social opposition and resistance are prevalent in Western societies (for a discussion of deception as resistance in non-Western societies, see Turiel [2002]). The study with physicians (Freeman et al., 1999) shows that adults accept resistance of practices that are detrimental to the welfare of those (patients) for whom one is responsible (when serious harm can befall people, but not when serious consequences are not involved). The study that examined judgments about deception in marital relationships revealed that similar judgments in that deception on the part of a wife or husband is accepted when welfare is at stake (i.e., when a person seeks treatment for alcoholism). That study also showed that inequalities in power and control within a marriage are seen as legitimate reasons for resistance. The perceived inequalities are based not only on existing arrangements within marital relations, but also on existing power arrangements within the society.

Relations of power and control were also associated with adolescents' acceptance or rejection of deception as resistance of parents or peers (Perkins, 2003). We saw that there was acceptance of resistance to both parental commands to engage in acts considered morally wrong and acts considered, by adolescents, part of their personal jurisdiction. We also saw that such defiance is not across the board in that restrictions on prudential matters were accepted and in that relationships of equality (with peers) are judged differently from relationships involving power differences (with parents).

Opposition and resistance originate in childhood. Children's social development involves a combination of cooperative and oppositional orientations. Evidence of the origins of opposition and resistance in early childhood comes from studies showing that young children do not accept rules or authority dictates that are in contradiction with their judgments of what is morally right or wrong (Laupa, 1991; Laupa & Turiel, 1986; Weston & Turiel, 1980). Specifically, children judge that rules and authorities should not be followed insofar as they prescribe actions that are harmful to people or unfair. There is a coexistence of positive, prosocial actions and opposition to, and conflicts with, parents, siblings, and peers (Dunn, 1987, 1988; Dunn, Brown, & Maguire, 1995; Dunn & Munn, 1985, 1987; Dunn & Slomkowski, 1992). This combination reflects the multiple judgments that children develop. They make moral judgments producing acts of cooperation and helping. Children's moral judgments also produce acts of defiance or opposition when they perceive unfairness and harm inflicted on themselves or others (including the judgment that exclusion based on gender or race is unfair; see Killen, Lee-Kim, McGlothlin, & Stagnor, 2002). Children's developing judgments about the realm of personal jurisdiction also produce opposition insofar as there are infringements on what are considered legitimate personal choices (Nucci, 2001; Nucci & Turiel, 2000; Smetana, 1997).

These patterns of opposition and resistance are evident among adults in positions of lesser power in the social hierarchy in many cultures, including non-Western cultures where cultural practices sometimes serve to subjugate groups like those of lower social castes or classes and women. The dynamics of relationships between people in different positions on the social hierarchy further demonstrate there is flexibility of thought in reciprocal interactions. In non-Western societies that might, through public ideologies and religious doctrine, attempt to foster group or collective interdependence and downplay independence and individual autonomy, people nonetheless are committed to both individual and group goals (Mensing, 2002; Neff, 2001; Spiro, 1993; Wainryb & Turiel, 1994). Adolescents and adults in patriarchal societies recognize that greater individual autonomy is accorded to men and boys than to women and girls.

In turn, most women and girls do no simply accept practices granting greater autonomy to men; they judge such practices to be unfair (Wainryb & Turiel, 1994). Anthropological research with women and the poor in rural and urban communities in Egypt has shown that people act on their discontents and their judgments that cultural practices are unfair. In one of these studies (Abu-Lughod, 1993), observations were made and interviews conducted of Bedouin families in a small hamlet on the northwest coast of Egypt. Women in that patriarchal culture attempted to shape their own lives, opposed the decisions men made for them, and attempted to circumvent practices of various kinds that affected their lives. The women plotted and employed various strategies, including subterfuge, to engage in desired activities and circumvent cultural practices pertaining to, as examples, arranged marriages and polygamy.

The conflicts, struggles, and efforts at subverting cultural practices evident among the Bedouin women were also observed in urban Egyptian areas (Wikan, 1996). In the poor areas of Cairo, as well, women protest inequalities in their relationships with men and express unhappiness with practices like polygamy. As summarized by Wikan, "these lives I depict can be read as exercises in resistance against the state, against the family, against one's marriage, against the forces of tradition or change, against neighborhoods and society—even against oneself. But it is resistance that seems to follow a hidden agenda and to manage and endure in ways that respect the humanity of others" (1996, pp. 6–7; for additional examples of studies in India and Bangladesh, see Chen, 1995; Chowdry, 1994; and Mencher, 1989).

CONCLUSIONS

People approach moral matters with strong convictions and morality has a seemingly binding aspect to it. As a consequence, there is a pervasive tendency in both academic and public discourse to focus on one aspect of morality, especially in efforts to capture its binding quality. Psychological explanations often entail a form of "something makes us act in certain ways." There is a fairly long list: our genes makes us do it; our built-in intuitions make us do it; our conscience makes us do it; traits of character or acquired virtues make us do it; our internalized parental authority makes us do it; our internalized societal values/norms/rules make us do it; our identification with, and commitment to, cultural ways (fostering certain ideas, emotions, or intuitions) makes us do it. In some of these explanations, there is an explicit or implicit absolutism. Genes are fixed; conscience, traits of character, and virtues need to be unvarying. In other explanations, there is some degree of relativism. Different parents, societies, or cultural ways can result in different groups having to do it in different ways.

Sometimes we do focus on the variable aspects of morality. It is noted that people say one thing and sometimes do another, or that people act one way in some situations and another way in other situations. Psychological explanations focusing on that aspect of morality lead to the proposition that context or the situation makes us do it.

There is, indeed, a binding quality to people's morality. People do have strong feelings about their moral convictions and do go to great lengths to implement their moral views. Furthermore, a consistent finding in research conducted over many years in many places is that children, adolescents, and adults judge certain issues (having to do with harm, theft, and unfair treatment) to be wrong regardless of existing rules, authority dictates and expectations, or common practices. However, these judgments are not applied in rigid or absolutistic ways. The research has also consistently shown that people make distinctions between such moral issues and the conventional and customary. Even though conventions are judged to be important aspects of group functioning, they are conceptualized differently and seen as contingent upon rules, authority, and common practice. These types of distinctions among social norms exist because humans are reasoning beings. And because humans are reasoning beings, the idea that "X (fill in the favored one) makes us do it" fails to capture the essence of morality.

That humans are reasoning beings, with emotional commitments and flexibility of thought, accounts for the type of morality evidenced in the research discussed in this chapter. It accounts for the contextual variations in judgments about issues of honesty, rights, and harm. It also accounts for the social opposition, resistance, and acts of subversion so prevalent in the world. Moral functioning, as described in this chapter, with substantial research support, rests on core judgments about welfare, justice, and rights that are considered important and necessary. However, such judgments do not have the fixed or absolutistic quality inherent in notions of conscience, character, and virtue. People struggle with moral issues in social lives that are neither neat nor tidy. Social conditions often pose problems that require a great deal of emotional and conceptual work. For one thing, it is often the case that different aspects of moral considerations conflict. This is why honesty and rights, as examples, are not upheld across all situations. As we have seen, there can be conflicts between the need to maintain honesty and to promote people's welfare. Similarly, people's strong commitments to justice and rights pose difficult conflicts and choices insofar as there are injustices in one's world. The result is that social interactions entail as much social conflict and struggle as social harmony and cooperation.

A metaphor for morality more adequate than "X makes us do it" would be "morality is in the trenches." This is to say that moral development occurs through children's continual reciprocal relationships, in their everyday lives, with adults and other children. It also occurs in the context of dealing with events that include social problems, conflicts, and struggles. Social interactions are complex and multifaceted. Some of the time there is cooperation, harmony, helping and being helped, sharing, and good will. Some of the time there is conflict, disagreement, disputes, harming and being harmed, and experiences of unfair treatment. Morality is in the trenches in the sense that people experience societal arrangements, cultural practices, and material conditions that make them aware of inequalities and injustices. An awareness of inequalities and injustices, along with acts of opposition and resistance, are part of most people's everyday lives (Turiel, 2003a). Strong moral concerns and moral resistance are not solely the province of people with special personal characteristics or of those at highly advanced levels of development. Morality is important in most people's lives in ways that result in actions largely in line with their moral judgments and emotions (Turiel, 2003b).

It is, therefore, misleading to categorize people's morality as either absolute or relative, although there are ways it appear so. Morality appears absolute because issues of welfare, justice, and rights, as we have seen, are not judged as arbitrary, but as obligatory across settings. Morality appears relative because issues of welfare, justice, and rights, as we have seen, are not applied uniformly in all situations. These categories can impede our efforts at understanding and explaining morality and its development because they fail to account for how people think about and struggle with issues of right and wrong. Research examining the development of a multiplicity of judgments in relation to a heterogeneous social world has provided understandings of how people think about social relationships. It certainly seems to be the case that moral judgments of welfare, justice, and rights are similar across cultures. People conceptualize these matters in ways that lead them to draw priorities, apply them selectively in different contexts, and attempt to change societal arrangements and cultural practices that fail to meet moral ends.

REFERENCES

Abu-Lughod, L. (1991). Writing against culture. In R. E. Fox (Ed.), *Recapturing anthropology: Working in the present* (pp. 137–162). Santa Fe, New Mexico: School of American Research Press.

Abu-Lughod, L. (1993). *Writing women's worlds: Bedouin stories.* Berkeley: University of California Press.

Antipoff, H. (1928). Observations sur la compassion et le sens de la justice chez l'enfant. *Archives de Psychologie, XXI.*

Aronfreed, J. (1968). *Conduct and conscience: The socialization of internalized control over behavior.* New York: Academic Press.

Astor, R. (1994). Children's moral reasoning about family and peer violence: The role of provocation and retribution. *Child Development, 65,* 1054–1067.

Brandt, R. B. (1959). *Ethical theory: The problems of normative and critical ethics.* Englewood Cliffs, NJ: Prentice–Hall, Inc.

Chen, M. (1995). A matter of survival: Women's right to employment in India and Bangladesh. In M. C. Nussbaum & J. Glover (Eds.), *Women, culture, and development: A study of human capabilities* (pp. 61–75). New York: Oxford University Press.

Chowdry, P. (1994). *The veiled women: Shifting gender equations in rural Haryana 1880–1990.* Delhi: Oxford University Press.

Damasio, A. R. (1994). *Descartes' error: Emotion, reason, and the human brain.* New York: Harper Collins.

Damasio, A. R. (2003). *Looking for Spinoza: Joy, sorrow, and the feeling brain.* New York: Harcourt, Inc.

Dunn, J. (1987). The beginnings of moral understanding: Development in the second year. In J. Kagan & S. Lamb (Eds.), *The emergence of morality in young children* (pp. 91–112). Chicago, IL: University of Chicago Press.

Dunn, J. (1988). *The beginnings of social understanding.* Cambridge, MA: Harvard University Press.

Dunn, J., Brown, J. R., & Maguire, M. (1995). The development of children's moral sensibility: Individual differences and emotion understanding. *Developmental Psychology, 23,* 791–798.

Dunn, J., & Munn, P. (1985). Becoming a family member: Family conflict and the development of social understanding in the second year. *Child Development, 56,* 480–492.

Dunn, J., & Munn, P. (1987). Development of justification in disputes with mother and sibling. *Developmental Psychology, 23,* 791–798.

Dunn, J., & Slomkowski, C. (1992). Conflict and the development of social understanding. In C. U. Shantz & W. W. Hartup (Eds.), *Conflict in child and adolescent development* (pp. 70–92). Cambridge, England: Cambridge University Press.

Dworkin, R. (1977). *Taking rights seriously.* Cambridge, MA: Harvard University Press.

Eisenberg, N., & Fabes, R. (1998). Prosocial development. In W. Damon (Ed.), *Handbook of child psychology* (5th ed., Vol. 3): N. Eisenberg (Ed.), *Social, emotional, and personality development* (pp. 710–778). New York: Wiley.

Frankena, W. K. (1963). *Ethics.* Englewood Cliffs, NJ: Prentice-Hall, Inc.

Freeman, V. G., Rathore, S. S., Weinfurt, K. P., Schulman, K. A., & Sulmasy, D. P. (1999). Lying for patients: Physician deception of third-party payers. *Archives of Internal Medicine, 159,* 2263–2270.

Freud, S. (1923). *The ego and the id.* New York: Norton.

Freud, S. (1930). *Civilization and its discontents.* New York: Norton.

Gewirth, A. (1982). *Human rights: Essays on justification and applications.* Chicago: University of Chicago Press.

Habermas, J. (1993). *Justification and application.* Cambridge, MA: MIT Press.

Haidt, J. (2001). The emotional dog and its rational tail: A social intuitinist approach to moral judgment. *Psychological Review, 108,* 814–834.

Hochschild, A. (1989). *The second shift.* New York: Avon Books.

Hoffman, M. L. (1970). Moral development. In P. H. Mussen (Ed.), *Carmichael's manual of child psychology* (Vol. 2, pp. 261–359). New York: Wiley.

Hoffman, M. L. (1984). Empathy, its limitations, and its role in a comprehensive moral theory. In J. L. Gewirtz & W. M. Kurtines (Eds.), *Morality, moral development, and moral behavior* (pp. 283–302). New York: Wiley.

Hoffman, M. L. (2000). *Empathy and moral development: Implications for caring and justice.* Cambridge, England: Cambridge University Press.

Hyman, H. H., & Sheatsley, P. B. (1953). Trends in public opinion on civil liberties. *Journal of Social Issues, 9,* 6–16.

Killen, M., Lee-Kim, J., McGlothlin, H., & Stangor, C. (2002). How children and adolescents evaluate gender and racial exclusion. *Monographs for the Society for Research in Child Development.* Serial No. 271, Vol. 67, No. 4. Oxford, England: Blackwell Publishers.

Kohlberg, L. (1963). The development of children's orientations toward a moral order: 1. Sequence in the development of moral thought. *Vita Humana, 6,* 11–33.

Kohlberg, L. (1968). The child as a moral philosopher. *Psychology Today, 2,* 25–30.

Kohlberg, L. (1969). Stage and sequence: The cognitive-developmental approach to socialization. In D. Goslin (Ed.), *Handbook of socialization theory and research* (pp. 347–480). Chicago: Rand McNally.

Kohlberg, L. (1971). From is to ought: How to commit the naturalistic fallacy and get away with it in the study of moral development. In T. Mischel (Ed.), *Psychology and genetic epistemology* (pp. 151–235). New York: Academic Press.

Kohlberg, L. (1984). *Essays on moral development: The psychology of moral development.* San Francisco: Harper & Row.

Laupa, M. (1991). Children's reasoning about three authority attributes: Adult status, knowledge, and social position. *Developmental Psychology, 27,* 321–329.

Laupa, M., & Turiel, E. (1986). Children's conceptions of adult and peer authority. *Child Development, 57,* 405–412.

Markus, H. R., & Kitayama, S. (1991). Culture and the self: Implications for cognition, emotion, and motivation. *Psychological Review, 98,* 224–253.

McClosky, H. (1964). Consensus and ideology in American politics. *American Political Science Review, 58,* 361–382.

McClosky, M., & Brill, A. (1983). *Dimensions of tolerance: What Americans believe about civil liberties.* New York: Russell Sage.

Mencher, J. P. (1989). Women agricultural labourers and landowners in Kerala and Tamil Nadu: Some questions about gender and autonomy in the household. In M. Krishnaraj & K. Chanana (Eds.), *Gender and the household domain: Social and cultural dimensions* (pp. 117–141). London: Sage Publications.

Mensing, J. F. (2002). Collectivism, individualism, and interpersonal responsibilities in families: Differences and similarities in social reasoning between individuals in poor, urban families in Colombia and the United States. Unpublished doctoral dissertation, University of California, Berkeley.

Milgram, S. (1974). *Obedience to authority.* New York: Harper & Row.

Neff, K. D. (2001). Judgments of personal autonomy and interpersonal responsibility in the context of Indian spousal relationships: An examination of young people's reasoning in Mysore, India. *British Journal of Developmental Psychology, 19,* 233–257.

Nucci, L. P. (2001). *Education in the moral domain.* Cambridge, England: Cambridge University Press.

Nucci, L. P., & Nucci, M. S. (1982a). Children's reponses to moral and social conventional transgressions in free-play settings. *Child Development, 53,* 1337–1342.

Nucci, L. P., & Nucci, M. S. (1982b). Children's social interactions in the context of moral and conventional transgressions. *Child Development, 53,* 403–412.

Nucci, L. P., & Turiel, E. (1978). Social interactions and the development of social concepts in preschool children. *Child Development, 49,* 400–407.

Nucci, L. P., & Turiel, E. (2000). The moral and the personal: Sources of social conflicts. In L. P. Nucci, G. Saxe, & E. Turiel (Eds.), *Culture, thought, and development* (pp. 115–137). Mahwah, NJ: Erlbaum.

Nucci, L. P., Turiel, E., & Encarnacion-Gawrych, G. (1983). Children's social interactions and social concepts: Analyses of morality and convention in the Virgin Islands. *Journal of Cross-Cultural Psychology, 14,* 469–487.

Nucci, L. P., & Weber, E. (1995). Social interactions in the home and the development of young children's conceptions of the personal. *Child Development, 66,* 1438–1452.

Nussbaum, M. C. (1995). Human capabilities, female human beings. In M. C. Nussbaum & J. Glover (Eds.), *Women, culture, and development: A study of human capabilities* (pp. 61–104). New York: Oxford University Press.

Nussbaum, M. C. (1999). *Sex and social justice.* New York: Oxford University Press.

Nussbaum, M. C. (2000). *Women and human development: The capabilities approach.* Cambridge, England: Cambridge University Press.

Okin, S. M. (1989). *Justice, gender, and the family.* New York: Basic Books.

Perkins, S. A. (2003). Adolescent reasoning about lying in close relationships. Unpublished doctoral dissertation. University of California, Berkeley.

Piaget, J. (1932). *The moral judgment of the child.* London: Routledge and Kegan Paul.

Piaget, J. (1951/1995). Egocentric thought and sociocentric thought. In J. Piaget, *Sociological studies* (pp. 270–286). London: Routledge.

Piaget, J. (1960/1995). Problems of the social psychology of childhood. In J. Piaget, *Sociological studies* (pp. 287–318). London: Routledge.

Rawls, J. (1971). *A theory of justice.* Cambridge, MA: Harvard University Press.

Shantz, C. U., & Hartup, W. W. (1992). Conflict and development: An introduction. In C. U. Shantz & W. W. Hartup (Eds.), *Conflict in child and adolescent development* (pp. 1–35). Cambridge, England: Cambridge University Press.

Shweder, R. A., Much, N. C., Mahapatra, M., & Park, L. (1997). The "Big Three" of morality (Autonomy, Community, and Divinity) and the "Big Three" explanations of suffering. In A. Brandt & P. Rozin (Eds.), *Morality and health* (pp. 119–169). New York: Routledge.

Skinner, B. F. (1971). *Beyond freedom and dignity.* New York: Knopf.

Smetana, J. G. (1982). *Concepts of self and morality: Women's reasoning about abortion.* New York: Praeger.

Smetana, J. G. (1995). Morality in context: Abstractions, ambiguities, and applications. In R. Vasta (Ed.), *Annals of Child Development, Vol. 10* (pp. 83–130). London: Jessica Kingsley Publishers.

Smetana, J. G. (1997). Parenting and the development of social knowledge reconceptualized: A social domain analysis. In J. E. Grusec & L. Kuczynski (Eds.), *Parenting and children's internalization of values* (pp. 162–192). New York: Wiley.

Spiro, M. (1993). Is the Western conception of the self "peculiar" within the context of the world cultures? *Ethos, 21,* 107–153.

Stouffer, S. (1955). *Communism, conformity and civil liberties.* New York: Doubleday.

Tisak, M. S. (1995). Domains of social reasoning and beyond. In R. Vista (Ed.), *Annals of Child Development, Vol. 11* (pp. 95–130). London: Jessica Kingsley Publishers.

Turiel, E. (1975). The development of social concepts: Mores, customs, and conventions. In J. M. Foley & D. J. DePalma (Eds.), *Moral development: Current theory and research* (pp. 7–38). Hillsdale, NJ: Lawrence Erlbaum Associates.

Turiel, E. (1978). The development of concepts of social structure: Social-convention. In J. Glick & A. Clarke-Stewart (Eds.), *The development of social understanding* (pp. 25–107). New York: Gardner Press.

Turiel, E. (1979). Distinct conceptual and developmental domains: Social-convention and morality. In H. E. Howe & C. B. Keasey (Eds.), *Social Cognitive Development. Nebraska Symposium on Motivation, 1977, Vol. 25. Social cognitive development* (pp. 77–116). Lincoln: University of Nebraska Press.

Turiel, E. (1983a). Domains and categories in social-cognitive development. In W. Overton (Ed.), *The relationship between social and cognitive development* (pp. 53–89). Hillsdale, NJ: Erlbaum Associates.

Turiel, E. (1983b). *The development of social knowledge: Morality and convention.* Cambridge, England: Cambridge University Press.

Turiel, E. (1998). The development of morality. In W. Damon (Ed.), *Handbook of child psychology* (5th ed., Volume 3): N. Eisenberg (Ed.). *Social, emotional, and personality development* (pp. 863–932). New York: Wiley.

Turiel, E. (2002). *The culture of morality: Social development, context, and conflict.* Cambridge, England: Cambridge University Press.

Turiel, E. (2003a). Resistance and subversion in everyday life. *Journal of Moral Education, 32,* 115–130.

Turiel, E. (2003b). Morals, motives, and actions. *British Journal of Educational Psychology, Monograph Series II: Psychological Aspects of Education—Current Trends, No. 2.* L. Smith, C. Rogers, & P. Tomlinson (Eds.). *Development and motivation: Joint Perspectives* (pp. 29–40). Leicester, England: The British Psychological Society.

Turiel, E., Hildebrandt, C., & Wainryb, C. (1991). Judging social issues: Difficulties, inconsistencies and consistencies. *Monographs of the Society for Research in Child Development, 56* (Serial No. 224).

Turiel, E., Killen, M., & Helwig, C. C. (1987). Morality: Its structure, functions and vagaries. In J. Kagan & S. Lamb (Eds.), *The emergence of moral concepts in young children* (pp. 155–244). Chicago: University of Chicago Press.

Turiel, E., & Perkins, S. A. (2004). Flexibilities of mind: Conflict and culture. *Human Development, 47,* 158–178.

Turiel, E., Perkins, S. A., & Mensing, J. F. (in preparation). Judgments about deception in marital relationships. University of California, Berkeley.

Turiel, E., & Smetana, J. G. (1998). Limiting the limits on domains: Comments on Fowler and heteronomy. *Merrill-Palmer Quarterly, 44,* 293–312.

Turiel, E., & Wainryb, C. (1998). Concepts of freedoms and rights in a traditional hierarchically organized society. *British Journal of Developmental Psychology. 16,* 375–395.

Wainryb, C. (1991). Understanding differences in moral judgments: The role of informational assumptions. *Child Development, 62,* 840–851.

Wainryb, C., & Turiel, E. (1994). Dominance, subordination, and concepts of personal entitlements in cultural contexts. *Child Development, 65,* 1701–1722.

Weston, D. R., & Turiel, E. (1980). Act-rule relations: Children's concepts of social rules. *Developmental Psychology, 16,* 417–424.

Wikan, U. (1991). Toward an experience-near anthropology. *Cultural Anthropology, 6,* 285–305.

Wikan, U. (1996). *Tomorrow, God willing: Self-made destinies in Cairo.* Chicago: University of Chicago Press.

Wikan, U. (2002). *Generous betrayal: Politics of culture in the new Europe.* Chicago: University of Chicago Press.

Wynia, M. K., Cummins, D. S., VanGeest, J. B., & Wilson, I. B. (2000). Physician manipulation of reimbursement rules for patients: Between a rock and a hard place. *Journal of the American Medical Association, 283,* 1858–1865.

2

MORAL STAGE THEORY

DANIEL K. LAPSLEY
BALL STATE UNIVERSITY

The history of science will record the latter decades of the twentieth century as the apotheosis of the cognitive–developmental tradition in developmental psychology. This tradition has its obvious source in Piaget's genetic epistemology and in his remarkable research program on the ontogenesis of children's logicomathematical and scientific reasoning. But the extension of the tradition's influence to matters of socialization, and to domains of social cognitive development, owe as much to the work of Lawrence Kohlberg and his colleagues. Piaget (1932/1965) did, of course, pioneer the study of moral judgement in children, yet it was Kohlberg's work that galvanized a whole generation of scholars to pursue the developmental features of moral reasoning in its several sociomoral manifestations, and to explore the implications of sociomoral development for educational (e.g., Power, Higgins, & Kohlberg, 1989) and clinical (e.g., Selman, 1980) practice.

Indeed, no developmental psychologist trained in the 1970s and 1980s could safely enter the professional guild without close study of two seminal papers, "Stage and Sequence" (Kohlberg, 1969) and "From Is to Ought" (Kohlberg, 1971). These chapters are the twin pillars on which rest the theoretical aspirations of the cognitive–developmental approach to morality and socialization. Here Kohlberg attempted to show not only that the cognitive–developmental approach was a progressive problem shift over rival accounts (maturationism, associationism, psychoanalysis) of socialization, but that the "doctrine of cognitive stages" (Kohlberg, 1969, p. 352) could also provide the resources to resolve fundamental problems in ethical theory, such as the problem of ethical relativism and how to defeat it. The scope of the doctrine—its range of application and sheer audacity— defined the problematic of its time and established the terms of debate over fundamental developmental questions that still resonate today, if only in vestigial forms.

And yet to speak of an apotheosis that is now past, and of an era in moral psychology that is post-Kohlberg, is to suggest that something has happened to the status of moral stage theory. Indeed, the claim that moral psychology is at an important crossroad is now being voiced with increasing frequency (e.g., Lapsley & Narvaez, 2005). One senses, given the slight and perfunctory treatment of moral stage theory in contemporary textbooks, and its relative obscurity at professional meetings, that the topic is more a matter of faint historical interest than a source of animated research activity on the cutting edge of developmental science.

Certainly part of the story of the declining influence of Kohlberg's moral stage theory can be traced to the general decline of Piaget's approach in developmental psychology. The influence of Kohlberg's theory has always been inextricably linked to the prestige and authority of the Piagetian paradigm. When Kohlberg talked about stage and sequence, invoked the doctrine of cognitive stages, and articulated the cognitive–developmental position on matters of socialization and education, it was with Piaget's armamentarium of conceptual tools that he staked his claims. Moreover, there is the intimation that Kohlberg's moral stage theory was the completion of Piaget's own intentions in the moral domain were Piaget not to put aside this work for other topics, which is to say that Kohlberg found the "hard" moral stages that somehow eluded Piaget (1932/1965) in his preliminary study of children's moral judgment. Kohlberg's reliance on Piaget's theory to give sense and direction to his project also meant, however, as Piaget's theory waned in influence, or was eclipsed by alternative conceptualizations of intellectual development, that Kohlberg's theory became deprived of much of its paradigmatic support.

Yet lack of paradigmatic support is not the only explanation for the current reduced status of moral stage theory (and, indeed, only shifts the argument to why Piaget's theory has drifted from view; see Lourenço & Machado, 1996). Factors internal to Kohlberg's theory, including its empirical warrant, and doubts about how to understand fundamental concepts, such as stage and structure, also must be part of the story.

This chapter describes the development of moral stage theory as it emerged within the cognitive–developmental tradition. Although the initial focus is largely on the work of Piaget and Kohlberg, as the principle architects of the cognitive developmental tradition, it would be a mistake to limit the consideration of moral stage theory to these pioneers. Indeed, a number of additional sociomoral stage progressions emerged within this tradition describing, for example, distributive justice and prosocial reasoning, along with other stage sequences that have implications for sociomoral judgment, including perspective taking, self-understanding, and interpersonal understanding. The consideration of these stages highlight issues critical to understanding social cognitive–development and the diversity of ways that stage theory has been used to describe it. Some observations about the contours of the next generation of research in moral psychology are also offered.

PIAGET'S THEORY

The Cognitive–Developmental Project

Piaget's life's work was an attempt to resolve fundamental problems of epistemology by appealing to the empirical record of how children reason about logical, mathematical, and scientific concepts. Similarly, Kohlberg hoped to undermine the claims for ethical relativism by examining how individuals construct moral meaning when faced with moral dilemmas. Their worked showed that reasoning about scientific and ethical concepts conform to systematic ontogenetic variation that can be characterized as *stages*. If one is to discern criteria for judging progress in science and philosophy (Piaget), or for deciding when some moralities are inadequate or unworthy of us (Kohlberg), then the data of child development would have to matter. Of course, the stage concept had to be of a certain kind to pull this off. The naturalizing approach to ethics and epistemology required that the concept of stage be fortified with certain stringent criteria that governed when it could be used legitimately to perform the task put to it. These criteria prove less important for developmental researchers who are not as interested in resolving philosophical questions with empirical data.

Three Key Concepts

Structured Wholes.   The stage concept in the cognitive–developmental tradition is inextricably linked to notions of structure and organization. Piaget's view of structure and organization was heavily influenced by his biological approach to intelligence. In every organized totality, at every level of reality, from the organization of biological and psychological systems to the workings of sociological entities (families, society), there exists a relationship between the structured whole (*structure d'ensemble*) and its constituent parts. Hence, part–whole relationships are evident in logic (between concepts and instances of the concept); in science generally (between facts and theory); in biology (between cells and the whole organism, or between a species type and instances of a species); in psychology (between cognitive operations and the structure of cognition); in sociology (between individuals and society); and in family life (between children and the parental and family system).

But the part–whole relationship is not, however, a static feature of organized totalities. Indeed, part–whole relationships are unstable, resulting in imperfect forms of equilibrium. For example, sometimes the whole predominates over the parts (*syncretism*), and sometimes the parts predominate over the whole (*juxtaposition*). Yet unstable equilibria are capable of transforming and evolving into more stable forms. The basic relationship between parts and the whole is transformative. It is the relationship between parts and the whole that is of primary importance. What is a structured totality at one stage becomes an element or part in a new configuration at a succeeding stage, a transformation that moves the structured totality from a less stable and imperfect equilibrium between parts and whole to an equilibrium that is more stable and more agile in its adaptive operations.

Two implications should be emphasized. One is that the boundary between structure and elements, between whole and parts, is a developmental construction. Hence different structural organization cannot be understood apart from the constructive, transformative operations that generate them (Broughton, 1981). A second implication is that the relationship between parts and whole is an evolving equilibrium that tends toward ideal forms that are perfected, stable, and adaptive. In its ideal form, the part–whole configuration is conserved in a dynamic system of perfect compensations that makes successful adaptation possible across a wide range of perturbations. Once more, examples abound at multiple levels of reality. The relationship between organisms (part) and the species (whole) can be described as an evolving equilibrium that tends toward perfected adaptation. In psychology, cognitive operations are organized into *structures d'ensemble* that are increasingly stable with development. In society, an ideal equilibrium between individuals (parts) and society (whole) is characterized by the operations of justice and morality.

An Evaluative Criterion.   The tendency of organized totalities to develop in the direction of increasing structural adequacy and more perfected modes of operation provided Piaget with an epistemological criterion by which to make evaluative judgments: Structured totalities that come later are better than earlier forms if the later form is a product of development. To say that something has developed is to say that its mode of operation is better, because it is more stable, more powerful, and more capable of complex adaptations. Hence, development has an internal standard of adequacy. The developmental process transforms part–whole relations in the direction of increasing articulation and differentiation (Werner, 1957) bringing the transformed *structure d'ensemble* into closer approximation to an ideal equilibrium. Structural organizations that approach the ideal equilibrium are judged more adequate than are organizations that are far from ideal. The developmental criterion of adequacy, then, distinguishes temporally early modes of operation that are unstable and less adaptive from later operations that are enduring, perfected, and adaptive.

Note that statements about development always make two claims. To say that the goal of development is to attain a particular endpoint, say, the endpoint at which a structured totality reaches its perfected mode of operation, its ideal equilibrium, is to make not only an empirical claim about the natural course of development, but also an evaluative or normative claim. One is making implicit reference to a standard that allows one to distinguish progressive development from mere change, and the standard is instantiated in one's conceptualization of the endpoint. Developmental change, if it is to count as an instance of development, is evaluated in terms of how closely it approximates the ideal equilibrium represented by the final stage of the developmental process (Kitchener, 1983). "Thus, the developmental end-state is a normative standard of reference by means of which we can evaluate the direction of development and its degree of progress towards this goal" (Kitchener, 1986, p. 29).

Note, too, that one cannot help conflating empirical claims about what is the case in the natural course of development from value-laden claims about what counts as good development. Our understanding of the end-state of development functions as a touchstone for evaluating progress in the evolution of structured totalities. To make a claim about development is to say that a structured totality has progressed to a more desirable and better mode of operation. It is good and better for *structures d'ensemble* to be adaptive rather than nonadaptive; to be ideal rather than partial; to be enduring rather than temporary; to be stable rather than unstable. In this way, factual–empirical (what is the case) and evaluative–normative (what is good or ought to be the case) issues are always mutually implicated in developmental studies. Kohlberg (1971, 1973a) made use of these claims to assert that later occurring moral stages are better than developmentally prior stages on both psychological (factual–empirical) and ethical (evaluative–normative) grounds, and that the study of moral development necessarily entails mixing factual (*is*) and normative (*ought*) claims, a position that has been denounced as the *naturalistic fallacy* in ethical theory.

Genetic Epistemology.   Piaget's developmental criterion was also crucial to his genetic epistemology, which was an attempt to "explain knowledge on the basis of its history, its sociogenesis and especially the psychological origins of the notions and operations on which it is based" (Piaget, 1970, p. 1). It attempts, in other words, to discover the developmental origins of knowledge to sustain rational claims as to why one system of philosophy, or one branch of logic, or one scientific theory, should be preferred over another. In Piaget's view, there is a complementary relationship between the psychological formation of knowledge as it might occur during the course of child development and the formation of knowledge as it might occur in the history of science. The very criteria that one uses to ascertain progressive change in cognitive development could also be applied, in turn, to explain progressive change in metaphysics, logic, and science. What counts as growth and progress in the developmental history of children's understanding of reality could also serve as criteria for what is to count as growth and progress in the historical development of the sciences. In this way, epistemological questions about the adequacy of knowledge claims, about the comparability of theoretical systems and the possibility of progress and growth, are turned into psychological questions about children's cognitive development (where *cognitive development* is understood biologically, in terms of structure, equilibrium, and adaptation). In this way, epistemology is naturalized by biologically informed studies of intellectual development.

In his seminal early studies, for example, Piaget showed that children's understanding of reality begins in an egocentric confusion of subjective and objective, but ends with a more scientific understanding of physical objects and causal events. But these developmental facts also bear on the theory of knowledge. Indeed, Piaget argued that two epistemological options are undermined by these stage progressions. The *empiricist* option suggests that children acquire their notions of reality as a result of environmental influence. Children are molded by their context from the outside in. One imagines Bacon's naked facts of nature impressed on Locke's tabula rasa. Yet the empiricist option is refuted by the fact that children assimilate objective facts to their own subjective schemes. As Chapman put it, "If all knowledge were directly impressed on children's minds by the external world, then their initial conception of reality would not be intermingled with subjective elements" (1988, p. 56).

A second option suggests that individuals make sense of the world because of preexisting schemas. In the manner of Kant, there exist a priori categories of the mind that structure our experience of the world. As a result sensibility is imposed on the world from the inside out. But a priorism cannot account for the fact that children's conception of reality develops. Surely children assimilate objective reality to subjective schemes, but schemas also change as a result of experience and, indeed, come to reflect completely accurate conceptions of reality.

From Piaget's perspective, then, both empiricism and a priorism are inadequate epistemological options. Empiricism is confounded by evidence of assimilation, a priorism by evidence of imitation and accommodation. In terms of Piaget's developmental criterion both options are examples of partial equilibria, of unstable part–whole configurations. A priorism is an example of syncretism, where the whole predominates over the parts—that is, where one's ideology, one's subjective preferences, one's world view, theory or perspective, deforms reality in acts of cognitive assimilation. In turn, empiricism is an example of juxtaposition, where the parts predominate over the whole. The pattern is missed but for isolated perceptions, impressions, and facts that are not coordinated. We are deceived by whatever isolated fact momentarily dominates our perceptions (what Piaget called *phenomenalism*). The challenge for the theory of knowledge is to develop alternative positions that coordinate these partial and unstable options in ways that approach an ideal equilibrium.

Piaget's naturalized approach to the theory of knowledge held an obvious appeal for Kohlberg. In the way that Piaget appealed to developmental criteria to dispense with unstable and inadequate epistemological positions (a priorism, empiricism), so too did Kohlberg press developmental claims against inadequate psychological positions (maturationism, associationism). For example, because a priorism is false, one cannot claim that moral structures are innate categories. They are not Kantian forms into which specific experiences are molded (or else how to account for their developmental transformation?). Moreover, because empiricism is false, one cannot account for moral structures by appealing to direct adult instruction, specific parings of objects and responses, or to reinforcement history, because this sort of learning is merely assimilated to children's moral structures but cannot change them (Kohlberg, 1969, 1987).

But, more importantly, Kohlberg could use Piaget's developmental criterion to show why some forms of moral reasoning are to be preferred and some rejected. Kohlberg could now take on the ethical relativist who asserts that no such criterion is possible and that moral perspectives are incommensurable. Indeed, one can view movement through Kohlberg's stages as the dawning awareness that some moral perspectives are errant and inadequate, that others are preferred, and that there is a way to know the difference. It is the growing realization, as one approaches the moral ideal, as one closes in on the final stage, that moral dilemmas are not insolvable, that moral conflict is not intractable, and that consensus is possible if disputants are motivated by the moral point of view.

Piaget's Moral Judgment of the Child

As a genetic epistemologist, Piaget (1932/1965) was interested in how children come to understand and respect moral rules, and whether these developmental facts can help us to understand the form and transformation of ethical codes in society. One standard view is that children are socialized into morality by the exertion of parents and authorities—a folk theory of parenting that favors empiricism. Children are raised, brought up, or socialized by others. It is something that happens to children from the outside in. So, under this view children become morally socialized when they are suitably constrained by the greater power of adults. Children become morally socialized when they accept the discipline and authority of the group, when they come to respect its rules and fear its sanctions. Moral socialization is a matter of one generation imposing its will on the next.

Piaget (1932/1965) argued, however, that this view of moral socialization was partial and one sided (just as empiricism is partial and one sided). This view of socialization does not allow for reciprocity and coordination of parts and wholes, and hence is an unstable equilibrium. Although he did not deny that moral socialization inevitably begins with children accepting the authority of adults, he also claimed that moral socialization does not end there; children eventually engage in new forms of social relationships that are reciprocal and equal, where relationships are balanced and in stable equilibrium, and where rules take on new meaning. In the context of peers, for example, one constructs ideas about fairness, justice, and moral responsibility, and about the function of rules in social life, that are at once different and developmentally advanced over the sort of moral understandings coerced by the huff and puff of adult authority.

Hence, the sense of moral obligation has two sources, each derived from a particular form of social relationship, and one is better than the other. The heteronomous orientation emerges within the context of adult–child relationships, and yields a morality of constraint that confirms and sustains childish egocentrism and moral realism. The autonomous orientation emerges within a peer society of equals, and yields a morality of cooperation that makes possible a more equilibrated understanding of justice.

Heteronomy.   In the *heteronomous stage*, the young child has unilateral respect for the power and magnificence of adults and is thereby constrained. The inherent inequality of this relationship requires children to subordinate their interests to the perspective of adults (syncretism), but this results in a cluster of moral notions that reveal the tendency of young children to subordinate the social interest to their own subjective point of view (juxtaposition). Put differently, the more completely a child's interest is subordinated to the often opaque and inscrutable perspective of adults, the more completely does the child subordinate adult strictures to her or his idiosyncratic point of view. The more a child feels the grip of adult constraint (syncretism), the more likely is her or his moral thinking to be infused with subjectivity, egocentrism, and realism (juxtaposition).

The heteronomous stage, then, is a partial and unstable equilibrium, characterized by syncretism and juxtaposition, and a lack of reciprocity between parts (children) and whole (parents). On the one hand parents constrain children by their greater social power, yielding a moral perspective that, for the child, reduces moral duty to obedience. And yet, on the other hand, childish cognitive notions persist that subordinate adult interests to a personal and subjective point of view. It encourages, for example, moral realism and a belief that justice is immanent in the workings of nature. It identifies fairness with egocentric desires ("sharing is fair if I get more"). It judges moral culpability by objective consequences rather than by intentions, and by physicalistic criteria (e.g., saying that a dog is as big as a cow is a more grievous "lie" than is fibbing about the marks one gets in school).

Hence the child submits to moral rules out of deference to adult constraint, and yet does not understand them. Rules are binding but do not constrain. The child intends to conform as moral duty requires but for subjective adherences, deforming assimilations and egocentrism. As Piaget put it, "The child is, on the one hand, too apt to have the illusion of agreement when actually he is only following his own fantasy; the adult, on the other, takes advantage of the situation instead of seeking 'equality'" (1932/1965, pp. 61–62). In this way does constraint act as an ally of egocentrism (and equality as its adversary).

This illusion of agreement is evident in Piaget's analysis of children's practice and understanding of the rules to the game of marbles. Young children are aware that marbles is played according to a set of rules and that these rules are inviolable, unchanging, and sacred, insofar as they have been handed down by Noah, by God, the elders, or some other external authority. But in practice children assimilate these inviolable rules to subjective schemes, resulting in idiosyncratic play that is uncoordinated with playmates. So, there is only the illusion of agreement with rules. Children feel the constraint of rules but rules do not govern conduct. Rules are sacred and unchanging, but play is idiosyncratic and variable, assimilated to individual schemes. Later, in the morality of cooperation, children come to see that rules are flexible, cooperative arrangements that have their source in mutual consent (rather than external authority) and serve the cause of solidarity (rather than the interests of constraint).

Autonomy. In contrast to heteronomy, then, the morality of cooperation emerges within a context of peer solidarity among equals. Notions of equality and mutual respect drive it. In the society of equals one must negotiate, settle conflicts, win over friends with reason, and otherwise sort out the benefits and burdens of cooperation in ways that are judged fair and equitable (Rest, 1983). In social relationships marked by equality there emerges a sense of moral obligation that warrants cooperation and reciprocity. Indeed, peer relations are a more perfect social equilibrium, and moral notions forged in the heat of mutual respect are hence more rational than the moral realism and heteronomy of the previous stage.

For Piaget, rational development is movement away from external imposition of inviolable injunctions, sacred laws, or the strictures of elders or of tradition, away from heteronomy and unilateral respect, to autonomy, mutual respect, and democratic cooperation. And this holds not just in ontogenesis but in political development as well. That is, rational development in the organization of societies is movement away from unstable equilibrium to more stable forms, away from the syncretism and unilateral respect of theocracy and gerontocracy to the mutual respect and reciprocity of political democracy. Rationality in political governance is the moral judgment of the child writ large.

The Empirical Warrant

Piaget's moral stage theory was the center of contention among three clashing psychological paradigms. Researchers in the cognitive–developmental tradition undertook studies to document the stage properties of the theory. Social learning theorists wanted to show that performance on Piaget's tasks revealed not the progressive articulation of cognitive structures but rather the "laws of learning" governing reinforcement, imitation, and modeling. Information-processing researchers wanted to show that moral judgment is better explained by the mechanisms of encoding and memory retrieval. Each camp could claim its share of vindication.

The cognitive–developmental literature, for its part, showed that the various features of moral judgment investigated by Piaget (1932/1965) did not coalesce into tightly knit stages. This is a lethal finding only if one insists on a strong reading of what *structures d'ensemble* entail. Piaget (1932/1965) did not seem to have a strong reading in mind. "There are," he writes, "no inclusive stages which define the whole of a subject's mental life at a given point in his evolution" (Piaget, 1932/1965, p. 85). Indeed, Piaget's findings pointed to significant stage overlap in children's responses. In his studies of children's understanding of the rules of the game, Piaget concluded "the mixture of elements is a further bar to our arranging these phenomena in a strict sequence" (p. 86).

Moreover, he complained that too much emphasis is placed on the expectation of discontinuity in moral judgment. "Let it be understood once and for all," he writes, "that any over-sharp discontinuities are analytical devices and not objective results" (Piaget, 1932/1965, p. 87). In later investigations of adult constraint and moral realism, he could not point to any stages "properly so called which followed one another in a necessary order" although there were processes evident that represented "the broad divisions of moral development" (p. 175). And in numerous places throughout the book Piaget noted that the results of his investigation might turn out quite differently if conducted among children with a different socio-economic background or different educational or religious upbringing than the "children from the poorer parts of Geneva" (p. 46) that were his subjects.

Subsequent research tended to support Piaget's developmental account of moral judgment, at least in broad outline. Indeed, Lickona suggested that the verdict of a generation of research is that more research is not needed and that Piaget's intuition "is probably sound" (1976, p. 239). A number of studies showed, for example, that young children do seem to believe in immanent justice, and that this belief attenuates with age, a developmental phenomena that is "real and robust" (Jose, 1991, p. 611). Moral judgment is improved with advances in perspective-taking (DeRemer & Gruen, 1979) and peer group participation (Brody & Shaffer, 1982; Enright & Sutterfield, 1980). The claim that children gradually come to understand intentions and to forsake objective responsibility when judging moral culpability is "the best documented of all of Piaget's moral judgment dimensions" (Lickona, 1976, p. 224).

Other aspects of Piaget's moral stage theory have not fared as well. The moral realism characteristic of the heteronomous stage is supposed to lead children to (a) define moral duty in terms of obedience to authority; (b) view rules as immutable and unchangeable insofar as they are invested with the prestige of adult authority; and (c) call for punishment the violation of any rule. There are empirical reasons to doubt each of these features of moral realism (Killen, 1991; Turiel, 1983). Children appear to make differentiated judgments about the legitimacy of punishment (Smetana, 1981, 1983) and parental injunctions (Tisak, 1986) depending on whether the rule concerns moral or social conventional violations. Moreover, children do not view rules as sacred and immutable, nor do they regard everything that the adult commands as moral (Weston & Turiel, 1980). Children are sensitive to the distinction between moral and conventional rules from an early age (Smetana, 1983), and their judgment about obligation, legitimacy, and punishment depend on the nature of the social events in question. Indeed, Turiel (1983) argued that Piaget's moral judgment research got off on the wrong foot by studying children's understanding of the rules to the game of marbles, which by its very nature involves considerations of social convention and not of morality.

Social learning research appeared to show that children's moral orientation could be influenced by exposure to live (Bandura, 1991; Bandura & McDonald, 1963; Cowan, Langer, Heavenrich, & Nathanson, 1969) and even narrated (Walker & Richards, 1976) models. In the Bandura and McDonald (1963) studies, for example, children changed their judgments about moral culpability in the direction modeled by adults. The fact that children's moral judgment could be readily modified through adult modeling cues was thought to undermine Piaget's "demarcated sequential stages of moral development" (Bandura & McDonald, 1963, p. 280), a conclusion that Turiel (1966) contested.

Finally, the information-processing paradigm generated a voluminous literature attempting to show that children's performance on the various dimensions of moral judgment can be explained in terms of how children come to encode, store, process, and retrieve information, rather than by the Piagetian notions of stage and structure. This research is reviewed elsewhere (Lapsley, 1996), but its general conclusion can be noted here, which is that appeal to global cognitive developmental variables, such as realism and egocentrism, are unnecessary encumbrances, and that developmental differences in moral judgment can often be attributed to the complex nature of Piagetian tasks that overtax the information-processing capabilities of young children.

KOHLBERG'S THEORY

One might suppose that because of the convergence of their respective intellectual projects that Piaget and Kohlberg also shared the same understanding of stage development. But Kohlberg appeared to have a more stringent reading of what *structures d'ensemble* required than did Piaget. According to Kohlberg (1969) cognitive stages, if they are to count as true stages, must meet the following exacting criteria:

1.   Stages must describe qualitative differences in modes of reasoning.

2.   Stages must follow an invariant sequence, which is to say, a constant order of succession: "Stage theory holds that every single individual, studied longitudinally, should only move one step at a time through the stage sequence and always in the same order. Any deviations from this order not due to obvious errors in observation or to dramatic regression-inducing stress or damage questions the validity of the stage sequence itself" (Kohlberg, 1987, p. 30).

3.   Each stage must describe an underlying thought-organization or structured whole (Piaget's *structure d'ensemble*). These *structures d'ensemble* should underwrite the manifestation of a "logically and empirically related cluster of responses in development" (Kohlberg, 1969, p. 353).

4.   The structured totality characteristic of a given stage is not simply replaced by emergent thought-organizations during the course of development but is instead taken up within the new structure by a process of hierarchical integration. Although hierarchical integration displaces the structures of earlier stages, these early structures are not entirely lost and, indeed, may be used when a situation warrants (made available or deployed, one gathers, from the perspective of the higher

stage) or when attempts to use a higher form of reasoning is unavailing. Nonetheless, "there is a hierarchical preference within the individual, i.e., a *disposition to prefer* a solution of a problem at the highest level available to him" (Kohlberg, 1969, p. 353, emphasis added).

Kohlberg argued that the stages of moral judgment identified by Piaget (1932/1965) do not meet these criteria. Piaget's stages are ideal–typical and age–developmental but not true structural–developmental stages. By ideal-typical, he means that the stages are defined by certain clusters of themes that hang together to form orientations or ideal types, but are not organized structurally (in the sense that content–function and form–structure are cleanly distinguished). These orientations are also age–developmental in the sense that the heteronomous orientation tends to give way to the autonomous type with age, although a heteronomous orientation may persist even into adulthood.

But Kohlberg does not consider these to be true structural–developmental stages for two reasons. First, the progression from heteronomy to autonomy lacks an inner logic. That is, the autonomous stage is not a transformation or hierarchical integration of the heteronomous stage. Rather, the two moralities are simply in opposition, with the autonomous orientation replacing heteronomy but not growing out of it. Second, the two moralities are linked to certain forms of social relationship, and, in addition, are influenced by other forms of social influence, such as social class, religious upbringing, forms of education, and the like. For Kohlberg, this means that structure is contaminated with content, or that the highest form of moral judgment "is dependent upon the kind of social relations or society in which the child lives" (Kohlberg, Higgins, Tappan, & Schrader, 1984, p. 655), which is precisely what one does not want to see in a stage sequence if one's purpose is to frustrate moral relativism.

Still, the movement from heteronomy to autonomy does represent movement from partial to more stable equilibrium. It does appeal to reciprocity as the mechanism that transforms part–whole relations in the direction of greater equilibrium. Its ontogenetic insights about the moral judgment of children are pressed into the service of genetic epistemological conclusions about ethical development in society. Whether the sequence is also true, logical or hard may be more of a concern to Kohlberg's project than to Piaget's.

Levels and Stages

Kohlberg describes the development of justice reasoning as the progressive elaboration of a sociomoral perspective across three levels of development (see Gibbs [2003] for a criticism of Kohlberg's use of levels). Within each level are two stages, the second of which is a more complete articulation of the sociomoral perspective than the first.

The preconventional level begins with a sociomoral perspective that is egocentric and heteronomous (Stage 1) and ends with a perspective that values the pursuit of self-interest by striking pragmatic exchanges with like-minded others (Stage 2). Preconventional justice, then, is an exchange system of favors, goods, and sanctions that are engaged to meet selfish, concrete-individualistic goals, quite apart from the norms and expectations of the larger group. At the next level there is a marked awareness of group membership and of the value of shared relationships (Stage 3). Indeed, the self identifies with conventional expectations that attach to social roles (e.g., being the good husband, the dutiful son, the loving wife, the loyal friend, etc.), and accepts the necessity of subordinating one's concrete-individualistic preferences for the needs of the shared relationship. This perspective is more fully realized at Stage 4, when the expectations that attach to being a good member of the shared relationship expand to include the impersonal collectivity of citizens in a shared polity. What regulates conduct here is not a set of shared expectations of "us friends," as in Stage 3, but rather a perspective that takes on the perspective of the system as whole, a perspective that is reflected in shared support for social institutions and equal treatment of citizen-strangers before the law.

In contrast to preconventional morality, then, the hallmark of conventional morality is the fact that self-interest is subordinated to the interests of the shared relationship (Stage 3) and of society itself (Stage 4). One conforms to these expectations and identifies with them just because they are conventional. At the final level, however, one identifies not with rules, laws, expectations or conventions per se, but rather with the general moral principle(s) that motivate them. One differentiates a commitment to uphold moral principles from the requirements of being a member of society, which is to say that one differentiates moral and legal points of view. Laws and conventions make sense only to the extent that they are staked to defensible moral considerations. A moral point of view is considered prior to social conventions and legal regulation, so that when principle and legality clash, the moral point of view bids one to uphold the former and reject the latter (Stage 5). At Stage 6, this perspective is formalized in terms of universal moral obligations, and the self-conscious use of procedural justice checks on the validity of one's moral deliberation. It is at this principled level of justice reasoning where moral consensus and agreement become a real possibility (because it transcends commitments to conventionality and because it seeks prescriptive, universalizable moral judgments). It is at this stage where ethical relativism is most firmly rejected.

Stage Scoring and Validation.   In addition to the level of sociomoral reflection, each stage can also be described in terms of how certain justice operations (e.g., equality, reciprocity, equity, prescriptive role taking, and universalizability) are understood and deployed. The description of moral stages in terms of level of sociomoral perspective and of justice operations is the result of an evolution in the method of scoring interview protocols (Colby, 1978; Colby & Kohlberg, 1987). The early protocol scoring systems (Sentence Scoring and Global Story Rating) generated anomalous data at odds with the assumptions of invariant sequence and holistic consistency. As Rest put it, "Given the clash between his hard-line stage model and the disconfirming data, rather than soften his stage model, Kohlberg's response was to revise the scoring system, assuming that the fault must be in confusing content with structure" (1985, p. 461).

Hence later scoring systems (Structural Issue and Standard Issue Scoring) were designed to dissolve these anomalies by making a cleaner differentiation between structure and content. In effect, what the previous scoring systems considered structure was now deemed content in the new systems. For example interview, material is parsed into four levels of classification before a stage score is assigned. Take the famous Heinz dilemma. First the protocol is sorted into one of two issues (saving a life versus upholding the law) then into norms (12 possible for each issue) that represent the areas of concern for the subject in justifying why Heinz should or should not steal the drug; then into elements (17 possible for each norm), which identify why the norm has value. So, one might argue that Heinz should steal the drug (issue: life) because he loves his wife (norm: affiliation) and could not live with himself if he did not try his best (element: upholding self-respect). Once one makes these decisions the Standard Issue Scoring Manual presents options for stage assignment.

Empirical Validity of Stages.   Kohlberg argued "the most important validity criterion of a stage test is evidence for it meeting the criterion of invariant sequence" (1987, p. 300). This implies no stage skipping and no stage regression. The second most important criterion is structured wholeness. By these criteria the results of validation research (e.g., Colby, Kohlberg, Gibbs, & Lieberman, 1983) are said to be "spectacular" (Rest, 1986, p. 466). Rest (1986) continues:

> The studies on these aspects of the new scoring system are very impressive—the findings are without parallel in all of social-cognitive development. For no other measurement procedure in the field have such strong confirmatory trends been reported (p. 464).... If one is not favorably impressed with these findings, it is difficult to know what would be impressive in all of social development literature. (p. 466)

But Rest (1986) also notes that developmental progress through the sequence is glacial; that the principled stages have largely disappeared from the empirical record; that evidence of holistic consistency might be an artifact of certain decision rules of standard issue scoring (see also Krebs, Denton, Vermeulen, Carpendale, & Bush, 1991). Hence, "one must be wary of how strong a claim can be made for the 'hard stage model' of development based on the longitudinal data" (Rest, 1985, p. 467).

Stage Six and Substages. It is a matter of significance for a structural developmental stage theory that some doubt attaches to the empirical reality of its final stage. After all, the final stage is the ideal equilibrium that makes developmental explanation possible. Stage transition makes sense only as gradual approximations of the ideal form instantiated as the final stage (Kitchener, 1983). If the final stage is not well attested, then one has grounds for doubting the coherence of the developmental model. One consequence of standard issue scoring, however, was that Stage 6 was dropped from the scoring manual and treated as a hypothetical endpoint of the sequence (but revised to include sympathy operations as well as justice operations; see Kohlberg, Boyd, & Levine, 1990). Moreover, the estrangement of Stage 6 was accompanied by a second theoretical development, which was the discovery of A and B substages at the remaining stages. Both the attenuation of Stage 6 and the appearance of substages were consequences of Kohlberg's attempt to tame unruly developmental trends in justice reasoning with the discipline of hard stage criteria.

Kramer (1968) reported, for example, that interviews scored with the early scoring systems did not coalesce around internally consistent stages (casting doubt on the structured whole assumption). Moreover, adolescents who were once classified at the principled levels (Stage 5 and Stage 6) in high school were found to embrace a kind of relativism more characteristic of Stage 2 upon entering college (a stage regression that violates the invariant sequence assumption). Recall that invariant sequence and holistic consistency are the only evidence of construct validity of interest to the structural developmental tradition. Hence these data presented Kohlberg with a prima facie refutation of his moral stage theory.

However, on further examination of the protocols (and with new scoring procedures) Kohlberg concluded that the relativism of the university students was quite different from the concrete-individualistic thinking of Stage 2 subjects. The university subjects seemed to be wrestling with relativism as part of an overall moral theory. Although these subjects were once considered principled reasoners in high school, their reasoning could not now be considered principled (because it embraced relativism), although it seemed more sophisticated than conventional reasoning (because it was theoretical). Hence Kohlberg deemed their reasoning to be at a transitional stage $4^1/_2$ (Kohlberg, 1973b, 1984; Kohlberg & Kramer, 1969). But the appearance of a transition stage forced other revisions. For example, if transitional stage subjects were wrestling with relativistic moral notions but in a theoretical way, should we not also expect principled subjects to be more theoretical in their moral reflection?

The problem was resolved by defining the principled stages in a philosophical–theoretical way (with the consequence that Stage 6 receded from empirical view), and the theoretical discourse of transitional subjects was downsized into a species of conventional reasoning. This meant that the universalizing tendencies once considered the sole province of principled reasoning could now be found among conventional subjects who otherwise have a member-of-society perspective. To make room for this sort of reasoning at the conventional level required the creation of A and B substages. The traditional description of conventional reasoning was relegated to the A substage, and the more theoretical kind was denoted as substage B.

The B substage reflects a better appreciation of the prescriptive and universalizable nature of moral judgments, and is oriented toward fairness, equality, and reciprocity, much like Piaget's autonomous orientation. In turn, the A substage was linked with the heteronomous orientation to rules, authority, and conventions. This means that the B substage is more equilibrated than the A substage, and that moral development can now be said to occur within stages (e.g., moving from Stage 3A to 3B) as well as between stages.

Kohlberg believed that the anomalous data reported by Kramer (1968) could be resolved by changing the scoring systems to allow a cleaner distinction between structure and content. The more effectively this was done the more Stage 6, the moral ideal, faded from view as an empirical possibility. As Gibbs (1979) put it, Stage 6 became "stranded" in an ethereal philosophical realm that made it difficult to see how it could be understood in terms of Piagetian structures. Indeed, even Stage 5 is vanishingly rare in the extant longitudinal data. But now the existence of the B substage provides a way of reintroducing ethical criteria of moral adequacy into a stage theory that has seemingly lost its moral ideal.

Moreover, it is hard not to see the attenuation of Stage 6 and the emergence of the B substage as a related development. Just when Kantian moral adequacy is lost as an empirical possibility with the reduction of Stage 6 to a hypothetical endpoint, it is regained with the discovery of the B substage. Although Stage 6 seems beyond the pale of most reasoners, some of its properties seep down into the B substages of lower stages. In this way, some semblance of moral rationality is recovered, indeed, is made more generally available even at conventional levels of moral reasoning. The more Stage 6 receded from view, stranded in a philosophical realm, the more its key features became a real possibility in the B substages of conventional reasoning. Curiously, then, principled reasoning, or some semblance of it, is at once exceedingly rare, yet quite common (Lapsley, 1996).

Decalage and the Structured Whole Assumption. Kohlberg interpreted Piaget's notion of *structure d'ensemble* to require the observation of synchrony in development. A cognitive structure is supposed to organize diverse content just because it is a structured whole. It is supposed to underwrite behavioral consistency among clusters of related content domains, providing for consistency in problem solving, reasoning, and judgment. This is a misinterpretation of Piaget's intention (Chapman, 1988). Yet testing the structured whole assumption was a vast empirical enterprise for almost three decades, peaking in the 1970s.

Two issues were symptomatic of this period. First, there was the matter of *content decalage*—tasks that shared the same underlying logical structure were nonetheless solved at different ages. Indeed, some researchers were so exercised by evidence of content decalage that they devised elaborate neo-Piagetian theories to account for them, suggesting, for example, that asynchronous mastery of different content manifestations of an underlying structure could be accounted for by the differential demands these tasks place on working memory, attentional resources, and mental capacity (e.g., Case, 1985; Pascual-Leone, 1970). Second, there was the matter of *procedural decalage*—when tasks are simplified, stripped of unnecessary performance demands, children could be shown to solve cognitive tasks at ages inexplicable from Piaget's developmental expectations. Both content and procedural decalage were thought to undermine the structured whole assumption of stages, which meant that it had important implications for the moral domain as well.

In the moral domain, Kohlberg held out for the received view on the structured whole assumption. It requires consistency across content domains. He writes that "stages must meet the criterion of consistency implied by the notion of 'structured whole'" (1969, p. 388). Indeed, tracking variations of stage usage by type of dilemma (e.g., hypothetical versus real life) has been an important line of moral development research that has not typically favored a strong reading of the structured whole assumption (Carpendale & Krebs, 1992; Krebs, Denton et al., 1991; Krebs, Vermeulen, Carpendale, & Denton, 1991; Leming, 1978). Substantial stage variation as a function of dilemma type was often reported, sometimes on the same dilemma argued from opposite sides of the issue (de Vries & Walker, 1986).

The issue of procedural decalage was also explored in studies that showed that the incidence of principled reasoning varies depending on the mode of assessment (e.g., Rest, Cooper, Coder, Masanz, & Anderson, 1974; Rest, Davison, & Robbins, 1978). The most commonly used alternative assessment of moral judgment is the Defining Issues Test (DIT), a standardized procedure that requires subjects first to read a moral dilemma, then a series of statements prototypic of moral stages that one might consider in resolving the dilemma, then, finally, to rank order the top four statements by importance. These four preferences are then scored to yield a percentage score (the p-score) of postconventional reasoning.

Note that the DIT is a comprehension and preference task. Individuals have to comprehend the moral stage statements in the list provided for them, and then rank order their top four preferences. This is in stark contrast to the Kohlberg assessment, which requires individuals to produce moral judgments during the course of an oral interview. Indeed, Rest (1973) considered the three tasks of production, comprehension and preference as a kind of Piagetian decalage, with production being more difficult than comprehension, which is more difficult than merely indicating a preference. Not surprisingly, the DIT literature typically shows a far greater incidence of postconventional reasoning than does research using clinical interview methods (e.g., Rogers, 2002).

But these findings have important implications for the structured whole assumption of moral stages. One enduring problem that plagues the cognitive–developmental tradition is how to determine the proper extension of a holistic structure. Colby and Kohlberg (1987) concluded that spontaneous production of moral judgments (as in an oral interview) could be characterized by hard stages, with hierarchical transformation, integration, and displacement, and all the rest, but that hard stages do not characterize comprehension and preference. In their view, "the development of moral judgment as a whole (including comprehension and preference as well as spontaneous production) is too broad in scope to be described by a single model" (Colby & Kohlberg, 1987, p. 7).

In other words, *structures d'ensemble* of justice reasoning are not so structured, or so holistic, as to encompass the sort of judgments assessed by the DIT. Apparently the justice structure does not respond to dilemmas that pull for caring and benevolence issues, either (Kohlberg, Levine, & Hewer, 1983). The structure of justice reasoning, and its ontogenesis, is specific to spontaneous production data that result from oral interviews, and not to moral judgments derived in any other way. This means that production, comprehension, and preference (let alone benevolence and caring) cannot even be considered a content decalage of the same deep justice structure, because only moral judgments that are spontaneous derivations of oral interviews qualify for hard stage classification (although perhaps the decalage evident here is procedural rather than contextual). In this way, the moral domain is narrowed to only those aspects that can be stage typed, and with the most stringent understanding of stage, and this provides the most secure basis for confronting ethical relativism.

Hierarchical Integration and the Structured Whole Assumption. The discussion of the size of the unit over which a structured whole extends also entails taking a stand on how to interpret the claim that stage developmental requires hierarchical integration. The Kohlberg group interprets hierarchical integration to mean that earlier moral structures are displaced or transformed and are no longer accessible once one has developed to a higher stage. This transformative–displacement model is in contrast to an *additive stage model* (e.g, Rest, 1979), whereby lower stages are still accessible, even when one advances to a higher stage. Additive models further assume that actual stage usage may depend on a number of variables, including the demand characteristics of situations, the pull of different types of dilemmas, the nature of the testing instrument, the response mode it requires, the way it is scored, and other contextual sources of influence. Clearly, the additive model has greater tolerance for stage heterogeneity than does the transformative model, which assumes "*very great* internal consistency of reasoning" (Colby & Kohlberg, 1987, p. 7, my emphasis) as befits strongly holistic stages.

However, as noted, "very great internal consistency" of moral reasoning is restricted to spontaneous production of moral arguments, and does not include comprehension or evaluation of moral arguments made by others or to preference judgments. "In fact, it is quite clear," write Colby and Kohlberg (1987, p. 7), "that a transformational model entailing a great degree of structured wholeness is not appropriate to describe comprehension and preference of moral judgments."

Fortified Stages. One notices that, as the Kohlberg research program developed over time, the insistence on hard stage criteria also entailed a narrowing of the range of extension of a moral structure to something narrow and cramped, so long as it could be stage typed, and with the most rigorous understanding of stage. This methodological commitment must be understood as part of the larger project to provide the developmental resources with which to confront the ethical relativist. Along similar lines, Kohlberg made certain claims about the logical status of cognitive developmental stages, although his use of *logic* and its cognate terms was varied and sometimes problematic (see, e.g., Locke, 1986; Phillips & Nicolayev, 1978). The order of stages is one of logical necessity, it was claimed, just because the sequence is defined in terms of increasing articulation, differentiation, and integration. Clearly, if later stages are partly defined in terms of the elements of earlier stages, then, of course, later stages must follow early stages by definition. This is a matter of logic, not of psychological theory (Kohlberg, 1984).

But Kohlberg also suggested that stages are defined by a logical analysis of what children say, which is quite different from the claim that the sequence of stages is attested by logical necessity. When one makes the internal connections in children's ideas, when one puts it all together into some sensible form, then the coherence of a stage is revealed. He writes "The ideas used to define the stages are the subjects', not ours. The logical analysis of the connections in a child's thinking is itself theoretically neutral" (Kohlberg,

1984, p. 196). And, for good measure, he adds, *"the stages themselves are not a theory"* (Kohlberg, 1984, p. 196, emphasis in original).

Kohlberg (1987) seems to be claiming that one can discern the meaning of a child's interview without prior theoretical commitments. The stages are not theoretical, cannot be derived from hypothetical constructs, and are plainly evident to anyone who cares to analyze the text of child's mind. This claim for stages is unfortunate. The claim that the stage sequence is vouchsafed by logical necessity, or that the stages themselves are not theoretical (and hence not open to question), are maneuvers to secure the foundations of justice reasoning against skeptics and relativists. The notion that scientific analysis is possible without theory is a Baconian fantasy long discarded in modern science and philosophy of science. It is a fantasy of positivist behavioral science that Kohlberg rejected on other grounds. Other stage theories of justice reasoning were disinclined to use Kohlberg's highly fortified notion of hard stages, perhaps because these were not intended to address problems in ethics.

POSITIVE JUSTICE STAGE THEORIES: DISTRIBUTIVE JUSTICE AND PROSOCIAL REASONING

Positive Justice

The sort of concerns that Kohlberg targets in his theory is sometimes called *prohibition moral reasoning* (Eisenberg, 1982) because it focuses on rights, duties, norms, and formal obligations. It focuses on issues (e.g., property rights versus the right to life) that are some distance from the moral world of young children. In contrast, the domain of positive justice focuses on issues of fairness that arise in the context of prosocial interactions. Sharing is the prototypic prosocial behavior that arises naturally in the social ecology of children. Indeed, children are often enjoined to share their belongings to benefit another, yet it is not often clear how to do this when there are many claimants and resources are few. To develop a scheme of sharing that is fair, then, is a problem of distributive justice.

Damon (1973, 1975) investigated children's understanding of the fair distribution of property, presenting sharing dilemmas to youngsters who ranged in age from 4 to 10 years. In the course of a clinical interview children are confronted with various distributive criteria. Should sharing be governed by strict equality (everyone gets the same), merit (whoever does the best or the most should get more), equity (should we permit special allowances for extenuating need), self-interest (whoever wants it most should get it), or other behavioral (best behaved) or physicalistic (all the girls get more, or the oldest ones)?

Stages of Distributive Justice Reasoning. Damon showed that children's reasoning about fair sharing followed a stage progression. At level 0-A, self-interest is the governing distributive criteria ("I should get more because that is what I want."). At 0-B, self-interest is backed up with an appeal to external, physicalistic, and observable features, such as size, age, and gender ("All us boys should get more"). At 1A, notions of strict equality ("Everyone should get the same") govern sharing. At 1B, merit and just deserts enters the distributive calculation ("If you did the best, you should get more; if you were lazy or did a lousy job, you should get less"). At 2A, one attempts to balance competing claims to merit by working out some equitable compromises. At 2B, the compromise between equity and reciprocity is worked out in light of the demands of the situation or the larger goals and purposes of the group.

One notices first that the three levels of Damon's sequence align tolerably well with the general progression noted by Piaget: from egocentrism and physicalistic notions of fairness (Level 0), to notions of strict equality (Level 1), and then equity (Level 2). A crucial research goal was to show that distributive justice reasoning was related to general cognitive development and displayed the requisite sequential properties. In one study, Damon (1975) showed a strong association between distributive justice reasoning and performance on operational tasks involving classification, logical compensation, coordination of perspectives and ratio, and proportions. Moreover, the three levels of distributive justice reasoning could be aligned with pre-operations (Level 0), concrete operations (Level 1), and transitional formal operations (Level 2). Hence, there is something distinctly Piagetian about the sequence. However, there was no indication that reasoning in the logical domain was a prerequisite for reasoning in the distributive justice domain. Although logical and moral reasoning are strongly associated, "the priority of logical and moral reasoning does not appear to be necessary in development: even among normal subjects the pattern may be quite the reverse" (Damon, 1975, p. 312).

The developmental properties of the sequence were explored in two longitudinal studies. In one study (Damon, 1977), children who showed change over 1 year tended to move to the next highest stage. But many children showed no change at all during this interval, and some reported a lower stage of reasoning. One explanation for the turgid pace of developmental change was that a 1-year interval was simply not sufficient to capture social–cognitive development in middle childhood. Perhaps testing children after a 2-year interval would see more instances of upward stage movement. This was indeed reported by Damon (1980) in a second longitudinal assessment. In this study, nearly 86% of children who changed showed progressive development over the 2-year interval. Moreover, children who showed an initial downward reversal after 1 year corrected themselves by the second year. Damon (1980) also showed that the best predictor of stage transition was not consolidation of reasoning at one's current stage but rather stage mixture as determined by the spread of scores above the mode. This finding, along with more recent studies (Walker, Gustafson, & Hennig, 2001; Walker & Taylor, 1991), supports Turiel's (1974) contention that stage mixture is an indication of readiness to develop, especially if the distribution of scores is tilted in favor of the next highest stage.

Distributive Justice Scale. Enright, Franklin, and Manheim (1980) opened up a second research front by designing a standardized, objective assessment of distributive justice reasoning called the Distributive Justice Scale (DJS), consisting of two sharing dilemmas that are similar to Damon's (1977). After an initial attempt to resolve the dilemma the child is shown pairs of pictures, each representing a particular stage in the sequence. All combinations of stages are paired in this way, and the child is asked to select the picture that resolves the sharing dilemma in the fairest way.

Research using the DJS reported strong age trends and an association with logical reciprocity (Enright, Franklin, & Mannheim, 1980), a pattern that was replicated in Sweden (Enright et al., 1984). When distributive justice issues involve family members rather than peers, reasoning is typically at higher levels (Enright et al., 1984, Study Two). Longitudinal comparisons documented upward stage progression that is uncontaminated by cohort effects and reveals a more rapid pace to development at younger ages than in middle childhood (Enright et al., 1984, Study 3). Social class differences were also evident, with lower class children lagging behind their middle-class peers regardless of race (Enright, Enright, & Lapsley, 1981). This suggests that children's understanding of distributive fairness is sensitive to contextual factors.

What is striking about this literature is the convergence of findings revealed by Damon's clinical method and the findings the DJS yields. Clearly the sequence enjoys strong empirical support. There are strong longitudinal age trends: The sequence is associated with other indices of cognitive development, is evident in at least two cultures, and shows an interesting sensitivity to contextual factors. Although there is some inevitable warble in findings across the two methodologies, one is more impressed by the similarity than by the differences. Hence, unlike the studies of moral reasoning conducted with Kohlberg's clinical interview and objective measures like the DIT, there appears to be little evidence of significant procedural decalage between Damon's clinical assessment of distributive justice and Enright's use of a standardized, objective instrument.

The Partial Structures Issue. The distributive justice sequence represents yet another option in moral stage theory. Damon (1977) argued that moral structures always maintain an element of content specificity, which means that different moral domains or concepts may be organized in different ways. Along similar, lines Turiel argued, "Cognitive structures are partial in that they encompass delimited domains of knowledge; thinking is organized within the boundaries of fundamental categories" (1983, p. 20).

According to Rest (1983), however, this agnostic position with respect to general structures is problematic because it pays insufficient attention to the systemic qualities of thought. Thought is not, in his view, a jumble of disconnected concepts. Damon's sequence certainly tells us something about how children come to resolve specific problems of sharing, but how does this help us to understand

> children's moral thinking regarding lying, promise-keeping, fighting and self-defense, punishment, cheating on games or school tests, being disruptive and unruly, special responsibilities to family and kin, performing assigned chores, and all the other situations in a child's life that involve moral issues. (Rest, 1983, p. 604)

This would be quite a general structure that could meet this exacting standard, although the main point is well taken: that as much effort go into specifying the system of organization as in identifying partial-structure domains. Another criticism is that the distributive justice sequence lacks an inner logic. It lacks a clear notion of hierarchical integration, or an explanation as to why one way of resolving a distributive dilemma should override another (Rest, 1983). Why, for example, should a compromise between merit and equality trump a reliance on equality or equity alone as a distributive criterion? On what grounds are succeeding levels of reasoning more adequate than lower levels (and in what sense are they lower)?

Hence our look at the distributive justice sequence illustrates the key debates about stage theory in the moral domain. Are stages general or partial? Is there an inner logic? Is development additive or transformative? How is the internal standard of adequacy to be understood in both psychological and moral terms? Whether the partial-structures perspective is an adequate conceptualization of development depends largely on how one understands Piaget's notion of *structure d'ensemble*. There is a case to be made that the partial-structures notion is closer to the Piagetian mark than the ostensible Piagetian orthodoxy that has grown up around hard stage criteria. Stages are bounded, delimited by domains, and content specific, but this does not commit one to the view that stages are a messy jumble of disconnected domains either, or that they constitute "autonomous, self-contained units manifested across tasks and situations" (Turiel, 1983, p. 21). In the next section, we see how another positive justice stage progression pushes even the notion of partial structure and loose readings of *structures d'ensemble* to the extreme.

Prosocial Moral Reasoning

Prosocial moral reasoning is another aspect of positive justice (Eisenberg-Berg, 1979). It emerges when we face the problem of whether to help others, typically at some cost to ourselves, when there is no formal obligation to do so. Take the problem facing the poor farmers of Circleville. Should they give most of their harvest to a neighboring community whose farmlands had been flooded, even if it meant that the residents of Circleville might go hungry? Should one donate blood even if one is physically weak or if it interferes with one's studies or costs one a job? Should one come to the aid of a victim even if it might be dangerous to do so?

Moral Consideration Categories.   Children presented with prosocial dilemmas like these generate a large number of moral considerations that can be taxonomically organized (Eisenberg-Berg, 1979). Some moral considerations include punishment and obedience (one might get punished if one does not help); hedonistic reasoning involving pragmatic self-gain ("I wouldn't help because I might be hungry") or direct reciprocity ("She'd help because they'd give her food the next time"); a needs orientation that shows a concern for another's physical-material ("He needs blood") or psychological ("They'd be happy if they had food") needs; stereotyped reasoning ("It's only natural to help"); an empathic orientation involving sympathetic caring ("He would feel sorry for them") or role taking ("I'm trying to put myself in their shoes"); a concern for social approval and acceptance ("His parents would be proud of him if he helped"), internalized affect ("Seeing the villagers fed would make her feel good"), and abstract reasoning that invokes internalized norms, laws, and values ("She has a duty to help others"), the rights of others ("I'd help because she has the right to walk down the street without being mugged"), generalized reciprocity ("If everyone helps one another, we'd all be better off"), or the conditions of society ("If everybody helps, society would be a lot better").

Developmental Trends.   In an early cross-sectional study, Eisenberg-Berg (1979) showed that the prosocial reasoning of elementary school children tended to focus on hedonistic, stereotyped, and needs-oriented concerns. High school students also invoked these considerations, but more often included abstract reasoning and internalized values and norms as considerations. The developmental trend was clarified by two longitudinal studies that tracked prosocial reasoning from preschool to ages 7 or 8. These data showed that the use of hedonistic reasoning steadily declined over this period, while empathic needs- and approval-oriented reasoning increased (Eisenberg, Lennon, & Roth, 1983; Eisenberg-Berg & Roth, 1980).

Subsequent longitudinal follow-up studies tracked changes in prosocial reasoning after 7 years (Eisenberg et al., 1987), 11 years (Eisenberg, Miller, Shell, McNalley, & Shea, 1991), and 15 years (Eisenberg, Carlo, Murphy, & Van Court, 1995), ranging from middle childhood to the cusp of early adulthood. Across this period, hedonistic reasoning decreased until adolescence, but then increased somewhat by late adolescence and early adulthood. Needs-oriented and stereotyped reasoning increased until middle childhood and early adolescence, and then declined in use. Direct reciprocity and approval reasoning declined until middle adolescence, but remained stable thereafter. Several modes of higher level reasoning, such as internalized norms and generalized reciprocity, emerged in late childhood and increased in use across adolescence and early adulthood.

Levels of Prosocial Reasoning.   It became clear that age-related changes in the use of the various moral consideration categories could be conceptualized as levels of prosocial reasoning (Eisenberg, 1986). At Level 1 (Hedonistic and Self-Focused Orientation) the motive for helping is linked to self-interest or possible consequences for the self. At Level 2 (Needs Oriented), a concern is expressed for the needs of others, even when it conflicts with one's own, although the concern is expressed without clear evidence of sympathy, guilt, or self-reflection. At Level 3 (Approval-Interpersonal Orientation and/or Stereotypic Orientation), prosocial intentions are judged in light of stereotypic notions of good and bad persons; one should help persons who are nice or good, but not persons who are not nice or bad. Prosocial behavior should also secure approval or acceptance. At Level 4 (Self-Reflective Empathic Orientation), there is evidence of self-reflective role taking, an empathic concern for the other's humanity, and whether one's actions would engender positive feelings or incur guilt. A transitional level (4B) follows where one's self-reflection begins to consider internalized norms and a sense of duty or responsibility. There is an inarticulate concern for the welfare of society or the dignity of persons. These concerns are better articulated at Level 5 (Strongly Internalized Stage). At this level, the appeal to internalized norms, duties, responsibilities, and rights is clearly stated. Issues of self-respect and living up to one's values are also commonly expressed at this stage.

Stage Issues.   Prosocial reasoning begins, then, in a fog of hedonism and egoism, but then expands to take an ever-widening social perspective that duly considers the needs and welfare of society. The developmental movement is from self-preoccupation to other-regard, from internal and private concerns to external and social concerns. But prosocial reasoning also moves in the opposite direction, from an external preoccupation with social stereotypy, approval, and acceptance, to strongly internalized commitments where the sense of self hangs in the balance.

Eisenberg's impressive commitment to longitudinal research has demonstrated amply the age-related changes in prosocial reasoning. The sequence conforms to an additive model, and is age–developmental rather than structural–developmental. Indeed, Eisenberg (1986) does not make strong hard stage assumptions about the sequence, nor has she shown much interest in the usual conceptual desiderata of moral stage theory. There is no attempt, for example, to differentiate structure and content, a goal that animated the Kohlberg team for decades. Instead the prosocial sequence was identified inductively from a taxonomy of motives that emerged in the content responses. There is little concern with whether each developmental level is a structured whole. Indeed, wondering whether prosocial reasoning is governed by general or partial structures seems hardly the right question in a sequence where children appeal to prosocial justifications from a variety of levels. There is little concern, too, with whether levels of prosocial reasoning conform to an invariant sequence. Notice, for example, how hedonistic motives decline in importance from early childhood to adolescence, but then are reasserted in late adolescence and early adulthood.

So here we have levels of prosocial moral judgment contaminated by content, without proper structural foundation, aligned in a sequence with shifting emphases and absent an inner logic that gives rise to hierarchical integration. From the perspective of cognitive–developmental orthodoxy this is quite alarming. This is sure to fail Kohlberg's test of what is to count as true structural–developmental stages. Yet stringent orthodoxy about these matters seems only required when the aim of research is other than simply documenting empirical realities but for also wanting to use data to score philosophical points.

Two Promising Directions. Two additional features of this research program should be noted briefly. First, there is now promising research on standardized assessments of prosocial reasoning (PROM; Carlo, Eisenberg, & Knight, 1992) and prosocial behavior (PTM; Carlo & Randall, 2002; Carlo, Hausmann, Christiansen, & Randall, 2003) in adolescents. Second, unlike any other research program in the moral domain, the study of prosocial reasoning has always been conducted in concert with studies of prosocial emotion, such as empathy, caring, and sympathetic concern (Eisenberg, in press, 1986; Eisenberg & Miller, 1987; Eisenberg & Morris, 2004). In recent years, this has led to important investigations of whether there is a dispositional or personological basis for prosocial behavior. In one study, spontaneous, other-oriented prosocial sharing behavior (but not low-cost helping or compliant prosocial behavior) observed at ages 4 and 5 predicted actual and self-reported prosocial behavior up to 17 years later, a relationship that was partially mediated by sympathy (Eisenberg et al., 1999). Similarly, self-reports of prosocial dispositions in early adulthood often related to self-reports of sympathy, empathy, and prosocial behavior 10 to 16 years earlier (Eisenberg et al., 2002). These studies support the claim that there is a prosocial personality disposition that emerges in early childhood and is consistent over time, although the manifestation of the altruistic personality may vary with the demand characteristics of social contexts (Carlo, Eisenberg, Troyer, Switzer, & Speer, 1991).

OTHER SOCIAL COGNITIVE STAGE MODELS

As we have seen, the stage concept has been used in varying ways in the moral development domain, from Kohlberg's structural developmental model, with its exacting demand for qualitative change, structural unity, and invariant sequence, to the partial-structure model of distributive justice reasoning, to the additive age-developmental models of prosocial reasoning and Piagetian moral judgment. Moral judgment, positive justice, and prosocial reasoning do not exhaust the domains to which the stage concept has been deployed within the study of social cognitive development. One could also point to stage theories of self-development (Kegan, 1982; Noam, 1985, 1988), self-understanding (Damon & Hart, 1982; Hart & Damon, 1986), perspective taking, interpersonal understanding (Selman, 1980), social conventional reasoning (Turiel, 1983), religious judgment (Oser, 1985), and faith development (Fowler, 1981), among others. The accounts of stage development in these domains contend with the same sort of issues that were evident in the moral domain, although some of them also introduce additional options for characterizing developmental change.

Social Conventional Reasoning

For example, the social conventional stage sequence formalizes the disequilibrating role of cognitive conflict in developmental growth by inserting negation stages throughout the sequence, so that developmental change unfolds dialectically through successive phases of affirmation and negation (Turiel, 1983). For example, at Stage 1 (age 6 to 7) a child is aware of broad social uniformities ("men are doctors, women are nurses"), but these are thought natural of the social order and the conventional uniformity is affirmed for this reason. At Stage 2 (age 8 to 9), however, this understanding is negated. Conventional acts are arbitrary and the fact that everybody does it is not sufficient to maintain the convention. At Stage

3 (age 10 to 11), conventional uniformities affirm the system of rules. Although rules are arbitrary, we follow them because this is what those in authority expect of us. At Stage 4 (age 12 to 13), this affirmation is negated. Conventions are nothing but social expectations that have no rule-like hold over us. At Stage 5 (age 14 to 16), conventions are affirmed as social norms characterized by fixed roles in a static hierarchical organization. Society is a complex organization of role statuses, some have more than others, and there is a system of conventions that regulate interactions among individuals who vary in status. These social conventions affirm the status hierarchy because codified standards of conduct maintain the social group. At Stage 6 (age 17 to 18), this understanding is negated. Conventions are nothing but societal expectations that have become codified through habitual use and inertia, but otherwise serve no function with respect to maintaining the social system. Finally, at Stage 7 (age 18 to 25), social convention is reaffirmed. Here one understands that social conventions are not societal codes that define the social group or regulate the distribution of status (Stage 5), but rather are shared, agreed upon uniformities that serve a functional purpose, such as the need for efficiency and coordination.

Perspective Taking

The root developmental achievement that underlies every domain of social cognitive development is perspective taking. It unfolds along two fronts—conceptions of relations and conceptions of persons (Selman, 1980). For example, with respect to conceptions of social relations, the young child, beset by egocentrism, is unable to infer another's perspective (Level 0). At Level 1, the child can accurately infer the other's point of view. At Level 2, the child can reciprocally assume self–other perspectives; at Level 3, a third-party perspective of the dyadic interaction; and at Level 4, the perspective of the social system as a whole. The developing capacity to take ever-widening social perspectives, from the preoccupation of the egocentric self, to local self–other perspectives, to third-party and then systems perspectives, is what underlies the growing sophistication of justice and prosocial reasoning (and every other instance of social cognitive development).

In addition to describing developing conceptions of relationships, from egocentric (Level 0) to societal perspective taking (Level 4), the sequence also charts parallel conceptions of persons. At Level 0, the egocentric child is unable to differentiate a psychological self from physicalistic qualities, and confuses what is subjective–psychological with what is objective–physical. At Level 1, this differentiation is now a possibility. One is aware of subjective states of both self and other and can differentiate intentional and unintentional actions, although the subjective life of persons (thoughts, feelings, opinions) is considered a unitary whole. At Level 2, one can be self-reflective about one's subjective–psychological life, and one realizes that others can do this as well. Persons are understood to have a covert inner life that reflects the true self, which can differ from the overt self presented to others. Deception, then, is now a possibility. Moreover, the subjective life of persons is conceived more complexly; it is possible, for example, to have multiple and conflicting thoughts and feelings, although these are mostly grouped, weighted, or isolated with respect to each other (e.g., "mostly happy but sometimes scared"). At Level 3, the person is understood as a fairly stable system of attitudes and values. One is able to monitor and reflect on the self by assuming the third-party perspective of the observing ego. This allows one to simultaneously perceive oneself as actor and object in ongoing interactions. At Level 4, there is a keen awareness of the subjective–psychological basis of behavior, that the self has an interior depth that cannot always be penetrated by a self-reflective observing ego. We sometimes have conflicting motives and contradictory subjective states that are opaque to self-reflection. Moreover, there is a new notion of personality as a product of dispositions that have a developmental history.

At the summit of social perspective taking, then, one can assume both a societal and in-depth perspective. There is simultaneous awareness of the broadest social point of view, of the social system as a whole (*conception of relations*), but also of the deepest complexities of the subjective self (*conception of persons*). The developing sophistication of one's understanding of selfhood, personality, and subjectivity is reciprocally linked to one's developing understanding of relations. This clearly matters to moral functioning. To monitor just how our decisions and actions influence the broadest social polity while being simultaneously aware of our intentions and motives, and how our actions reflect the sort of person we have come to be, should be one mark of moral maturity. We saw this dual movement of social perspective taking most clearly in the levels of prosocial reasoning, although it is clear that advances in social perspective taking should underwrite mature functioning across all of the moral domains. Indeed, the traditional formula is that advances in social perspective taking are necessary but not sufficient for advances in moral judgment, although the empirical basis for the interdependency formula has not always been demonstrated conclusively (Lapsley, 1996).

Self-Understanding

A similar point can be made with respect to the stage sequences that describe self-understanding. According to Hart and Damon (1986; Damon & Hart, 1982), *self-understanding* is a conceptual system that focuses on "the totality of characteristics that define the self and distinguish the self from others" (p. 388). The self-as-subject, the I-self, includes one's sense of continuity, distinctiveness, volitional agency, and self-reflectivity (see Blasi [1988], for a similar scheme). The self-as-object, the me-self (the self-concept), includes four schemes that define the self: physical self (bodily and material possessions), active self (activities and abilities), social self (social personality characteristics), and the psychological self (emotions, thoughts, cognitive processes). Developmental change in self-understanding in each of these domains unfolds across four levels.

Take the physical self, for example (all stage descriptions and prototypic statements are from Hart and Damon, 1986). Across development the physical self is understood in terms of bodily properties or material possessions (Level 1); then as activity related physical attributes (Level 2); then in terms of physical attributes that influence social appeal and social interactions (Level 3); and then finally as physical attributes reflecting volitional choices and moral standards (Level 4: "It's not fair to have a lot of things when some people don't have anything").

Similarly, one's first understanding of the active self is in terms of typical behaviors (Level 1), then capabilities relative to others (Level 2), then as attributes that influence social standing (Level 3), then finally as active attributes that reflect choices and personal or moral standards (Level 4: "I want to be a faithful Christian."). The social self is first understood by the fact of one's membership in a particular group or social relationship (Level 1); then by activities that are considered with reference to the approval or disapproval of others (Level 2), then by social-personality characteristics (Level 3), then by moral or personal choices concerning social relations or social-personality characteristics (Level 4: "I try not to hurt my friends because you should treat people with respect"). Finally, the psychological self is first linked with momentary moods, feelings, preferences, and aversions (Level 1); then with knowledge, learned skills, or activity related emotional states (Level 2); then with psychologically related social skills (e.g., social sensitivity, communicative competence; Level 3); then with belief systems that reflect a personal philosophy (Level 4: "I believe in world peace. I don't think wars solve anything and we should try to keep from fighting.").

What is strikingly obvious about these developmental trends is that progress in self-understanding, no matter the domain, leads one to morality. Mature self-understanding, at the highest level of developmental complexity, reflects on the moral implications of selfhood. Social cognitive development leads us, in other words, to the moral self, to a self that cannot be understood apart from the moral point of view. This suggests that the formation of the moral self is the clear goal of self-development. And this is true not just in social cognitive development but in psychosocial development as well. Erik Erikson argued, for example, that morality and identity stand in a mutually supportive relationship. An ethical capacity is the "true criterion of identity" (Erikson, 1968, p. 39), but also "identity and fidelity are necessary for ethical strength" (Erikson, 1964, p. 126). This suggests that the formation of moral identity is the clear goal of both moral and identity development, too, just as it is for the moral self, and that the trajectories of moral and self-identity development are ideally conjoined in the moral personality (Lapsley & Lasky, 2001).

SUMMARY AND PROSPECTS

In this chapter, we considered the variety of ways that stage theory has been used within the moral domain. The concept of stage played an important role in the larger aims of both Piaget and Kohlberg. For Piaget, the stage concept was an analytical device that allowed him to draw certain conclusions with respect to genetic epistemology. For this purpose an age-development or ideal-typical sequence was sufficient. For Kohlberg, quite a different stage concept was required to provide a developmental grounding to the moral point of view, and to undermine philosophical positions that were incompatible with it. The orthodoxy that has grown up around this notion of hard stages must be understood in light of this project. To pull this off required not only exacting criteria to determine when structural developmental change is true, but also a narrowing of the field of study to that aspect of moral judgment that could satisfy it. Kohlberg's use of stage theory to address philosophical problems, indeed, his insistence that ethical theory be part of the very conceptualization of moral stages, had the effect of promoting productive reflection on ethics and philosophy, although it also involved the field with the sort of issues that psychologists are ill-equipped to address with the empirical and conceptual tools of their discipline. Indeed, it is doubtful that psychological data can ever resolve philosophical problems (Blasi, 1990).

In contrast to the transformative developmental stage model embraced by Kohlberg we also examined a partial-structure stage model in the positive justice domain, and the age-developmental approach to prosocial reasoning. These models are some distance from the strict notions of invariant sequence, hierarchical integration, and structural unity Kohlberg laid down, although perhaps apostasy in these matters simply reflects the lack of philosophical ambition evident in these stage theories.

In addition to distributive justice and prosocial reasoning, three additional stage theories were considered. The social-conventional stage sequence was examined to illustrate another option for characterizing transformative stage development. This sequence is distinctive for the way that it characterizes developmental growth in terms of successive periods of affirmation and negation. In this way, cognitive disequilibria are built into the very core of the stage theory. Finally, the stage sequences describing social perspective taking and self-understanding were reviewed, and both were found critical for understanding moral selfhood and identity. Indeed, we concluded that moral and self-development aim for the same goal, and are ideally conjoined in the moral personality.

One evident trend in the moral domain is the effort to supplement clinical interviews with standardized and objective assessments of moral judgment. Kohlberg's elaborate methodology for interviewing participants and assigning stage scores is joined by Rest's Defining Issues Test. Enright's Distributive Justice Scale stands alongside Damon's oral assessment of children's understanding of fair sharing. And Carlo and his colleagues' recent development of objective measures of prosocial reasoning (PROM) and behavior (PTM) complete the trend in the prosocial domain. The DIT has generated a substantial literature over the years, and is the core of a neo-Kohlbergian view of moral judgment development that has modified stage theory to schema theory, integrating notions from cognitive science (Narvaez & Bock, 2002; Rest, Narvaez, Bebeau, & Thoma, 1999). The availability of objective measures should facilitate new lines of research in the prosocial domain as well.

A related trend is that researchers are showing increased interest with individual differences in moral thought and behavior, perhaps eclipsing the more traditional concern with mapping developmental change. This is perhaps seen most clearly in the prosocial domain, where a full range of methodologies, including laboratory experimental manipulations, are probing for the dispositional basis of prosocial behavior. What is telling about this research is that it is informed by the best insights of developmental science, or at least an ecological-contextualist version of it, in its insistence of locating dispositional consistency at the intersection of person–context interactions.

But it is also clear that the desire to understand moral functioning in the context of larger developmental processes, including self, identity, and personality development, is now the unmistakable next wave in moral psychological research. Indeed, we have seen how advances in social perspective taking and self-understanding point in the direction of moral maturity, and attempts to articulate the parameters of moral self and moral identity are increasingly common (Blasi, 1995; Lapsley & Narvaez, 2004).

Finally, as the present volume illustrates, the moral domain has expanded its interest beyond a concern with the sort of reasoning that can be captured by stage theory. Indeed, it is now clear that findings regarding the stage-developmental patterning of moral reasoning must be understood in the context of what we know from other developmental literatures regarding, say, motivational processes, self-regulation, the construction of autobiographical memory, self-development, social information processing, and expertise, among other literatures. Research on social-contextual variation, including cultural studies, will provide new insights concerning the moral formation of children (e.g., Killen & Hart, 1995; Turiel, 1997). All of this makes clear that research in the post-Kohlberg era is far from reaching its final stage.

REFERENCES

Bandura, A. (1991). Social cognitive theory of moral thought and action. In W. M. Kurtines & J. L. Gewirtz (Eds.), *Handbook of moral behavior and development: Vol. 1. Theory* (pp. 45–104). Hillsdale, NJ: Lawrence Erlbaum Associates.

Bandura, A., & McDonald, F. J. (1963). The influence of social reinforcement and the behavior of models in shaping children's moral judgments. *Journal of Abnormal and Social Psychology, 67,* 274–281.

Blasi, A. (1988). Identity and the development of the self. In D. K. Lapsley & F. Clark Power (Eds.), *Self, ego, and identity: Integrative approaches* (pp. 226–242). New York: Springer.

Blasi, A. (1990). How should psychologists define morality? Or, the negative side effects of philosophy's influence on psychology. In T. Wren (Ed.), *The moral domain: Essays on the ongoing discussion between philosophy and the social sciences* (pp. 38–70). Cambridge, MA: MIT Press.

Blasi, A. (1995). Moral understanding and the moral personality: The process of moral integration. In W. M. Kurtines & J. L. Gewirtz (Eds.), *Moral development: An introduction* (pp. 229–253). Boston: Allyn & Bacon.

Broughton, J. (1981). Piaget's structural developmental psychology. I. Piaget and structuralism. *Human Development, 24,* 78–109.

Carlo, G., Eisenberg, N., & Knight, G. P. (1992). An objective measure of adolescents' prosocial moral reasoning. *Journal of Research on Adolescence, 2,* 331–349.

Carlo, G., Eisenberg, N., Troyer, D., Switzer, G., & Speer, A. L. (1991). The altruistic personality: In what contexts is it apparent? *Journal of Personality and Social Psychology, 61,* 450–458.

Carlo, G., Hausmann, A., Christiansen, S., & Randall, B. A. (2003). Sociocognitive and behavioral correlates of a measure of prosocial tendencies for adolescents. *Journal of Early Adolescence, 23,* 107–134.

Carlo, G., & Randall, B. A. (2002). The development of a measure of prosocial behaviors for late adolescents. *Journal of Youth and Adolescence, 31,* 31–44.

Carpendale, J., & Krebs, D. (1992). Situational variation in moral judgment: In a stage or on a stage? *Journal of Youth and Adolescence, 21,* 203–224.

Case, R. (1985). *Intellectual development: Birth to adulthood.* Orlando, FL: Academic Press.

Chapman, M. (1988). *Constructive evolution: Origins and development of Piaget's thought.* Cambridge, UK: Cambridge University Press.

Colby, A. (1978). *Logical operational limitations in the development of moral judgment.* Unpublished doctoral dissertation, Columbia University, New York.

Colby, A., & Kohlberg, L. (1987). *The measurement of moral judgment: Vol. 1. Theoretical foundations and research validation.* Cambridge: Cambridge University Press.

Colby, A., Kohlberg, L., Gibbs, J., & Lieberman, M. (1983). A longitudinal study of moral judgment. *Monographs of the Society for Research in Child Development, 48* (1–2, Serial No. 200). Chicago: University of Chicago Press.

Cowan, P., Langer, J., Heavenrich, J., & Nathanson, M. (1969). Social learning and Piaget's cognitive theory of moral development. *Journal of Personality and Social Psychology, 11,* 261–274.

Damon, W. (1973). *Early conceptions of justice as related to the development of operational reasoning.* Unpublished doctoral dissertation, University of California—Berkeley.

Damon, W. (1975). Early conceptions of positive justice as related to the development of logical operations. *Child Development, 46,* 301–312.

Damon, W. (1977). *The social world of the child.* San Francisco: Jossey-Bass.

Damon, W. (1980). Patterns of change in children's social reasoning: A two-year longitudinal study. *Child Development, 51,* 1010–1017.

Damon, W., & Hart, D. (1982). The development of self-understanding from infancy through adolescence. *Child Development, 51,* 1010–1017.

DeRemer, P. A., & Gruen, G. E. (1979). Children's moral judgments: The relationship between intentionality, social egocentrism and development. *Journal of Genetic Psychology, 134,* 207–217.

deVries, B., & Walker, L. (1986). Moral reasoning and attitudes toward capital punishment. *Developmental Psychology, 22,* 509–513.

Eisenberg, N. (Ed.). (1982). *The development of prosocial behavior*. New York: Academic Press.

Eisenberg, N. (1986). *Altruistic emotion, cognition and behavior*. Hillsdale, NJ: Lawrence Erlbaum Associates.

Eisenberg, N. (in press). The development of empathy-related responding. In C. Pope-Edwards & G. Carlo (Eds.), *Nebraska symposium on motivation, 2003, Vol. 51*. Lincoln: University of Nebraska Press

Eisenberg, N., Carlo, G., Murphy, B., & Van Court, P. (1995). Prosocial development in late adolescence: A longitudinal study. *Child Development, 66,* 1179–1197.

Eisenberg, N., Guthrie, I. K., Cumberland, A., Murphy, B. C., Shepard, S. A., Zhou, Q., & Carlo, G. (2002). Prosocial development in early adulthood: A longitudinal study. *Journal of Personality and Social Psychology, 82,* 993–1006.

Eisenberg, N., Guthrie, D. K., Murphy, B. C., Shepard, S. A., Cumberland, A., & Carlo, G. (1999). Consistency and development of prosocial dispositions: A longitudinal study. *Child Development, 70,* 1360–1372.

Eisenberg, N., Lennon, R., & Roth, K. (1983). Prosocial development: A longitudinal study. *Developmental Psychology, 19,* 846–855.

Eisenberg, N., & Miller, P. A. (1987). The relation of empathy to prosocial and related behaviors. *Psychological Bulletin, 101,* 91–119.

Eisenberg, N., Miller, P. A., Shell, R., McNalley, S., & Shea, C. (1991). Prosocial development in adolescence: A longitudinal study. *Developmental Psychology, 27,* 849–857.

Eisenberg, N., & Morris, A. S. (2004). Moral cognitions and prosocial responding in adolescence. In R. Lerner & L. Steinberg (Eds.), *Handbook of adolescent psychology* (2nd ed.). (pp. 155–188). New York: Wiley.

Eisenberg, N., Shell, R., Pasternack, J., Lennon, R., Beller, R., & Mathy, R. (1987). Prosocial development in middle childhood: A longitudinal study. *Developmental Psychology, 23,* 712–718.

Eisenberg-Berg, N. (1979). Development of children's prosocial moral judgment. *Developmental Psychology, 15,* 128–137.

Eisenberg-Berg, N., & Roth, K. (1980). Development of young children's prosocial moral judgment: A longitudinal follow-up. *Developmental Psychology, 16,* 375–376.

Enright, R. D., Bjerstedt, A., Enright, W., Levy, V., Lapsley, D., Buss, R. R., Harwell, M., & Zindler, M. (1984). Distributive justice development: Cross-cultural, contextual and longitudinal evaluations. *Child Development, 55,* 1737–1751.

Enright, R. D., Enright, W., & Lapsley, D. (1981). Distributive justice development and social class. *Developmental Psychology, 17,* 826–832.

Enright, R. D., Franklin, C. C., & Manheim, L. A. (1980). Children's distributive justice reasoning: A standardized and objective scale. *Developmental Psychology, 16,* 193–202.

Erikson, E. (1964). *Insight and responsibility*. New York: Norton.

Erikson, E. (1968). *Identity, youth and crisis*. New York: Norton.

Fowler, J. (1981). *Stages of faith: The psychology of human development and the quest for meaning*. San Francisco: Harper & Row.

Gibbs, J. (1979). Kohlberg's moral stage theory: A Piagetian revision. *Human Development, 22,* 89–112.

Gibbs, J. (2003). *Moral development and reality: Beyond the theories of Kohlberg and Hoffman*. Thousand Oaks, CA: Sage.

Hart, D., & Damon, W. (1986). Developmental trends in self-understanding. *Social Cognition, 4,* 388–407.

Jose, P. E. (1991). Measurement issues in children's immanent justice judgments. *Merrill Palmer Quarterly, 37,* 601–617.

Kegan, R. (1982). *The evolving self.* Cambridge, MA: Cambridge University Press.

Killen, M. (1991). Social and moral development in early childhood. In W. M. Kurtines & J. Gewirtz (Eds.), *Handbook of moral behavior and development. Vol. 2. Research* (pp. 115–138). Hillsdale, NJ: Lawrence Erlbaum Associates.

Killen, M., & Hart, D. (Eds.). (1995). *Morality in everyday life: Developmental perspectives.* Cambridge, UK: Cambridge University Press.

Kitchener, R. (1983). Developmental explanations. *Review of Metaphysics, 36,* 791–818.

Kitchener, R. (1986). *Piaget's theory of knowledge: Genetic epistemology and scientific reasoning.* New Haven, CT: Yale University Press.

Kohlberg, L. (1969). Stage and sequence: The cognitive developmental approach to socialization. In D. Goslin (Ed.), *Handbook of socialization theory and research* (pp. 347–480). New York: Rand McNally & Company.

Kohlberg, L. (1971). From is to ought: How to commit the naturalistic fallacy and get away with it in the study of moral development. In T. Mischel (Ed.), *Cognitive development and epistemology* (pp. 151–284). New York: Academic Press.

Kohlberg, L. (1973a). The claim to moral adequacy of the highest stage of moral development. *Journal of Philosophy, 70,* 630–646.

Kohlberg, L. (1973b). Continuities in childhood and adult moral development research. In P. B. Baltes & K. W. Schaie (Eds.), *Lifespan developmental psychology: Personality and socialization.* New York: Academic Press.

Kohlberg, L. (1984). Moral stages and moralization: The cognitive developmental approach. In L. Kohlberg (Ed.), *The psychology of moral development: The nature and validity of moral stages* (pp. 170–205). San Francisco: Harper & Row.

Kohlberg, L. (1987). The young child as a philosopher. In L. Kohlberg (Ed.), *Child psychology and childhood education: A cognitive-developmental view* (pp. 13–44). New York: Longman.

Kohlberg, L., Boyd, D., & Levine, C. (1990). The return of Stage 6: Its principle and moral point of view. In T. Wren (Ed.), *The moral domain: Essays in the ongoing discussion between philosophy and the social sciences* (pp. 151–181). Cambridge, MA: MIT Press.

Kohlberg, L., Higgins, A., Tappan, M., & Schrader, D. (1984). From substages to moral types: Heteronomous and autonomous morality. In L. Kohlberg (Ed.), *Essays on moral development* (Vol. II, App. C, pp. 652–683). San Francisco: Harper & Row.

Kohlberg, L., & Kramer, R. (1969). Continuities and discontinuities in childhood and adult moral development. *Human Development, 12,* 93–120.

Kohlberg, L., Levine, C., & Hewer, A. (1983). *Moral stages: A current formulation and a response to critics.* In J. A. Meacham (Ed.), *Contributions to human development* (Vol. 10). Basel: Karger.

Kramer, R. (1968). *Moral development in young adulthood.* Unpublished doctoral dissertation, University of Chicago.

Krebs, D., Denton, K. L., Vermeulen, S. C., Carpendale, J., & Bush, A. (1991). Structural flexibility of moral judgment. *Journal of Personality and Social Psychology, 61,* 1012–1023.

Krebs, D., Vermeulen, S. C., Carpendale, J., & Denton, K. L. (1991). Structural and situational influences on moral judgment: An interaction between stage and dilemma. In W. M. Kurtines & J. L. Gewirtz (Eds.), *Handbook of moral behavior and development: Vol. 2. Research* (pp. 139–170). Hillsdale, NJ: Lawrence Erlbaum.

Lapsley, D. K. (1996). *Moral psychology.* Boulder, CO: Westview Press.

Lapsley, D. K., & Lasky, B. M. (2001). Prototypic moral character. *Identity, 1,* 345–464.

Lapsley, D. K., & Narvaez, D. (2004). A social cognitive approach to the moral personality. In D. K. Lapsley & D. Narvaez (Eds.), *Moral development, self and identity: Essays in honor of Augusto Blasi* (pp. 189–212). Mahwah, NJ: Lawrence Erlbaum Associates.

Lapsley, D. K., & Narvaez, D. (2005). Moral psychology at the crossroads. In D. K. Lapsley & F. C. Power (Eds.), *Character psychology and character education.* Notre Dame, IN: University of Notre Dame Press.

Leming, J. (1978). Intrapersonal variations in stage of moral reasoning among adolescents as a function of situational context. *Journal of Youth and Adolescence, 7,* 405–416.

Lickona, T. (1976). Research on Piaget's theory of moral development. In T. Lickona (Ed.), *Moral development and behavior* (pp. 219–240). London: Holt, Rinehart & Winston.

Locke, D. (1986). A psychologist among the philosophers: Philosophical aspects of Kohlberg's theory. In S. Modgil & C. Modgil (Eds.), *Lawrence Kohlberg: Consensus and controversy* (pp. 21–38). Philadelphia: Falmer Press.

Lourenço, O., & Machado, A. (1996). In defense of Piaget's theory: A reply to 10 common criticisms. *Psychological Review, 103,* 143–164.

Narvaez, D., & Bock, T. (2002). Moral schemas and tacit judgment, or how the Defining Issues Test is supported by cognitive science. *Journal of Moral Education, 31,* 297–314.

Noam, G. (1985). Stage, phase and style: The developmental dynamics of the self. In M. Berkowitz & F. Oser (Eds.), *Moral education: Theory and application* (pp. 321–346). Hillsdale, NJ: Lawrence Erlbaum Associates.

Noam, G. (1988). The self, adult development, and the theory of biography and transformation. In D. K. Lapsley & F. Clark Power (Eds.), *Self, ego, and identity: Integrative approaches* (pp. 3–29). New York: Springer.

Oser, F. (1985). Stages of religious judgment. In C. G. Harding (Ed.), *Moral dilemmas.* Chicago: Precedent.

Pascual-Leone, J. (1970). A mathematical model for the transition rule in Piaget's developmental stages. *Acta Psychologica, 32,* 301–345.

Phillips, D. C., & Nicolayev, J. (1978). Kohlbergian moral development: A progressive or degenerating research program? *Educational Theory, 28,* 286–301.

Piaget, J. (1932/1965). *The moral judgment of the child.* New York: The Free Press.

Piaget, J. (1970). *Genetic epistemology.* New York: Norton.

Power, F. C., Higgins, A., & Kohlberg, L. (1989). *Lawrence Kohlberg's approach to moral education.* New York: Columbia University Press.

Reed, D. R. C. (1997). *Following Kohlberg: Liberalism and the practice of democratic community.* Notre Dame, IN: University of Notre Dame Press.

Rest, J. R. (1973). The hierarchical nature of moral judgment: A study of patterns of comprehension and preference of moral stages. *Journal of Personality, 41,* 86–109.

Rest, J. R. (1979). *Development in judging moral issues.* Minneapolis: University of Minnesota Press.

Rest, J. R. (1983). Morality. In J. H. Flavell & E. Markman (Eds.), *Handbook of child psychology* (4th ed.). *Vol. 3. Cognitive development.* New York: Wiley.

Rest, J. R. (1986). Moral research methodology. In S. Modgil & C. Modgil (Eds.), *Lawrence Kohlberg: Consensus and controversy* (pp. 455–470). Philadelphia: Falmer Press.

Rest, J. R., Cooper, D., Coder, R., Masanz, J., & Anderson, D. (1974). Judging the important issues in moral dilemmas—an objective test of development. *Developmental Psychology, 10,* 491–501.

Rest, J. R., Davison, M., & Robbins, S. (1978). Age trends in judging moral issues: A review of cross-sectional, longitudinal and sequential studies of the Defining Issues Test. *Child Development, 49,* 263–279.

Rest, J. R., Narvaez, D., Bebeau, M. J., & Thoma, S. J. (1999). *Postconventional moral thinking: A neo-Kohlbergian approach.* Mahwah, NJ: Lawrence Erlbaum Associates.

Rogers, G. (2002). Rethinking moral growth in college and beyond. *Journal of Moral Education, 31,* 325–338.

Selman, R. (1980). *The growth of interpersonal understanding: Developmental and clinical analyses.* New York: Academic Press.

Smetana, J. (1981). Pre-school children's conceptions of moral and social rules. *Child Development, 52,* 1333–1336.

Smetana, J. (1983). Social-cognitive development: Domain distinctions and coordinations. *Developmental Review, 3,* 131–147.

Turiel, E. (1966). An experimental test of the sequentiality of developmental stages in the child's moral judgments. *Journal of Personality and Social Psychology, 41,* 235–245.

Turiel, E. (1974). Conflict and transition in adolescent moral development. *Child Development, 45,* 14–29.

Turiel, E. (1983). Domains and categories in social cognitive development. In W. Overton (Ed.), *The relationship between social and cognitive development* (pp. 53–89). Hillsdale, NJ: Lawrence Erlbaum Associates.

Turiel, E. (1997). The development of morality. In W. Damon (Ed.) & N. Eisenberg (Vol. Ed.), *Social, emotional and personality development: Vol. 3. Handbook of child psychology* (5th ed., pp. 863–932). New York: Wiley.

Walker, L., Gustafson, P., & Hennig, K. H. (2001). The consolidation/transition model in moral reasoning development. *Developmental Psychology, 37,* 187–197.

Walker, L., & Richards, B. S. (1976). The effects of narrative model on children's moral judgments. *Canadian Journal of Behavioural Science, 8,* 169–177.

Walker, L., & Richards, B. S. (1979). Stimulating transitions in moral reasoning as a function of stage of moral development. *Developmental Psychology, 15,* 95–103.

Walker, L., & Taylor, J. H. (1991). Stage transitions in moral reasoning: A longitudinal study of developmental processes. *Annals of Child Development, 5,* 33–78.

Werner, H. (1957). The concept of development from a comparative and organismic point of view. In D. B. Harris (Ed.), *The concept of development* (pp. 125–148). Minneapolis: University of Minnesota Press.

Weston, D. R., & Tunel, E. (1980). Act-rule relations: Children's concept of social rules. *Developmental Psychology, 16,* 417–424.

CHAPTER

3

RESEARCH ON THE DEFINING ISSUES TEST

STEPHEN J. THOMA
UNIVERSITY OF ALABAMA

RESEARCH USING THE DEFINING ISSUES TEST

This chapter reviews recent research on the Defining Issues Test (DIT), developed in the early 1970s by James Rest as a paper-and-pencil alternative to Lawrence Kohlberg's own semistructured interview measure of moral judgment development (Rest, 1979). Heavily influenced by Kohlberg's six-stage theory of moral reasoning (see Lapsley, chap. 2, this volume), Rest developed the DIT as an assessment of how adolescents and adults come to understand and interpret moral issues. Like Kohlberg, Rest viewed moral judgment development as a social and cognitive construct that followed a developmental progression from a narrow self-focused interpretation of moral issues, through an understanding of the broader social world and associated group-based claims on moral decisions, to a reliance on postconventional moral principles. Rest viewed the cognitive features of moral judgments as central to an understanding of moral actions and emotions. At its conception, therefore, the DIT was designed to assess Kohlberg's developmental sequence and contribute to the development of moral judgment theory in adolescent and adult populations.

As a measurement process, the DIT was also heavily influenced by the Kohlberg interview method. Similar to Kohlberg's moral judgment interview, the DIT assessment process begins by presenting participants with stories that highlight a moral dilemma, many of which were originally used by Kohlberg and his students (e.g., the story of Heinz and the drug). Further, many of the items used on the DIT were distillations of themes found in Kohlberg interview data. However, unlike the Kohlberg interview process in which the participant must produce a response, the task on the DIT is to rate and then rank 12 short issue statements the majority reflecting Kohlberg's six stages (Rest, 1979). Specifically, participants taking the DIT read the story and then decide on a 3-point scale what the protagonist ought to do (e.g., on the Heinz dilemma the choices are steal the drug, not steal, and can't decide). Following the action choice, 12 items are presented and rated on a 5-point scale (from very important to not very important). These ratings are followed by a ranking task in which the participant is asked to rank the four items that best reflect their thinking about how the protagonist ought to solve the dilemma. This process is repeated for the remaining stories. Thus, as a recognition task, the DIT only requires the participant to recognize and select issue statements that best reflect their understanding of the moral dilemma.

By focusing the index of moral judgment development on the four items ranked as most important by participants, Rest and his colleagues were able to demonstrate that the DIT produced results that were quite consistent with theoretical expectations based on Kohlberg's model (e.g., Kohlberg, 1969). As described in more detail later, research using the DIT supported Kohlberg's claim that moral judgment developed rapidly over the high school and college years, the DIT was able to distinguish known groups who ought to differ on moral judgment development, while also demonstrating that the measure was sensitive to educational interventions, moral actions and choices, and other validating criteria. Thus, Rest claimed, one could measure moral judgment development without having to interview, interpret, or score participants verbal protocols.

Given the close ties to Kohlberg's model, the DIT was often viewed as simply a methodological alternative to the interview method. However, over time, the DIT research program evolved into a distinct branch in the field (Rest, Narvaez, Bebeau, & Thoma, 1999). Since the mid-to-late 1990s changes to the theory and measurement process have accelerated. Currently, DIT researchers have a new version of the DIT at their disposal (DIT-2; Rest, Narvaez, Thoma, & Bebeau, 1999), an expanded set of indices, a more elaborate validation strategy, and an underlying theory that is increasingly aligned with aspects of schema theory. Given the extent of these changes, this chapter focuses on what makes the DIT measurement process and underlying theory distinct from other branches in the field of moral psychology and to describe recent adjustments to the DIT along with associated shifts in theory.

CURRENT THEORETICAL CONSIDERATIONS—THE NEO-KOHLBERGIAN MODEL

A hallmark of DIT research and theory building is the very tight link between measurement issues and the underlying theory of the DIT. Since its inception, DIT researchers have refrained from modifying the measure, choosing instead to make modifications to theory guided by the growing body of empirical data. By contrast, others such as Kohlberg and colleagues viewed the measurement process as a direct extension of theory. Thus, the primary focus of Kohlberg's efforts was to modify the measurement process in the service of producing data that conformed to the theory (e.g., Colby & Kohlberg, 1987). DIT researchers' willingness to alter the supporting theory in the face of empirical evidence has led to a fairly rapid evolution of the moral judgment construct assessed by the DIT. The recent shifts in theory and measurement addressed by this chapter attest to the extent of these changes.

Recently, DIT researchers have described their current theory as neo-Kohlbergian, signaling a significant shift away from the original theory proposed by Kohlberg (Rest, Narvaez, Bebeau, & Thoma, 1999; see also Rest, Narvaez, Thoma, & Bebeau, 2000). A central feature of this work is the authors' attempt to locate the theory supporting the DIT within the current issues and debates in the field as well as to highlight its theoretical roots. Because the details of this work are rather extensive and accessible, they will be only summarized here in.

Similarities With Kohlberg's Model

At its core, the neo-Kohlbergian model assumes that the best way to understand morality is to focus on its cognitive component. Obviously, this choice does not preclude other entry points into moral functioning such as emotions (e.g., Haidt, 2001), human biology (Krebs, 2001), or prosocial behavior (Eisenberg & Fabes, 1998). However, as with any exploration into a phenomena one must make a choice of priorities and make compromises, all in the hope that the result is informative and provides significant contributions to the broader field. To neo-Kohlbergians, the choice of focusing on cognition continues to be a plausible entry point into the study of moral functioning. That is, Rest and his colleagues reaffirm the view that attending to how the individual comes to understand the social world generally and moral issues, in particular, is central to a theory of moral functioning and its developmental features.

Specifically, like Kohlberg, neo-Kohlbergians view growth in terms of development. That is, new forms of moral thinking develop over time and these new developments are improvements over the older conceptions. These newer conceptions are better in both the philosophical sense of leading to more justifiable applications, and in terms of the complexity of the resulting cognitive structures.

Like Kohlberg, neo-Kohlbergians accept the view that the individual constructs his or her own view of the social world and in so doing comes to understand cooperation and the social structures that support it. Neo-Kolbergians do not discount the role of culture in the individuals' development; however, the unit of measure is firmly set on the conceptions of cooperation formed by the individual. In this view, culture serves as a moderator in the process of development. In some circumstances culture may intensify the construction of some aspects of understanding cooperation (e.g., for individuals residing within a culture that places an emphasis on the free expression of ideas). By contrast, other cultures may potentially impede moral judgment development (e.g., when culture defines social conventions in religious terms, thereby making it more difficult for the individual to critically evaluate social structures and progress to a postconventional understanding of morality).

Finally, consistent with Kohlberg's view, neo-Kohlbergians focus on the shift from a conventional view of cooperation to a postconventional perspective and describe it as a central feature of adolescent and adult development. Clearly, there are many factors prior to adolescence that form the foundation for moral judgment development throughout the lifespan (e.g., Kagan & Lamb, 1987). However, neo-Kohlbergians argue that there is great significance in understanding how the adolescent comes to understand social conventions and eventually to recognize and debate the more subtle underpinnings of the social world.

Differences From Kohlberg's Model

There are also significant differences between the neo-Kohlbergian view and Kohlberg's theory. Reaffirmed in the neo-Kohlbergian view is the rejection of the strong stage model of development in which individuals move from stage to stage, one stage at a time. Instead, the model defines development as a gradual shifting from lower to more complex conceptions of social cooperation. Further, the neo-Kolbergian model assumes at any given time there are multiple conceptions available to the individual. Thus, appropriate measurement strategies must assess not only which conceptions are available, but the most preferred system.

Second, the neo-Kohlbergian approach reemphasizes the differences in data collection strategies from the Kohlberg system. As mentioned in the introduction, Kohlberg's measurement approaches asks participants to reason about moral dilemmas and explain their choices, whereas the DIT asks participants to rate and rank a set of items. Traditionally, this choice of measurement system was viewed in practical terms—it is easier to collect paper-and-pencil data than to conduct extensive interviews. However, neo-Kohlbergians note the growing concerns about interview data as a window into cognitive processing and particularly the use of this method as an accurate assessment of the level of processing used in real-life contexts (e.g., Narvaez & Bock, 2002). Pointing to the growing body of data originating from cognitive science perspectives, neo-Kohlbergians suggest that self-reported explanations of one's own cognitive processes have severe limitations (e.g., Narvaez & Bock, 2002; Nisbett & Wilson, 1977). Further, they note that assessing implicit understandings of moral situations may result in more accurate representations of real-time cognitive functioning. As such, the DIT with its emphasis on a tacit understanding of moral issues may actually have an advantage over interview-based systems. This argument is a work in progress, but the basic idea is that DIT stories and items are an efficient method for activating moral schemas. When an individual reads moral dilemmas (and the DIT sentence fragments) moral schemas are activated. The actual schemas activated are, of course, limited to the extent that a person has developed them. When an item is rated and ranked highly, we assume that the rater both understands the item and that it represents a preferred schema. By contrast, when the individual rates an item as low and does not rank it, then the assumption is that the item either does not make sense or seems simplistic and unconvincing; that is, it does not activate the individuals preferred schema. Sentence fragments are particularly good at evoking preferred schema because they balance bottom-up processing (stating just enough of a line of argument to activate a schema) with top-down processing (leaving the argument incomplete so that the participant has to fill in the meaning from schemas already in long-term memory).

Recently, Narvaez and Bock (2002) have argued that not only does the DIT work well to elicit moral schema, it also taps a level of processing that is most closely tied to everyday moral thinking. That is, we tend to make judgments with little evidence of direct or conscious reflection. The DIT, presumably, is very close to a measure of tacit understanding of moral issues because it is free from verbal demands and a heavy reliance on conscious reflection. Narvaez and her colleagues are currently engaged in a program of research to assess these claims. At the very least, these researchers suggest that interview data do not necessarily have an advantage over other measurement systems and argue that the decision whether or not to use any form of assessment is an empirical question.

In addition to reaffirming differences in stage models and measurement systems, a number of additional distinctions from Kohlberg's system were elaborated in the formulation of the neo-Kohlbergian perspective. One major departure is the definition of postconventional reasoning. In Kohlberg's view, postconventional reasoning is best defined by philosophers associated with the deontological theories of the Liberal Enlightenment and by John Rawls' work in particular. When Kohlberg was developing his theory in the 1960s, Rawls' work was a very plausible starting point in defending the view that postconventional reasoning is logically an advance over conventional reasoning. However, much has changed in both applied and theoretical philosophy that calls into question the clear superiority of deontological theories and perspectives (see Beauchamp & Childress, 1994, 2002). Thus, the philosophical foundations for postconventional reasoning are no longer as secure as Kohlberg defined them.

Using a "big-tent" approach, the neo-Kohlbergian description of postconventional reasoning is no longer tied to a particular philosophical theory or perspective. In its place, and to guard against the claim that the model is slipping back into moral relativism, a series of criteria were developed that must be met to qualify as a postconventional system. In short, these criteria include (a) the central role of moral criteria in the formulation and understanding of laws and norms, (b) the appeal to an ideal—that is, the system— must convey some idealized view of how the community ought to be ordered. Further, (c) a postconventional system must present a clear sense that moral ideals are open, subject to critique and thus sharable with the larger community. Finally, (d) the system is fully reciprocal, that is, developed to address the community as a whole and then uniformly applied.

Many of the traditional philosophical approaches fit these criteria; therefore, there is no need take a partisan position and tie the psychological model to a particular philosophical tradition. However, neo-Kolbergians are clear that not all philosophical traditions are consistent with these criteria. Absent from a list of qualifying approaches are those who reject human cooperation as a ploy of the strong to control the weak (e.g., Nietzsche, 1968/1986), who view morality as simply a language that conveys personal likes and dislikes (e.g., Stevenson, 1937), or whose moral systems are based on religious doctrine that is not open to debate or scrutiny (see Rest, Narvaez, Bebeau, & Thoma [1999]; also Beauchamp & Childress [1994] for a discussion of the relative adequacy of moral theories).

Second, the neo-Kohlbergian model breaks with the Kohlberg system on the claim that moral stages are universal. Kohlberg had very strong views concerning the universality question, arguing that all normal functioning individuals in all cultures move through the same developmental sequence albeit at different rates and perhaps terminating at different levels (Kohlberg, 1984). Rest notes in his remembrances of Kohlberg that the universality claim was particularly important to Kohlberg because it provided the strongest buffer against claims of moral relativism, which he viewed as a slippery slope toward immoral systems and practices legitimized simply because of their existence (Rest, 1999; see also Reed, 1997).

Drawing from recent work in the professional ethics education area (e.g., Bebeau, 2002), the neo-Kohlbergian model adopts a common morality viewpoint somewhat similar to the notion of common law. Common law can be identified across cultures and regions serving similar ends and sharing many features. However, due to particular circumstances and prototype cases, common law develops noticeable differences across cultures and contexts in both emphases and precedents.

The neo-Kohlbergian view is that common morality may develop in a similar fashion across cultures and settings. On the one hand, cross-cultural similarities may be evident given that circumstances and histories overlap as well as the expectation that there are some basic cooperative presses common to all social groupings. Conversely differences may appear for similar reasons: different histories and different circumstances that serve to emphasize particular issues (e.g., the U.S. views on the separation of church and state). Put another way, the notion of common morality adopted by neo-Kohlbergians is one that views morality as the product of society, its history, and its formalized structures that promote discussion of social issue. Furthermore, the evolution of common morality is driven by debate and negotiation, and achieves permanency only by garnering general support from the larger community. This last point is important in that it attempts to deal with the notion of moral relativism, which is always a concern for moral judgment researchers. In short, the notion of common morality is not simply a retreat to relativism because the moral systems that it describes develop out of a process of deliberation that is community wide and generally applicable. The major implication of this view for researchers is that the universality question is now an empirical one that asks whether and to what degree there are overlaps in moral conceptions across culture. It does not begin with the assumption that none exist.

Finally, neo-Kohlbergians adopt a schema view of moral judgment development. The shift in terminology signals an abandonment of cognitive operations as the defining features of moral stages that were so central to Kohlberg's stage definitions. In their place, the neo-Kohlbergian model suggests that schemas represent a network of knowledge that is organized around particular life events and exists to help individuals understand new information based on prior experiences (Rest, Narvaez, Bebeau, & Thoma, 1999). Schemas are, therefore, highly contextual, often automatic, and less reflective than Kohlberg's stages. Consistent with this view and current thinking in cognitive psychology (e.g., Rummelhart, 1980) is a companion position suggesting that schemas may not be explicitly understood by the individual and may operate at the tacit level. As mentioned, the DIT may be particularly well-suited to assess moral schemas at the schema level.

Locating the DIT in the Neo-Kohlbergian Model of Moral Functioning

The attention to theory has had a direct effect on how the information supplied by the DIT is interpreted. Part of this reevaluation occurred in the 1980s during the development of the Four Component Model, which was originally created as a means to organize the field of moral development for a major review chapter (Rest, 1983). However, the Four Component Model continues to be used as a means to understand and explain the construct measured by the DIT.

The Four Component Model.   The Four Component Model suggests that moral functioning is the result of at least four component processes: moral sensitivity, moral judgments, moral motivation, and moral character operating together and in interaction. As defined by the model, each of these components has a unique contribution to moral functioning and is best viewed as defining a set of processes that serve the same ends. One major implication of this model is that moral judgment development in the Kohlberg tradition, including the neo-Kohlbergian perspective, is contained within Component II (moral judgment) of the Four Component Model. Further, moral judgment development is viewed as only one of a set of processes leading to the judgment of what one ought to do (i.e., the output of Component II moral judgments). In short, the primary effect of the Four Component Model on clarifying what the DIT measured was to clearly locate the construct within the second component.

Perhaps less apparent was the Four Component Model's role in delimiting moral judgment development within the psychological space related to moral functioning. Thus, following the development of the Four Component Model, it was very difficult to claim that the DIT was a sufficient measure of moral thinking. This shift in perspective of what the DIT measured was significant and had a direct effect on the ways in which the DIT was used. For example, consider the moral judgment and action studies of the 1980s (e.g., Rest, 1986). Prior to the Four Component Model, DIT researchers interested in the link between moral judgment and action tended to design studies in which the primary goal was to estimate the direct effect of DIT scores on moral action. After the Four Component Model became well known, researcher interest shifted to studies that adopted a multimeasure approach in which attention to the contributions of other components was included in the study design (Rest, 1986).

Codes, Intermediate Concepts, and Bedrock Schema. More recently, the neo-Kohlbergian view of the Four Component Model has prompted a reinterpretation of the construct measured by the DIT. Driven in part by DIT researchers working within professional school settings, Component II has been further elaborated by proposing three levels of Component II functioning: codes of conduct, intermediate concepts, and bedrock schema (Bebeau, 1994, 2002; Rest & Narvaez, 1994). As Fig. 3.1 indicates, these three levels differ in the degree of specificity with codes representing the most specific form of Component II functioning and bedrock schema the most broadbased. Although research indicates that DIT scores relate to measures at all three levels, findings also indicate that there is room for improvement, particularly among measures that directly target the concept (Bebeau, 2002; Bebeau & Thoma, 1999). Thus, interest has grown in clarifying the measurement of the three levels, particularly the intermediate level (Bebeau, 2002). At the same time, DIT scores are increasingly viewed as directly assessing only the most general bedrock level of functioning (e.g., Rest, Narvaez, Bebeau, & Thoma, 1999).

More specifically, codes are highly prescriptive and require less extensive interpretation. For example, a professional finding him- or herself in a particular situation covered by a code has very little leeway in constructing an action because the required action is explicit in the code (e.g., When *x* occurs, you must do *y*). Thus, the most difficult aspect of this form of Component II reasoning is to identify the situation as falling under the purview of a code. Once identified, however, the processing demands leading to the component II outcome seem relatively straightforward.

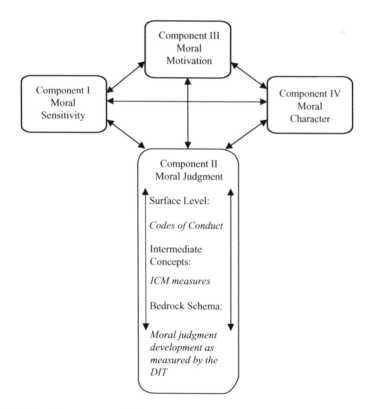

FIG. 3.1 The Four Component Model.

The second level—intermediate concepts—represents ethical concepts that are often tied to a particular setting or profession. These concepts are abstract and require interpretation and the self-constructed means for implementation and evaluation. So, for instance, the concept of informed consent, beneficence, and professional authority are standard topics within many health and social science professional ethics education programs. These topics are usually described within particular contexts and rely on sets of precedents for interpretation and resolution. Many of these concepts represent day-to-day morality and are often interpersonal in nature (see also Bebeau & Thoma, 1999).

Finally, bedrock schema, the most general and context-free system for interpreting moral situations, is the construct measured by the DIT. Recent interpretations of these schemas suggest that it is used as a default system and exists when other, more automatic and context-specific, interpretive systems fail or provide incomplete or inconsistent information. It is important to note that by defining the construct measured by the DIT as default and serving some backup function does not mean that the practical relationship between DIT scores and external criteria is minimal. Given the hypothesized influence of these default schema on the development of reasoning about intermediate concepts, DIT scores represent multiple sources, both direct and indirect. That is, DIT scores directly assess default schema and indirectly the influence of the default schema on systems at the additional higher levels.

Micro Versus Macro Morality.   One final reinterpretation of the construct measured by the DIT deserves mention. Much as has been made of the distinction between everyday morality or micromorality and society-wide morality or macromorality (e.g., Rest, Narvaez, Bebeau, & Thoma, 1999; Thoma, 2002). DIT researchers have been clear that as a measure of the default schema within Component II of the Four Component Model the DIT assesses macromorality. As such, these default, macromoral processes form the basis of how the individual views social cooperation in terms of justice and fairness within law and the mechanisms of government and other social institutions. Obviously, the distinction between micro- and macromorality is not complete and how one understands morality in terms of social structures must relate in some way to everyday morality. However, the claim advanced by the model is that everyday morality is much more contextual than macromorality and driven by multiple sources (e.g., as defined by the other components in the Four Component Model), only one of which is the default system measured by the DIT).

Although the distinction between macro- and micromorality may appear to place limits on the impact of macromorality on moral function, its significance during the second decade of life and beyond is often noted (e.g., Adelson, 1971; Torney-Purta, 1990). Indeed, the DIT measurement system assumes that the major developmental shifts during adolescence and beyond are the growing understanding of macromoral conceptions of social cooperation in conventional and postconventional terms (Rest, Narvaez, Bebeau, & Thoma, 1999).

In summary, recent attention has been given to the theoretical location of the construct measured by the DIT. At present, the interpretation of various sources of empirical data and theoretical discussions suggest that the measurement focuses not only on a specific member of the set of Component II processes, but that it resides at the most general level. Further, it is assumed that the DIT assesses the system that is used as a default interpretive system. As such, the construct measured by the DIT focuses on macromoral features of moral judgment development with the expectation that it will provide both direct and indirect (e.g., through intermediate concepts) paths of influence on moral choices and actions.

Construct Validity and the DIT

One strength of the DIT research program is its focus on construct validity studies (e.g., Thoma, 2002). The number and types of studies supporting the DIT as a measure of moral judgment development are both broad and deep (see Rest, 1979, 1986; Rest & Narvaez, 1994; Rest, Narvaez, Bebeau, & Thoma, 1999). A well-articulated set of validity criterion was essential in the development of the DIT and contributed to the theoretical shifts mentioned in previous sections. Further, these criteria served as the testing ground for new indexes and for dealing with criticisms of the measure. Over time, a series of studies were identified that represented different aspects of the criterion categories used to validate the DIT. These studies became the laboratory for testing new ideas. To be a worthy addition or scoring modification, the experimental variable had to produce significantly better trends across criteria and studies than the trends produced by its older counterpart.

In a similar manner, criticisms of the DIT were addressed through the use of the validity criteria. For example, when it was claimed that the DIT actually measured verbal ability (Sanders, Lubinski, & Benbow, 1995), the response from DIT researchers was to find studies that could both represent the different types of criterion studies and contain a measure of verbal ability or some reasonable proxy of it. The procedure to test the claim then becomes very straightforward: reanalyze these data while controlling for verbal ability and observe whether the trend remains (i.e., when verbal ability is controlled can DIT scores, still produce age trends, differentiate know groups, relate to political attitudes and choices and so on). In this case, Thoma, Narvaez, Rest, and Derryberry (1999) found that the dominant trends remained—verbal ability could not account for findings using DIT scores.

The specific criteria used to validate the DIT include the following: (1) differentiation of various age and education groups; (2) longitudinal gains; (3) correlation with cognitive capacity measures; (4) sensitivity to moral education interventions; (5) correlation with behavior and professional decision making; and (6) predicting to political choice and attitude. Briefly, differentiation of various age and education groups suggests that the DIT is able to distinguish between groups who ought to differ on a measure of moral judgment development. For instance, graduate students in political science and philosophy should score higher than other graduate students who are not so well versed in political and ethical theory. Similarly, college students should score higher than high school students, and so on. The use of naturally occurring groups became a particularly popular study especially in the early years of the DIT. Large composite samples (thousands of subjects) show that 30% to 50% of the variance of DIT scores is attributable to level of education in samples ranging from those with a junior-high education to those with a PhD.

The longitudinal gains criteria suggest that the DIT should produce evidence of upward movement across time. This criterion basically mirrors the traditional claim that a developmental measure ought to describe change in an upward manner. For instance, a 10-year longitudinal study shows significant gains for men and women, for college students and people not attending college, from diverse walks of life (Rest, 1986). A review of a dozen studies comparing freshman to senior college students ($n = 755$) shows effect sizes (expressed as Cohen's d statistic) of .80 (large gains). In short, DIT gains are one of the most dramatic longitudinal gains in college of any variable studied in college students (Rest & Narvaez, 1994).

Criterion 3 suggests that DIT scores ought to be related to measures of moral comprehension and other cognitive measures. Relationships with cognitive measures should not be excessive and thus raise the possibility that DIT scores are actually measuring general cognitive skills. Nor should cognitive measures subsume the relationship between DIT scores and other criterion variables (as claimed by the Sanders et al. [1995] study). In general, findings indicate that DIT scores are significantly related to cognitive capacity measures of moral comprehension ($r = .60$s), to recall and reconstruction of postconventional moral argument, to Kohlberg's measure, and (to a lesser degree) to other cognitive–developmental measures (Rest, 1979).

The fourth criterion suggests that DIT scores should be related to specific experiences that ought to stimulate development. Intervention studies are the prototype for this criterion (e.g., presence or absence of a dilemma discussion condition). For example, Rest (1986) describes a review of over 50 intervention studies and reports an effect size for dilemma discussion interventions to be .41 (moderate gains), whereas the effect size for comparison groups was only .09 (small gains).

The fifth criterion proposes that DIT scores should be linked to prosocial behaviors and to desired professional decision making. One review reports that 32 out of 47 measures were statistically significant (Rest, 1986). Further, Rest and Narvaez (1994) link DIT scores to many aspects of professional decision making.

Finally, criterion 6 focuses on the link between DIT scores and social and political variables. The claim associated with criterion 6 is that DIT scores should be significantly linked to political attitudes and political choices, particularly because it is a measure of macromorality and as such ought to relate to political knowledge and understanding. In a review of several dozen correlates with political attitude, DIT scores it was found that they typically correlate in the range of $r = .40$ to $.65$ (Thoma et al., 1999). When DIT scores are combined in multiple regression with measures of cultural ideology, the overall prediction increased to up to two thirds of the variance in opinions about controversial public policy issues (such as abortion, religion in public schools, women's roles, rights of the accused, rights of homosexuals, and free speech issues). Because such issues are among the most hotly debated issues of our time, the DIT's predictability to these issues is important and worthy of future study. (Narvaez, Getz, Rest, & Thoma, 1999).

In addition to these validity criteria, the Minnesota group also focused on traditional enabling standards for tests and measures such as acceptable psychometric evidence as well as response stability across different test-taking sets. In addition, DIT scores show discriminant validity from a host of competing variables such as verbal ability/general intelligence and from conservative/liberal political attitudes (see review of more than 20 studies in Thoma et al., 1999). Moreover, the DIT is equally valid for men and women, because gender accounts for less than one half of a percent of the variance of the DIT, whereas education is 250 times more powerful in predicting DIT variance (Thoma, 1986).

Recent Changes to the DIT Measurement System

Development of the DIT-2.   Concurrent with the discussion about the location of the moral judgment construct measured by the DIT, there has been significant work on the measurement process as well. Chief among these changes is the development of a new DIT (hereafter DIT-2). It is now well known that the DIT is a paper and pencil measure in which participants are asked to read six stories and then for each story, rate and rank 12 items the majority of which are written to reflect Kohlberg stages two through six, as described by Kohlberg in 1973 (see Rest, 1979; Thoma, 2002). Responding to criticism that the content of the original DIT was becoming outdated and stale, the DIT-2 was created with new stories and items. Specifically, the original DIT had stories that focused on issues that were no longer as current such as protesting the Vietnam War and items that included terminology no longer used (e.g., the label *Oriental*). Unlike the original DIT, which had its roots in the Kohlberg interview system, the DIT-2 was written to mirror the basic features of the DIT shifting only the content of the stories and items. Thus, the stories all presented the same dilemma with a different context. For example, in place of Heinz and the Drug, the equivalent DIT-2 story asks whether a poor farmer should break into a rich store owner's food warehouse to feed his starving family.

The only major change in developing the DIT-2 was the elimination of the content associated with the Webster story, the story of a repair shop owner considering hiring an Asian-American mechanic. This story was always considered the weakest of the original six because it was the least controversial (almost everyone agreed that the owner should hire the minority mechanic), and empirically it was not as strongly related to the other five story summary scores (Minnesota Center for the Study of Ethical Development, personal communication). Therefore, no attempt was made to create a parallel version of the Webster story.

The procedures used to develop the DIT-2 represented a significant break from the original process of creating a measure of moral thinking. As described by Rest (1979), the initial DIT stories were derived from similar stories used by Kohlberg and his colleagues (e.g., Lockwood, 1970). The corresponding items on the DIT were written by Rest based on the distillations of interview data. Thus, if few participants generated a particular argument in response to a story, then no attempt was made to create one for the DIT. The close connection between interview data and item development ensured a level of psychological reality in the task that is unusual for a paper-and-pencil measure.

The DIT-2, by contrast, piggybacks off of the work leading to the DIT by creating stories to match the underlying dilemmas in the original without the reliance on previous interview data. In addition, DIT-2 items were written to reflect the same stage and sentence structure as well as to provide the same mix of stage-based items and reliability check items, the latter of which are designed to identify participants using an alien test-taking set (the *M* or meaningless items). Prior to the validation studies, experts in the field assessed the match between each DIT and DIT-2 item. All DIT-2 items that failed this check were written until all were independently found to reasonably match the original.

Interestingly, these validation studies found that the correlation between DIT and DIT-2 summary indexes was r (505) = .79; $p < .01$, a figure very close to the typical test–retest reliability correlations found with the DIT. Indeed, if the correlation between versions is corrected for the unreliability of the two measures (both ranging from the mid-.70s to low .80s in age heterogeneous samples), the adjusted correlation is a very respectable .98 (see Rest, Narvaez, Thoma, & Bebeau, 1999). Taken together, these findings suggest not only that the DIT and DIT-2 can be viewed as parallel forms, but that there is a particular measurement advantage in having subjects rate and rank items. That is, having participants assess all items twice, once during the rating task and a second time when determining the ranking, produces a highly stable measure with respectable reliability and validity coefficients (Rest, Narvaez, Thoma, & Bebeau, 1999).

Reinterpreting the Internal Composition of the DIT. Concurrent with the process of updating the measure, DIT researchers have also focused on the characteristics of the developmental dimension the measure is supposed to assess. As originally conceived, the developmental dimension was defined in terms of Kohlberg's stages as presented in the early 1970s. This definition remained constant for over 20 years in spite of the revisions to Kohlberg's theory during the late 1970s and 1980s. In addition, as the Kohlberg group worked on revisions to their model, the supporting theory presupposed by DIT researchers increasingly diverged, further eroding the motivation to revise the model to keep it in line with the Kohlbergian view. Thus, the definition of the developmental dimension remained constant throughout the 1980s and early 1990s.

More recently, however, the need to better understand participants' location on developmental dimension has lead to a renewed interest in how best to define development. Part of the motivation to explore new indices was the ability to create data sets with sufficient numbers (some as large as 44,000) and diversity to assess empirically the fit of the Kohlberg's model to DIT data. Further, there was some empirical work that suggested that some of the lower stage items on the DIT clustered together in ways not predicted by Kohlberg's theory (Center for the Study of Ethical Development, 1998).

It is interesting to note that some of this work was presaged by Davison (in Rest [1979]) who, with limited data, found that the psychological space between Kohlberg's Stages 2 and 3 as assessed by the DIT was smaller than between Stages 3 and 4. Further, Stage 4 seemed distant from Stages 5 and 6 which tended to parallel each other. Overall, Davison found support for Kohlberg's ordering of the stages on the DIT. However, Davison also noted that the lower stages were more closely aligned than expected. That is, one could argue that three clusters of items were evident in the data (Stages 2 and 3 combined, Stage 4 and the Postconventional items, Stages 5 and 6).

Using the larger and more diverse samples empirical estimates of the number of item clusters do suggest three distinct groupings: Stages 2 and 3, Stage 4, and Stages 5 and 6. This finding is especially clear when using a broadbased high school through adult sample (e.g., Thoma & Rest, 1999). Only when samples are constructed to emphasize a junior high school population, the youngest group appropriate for the DIT, did the Stages 2 items become distinct from Stage 3 items. In short, the developmental scheme that best fits DIT data is no longer the six Kohlberg stages. Instead, a three-level model loosely informed by Kohlberg's model seems more appropriate.

No doubt this structure is due in part to the populations typically under study and the properties of the measure itself. However, empirically, participants tend to view items representing Stages 2 and 3 as less important reasoning and treat them similarly. As a group, these items are not often ranked. That is, items that speak of self-preservation, self-interest, and personal relationships are viewed together as lesser personal concerns that do not seem as central as other, more system-wide concerns represented by the Stage 4 items and those that constitute the postconventional cluster. These items are viewed as highly important and are often ranked. Consistent with the view that the DIT items are tapping into the more macromoral aspects of moral reasoning, the engine of the DIT is clearly derived from the Stage 4 conventional items and the postconventional items.

Interpreting the Three Clusters of Items.   Following from the shift to a more contextualized, schema-based view of moral judgment development, the three empirical clusters of items have been interpreted as representing three ordered moral schema: the Personal Interest schema (drawing from Kohlberg's descriptions of Stages 2 and 3); the Maintaining Norms schema (drawing from Kohlberg's Stage 4); and the Postconventional schema (drawing from Kohlberg's Stages 5 and 6—the old P score items). A description of each schema is presented below.

Personal Interest Schema.   Rest, Narvaez, Bebeau, and Thoma (1999) describe the personal Interest schema as fully developed by the time participants are able to reliably complete the DIT (typically defined as a 9th-grade reading level). As the label implies, the main considerations highlighted by the scheme are the gains and losses each participant may personally experience within a moral dilemma. No appeal to the broader social systems are included within this schema. It is as if the social world was a network of micromoral considerations linking close relationships and individual interests. Unfortunately, the DIT can say little about the development of the schema within childhood, except to say that empirically participants recognized it as, at best, a secondary consideration by the time reach adolescence.

The Maintaining Norms Schema.   The Maintaining Norms schema represents the first entry into a society-wide moral perspective by directly focusing on the moral basis of society; it addresses the question of how to organize cooperation on a society-wide basis. The organization of society this schema promotes is based on an understanding of rules, roles, and the importance of authorities. As such, it draws heavily from Kohlberg's Stage 4. However, it is also informed by Adelson's (1971) notion of the adolescents' developing understanding of political thought and in particular his views on adolescent authoritarianism. More specifically the Maintaining Norms schema has the following elements: (a) the perceived need for generally accepted social norms to govern a collective. (b) The necessity that the norms apply society wide, to all people in a society. (c) The need for the norms to be clear, uniform, and categorical (i.e., that there is "the rule of law"). (d) The norms are seen as establishing a reciprocity (each citizen obeys the law, expecting that others will also obey). (e) The establishment of hierarchical role structures, chains of command, and authority and duty. That is, in an organized society, there are hierarchical role structures (e.g., teacher–pupil, parent–child, general–soldier, doctor–patient; see Rest, Narvaez, Bebeau, & Thoma [1999, p. 37]).

In short, the Maintaining Norms schema explicitly views maintaining the established social order as a moral obligation. As in Kohlberg's stage four, the schema suggests that without law there would be no order, people would instead act on their own special interests and the result would be chaos. For this schema, no further rationale for defining morality is necessary beyond simply asserting that an act is prescribed by the law, is the established way of doing things, or is the established will of God.

Postconventional Schema.   The neo-Kohlbergian model assumes a different definition of what constitutes a postconventional system. Following from many philosophical traditions, the essential feature of postconventional thinking is that moral obligations are to be based on shared ideals, are fully reciprocal, and are open to scrutiny (i.e., subject to tests of logical consistency, experience of the community, and coherence with accepted practice (see above and Rest, Narvaez, Bebeau, & Thoma [1999, p. 38] for a more detailed description).

In short, the major distinctions measured by the DIT are the differences between conventionality and postconventionality (e.g., what Kohlberg regarded as the distinction between Stage 4 and Stage 5; and Adelson's description of the development of political thought). Although the focus of the DIT is more limited in scope than these earlier models, the significance of the shift from conventional to postconventional reasoning is quite compelling. For instance, the distinction between conventional and post-conventionality is what tends to drive so many public policy disputes such as the reactions to the Gulf wars, minority rights, religion in the schools, medical policy, and so on. Further, and perhaps most importantly given the events following 9/11, conventional and postconventional reasoning addresses the divide between religious fundamentalism and secular modernism (see Marty & Appleby, 1993).

New Indices and Measures

In addition to the development of an updated measure, a number of new indices regarding the DIT have developed in the last 5 years. Most notably and after a number of failed attempts, a new overall index was identified that could rival the traditional *P*-score, and it was added to the standard set of indices provided by the measure (Rest, Thoma, Narvaez, & Bebeau, 1997). For many years, the primary DIT index was the *P*-score, which is derived from the participant's ranking of postconventional items. This score has been criticized for at least two reasons: for treating qualitative data as continuous, and for throwing away subject responses to stage-based items other than the postconventional items. Much has been written about the first criticism (e.g., Rest, 1979, 1986; Rest et al., 1997). Suffice it to say that DIT researchers acknowledge the qualitative distinctions between different conceptions of moral thinking, but argue strongly that the assessment process must be quantitative to measure the relative differences in responses to types of moral thinking. *P*-scores, therefore represent the participant's relative location on the developmental continuum (defined by qualitatively different markers). As *P*-scores build, the assumption is that the individual's developmental location is increasingly toward higher levels of moral thinking.

The second criticism of the *P*-score questions the advisability of an overall index that does not use all of the information available. As mentioned, *P*-scores infer the use of lower stage-based items by the relative use of *P* items, but the measurement of *P* does not directly incorporate other items in the computation of the score. This characteristic of the DIT's main index of development has been a concern from many because it violates the basic tenant of classical measurement theory—you do not throw away useful data (e.g., Loevinger, 1976). Although the *P*-score has demonstrated its worth for many years, there have been a number of attempts to improve on *P* by adding the additional missing information. Unfortunately, these attempts have failed in the sense that the information supplied by the experimental indices did not provide superior trends when pitted against the *P*-score (Davison, in Rest, 1979; Evens, 1995; Rest et al., 1997). That is, until the N2 score was identified.

The N2 Score. Recently, however, a new index, N2, has been developed that has shown promise in unseating the *P*-score. Interestingly, the N2 scores uses the *P*-score as its starting point and then adjusts the *P*-score based on the participants' ability to discriminate between *P* items and lower stage items. In short, *P*-scores are adjusted in a positive direction if the participant discriminates high and low items (i.e., rates the higher items as more important than the lower stage items). Failure to make this discrimination, results in the downward adjustment of the *P*-score. Typically, the correlation between *P* and N2 is high and ranges from the mid 80s to the lower 90s (see Rest et al., 1997). However, the major impact of the N2 score is with older and presumably more developed individuals because it should be most helpful in discriminating at the high end of the developmental scale. Thus, researchers using the DIT on graduate and professional school populations should find the N2 score an improvement over *P*-score. Current observations of high school and college samples suggest that *P*-scores and N2 scores tend to behave very similarly (Center for the Study of Ethical Development, November 11, 2003, personal communication).

Additional Measures Derived From the DIT and DIT-2. Two additional classes of measures have been recently developed and are under current use. The first represents additional ways to capture aspects of moral judgment development not directly assessed by using the common overall indices. These measures include an index of consolidation and transition, and a moral type index. The second class of measures includes nonmoral development indices that can be derived from responses to the DIT.

Developmental Phase Indicators. The first class of the additional measures of moral judgment development was created to explore the role of consolidation and transition on moral judgment development (Thoma & Rest, 1999). Following the consolidation and transition developmental phase model of Snyder and Feldman (1984), and noting Walker and Taylor's (1991) application of the this model within the moral judgment domain, Thoma and Rest (1999) attempted to measure the degree to which participants were transitional (i.e., evidences little preference for the various stage-based items and, thus, presents a flat response profile) or consolidated (evidences a clear preference for a particular stage-based items and, thus, a peaked response profile) on the DIT.

The main difficulty Thoma and Rest (1999) faced was that Snyder and Feldman developed their theory of consolidation and transition assuming an orthodox stage model. In this view, development is described by locating the participant directly on the developmental continuum (e.g., Kohlberg's stages fit this description). Thus, to make the system applicable to DIT data, it was necessary to translate the basic ideas of the Snyder and Feldman model into the more continuous model presupposed by the DIT. The method used by Thoma and Rest (1999) defined consolidation and transition by assessing the variance accounted for in participant's item ratings by the item's stage assignment. That is, if the variance accounted in item ratings by stage assignment reached a statistically significant level, then the participant was labeled in the consolidated phase. Note that as the variance accounted for index increases the profile of stage responses must become more peaked. Thus, the statistical test is simply an objective decision rule for defining when a profile is peaked. Conversely, when the statistical test indicated that there was little variance accounted for by stage assignment, then transitional status was assigned. Under these conditions, the item response pattern would have to be flat. In short, by attending to item response patterns it was possible to develop a continuous stage model equivalent for the Snyder and Feldman model.

Using the index of developmental phase, Thoma and Rest were able to replicate findings (e.g., Walker & Taylor, 1991) indicating that change in moral judgments varies as a function of consolidation and transition. Specifically, participants moving from a transitional to consolidated phase changed at a faster rate than all other patterns. Further, they found that moral information is more salient in the decision-making process during the consolidation phase regardless of developmental level. More recently, developmental phase has been shown to relate to the time it takes to arrive at decisions about moral issues (Thoma, Narvaez, Endicott, & Derryberry, 2001). Consolidated subjects took longer to judge the moral issues, suggesting a deeper processing of these issues. Further, Derryberry (2000) found that developmental phase indicators, when included in the analysis as a moderator, increased the magnitude of the relationship between moral judgment and action. Indeed, the common finding across these studies is that developmental phases help to moderate the relationship between DIT scores and external variables. Generally speaking, if an effect is observed using the DIT, the effect is stronger if computed for participants in the consolidated groupings.

Developmental Types. One of the frustrations in using developmental phase information is incorporating it with developmental level when presenting study results. Typically

TABLE 3.1
Description of the Type Variable

Type	Consolidation?	Modal Schema	Off-Modal Schema
1	Yes	2/3	N/A
2	No	2/3	4
3	No	4	2/3
4	Yes	4	N/A
5	No	4	5/6
6	No	5/6	4
7	Yes	5/6	N/A

Note. N/A, not applicable.

in the studies mentioned, the influence of developmental phase is assessed after controlling for developmental level. This approach maintains the continuous nature of the developmental level variables and supports the view that developmental phase has a unique effect on the variable of interest. Conversely, some studies have attempted to add both sources of information within a mixed-model regression (i.e., developmental phase carried by a dichotomous variable, and developmental level as a continuous variable). Although this approach is consistent with the measurement properties of both variables, it is not always easy to present the data in a meaningful way. To circumvent this difficulty, a new variable labeled *Type* was created that reflects both developmental phase and developmental level.

As Table 3.1 indicates, Type has seven levels defined by developmental phase (i.e., consolidation or transition) and developmental level, which in turn is defined by modal ratings on the three-item cluster (i.e., Stage 2/3 items—personal interest schema, Stage 4 items—maintaining norms schema, and *P* items—the postconventional schema). In the seven-point system, consolidated types are 1, 4, and 7 based on developmental phase status and dominant schema.

Transitional types are a bit more difficult to define. Like consolidated subjects, the preferred schema is identified by highest use. In addition, however, the second most preferred schema is also identified. The latter is used to calibrate whether the individual is moving toward a consolidated phase or away from it. For instance, consider Types 3 and 5. Both of these types are transitional, and both are characterized as having a preference for the maintaining norms schema. What separates Types 3 and 5 from each other is the second highest rating cluster. For Type 3, the developmentally lower personal interest cluster is the second highest rated cluster. By contrast, the *P* item cluster is the second most important schema that defines Type 5. One can view the two transitional types as moving toward consolidation on the conventional items (Type 3) and moving away from consolidation on conventional items (Type 5).

Figure 3.2 indicates the anticipated strong relationship between Type and the *P* and N2 scores. Although it is clear that type is a very useful way of presenting both developmental phase and level information, it is not without its problems. Chief among these difficulties is the statistical issue of categorizing a continuous variable (see also Walker [2002], who notes this difficulty as well). As DIT researchers have argued for many years, the primary measure of development provided by the DIT is continuous. Thus it seems to be a bit of backsliding to advocate for a categorical measure like Type when it is derived from DIT data. On the other hand, consider that the intent of the Type variable is not to supplant *P*- or N2 scores as the main developmental indices of the DIT, but rather to provide an

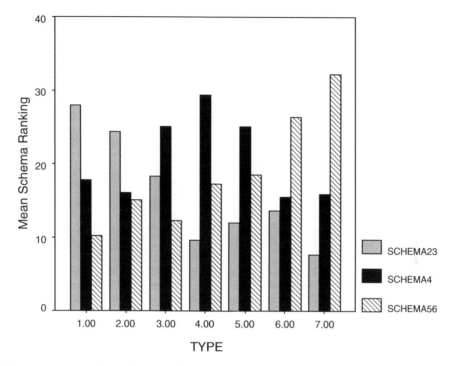

FIG. 3.2 **Mean DIT item ratings as a function of moral type.**

efficient way of presenting a picture of development together with developmental phase information. Consistent with this purpose, in most cases it would inappropriate to rely on Type as the primary analysis strategy for a study using the DIT. However, it would be quite appropriate to supplement the main analyses by presenting an overall picture of the data using the Type indicators.

Nonmoral Judgment Measures Derived From the DIT. The second cluster of variables mentioned was developed to serve as proxies of other nonmoral variables. For the most part, these variables are attempts at deriving additional information from the DIT without relying on other measures and to minimize the demands on participants' time (Thoma, 2002). Specifically, these variables capture the degree of decisiveness on the DIT story action choices, agreement with action choice decisions made by a liberal group of graduate students in philosophy and political science, and an item rating and ranking pattern that is consistent with a religious orthodoxy orientation. Not only are these variables readily available for researchers using the DIT, they also serve as a template for others wishing to create variable proxies for their own use.

Number of Can't Decides. The Can't Decide variable was created to represent the decisiveness with which an individual selects action choices on the DIT. The computation of this variable is rather straightforward. For each of the six (or five on the DIT-2) stories, participants must choose whether the protagonist should or should not act in a particular way (e.g., should steal or not steal on the Heinz dilemma). Participants may also select the Can't Decide option. To compute this variable, the researcher counts the number of times the participant selects the Can't Decide option, resulting in a measure ranging from

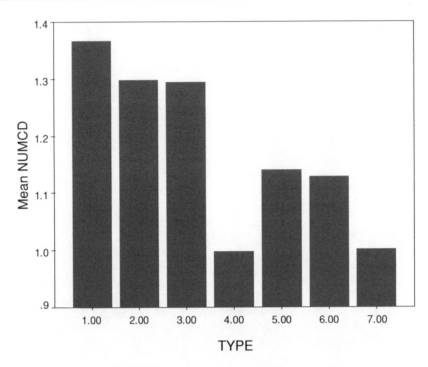

FIG. 3.3   Mean number of Can't Decide action choices (NUMCD) by moral type.

0 to 6 on the DIT and 0 to 5 on the DIT-2. The interest in this variable centers around the notion that indecision is in part a product of the ease with which moral information is processed. Further, based on the Thoma and Rest (1999) study, there is the expectation that indecision may covary with developmental phase. Specifically, transitional phases should be associated with increased indecision given the multiple and potentially conflicting interpretations associated with transition. For example, Fig. 3.3 plots average Can't Decide scores (labeled NUMCD) by Type for a large sample ($N = 45,829$; see Evens, 1995). This sample is a mixed-gender composite sample of all U.S. regions and age ranges representing 10 years of DIT data scored by the Minnesota Center for the Study of Ethical Development. As can be observed, the consolidated Types—4 and 7—are associated with the lowest frequency of Can't Decides. Type 1—also a consolidated type—does not fit this pattern. However, it is a relatively small and unstable group. Further, it may be that individuals consolidated on the personal interest cluster may be limited in the moral information they can readily absorb and apply to the various situations. Note too how useful the Type information is in clarifying the relationship between moral judgment development and the processing of moral information.

Humanitarian/Liberal Perspective.   This variable is a proxy for a humanitarian/liberal perspective on moral issues. Early in the development of the DIT, it was noted that professionals in political science and philosophy obtained the highest P-scores. So high, in fact that this group was presented as experts in the domain and used to anchor the upper end of the measure (Rest, 1979). Less well known, however, is that not only were these subjects obtaining high scores on the DIT, but they were also quite consistent in their action choices. For instance, these subjects strongly endorsed the position that Heinz should

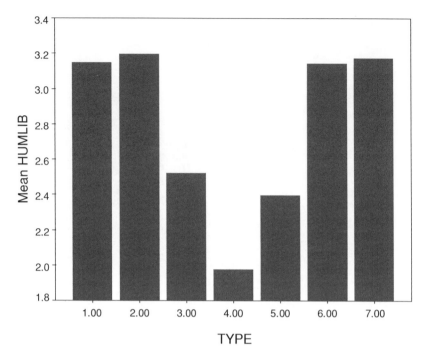

FIG. 3.4 Mean humanitarian liberal perspective (HUMLIB) scores by moral type.

steal the drug for his dying wife, that the neighbor should not turn in the escaped prisoner now leading an exemplary life, that the principal should not shut down the student newspaper for publishing controversial topics, that the doctor should acquiesce to the will of a coherent terminally ill patient and provide a fatal dose of pain killer, that the owner should hire the minority applicant even if some customers stop doing business with the firm, and agreeing that students were within their rights to take over the administration building to further their protest. Given these clear choice patterns, a variable was created that simply counts the number of times a participant's choice matches this high scoring group (Rest, 1979; Thoma, 2002). The score can range from 0 (no matches) to 6 (all matches).

Figure 3.4 presents humanitarian liberal perspective scored (labeled HUMLIB) as a function of Type. Most noticeable is the curvilinear pattern with low and high Types associated with a higher congruence with the expert group. The conventional Types (3–5) are significantly lower with the consolidated version (Type 4) the lowest of all.

Religious Orthodoxy.   The religious orthodoxy variable represents the sum of the rates and ranks for item 9 in the doctor's dilemma. As mentioned, this story is based around the dilemma whether or not to provide a drug to a dying woman that will hasten her death. Item 9 evokes the notion that only God can determine whether or not someone should live or die. It was found (most recently in Narvaez et al., 1999) that the ratings and ranking of this single item correlates very strongly with the summary scores on religious orthodoxy measures such as the Brown and Lowe Inventory of Religious Beliefs (1951). Specifically, the religious orthodoxy score is computed by adding the rating given to item 9 with the ranking value. Considering that the ratings are computed on a scale of 1 to 5 and four items are ranked per story, then the top score for this variable is 9 (rated most important and ranked first) and the lowest is 1 (rated not important and unranked).

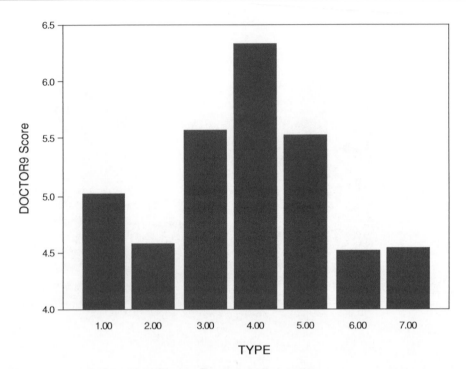

FIG. 3.5   Mean religious orthodoxy (DOCTOR9) scores by moral type.

Figure 3.5 presents the religious orthodoxy score (labeled DOCTOR9) by Type. It is interesting to note that the pattern of means is the mirror image of the humanitarian/liberal perspective score. That is, when the focus is on religious orthodoxy, participants scoring at the consolidated conventional level are highest in religious orthodoxy and the low and high Types score significantly lower.

Empirical Support for Moral Schemas

As mentioned, the basic idea behind the shift to schema theory is to signal the shift to a more contextualized, tacit view of cognitive structures. Consistent with this view is the expectation that moral schema facilitate the processing of moral information. Although empirical support for this claim is preliminary, there are some consistent findings that suggest that it is a research direction worth pursuing. The basic approach thus far has been to explain why some people have an easier time making moral judgments than others. For the most part, studies addressing this question focus on whether some people are more certain of their judgments, are more consistent, and seem to approach the task of handling moral dilemmas with a definite and coherent point of view.

The Can't Decide variable mentioned was created just for this purpose: The expectation is that participants who have more difficulty processing the moral content of the DIT should also have an increased number of Can't Decide choices. That is, for whatever reason, participants with high Can't Decide scores have moral schema that are not providing a clear interpretation of the story situation nor helping to formulate an action choice (Thoma & Narvaez, in preparation).

Referring to Fig. 3.3 and the plot of the Can't Decide score by Type, one can observe the main findings of this line of study. The Can't Decide score was found to covary with development (i.e., lower Can't Decide scores are associated with higher P- and N2 scores). However, the consolidated Type 4 and Type 7 were significantly lower than all other types. That is, the more consolidated a person is in one of the schemas (i.e., Maintaining Norms, or Postconventional), the greater the ease and consistency in information processing. Conversely, the greater the mix of schemas (potentially conflicting and contradictory sources of information), the more difficulty the person has in making a decision. Note that this finding links the particular definitions of moral schemas with specific effects, and thus supports the claim that the proposed schema has some psychological reality (otherwise, the measure of consolidation and schema predominance would have failed to produce the expected pattern).

Corroborating this finding using data outside the DIT, Thoma, Narvaez, Endicott, and Derryberry (2001), found that the time it took to rate the importance of moral issues is related to consolidation and transition. Using a standard reaction time methodology, both Type 4 and 7 participants (there were no Type 1s in this study), took longer overall to process moral issues. This finding suggests that moral schema may be nested within a broader network of knowledge structures such as the self-system. In addition, within-subject analyses found that conventional reasoning (Type 4) was associated with faster processing of the maintaining norms items. Similarly, participants reasoning at the postconventional level were faster at processing postconventional items. Again, the clarity of the schema (defined by developmental phase), influenced the processing of moral information.

Note also that being clear about moral information does not lead to the same decision. For instance, Fig. 3.4 shows that the consolidation on the maintaining norms schema is associated with a strong endorsement of religious orthodoxy. By contrast, consolidation on Type 7 rejects this view. In general, and using variables not associated with the DIT, the maintaining norms schema tends to be more strongly associated with a conservative political ideology and religious orthodoxy than the postconventional schema (Thoma & Narvaez, in preparation).

SUMMARY AND CONCLUSIONS

As outlined in the current chapter, the last 5 years have seen a number of significant changes to the DIT and the theory of moral judgment development it claims to measure. It is now proposed that the DIT measures the default schema by which individuals interpret moral issues. Pitched at the macromoral level, these default schemas inform the individual's understanding of social structures and their mechanisms. Further, it is claimed that the development of these schemas is ordered such that, starting during the second decade of life, a focus on understanding and maintaining norms gives way to a postconventional understanding.

This period of change for the DIT research tradition is also associated with a further distancing of the theory presupposed by the DIT from the Kohlberg system. Chief among these changes is the reinterpretation of the developmental continuum from six stages to three moral schemas. The latter is now more aligned with modern schema theory than Kohlberg's stage theory. Further, the adoption of schema notions to define development signal additional shifts in basic assumptions such as abandoning the universality claim as an a priori assumption, abandoning the strong view on the content and structure distinction, and accepting the view that a focus on the tacit understanding of moral issues may be a better representation of real-life decision making than other, more verbally based assessment systems.

Concurrent with these theoretical shifts, considerable effort has been directed to the creation of a new version of the DIT and a number of new variables. DIT researchers now have the means to assess development, developmental phase—independently and together—the decisiveness in making moral decisions, a proxy for a humanitarian/liberal perspective and for religious orthodoxy.

Despite these rather significant changes, the DIT research tradition has also been a force of stability in reaffirming Kohlberg's key insights. Like Kohlberg, DIT researchers believe that moral judgments are cognitive and developmental. Further, the broad outlines of the three moral schemas reflect Kohlberg's stages and core ideas about adolescent and youth moral judgment development. Kohlberg's legacy in the current thinking of DIT researchers is explicitly acknowledged through the use of the neo-Kohlbergian label to define this perspective. In addition to the theoretical connections with Kohlberg' theory, the empirical data generated by the DIT have supported many of the main Kohlbergian predictions. Indeed, one would be hard pressed to find a consistent finding using the DIT that was not mirrored in research using Kohlberg's interview approach.

Taken together, these efforts support the view that DIT research is a progressive force in the field and it has been efficient in suggesting new directions for study, particularly in the more applied areas such as higher educational outcomes and professional ethics (Bebeau, 2002; King & Mayhew, 2002) or on methodological concerns (Lind, 1995) and strategies (Carlo, Eisenberg, & Knight (1992). It seems plausible that as an increasingly distinct branch within the field, the DIT is now better poised to make specific contributions to other traditions. For instance, the current interest in developmental phase as measured by the DIT (Thoma & Rest, 1999) has the potential for furthering our understanding of how different social/moral systems (e.g., social domains) take precedence in ambiguous situations. It may be that those participants who are consolidated on moral schema process moral information differently than social convention information particularly when compared to transitional subjects (e.g., Thoma, Narvaez, Endicott, & Nucci, 2002).

The DIT research program's current and potential contributions notwithstanding, this perspective on moral judgment research is not without its critics. For instance, some have wondered whether the process of change is too empirically driven, leading to a construct that owes as much to the vagaries of different samples and researcher interests and less to a logically consistent set of defining characteristics (e.g., Nucci, 2002). To counter these claims, DIT researchers point to the broad-based and well-articulated set of validating criteria through which all proposed modifications are tested. Through this vetting process, they argue, new measures and theoretical propositions gain acceptance only when they consistently show a significant improvement over existing measures and explanations. Although the process is clearly empirically driven, it is not haphazard. The hope is that through these efforts the DIT and associated neo-Kohlbergian model can continue to offer the field a theoretical model and research strategy that serves to further moral judgment research.

REFERENCES

Adelson, J. (1971) The political imagination of the young adolescent. *Daedalus, 100*, 1013–1050.

Beauchamp, T. L., & Childress, J. F. (1994). *Principles of biomedical ethics* (4th ed). New York: Oxford University Press.

Beauchamp, T. L., & Childress, J. F. (2002). *Principles of biomedical ethics* (5th ed.). New York: Oxford University Press.

Bebeau, M. (1994). Influencing the moral dimension of dental practice. In J. Rest, & D. Narvaez (Eds.), *Moral development in the professions*. Hillsdale, NJ: Lawrence Erlbaum Associates.

Bebeau, M. (2002). The Defining Issues Test and the Four Component Model: Contributions to professional education. *Journal of Moral Education, 31,* 271–298.

Bebeau, M. J., & Thoma, S. J. (1999). Intermediate concepts and the connection to moral education. *Educational Psychology Review,* 11, 343–360.

Brown, D. G., & Lowe, W. L. (1951). Religious beliefs and personality characteristics of college students. *Journal of Social Psychology, 33,* 103–129.

Carlo, G., Eisenberg, N., & Knight, G. P. (1992). An objective measure of adolescents' prosocial moral reasoning. *Journal of Research on Adolescence, 2*(4), 331–349.

Colby, A., & Kohlberg, L. (1987). *The measurement of moral judgment.* Cambridge: Cambridge University Press.

Derryberry, W. P. (2000). *The relationship of moral reasoning and self-understanding and their influences on moral action.* Unpublished doctoral dissertation, University of Alabama. Tuscaloosa, AC.

Eisenberg, N., & Fabes, R. (1998). Prosocial development. In W. Damon (Series Ed.) & N. Eisenberg (Vol. Ed.), *Handbook of child psychology. Vol. 3. Social, emotional, and personality development* (5th ed., pp. 701–778). New York: John Wiley.

Evens, J. (1995). *Indexing moral judgment using multidimensional scaling.* Unpublished doctoral dissertation, University of Minnesota, Minneapolis.

Haidt, J. (2001). The emotional dog and its rational tail: A social intuitionist approach to moral judgment. *Psychological Review, 108,* 814–834.

Kagen, J., & Lamb, S. (1987). *The emergence of morality in young children.* Chicago: The University of Chicago Press.

King, P. M., & Mayhew, M. (2002). Moral judgment development in higher education: Insights from the Defining Issues Test. *Journal of Moral Education, 31,* 247–270.

Kohlberg, L. (1969). Stage and sequence. The cognitive-developmental approach to socialization. In D. A. Goslin (Ed.), *Handbook of socialization theory and research*. Chicago: Rand McNally.

Kohlberg, L. (1984). *Essays on moral development: The nature and validity of moral stages* (Vol. 2). San Francisco: Harper & Row.

Krebs, D. (2001). *The evolution of morality: Reconceptualizing Kohlbergian structures of moral development.* Paper presented to the Annual meeting of the Association for Moral Education, Vancouver, BC, Canada.

Lind, G. (1995, April). The meaning and measurement of moral competence revisited. Paper presented at the Annual Meeting of the American Educational Research Association, San Francisco, CA.

Loevinger, J. (1976). *Ego development.* San Francisco: Jossey-Bass.

Lockwood, A. (1970). *Relations of political and moral thought.* Unpublished doctoral dissertation, Harvard University, Cambridge, MA.

Marty, M. E., & Appleby, R. S. (Eds.). (1993). *Fundamentalism and the state.* Chicago: University of Chicago Press.

Narvaez, D., & Bock, T. (2002). Moral schemas and tacit judgments or how the Defining Issues Test is supported by cognitive science. *Journal of Moral Education, 31,* 297–314.

Narvaez, D., Getz, I., Rest, J., & Thoma, S. (1999). Individual moral judgment and cultural ideologies. *Developmental Psychology, 35,* 478–488.

Nietzsche, F. (1968/1986). *Beyond good and evil*. In W. Kaufman (Trans.). *The portable Nietzsche* (pp. 443–447). New York: Viking Press.

Nisbett, R. E., & Wilson, T. D. (1977). Telling more than we can know: Verbal reports on mental processes. *Psychological Review, 84*(3), 231–259.

Nucci, L. (2002). Goethe's Faust revisited: Lessons from DIT research. *Journal of Moral Education, 31,* 315–324.

Reed, D. R. C. (1997). *Following Kohlberg: Liberalism and the practice of the democratic community.* Notre Dame, IN: University of Notre Dame Press.

Rest, J. (1979). *Development in judging moral issues.* Minneapolis: University of Minnesota Press.

Rest, J. (1983). *Morality.* In P. H. Mussen (Series Ed.), J. Flavell, & E. Markman (Vol. Ed.), *Handbook of child psychology. Vol. 3: Cognitive development* (4th ed., pp. 556–629). New York: Wiley.

Rest, J. (1986). Moral development: Advances in research and Theory. New York: Praeger.

Rest, J. (1999). Stories about Larry Kohlberg. Unpublished manuscript, available from The Center for the Study of Ethical Development, The University of Minnesota.

Rest, J., & Narvaez, D. (1994). *Moral development in the professions.* Hillsdale, NJ: Lawrence Erlbaum Associates.

Rest, J., Narvaez, D., Bebeau, M., & Thoma, S. (1999). *Post-conventional moral thinking: A neo-Kohlbergian approach.* Mahwah, NJ: Lawrence Erlbaum Associates.

Rest, J., Narvaez, D., Thoma, S. J., & Bebeau, M. J. (1999). DIT2: Devising and testing a revised instrument of moral judgment. *Journal of Educational Psychology, 91,* 644–659.

Rest, J., Narvaez, D., Thoma, S. J., & Bebeau, M. J. (2000). A neo-Kohlbergian approach to morality research. *Journal of Moral Education, 29,* 381–396.

Rest, J., Thoma, S. J., Narvaez, D., & Bebeau, M. J. (1997). Alchemy and beyond: Indexing the Defining Issues Test. *Journal of Educational Psychology, 89*(3), 498–507.

Rummelhart, D. E. (1980). Schemata: The building blocks of cognition. In R. Spiro, B. Bruce, & W. Brewer (Eds.), *Theoretical issues in reading comprehension* (pp. 33–58). Hillsdale, NJ: Erlbaum.

Sanders, C. E., Lubinski, D., & Benbow, C. P. (1995). Does the Defining Issues Test measure psychological phenomena distinct from verbal ability? *Journal of Personality and Social Psychology, 69,* 498–504.

Snyder, S. S., & Feldman, D. H. (1984). Phases of transition in cognitive development: Evidence from the domain of spatial representation. *Child Development, 55,* 981–989.

Stevenson, C. L. (1937). The emotive meaning of ethical terms. *Mind, XLVI,* 14–31.

Thoma, S. J. (1986). Estimating gender differences in the comprehension and preferences of moral issues. *Developmental Review, 6,* 165–180.

Thoma, S. J (2002). An overview of the Minnesota approach in moral development. *Journal of Moral Education, 31,* 225–246.

Thoma, S. J., & Rest, J. (1999). The relationship between moral decision-making and patterns of consolidation and transition in moral judgment development. *Developmental Psychology, 35,* 323–333.

Thoma, S. J., & Narvaez, D. (unpublished manuscript). *Evidence supporting a schema view of the Defining Issues Test.* The University of Alabama, Tuscaloosa.

Thoma, S. J., Narvaez, D., Endicott, L., & Derryberry, P. (2001, April). *Developmental phase indicators and moral information processing.* Paper presented to the American Educational Research Association, New Orleans, LA.

Thoma, S., Narvaez, D., Endicott, L., & Nucci, L. (2002, November). *Judging social issues: The influence of domain and developmental phase indicators.* Paper presented to the Association for Moral Education, Chicago, IL.

Thoma, S. J., Narvaez, D., Rest, J., & Derryberry, P. (1999). The distinctiveness of moral judgment. *Educational Psychology Review, 11,* 361–376.

Torney-Purta, J. (1990). Youth in relation to social institutions. In S. Feldman & G. R. Elliott (Eds.), At the threshold: The developing adolescent (pp. 457–478). Cambridge, MA: Harvard University Press.

University of Minnesota, Center for the Study of Ethical Development. (1998). Norming Data for the DIT. Unpublished data.

Walker, L. J. (2002). The model and the measure: An appraisal of the Minnesota approach to moral development. *Journal of Moral Education, 31,* 353–367.

Walker L. J., & Taylor, J. H. (1991). Stage transitions in moral reasoning: A longitudinal study of developmental processes. *Developmental Psychology, 27,* 330–337.

4

GENDER AND MORALITY

LAWRENCE J. WALKER
UNIVERSITY OF BRITISH COLUMBIA

Issues surrounding gender and morality have attracted considerable interest over the past two decades, not only within the field of moral psychology, where they have been a central preoccupation, but also across the social sciences, humanities, and, indeed, in broader society. Much of the heated debate has subsided in recent years, and it would now seem to be an appropriate time to review where we stand in regard to these issues. That is the intent of this chapter.

At the outset, it is important to acknowledge the appropriately contentious nature of the issue. Claims and allegations regarding gender and morality have been widely voiced and popularized over the past couple of decades. Given that the moral domain is so central to our self-definition (most people regard themselves as being moral) and is so clearly evaluative, claims of difference on this dimension ought to be examined with particular caution and scrutiny, not only with attention to conceptual and empirical concerns, but also to the broader ideological and practical implications. A careful review of relevant psychological theories and empirical evidence contributes in a positive way to continued dialogue on these issues.

The current controversies regarding gender and morality stem from past debates around the work of two theorists who have, in some respects, come to dominate contemporary moral psychology: Lawrence Kohlberg (1969, 1981, 1984) and Carol Gilligan (1977, 1982). Despite this recent Kohlberg–Gilligan debate, as it has come to be known by some, it should be kept in mind that the issue is actually a rather longstanding one. Historically, men and women have often been accorded or have claimed different moral qualities (and sometimes, different moral worth). The predominance of patriarchal societies illustrates the frequent denial to women of public, institutional positions of moral leadership; being relegated instead to roles within the domestic sphere. Women remain underrepresented in our society among leadership in the judicial, political, religious, business, academic, and other domains (although these domains are not entirely synonymous with moral leadership). In contrast to the historical view implying male moral superiority and leadership, it should be recalled that women have initiated and fostered many movements in an attempt to impart their claimed higher moral standards into public life—for example, the movement to promote children's welfare during the time of the industrial revolution (which resulted in child labor laws and universal education), the suffragist movement, and the temperance movement (Tronto, 1993). Similarly, in contemporary society, women and men often hold divergent attitudes on many pressing moral issues such as capital punishment, abortion, domestic violence, gun control, and war.

Moral philosophers over the ages (e.g., Philo, Augustine, Aquinas, Descartes, Kant, Rousseau, Hegel) have similarly perpetuated the notion of gender differences in morality, with men typically being characterized as having a more rational sense of morality and women as possessing a more emotional sense of morality (see Lloyd [1983] for a review).

Perhaps philosophers can be somewhat forgiven for their well-articulated but poorly informed armchair observations; however, psychologists have the additional guidance of empirical data on the issue. Freud (1927) came to the following conclusion regarding gender and morality, a comment that garnered him considerable notoriety.

> I cannot escape the notion (though I hesitate to give it expression) that for women the level of what is ethically normal is different from what it is in men. Their super-ego is never so inexorable, so impersonal, so independent of its emotional origins as we require it to be in men. Character-traits which critics of every epoch have brought up against women—that they show less sense of justice than men, that they are less ready to submit to the great necessities of life, that they are more often influenced in their judgments by feelings of affection or hostility—all of these would be amply accounted for by the modification in the formation of their super-ego which we have already inferred. (pp. 141–142)

Freud attributed women's relative moral immaturity to deficiencies in same-sex parental identification and consequent superego formation—an inherent part of his model of psychosexual development—but he also acknowledged that his views were speculative, based on a handful of cases, and required empirical verification. Freud's explanatory notions of the Oedipal and Electra complexes eventually came to be regarded as largely untestable, and, with the demise of psychoanalytic theory, the notion of gender differences in the moral domain subsided within psychology for several decades. Until recently, no other major theorist in the moral development field has posited gender differences as an integral part of his or her model.

The issue was resurrected by Carol Gilligan in an influential article in the *Harvard Educational Review* (1977) and in her best-selling book, *In a Different Voice* (1982), and occurred in the context of the ascendancy of feminism in America. Gilligan's primary claim was that the morality of women is qualitatively different from that of men; she characterized women's moral reasoning by an ethic of care and men's moral reasoning by an ethic of justice. These divergent moral orientations are held to be a reflection of a profound gender difference in basic life orientation. Gilligan's perhaps secondary claim was that influential theories of human development (and she identified those posited by Freud, Piaget, Erikson, Levinson, McClelland, and notably Kohlberg) are biased against women's experiences. In particular, and most relevant for moral psychology, she argued that Kohlberg's theory misses or misconstrues women's different voice on morality and characterizes them as morally deficient.

In the following section, Gilligan's theory of moral orientations is briefly explicated. Then, the evidence regarding her allegation of gender bias against Kohlberg's theory is reviewed, and, in the final section, the empirical validity of Gilligan's model is considered in some detail.

GILLIGAN'S THEORY OF MORAL ORIENTATIONS

Gilligan (1977, 1982, 1986b, 1987; Gilligan & Attanucci, 1988; Gilligan, Brown, & Rogers, 1990; Gilligan, Lyons, & Hanmer, 1990; Gilligan, Ward, & Taylor, 1988; Gilligan & Wiggins, 1987) proposed that men and women typically differ in their basic life orientation, especially in conceptions of self and morality, and that they follow different developmental pathways. A *moral orientation* is a conceptually distinctive framework for organizing and understanding the moral domain. Gilligan claims that there is something of a gestalt shift between the care and justice orientations and sometimes uses the classic face–vase illusion to illustrate the relationship between them.

Gilligan believes that men typically have a justice orientation (sometimes also referred to as a rights orientation) because of their individualistic and separate conception of self, detached objectivity, basing of identity on occupation, and proclivity for abstract and impartial rules or principles. Thus, she holds that men typically regard moral conflicts as entailing issues of conflicting rights. Gilligan holds that this moral orientation has been well represented in both moral philosophy and moral psychology.

On the other hand (and she does describe the difference as if it were a dichotomy, representing fundamentally incompatible perspectives; Stocker, 1987), she believes that women typically have a care orientation (sometimes referred to as a response orientation) because of their perception of self as connected to and interdependent with others, basing of identity on intimate relationships, sensitivity not to endanger or hurt, concern for the well-being of self and others, and concern for harmonious relationships in concrete situations. Thus, she holds that women typically recognize moral conflicts as entailing issues of conflicting responsibilities. It is this "feminine" ethic of care, Gilligan argues, that has not been adequately represented in moral philosophy and theories of human development. It is important to note (and Gilligan is insistent on this point) that the moral orientations are gender related, but not gender specific.

Gilligan's (1982) theory also entails a methodological consideration; in particular, she holds that the care orientation is best revealed in reasoning about real-life moral dilemmas and that it may be obscured by hypothetical moral dilemmas, perhaps the standard paradigm in the assessment of moral reasoning (e.g., Colby & Kohlberg's [1987] Moral Judgment Interview and Rest's [1979] Defining Issues Test). Gilligan's argument is that hypothetical dilemmas are abstract, depersonalized, limited in contextual information, not emotionally engaging, and with the moral issue preconstructed (by the researcher, often in terms of conflicting rights). On the other hand, personally generated real-life dilemmas, arising from one's own experience, are held to be more appropriate contexts for revealing care reasoning because they are particular, contextually rich, personally relevant and relational, and open ended in terms of their framing.

Gilligan's proposal of gender-related moral orientations received widespread attention and eventually prompted questions as to the developmental origins of these orientations. How is it that these moral orientations become gendered in development? Gilligan in her later writings (1986b, 1987; Gilligan et al., 1988; and especially Gilligan & Wiggins, 1987) argued that the origins of these moral orientations are firmly embedded within the family, in young boys' and girls' differential experiences with parents. As is common among scholars in the feminist "differences" tradition (Kimball, 1994), Gilligan relies on neopsychoanalytic theory (Chodorow, 1978) to explain the gender asymmetry in moral reasoning by reference to early parent–child relationships.

Gilligan and Wiggins (1987) believe that relationships with other people lie at the heart of moral functioning and thus that a perspective on relationships should frame any conception of morality. They propose that the awareness of self in relation to others is best characterized in terms of the two dimensions of equality–inequality and attachment–detachment (akin to the primary interpersonal dimensions of dominance and nurturance, posited by circumplex theorists in personality; Wiggins, 1991). They premised their proposal on the assumptions that mothers are the primary caregivers for young children and that children come to identify with the same-sex parent. Thus, early differences along these two dimensions in relationships with parents are held to account for the differential moral orientations that arise in early childhood and that persist across the lifespan.

The dimension of equality–inequality reflects children's acute awareness of being dependent, smaller, less powerful, and less competent than adults. Developmental progress (at least within a justice framework) is toward a position of equality with, and independence from, others. The orthogonal dimension of attachment–detachment reflects children's sense of being cared for, their affection for their caregivers, and their awareness of having an effect on others and of connecting with them. Gilligan argued that the dynamics of attachment relationships induce a very different sense of self and that the moral implications of such attachments have been largely overlooked in developmental psychology.

Gilligan hypothesized that boys' and girls' differential experiences of inequality and attachment form the bases for the moral orientations of justice and care. She argued that girls are both attached to, and identify with, their mothers. Girls' identity develops in the context of maintaining this relationship with the mother. Thus, the experience of inequality is not so salient, whereas the experience of attachment, of sustaining connections with others, is more central to their self-definition. The result is an interdependent sense of self and a moral orientation toward care and the maintenance of relationships. In contrast, boys are initially attached to their mothers but identify with their fathers. Boys' identity develops in the context of detachment from the mother while, at the same time, relating to the father's power and authority. Thus, the experience of inequality is more salient and the need for separation and independence is more central to their self-definition. The result is an individualistic sense of self and a moral orientation toward justice and rights.

Gilligan (1977, 1982) originally proposed developmental stages in the ethic of care, although she never integrated these developmental stages with her later theorizing on the origins of moral orientations. Her developmental sequence for care reasoning has three distinct levels along with two intermediary transition points. The initial level has an egocentric focus on the self, where moral concerns are pragmatic and entail ensuring one's own happiness and avoiding being hurt. The second level has a normative or conventional focus on goodness, which is equated with self-sacrificial caring for others. The third level entails an ethic of care for both self and others through a balanced understanding of their interconnection; there is a focus on the principle of nonviolence (the injunction against hurting) and the assertion of a moral equality between responsibility to self and other.

This section has briefly explained Gilligan's theory of moral orientations. The extant empirical evidence regarding moral orientations is examined later in the chapter, after first turning to Gilligan's other, quite separable, claim that Kohlberg's theory of moral judgment development has not heard women's different voice on morality and has falsely caricatured women as morally deficient and aberrant.

GENDER BIAS IN KOHLBERG'S THEORY

Gilligan's second major claim is that influential theories of human development, particularly the one that has most recently dominated moral psychology—Kohlberg's—are insensitive to women's ethic of care. She argues that Kohlberg's conception of morality emphasizes (particularly at the higher stages) traditional masculine traits and values such as rights, individuality, rationality, impersonality, and principles of justice. And she holds that traditional feminine concerns, such as the maintenance of relationships, care, and commitment, when they are tapped, are typically relegated to the lower stages of moral development. Thus, Gilligan alleges that Kohlberg's approach falsely yields evidence that women (and those with an ethic of care) are deficient in their level of moral reasoning and that this gender difference is indicative of the pervasive gender bias of the model.

The foundation for Gilligan's claim of gender bias is twofold: (a) One potential source of bias is the ideological basis for the moral theory. The self-admitted intellectual roots of Kohlberg's (1984) theory are in a tradition of formalist moral philosophy and liberal social science. (b) The second potential source of bias relates to the characteristics of the original sample upon which the theory's constructs were originally derived and validated (although it is recognized that theories are not based exclusively on research data). Kohlberg's moral stage model and scoring system were constructed, in large part, from the longitudinal data of an exclusively male sample (Colby, Kohlberg, Gibbs, & Lieberman, 1983).

Gilligan (1982) and others (e.g., Baumrind, 1986) have argued that findings of difference confirm gender bias. However, it is not always that straightforward. Findings of gender difference support the allegation of bias only if they do not appropriately reflect reality. It is possible that gender differences may simply be a reflection of a sexist society that denies opportunities to women rather than an indication of a biased theory. To illustrate: men are taller than women on average, but that finding does not necessarily challenge our systems of measurement. The foundation for an interpretive claim of bias against a theory would be empirical evidence indicating that its claims regarding gender and morality cannot be substantiated.

Kohlberg's (1984) theoretical perspective on gender differences in moral development differs considerably from Gilligan's. His approach neither predicts nor requires gender differences in either "developmental pathway" or rate of development. Kohlberg's moral stage model is well known (for both theoretical and methodological explication, see Colby and Kohlberg [1987]). Kohlberg claimed that the order of stage acquisition was invariant and universal, but predicted variability in rate and eventual endpoint of development as a function of exposure to appropriately disequilibrating social experiences. Considerable evidence has been accumulated to indicate that a variety of social experiences predict moral reasoning development (Walker & Hennig, 1997). Kohlberg argued that these determinants of moral development explain variability among individuals and between groups, including the sexes. Thus, his position is that, if gender differences on his measure are revealed, they should be fully attributable to differences in terms of these influences on moral development.

There is now a considerable body of evidence regarding gender differences in stage of moral reasoning development, given the widespread research interest in Kohlberg's model. It should be noted that the true incidence of gender differences is probably somewhat overestimated by the extant research literature, because such differences were not of primary interest (prior to Gilligan's popularization of the notion), and reporting and publication biases often preclude the reporting of nonsignificant findings—the file-drawer problem (Rosenthal, 1991).

Walker (1984, 1986b, 1991) reported reviews of the literature that included all studies using Kohlberg's measure in which gender differences were, or could be examined (very few studies using Kohlberg's measure have been published more recently, so this review does not require updating). The review included 80 studies with 152 samples, and involved 10,637 participants. Of these 152 separate samples, nonsignificant gender differences were reported for the vast majority (86%); of the balance, females scored higher in 6% of the samples and males in 9%. The few differences favoring women tended to occur in homogeneous samples of students, whereas the few differences favoring men tended to occur in heterogeneous samples of adults (heterogeneous in that men and women differed, on average, in level of education and occupation, as is sometimes found in contemporary society). Interestingly, in every case where researchers controlled in some way for education, occupation, or both, gender differences in moral reasoning disappeared. This is not an attempt to explain away these findings—there is no need given the overall nonsignificant pattern—but to illustrate Kohlberg's point that such experiences influence rate of development.

One limitation of the traditional vote-counting (significant or not) method of integrating findings is that it fails to take account of the size of the effect. If the effect is a modest one, then differences in individual studies may tend not to reach significance although they may cumulatively favor a given direction. Meta-analysis is an objective and powerful means by which to statistically combine the results of a set of studies, overcoming the limitations of the traditional review method. It can determine the probability level for the overall pattern of findings, the effect size, and the relevance of various moderator variables. Walker's (1984, 1986b) meta-analysis indicated that the overall pattern of findings was not significant and that the effect size was minuscule ($d = .046$; which means that gender explains 1/20 of 1% of the variability in moral reasoning development). One explanation proffered for the occasional finding of gender differences among older studies is that earlier versions of Kohlberg's scoring system (which underwent considerable revision before being finalized; Colby & Kohlberg, 1987) were inadequate, confusing content and structure. Walker (1991) examined earlier versus current scoring system as a moderator variable, but found no significant differences.

There is another comprehensive meta-analysis of gender differences in moral reasoning to note. Thoma (1986) examined gender differences on the Defining Issues Test (DIT), a measure derived from Kohlberg's theory (with somewhat different stage descriptions and a very different methodology) and hence vulnerable to Gilligan's criticisms. Thoma reviewed 56 samples in which gender differences on the DIT were examined and found a significant difference favoring women but again the effect size was extremely small, accounting for less than half of 1% of the variability in moral reasoning.

Given the miniscule effect sizes in these meta-analyses, one is forced to conclude that no meaningful relation exists between gender and moral stage. There is no empirical support for Gilligan's claim that Kohlberg's model downscores the moral thinking of women; that notion has been "convincingly debunked" (Jaffee & Hyde, 2000, p. 707).

Gilligan's criticisms of Kohlberg's model, however, were not only that his approach downscores the moral reasoning of women, but also that his approach undervalues the ethic of care, categorizing such reasoning at lower stages (for Gilligan, women's moral reasoning and an ethic of care are essentially synonymous, but this, as shall be seen, may be an unwarranted assumption). Gilligan noted that "the primary use of the care orientation thus creates a liability within Kohlberg's framework" (1986b, p. 45).

There is relatively little evidence regarding that claim, and the few available findings are not consistent. Krebs, Vermeulen, Denton, and Carpendale (1994) had university students provide written responses to Kohlberg's Moral Judgment Interview (MJI), which were coded for both moral stage and Gilligan's moral orientation (note that the MJI is not Gilligan's preferred vehicle for assessing her moral orientations). The predicted negative correlation between moral stage and care reasoning was found for men, but not for women. Pratt, Golding, Hunter, and Sampson (1988, Study 1) had adults respond to Kohlberg's MJI, which was coded for moral stage, and also discuss a real-life dilemma, which was coded for Gilligan's moral orientation. Pratt and co-workers' findings did not support Gilligan's allegation of bias against the ethic of care in Kohlberg's model: For women, higher stage reasoning was associated with greater use of care reasoning; whereas for men, there was no significant relationship, a finding later replicated by Skoe, Pratt, Matthews, and Curror (1996). Two studies have assessed moral stages and moral orientations in reasoning about dilemmas related to sexual behavior and diseases and found no relationship (Conley, Jadack, & Hyde, 1997; Jadack, Hyde, Moore, & Keller, 1995), although not all participants may have considered these to be moral issues.

Similarly, in my own research on this issue (Walker, 1989; Walker, de Vries, & Trevethan, 1987), participants responded to both the MJI and a real-life moral dilemma at two different interview times (over a 2-year longitudinal interval). Both types of dilemmas (hypothetical and real life) were scored for both moral stage and moral orientation. If Gilligan's arguments are correct, then participants with a care orientation should score lower in moral stage than those with a justice orientation (which is presumably favored in Kohlberg's model). The analyses for the relation between stage and orientation on the hypothetical dilemmas indicated no significant effects; however, the analyses for the real-life dilemmas indicated that individuals with a care orientation scored higher in moral stage than those with a justice orientation. There is limited empirical support for Gilligan's claim that the ethic of care is undervalued in Kohlberg's model; rather the indications are that it is advantaged.

In summary, Gilligan's concerns about Kohlberg's moral stage model cannot be empirically substantiated. Nevertheless, interest in Kohlberg's approach has waned, although for other reasons. Despite the considerable empirical support that has been amassed regarding the validity of the moral stage model and its explanations for development, it is becoming increasingly evident that the approach entails a somewhat constricted, even inadequate, view of moral functioning (Walker, 1996; Walker & Pitts, 1998). This does not in any way deny the considerable contributions of the approach, but rather attempts to place these contributions within an appropriate framework. It can be argued that morality, properly understood, has both interpersonal and intrapersonal components. The interpersonal component involves the regulation of social interactions and, in particular, the adjudication of conflicts regarding people's rights and welfare; this aspect of morality has been well represented in Kohlberg's moral psychology (reflecting a formalist, deontological perspective in moral philosophy). The intrapersonal component involves one's basic values, identity, goals, and character, and has been ignored in the Kohlbergian paradigm. The circumscribed nature of Kohlberg's model also is apparent if one accepts a definition of moral functioning that acknowledges its truly multifaceted psychological nature, entailing the dynamic interplay of thought, emotion, and behavior. His approach hives off cognitive reasoning abilities as representing the essence of morality and excludes serious consideration of other aspects of moral functioning. Despite the lack of evidence for Gilligan's allegations of gender bias within Kohlberg's approach, her theorizing has contributed to the growing realization that his paradigm does not represent the full scope of the moral domain.

Regardless of the veracity of Gilligan's allegations about other theories, her claims regarding the ethic of care are separable and can be evaluated on their own terms. The next section provides an empirical review and evaluation of Gilligan's theory of moral orientations.

EMPIRICAL EVIDENCE AND CONCEPTUAL ISSUES REGARDING THE ETHIC OF CARE

Gilligan has advanced various claims regarding her theory of moral orientations. This section reviews the available empirical evidence regarding these claims, many of which are interrelated, and also raises some conceptual issues regarding aspects of the model.

Assessment

Basic to any evaluation of the empirical evidence relevant to Gilligan's model is some consideration of how moral orientations are assessed and whether such measures are reliable and valid. Gilligan's (1982) book provides only anecdotal and informal evidence regarding moral orientations and does not address issues of assessment. However, Lyons (1982), a student of Gilligan's, did develop a coding system for classifying justice and care considerations (i.e., scorable thought units) in reasoning about real-life moral dilemmas. In Lyons's system, the relative number of considerations for each orientation within the interview determines the modal moral orientation. This is the coding system that Gilligan used in the only empirical study she authored on moral orientations that appeared in a refereed psychology journal (Gilligan & Attanucci, 1988). Johnston (1988) later adapted Lyons's coding system to score moral orientations in responses to hypothetical dilemmas (viz., two of Aesop's fables).

Gilligan's coding system for moral orientations further evolved with the development of a *Reader's Guide* (Brown, 1987; Brown, Debold, Tappan, & Gilligan, 1991; Brown, Tappan, Gilligan, Miller, & Argyris, 1989), which provides interpretive procedures for identifying self in narratives and for listening to the moral voices of care and justice. This explicitly reader-response and feminist method eschews objectivity and seeks instead to create meaning within a particular "interpretative community" (Brown et al., 1991, pp. 27, 33).

The inaccessibility and subjectivity of the coding systems developed within Gilligan's group precluded their widespread adoption by other researchers; hence the development of several other measures intended to tap these moral orientations. Skoe and Marcia (1991) developed and, in later research, validated the Ethic of Care Interview (ECI), which assesses Gilligan's levels of care reasoning (note that this measure taps the care but not the justice orientation). The ECI consists of three standard interpersonal dilemmas and one real-life one.

The above measures are interview measures, but self-report objective measures have also been developed. Some researchers have simply asked participants to rate their own use of each moral orientation in resolving moral conflicts (Ford & Lowery, 1986; Galotti, Kozberg, & Farmer, 1991). The Moral Orientation Scale (Yacker & Weinberg, 1990) presents a series of childhood dilemmas and asks participants to rank moral considerations (reflecting the justice and care orientations) in resolving each. The Measure of Moral Orientation (Liddell & Davis, 1996; Liddell, Halpin, & Halpin, 1992) similarly presents a series of dilemmas relevant to the lives of college students and asks participants to rate moral considerations (reflecting both orientations) in resolving each dilemma. A second part of this measure taps self-perceptions by asking participants to rate themselves, in general, on 14 items designed to reflect the two orientations.

A critical issue, given the diversity of measures that have been developed to assess Gilligan's moral orientation construct, is their convergent validity. Are these comparable measures and do they assess moral orientations as conceptualized by Gilligan? There is very little evidence as yet in this regard. However, Liddell (1998) compared her objective Measure of Moral Orientation to the moral reasoning evident in a moral-conflict interview, which was scored using Lyons's (1982) coding system. Liddell found no significant relationship between the moral orientation scores yielded by the two measures. This lack of convergent validity signals that caution should be exercised in interpreting the results of studies purporting to assess Gilligan's model but not using her measures and coding system. As Jaffee and Hyde (2000) have noted, "researchers have seldom agreed on how Gilligan's care and justice orientations should be defined or how they should be measured" (p. 703). Of course, the problem is compounded by Gilligan's relative lack of attention to measurement issues.

Intrapsychic Consistency

The ethic of care and the ethic of justice are, in Gilligan's theorizing, "distinct moral orientations—i.e., two frameworks that organize thinking about what constitutes a moral problem and how to resolve it" and that "most people . . . focus on one orientation and minimally represent the other" (Gilligan, 1986a, p. 10). If moral orientations do indeed represent distinctive frameworks for understanding morality and are as basic and pervasive in our functioning as Gilligan claims, then individuals should focus on one orientation or the other, a preference that generalizes across moral situations and is stable over time. Gilligan's claim of focus empirically means that a substantial proportion of an individual's reasoning should reflect one orientation with relatively little reasoning reflecting the other. The question then becomes: What is a reasonable level of consistency? Gilligan (1986a) proposed a criterion of 75% or more of reasoning reflecting the modal moral orientation, either justice or care (given that 50% represents equal use of the two orientations and 100% represents exclusive use of one orientation).

Using this criterion, Gilligan and Attanucci (1988) reported that only 66% of their participants evidenced a focus on one orientation or the other in their reasoning about a single real-life dilemma. Similarly, Walker and associates (1987) found that only 53% of their sample was consistent in orientation usage on a real-life dilemma. Pratt and colleagues (1988, Study 2) addressed the issue of consistency by having their participants discuss two real-life dilemmas, each of which was globally scored for moral orientation. Only 60% of their sample used the same modal orientation on the two dilemmas, a level of consistency not significantly different from chance. Walker (1989) examined the stability of individuals' moral orientations in their reasoning about real-life dilemmas over a 2-year longitudinal interval and found that 50% evidenced a different modal orientation on the retest than the initial interview. Thus, even when using Gilligan's preferred paradigm of real-life moral dilemmas, there is minimal evidence of focus or preference; indeed, low levels of consistency in orientation usage within and across contexts seem to be the norm.

The focus phenomenon should not only be evident in reasoning about idiosyncratic real-life dilemmas, but also standard hypothetical ones; and, although Gilligan decried the use of hypothetical dilemmas (for reasons already articulated), her 1982 book is replete with illustrations of both orientations in responses to Kohlberg's MJI. Thus, Walker (1989; Walker et al., 1987) examined the consistency in orientation usage in responses between the MJI and a real-life dilemma and found than less than 20% were consistent in their modal moral orientation between these two dilemma contexts. The correlations in care reasoning scores between the two dilemma contexts were very weak (less than .15). Finally, Wark and Krebs (1996) assessed orientation consistency using a somewhat different criterion. They had university students respond to Kohlberg's MJI and two real-life moral dilemmas and assessed moral orientation usage on a 5-point scale (exclusively justice, predominantly justice, mixed justice and care, predominantly care, and exclusively care). They considered participants to be consistent if their reasoning was classified at the same or the adjacent point on this scale across the three types of dilemmas; only 29% met this consistency criterion. In short, many individuals use a considerable mix of both orientations, evidencing no clear focus or preference. As such, the classification of individuals simply on the basis of modal moral orientation may be misleading and the use of the term *orientation* seems unwarranted.

Origins of the Moral Orientations

Gilligan and Wiggins (1987) proposed that the developmental origins for the moral orientations of justice and care are in boys' and girls' differential experiences of inequality and attachment with their parents. However, Gilligan did not allude to any research relevant to such claims and her arguments in this regard have received minimal empirical examination, despite their centrality in her model. Although, in her more recent writings, Gilligan has somewhat moderated her claims regarding gender differences in moral orientations (given the compelling evidence, to be reviewed, that they are minimal), her notion that they arise in the context of fundamental dimensions of early parent–child relationships belies that view and instead implies a strong bifurcation between boys and girls, and men and women.

One study, by Lollis, Ross, and Leroux (1996), however, has provided evidence relevant to Gilligan's notions regarding the gender-based origin of moral orientations. Their research examined whether parents do, indeed, socialize girls for care and boys for justice. They obtained direct observations of interactions in the home with a sample of two-parent families with preschoolers (the critical age range in Gilligan's theorizing), and parental interventions were coded for moral orientation. Although there was a tendency for mothers to direct more care- than justice-oriented reasoning to children, in general, and for fathers to do the converse, there was no evidence that girls received more care-oriented reasoning or that boys received more justice-oriented reasoning from either parent. In other words, although parents themselves displayed a gender-related pattern of moral orientations, they did not socialize boys and girls differentially. These data fail to support for Gilligan's proposition regarding the origins of moral orientations in early parent–child relationships.

It should be pointed out that Lollis and associates (1996) did not examine Gilligan's claim directly. Their design involved the assessment of patterns of parental moral orientation use in their interactions with children, whereas Gilligan's proposal entailed something a bit different—the dimensions of inequality and attachment and the related patterns of identification, as framed by neopsychoanalytic theory. It is possible that these dimensions in parent–child relationships are relevant to children's developing morality without them being evidenced in the direct differential socialization of moral orientations. The empirical issue, as yet not addressed by Gilligan, is how to directly assess these two dimensions in early parent–child relationships. One would not expect that they would be easy to quantify with validity and reliability. Then longitudinal research would need to be conducted to relate these early parent–child relationships to later moral orientations.

Further questions arise regarding Gilligan's model of the developmental origin of moral orientations: Are inequality and attachment the only or even the most salient dimensions of parent–child relationships? Are these dimensions of relationships as strongly linked to gender as Gilligan claims? Are relationships with peers and other adults really irrelevant to moral development? The notion that care and justice are based on two dimensions of relationships strongly related to two genders implies that there two and only two moral orientations. Some moral philosophers (e.g., Flanagan, 1991) would regard such a claim as contentious. The notion that these dimensions are strongly linked to gender has similarly been challenged by Turiel (1998), who noted that the issue of inequality is one that is particularly salient and acute for girls and women as they encounter the inequities and power imbalance that permeate home, school, and work experiences (Okin, 1989). Likewise, for boys, issues of attachment are salient in their experiences of groups, team sports, and gangs that involve cooperation, solidarity, and connection. Turiel's arguments further imply the significance for moral development of interpersonal relationships with other people beyond Gilligan's exclusive focus on parents.

Developmental Trends and Levels

Gilligan (1986b; Gilligan & Wiggins, 1987) claimed that the contrasting moral orientations emerge in early childhood and are then evident across the lifespan. She (1977, 1982) also proposed a three-level developmental sequence in the ethic of care. Unfortunately, she never integrated her theorizing regarding the origins of the orientations with this developmental sequence. The unstated implication is that, if moral orientations originate in parent–child relationships in early to mid-childhood, then there is no need to account for subsequent development. Surprisingly, Gilligan eventually abandoned the concept of developmental progression through these levels in the care orientation. One rationale for this retreat was her observation (1990, p. 9) that the developmental sequence did not reflect the moral experiences of girls (given that the initial levels had been rooted in the reasoning of women considering a problematic pregnancy). Her more ideological rationale was her increasing discomfort with the concepts of developmental psychology (such as stages) and her preference for describing these moral orientations using literary or musical analogies (Gilligan, Brown, & Rogers, 1990, pp. 111–112).

Despite Gilligan's abandonment of her developmental stages, Skoe, in her program of research, has pursued their validity. Skoe and Marcia (1991) developed the ECI and a reliable coding system to assess levels of care reasoning. In cross-sectional studies of adolescents and young adults, it was found that age and level of care reasoning were positively associated (Skoe, 1995; Skoe & Marcia, 1991), but no such relationship was found among samples of older adults (Skoe et al., 1996, Studies 1 and 2). A 4-year longitudinal study, again with older adults, failed to reveal any developmental progression in levels of care reasoning (Skoe et al., 1996, Study 2). Although research using the ECI has been conducted with preadolescents as well (Skoe et al., 1999; Skoe & Gooden, 1993), developmental trends in that age group have not been explored. Thus, there is limited evidence to date regarding developmental progression in levels of care reasoning as assessed by the ECI, and there is no evidence regarding the sequentiality of these levels.

There is some evidence regarding developmental patterns in care reasoning as assessed by one of the coding systems developed within Gilligan's group. Several studies—including those by Langdale (1986) with samples of children, adolescents, and adults; Garrod, Beal, and Shin (1990) with children in Grades 1 through 5; and Pratt, Diessner, Hunsberger, Pancer, and Savoy (1991) with a sample of middle-aged and older adults—have failed to find significant relationships between age and moral orientations. The most comprehensive study of developmental trends was reported by Walker (1989) in a 2-year longitudinal study with a large sample of children, adolescents, and adults. He found a significant developmental pattern with the proportion of care reasoning increasing across age groups, although there was no evidence of development over the longitudinal interval.

The extant evidence is rather equivocal regarding developmental trends and levels, and suggests the need for a more elaborated description of developmental changes in moral orientations across the lifespan. The challenge here is not only to describe development, but also to explain how and why it occurs, because a developmental model is incomplete without the specification of the causal mechanism(s) underlying development (Auerbach, Blum, Smith, & Williams, 1985; Puka, 1989a). The implication from some of Gilligan's writing (Blackburne-Stover, Belenky, & Gilligan, 1982; Gilligan, 1982) is that experiences of crisis and conflict can prompt moral growth, akin to the cognitive–developmental mechanism of disequilibrium, but her more recent theorizing regarding the developmental origins of the orientations (Gilligan & Wiggins, 1987) is aligned more closely with neopsychoanalytic notions of identification. Given the abundant evidence from decades of research that there are significant developmental changes in moral functioning across the lifespan, it would seem that the developmental aspects of Gilligan's model require further elaboration and clarification.

Definition of Moral Maturity

A basic question in evaluating Gilligan's model concerns her definition of moral maturity. Although it is widely recognized that the developmental endpoint is critical to evaluating a model of human development (particularly one that is so clearly value laden), it is unclear from Gilligan's work what she holds out to be moral maturity. Gilligan has proffered a variety of conflicting possibilities on this issue (see Flanagan & Jackson [1987] and Mason [1990] for further discussion).

1.   She sometimes argues that moral maturity involves the primary acquisition of the care orientation rather than the justice orientation (which is described in pejorative terms), and clearly she aligns herself with the ethic of care. "Admittedly, we stand more firmly in the care perspective" (Gilligan, Brown, & Rogers, 1990, p. 123). It is possible that this argument may represent a rhetorical device on her part to promote the value of care reasoning. The implication of this view is that women are typically more moral than are men.

2.   Gilligan also argues, on occasion, that moral maturity could be represented by either of the orientations, which are equally valid and acceptable as moral frameworks and perhaps differentially appropriate for different types of moral problems (although she does not offer any guidelines for determining which orientation is more appropriate in different situations). This view is reinforced by her argument that the orientations are both logically and psychologically incompatible and that they originate in differential gender socialization (Gilligan, 1982, p. 20; Gilligan & Wiggins, 1987, p. 295). This position is also reflected in her frequent allusions to the gestalt shift metaphor to illustrate the orientations (alternate perspectives that cannot be reconciled). She uses the ambiguous figure analogy to argue "against the implication that these two perspectives are readily integrated or fused" (1987, p. 30).

3.   Another of Gilligan's responses to the issue of moral maturity was to argue that these two orientations are actually complementary perspectives that could be maintained in some kind of dynamic tension (Gilligan, 1982, pp. 33, 100).

4.   A final possibility that Gilligan has advanced is that moral maturity is represented by a synthesis or an integration of these orientations (Gilligan, 1982, p. 174); that is, that both unjust caring and uncaring justice are morally deficient without the other.

There is some limited empirical evidence regarding this issue of moral maturity, which tends to accord with the position that moral maturity entails the ability to integrate justice and care reasoning. Garrod and colleagues (1990) found that children's ability to explain both orientations and to switch between them when prompted was associated with advanced cognitive and perspective-taking development. In Walker and associates' (1987) research, it was found that individuals at the higher stages of moral development (as indexed by Kohlberg's well-validated model) were more likely to be split in their moral orientation—that is, to evidence substantial amounts of both care and justice reasoning. This split orientation suggests an attempt to integrate or coordinate both types of reasoning. The association with moral stage indicates that mature moral thinking does entail such an integration. Incidentally, this finding is also consistent with the notion that principled moral thinking, as conceptualized by Kohlberg, does entail the reasoning of both care and justice orientations (Kohlberg, Boyd, & Levine, 1990). There is no reason to assume that an ethic of justice and an ethic of care are mutually exclusive. Assuming that this view of maturity in moral orientations prevails, the question becomes: How, and at what level, does this integration occur?

Limitations to the Ethic of Care

Gilligan's arguments that the moral orientations are fundamentally incompatible and that they originate in early gender-typed relationships with parents implies a strong bifurcation between boys and girls and between men and women. These arguments are ones that many feminists regard as fraught with political dangers for women and unhelpful for their cause. Although the value of a "woman-centered analysis" (Brabeck, 1989) and of women's "epistemic privilege" to interpret oppression (Boyd, 1990) are acknowledged, it should be recognized that Gilligan's theory reinforces traditional and restrictive stereotypes about the sexes (Henley, 1985). As such, it does little to challenge the status quo in patriarchal societies where women remain in a disadvantaged and subordinate position, and it does not challenge either individuals or social structures to change (Hare-Mustin, 1987; Tronto, 1993). For example, Gilligan's theorizing has been used in arguments for maintaining exclusively male public schools (as in the case of the Virginia Military Institute; Kaminer, 1998). This dichotomization on the basis of gender reflects what has been labeled the *alpha bias* (Hare-Mustin & Marecek, 1988). This bias, which minimizes within-gender variability and maximizes between-gender differences, caricatures human experience and creates a false dichotomy. (For a helpful discussion of the science and politics of the alpha bias [reflecting the differences tradition] and its counterpart, the beta bias [reflecting the similarities tradition], see Eagly [1995] and Kimball [1994].)

Several commentators (Brabeck, 1987; Card, 1990; Kimball, 1994; Okin, 1989; Puka, 1989b; Tronto, 1993; Turiel, 1998) have noted that the ethic of care is essentially a sexist service orientation that represents the type of thinking that is adaptive in dealing with oppression. It is argued that persons in power advocate rights and rationality, whereas persons in subordinate positions, of necessity, advocate compassion and connection (Hare-Mustin & Marecek, 1988). Furthermore, the argument that the orientations arise in the context of gendered parent–child relationships ignores the role played by social, political, and economic structures in creating and maintaining the orientations as gender related (Turiel, 1998), as well as that of culture (Haste, 1994). Herein lies a potential paradox: If women's essential qualities, such as caring and compassion, are to be valued (as Gilligan claims), but arise primarily through subordination, how can these qualities be advanced without also endorsing inequality (Houston, 1989)?

There are also some significant moral limitations to an ethic of care that need to be addressed. Although care is unarguably an important aspect of moral functioning, it seems incomplete and deficient in itself (Held, 1987). For example, it does not include the concepts of impartiality and universalizability that have been regarded as important to mature moral decision making (Flanagan & Adler, 1983). This notion of impartiality has been maligned by Gilligan and others. It does not imply that one should be cold, calculating, and blind to the context (Hill, 1987; Mason, 1990); rather, it focuses one on the contextual features of the situation that are morally relevant and excludes those which are not (Sher, 1987). The real conundrum is to determine what is morally relevant (Houston, 1989). Another limitation to the ethic of care is its focus on interpersonal relationships and relative exclusion of moral responsibility beyond this sphere of personal interactions. Likewise, the ethic of care has no inherent mechanism to resolve the conflicts of responsibilities that are inherent in everyday living (Flanagan & Jackson, 1987).

Finally, it is important to recognize that care, like any other virtue including justice, can be maladaptive or morally questionable in some contexts. As Flanagan argued, "Care comes in self-effacing, autonomy-undermining forms. Furthermore, it can support and engender chauvinism if insufficiently principled or context-sensitive, and it can involve the nurturance of all manner of suspect types of persons and projects" (1991, p. 202). Hennig and Walker (2004) used techniques of personality assessment to map the ethic of care domain. Their focus was on aspects of the care where it has in some sense gone awry—being dysfunctional for either the one caring, the one being cared for, or both. For example, one problematic form of care that was identified was self-sacrificial care, which can justify self-neglect and overinvolvement in others' lives and, thus, compromise the quality of care undertaken (see the related research on unmitigated communion; Helgeson & Fritz, 1998). Another problematic pattern identified was submissive care, where care for the other is anxiously motivated by fear of negative evaluation and where one's self-expression is inhibited in deference to others' opinions. In other words, the virtue of caring can take on less-than-authentic manifestations, and both conceptual and empirical analyses are required to provide a more adequate description of its development and expression.

Gender Differences in Moral Orientations

Gilligan's primary claim, and the one which has attracted the most attention, is that men and women typically diverge in their moral orientations, with men relying on an ethic of justice and women relying on an ethic of care. She was careful to note that the association of orientation to gender is not absolute, but a strong gender polarity is certainly predicted by her neopsychoanalytic theorizing regarding the origin of the orientations.

Reviews of gender differences in moral orientations have been provided before (Walker, 1991, 1995) and are not duplicated here, in large part because those earlier reviews have been supplanted by a comprehensive meta-analysis recently reported by Jaffee and Hyde (2000). Their database search yielded a total of 113 studies (both published and unpublished) that met inclusion criteria. Of these studies, there were 160 samples in which gender differences in the care orientation were reported or could be determined and 95 samples in which gender differences in the justice orientation were assessed. Note that Gilligan's justice orientation is not synonymous with Kohlberg's moral stages, and, indeed, the empirical evidence is that they are weakly related (Walker, 1989). Thus, a meta-analysis of the justice orientation may yield quite different findings from my earlier meta-analyses of gender differences in moral stage (Walker, 1984, 1986b, 1991).

Of the 160 samples in which gender differences in the care orientation were assessed, 73% reported nonsignificant findings, a pattern clearly inconsistent with Gilligan's strong claim of gender polarity. Jaffee and Hyde's meta-analysis yielded an overall effect size for gender differences in care reasoning that would be considered small ($d = -.28$). One

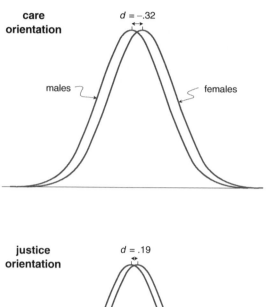

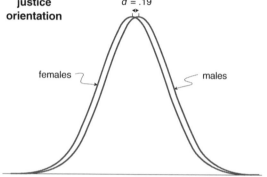

FIG. 4.1 **Illustration of the effect sizes for gender differences in moral orientations.**

problem with their meta-analysis is that they included a large number of measures that were not meant to tap Gilligan's conceptualization of care although they could be considered relevant to it; for example, Kohlberg's measure of moral orientations (viz., the utilitarianism and perfectionism orientations; see Colby & Kohlberg, 1987) and Eisenberg's measure of stages in prosocial moral reasoning (Eisenberg, Fabes, & Shea, 1989). But even when the studies under consideration were restricted to those that assessed the care orientation as conceptualized by Gilligan—probably a more legitimate test of her model—the average effect size remained relatively modest ($d = -.32$). Effect sizes are somewhat difficult to interpret, so I calculated a couple of other statistics (the r^2 and U_1 statistics) that may have greater intuitive meaning: This effect size ($d = -.32$) means that gender explains only 2.4% of the variance in care orientation scores and that, of the combined area of the two distributions of scores for males and females, only 22.6% is not overlapped. In other words, the distributions are pretty much superimposed, as is evident in Fig. 4.1, which provides a graphic representation of this gender difference.

Similarly, of the 95 samples in which gender differences in the justice orientation were assessed, 72% were reported as not significant. Jaffee and Hyde's (2000) meta-analysis yielded a small overall effect size for gender differences in the justice orientation ($d = .19$; the same effect size was found regardless whether the studies assessed the justice orientation as conceptualized by Gilligan or by some other model). Again, I calculated the r^2 and U_1 statistics that are somewhat more interpretable: This effect size means that gender explains only 0.9% of the variance in justice orientation scores and that of the combined area of the two distributions of scores for males and females, only 14.1% is not overlapped (see the lower panel of Fig. 4.1).

Jaffee and Hyde's (2000) summary of their meta-analysis was unequivocal: "The small magnitude of these effects, combined with the finding that 73% of the studies that measured care reasoning and 72% of the studies that measured justice reasoning failed to find significant gender differences, leads us to conclude that these orientations are not strongly associated with gender" (p. 719). They further argued that "the field should move beyond the debate about gender differences" (p. 721).

Dispositional Versus Situational?

Jaffee and Hyde's (2000) meta-analysis also examined to what extent the magnitude of the effect sizes for gender differences was moderated by other variables. For both care and justice orientations, the type of dilemma under consideration was found to be a significant moderator variable. When participants were responding to any type of hypothetical dilemma (standard hypothetical dilemmas, hypothetical dilemmas that are more realistic or familiar, hypothetical dilemmas pulling for care, or ones pulling for justice), the effect sizes for gender differences in care and justice were uniformly small or negligible ($ds \leq \pm.20$), whereas when participants were reasoning about a real-life dilemma generated from their personal experience, the effect sizes were significantly stronger although still far from substantial ($d = -.37$ for the care orientation and $d = .42$ for the justice orientation).

There is a notable methodological problem in studies of moral orientations that rely on real-life dilemmas from personal experience. Participants are simply recounting one of their own moral problems; thus, these dilemmas are idiosyncratic, and may not accord with the underlying criteria for morality as articulated by a wide range of philosophers and social scientists. This suggests the possibility that the gender differences in these studies might be an artifact of the differing moral problems that men and women typically encounter or choose to relate, rather than a fundamental difference in basic moral framework (Walker, 1986a).

The importance of the nature of the dilemma in influencing moral orientation has been illustrated in several studies (Pratt et al., 1988, 1991; Walker, 1989; Walker et al., 1987). In these studies, participants were asked to recall and discuss real-life dilemmas from their own experience, and their moral orientations were determined. These researchers conducted content analyses of these real-life dilemmas: Walker distinguished between personal and impersonal dilemmas, whereas Pratt and co-workers distinguished relational and nonrelational dilemmas. *Personal* or *relational dilemmas* involve conflicts among people who have a significant, ongoing relationship; *impersonal* or *nonrelational dilemmas* involve conflicts among relative strangers, or with institutions or generalized others, or are primarily intrinsic to the self. Both Walker and Pratt and colleagues examined the relationship between dilemma content and moral orientation and found that personal/relational dilemmas, not surprisingly, tended to be discussed in terms of the ethic of care, whereas impersonal/nonrelational dilemmas were more likely to be reasoned about in terms of the ethic of justice. Thus, the nature of the dilemma exerts a considerable influence on the mode of moral reasoning used (for other analyses of the content of real-life dilemmas, see Walker, Pitts, Hennig, & Matsuba [1995] and Wark & Krebs [2000]).

Further, when Pratt and associates (1988, 1991) and Walker (1989; Walker et al., 1987) examined gender differences within types of real-life dilemmas, none were evident. Thus, variability in moral orientations can be better attributed to the types of dilemma that people typically encounter than to their gender. Clopton and Sorell (1993) argue that Gilligan has made a fundamental attribution error in underestimating the significance of situational factors and overestimating the role of dispositional ones. The extant evidence is that people do not focus on, or have a clear preference for, a single moral orientation, but rather use a considerable mix of both orientations, a pattern strongly influenced by the nature of the moral problem under consideration. The general absence of gender differences in moral orientations in responses to hypothetical dilemmas or within types of real-life dilemmas suggests that the initial evidence regarding the gender-relatedness of moral orientations was based on a methodological artifact. Seigfried (1989) and Turiel (1998), among others, have noted the philosophical and political advantages to women for locating moral orientations in situational rather than dispositional factors.

CONCLUSIONS

The issue of gender and morality has rightly been contentious. The controversy has revolved around Kohlberg's and Gilligan's theories for the past couple of decades, but it is important to keep in mind that there are many other significant theoretical perspectives in moral psychology that have remained untouched and unscathed by the issue. Most models of moral development make no claims about gender differences. The intent of this chapter was to provide a careful review of the extant evidence and a balanced discussion of the conceptual issues involved. What this chapter reveals is that gender explains a negligible amount of the variability in moral reasoning development. It is time to set this issue aside and to focus instead on more significant conceptual and practical concerns that confront moral psychology.

This is not to negate the many positive contributions that Gilligan's model has engendered. Her theorizing has expanded our understanding of moral psychology and moral philosophy with her emphasis on care, response, interdependence, and relationships. She has introduced a new methodology to assess moral reasoning with her reliance on self-generated real-life dilemmas, an approach that has yielded numerous new insights. And she has clearly helped to focus attention on the need to represent more carefully the experience of females in psychological theories.

However, the accumulated evidence regarding Gilligan's claims of gender differences and gender bias indicates that she is substantially incorrect in that regard. She argued that there are two gender-related moral orientations, an ethic of care and an ethic of justice, which arise in early childhood experiences with parents of attachment and inequality, and she further argued that Kohlberg's theory is biased against women and their ethic of care.

The abundant empirical evidence indicates that there is no support for the notion that Kohlberg's model downscores the reasoning of women and those with a care orientation. Similarly, Gilligan's claim of gender polarity in moral orientations cannot be sustained in light of the small effect sizes in analyses of gender differences. Gilligan's model is further plagued by other methodological and conceptual concerns. For example, her failure to develop a reliable and valid coding system reflects her disinterest in measurement issues and compromises other researchers' ability to examine her theory, as reflected in the lack of convergent validity among various measures. Almost no research has examined her claim regarding the developmental origins of the orientations and, given the nature of the constructs she proposed in this regard, it is difficult to imagine how they could be tested. The claim that people typically show a strong preference for one orientation also could not be supported; rather, the evidence is that most people use a considerable mixture of both orientations, a pattern readily influenced by situational factors such as the nature of the moral problem. Finally, Gilligan's advocacy of gender polarity has served to reify traditional (and restrictive) stereotypes that seem unhelpful for women's cause (men's, as well).

Gilligan's model aside, there are several other broad questions and future directions to note in the area of gender and morality. Gender is a rapidly evolving social category of considerable significance that entails multiple layers of meaning and that interacts in powerful ways with culture. Undoubtedly, many morally relevant issues continue to arise at the interface of gender and morality. The conceptual skew in contemporary moral psychology, well exemplified in the current Kohlberg–Gilligan debate, entails a focus on moral reasoning as applied to interpersonal conflicts with concomitant inattention to other aspects of the moral domain (Walker, 2004). For example, morality not only involves the adjudication of conflicts and regulation of interactions, but also the intrapsychic aspects that pertain more to our fundamental goals and values, lifestyle, and identity. There may very well be important gender variability in these aspects that reference moral character and virtue. Likewise, morality is inherently multifaceted, involving the dynamic interplay of thought, emotion, and behavior. Recent debates about gender and morality have focused on claims of gender differences in the area of moral cognition, again with minimal consideration of the emotional and behavioral aspects of moral functioning and to the interrelationships among these various components. Future research could be focused on a more comprehensive perspective on moral functioning and on the range of psychological processes that engender moral maturity.

REFERENCES

Auerbach, J., Blum, L., Smith, V., & Williams, C. (1985). Commentary on Gilligan's "In a Different Voice." *Feminist Studies, 11,* 149–161.

Baumrind, D. (1986). Sex differences in moral reasoning: Response to Walker's (1984) conclusion that there are none. *Child Development, 57,* 511–521.

Blackburne-Stover, G., Belenky, M. F., & Gilligan, C. (1982). Moral development and reconstructive memory: Recalling a decision to terminate an unplanned pregnancy. *Developmental Psychology, 18,* 862–870.

Boyd, D. R. (1990, April). *One man's reflection on a masculine role in feminist ethics: Epistemic vs. political privilege.* Paper presented at the meeting of the Philosophy of Education Society, Miami, FL.

Brabeck, M. M. (1987). Gender and morality: A response to Philibert and Sayers. *New Ideas in Psychology, 5,* 209–214.

Brabeck, M. M. (1989). Introduction: Who cares? In M. M. Brabeck (Ed.), *Who cares? Theory, research, and educational implications of the ethic of care* (pp. xi–xviii). New York: Praeger.

Brown, L. M. (Ed.). (1987). *A guide to reading narratives of moral conflict and choice for self and moral voice.* Unpublished manuscript, Harvard University Graduate School of Education GEHD Study Center, Cambridge, MA.

Brown, L. M., Debold, E., Tappan, M., & Gilligan, C. (1991). Reading narratives of conflict and choice for self and moral voices: A relational method. In W. M. Kurtines & J. L. Gewirtz (Eds.), *Handbook of moral behavior and development: Research* (Vol. 2, pp. 25–61). Hillsdale, NJ: Erlbaum.

Brown, L. M., Tappan, M. B., Gilligan, C., Miller, B. A., & Argyris, D. E. (1989). Reading for self and moral voice: A method for interpreting narratives of real-life moral conflict and choice. In M. J. Packer & R. B. Addison (Eds.), *Entering the circle: Hermeneutic investigations in psychology* (pp. 141–164). Albany: State University of New York Press.

Card, C. (1990). Gender and moral luck. In O. Flanagan & A. O. Rorty (Eds.), *Identity, character, and morality: Essays in moral psychology* (pp. 199–218). Cambridge, MA: MIT Press.

Chodorow, N. (1978). *The reproduction of mothering: Psychoanalysis and the sociology of gender*. Berkeley: University of California Press.

Clopton, N. A., & Sorell, G. T. (1993). Gender differences in moral reasoning: Stable or situational? *Psychology of Women Quarterly, 17,* 85–101.

Colby, A., & Kohlberg, L. (1987). *The measurement of moral judgment* (Vols. 1–2). New York: Cambridge University Press.

Colby, A., Kohlberg, L., Gibbs, J., & Lieberman, M. (1983). A longitudinal study of moral judgment. *Monographs of the Society for Research in Child Development, 48*(1–2, Serial No. 200).

Conley, T. D., Jadack, R. A., & Hyde, J. S. (1997). Moral dilemmas, moral reasoning, and genital herpes. *Journal of Sex Research, 34,* 256–266.

Eagly, A. H. (1995). The science and politics of comparing women and men. *American Psychologist, 50,* 145–158.

Eisenberg, N., Fabes, R., & Shea, C. (1989). Gender differences in empathy and prosocial moral reasoning: Empirical investigations. In M. M. Brabeck (Ed.), *Who cares? Theory, research, and educational implications of the ethic of care* (pp. 127–143). New York: Praeger.

Flanagan, O. J. (1991). *Varieties of moral personality: Ethics and psychological realism.* Cambridge, MA: Harvard University Press.

Flanagan, O. J., & Adler, J. E. (1983). Impartiality and particularity. *Social Research, 50,* 576–596.

Flanagan, O. J., & Jackson, K. (1987). Justice, care, and gender: The Kohlberg–Gilligan debate revisited. *Ethics, 97,* 622–637.

Ford, M. R., & Lowery, C. R. (1986). Gender differences in moral reasoning: A comparison of the use of justice and care orientations. *Journal of Personality and Social Psychology, 50,* 777–783.

Freud, S. (1927). Some psychological consequences of the anatomical distinction between the sexes. *International Journal of Psycho-Analysis, 8,* 133–142.

Galotti, K. M., Kozberg, S. F., & Farmer, M. C. (1991). Gender and developmental differences in adolescents' conceptions of moral reasoning. *Journal of Youth and Adolescence, 20,* 13–30.

Garrod, A., Beal, C., & Shin, P. (1990). The development of moral orientation in elementary school children. *Sex Roles, 22,* 13–27.

Gilligan, C. (1977). In a different voice: Women's conception of the self and of morality. *Harvard Educational Review, 47,* 481–517.

Gilligan, C. (1982). *In a different voice: Psychological theory and women's development.* Cambridge, MA: Harvard University Press.

Gilligan, C. (1986a, Spring). Letter to D. Baumrind. *Newsletter of the APA Division on Developmental Psychology,* pp. 10–13.

Gilligan, C. (1986b). Remapping development: The power of divergent data. In L. Cirillo & S. Wapner (Eds.), *Value presuppositions in theories of human development* (pp. 37–53). Hillsdale, NJ: Erlbaum.

Gilligan, C. (1987). Moral orientation and moral development. In E. F. Kittay & D. T. Meyers (Eds.), *Women and moral theory* (pp. 19–33). Totowa, NJ: Rowman & Littlefield.

Gilligan, C. (1990). Teaching Shakespeare's sister: Notes from the underground of female adolescence. In C. Gilligan, N. P. Lyons, & T. J. Hanmer (Eds.), *Making connections: The relational worlds of adolescent girls at Emma Willard School* (pp. 6–29). Cambridge, MA: Harvard University Press.

Gilligan, C., & Attanucci, J. (1988). Two moral orientations: Gender differences and similarities. *Merrill-Palmer Quarterly, 34,* 223–237.

Gilligan, C., Brown, L. M., & Rogers, A. G. (1990). Psyche embedded: A place for body, relationships, and culture in personality theory. In A. I. Rabin, R. A. Zucker, R. A. Emmons, & S. Frank (Eds.), *Studying persons and lives* (pp. 86–147). New York: Springer.

Gilligan, C., Lyons, N. P., & Hanmer, T. J. (Eds.). (1990). *Making connections: The relational worlds of adolescent girls at Emma Willard School.* Cambridge, MA: Harvard University Press.

Gilligan, C., Ward, J. V., & Taylor, J. M. (Eds.). (1988). *Mapping the moral domain: A contribution of women's thinking to psychological theory and education.* Cambridge, MA: Harvard University Graduate School of Education.

Gilligan, C., & Wiggins, G. (1987). The origins of morality in early childhood relationships. In J. Kagan & S. Lamb (Eds.), *The emergence of morality in young children* (pp. 277–305). Chicago: University of Chicago Press.

Hare-Mustin, R. T. (1987). The gender dichotomy and developmental theory: A response to Sayers. *New Ideas in Psychology, 5,* 261–267.

Hare-Mustin, R. T., & Marecek, J. (1988). The meaning of difference: Gender theory, postmodernism, and psychology. *American Psychologist, 43,* 455–464.

Haste, H. (1994). "You've come a long way, babe": A catalyst of feminist conflicts. *Feminism & Psychology, 4,* 399–403.

Held, V. (1987). Feminism and moral theory. In E. F. Kittay & D. T. Meyers (Eds.), *Women and moral theory* (pp. 111–128). Totowa, NJ: Rowman & Littlefield.

Helgeson, V. S., & Fritz, H. L. (1998). A theory of unmitigated communion. *Personality and Social Psychology Bulletin, 2,* 173–183.

Henley, N. M. (1985). Psychology and gender. *Signs, 11,* 101–119.

Hennig, K. H., & Walker, L. J. (2004). *Thinking too much about others: Risks associated with a relational self-construal.* Manuscript submitted for publication.

Hill, T. E., Jr. (1987). The importance of autonomy. In E. F. Kittay & D. T. Meyers (Eds.), *Women and moral theory* (pp. 129–138). Totowa, NJ: Rowman & Littlefield.

Houston, B. (1989). Prolegomena to future caring. In M. M. Brabeck (Ed.), *Who cares? Theory, research, and educational implications of the ethic of care* (pp. 84–100). New York: Praeger.

Jadack, R. A., Hyde, J. S., Moore, C. F., & Keller, M. L. (1995). Moral reasoning about sexually transmitted diseases. *Child Development, 66,* 167–177.

Jaffee, S., & Hyde, J. S. (2000). Gender differences in moral orientation: A meta-analysis. *Psychological Bulletin, 126,* 703–726.

Johnston, D. K. (1988). Adolescents' solutions to dilemmas in fables: Two moral orientations—Two problem solving strategies. In C. Gilligan, J. V. Ward, & J. M. Taylor (Eds.), *Mapping the moral domain: A contribution of women's thinking to psychological theory and education* (pp. 49–71). Cambridge, MA: Harvard University Graduate School of Education.

Kaminer, W. (1998, April). The trouble with same-sex schools. *The Atlantic Monthly, 281*(4), 22–36.

Kimball, M. M. (1994). The worlds we live in: Gender similarities and differences. *Canadian Psychology, 35,* 388–404.

Kohlberg, L. (1969). Stage and sequence: The cognitive-developmental approach to socialization. In D. A. Goslin (Ed.), *Handbook of socialization theory and research* (pp. 347–480). Chicago: Rand McNally.

Kohlberg, L. (1981). *Essays on moral development: Vol. 1. The philosophy of moral development*. San Francisco: Harper & Row.

Kohlberg, L. (1984). *Essays on moral development: Vol. 2. The psychology of moral development*. San Francisco: Harper & Row.

Kohlberg, L., Boyd, D. R., & Levine, C. (1990). The return of Stage 6: Its principle and moral point of view. In T. Wren (Ed.), *The moral domain: Essays in the ongoing discussion between philosophy and the social sciences* (pp. 151–181). Cambridge, MA: MIT Press.

Krebs, D. L., Vermeulen, S. C., Denton, K. L., & Carpendale, J. I. (1994). Gender and perspective differences in moral judgement and moral orientation. *Journal of Moral Education, 23,* 17–26.

Langdale, C. J. (1986). A re-vision of structural-developmental theory. In G. L. Sapp (Ed.), *Handbook of moral development: Models, processes, techniques, and research* (pp. 15–54). Birmingham, AL: Religious Education Press.

Liddell, D. L. (1998). Comparison of semistructured interviews with a quantitative measure of moral orientation. *Journal of College Student Development, 39,* 169–178.

Liddell, D. L., & Davis, T. L. (1996). The measure of moral orientation: Reliability and validity evidence. *Journal of College Student Development, 37,* 485–493.

Liddell, D. L., Halpin, G., & Halpin, W. G. (1992). The measure of moral orientation: Measuring the ethics of care and justice. *Journal of College Student Development, 33,* 325–330.

Lloyd, G. (1983). Reason, gender, and morality in the history of philosophy. *Social Research, 50,* 490–513.

Lollis, S., Ross, H., & Leroux, L. (1996). An observational study of parents' socialization of moral orientation during sibling conflicts. *Merrill-Palmer Quarterly, 42,* 475–494.

Lyons, N. P. (1982). *Conceptions of self and morality and modes of moral choice: Identifying justice and care in judgments of actual moral dilemmas.* Unpublished doctoral dissertation, Harvard University, Cambridge, MA.

Mason, A. (1990). Gilligan's conception of moral maturity. *Journal for the Theory of Social Behaviour, 20,* 167–179.

Okin, S. M. (1989). *Justice, gender, and the family.* New York: Basic.

Pratt, M. W., Diessner, R., Hunsberger, B., Pancer, S. M., & Savoy, K. (1991). Four pathways in the analysis of adult development and aging: Comparing analyses of reasoning about personal-life dilemmas. *Psychology and Aging, 6,* 666–675.

Pratt, M. W., Golding, G., Hunter, W., & Sampson, R. (1988). Sex differences in adult moral orientations. *Journal of Personality, 56,* 373–391.

Puka, B. (1989a). Caring—In an interpretive voice. *New Ideas in Psychology, 7,* 295–314.

Puka, B. (1989b). The liberation of caring: A different voice for Gilligan's "different voice." In M. M. Brabeck (Ed.), *Who cares? Theory, research, and educational implications of the ethic of care* (pp. 19–44). New York: Praeger.

Rest, J. R. (1979). *Development in judging moral issues.* Minneapolis: University of Minnesota Press.

Rosenthal, R. (1991). *Meta-analytic procedures for social research* (rev. ed.). Newbury Park, CA: Sage.

Seigfried, C. H. (1989). Pragmatism, feminism, and sensitivity to context. In M. M. Brabeck (Ed.), *Who cares? Theory, research, and educational implications of the ethic of care* (pp. 63–83). New York: Praeger.

Sher, G. (1987). Other voices, other rooms? Women's psychology and moral theory. In E. F. Kittay & D. T. Meyers (Eds.), *Women and moral theory* (pp. 178–189). Totowa, NJ: Rowman & Littlefield.

Skoe, E. E. (1995). Sex role orientation and its relationship to the development of identity and moral thought. *Scandinavian Journal of Psychology, 36,* 235–245.

Skoe, E. E., & Gooden, A. (1993). Ethic of care and real-life moral dilemma content in male and female early adolescents. *Journal of Early Adolescence, 13,* 154–167.

Skoe, E. E., Hansen, K. L., Mørch, W., Bakke, I., Hoffman, T., Larsen, B., & Aasheim, M. (1999). Care-based moral reasoning in Norwegian and Canadian early adolescents: A cross-national comparison. *Journal of Early Adolescence, 19,* 280–291.

Skoe, E. E., & Marcia, J. E. (1991). A measure of care-based morality and its relation to ego identity. *Merrill-Palmer Quarterly, 37,* 289–304.

Skoe, E. E., Pratt, M. W., Matthews, M., & Curror, S. E. (1996). The ethic of care: Stability over time, gender differences, and correlates in mid- to late adulthood. *Psychology and Aging, 11,* 280–292.

Stocker, M. (1987). Duty and friendship: Toward a synthesis of Gilligan's contrastive moral concepts. In E. F. Kittay & D. T. Meyers (Eds.), *Women and moral theory* (pp. 56–68). Totowa, NJ: Rowman & Littlefield.

Thoma, S. J. (1986). Estimating gender differences in the comprehension and preference of moral issues. *Developmental Review, 6,* 165–180.

Tronto, J. C. (1993). *Moral boundaries: A political argument for an ethic of care.* New York: Routledge.

Turiel, E. (1998). The development of morality. In W. Damon (Series Ed.) & N. Eisenberg (Vol. Ed.), *Handbook of child psychology: Vol. 3. Social, emotional, and personality development* (5th ed., pp. 863–932). New York: Wiley.

Walker, L. J. (1984). Sex differences in the development of moral reasoning: A critical review. *Child Development, 55,* 677–691.

Walker, L. J. (1986a). Experiential and cognitive sources of moral development in adulthood. *Human Development, 29,* 113–124.

Walker, L J. (1986b). Sex differences in the development of moral reasoning: A rejoinder to Baumrind. *Child Development, 57,* 522–526.

Walker, L. J. (1989). A longitudinal study of moral reasoning. *Child Development, 60,* 157–166.

Walker, L. J. (1991). Sex differences in moral reasoning. In W. M. Kurtines & J. L. Gewirtz (Eds.), *Handbook of moral behavior and development* (Vol. 2, pp. 333–364). Hillsdale, NJ: Erlbaum.

Walker, L. J. (1995). Sexism in Kohlberg's moral psychology? In W. M. Kurtines & J. L. Gewirtz (Eds.), *Moral development: An introduction* (pp. 83–107). Boston: Allyn & Bacon.

Walker, L. J. (1996). Kohlberg's cognitive-developmental contributions to moral psychology. *World Psychology, 2,* 273–296.

Walker, L. J. (2004). Progress and prospects in the psychology of moral development. *Merrill-Palmer Quarterly, 50,* 546–557.

Walker, L. J., de Vries, B., & Trevethan, S. D. (1987). Moral stages and moral orientations in real-life and hypothetical dilemmas. *Child Development, 58,* 842–858.

Walker, L. J., & Hennig, K. H. (1997). Moral functioning in the broader context of personality. In S. Hala (Ed.), *The development of social cognition* (pp. 297–327). East Sussex, England: Psychology Press.

Walker, L. J., & Pitts, R. C. (1998). Naturalistic conceptions of moral maturity. *Developmental Psychology, 34,* 403–419.

Walker, L. J., Pitts, R. C., Hennig, K. H., & Matsuba, M. K. (1995). Reasoning about morality and real-life moral problems. In M. Killen & D. Hart (Eds.), *Morality in everyday life: Developmental perspectives* (pp. 371–407). Cambridge, UK: Cambridge University Press.

Wark, G. R., & Krebs, D. L. (1996). Sex and dilemma differences in real-life moral judgment. *Developmental Psychology, 32,* 220–230.

Wark, G. R., & Krebs, D. L. (2000). The construction of moral dilemmas in everyday life. *Journal of Moral Education, 29,* 5–21.

Wiggins, J. S. (1991). Agency and communion as conceptual coordinates for the understanding and measurement of interpersonal behavior. In D. Cicchetti & W. M. Grove (Eds.), *Thinking clearly about psychology: Essays in honor of Paul E. Meehl* (Vol. 2, pp. 89–113). Minneapolis: University of Minnesota Press.

Yacker, N., & Weinberg, S. L. (1990). Care and justice moral orientation: A scale for its assessment. *Journal of Personality Assessment, 55,* 18–27.

III

SOCIAL DOMAIN THEORY AND SOCIAL JUSTICE

This section describes research and theory on the social–cognitive domain model, which was influenced by the structural–developmental approach, and how a social judgment model has been extended into such areas as intergroup relationships, rights, and culture. Chapter 5, written by Judith Smetana, provides an overview of social domain theory and research. She contrasts the social domain model to the global stage theories of Piaget and Kohlberg and then describes how the model has been used to understand early moral development, peer relationships, parent–adolescent relationships, and culture. Smetana describes research on developmental changes within the moral domain, how individuals use moral and social knowledge to evaluate complex situations, and recent findings on differences in judgments regarding hypothetical and actual situations. Her chapter provides readers with an in-depth and theoretical overview of the social–cognitive domain model and the research avenues it has generated in a diverse array of morally relevant areas.

In Chapter 6, Melanie Killen, Nancy Margie, and Stefanie Sinno apply the social domain model to examine morality in the context of intergroup relationships. Social psychological research on intergroup relationships has studied adult attitudes about prejudice, biases, and discrimination, all morally relevant constructs, with few analyses of how these concepts manifest and are acquired in development. Killen, Margie, and Sinno describe developmental research on children's and adolescents' concepts of gender, ethnicity, and race and how individuals weigh fairness, justice, and equality when confronted with situations, such as exclusion, that often evoke stereotypic knowledge as well as moral knowledge.

In Chapter 7, Charles Helwig discusses research focusing on children's and adolescents' concepts of rights, civil liberties, and democracy. He describes cross-cultural research, particularly in China, that challenges cultural stereotypes about the valuing of rights in different cultures. Helwig articulates the multiple dimensions of rights and civil liberties and demonstrates the developmental emergence of these concepts in a range of cultures.

Finally, in Chapter 8, Cecilia Wainryb focuses on the complex issue of culture. She posits that cultures are not homogeneous "totalities," as has often been asserted in the literature and describes an extensive set of empirical studies that demonstrates that individuals in a wide range of cultures value autonomy, rights, interpersonal obligations, authority, conventions, customs, and fairness. She asserts that these values are not culturally specific, but rather are universal, even though the manifestation of these values takes multiple trajectories. She describes the ways in which characterizations of culture have perpetuated stereotypic viewpoints and served to maintain unfair hierarchical arrangements in cultures, such as those in which girls and women are denied autonomy and rights.

Together, these chapters provide a bridge among philosophical, anthropological, and psychological characterizations of moral development. An underlying theme in this section is the notion that social life is multifaceted and that empirical research on morality needs to take into account these multiple dimensions to provide comprehensive characterizations of the emergence and transformation of morality over the lifespan.

5

SOCIAL–COGNITIVE DOMAIN THEORY: CONSISTENCIES AND VARIATIONS IN CHILDREN'S MORAL AND SOCIAL JUDGMENTS

JUDITH G. SMETANA
UNIVERSITY OF ROCHESTER

The social world is complex. It is structured by many social expectations and rules, which are enforced in diverse social situations and in the context of different social relationships and societal arrangements. Through the process of development, children must acquire an understanding of these different social expectations and rules, including an awareness of the regularities that are specific to particular social contexts, as well as an understanding of which expectations and rules are more broadly applicable and obligatory across contexts. Moreover, although morality regulates social relationships, not all social rules are moral; some rules may be functional in regulating social interactions but lack the prescriptive and obligatory basis of moral rules. This chapter describes theory and research from the social–cognitive domain perspective on moral and social development (Helwig & Turiel, 2003; Nucci, 2001, 2002; Smetana, 1995b; Turiel, 1998, 2002, chap. 1 this volume) that describes how children come to understand, interpret, accept, and sometimes reject these diverse aspects of their social world.

Most psychological approaches to moral development view morality as multifaceted and as having affective, cognitive, and behavioral components, but theoretical perspectives have varied in the extent to which they have prioritized the different components. Like other structural–developmental theories of moral judgment development, researchers from the social–cognitive domain perspective (hereafter referred to as *domain theory*) propose that moral development is best understood through psychological analyses of moral judgments, but as discussed in this chapter, emotion and behavior have not been neglected. Emotion is seen as inseparable from and providing one motivational or energetic force for judgments, and behavior is seen as following from individuals' interpretations of situations. Also consistent with other structural–developmental theories of moral judgment development, domain theory proposes that morality is constructed out of reciprocal individual–environment interactions (Turiel, 1983, 1998).

Domain theory differs from other structural developmental theories; however, in viewing morality as one of several strands of children's developing social knowledge. Thinking about the social world is seen as characterized by heterogeneity and the coexistence of different social orientations, motivations, and goals. Thus, concerns with justice, welfare, and rights—all moral issues—coexist with concerns with authority, tradition, and social norms (viewed as *social-conventional issues*) and concerns with privacy, bodily integrity and control, and a delimited set of choices and preferences (described as *personal issues*). Domain theory proposes that each of these constitutes an organized system, or domain, of social knowledge that arises from children's experiences of different types of regularities in the social environment (Turiel, 1983, 1998). This view differs from other structural–developmental stage models of moral judgment development, which have described the process of moral development as entailing the gradual differentiation of principles of justice or rights from nonmoral concerns with conventions, pragmatics, and prudence (Kohlberg, 1984; Piaget, 1932/1965). Rather, these social knowledge domains are seen as differentiated in early experience and following different developmental trajectories. Thus, a full understanding and appreciation of the complexity and diversity of social life entails a consideration of moral knowledge as distinct from, and sometimes in coordination with (or subordinated to) other types of social knowledge.

Since the initial theoretical formulations (Nucci & Turiel, 1978; Turiel, 1979, 1983), domain theory has expanded in many different directions, far too many to summarize concisely in a single chapter. Fortunately, however, a number of excellent and comprehensive reviews have been published elsewhere (Helwig & Turiel, 2003; Killen, Lee-Kim, McGlothlin, & Stangor, 2002; Nucci, 2001, 2002; Tisak, 1995; Turiel, 1983, 1998, 2002; see also Smetana, 1995b, 1997, 2002; Smetana & Turiel, 2003); many of these research directions are described in this handbook.

This chapter takes as its focus the basic proposition that children's moral and social knowledge is constructed out of reciprocal individual–environment interactions (Turiel, 1983, 1998) and considers how aspects of those interactions lead to consistencies and variations in moral and social judgments. The chapter begins with an overview of domain theory. Morality as a distinct developmental and conceptual domain is defined in distinction to other types of social knowledge, and methods for assessing children's moral and social knowledge are described. Then, evidence for the differentiation of moral, social, and nonsocial judgments in hypothetical and actual contexts and in straightforward and multifaceted situations is presented.

The next section focuses on how regularities in the environment, including characteristics and features of social interactions, lead to consistencies and variations in moral and social judgments. This is followed by a consideration of the influence of characteristics of individuals (such as gender, social class, and ethnicity) on moral and social judgments. Despite the criticism that structural–developmental theories of moral judgment development (particularly Kohlberg's theory) have neglected the influence of context (Shweder, 1982; Simpson, 1973), domain researchers have given a great deal of attention to contextual and particularly cultural variations in judgments. In the following sections, we return to a consideration of the environmental side of individual–environment interactions, but with a broader lens: we consider how different contexts, including social roles and social relationships, influence judgments. Broadening the lens still further, consistencies and variations in judgments due to cultural influences are discussed. The chapter concludes with some future directions for research.

DEFINING THE MORAL DOMAIN

Morality as a Distinct Domain of Social Knowledge

Social–cognitive domain theory has drawn on philosophical definitions of morality (Dworkin, 1978; Gewirth, 1978; Rawls, 1971) and psychological research to define morality in terms of the obligatory and generalizable norms, based on concepts of welfare (harm), fairness, and rights, that regulate social relationships (Helwig & Turiel, 2003; Turiel, 1983, 1998). Moral transgressions are hypothesized to be wrong because they have intrinsic effects for others' rights and welfare. Therefore, moral concepts are hypothesized to be obligatory, universally applicable, impersonal, and normatively binding.

Children's prescriptive understanding of their social relationships differs from their descriptive understanding of social systems, social organization, and social conventions. Social conventions have been defined as contextually relative, shared uniformities and norms (like etiquette or manners) that coordinate individuals' interactions in social systems. Social conventions provide individuals with expectations regarding appropriate behavior in different social contexts and thus help to facilitate the smooth and efficient functioning of the social system. Thus, social-conventional concepts are hypothesized to be contextually relative, consensually agreed on, contingent on specific rules or authority commands, and alterable.

Moral and social conventions have been further differentiated from individuals' descriptive understanding of persons as psychological systems, including their understanding of and attributions for their own and others' behavior and their knowledge of self, personality, and identity. Psychological knowledge pertains to individuals' attempts to understand psychological causes and to infer meaning that is not given in social interactions. Although the psychological domain is a distinct conceptual and developmental system of social knowledge, it bears on the scope and nature of morality in that the notion of rights is grounded in notions of the self and personal agency (Dworkin, 1978; Gewirth, 1978; Nucci, 1996, 2001).

In turn, Nucci (1996, 2001) has proposed that individuals exercise personal agency when asserting control over personal issues. Personal issues include preferences and choices regarding issues such as control over one's body, privacy, and choice of friends or activities (Nucci, 1996, 2001; Nucci & Turiel, 2000). Because personal issues pertain only to the actor and the private aspects of one's life, they are considered to be outside the realm of conventional regulation and moral concern. Thus, asserting claims to an issue as personal is an important aspect of individuals' developing autonomy or distinctiveness from others (Nucci, 2001), and the right to make autonomous decisions forms the boundary between the self and the social world. Children and adolescents typically categorize personal issues as up to the individual (rather than as acts that are right or wrong), based on justifications that the action's consequences only affect the actor or that the acts are personal matters and should be the actor's own business (Killen & Smetana, 1999; Nucci, 1981; Nucci & Weber, 1995; Smetana & Asquith, 1994).

Criteria for Identifying Morality as a Domain of Social Knowledge

Much of the early research from the social–cognitive domain perspective focused on testing the proposition that children are able to distinguish morality from social convention. This research examined whether children made consistent distinctions using theoretical criteria hypothesized to distinguish the domains. Accordingly, these studies examined children's judgments about hypothetical situations that are considered prototypical of the domains. Moral events, rules, or transgressions typically have been presented in story vignettes or pictures that depict straightforward events (in that the acts are not depicted as being in conflict with other types of goals, motivations, or events), and the moral stimuli usually are depicted as intentional and voluntary acts that have consequences for others' welfare or rights.

Domain distinctions have been examined using two types of assessments. First, children's criterion judgments have been assessed using the theoretical dimensions that are hypothesized to differentiate morality from other types of social knowledge. The criteria for morality include generalizability, obligation, inalterability, and independence from rules and authority sanctions, whereas the criteria for convention include contextual relativity, alterability, and contingency on rules and authority. *Generalizability* has been operationalized in terms of whether events or transgressions are judged to be wrong or permissible in different social contexts, such as at home, in another school, or in other countries. *Moral obligation* has been assessed by children's judgments as to whether individuals are obligated to perform requested actions or obey rules. *Judgments of rule and authority independence* have been operationalized in terms of children's evaluations of whether acts or transgressions would be wrong in the absence of rules or if the authority (teacher, parent, etc.) did not see or know about the rule violation.

In addition, studies also have included quantitative assessments of the seriousness and amount of punishment deserved for different transgressions and the importance of different types of rules. Although moral transgressions typically are treated as more serious and more punishable than conventional transgressions and moral rules are rated as more important than conventional rules, these quantitative dimensions are seen as correlated with, rather than as formal criteria for, distinguishing the domains (see Tisak & Turiel [1988] for an example of how seriousness can be disentangled from event domain).

Children's justifications for their judgments, or the types of reasons individuals provide to explain their evaluations of social actions, also have been used as criteria for domain distinctions. *Moral justifications* pertain to the intrinsic consequences of acts for others, including concerns with others' harm or welfare, fairness or rights, and obligations, whereas *social-conventional justifications* pertain to authority (including concerns with punishment, rules, or authority commands), social expectations and social regularities (e.g., social and cultural norms), and social organization or social order (e.g., the need to maintain social order, avoid disorder, or coordinate social interactions).

Over the last 30 years, numerous studies have examined whether children across a broad age range distinguish between moral and conventional acts in their judgments and justifications. The results of this research have been reviewed extensively elsewhere (see Killen, McGlothlin, & Lee-Kim, 2002; Nucci, 2001; Smetana, 1995b, 1997; Tisak, 1995; Turiel, 1998) and thus are not reviewed in detail here. But, as Killen, McGlothlin, and Lee-Kim (2002) have noted, the results of more than 100 studies provide strong support for the proposition that from early ages on, children distinguish morality and social convention using these theoretical criteria. Research (conducted in the United States and elsewhere) examining evaluations of prototypical hypothetical moral events have found that individuals from early childhood on evaluate straightforward moral transgressions as prescriptively and generalizably wrong, based on moral concerns with others' welfare or rights. Children generally are act oriented and focus on the consequences of acts for others when evaluating moral events, whereas they are rule oriented when evaluating social conventional events. Furthermore, children as young as 3 years of age make rudimentary distinctions between moral and social events (Smetana, 1981a; Smetana & Braeges, 1990), and young children apply the distinction more for familiar than unfamiliar events (Davidson, Turiel, & Black, 1983). With increasing age, the distinction becomes applied more reliably and to a broader range of social events. Development proceeds from a reliance on specific personal experiences to the ability to apply the criteria to more abstract and unfamiliar social events.

Coordinations and Overlaps in Moral and Social Concepts

Not all events or situations can be cleanly separated into moral and conventional components (Smetana, 1983; Turiel, 1983; Turiel, Killen & Helwig, 1987). Many events or situations are multifaceted and entail overlapping concerns with morality, social conventions, prudence, pragmatics, or personal issues, sometimes in conflict with one another and sometimes in synchrony. These mixed domain (or multifaceted) events have been the focus of much recent research, as they are the source of much developmental and contextual variability and inconsistency in judgments. That is, the way individuals weigh and coordinate moral and nonmoral considerations in making judgments may vary across contexts, cultures, and development. Indeed, an adequate explanation of development must include analyses of how individuals coordinate moral and nonmoral issues in their thinking (Helwig & Turiel, 2003; Smetana & Turiel, 2003; Turiel, 1983, 1998).

In the research examining judgments about multifaceted situations, participants typically are asked to evaluate hypothetical situations where different types of concerns conflict. Some studies have examined children's judgments about different mixed domain situations (e.g., Killen, 1990; Smetana, Killen, & Turiel, 1991), or judgments about straightforward (single-domain) events have been compared to judgments about mixed-domain situations (e.g., Helwig, 1995; Turiel, Hildebrandt, & Wainryb, 1991). These types of comparisons demonstrate that although children may understand and apply moral concepts in straightforward situations, they sometimes subordinate morality to other concerns (e.g., law or social convention) when they are contextualized in more complex situations. These studies demonstrate clearly that children's reasoning in such complex situations does not reflect a general failure to distinguish morality from social convention (as global stage models of moral judgment development have assumed), but rather reflects the salience of different concerns in multifaceted situations. The findings from numerous studies reflect considerable variation both between and within individuals in how they coordinate morality with other social concepts. In some situations, children subordinate concepts in one domain to another domain, either because they explicitly consider but reject one type of concern as less salient or less valid, or because they do not recognize the competing concerns. In other situations, children may coordinate different social concepts, or they may view them as in conflict. Much research remains to be done to understand the nature of these coordinations at different ages and whether there are general developmental patterns in children's ability to coordinate different social concepts. In the following section, within-domain variations in children's moral judgments and judgments about moral versus different types of nonmoral acts are considered.

CHARACTERISTICS OF ACTS AS SOURCES OF CONSISTENCY AND VARIATIONS IN JUDGMENTS

Some of the studies examining children's judgments of prototypical moral and social-conventional events also have systematically varied the moral stimuli, yielding analyses of moral judgments regarding different types of moral issues. There has been substantially less attention to studying development within the moral domain, although the available research does provide some evidence of developmental change in moral concepts with age. Other studies have compared moral or conventional events (or both) with nonsocial events, such as physical or logical regularities, or have examined judgments about hypothetical versus actual events. The findings from these studies are reviewed next.

Within-Domain Variations

Moral Judgments of Physical Harm, Psychological Harm, and Fairness. Most of the research examining distinctions in children's and adolescents' moral and conventional understanding has included different types of moral events, although the analyses have focused on comparing moral and conventional (or other nonmoral) judgments. Several studies have systematically examined children's judgments of different types of moral events, however, including those entailing fairness (e.g., not sharing or taking turns), psychological harm or distress (e.g., teasing, calling a child names, or being mean), and physical harm (e.g., hitting or kicking) along with their evaluation of social-conventional items (Smetana, Kelly, & Twentyman, 1984; Smetana, Schlagman, & Adams, 1993). Moral transgressions of all kinds are seen as more serious, more deserving of punishment, more independent of rules, and more generalizably wrong than social-conventional transgressions. But young children also view unfairness, psychological distress, and physical harm as increasingly serious transgressions (Smetana et al., 1984).

Furthermore, young children (primarily preschoolers) more consistently apply moral criteria to events entailing physical harm (hitting and hurting) than unfairness (such as not sharing a toy; Smetana, 1981a). The findings for young children's moral judgments of fairness regarding sharing are inconsistent, but differences among studies of preschoolers may be due to ambiguity in the depiction of sharing and resource distribution. The stimuli in these studies do not always clearly indicate whether the objects are personal possessions (where rights of ownership dictate that sharing may be more discretionary) or communal property, where rights of possession may dominate (e.g., Ross, Tesla, Kenyon, & Lollis, 1990). Furthermore, because mothers of toddlers have been found to be inconsistent in supporting rights of ownership versus rights of possession (Ross et al., 1990), children may have difficulty constructing an understanding of fairness in these situations.

More generally, however, studies with slightly older children confirm that children's understanding within the moral domain develops from a focus on concrete harm and others' welfare in early childhood to an understanding of fairness, defined in terms of equality and equal treatment between persons, in middle childhood (Damon, 1977; Davidson et al., 1983; Kahn, 1992; Nucci, 2001; Tisak & Turiel, 1988). During preadolescence, concerns with equality are transformed into a concern with equity, or an understanding that fair treatment entails a consideration of individual differences in needs and statuses (Damon, 1977; Nucci, 2001, 2002). Finally, during adolescence, concepts of fairness become more broadly comprehensive, universally applicable, and generalizable across situations as well as more able to take situational variations into account (Nucci, 2001, 2002).

Children have been found to apply concepts of welfare to situations entailing physical harm at earlier ages than to situations entailing psychological harm (Davidson et al., 1983; Smetana et al., 1993), most likely because situations involving physical harm are more immediate and concrete to young children than psychological harm. In situations entailing psychological harm, victims must first interpret the situation to experience the harmful consequences, whereas physical harm is more direct and does not require symbolic mediation (Helwig, Hildebrandt, & Turiel, 1995).

These studies provide some evidence that children's moral concepts as defined within domain theory change qualitatively with age, but the research evidence thus far has been based on relatively small and homogeneous samples studied in exclusively cross-sectional designs. Moreover, the studies have tended to focus on specific moral concepts (e.g., distributive justice or physical harm versus psychological harm). There is a need for longitudinal research that uses more heterogeneous samples and that more comprehensively examines qualitative changes in moral concepts as defined within domain theory.

Religious Versus Moral Rules.   Distinctions between morality and social convention are not restricted to secular contexts but can be applied to religious rules as well. Nucci and Turiel (Nucci, 1985; Nucci & Turiel, 1993) examined conceptions of moral and religious rules in adolescents of different religious faiths (Catholic, Dutch Reform Calvinist, Amish-Mennonite, Orthodox Jewish, and Conservative Jewish). In addition to the usual domain assessments, the studies examined whether the permissibility of a given act is contingent on the presence or absence of a specific command from God and whether God's commands could make an act like stealing right that most children treat as morally wrong. As expected, regardless of religious affiliation, most adolescents treated moral issues (like stealing, hitting, and property damage) as wrong in the absence of a rule from God, whereas religious conventions, such as day of worship, expectations regarding appropriate dress (for Amish participants), and diet (for Jewish participants) were treated as acceptable. In addition, most children rejected the notion that God's commands could make a moral violation (such as stealing) morally right, and nearly all of the participants rejected the notion that God would make such a commandment. Thus, children of different religious faiths apply moral criteria to religious rules pertaining to fairness and rights and differentiate religious conventions from moral issues.

Judgments of Moral and Conventional Versus Other Social and Nonsocial Acts

Prudential and Personal Issues.   Children's and adolescents' understanding of moral and conventional events has been compared to their understanding of *prudential issues,* which are nonsocial acts pertaining to safety, harm to the self, comfort, and health (Tisak, 1993; Tisak & Turiel, 1984). Children differentiate between situations involving (moral) harm to others (such as when a child pushes another child off a swing), and (prudential) harm to the self (such as when a child purposely jumps off a swing), even when violations are depicted as having similar consequences (e.g., a child getting hurt; Tisak, 1993). Furthermore, children judge moral transgressions to be more wrong than prudential transgressions, even when the consequences are depicted as more severe for the prudential than the moral rule violations or when the consequences of moral violations are depicted as minor (Tisak, 1993). Thus, children's judgments reflect a concern with the type of harm, rather than its severity.

As early as 3 years of age, children also distinguish moral and conventional issues from personal issues in both home and preschool contexts (Killen & Smetana, 1999; Nucci & Weber, 1995; Weber, 1999). Children typically categorize personal issues as up to the individual (rather than as acts that are right or wrong), based on justifications that the consequences only affect the actor or that the acts are personal matters and should be the actor's own business (Killen & Smetana, 1999; Nucci, 1981; Nucci & Weber, 1995).

Logical and Physical Issues.   Although children of all ages treat moral laws as more unalterable than conventions, young children's ability to distinguish conventional and physical regularities (such as gravity) increases with age in middle childhood (Komatsu & Galotti, 1986; Lockhart, Abrahams, & Osherson, 1977). Komatsu and Galotti (1986) also manipulated whether the events were depicted in this world versus a presumably dissimilar world ("E.T.'s world"); by third grade, most children understood that conventions are alterable in both worlds. In contrast, children viewed physical facts as unalterable in this world, but increasingly alterable in another world. Thus, children's understanding of different types of social and nonsocial regularities increases with age during middle childhood.

These distinctions have been expanded to include intellectual conventions (like how to draw certain letters) and personal intellectual matters (like preferences for particular books; Nicholls & Thorkildsen, 1988), as well as logical problems (Laupa, 2000). Children judge intellectual conventions to be more alterable than physical and logical laws, and they view children as having autonomy over personal issues, whereas teachers are seen as having the legitimate authority to set standards over other types of issues (logic and conventions).

Judgments Regarding Hypothetical Versus Actual Situations

The research discussed in the previous sections has focused primarily on children's judgments and justifications in hypothetical, prototypical situations. Studies using prototypical examples are designed to depict the features of moral actions in unambiguous and straightforward ways. In actual situations, transgressions also may be straightforward, but they may be more fleeting and more nuanced, and actors' intentions, the victim's role in instigating the events, and the extent of the negative consequences experienced by the victim all may be ambiguous or difficult to discern. In addition, actual situations may entail mixtures of different domains, for instance, when rules or authority pertain to unfair practices (Turiel, 2002). These factors all may lead to variations in judgments of actual situations.

Children's judgments of prototypical and hypothetical and actual, witnessed transgressions have been compared (Smetana et al., 1993; Smetana, Toth et al., 1999; Turiel, 2002). In one study (Smetana et al., 1993), preschool children made judgments about prototypical moral and conventional transgressions using standard assessment procedures. The novel aspect of this study was that preschool classrooms also were observed until a moral or conventional transgression occurred, and then bystanders, or witnesses to the transgressions, were interviewed about the events. Few differences in judgments about hypothetical and actual transgressions were observed, although children made clearer distinctions between moral and conventional events in their judgments of authority independence when judging hypothetical than actual transgressions.

A second study (Smetana, Toth et al., 1999) employed the same methods but interviewed actual victims and transgressors instead of bystanders. Again, children's judgments about prototypical moral transgressions were compared to judgments about straightforward moral transgressions. Children did not differ in their ratings of the severity of hypothetical and actual transgressions, but they viewed hypothetical transgressions as more deserving of punishment than actual transgressions. Children also focused more on the intrinsic features of acts when justifying hypothetical than actual transgressions, whereas they more often did not know why transgressions were wrong when justifying actual than hypothetical transgressions. Thus, children clearly judged the actual moral transgressions using moral criteria, but the hypothetical events appeared to elicit more clearcut moral evaluations.

Perhaps the most detailed description of judgments in hypothetical and actual situations comes from an observational study described by Turiel (2002). Observations of moral, conventional, and mixed-domain events were conducted in several contexts in different schools. Children of varying ages were interviewed about the actual events shortly after they occurred; they were also administered standard interviews about hypothetical moral and conventional events about a month following the observations. As found in the previous studies, children of all ages distinguished actual moral from conventional events, but judgments about the hypothetical events were more clearcut and uniform than judgments about the actual events (Turiel, 2002). Thus, when children encounter straightforward moral transgressions in everyday life, the situations may be more ambiguous and the features of the events may not be as well specified and detailed as the situations that are presented in hypothetical interviews, leading to some variation in moral judgments.

Facts and Values: Informational Assumptions

A series of studies by Wainryb (1991, 2000; Wainryb & Ford, 1998) has illuminated the importance of distinguishing between children's factual beliefs and moral evaluations (for a discussion of this issue from an anthropological perspective, see Hatch [1983]; for a developmental discussion, see Turiel [2002] and Turiel et al. [1987]). Wainryb has proposed that apparent differences in moral evaluations may be due to differences in children's descriptive understanding of the nature of reality (which she refers to as *informational assumptions*), rather than in moral concepts or principles. Her research has demonstrated that children consistently take into account both moral and factual beliefs when making moral judgments.

In an initial study, Wainryb (1991) found that although adolescent and college-age students had similar moral beliefs about the wrongness of inflicting harm on others, they varied in their evaluations of particular situations (like whether it is permissible for a father to administer corporal punishment), because they disagreed about what they believed to be true (whether causing pain in the context of corporal punishment promotes learning or not). Differences in these factual beliefs informed their moral evaluations of the permissibility of corporal punishment. Attitudes about corporal punishment were more positive among those who believed that pain facilitates learning, whereas attitudes were more negative among those with more negative or uncertain beliefs about the value of pain in learning. Moreover, manipulating the informational assumptions led to changes in individuals' moral evaluations of the acts. Similar relationships between informational assumptions and moral evaluations have been found for other social practices as well (Turiel et al., 1991; Wainryb, 1991).

Factual or informational beliefs also have been found to inform real-life decisions about unwanted pregnancy through their influence in structuring judgments. Variations in adolescent and young adult women's beliefs about personhood (including when during a pregnancy a fetus becomes a person and the criteria for defining personhood) informed women's concepts of abortion as a moral or personal issue, which in turn, influenced their decisions whether or not to terminate an unwanted pregnancy (Smetana, 1981b, 1982). Indeed, domain orientation was a better predictor of pregnancy decisions than either religious background or developmental level of moral reasoning, as assessed using hypothetical Kohlbergian moral judgment dilemmas, although religious background influenced women's definitions of personhood. Thus, factual beliefs have a bearing on how individuals construe social practices and act on their beliefs. As these studies suggest, informational assumptions or factual beliefs come from a variety of sources, including science and religion, and may change (e.g., when sientific knowledge advances), or be contested by different groups within a culture (e.g., different religious beliefs about when a fetus becomes a person).

In an interesting extension of these studies, Wainryb and her colleagues have examined judgments of tolerance, or how children's factual beliefs inform their evaluations of the legitimacy of beliefs different than their own. Shaw and Wainryb (1999) asked college students to evaluate social practices that were described as typically practiced by most members of another culture but that entailed harm (e.g., knocking out boys' front teeth with a rock as boys turned 14). Most study participants stated that individuals in this other culture must have factual beliefs that make these practices beneficial rather than harmful. Moreover, the researchers manipulated both the type of belief (moral versus factual) and whether or not there was societal consensus about the belief. They found that the practice was evaluated positively only when members of the society were said to hold the same factual beliefs (e.g., that the practice has beneficial consequences) and to have consensual agreement about the practice. When members of the society were described as disagreeing about the underlying facts or whether the behavior was immoral or agreeing that the practice was immoral, it was assessed negatively as having unfair or harmful consequences. Thus, individuals judge acts that they view as harmful or unfair to be acceptable if they appear to be based on divergent factual beliefs. Wainryb, Shaw, and Maianu (1998) concluded that an understanding that beliefs are matters of interpretation and that individuals may interpret the facts differently leads to tolerance of other people and their behavior. Individuals in such societies are viewed as misinformed but well intentioned.

Another set of studies has drawn on the extensive literature on theory of mind and children's understanding of false beliefs to examine when children begin to understand that individuals have moral and factual beliefs different than their own. An initial study (Flavell, Mumme, Green, & Flavell, 1992) reported that 3-year-olds' difficulty in a standard theory of mind false belief task (which focuses on factual beliefs) also extends to their inability to understand that others might have divergent moral beliefs. By 5 years of age, however, children in this study understood that others might have different factual and moral beliefs. However, as Wainryb and Ford (1998) noted, accurately attributing false moral beliefs alone does not predict how individuals judge the permissibility of others' social practices. Therefore, Wainryb and Ford (1998) extended this research to examine young children's evaluations of divergent social practices. Like Flavell and co-workers (1992), Wainryb and Ford (1998) found that 3-year-olds do not understand that other people have beliefs different than their own, and thus are intolerant. As with older children, however, Wainryb and Ford (1998) found that 5- and 7-year-olds more positively evaluated potentially immoral (e.g., harmful or unfair) practices when they disagreed with the informational beliefs than the moral beliefs. In other words, young children were more tolerant when they used informational beliefs different from their own to reconceptualize the meaning of the acts.

Summary.   Substantial empirical evidence indicates that young children apply moral criteria to familiar moral issues and distinguish them from conventional, personal, and prudential issues in their judgments and justifications. In early childhood, moral criteria such as generalizability and rule independence are applied more consistently to moral issues pertaining to concrete harm and welfare than to fairness and psychological harm. During middle childhood, children also are increasingly able to apply moral criteria to unfamiliar moral events and to a broader range of moral concepts. Cross-sectional studies have yielded evidence that children's moral reasoning changes with age from early childhood to adolescence, but longitudinal research examining normative changes in moral concepts as defined within domain theory is needed to provide evidence of qualitative changes in the moral domain. Longitudinal research also is needed to inform our understanding of age-related increases in children's application of the different criteria underlying their moral judgments.

During middle childhood, children's understanding of different types of regularities expands to include distinctions among moral concepts, intellectual and social-conventional uniformities, physical regularities, and logical rules. An understanding of distinctions between morality and social convention is not limited to secular contexts, but is applied to religious issues as well. Children's understanding of factual beliefs, which develops during early childhood, also influence moral evaluations and may be an important source of variation in children's moral judgments.

FEATURES OF SOCIAL INTERACTIONS AS SOURCES OF CONSISTENCY AND VARIATION IN JUDGMENTS

The hypothesis that moral and social knowledge is constructed from reciprocal individual–environment interactions has been examined in at least three types of studies. *Experimental studies* have varied features of acts associated with different types of transgressions to examine whether these features lead to differentiations in moral and social judgments. *Observational research* has examined children's and adults' responses to naturally occurring transgressions in different domains. Finally, research on *emotion attributions* has been examined in terms of its role in differentiating moral from nonmoral concepts. Evidence from these three lines of research is summarized in the following sections.

Features of Acts

Experimental designs have been used to explicitly test the proposition that children make moral judgments based on the features of social events. Smetana (1985) examined preschool children's judgments about familiar and unspecified moral and conventional events. The unspecified events were labeled by nonsense words, but they varied in the consistency of the prohibitions and the types of responses to the actions. Preschool children differentiated between familiar moral and conventional transgressions in the expected ways; they also differentiated the unspecified events on the basis of their features. Acts that were depicted as generalizably wrong and having consequences for others' welfare ("moral" acts) led to moral judgments, whereas acts that were depicted as contextually relative and prohibited by adults but that did not entail apparent harm or violations of rights ("conventional" acts) led to conventional judgments. Thus, children evaluated the features of interactions independent of children's knowledge of the content of specific events.

Using a different methodology, Zelazo, Helwig, and Lau (1996) assessed preschool children's judgments in different conditions that varied actors' intentions, as well as the relation between acts and their associated outcomes. For instance, children considered conditions under which hitting either caused harm (a normal or canonical causal relation) or pleasure (an unexpected or noncanonical causal relation) and where the actors either intended or did not intend to cause harm. Although young children had more difficulty with the unexpected than the normal causal relations, children's judgments of act acceptability were primarily based on the outcomes (whether or not someone got hurt), not on associations between the acts (such as hitting) and factors external to the acts, such as adult punishment or sanctions. These findings have been replicated in 3-year-olds, demonstrating that they make similar judgments about psychological harm (Helwig, Zelazo, & Wilson, 2001). Thus, these studies provide convincing evidence that children use the specific features of moral actions, such as whether they cause harm to others, to construct generalizable moral judgments (as well as contextually relative conventional judgments).

Shaw and Wainryb (2003) took a somewhat different approach. They examined whether nonprototypical responses to transgressions (compliance or subversion rather than opposition in response to a hypothetical transgressor's demands) lead children to evaluate moral transgressions pertaining to unfairness as permissible or acceptable. Compliance and subversion can be seen as nonprototypical responses, because victims typically respond to unfairness with protest or resistance. Thus, compliant victims might be seen as willing participants. Contrary to expectations, 7- to 15-year-olds evaluated the transgressor's behavior to be morally wrong, regardless of the victim's responses. Children constructed an understanding of victimization and unfairness without explicit behavioral cues (like protests or cries from victims). The authors interpreted these findings as suggesting that the participants brought information and judgments from their own experience to bear on their evaluations of the events. Even when the hypothetical victims complied or subverted the transgressor's demands, most study participants evaluated victims as having negative emotional responses to their victimization. Thus, in addition to their moral evaluations of the transgressors, children displayed a sophisticated understanding that the victim's behavior may not accurately reflect their psychological states or internal feelings.

Characteristics of Social Interactions

Children ranging in age from infancy through middle school have been observed in different naturalistic contexts, including homes, day care centers and nursery schools, school classrooms, and playgrounds to examine characteristics of their moral, conventional, personal, and prudential interactions (see Smetana [1995b, 1997] and Turiel [1998] for reviews). The results of at least 10 observational studies (Blumenfeld, Pintrich, & Hamilton, 1987; Killen & Smetana, 1999; Much & Shweder, 1978; Nucci & Nucci, 1982a, 1982b; Nucci & Turiel, 1978; Nucci, Turiel, & Gawrych, 1983; Nucci & Weber, 1995; Smetana, 1984, 1989b; Tisak, Nucci, & Jankowski, 1996) using the same observational paradigm and highly similar coding systems (and at least 10 more studies that have modified the standard protocol to examine conflict resolution, discourse, and family, peer, and teacher–child interactions) have indicated that social interactions in the context of moral, conventional, and prudential transgressions differ, both in terms of who responds to transgressions, as well as in the type of response to misdeeds.

In these studies, observers first used behavioral definitions (e.g., object conflicts or aggression) to reliably identify and classify observed transgressions as moral or conventional (or in a few cases, prudential or personal). Then, observers coded who responded to the transgressions (e.g., the victim, other peers, or adults) and the type of response using a category system that included behavioral responses (such as physical retaliation), emotional reactions, ridicule, commands, and different types of statements (e.g., disorder versus rights statements).

These studies yielded highly consistent results. Both adults and children (primarily the victims) respond to moral transgressions in ways that provide feedback about the effects of acts for others' rights or welfare (e.g., requests by adults to take the victim's perspective, attempts by both children and adults to evaluate rights, victims' emotional reactions, or claims of injury or loss). Both children and adults also responded to all violations with commands or sanctions, but most of the responses were consistent with the notion that children's moral understanding can be derived from the acts themselves rather than from the rules that regulate the acts. Furthermore, these studies suggested that although children's moral development may be of great concern to adults, many moral conflicts occur and are resolved in the absence of parents or other adults. Indeed, adult intervention in children's moral conflicts decreases from the early years to middle childhood (see Smetana, 1997). In contrast, adults primarily responded to children's conventional violations, especially until middle childhood, with information about what is acceptable in different contexts and what is not (e.g., statements about the disorder the acts caused, sanctions, rule statements, and commands). These findings provide behavioral evidence for how adults and children treat moral and social-conventional conflicts and transgressions. Moreover, the research provides support for the claim that social interactions form the experiential basis for the construction of social knowledge.

Affective Consequences of Transgressions

There has been increasing interest in the role of emotions in moral development (see Arsenio, Gold, & Adams, chap. 21, this volume; Arsenio & Lemerise, 2004; Arsenio & Lover, 1995; Lemerise & Arsenio, 2000). Theoretical approaches that give priority to emotions assert that the socialization of moral principles is accomplished through associations with (parents') negative emotions or that affective processes (such as empathy) drive changes in moral principles. In contrast, following Piaget (1967), domain theory researchers have viewed emotions as the energy that drives and organizes judgments; children's affective experiences are "grist for the social–cognitive mill" (Smetana, 1997, p. 122) in that they influence children's understanding, encoding, and memory of moral transgressions. Thus, in this view, moral knowledge, not emotional response, changes qualitatively with age (Nucci, 2001; Smetana, 1997; Turiel, 1998).

Arsenio's research program provides some support for this assertion (see Arsenio, Gold, & Adams, chap. 21, this volume). His research has shown that different emotions are associated with different types of transgressions. In middle childhood, moral events are evaluated as affectively negative, whereas conventional transgressions are viewed as affectively neutral, and these ratings are highly correlated with judgments of obligatoriness and alterability (Arsenio & Ford, 1985). Furthermore, children's expectancies of the emotional consequences of moral and social judgments are highly differentiated and increase in complexity with age; children use information about situational affective consequences (e.g., whether actors or victims are happy, sad, angry, fearful, or neutral) to infer whether initiating events are moral, conventional, or personal (Arsenio, 1988). These findings led Arsenio to propose that differences in the tendency of moral and conventional events to elicit emotional arousal may promote differential encoding of these events; highly arousing moral events may be considered "immoral" in part because they are more affectively salient than less arousing events. Thus, these studies suggest that affective reactions are a salient feature of children's experiences of transgressions that influence their ability to understand, differentiate, and remember moral and other types of social events.

Although children of all ages consistently attribute negative emotions to the victims of transgressions, most young children are "happy victimizers." That is, children attribute positive emotions (like happiness) to transgressors (Arsenio & Kramer, 1992). With advancing age (beginning at about 6 years), children also attribute conflicting emotions (happiness due to their gains as a result of the behavior as well as negative emotions due to their understanding of their victim's plight) to victimizers. Arsenio and Lover (1995) proposed that with age, and as a consequence of positive peer relationships, normally developing children shift from viewing victimizers as feeling strictly happy to focusing on the negative consequences for the victim. This model helps to explain the apparent inconsistency between young children's relatively sophisticated moral evaluations (at least while focusing on victims) and the frequency of moral misbehaviors and transgressions in early childhood (because children also focus on the gains achieved through victimization). In Arsenio and Lover's (1995) conceptualization, stable individual differences in children's peer relationships combine with developmental changes to influence children's moral understanding.

Summary.   The studies reviewed in this section bear on the claim that there are consistencies in children's moral judgments and that morality can be universalized. Using different methodologies, the studies provide evidence that children's moral and social judgments are inferred from features of the acts rather than from knowledge of the prohibitions regarding particular acts. Research on children's emotional expectancies and attributions for different types of transgressions suggests that the ability to coordinate the negative consequences of victimization with the potentially positive gains for perpetrators increases with age and that an attributional shift may account for discrepancies between children's moral evaluations and behavior.

Moreover, observational research indicates that adults and children use different conflict resolution strategies and have different responses to moral and social-conventional conflicts and transgressions. This research demonstrates that there are observable regularities in social interactions that map onto the distinctions that have been found in children's moral and social judgments. Research is needed to explicitly test these hypothesized connections between patterns of social interactions and the development of moral and social judgments.

CHARACTERISTICS OF SOCIAL ROLES AND SOCIAL RELATIONSHIPS AS SOURCES OF CONSISTENCY AND VARIATION IN JUDGMENTS

The proposition that moral and social judgments are actively constructed from reciprocal social interactions implies that individuals are constantly interpreting situations and ascribing meaning to their interactions. This process of interpretation has been referred to as *social construal* (Saltzstein, 1994; Turiel et al., 1987, 1991) and has been the focus of much recent research. Although the steps involved in social construal have not been well specified in domain research (but see Arsenio & Lemerise [2004]), the steps in children's real-time social–cognitive processing of information and social cues during social situations have been examined from social information processing (SIP) models of social behavior. The initial steps are described as entailing coding and interpreting of social situations (Coie & Dodge, 1998). SIP models propose that because social situations typically are complex and too much information is available, individuals use heuristics (including biases and deficits) to encode the relevant portions of the interactions. Social construal, including evaluating the morally relevant aspects of situations, is part of this process and may be particularly important in evaluating mixed domain or multifaceted events (Arsenio & Lemerise, 2004). The research reviewed in the following sections indicates that elements of the situation, such as one's role in the interaction or the social relationships among the participants, may influence individuals' social construal of morally relevant situations.

Children's Roles in Situations

Not surprisingly, when preschool children are asked to evaluate hypothetical moral and conventional transgressions that are described as either committed by the self or by others, children view transgressions committed by the self as more permissible than those committed by others (Slomkowski & Killen, 1992; Smetana et al., 1984). Children's judgments also differ as a function of whether they are victims or perpetrators in a transgression. Dunn, Cutting, and Demetriou (2000) found that preschoolers gave more interpersonal justifications when the child-participant was described as the victim of a moral transgression than when the child was described as the violator. In real-life situations, preschool victims judge actual moral transgressions to be more serious and more deserving of punishment than did (actual) violators, whereas transgressors view their behavior to be more justified than do victims (Smetana, Toth et al., 1999). These perspective differences could be attributed to self-interest, but social psychological research on actor/observer differences has demonstrated that individuals have more information about the situational factors affecting their own than others' behavior and thus are more likely to consider mitigating and situational circumstances when making attributions about their own behavior.

This is consistent with the findings from Turiel's (2002) study of social judgments and social action. He also found role-related differences in evaluations, but importantly, victims and transgressors did not differ in their domain assessments of the same event as moral. Transgressors and victims had disagreements over who instigated a moral transgression or why a transgression occurred, but victims and transgressors almost always both viewed such events as moral (whereas for conventional transgressions, transgressors viewed the acts less negatively than did observers).

Recent research by Wainryb and Langley (2003) further illuminates these issues. These researchers examined 6-, 10-, and 15-year-old children's retrospective narrative descriptions of their intentions and reasons in situations of where children had been either a perpetrator or a victim of a moral transgression. When narrating experiences of victimization, children (and particularly younger children) were more likely to view the harm as intentional. Perpetrators typically described their behavior as a response to provocation, whereas victims typically described the perpetrator as wanting to harm or anger them, although with age, children more frequently referred to mitigating circumstances, misunderstandings, and negligence. Importantly, because most of these studies (Dunn et al., 2000; Smetana, Daddis et al., 1999; Wainryb & Langley, 2003) utilized within-subjects designs, differences between victims' and perpetrators' responses cannot be due to individual differences in children. Rather, there appear to be systematic differences in children's social construal depending on their role in the situation.

Social Relationships With Peers and Siblings

Piaget (1932) first proposed that the mutual nature of peer relationships allows for experiences of cooperation, conflict, and negotiation that may facilitate moral development. Others (Damon, 1977; Youniss, 1980) have likewise assumed that relationships with peers allow for reciprocity and mutual give-and-take, which may lead to the co-construction of knowledge. Consistent with this assertion, children have been found to have different social experiences with age mates and near age mates (e.g., siblings) than with parents. Based on a review of studies, Smetana (1997) concluded that moral conflicts, including disputes over possessions, rights, taking turns, hurting, aggression, psychological harm, and unkindness, occur primarily in interactions with peers and siblings rather than with adults, whereas at least among young children, conflicts over social conventions occur primarily in interactions with adults (because adults have a stake in maintaining conventional regularities). By middle childhood, children also participate in conflicts over the conventions of a particular social context (and at younger ages when cultural conventions are involved).

Although moral conflicts have been found to be more frequent in peer than in parent–child interactions, little research from the social–cognitive domain perspective has examined whether the quality (or extent) of social experience with peers influences the developmental maturity of children's moral and social reasoning. An exception is a study by Sanderson and Siegal (1988). These researchers hypothesized that more socially skilled children would have more highly developed conceptions of social rules than their less socially skilled peers. They assessed judgments of moral and conventional transgressions in 4- and 5-year-olds, who were designated as controversial, popular, average, neglected, and rejected based on peer group nominations. Consistent with previous research, children distinguished the domains using a variety of criteria. Controversial children, however, rated moral transgressions as more deserving of punishment than did their popular peers. Because controversial children are more interpersonally skilled than other children, this finding was interpreted as demonstrating that more socially skilled children are more advanced in their moral maturity. Although these findings are suggestive, their hypotheses regarding popular children were not confirmed, nor were there consistent differences in other criterion judgments. Thus, further research is needed to replicate this finding.

Friendships.   Several researchers have further proposed that early friendships may be particularly important in moral development (Arsenio & Lover, 1995; Dunn et al., 2000). Dunn and colleagues (2000) have asserted that interactions between friends provide an important context for a developing understanding of self and others through the opportunity for discourse about inner states and emotions, which may influence children's moral evaluations. Preschool children have been found to view moral transgressions as more permissible when they involve a friend than a nonfriend (Slomkowski & Killen, 1992). Moreover, children referred to interpersonal considerations more when justifying moral transgressions among friends, whereas they used moral justifications more to justify transgressions among nonfriends. Because the majority of children viewed hypothetical moral transgressions as wrong, the findings suggest that friendship influenced children's willingness to consider situational circumstances that mitigated the wrongness of the acts. Furthermore, research shows that young adolescents have different beliefs about appropriate resolution strategies in response to friends' versus acquaintances' moral transgressions (Tisak & Tisak, 1996).

Peer Groups.   Horn, Killen, and Stangor (1999) have shown that stereotypes about adolescent social reference groups, or crowds (such as jocks or techies) influence adolescents' judgments about ambiguous situations in which blame for a moral transgression is unclear. Adolescents focused more on social-conventional concerns and less on moral concerns when moral transgressions were consistent rather than inconsistent with stereotypical expectations about different reference groups (Horn et al., 1999). In other words, social-conventional reasoning was activated more often when behavior was depicted as stereotype consistent, but judgments also varied according to the social reference group. Horn (2003) has further demonstrated that adolescents treat exclusion from social groups as multifaceted and having moral and conventional components. She found that adolescents who belonged to high status groups (cheerleaders, jocks, or preppies) judged exclusion from peer groups as less wrong than did adolescents who either did not belong to a group or who belonged to low status groups (dirties, druggies, and gothics). Thus, moral concepts of fairness or equal treatment were influenced both by the moral parameters of the situation as well as adolescents' position in the social hierarchy (see Killen, Margie, and Sinno [chap. 6, this volume] for more elaboration on judgments regarding social exclusion).

Siblings. Siblings, like friends, provide a context for moral experience and interactions (Dunn & Munn, 1987). Children learn moral behavior (such as empathy), as well as immoral behavior, including experiences of hurting and upsetting others, from their siblings. During the second year of life, there is an increase in teasing, including an increased understanding of "how to provoke and annoy the sibling during confrontation" (Dunn, 1987, p. 94). Dunn (1987) found that 2-year-olds demonstrating greater sibling rivalry had a better moral understanding of how to hurt and upset others, whereas close and affectionate sibling relationships were associated concurrently with children's ability to cooperate, conciliate, and role play (Dunn, 1987) and longitudinally with a more mature moral orientation (Dunn, Brown, & McGuire, 1995).

Four-year-olds showed a greater understanding of others' mental states in naturally occurring conversations with siblings and friends than with mothers, and children who used more mental state terms engaged in more cooperative interactions (Brown, Donelan-McCall, & Dunn, 1996). Thus, social interactions between equals and near-equals provide contexts for gaining a psychological understanding of others, which may facilitate moral judgment development.

Relationships With Parents and Other Adults

Piaget (1932/1965) first called attention to the importance of power in social relationships. Whereas the mutual nature of peer relationships was seen as leading to cooperation and advances in moral judgment development, the imbalances in power that characterize parent–child (or more generally, adult–child) interactions were hypothesized to lead to relationships of constraint that impede moral development. This has led to a relative neglect of the influence of parents in facilitating moral judgments in early structural developmental research (but see Walker & Taylor [1991] for an exception). Domain theory researchers have examined several issues pertaining to the role of parents, including the types of family interactions and discipline methods that facilitate moral development and children's and adolescents' judgments of parental and teacher authority. Findings from this research are discussed briefly in the following sections.

Parental Discipline. Researchers from socialization perspectives have focused on the influence of parental discipline on moral development. A consistent finding is that induction, or parents' use of reasoning, explanations, and rationales, is associated with more mature morality, as assessed in a variety of ways (Hoffman, 1991; Thompson & Meyer, chap. 10, this volume). Traditional socialization theories have paid insufficient attention, however, to the content of those messages and the values to be internalized. Research reviewed extensively by Grusec and Goodnow (1994) has shown that the types of reasons parents use vary according to the nature of the misdeed. As noted, mothers tend to reason about others' needs and rights in response to acts entailing welfare and harm, and social order and rules in response to conventional transgressions. Furthermore, parental responses to moral (and conventional) transgressions are direct, explicit, and typically do not entail negotiation, whereas responses to personal issues entail more tacit forms of communication, including greater negotiation and more opportunities for children to make choices (Nucci & Weber, 1995).

According to domain theory, interactions with parents (as well as peers) are important contexts for moral judgment development. Children's direct experiences (as victims and observers of transgressions) provide one source of knowledge about the intrinsic consequences of acts for others' welfare and rights, but parental statements, reactions, and responses to transgressions provide another source. Inductive discipline methods, including parents' domain-specific explanations and reasoning, facilitate children's moral and social development by providing information about the nature of transgressions and by stimulating children to think reflectively about their actions. As an illustration, sequential analyses of middle-class European American children's responses to transgressions demonstrated that young child victims reacted to moral transgressions with statements regarding the injury or loss they experienced or with emotional reactions; these were either followed sequentially by parental commands to stop the misbehavior or parental statements focusing on rights or requests to take the victims' perspectives (Smetana, 1989b). Thus, at least in the latter case, parents' reactions provided a complementary source of information about children's experiences that can be used to construct moral concepts. Parents' reasoning and explanations may help children to translate their immediate and potentially highly emotional reactions and responses into more generalizable, abstract principles regarding justice, fairness, and rights. Reasoning has been criticized as an overly broad and amorphous category (Grusec & Goodnow, 1994), but studies focusing specifically on parents' other-oriented reasoning have found that these explanations do facilitate moral development (Kuczynski, 1982; Zahn-Waxler & Chapman, 1982) and are associated with fewer moral transgressions (unpublished analyses reported in Smetana, 1997).

Conversely, power-assertive methods may be ineffective in facilitating moral maturity because they fail to provide information that can be used to construct generalizable moral concepts. Indeed, research has shown that power assertion is effective in inducing short-term compliance, but it does not facilitate moral development (Kuczynski, 1984). Parental responses that are extremely negative, angry, or coercive may be especially detrimental to the development of moral and social understanding because they are too negatively arousing, which may scare the child, threaten his or her sense of security, and lead to a focus on the child's rather than on others' feelings (Grusec & Goodnow, 1994; Zahn-Waxler & Chapman, 1982). Consistent with the claim that affect influences the salience and encoding of moral events (Arsenio & Lover, 1995); however, moderate anger and negative affect in conjunction with explanations that focus on others' welfare and rights, appear to increase the effectiveness of parental reasoning, perhaps because they help to focus the child on the harm or injustice caused (Grusec & Goodnow, 19994; Smetana, 1997; Zahn-Waxler & Chapman, 1982).

Furthermore, the process of discipline is interactive (Turiel, 1998), and thus, it is important to focus not just on the parental message, but how children interpret those messages. Children evaluate the appropriateness of adult responses to their actions and have clear preferences for domain-appropriate over domain-inappropriate responses (Killen, Breton, Ferguson, & Handler, 1994; Nucci, 1984). Although the observational research suggests that parents and other adults naturally coordinate their responses to transgressions with the nature of the act, children may be more responsive to parental directives when they are consistent with children's understanding of the actions.

Parental and Teacher Authority. Traditional approaches to moral internalization have focused on children's compliance as an indicator of successful socialization. More recently,

Grusec and Goodnow (1994) have recognized that, although compliance may be desirable in some circumstances, parents may have other goals for their children, including facilitating their child's autonomy or initiative. Thus, greater compliance or submissiveness to parental requests may not always indicate greater moral maturity or developmental competence, even when compliance is mutual or freely chosen (what Kochanska [1997] has referred to as committed compliance) rather than externally coerced (or situational compliance; Kochanska [1997]).

From the domain perspective, the proposition that discipline situations are interactive also implies that children or adolescents evaluate the legitimacy of adults' authority to make rules or request compliance. An extensive body of research (summarized in Laupa, Turiel, & Cowan [1995], Smetana [1995a, 1995b, 2002], Tisak [1995], and Turiel [1998]) has examined children and adolescents' conceptions of legitimate parental (and teacher) authority. Contrary to Piaget's (1932/1965) claims, even young children do not have unilateral respect for adult authority; they critically evaluate its legitimacy along several dimensions, including the domain and nature of the request, as well as the attributes of the authority source. From early childhood to late adolescence, children judge both moral and conventional issues as legitimately regulated by adults, as long as their authority is contextually appropriate (teachers are not seen as having legitimate authority to enforce conventions in the home and mothers have less authority to regulate conventions at school than at home; Laupa, 1991; Weber, 1999) and when they have the requisite knowledge (Laupa, 1991). Children reject adults' authority to make immoral requests, such as to steal or hurt others (Damon, 1977).

American children and adolescents also draw boundaries to legitimate parental and adult authority and consistently view personal issues as beyond the bounds of legitimate parental and teacher authority. Although parents and teachers also endorse the view that children and adolescents should have some personal jurisdiction over certain issues, such as choice of food, clothes, friendships, and activities (see Smetana [1995a, 2002] for a review) and among older adolescents, career decisions (Bregman & Killen, 1999), parents consistently view themselves as having more authority over personal issues than their children are willing to grant them. Parents (as well as teachers) and adolescents also consistently disagree over parents' legitimate authority to regulate issues that entail overlaps between the domains (e.g., events that include both conventional and personal components). Disagreements over where to draw the boundaries between parents' legitimate authority and adolescents' personal discretion has been found to lead to conflict in adolescent–parent relationships, and conflict, in turn, has been found to broaden the boundaries of adolescents' personal domains (Smetana, 1989a, 2002). Thus, disagreement and rejection of parents' control of personal issues are characteristic of children's social relations with parents throughout childhood and adolescence. Children and adolescents actively claim events as personal, resisting regulation and challenging adult authority. Although socialization research typically has treated children's resistance to adult authority as a characteristic of the child and as evidence of failure in socialization, these findings suggest that resistance may be systematically related to domains of social knowledge and beliefs about who should legitimately control and regulate different types of issues.

Finally, how adolescents and parents draw boundaries among the domains is related to children's psychological adjustment. Hasebe, Nucci, and Nucci (2004) have found that middle-class American and Japanese adolescents' evaluations of parental overcontrol of personal issues (but not conventional or prudential issues) is associated with self-reported symptoms of psychopathology (particularly internalizing symptoms like depression and anxiety) and that symptoms are more acute with age, as adolescents expand their claims to a personal sphere. African-American adolescents' perceptions of greater parental control of decision making over personal and multifaceted issues was found to be associated with better adjustment (including better academic performance, more positive self-worth, and less deviance) in early adolescence, but increases in adolescent decision making over personal and multifaceted issues from middle to late adolescence were associated with better adjustment, including better self-worth and less depression (Smetana, Campione-Barr, & Daddis, 2004). Adolescents also view overcontrol of the personal domain as psychologically intrusive (Smetana & Daddis, 2002). However, the findings also indicate that granting adolescents autonomy needs to be developmentally appropriate, because too-early or contextually inappropriate autonomy is associated with poorer psychosocial adjustment (Smetana et al., 2004).

Summary.   Social construal entails interpretations of social interactions, including whether children view acts as being morally relevant (e.g., in the moral domain) or not. Perpetrators are more likely to view their behavior as a response to provocation, whereas victims are more likely to view harm as intentional. Because most of the research has used within-subjects designs, there is compelling evidence that these differences are due to children's roles in the situation rather individual differences in children (and the likelihood that they will be victims versus transgressors in social situations). With age, child victims are more likely to consider mitigating circumstances, but more research is needed on normative shifts in children's understanding of these mitigating circumstances and on coordinations between knowledge obtained in victim versus violator roles.

Moral conflicts and transgressions occur more frequently in interactions with peers and siblings than with adults. Dunn's (1987) research has shown that interactions with siblings provide children with opportunities to learn both moral and immoral behavior. Developmentally appropriate parental reasoning and explanations help children to construct moral understandings of right and wrong, but discipline is interactive, and children also interpret the messages they receive. Thus, children are more responsive to parental (and more broadly, adult) directives that are domain-appropriate and consistent with their understanding of the events and when the adult authority is contextually appropriate and knowledgeable.

CHARACTERISTICS OF INDIVIDUALS AS SOURCES OF VARIATION IN CHILDREN'S JUDGMENTS

Because structural–developmental theories of moral judgment development focus on normative development, there has been relatively little attention to individual differences in moral judgment development. Although domain theory also assumes that there are qualitative changes with age in moral reasoning, the focus on how moral understanding is coordinated with other types of social knowledge leaves room for examining individual differences in judgments. In the following section, differences in moral and social judgments according to gender, social class, and race/ethnicity are discussed, followed by a review of research on atypical children's development.

Individual Differences

Gender.   The issue of sex differences in moral development has been a longstanding source of controversy, from early moral theorists (like Freud) who claimed that girls have a weaker moral sense, to Gilligan (1982), who has claimed that boys and girls develop different moral orientations. Gilligan also asserts that boys' morality is oriented toward rules, rights, and the self as an autonomous agent, whereas girls' morality is structured by care, responsibility, and the need to avoid harm. These claims have been extensively debated (see Walker, chap. 4, this volume).

In light of these controversies, it is notable that few sex differences have emerged in research from the domain approach. Boys and girls do not appear to differ systematically in their ability to apply moral criteria to situations or to use moral reasoning. One study, specifically designed to examine the balance between justice and welfare (care) in children and adolescents' moral reasoning (Smetana et al., 1991) indicated that whether boys and girls give greater priority to maintaining interpersonal obligations or justice depends on the features of the situations. Children and adolescents favored maintaining interpersonal obligations in situations depicting close interpersonal relationships (a friend rather than acquaintance) or when unfairness was minimized. However, when fairness was made more salient, adolescents gave less priority to maintaining interpersonal relationships. There were considerable inconsistencies both within and across individuals in their reasoning that were not simply due to gender. Rather, much as Walker (1991, chap. 4, this volume) has concluded, the situational features of the dilemmas accounted for the variations.

Gender has been considered in more complex ways in recent research. Okin (1989) and Turiel (1998) have called attention to the way that gender inequalities in the distribution of power and resources in the family may influence children's moral understanding as well as social roles and relationships. This has led to an emerging body of research (discussed in following sections) on how gender inequalities inform children's moral and social evaluations.

Ethnicity and Social Class

Socioeconomic Status. Although much research on children's moral and social judgments has focused on middle-class children, an increasing number of studies have examined the judgments of children living in poverty. Jagers, Bingham, and Hans (1996) examined moral and social judgments as well as relationships between judgments and socialization experiences in African-American preschoolers from lower socioeconomic backgrounds. In contrast to the vast majority of studies, Jagers and associates (1996) found mixed support for children's ability to make domain distinctions. Children generalized the wrongness of moral (but not conventional) transgressions from school to home and judged moral transgressions to be more independent of rules than conventional transgressions, but they did not differentiate between moral and conventional transgressions in their ratings of seriousness and deserved punishment or in judgments of generalizability across school contexts. The authors speculated that in an environment where violence is endemic, children may view moral transgressions such as hitting as relatively innocuous offenses and therefore may not differentiate morality from social convention for what may be perceived as relatively minor violations. Children who distinguished the domains, however, had mothers who reasoned more with their children and denied privileges and ignored transgressions less. Thus, children's failure to apply moral criteria to moral events and differentiate morality from social convention can be attributed at least partly to differences in parents' child-rearing practices. Lower socioeconomic status has been associated with the greater use of harsh, power-assertive, and more parent-centered methods of discipline (Hoff, Laursen, & Tardif, 2002), which may stem from different cultural or social class-based (informational) assumptions about the efficacy of those practices. It should be noted, however, that other research including children living in poverty (e.g., Astor,

1994; Smetana, Toth et al., 1999) did not find similar deficits in children's moral and social understanding.

Nucci, Camino, and Sapiro (1996) explicitly examined the influence of socioeconomic status on Brazilian children's moral, conventional, prudential, and personal justifications and judgments across a range of criteria. Comparing lower versus middle-class northeastern Brazilian children, these researchers found no effects for socioeconomic status, except that lower class children were more likely to generalize the effects of conventions across contexts and to justify conventions by appealing to rules. Claims to a personal domain also were more frequent in middle-class than in lower class children, but these social class effects disappeared by middle adolescence. Thus, the emergence of claims to a personal sphere was attributed to developmental factors. Nucci and his colleagues proposed that social class effects, particularly in judgments of personal issues, are linked to opportunities to express personal freedoms, which may be more limited for children living in poverty.

Smetana and Gaines (1999) compared reasoning at the other end of the income distribution—among middle-class versus upper class African American families—and found few differences in reasoning according to income (but a number of differences in how parent–adolescent conflict was experienced and resolved). There were some subtle differences in the types of conventional justifications used; upper class parents appealed more to traditions and cultural norms and to responsibility than did middle-income parents. However, the two groups did not differ in their overall use of conventional justifications.

Race and Ethnicity.   Although many of the studies cited in previous sections have included ethnic minority children, only a few studies have explicitly examined the influence of race or ethnicity on children's judgments. Few race or ethnic differences have been found. Killen and associates (2002) found that African-American, Asian-American, European-American, and Latin-American adolescents did not differ in their evaluations of straightforward moral transgressions; ethnic differences were found only for elaborations of the wrongfulness of exclusion, a multifaceted issue. Fuligni (1998) also found few differences among American adolescents from European, Chinese, Filipino, and Mexican backgrounds in their conceptions of parents' legitimate authority to make rules about conventional and personal issues (moral issues were not studied).

Likewise, Smetana (2000) found much the same pattern in African-American adolescents' and parents' judgments of legitimate parental authority regarding moral, conventional, personal, prudential, and overlapping issues as has been observed in European-American families. Comparing across studies, Smetana (2002) concluded that African-American parents appear to be somewhat more restrictive of adolescents' freedom to make choices over personal and multifaceted events than are European-American parents, although African-American children, like their European-American counterparts, assert their personal jurisdiction in opposition to parents' claims. Like Nucci and co-workers (1996), Smetana linked African-American parents' greater restrictiveness to their concerns for their children's well-being in an environment where racism and prejudice remain pervasive and where too-early autonomy may carry substantial risks for their children's safety.

Atypical Populations

Moral and social-conventional reasoning and judgments have been examined extensively in atypically developing children. These studies provide useful insights into the role of social experience in development. In some of these studies, the hypothesis has been that children's moral and social understanding would follow the same progression or process but at a different rate, due to the nature of their disability. For instance, Schmidt, Nucci, and Kahn (1991) hypothesized that retarded adolescents' judgments would be more consistent with their mental age than with their chronological age. The results confirmed this expectation in that, as assessed through interviews, the mildly mentally retarded adolescents' developmental levels of conventional reasoning were consistent with their mental age rather than their chronological age. Retarded adolescents distinguished moral and social rules on a number of criteria, but they also judged a higher proportion of conventional items as wrong in the absence of rules and gave justifications that were more dependent on appeals to authority or the absence of rules than has been found in research with same-age normally developing children.

Blair (1996) hypothesized that autistic children's ability to make moral evaluations would be associated with their understanding of theory of mind. Therefore, he examined a sample of autistic children who were divided between those who had passed or failed a standard theory of mind false belief task, as compared to normally developing children and children with moderate learning difficulties. Contrary to the hypotheses, all children distinguished between moral and conventional issues in their judgments; level of ability on the false belief tasks was not associated with children's ability to make moral and conventional judgments.

Smetana and her colleagues have hypothesized that the aberrant social experiences associated with maltreatment might lead to different moral evaluations (Smetana et al., 1984; Smetana, Toth et al., 1999). In two separate studies, abused and neglected preschoolers (who were compared to nonmaltreated children matched in age, gender, socioeconomic status, and race) were found to differentiate moral and conventional transgressions in their judgments of hypothetical transgressions and evaluate moral events according to the hypothesized moral criteria. One study (Smetana et al., 1984) suggested that compared to nonmaltreated children, abused and neglected children were more sensitive to the intrinsic wrongness of moral events most closely connected to their experiences of maltreatment than were nonmaltreated children, but these findings were not replicated in later research (Smetana, Toth et al., 1999). In general, moral judgments did not differ as a function of maltreatment status (Smetana, Daddis et al., 1999; Smetana, Toth et al., 1999), although maltreated and nonmaltreated children differed in their emotional attributions for transgressions.

Research with children and adolescents (as well as adults, e.g., Blair [1995]) with conduct problems has examined whether children and adolescents who are identified as acting out or behaving aggressively have deficits in their moral reasoning (an assumption that also has received extensive empirical examination in research employing Kohlbergian stages of moral judgment development). In these studies, conduct problems have been assessed in a variety of ways, including high scores on measures of psychopathy (Blair, 1995, 1997; Blair, Monson, & Frederickson, 2001), children identified as disruptive and hard to manage (Hughes & Dunn, 2000), diagnoses of behavioral or conduct disorder (Arsenio & Fleiss, 1996; Nucci & Herman, 1982), and adjudication as a juvenile felon and misdemeanant (Tisak & Jankowski, 1996). The findings demonstrate that conduct disordered or adjudicated children and adolescents evaluate moral transgressions using moral criteria and successfully distinguish morality from social convention in their judgments and justifications (Blair, 1997; Blair et al., 2001; Nucci & Herman, 1982; Tisak & Jankowski, 1996); they also distinguish morality and social conventions from personal issues (Nucci & Herman, 1982; Tisak & Jankowski, 1996).

Nevertheless, some consistent differences in conduct-disordered and typically developing children's judgments have been observed. Behaviorally disturbed or adjudicated adolescents are more likely to judge moral transgressions to be permissible (or less wrong) in the absence of rules (Blair, 1997; Blair et al., 2001; Nucci & Herman, 1982) and also are more likely than typically developing children to focus on conventional aspects of moral transgressions, reasoning that moral transgressions are wrong because the acts could lead to punishment. Conduct-disordered children also are less likely than normally developing children to treat personal issues as within their personal discretion (Nucci & Herman, 1982). Similarly, felons rated rules regarding personal issues to be more important than did misdemeanants (Tisak & Jankowski, 1996). This suggests that behaviorally disordered children have some difficulty in understanding the intrinsic basis of moral transgressions. They also lack clarity about the boundaries between societal regulation and personal autonomy, and have difficulty in identifying areas of personal responsibility. The research to date has not examined the developmental factors that lead to these differences in judgments, however. Intriguingly, one study found that greater behavioral disturbance was associated with greater deficits in making moral/conventional distinctions (Blair et al., 2001), but whether these differences in judgments are causes or consequences of children's behavioral problems has not been examined.

More recent research has focused on another potential source of variability in moral judgments. Astor (1994) examined differences between aggressive and nonaggressive children in their judgments of provocation. He found that although both violent and nonviolent children both used moral reasoning in hypothetical situations that were depicted as provoked, aggressive children focused more on the immorality of provocation and viewed hitting back as morally justified, whereas nonviolent children used moral reasoning to condemn retaliation. These findings are consistent with Nucci and Herman's (1982) observation that behaviorally disordered children understood that moral transgressions like hitting caused harm but often referred to mitigating circumstances (e.g., that "she wasn't really hurt" or "she deserved it") to excuse the moral transgressions. They also elaborate on earlier findings (Slaby & Guerra, 1988) that compared to aggressive or nonaggressive high school students, violent juveniles who were incarcerated for violent crimes (like rape, robbery, and murder) were more likely to believe in the legitimacy of aggression and to ignore the sufferings of their victims.

These studies suggest that there is a social–cognitive bias in conduct-disordered and adjudicated children's and adolescents' construal of situations. This claim is not novel; Dodge and his colleagues have provided extensive evidence of information processing deficits in aggressive children's evaluations of ambiguous situations (see Coie & Dodge [1998] for a review). But social domain research adds the insight that although aggressive and conduct-disordered children are capable of making moral evaluations, they focus on the perspective of the perpetrator and view provocation as a moral justification for their behavior, rather than focusing on the effects of the act on the victim. In addition, much as has been found with maltreated children (Smetana, Toth et al., 1999), behaviorally disordered children made different attributions (for both victims and perpetrators) about the emotional consequences of transgressions than normally developing children. These findings need to be considered along with studies reviewed earlier that indicate that typically developing children also show biases in their judgments according to their role in the situation and that perpetrators are more likely to attribute provocation to their actions than are victims (Smetana, Toth et al., 1999; Wainryb & Langley, 2003). Further research should examine developmental differences between typically developing and aggressive or conduct-disordered children in their ability to focus on victims' versus perpetrators' perspectives.

Summary. Few systematic gender differences in judgments about prototypical moral and social events have been observed. Contrary to Gilligan's (1982) claims, judgments about multifaceted situations that entail conflicts between interpersonal needs and justice reveal variations according to situations rather than gender. Socioeconomic status and racial and ethnic differences are more evident in how children and adolescents construct the boundaries between legitimate personal control and conventional and moral regulation; variations in these evaluations appear to be related to differences in social experiences (such as childrearing practices), informational assumptions, and opportunities, although more research explicitly examining these issues is needed.

Compared to typically developing children, research on atypical samples, including autistic children and maltreated children, have found relatively few differences in moral evaluations and in their ability to differentiate the domains, although maltreated and non-maltreated children appear to differ in their understanding and attributions of emotions. As hypothesized, developmental delays consistent with their developmental rather than chronological age have been found in retarded adolescents' developmental levels of conventional understanding.

Numerous studies of conduct-disordered and aggressive youth indicate that they apply moral concepts to moral violations and distinguish them from conventional regularities on some dimensions, although there is some evidence that they conventionalize moral transgressions and focus more on the immorality of provocation than on the consequences of transgressions for victims. As research suggests that there are developmental changes in typically developing children's understanding of provocation, longitudinal research should determine whether developmental delays in understanding provocation or differences in social construal of situations contribute to the development of conduct problems.

CHARACTERISTICS OF CULTURES AS SOCIAL CONTEXTS

The cross-cultural application of theories of moral reasoning development has generated a great deal of interest and controversy and has been an ongoing concern to researchers from the domain perspective. The following section briefly considers culture as a source of both consistency and variation in moral and social judgments from a domain perspective (for more extensive treatment, see chapters by Wainryb, chap. 8, and Turiel, chap. 1, this volume).

One currently popular approach to understanding culture has been to describe cultures as varying on global dimensions, like individualism and collectivism (Shweder et al., 1998). According to this view, individualistic cultures stress self-sufficiency, the attainment of personal goals, autonomy, detachment from others, and, in the moral realm, a concern with individual rights. In contrast, collectivist cultures are said to stress interdependence, harmony, and connectedness in interpersonal relationships, a focus on statuses, roles, relationships, and, in the moral realm, concerns with authority, tradition, and duty.

In contrast, domain theory researchers have adopted a more differentiated view that takes into consideration the diversity of orientations within cultures. Individuals across cultures develop heterogeneous orientations that entail the coexistence of different kinds of concerns (Killen & Wainryb, 2000; Nucci & Turiel, 2000; Smetana, 2002; Turiel, 1998, 2002; Wainryb, 1997), including the importance of maintaining traditions and group goals (social conventions), concerns for others' rights and welfare (morality), and concerns with personal choice, personal entitlements, and autonomy (personal issues). Thus, like other structural developmental theories (e.g., Colby & Kohlberg, 1987; Kohlberg, 1984), the domain theory claim is that moral concepts are universally applicable, but so are concepts of social convention and personal jurisdiction. Social conventions serve the same function of structuring and facilitating social interactions in all cultures, although their form is expected to be cross-culturally variable. Furthermore, because notions of the personal domain are grounded in underlying psychological realities that are cross-culturally applicable (Killen & Wainryb, 2000; Nucci, 1996; Nucci & Turiel, 2000; Turiel & Wainryb, 2000; Wainryb, 1997), all cultures are hypothesized to treat some issues as fundamentally within the boundaries of the self and personal agency, although cultural variations are expected in both the scope and content of the personal domain (Nucci 1996; Smetana, 2002).

These assertions have been examined in numerous studies. Children in a wide range of cultures in North and South America, Asia, Africa, the Middle East, and Australia have been found to differentiate moral from social-conventional issues on a variety of criteria, although some differences in justifications have been observed. Although there have been fewer studies, research has shown that appeals to personal choice are not restricted to children in individualistic cultures, but are found in children's judgments in diverse cultures in Europe, Asia, South America, and the Middle East (see Killen, McGlothlin et al. [2002], Nucci [2001], and Smetana [2002] for reviews).

There has been a growing interest (discussed extensively in Turiel [2002]) in examining moral and social judgments as a function of individuals' position in the social hierarchy. Individuals construct notions of the fairness of different social and societal arrangements. Thus, individuals in more subordinate roles (e.g., women, children, individuals living in poverty) may experience greater restrictions in their choices and freedoms as a function of their social position, as well as inequalities in the distribution of power, the way resources are allocated, and their available opportunities. All of these may be potent sources of variation in moral and social judgments (Turiel, 1998, 2002).

This has led to research examining children's, adolescents', and adults' judgments about the rights, entitlements, and choices accorded to men and women in traditional societies. For instance, an extensive series of studies by Wainryb and Turiel (1994; Turiel & Wainryb, 1998, 2000) have examined the social judgments of the Druze, a small, hierarchically organized, highly inbred Arab community in Israel, where women occupy subordinate roles and also experience greater restrictions in their choices and freedoms as a function of their social position. Druze-Arab women desire more control over personal issues, but they view decisions not to oppose the existing conventional order and to express their desires for more personal jurisdiction as more appropriate or more pragmatically wise. Nevertheless, in such situations, women tend to evaluate social practices as more unfair than do those in more dominant positions, who are accorded more entitlements and choices. Thus, gender differences were linked to individuals' position in the social hierarchy. Therefore, even in collectivistic cultures, where individuals are said to value interdependence rather than independence and where social relationships are more hierarchically organized, different social concepts, including justice, interpersonal obligations, conventions, personal choice, and personal entitlements, coexist. At the same time, cultural orientations do affect social judgments. Furthermore, drawing on ethnographic research in cultural anthropology as well as psychological studies, researchers have shown that individuals in subordinate positions contest, resist, and attempt to transform social practices.

It should be clear that this perspective also informs the research on gender, ethnicity, and socioeconomic status differences in moral and social evaluations described in the previous section (see Nucci and colleagues' [1996] discussion of social class differences in personal choices in Brazil as an example), as social inequalities and restrictions in choices and freedoms may be a powerful sources of variation in moral, social, and personal judgments.

CONCLUSIONS AND FUTURE DIRECTIONS

The domain model has expanded and revitalized the study of moral judgment development. It has provided a complex way of conceptualizing the different concerns of individuals within cultures, including concerns with justice, welfare, rights, social conventions, traditions, authority, personal choice, and personal entitlements. These different concerns coexist in individuals' reasoning because they are all aspects of social life within cultures, yet they may be coordinated in different ways depending on individual development, social contexts, and particular cultural arrangements.

Although early social domain research focused on validating the claim that children of different ages distinguish between moral and social-conventional concepts, more recent research has examined children's, adolescents', and adults' reasoning in multifaceted situations that entail overlapping or conflicting concerns. This approach has generated much research on a variety of topics, including children's rights, aggression, concepts of tolerance, peer exclusion, stereotyping, and adolescent–parent relationships. The domain approach provides a powerful way of understanding reasoning in such contextualized situations that does not reduce all thinking to global stages of moral judgment development, but rather considers how individuals evaluate the salience of different moral, conventional, and personal concerns. Moreover, this approach has shown that considering individuals' (domain-related) interpretations of situations leads to associations between domain orientations and social behavior.

Despite the progress that has been made in understanding morality as one strand of children's social reasoning, there still are many gaps in our knowledge. The qualitative, normative developmental shifts in children's moral reasoning that have emerged from cross-sectional studies, as well as the apparent sequencing with age in children's understanding of different moral concepts, need further specification using longitudinal research. We also need to understand how these developmental changes intersect with children's ability to coordinate morality with other social concepts, and more generally, how children's ability to coordinate moral and nonmoral concepts changes with age and may be moderated by features of the social context.

The research thus far has provided some important insights into how interactions with siblings, friends, peers, parents, and other adults facilitate moral reasoning development, but more research using heterogeneous samples is needed to fully understand the processes that influence children's construction of moral concepts in different social contexts and the causal links (which have been inferred but not directly tested) between social interactions and the development of moral and social judgments. Furthermore, not much is known about how children's developing ability to distinguish morality from other social concepts is related to other moral or psychological characteristics, including psychological adjustment. The studies of atypically developing children suggest that difficulties in understanding the intrinsic basis of morality are related to conduct problems, but more research on the processes leading to difficulties in development and variations in normally developing children is needed.

The research on children's moral and social reasoning in actual situations and the different perspectives of victims versus transgressors in the context of different social relationships (such as friendship or peer relationships) has begun to inform our understanding of within-individual variations in moral reasoning. Future research should examine how children at different ages evaluate provocation and coordinate the perspectives of victims and transgressors in their moral and social judgments in hypothetical and actual situations and in their understanding of and attributions for emotions. This research is likely to inform our understanding of problematic development, such as in the case of aggressive or conduct-disordered children, as well as normative development in different contexts.

Finally, the recent focus on hierarchical structures and societal arrangements in different cultures opens many new avenues of investigation, not just for cross-cultural research, but for developmental research as well. The notion that hierarchical structures can lead to dominance, subversion, and resistance in social life can be fruitfully applied to studying morality in other cultures, as well as variations in moral development in American culture. The social–cognitive domain approach provides a rich theoretical framework for further research on developmental variations and consistencies in moral and social judgments both within and across cultures.

REFERENCES

Arsenio, W. (1988). Children's conceptions of the situational affective consequences of sociomoral events. *Child Development, 59,* 1611–1622.

Arsenio, W., & Fleiss, K. (1996). Typical and behaviourally disruptive children's understanding of the emotional consequences of sociomoral events. *British Journal of Developmental Psychology, 14,* 173–186.

Arsenio, W., & Ford, M. (1985). The role of affective information in social-cognitive development: Children's differentiation of moral and conventional events. *Merrill-Palmer Quarterly, 31,* 1–18.

Arsenio, W., & Kramer, R. (1992). Victimizers and their victims: Children's conceptions of the mixed emotional consequences of victimization. *Child Development, 63,* 915–927.

Arsenio, W., & Lemerise, E. (2004). Aggression and moral development: Integrating social information processing and moral domain models. *Child Development, 75,* 987–1002.

Arsenio, W., & Lover, A. (1995). Children's conceptions of sociomoral affect: Happy victimizers, mixed emotions and other expectancies. In M. Killen & D. Hart (Eds.), *Morality in everyday life: Developmental perspectives* (pp. 87–128). Cambridge, UK: Cambridge University Press.

Astor, R. A. (1994). Children's moral reasoning about family and peer violence: the role of provocation and retribution. *Child Development, 65,* 1054–1067.

Blair, R. J. R. (1995). A cognitive developmental approach to morality: Investigating the psychopath. *Cognition, 57,* 1–29.

Blair, R. J. R. (1996). Morality in the autistic child. *Journal of Autism and Developmental Disorders, 26,* 571–579.

Blair, R. J. R. (1997). Moral reasoning in the child with psychopathic tendencies. *Personality and Individual Differences, 22,* 731–739.

Blair, R. J. R., Monson, J., & Frederickson, N. (2001). Moral reasoning and conduct problems in children with emotional and behavioural difficulties. *Personality and Individual Differences, 31,* 799–811.

Blumenfeld, P. C., Pintrich, P. R., & Hamilton, V. L. (1987). Teacher talk and students' reasoning about morals, conventions, and achievement. *Child Development, 58,* 1389–1401.

Bregman, G., & Killen, M. (1999). Adolescents' and young adults' evaluations of career choice and the role of parental influence. *Journal of Research on Adolescence, 9,* 253–275.

Brown, J. R., Donelan-McCall, N., & Dunn. J. (1996). Why talk about mental states: The significance of children's conversations with friends, siblings, and mothers. *Child Development, 67,* 836–849.

Coie, J. D., & Dodge, K. A. (1998). Aggression and antisocial behavior. In N. Eisenberg (Ed.), *Handbook of Child Psychology, 5th Edition, Volume 3: Social, Emotional, and Personality Development* (William Damon, Series Editor) (pp. 779–862). New York: Wiley.

Colby, A., & Kohlberg, K. (Eds.). (1987). *The measurement of moral judgment* (Vols. 1–2). New York: Cambridge University Press.

Damon, W. (1977). *The social world of the child*. San Francisco: Jossey-Bass.

Davidson, P., Turiel, E., & Black, A. (1983). The effect of stimulus familiarity of criteria and justifications in children's social reasoning. *British Journal of Developmental Psychology, 1*, 49–65.

Dunn, J. (1987). The beginnings of moral understanding: Development in the second year. In J. Kagan & S. Lamb (Eds.), *The emergence of morality in young children* (pp. 91–112). Chicago: University of Chicago Press.

Dunn, J., Brown, J. R., & Maguire, M. (1995). The development of children's moral sensibility: Individual differences and emotion understanding. *Developmental Psychology, 31*, 649–659.

Dunn, J., Cutting, A. O., & Demetriou, H. (2000). Moral sensibility, understanding others, and children's friendship interactions in the preschool period. *British Journal of Developmental Psychology, 18*, 159–177.

Dunn, J., & Munn, P. (1987). Development of justification in disputes with mothers and siblings. *Developmental Psychology, 23*, 791–798.

Dworkin, R. (1978). *Taking rights seriously*. Cambridge, MA: Harvard University Press.

Flavell, J. H., Mumme, D. L., Green, F. L., & Flavell, E. R. (1992). Young children's understanding of different types of beliefs. *Child Development, 63*, 960–977.

Fuligni, A. J. (1998). Authority, autonomy, and parent-adolescent conflict and cohesion: A study of adolescents from Mexican, Chinese, Filipino, and European backgrounds. *Developmental Psychology, 34*, 782–792.

Gewirth, A. (1978). *Reason and morality*. Chicago: University of Chicago Press.

Gilligan, C. (1982). *In a different voice*. Cambridge, MA: Harvard University Press.

Grusec, J. E., & Goodnow, J. J. (1994). Impact of parental discipline methods on the child's internalization of values: A reconceptualization of current points of view. *Developmental Psychology, 30*, 4–19.

Hasebe, Y., Nucci, L., & Nucci, M. S. (2004). Parental control of the personal domain and adolescent symptoms of psychopathology: A cross-national study in the United States and Japan. *Child Development, 75*, 815–826.

Hatch, E. (1983). *Culture and morality: The relativity of values in anthropology*. New York: Columbia University Press.

Helwig, C. C. (1995). Adolescents' and young adults' conceptions of civil liberties: Freedom of speech and religion. *Child Development, 66*, 152–166.

Helwig, C.C., Hildebrandt, C., & Turiel, E. (1995). Children's judgments about psychological harm in social context. *Child Development, 66*, 1680–1693.

Helwig, C. C., & Turiel, E. (2003). Children's social and moral reasoning. In P. K. Smith & C. H. Hart (Eds.), *Blackwell handbook of childhood social development* (pp. 475–490). Oxford: Blackwell.

Helwig, C. C., Zelazo, P. D., & Wilson, M. (2001). Children's judgments of psychological harm in normal and noncanonical situations. *Child Development, 72*, 66–81.

Hoff, E., Laursen, B., & Tardif, T. (2002). Socioeconomic status and parenting. In M. H. Bornstein (Ed.), *Handbook of parenting: Vol. 2: Biology and ecology of parenting* (2nd ed., pp. 231–252). Mahwah, NJ: Lawrence Erlbaum Associates.

Hoffman, M. L. (1991). Empathy, social cognition, and moral action. In J. L. Gewirtz & W. M. Kurtines (Eds.), *Handbook of moral behavior and development, Vol. 1: Theory* (pp. 275–301). Hillsdale, NJ: Lawrence Erlbaum Associates.

Horn, S. S. (2003). Adolescents' reasoning about exclusion from social groups. *Developmental Psychology, 39,* 71–84.

Horn, S. S., Killen, M., & Stangor, C. (1999). The influence of group stereotypes of adolescents' moral reasoning. *Journal of Early Adolescence, 19,* 98–113.

Hughes, C., & Dunn, J. (2000). Hedonism or empathy?: Hard-to-mange children's moral awareness and links with cognitive and maternal characteristics. *British Journal of Developmental Psychology, 18,* 227–245.

Jagers, R. J., Bingham, K., & Hans, S. L. (1996). Socialization and social judgments among inner-city African-American kindergartners. *Child Development, 67,* 140–150.

Kahn, P. H., Jr. (1992). Children's obligatory and discretionary moral judgments. *Child Development, 63,* 416–430.

Killen, M. (1990). Children's evaluations of morality in the context of peer, teacher–child, and family relations. *Journal of Genetic Psychology, 151,* 395–410.

Killen, M., Breton, S., Ferguson, H., & Handler, K. (1994). Preschoolers' evaluations of teacher methods of intervention in social transgressions. *Merrill-Palmer Quarterly, 40,* 399–416.

Killen, M., Lee-Kim, J., McGlothlin, H., & Stangor, C. (2002). How children and adolescents evaluate gender and racial exclusion. *Monographs for the Society for Research in Child Development.* Serial No. 271, Vol. 67, No. 4. Oxford, UK: Blackwell.

Killen, M., McGlothlin, H., & Lee-Kim, J. (2002). Heterogeneity in social cognition and culture. In H. Keller, Y. Poortinga, & A. Schoelmerich (Eds.), *Between biology and culture: Perspectives on ontogenetic development* (pp. 159–190). Cambridge, UK: Cambridge University Press.

Killen, M., & Smetana, J. G. (1999). Social interactions in preschool classrooms and the development of young children's conceptions of the personal. *Child Development, 70,* 486–501.

Killen, M., & Wainryb, C. (2000). Independence and interdependence in diverse cultural contexts. In S. Harkness, C. Raeff, & C. M. Super (Eds.), *Variability in the social construction of the child: New directions for child and adolescent development* (Vol. 87, pp. 5–21). San Francisco: Jossey-Bass.

Kochanska, G. (1997). Mutually responsive orientation between mothers and their young children: Implications for early socialization. *Child Development, 68,* 94–112,

Kohlberg, L. (1984). *Essays on moral development: Vol. 2. The psychology of moral development.* San Francisco: Harper and Row.

Komatsu, L. K., & Galotti, K. M. (1986). Children's reasoning about social, physical, and logical regularities: A look at two worlds. *Child Development, 57,* 413–420.

Kuczynski, L. (1982). Intensity and orientation of reasoning: Motivational determinants of children's compliance to verbal rationales. *Journal of Experimental Child Psychology, 34,* 357–370.

Kuczynski, L. (1984). Socialization goals and mother-child interaction: Strategies for long-term and short-term compliance. *Developmental Psychology, 20,* 1061–1073.

Laupa, M. (1991). Children's reasoning about three authority attributes: Adult status, knowledge, and social position. *Developmental Psychology, 27,* 321–329.

Laupa, M. (2000). Similarities and differences in children's reasoning about morality and mathematics. In M. Laupa (Ed.), *Rights and wrongs: How children and young adults evaluate the world. New directions for child development* (Vol. 89, pp. 19–31). San Francisco: Jossey-Bass.

Laupa, M., Turiel, E., & Cowan, P. (1995). Obedience to authority in children and adults. In M. Killen & D. Hart (Eds.), *Morality in everyday life: Developmental perspectives* (pp. 131–165). Cambridge, UK: Cambridge University Press.

Lemerise, E., & Arsenio, W. (2000). An integrated model of emotion processes and cognition in social information processing. *Child Development, 71,* 107–118.

Lockhart, K. L., Abrahams, B., & Osherson, D. N. (1977). Children's understanding of uniformity in the environment. *Child Development, 48,* 1521–1531.

Much, N., & Shweder, R. A. (1978). Speaking of rules: The analysis of culture in breach. In W. Damon (Ed.), *New directions for child development. Vol. 1: Moral development* (pp. 19–40). San Francisco: Jossey-Bass.

Nicholls, J. G., & Thorkildsen, T. A. (1988). Children's distinctions among matters of intellectual convention, logic, fact, and personal preference. *Child Development, 59,* 939–949.

Nucci, L. (1981). The development of personal concepts: A domain distinct from moral or societal concepts. *Child Development, 52,* 114–121.

Nucci, L. (1984). Evaluating teachers as social agents: Students' ratings of domain appropriate and domain inappropriate teachers' responses to transgressions. *American Educational Research Journal, 21,* 367–378.

Nucci, L. (1985). Children's conceptions of morality, social conventions, and religious prescription. In C. Harding (Ed.), *Moral dilemmas: Philosophical and psychological reconsiderations of the development of moral reasoning* (pp. 137–174). Chicago: Precedent Press.

Nucci, L. P. (1996). Morality and personal freedom. In E. S. Reed, E. Turiel, & T. Brown (Eds.), *Values and knowledge* (pp. 41–60). Mahwah, NJ: Lawrence Erlbaum Associates.

Nucci, L. (2001). *Education in the moral domain.* Cambridge: Cambridge University Press.

Nucci, L. (2002). The development of moral reasoning. In U. Goswami (Ed.), *Blackwell handbook of child cognitive development* (pp. 303–325). Oxford: Blackwell.

Nucci, L. P., Camino, C., & Sapiro, C. M. (1996). Social class effects on Northeastern Brazilian children's conceptions of areas of personal choice and social regulation. *Child Development, 67,* 1223–1242.

Nucci, L. P., & Herman, S. (1982). Behavioral disordered children's conceptions of moral, conventional, and personal issues. *Journal of Abnormal Child Psychology, 10,* 411–426.

Nucci, L. P., & Nucci, M. S. (1982a). Children's responses to moral and social-conventional transgressions in free-play settings. *Child Development, 53,* 1337–1342.

Nucci, L. P., & Nucci, M. S. (1982b). Children's social interactions in the context of moral and conventional transgressions. *Child Development, 53,* 403–412.

Nucci, L. P., & Turiel, E. (1978). Social interactions and the development of social concepts in preschool children. *Child Development, 49,* 400–407.

Nucci, L. P., & Turiel, E. (1993). God's word, religious rules, and their relation to Christian and Jewish children's concepts of morality. *Child Development, 64,* 1475–1491.

Nucci, L. P., & Turiel, E. (2000). The moral and the personal: Sources of social conflict. In L. P. Nucci, G. Saxe, & E. Turiel (Eds.), *Culture, thought, and development* (pp. 115–137). Mahwah, NJ: Lawrence Erlbaum Associates.

Nucci, L. P., Turiel, E., & Gawrych, G. (1983). Children's social interactions and social concepts: Analyses of morality and convention in the Virgin Islands. *Journal of Cross-Cultural Psychology, 14,* 468–487.

Nucci, L. P., & Weber, E. K. (1995). Social interactions in the home and the development of young children's conceptions of the personal. *Child Development, 66,* 1438–1452.

Okin, S. M. (1989). *Justice, gender, and the family.* New York: Basic Books.

Piaget, J. (1932/1965). *The moral judgment of the child.* New York: The Free Press.

Piaget, J. (1967). *Six psychological studies.* New York: Vintage.

Rawls, J. (1971). *A theory of justice*. Cambridge, MA: Cambridge University Press.

Ross, H., Tesla, C., Kenyon, B., & Lollis, S. (1990). Maternal intervention in toddler peer conflict: The socialization of principles of justice. *Developmental Psychology, 26*, 994–1003.

Saltzstein, H. D. (1994). The relation between moral judgment and behavior: A social-cognitive and decision-making analysis. *Human Development, 37*, 299–312.

Sanderson, J. A., & Siegal, M. (1988). Conceptions of moral and social rules in rejected and nonrejected preschoolers. *Journal of Clinical Child Psychology, 17*, 66–72.

Schmidt, M. F., Nucci, L., & Kahn, J. V. (1991). *Development of conventional reasoning in trainable mentally retarded adolescents*. Unpublished manuscript, University of Illinois, Chicago.

Shaw, L., & Wainryb, C. (1999). The outsider's perspective: Young adults' judgments of social practices of other cultures. *British Journal of Developmental Psychology, 17*, 451–471.

Shaw, L., & Wainryb, C. (2003). *Children's and adolescents' thinking about victimization and consent*. Unpublished manuscript, University of Utah Salt Lake City.

Shweder, R. A. (1982). Liberalism as destiny. *Contemporary Psychology, 27*, 421–424.

Shweder, R. A., Goodnow, J. J., Hatano, G., LeVine, R. A., Markus, H., & Miller, P. (1998). The cultural psychology of development: One mind, many mentalities. In R. M. Lerner (Ed.) & W. Damon (Series Ed.), *Handbook of child psychology, Vol. 1: Theoretical models of human development* (5th ed., pp. 865–937). New York: Wiley.

Simpson, E. L. (1973). Moral development research: A case study of scientific cultural bias. *Human Development, 17*, 81–106.

Slaby, R. G., & Guerra, N. G. (1988). Cognitive mediators of aggression in adolescent offenders I. Assessment. *Developmental Psychology, 24*, 580–588.

Slomkowski, C., & Killen, M. (1992). Young children's conceptions of transgressions with friends and nonfriends. *International Journal of Behavioral Development, 15*, 247–258.

Smetana, J. G. (1981a). Preschool children's conceptions of moral and social rules. *Child Development, 52*, 1333–1336.

Smetana, J. G. (1981b). Reasoning in the personal and moral domains: Adolescent and young adult women's decision-making about abortion. *Journal of Applied Developmental Psychology, 2*, 211–226.

Smetana, J. G. (1982). *Concepts of self and morality: Women's reasoning about abortion*. New York: Praeger.

Smetana, J. G. (1983). Social-cognitive development: Domain distinctions and coordinations. *Developmental Review, 3*, 131–147.

Smetana, J. G. (1984). Toddlers' social interactions regarding moral and conventional transgressions. *Child Development, 55*, 1767–1776.

Smetana, J. G. (1985). Preschool children's conceptions of transgressions: The effects of varying moral and conventional domain-related attributes. *Developmental Psychology, 21*, 18–29.

Smetana, J. G. (1989a). Adolescents' and parents' reasoning about actual family conflict. *Child Development, 60*, 1052–1067.

Smetana, J. G. (1989b). Toddlers' social interactions in the context of moral and conventional transgressions in the home. *Developmental Psychology, 25*, 499–508.

Smetana, J. G. (1995a). Context, conflict, and constraint in adolescent-parent authority relationships. In M. Killen & D. Hart (Eds.), *Morality in everyday life: Developmental perspectives* (pp. 225–255). Cambridge, UK: Cambridge University Press.

Smetana, J. G. (1995b). Morality in context: Abstractions, ambiguities, and applications. In R. Vasta (Ed.), *Annals of child development, Vol. 10* (pp. 83–130). London: Jessica Kingsley.

Smetana, J. G. (1997). Parenting and the development of social knowledge reconceptualized: A social domain analysis. In J. E. Grusec & L. Kuczynski (Eds.), *Parenting and the internalization of values* (pp. 162–192). New York: Wiley.

Smetana, J. G. (2000). Middle class African American adolescents' and parents' conceptions of parental authority and parenting practices: A longitudinal investigation. *Child Development, 71*, 1672–1686.

Smetana, J. G. (2002). Culture, autonomy, and personal jurisdiction in adolescent-parent relationships. In H. W. Reese & R. Kail (Eds.), *Advances in child development and behavior* (Vol. 29, pp. 51–87). New York: Academic Press.

Smetana, J. G., & Asquith, P. (1994). Adolescents' and parents' conceptions of parental authority and adolescent autonomy. *Child Development, 65*, 1147–1162.

Smetana, J. G., & Braeges, J. L. (1990). The development of toddlers' moral and conventional judgments. *Merrill-Palmer Quarterly, 36*, 329–346.

Smetana, J., Campione-Barr, N., & Daddis, C. (2004). Developmental and longitudinal antecedents of family decision-making: Defining healthy behavioral autonomy for middle class African American adolescents. *Child Development, 75*, 932–947.

Smetana, J. G., & Daddis, C. (2002). Domain-specific antecedents of psychological control and parental monitoring: The role of parenting beliefs and practices. *Child Development, 73*, 563–580.

Smetana, J. G., & Gaines, C. (1999). Adolescent-parent conflict in middle-class African-American families. *Child Development, 70*, 1447–1463.

Smetana, J., Daddis, C., Toth, S., Cicchetti, D., Bruce, J., & Kane, P. (1999). Effects of provocation on preschoolers' understanding of moral transgressions. *Social Development, 8*, 335–348.

Smetana, J. G., Kelly, M., & Twentyman, C. T. (1984). Abused, neglected, and nonmaltreated children's conceptions of moral and conventional transgressions. *Child Development, 55*, 277–287.

Smetana, J. G., Killen, M., & Turiel, E. (1991). Children's reasoning about interpersonal and moral conflicts. *Child Development, 62*, 629–644.

Smetana, J. G., Schlagman, N., & Adams, P. (1993). Preschoolers' judgments about hypothetical and actual transgressions. *Child Development, 64*, 202–214.

Smetana, J. G., Toth, S., Cicchetti, D., Bruce, J., Kane, P., & Daddis, C. (1999). Maltreated and nonmaltreated preschoolers' conceptions of hypothetical and actual moral transgressions. *Developmental Psychology, 35*, 269–281.

Smetana, J. G., & Turiel, E. (2003). Morality during adolescence. In G. R. Adams & M. Berzonsky (Eds.), *The Blackwell handbook of adolescence* (pp. 247–268). Oxford, UK: Blackwell.

Tisak, M. (1993). Preschool children's judgments of moral and personal events involving physical harm and property damage. *Merrill-Palmer Quarterly, 39*, 375–390.

Tisak, M. (1995). Domains of social reasoning and beyond. R. Vasta (Ed.). *Annals of child development* (Vol. 11, pp. 95–130). London: Jessica Kingsley.

Tisak, M. S., & Jankowski, A. M. (1996). Societal rule evaluations: Adolescent offenders' reasoning about moral, conventional, and personal rules. *Aggressive Behavior, 22*, 195–207.

Tisak, M. S., Nucci, L. P., & Jankowski, A. M. (1996). Preschool children's social interactions involving moral and prudential transgressions: An observational study. *Journal of Early Education & Development, 7*, 137–148.

Tisak, M. S., & Tisak, J. (1996). My sibling's but not my friend's keeper: Reasoning about responses to aggressive acts. *Journal of Early Adolescence, 16*, 324–339.

Tisak, M. S., & Turiel, E. (1984). Children's conceptions of moral and prudential rules. *Child Development, 55,* 1030–1039.

Tisak, M. S., & Turiel, E. (1988). Variation in seriousness of transgressions and children's moral and conventional concepts. *Developmental Psychology, 24,* 352–357.

Turiel, E. (1979). Distinct conceptual and developmental domains: Social convention and morality. In C. B. Keasey (Ed.), *Nebraska symposium on motivation* (pp. 77–116). Lincoln: University of Nebraska Press.

Turiel, E. (1983). *The development of social knowledge: Morality and convention.* Cambridge, UK: Cambridge University Press.

Turiel, E. (1998). Moral development. In N. Eisenberg (Ed.) & W. Damon (Series Ed.), *Handbook of child psychology, Vol. 3: Social, emotional, and personality development* (5th ed., pp. 863–932). New York: Wiley.

Turiel, E. (2002). *The culture of morality: Social development, context, and conflict.* New York: Cambridge University Press.

Turiel, E., Hildebrandt, C., & Wainryb, C. (1991). Judging social issues: Difficulties, inconsistencies, and consistencies. *Monographs of the Society for Research on Child Development, 56* (2, Serial No. 224).

Turiel, E., Killen, M., & Helwig, C. (1987). Morality: Its structure, functions, and vagaries. In J. Kagan & S. Lamb (Eds.), *The emergence of morality in young children* (pp. 155–243). Chicago: University of Chicago Press.

Turiel, E., & Wainryb, C. (1998). Concepts of freedoms and rights in a traditional, hierarchically-organized society. *British Journal of Developmental Psychology, 16,* 375–395.

Turiel, E., & Wainryb, C. (2000). Social life in cultures: Judgments, conflict, and subversion. *Child Development, 71,* 250–256.

Wainryb, C. (1991). Understanding differences in moral judgments: The role of informational assumptions. *Child Development, 62,* 840–851.

Wainryb, C. (1997). The mismeasure of diversity: Reflections on the study of cross-cultural differences. In E. Turiel (Ed.), *Development and cultural change: Reciprocal processes. New directions for child development* (Vol. 83, pp. 51–76). San Francisco: Jossey-Bass.

Wainryb, C. (2000). Values and truths: The making and judging of moral decisions. In M. Laupa (Ed.), *Rights and wrongs: How children evaluate the world. New directions for child development* (Vol. 89, pp. 33–46). San Francisco: Jossey-Bass.

Wainryb, C., & Ford, S. (1998). Young children's evaluations of acts based on beliefs different from their own. *Merrill-Palmer Quarterly, 44,* 484–503.

Wainryb, C., & Langley, M. (2003). *Victims and perpetrators: Children's narrative accounts of their own interpersonal conflicts.* Unpublished manuscript, University of Utah, Salt Lake City.

Wainryb, C., Shaw, L., & Maianu, C. (1998). Tolerance and intolerance: Children's and adolescents' judgments of dissenting beliefs, speech, persons, and conduct. *Child Development, 69,* 1541–1555.

Wainryb, C., & Turiel, E. (1994). Dominance, subordination, and concepts of personal entitlements in cultural contexts. *Child Development, 66,* 390–401.

Walker, L. J. (1991). Sex differences in moral reasoning. In W. M. Kurtines & J. L. Gewirtz (Eds.), *Handbook of moral behavior and development* (Vol. 2, pp. 333–364). Hillsdale, NJ: Erlbaum.

Walker, L., & Taylor, J. H. (1991). Family interactions and the development of moral reasoning. *Child Development, 62,* 264–283.

Weber, E. K. (1999). Children's personal prerogative in home and school contexts. *Early Education and Development, 10,* 499–515.

Youniss, J. (1980). *Parents and peers in social development: A Sullivan-Piaget perspective.* Chicago: University of Chicago Press.

Zahn-Waxler, C., & Chapman, M. (1982). Immediate antecedents of caretakers' methods of discipline. *Child Psychiatry & Human Development, 12,* 179–192.

Zelazo, P., Helwig, C. C., & Lau, A. (1996). Intention, act, and outcome in behavioral prediction and moral judgment. *Child Development, 67,* 2478–2492.

6

Morality in the Context of Intergroup Relationships

Melanie Killen
Nancy Geyelin Margie
Stefanie Sinno
University of Maryland

We must have the moral courage to stand up and protest against injustice wherever we find it.

—Martin Luther King, Jr. (1957/1986)

Throughout history it is not difficult to find examples in society in which entire segments of the population have not received just, fair, and equal treatment; that is, principles of morality are applied to some, but not all, members of societies and cultures. Social commentators have extensively analyzed and scrutinized examples of both consistencies and inconsistencies in individual social and moral decision making throughout history. One such example is the recent reexamination of the private lives and famous words espoused by the founding fathers of the United States, who, on the one hand, argued for a new nation in which all people should be treated equally, with unalienable rights, such as life, liberty and the pursuit of happiness, and on the other hand, were slaveowners (see the *New York Times* [December 14, 2003] for a review of recent books on this topic). This example raises a number of compelling questions about human nature and morality: How can individuals who believe in equality for all treat others in such a manner that violates basic principles of fairness and justice? Does the violation then indicate a lack of understanding about the principles of fairness and justice or is it something else?

Although there is extensive evidence that individuals hold, act on, and value moral principles about equality, justice, and fairness, there is also overwhelming evidence that individuals hold stereotypic expectations about others based on their group membership.

These stereotypic expectations are reflected in negative intergroup relationships and interactions, resulting in prejudice and intergroup biases. This chapter addresses several related conceptual and empirical issues revolving around morality within the context of intergroup relationships. These issues have direct implications for developmental theories of morality and social psychological theories of intergroup relationships. Research examining the types of competing judgments and principles involved in moral decision-making about intergroup relationships and its developmental trajectory, particularly in terms of the acquisition and emergence of moral principles and attitudes about intergroup relationships, is reviewed.

The extent to which children and adolescents apply their principles of justice to all members of society is clearly within the moral domain of development. Yet, the specific focus on the application of moral principles to individuals from different social, ethnic, and cultural groups has only recently undergone systematic and empirical scrutiny. Only in the past decade have developmental psychologists extensively examined whether, how, and when children apply their emerging principles of justice to individuals belonging to an array of different social groups and the extent to which children are aware of the complexities involved in decisions regarding fairness within and between cultures.

To some extent, this gap in the literature may be the result of two well-developed lines of research that have rarely intersected or overlapped. These lines of research include *moral development*, which encompasses children's evolving concepts of fairness and justice in the context of peer, family, and school interactions, and *intergroup relationships,* which includes topics such as stereotypes, prejudice, discrimination, ingroup/outgroup attitudes, and implicit and explicit intergroup biases in adult populations.

This chapter is divided into four sections. The first describes the ways in which moral developmental theories have considered intergroup relationships. In the second section, theory and research on racial, ethnic, and gender stereotyping and intergroup attitudes are discussed in terms of developmental emergence, concepts about discrimination and fairness, and intergroup contact considerations. The third section examines theory and research that has drawn on both moral developmental frameworks and intergroup relationship constructs. In the last section, we conclude with reflections on future directions. Although group membership includes a wide range of categories (i.e., race, ethnicity, gender, sexuality, religion, handicapped, weight), the focus here is on race or ethnicity and gender. These categories constitute the most robust areas in terms of research findings and are the most pervasive issues in the United States and other regions of the world. We discuss this work as it reveals aspects of moral development and is informative about the emergence of concepts of intergroup relationships and moral reasoning, including fairness, equality, and justice.

TWO LINES OF RESEARCH: MORAL DEVELOPMENT AND INTERGROUP RELATIONSHIPS

For the most part, moral developmental researchers have examined how children from a wide range of groups, who vary in their cultural, ethnic, socioeconomic, and religious dimensions, evaluate fairness, rights, and others' welfare. To this extent, the moral developmental research program has concentrated on documenting the universality of conceptual categories and distinctions, such as the extent to which children differentiate moral rules from social-conventional ones (see Nucci, 2001; Smetana, 1995, chap. 5, this volume; Turiel, 1983, 1998), understand inhibitive morality as distinct from prohibitive (Tisak, 1986), make prosocial judgments (Carlo, chap. 20, this volume; Eisenberg, chap. 19, this volume; Eisenberg & Fabes, 1998), understand distributive justice (Damon, 1977), evaluate sociomoral emotions (Arsenio & Lover, 1995), and distinguish rights and freedoms (Helwig & Turiel, 2002; Nucci, 2001; Ruck, Abramovitch, & Keating, 1998; Wainryb & Turiel, 1994).

Research on the universality of these principles has demonstrated that children and adolescents in a wide range of cultures believe that equality, justice, and fairness apply to individuals everywhere. In moral judgment research, universality or generalizability is typically examined in terms of whether individuals in one culture believe that moral values should be upheld by members of another culture or whether these values are culturally specific. For example, cross-cultural studies in India and the United States have posed it this way: Do individuals in the United States and India believe that free speech is a universal right? Answers to this question address theories about moral universalism and moral relativism.

Another way to address the question of universality of principles, however, is to ask whether individuals include members of other groups (defined by culture, race, ethnicity, gender) when making judgments about equality and fairness. Do individuals believe that resources should be divided equitably among individuals regardless of group membership? Does the fair distribution of resources depend on one's majority or minority status, and is this judgment applied similarly to members of the ingroup and the outgroup? What are the contexts in which this judgment is clearly answered in the affirmative, and when do stereotypes about the other influence these types of judgments? These questions concern intergroup relationships, which bear on the universality of morality from the viewpoint of the individual.

Most research on moral development has examined how children apply their moral principles to members of their own cultural, ethnic, or gender group. In fact, most research by design involves interviewing children and adolescents about others who are just like them, typically to increase the comfort level of the interviewee (e.g., children are shown picture cards that match the gender and race or ethnicity of the participant). Nonetheless, there is an underlying assumption about intergroup relationships in moral developmental theories to the extent that morality is about being impartial and applying concepts of justice and rights to everyone, regardless of group membership. Until very recently, however, moral development research has not directly tested these assumptions, nor have moral developmental hypotheses included considerations about the influence of intergroup attitudes on moral judgments.

In contrast, researchers from the intergroup relationships and intergroup processes perspectives rarely focus on the moral developmental implications of stereotyping or ingroup or outgroup biases in childhood and adolescence. Research on intergroup relationships, which has been most closely investigated by social psychologists studying adult populations, has examined such topics as stereotypes, intergroup bias, implicit and explicit attitudes, discrimination, minority–majority relations, prejudice, and social categorization (see Brown & Gaertner, 2001; Oskamp, 2000). Most studies of intergroup relationships and intergroup contact are conducted with college student samples and have employed artificial groups created in the laboratory or nonracial, nongendered groups (i.e., college majors such as engineers versus English majors) to examine intergroup attitudes and intergroup processes.

Many of the issues examined in the area of intergroup relationships are clearly within the moral realm (e.g., discrimination, by definition, refers to negative interindividual treatment). Yet, intergroup researchers do not typically examine the extent to which individuals reflect on the moral implications of these constructs; that is, is it right or wrong to hold biases or to act in a discriminatory way? This has to do with a different theoretical orientation as well as a different methodological approach. Whereas most moral judgment work has relied on in-depth interviews in which social reasoning is probed and analyzed, social psychology research typically employs attitude surveys or questionnaires in which participants respond to scale ratings that do not assess complex reasoning responses. In addition, social desirability is viewed as a limitation of social psychology self-report data (Dovidio, Kawakami, & Beach, 2001). In fact, few studies have assessed the in-depth pattern of moral reasoning about intergroup relationships, which is less vulnerable to so-cial desirability because the interviewer counterprobes interviewee responses. In addition, some researchers posit that stereotypic judgments are efficient means for categorizing the world and do not assume that these judgments are within the moral realm (see Stangor & Schaller, 1996). Only in the last 5 to 7 years has research been designed to address the intersection of these issues, revealing significant progress toward an understanding of the development of morality in the context of intergroup relationships.

Moral Development

In this section, we discuss the extent to which moral developmental theories, stemming from Piaget's (1932) foundational work, have been concerned with or have addressed intergroup relationships. The moral philosophical theories that have informed cognitive–developmental theories of moral development include principles of fairness, justice, and rights (Dworkin, 1986; Gewirth, 1978; Rawls, 1971). The empirical programs stemming from these perspectives provide a basis for documenting children's construction of morality and for investigating how moral judgments emerge out of social interactions (Killen & de Waal, 2000). Piaget relied on Kantian morality (see Kant, 1785/1959), particularly the categorical imperative, "act only on that maxim which you can, at the same time, will to become a universal law," (p. 38) to study moral judgment in the child. Clearly, this definition assumes that principles of justice apply to all individuals, even those representing different group memberships. Yet, Piaget's (1952) set of sociological studies, in which he examined children's notions of other cultures by interviewing them about where they lived and how their own culture fit into the larger category of the world's cultures, was his closest empirical attempt to consider the child's view of intergroup relationships. His empirical program did not focus on the extent to which children's concepts of fairness were applied to the treatment of others from different cultural and ethnic backgrounds (or of a different gender). He was also not interested in how it applied to the development of prejudice or discrimination. Instead, Piaget's interest was in investigating the logical and cognitive underpinnings of a child's understanding that an individual is simultaneously a member of a city and of a country (Geneva and Switzerland).

Kohlberg's (1971, 1984) work was more focused on intergroup relationships than Pi-aget's in the way that he conceptualized moral reasoning and the examples that defined his highest stage of moral development. Kohlberg identified *moral exemplars*—those at the highest stage of morality—as individuals who devoted their lives to fostering positive intergroup relationships, specifically, Martin Luther King, Jr. and Mahatma Gandhi. In Kohlberg's system, the highest stage of moral reasoning, Stage six or postconventional reasoning, involved a systematic application of the universal ethical principle to one's life endeavors. Very few individuals reach this stage of moral reasoning. He proposed that individuals obtained this stage when they followed self-chosen ethical principles, which consisted of principles pertaining to the equality of human rights and respect for the dignity of human beings as individual persons (Colby & Kohlberg, 1987, see Table 1.1, p. 19; Lapsley, chap. 2, this volume). Much more explicitly than Piaget, Kohlberg drew on Kantian ethics to define morality, and he utilized Rawls' (1971) theory of justice framework to formulate his stage theory of morality. However, like Piaget, Kohlberg defined morality as distinct from cultural norms and customs, and he did so by identifying principled morality as postconventional (independent of culture) and pertaining to humankind.

In his seminal paper on moral development, Kohlberg (1971) gave examples of Stage six reasoning as acts of civil disobedience, such as "helping slaves escape before the Civil War" (p. 171). Nonetheless, his empirical research program was not designed to directly assess individuals' evaluations of wrongful intergroup treatment. Instead, the program was designed to demonstrate that reasoning about moral dilemmas progressed toward a stage in which universal ethical principles were applied to all human beings.

Thus, Kohlberg's theoretical formulation of morality included the fostering of positive intergroup relationships even though this dimension was not explicitly examined in his empirical research program. Rather, his research was designed to formulate a cognitive-developmental psychological theory of morality. This was in contrast to prevailing theories at the time, which focused on behavioral aspects of morality (not judgments), culturally specific definitions of morality (not universalism), and psychoanalytic theories of internalization (see Lapsley, chap. 2, this volume).

The most current cognitive-developmental moral theory to include intergroup relationships is one proposed by Turiel (1998, 2002). Turiel also draws from moral philosophical theories to define morality and to generate criteria for empirically investigating moral reasoning in childhood, adolescence, and adulthood (Turiel, 1983, 1998, 2002). He argued for distinguishing between moral principles (which are universalizable) and conventional rules (which are accepted by agreement). He applied Gewirth's (1978) ethical criteria for determining how individuals differentiate morality from social-conventional regulations. Moral criteria include obligatoriness, generalizability, unalterability, and impersonality, whereas social-conventional criteria include rule contingency, alterability, context specificity, and authority jurisdiction (for definitions of these criteria, see Smetana, 1995, chap. 5, this volume).

Most pertinent to the issue of intergroup relationships, Turiel and his colleagues have analyzed how individuals evaluate the moral, societal, and psychological dimensions of gender hierarchies, statuses, and social power in different parts of the world (Turiel, 2002, chap. 1, this volume; Turiel & Neff, 2000; Wainryb & Turiel, 1994, 1995). Social–cognitive domain research has examined the ways in which cultural ideologies serve to perpetuate discriminatory and prejudicial cultural practices, many of which have had negative consequences for women's freedoms, rights, and liberties (as documented by Nussbaum [1999] and Okin [1989]). To this end, the findings have demonstrated the ways in which individuals in so-called collectivistic cultures value autonomy, fairness, and justice, contrary to the cultural characterization of collectivism, which emphasizes duty, hierarchy, and interdependence.

Using the social–cognitive domain model, other researchers have extended this direction by studying children's and adolescents' evaluations of tolerance of different ideas (Wainryb, Shaw, Laupa, & Smith, 2001), the support of rights in collectivistic cultures (Helwig, Arnold, Tan, & Boyd, 2003; Ruck et al., 1998), and the value of freedoms in collectivistic cultures (Nucci, Camino, & Milnitsky-Sapiro, 1996). The findings have revealed that culture alone does not account for whether an individual values rights, freedoms, and tolerance. In fact, many of the results are counterintuitive, such as Chinese children and adolescents supporting the right of an individual to protest against the government (Helwig et al., 2003). These studies bear on intergroup relationships to the extent that the findings debunk cultural stereotypes (e.g., Chinese are not solely group oriented, and, at times, value individual rights). Yet, these researchers have not directly assessed attitudes about intergroup judgments in their measures of social values.

To investigate morality in the context of intergroup relationships, it is necessary to understand children's social reasoning about race, ethnicity, gender, and culture as well as the extent to which stereotypes and prejudiced notions about others bear on social and moral judgments. As recent research has revealed, answers to these questions are complex. Giving priority to morality or to stereotypic expectations depends on the context and the target (gender, race, ethnicity) as well as the age, gender, and ethnicity of the individual making the decisions. As social psychology research findings with adults have indicated, individuals appear to hold both egalitarian views and intergroup biases (Fiske, 2002; Gaertner & Dovidio, 1986, 2000). Understanding the contexts and variables that contribute to the predominance of these diverse forms of judgments is the key to determining when various types of judgments take priority in decision making.

Overall, the moral development literature has shown that, although children form concepts of fairness and equality early in life (as young as $2^{1}/_{2}$ years of age; see Smetana, 1985), children's moral understanding lacks a sensitivity to context differences and is limited by an inability to evaluate complex and ambiguous problems. Like moral knowledge, children's knowledge about society, culture, and people changes throughout childhood, and these changes intersect and bear on how children apply moral principles to everyday situations, events, and social encounters. Children are young moral philosophers and they are also young sociologists (forming theories and beliefs about societal norms, expectations, and traditions), anthropologists (forming theories of culture), and psychologists (developing theories of people and theories of mind). Coordinating these diverse areas of knowledge is difficult, and this difficulty is reflected in their application of judgments of fairness to situations involving stereotypes and cultural expectations about members of other groups. Before turning to current research on moral development and intergroup relationships, it is necessary to identify some of the central theoretical constructs identified by researchers in the area of intergroup relationships (Brown & Gaertner, 2001).

Intergroup Relationships and Attitudes

Intergroup relationships are the attitudes, judgments, biases, and dispositions that a member of one group holds about a member of another group (Allport, 1954). Social psychologists have documented that, when using minimal group paradigms in which artificial groups are created in the laboratory, most individuals readily favor their ingroup and exhibit negative outgroup biases (Bourhis & Gagnon, 2001; Tajfel, 1978; Tajfel & Turner, 1979), even attributing stereotypes, biases, and prejudices toward members of outgroups (Devine, Plant, & Blair, 2001). *Stereotypes,* defined as the attribution of a label to a member of a group without consideration of intragroup variation, are very difficult to change, particularly in adulthood (Macrae, Stangor, & Hewstone, 1996). Thus, understanding how stereotypes emerge in childhood is crucial to combating their use and transmission in social life.

Intergroup theorists study explicit as well as implicit intergroup attitudes (Brown & Gaertner, 2001). In the social psychology literature, explicit attitudes "operate in a conscious mode and are exemplified by traditional, self-report measures of these constructs" (Dovidio et al., 2001, p. 176). Assessments of explicit biases with adults have included survey measures of egalitarian attitudes, which reflect judgments in the moral domain in adulthood, judgments that support equality and fairness norms. Implicit attitudes are "evaluations and beliefs that are automatically activated by the mere presence of the attitude object" (Dovidio et al., 2001, p. 176). There is extensive research on implicit biases with adults.

Although explicit and outward intergroup biases have diminished substantially over the past 50 years, possibly because they have been legally challenged through desegregation orders and civil rights legislation, implicit biases are still quite pervasive (Gaertner & Dovidio, 1986). Explicit biases about other group membership categories, such as gender and sexual identity, have not diminished to the same extent, but they are also clearly less condoned than they were several decades ago (Dovidio et al., 2001; Fiske, 2002). Despite the decrease in explicit racial bias, recent findings have shown that individuals who consider themselves to be unprejudiced actually reveal implicit biases. In the area of racial prejudice, this phenomenon of *aversive racism* is revealed by individuals who openly support egalitarian principles but unconsciously demonstrate racial biases (Gaertner & Dovidio, 1986).

There are different views on whether implicit biases reflect attitudes that underlie explicit judgments, meaning that they are part of the same set of values, or whether implicit and explicit attitudes reflect different types of intergroup judgments (see Dovidio et al., 2001; Greenwald et al., 2002; Karpiniski & Hilton, 2001). For example, implicit attitudes may be associations acquired as a result of exposure to the media and are not reflective of an individuals' intergroup orientation. There is much debate about this issue in the social psychology literature centering on the origins of implicit biases and their connections to explicit judgments (see Dovidio et al., 2001; Fazio, Jackson, Dunton, & Williams, 1995; Greenwald et al., 2002). This issue is relevant to the moral development literature because most moral development work has documented explicit judgments and attitudes. If implicit racial biases are related to explicit judgments about racial exclusion then this would be an important aspect of children's and adolescents' judgments to document, because it would provide additional information about how to understand the developmental trajectory of moral reasoning.

The handful of studies that have examined implicit bias in children have used the Implicit Associations Test (IAT) and ambiguous pictures assessments. The IAT has been used extensively with adults to demonstrate that negative adjectives are associated much faster with pictures of outgroup members than with those belonging to their ingroup (through word priming techniques administered on computer screens). Findings with adults with the IAT have raised a number of issues and controversies involving issues of internal and external reliability and validity (see Dovidio et al., 2001; Greenwald et al., 2002; Rudman, 2004). Concerns about the IAT with children pertain to the appropriateness of the techniques due to the verbal demands and fatigue associated with the procedure (Skowronski & Lawrence, 2001).

Indirect measures of racial attitudes, such as asking children to evaluate ambiguous situations involving characters from different ethnic backgrounds, are situated in the context of children's everyday, familiar interactions (see Lawrence, 1991; Margie, Killen, Sinno, & McGlothlin, 2005; McGlothlin, Killen, & Edmonds, 2005; Sagar & Schofield, 1980). These measures involve asking children to interpret a potential perpetrator's motives in two picture cards identical except for the race of the potential perpetrator (e.g., one child stands behind a swing and the second child is on the ground looking hurt; the ambiguity lies with whether the child pushed the second child off the swing).

The findings have shown that implicit racial biases emerge as a function of age, gender, and context. That is, with advancing age, children attribute negative intentions to peers as a function of race, but even when this occurs, it does not occur across the board. Children who display racial bias in one context (e.g., friendship) do not do so in another context (e.g., group interactions; McGlothlin et al., 2005). Further, focusing on race depends on the race of the target and the race of the participant (Margie et al., 2005).

The use of ambiguous picture cards to assess the attribution of intentions has been used in social information processing research, which finds that aggressive children over-attribute hostile intentions of others (see Arsenio & Lemerise, 2004; Crick & Dodge, 1994). The difference in the racial bias literature is that evaluations of ambiguous pictures provide an assessment of the attribution of hostile intentions as a function of the race of the potential perpetrator. Further, the findings reveal biases found in "normative" populations, in contrast to the work in social information processing, which serves as a diagnostic for aggressive and overly hostile children. The next steps for research on implicit racial bias in children are to examine whether children's judgments about fair treatment are related to implicit biases, and if so, how.

Another phenomenon established by social psychologists refers to the *outgroup homogeneity effect* (Judd & Park, 1993; Park & Rothbart, 1982), the tendency to recognize the heterogeneity of the ingroup, while assuming homogeneity of the outgroup. For example, a woman recognizes that women are quite diverse (i.e., loud, quiet, aggressive, passive) but, nonetheless, assumes that men are all the same (aggressive). This phenomenon contributes to stereotyping (lack of recognition of intragroup variation) and to cultural biases (lack of familiarity with a group leads to an assumption of homogeneity). As Oakes (2001) states, the principle of outgroup homogeneity combined with the principle of ingroup favoritism produces negative outgroup stereotypes and intergroup conflict. Research on the outgroup homogeneity effect with children has been minimal. A few studies indicate that between 5 and 12 years of age, children's outgroup homogeneity judgments are linked to prejudiced responses (Aboud & Amato, 2001). This means that children who judge the outgroup to be similar (while recognizing variation with the ingroup) are likely to display prejudiced responses. The morality of this phenomenon lies with the stereotypes that are applied to individuals when intragroup variation is not recognized, which potentially results in discriminatory attitudes and behavior.

In the area of gender biases, Biernat (2003) has documented the *shifting standards phenomenon*. Biernat shows how individuals use a different "ruler" to evaluate gender-related expectations. For example, a woman who jogs three times a week is viewed as "highly athletic," whereas a man who jogs three times a week is viewed as "somewhat athletic." The fact that individuals vary in their expectations indicates that there are underlying stereotypic expectations (e.g., "Women are not very athletic"). Again, this phenomenon has not been studied by developmental psychologists, nor have the moral implications been investigated. One line of research to be examined is to assess whether children use a shifting standard to evaluate gender roles in the family and their fairness judgments about these different roles. As an illustration, recent findings by Sinno and Killen (2004), who assessed children's judgments about mother's and father's roles in the home (e.g., working full time and staying at home to take care of a baby), revealed that children used both fairness and stereotypical expectations when evaluating these types of decisions by parents. Relating these judgments to children's ruler regarding mothers' roles in contrast to fathers' roles in the home would provide insight into when stereotypes are activated. For example, children who view a father who cooks three nights a week as highly domestic also view a mother who cooks three nights a week as moderately domestic, revealing an underlying stereotypical expectation that mothers cook dinner. There are a number of implications of this phenomenon for children's biases in the area of gender, and other stigmatized social groups.

Although social psychologists have researched a wealth of complex aspects of stereotyping, prejudice, discrimination, and biases, we have only reviewed a few key constructs in this chapter because of our overall focus on moral development in the context of intergroup relationships. Nonetheless, these constructs are quite revealing and provide heuristics for understanding how children and adolescents sort out fairness and justice from stereotypes and biases. In the next sections, we discuss developmental studies on race, ethnicity and gender, and then conclude with an analysis of current work designed to integrate intergroup theory and moral judgment perspectives.

DEVELOPMENTAL RESEARCH ON RACIAL AND ETHNIC STEREOTYPES

Stereotypes are defined in the literature as the generalized attribution of labels to individuals based solely on group membership, such as race, ethnicity, or gender, without consideration for intragroup variation (Stangor & Schaller, 1996). Researchers often conceptualize stereotypes and prejudice separately, with stereotypes dependent on cognition and prejudice based on negative affect (Aboud, 1988). In keeping with this conceptualization, most research on children's stereotypes has focused on cognitive aspects of stereotypes, rather than social–cognitive or moral dimensions. Yet, holding stereotypes about individuals based on racial and ethnic categories can lead to actions that would be viewed as wrong from a moral viewpoint. Thus, it is important to understand when stereotypes emerge in development, and what changes take place over time.

It has been shown, for example, that children's ability to remember information is influenced by stereotypes. Bigler and Liben (1993) examined children's ability to categorize social stimuli and their memory for stereotypic and counterstereotypic information. Results showed that children remember stereotypic information better than counterstereotypic information and stories about traits better than stories about social relationships. In addition, children who endorsed more stereotypes and children who could not recategorize social stimuli on multiple dimensions had worse memories for counterstereotypic information (Bigler & Liben, 1993). Five- to 7-year-old African-American children were better at remembering stereotypic information about skin tone than counterstereotypic information, but this varied depending on their ratings of their own skin color and how much they agreed with negative stereotypes of African Americans (Averhart & Bigler, 1997). Theories about how children acquire negative biases based on skin color are few, but stereotypic images in the media clearly play a role (Rudman, 2004).

With age, children become better able to distinguish between societal stereotypes and their own personal beliefs. Five- and 6-year-old children were not able to make this distinction and reported personal beliefs that were similar to the negative stereotypes (Augoustinos & Rosewarne, 2001). In contrast, 8- and 9-year-old children who were aware of negative stereotypes about an outgroup were able to distinguish between the stereotypes and their personal beliefs when given the opportunity. Whether this age-related change is due to age-related changes in moral understanding is not known and requires investigation.

To understand the basic processes underlying stereotyping reasoning, researchers have examined stereotypes as linked to children's conceptions of others' personalities. Children who view others' personal qualities as static and traits as causes of behavior are also more likely to stereotype an unknown member of a novel group. In contrast, children who see others' traits as malleable and believe the context is an important influence on behavior are less likely to stereotype (Levy & Dweck, 1999; Levy, Plaks, Hong, Chiu, & Dweck, 2001). This distinction has been related to "stereotype threat" research, which has shown that students who hold static views of traits are more susceptible to the detrimental effects of stereotypic attitudes than are students who hold dynamic views of traits (Good, Aronson, & Inzlicht, 2003). Extensive research has demonstrated that the wariness of conforming to a negative stereotype can also directly and indirectly influence performance on academic assessments and academic motivation (Aronson, Fried, & Good, 2002; Steele, 1997). Moreover, racial and ethnic stereotypes influence the activities adolescents engage in, the peers they associate with, and how they view their capacity for success (Kao, 2000). Clearly, an implication of the employment of racial and ethnic stereotyping is unfair treatment of others.

Most developmental literature on stereotypes focuses on cognitive processes, however, and few studies have examined the implications of stereotypical knowledge on moral reasoning. Clearly, stereotypical knowledge becomes a moral issue when stereotypes turn into negative racial attitudes and influence prejudice and discrimination. From a moral viewpoint, stereotypes in themselves involve unfairness, in that it is unfair to categorize someone based solely on their group membership, whether or not the categorization is positive or a negative. Although stereotypes may provide for more efficient social categorization, how individuals perceive the rightness or wrongness of stereotyping, independent of prejudice, should be studied empirically.

Developmental Emergence of Racial and Ethnic Prejudice

The literature on racial attitudes and prejudice are tightly interwoven, because much of the research on racial attitudes focuses on negative attitudes or prejudice. In addition, when positive attitudes are examined, it is usually in relation to negative attitudes. *Prejudice* is generally defined as a predisposition to respond in an unfavorable manner to members of a racial group (Aboud, 1988). However, prejudice is operationally defined in most studies, especially those with young children, as the tendency to attribute negative characteristics to members of an outgroup (Aboud & Amato, 2001). In studies of older children, the experience of prejudice is also sometimes examined.

Research on ethnic attitudes has shown that the simultaneous assignments of negative characteristics to both the ingroup and the outgroup increase with age (Bigler & Liben, 1993; Doyle, Beaudet, & Aboud, 1988), as does the flexibility of children's attitudes (i.e., they are better able to recognize and acknowledge between-group similarity; Powlishta, Serbin, Doyle, & White, 1994). In addition, as children's perspective-taking abilities mature, they are able to understand that different perspectives are acceptable. This understanding, called *reconciliation*, increases from age 5 to age 9 (Aboud, 1981). Doyle and Aboud (1995) found that 6- to 9-year-old children who showed increases in *counterbias* (positive attitudes toward outgroups and negative attitudes toward the ingroup) also evidenced increases in perception of between-race similarity, decreases in perception of within-race similarity, and increases in reconciliation. Also, the more similar a child perceived two children of the same race to be, the higher the child's prejudice score was (Doyle & Aboud, 1995).

Although minority children's ethnic attitudes also start to develop around age 3, age trends for racial and ethnic attitude development after that are more variable. Some measures have documented negative biases toward the ingroup among African-American children, and others do not (Aboud, 1988; Margie et al., 2005). Mexican-American and Asian-American children show the same variability (Aboud & Amato, 2001; Bernal, Knight, Ocampo, Garza, & Cota, 1993; Margie et al., 2005; Morland & Hwang, 1981). Between 7 and 10 years of age, though, children from racial and ethnic minority groups display neither an ingroup nor an outgroup bias (Aboud & Doyle, 1995; Bernal et al., 1993; Kelly & Duckitt, 1995).

Interpersonal relationships are an important context for examining racial prejudice and biases. Whereas children's negative outgroup bias tends to decline with age, research has found that children and adolescents have negative racial or ethnic attitudes and prejudice in the area of social relationships. One study with 6th to 10th grade African-American and European-American children found that European Americans were more prejudiced than African Americans concerning situations involving prolonged interracial contact (i.e., dating, marriage), whereas there were no ethnic or racial differences concerning less intimate social relationships (i.e., interaction in school, racial interactions in restaurants; Moore, Hauck, & Denne, 1984). Research with young adults indicates that using race to make a decision about who to vote for for student council president was wrong from a moral viewpoint (unfair treatment) but that using race as a reason to make a decision about who to date was a mixture of moral ("It's unfair to use race as a reason for deciding who to date"), personal ("It's up to the individual to decide"), and social-conventional reasons ("His friends might think differently about him if he dates her") (Killen, Stangor, Price, Horn, & Sechrist, 2004).

Additional studies have found that young children are capable of categorizing others by race (Aboud, 1988; Levy, 2000; Ramsey, 1991; Ramsey & Myers, 1990), and that race-related cues are more salient than non-race-related cues for high-prejudice children (Katz, Sohn, & Zalk, 1975). Powlishta and colleagues (1994) found that Kindergarten through 6th grade Canadian children who were biased in one domain (gender, ethnic or language group, or body type) were not necessarily biased in another domain. Flexibility in attitudes concerning one domain, however, was indicative of flexibility in other domains, and flexibility in the ethnic or language group domain was related to a reduced attribution bias. (Extensive research from Europe has demonstrated the complexities of ingroup and outgroup biases regarding national identities; this work is outside the scope of this chapter; see Bennett & Sani, 2004; Rutland, 2004.)

Although studies of racial attitudes and prejudice have generally assumed that a child who shows ingroup favoritism is also likely to exhibit negative bias toward an outgroup, these two attitudes are not necessarily reciprocal (Brewer, 1999) and may be a method-ological artifact (Aboud, 2003). In fact, a recent study examining this issue had mixed findings (Aboud, 2003). Positive ingroup bias was, at times, reciprocally related to negative outgroup bias in a sample of 4- to 7-year-old children attending a racially homogeneous school, but were not reciprocally related in a sample of 4- to 7-year-old children attending a racially heterogeneous school.

Aboud (2003) also found that ingroup favoritism developed more rapidly and was stronger than outgroup prejudice. She concludes that "ingroup attachment is [young children's] primary concern. Outgroup members suffer more from comparison than from outright hostility" (2003, p. 56). Also, prejudice was seen in a smaller proportion of the children than was ingroup favoritism, highlighting the need to consider and examine ingroup and outgroup bias separately (Aboud, 2003).

Discrimination and Fairness: Race and Ethnicity

Discrimination is the behavioral manifestation of prejudice. It is defined in the literature as negative behavior toward outgroups (Romero & Roberts, 1998). Although there are few studies on children's experiences with discrimination, those that do exist suggest that discrimination is a common experience for children and adolescents, especially those from minority groups (Biafora et al., 1993). Perception of discrimination has also been related to ethnic identity and negative outgroup bias (Romero & Roberts, 1998). Overall, though, the literature on discrimination has examined the detrimental effects of discrimination and how adolescents cope with discrimination. Adolescents of all ethnicities report experiencing distress when they perceive being discriminated against in educational situations (Fisher, Wallace, & Fenton, 2000).

Only one study examined children's moral judgments about discrimination (Verkuyten, Kinket, & van der Wielen, 1997). In this study, 10- to 13-year-old children living in the Netherlands were asked to explain discrimination. Most of the participants defined discrimination as a situation involving name calling; others said that it involved unequal distribution of goods or exclusion from play. This study found that ethnic majority and minority children's understandings of discrimination were very similar, suggesting a form of universality as found in the moral development literature.

Most of the studies focusing on fairness do not examine issues of race or ethnicity specifically, but instead they look at children's perceptions of fairness in general (e.g., Astor, 1994; Dalbert & Maes, 2002; Evans, Galyer, & Smith, 2001; Konstantareas & Desbois, 2001; Vandiver, 2001). Overall, these studies show that children have definite ideas about fairness and take context into account when reasoning about fairness, but how children think about fairness in relation to race or ethnicity has not been explored separately. Fairness concerning race or ethnicity appears to be addressed somewhat within the literature on discrimination and exclusion. For instance, Verkuyten and colleagues (1997) reported that participants appealed to fairness as a reason for why discrimination is wrong. Similarly, Killen and colleagues (Killen, Lee-Kim, McGlothlin, & Stangor, 2002; Killen & Stangor, 2001) and Phinney and Cobb (1996) found that children and adolescents use fairness as a reason to not exclude someone of another race or ethnicity from various activities. Interestingly, the studies that discuss fairness specifically in relation to racial and ethnic issues (i.e., Killen, Lee-Kim, et al., 2002; Phinney & Cobb, 1996; Verkuyten et al., 1997) are also the ones that explicitly examine children's reasoning about these issues. In addition, the Killen, Lee-Kim, and associates (2002) and Verkuyten and co-workers (1997) studies also are explicitly interested in the moral aspects of exclusion and discrimination, respectively, based on race and ethnicity.

The evidence shows that children have racial attitudes and often exhibit prejudicial beliefs. The acquisition question (that is, how do children acquire their racial attitudes?) is complex. Social learning theorists suggest that children get them from their parents, peers, or both (Allport, 1954; see also Aboud & Amato, 2001). Studies have found, however, that social learning theory does not adequately explain how children acquire their racial attitudes. Although children assume that their parents and friends hold the same views they do, there is little correspondence between the racial attitudes of children and their parents or their friends (Aboud & Doyle, 1996). In addition, adolescent friends do not necessarily share the same racial attitudes, stereotypes, or prejudices either (Ritchey & Fishbein, 2001). Cognitive-developmentalists, however, propose that young children's prejudice is due to their limited cognitive abilities (Aboud & Doyle, 1996) and not to the imitation of parental attitudes.

Social-cognitive domain theory predicts that children's prejudicial attitudes are a product of their reflection on their social experiences, which includes a wide array of social influences, and that these judgments manifest in different ways, depending on the context, target, and meaning attributed to the situation (Killen, McGlothlin, & Lee-Kim, 2002). What is not fully understood is how racial prejudice is connected to moral judgment. During the elementary school years, children evaluate moral transgressions, such as harming others or refusing to share, as wrong. Their reasons are based on fairness, justice, and equality. Equality judgments should extend to all people, regardless of racial and ethnic backgrounds.

One link between racial prejudice and moral judgments is peer interaction. Moral judgment theory predicts that peer interaction facilitates moral judgment (Piaget, 1932;

Turiel, 1983). This is because children infer, through reciprocal interactions, that one should act toward others as they would want others to act toward them (the "Golden Rule"). Similarly, in the area of racial prejudice, interracial contact (under the right conditions; Allport, 1954) and cross-ethnic friendships are theorized to reduce prejudice (Pettigrew, 1997; Pettigrew & Tropp, 2000). In the next section, we discuss how peer interactions and friendship are part of intergroup contact theory.

Intergroup Contact and Cross-Race Friendships

What is it about intergroup contact that contributes to a reduction in implicit biases and prejudices? Meta-analyses using mostly adult samples have revealed that cross-race friendships are the best predictor of a reduction in prejudice (Pettigrew & Tropp, 2000). Friendship, in particular, gives individuals the opportunity to see that there are similarities between people of different ethnicities and that people of other ethnicities are not all the same, thus increasing feelings of sympathy for unfair treatment of a person of another ethnicity (Pettigrew & Tropp, 2000).

Developmental research has shown that children report having fewer cross-race than same-race friendships (i.e., Aboud, Mendelson, & Purdy, 2003; Clark & Ayers, 1992; Hallinan & Smith, 1985), and this trend generally increases with age (Aboud et al., 2003; for an exception, see Howes & Wu, 1990). Children's and adolescents' reports of the number of cross-ethnic friends they have also vary by the ethnicity of the reporter. For instance, in a study of European-American and African-American middle school students, European-American children were more likely than African-American children to report having same-ethnic friends (Clark & Ayers, 1992). What is not known is why these trends exist. Do children prefer same-ethnic peers to cross-ethnic peers out of a response to societal expectations, cultural norms, or stereotypic classifications? Understanding the reasons for these preferences would provide a framework for addressing the origins of these preferences, and understanding the moral developmental implications of these patterns of social interaction.

Another characteristic children bring with them to cross-ethnic friendships is their racial attitudes. A recent study of first-, third-, fifth-, and sixth-grade children examined the relation between children's cross-ethnic friendships and racial attitudes (Aboud et al., 2003). In European-American children, those with higher prejudice scores reported higher numbers of cross-ethnic nonfriends, but not lower numbers of cross-ethnic friends. Of the European-American children with cross-ethnic friends, however, those children with higher prejudice scores rated their cross-ethnic friendships lower on quality overall. For African-American children, there was no relation between prejudice scores and cross-ethnic friendships (Aboud et al., 2003). In addition, this study found that children rate their same-ethnic friends slightly higher in intimacy than their cross-ethnic friends (Aboud et al., 2003). Again, these findings provide a number of research avenues to pursue from a moral developmental perspective. If children report higher intimacy with same-race than cross-race friendships, does this mean that they treat others differently depending on their race? What factors contribute to different qualities of relationships based on race if, in fact, children's reports are accurate? Perhaps children's cross-race and same-race relationships do not differ in quality and that their self-report data reflect stereotypic perceptions rather than reality.

Finally, studies have examined aspects of school environment that can encourage or discourage cross-ethnic friendships. Ethnically balanced classrooms are best for the promotion of cross-ethnic friendships because they provide students with the maximum opportunity for interethnic interaction (Hallinan & Smith, 1985). Findings are less clear concerning the ethnic composition of the school. Using a nationally representative sample of 7th through 12th graders, Moody (2001) found that friendship segregation, which is defined as fewer cross-ethnic friendships than the number of opportunities for cross-ethnic friendships, is lowest when a school is either homogeneous or very heterogeneous. Carlson, Wilson, and Hargrave (2003), however, found that for sixth- to eighth-grade Latinos, the ethnic composition of the school did not affect the number of cross-ethnic friendships reported. In addition, Carlson and colleagues (2003) found that participants' other-group orientation and their reports of how comfortable their friends were with cross-ethnic interaction did differ by ethnic composition of the school.

Thus, the studies that have been conducted in this area suggest that cross-race and cross-ethnic friendships provide an essential source of experience for children with respect to understanding the wrongfulness of racism, bigotry, and prejudice. Piaget's (1932) theory that peer interaction facilitates moral judgment was based on the concept that perspective taking and reciprocity occurs between "relations of equals," that is, peer relationships. Extending Piaget's theory, it is proposed that children's and adolescents' friendships with others who are different from themselves, in terms of group membership categories, facilitates the awareness of who is to be included when making decisions concerning equality and justice. (This may be true for gender as well, as discussed in the section on gender stereotypes.)

To date, few studies have investigated children's moral judgments about the decision to not become friends with someone solely because of their ethnicity. As part of a study by Killen, Lee-Kim, and associates (2002), 4th-, 7th-, and 10th-grade students were asked to evaluate the permissibility of not becoming friends with someone based on race. Killen, Lee-Kim, and co-workers (2002) found that most children and adolescents thought it would be unfair to not be friends with someone just because they were African American. Children and adolescents were also more likely to say that excluding someone from friendship was a personal choice in comparison to excluding someone from a club or denying them access to school, even if the reason they were being excluded from friendship was because of their ethnicity.

In a follow-up study, Killen, Crystal, and Ruck (2004) interviewed 4th-, 7th-, and 10th-grade students from majority and minority backgrounds (attending both homogeneous and heterogeneous schools) about their moral evaluations of cross-race relationships on three levels of intimacy: befriending a new student at school, bringing a friend home for a sleepover party, and bringing a date to a school dance. In each of these scenarios, there were two considerations, one based on race (the person making the decision was European American and the recipient was African American) and one based on nonracial considerations (a new student does not share the same sports interest; parents are uncomfortable with someone they have not yet met coming over for a sleepover party; and bringing a date to a school dance from a rival high school). The assessments were designed to measure whether participants focused on the race or the nonrace consideration when evaluating the decision to exclude someone, and what is it about being a different race that potentially makes people feel uncomfortable. In addition, participants were asked to respond to a set of general questions about their personal experiences of discrimination based on race and gender.

Analyses revealed that students who report having experienced personal discrimination are much more likely than students who have not experienced discrimination to view exclusion in intergroup contexts as being influenced by racial prejudice. Students who have not experienced discrimination tend to view exclusion in personal terms ("It's up to you to decide who you want to be friends with") as opposed to moral terms ("It's unfair to exclude"). Children who do not recognize the existence of racial or gender discrimination are also less likely to use moral reasoning to reject exclusion and more likely to use personal and social-conventional reasoning to justify exclusion. Further, children and adolescents attending heterogeneous schools (minority and majority) were more likely to use moral reasoning to evaluate the wrongfulness of racial exclusion than were majority students attending homogeneous schools.

DEVELOPMENTAL RESEARCH ON GENDER STEREOTYPES

We now turn to gender in the context of intergroup relationships. Although gender and race are quite different constructs, both reflect group membership categories that have been subjected to status differences that have led to morally relevant relationships involving issues of fairness, justice, and equality. There are ways in which gender equality has made more progress in the United States than has racial equality, particularly in terms of equal pay, education, and representation in political arenas. Yet, at the same time, gender stereotypes are much more readily condoned than are racial stereotypes. Further, there are many parts of the world in which gender inequality is extreme. For example, in much of the Middle East, Africa, and Asia, women are denied basic rights, are subjected to persecution, mistreatment, and torture, and are forced to live in segregated conditions (see Nussbaum, 1999; Turiel, 2002).

Thus, the developmental trajectories that lead to the application of moral principles in the context of intergroup relationships may be quite different for gender and race in different parts of the world. Given the relative absence of research on gender attitudes in children from other parts of the world, this chapter covers research on gender attitudes in the United States, and interprets these findings with respect to the moral development literature. As with research on racial and ethnic attitudes, most of the research on gender stereotyping and discrimination is not well linked to the moral development literature. Yet, there are clear implications for children's and adolescents' moral development when individuals are limited by stereotypical expectations of their behavior, attitudes, and abilities. The differences between judgments about gender and those about race and ethnicity lie with the wider range of contexts in which gender stereotypes are condoned and articulated. Thus, the subsection "Discrimination and Fairness" encompasses research on judgments about gender stereotyping and morality regarding play activities, division of labor in the home, and classroom/teacher expectations.

Developmental Emergence of Gender-Specific Categories

A vast amount of research indicates that children are aware of gender stereotypes as early as the preschool period (Liben & Bigler, 2002; Ruble & Martin, 1998). Cross-sectional work has shown that gender stereotyping increases with age. For instance, 4- to 6-year-olds were compared to 8- to 10-year-olds in their use of gender stereotyping to predict the likelihood of other stereotypically feminine or masculine characteristics, when they knew one characteristic of a child whose gender was not mentioned (Martin, Wood, & Little, 1990). For younger children, the target characteristic was toy preference. For older children, the characteristic referred to appearance, personality, occupation, or toys. Children in the younger age group had an easier time making associations about toy preferences when the characteristic was one common to their own gender. Older children were able to make associations for their own gender as well as opposite gender. Also, older children who were in middle childhood were found to be more extreme in their stereotypical judgments.

These results show that children use gender stereotypes to make interpretations about activities and behaviors. From a moral viewpoint, these types of judgments have the potential to conflict with concepts of equality, justice, and fairness. What needs to be known to determine the moral status of stereotypical judgments is the extent to which children use this knowledge when making decisions that involve sharing toys, allocating resources, or interacting with others in a range of social situations. Killen, Pisacane, Lee-Kim, and Ardila-Rey (2001) interviewed preschool-aged children about their fairness judgments in the context of gender stereotypic play activities. Children at $3\frac{1}{2}$, $4\frac{1}{2}$, and $5\frac{1}{2}$ years of age were asked whether it was all right for girls to exclude a boy from playing with dolls or for boys to exclude a girl from playing with trucks. With age, children judged it wrong because it would be unfair. Yet, when children were asked to make a forced choice judgment ("What if there is only room for one more to play then who should the group pick, a boy or a girl?"), stereotypical expectations increased with age as well. In addition, children's stereotypical judgments were more malleable than were their fairness judgments. Thus, in a straightforward context, children gave priority to fairness, despite the fact that they knew the stereotypes associated with doll and truck playing. The next step for this research is to examine how children's judgments about cross-gender attitudes and reasoning reveal their awareness of issues of discrimination and fairness. This includes studies on actual social reasoning and attitudes in the home as well as school.

Discrimination and Fairness: Gender

Differential treatment in the home context has been related to egalitarian attitudes. In families where girls held much more responsibility for chores than did boys, a large gap in sibling gender-role attitudes emerged, with boys having more traditional beliefs (Crouter, Head, Bumpus, & McHale, 2001). For boys, there were positive correlates to egalitarian views if and only if the son's gender role behavior was congruent with their father's gender-role behavior and attitudes (McHale, Bartko, Crouter, & Perry-Jenkins, 1990). In addition, it has been found that parental encouragement of both feminine and masculine tasks led to an increased involvement by children in cross-gendered activities (Antill, Goodnow, & Russell, 1996). For boys, the impact was stronger for same-sex parent, in that, if the father participated in typically "female" chores, such as the laundry, then his son was more likely to participate in these types of tasks also.

Further, research has shown that adolescents exhibit an increase in sex-typed patterns of involvement in feminine tasks when parents divided work along traditional gender lines and when there is a younger opposite-sex sibling present (Crouter, Manke, & McHale, 1995). Although these findings enhance an understanding of the family patterns that contribute to differential treatment, it is also important to determine how adolescents evaluate gender-related patterns and expectations in the home. As Biernat (2003) has indicated, there are different standards for expectations about gender-related abilities, and stereotypical assumptions often underlie these expectations. Moreover, there has been very little developmental work on the moral or "justice" implications of differential gender expectations in the home (see Goodnow, 1988). Do children and adolescents view gender-related patterns of expectations as fair or legitimate? To what extent do gender expectations reflect stereotypical attitudes? Addressing these questions would add a moral developmental perspective to this type of research.

From a social-cognitive domain perspective, it is important to examine how children reason about gender stereotypes. Carter and Patterson (1982) asked children to reason about the flexibility and cultural implications of gender-stereotypical toys and occupations, as well as table manners and a natural law. This study showed that children evaluated cross-gender behavior from a social-conventional perspective, not a moral one. Thus, a girl playing football was evaluated with criteria similar to how children evaluated a violation of table manners rather than to how children evaluated denying resources. Moreover, there was an increasing flexibility with age in both the use of toys for both genders and occupations for both genders. An implication of this research is that children view cross-gender behavior as a matter of choice or consensus, and not a matter of morality (universally applied principles). The next step is to examine how children evaluate the denial of the opportunity to engage in cross-gender behavior. For example, research by Horn and Nucci (2003) has shown that adolescents view it as unfair and discriminatory when individuals are denied the opportunity to decide an activity or way of dressing that reflects one's gender identity.

A study conducted with children 5 through 13 years old found a U-shaped curve in children's acceptance of cross-gender activity (Stoddart & Turiel, 1985). Children in the youngest age group, as well as children in the oldest age group, thought that participation in a gender-atypical activity was more wrong than children in middle childhood. The authors concluded that in kindergarten the maintenance of gender identity is defined in physical terms, so if a girl was to play a male-stereotypical game, other children might question her gender. As for adolescents, gender identity becomes closely linked to psychological characteristics and behaving in a gender-atypical manner may lead to exclusion.

Furthermore, the extent to which stereotypical expectations influence parental decisions regarding children's gender-related behavior remains to be better understood. In a recent study by Killen, Park, Lee-Kim, and Shin (2005), parents and nonparental adults were interviewed regarding whether it was all right to allow a son but not a daughter to play baseball, or a daughter but not a son to take ballet. Parents were more likely than nonparental adults to view the decision in social-conventional terms whereas nonparental adults were more likely to view the issue in moral terms (unfairness). Thus, gender expectations may influence parental decisions, and may impact on the decisions to grant autonomy and treat children differently based on gender.

Judgments about gender equality in the home are also influenced by father-child relationships. Young adults in intact families whose fathers were highly involved in childrearing and housework had more egalitarian views about gender roles in career and family contexts than those peers who were raised in a more traditional home, with dad working and mom staying home (Williams & Radin, 1999). Moreover, maternal employment and egalitarian roles in the family had positive effects on daughters, such as in the display of more independent coping skills and higher achievement test scores (Hoffman & Kloska, 1995). For both sons and daughters, paternal attention and intimacy are positively correlated with children's self-esteem, indicating that children's prosocial development is influenced by counterstereotypical father involvement. Sons of egalitarian fathers are more accepting of female activities and are less likely to associate such activities with a negative stigma than are daughters of egalitarian fathers. Again, children's moral development, that is, judgments about equal opportunity, was shown to be positively influenced by paternal expectations for gender equality and equity. Researchers studying father involvement have lamented the relative absence of a focus on the father's role in developmental research (see Tamis-LaMonda & Cabrera, 2003). In addition, more research on how father's roles contribute to children's and adolescents' interpretations of discrimination and fairness in the home is needed.

As we have described, parents' own beliefs about gender differences impact the socialization of gender stereotypes in their children and influence children's social development. One such way that this occurs is through their expectancies for their children's success in the academic and sports arenas. Eccles, Jacobs, and Harold (1990) found that when parents held gender-stereotyped beliefs about one gender being more talented in a particular domain, they were more likely to have lower expectations of their child of the opposite gender, and this in some ways affected how the child performed. For example, a mother who believes that boys are naturally more talented than girls in mathematics expects less from her daughter, resulting in a self-fulfilling prophecy for the daughter. Obviously, this has an impact on equality and equal opportunities for girls and women.

Children often have their own self-beliefs and competence beliefs about academics and also about sports activities. Younger children (first grade) are found to have more positive outlooks about their capability in various arenas. As children grow older (fourth grade), their concept of personal abilities becomes divided by gender. Boys tend to have a more positive competence belief in sports and mathematics than girls, and girls tend to have a more positive competence belief in reading and music than boys (Eccles, Wigfield, Harold, & Blumenfeld, 1993). This differentiation is seen as early as fourth grade. Further, girls are less likely than boys to believe that they can work to be the best in their weakest academic subject (usually math). Boys are less likely to think that they can improve to be the best in areas such as music or art (Freedman-Doan et al., 2000).

To the extent that teachers and parents hold stereotypical expectations based on gender, these expectations may inhibit children from exploring their potential in academics and nonacademic interests, which, in turn, could limit their future career choices and occupations. As an example, children make links between occupations, job status, and gender (Liben, Bigler, & Krogh, 2001). In research by Liben and colleagues (2001), children, aged 6 to 11 years, rated occupations that they interpreted as male oriented, such as being a doctor, as higher in status than an occupation they interpreted as female oriented, such as being a teacher. Further, this study found that children preferred occupations that were associated with their own gender. Girls preferred occupations such as teacher and nurse, whereas boys preferred occupations such as doctor and lawyer. Gender-differential expectations, then, may lead to gender-segregated occupations and opportunities.

Intergroup Contact and Gender Equality

Intergroup theory from social psychology (see Pettigrew & Tropp, 2000), discussed previously, can also help to interpret findings about gender equality and moral development. Because most children attend coeducational schools, it has been suggested that intergroup contact does not apply to gender equality. Yet, the extensive documentation on the sex-segregated play and interactions of children in middle childhood (Ruble & Martin, 1998) suggests that the conditions under which children interact are not ideal for promoting equality and prejudice reduction in the area of gender-based discrimination. For example, one central condition that facilitates a reduction in prejudice is authority sanctioning, which refers to the extent that individuals in authority positions, such as teachers and parents, encourage principles of mutual respect, equal opportunity, and justice. As Bigler, Brown, and Markell (2001) have shown, however, teachers routinely differentiate boys and girls through explicit and implicit messages about gender-specific abilities. Eccles and co-workers (1993) have demonstrated that girls are not granted equal status in the arena of math and science, and personalized interactions are often discouraged as exemplified by sex-segregated play patterns (Ruble & Martin, 1998). Thus, extensive sex-segregated interactions, gender-specific expectations, and gender-related career opportunities may inhibit the development of gender equality principles as well as ideas of fairness, leading to discriminatory practices, just as lack of intergroup contact in the area of race and ethnicity contributes to prejudicial responses. Deemphasizing gender differences in elementary school may serve not only to encourage girls to succeed in math and science, but it may also contribute to the facilitation of equality and fairness concepts for all children.

DEVELOPMENTAL STUDIES OF MORALITY AND INTERGROUP ATTITUDES

As indicated, much of the work in the area of moral judgment has focused on reasoning about fairness and justice without directly including intergroup categories in the research design. When including intergroup categories in assessments of straightforward moral transgressions, however, research has shown that the vast majority of children and adolescents view it as wrong and unfair. For example, Horn (2003) demonstrated that adolescents evaluated the denial of resources to individuals based on group membership, such as belonging to a clique as wrong (e.g., denying a scholarship to a jock is unfair). Similarly, Killen, Lee-Kim, and associates (2002) reported that over 95% of children and adolescents rejected gender and racial exclusion in the context of denying educational opportunities, such as going to school. Yet, as indicated by Dovidio and co-workers (2001), when discussing the complex attitudes in the context of multifaceted situations in which moral, social-conventional, and personal considerations are involved, the patterns of responses look very different from those in the context of straightforward situations. Findings from Horn (2003) and Killen, Lee-Kim, and colleagues (2002) indicate that whereas straightforward acts of exclusion were evaluated as wrong, acts of exclusion in complex situations revealed stereotypical expectations and an increased reliance, with age, on group functioning as the basis for legitimizing exclusion.

In most developmental research, peer exclusion is examined in terms of the individual social deficits of children who typically exclude others or who are excluded (Arsenio & Lemerise, 2004; Asher & Coie, 1990; Rubin, Bukowski, & Parker, 1998). These variables include bullying and aggressiveness on the part of the excluder, and wariness and fearfulness on the part of the one who is excluded. More recently, peer exclusion has been studied as a distinct form of relational aggression (Crick & Grotpeter, 1995). Yet, there are times in which children exclude others for reasons that have very little to do with the social deficits of the child who is excluded (or the excluder). Some children are excluded because of their group membership, such as because they are a girl or African American or Muslim. In addition, studies have demonstrated that children from minority racial and ethnic groups report experiencing exclusion because of their race or ethnicity more often than children from majority racial and ethnic groups (Phinney & Cobb, 1996; Verkuyten & Thijs, 2002).

Results described in this chapter clearly demonstrate the ways in which children's and adolescents' evaluations of exclusion in peer group contexts involve moral reasoning as well as stereotypical expectations about gender and race (Killen et al., 2001; Killen & Stangor, 2001; Theimer, Killen, & Stangor, 2001). When ambiguity is introduced into the situation, participants often used social-conventional reasoning and rely on stereotypic expectations. These results support claims by Gaertner and Dovidio (1986) (see also Dovidio et al., 2001) that adults use egalitarian justifications in straightforward situations and rely on stereotypes in situations involving ambiguity, complexity, and unfamiliarity;

this also appears to be the case for children and adolescents. Thus, these developmental findings, so far, indicate that, in specified contexts, children and adolescents apply moral principles to situations involving intergroup relationships. Yet, much more information is needed regarding the wide range of contexts in which stereotypical beliefs conflict with moral principles.

Overall, gender exclusion is typically more readily condoned than racial exclusion. Furthermore, there are significant differences depending on the gender, age, and ethnicity of the participants. For example, in some studies, majority girls and minority students (girls and boys) view exclusion as more wrong than do majority boys (Killen, Lee-Kim, et al., 2002). These latter findings may be a function of the extent to which children have personally experienced exclusion. The few differences for the ethnicity of the participant were revealed in the elaboration of the moral reasoning responses. Whereas majority students viewed gender and racial exclusion as wrong ("It's not fair to exclude someone for that type of reason"), the minority students were more likely to extend their reasoning about the wrongfulness beyond the immediate situation, and to talk about what makes it wrong when members of a culture exclude on the basis of ethnicity. In the words of a 10th-grade African-American girl:

> People do come from different places, and yes, they do speak different languages. But every- body has a heart, and they also have feelings, and they also know how it is to be put down. And it hurts. So I mean if you're the type of person who says "Okay, I don't like you because of your race," it's just wrong. (Killen, Lee-Kim, et al., 2002, p. 55)

In general, nonmoral reasons for exclusion increase with age and are more prevalent among majority boys than among majority girls or minority individuals. Thus, individuals' evaluations of exclusion as a moral transgression depends on the target of exclusion (gender or race), the context (friendship, peer club, social institution), and their own interpretation of the situation (their justifications). The developmental picture emerging regarding morality in the context of intergroup relationships indicates that both moral and stereotypic norms influence social reasoning very early, and that with age, fairness and stereotypic norms are differentially influential on children's decision making about social relationships.

CONCLUSIONS

Studying morality in the context of intergroup relationships reveals how fairness, equality, and justice play out in children's lives and the ways in which their experiences hinder or foster an appreciation for the application of moral and ethical principles to individuals from a wide range of backgrounds. Further, this approach widens the types of nonmoral judgments that bear on moral evaluations. In this chapter, we demonstrated that nonmoral social judgments, such as group functioning and stereotypical expectations, influence moral decision making. Social-cognitive domain theory has provided a model by which to examine how individuals weigh moral considerations (e.g., fairness, equality, justice), with social-conventional issues (e.g., group functioning, group identity, traditions, cultural expectations) and psychological concerns (e.g., personal choice and autonomy). This model, which is quite different from traditional moral development theories that postulate global stages of moral judgments, provides a framework for examining the different forms of reasoning, moral and nonmoral, that are used by individuals to evaluate interindividual and intergroup behavior.

There are several avenues of research that can enrich the understanding of the emergence of morality in the context of intergroup relationships. Developmental social cognition theory proposes that children make inferences about their own experiences, and that these interpretations form the basis, in part, of their social judgments (Smetana, 1995, chap. 5, this volume; Turiel, 1983, chap. 1, this volume). Thus, researchers should analyze the relationships between children's and adolescents' personal experiences with discrimination and unfair treatment with their evaluations of exclusion and discrimination. There are indications that children's personal experiences contribute to their evaluations of the fairness of differential treatment, but little is known about this connection (Fisher, Jackson, & Villarruel, 1998). Further, the role of majority or minority status in a group influences how individuals evaluate intergroup relationships. This is a unique form of social experience that has received extensive investigation in the adult social psychology literature (Brown & Gaertner, 2001) with very little scrutiny in the child development literature. More research is needed to understand how the experience of being a majority or minority member of a culture influences children's judgments about discrimination, fairness, and exclusion.

There are clear indications that implicit biases are pervasive in adult social attitudes (Dovidio et al., 2001); more research is needed on implicit attitudes in childhood and adolescence. In addition, the relationship between implicit and explicit biases in childhood needs to be better understood. Do children who have strong beliefs about the unfairness of prejudice nonetheless demonstrate implicit biases? If so, what does this tell us, and when do these implicit biases emerge?

Recent work on implicit biases has focused on race more often than on gender. To some extent, explicit biases about gender are viewed as more socially acceptable than are explicit biases about race and ethnicity (certainly over the past 25 years). Thus, researchers may feel a more pressing need to examine implicit racial biases. Still, little is known about individuals view different types of intergroup relationships. Do individuals who view gender exclusion as wrong also view racial exclusion as wrong? What about other group membership categories, such as religion, cultural membership, and handicapped status? Individuals perceive some forms of exclusion as more wrong from a moral viewpoint than other forms of exclusion, and investigating comparisons among different forms of intergroup bias could contribute to an understanding of what underlies prejudicial judgments.

Pertinent to moral development perspectives, researchers should examine how different forms of moral reasoning, such as fairness, equality, justice, and rights, are applied to intergroup contexts. Children refer to fairness concerns in the context of straightforward exclusion, for example, but make reference to equality and equal opportunity in more complex situations. Developmental analyses of different forms of moral explanations remain fairly general. Yet, moral philosophers differentiate what it means to argue from a fairness position in contrast to an equality or rights perspective (Gewirth, 1978; Nussbaum, 1999). Translating these abstract criteria for developmental analyses remains a fundamental goal for moral development research. Finally, the relation between culture, local (i.e., school) as well as global (i.e., nationality, religion, and modernity), and intergroup attitudes has to be further examined (Turiel, 2002). These different sources of influence clearly have an impact on children's priority of fairness or stereotypic expectations in social decision-making situations, and yet little is known about how these cultural variables bear on children's moral reasoning about intergroup relationships.

Despite strides toward greater racial and gender equality, interactions between individuals from different backgrounds continue to involve stereotypes, biases, discriminatory practices, and prejudices, which contribute to tensions, stress, and conflict in social life. It is essential to understand the developmental origins, emergence, and trajectory for these types of judgments. Because stereotypical beliefs are deeply entrenched and difficult to change in adulthood, it is paramount that we understand how stereotypes emerge in childhood, as well as how children use stereotypes to make decisions about social relationships in school and home contexts. Research uncovering the root causes of negative intergroup attitudes in adulthood contributes to facilitating positive social relationships, academic success, and productive workforce environments. Ultimately, a better understanding of these issues could identify the sources of influences that contribute to a just and fair society.

ACKNOWLEDGMENTS

We thank Christy Edmonds, Heidi McGlothlin, Judith G. Smetana, and Elliot Turiel for feedback on the manuscript. Part of the research described in this chapter was supported, in part, by grants from the National Science Foundation (#BCS0346717) and the National Institute of Child Health and Human Development (#1R01HD04121-01).

REFERENCES

Aboud, F. E. (1981). Egocentrism, conformity, and agreeing to disagree. *Developmental Psychology, 17,* 791–799.

Aboud, F. E. (1988). *Children and prejudice.* New York: Blackwell.

Aboud, F. E. (2003). The formation of in-group favoritism and out-group prejudice in young children: Are they distinct attitudes? *Developmental Psychology, 39*(1), 48–60.

Aboud, F. E., & Amato, M. (2001). Developmental and socialization influences on intergroup bias. In R. Brown & S. Gaertner (Eds.), *Blackwell handbook of social psychology: Intergroup relations* (pp. 65–85). Oxford, UK: Blackwell.

Aboud, F. E., & Doyle, A. B. (1995). The development of in-group pride in Black Canadians. *Journal of Cross-Cultural Psychology, 26*(3), 243–254.

Aboud, F. E., & Doyle, A. B. (1996). Parental and peer influences on children's racial attitudes. *International Journal of Intercultural Relations, 20*(3–4), 371–383.

Aboud, F. E., Mendelson, M. J., & Purdy, K. T. (2003). Cross-race peer relations and friendship quality. *International Journal of Behavioral Development, 27*(2), 165–173.

Allport, G. W. (1954). *The nature of prejudice.* Reading, MA: Addison-Wesley.

Antill, J. K., Goodnow, J. J., & Russell, G. (1996). The influence of parents and family context on children's involvement in household tasks. *Sex Roles, 34*(3–4), 215–236.

Aronson, J., Fried, C. B., & Good, C. (2002). Reducing the effects of stereotype threat on African American college students by shaping theories of intelligence. *Journal of Experimental Social Psychology, 38*(2), 113–125.

Arsenio, W. F., & Lemerise, E. A. (2004). Aggression and moral development: Integrating social information processing and moral domain models. *Child Development, 75,* 987–1002.

Arsenio, W. F., & Lover, A. (1995). Children's conceptions of sociomoral affect: Happy victimizers, mixed emotions, and other expectancies. In M. Killen & D. Hart (Eds.), *Morality in everyday life* (pp. 87–128). Cambridge, UK: Cambridge University Press.

Asher, S., & Coie, J. (1990). *Peer rejection in childhood.* Cambridge, UK: Cambridge University Press.

Astor, R. A. (1994). Children's moral reasoning about family and peer violence: The role of provocation and retribution. *Child Development, 65*(4), 1054–1067.

Augoustinos, M., & Rosewarne, D. L. (2001). Stereotype knowledge and prejudice in children. *British Journal of Developmental Psychology, 19,* 143–156.

Averhart, C. J., & Bigler, R. S. (1997). Shades of meaning: Skin tone, racial attitudes, and constructive memory in African American children. *Journal of Experimental Child Psychology, 67*(3), 363–388.

Bennett, M., & Sani, F. (Eds.). (2004). *The development of the social self.* New York: Psychology Press.

Bernal, M. E., Knight, G. P., Ocampo, K. A., Garza, C. A., & Cota, M. K. (1993). Development of Mexican-American identity. In M. E. Bernal & G. P. Knight (Eds.), *Ethnic identity: Formation and transmission among Hispanics and other minorities* (pp. 31–46). Albany: State University of New York Press.

Biafora, F. A., Warheit, G. J., Zimmerman, R. S., Gil, A. G., Apospori, E., Taylor, D., & Vega, W. A. (1993). Racial mistrust and deviant behaviors among ethnically diverse Black adolescent boys. *Journal of Applied Social Psychology, 23,* 891–910.

Biernat, M. (2003). Toward a broader view of social stereotyping. *American Psychologist, 58*(12), 1019–1027.

Bigler, R. S., & Liben, L. S. (1993). A cognitive-developmental approach to racial stereotyping and reconstructive memory in Euro-American children. *Child Development, 64,* 1507–1518.

Bigler, R. S., Brown, C. S., & Markell, M. (2001). When groups are not created equal: Effects of group status on the formation of intergroup attitudes in children. *Child Development, 72,* 1151–1162.

Bourhis, R. Y., & Gagnon, A. (2001). Social orientations in the minimal group paradigm. In R. Brown & S. Gaertner (Eds.), *Intergroup processes: Blackwell handbook in social psychology* (Vol. 4, pp. 89–111). Oxford: Blackwell.

Brewer, M. B. (1999). The psychology of prejudice: In-group love or out-group hate? *Journal of Social Issues, 55,* 429–444.

Brown, R., & Gaertner, S. (Eds.). (2001). *Blackwell handbook in social psychology. Vol. 4: Intergroup processes.* Cambridge, MA: Blackwell.

Carlson, C. I., Wilson, K. D., & Hargrave, J. L. (2003). The effect of school racial composition on Hispanic intergroup relations. *Journal of Social and Personal Relationships, 20*(2), 203–220.

Carter, D. B., & Patterson, C. J. (1982). Sex roles as social conventions: The development of children's conceptions of sex-role stereotypes. *Developmental Psychology, 18,* 812–824.

Clark, M. L., & Ayers, M. (1992). Friendship similarity during early adolescence: Gender and racial patterns. *The Journal of Psychology, 126*(4), 393–405.

Colby, A., & Kohlberg, L. (1987). *The measurement of moral judgment. Vol. 1: Theoretical foundations and research validation.* New York: Cambridge University Press.

Crick, N., & Dodge, K. A. (1994). A review and reformulation of social information-processing mechanisms in children's social adjustment. *Psychological Bulletin, 115,* 74–101.

Crick, N., & Grotpeter, J. (1995). Relational aggression, gender, and social psychological adjustment. *Child Development, 66,* 710–722.

Crouter, A. C., Head, M. R., Bumpus, M. F., & McHale, S. M. (2001). Household chores: Under what conditions do mothers lean on daughters? In A. Fuligni (Ed.), *Family assistance and obligation during adolescence.* New Directions in Child Development Monograph. San Francisco: Jossey-Bass.

Crouter, A. C., Manke, B., & McHale, S. M. (1995). The family context of gender intensification in early adolescence. *Child Development, 66,* 317–329.

Dalbert, C., & Maes, J. (2002). Belief in a just world as a personal resource in school. In M. Ross & D. T. Miller (Eds.), *The justice motive in everyday life* (pp. 365–381). New York: Cambridge University Press.

Damon, W. (1977). *The social world of the child.* San Francisco: Jossey-Bass.

Devine, P. G., Plant, E. A., & Blair, I. V. (2001). Classic and contemporary analyses of racial prejudice. In R. Brown & S. L. Gaertner (Eds.), *Blackwell handbook in social psychology: Vol. 4: Intergroup processes* (pp. 198–217). Oxford, UK: Blackwell.

Dovidio, J. F., Kawakami, K., & Beach, K. R. (2001). Implicit and explicit attitudes: Examination of the relationship between measures of intergroup bias. In R. Brown & S. Gaertner (Eds.), *Blackwell handbook in social psychology. Vol. 4: Intergroup processes* (pp. 175–197). Oxford, UK: Blackwell.

Doyle, A. B., & Aboud, F. E. (1995). A longitudinal study of White children's racial prejudice as a social-cognitive development. *Merrill-Palmer Quarterly, 41*(2), 209–228.

Doyle, A. B., Beaudet, J., & Aboud, F. E. (1988). Developmental patterns in the flexibility of children's ethnic attitudes. *Journal of Cross-Cultural Psychology, 19,* 3–18.

Dworkin, R. (1986). *Law's empire.* Cambridge, MA: Harvard University Press.

Eccles, J., Jacobs, J., & Harold, R. (1990). Gender role stereotypes, expectancy effects, and parents' socialization of gender differences. *Journal of Social Issues, 46,* 183–201.

Eccles, J., Wigfield, A., Harold, R. D., & Blumenfeld, P. (1993). Age and gender differences in children's self- and task perceptions during elementary school. *Child Development 64*(3), 830–847.

Eisenberg, N., & Fabes, R. A. (1998). Prosocial development. In W. Damon (Series Ed.) & N. Eisenberg (Vol. Ed.), *Handbook of child psychology. Vol. 3: Social, emotional, and personality development* (5th ed., pp. 701–778). New York: Wiley.

Evans, I. M., Galyer, K. T., & Smith, K. J. H. (2001). Children's perceptions of unfair reward and punishment. *Journal of Genetic Psychology, 162*(2), 212–227.

Fazio, R. H., Jackson, J. R., Dunton, B. C., & Williams, C. J. (1995). Variability in automatic activation as an unobtrusive measure of racial attitudes: A bona fide pipeline? *Journal of Personality and Social Psychology, 69,* 1013–1027.

Fisher, C. B., Jackson, J. F., & Villarruel, F. A. (1998). The study of African-American and Latin-American children and youth. In W. Damon (Series Ed.) & R. Lerner (Vol. Ed.), *Handbook of child psychology. Vol. 1: Theoretical models of human development* (5th ed., pp. 1145–1207). New York: Wiley.

Fisher, C. B., Wallace, S. A., & Fenton, R. E. (2000). Discrimination distress during adolescence. *Journal of Youth & Adolescence, 29*(6), 679–695.

Fiske, S. (2002). What we know now about bias and intergroup conflict, the problem of the century. *Current Directions in Psychological Science, 11,* 123–128.

Freedman-Doan, C., Wigfield, A., Eccles, J., Blumenfeld, P., Arbreton, A., & Harold, R. (2000). What am I best at? Grade and gender differences in children's beliefs about ability improvement. *Journal of Applied Developmental Psychology, 21,* 379–402.

Gaertner, S. L., & Dovidio, J. F. (1986). The aversive form of racism. In J. F. Dovidio & S. L. Gaertner (Eds.), *Prejudice, discrimination, and racism* (pp. 61–89). Orlando, FL: Academic Press.

Gaertner, S. L., & Dovidio, J. F. (2000). *Reducing intergroup bias: The Common Ingroup Identity Model.* Philadelphia: The Psychology Press.

Gewirth, A. (1978). *Reason and morality.* Chicago: University of Chicago Press.

Good, C., Aronson, J., & Inzlicht, M. (2003). Improving adolescents' standardized test performance: An intervention to reduce the effects of stereotype threat. *Journal of Applied Developmental Psychology, 24*(6), 645–662.

Goodnow, J. J. (1988). Children's household work: Its nature and functions. *Psychological Bulletin, 103*(1), 5–26.

Greenwald, A. G., Banaji, M. R., Rudman, L. A., Farnham, S. D., Nosek, B. A., & Mellott, D. S. (2002). A unified theory of implicit attitudes, stereotypes, self-esteem, and self-concept. *Psychological Review, 109,* 3–25.

Hallinan, M. T., & Smith, S. S. (1985). The effects of classroom racial composition on students' interracial friendliness. *Social Psychological Quarterly, 48*(1), 3–16.

Helwig, C. C., Arnold, M. L., Tan, D., & Boyd, D. (2003). Chinese adolescents' reasoning about democratic and authority-based decision making in peer, family, and school contexts. *Child Development, 74*, 783–800.

Helwig, C. C., & Turiel, E. (2002). Rights, autonomy, and democracy: Children's perspectives. *International Journal of Law and Psychiatry, 25*, 253–270.

Hoffman, L. W., & Kloska, D. (1995). Parents' gender-based attitudes toward marital roles and child rearing: Development and validation of new measures. *Sex Roles, 32*, 273–295.

Horn, S. S., (2003). Adolescents' reasoning about exclusion from social groups. *Developmental Psychology, 39*, 71–84.

Horn, S. S., & Nucci, L. P. (2003). The multidimensionality of adolescents' beliefs about and attitudes toward gay and lesbian peers in school. *Equity and Excellence in Education, 36*, 136–147.

Howes, C., & Wu, F. (1990). Peer interactions and friendships in an ethnically diverse school setting. *Child Development, 61*(2), 537–541.

Judd, C. M., & Park, B. (1993). Definition and assessment of accuracy in social stereotypes. *Psychological Review, 100*, 109–128.

Kant, I. (1785/1959). *Foundations of the metaphysics of morals.* New York: Bobbs-Merrill.

Kao, G. (2000). Group images and possible selves among adolescents: Linking stereotypes to expectations by race and ethnicity. *Sociological Forum, 15*(3), 407–430.

Karpiniski, A., & Hilton, J. (2001). Attitudes and the Implicit Association Test. *Journal of Personality and Social Psychology, 81*, 774–488.

Katz, P. A., Sohn, M., & Zalk, S. R. (1975). Perceptual concomitants of racial attitudes in urban grade-school children. *Developmental Psychology, 11*(2), 135–144.

Kelly, M., & Duckitt, J. (1995). Racial preference and self-esteem in Black South African children. *South African Journal of Psychology, 25*, 217–223.

Killen, M., Crystal, D., & Ruck, M. (2004, June 3). *Children's and adolescents' intergroup biases in the context of peer relationships.* Paper presented at the Annual Symposium of the Jean Piaget Society: Society for the Study of Knowledge and Development, Toronto, Canada.

Killen, M., & de Waal, F. B. M. (2000). The evolution and development of morality. In F. Aureli & F. B. M. de Waal (Eds.), *Natural conflict resolution* (pp. 352–372). Berkeley: University of California Press.

Killen, M., Lee-Kim, J., McGlothlin, H., & Stangor, C. (2002). How children and adolescents evaluate gender and racial exclusion. *Monographs of the Society for Research in Child Development, 67*(4, Serial No. 271).

Killen, M., McGlothlin, H., & Lee-Kim, J. (2002). Between individuals and culture: Individuals' evaluations of exclusion from social groups. In H. Keller, Y. Poortinga, & A. Schoelmerich (Eds.), *Between biology and culture: Perspectives on ontogenetic development.* Cambridge, UK: Cambridge University Press.

Killen, M., Park, Y., Lee-Kim, J., & Shin, Y. (2005). Evaluations of children's gender stereotypic activities by Korean parents and nonparental adults residing in the United States. *Parenting: Science and Practice, 5*, 57–89.

Killen, M., Pisacane, K., Lee-Kim, J., & Ardila-Rey, A. (2001). Fairness or stereotypes?: Young children's priorities when evaluating group exclusion and inclusion. *Developmental Psychology, 37*, 587–596.

Killen, M., & Stangor, C. (2001). Children's social reasoning about inclusion and exclusion in gender and race peer group contexts. *Child Development, 72*, 174–186.

Killen, M., Stangor, C., Price, B. S., Horn, S., & Sechrist, G. (2004). Social reasoning about racial exclusion in intimate and non-intimate relationships. *Youth and Society, 35,* 293–322.

King, M. L. (1957/1986). Facing the challenge of a new age. In J. M. Washington (Ed.), *I have a dream: Writings and speeches that changed the world* (pp. 14–28). San Francisco: Harper Press.

Kohlberg, L. (1971). From is to ought: How to commit the naturalistic fallacy and get away with it in the study of moral development. In T. Mischel (Ed.), *Psychology and genetic epistemology* (pp. 151–235). New York: Academic Press.

Kohlberg, L. (1984). *Essays on moral development. Vol. 2: The psychology of moral development—The nature and validity of moral stages.* San Francisco: Harper & Row.

Konstantareas, M. M., & Desbois, N. (2001). Preschoolers perceptions of the unfairness of maternal disciplinary practices. *Child Abuse & Neglect, 25*(4), 473–488.

Lawrence, V. W. (1991). Effect of socially ambiguous information on White and Black children's behavioral and trait perceptions. *Merrill-Palmer Quarterly, 37,* 619–630.

Levy, G. D. (2000). Individual differences in race schematicity as predictors of African American and White children's race-relevant memories and peer preferences. *The Journal of Genetic Psychology, 161*(4), 400–419.

Levy, S. R., & Dweck, C. S. (1999). The impact of children's static versus dynamic conceptions of people on stereotype formation. *Child Development, 70*(5), 1163–1180.

Levy, S. R., Plaks, J. E., Hong, Y. Y., Chiu, C. Y., & Dweck, C. S. (2001). Static vs. dynamic theories and the perception of groups: Different routes to different destinations. *Personality and Social Psychology Review, 5,* 156–168.

Liben, L. S., & Bigler, R. S. (2002). The developmental course of gender differentiation. *Monographs of the Society for Research in Child Development, 67* (2, Serial No. 269).

Liben, L. S., Bigler, R. S., & Krogh, H. R. (2001). Pink and blue collar jobs: Children's judgments of job status and job aspirations in relation to sex of worker. *Journal of Experimental Child Psychology, 79,* 346–363.

Macrae, C. N., Stangor, C., & Hewstone, M. (1996). *Stereotypes and stereotyping.* New York: The Guilford Press.

Margie, N. G., Killen, M., Sinno, S., & McGlothlin, H. (2005). Minority children's intergroup attitudes about peer relationships. *British Journal of Developmental Psychology, 23,* 251–269.

Martin, C. L., Wood, C. H., & Little, J. K. (1990). The development of gender stereotype components. *Child Development, 61,* 1891–1904.

McGlothlin, H., Killen, M., & Edmonds, C. (2005). European-American children's intergroup attitudes about peer relationships. *British Journal of Developmental Psychology, 23,* 227–249.

McHale, S. M., Bartko, W. T., Crouter, A. C., & Perry-Jenkins, M. (1990). Children's housework and psychosocial functioning: The mediating effects of parents' sex role behaviors and attitudes. *Child Development, 61,* 1413–1426.

Moody, J. (2001). Race, school integration, and friendship segregation in America. *American Journal of Sociology, 107*(3), 679–716.

Moore, J. W., Hauck, W. E., & Denne, T. C. (1984). Racial prejudice, interracial contact, and personality variables. *Journal of Experimental Education, 52*(3), 168–173.

Morland, J. K., & Hwang, C. H. (1981). Racial/ethnic identity of preschool children: Comparing Taiwan, Hong Kong and the United States. *Journal of Cross-Cultural Psychology, 12,* 409–424.

Nucci, L. P. (2001). *Education in the moral domain.* Cambridge, UK: Cambridge University Press.

Nucci, L. P., Camino, C., & Milnitsky-Sapiro, C. (1996). Social class effects on Northeastern Brazilian children's conceptions of areas of personal choice and social regulation. *Child Development, 67,* 1223–1242.

Nussbaum, M. (1999). *Sex and social justice.* Oxford: Oxford University Press.

Oakes, P. (2001). The root of all evil in intergroup relations? Unearthing the categorization process. In R. Brown & S. Gaertner (Eds.), *Blackwell handbook of social psychology. Vol. 4: Intergroup relations* (pp. 3–21). Oxford, UK: Blackwell.

Okin, S. M. (1989). *Justice, gender, and the family.* New York: Basic Books.

Oskamp, S. (Ed.). (2000). *Reducing prejudice and discrimination.* Hillsdale, NJ: Lawrence Erlbaum Associates.

Park, B., & Rothbart, M. (1982). Perception of out-group homogeneity and levels of social categorization: Memory for the subordinate attributes of in-group and out-group members. *Journal of Personality & Social Psychology, 42*(6), 1051–1068.

Pettigrew, T. F. (1997). Generalized intergroup contact effects on prejudice. *Personality and Social Psychological Bulletin, 23,* 173–185.

Pettigrew, T. F., & Tropp, L. (2000). Does intergroup contact reduce prejudice?: Recent meta-analytic findings. In S. Oskamp (Ed.), *Reducing prejudice and discrimination* (pp. 93–114). Mahwah, NJ: Lawrence Erlbaum Associates.

Phinney, J. S., & Cobb, N. J. (1996). Reasoning about intergroup relations among Hispanic and Euro-American adolescents. *Journal of Adolescent Research, 11*(3), 306–324.

Piaget, J. (1932). *The moral judgment of the child.* Oxford, UK: Harcourt, Brace.

Piaget, J. (1952). *The origins of intelligence in children.* New York: International Universities Press.

Powlishta, K. K., Serbin, L. A., Doyle, A., & White, D. R. (1994). Gender, ethnic, and body type biases: The generality of prejudice in childhood. *Developmental Psychology, 30*(4), 526–536.

Ramsey, P. G. (1991). The salience of race in young children growing up in an all-White community. *Journal of Educational Psychology, 83*(1), 28–34.

Ramsey, P. G., & Myers, L. C. (1990). Salience of race in young children's cognitive, affective, and behavioral responses to social environments. *Journal of Applied Developmental Psychology, 11*(1), 49–67.

Rawls, J. (1971). *A theory of justice.* Cambridge, MA: Harvard University Press.

Ritchey, P. N., & Fishbein, H. D. (2001). The lack of an association between adolescent friends' prejudices and stereotypes. *Merrill-Palmer Quarterly, 47*(2), 188–206.

Romero, A. J., & Roberts, R. E. (1998). Perception of discrimination and ethnocultural variables in a diverse group of adolescents. *Journal of Adolescence, 21*(6), 641–656.

Rubin, K. H., Bukowski, W., & Parker, J. (1998). Peer interactions, relationships and groups. In W. Damon (Series Ed.) & N. Eisenberg (Vol. Ed.), *Handbook of child psychology. Vol. 3: Social, emotional, and personality development* (5th ed., pp. 619–700). New York: Wiley.

Ruble, D. N., & Martin, C. L. (1998). Gender development. In W. Damon (Series Ed.) & N. Eisenberg (Vol. Ed.), *Handbook of child psychology. Vol. 3: Social, emotional, and personality development* (5th ed., pp.933–1016). New York: Wiley.

Ruck, M. D., Abramovitch, R., & Keating, D. P. (1998). Children's and adolescents' understanding of rights: Balancing nurturance and self-determination. *Child Development, 69,* 404–417.

Rudman, L. A. (2004). Sources of implicit attitudes. *Current Directions in Psychological Science, 13,* 79–82.

Rutland, A. (2004). The development and self-regulation of intergroup attitudes in children. In M. Bennett & F. Sani (Eds.), *The development of the social self* (pp. 247–265). East Sussex, UK: Psychology Press.

Sagar, H. A., & Schofield, J. W. (1980). Racial and behavioral cues in Black and White children's perceptions of ambiguously aggressive acts. *Journal of Personality and Social Psychology, 39,* 590–598.

Sinno, S., & Killen, M. (2004). *Children's evaluations of working mothers and caretaking fathers: Evidence for shifting standards in childhood.* University of Maryland.

Skowronski, J. J., & Lawrence, M. A. (2001). A comparative study of the implicit and explicit gender attitudes of children and college students. *Psychology of Women Quarterly, 25,* 155–165.

Smetana, J. G. (1985). Preschool children's concepts of transgressions: The effects of varying moral and conventional domain-related attributes. *Developmental Psychology, 21,* 18–29.

Smetana, J. G. (1995). Morality in context: Abstractions, ambiguities, and applications. In R. Vasta (Ed.), *Annals of child development* (Vol. 10, pp. 83–130). London: Jessica Kinglsey.

Stangor, C., & Schaller, M. (1996). Stereotypes as individual and collective representations. In C. N. Macrae, M. Hewstone, & C. Stangor (Eds.), *Foundations of stereotypes and stereotyping* (pp. 3–37). New York: Guilford Press.

Steele, C. M. (1997). A threat in the air: How stereotypes shape intellectual identity and performance. *American Psychologist, 52*(6), 613–629.

Stoddart, T., & Turiel, E. (1985). Children's concepts of cross-gender activities. *Child Development, 56,* 1241–1252.

Tajfel, H. (1978). *Differentiation between social groups: Studies in the social psychology of intergroup relations.* London: Academic Press.

Tajfel, H., & Turner, J. C. (1979). An integrative theory of intergroup conflict. In W.G. Austin & S. Worchel (Eds.), *The social psychology of intergroup relations* (pp. 33–47). Monterey, CA: Brooks-Cole.

Tamis-LaMonda, C. S., & Cabrera, N. (Eds.). (2003). *Handbook of father involvement: Multidisciplinary perspectives.* Hillsdale, NJ: Lawrence Erlbaum Associates.

Theimer, C. E., Killen, M., & Stangor, C. (2001). Preschool children's evaluations of exclusion in gender-stereotypic contexts. *Developmental Psychology, 37,* 1–10.

Tisak, M. S. (1986). Children's conceptions of parental authority. *Child Development, 57,* 166–176.

Turiel, E. (1983). *The development of social knowledge: Morality and convention.* Cambridge, UK: Cambridge University Press.

Turiel, E. (1998). The development of morality. In W. Damon (Ed.), *Handbook of child psychology. Vol. 3: Social, emotional, and personality development* (5th ed., pp. 863–932). New York: Wiley.

Turiel, E. (2002). *The culture of morality.* Cambridge, UK: Cambridge University Press.

Turiel, E., & Neff, K. D. (2000). Religion, culture, and beliefs about reality in moral reasoning. In K. Rosengren, C. Johnson, & P. Harris (Eds.), *Imagining the impossible: The development of magical, scientific and religious thinking in contemporary society.* Cambridge, UK: Cambridge University Press.

Vandiver, T. (2001). Children's social competence, academic competence, and aggressiveness as related to ability to make judgments of fairness. *Psychological Reports, 89*(1), 111–121.

Verkuyten, M., Kinket, B., & van der Wielen, C. (1997). Preadolescents' understanding of ethnic discrimination. *Journal of Genetic Psychology, 158*(1), 97–112.

Verkuyten, M., & Thijs, J. (2002). Racist victimization among children in The Netherlands: The effect of ethnic group and school. *Ethnic and Racial Studies, 25*(2), 310–331.

Wainryb, C., Shaw, L., Laupa, M., & Smith, K. R. (2001). Children's, adolescents', and young adults' thinking about different types of disagreements. *Developmental Psychology, 37,* 373–386.

Wainryb, C., & Turiel, E. (1994). Dominance, subordination, and concepts of personal entitlements in cultural contexts. *Child Development, 65,* 1701–1722.

Wainryb, C., & Turiel, E. (1995). Diversity in social development: Between or within cultures? In M. Killen & D. Hart (Eds.), *Morality in everyday life: Developmental perspectives* (pp. 283–316). Cambridge, UK: Cambridge University Press.

Williams, E., & Radin, N. (1999). Effects of father participation in child rearing: Twenty-year follow-up. *American Journal of Orthopsychiatry, 69*(3), 328–336.

Wood, G. S. (2003, December 14). Slaves in the family. *The New York Times,* p. 10.

7

Rights, Civil Liberties, and Democracy Across Cultures

Charles C. Helwig
University of Toronto

Recently there have been extensive debates and discussions about human rights and democracy. The meaning of these terms, and their applicability to diverse nations and cultural settings, are matters of disagreement within academic circles and in public and international foreign policy debates. On the one hand, the historian Michael Ignatieff has labeled the current widespread interest in human rights as a "Rights Revolution" (Ignatieff, 2000). Evidence of the universal appeal of human rights may be seen in the endorsement of the United Nations Universal Declaration of Human Rights across the globe by nations with different political and cultural systems, together with recent efforts at its implementation in international law. On the other hand, others have charged that notions of rights and democracy are mere ideological red herrings, used to promote the hegemonic political interests of powerful Western nations by imposing Western-style political systems on cultures where these ideas are foreign and unwanted.

Are rights and democracy uniquely Western notions, and therefore limited in their appeal, or do they, in at least some aspect, have validity and currency beyond Western cultural traditions and peoples? Commentators on both sides of this issue frequently claim to know what people think and believe without directly consulting the available empirical evidence. This chapter examines research on the development of concepts of rights, civil liberties, and democracy conducted in both Western and non-Western cultures. Attempts to account for the development of notions of rights and democracy by theoretical perspectives such as global stage theories of moral judgment (Kohlberg, 1981) and cultural psychology (Shweder, 1999) are critically evaluated. Such perspectives draw on global stages or broad, culturally defined orientations and are unable to account for several aspects of the research findings, including (a) contextual variations in judgments about rights and democracy found within cultures, and (b) important commonalities in reasoning about these concepts uncovered throughout development and in diverse cultures. An alternative account is described that explains these commonalities and variations by drawing on models of social development that propose that individuals develop distinct moral concepts of rights and democracy early in childhood, and coordinate these ideas in their reasoning with other features of social situations in increasingly sophisticated ways throughout development.

RESEARCH ON CIVIL LIBERTIES AND RIGHTS IN WESTERN CULTURAL CONTEXTS: SURVEY AND GLOBAL STAGE APPROACHES

Research has been conducted over the last several decades on attitudes and reasoning about rights and civil liberties such as freedom of speech and religion, along with other aspects of democratic political systems. Initial research on these topics was carried out in the 1950s, 1960s, and 1970s by political scientists who conducted large-scale surveys of the attitudes of American adults and children toward civil liberties and rights (McClosky & Brill, 1983; Prothro & Grigg, 1960; Sarat, 1975; Stouffer, 1955; Zellman & Sears, 1971), and by developmental psychologists who generally adhered to global stage perspectives such as those of Piaget or Kohlberg (e.g., Gallatin & Adelson, 1970, 1971; Melton, 1980). Both of these general lines of research have led to the conclusion that conceptions of rights and civil liberties are often poorly understood by many individuals, including children, adolescents, and the general public. In this section, research stemming from each of these paradigms is discussed, to illustrate the findings that have led to this pessimistic view, before turning to recent theoretical formulations and research that has called into question some of these conclusions.

In survey research, political scientists have pursued a research strategy of posing individuals with questions examining their support for civil liberties in general or in the abstract (e.g., "I believe in freedom of speech for all no matter what their view might be") and in a series of concrete situations. A consistent finding of these surveys is that although high levels of support for civil liberties is found when questions are abstract, much less support for civil liberties is found in concrete situations. For example, only 29% of adult respondents thought that members of the Nazi Party or Ku Klux Klan should be allowed to appear on television to state their views, and only 14% thought that books showing terrorists how to build bombs should be available in the public library (McClosky & Brill, 1983). Similarly, Zellman and Sears (1971) found little correlation between children's endorsement of values such as freedom of speech in general and their judgments about whether Nazis, Communists, or Viet Cong supporters should be allowed to give public speeches or to appear on television. Instead, Zellman and Sears (1971) found that judgments in concrete situations were most related to the strength of the attitude (positive or negative) held toward the group attempting to exercise its freedom of expression. Studies of attitudes held by elites, such as highly educated professionals, however, reveal more consistency between judgments in the abstract and in concrete situations (McClosky & Brill, 1983). A common interpretation of these survey findings is that, for the general public at least, civil liberties such as freedom of speech are appealed to only as general "slogans" that are held without conviction or true understanding (Prothro & Grigg, 1960; Sarat, 1975; Zellman & Sears, 1971).

Somewhat similar conclusions were reached by some developmental psychologists conducting research on children's and adolescents' moral judgments, including their understandings of concepts of rights and civil liberties. Much of this research was influenced by Kohlberg's moral developmental theory, which postulates a series of six stages, organized within three broad levels, in the development of moral understandings. Beginning in childhood, a concrete, punishment orientation is held, in which moral rightness or wrongness initially is determined by authority or power. In adolescence, an intermediate, conventional level is usually reached, in which right action is defined as that which upholds the existing social organization or adheres to laws or social customs. The sequence culminates in a principled level, reached by a minority of adults, in which morality is defined in terms of abstract principles of justice, universal rights, and human dignity (Kohlberg, 1981). Research employing the Kohlbergian paradigm examined children's and adults' moral reasoning about a series of dilemmas, such as whether or not a husband should steal a drug to save the life of his dying wife (the Heinz dilemma). The normative moral orientation of individuals in both Western and non-Western societies has been found to be Stage four of the conventional level of Kohlberg's system, with its emphasis on upholding the social order and its existing laws, customs, and social conventions, often at the expense of individual rights, due process, and equality (Snarey, 1985).

Although Kohlberg's formulation draws conclusions about the concept of rights held at each of the levels from responses to such general moral dilemmas, concepts of rights themselves were not directly investigated. Others, however, have drawn on Kohlberg's system as a guide to interpret the findings of their own studies that directly investigated the development of notions of rights. For example, Melton (1980) investigated children's conceptions of their own rights, both through probes asking children to define *rights,* and by examining their judgments and reasoning in a series of dilemmas in which children's rights (including rights to freedom of expression, privacy, work, and due process) conflicted with the demands of school authorities, parents, or older peers. Melton (1980) found three broad levels in children's understanding of rights, paralleling Kohlberg's stage sequence. At younger ages (6 to 8 years), rights were conceptualized as simply equivalent to powers or privileges granted to children and revocable by authority figures. Older participants (8 to 13 years old) increasingly viewed rights as based on fairness and serving to uphold the social order; only a minority of adolescents (and even adults, see Melton & Limber, 1992) reached the third level, in which rights are based on universal, abstract ethical principles and conceptualized as natural rights that cannot be revoked by authority figures.

Other research has examined children's and adolescents' conceptions of rights in political settings, such as that of government and society (Gallatin & Adelson, 1970, 1971). Gallatin and Adelson (1970, 1971) investigated American, German, and British children's and adolescents' conceptions of individual rights and civil liberties in situations in which these rights conflicted with broader societal concerns, such as public welfare, societal order, or national defense. For example, participants were asked whether freedom of speech should be rescinded in a national emergency or war time, whether members of a religion opposed to vaccination should be required by the state to undergo the procedure, or whether men over age 45 should be required to submit to a yearly medical examination. They were also asked to give examples of laws that should be unchangeable, as in a constitutional Bill of Rights.

Gallatin and Adelson (1970, 1971) found developmental differences in judgments of some situations, in the kinds of reasoning used to support decisions in the conflicts, and in the types of laws judged to be unchangeable. Older adolescents were more likely than younger or pre-adolescents to view laws such as those requiring medical examinations as infringing on individuals' freedom and privacy. In their reasoning about conflicts between individual rights and the public good, older adolescents were more likely to articulate general principles, such as protection of individuals' privacy or freedom, or societal interests such as "the public welfare," or "the national good," whereas younger adolescents and pre-adolescents were more likely to appeal to concrete consequences, such as the immediate threat of disease or other negative effects of actions. As well, older adolescents were more likely to identify civil liberties, such as freedom of speech or religion, as areas that should be protected by permanent laws. Although there were some minor national differences in responding—most notably a tendency for Americans to give priority to individual freedom in some conflicts—these general developmental patterns held up across the three nationalities studied. Gallatin and Adelson (1970) conclude that pre-adolescents possess "only a dim grasp of abstract political concepts" (p. 226) and that abstract conceptions of individual liberty develop in mid-adolescence and are probably related to global shifts in reasoning associated with cognitive development, such as the attainment of formal operations and hypotheticodeductive reasoning (Inhelder & Piaget, 1958).

GLOBAL STAGE APPROACHES AND SURVEY RESEARCH: SOME CONCEPTUAL AND METHODOLOGICAL PROBLEMS

The research reviewed in the previous section has led to the conclusions that abstract concepts of civil liberties develop either, at best, later in adolescence (e.g., Gallatin & Adelson, 1970), or at worst, not at all in the majority of the population (e.g., McClosky & Brill, 1983; Melton, 1980; Melton & Limber, 1992; Sarat, 1975). However, these conclusions about the judgments and reasoning of younger children and adolescents and the general public need to be reconsidered in the light of several limitations that have been identified regarding this research (Helwig, 1995a; Helwig & Turiel, 2002; Turiel, Killen, & Helwig, 1987). First, some of the assessments used in this research required children to provide definitions of abstract terms such as *rights*, or to generate examples, such as laws that should be constitutionally guaranteed (Gallatin & Adelson, 1971; Melton, 1980). Research in other areas has shown that people can possess considerable implicit knowledge of concepts such as social causality, number, and the structural principles of language, even though they are not able to articulate these principles when asked directly about them, or generate relevant examples (e.g., Nisbett & Wilson, 1977; Shweder, Mahaptra, & Miller, 1987). Correspondingly, many of the methods used in the prior research on rights probably elicited strong production demands that may have led to a bias against less verbally articulate younger children, or even older adolescents and adults in some instances. These methods may draw on the development of moral reflection and metacognitive abilities that would be expected to develop only in adolescence, and that may vary by individuals, even in adulthood (Moshman, 1998).

Second, the model of social reasoning that appears to underlie much of this research may be problematic and incomplete. In both the survey and developmental psychological research, participants were presented with situations that entailed applications of these rights in conflict with other social and moral issues (e.g., law, public welfare or harm, equality). An underlying (and sometimes explicit) assumption of this model is that notions of civil liberties or rights are seen as abstract, principled, or genuine only if they override other social and moral concerns in contextualized judgments. Thus, commitment to civil liberties or individual rights is questioned if individuals are found to give priority to other issues in some situations (e.g., Sarat, 1975; Zellman & Sears, 1971). However, this model assumes that rights and civil liberties must be absolute to be genuinely held, a position that fails to take into account potential exceptions to moral principles, such as when rights conflict with other important moral and social concerns implicated in certain situations. Many of the survey examples and conflicts used in the research appear to be of this nature; they raise important conflicting moral issues, such as the dissemination of racial hatred (e.g., speeches by the Nazis or Ku Klux Klan), perceived threats to the democratic political system or the nation state (e.g., as in war or national emergency), or even physical harm or violence (e.g., terrorism). Moral philosophers have argued that genuinely held concepts of rights may be legitimately overridden by other concerns in some circumstances (Dworkin, 1977; Meldon, 1977). Both the survey and global stage approaches thus may have missed or underestimated important conceptions of rights or civil liberties by focusing mainly or exclusively on reasoning and judgments about rights in difficult conflicts.

ACCOUNTING FOR CONTEXTUAL VARIATIONS: RECENT RESEARCH ON RIGHTS AND CIVIL LIBERTIES IN ADOLESCENCE

More recent research has explored the development of understandings of individual freedom and rights by examining the general criteria by which children and adolescents reason about these concepts, such as their independence from authority or laws, and how concepts of rights and freedoms are applied to a variety of situations, including both conflicts of different types and in more straightforward situations (Helwig, 1995a, 1997, 1998). In Helwig (1995a), participants (7th and 11th graders and college students) were presented with a series of general questions about freedoms and their applications in a variety of situations. The general questions were meant to assess criterial aspects of concepts of freedoms, such as whether these rights would be seen as moral rights (Gewirth, 1978) and judged to be universal across cultures, and, correspondingly, whether general legal restrictions placed on these rights by governments would be viewed as wrong. The applications in concrete situations were designed to determine whether individuals understand basic applications of freedoms in straightforward situations (e.g., an individual giving a public speech critical of the government's economic policy) and how they would reason about freedoms when in conflict with other social and moral issues as, for example, in speech that contains racial slurs or advocates violence, or in religious rituals in which psychological or physical harm was inflicted on consenting participants.

The findings indicated that at all ages, concepts of freedom of speech and religion were held as "natural rights" independent of authority and laws and generalized across cultural contexts (Helwig, 1995a). In their reasoning, adolescents appealed to a number of rationales typically used by moral and political philosophers to justify these rights (Emerson, 1970). Freedom of speech was seen as important in fulfilling individual psychological needs for self-expression and autonomy, in ensuring access to and free flow of information, in leading to societal progress by facilitating the discovery of useful innovations, and in fulfilling democratic moral functions of political representation and voice (e.g., by ensuring that minority voices are expressed in a democratic political order). In contrast, freedom of religion was conceived as an important avenue for individual self-expression within a shared identity and group tradition. All of these rationales were used to support these freedoms by even the youngest adolescents (13-year-olds).

Participants at all ages in Helwig (1995a) applied these concepts to straightforward situations and rejected government laws or restrictions on exercising civil liberties as wrong; they also applied freedoms in some, although not all, conflicts. They were especially inclined to argue that civil liberties should not be given priority in situations in which physical harm was seen as a likely consequence. There were also age differences in whether or not freedoms were seen to override certain conflicting issues. Younger adolescents were more likely than older adolescents to support restrictions on civil liberties when they conflicted with issues of equality, as in speech advocating exclusion of low-income people from political parties, or in the case of a religion that prohibits low-income people from holding important positions in the organization. Younger adolescents also were more likely than older adolescents to judge that hypothetical laws restricting civil liberties should be followed, even though they judged these restrictive laws to be wrong and unjust. It appears that evaluations of laws restricting civil liberties and judgments of compliance to these unjust laws become better integrated and coordinated in individuals' reasoning with development (Helwig, 1995b).

The latter finding may help to shed light on the conventional orientation that proponents of global stage approaches claim to be normative of moral reasoning in adolescence and adulthood (Kohlberg, 1981). Recall that the conclusion in Kohlbergian theory that individuals are "conventional" in their moral orientation, and in their corresponding conceptions of rights, is drawn from studies of judgments and reasoning about situations in which individuals may be required to violate laws to uphold rights (e.g., the Heinz dilemma). However, as the findings from Helwig (1995a) indicate, it would be problematic to conclude that individuals who advocate compliance with such laws do not distinguish rights from social conventions or authority, or that they see rights as deriving solely from these sources. Instead, individuals sometimes make judgments of rights independent of authority and law, such as when they are asked to make judgments about the criteria that define rights or to apply them in straightforward situations, and at other times they subordinate rights to laws, such as when making judgments of obedience or compliance to unfair laws. A methodology that does not allow for the separation of these different dimensions of judgments is thus likely to underestimate or misrepresent individuals' ability to distinguish rights from social conventions and legal norms.

The same general pattern of endorsement of rights and freedoms in some situations but subordination of rights to other social and moral issues in other situations has been found in other cross-national and cross-cultural studies. Clemence, Doise, de Rosa, and Gonzalez (1995) investigated judgments of rights in Costa Rica, France, Italy, and Switzerland. In this study, participants ranging in age from 13 to 20 years were presented with a set of situations and asked to judge whether or not each example constituted a violation of human rights. Some situations, such as imprisoning individuals for protesting against the government or discrimination against ethnic minorities, were judged to be human rights violations by the majority of individuals in all countries. However, in other situations, concern for community welfare or issues of law and order were judged to override individual rights and freedoms. This occurred for situations such as government tapping of phone conversations, capital punishment, or laws requiring that individuals with infectious diseases be admitted to hospitals.

Some research has begun to investigate judgments of civil liberties and other rights in non-Western, traditional societies. One study examined adolescents' and adults' judgments and reasoning about rights in the Muslim society of the Druze (Turiel & Wainryb, 1998). The Druze are a religious community based on the Koran, living in segregated and isolated villages in Israel. The research used a similar methodology as Helwig (1995a), examining civil liberties such as freedom of speech and religion and other rights both in general and in a variety of situations in which freedoms conflicted with other concerns, such as avoiding harm, community interest, and paternal authority. It was found that civil liberties were endorsed in general and in some situations, especially when the conflicting interest was not strong. However, in other situations in which the salience of the conflicting concern was strong—such as when making judgments about religious practices that entailed harm or about the reproductive freedom of a couple with a past history of neglecting their children—rights were often subordinated to other issues. Several specific parallels were found between the reasoning of the Druze adolescents in this study and the

American adolescents in Helwig (1995a). Adolescents in both cultures appealed to similar rationales to justify rights like freedom of speech, such as psychological justifications (or beliefs about universal human needs for autonomy and self-expression) and democratic principles served by these rights. In both cultures, there was also an increasing tendency with age to judge violations of unjust laws restricting civil liberties to be acceptable, suggesting that legal and moral obligations become coordinated in development in ways that tend toward giving priority to civil liberties over obedience to existing laws. Turiel and Wainryb's (1998) findings show that individuals in a traditional, non-Western society develop sophisticated concepts of civil liberties that they apply to situations in meaningful ways, and they further suggest that at least some of the age-related variation in judgments and reasoning about these concepts may follow culturally general developmental patterns.

In sum, the findings of the recent research reviewed illustrate the importance of separating different dimensions of judgment in studies of reasoning about rights and civil liberties, including accounting for similarities and differences in judgments of rights in the abstract and in contextualized situations of different types. By directly examining the role of criteria believed to define the moral domain (e.g., universality and non contingency on laws and authority), several aspects of reasoning about civil liberties and rights were identified that appear to be continuous across development in adolescence. These include the conceptualization of civil liberties as universal rights believed to be independent of social convention and law, and their association with substantive rationales that historically have been invoked to justify and support these rights in philosophical and political theorizing. At the same time, although individuals have been found to apply these rights in many situations (both straightforward situations and in conflict with other issues), they sometimes subordinate rights to other social and moral concerns, including issues such as compliance with laws and conflicting moral norms and values, such as avoidance of harm and the unequal treatment of individuals. However, rather than indicating that people do not understand civil liberties, as suggested by some political scientists (e.g., Prothro & Grigg, 1960), recent research demonstrates both a genuine understanding of, and commitment to, civil liberties among individuals of a variety of ages, nationalities, and cultures, coupled with the recognition that civil liberties are not the only social and moral concern operating in individuals' moral judgments (Helwig, 1995a; Helwig & Turiel, 2002).

The contextual variation found in this research is not compatible with global stage approaches that characterize the reasoning of adolescents as based on a purely social conventional understanding of rights and civil liberties (Kohlberg, 1981; Melton, 1980). However, the overall pattern of results is consistent with models of social reasoning that postulate the early differentiation of domains of social and moral concepts, such as morality and social convention, and their interrelation in increasingly complex ways throughout development (Helwig, 1995b; Turiel, 1998). This perspective, commonly termed the *domain approach,* postulates that children construct multiple forms of social understanding through their encounters with different types of social experiences. These understandings include moral conceptions based on a concern with justice, fairness, and harm, as well as social-conventional conceptions based on authority, tradition, and explicit social rules and customs. According to this perspective, the reasoning of individuals cannot be described in terms of a global or central tendency to emphasize one form of social reasoning over the other at different points in development. Rather, individuals give priority to different concerns depending on a variety of factors, such as the particular features of situations that are perceived to be salient and the way that different types of conflicting concerns are coordinated at different points in development (Helwig, 1995b; Neff & Helwig, 2002; Turiel, 1998).

ORIGINS AND PRECURSORS: CONCEPTIONS OF RIGHTS AND CIVIL LIBERTIES IN CHILDHOOD

One issue raised by the research described in the previous section is whether concepts of rights, personal autonomy, and civil liberties develop prior to adolescence. Several lines of research have begun to explore judgments of rights and civil liberties in childhood (Helwig, 1997, 1998; Nucci, 1981, 2001; Ruck, Abramovitch, & Keating, 1998). One line of research, conducted within the social domain approach (see also Turiel, chap. 1, and Smetana, chap. 2, this volume) has explored children's understandings of *personal issues*, areas over which children are believed to have personal decision-making autonomy. Conceptions of rights have been connected to the development of an area or domain of personal autonomy over which persons, including sometimes children, are judged to be free from the interference of other individuals or authorities (Gewirth, 1978; Nucci & Lee, 1993). In research on personal issues, children are typically presented with examples of different kinds of choices and asked to judge whether they should be up to children to decide, or they are asked to evaluate the appropriateness of hypothetical rules or restrictions placed on children's choices by authorities such as parents or teachers. This method contrasts with the dilemma methodology used in the global stage approach described previously.

Studies with American children and adolescents (e.g., Nucci, 1981; Smetana, 1989) have found that rules by authorities restricting or prohibiting children from making their own decisions about matters such as choice of friends, recreational activities, and appearance (e.g., hairstyles or choices over clothing) are judged by even young children to be wrong or illegitimate. These judgments are typically justified by references to children's desires or needs for personal choice or autonomy, or by explicit appeals to their rights. The personal domain appears to develop, beginning in the preschool years and continuing throughout adolescence, in the context of situations in which children claim for themselves decision-making autonomy over increasingly greater areas of their lives (Nucci, 2001; Smetana, 2002). The construction of a personal domain has been found in a variety of other cultural settings, including Brazil (Nucci, Camino, & Sapiro, 1996), Columbia (Ardila-Rey & Killen, 2001), Japan (Killen & Sueyoshi, 1995), and Hong Kong (Yau & Smetana, 2003a). The finding that children develop an area of personal decision-making autonomy that leads them to reject authority dictates or control in some situations contrasts with the conclusion reached by proponents of global stage perspectives that young children define their own rights or autonomy solely in the form of privileges granted to them by adults (e.g., Melton, 1980).

The development of conceptions of personal autonomy would be expected to be a prerequisite for notions of civil liberties, such as freedom of speech and religion. Recall that one of the underlying rationales for civil liberties such as freedom of speech found among the reasoning of adolescents was that these rights should be protected because they are associated with basic, universal, psychological needs for autonomy and self-expression. These perceived universal human needs may provide one source of grounding for a generalized concept of universal or human rights that can be used to place limits on the actions of governments or other authorities.

Research investigating Canadian elementary school age children's judgments of freedom of speech and religion has found that understandings of these general features of moral rights appear to have developed by early childhood. For example, children as young as 6 years of age view freedom of speech and religion as universal rights that should apply in all cultures, and they negatively evaluate general restrictions placed on these rights by governments as wrong or illegitimate (Helwig, 1997, 1998). In these studies, developmental differences were found in the kinds of rationales used to support freedom of speech and religion in childhood. Younger children (6-year-olds) tended to support civil liberties by appeals to needs for personal choice and individual expression, suggesting that they link rights like freedom of speech and religion to their developing notions of a personal sphere at an early age. However, beginning around 8 years of age, children also begin to perceive broader societal, cultural, and democratic implications of these rights. For example, older children saw freedom of speech as fostering communication among individuals that could lead to societal innovations, or they perceived it as an important means by which societal injustices could be corrected through enabling individuals to voice their concerns in protests or petitions (Helwig, 1998). As children develop a more sophisticated concept of the political sphere and the possibilities of different types of political action, their understanding of the value and function of civil liberties within a democratic political order is enhanced. At no age in these studies were children's conceptions of civil liberties found to be defined by authority, existing societal laws, or culturally specific forms of social organization.

This research suggests that the basic features of civil liberties as moral rights have developed by early childhood. This does not suggest that important developments in reasoning about rights and civil liberties do not occur during childhood or beyond. Age differences have been found in how these rights are applied in different social contexts that are related to development in children's understanding of the features of situations and the role played by factors such as perceptions of the competence and maturity of agents to exercise their rights. For example, in one study (Helwig, 1997), children, adolescents, and adults were asked to evaluate whether it would be acceptable for different authorities (e.g., the government, a school principal, parents) to prohibit either adults or children from exercising their free speech rights (e.g., by talking about rock music) or practicing a religion different from that of the authority when the authority disapproves. Younger children tended not to draw distinctions between the rights of adults and children or between the social contexts of the family, the school, or society at large, using general concepts of personal choice and individual autonomy to argue in support of both children's and adults' rights to freedom of speech and religion. However, starting at around 11 years of age, distinctions began to be made between the rights of children and adults in different social contexts. For example, many older children and adults judged it as acceptable for parents to restrict their young child's right to practice a religion different from that of the parents, while at the same time they did not believe that school principals or the government could similarly restrict children's rights. It was viewed also as unacceptable for parents to restrict their offsprings' rights to practice a different religion once their child became an adult. These distinctions were justified by beliefs about young children's lack of competence to make decisions about matters such as religion, and by beliefs about the special role of parents in children's socialization, including their "right" to socialize their children in accordance with their own religious beliefs. These age-related patterns in judgments and reasoning suggest that older children and adults were weighing and considering a broader set of factors in making judgments about children's rights, leading to applications of rights in context that were more nuanced, discriminative, and context sensitive than those of younger children.

Similar contextual variations in applications of rights have been found in other recent research on children's conceptions of their own rights. Researchers (Cherney & Perry, 1996; Ruck et al., 1998) have distinguished between two types of rights pertinent to children: nurturance and self-determination rights. *Nurturance rights* refer to children's rights to care and protection and include such issues as parental provision of food and clothing, protection, and emotional support. *Self-determination rights* refer to children's rights to autonomy and control over their lives and include many of the types of rights we have discussed up to this point, such as those covered by the research on personal issues (Nucci, 1981) and civil liberties (Helwig, 1995b, 1997). Ruck and colleagues (1998) found that children and adolescents distinguished between the two types of rights in ways that showed developmental patterns. Children and younger adolescents were more likely to support children's nurturance rights than self-determination rights; however, this difference disappeared by mid-adolescence, when support for self-determination rights increased. Responses were found to vary by the specific situation that children were asked to judge within each of these types of rights, however. For example, although 100% of 14-year-olds believed that children had a right to keep a secret diary, only 20% believed that children should have the right to vote. Ruck and co-workers (1998) concluded that this pattern of variation in judgments and reasoning by different types of rights and situations "does not support a strong global stage interpretation of children's reasoning about their rights" (p. 413).

The findings reviewed thus far suggest that concepts of rights and freedoms emerge in early childhood and are linked, at least initially, to developing conceptions of autonomy and personal choice (and in the case of nurturance rights, to children's welfare). The development of notions of rights and freedoms does not follow a pattern of the differentiation of rights from the dictates of authority, social convention, or legal rules (Kohlberg, 1981), but instead may be better understood in terms of increasingly sophisticated applications of rights in complex social situations. As children consider a broader range of issues implicated in different situations, including conflicting moral or legal concerns, the competence of agents to exercise their rights, and the functions and purposes of rights within a democratic political order, their judgments and reasoning become more sophisticated and sensitive to myriad features of social context.

Civil liberties and freedoms are generally believed to be important aspects of democratic political systems, and historically ideas about freedoms and democracy have been seen as developing in parallel (Held, 1996). The preceding review illustrated how democratic principles have been invoked both as an important rationale for civil liberties such as freedom of speech, and sometimes to circumscribe these rights when they conflict with other democratic ideals, such as equality. In the next section, the development of conceptions of democracy and democratic decision making is considered.

DEMOCRACY AND DEMOCRATIC DECISION MAKING: RESEARCH IN SOCIETIES WITH WESTERN-STYLE POLITICAL SYSTEMS

Democracy comprises forms of social organization in which individuals are given a say in decisions that affect them (Cohen, 1971). Democracy, in its varied forms, is frequently justified as serving general or universal moral aims of justice and respect for persons (Cohen, 1971; Richardson, 2002). Democratic procedures of social decision making that allow individuals from various segments of society to express their viewpoints (either directly or through their elected representatives), and to have an impact on social policies or decisions, have been argued to help protect individuals from the arbitrary exercise of political power and to provide a means for correcting existing injustices in policies or practices.

Early research on the development of concepts of government and democracy, conducted in Western cultures, examined children's and adolescents' understandings of political terms, including *government, representation,* and *democracy* (Connell, 1971; Greenstein, 1965). Greenstein (1965), for example, asked children to define abstract terms such as democracy or to explain the functions and roles of different branches of government. Children's ability to define these terms or to identify the roles of different branches of government was found to be very limited prior to adolescence, and their political understandings were characterized as concrete, fragmentary, and largely based on affect (Greenstein, 1965).

This research, however, may be subject to many of the same sorts of criticisms leveled at the research on rights discussed earlier, given the reliance on children's ability to define abstract terms such as democracy or to explain the functioning of complex political systems. Recent research (Helwig, 1998) examining judgments and reasoning about democracy under less strenuous task demands, however, has indicated that even young children comprehend many of the basic features of democracy, suggesting that children's understandings were underestimated in the earlier research.

In Helwig (1998), Canadian children's (6 to 11 years of age) conceptions of democratic government were investigated, not by asking them to provide definitions of democracy, but rather by requiring them to make judgments about the fairness of "classic" systems of government that either possessed, or did not possess, critical features of democracy. Each of the examples was presented in the context of a scenario in which the people of a new country are deciding on the form of their government. Among the democratic systems contrasted were (a) a representative government, or government by officials elected by the people in regular elections; (b) a direct democracy, in which the entire population participates directly in decision making and decisions are made by majority rule; and (c) a democracy by strict consensus, in which everyone in the nation must agree on all decisions. All of these democratic systems serve the essential democratic function of voice, or allowing the people as a whole to have input into decision making and governance, although the means by which this is accomplished varies across these examples. The nondemocratic systems included (a) a meritocracy, or government by the smartest or most capable individuals (as determined by a test of knowledge), and (b) an oligarchy in which the most wealthy ruled the country. The nondemocratic systems fail to meet democratic standards of voice and equal representation of citizens in political decision making, although they may be perceived to have pragmatic advantages (e.g., as in government by the most knowledgeable).

It was found that, at all ages, democratic systems were preferred and judged as more fair than nondemocratic systems (Helwig, 1998). In supporting democratic systems, children appealed to fundamental democratic principles such as voice, or the necessity of everyone having a say in decision making, and to notions of fairness based on majority rule. The nondemocratic systems were rejected as unfair because of their partiality and failure to represent the views of the people as a whole. Developmental differences were found within evaluations of the democratic systems. A substantial proportion of younger children (6-year-olds) preferred democracy by consensus, in which everyone in a nation had to agree on every decision, whereas older children tended to reject this system as impractical because of the impossibility of achieving consensus in a large and diverse nation state. Older children, instead, tended to prefer majority rule (direct democracy). Subsequent research with Canadian adolescents (Helwig, 2003) indicates that preferences for majority rule tend to be replaced in mid-adolescence by preferences for representative democracy, as older adolescents begin to identify practical problems with entrusting decision making to the majority of the population, who may not have the time or expertise to devote to making properly informed decisions.

Several aspects of these findings are noteworthy. First, they reveal that even in the early elementary school years, children are aware of and committed to fundamental democratic principles such as voice and representation, to the point that they give priority to these

principles over other, more pragmatic functions of government, such as decision making by the most knowledgeable. Second, the findings cannot be accounted for merely in
terms of political socialization or the absorption of learned political content. At the same
time that these Canadian children are first being exposed in formal education to the representative Parliamentary system (around late childhood), they nonetheless prefer direct
democracy as an ideal. A preference for representative democracy only clearly emerges
in mid-adolescence, well after they have been exposed to the features of their own system
of government in their formal education and general experience. Conceptions of group
decision-making fairness based on majority rule, and not mere identification with the political system of their own society, appear to account for important aspects of children's
judgments of political fairness. These findings suggest that children do not simply directly
assimilate moral–political judgments from the surrounding political structure, but rather
use their emerging conceptions of the fairness of group decision-making procedures to
evaluate alternative forms of government, including that of the society in which they live.

This interpretation is supported by findings from a small body of research on children's
judgments of the fairness of decision-making procedures such as majority rule in other
social contexts, besides that of government (Helwig & Kim, 1999; Kinoshita, 1989; Mann
& Greenbaum, 1987; Moessinger, 1981). In these studies, children were presented with
a set of decisions that needed to be made by a group of children, such as where a school
class would go on a field trip. This research has found that elementary school age children
from a variety of countries, including Canada, Switzerland, Australia, Israel, and Japan,
uphold majority rule as a fair procedure for making a variety of decisions in social groups.
Majority rule appears to be a strong determinant of fair group decision making in childhood.
Children's preferences for direct democracy in judgments of political fairness therefore
may be due to a generalization from other, more local contexts, such as the peer group
or school, where majority rule is judged as fair. However, by mid-adolescence, once
the special problems of applying majority rule at the national level are recognized and
appreciated, other forms of democratic political decision making, such as representative
democracy, begin to replace majority rule in judgments and reasoning about political
fairness.

Indeed, research on elementary school age children's judgments of decision making
in an array of social contexts has shown that children appear to become increasingly
proficient with age at distinguishing when and where majority rule or other decision-
making procedures are appropriate for decisions that involved children (Helwig & Kim,
1999). Helwig and Kim (1999) contrasted Canadian children's judgments about decision
making within more egalitarian social contexts, such as the peer group, with decision
making in more hierarchical social contexts such as the family or school classroom. It was
expected that decision-making procedures such as majority rule or consensus that gave
children the same input into group decision making as adults, would be more likely to
be endorsed in egalitarian than hierarchical social contexts, and decision making by adult
authorities alone would be more likely to be preferred in the hierarchical social contexts.
However, it was also expected that the type of decision being made would play an important
role, such that children's own decision-making autonomy would be endorsed for some
decisions made even in hierarchical social contexts, especially when these decisions did
not implicate the potential for harm or conflict with other important social goals, such as
education.

The findings of Helwig & Kim (1999) largely bore out these expectations. Judgments
of decision-making procedures varied by social context, with procedures such as majority
rule and consensus more likely to be endorsed in decisions in the peer group than in the

family or school. Evaluations of procedures also varied within social contexts, in ways that revealed support both for democratic decision making and decision making by adult authority for different decisions. For example, in the school context, children judged that decisions about where a school class should go on a field trip should be made by the vote of the class (majority rule), but not for decisions about the curriculum, which they believed should be up to the teacher to decide. Similar distinctions between decisions were found in other social contexts, such as the family, where, for example, children tended to believe that a decision about a family vacation should be made democratically, by majority rule or consensus, but decisions about other matters, such as what school a child should attend, were more likely to be seen as best decided by parents. In deciding whether or not children should have the right to input in decision making, participants considered the competence of children to make informed decisions about the matter in question, as well as the general goals of the social organizational context (Helwig & Kim, 1999). For example, children were seen as competent to make decisions about school field trips, which were generally seen as largely recreational in nature and thus dependent on children's interests and wishes, whereas broader curriculum decisions were seen as serving educational goals and outside the scope of children's competence, and thus best left to more qualified adults.

Children's reasoning about the suitability of different democratic procedures (i.e., majority rule versus consensus) also showed subtle discriminations by social context (Helwig & Kim, 1999). One issue children considered when reasoning about which decision-making procedure was appropriate was the likelihood of reaching agreement in different social contexts. For example, consensus was seen as more appropriate for decisions made in small groups, such as the family or the peer group, where differences of opinion were fewer and could be resolved through discussion. However, in larger groups such as the classroom, where divergence of opinion might be greater and compromise more difficult to achieve, children preferred more formal democratic procedures such as voting or majority rule.

The ability to coordinate different types of decisions and social contexts developed with age (Helwig & Kim, 1999). Older children made more distinctions between social contexts and decision-making procedures than younger children. Interestingly, however, younger children were not found to be more heteronomous, or more likely to endorse decision making by adult authority, than older children (Piaget, 1932). In fact, younger children were more likely than older children to endorse decision-making procedures that gave children more autonomy, such as consensus, across social contexts and decisions. In this research, younger children displayed an exaggerated sense of their own autonomy that appears to become tempered in development by a better realization of their own limitations and capabilities.

The findings of the research on democratic decision making bear several similarities to those of the research on rights reviewed earlier. First, the research shows that even young children possess understandings of basic features of democratic norms and procedures, including norms of fairness based on majority rule and the importance of voice, or allowing people to have a say in group decision-making processes. These democratic principles or norms were seen to apply not only to adults but also to children. Furthermore, there was no evidence that the development of democratic understandings follows a pattern of differentiation of truly democratic understandings from those based on punishment, authority, or social custom or convention (Kohlberg, 1981). Rather, even young children seem to understand the basic functions and rationales that underlie democratic norms and procedures, and they even apply them to social situations at different points in development in ways that sometimes deviate from their own social experience or cultural norms. With development, applications of democratic concepts appear to become more sophisticated as children and adolescents consider different features of social contexts, including the competence of different agents to exercise democratic decision-making autonomy, the goals and functions of different types of social organizations, and the practical implications of implementing democratic decision making in groups of different sizes and compositions. Accounting for how these and other features of social contexts are implicated in judgments and reasoning about rights and democracy across the age span should be a major goal of emerging theories of the development of moral cognition. Existing global stage theories of moral judgment, such as those of Piaget and Kohlberg, have proven to be ill suited to explaining these sorts of variations in judgments and reasoning across different social contexts.

NON-UNIVERSALIST PERSPECTIVES: CULTURAL PSYCHOLOGY AND INDIVIDUALISM/COLLECTIVISM

The research on conceptions of rights and democracy described in the previous sections has come mostly from Western societies, or at least those with Western-style democratic political systems. The extent to which these findings may generalize to other cultures with different political and social organizations is an important question. This question is of prime significance for theorizing in moral development, because of the current popularity of theoretical perspectives such as cultural psychology that propose that cultures vary over their commitment to rights and democratic values and beliefs.

Cultural psychologists (e.g., Shweder, 1999; Shweder & Sullivan, 1993) maintain that conceptions of self and morality are largely transmitted to individuals through cultural ideology and participation in shared rituals and practices. One of the distinctions proposed by cultural psychologists to make sense of cultural differences is that of individualism/collectivism (Triandis, 1989). Cultural psychologists maintain that different conceptions of the self and morality are held in individualistic and collectivistic societies. In individualistic societies, such as those in North America and Europe, the self is seen as autonomous and separate from others, leading to a moral focus on individual rights, personal freedom, and equality. In contrast, in collectivist societies, which include Asia, South America, and Africa, a sociocentric or interdependent conception of the self is held (Markus & Kitayama, 1991), in which individuals subordinate personal interests and desires to social norms, duties, and the needs of the collective. The sociocentric self is compatible with the hierarchical social organization found in collectivist societies, and produces a duty-based moral orientation (Shweder, Mahapatra, & Miller, 1987), characterized by acceptance of inequality, adherence to role obligations and duties, the necessity of obedience to authority, and maintenance of the existing social order. Examples of evidence that cultural psychologists have drawn on to support their argument are that individuals from collectivist societies (in contrast to those from individualist societies) tend to emphasize interpersonal obligations over personal autonomy and choice when making decisions about helping others (Miller, 1994), or that they more often define the self using contextually embedded, relational terms (Shweder & Bourne, 1982).

The individualism/collectivism construct, and the notion that cultures can be characterized through the use of such general templates or cultural ideologies, have been extensively critiqued elsewhere (e.g., Bond, 2002; Helwig, 2005; Killen, 1997; Oyserman, Coon, & Kemmelmeier, 2002; Smetana, 2002; Takano & Osaka, 1999; Turiel, 2002; Turiel et al., 1987; Wainryb, chap. 8, this volume; Wainryb & Turiel, 1994). Here, the specific instance of Asia, with a focus on China in particular, is discussed to illustrate some of the problems with general cultural orientations as they bear on the question of the universality of notions of rights and democracy. Then, emerging new research findings on rights and democracy in Asian societies such as Mainland China, is reviewed.

Confucianism, Filial Piety, and Asian Values

The idea that Asian societies are collectivistic, and that concepts such as rights and democracy may be less relevant or even alien to these societies, is not only found within social scientific accounts such as cultural psychology and adherents to the individualism/collectivism dichotomy. Proponents of *Asian values*, a political and cultural movement advanced over the last decade by some East Asian and Southeast Asian leaders and governments, such as Singapore's former Prime Minister Lee Kuan Yew, have asserted that democracy and individual rights and freedoms are a Western imposition that is in tension with indigenous Asian values giving priority to the community over the individual, the maintenance of social harmony and order, and the centrality of the family and other social hierarchies based on authority and obedience (Zakaria, 1994).

Historically, Chinese social and moral thinking, and that of some other Asian cultures, has been viewed as dominated by the philosophy of Confucianism (Dien, 1982; Pye, 1992). According to a common construal by many Western and Asian scholars, Confucianism emphasizes the maintenance of existing hierarchical social structures, along with their inherent inequalities, as expressed through Confucianism's focus on the proper adherence to social duties or rites through which it is claimed that the moral worth of the person is defined (Pye, 1992). One of the prime virtues in Confucianism is *filial piety*, the fostering of strict obedience toward or respect for parents and elders. The patriarchal family is seen as the primary social unit, and obedience to the authority of the father is paramount. According to Pye (1992), in classical Confucian teachings, "filial piety is an absolute requirement and exists without regard to the quality of parental behavior" (p. 92). The hierarchical family, with its inequalities and distinct role obligations, is held as a model for the individuals' other social relations and obligations, such as those involving the state. This construal of Confucianism is one of the primary reasons why China is labeled a collectivist society by cultural psychologists; it also underlies the claim by proponents of the Asian values movement that conceptions of human rights and democracy are in opposition to traditional Chinese values.

However, a wealth of scholarship from the disciplines of political philosophy and Asian studies over the last decade or so has begun to qualify the conclusion that human rights and democracy are purely Western notions having little resonance with traditional Chinese thought and values (e.g., Angle, 2002; Ching, 1998; de Barry, 1998; Friedman, 2002; Gangjian & Gang, 1995; Jung, 1994; Roetz, 1993; Svensson, 2002). This scholarship bears some discussion here as, surprisingly, it has not had much impact on current psychological theorizing and research pertaining to Asian cultures, when compared to its influence on scholarship in other disciplines.

One line of scholarship has examined the development of theorizing about rights and democracy in Chinese political and philosophical writings over the last 150 years. A comprehensive historical survey by Svensson (2002) reveals both influences from the West, as classic Western political and philosophical works were translated into Chinese in the latter half of the 19th century, as well as indigenous influences as Chinese thinkers adapted these concepts to suit their own purposes and society. In early Chinese rights discourse of the late 19th and early 20th century, human rights were seen as based on inborn human nature, as supporting universal human needs for autonomy, and as a means for persons to realize their full potential and human dignity in a context of democratic political participation and freedom (Angle & Svensson, 2001). These rationales are similar to those used to justify concepts of rights in the development of Western political thought (Emerson, 1970), and by contemporary Western adolescents in the research on reasoning about rights reviewed earlier (Helwig, 1995a). But, as Svennson (2002) concludes, "the concept of human rights was not imposed on China by the West" (p. 73). Instead, human rights were frequently invoked to support Chinese national self-determination and to resist colonialism and domination by the West. Human rights and democracy were also invoked by Chinese writers as a way of addressing matters of social injustice internal to China, such as the problem of Imperial tyranny and the pernicious effects of social inequalities, including concerns over the unequal power and status of men and women. In contemporary Asian discourse on human rights, the Asian values movement itself has been criticized as a cover for authoritarian regimes to legitimize their political systems and to stave off local and international criticisms of human rights records (Jung, 1994; Sen, 1999; Svensson, 2002). The concordance in the kinds of justifications believed to underlie notions of rights and democracy among Chinese and Western political thinkers and philosophers, and their application to similar sorts of political and social problems occurring within Western and Asian societies, points to the utility and relevance of these concepts beyond Western cultures.

A substantial body of scholarship over the last couple decades has also criticized the historical depiction of Confucianism as oriented to unquestioned obedience to authority and the maintenance of existing social hierarchies at the expense of social justice or equality. Roetz (1993), for example, points out that the highest human value in Confucianism is that of *ren,* or humaneness, construed as a universal human dignity that comes from acting in accordance with justice or truth, as apart from the lesser form of dignity that stems from simply following one's proper role or station. Confucius himself explicitly expressed the equality of all by nature ("all men are brothers") well before these ideas were commonplace among Western thinkers. As well, Confucius articulated a notion of justice as reciprocity in the form of the Golden Rule.

Most telling, however, are the constraints placed on filial piety by Confucian philosophers. Confucius and his followers recognized the potential for conflict arising between the demands of role obligations of respect and obedience to authority and higher moral principles based on justice, and they generally gave priority to justice over obedience in such conflicts. For example, Confucius maintained that when a child believes that his parents are doing something wrong, the child should gently remonstrate with them (all the while in a respectful fashion) to try to get them to change their ways (Roetz, 1993). The very meaning of *filial* often was equated with following the requirements of justice, rather than simple obedience. Here is an example from the Xiaojing, a traditional Confucian text (quoted in Roetz, 1993, p. 64):

> Therefore, faced with an injustice, a son cannot but quarrel with the father, and a subordinate cannot but quarrel with his ruler. Faced with an injustice, one has to take up the quarrel. How can it count for filial if one . . . simply follows the order of the father!

Note that this duty to speak out against the potential injustices of authorities extends to relations between ministers or government officials and the ruler. If a ruler behaves immorally or in a way that harms the public good, ministers were urged first to speak out in an attempt to change the rulers's mind and, failing that, to resign, rather than to carry out an unjust order (Gangjian & Gang, 1995).

The value that Confucianism places on expression as a means of influencing the dictates and policies of the ruler—and indeed, as a moral duty in the case of confronting political injustice—has been seen by some as evidence of a nascent appreciation of the importance of freedom of speech in traditional Chinese political thought (de Barry, 1998; Gangjian & Gang, 1995; Jung, 1994). Although this freedom was usually spoken of in the context of ministers, and not the general public, there are even some instances in ancient Confucian writings where public dissent was condoned (Roetz, 1993, p. 44). The most striking instance is in the context of ancient Chinese theories of the foundations of political power. Chinese political philosophers espoused a form of social contract theory of political governance (Gangjian & Gang, 1995; Jung, 1994; Roetz, 1993). According to the prominent Confucian philosopher Mencius, the ruler must follow a "Mandate of Heaven," conceived as a form of reciprocity in which the ruler is required to provide for the welfare of the people in return for their loyalty and obedience. However, if the ruler were to abuse this mandate by governing with extreme injustice and to ignore the people's protests and complaints, the people were granted a "right of revolution" to rise up and overthrow the ruler in the name of Heaven (Ching, 1998). As Gangjian and Gang (1995) and Ching (1998) point out, a similar right of rebellion was not mentioned in the West until much later (the 16th century), becoming formally enshrined in the French Declaration of the Rights of Man of 1789 and the American Declaration of Independence.

This brief discussion of ancient Chinese moral philosophy and traditions illustrates that even in an ancient Asian society, moral obligation or worth was not defined purely in terms of obedience to authority or solely through the fulfillment of social duties. Moreover, there appear to be moral intuitions within ancient Chinese philosophical texts similar to those that have formed the basis of the development of Western theories of rights and democracy (Ching, 1998; de Barry, 1998; Jung, 1994; Roetz, 1993). These include a recognition of the moral equality of all individuals (at least, in principle), the idea that government is founded on a social contract between the ruler and the people with the requirement that rulers should consider the interests of the people as a whole in governance, and the necessity of some form of respect for freedom of speech and dissent.

However, ancient Chinese philosophers did not elaborate on and develop these ideas into institutional mechanisms promoting the people's full participation in politics and safeguarding basic rights and freedoms, such as electoral democracy and formal, constitutional guarantees of civil liberties such as freedom of speech, as occurred much later in the West (de Barry, 1998; Jung, 1994). Instead, political justice in Confucianism depends on the good will or virtue of leaders to act in accordance with the people's best interests, and on ministers to speak up on the people's behalf, conditions that surely have, in practice, led to despotism or abuse of authority and injustice. Yet, this brief survey of the more recent scholarship illustrates two important points pertinent to the current topic. First, it shows that many of the values and principles used to justify democratic concepts and rights in Western cultures are relevant in both contemporary and historical Chinese moral discourse, including conceptions of universal human dignity, the importance of government that takes into consideration the interests of the people or serves some basic conception of voice, and the independence of justice from mere social conventional values or the dictates of authority. Second, it illustrates that broad cultural orientations such as individualism or collectivism are insufficient for characterizing the complexity of cultural traditions and the diverse array of values expressed there, as seen in the example of Confucianism, a belief system often held to represent one of the most pure incarnations of collectivist morality.

The central psychological question raised by this analysis is an empirical one, that is, whether democratic values or understandings of any sort may also be held by the general population in these societies, rather than just among moral philosophers and political theorists. Psychologists have begun to examine the development of conceptions of rights and democratic concepts in Asian societies, including those believed by some to be under the sway of collectivism and Asian values, such as mainland China and Malaysia. In the next section, findings from this recent research is reviewed.

Judgments of Rights and Democratic Decision Making in Asian Societies

One important area shown previously to form the basis of conceptions of rights is the construction of a personal sphere of individual autonomy. As noted, recent research has shown that children in Hong Kong distinguish personal issues from moral or social conventional issues in ways broadly similar to that found in studies of children in North American and other cultural contexts (Yau & Smetana, 2003a). A developmental pattern found in research in Western cultural contexts is that children and adults are more likely to grant personal decision-making autonomy to children over a broader set of issues as they get older, reflecting the role of judgments about children's developing competence to handle greater autonomy over wider areas of their lives. This process, however, is often characterized by disputes, disagreements, and conflict between children and adults, as children (especially in adolescence) often attempt to claim personal autonomy over issues that parents still view as within their discretion (Smetana, 1989).

Yau and Smetana (2003b) examined adolescents' reports of experiences of conflict and disagreement with their parents, and their reasoning about these events, in Hong Kong and Shenzhen, a city in mainland China. It was found that in both cities, conflicts between adolescents and their parents were not infrequent, a finding that contrasts with collectivist characterizations of Chinese family life and culture as reflecting mainly social harmony and submission to parental authority. Although conflicts were less frequent in Shenzhen than in Hong Kong overall, conflicts over school work were more frequent in Shenzhen. Similarities were found between the findings of this study and those of previous research with Western samples (Smetana, 1989) in the kinds of issues that lead to conflict (e.g., chores, regulation of activities, interpersonal relationships) and, most significantly, in the kinds of justifications used by adolescents to support their position in disputes. Adolescents in Hong Kong and Shenzhen appealed to concepts such as personal choice and the pursuit of individual needs and desires to challenge parental authority and control. Moreover, appeals to personal choice increased with age in both Hong Kong and Shenzhen, consistent with the developmental progression toward greater concern with autonomy issues in adolescence identified by Western researchers and theorists (Dornsbusch et al., 1985; Erikson, 1968).

The role of beliefs about children's autonomy is also evident in a cross-national study of conceptions of children's rights that included a sample of Chinese ethnic minority adolescents living in Malaysia (Cherney & Shing, 2003). The study focused on reasoning about a variety of self-determination and nurturance rights and revealed very few cross national differences between the Chinese-Malaysian adolescents and those from Switzerland, the United States, and Canada. Chinese-Malaysian adolescents were no more likely to endorse nurturance rights than children from Western cultures, nor were they less likely to endorse self-determination rights, as the individualism-collectivism dichotomy might suggest (along with the Asian values argument). Especially salient in this regard was the finding that Chinese-Malaysian adolescents supported a variety of self-determination rights for children, such as their right to choose their own religion, even when it differed from that of their parents; their right to choose which parent should have custody after a divorce; their right to be heard and to give evidence when accused of violating school rules about fighting (due process); and their rights to keep a private diary or to chose their own friends even over the objections of their parents. At the same time, Chinese-Malaysian adolescents, like those from Western nations, did not believe that children should have other rights, such as the right to vote or to work. As noted by Cherney and Shing (2003), broad cultural orientations such as individualism and collectivism were of little use in explaining these patterns. Instead, when making judgments about the rights of children, adolescents across a variety of cultures considered the specific rights implicated in situational contexts, taking into account the psychological competencies presumed to be inherent in the ability to exercise different kinds of rights. Common conceptions of children's developmental capacities appear to underlie these similarities in judgments about rights across cultures, a conclusion similar to that reached in explaining contextual variations in the research on rights and decision making in Western cultural contexts reviewed earlier.

Other studies (Helwig, Arnold, Tan, & Boyd, 2003a, 2003b) have investigated judgments of democratic decision making in a variety of settings in mainland China, including modern, urban settings (Nanjing) and in more traditional, rural environments. One study (Helwig et al., 2003a), was based on the design of Helwig and Kim (1999) but used a confidential paper-and-pencil assessment rather than a face-to-face interview. It examined Chinese adolescents' (ages 13 to 18 years) reasoning about democratic and authority-based group decision making in the peer group, family, and school for decisions that involved children. The findings revealed both strong support for democratic decision making, in which children's autonomy and right to participate in decisions was acknowledged and supported, as well as variations in judgments of decision-making procedures by different situations and social contexts, as found in research with Canadian participants. Chinese adolescents justified their support for democratic decision-making procedures, such as majority rule and consensus, by explicit appeals to children's autonomy and right to be involved in decision making, and by conceptions of fairness based on majority rule. These justifications accounted for nearly half of all responses. For most decisions, Chinese adolescents rejected decision making by adult authorities, seeing it as unfair and restrictive of children's autonomy. For other decisions, such as decisions about school curriculum, many adolescents (although not the majority) believed that adult authorities such as teachers should decide, because of their greater knowledge and competence to make better decisions.

The patterns of variation across context and types of decision, including developmental differences, largely followed that found in the earlier studies with Canadian children and adolescents. For example, with development, Chinese adolescents were more likely to make distinctions regarding when consensus or majority rule would be appropriate, preferring consensus in smaller groups such as the family but majority rule for decisions made in larger groups, such as the school classroom. Although decision making favoring adult authority was more likely to be endorsed by rural than urban participants, regional differences were quite small, and the same pattern of variations in judgments across contexts and decisions was found in all settings.

One surprising finding in this study involved an example, presented in the family context, of a decision that was expected to pull more for responses favoring adult authority. The example involves a decision about whether a child in a family should receive special tutoring on weekends to boost the child's grades in school. Given the greater involvement of parents in children's academic life in China (Chao & Sue, 1996; Wu, 1996), it was expected that this example might generate more responses supporting adult (parental) decision making than in other decisions. However, Chinese adolescents were found to reject adult authority for this decision and to support decision making by consensus instead. Their support for consensus was based on the necessity of securing the child's agreement, even over the wishes of the child's parents, a position that tended to be justified by the requirement to respect children's autonomy and their right to make academic decisions on their own.

Chinese participants also appealed to children's rights, personal autonomy, and the importance of fostering individual motivation to critique decision making by adult educational authorities in the school context. Although there was greater support for decision making by adult authority in curriculum decisions than in other decisions, most Chinese participants from both urban and rural settings still preferred curriculum decisions to be made democratically, by majority rule in the classroom. This contrasts with the majority of participants in the Canadian research (Helwig & Kim, 1999), who tended to accept adult authority because of concerns over children's competence to make appropriate curriculum decisions. The strong support for democratic decision making regarding curriculum issues found among Chinese adolescents appears to result from their unease and distrust of certain educational practices currently in use in China, such as standardized curricula and nationwide achievement examinations. As one adolescent put it: "Education authorities' decisions are only based on examinations, and make us learn the boring texts. As to today's quality education, it develops one's interest. No to education authorities' decision!"

The support for democratic decision making in the curriculum context is striking not only because of its departure from collectivist characterizations of Chinese psychology emphasizing harmony and acceptance of social hierarchy and authority, but also for its willingness to extend to children a degree of autonomy that might be considered extreme even in many Western educational contexts. The perspective of these Chinese adolescents is likely to diverge from that of many adults in the society, especially those in positions of authority in the educational system. Although some Chinese commentators have called for children to have more rights and autonomy in schools (e.g., Chen & Su, 2001), a comparative study of the views of early childhood educators in the United States and China has shown that Chinese teachers were more likely to endorse top-down or hierarchical teaching methods based on respect for the teachers' authority, whereas U.S. teachers were more likely to endorse methods that they saw as giving children more choice and say over educational decisions (Wang, Elicker, McMullen, & Mao, 2001). The responses of Chinese adolescents may indicate that under an atmosphere of severe restrictions on children's educational decision making autonomy by parents and educators, a heightened sense of autonomy may ensue that may enhance or even exaggerate appeals to democratic voice and participation. These findings also illustrate how judgments of democratic decision making and rights may vary depending on the perspectives of individuals within social systems, a point made by others when considering the social and moral judgments made by males and females within gender hierarchies (Wainryb & Turiel, 1994; Neff & Helwig, 2002).

A follow-up study investigating Chinese adolescents' conceptions of democratic government provides further evidence that conceptions of democracy held in China bear important similarities to those found in Western cultures (Helwig et al., 2003b). This study, based on Helwig (1998), examined Chinese adolescents' reasoning about democratic and nondemocratic systems of government. Like the Canadian participants of Helwig (1998), Chinese adolescents (from both rural and urban settings) preferred democratic systems such as representative democracy and majority rule to nondemocratic systems such as a meritocracy or oligarchy. In their justifications, Chinese adolescents appealed to a wide array of reasons and principles commonly invoked to support democratic government in modern political theorizing (Cohen, 1971; Richardson, 2002) and found in the prior work with Canadian children and adolescents. These included the principle of voice or having a say, the notion that government should represent the interests of a variety of segments of society, the principle of political accountability afforded by free and regular elections, conceptions of democracy based on the will of the majority, and concern over the protection of the rights of minorities in political systems. As one Chinese adolescent put it: "(Representative Democracy) is fair because these representatives are selected by the ordinary people, so they represent the interests of the ordinary people. If any of them do not speak for the ordinary people, they are going to be left out in a couple years."

The developmental patterns found in this research also paralleled those found in the research with Canadian adolescents. Preferences for nondemocratic systems, such as meritocracy, declined with age (although democratic systems were rated as most fair and preferred at all ages). By mid-adolescence (15 years), judgments of political fairness tended to settle around representative democracy as the most fair. An analysis of justifications indicates that these developmental patterns appear to be driven by the perception, with increasing age, of representative democracy as an ideal form of government that best balances the moral aim of representation and the practical aim of delegation of decision making to elected officials who have the time to devote to formulating and debating policy issues.

As in the previous Chinese study on democratic decision making in nongovernmental contexts (Helwig et al., 2003a), there were very few regional differences. Rural and urban adolescents were equally likely to endorse democratic government and to reject the other systems as unfair. This research shows that democratic forms of government, and the reasons and principles characteristically used to defend these systems, are appreciated and accepted across diverse cultures (Canada, China), and throughout areas of China that differ markedly in modernization, exposure to Western influences, and traditionality. The findings of this research provide strong evidence that fundamental democratic conceptions have universal moral appeal and transcend dichotomies between individualistic or collectivistic cultures, or Western and Asian values.

CONCLUSION

The research findings described in this chapter suggest that conceptions of rights, civil liberties, and democracy begin to develop in early childhood and are found across a variety of cultures. Prior theoretical perspectives emphasizing global stages of moral reasoning (Kohlberg, 1981) or broad cultural orientations of individualism and collectivism (Shweder, 1999) are insufficient in accounting for the existing body of findings. Global stage theories fail to anticipate or explain both important continuities in the basic rationales invoked to support rights and democratic principles throughout development and the variations uncovered in applications of rights and civil liberties across situations. Even young children hold conceptions of rights and democracy that are differentiated from punishment, authority, or social conventions, although these concepts are not always understood or given priority in complex social situations or applied in the same way throughout development. To account for these commonalities and variations in judgments and reasoning about rights and democracy, a differentiated model of social development is needed that examines the development of these concepts both in and of themselves and in complex situations entailing conflicts with other social and moral concepts.

The evidence shows that conceptions of personal autonomy, rights, and democracy are not tied to Western cultural traditions but appear in a variety of cultures, including Asian societies often characterized as collectivist and oriented to obedience to authority and the maintenance of hierarchy and tradition. The findings are inconsistent with perspectives on social and moral development, such as cultural psychology, that trace the source of social and moral understandings primarily to the influence of varying cultural traditions or doctrines (Shweder, 1999). The source of notions of personal autonomy, rights, and democratic concepts appears to rest instead on common conceptions of universal human needs and the exigencies of social life experienced in different cultures. Individuals from a variety of cultures find compelling the idea that people should have a say in the institutions that govern them, and they believe that needs for personal autonomy are vital and must be taken into account when considering and evaluating social practices and norms. The developmental patterns emerging from findings of studies conducted in a variety of nations and cultures show that, as children develop, they consider in increasingly complex ways an array of factors such as the goals and structure of different social contexts (e.g., peer groups, family, school, government), the competence of different agents (e.g., children or adults) to act on autonomy and rights, and the presence of other social and moral concerns, such as issues of harm or legal requirements. Such factors, and not general cultural orientations, were far more informative in explaining the applications of concepts of rights and democratic decision making in the cultures examined so far.

This is not to say that we have anything approaching a complete account of the role of culture in reasoning about rights and democracy, or that there are no important cultural differences yet to be uncovered. For instance, we need to know more about how conceptions of freedom of speech and other civil liberties are reasoned about and applied across a variety of cultures, especially in authoritarian societies or those without a formal democratic tradition. Although it is clear now that both beliefs about personal autonomy and democratic conceptions of group decision making are held in Asian societies such as mainland China, we also need to know more about how the potential tradeoff between these concepts is understood. For example, are the boundaries between democratic notions of majority rule and individual freedom drawn differently in China than in the West? Can the group make decisions over broader (or different) areas of the lives of individuals in societies such as China, so long as such decisions are perceived to be made in ways that can be justified as democratic? We can probably expect future research to yield both patterns of similarity and differences in judgments by situation and by culture. However, the answers to these and other important questions can be found only if we abandon the misleading heuristic of global cultural orientations and look more closely at how concepts of rights and democracy are applied and coordinated in different social contexts both within and across cultures.

ACKNOWLEDGMENTS

Preparation of this chapter was supported by a grant from the Social Sciences and Humanities Research Council of Canada to the author. I would like to thank Christopher Lo, Angela Prencipe, Rachel Ryerson, Elliot Turiel, and the Editors for comments on an earlier version of this chapter.

REFERENCES

Angle, S. C. (2002). *Human rights and Chinese thought: A cross-cultural inquiry*. Cambridge, UK: Cambridge University Press.
Angle, S. C., & Svensson, M. (2001). *The Chinese human rights reader: Documents and commentary, 1900–2000*. New York: M. E. Sharpe.

Ardila-Rey, A., & Killen, M. (2001). Middle-class Columbian children's evaluations of personal, moral, and social conventional interactions in the classroom. *International Journal of Behavioral Development, 25,* 246–255.

Bond, M. H. (2002). Reclaiming the individual from Hofstede's ecological analysis—A 20 year odyssey: Comment on Oyserman et al. (2002). *Psychological Bulletin, 128,* 73–77.

Chao, R. K., & Sue, S. (1996). Chinese parental influence and their children's school success: A paradox in the literature on parenting styles. In S. Lau (Ed.), *Growing up the Chinese way: Chinese child and adolescent development* (pp. 93–120). Hong Kong: The Chinese University Press.

Chen, H., & Su, L. (2001). Child protection and development in China. *International Society for the Study of Behavioral Development Newsletter, 2,* 7–8.

Cherney, I., & Perry, N. W. (1996). Children's attitudes toward their rights–an international perspective. In E. Verhellen (Ed.), *Monitoring children's rights* (pp. 241–250). Boston: Martinus Nijhoff.

Cherney, I. D., & Shing, Y. L. (2003, April). *Children's attitudes toward their rights: A cross-cultural perspective.* Poster presented at the meeting of the Society for Research in Child Development, Tampa, FL.

Ching, J. (1998). Human rights: A valid Chinese concept? In W. de Barry & T. Weiming (Eds.), *Confucianism and human rights* (pp. 67–82). New York: Columbia University Press.

Clemence, A., Doise, W., de Rosa, A. S., & Gonzalez, L. (1995). Le representation sociale des droites de l'homme: Une recherche internationale sur l'entendue et les limites de l'universalité. [Social representations of human rights: International research on the extent and limits of their universality.] *Journal Internationale de Psychologie, 30,* 181–212.

Cohen, C. (1971). *Democracy.* New York: The Free Press.

Connell, R. W. (1971). *The child's construction of politics.* Melbourne, Australia: Melbourne University Press.

de Barry, W. (1998). *Asian values and human rights: A Confucian communitarian perspective.* Cambridge, MA: Cambridge University Press.

Dien, D. S. (1982). A Chinese perspective on Kohlberg's theory of moral development. *Developmental Review, 2,* 331–341.

Dornbusch, S. M., Carlsmith, J. M., Bushwall, S. J., Ritter, P. L., Leiderman, H., Hastorf, A. H., & Gross, R. T. (1985). Single parents, extended households, and the control of adolescents. *Child Development, 56,* 326–341.

Dworkin, R. (1977). *Taking rights seriously.* Cambridge, MA: Harvard University Press.

Emerson, T. (1970). *The system of freedom of speech.* New York: Random House.

Erikson, E. (1968). *Identity, youth, and crisis.* New York: W. W. Norton.

Friedman, E. (2002). On alien western democracy. In C. Kinwall & K. Sönsson (Ed.), *Globalization and democratization in Asia* (pp. 53–72). London: Routledge.

Gallatin, J., & Adelson, J. (1970). Individual rights and the public good: A cross-national study of adolescents. *Comparative Political Studies, 2,* 226–244.

Gallatin, J., & Adelson, J. (1971). Legal guarantees of individual freedom: A cross-national study of the development of political thought. *Journal of Social Issues, 27,* 93–108.

Gangjian, D., & Gang, S. (1995). Relating human rights to Chinese culture: The four paths of the Confucian Analects and the four principles of a new theory of benevolence. In M. C. Davis (Ed.), *Human rights and Chinese values: Legal, philosophical, and political perspectives* (pp. 35–56). New York: Oxford University Press.

Gewirth, A. (1978). *Reason and morality.* Chicago: University of Chicago Press.

Greenstein, F. (1965). *Children and politics.* New Haven, CT: Yale University Press.

Held, D. (1996). *Models of democracy*. Cambridge, UK: Polity Press.

Helwig, C. C. (1995a). Adolescents' and young adults' conceptions of civil liberties: Freedom of speech and religion. *Child Development, 66,* 152–166.

Helwig, C. C. (1995b). Social contexts in social cognition: Psychological harm and civil liberties. In M. Killen & D. Hart (Eds.), *Morality in everyday life: Developmental perspectives* (pp. 166–200). Cambridge, UK: Cambridge University Press.

Helwig, C. C. (1997). The role of agent and social context in judgments of freedom of speech and religion. *Child Development, 68,* 484–495.

Helwig, C. C. (1998). Children's conceptions of fair government and freedom of speech. *Child Development, 69,* 518–531.

Helwig, C. C. (2003). [Judgments and reasoning about the fairness of government systems in adolescence]. Unpublished raw data.

Helwig, C. C. (2005). Culture and the construction of concepts of personal autonomy and democratic decision-making. In J. E. Jacobs & P. A. Klaczynski (Eds.), *The development of judgment and decision making in children and adolescents* (pp. 181–212). Mahwah, NJ: Lawrence Erlbaum Associates.

Helwig, C. C., Arnold, M. L., Tan, D., & Boyd, D. (2003a). Chinese adolescents' reasoning about democratic and authority-based decision making in peer, family, and school contexts. *Child Development, 74,* 783–800.

Helwig, C. C., Arnold, M. L., Tan, D., & Boyd, D. (2003b, June). *Mainland Chinese adolescents' judgments and reasoning about democratic government.* Poster presented at the annual meeting of the Jean Piaget Society, Chicago, IL.

Helwig, C. C., & Kim, S. (1999). Children's evaluations of decision making procedures in peer, family, and school contexts. *Child Development, 70,* 502–512.

Helwig, C. C., & Turiel, E. (2002). Civil liberties, autonomy, and democracy: Children's perspectives. *International Journal of Law and Psychiatry, 25,* 253–270.

Ignatieff, M. (2000). *The rights revolution*. Toronto: Anansi.

Inhelder, B. & Piaget, J. (1958). *The growth of logical thinking from childhood to adolescence*. New York: Basic Books.

Jung, K. D. (1994). Is culture destiny?: The myth of Asia's anti-democratic values; a response to Lee Kuan Yew. *Foreign Affairs, 73*(6), 189–194.

Killen, M. (1997). Culture, self, and development: Are cultural templates useful or stereotypic? *Developmental Review, 17,* 239–249.

Killen, M., & Sueyoshi, L. (1995). Conflict resolution in Japanese social interactions. *Early Education and Development, 6,* 313–330.

Kinoshita, Y. (1989). Developmental changes in understanding the limitations of majority decisions. *British Journal of Developmental Psychology, 7,* 97–112.

Kohlberg, L. (1981). *Essays on moral development. Vol. 1: The philosophy of moral development*. San Francisco: Harper & Row.

Mann, L. & Greenbaum, C. W. (1987). Cross-cultural studies of children's decision rules. In C. Kagitcibasi (Ed.), *Growth and progress in cross-cultural psychology* (pp. 130–137). Berwyn, PA: Swets North America.

Markus, H. R., & Kitayama, S. (1991). Culture and the self: Implications for cognition, emotion, and motivation. *Psychological Review, 98,* 224–253.

McClosky, H., & Brill, A. (1983). *Dimensions of tolerance: What Americans believe about civil liberties*. New York: Russell Sage.

Meldon, A. I. (1977). *Rights and persons*. Berkeley: University of California Press.

Melton, G. B. (1980). Children's concepts of their rights. *Journal of Clinical Child Psychology, 9,* 186–190.

Melton, G. B., & Limber, S. P. (1992). What children's rights mean to children: Children's own views. In M. Freeman & P. Veerman (Eds.), *The ideologies of children's rights* (pp. 167–187). Dordrecht: The Netherlands: Kluwer.

Miller, J. G. (1994). Cultural diversity in the morality of caring: Individually-oriented versus duty-based interpersonal moral codes. *Cross Cultural Research, 28,* 3–39.

Moessinger, P. (1981). The development of the concept of majority decision: A pilot study. *Canadian Journal of Behavioral Science, 13,* 359–362.

Moshman, D. (1998). Cognitive development beyond childhood. In W. Damon (series Ed.) & D. Kuhn & R. Siegler (Vol. Eds.), *Handbook of child psychology. Vol. 2: Cognition, perception, and language* (5th ed., pp. 947–978). New York: Wiley.

Neff, K. D., & Helwig, C. C. (2002). A constructivist aproach to understanding the development of reasoning about rights and authority within cultural contexts. *Cognitive Development, 17,* 1429–1450.

Nisbett, R. E., & Wilson, T. D. (1977). Telling more than we can know: Verbal reports on mental processes. *Psychological Review, 84,* 231–259.

Nucci, L. P. (1981). The development of personal concepts: A domain distinct from moral and social concepts. *Child Development, 52,* 114–121.

Nucci, L. (2001). *Education in the moral domain.* Cambridge, UK: Cambridge University Press.

Nucci, L. P., Camino, C., & Sapiro, C. (1996). Social class effects on northeastern Brazilian children's conceptions of areas of personal choice and social regulation. *Child Development, 67,* 1223–1242.

Nucci, L. P., & Lee, J. (1993). Moral and personal autonomy. In G. Noam & T. Wren (Eds.), *Morality and the self* (pp. 123–148). Cambridge, MA: MIT Press.

Oyserman, D., Coon, H. M., & Kemmelmeier, M. (2002). Rethinking individualism and collectivism: Evaluation of theoretical assumptions and meta-analysis. *Psychological Bulletin, 128,* 3–72.

Piaget, J. (1932). *The moral judgment of the child.* London: Routledge & Kegan Paul.

Prothro, J. W., & Grigg, C. M. (1960). Fundamental principles of democracy: Bases of agreement and disagreement. *Journal of Politics, 22,* 276–294.

Pye, L. W. (1992). *The spirit of Chinese politics.* Cambridge, MA: Harvard University Press.

Richardson, H. S. (2002). *Democratic autonomy: Public reasoning about the ends of policy.* New York: Oxford University Press.

Roetz, H. (1993). *Confucian ethics of the axial age.* Albany: SUNY Press.

Ruck, M. D., Abramovitch, R., & Keating, D. P. (1998). Children's and adolescents' understanding of rights: Balancing nurturance and self-determination. *Child Development, 69,* 404–417.

Sarat, A. (1975). Reasoning in politics: The social, political, and psychological bases of principled thought. *American Journal of Political Science, 19,* 247–261.

Sen, A. (1999). *Development as freedom.* Random House: New York.

Shweder, R. A., (1999). Why cultural psychology? *Ethos, 27,* 62–73.

Shweder, R. A., & Bourne, E. J. (1982). Does the concept of the person vary cross-culturally? In A. J. Marsella & G. M. White (Eds.), *Cultural conceptions of mental health and therapy* (pp. 97–137). Boston: Reidel.

Shweder, R. A., Mahapatra, M., & Miller, J. G. (1987). Culture and moral development. In J. Kagan & S. Lamb (Eds.), *The emergence of morality in young children* (pp. 1–83). Chicago: University of Chicago Press.

Shweder, R. A., & Sullivan, M. A. (1993). Cultural psychology: Who needs it? *Annual Review of Psychology, 44,* 497–523.

Smetana, J. G. (1989). Adolescents' and parents' reasoning about actual family conflict. *Child Development, 60,* 1052–1067.

Smetana, J. G. (2002). Culture, autonomy, and personal jurisdiction in adolescent-parent relationships. In H. W. Reese, & R. Kail (Eds.), *Advances in Child development and behavior* (Vol. 29, pp. 51–87). New York: Academic Press.

Snarey, J. (1985). Cross-cultural universality of moral development: A critical review of Kohlbergian research. *Psychological Bulletin, 97,* 202–232.

Stouffer, S. (1955). *Communism, conformity and civil liberties.* New York: Doubleday.

Svensson, M. (2002). *Debating human rights in China: A conceptual and political history.* New York: Rowman & Littlefield.

Takano, Y., & Osaka, E. (1999). An unsupported common view: Comparing Japan and the U.S. on invidualism/collectivism. *Asian Journal of Social Psychology, 2,* 311–341.

Triandis, H. C. (1989). The self and social behavior in differing cultural contexts. *Psychological Review, 96,* 506–520.

Turiel, E. (1998). The development of morality. In W. Damon (Series Ed.) & N. Eisenberg (Vol. Ed.), *Handbook of child psychology. Vol. 3: Social, emotional, and personality development* (5th ed., pp. 863–932). New York: Wiley.

Turiel, E. (2002). *The culture of morality: Social development, context, and conflict.* Cambridge, UK: Cambridge University Press.

Turiel, E., Killen, M., & Helwig, C. C. (1987). Morality: Its structure, functions and vagaries. In J. Kagan & S. Lamb (Eds.), *The emergence of morality in young children* (pp. 155–244). Chicago: University of Chicago Press.

Turiel, E., & Wainryb, C. (1998). Concepts of freedoms and rights in a traditional, hierarchically organized society. *British Journal of Developmental Psychology, 16,* 375–395.

Wainryb, C., & Turiel, E. (1994). Dominance, subordination, and concepts of personal entitlement in cultural context. *Child Development, 65,* 1701–1722.

Wang, J., Elicker, J., McMullen, M., & Mao, S. (2001, April). *American and Chinese teachers' beliefs about early childhood curriculum.* Poster presented at the biennial meeting of the Society for Research in Child Development, Minneapolis, MN.

Wu, D. Y. H. (1996). Parental control: Psychocultural interpretations of Chinese patterns of socialization. In S. Lau (Ed.), *Growing up the Chinese way: Chinese child and adolescent development* (pp. 1–28). Hong Kong: The Chinese University Press.

Yau, J., & Smetana, J. G. (2003a). Conceptions of moral, social-conventional, and personal events among Chinese preschoolers in Hong Kong. *Child Development, 74,* 1–12.

Yau, J., & Smetana, J. G. (2003b). Adolescent-parent conflict in Hong Kong and Shenzhen: A comparison of youth in two cultural contexts. *International Journal of Behavioral Development, 27,* 201–211.

Zakaria, F. (1994). Culture is destiny: A conversation with Lee Kuan Yew. *Foreign Affairs, 73*(2), 109–127.

Zellman, G. L., & Sears, D. O. (1971). Childhood origins of tolerance for dissent. *Journal of Social Issues, 27,* 109–136.

8

Moral Development in Culture: Diversity, Tolerance, and Justice

Cecilia Wainryb
University of Utah

PERSPECTIVES ON MORAL DEVELOPMENT AND MORAL DIVERSITY

The propositions that persons develop in cultures and that cultural arrangements frame their moral lives are not controversial. Deep disagreements do exist, however, concerning what cultures are like and what it means to say that culture frames moral development. Divergent views on these issues translate, in turn, into different understandings of the nature of the diversity of moral experiences across cultures.

The perspective on moral development in culture presented in this chapter is grounded on a developmental theory that posits that persons develop moral and other social concepts within their culture through participation in and reflection on social interactions of different kinds (Turiel, 1983; 1998a). This perspective is also informed by contemporary scholarship in cultural anthropology (Abu-Lughod, 1991; Wikan, 1991) positing that cultures are historical constructs created and sustained in the context of collaborations, disagreements, power clashes, and contested meanings among individuals—men and women, adults and children, haves and have nots. This view holds that cultures do not have the power to make people feel, think, or act certain ways; they are multifaceted environments offering opportunities for diverse kinds of social interactions. Persons, including children, are capable of reflecting on social interactions embedded in the practices and traditions of their culture; disagreements about what is right or valuable are common. Rather than being products of their culture and exchangeable copies of other members of their culture, people in cultures "are confronted with choices, struggle with others, make conflicting statements, argue about points of view on the same events, undergo ups and downs in various relationships and changes in their circumstances and desires, face new pressures, and fail to predict what will happen to them or those around them" (Abu-Lughod, 1991, p. 154).

This perspective contrasts with propositions centered on the cultural determination of development, propositions typically grouped under the broad umbrella of *cultural psychology* (Bruner, 1990; Cole, 1990; Markus & Kitayama, 1991; Shweder, 1990; Shweder & Sullivan, 1993). Although those propositions differ in meaningful ways, they also share key assumptions about culture and development that are of consequence to the study of moral development in culture. From the viewpoint of cultural psychology, cultures are presumed to be all-embracing constructs that form relatively coherent patterns of thought and action, with the patterns of one culture differing from those of another. The psychology of individuals is said to be structured in accord to the culture's dominant pattern or orientation, and persons are generally believed to be predisposed to participate in culture and to accept and reproduce their culture's main features. Although the means by which cultures achieve *enculturation* (Herskovits, 1947, 1955) has not been specified in much detail, the assumption of cultural psychologists is that a culture's orientation is explicitly or tacitly communicated to, and acquired by, the members of a culture through top-down processes of cultural transmission by "local guardians of the moral order" (Shweder, Mahapatra, & Miller, 1987) or through participation in cultural practices and socially prescribed forms of behavior (Rogoff, 1990). As a result of these processes, members of cultures are assumed to have a shared commitment to goals, values, and developmental paths, indeed, a shared culture.

Cultural psychologists' notion of coherent and consistent patterns of cultural organization is best exemplified by the proposition that patterns of culture can be broadly sorted into individualistic or collectivistic. According to this formulation, cultures with an *individualistic* orientation (e.g., the United States, Canada, Western Europe, Australia, and New Zealand) structure social experience around autonomous persons, relatively detached from their relationships and community, and motivated to attain freedom and personal goals. Cultures whose core is *collectivistic* (e.g., much of Asia, Africa, and South America) structure social experience around collectives such as the family or the community; members of collectivistic cultures are identified largely by their interdependent roles and by the duties prescribed to them by the collective social system (Hofstede, 1980; Markus & Kitayama, 1991; Triandis, 1989, 1990). Within the realm of moral development, individualistic and collectivistic cultures have been described as maintaining fundamentally divergent conceptions of morality (Shweder et al., 1987). Morality in individualistic cultures is rights based, and is structured by concerns with furthering and protecting the independence of the individual; rights, equality, justice, and individual freedoms make up individualistic moral codes and social practices. By contrast, collectivistic cultures have a more interdependent duty-based morality, in which the organizing features are the actions dictated by the rules and duties assigned by one's role in the social system, to the exclusion of concerns with rights, freedoms, and personal agency.

Although the construct of individualism/collectivism has enjoyed tremendous popularity as a model of variability in human thought, emotion, and behavior, and generated a great deal of research across many cultures and across a wide array of domains (for overviews, see Kagitcibasi & Berry, 1989; Triandis, 1990, 1995), its focus on differences *between* cultures has led to the overlooking or downplaying of differences *within* cultures. Entire cultures (indeed, entire continents) have been characterized according to their presumably uniform orientation to individualism or collectivism, to rights or duties, to independence or interdependence (Markus & Kitayama, 1991; Triandis, 1989). This emphasis on cultural homogeneity became the target of criticism by anthropologists and developmental psychologists, who argued that autonomy and interdependence are not mutually exclusive but interwoven in development, coexisting in the thoughts and actions of people in Western and non-Western societies (Holloway, 2000; Killen & Wainryb, 2000; Spiro, 1993; Strauss, 2000; Turiel, 1998a, 2002; Turiel &Wainryb, 1994, 2000; Wainryb, 1997; Wainryb & Turiel, 1995). A recent meta-analysis of both cross-national research and research conducted in the United States since 1980 (Oyserman, Coon & Kemmelmeir, 2002) confirmed that differences between individualistic and collectivistic societies are neither large nor systematic, and that societies and individuals cannot be accurately characterized in terms of a single orientation.

Over the years, descriptions of cultures as individualistic or collectivistic gave way to portrayals allowing a mixture of individualistic and collectivistic elements (compare, for example, Markus & Kitayama [1991] with Markus, Mullally, & Kitayama [1997] and Shweder et al. [1987] with Shweder, Much, Mahapatra & Park [1997]). Nevertheless, even those propositions presuppose a substantial level of cultural homogeneity and a process of cultural patterning of psychological development. In one such formulation, individualism and collectivism are conceptualized as ideal types at opposite poles of a continuous dimension. Although cultures are portrayed as striking a specific balance between the two ideal types with different proportions of individualistic and collectivistic elements (Greenfield, 1994; Sinha & Tripathi, 1994), they are still thought to cohere around a dominant orientation. For example, the particular mixture of individualistic and collectivistic elements in Japanese society has been described as indicative of a set point on the collectivistic side of the dimension, whereas the mixture of orientations in American society is said to be indicative of a set point on the individualistic side (Greenfield, 1995). A different argument has been that cultures may be heterogeneous insofar as smaller cultural communities or subcultures—each with its own cultural orientation—coexist within a larger society. This formulation, too, leaves intact the assumption that cultures (although smaller in size) are entities with a dominant and relatively homogeneous core of shared meanings, values, traditions, and practices; in this view, too, persons are locked into enacting (multiple) cultural scripts.

Although formulations that allow for the coexistence of mixed orientations capture some aspects of the multifaceted experiences that make up social life within cultures, all cultural analyses downplay the scope of social and moral diversity within cultures. For example, some such formulations recognize that conflicts might arise between the values of different subcultures within a society. Those conflicts, however, are considered to be conflicts *between* cultural groups—a move that allows for retaining the assumption of homogeneity and harmony *within* cultural groups. Because persons' goals and perspectives are thought to be shaped by their culture's dominant orientation, the possibility that individuals within a culture (or subculture) may develop different perspectives or enter into significant conflict with each other is not a central consideration. The resulting view is one where people's concerns mirror their culture's orientation, with little substantial conflict among people within a culture.

In a provocative critique of cultural psychology, Gjerde (2004) has noted that underlying cultural analyses of this type is an essentialist belief that:

> There exist natural entities—often described as tribes, ethnicities or cultural groups—that share essences such as language, blood, kinship, or customs, and whose affinity is real, natural and overpowering. In this view, each individual possesses the properties of his or her culture and groups can take on the status of independent variables and operate as causative factors. These characteristics are presumed to be so deeply inscribed that each person within the 'cultural unit' can be treated as an exchangeable item ... [and] peoples are reduced to miniature representations of their societies, cultures, and continents. (p. 142)

Gjerde's depiction of the position of cultural psychology as essentialist is likely to meet with some resistance on the part of cultural psychologists who, instead, claim to acknowledge the central role of individual agency (e.g., Shweder & Sullivan, 1993). Whether the label of essentialism does or does not fit them, it is a fact that cultural analyses have consistently neglected to specify developmental processes by which individuals might come to resist, or even disagree with, cultural norms and practices. Their inattention to those aspects of development is unlikely to be an oversight. On the contrary, the emphasis placed by cultural analyses on the cultural shaping of psychological processes implicates, by definition, both the tendency to overestimate a culture's power to dictate meanings and the tendency to underestimate individual agency.

The view of cultures as speaking in a collective, shared, voice is inconsistent with evidence pointing to the plurality of concerns of persons within cultures, to the conflicts and disagreements among persons within cultures, and to the multiple interpretations and critical judgments that persons make about their culture's norms and practices. This type of heterogeneity cannot be fully accounted for by formulations emphasizing the cultural determination or patterning of development, even if those formulations allow for the co-existence of multiple cultural templates within a society. As discussed more fully in the next section, explanations of cultural heterogeneity require more than determining the specific proportions of collectivistic and individualistic elements. Orientations to both autonomy and interdependence are central in social relationships; persons develop multiple goals and concerns (some individualistic-like and some collectivistic-like), and make different—often conflict ridden—judgments and decisions depending on their interpretation of specific contexts within culture.

In the developmentally grounded perspective on morality and culture presented in this chapter (see also Turiel & Wainryb, 1994, 2000), the analysis shifts away from the cultural patterning of development to focus instead on the diverse experiences of persons in multiple contexts within culture. Wouldn't such an *acultural discourse*—a discourse that downplays the impact of cultural meanings and practices on the development of morality—yield data about "highly general and somewhat vacuous commonalities" in moral outlook (Miller, 2001, p. 159) and render moral and social life homogeneous, human only in a generic sense? Cultural psychologists might think so, for they view the notion of culture as critical for anchoring the idea of human diversity and for giving voice to diverse cultural outlooks. From a developmental perspective, however, it is *moving away from culture* as the main anchor of diversity that allows capture of the full range of human diversity.

The study of social and moral development in culture is inevitably tied to questions about the nature of moral diversity, questions whose import extends beyond academia (Wainryb, 2004b). Democratic societies in North America and Western Europe, increasingly multicultural in their composition, face the serious challenges of deciding whether to accommodate and how to best respond to the social and moral practices and values of immigrants coming from diverse cultures. At stake are concerns with human rights, equality, and respect for human diversity.

Propositions emphasizing the cultural patterning of social and moral development have emerged largely in response to the perceived ethnocentricity and Western biases of explanations that emphasize universal characteristics, and have been advanced with the explicit goal of promoting a richer view of human development. As recently as the 1980s, cultural psychologists spoke of "an intellectual climate suspicious of a one-sided emphasis on fixed essences, intrinsic features, and universally necessary truths" (Shweder & Sullivan, 1993, p. 500). In response, they championed culture as the main source of development—the origin and organizer of the self, emotion, cognition, and values. Their intellectual agenda included studying "the way cultural traditions and social practices regulate, express, trans-form, and permute the human psyche, resulting less in psychic unity for humankind than in ethnic divergences in mind, self, and emotion" (Shweder, 1990, p. 1), "examin[ing] ethnic and cultural sources of psychological diversity in emotional and somatic functioning, self organization, moral evaluation, social cognition, and human development" (Shweder & Sullivan, 1993, p. 497), and developing "a credible theory of psychological pluralism" (p. 498).

Traditionally, then, propositions emphasizing the cultural patterning of social and moral development have been associated with the fight against racism and, more recently, with the promotion of multiculturalism and the rights of cultures. Their underlying assumption, that each culture has a distinctive point of view that makes sense within the culture, has been typically taken to imply that each cultural point of view is deserving of respect or, at the very least, tolerance by those outside the culture (Shweder, 2000, 2002). Seldom has it been acknowledged, however, that this call for respect and tolerance also presupposes that cultures have only *one* distinctive point of view—*one* insider perspective, *one* local voice.

By contrast, the perspective presented in this chapter points to the multiple and conflict-ing social and moral viewpoints found within cultures, and it underscores that the range of human diversity cannot be fully represented in terms of differences between cultures. Therefore, the construct of culture cannot plausibly serve as the basis for promoting re-spect for human diversity and justice. Why? Because propositions concerning the cultural patterning of development highlight *participation* in culture and *acceptance* of cultural norms and practices and make light of the possibility that individuals within a culture might dislike and wish to change some aspects of their culture. Therefore, analyses that rely on the notion of culture as the main anchor of human diversity are bound to overlook the experiences of some of the very groups and individuals that the notion of culture was meant to give voice to.

MORAL LIFE IN CONTESTED CULTURAL LANDSCAPES: A DEVELOPMENTAL APPROACH

Persons—adults and children—live and develop in multifaceted social environments, try to make sense of their diverse social experiences, disagree with one another about the meanings of social practices and the norms and values that regulate them and, at times, assume critical attitudes toward aspects of their social environment and resist or even attempt to change them. Persons occupying social positions with more or less power often have different experiences and develop different goals and interests which, at times, come into conflict with each other. It is the diverse, and often conflict-ridden, social experiences of persons in culture—rather than dominant cultural configurations or templates—that influence social and moral development (Turiel & Wainryb, 1994, 2000).

Descriptions of social and moral development in terms of global cultural orientations, such as right-based and duty-based moral codes, cannot capture the multiplicity of con-cerns and goals that are part of the social and moral lives of individuals in cultures, or the varied ways in which individuals prioritize those concerns and goals in specific con-texts, or disagree with one another about those priorities. This is not to say that culture is unimportant or that social and moral development does not take place in cultural contexts. Rather, it is argued that to account for the full range of variation in cultural contexts and, in turn, to allow for meaningful cross-cultural comparisons, it is necessary to avoid char-acterizing cultures in terms of opposites or dualisms (Killen & Wainryb, 2000; Turiel, 1998a, 2002; Turiel & Wainryb, 1994, 2000; Wainryb, 1997; Wainryb & Turiel, 1995).

Although it may be possible to draw comparisons between cultural groups, such comparisons must be made in ways that recognize the complexity of social experiences within societies. Cultural discourse and ideology are subject to interpretation and even criticism by members of society. To fully account for the full range of social and moral diversity within cultural contexts, research must extend its focus beyond cultural symbols and shared understandings, and recognize the active role of individuals in attributing meanings to their experience, reinterpreting cultural ideologies, and making judgments at variance with cultural practices.

A large body of programmatic research conducted over the last 25 years has yielded reliable evidence concerning the multifaceted social and moral experiences of children and adults in different cultural settings. Although research was first conducted largely in North America, to date studies have been conducted in many countries in Asia, Africa, and Central and South America. Two distinct, though related and mutually informative, sets of findings bear evidence to the heterogeneity of moral life and to the developmental roots of such heterogeneity. One set of findings documents the multiple social and moral concerns that persons across cultures develop, and the diverse ways in which persons weigh those concerns as they make sense of specific social contexts within their cultures. The other set of findings points to the conflicting perspectives developed by individuals occupying different positions in society. The view of persons, including children, as agents capable of reflection and interpretation, likely to engage in cooperation with others as well as in conflict and subterfuge, underlies both sets of findings.

Multiple Social and Moral Concerns Within Cultures

The diversity of children's social and moral concerns has been amply documented among members of both Western and non-Western societies. Extensive research carried out in North America has demonstrated that children begin to form differentiated social concepts at an early age. Children develop concerns with the self and the person's autonomy, entitlements, and rights—concerns that might be thought of as individualistic. Multiple experimental and observational studies have shown that areas of personal autonomy are demarcated largely in the context of conflicts, tensions, and negotiations with authority figures such as parents. Even at ages 4 and 5 years, preschool children have been shown to negotiate with parents over issues they believe to be within their own personal jurisdiction, and reject adult rules and intervention as illegitimate (Killen & Smetana, 1999; Nucci, 1981; Nucci & Weber, 1995; Smetana, 1989; Weber, 1999). Research has also shown that conflicts between children and their parents over the definition of the personal domain become more frequent in adolescence, as teens increasingly challenge the legitimacy of their parents' control over matters such as their personal appearance, cleaning their room, and curfew (Smetana, 1988, 1989, 2000; Smetana & Asquith, 1994; Smetana & Gaines, 1999).

In addition to concerns with a realm of personal choice, children also develop concerns with individual freedoms and rights. In studies conducted in the United States and Canada (Helwig, 1995, 1997, 1998; see also Helwig, chap. 7, in this volume; Ruck, Abramovitch & Keating, 1998), for example, children as young as 6 or 7 years conceptualize freedoms of speech and religion as universal moral rights, which hold across cultural contexts even in the face of laws denying these rights. In justifying those rights as universal, children and adolescents appeal to conceptions of human agency and personal choice; adolescents also refer to the importance of these rights for maintaining democratic social and political organizations that guarantee all individuals a voice (Helwig, 1998). Similar findings were obtained in various European countries (Doise, Clemence & Spini, 1996).

In spite of the centrality that notions of personal autonomy and rights have for children in Western societies, research has reliably shown that children are also concerned with the well-being of others, justice, and fairness—concerns that could be seen as inconsistent with the individualistic characterization of Western societies. Children also develop collectivistic-like concerns with authority and obedience (Damon, 1977; Laupa, 1991; Laupa & Turiel, 1986; Tisak, 1986), social roles and conventions (Nucci & Nucci, 1982; Smetana, 1981, 1985; Smetana & Braeges, 1990; Tisak & Turiel, 1988; Turiel, 1983), as well as with interpersonal obligations (Killen & Turiel, 1998; Neff, Turiel & Anshel, 2002; Smetana, Killen, & Turiel, 1991).

When social interactions bear simultaneously on concerns with the individual (e.g., personal choice, rights, autonomy) and the collective (obedience, mutuality, collective interests), children do not merely place individualistic goals ahead of group goals. Instead, they appraise and interpret the specific features of those contexts and make judgments that vary by context, giving priority to individualistic concerns in some situations and to collectivistic concerns in others. Research conducted in the Unites States and Canada has shown that North American children (and adults) often uphold personal autonomy and rights, but are also responsive to other features of social situations and, in many contexts, subordinate the concerns with autonomy and rights to concerns bearing on the prevention of harm to others (Helwig, 1995, 1997), interpersonal obligations (Neff et al., 2002; Smetana et al., 1991), friendship and mutuality (Kahn & Turiel, 1988), group goals (Killen, 1990), and even authority (Fuligni, 1998; Laupa, 1991; Laupa & Turiel, 1986, 1993; Smetana, 1988, 1989; Smetana & Asquith, 1994; Smetana & Bitz, 1996; Tisak, 1986).

Similar findings were observed among members of traditional societies, where one might have expected that concerns with autonomy and individual rights would be systematically subordinated to the maintenance of social harmony, the preservation of hierarchy, and the upholding of traditional roles and duties. Although research with members of traditional cultures has been less extensive, a substantial body of research in Asia (e.g., China [Helwig, Arnold, Tan, & Boyd, 2003]; Hong Kong [Yau & Smetana, 1996, 2003a, 2003b], India [Madden, 1992; Neff, 2001], Indonesia [Carey & Ford, 1983], Japan [Crystal, 2000; Crystal, Watanabe, Weinfurt, & Wu, 1998; Killen & Sueyoshi, 1995], Korea [Kim, 1998; Kim & Turiel, 1996; Song, Smetana, & Kim, 1987], Taiwan [Killen, Ardila-Rey, Barakkats & Wang, 2000]), the Middle East (Turiel & Wainryb, 1998; Wainryb, 1995; Wainryb & Turiel, 1994), Africa (e.g., Benin [Conry, 2004], Nigeria [Hollos, Leis, & Turiel, 1986], Zambia [Zimba, 1987]), and Central and South America (e.g., Brazil [Nucci, Camino, & Sapiro, 1996], Colombia [Ardila-Rey & Killen, 2001; Killen et al., 2000; Mensing, 2002], and El Salvador [Killen et al., 2000]) has demonstrated that children in traditional cultures form a mixture of judgments on the dimensions of morality, social convention, and interpersonal obligation, while also maintaining concepts of persons as autonomous agents with choices, entitlements, and rights. Research examining the ways in which concerns with autonomy and interdependence are weighed and played out when they come into conflict indicated that children and adults in traditional societies do not subordinate individualistic goals to the concerns of the collective (as had been suggested by Triandis, 1990), but make judgments that account for and vary with the features of the context.

The conceptualization of persons in traditional societies as autonomous agents, with personal jurisdiction, personal choices, entitlements, and rights is of particular importance because of the common presumption that members of such cultures form sociocentric and interdependent concepts that override concerns with personal autonomy and independence. As put by Triandis, "In the case of extreme collectivism individuals do not have personal goals, attitudes, beliefs, or values, but only reflect those of the ingroup. One's behavior is totally predictable from social roles . . ." (1990, p. 52; see also Cousins, 1989; Markus & Kitayama, 1991; Shweder & Bourne, 1982; Triandis, 1989).

Research in several countries has demonstrated that persons in traditional societies develop concepts of personal agency including a sense of self, personal goals and interests, as well as an understanding that other persons also have personal goals and interests. Preschoolers in Hong Kong (Yau & Smetana, 2003a), children in Brazil (Nucci et al., 1996), and Colombia (Ardila-Rey & Killen, 2001), and adolescents in Japan (Crystal, 2000; Crystal et al., 1998; Gjerde & Onishi, 2000; Holloway, 1999, 2000; Killen & Sueyoshi, 1995), Hong Kong (Yau & Smetana, 1996, 2003b), and mainland China (Helwig et al., 2003) carve up areas of personal autonomy, including regulation of activities, schoolwork, personal appearance, chores, and friendships, which they think should be outside parental and societal regulation and subject exclusively to personal discretion. Children have disagreements with their parents over those issues, attempt to balance personal autonomy with other goals, and in many contexts uphold autonomy even in the face of conflicts with important competing social concerns, such as family harmony, the preservation of hierarchy, and obedience to roles and duties. Children in traditional societies appeal to individualistic concepts such as personal choice, freedom from adult interference, and the pursuit of individual desires and wants. Research with the Druze (Wainryb, 1995) and in India (Neff, 2001) has similarly suggested that in many contexts children and adolescents uphold the primacy of personal choice over interpersonal obligations.

Noteworthy are also the findings that adults in traditional societies recognize a realm of personal choice for their children. Several studies have shown that Chinese mothers from Taiwan and from mainland China residing in North America, and mothers in Japan and Brazil believe that children should be allowed some independent decision making (e.g., Chuang [2000] in Taiwan; Xu [2000] in mainland China) largely because they perceive the need to foster the child's developing autonomy and sense of individuality. Similarly, preschool teachers in Colombia, El Salvador, and Taiwan list among their important goals not only teaching cooperation, but also fostering the child's autonomy and self-reliance (Killen et al., 2000).

In addition to concepts bearing on a realm of personal jurisdiction, children in traditional societies also develop concepts of individual rights and freedoms (see also Helwig chap. 7, in this volume). As examples, children and adolescents in China (Helwig et al., 2003) and among the Druze in northern Israel (Turiel & Wainryb, 1998) maintain that freedom of speech, religion, and reproduction are basic human rights not contingent on existing laws and, in general, generate obligations of noninterference on the part of the government. Furthermore, they uphold those rights in many conditions, even in the face of conflicts with parental authority or other collective concerns. Not unlike the findings among North American children and adolescents, considerations with the prevention of harm, rather than with duty and obedience, are seen as consistently overriding individual rights.

When considered as a whole, research indicates that persons in traditional cultures judge in accord with roles, duties, and traditions in the social system, and also have a pervasive sense of persons as independent agents, with autonomy, entitlements, and rights. They draw boundaries on the jurisdiction of authority commands, and are aware of personal choice, entitlements, and rights as components of their social interactions. In exercising personal autonomy, they weigh their freedoms against other social considerations, such as the goals of the group, the welfare of others, and the hierarchical roles in the cultural system, revealing a complex picture of priorities and preferences.

Two systematic age-related patterns were observed in both Western and non-Western societies. Concerns with autonomy and personal choice were seen to increase systematically with age in all cultures, and across societies, children's judgments became more discriminative, nuanced, and context sensitive with age. Together, these findings suggest that the shift toward increased autonomy in adolescence and the increased understanding and concern with features of the social context reflect general developmental shifts rather than the manifestation of specific cultural orientations.

The finding that personal goals and individual rights are part of the thinking of members of hierarchically organized societies should not be taken to mean that those concerns are manifested identically across societies. The proposition, rather, is that irrespective of the type of cultural arrangements, interpersonal relationships are never merely the context for the enactment of cultural scripts. Relationships are multifaceted and involve mutual expectations, conflicts, and negotiations over issues of personal preference, rights, and fairness. It is argued, therefore, that in the context of most relationships some persons might attempt to impose their own personal choices and decisions on others; others might attempt to pursue their own personal goals and desires, try to assert their rights and entitlements, and arrive at compromises. How those issues are manifested may well vary (Turiel, 1994, 1996, 1998b).

Developmental and anthropological research illustrates the diverse ways in which personal autonomy is manifested in societies that are more restrictively organized around hierarchical systems. Research conducted with the hierarchically organized Israeli Druze community (Wainryb & Turiel, 1994), for example, has shown that persons occupying dominant positions in society have a strong sense of personal prerogative and entitlement. The experiences of autonomy for persons in subordinate positions, by contrast, are constrained and narrowed by society's demands for conformity. In most cases, persons in subordinate positions judge that not expressing their desires for personal freedom is preferable or necessary. Nonetheless, they are aware of their own goals and agendas, and view their roles and duties as unfairly restricting their autonomy and rights. Similarly, adult men and women from all strata of Indian society (Mines, 1988) describe themselves as having personal goals (e.g., occupational interests, economic goals) separate from the goals of their social group, many describe such goals as being in clear opposition to societal expectations, and most report postponing pursuing their goals until later in life, when the consequences of asserting their autonomy are less extreme (e.g., when disinheritance is no longer a threat). Further evidence of the diverse ways in which the striving for autonomy is manifested within the context of society's demands for conformity can be seen in the more or less covert processes of maneuvering and negotiation typical of persons in subordinate positions within societies; examples are the behaviors of South Asian women (Ewing, 1990, 1991), and of women in harems (Mernissi, 1994) and polygynous Bedouin societies (Abu-Lughod, 1993). Developmental research across cultures (Smetana, 2002) similarly indicate that although adolescents in traditional and Western societies express desires for personal autonomy, overt conflict between adolescents and parents in traditional societies is more muted—is reported to be less frequent and less intense—than among adolescents and their parents in Western societies.

The findings considered in this section indicate that children and adults across societies develop multiple social and moral concerns. These findings also indicate that children and adults across societies apply those concerns differently in different social contexts, giving priority sometimes to autonomy and rights and sometimes to tradition and social harmony. The proposition that *social contexts* have an influence on social judgments and actions is neither novel nor controversial. Findings from disparate perspectives, including social psychological research on conformity (Asch, 1952), obedience (Milgram, 1963), and prosocial behavior (Darley & Latane, 1968; Latane & Darley, 1970), as well as large-scale public opinion surveys dealing with attitudes toward personal freedoms and rights

(McClosky & Brill, 1983; Stouffer, 1955), and behavioristic studies dealing with learning and conditioning (Gewirtz, 1972) have long ago indicated that contextual variations are associated with significant shifts in judgments and actions. As examples, large-scale opinion surveys have shown persons endorse freedoms of speech and religion, freedom of assembly, the right to privacy and to divergent lifestyles in many situations; in other situations they subordinate those rights and freedoms to considerations of tradition, the maintenance of public order, or the welfare of others. Similarly, bystander intervention studies have shown that persons display a sense of interdependence and altruism in some contexts and a detached or individualistic tendency in others (for a more extensive discussion of these and similar findings, see Turiel & Wainryb [1994]).

One interpretation of the findings obtained in various types of psychological research concerning the contextual shifts in judgments and behaviors is that variations in judgments and behavior are mechanically elicited by variations in contextual features. An alternative interpretation—one that better captures the interactive process by which persons come to know and make decisions about their social world—is that the variations in contextual features alter the meaning of the situations being perceived and judged. This interpretation rests on the idea that persons make judgments about the total context experienced (Asch, 1952; Ross & Nisbett, 1991; Turiel & Wainryb, 1994). When viewed this way, the evidence of contextual variations in judgments and behaviors is consistent with the developmental proposition that social and moral understandings stem from an interactive process between the individual and diverse aspects of the social environment, a process entailing what Turiel recently labeled *flexibilities of mind* (Turiel & Perkins, 2004; see also Turiel, chap. 1, in this volume).

Regardless of their cultural background, children (and adults) are flexible in their approach to their social experiences and relationships: They continuously appraise the features of the social contexts in which they participate, adjust their understandings and behaviors, and make judgments that vary systematically in accord to the meanings and interpretations they attribute to those contexts. Research conducted over the last 15 years has documented aspects of the interactive and interpretive process that goes into making social and moral judgments (Wainryb, 2000, 2004a). This research has shown that when children (and adults) make social and moral judgments, they do so in reference to their interpretations of specific features of social contexts, such as their understandings of the relevant facts (Wainryb, 1991, 1993; Wainryb & Ford, 1998; Wainryb, Shaw, Langley, Cottam, & Lewis, 2004; Wainryb, Shaw, Laupa, & Smith, 2001; Wainryb, Shaw, & Maianu, 1998), the covert and overt responses of the persons involved (Shaw & Wainryb, 2004), their psychological states (Brehl & Wainryb, 2004; Chandler, Sokol, & Wainryb, 2000; Wainryb & Ford, 1998), and roles (Wainryb, Brehl, & Matwin, 2004), as well as the shared or contested nature of those understandings (Shaw & Wainryb, 1999).

Altogether, the research considered in this section indicates that persons in traditional and Western societies alike develop concerns with autonomy and rights, with group goals, harmony, and tradition, with human welfare, and with justice. The research also shows that rather than enacting cultural scripts, persons across societies approach social contexts within their cultures with flexibility.

Power and Conflicting Perspectives Within Cultures

The diversity of concerns that persons (children and adults) bring to bear on their sociomoral interactions in different contexts is one indication of the flexibility with which they approach their social environment. In addition, persons within a culture may also attribute different meanings to the same social contexts; this is especially evident, and especially meaningful, among individuals with unequal power. In fact, analyses of power and conflict within cultures are extremely significant for cultural analyses because they reveal that the meanings of cultural norms and practices are not shared among people in different roles (Turiel, 1994, 1996, 2002).

Social life in cultures includes not only collaboration among individuals, but also power clashes. In most societies, disagreements about what is right and valuable are common. Cultural practices and traditions are not authentic representations of the past handed down from one generation to the next; they are shaped, contested, and changed in the context of overt and convert disagreements and conflicts (Gjerde, 2004; Wikan, 2002). As mentioned, persons across cultures—even in traditional, hierarchically organized cultures—carve up a realm of personal goals and interests, and strive to achieve and maintain control over their own goals and interests even in the face of competing social considerations. It makes sense, therefore, that rather than (or at the least, in addition to) developing shared understandings about aspects of their culture, persons occupying social positions with more or less power interpret their experiences differently, develop different goals, interests, and perspectives, and find themselves in conflict with each other.

The contested nature of cultural meanings and practices, and the ubiquity of discontent and conflict among individuals in subordinate positions in traditional societies have been amply documented in journalistic accounts and ethnographic studies. Bumiller's (1990) account of the perspectives of women in India, Goodwin's (1994) interviews with women in Islamic countries, and Mernissi's (1994) account of women's and children's life in a harem in Morocco, show that women are aware of the burdens and injustices they experience as a consequence of cultural practices that accord men control over them. Abu Lughod's (1993) ethnographic studies of Bedouin women in Egypt illustrate the many ways in which women deliberately disobey and subvert practices they consider unfair, such as arranged marriages and polygamy. Similarly, Chen's (1995) work in Bangladesh and India documents defiant acts against traditions restricting employment for women and people of lower social castes. Conflict and discontent are also present in Western societies, as evidenced by the ubiquity of social movements challenging existing arrangements bearing on racial, economic, and gender relations (e.g., Okin, 1989). Across cultures, individuals often resist cultural practices and traditions that oppress them or, at the least, express discontent and give voice to their thwarted wishes. Sometimes resistance takes the form of organized political and social movements, but persons also challenge cultural meanings in everyday life through overt and covert activities (Turiel, 1994, 1996, 2002, 2003; see also Turiel, chap. 1, in this volume).

To understand moral and social development it is, therefore, not sufficient to attend to the perspectives of those with power—the very perspectives that are predominant in a culture's public discourse. The perspectives of those who lack the power to make their views count as culture must be documented as well. Systematic research into the perspectives held by people occupying subordinate positions in regard to their culture's practices revealed several layers of interpretation and conflict associated with power differentials in culture. Consider a series of studies conducted among the Israeli Druze community, a traditional and hierarchically organized society arranged around a patrilineal and patriarchal family structure (for comprehensive descriptions of this society, see Turiel & Wainryb [1994] and Wainryb & Turiel [1994]). This research, focused on conflicts between men and women or girls within the family, indicated that persons in different roles, with more or less power, had different experiences of and made different judgments about what were, ostensibly, the same situations.

For example, when considering conflicts between husbands and wives or between fathers and daughters in which the person in the dominant position objected to the behaviors of the person in the subordinate position, male and female participants attributed a great deal of decision making power to husbands and fathers, and judged that those conflicts should be resolved by the wife or daughter acquiescing to the man's wishes. As would be expected from a patriarchal society, their reasoning revolved around concerns with duties, social roles, and interdependence in the hierarchical system. However, the same participants approached conflicts between husband and wife or father and daughter differently when it was the person in the subordinate position who objected to the behaviors of the person in the dominant position. In that context, they stated that a wife or daughter should not interfere with a man's decisions, and accorded to men autonomy and entitlements. Thus, what appears to be one social context—disagreements between husband and wife or father and daughter—was interpreted in terms of status, roles, and interdependence in one condition (when a man objects to his wife's or daughter's choice), and in terms of independence, individual choice, and autonomy in the other condition (when a wife or daughter objects to her husband's or father's choice). Similar findings documenting the different perspectives concerning the freedoms and entitlements of those in dominant and subordinate positions have been obtained in India (Neff, 2001), Colombia (Mensing, 2002), and Benin (Conry, 2004).

Another important finding in these studies was that the experience of disagreeing with another family member had a different quality and carried distinctly different consequences for different persons. Whereas family disagreements carried a strong sense of entitlements for men, Druze women and girls described the serious negative consequences to a woman's welfare if she failed to acquiesce to her husband's or father's wishes: the husband might divorce the wife, throw the wife or daughter out of the house, or cause her physical harm. The importance of this finding is twofold. First, it shows that members of a society might have different experiences. Furthermore, it suggests that members of a society might adhere to cultural practices not only out of commitment to their culture, but also out of fear of the consequences likely to ensue from their failure to do so. This is of tremendous consequence for the study of social and moral development and culture, because it demonstrates that even when people go along with and participate in presumable shared cultural practices and traditions, the meaning of their participation in those practices is not transparent. It is indeed likely that participation in shared cultural practices and traditions more often than not conceals struggles over meaning, disagreement, and discontent. In the research with the Druze, for example, the majority of girls and women did not merely accept or identify with the hierarchy of roles and status common in their society; rather, they stated that the father's or husband's demands were unfair and violated the rights and entitlements of wives and daughters.

Altogether, the findings concerning the perspectives of those in subordinate positions in society underscore the contested nature of social and moral life and are suggestive of the critical role that disagreement, opposition, and resistance might play in social and moral development. Cultural psychologists, however, have made light of those perspectives and of the possibility that they reflect opposition and resistance (e.g., Miller, 2001; Menon & Shweder, 1998).

In the last several years, cultural psychologists have come to acknowledge that persons occupying subordinate positions in traditional societies might express discontent with their life, complain about the burdens imposed on them, and engage in behaviors meant to communicate their dissatisfaction. Cultural psychologists nevertheless deny that such behaviors implicate genuine concerns with personal autonomy, rights, and justice, or that they are meant to challenge or subvert fundamental aspects of cultural norms and practices. Rather, their argument has been that "dissent is frequently directed at relatively superficial or overt aspects of cultural practices, with more fundamental cultural commitments remaining unchallenged" (Miller, 2001, p. 166; see also Menon & Shweder, 1998).

Consider, as an example, the interpretations given by cultural psychologists to the findings from an ethnographic study conducted with Oriya Hindu women of the temple town of Bhubaneswar (Menon & Shweder, 1998). Women, it was found in that study, are discontent with their everyday lives, feel unappreciated, and make their feelings of displeasure known by dragging their feet, complaining loudly, and withholding their advice. These behaviors, we are told, do not suggest resistance or subversion. Rather, "in Old Town they are just the ways in which confident women express their dissatisfaction or displeasure with what is happening within the family" (Menon & Shweder, 1998, p. 179). Oriya Hindu women are not "subversive rebels, but rather active upholders of a moral order that Western feminists have largely failed to comprehend. High on the list of virtues and values in the moral order upheld by Oriya women are chastity, modesty, duty, self-discipline, the deferment of gratification, self-improvement, and the ideal of domestic 'service'. Low on the list are liberty and social equality" (p. 156). This cultural interpretation, it should be noted, fails to articulate what *does* constitute credible evidence of genuine expressions of resistance and opposition. (Might cultural psychologists count the discontents that fueled Blacks' and women's opposition to the cultural values and practices prevailing in the United States in the 1960s as credible expressions of thwarted autonomy and violated rights? It is possible that they would, insofar as those behaviors occurred in the context of an *individualistic* society oriented to the pursuit of individual goals, rights, and freedoms. If they did, however, it would be upon them to justify the basis on which a society that denied rights to Blacks and women can be said to be "rights oriented"). More important, this interpretation minimizes and trivializes the behaviors and perspectives of those who occupy subordinate positions in traditional societies.

The judgments and behaviors of persons in subordinate positions, including the evidence pointing to discontent, resistance, opposition, and subversion, reveal their deep understanding of personal goals, entitlements, and autonomy as well as their concern with justice and rights. They also reveal their willingness and readiness to participate in the life of their communities while also engaging in cultural critique. The descriptions emerging from journalistic accounts and research indicate that discontent, resistance, opposition, and subversion not only are part of the everyday lives of persons in subordinate positions, but often involve nontrivial physical and emotional commitments and risks on their side. When women in traditional societies engage in overt and covert behaviors meant to circumvent and subvert those aspects of their culture's practices and norms they consider unfair or overly restrictive, their behavior is not limited to complaining or dragging their feet. They form alliances with other women in an effort to gain power that allows them to manipulate circumstances in ways that are beneficial to them; they engage in deception about their own and other women's whereabouts and secretly take and horde resources for the purpose of pursuing forbidden goals and activities; they bargain, complain, pretend, hide, and run away to avoid being forced into marriages or arrangements they do not desire; and they engage in open confrontation and defiance—and at times form political organizations—to protect their own and other women's freedoms and integrity. In doing so, they risk being ostracized, cut off from their children, beaten, burned, and killed. Members of lower and disenfranchised castes within traditional societies make demands and engage in confrontations, including physical confrontations, thereby risking their livelihoods and lives.

By dismissing or minimizing those judgments and behaviors, cultural analyses over-look the sincerity and depth of the pain afflicting people in subordinate positions, the genuineness and legitimacy of their resentment and anger, the seriousness of their en-gagement, and the complexity of their moral commitments. Dismissing or minimizing the perspectives of those in subordinate positions, however, might be an unavoidable el-ement of psychological theories that view participation in culture, and identification and compliance with culture, as explanations for development.

The reliance on processes of participation in culture and identification with culture as explanations for social and moral development ignores the crucial roles that dis-agreement, conflict, and subversion may have in social and moral development. It also ignores that compliant behaviors and attitudes might conceal the workings of power within hierarchical contexts. "One aspect of power is the ability to define what counts as knowledge and to make definitions of knowledge appear *natural* rather than artificially constructed . . . [power] is not necessarily experienced as directly coercive, but frames, molds and structures the settings in which people live their lives and what they can and cannot do without being subject to coercive violence" (Gjerde, 2004, p. 145). The absence of discontent and opposition cannot be merely presumed to indicate that persons have freely chosen to participate in, or genuinely identified with, their culture's practices and traditions. Instead, the absence of discontent and opposition might reflect the very con-ditions of deprivation and injustice in which those cultural practices and traditions arise (Baumrind, 1998; Nussbaum, 1999; Okin, 1999).

The absence of discontent and opposition may be manifested not only in those instances (well documented in developmental research) in which individuals in subordinate positions judge that they (and others) should acquiesce to the demands of cultural norms even though they judge them to be unjust (Wainryb & Turiel, 1994), but also in situations in which individuals do not seem to recognize the unfairness of the arrangements by which they live. In an article suggestively entitled *God created me to be a slave*, Burkett (1997) reports on Mauritania's 90,000 slaves. Based on conversations with members of this community, Burkett notes that "the possibility of rebellion, like the possibility of a world made up entirely of free men and women, is inconceivable among people who have lost their collective memory of freedom" (p. 57). The acceptance of oppression might result also from conditions of injustice much less extreme than slavery. Having lacked even minimal access to education or employment, women might no longer express a desire for it. Having been subjected to veiling, purdah, or genital mutilation, women might endorse, and even enforce, those practices. Because people who have had "such a reduced menu of options . . . can be said to have chosen only in a reduced sense" (Nussbaum, 1999, p. 23), it cannot be assumed that those individuals have freely chosen or consented to their conditions (Baumrind, 1998; Okin, 1999; Sunstein, 1999).

The notion of false consciousness or, in Nussbaum's (1999) terms, "deformation of desire," is complex and besieged by controversy. At the heart of the problem is whether a practice or tradition can be deemed unjust or oppressive if the presumed victims do not ex-perience it as unjust or oppressive. Some contend that it is "patronizing, even impertinent" (Parekh, 1999, p. 73) to view individuals as misguided victims of false consciousness, and that doing so disempowers them and reinforces the very images of vulnerability and unfitness that are commonly used to justify their curtailed choices (Bhabha, 1999; Minow, 2002; Parekh, 1999). It may, on the other hand, be argued that the perspectives of outsiders should not be dismissed outright, especially in those situations in which oppression and injustice have been longstanding and pervasive, as they may point to possibilities that—as in the case of Mauritania's slaves—are no longer recalled or contemplated. "A voice that is in some sense foreign [may be] essential to the self expression of a marginalized or oppressed group: for people often appropriate good ideas from outside and vindicate their dignity by pointing to examples of respect elsewhere" (Nussbaum, 1999, p. 8).

The dismissal of the proposition that persons occupying subordinate positions may genuinely be concerned with autonomy and justice, as well as the acceptance of the proposition that persons might freely choose oppression over freedom, are neither desultory nor incoherent. Such views do, in fact, make sense within certain assumptions about the nature of culture and development. If cultures are integrated, coherent, and harmonious, and a person's thoughts, emotions, and morality—her preferences and desires—are shaped by culture, "resulting less in psychic unity for humankind than in ethnic divergences in mind, self, and emotion" (Shweder, 1990, p. 1), it would make sense that persons choose or cherish cultural conditions that, from an outsider's point of view, curtail their freedom and choices. After all, from such a cultural perspective, the preference of autonomy and rights is merely a product of culture, neither more nor less in tune with human nature than the preference of submission and inequality (or "chastity, modesty, duty, self-discipline, the deferment of gratification, self-improvement, and the ideal of domestic service"; Menon & Shweder, 1998, p. 156).

As evidenced in the research and other accounts considered thus far, cultures are not harmonious monoliths, and the strive for agency and autonomy (along with the strive for justice, mutuality, and friendship) is not a parochial, Western invention. Both the recognition of culture as a nucleus of power and conflict, and the idea of a common human nature—albeit one that is liable to being constrained by features of social and cultural organization—make a person's choice of subjugation over freedom opaque and begging explanation. Although it would be naive to claim that the question of false consciousness is straightforward, it makes sense to remain skeptical about the meanings of compliance and consent on the part of persons living lives of deprivation.

Even as they acknowledge that there is some diversity within all cultures, cultural psychologists have assumed that there is, within cultures, substantial homogeneity in cultural meanings and practices. Indeed, their assumption has been that the homogeneity in cultural meanings and practices is substantial enough to allow for meaningful comparisons among the main orientations of different cultures. As reviewed thus far, the varied social and moral perspectives of people within cultures, the contextual variations observed in their judgments and behaviors, and the critical judgments they make about their culture's norms and practices challenge cultural psychologists' conceptualization of culture.

The data considered in this chapter indicate strongly that there is little homogeneity to cultural meanings and cultural practices. Social and moral life within cultures features many layers and levels of diversity, plurality, and conflict. Significant variations in social reasoning and social behavior occur within cultures and within individuals. Adults and children, in traditional and Western societies alike, develop multiple social and moral concerns, and approach social contexts within their cultures with flexibility. Orientations to *both* autonomy and interdependence are central to their social relationships. Adults and children reflect on their culture's norms and practices, and often take critical positions with respect to some of them and attempt to subvert or change them. Power differences constitute a central dimension along which substantial heterogeneity, rather than homogeneity, emerges within cultures. This heterogeneity becomes instantiated in diverse experiences of seemingly identical situations, different perspectives on cultural practices, and conflicting goals and interest. It is hard to see how any one set of substantially homogeneous cultural meanings can be identified within such heterogeneous environments. Instead, the many specific social contexts in which individuals participate within their culture, and their varied and conflicting interpretations and evaluations of such contexts, ought to be the focus of the study of social and moral development.

It should be noted, however, that the notion of culture has long been viewed as critical for anchoring the idea of human diversity. Cultural differences (differences among cultures) have been intricately associated with the fight against racism and, more recently, with the promotion of multiculturalism and the rights of cultures. It could therefore be argued that, in downplaying differences among cultures, the acultural discourse proposed here—a discourse that focuses on the multiple contexts, diverse experiences, and heterogeneous perspectives of persons within cultures—obscures the range of human diversity. The opposite view is argued herein. Not only, as indicated by the data considered, is the range of human diversity not fully represented in terms of cultural differences, but the construct of culture—as typically used in cultural analyses—cannot serve as the basis for promoting respect for human diversity and justice. These issues are addressed in the next section.

CAPTURING MORAL DIVERSITY, AND THE PROBLEMS OF CULTURE

The concept of culture has been associated with struggles against social hierarchies and racism, and with the promotion of tolerance for diversity. As typically used in the social sciences, however, the construct of culture has been implicated in the perpetuation of various forms of violence, discrimination, and oppression. To understand why this has been so, it is necessary to review, even if cursorily, the social and historical circumstances surrounding the rise of the idea of culture (for more comprehensive socio-historical accounts, see Finkielkraut, 1995; Hatch, 1983).

Culture first emerged as an alternative to the concept of race early in the 20th century. Breaking with traditional anthropology, Boas (1908, 1938) disputed the 19th-century evolutionist view that races exhibit fixed moral and intellectual differences and proposed, instead, that those differences can be explained in terms of cultural conditioning. Whereas evolutionists thought in terms of a single direction in history, one of "progress," which led them to rank societies relative to one another, Boas and others (e.g., Benedict, 1934; Herskovits, 1955) advanced the idea that each culture has its own unique pattern of development and pursues its own goals, thereby challenging the belief in the superiority of Western civilization. Soon, Boasian thought became standard anthropological thought; anthropologists no longer spoke of savages and civilized peoples but of *cultures*, a term that carried no evaluative implications. Along with the idea of cultures came the idea of *tolerance*—the belief that all cultures ought to be given equal respect. This idea of tolerance was a much welcome alternative to the Victorian proposition concerning the superiority of Western civilization, a proposition used to justify Western expansionism and the imposition of civilized Western standards on savages.

It is not difficult to see why culture became not only a central feature of anthropological thinking, but also a concept of tremendous sociopolitical importance. It is likely, in fact, that the notion of tolerance, and the related ideas of human dignity and self-determination, have always been at the basis of the strong appeal enjoyed by the construct of culture in the social sciences. Few would disagree with the proposition that the peremptory criticism of the traditions of other cultures is unjustified. However, the equally peremptory expectation that all aspects of a culture be judged as acceptable is also unjustified. Such an expectation is inconsistent with the driving force behind tolerance; positive judgments "on demand" are not genuine expressions of respect. More significantly, the presumption that all aspects of cultures are acceptable, and the demand that the integrity of cultures be protected, overlook (or dismiss) the possibility that some cultural practices might be unjust and oppressive (Hatch, 1983).

The import of these issues is far from being merely academic. In recent years, cultural traditions and practices such as female genital mutilation, footbinding, forced marriages, honor-related violence, seclusion/purdah, and polygamy have generated complex debates across the world. Consider, as one example, the practice of female genital mutilation[1] (hereafter referred to as FGM), which although widely resisted, is still common in many African countries. The devastating short- and long-term effects of FGM on women's health and sexuality have been amply documented (Amnesty International, 1995; World Health Organization, 1994). Nonetheless, in the view of proponents of tolerance, diversity, and cultural integrity, FGM is, in the countries where it is practiced, "not only popular but fashionable" (Shweder, 2002) and no different from Western practices such as breast augmentation and other medically unnecessary and potentially harmful procedures promoted by Western conceptions of female beauty (see also Tamir, 1996). Western criticisms of FGM—it is further argued—are merely emotional responses of disgust ("yuck responses"; Shweder, 2002, p. 222), that violate the right of individuals to perpetuate their culture (Gilman, 1999; Parekh, 1999).

The likening of FGM to matters of taste or aesthetics ignores crucial distinctions between procedures such as FGM and breast augmentation. FGM is carried out by force on small girls as young as 4 or 5 years, and even when the girls are older their consent is not solicited; the preferences and decisions of the women who perform the operation are constrained by conditions such as illiteracy, malnutrition, economic dependency, intimidation, and lack of political power. By contrast, procedures common in Western societies, such as breast augmentation, are undergone largely by adults whose menu of choices is considerably richer; the misinformation and social pressure that may affect their decision to undergo such procedures, although deplorable, are not the same as physical force and coercion. In overlooking those distinctions, proponents of tolerance trivialize the experiences of the girls and women who are subjected to FGM. It is the dismissal of the experiences and perspectives of some people in a culture and their right to decide which aspects of their culture they wish to perpetuate, that makes it possible to endorse practices such as FGM as well as the position that all aspects of culture are acceptable and valuable.

The debates concerning FGM and other such cultural practices have come even closer to home, as thousands of individuals have emigrated from the Middle East, North Africa, and South Asia, bringing their cultural practices along with them into European and North American societies. Although most agree that immigrants ought to be treated with the same respect as everyone else, there is little agreement concerning what, precisely, that means. Should immigrants be allowed to continue practicing, in Western societies, cultural practices such as FGM, footbinding, or polygamy? Should they be allowed to take their

---

[1] Although various terms, such as *female circumcision, clitoridectomy, infibulation,* and *female genital mutilation* (FGM) are often used indistinctly, they represent distinctly different procedures; FGM is the standard term for all those procedures in the medical literature. *Female circumcision* has been rejected by international medical practitioners because it suggests the analogy to male circumcision, which is generally believed to have no harmful effects on health and sexual functioning. Although there are some cases of symbolic procedures among girls and women that involve no removal of tissue, those procedures are not included in the category of FGM by international agencies. On the other hand, the male equivalent of clitoridectomy is the amputation of most of the penis; the male equivalent of infibulation is the removal of the entire penis and part of the scrotal skin. Approximately 85% of women who undergo FGM have clitoridectomy. Although infibulation accounts for only 15% of the total, 80% to 90% of all operations in Sudan and Somalia are of this kind (for more details, see Nussbaum, 1999, Chap. 4).

children, who may have been born and raised in a Western country, back to their country of origin to be married against their will? More generally, should respect for their culture take precedence over civil rights and the principle of equality?

Advocates of cultural diversity are likely to answer in the affirmative. In fact, "cultural defenses" are now increasingly invoked in the United States (Maslow-Cohen & Bledsoe, 2002) and in other Western countries (Wikan, 2002) on behalf of members of immigrant groups charged with committing domestic crimes. Underlying this strategy is the presumption that persons socialized in a foreign culture should not be held fully accountable for behavior that violates official law, if their behavior conforms to their own culture's norms (Maslow-Cohen & Bledsoe, 2002). Furthermore, the argument is that only a defense that allows evidence of the act's cultural ground can provide a person with an opportunity to be understood in authentic terms (Honig, 1999). The cultural defense ("my culture made me do it") is being used in the United States more widely than it is generally recognized and, often with success, in cases involving FGM, murder of wives presumed to have committed adultery by male immigrants from Asian and Middle Eastern countries, kidnap and rape by Hmong Laotian men alleging that their actions are part of their cultural practice of "marriage by capture" (*zij poj niam*), and murder of children by Japanese or Chinese mothers (who also attempt to take their own lives) alleging that mother–child suicide is meant to rectify the shame and damage caused by a husband's infidelity (Maslow-Cohen & Bledsoe, 2002; Okin, 1999).

Inevitably, the notion of cultural defense as it relates to the understanding of moral diversity raises difficult issues. Cultural defenses entail the recognition that to fully understand a person's behavior it is necessary to understand the meanings within which he or she functions and makes decisions. However, cultural defenses also privilege the status of culture by denigrating the equal status of victims. Furthermore, because the promotion of cultures' survival tends to implicate largely the behavior of women and children ("how far would an Algerian immigrant get, I wonder, if he refused to pay the interest on his Visa bill on the grounds that Islam forbids interest on borrowed money," asks Katha Pollitt [1999, p. 29]), it is *they* who most often pay the price for tolerance and respect for culture. Consider Wikan's (2002) report of the deeply disturbing events surrounding instances of abductions and "honor killings" among immigrants in Norway. By her report, girls and young women from immigrant communities often come to serious harm at the hand of their male relatives. They are beaten or killed because they had presumably acted in disregard for "their culture," even though these young women were raised, and many were even born, in Norway. How should it be decided, and who should decide, what their culture is? "Who is the quintessential 'immigrant' . . . is he or she a first generation immigrant only, or are the children of immigrants also included? If so . . . how many generations does it take? . . . What is the identity of a girl, or a boy, who has grown up in historical circumstances different from those of the parents?" (Wikan, 2002, p. 72).

The criticism of the proposition that practices such as FGM and honor killings should be tolerated (whether carried out in the cultures of origin or in the midst of Western societies) need not be taken to mean that concerns with ethnocentrism and racism are trivial: those are significant concerns that merit close consideration. Neither does this criticism imply that the task of distinguishing between cultural practices that (although unpalatable) should be tolerated and those that should be resisted is uncomplicated: that task is vexing, and reasonable people could reach different conclusions about particular cases. The critical discussion of cultural practices such as FGM and honor killings is, instead, meant to underscore that the force of arguments for tolerance of diversity and for the perpetuation of cultural traditions rests largely on the assumption that cultures are organic totalities whose members speak in a single voice (whether or not it is *their* genitals that are being mutilated, or *their* freedom to participate in society that is being restricted). This assumption is mistaken. Cultures comprise multiple and conflicting goals and perspectives, including some that may be distorted or silent. The construct of culture as typically used by cultural psychologists, and the associated notions of cultural integrity and tolerance, tend to promote or legitimize the perspectives of some members of a society at the expense of the perspectives of others. The notion of culture, it is argued here, is not well suited for capturing the diversity of human experience or for furthering respect for persons and justice.

Thinking of diversity in terms of cultural differences fails to acknowledge the fact that people are—or should be—free to decide "which traditions they want to perpetuate and which they want to discontinue, how they want to deal with their history, with one another, and so on" (Habermas, 1994, p. 125). This problem, namely that the anchoring of diversity in terms of cultural differences can lead to trampling with individuals' freedom to decide what aspects of their culture they wish to preserve and which they wish to reject, is also evidenced in discussions about multiculturalism.

Unlike the cases described, bearing on cultural practices that entail inflicting harm or restricting the freedoms of some members of a culture, the notion of multiculturalism does not suggest internal conflicts or the silencing of certain voices. On the contrary, the idea of multiculturalism calls to mind instances in which persons speak in a collective cultural voice for the explicit purpose of articulating overlapping experiences, meanings, and identities in response to situations of injustice and inequality. Toward the end of the 20th century, many such collective voices emerged under the banner of multiculturalism and identity politics. In the United States, for example, the 1960s universalistic discourse of racial desegregation and civil rights gave way, by the late 1970s, to a discourse on culture and cultural identity. A collective voice—a call for black power, for example—was articulated as a means for contesting racism; the very act of rediscovering and celebrating African-American culture was seen as a powerful means for discrediting wholesale racist scripts (Boykin, 1983; Boykin & Toms, 1985; McLoyd, 2004). The expectation underlying identity politics was that public recognition of collective identities would contribute to the empowerment and advancement of previously disenfranchised groups (Taylor, 1994). By articulating collective identities and demanding that their culture be recognized and respected for its particularity (e.g., as African Americans), underprivileged groups were expected to "turn into an object of pride what they had been taught to be ashamed of" (Finkielkraut, 1995, p. 68).

Insofar as those collective cultural identities are acknowledged as partially overlapping representations that become articulated at a specific time and around specific shared experiences and goals (Gjerde, 2004), they may be of considerable social and political (perhaps also psychological) value for furthering the rights of individuals and groups. However, under the banner of multiculturalism and identity politics, cultural identities have been typically reified and made into bounded and transhistorical realities.

> Ethnopolitics stresses, ideologizes, reifies, modifies, and sometimes virtually recreates the putatively distinctive and unique cultural heritages of the ethnic groups that it mobilizes. Ethnic categories are thus validated as forming ethnic groups, and these groups are defined with reference to a culture they are assumed to share.... [The abstract notion of culture] is replaced by a reified entity that has a definite substantive content and assumed the status of a thing that people "have" or "are members of"... a substantive heritage that is normative, predictive of individuals' behavior, and ultimately a cause of social action." (Baumann, 1996, pp. 11–12).

This move into a reified notion of culture, although perhaps necessary to effect social and political change, holds grave danger to the autonomy of members of those collectivities both at the individual and at the societal levels. For culture does not capture the multiplicity of experiences (concerns, goals, perspectives) of persons within societies, and people, regardless of their group of origin, have the right to be regarded as individuals and not just as a part of a group. In a compelling response to Taylor's (1994) "The Politics of Recognition," a strong endorsement of multiculturalism and group rights, Appiah (1994) pointed to the perils that collective identities have for individuals, even as he recognized the urgent historical circumstances in which those identities emerge:

> In our current situation in the multicultural West . . . certain individuals have not been treated with equal dignity because they were, for example, women, homosexuals, blacks. . . . In order to construct a life with dignity, it seems natural to take the collective identity and construct positive life-scripts instead. An African-American after the Black Power movement takes the old script of self-hatred, the script in which he or she is a nigger, and works, in community with others, to construct a series of positive Black life-scripts . . . It may even be historically, strategically necessary for the story to go this way. But I think we need to . . . ask whether the identities constructed in this way are ones we . . . can be happy with in the longer run. Demanding respect for people as blacks and as gays requires that there are some scripts that go with being an African-American or having same-sex desires. There will be proper ways of being black and gay, there will be expectations to be met, demands will be made. It is at this point that someone who takes autonomy seriously will ask whether we have not replaced one kind of tyranny with another. . . . If I had to choose between the world of the closet and the world of gay liberation, or between the world of *Uncle Tom's Cabin* and Black Power, I would, of course, choose in each case the latter. But I would like not to have to choose. (pp. 160–163)

Further evidence that collective identities such as those defined by culture or ethnicity may pose dangers to the individual are the longstanding debates about gender as a collective category, the role of power in defining gender identities, and the situation of women who have been constrained by their collective identity as "nothing but women." In turn, consideration of gender categories serves to illustrate how, for example, African Americans, immigrants, or gays, could feel constrained by the expectation that they make their ethnic identity, country of origin, or sexual orientation the central part of their lives (Wolf, 1994).

None of these considerations, however, are meant to suggest that the diversity of human experience is unimportant. Arguably, the construct of culture, as instantiated in cultural identities, can serve as a means for self-determination and resistance. Nevertheless, when reified into integrated and harmonious entities capable of dictating meaning, cultural categories also have the potential for becoming a repressive straightjacket.

At the societal level, concerns with diversity and cultural identities have become instantiated in the notion of multiculturalism and the demands for cultural rights. By the end of the 20th century, the demands for the recognition of cultural identities and cultural rights had become a main staple in the political discourse of liberal democracies. In an effort to articulate the danger that the movement toward multiculturalism and cultural rights holds for Western democracies, Habermas (1994) underscored the distinction between the obligation of a society to grant rights to cultures (an enterprise he likened to "the preservation of species by administrative means") and its obligation to ensure that persons have the freedom to live according to the prescription of their cultural heritage without suffering discrimination because of it. The challenging of culture neither equals nor implies indifference toward human diversity. On the contrary, the challenging of the construct of culture reflects the belief that persons should have "the opportunity to confront [their own] culture and to perpetuate it in its conventional form or transform it; as well as the opportunity to turn away from its commands with indifference, or break with it self-critically and then live spurred on by having made a conscious break with tradition, or even with a divided identity" (Habermas, 1994, p. 132).

Proponents of cultural rights and of tolerance of cultural diversity—proponents, that is, of culture as *the* measure of diversity—might argue that the failure to recognize human diversity as enshrined in cultures blends the distinctiveness of persons' experiences across the world into a homogeneous and unauthentic mold (Taylor, 1994). The argument put forth here is that the idea of culture, as typically understood, underscores participation in culture and acceptance of cultural norms and practices while dismissing the possibility that some members of cultures might dislike, resent, resist, or wish to change some aspects of their culture. Although meant to be liberating in its acceptance and respect for divergent traditions, the notion of culture has been used to implicitly and explicitly justify norms, arrangements, and practices that are unjust and oppressive. The reliance on the notion of culture as a main anchor of human diversity obstructs the promotion of both respect for diversity and justice (Wainryb, 2004b). An approach that recognizes the multiple and conflicting perspectives within cultures is better suited for the task.

CONCLUDING THOUGHTS: MORAL DIVERSITY AND UNIVERSALITY IN CULTURE

The discourse about culture has enjoyed a sort of conceptual and communicative hegemony in the world of psychological research. This discourse has centered on an understanding of culture stamped with assertions of holism and integration. This view of culture ignores systems of inequality within societies and conceals the varied and complex experiences of individuals. It overestimates the power of society to dictate meaning and underestimates individual agency, rendering the process of development as one of conservative adaptation to culture, and individuals as cultural imprints. Adopting a more critical understanding of culture implies discarding the language of coherence and harmony, and acknowledging that cultures are made up of individuals who have diverse concerns and goals, and are capable of reflecting on values, practices, and traditions, embracing some and rejecting others. It also implies acknowledging that, in any community, persons, especially those in unequal positions, are bound to develop different, and often conflicting, perspectives. Hence, the study of social and moral development in culture must attend to the many contexts of social life in cultures and to the varied ways in which individuals make sense of their experiences in those social contexts. This is not to say that the social and moral lives of persons in culture are devoid of pattern. Rather, within cultures, multiple partial and overlapping patterns assert themselves to varying degrees, in different social contexts, and different realms of experience.

Speaking about the diversity within cultures does not imply that differences among cultures do not exist or are trivial. To be sure, historical, social, and political circumstances shape and frame extremely different developmental contexts for people in different parts of the world. Moreover, societies differ substantially in regard to the realms of life that are organized around hierarchical relations (e.g., economic, family, religious), the extent to which hierarchical differences are sanctioned and institutionalized, and the opportunities for individuals to gain (or lose) power and status. In some cultures, for example, there are sharp status distinctions between men and women within the family, and strong sanctions associated with disobedience or transgressions. Some of the research considered in this chapter indicated that concerns with, for example, autonomy and rights, or parent–child conflicts, are manifested differently in such societies. At the same time, the research indicated that multiple social and moral considerations other than hierarchical distinctions *also* apply in such hierarchically organized cultures, including concerns with personal autonomy and conflicts between people of different status. It also showed that less hierarchically organized societies are not free of status distinctions and inequalities. Analyses of social and moral development in cultures must, therefore, be sensitive to the variety of cultural conditions and arrangements; indeed, it is the homogenizing effect of culture and its tyrannical ways that need resisting. While attending to the complexity within societies, research must remain alert to potential differences between societies, including the multiple and distinct ways in which persons and groups are being mistreated or oppressed within their culture.

Urging sensitivity to contextual specificity and cultural conditions, however, is not the same as posing distinct, essential, human natures, or arguing for moral relativism. Nussbaum (1999) has made a strong case for why universalism is the best path to promote diversity, pluralism, and tolerance, as have other political philosophers (e.g., Okin, 1999), anthropologists (e.g., Hatch, 1983; Wikan, 2002), and psychologists (e.g., Turiel, 2002; Wainryb, 2004b). Appiah (1992) put it succinctly: "We shall solve our problems if we see them as human problems arising out of a special situation, and we shall not solve them if we see them as African problems, generated by our being somehow unlike others" (pp. 179). Although he made this comment in reference to the challenges inherent to Pan-African politics, Appiah's call to resist the essentialization of cultural differences is of foremost importance to the study of social and moral development.

This can be accomplished by being at once alert to patterns of differences between and within cultures and skeptical of the coherence of culture. As illustrated by the research considered in this chapter, persons in different cultures experience both autonomy and connectedness in the context of their multiple, more or less hierarchically organized, relationships. Persons in different cultures also negotiate the intrapersonal and interpersonal conflicts that unavoidably result from the coexistence of multiple social goals and types of relationships. Cooperation, submission, opposition, and subversion all coexist within contested cultural landscapes. To capture the diversity of social and moral life across cultures while both steering clear from dangerous essentializations and giving voice to the multiple and dynamic perspectives that coexist within cultures, research on social and moral development should focus its attention on the local ways in which goals and concerns with matters of justice, autonomy, friendship, mutuality, and tradition are played out in harmony or conflict, in distinct contexts, within different cultures. Research must also question presumptions about children's and adults' acceptance of cultural norms and practices and, instead, try to identify the local forms that cooperation, submission, opposition, and subversion take in different societies. In moving away from the construct of culture as the main anchor of human diversity, research on social and moral development has the potential for documenting the range of diversity in human development—not the different moral outlooks of different cultures, but the multiple and conflicting outlooks of different people within different cultures.

REFERENCES

Abu-Lughod, L. (1991). Writing against culture. In R. E. Fox (Ed.), *Recapturing anthropology: Working in the present* (pp. 137–162). Santa Fe, NM: School of American Research Press.
Abu-Lughod, L. (1993). *Writing women's worlds: Bedouin stories.* Berkeley: University of California Press.

Amnesty International. (1995). *Human rights are women's rights* (pp. 131–134). London: Amnesty International.

Appiah, K. A. (1992). *In my father's house: Africa in the philosophy of cultures.* Oxford: Oxford University Press.

Appiah, K. A. (1994). Identity, authenticity, survival: Multicultural societies and social reproduction. In A. Gutmann (Ed.), *Multiculturalism* (pp. 149–164). Princeton: Princeton University Press.

Ardila-Rey, A., & Killen, M. (2001). Colombian preschool children's judgments about autonomy and conflict resolution in the classroom setting. *International Journal of Behavioral Development, 25,* 246–255.

Asch, S. (1952). *Social psychology.* Englewood Cliffs, NJ: Prentice-Hall.

Baumann, G. (1996). *Contesting culture: Discourse of identity in multi-ethnic London.* New York: Cambridge University Press.

Baumrind, D. (1998). From ought to is: A neo-Marxist Perspective on the use and misuse of the culture construct. *Human Development, 41,* 45–65.

Benedict, R. (1934). *Patterns of culture.* Boston: Houghton Mifflin.

Bhabha, H. K. (1999). Liberalism's sacred cow. In J. Cohen, M. Howard, & M. Nussbaum (Eds.), *Is multiculturalism bad for women?* (pp. 79–84). Princeton: Princeton University Press.

Boas, F. (1908). *Anthropology.* New York: Columbia University Press.

Boas, F. (1938). *The man of primitive man.* New York: Free Press.

Boykin, A. W. (1983). The academic performance of Afro-American children. In J. T. Spence (Ed.), *Achievement and achievement motives* (pp. 324–371). San Francisco: Freeman.

Boykin, A. W., & Toms. F. D. (1985). Black child socialization: A conceptual framework. In H. P. McAdoo & J. L. McAdoo (Eds.), *Black children: Social, educational, and parental environments* (pp. 33–52). Newbury Park, CA: Sage.

Brehl, B., & Wainryb, C. (2004). *Children's explanations of harmful behavior: Naive realism and interpretation.* Unpublished manuscript, University of Utah.

Bruner, J. (1990). *Acts of meaning.* Cambridge, MA: Harvard University Press.

Bumiller, E. (1990). *May you be the mother of a hundred sons: A journey among the women of India.* New York: Fawcetts Columbine.

Burkett, E. (1997, October 12). God created me to be a slave. *New York Times Magazine,* pp. 56–60.

Carey, N., & Ford, M. (1983, August). *Domains and social and self-regulation: An Indonesian study.* Presented at the meeting of the American Psychological Association, Los Angeles.

Chandler, M. J., Sokol, B. W., & Wainryb, C. (2000). Beliefs about truth and beliefs about rightness. *Child Development, 71,* 91–97.

Chen, M. (1995). A matter of survival: Women's right to employment in India and Bangladesh. In M. C. Nussbaum & J. Glover (Eds.), *Women, culture, and development: A study of human capabilities* (pp. 61–75). New York: Oxford University Press.

Chuang, S. S. (2000). *Chinese mothers' parenting beliefs about the personal domain for young children.* Unpublished doctoral dissertation, University of Rochester.

Cole, M. (1990). Cultural psychology: A once and future discipline? In J. J. Berman (Ed.), *Nebraska Symposium on Motivation: Vol. 38. Cross-cultural perspectives* (pp. 279–335). Lincoln: University of Nebraska Press.

Conry, C. (2004). *Moral reasoning about traditional and everyday gender hierarchy in Benin West Africa: The roles of informational assumptions about capabilities and pragmatic concerns.* Unpublished manuscript, University of California, Berkeley.

Cousins, S. D. (1989). Culture and self-perception in Japan and the United States. *Journal of Personality and Social Psychology, 56,* 124–131.

Crystal, D. (2000). Concepts of deviance and disturbance in children and adolescents: A comparison between the United States and Japan. *International Journal of Psychology, 35,* 207–218.

Crystal, D. S., Watanabe, H., Weinfurt, K., & Wu, C. (1998). Concepts of human differences: A comparison of American, Japanese, and Chinese children and adolescents. *Developmental Psychology, 34,* 714–722.

Damon, W. (1977). *The social world of the child.* San Francisco: Jossey-Bass.

Darley, J. M., & Latane, B. (1968). Bystander intervention in emergencies: Diffusion of responsibility. *Journal of Personality and Social Psychology, 8,* 377–383.

Doise, W., Clemence, A., & Spini, D. (1996). Human rights and social psychology. *The British Psychological Society Social Psychology Section Newsletter, 35,* 3–21.

Ewing, K. (1990). The illusion of wholeness: Culture, self and the experience of inconsistency. *Ethos, 18,* 251–278.

Ewing, K. (1991). Can psychoanalytic theories explain the Pakistani woman? Intrapsychic autonomy and interpersonal engagement in the extended family. *Ethos, 19,* 131–160.

Finkielkraut, A. (1995). *The defeat of the mind.* New York: Columbia University Press.

Fuligni, A. J. (1998). Authority, autonomy, and parent-adolescent conflict and cohesion: A study of adolescents from Mexican, Chinese, Filipino, and European backgrounds. *Developmental Psychology, 34,* 782–792.

Gewirtz, C. (1972). Some contextual determinants of stimulus potency. In R. D. Parke (Ed.), *Recent trends in social learning theory* (pp. 7–33). New York: Academic Press.

Gilman, S. L. (1999). "Barbaric" rituals?. In J. Cohen, M. Howard, & M. Nussbaum (Eds.), *Is multiculturalism bad for women?* (pp. 53–56). Princeton: Princeton University Press.

Gjerde, P. F. (2004). Culture, power, and experience: Toward a person-centered cultural psychology. *Human Development, 47,* 138–157.

Gjerde, P. F., & Onishi, M. (2000). Selves, cultures, and nations: The psychological imagination of "the Japanese" in the era of globalization. *Human Development, 43,* 216–226.

Goodwin, J. (1994). *Price of honor: Muslim women lift the veil of silence on the Islamic world.* New York: Penguin.

Greenfield, P. M. (1994). Independence and interdependence as developmental scripts. In P. M. Greenfield, & R. R. Cocking (Ed.), *Cross-cultural roots of minority child development* (pp. 1–40). Hillsdale, NJ: Lawrence Erlbaum Associates.

Greenfield, P. M. (1995, March). Discussant's remarks. In C. Raeff (Chair), *Individualism and collectivism as cultural contexts for developing different modes of independence and interdependence.* Society for Research in Child Development, Indianapolis, IN.

Habermas, J. (1994). Struggles for recognition in the democratic constitutional state. In A. Gutmann (Ed.), *Multiculturalism* (pp. 107–148). Princeton: Princeton University Press.

Hatch, E. (1983). *Culture and morality: The relativity of values in anthropology.* New York: Columbia University Press.

Helwig, C. C. (1995). Adolescents' and young adults' conceptions of civil liberties: Freedom of speech and religion. *Child Development, 66,* 152–166.

Helwig, C. C. (1997). The role of agent and social context in judgments of freedom of speech and religion. *Child Development, 68,* 484–495.

Helwig, C. C. (1998). Children's conceptions of fair government and freedom of speech. *Child Development, 69,* 518–531.

Helwig, C. C., Arnold, M. L., Tan, D., & Boyd, D. (2003). Chinese adolescents' reasoning about democratic and authority-based decision making in peer, family, and school contexts. *Child Development, 74,* 783–800.

Herskovits, M. J. (1947). *Man and his work: The science of cultural anthropology.* New York: Knopf.

Herskovits, M. J. (1955). *Cultural anthropology.* New York: Knopf.

Hofstede, G. (1980). *Culture's consequences: International differences in work-related values.* Beverly Hills, CA: Sage.

Hollos, M., Leis, P. E., & Turiel, E. (1986). Social reasoning of Ijo children and adolescents in Nigerian communities. *Journal of Cross-Cultural Psychology, 17,* 352–374.

Holloway, S. D. (1999). Divergent cultural models of child rearing and pedagogy in Japanese preschools. In E. Turiel (Ed.), *New directions for child development. Vol. 83: Development and cultural change: Reciprocal processes* (pp. 61–75). San Francisco: Jossey Bass.

Holloway, S. D. (2000). *Contested childhood: Diversity and change in Japanese preschools.* New York: Routledge.

Honig, B. (1999). "My culture made me do it." In J. Cohen, M. Howard, & M. Nussbaum (Eds.), *Is multiculturalism bad for women?* (pp. 35–40). Princeton: Princeton University Press.

Kagitcibasi, C., & Berry, J. W. (1989). Cross-cultural psychology: Current research and trends. *Annual Review of Psychology, 40,* 493–531.

Kahn, P. H., & Turiel, E. (1988). Children's conceptions of trust in the context of social expectations. *Merrill Palmer Quarterly, 34,* 403–419.

Killen, M. (1990). Children's evaluations of morality in the context of peer, teacher-child, and family relations. *Journal of Genetic Psychology, 151,* 395–410.

Killen, M., Ardila-Rey, A., Barakkatz, M., & Wang, P. (2000). Preschool teachers' perceptions about conflict resolution, autonomy, and the group in four countries: United States, Colombia, El Salvador, and Taiwan. *Early Education and Development, 11,* 73–92.

Killen, M., & Smetana, J. G. (1999). Social interactions in preschool classrooms and the development of young children's conceptions of the personal. *Child Development, 70,* 486–501.

Killen, M., & Sueyoshi, L. (1995). Conflict resolution in Japanese preschool interactions. *Early Education and Development, 6,* 313–330.

Killen, M., & Turiel, E. (1998). Adolescents' and young adults' evaluations of helping and sacrificing for others. *Journal on Adolescence, 8,* 355–375.

Killen, M., & Wainryb, C. (2000). Independence and interdependence in diverse cultural contexts. In S. Harkness & C. Raeff (Eds.), *Individualism and collectivism as cultural contexts for development. New directions for child development, 87* (pp. 5–22). San Francisco: Jossey-Bass.

Kim, J. A. (1998). Korean children's concepts of adult and peer authority and moral reasoning. *Developmental Psychology, 34,* 947–955.

Kim, J. M., & Turiel, E. (1996). Korean children's concepts of adult and peer authority. *Social Development, 5,* 310–329.

Latane, B., & Darley, J. M. (1970). *The unresponsive bystander: Why doesn't he help?* New York: Appleton-Crofts.

Laupa, M. (1991). Children's reasoning about three authority attributes: Adult status, knowledge, and social position. *Developmental Psychology, 27,* 321–329.

Laupa, M., & Turiel, E. (1986). Children's conceptions of adult and peer authority. *Child Development, 57,* 405–412.

Laupa, M., & Turiel, E. (1993). Children's concepts of authority and social contexts. *Journal of Educational Psychology, 85,* 191–197.

Madden, T. (1992). *Cultural factors and assumptions in social reasoning in India.* Unpublished doctoral dissertation, University of California, Berkeley.

Markus, H. R., & Kitayama, S. (1991). Culture and the self: Implications for cognition, emotion, and motivation. *Psychological Review, 98,* 224–253.

Markus, H. R., Mullally, P., & Kitayama, S. (1997). Selfways, Diversity in modes of cultural participation. In U. Neisser & D. Jopling (Eds.), *The conceptual self in context: Culture, experience, self-understanding* (pp. 13–61). Cambridge, MA: Cambridge University Press.

Maslow-Cohen, J., & Bledsoe, C. (2002). Immigrants, agency, and allegiance: Some notes from anthropology and from law. In R. A. Shweder, M. Minow, & H. R. Markus (Eds.), *Engaging cultural differences: The multicultural challenge in liberal democracies* (pp. 99–127). New York: Russell Sage Foundation.

McClosky, M., & Brill, A. (1983). *Dimensions of tolerance: What Americans believe about civil liberties.* New York: Russell Sage.

McLoyd, V. C. (2004). Linking race and ethnicity to culture: Steps along the road from inference to hypothesis testing. *Human Development, 47,* 185–191.

Menon, U., & Shweder, R. A. (1998). The return of the "white man's burden": The moral discourse of anthropology and the domestic life of Hindu women. In R. A. Shweder (Ed.), *Welcome to middle age!: (And other cultural fictions)* (pp. 139–188). Chicago: University of Chicago Press.

Mensing, J. F. (2002). Collectivism, individualism, and interpersonal responsibilities in families: Differences and similarities in social reasoning between individuals in poor, urban families in Colombia and the United States. Unpublished doctoral dissertation, University of California, Berkeley.

Mernissi, F. (1994). *Dreams of trespass: Tales of a Harem girlhood.* Reading, MA: Addison-Wesley.

Milgram, S. (1963). Behavioral study of obedience. *Journal of Abnormal and Social Psychology, 67,* 371–378.

Miller, J. G. (2001). Culture and moral development. In D. Matsumoto (Ed.), *The handbook of culture and psychology* (pp. 151–169). New York: Oxford University Press.

Mines, M. (1988). Conceptualizing the person: Hierarchical society and individual autonomy in India. *American Anthropologist, 90,* 568–579.

Minow, M. (2002). About women, about culture: About them, about us. In R. A. Shweder, M. Minow, & H. R. Markus (Eds.), *Engaging cultural differences: The multicultural challenge in liberal democracies* (pp. 252–268). New York: Russell Sage Foundation.

Neff, K. D. (2001). Judgments of personal autonomy and interpersonal responsibility in the context of Indian spousal relationships: An examination of young people's reasoning in Mysore, India. *British Journal of Developmental Psychology, 19,* 233–257.

Neff, K. D., Turiel, E., & Anshel, D. (2002). Reasoning about interpersonal responsibility when making judgments about scenarios involving close personal relationships. *Psychological Reports, 90,* 723–742.

Nucci, L. (1981). The development of personal concepts: A domain distinct from moral or societal concepts. *Child Development, 52,* 114–121.

Nucci, L. P., Camino, C., & Sapiro, C. M. (1996). Social class effects on Northeastern Brazilian children's conceptions of areas of personal choice and social regulation. *Child Development, 67,* 1223–1242.

Nucci, L. P., & Nucci, M. S. (1982). Children's responses to moral and social-conventional transgressions in free-play settings. *Child Development, 53,* 1337–1342.

Nucci, L. P., & Weber, E. K. (1995). Social interactions in the home and the development of young children's conceptions of the personal. *Child Development, 66,* 1438–1452.

Nussbaum, M. C. (1995). Human capabilities, female human beings. In M. C. Nussbaum & J. Glover (Eds.), *Women, culture, and development: A study of human capabilities* (pp. 61–104). New York: Oxford University Press.

Nussbaum, M. C. (1999). *Sex and social justice.* New York: Oxford University Press.

Nussbaum, M. C. (2000). *Women and human development: The capabilities approach.* Cambridge, UK: Cambridge University Press.

Okin, S. M. (1989). *Justice, gender, and the family.* New York: Basic Books.

Okin, S. (1999). Is multiculturalism bad for women? In J. Cohen, M. Howard, & M. Nussbaum (Eds.), *Is multiculturalism bad for women?* (pp. 7–26, 115–132). Princeton: Princeton University Press.

Oyserman, D., Coon, H., & Kemmelmeier, M. (2002). Rethinking individualism and collectivism: Evaluation of theoretical assumptions and meta-analyses. *Psychological Bulletin, 128,* 3–72.

Parekh, B. (1999). A varied moral world. In J. Cohen, M. Howard, & M. Nussbaum (Eds.), *Is multiculturalism bad for women?* (pp. 69–75). Princeton: Princeton University Press.

Pollitt, K. (1999). Whose culture? In J. Cohen, M. Howard, & M. Nussbaum (Eds.), *Is multiculturalism bad for women?* (pp. 27–30). Princeton: Princeton University Press.

Rogoff, B. (1990). *Apprenticeship in thinking: Cognitive development in social context.* New York: Oxford University Press.

Ross, L., & Nisbett, R. M. (1991). *The person and the situation: Perspectives on social psychology.* Philadelphia: Temple University Press.

Ruck, M. D., Abramovitch, R., & Keating, D. P. (1998). Children's and adolescents' understandings of rights. *Child Development, 69,* 404–417.

Shaw, L., & Wainryb, C. (1999). The outsider's perspective: Young adults' judgments of social practices of other cultures. *British Journal of Developmental Psychology, 17,* 451–471.

Shaw, L., & Wainryb, C. (2004). *Children's and adolescents' thinking about victimization and consent.* Unpublished manuscript, University of Utah.

Shweder, R. A. (1990). Cultural psychology—What is it? In J. W. Stigler, R. A. Shweder, & G. Herdt (Eds.), *Cultural psychology: Essays on comparative human development* (pp. 27–66). New York: Cambridge University Press.

Shweder, R. A. (2000). The psychology of practice and the practice of the three psychologies. *Asian Journal of Social Psychology, 3,* 207–222.

Shweder, R. A. (2002). "What about female genital mutilation?" and why understanding culture matters in the first place. In R. A. Shweder, M. Minow, & H. R. Markus (Eds.), *Engaging cultural differences: The multicultural challenge in liberal democracies* (pp. 216–251). New York: Russell Sage Foundation.

Shweder, R. A., & Bourne, E. J. (1982). Does the concept of person vary cross-culturally? In A. J. Marsella & G. M. White (Eds.), *Cultural conceptions of mental health and therapy.* Boston: Reidel.

Shweder, R. A., Mahapatra, M., & Miller, J. G. (1987). *Culture and moral development. The emergence of morality in young children* (pp. 1–83). Chicago: University of Chicago Press.

Shweder, R. A., Much, N. C., Mahapatra, M., & Park, L. (1997). The "big three" of morality (autonomy, community, divinity) and the "big three" explanations of suffering. In A. M. Brandt (Ed.), *Morality and health* (pp. 119–169). New York: Routledge.

Shweder, R. A., & Sullivan, M. A. (1993). Cultural psychology: Who needs it? *Annual Review of Psychology, 44,* 497–527.

Sinha, D., & Tripathi, R. (1994). Individualism in a collectivistic culture: A case of coexistence of opposites. In U. Kim, H. C. Triandis, C. Kagitcibasi, S. Choi, & G. Yoon (Eds.), *Individualism and collectivism: Theory, method, and applications.* Beverly Hills, CA: Sage.

Smetana, J. G. (1981). Preschool children's conceptions of moral and social rules. *Child Development, 52,* 1333–1336.

Smetana, J. G. (1985). Preschool children's conceptions of transgressions: The effects of varying moral and conventional domain-related attributes. *Developmental Psychology, 21,* 18–29.

Smetana, J. G. (1988). Adolescents' and parents' conceptions of parental authority. *Child Development, 59,* 321–335.

Smetana, J. G. (1989). Adolescents' and parents' reasoning about actual family conflict. *Child Development, 60,* 1052–1067.

Smetana, J. G. (2000). Middle class African American adolescents' and parents' conceptions of parental authority and parenting practices: A longitudinal investigation. *Child Development, 71,* 1672–1686.

Smetana, J. G., & Asquith, P. (1994). Adolescents' and parents' conceptions of parental authority and adolescent autonomy. *Child Development, 65,* 1147–1162.

Smetana, J. G., & Bitz, B. (1996). Adolescents' conceptions of teachers' authority and their relations to rule violations in school. *Child Development, 67,* 1153–1172.

Smetana, J. G., & Braeges, J. L. (1990). The development of toddlers' moral and conventional judgments. *Merrill-Palmer Quarterly, 36,* 329–346.

Smetana, J. G., & Gaines, C. (1999). Adolescent-parent conflict in middle-class African-American families. *Child Development, 70,* 1447–1463.

Smetana, J. G., Killen, M., & Turiel, E. (1991). Children's reasoning about interpersonal and moral conflicts. *Child Development, 62,* 629–644.

Song, M. J., Smetana, J. G., & Kim, S. Y. (1987). Korean children's conceptions of moral and conventional transgressions. *Developmental Psychology, 23,* 577–582.

Spiro, M. (1993). Is the Western conception of the self "peculiar" within the context of the world cultures? *Ethos, 21,* 107–153.

Stouffer, S. (1955). *Communism, conformity and civil liberties.* New York: Doubleday.

Strauss, C. (2000). The culture concept and the individualism-collectivism debate: Dominant and alternative attributions for class in the United States. In L. Nucci & G. E. Saxe (Eds.), *Culture, thought, and development* (pp. 85–114). Mahwah, NJ: Lawrence Erlbaum Associates.

Sunstein, C. R. (1999). Should sex equality law apply to religious institutions? In J. Cohen, M. Howard, & M. Nussbaum (Eds.), *Is multiculturalism bad for women?* (pp. 85–94). Princeton: Princeton University Press.

Tamir, Y. (1996). Hand off clitoridectomy: What our revulsion reveals about ourselves. *The Bostom Review, 21,* 3/4.

Taylor, C. (1994). The politics of recognition. In A. Gutmann (Ed.), *Multiculturalism* (pp. 25–74). Princeton: Princeton University Press.

Tisak, M. (1986). Children's conceptions of parental authority. *Child Development, 57,* 166–176.

Tisak, M. S., & Turiel, E. (1988). Variation in seriousness of transgressions and children's moral and conventional concepts. *Developmental Psychology, 24,* 352–357.

Triandis, H. C. (1989). The self and social behavior in differing cultural contexts. *Psychological Review, 96,* 506–520.

Triandis, H. C. (1990). Cross-cultural studies of individualism and collectivism. In J. J. Berman (Ed.), *Nebraska Symposium on Motivation 1989,* Vol. 37 (pp. 41–133). Lincoln: University of Nebraska Press.

Triandis, H. C. (1995). *Individualism and collectivism.* Boulder, CO: Westview Press.

Turiel, E. (1983). *The development of social knowledge: Morality and convention.* Cambridge, UK: Cambridge University Press.

Turiel, E. (1994). Morality, authoritarianism, and personal agency. In R. J. Sternberg & P. Ruzgis (Eds.), *Personality and intelligence.* Cambridge, UK: Cambridge University Press.

Turiel, E. (1996). Equality and hierarchy: Conflict in values. In E. S. Reed, E. Turiel, & T. Brown (Eds.), *Values and knowledge* (pp. 75–102). Mahwah, NJ: Lawrence Erlbaum Associates.

Turiel, E. (1998a). The development of morality. In W. Damon (Series Ed.) & N. Eisenberg (Vol. Ed.), *Handbook of child psychology* (5th ed.). *Vol. 3: Social, emotional, and personality development* (pp. 863–932). New York: Wiley.

Turiel, E. (1998b). Notes from the underground: Culture, conflict, and subversion. In J. Langer & M. Killen (Eds.), *Piaget, evolution, and development* (pp. 271–296). Mahwah, NJ: Erlbaum.

Turiel, E. (2002). *The culture of morality: Social development, context, and conflict.* Cambridge, UK: Cambridge University Press.

Turiel, E. (2003). Resistance and subversion in everyday life. *Journal of Moral Education, 32,* 115–130.

Turiel, E., & Perkins, S. A. (2004). Flexibilities of mind: Conflict and Culture. *Human Development, 47,* 158–178.

Turiel, E., & Wainryb, C. (1994). Social reasoning and the varieties of social experience in cultural contexts. In H. W. Reese (Ed.), *Advances in child development and behavior, Vol. 25* (pp. 289–326). New York: Academic Press.

Turiel, E., & Wainryb, C. (1998). Concepts of freedoms and rights in a traditional, hierarchically-organized society. *British Journal of Developmental Psychology, 16,* 375–395.

Turiel, E., & Wainryb, C. (2000). Social life in cultures: Judgments, conflict, and subversion. *Child Development, 71,* 250–256.

Wainryb, C. (1991). Understanding differences in moral judgments: The role of informational assumptions. *Child Development, 62,* 840–851.

Wainryb, C. (1993). The application of moral judgments to other cultures: Relativism and universality. *Child Development, 64,* 924–933.

Wainryb, C. (1995). Reasoning about social conflicts in different cultures: Druze and Jewish children in Israel. *Child Development, 66,* 390–401.

Wainryb, C. (1997). The mismeasure of diversity: Reflections on the study of cross-cultural differences. In E. Turiel (Ed.), *Development and cultural change: Reciprocal processes new directions for child development, Vol. 83* (pp. 51–76). San Francisco: Jossey-Bass.

Wainryb, C. (2000). Values and truths: The making and judging of moral decisions. In M. Laupa (Ed.), *Rights and wrongs: How children evaluate the world, new directions for child development, Vol. 89* (pp. 33–46). San Francisco: Jossey-Bass.

Wainryb, C. (2004a). Is and ought: Moral judgments about the world as understood. In J. Baird & B. Sokol (Eds.), *Mind, morals, and action. New directions for child development.* San Francisco: Jossey-Bass.

Wainryb, C. (2004b). The study of diversity in human development: Culture, urgencies, and perils. *Human Development, 47,* 131–137.

Wainryb, C., Brehl, B., & Matwin, S. (2004). *Being hurt and hurting others: Children's narrative accounts and moral judgments of their own interpersonal conflicts.* Unpublished manuscript, University of Utah.

Wainryb, C., & Ford, S. (1998). Young children's evaluations of acts based on beliefs different from their own. *Merrill-Palmer Quarterly, 44,* 484–503.

Wainryb, C., & Langley, M. (2003). *Victims and perpetrators: Children's narrative accounts of their own interpersonal conflicts.* Unpublished manuscript, University of Utah.

Wainryb, C., Shaw, L., Langley, M., Cottam, K., & Lewis, R. (2004). Children's thinking about diversity of belief in the early school years: Judgments of relativism, tolerance, and disagreeing persons. *Child Development, 75,* 687–703.

Wainryb, C., Shaw, L., Laupa, M., & Smith, K. R. (2001). Children's, adolescents', and young adults' thinking about different types of disagreements. *Developmental Psychology, 37,* 373–386.

Wainryb, C., Shaw, L., & Maianu, C. (1998). Tolerance and intolerance: Children's and adolescents' judgments of dissenting beliefs, speech, persons, and conduct. *Child Development, 69,* 1541–1555.

Wainryb, C., & Turiel, E. (1994). Dominance, subordination, and concepts of personal entitlements in cultural contexts. *Child Development, 65,* 1701–1722.

Wainryb, C., & Turiel, E. (1995). Diversity in social development: Between or within cultures? In M. Killen & D. Hart (Eds.), *Morality in everyday life: Developmental perspectives* (pp. 283–316). Cambridge, UK: Cambridge University Press.

Weber, E. K. (1999). Children's personal prerogative in home and school contexts. *Early Education and Development, 10,* 499–515.

Wikan, U. (1991). Toward an experience-near anthropology. *Cultural Anthropology, 6,* 285–305.

Wikan, U. (2002). *Generous betrayal: Politics of culture in the new Europe.* Chicago: University of Chicago Press.

Wolf, S. (1994). Commentary to Charles' Taylor "The politics of recognition." In A. Gutmann (Ed.), *Multiculturalism* (pp. 75–86). Princeton: Princeton University Press.

World Health Organization (1994). WHO leads action against female genital mutilation. *World Health Forum, 15.*

Xu, F. (2000). *Chinese children's and mothers' concepts regarding morality, social convention, and children's personal autonomy.* Unpublished doctoral dissertation, University of Illinois, Chicago.

Yau, J., & Smetana, J. G. (1996). Conceptions of moral, social-conventional, and personal events among Chinese preschoolers in Hong Kong, *Child Development, 74,* 647–658.

Yau, J., & Smetana, J. G. (2003a). Adolescent-parent conflict among Chinese adolescents in Hong Kong, *Child Development, 67,* 1262–1275.

Yau, J., & Smetana, J. G. (2003b). Adolescent-parent conflict in Hong Kong and Shenzhen: A comparison of youth in two cultural contexts. *International Journal of Behavioral Development, 27,* 201–211.

Zimba, R. F. (1987). *A study of forms of social knowledge in Zambia.* Unpublished doctoral dissertation, Purdue University.

IV

Conscience and Internalization

The chapters in this section reflect approaches to moral development that focus on the child's internalization of societal values and standards and the acquisition of conscience. As described in Chapter 9 by Joan Grusec, internalization approaches have a long history in the field of moral development. Grusec provides a historical overview of research by socialization theorists, tracing the evolution of both psychoanalytic and behaviorist approaches to the internalization of social standards. She lucidly describes the connection between these earlier theoretical perspectives and more recent approaches to parenting and moral development, including information processing and attribution theories, which has reflected a successful integration of multiple theoretical approaches.

Beginning with Freud, conscience had been a central construct in both psychoanalytic and behaviorist approaches to moral development. *Conscience* refers to an internalized mechanism that regulates children's behavior by exerting control over impulses and regulating conduct consistent with societal values, norms, and expectations. Children are said to have successfully acquired a conscience when they are able to comply with rules, even in the absence of supervision or surveillance by parents or other socialization agents. After falling into disfavor for many decades, there has been a resurgence of interest over the last decade in the construct of conscience. In Chapter 10, Ross Thompson, Sara Meyer, and Meredith McGinley describe this recent research on conscience. In their view, conscience is the central mechanism governing young children's moral development and provides the foundations for the development of interpersonal relationships. They provide an integrative conceptualization of conscience that draws on recent research in emotional development, social understanding, and mental schemas. Drawing on attachment theory, they describe the relational influences that impact conscience development.

Chapter 11, by Leon Kuczynski and Geoffrey Navara, also picks up the narrative thread described by Grusec by providing a contemporary reconceptualization of socialization theories. In the face of overwhelming empirical evidence that socialization is bidirectional between parents and children (rather than proceeding in a top-down and unidirectional fashion) and that children have an active role in the socialization process, Kuczynski and Navara present a new conceptualization of socialization in the family that stresses its transactional nature and the active attempts of the child to interpret and evaluate the messages they receive. They expand their dialectical view by attempting to link transactional processes of socialization within the family with the larger social system by examining families in the context of culture and social change. Thus, these chapters demonstrate how the study of conscience and socialization in the family has been revitalized and transformed in current theories and research.

9

THE DEVELOPMENT OF MORAL BEHAVIOR AND CONSCIENCE FROM A SOCIALIZATION PERSPECTIVE

JOAN E. GRUSEC
UNIVERSITY OF TORONTO

This chapter describes the approach of socialization theorists to the study of moral development. The chapter is historical in its orientation, noting how the ideas of socialization theorists about children's acquisition of the values and standards of society, including moral values and standards, have evolved over time. It begins with Freud and ends with examples of current thinking about the socialization process that include, but are not limited to, the socialization of morality. It describes a tradition in which researchers and theorists have been concerned with how children learn rules and standards of behavior and how this learning is manifested in conscience. Conscience includes adherence to societal requirements; feelings of guilt, confession, and attempts at reparation after deviation from those requirements; and compliance with rules in the absence of surveillance by agents of socialization. The rules encompass a wide range of actions that include what Turiel and his colleagues (Turiel, 1998) have labeled as *moral* (involving prescriptive understanding of how individuals should behave toward one another) but extend beyond them to include any deviations from societal demands, including arbitrary rules of social behavior or social conventions. Indeed, little attention has been paid until recently (e.g., Bugental & Goodnow, 1998) to the possibility that different domains of rules might call for different socialization practices.

Directed in part by the model of socialization provided by Freud (see, for example, Freud, 1930/1955, 1937) research and theory have focused on behavioral and emotional manifestations of conscience and on the internalization or taking over of societal values as the individual's own. Internalization implies that moral conduct occurs not because of external pressure such as hope of reward or fear of punishment, but because the values underlying it are apparently self-generated or intrinsically motivated. Attention has centered on the understanding of socialization, that is, of the process by which individuals acquire a set of standards, values, attitudes, beliefs, and behaviors that they accept as their own and that are based on or derived from the standards of one or more groups of which they are a member. Individuals are seen to be assisted in this acquisition by the actions of more experienced group members including parents, teachers, peers, and siblings as well as by information they receive from the media, including television and the Internet, although it should be noted that the greatest interest has been in the role of parents as agents of socialization. Socialization does not involve the transmission or simple passing on of moral and other values. Although Freud emphasized a "social mold" model whereby children incorporate or take over the values of their parents as their own, the model evolved into a bidirectional one that saw the child as active in the socialization process, co-constructing with agents of socialization a set of guidelines for acceptable behavior. More recently, some (e.g., Kuczynski, 2003) have moved to a transactional model that emphasizes the agency of the child in socialization, with a focus on the considerable powers that children have in their interactions with their parents.

PSYCHOANALYTIC THEORY AND MORAL DEVELOPMENT

Freud's analysis of psychosocial stages provided the underpinnings of early theories of conscience and moral development. According to Freud (1930/1955), in each psychosexual stage children are faced with the problem of how to solve a conflict between the desire to satisfy bodily desires and the need to comply with the demands of society. The manner in which that conflict is resolved directs their life-long social and emotional functioning. With respect to moral development, the most important childhood events are those that happen during the phallic stage which begins around the fourth year of life. For boys, mothers, initially viewed as loved objects because of their provision of food and security, now become desirable as sexual objects. Consequently the Oedipus complex develops and boys see themselves as rivals with their fathers for their mother's love. Fear of castration by the father, however, defuses the situation. Thus, anxiety produced by the fear leads the boy to identify with or become similar to his father (or to his conception of what the father is like) as a way of gaining fantasy control over this dangerous person. By playing the role of the father the boy also sees himself as in a more competitive position for the mother's attention. Through identification with the aggressor, then, boys adopt or internalize the moral values of society as these values are revealed in the moral actions of the father. Their superego, or conscience, thereby develops through internalization or incorporation of paternal standards and paternal demands for compliance.

And what of girls? The mechanism for internalization obviously cannot be the same as that for boys. Girls are alleged to have sexual feelings for their fathers (the so-called Electra complex) and to view their mothers as rivals for their father's affection, but they cannot fear castration. The mechanism that operates for them involves the continuing loving relationship they already have with their mother: They wish to emulate her because she is a source of food and security. But anaclitic identification is not as powerful a mechanism as identification with the aggressor because it, unlike identification with the aggressor, is not separated from its emotional origins. As a result, moral behavior in girls is more likely to be guided by feeling, rather than by a sense of justice and an impersonal approach to moral issues characteristic of the male approach.

Although specific notions about children's incestuous desires have little empirical foundation, some of Freud's basic ideas have been elaborated by others. In a description of the central thrust of psychoanalytic theorists in the area of conscience development, Hoffman

(1970a) summarized these elaborations. Young children inevitably experience frustration resulting from control by their parents as well as from events such as physical discomfort and illness that are not caused by their parents. These frustrations promote the growth of hostility toward the parent, but the hostility is repressed because children are afraid they will be punished by their parents, particularly that their parents will stop loving them or abandon them. Adoption in relatively unmodified form of parental rules and prohibitions helps to maintain the repression as well as increases the likelihood of parental approval. Children also develop a generalized motive to emulate their parents' behavior and inner states, including assumption of the parents' role as disciplinarian. Thus the hostility they have felt for the parent is turned inward where it assumes the form of guilt. Under these conditions the only way they can avoid feelings of guilt is to conform to parental prohibitions and to defend against conscious awareness of desires to deviate from prescribed norms. In all of this, then, theoretical notions of identification, introjection, and internalization play a dominant role in attempts to understand conscience development, setting the stage for much subsequent thinking about moral development and conscience.

SOCIAL LEARNING THEORY AND MORAL DEVELOPMENT

Sears and the Yale Institute of Human Relations

Psychoanalytic theory was limited by its general lack of amenability to empirical testing. However, academic psychologists attempting to develop a theory of personality and human development during the 1930s and 1940s nevertheless saw its value for their work. Behaviorism and stimulus–response theory, at their peak of influence, provided the essence of scientific rigor. But Freud and the psychoanalysts provided clinically based material from which to fashion a general theory of human behavior. And so social learning theory emerged as a combination of research rigor and rich material about human experience. Mark May at the Yale Institute of Human Relations began to construct a unified science of behavior, with Clark Hull, Neal Miller, John Dollard, Leonard Doob, Neil Miller, O. Hobart Mower, and Robert Sears among those who joined in the enterprise (e.g., Dollard, Doob, Miller, Mowrer, & Sears, 1939). Their work involved essentially a reinterpretation of Freudian hypotheses within the framework of stimulus–response theory. In this way they produced a dynamic view of human functioning and development.

Robert Sears did the most to achieve an understanding of the development of moral behavior within this unified framework. For example, with his colleagues he proposed an account of the relation between frustration and aggression, including an analysis of how aggressive behavior is socialized in childhood (Dollard et al., 1939). The proposal (influenced by Freud's early writings on the topic) was of aggression as a drive, motivated by exposure to frustration, with its strength determined by the amount of frustration experienced. Although aggression was the dominant response to frustration, Sears (1941) proposed that dependency, regression, or increased problem solving could, through learning, replace the naturally dominant one. Aggression acquires (secondary) drive properties because aggressive responses are paired with the successful elimination of frustrating conditions as well as paired with possible elicitation of pain in the individual who is the source of frustration (a primarily reinforcing event).

Sears (Sears, Whiting, Nowlis, & Sears, 1953) expanded his analysis of socialization in the moral domain with the concept of a dependency drive. He suggested that proximity to the caregiver is secondarily reinforcing to the young child because the caregiver has been paired with the reduction of primary drives such as hunger, thirst, and the need for warmth and comfort. Dependency's move to the status of an acquired drive was necessitated by the fact that children behave in a dependent manner even when all primary drives are reduced: The mechanism proposed for its development was the conflict produced by inconsistent reward and punishment, which provides the necessary energy for maintaining operation of the drive. Moving from this point, Sears proposed a theory of identification. The inability of young children to discriminate between themselves and their mothers means that her actions are seen to be equivalent to their own actions. Reproduction of the mothers' behaviors, therefore, is reinforcing and so a habit of imitative responding develops, along with a secondary drive system whose goal is to act like the mother. In this way Sears managed to translate Freud's concept of anaclitic identification into learning theory terms. Moreover, he provided a way to understand how children acquire parental values through identification with, or becoming like, their caregivers. He had difficulty, however, in explaining how identification could acquire drive status (Grusec, 1992).

Sears, Maccoby, and Levin (1957) provided the first major test of social learning hypotheses with respect to conscience development and internalization of values. In a survey of 379 families living in the Boston area, they assessed a large number of variables relevant to childrearing and socialization, including the techniques of discipline mothers used when their children engaged in misdeeds and indices of their children's conscience development which included guilt, confession, and reparation. Here, then, conscience was operationalized in a way that included emotional responses to deviation as well as behavioral features such as resistance to temptation and taking over of the parental role (e.g., self-instruction with respect to forbidden activity). Note that successful socialization, then, required that children not comply with parental dictates because of obvious external pressure, a condition indicating they had not actually internalized values. Indeed, young children were seen as moving along a continuum from external control requiring constant parental surveillance and direct intervention to self-control based on fear of punishment or hope of reward to inner control appearing to come from acceptance of parental standards of conduct as their own.

Sears and associates (1957) divided discipline strategies into two categories: *love oriented*, which included praise, isolation, reasoning, and withdrawal of love, and *material*, which included tangible rewards, deprivation, and physical punishment. In support of their theory of identification, they found that mothers who used love-oriented techniques had children with higher levels of conscience development than did the children of mothers who used materially oriented techniques. Sears and colleagues suggested this was because children punished by withdrawal of love needed to practice parental actions, including moral actions, to provide themselves with the love that had been withdrawn. As well, conscience development was higher in children who had mothers who were relatively warm and used love withdrawal than in those who had relatively cold mothers or warm mothers who used little or no withdrawal of love. Clearly children of warm mothers who used withdrawal of love would gain more secondary reinforcement from rehearsing the actions, standards, and values of their mothers than would those of cold mothers and mothers who did not withdraw their love.

Although this study and later ones (e.g., Sears, Rau, & Alpert, 1964) were major steps forward in the empirical investigation of moral development, the social learning approach that borrowed heavily from the psychoanalytic perspective became mired down in the challenges it faced in trying to describe the development of secondary or acquired drives (Grusec, 1992) and was supplanted by a more parsimonious theory developed by Albert Bandura and Richard Walters (1963) that relied primarily on the behaviorist tradition.

Bandura and Social Cognitive Theory

Albert Bandura and Robert Sears were colleagues at Stanford University, and their mutual interest in a theory of human behavior guided by the principles of learning brought them to each other's attention. A link between them was also provided by Richard Walters, then a Stanford graduate student. Bandura and Walters' first book was very much in the tradition of social learning theory as it then existed. In *Adolescent Aggression* (1959), they argued that antisocial boys were suffering from dependency anxiety arising from rejection and punishment of dependent responses and that the frustration promoted by this anxiety accounted for their antisocial actions. They also spoke to the role played by identification in the internalization of control over behavior, with emphasis on parent warmth, use of withdrawal of love, and conscience development.

Even while *Adolescent Aggression* was being written, however, Bandura and Walters were growing dissatisfied with current social learning approaches to the understanding of human development. They were attracted by the ideas of behaviorism, which embodied the phenomena of learning without the complexities Sears and his collaborators encountered in their sometimes convoluted attempts to explain behavior in terms of drive and motivational constructs. They also were seeing examples of the successful application of operant conditioning principles to various domains of abnormal behavior (e.g., Ayllon & Haughton, 1962). In 1963, Bandura and Walters published *Social Learning and Personality Development* in which they presented a "sociobehavioristic" approach, devoid of psychoanalytic influence (except, of course, for the topics it addressed such as dependency, aggression, and conscience). They also argued that social learning theory to that point had relied too heavily on a narrow range of learning principles derived from the study of animals, and that the social nature of human functioning needed to be emphasized much more strongly. This was particularly evident in the area of identification, or what Bandura and Walters described as *imitation*. They maintained that the failure to consider the importance of social variables was most clearly revealed in the difficulties social learning theorists had experienced with understanding how novel responses are acquired.

The acquisition of novel responses in Skinner's approach was accounted for through the process of successive approximation. Miller and Dollard (1941) had suggested that imitation was a special case of instrumental conditioning, proposing that social cues served as discriminative stimuli and that imitation occurred when behavioral matches to these stimuli were reinforced. Bandura and Walters demonstrated empirically, however, that observational learning, which led to imitation, could take place even when matching responses had not been made and therefore could not have been reinforced. Thus they suggested that observational learning was the primary way in which novel responses were acquired and that it was, indeed, the central and most important form of learning. In essence, then, Bandura and Walters did away with the Freudian notion of identification, with the need for an identification drive, and with the idea of imitation as requiring reinforcement of matching responses. They also argued that observational learning was a more efficient technique of behavior change than either successive approximation or direct learning. In addition, they provided a more cognitive interpretation of socialization processes, reflected ultimately in the theory's change of name from *social learning* to *social cognitive* (e.g., Bandura, 1986).

During the 1960s Bandura and his colleagues published a large number of studies demonstrating the utility of their approach in the moral area (e.g., Bandura, Grusec, & Menlove, 1966; Bandura & Huston, 1961; Bandura & Mischel, 1965; Bandura, Ross, & Ross, 1965; Walters & Parke, 1964). They focused on inhibition of aggression, self-regulation (self-denial with respect to standards of performance), resistance to temptation, and delay of gratification—what they considered to be the essence of morality or conscience, demonstrating that models not only teach novel responses but also change the probability that previously learned behaviors will occur. They found as well that observers showed the same amount of observational learning whether or not they knew they would receive rewards for correct imitation (Bandura et al., 1966): After the capacity for observational learning has developed, then, people cannot be kept from learning what they have seen. Bandura also turned his attention briefly to the area of moral reasoning and judgment, an approach to moral development whose study began to be central in the 1960s. Thus Bandura and MacDonald (1963) had boys ranging in age from 5 to 11 years observe a model who was reinforced for stating moral judgments (using either intentions or consequences as an explanation for why a particular action was blameworthy) that were either more or less advanced than the boys'. They found that the boys subsequently changed their judgments either upward or downward in the direction of the model and argued (although not convincingly to some; e.g., Cowan, Langer, Heavenrich, & Nathason, 1969) that this finding called into question the idea that stages of moral judgment develop in an irreversible sequence directed by synthesis of current thinking and new experiences.

Bandura's answer to the central question of how control of the child's behavior shifts from consequences in the environment (punishment or reward from agents of socialization) to self-control was different from that of Sears and co-workers (1957). As described earlier, Sears and associates had handled this problem through the mechanism of identification or internalization of the actions and standards of the agent of socialization. For Bandura, the answer to conscience or internalization came in self-regulation, with the proposal that people maintain ideological positions in spite of changing situations (that is, they internalize values) because they judge their own actions, with these judgments learned through observations of others and through direct tuition. Those actions that conform to internal standards are judged positively and those that do not conform to these standards are judged negatively (Bandura, 1977). In other words, socialization agents respond differently to the child's various actions and these reactions are imitated. Also, children observe and adopt the self-evaluative standards they see others adopt for themselves, as well as being rewarded by others for engaging in self-regulation. With a history of these kinds of experiences, then, children come to develop control over their own behavior.

Bandura (e.g., 1977) was at pains to point out that standards of behavior are not passively absorbed (the "social mold" model). Children select from the often conflicting information they receive before they can generate rules or standards of behavior, with their selection depending on a wide variety of factors including differences in perceived competence between the model and the self, the value placed on a particular activity, and the degree to which behavior is seen as arising from one's own effort and ability rather than being a function of external factors over which one has little control.

Hoffman and Parental Discipline Strategies: A Cognitive Developmental Perspective

Bandura's research underlined the importance of observational learning in the socialization process. Nevertheless, its role in internalization of values and standards was questioned. Hoffman (1970a), in a review of the relevant literature on moral development, undertook an extensive analysis of the many studies of imitation that had been published in the previous few years. He concluded there was ample evidence that direct observation of a deviant model has a disinhibiting effect on the observer. He argued that the evidence was not conclusive, however, for the position that a model who behaves in an inhibitory or self-denying manner, or who is punished for antisocial action, has actually contributed to inhibition or self-denial in the observer. Rather, the research to date had not shown that punishment to the model raised the child's display of control beyond the baseline in existence before exposure to the model. Hoffman concluded, then, that modeling was essentially external morality in which motives are hedonistic in nature and therefore turned to an alternative socialization mechanism, parental discipline strategies and their role in the internalization of positive moral actions. From a cognitive–developmental perspective, he argued that children's changing views of rules as being external and arbitrary to views that they are objective and rational is brought about by agents of socialization who do not maintain excessive surveillance of the child and who make demands accompanied by reasoning that is comprehensible to the child. Internalization of values is also fostered by agents who encourage children to participate in decisions about their own actions. Accompanying this socialization climate are emotional reactions in the child that help to internalize standards of behavior: anxiety and guilt brought about when parents withhold love in response to their children's antisocial actions and a more positive form of guilt reaction that involves awareness of the harmful effects antisocial actions have on others. This latter form of guilt is engendered by parental reasoning that focuses on the impact of a child's negative actions on others. It is less irrational than guilt produced by parental withdrawal of love, builds on a child's empathic capacities, and is more likely to promote efforts at reparation or future consideration of others.

Hoffman classified morality as it had been studied to that point into four categories, with each assessed by some form of behavioral or emotional marker: (a) an internal moral orientation frequently assessed by a projective technique, that is, a vignette describing a hypothetical deviation with the child asked to describe the outcome, and with this outcome involving acceptance of responsibility, attempts at reparation, or a minimal focus on external concerns such as punishment; (b) guilt intensity, assessed through reactions to story completion tasks describing hypothetical deviation; (c) resistance to temptation assessed both with responses to stories and observation of the child's actual behavior in a temptation situation; and (d) confession and acceptance of blame as seen either from actual behavior exhibited in a temptation situation, fantasy responses in doll play, or parental report. He took the Sears and associates' (1957) division of discipline strategies or techniques into two categories, love oriented and material, and further refined them into three categories: (a) power assertion including physical punishment, deprivation of material objects and privileges, direct application of force, or the threat of any of these; (b) love withdrawal including nonphysical indications of anger or disapproval such as ignoring, refusing to communicate, isolation, and threat of abandonment; and (c) induction comprising explanations or reasons for why the child should behave differently, appeals to the child's pride or strivings for mastery, and, most important, other-oriented induction. By *other-oriented induction*, Hoffman meant reasoning that referred to the implications of the child's actions for others, pointed out the needs and desires of others, or involved an explanation of why another person engaged in an action that may have set the stage for the child's own misdeed.

Having made these distinctions, Hoffman (1970a, Table 3) surveyed the existing relevant research. He found modest support for a negative relation between power assertion and internalization and a positive one between induction and internalization (both of which held for mothers but not for fathers), and no clear relation between withdrawal of love and induction. He also noted some support for a relation between maternal affection and internalization.

Hoffman proposed several mechanisms for the linkages between the three forms of discipline and internalization. He suggested that power assertion produces anger in a child whose autonomy has been challenged as well as providing a model for antisocial ways of discharging anger. He also suggested that it focuses the child's attention on the self rather than on the object that has been harmed and that it leads to high levels of arousal that make it more difficult for the child to attend to cues in the surrounding environment. Finally, it does not take advantage of the child's ability to feel empathy for the needs of others. He offered a somewhat tempered conclusion when he suggested that all discipline interventions include components of power assertion, love withdrawal, and reasoning, with power assertion and love withdrawal providing the motivation to behave and reasoning providing the morally relevant cognitive structure. With optimal levels of arousal, then, children are in the best position to be influenced by the cognitive material involving attention to the harm done to others and to integrate this with their empathic capacities and knowledge of how their actions affect others. Hoffman's conclusion was a nuanced one, but it lost some of its subtlety over the years, often reduced to a simple assertion of the superiority of reasoning over power assertion (Grusec & Goodnow, 1994). Also lost was the notion that maternal warmth was a reasonable predictor of moral development, an idea that is revisited in this chapter.

MORAL DEVELOPMENT FROM AN ATTRIBUTIONAL PERSPECTIVE

Many theoretical orientations have guided the study of socialization. Discussed to this point are the contributions of social learning theory, social–cognitive theory, and cognitive–developmental theory. During the late 1970s and 1980s, a new theoretical perspective emerged in social psychology from the area of social cognition, namely, attribution theory. A number of researchers (e.g., Dienstbier, Hillman, Lehnhoff, Hillman, & Valkenaar, 1975; Grusec, 1983; Lepper, 1983; Walters & Grusec, 1977) quickly came to see the usefulness of this new theory in explaining socialization processes and, in particular, the way in which standards become internalized or taken over by individuals as their own. In an early study, Freedman (1965) had demonstrated that children who were punished mildly for playing with particular toys were more likely to refrain from playing with them at a later time when they were alone and believed themselves to be unobserved (a significant feature of internalization) than were children who had been severely punished. Lepper (1983) employed the minimal sufficiency principle (Nisbett & Valins, 1971) to account for this finding. The idea was that people look for reasons or explanations for their behavior. When there is an obvious explanation, for example, fear of punishment, they attribute their actions to external pressure and, when that external pressure is no longer present, they can behave in a different way. When there is no obvious explanation, for example, there was only minimal pressure for them to engage in the action in question (the kind of minimal pressure provided by reasoning), they seek the reason in their own beliefs and intrinsic motivation. Extrapolating to issues of internalization, the optimal strategy for the socialization of moral and other values would be to provide conditions under which children were induced to comply with the minimum of pressure—just sufficient to obtain compliance—and would therefore have to attribute their compliance to an internalized value system. When there was overly sufficient justification for compliance then attributions to external causality would be more likely and the behavior would not be internalized. Here, then, was another explanation, beyond those provided by Hoffman (1970a), for the superiority of reasoning over power assertion.

A number of studies fit with an attributional analysis of socialization. For example, Grusec and Redler (1980) provided noncoercive prompts to children to share their winnings from a game with others and then interpreted their behavior by telling them either that they must have done so because they were nice people who liked to help others whenever possible or because it was a nice thing to do. The latter was intended to provide a more external justification for prosocial behavior because it involved external social reinforcement for sharing, whereas attributions to internal motivation were deemed to be more likely to promote internalization. In keeping with expectation, children provided with an explanation that involved internal motives were subsequently more prosocial in a variety of situations than those whose actions had been followed with more external consequences in the form of social reinforcement.

EXPANSIONS OF THINKING ABOUT DISCIPLINE TECHNIQUES

From the publication of Sears and co-workers' (1957) highly significant assessment of child rearing practices through the influential analysis by Hoffman (1970a), as well as continued work in the field (see Maccoby & Martin [1983] for a review of relevant research), the accepted wisdom was that strongly power assertive parenting strategies were detrimental to children's internalization of values whereas reasoning and autonomy-supportive (noncoercive or nonpunitive) approaches were more conducive to internalization. Withdrawal of love was seen to lie somewhere between the two in terms of its impact on internalization. What came next was a refinement of this somewhat overly simplistic view and a further development of thinking about the nature of effective socialization. Specifically, it was recognized that reasoning, withdrawal of love, and power assertion are not monolithic constructs. Accordingly and not surprisingly, the evidence of differential effectiveness was not always consistent or convincing. Moreover, it became clear that any implication that parents who were most, or least, effective were those who consistently used one particular approach to discipline was probably incorrect. Finally, it was acknowledged that an adequate theory had to take into account developmental considerations as well as the significant role played by the child in socialization.

Discipline Strategies as Single Categories

Reasoning covers a gamut of approaches, including a discussion of the consequences of deviation for the self and for others, statements of normative behavior, and noninformative verbalizations. Each reason, which differs in its content, can have different outcomes: Other-oriented reasoning, for example, might depend on the ability of the child to take the perspective of the other, whereas statements of normative behavior would not. Children might believe some rationales to have greater "truth value" than others and hence be differentially affected by those rationales. Some reasons are more relevant to the child's particular ways of viewing the world and therefore more easily assimilated into existing cognitive structures. Mancuso and Lehrer (1986) distinguish reasons on the basis of structure as opposed to content. Thus some reasons are more general than others, with low-level, specific statements less likely to promote acceptance of a generalized directive concerning appropriate actions. Reasons also differ in their clarity and redundancy (Cashmore & Goodnow, 1985), although reasons that are more indirect (e.g., the statement "Who was your servant last year?" intended to convey the inappropriateness of a particular request) may serve a useful function in internalization as well because they require attention and decoding that ultimately make the desired action more evident.

Similarly, power assertion covers a wide variety of interventions. Even physical punishment needs to be broken down as a function of severity and whether, for example, it involves objects or the hand: Failure to do so has led to confusing debates about its harmfulness or lack of harmfulness (Gershoff, 2002). Punishment also includes withdrawal of privileges or material resources, expressions of anger, commands, disapproval, shame, and humiliation. As well, the context in which it is delivered matters. Is it done in public or in private? Is it administered by a loving or a rejecting parent, by a parent who is in control and assuming a stance of teacher or by a parent who has lost control and become unpredictable? Does it underline the child's loss of autonomy? Finally, withdrawal of love includes both a frightening threat of separation from the parent as well guilt aroused by failure to please a loved one, features that might have quite different consequences for the child.

Inconsistent Evidence

Findings with respect to the alleged superiority of reasoning over power assertion are not overwhelming. For example, the relation seems to hold for mothers but not for fathers, and for middle-class but not lower-class children (e.g., Brody & Flor, 1997; Brody & Shaffer, 1982). Children with fearful temperaments are more likely to display significant levels of conscience development when their mothers use inductive discipline, whereas those with fearless temperaments are not differentially affected by maternal discipline technique (Kochanska, 1997).

Parents as Consistent in Their Use of a Particular Discipline Strategy

Socialization theorists, as noted at the beginning of this chapter, did not pay much attention to the content of values children were acquiring, with little if any distinction made, for example, between aggression, dishonesty, showing consideration for others, and table manners. An exception appears in Hoffman (1970b) in his observation that different situations seemed to elicit different discipline strategies from agents of socialization, and that this was particularly the case among mothers of children who had a strong moral orientation. The idea was not pursued for some time, however, until a number of researchers reported that mothers not only use discipline strategies in combination, but that they vary them as a function of the misdeed to which they are responding. Thus Grusec and Kuczynski (1980) observed that mothers report using reasoning when their children inflict psychological harm on others, whereas they are more likely to be power assertive in the case of disobedience and harm to objects. Zahn-Waxler and Chapman (1982) reported that damage to physical objects and lapses in impulse control in young children elicited physical punishment and withdrawal of love, but that aggression did not. High arousal activity such as rough-and-tumble play is linked with power assertion alone and violations of social conventions (e.g., bad table manners) are linked with reasoning alone (Trickett & Kuczynksi, 1986). Grusec, Dix, and Mills (1982) found that mothers reacted to antisocial acts with a combination of reasoning and power assertion and to failures to show concern for others with reasoning. Mothers and teachers also use a variety of different reasons in response to different domains of misdeed (Smetana, 1997). These studies indicate, then, that mothers respond differently to their children's misdeeds as a function of the nature of that misdeed, although a clear pattern with respect to linkages between the nature of the misdeed and maternal reaction remains to be identified.

    One reason for the differential responsiveness may have to do with the goals that parents have when they are reacting to their children's transgressions. In some situations, for example, they may wish to teach a child about general standards or values whereas in other situations they may simply want obedience, cessation of a particular action, or both. Accordingly, Hastings and Grusec (1998) report that mothers who stated as their goal the desire to teach their children standards of behavior were more likely to reason with them. Mothers who wished simply to stop their children from engaging in the action in question were more likely to use punishment or threats of punishment, and those who were more focused on maintaining a positive relationship with their child were more likely to negotiate or even to accept their child's refusal to comply. Similarly, Kuczynski (1984) asked mothers to obtain cooperation on a utensil-sorting task while they were in the room with their children (a goal of immediate compliance), or to have their children continue with the task after being left alone (a goal of continued compliance). The latter group of mothers were more nurturant with their children during pretask play, gave more explanations, and made more positive statements about their children's character while working on the task. Presumably, to reach their goal of fostering responsible, unmonitored child behavior, these mothers used warmth and encouraged child receptivity to promote their children's feelings of self-motivation (Jensen & Moore, 1977; Miller, Brickman, & Bolen, 1975). Still unaddressed, of course, is the question of whether agents of socialization tend to have long-term goals of teaching general standards or gaining continued compliance when they are dealing with moral actions and more short-term goals when they are socializing other forms of behavior.

In addition to promoting different goals, however, differential reactions as a function of the nature of the misdeed may also be an indication of more effective parenting by socialization agents who realize that different domains of behavior require different interventions. Thus Trickett and Kuczynski (1986) found that abusive mothers were less flexible in their responding to children's misdeeds and Hoffman (1970b) reported that strong moral orientations were more prevalent among children whose mothers were more variable in their reactions. Thus matching strategy to misdeed (whatever the appropriate linkages might be) may be a functional approach to socialization.

Children do evaluate the content of adult reasoning as a function of its appropriateness to the domain of misbehavior (moral or social conventional; Smetana, 1997). Moreover, evidence indicates that children differ in their perceptions of how deserving transgressions are of punishment as a function of the nature of the transgression and of age. Thus, children from preschool years on consider moral transgressions as more serious and more deserving of punishment than social conventional transgressions. Even adolescents agree that parents should retain authority and the right to exert discipline over moral issues and, to a lesser extent, over conventional issues (Smetana & Asquith, 1994). Problems arise when parents see transgressions as falling within the conventional domain whereas adolescents see them as now outside the domain of parental intervention (Nucci, 1984; Smetana & Berent, 1993). Presumably there is a substantial correlation between a child's evaluation of the appropriateness of a parenting intervention and that child's willingness to comply with the parental demand.

SOCIALIZATION FROM AN INFORMATION-PROCESSING PERSPECTIVE

Grusec and Goodnow (1994), in response to problems of the sort described, proposed a reformulation of traditional approaches to socialization, particularly those involving discipline strategies. They argued that rather than a focus on strategies, socialization might be better understood in terms of the kind of information agents of socialization presented and the manner of its presentation. They suggested that greater similarity in the values (moral or otherwise) espoused by parent (or any agent of socialization) and child involves two steps: the child's accurate perception of the parent's message and the child's acceptance rather than rejection of that message. According to their analysis, accurate perception is facilitated when the standard or value the parent wishes to teach is expressed clearly. Redundancy and consistency are obviously two conditions, then, that promote clarity of expression. Some degree of power assertion or dramatic presentation may help in making messages clearer by drawing the child's attention to that message. Messages need to be fitted to the child's comprehension abilities, for example, taking into account the child's level of cognitive sophistication and ability to take the perspective of others. The extent to which messages are tangential or relevant to the issue at hand, and the level of generality at which they are pitched is also important. Implicit messages that require unpacking can be effective because they again draw attention to the message and make it more salient. Messages also contain information about the importance that a particular value holds for the parent and therefore how much attention should be paid to the content.

A few studies have focused on the conditions that facilitate accurate perception. Thus Cashmore and Goodnow (1985) found that agreement between parents about the importance of particular values, presumably a condition that made values more salient, facilitated accurate perception of those values. Okagaki and Bevis (1999) report that discussion by families about values increases the extent to which children perceive their parents' values accurately. In a study of Israeli high school students, Knafo and Schwartz (2003) found a number of variables to be positively related to the student's accurate perception of their parents' values, including the degree of warmth and responsiveness their parents displayed and the extent to which their parents agreed with each other about the importance of a value. Parental conflict over values and indifferent and autocratic parenting were negatively correlated with accurate perception and, with the exception of father–son dyads, withdrawal of love and consistency in parental value messages over time were positively related to accuracy. Knafo and Schwartz suggest that affectionate parenting increases the motivation of children to listen more closely to the values their parents espouse, and that consistency makes messages more understandable.

Acceptance of a parent's message, according to Grusec and Goodnow, involves three possible conditions: the extent to which the child believes that parental behavior is appropriate, the degree to which the child is motivated to comply with the wishes of the parent, and the extent to which the child sees the value expressed in the message as self-generated. With respect to perceived appropriateness, parental intervention must be seen as fitting well with the nature of the misdeed (reasons involving references to harm done to others, for example, may be seen as inappropriate when the misdeed is a violation of social convention), as well intentioned, and as fair. Perceived appropriateness is also affected by expectations having to do with cultural context—some actions are more normative among certain cultural groups or in a given social class, or from fathers as opposed to mothers, and may therefore be more acceptable. As well, the appropriateness of a particular intervention can change as a function of the child's age, mood, or temperament. Motivation that promotes acceptance must have as a priority that it not threaten the child's autonomy or be seen as strongly linked to external incentives. Empathic arousal, perceptions of how important the value is to the parent, and a desire to please the parent are all candidates for motivational states that increase the desire to accept a parental message. Threats to feelings of security, generated by withdrawal of love, also qualify as motivational forces, although this sort of motive is probably less conducive to healthy functioning. Finally, feeling that a value is self-generated certainly promotes internalization. Such a feeling comes from parental interventions that minimize the salience of external pressure and maximize the attribution of prosocial behavior to intrinsic motivation.

EFFECTIVE PARENTING AS SUCCESSFUL PROBLEM SOLVING

Analysis of internalization in terms of accurate perception and acceptance moves the understanding of moral socialization from a focus on the agent of socialization and on the strategies used by that agent to one that focuses on the child and the conditions that are most likely to facilitate desired behavior on the child's part. These conditions include the child's perception and evaluation of the situation, thus providing much more room for contributions from the child than previous analyses focused on parenting strategies per se. Thus effective parenting can be seen as "a matter of appraisal and flexible action in the face of constantly changing features of children and of situations" (Grusec, Goodnow, & Kuczynski, 2000, p. 206). This approach fits well with a growing body of research evidence pointing to the great variety of variables affecting the impact of specific parenting strategies on children's behavior. Already discussed are findings with respect to interactions between parenting strategy and the nature of the child's misdeed. Some additional variables that have been identified in the socialization literature include the parenting context in which the strategy is employed; the child's temperament; culture and social class; the presence of extenuating circumstances; the child's developmental status; and gender of child and parent. Each of these is briefly considered with respect to their interaction with approaches to parenting in promoting moral behavior.

Context

Of increasing interest to socialization theorists is the context in which parental interventions are delivered. Clearly, interventions assume different meanings as a function of the setting and background in which they occur. Two features of context that seem to be of particular importance are the quality of the relationship between socialization agent and child and the extent to which the intervention is autonomy supportive.

Relationship.   One relationship quality—warmth—of course, has a long history in socialization research (recall its importance in the findings of Sears et al. [1957]—withdrawal of love from a warm parent was found to be more conducive to conscience development than withdrawal of love from a cold parent). Warmth obviously serves a variety of functions. It motivates children to please the agent of socialization. It keeps children in the vicinity of parents so that they are more likely to hear their messages. A second relationship quality has to do with protection of the child by the parent. When the protection relationship is a positive one children are more likely to trust their parents not only to protect them from physical and psychological harm but also to guide them in acceptable and moral ways. As well, the validation of feelings provided by a parent who is responsive to and understanding of negative affect is also conducive to the internalization of standards (Bretherton, Golby, & Cho, 1997). Securely attached children appear to react differently than insecurely attached children to given parental interventions. Allen, Moore, Kuperminc, and Bell (1998), for example, noted that the adolescent children of mothers who exerted higher levels of control displayed fewer externalizing behaviors, presumably a reflection of impaired moral development, when they had an autonomous or preoccupied attachment status. In the case of adolescents with an insecure/nonpreoccupied attachment status there was no relation between maternal control and externalizing problems. As well, maternal control was correlated with lower levels of delinquency among adolescents who were securely attached. The conclusion is that securely attached children are more accepting of maternal control than are insecurely attached children, perhaps because they trust their parents more to make reasonable demands on them or because they do not perceive the behavior of their mothers in a negative light.

Autonomy Support. Feelings of self-generation are central in the internalization of positive social behaviors. Thus, agents of socialization who are intrusive and controlling in their influence attempts are much less likely to be effective than those who use the same influence techniques but who do so in a manner that promotes feelings of choice (Deci & Ryan, 1985). Reasoning, for example, can be used in a way that assists the child to take over standards in a way that is not seen as coercive. Or it can be used in a way that makes children feel they are being coerced into certain actions. Even power assertion can have less coercive qualities depending on the context in which it is delivered and the extent to which a deviating child is made to feel that he or she is still in control as opposed to being overwhelmed by nonresponsive adults. The negative impact of intrusive control in the moral domain is clear from studies demonstrating that coercive control is more likely to result in antisocial and delinquent behavior (Kerr & Stattin, 2000).

Child's Temperament

The search for gene–environment interactions has become a primary focus for socialization researchers (Collins, Maccoby, Steinberg, Hetherington, & Bornstein, 2000), and one form this pursuit takes is to look at the differential impact of environmental conditions in the form of parenting practices on children who have different temperaments (with *temperament* defined as constitutionally based and early appearing individual differences in characteristic emotional, motor, and attentional reactivity and self-regulation).

Temperament exhibits some degree of stability. For example, inhibition or fearfulness is linked to later internalizing behavior, whereas early impulsivity or unmanageability and irritability are linked more to externalizing problems (Rothbart & Bates, 1998). Nevertheless, stability is modest, an indication of the importance of experience. Children also evoke specific parenting behaviors as a function of their temperament, although evocative gene–environment correlations by no means account for a substantial portion of the links between parenting practices and child outcomes (e.g., O'Connor, Deater-Deckard, Fulker, Rutter, & Plomin, 1998). Thus, parenting makes an independent contribution to child outcomes, over and above those features of parenting determined by child temperament. Research indicates, however, that temperament and parenting can interact to produce identifiably different outcomes in a variety of areas of social development including the development of morality.

One of the first studies to demonstrate an interaction between temperament and parenting was reported by Kochanska (1997). She noted that fearful children (those who at an early age displayed discomfort in strange situations, stayed close to their mothers, and were reluctant to explore) showed the usual positive relation between maternal use of gentle discipline that deemphasizes power and conscience development. Those who were constitutionally fearless, however, did not: Their level of conscience development was better predicted by a mutually cooperative, responsive, and positive orientation on the part of the mother. Kochanska suggested that gentle discipline for fearless children does not arouse a level of discomfort that is optimal for internalization, but that greater levels of power assertion (which presumably would be closer to an optimal level) also arouse reactance and hostility and therefore discourage internalization. (Less clear is why a mutually cooperative relationship is not a predictor of conscience in fearful children.) Similar findings have been documented by Colder, Lochman, and Wells (1997), who found that boys who were temperamentally fearful and whose parents used harsh discipline were more aggressive according to their teachers' ratings than either children who were low in fear and had harsh parents or children who were high in fear and had gentle parents. The complexity of the situation, however, is demonstrated by a recently published failure to replicate these findings (van der Mark, Bakermans-Kranenberg, & van Ijzendoorn, 2002).

A number of other studies have also demonstrated interactions between parenting practices and child temperament in the production of antisocial or immoral behavior. Irritable infants with angry and punitive mothers are more likely to be angry and noncompliant when they are 2 years old than are irritable infants with less punitive mothers, with attenuated relations between maternal punitiveness and child outcomes observed for infants who are not irritable (Crockenberg, 1987). Maternal control and support have been more strongly linked to antisocial behavior for adolescents who are high on behavioral undercontrol and negative affectivity than for those with more moderate scores on these temperament markers (Stice & Gonzales, 1998). Similarly, children's dysregulated temperament (that is, anger) and aggression to peers are related when maternal negative control and hostility are high, but not related when mothers are low in negative control and hostility (Rubin, Hastings, Chen, Stewart, & McNichol, 1998). Although physical punishment is not correlated with the externalizing or antisocial behavior of flexible children, that is, children who are adaptable and low in reactivity, the two variables are correlated in the case of inflexible and reactive children (Paterson & Sanson, 1999).

Although this series of studies suggests that maternal control is detrimental for children who have a difficult temperament, other findings indicate that this is not always the case. Bates, Dodge, Pettit, and Ridge (1998), for example, studied children who were temperamentally high in resistance to control (who were strongly and excitedly attracted to rewarding stimuli had a relatively weak level of basic social agreeableness, and exhibited difficulties in effortful control of attention and vigilance). In the case of these children, they found that when mothers were low in restrictive control the children were more likely than their low resistance to control counterparts to have externalizing behavior problems in middle childhood, a linkage that did not exist when mothers were high in restrictive control. Indeed, in the case of high maternal restrictiveness, highly resistant children were sometimes very well behaved in their social and moral interactions and sometimes not at all well behaved.

The idea of temperament–parenting interactions is appealing, and certainly there is empirical support for its usefulness. Nevertheless much work still needs to be done in terms of determining the specific directions of interactions as well as conditions under which these interactions do not appear to occur.

Culture and Social Class

One important moderator of the effect of parenting practices on children's moral development is the cultural niche in which parent and child find themselves. Often the nature of this cultural niche is represented by differences in social class or country of origin. This cultural context has an impact on the way in which parenting practices are employed as well as how they are perceived and responded to. Rigid and power assertive parenting, for example, occurs more frequently among Asian and African American parents than those of Anglo-European background but it appears to be less harmful, relative to the same kind of parenting in the Anglo-European context (Chao, 1994). Parents from lower socioeconomic backgrounds also use more power assertive discipline techniques, but the outcomes do not always appear to have negative social and emotional outcomes similar

to those demonstrated in middle-class contexts (e.g., Brody & Flor, 1998). Physical discipline is linked to externalizing problems for Anglo-American children but not for African-
American children (Deater-Deckard, Dodge, Bates, & Pettit, 1996).

Part of the explanation for these differences may have to do with the different meanings
of rigid and power assertive parenting in different cultural contexts. In more collectivist
cultures such as the Chinese, for example, Chao (1994) has argued that power assertive
parenting reflects a focus on the centrality of training children and of parental responsibility
for being involved with and concerned and caring for one's offspring. This is in contrast
to the individualist (Western European) context, where such parenting is associated with
Puritan implications of harshness and breaking of the child's will to achieve morality,
approaches to socialization of children that are no longer considered acceptable. In a similar
vein, Rudy and Grusec (2001) found that collectivist (Egyptian-Canadian) mothers were
more power assertive in their approach to child rearing than were individualist (Anglo-
Canadian) mothers. However, the two groups did not differ on warmth and feelings of
self-efficacy in difficult childrearing situations, two variables that have been linked to
positive outcomes for children. Moreover, low levels of warmth and low feelings of self-
efficacy were correlated with punitive parenting in the Anglo-Canadian sample but not in
the Egyptian-Canadian sample, further evidence that harsh and power assertive parenting
takes on different meanings in different contexts. Similarly, in a study of largely poor, single
parent, African-American families, Brody and Flor (1998) observed mothers who were
highly controlling of their children and who used physical restraint, but who accompanied
their parenting practices with warmth. The children of these mothers demonstrated a
greater ability to regulate their own actions, that is, to plan ahead, stay on task, and think
ahead about the consequences of those actions, certainly prime requirements for moral
behavior.

The greater frequency of power assertive parenting in Asian cultures and in lower
socioeconomic class contexts has been attributed to a number of possibilities. In Asian
cultures, it may reflect a greater emphasis on respect for authority, whereas, in lower-class
settings, it may represent more adaptive reactions to a dangerous context where opportunities for antisocial behavior are more easily available. Whatever the reason, the empirical
evidence points to the strong possibility that power assertion in a positive emotional context is less detrimental to children's socialization than in a less positive emotional context
(as noted in the discussion about the context of parenting practices) and that its negative
impact in a Western middle-class context can be attributed to the emotional context in
which it is frequently employed.

Presence of Extenuating Circumstances

Children may behave badly for one of several reasons: They may not know any better.
They may understand what they have done is unacceptable but for some reason they still
knowingly engage in an antisocial action. Clearly the appropriate response depends on
why the misbehavior has occurred. In the former case, explanation and reasoning are
the methods of choice. In the latter case, a more power assertive intervention may be
appropriate.

Child's Developmental Status

Level of cognitive functioning obviously is a determinant of how different parenting
strategies are received. Young children are more likely to see physical punishment as an

acceptable strategy than are older children (Siegal & Cowen, 1984). As well, with age, children come to see increasing numbers of issues as personal ones over which parents have no right to exercise control (Smetana, 1997). Young children, because of their limited ability to decenter, find it difficult to deal with messages delivered in a sarcastic way (Bugental, Kaswan, & Love, 1970). Another example of age-dependent effects is the finding that the content of a message carries more weight than does the tone of voice in which it is expressed for younger than for older children, even though all age groups are able to provide a clear description of the conflicting messages (Morton & Trehub, 2001). Interestingly, in a meta-analysis, Rothbaum and Weisz (1994) found that associations between power assertive parenting behavior and externalizing problems were greater for older children and adolescents than for toddlers and preschoolers: One reason for this may well be that punitive parenting is seen as less fair and acceptable as children grow older.

Child's Gender

Girls react differently to the same parental intervention than do boys. Boys, for example, are generally more likely to exhibit externalizing behaviors than are girls and, as a result, may be more likely to be involved in the kinds of escalating cycles of coercive behavior that have been described by Patterson (1982). In other words, they are more inclined to begin an interaction with parents (more specifically, mothers) at a higher level of antisocial behavior and therefore more likely to be reactive to maternal intervention. Boys may also be more genetically predisposed to react negatively to the stress of parental pressures than are girls (Rothbaum & Weisz, 1994).

Parent's Gender

Another important moderator of parenting practices is parent gender. As noted, correlations between reasoning and conscience development are more likely to be seen for middle-class mothers than middle-class fathers. Maternal but not paternal communicativeness about misbehavior is related to resistance to temptation in adolescent boys (LaVoie & Looft, 1973). In their meta-analysis, Rothbaum and Weisz (1994) found a much stronger relation between parental responsivity and children's externalizing behavior for mothers than for fathers (although they also noted the opposite effect in clinic-referred samples; see Loeber & Stouthamer-Loeber, 1986). This gender difference might be explained simply by the fact that mothers are the primary caregivers, or that they are more likely to reason, to look for explanations for their children's actions, and to seek mutually acceptable resolutions for conflicts between themselves and their children (Grusec & Goodnow, 1994). Also, fathers tend to be more direct and power assertive in their approach to childrearing (Vuchinich, Emery, & Cassidy, 1988) and so children may come to consider power assertion as the norm for fathers and find it more acceptable. In fact, a number of studies (Dadds, Sheffield, & Holbeck, 1990; Siegal & Barclay, 1985; Siegel & Cowen, 1984) suggest that children consider physical punishment to be more acceptable when it is administered by fathers than by mothers.

CONCLUSION

This long list of moderating variables clearly requires a move beyond the notion of parenting strategies as monolithic conveyors of values to children. Different children and different situations demand different methods. Effective parents are those who know what to do at a particular point in time. This approach requires acknowledgement of the bidirectional nature of the parent–child interaction (Kuczynski, 2003) and specific recognition of the child's agency as an essential feature of parenting. Children and parents are involved in a continuing exchange, with children evaluating, comparing, and interpreting those things that parents do to them.

Of course these ideas are far from new. Sears (1951) argued that not only does the external world act on the individual, but the individual acts on the external world. As described, Bandura (1977) also was at pains to demonstrate that people are selective in what and whom they choose to imitate. What has happened is that socialization theorists have begun to elaborate or how and why individuals have different reactions to the same socialization input. And it is becoming increasingly clear that successful agents of socialization need to know how their children respond to given strategies. The importance of parental understanding in socialization, including the socialization of morality, has been argued by Grusec, Goodnow, and Kuczynski (2000) who pointed to the importance of clarifying variables and exploring processes governing the relations between parent understanding and child outcomes. Part of this understanding must involve a focus on conditions that lead to knowledge of the child's thinking and evaluation. These conditions include a context of warmth that promotes good dyadic relationships and a desire on the part of both members of the dyad to be together and to receive and impart information. They also include a context of acceptance and autonomy support that makes children more likely to freely impart information, a situation that is conducive to positive socioemotional outcomes including moral behavior (Kerr & Statin, 2000). In this sense, then, the study of internalization of values appears to have moved from a focus on strategy and technique to a focus on the child's reactions to strategies and to conditions that facilitate knowledge of those reactions as well, of course, as on the ability and willingness of agents of socialization to put that understanding to good use.

Additional Features of Socialization Research and the Study of Moral Development

A considerable amount is known about the conditions that facilitate children's acquisition of moral values, moral behavior, and conscience development. In the remainder of this chapter two other current directions of research activity are described. They are an extension of strategies important in the socialization process and a greater interest in domains of behavior and differential mechanisms underlying socialization in those domains.

Socialization Strategies.   Socialization theorists began with a focus on discipline strategies and the discipline context as the primary one in which the socialization of morality occurs. Identification and observational learning have also been included as central features of parenting behavior, although Hoffman's (1970a) argument that they promote behavior motivated only by hedonistic motives really has not been addressed. Rewards have generally been downplayed as significant methods of socialization because of the argument that they can undermine intrinsic motivation (e.g., Lepper, 1983).

Parental responsiveness to and compliance with the wishes and needs of their children (where this is appropriate) has also been identified as a precursor of conscience or morality. This orientation fosters a situation of mutual reciprocity whereby children, in turn, become responsive to and compliant with the wishes of their parents (Maccoby & Martin, 1983; Parpal & Maccoby, 1985). Parent–child relationships characterized by mutual compliance, harmony, and positivity have been shown to predict children's conscience including levels of guilt after deviation, resistance to temptation in the absence of surveillance, reluctance to violate rules, and maternal reports of moral and prosocial behavior (e.g., Kochanska & Murray, 2000).

Discussion of moral issues outside the bounds of specific conflicts or requests for compliance obviously is another important strategy for socialization. Routines, or everyday ways of acting, thinking, or feeling that are followed by most members of the social group, are another vehicle for the development of moral orientations (Goodnow, Miller, & Kessel, 1995). They are not modes of action that arise as a result of resolution of conflict, because of a desire to reciprocate, or as a result of discussion and teaching. Rather they appear simply as part of a natural order or way of doing things and, for that reason, may be resistant to challenge and questioning. Other strategies are discussed by Bugental and Goodnow (1998) and Grusec and colleagues (2000) and include cocooning or pre-arming. In the case of *cocooning*, children are protected from exposure to deviant behavior and thinking and therefore temptation. In the case of *pre-arming*, they are alerted to other ways of thinking and provided with ways of dealing with these alternate approaches. The role these sorts of strategies play in internalization of moral values and the development of moral behavior is not nearly so clearly elaborated as in the case of disciplinary strategies, but remains to be explored.

The Nature of Moral Behavior.   As noted throughout this chapter, socialization theory has, by and large, treated social outcomes including morality as a single class of behaviors and assumed that the same mechanisms govern development in all areas. Indications that this may not be appropriate come with the discovery that the impact of socialization interventions may depend on the nature of the misdeed. Bugental (2000) has proposed an evolutionary approach to the understanding of socialization that calls for distinctions between classes or domains of behavior (e.g., relationships where the emphasis is on protection, authority, reciprocity, or coalitions whose purpose is the sharing of resources and mutual defense) and argues that different mechanisms govern development in these different areas. Exploration in these directions will no doubt be a feature of future research activities as socialization theorists continue to deal with the challenge of how it is that children develop into moral human beings.

REFERENCES

Allen, J. P., Moore, C., Kuperminc, G., & Bell, K. (1998). Attachment and adolescent psychosocial functioning. *Child Development, 69,* 1406–1419.

Ayllon, T., & Haughton, E. (1962). Control of the behavior of schizophrenic patients by food. *Journal of the Experimental Analysis of Behavior, 5,* 343–352.

Bandura, A. (1977). *Social learning theory.* Englewood Cliffs, NJ: Prentice-Hall.

Bandura, A. (1986). *Social foundations of thought and action: A social cognitive theory.* Englewood Cliffs, NJ: Prentice-Hall.

Bandura, A., Grusec, J. E., & Menlove, F. L. (1966). Observational learning as a function of symbolization and incentive set. *Child Development, 37,* 499–506.

Bandura, A., & Huston, A. C. (1961). Identification as a process of incidental learning. *Journal of Abnormal and Social Psychology, 63,* 311–318.

Bandura, A., & McDonald, F. J. (1963). The influence of social reinforcement and the behavior of models in shaping childrens' moral judgments. *Journal of Abnormal and Social Psychology, 67,* 274–281.

Bandura, A., & Walters, R. H. (1959). *Adolescent aggression.* New York: Ronald Press.

Bandura, A., & Walters, R. H. (1963). *Social learning theory and personality development.* New York: Holt, Rinehart, & Winston.

Bates, J. E., Dodge, K. A., Pettit, G. S., & Ridge, B. (1998). Interaction of temperamental resistance to control and restrictive parenting in the development of externalizing behavior. *Developmental Psychology, 34,* 982–985.

Bretherton, I., Golby, B., & Cho, E. (1997). Attachment and the transmission of values. In J. E. Grusec & L. Kuczynski (Eds.), *Parenting and children's internalization of values* (pp. 103–134). New York: Wiley.

Brody, G. H., & Flor, D. L. (1998). Maternal resources, parenting practices, and child competence in rural, single-parent African American families. *Child Development, 69,* 803–816.

Brody, G. H., & Shaffer, D. R. (1982). Contributions of parents and peers to children's moral socialization. *Developmental Review, 2,* 31–75.

Bugental, D. B. (2000). Acquisition of the algorithms of social life: A domain-based approach. *Psychological Bulletin, 126,* 187–219.

Bugental, D., & Goodnow, J. J. (1998). Socialization processes: Biological, cognitive, and social-cultural perspectives. In W. Damon (Ed.), *Handbook of child psychology* (vol. 4, pp. 389–462). New York: Wiley.

Bugental, D. B., Kaswan, J. W., & Love, L. R. (1970). Perceptions of contradictory messages conveyed by verbal and nonverbal channels. *Journal of Personality and Social Psychology, 16,* 647–655.

Cashmore, J. A., & Goodnow, J. J. (1985). Agreement between generations: A two-process approach. *Child Development, 56,* 493–501.

Chao, R. K. (1994). Beyond parental control and authoritarian parenting style: Understanding Chinese parenting through the cultural notion of training. *Child Development, 65,* 1111–1119.

Collins, W. A., Maccoby, E. E., Steinberg, L., Hetherington, E. M., & Bornstein, M. H. (2000). Contemporary research on parenting: The case for nature and nurture. *American Psychologist, 55,* 218–232.

Colder, C. R., Lochman, J. E., & Wells, K. C. (1997). The moderating effects of children's fear and activity level on relations between parenting practices and childhood symptomatology. *Journal of Abnormal Child Psychology, 25,* 251–263.

Cowan, P. A., Langer, J., Heavenrich, J., & Nathanson, M. (1969). Social learning and Piaget's cognitive theory of moral development. *Journal of Personality and Social Psychology, 11,* 261–274.

Crockenberg, S. (1987). Predictors and correlates of anger toward and punitive control of toddlers by adolescent mothers. *Child Development, 58,* 964–975.

Dadds, M. R., Sheffield, J. K., & Holbeck, J. F. (1990). An examination of the differential relationship of marital discord to parents' discipline strategies for boys and girls. *Journal of Abnormal Child Psychology, 18,* 121–129.

Deater-Deckard, K., Dodge, K. A., Bates, J. E., & Pettit, G. S. (1996). Physical discipline among African-American and European-American mothers: Links to children's externalizing behaviors. *Developmental Psychology, 32,* 1065–1072.

Deci, E. L., & Ryan, R. M. (1985). *Intrinsic motivation and self-determination in human behavior.* New York: Plenum Press.

Dienstbier, R. A., Hillman, D., Lehnhoff, J., Hillman, J., & Valkenaar. M. C. (1975). An emotion-attribution approach to moral behavior: Interfacing cognitive and avoidance theories of moral development. *Psychological Review, 82,* 299–315.

Dollard, J., Doob, W. L., Miller, N. E., Mowrer, O. H., & Sears, R. R. (1939). *Frustration and aggression*. New Haven, CT: Yale University Press.

Dornbusch, S., Ritter, P., Leiderman, P., Roberts, D., & Fraleigh, M. (1987). The relation of parenting style to adolescent school performance. *Child Development, 58,* 1244–1257.

Freedman, J. L. (1965). Long-term behavioral effects of cognitive dissonance. *Journal of Abnormal and Social Psychology, 1,* 145–155.

Freud, S. (1930/1955). *Civilization and its discontents*. London: Hogarth Press.

Freud, S. (1937). *New introductory lectures on psychoanalysis*. London: Hogarth Press and Institute of Psychoanalysis.

Gershoff, E. T. (2002). Corporal punishment by parents and associated child behaviors and experiences: A meta-analytic and theoretical review. *Psychological Bulletin, 128,* 539–579.

Goodnow, J. J., Miller, P. M., & Kessel, F. (Eds.). (1995). *Cultural practices as contexts for development*. San Francisco: Jossey-Bass.

Grusec, J. E. (1983). The internalization of altruistic dispositions: A cognitive analysis. In E. T. Higgins, D. N. Ruble, & W. W. Hartup (Eds.). *Social cognition and social development* (pp. 275–293). New York: Cambridge University Press.

Grusec, J. E. (1992). Social learning theory and developmental psychology: The legacy of Robert Sears and Albert Bandura. *Developmental Psychology, 28,* 776–786.

Grusec, J. E., Dix, T., & Mills, R. (1982). The effects of type, severity and victim of children's transgressions on maternal discipline. *Canadian Journal of Behavioural Science, 14,* 276–289.

Grusec, J. E., & Goodnow, J. J. (1994). Impact of parental discipline methods on the child's internalization of values: A reconceptualization of current points of view. *Developmental Psychology, 30,* 4–19.

Grusec, J. E., Goodnow, J. J., & Kuczynski, L. (2000). New directions in analyses of parenting contributions to children's acquisition of values. *Child Development, 71,* 205–211.

Grusec, J. E., & Kuczynski, L. (1980). Direction of effect in socialization: A comparison of the parent vs. the child's behavior as determinants of disciplinary techniques. *Developmental Psychology, 16,* 1–9.

Grusec, J. E., & Redler, E. (1980). Attribution, reinforcement, and altruism: A developmental analysis. *Developmental Psychology, 16,* 525–534.

Hastings, P. D., & Grusec, J. E. (1998). Parenting goals as organizers of responses to parent-child disagreement. *Developmental Psychology, 34,* 465–479.

Hoffman, M. L. (1970a). Moral development. In P. H. Mussen (Ed.). *Carmichael's manual of child psychology* (vol. 2, pp. 261–360). New York: Wiley.

Hoffman, M. L. (1970b). Conscience, personality, and socialization techniques. *Human Development, 13,* 90–126.

Jensen, A. M., & Moore, S. G. (1977). The effect of attribute statements on cooperativeness and competitiveness in school-age boys. *Child Development, 48,* 305–307.

Kerr, M., & Stattin, H. (2000). What parents know, how they know it, and several forms of adolescent adjustment: Further support for a reinterpretation of monitoring. *Child Development, 36,* 366–380.

Knafo, A., & Schwartz, S. H. (2003). Parenting and adolescents' accuracy in perceiving parental values. *Child Development, 74,* 595–611.

Kochanska, G. (1997). Multiple pathways to conscience for children with different temperaments: from toddlerhood to age 5. *Developmental Psychology, 33,* 228–240.

Kochanska, G., & Murray, K. T. (2000). Mother-child mutually responsive orientation and conscience development: From toddler to early school age. *Child Development, 71,* 417–431.

Kuczynski, L. (1984). Socialization goals and mother-child interaction: Strategies for long-term and short-term compliance. *Developmental Psychology, 20,* 1061–1073.

Kuczynski, L. (Ed.). (2003). *Parent-child relationships as a dyadic process.* Thousand Oaks, CA: Sage.

LaVoie, J. C., & Looft, W. R. (1973). Parental antecedents of resistance-to-temptation behavior in adolescents. *Merrill-Palmer Quarterly, 19,* 107–116.

Lepper, M. (1983). Social control processes, attributions of motivation, and the internalization of social values. In E. T. Higgins, D. N. Ruble, & W. W. Hartup (Eds.), *Social cognition and social development: A sociocultural perspective* (pp. 294–330). New York: Cambridge University Press.

Loeber, R., & Stouthamer-Loeber, J. (1986). Family factors as correlates and predictors of juvenile conduct problems and delinquency. In M. Tonry and N. Morris (Eds.), *Crime and justice* (vol. 7, pp. 219–339). Chicago: University of Chicago Press.

Maccoby, E. E., & Martin, J. A. (1983). Socialization in the context of the family: Parent-child interaction. In E. M. Hetherington (Ed.). *Handbook of child psychology* (vol. 4, pp. 1–102). New York: Wiley.

Mancuso, J. C., & Lehrer, R. (1986). Cognitive processes during reactions to rule violation. In R. D. Ashmore & D. M. Brodzinsky (Eds.). *Thinking about the family: Views of parents and children* (pp. 67–93). Hillsdale, NJ: Lawrence Erlbaum Associates.

Miller, N. E., & Dollard, J. (1941). *Social learning and imitation.* New Haven, CT: Yale University Press.

Miller, R. L., Brickman, P., & Bolen, D. (1975). Attribution *versus* persuasion as a means for modifying behavior. *Journal of Personality and Social Psychology, 31,* 430–441.

Morton, B., & Trehub, S. (2001). Children's understanding of emotion in speech. *Child Development, 72,* 834–843.

Nisbett, R. E., & Valins, S. (1971). *Perceiving the causes of one's own behavior.* Morristown NJ: General Learning Press.

Nucci, L. (1984). Evaluating teachers as social agents: Students' ratings of domain appropriate and domain inappropriate teacher responses to transgression. *American Educational Research Journal, 21,* 367–378.

O'Connor, T. G., Deater-Deckard, K., Fulker, D., Rutter, M., & Plomin, R. (1998). Genotype-environment correlations in late childhood and early adolescence: Antisocial behavioral problems and coercive parenting. *Developmental Psychology, 34,* 970–981.

Okagaki, L., & Bevis, C. (1999). Transmission of religious values: Relations between parents' and daughters' beliefs. *Journal of Genetic Psychology, 160,* 303–318.

Parpal, M., & Maccoby, E. E. (1985). Maternal responsiveness and subsequent child compliance. *Child Development, 56,* 1326–1334.

Paterson, G., & Sanson, A. (1999). The association of behavioural adjustment to temperament, parenting and family characteristics among 5-year-old children. *Social Development, 8,* 293–309.

Patterson, G. R. (1982). *Coercive family process.* Eugene, OR: Castalia Press.

Rothbart, M., & Bates, J. (1998). Temperament. In W. Damon & N. Eisenberg (Eds.). *Handbook of child psychology: Social, emotional, and personality development* (vol. 3, pp. 105–176). New York: Wiley.

Rothbaum, F., & Weisz, J. R. (1994). Parental caregiving and child externalizing behavior in nonclinical samples: A meta-analysis. *Psychological Bulletin, 116,* 55–74.

Rubin, K. H., Hastings, P. D., Chen, X., Stewart, S., & McNichol, K. (1998). Intrapersonal and maternal correlates of aggression, conflict, and externalizing problems in toddlers. *Child Development, 69,* 1614–1629.

Rudy, D., & Grusec, J. E. (2001). Correlates of authoritarian parenting in individualist and collectivist cultures and implications for understanding the transmission of values. *Journal of Cross-Cultural Psychology, 32,* 202–212.

Sears, R. R. (1941). Non-aggressive reactions to frustration. *Psychological Review, 48,* 343–346.

Sears, R. R. (1951). A theoretical framework for personality and social behavior. *American Psychologist, 6,* 476–483.

Sears, R. R., Maccoby, E. E., & Levin, H. (1957). *Patterns of child rearing.* Evanston, IL: Row Peterson.

Sears, R. R., Rau, L., & Alpert, R. (1964). *Identification and child* rearing. Stanford, CA: Stanford University Press.

Sears, R. R., Whiting, J. W. M., Nowlis, V., & Sears, P. S. (1953). Some child-rearing antecedents of dependency and aggression in young children. *Genetic Psychology Monographs, 47,* 135–234.

Siegal, M., & Barclay, M. S. (1985). Children's evaluations of fathers' socialization behavior. *Developmental Psychology, 21,* 1090–1096.

Siegal, M., & Cowen, J. (1984). Appraisals of intervention: The mother's versus the culprit's behavior as determinants of children's evaluations of discipline techniques. *Child Development, 55,* 1760–1766.

Smetana, J. (1997). Parenting and the development of social knowledge reconceptualized: A social domain analysis. In J .E. Grusec and L. Kuczynski (Eds.). *Parenting and the internalization of values: A handbook of contemporary theory* (pp. 162–192). New York: Wiley.

Smetana, J., & Asquith, P. (1994). Adolescents' and parents' conceptions of parental authority and adolescent autonomy. *Child Development, 65,* 1147–1162.

Smetana, J., & Berent, R. (1993). Adolescents' and mothers' evaluations of justifications for disputes. *Journal of Adolescent Research, 8,* 252–273.

Stice, E., & Gonzales, N. (1998). Adolescent temperament moderates the relation of parenting to antisocial behavior and substance use. *Journal of Adolescent Research, 13,* 5–31.

Trickett, P., & Kuczynski, L. (1986). Children's misbehavior and parental discipline in abusive and non-abusive families. *Developmental Psychology, 22,* 115–123.

Turiel, E. (1998). The development of morality. In W. Damon (Ed.). *Handbook of child psychology* (vol. 4, pp. 863–932). New York: Wiley.

van der Mark, I. L., Bakermans-Kranenburg, M. J., & van Ijzendoorn, M. H. (2002). The role of parenting, attachment, and temperamental fearfulness in the prediction of compliance in toddler girls. *British Journal of Developmental Psychology, 20,* 361–378.

Vuchinich, S., Emery, R. E., & Cassidy, J. (1988). Family members as third parties in dyadic family conflict: Strategies, alliances, and outcomes. *Child Development, 59,* 1293–1302.

Walters, G. C., & Grusec, J. E. (1977). *Punishment.* San Francisco: Freeman.

Zahn-Waxler, C., & Chapman, M. (1982). Immediate antecedents of caretakers' methods of discipline. *Child Psychiatry and Human Development, 12,* 179–192.

10

UNDERSTANDING VALUES IN RELATIONSHIPS: THE DEVELOPMENT OF CONSCIENCE

ROSS A. THOMPSON
SARA MEYER
UNIVERSITY OF CALIFORNIA, DAVIS

MEREDITH MCGINLEY
UNIVERSITY OF NEBRASKA

Conscience consists of the cognitive, affective, relational, and other processes that influence how young children construct and act consistently with generalizable, internal standards of conduct. Conscience development in the early years was not, until recently, of central interest to students of moral development. Traditional approaches to moral growth (such as those of learning theory and the cognitive–developmental view pioneered by Piaget and Kohlberg) portrayed young children as egocentric and preconventional thinkers and as self-interested moralists who respond to the incentives and sanctions provided by other people. By contrast with older children who are concerned with maintaining good relations with others, and with adolescents who consider moral issues within a broader ethical framework, the morality of young children was viewed as an authoritarian, instrumental orientation guided by rewards, punishment, and obedience. In this regard, morality in early childhood was sharply distinguished from the morality of values, humanistic regard, and relationships of later years.

But as developmental scientists have reexamined traditional conclusions about thinking and reasoning in early childhood, they have also taken a fresh look at moral understanding. Young children are no longer regarded as egocentric but instead as being intensely interested in the thoughts, feelings, and beliefs of other people, and research on developing theory of mind has revealed the sophistication of young children's inferences about different mental and emotional states (Wellman, 2002; Wellman, Cross, & Watson, 2001). Young children's sensitivity to standards, developing conceptions of others' desires, intentions, and rules, and representations of behavioral expectations each contribute, beyond punishment, to the motivational bases of compliance and cooperation. And developmental relational theory, particularly the contributions of attachment theory, has shown how significantly young children's experience in close relationships shapes their views of themselves, conceptions of morality, and motivation to cooperate with others (Kochanska & Thompson, 1997; Maccoby, 1984; Thompson, Laible, & Ontai, 2003). Taken together, it is now becoming clear that conscience development in early childhood shares much in common with later moral development: the foundations for a relational, humanistic, and other-oriented morality are emerging in the preschool years.

New research on early conscience is important for another reason. By contrast with studies of moral development in later years, which sometimes focus narrowly on children's social-cognitive judgments about wrongdoing, research on conscience development is conceptually and methodologically multifaceted (e.g., Kochanska, Aksan, & Nichols, 2003; Laible & Thompson, 2002; Smetana, 1997; Zahn-Waxler & Robinson, 1995). Research in this area explores, for example, the development of moral affect (particularly the conditions eliciting salient feelings of guilt or shame, as well as empathy), the emergence of behavioral self-control, relational influences on the motivation to cooperate, the emergence of a "moral self" (and the facets of self-awareness that contribute to the growth of conscience), temperamental influences, as well as cognitive achievements in the representation of behavioral standards. By studying young children's moral judgments, affect, and behavioral compliance, students of conscience development bring much-needed breadth to the study of early moral development (see, e.g., Grusec, Goodnow, & Kuczynski, 2000; Harris & Nunez, 1996; Kochanska, Gross, Lin, & Nichols, 2002; Lagattuta, in press; Thompson et al., 2003). Doing so has required methodological creativity. Studies in this field enlist laboratory procedures to assess young children's compliance with a parent's requests, observations of children's behavioral and emotional reactions to rigged mishaps and resistance to temptation tasks, responses to hypothetical stories involving moral violation and compliance, parental questionnnaires of early conscience, parent–child conversations about misbehavior and good behavior, and a variety of other procedures to elucidate how young children understand, feel, and respond as intuitive moralists. The study of early conscience has required conceptual breadth and methodological creativity to examine the foundations of morality in the early years.

Our goal is to profile these new discoveries and to suggest directions for future inquiry. The first section is devoted to the conceptual foundations of early conscience. We consider how young children become intuitive moralists in their initial learning about behavioral expectations, their representations of behavioral standards, and their sensitivity to the violation of standards. One conclusion emerging from these literatures is that young children are attuned to behavioral expectations as part of their representations of what is expectable and normative in the world, but that moral standards pose special conceptual challenges for them. Because emotion is a potent motivator of moral understanding and compliance, the affective side of conscience development is considered in the section that follows. This includes influences on developing self-understanding and self-regulation, the development of moral emotions, and the importance of temperamental individuality and its relation to conscience development. The account that emerges from these literatures is that rather than having to be tutored in morality by the incentives and sanctions of parents, young children are attuned to moral issues because of the incentives that arise from developing self-awareness and children's emotional connections to others.

Thus the third section profiles relational contributions to conscience development. We consider the importance of the affective quality of the parent-child relationship and the significance of the security of attachment to a young child's motivation to cooperate with parental expectations. Then we unpack relational influences further to consider parental strategies of control and discipline and other influences that shape the development of conscience in the early years (e.g., Holden, Miller, & Harris, 1999; Kochanska, Aksan, & Nichols, 2003; Kuczynski, Marshall, & Schell, 1997). The conclusion that emerges from these literatures is that far more important than rewards and punishments are the relational incentives that exist within the family, including the young child's desire to maintain an environment of cooperation with each parent and to be perceived by the adult as a good (and competent) person. In turn, the parental strategies that contribute to conscience development are far more than the reliable enforcement of consistent behavioral standards, and involve also affection, conversation, and proactive efforts to help children develop as naive young moralists.

In a concluding section, we consider more broadly what these new perspectives to early conscience development mean for moral development theory and research.

CONCEPTUAL FOUNDATIONS OF CONSCIENCE

The study of moral development has always been closely tied to children's conceptual development because morality involves reasoning of various kinds. Morality entails understanding behavioral standards, for example, and their applications to personal behavior. Morality involves generalizing context-specific and act-specific sanctions and rewards into broader rules of conduct. Morality requires understanding others' needs, desires, and interests and relating them to one's own. It also requires anticipating the responses of others to one's actions. Morality involves many domains of understanding, and thus the study of conscience development is closely tied to research examining children's conceptual growth.

Learning About Behavioral Expectations

Conscience development has its origins in infancy, when the sanctions (and rewards) of adults in response to the child's actions have emotional and behavioral consequences (Kochanska & Thompson, 1997). A 12-month-old may avoid prohibited acts (such as touching forbidden objects), for example, because of simple associative learning or a conditioned response to past disapproval and the feelings of uncertainty or anxiety with which it is associated. The child quickly learns that certain actions are routinely followed by disapproval and anxiety. As a result, he or she feels uncertain in similar situations and tends to inhibit prohibited actions. During the second year, a toddler may also resist acting in a disapproved manner because of imitative learning from another who has been punished. In these instances, however, the young child's behavioral compliance arises from prior reward and punishment and not from an internal obligation to a generalized value, and these behaviors thus cannot be really considered "moral." Although infants and toddlers are beginning to develop the conceptual foundations of conscience, as we show next, these foundations are not sufficiently well developed to motivate genuinely moral conduct.

These experiences of disapproval and reward are important, however, because disapproval comes from an adult to whom the child has developed a close emotional attachment. Thus a parent's disapproval is a salient experience that elicits attention and efforts to comprehend. Moreover, the infant's experience with the behavioral sanctions of parents increases markedly by the end of the first year, especially with the growth of self-produced locomotion. As Campos, Kermoian, and Zumbahlen (1992) have found, once infants begin crawling or creeping they become more capable of goal attainment but also of acting in a dangerous or disapproved manner and of wandering away from the parent. Consequently, parents report that they more actively monitor the child's activity, increasingly use prohibitions and sanctions, and also expect greater behavioral compliance from their locomotor offspring (Biringen, Emde, Campos, & Appelbaum, 1995; Campos, Anderson, Barbu-Roth, Hubbard, Hertenstein, & Witherington, 1999; Campos et al., 1992). Thus, during the same period (9 to 12 months) that a secure or insecure attachment to the parent is becoming consolidated, infants increasingly find that their actions and intentions are being frustrated and disapproved by the attachment figure. From the beginning, therefore, young children learn about behavioral expectations in the context of salient relational incentives for doing so, and the manner in which parents monitor and guide the behavior of offspring is likely related to their broader relationship quality.

These experiences are important for conscience development because they are also occurring at a time that infants are developing a dawning awareness that others have intentional and subjective orientations toward events that may differ from the child's own (Tomasello, 1999; Tomasello & Rakoczy, 2003). In their communicative gestures, efforts to achieve joint attention with another, and imitative learning, 12-month-olds reveal their awareness that others are deliberate and subjective partners. One of the most widely studied manifestations of this awareness is the emergence of social referencing by the end of the first year (Baldwin & Moses, 1996; Feinman, Roberts, Hsieh, Sawyer, & Swanson, 1992). Social referencing is commonly observed when infants respond to novel or uncertain situations based on the emotional expressions they detect in others; young children respond with cautious wariness to a novel situation when a caregiver appears anxious or frightened, for example. Although it is unclear whether social referencing reflects self-initiated information seeking or is instead a correlate of affective sharing, comfort seeking, or other facets of secure-base behavior (Baldwin & Moses, 1996), the emergence of social referencing as another intersubjective capacity by the end of the first year suggests that infants are good consumers of emotional information from others and can use it to guide their own actions (Thompson, 1998a).

Social referencing is important to learning about behavioral expectations because parents signal anxiety or disapproval in circumstances when young children may be unaware or uncertain of dangerous or prohibited acts. A mother whose imperative "ahhh!" and anxious facial expression when the baby crawls toward the cat's litter box in another's home is endowing this activity with affective valence for the infant, and this becomes even more influential when the parent's emotional cues are accompanied by imperative language and action. Moreover, at somewhat older ages, social referencing may become deliberately enlisted by the child as part of the nonverbal negotiation between a parent and a toddler over permitted and prohibited actions through their exchange of looks, expressions, and gestures. A toddler who progressively approaches the VCR with sticky fingers while glancing back toward the parent is enlisting the parent's expressions in clarifying or confirming the child's expectations about sanctioned conduct (Emde & Buchsbaum, 1990). According to Emde and his colleagues, this kind of checking and rechecking the parent's emotional expressions is an important avenue toward the growth of self-control as young children compare their contemplated behavior with an external emotional cue before the behavioral standard has become fully internalized. Subsequently, as children progressively remember and internalize the parent's approving or disapproving expressions when considering acting in the parent's absence, they are "referencing the absent parent" as an avenue toward conscience development (Emde, Biringen, Clyman, & Oppenheim, 1991; Emde & Buchsbaum, 1990).

Much more research should be devoted to elucidating the influence of this kind of emotional cuing on the behavioral regulation of infants and toddlers. For example, although considerable research indicates that infants inhibit activity in the presence of a parent (or another trusted caregiver) who expresses fearful or anxious affect, many behavioral expectations are conveyed in the context of an angry, "warning" tone. It is less clear how very young children respond to the prosody of adult voice and facial expressions signaling angry affect, even though these are likely to be evoked discriminatingly to contexts involving the violation of the parent's behavioral expectations. There is also much more to be learned about how the adult's emotional cues have the influence they do on young children, including the frequently debated issue of whether they alter behavior through the information inherent in the caregiver's emotional display, or through the arousal of resonant affect in the child that facilitates or inhibits ongoing activity, or both.

By the first birthday, therefore, infants are learning about behavioral expectations within a relational context in which the caregiver's emotional cues, together with the child's awareness of the adult as a subjective, intentional agent, endows the adult's disapproval with normative informational value and behavioral incentive. But until the child begins to adopt behavioral standards as internalized rules within a broader understanding of expectations and values, it is difficult to regard the child's compliance as truly moral in nature.

Representing Behavioral Standards

As constructivist theorists argue, children are active interpreters of experience. This is true of children's encounters with the rules and values communicated to them by parents. As Grusec and Goodnow (1994) have noted, for example, whether children internalize the values conveyed in discipline encounters with parents depends significantly on how children perceive the appropriateness and relevance of the adult's intervention, the clarity of the parental message, the emotional effects of the parent's behavior on the child (e.g., threats to security or a sense of autonomy), as well as the general quality of the parent–child relationship. Although their analysis focused on older children (who have been the traditional focus of moral socialization studies), the same is true of young children. As we shall see, for example, a child's temperamental qualities can mediate the impact of parental discipline practices. Some children respond emotionally and behaviorally to specific disciplinary interventions, whereas other children respond to the broader quality of the parent–child relationship. In addition, developmental changes in how young children reason about desires, beliefs, and intentions in relation to external standards are important influences on how they mentally represent behavioral expectations.

Research on children's developing understanding of people's internal states, or "theory of mind," indicates that young children achieve significant insight into the psychological causes of behavior during the first 5 years of life (Wellman, 2002; Wellman et al., 2001). Theory of mind begins with the dawning realization that intentions, desires, and emotions underlie actions, which emerges during the first 18 months of life (e.g., Repacholi & Gopnik, 1997; Woodward, 1998). This is the basis for the development of a "desire psychology" that involves a richer understanding of the mental world. By age 3, therefore, children understand that people behave according to their intentions, desires, and feelings. At this age, however, children have still not yet grasped the representational nature of mental events and, as a result, cannot easily conceive how beliefs about events would be inconsistent with reality. By age 5, however, children have reconstructed a more adequate "belief–desire" theory of mind that incorporates an understanding that behavior can be motivated by false belief (e.g., mistakenly searching in a drawer for pencils that have been taken by someone else). Children of this age also begin to grasp corollary concepts of emotional display rules (producing mistaken beliefs in others about one's feelings) and social deception. There are further achievements in developing theory of mind after age 5. As Flavell, Miller, and Miller (2002) note, for example, a constructivist theory of mind likely emerges around age 6 when children appreciate how mental processes (like expectations and biases) shape knowledge and understanding, and somewhat later children become aware of how individual differences in background and experience shape psychological traits that, in turn, affect mental states. Nevertheless, the first 5 years witness the emergence of young children as naive psychologists who understand the mental origins of self-determined behavior in other people.

The problem is that much behavior is not self-determined: choices are constrained by rules, obligations, and prohibitions imposed on people. In an intriguing recent analysis, Wellman and Miller (2003) have argued that *deontic reasoning*—thinking concerning what someone may, should, or may not, should not do—is another important facet of psychological understanding related to theory of mind reasoning in early childhood. Like theory of mind, they argue, young children demonstrate an early grasp of obligation. In one study, for example, Harris and Nunez (1996) showed that 3-year-olds are highly accurate at appropriately applying a prescriptive rule (i.e., "Mom says if Cathy rides her bike she should put her helmet on") to different scenarios, even though children of the same age are not as skilled at applying a similar descriptive, but not prescriptive, maxim ("when Cathy rides her bike, she always wears her helmet"). The differences between the two situations not only involve whether an authority is involved, but also whether forbidden and permitted actions—rather than typical and atypical actions—are delineated. Obligations are especially salient to young children for these reasons, and Wellman and Miller (2003) argue that they are likely to have an imperative quality that is comparable to the compelling truth of reality that causes 3-year-olds to have difficulty conceptualizing false belief. In the case of obligation, they suggest, young children are prone to assert that rules cannot be broken and obligations must necessarily be discharged, which is similar to the moral absolutism observed in young children long ago by Piaget (1965). As Piaget himself noted, children's construal of rules as obligatory develops regardless of the manner in which these rules are conveyed by parents because they enlist young children's capacities for intuitive reasoning about compelling social realities (beliefs about events) and obligations (beliefs about rules).

Young children also conceptually distinguish between different obligatory domains. Adults readily differentiate moral rules (which are applicable in all situations and cannot be abrogated) from social-conventional rules (which are applicable in some locales but not others, and can be changed by parents and other authorities). Both are obligatory, in some sense, but differ in the origins, generality, and strength of the obligation. In a series of studies, Smetana has shown that even young children make such conceptual distinctions among domains entailing social regulation (Smetana, 1981, 1985; Smetana & Braeges, 1990). In her studies, children from age 2 through age 4 described as "bad" the violation of moral and social-conventional rules with which they were familiar. But although 2-year-olds did not distinguish between different kinds of violations, 3- and 4-year-olds viewed moral violations as more serious and less revocable (e.g., "Would it be OK if there was not a rule about it here?") than social-conventional violations. Smetana has shown that such domain distinctions are also incorporated into parents' socialization strategies at home (Smetana, 1989, 1997; Smetana, Kochanska, & Chuang, 2000). Young children are, in short, sensitive to obligatory expectations and distinguish between different obligatory domains in their thinking about the social world.

Remarkably, young children also make sophisticated judgments about the interplay between moral and social conventional standards in complex social situations. Killen, Pisacane, Lee-Kim, and Ardile-Rey (2001) and Theimer, Killen, and Stangor (2001) each assessed how preschoolers would evaluate common gender-based social exclusion probes in peer play (e.g., girls excluding a boy from doll play). They found that although preschoolers recognized that gender exclusion occurs based on conventional stereotypes, they also gave priority to fairness considerations in rejecting gender-based exclusion. In short, they appreciated both social-conventional norms and the moral imperative for equal treatment.

Conscience and morality are not, of course, merely cognitive capacities. They involve salient emotions evoked both by compliance and transgression. Lagattuta (in press) explored children's understandings of the emotions that are elicited when one complies (but resists fulfilling one's desires) or when one transgresses (to satisfy desire). Children ranging in age from 4 to 7 and adults were interviewed about how a story character would feel who wanted to act in a certain way (e.g., running into the street to retrieve a ball) that conflicted with a prohibitive rule (e.g., "You should not run into the street"). By contrast with the younger children, the majority of 7-year-olds and adults predicted that the story character would feel positive or mixed emotions when complying, and that the story character would feel negative or mixed emotions when transgressing. In each case, of course, the story character is responding emotionally in a manner inconsistent with the satisfaction of their underlying desire to retrieve the ball. By contrast, young children attributed more negative emotion to the compliant story character, and more positive emotions to the one who transgressed. Younger children had more difficulty looking beyond the satisfaction or frustration of personal desires to consider the future consequences of desire-related moral action. Such a view is consistent with the conclusions of Arsenio and his colleagues that children perceive victimizers as feeling positively about their misconduct because of their focus on the satisfaction of the victimizer's desires, not the victim's distress (Arsenio & Kramer, 1992; Arsenio & Lover, 1999). As Lagattuta notes, considering the future consequences of fulfilling present desires is a conceptual challenge for preschoolers when considering moral obligation and other activity, particularly when later consequences may conflict emotionally with the satisfaction of present desires. Such a conclusion is consistent with many observations of young children's difficulty in denying present pleasures to pursue long-term goals or obligations.

It is apparent from studies such as these that young children think deeply and with considerable insight about the rules and obligations that characterize everyday life. They not only make conceptual distinctions between different obligatory domains, but they do so within the context of representations of other people's desires, intentions, and beliefs that develop significantly in sophistication and scope. Obligations, in the form of rules, expectations, and standards, seem to have special salience to young children as part of their understanding of how the world normatively functions, even though they often have difficulty applying such rules consistently to their own actions or resisting the tendency to violate such rules when doing so enables the satisfaction of salient, present intentions and desires. Nevertheless, rules are conceptually compelling constructs to them, and their emergent conceptualization of rules in these ways inaugurates the transition from the behavioral compliance of the infant to the internalized conscience of the preschooler.

Children's developing representations of behavioral standards are also likely to be embedded within broader prototypical knowledge structures by which young children represent and understand common, recurrent experiences as well as predict their outcomes. These "scripts" constitute a foundation for event representation by enabling young children to inclusively represent familiar experiences and integrate them with other knowledge systems (Hudson, 1993; Nelson, 1978). Many of the moral and conventional standards affecting young children are related to routine events and are repeatedly conveyed in these contexts, whether consisting of prohibitions from touching dangerous objects at home; avoiding making messes and breaking things; self-control with respect to waiting, sharing, aggression, and eating; simple manners; self-care; and participation in family routines (Gralinski & Kopp, 1993; Smetana et al., 2000). Thus, behavioral expectations are likely to become incorporated into young children's early prototypical knowledge systems and assume normative value as a result. Young children's understanding of how things are done (mealtime, bedtime, daytime routines) includes standards for how one should act in these and other situations. Moreover, to the extent that young children use event scripts to represent novel as well as routine situations (such as using the mealtime script to describe the specific activities that happened at dinner last night), their understanding of behavioral standards is likely to be implicit in their memory and representation of many events of personal significance to them. Taken together, therefore, another reason why behavioral standards are salient and assume normative value to young children (i.e., Piaget's moral absolutism) is that early understanding of behavioral expectations becomes incorporated into children's developing representations of the normative structure of routine events. Expectations for how one acts may become perceived as normative and obligatory just as are expectations for how others will act in these prototypical situations.

As the studies described in this section illustrate, there is a considerable research agenda remaining for scientists interested in elucidating the nature of young children's representations of behavioral standards. In particular, it will be important to understand how young children think about behavioral norms by comparison with other normative events with which they are familiar (including events of the natural as well as the social world), and to explore further their conceptions of moral and conventional obligations by comparison with social events that are consistent but not necessarily obligatory (e.g., daily routines). It will be especially important to study young children's conceptions of normative obligations in a relational context, taking into account how these standards are conveyed to young children and the emotional incentives for compliance that inhere in parent–child interaction. As Smetana's research indicates, children likely appropriate considerable knowledge of the domains of social obligation in their interactions with caregivers. But do caregivers convey their behavioral expectations to young offspring in ways that also contribute to children's beliefs in their normative, obligatory quality?

Sensitivity to Standards

If young children are creating mental schemas for what is normative in their worlds, including the obligations that underlie behavioral standards, this tendency should also be apparent in other ways. Kagan (1981, in press) has argued that young children develop a heightened sensitivity to the standard violations they encounter late in the second year, which is apparent in their responses to obviously marred or disfigured objects. During this period (but not before), he argues, children become concerned when standards of wholeness and intactness have been violated, such as when they notice missing buttons from garments, torn pages from books, trash on the floor, broken toys, or misplaced objects. In his research, Kagan found that 19-month-olds, but not 14-month-olds, expressed concerned over broken toys either vocally (e.g., "It's yukky") or with a despondent expression and obvious concern (see also Lamb, 1993). Kagan has interpreted this phenomenon as an emerging moral sense because each event violated the implicit norms or standards that are typically enforced by parents through sanctions on broken, marred, or damaged objects. In a sense, children of this age have created an internal norm that is generalized from the specific standards they have received from parents. In addition, children of this age also spontaneously attribute human intentionality to these violations—inferring that someone is responsible for the disfigurement—that also contributes to the moral relevance of these reactions (Kagan, April 3, 2003, personal communication).

Kochanska, Casey, and Fukumoto (1995) explored this view further in a study with somewhat older children (26- to 41-month-olds). Children were presented with pairs of toys, with one toy intact and the other flawed (e.g., torn stuffed bear; torn or stained blanket), and their responses were observed. Kochanska and her colleagues reported that children were highly interested in the flawed objects, commenting on them (e.g., "broken," "I don't like it," "fix it") and trying to repair them. Several weeks later, children were observed in the laboratory in a series of rigged mishaps for which children believed they were responsible, and their subsequent emotional and reparative responses were observed. Girls who had earlier shown greater sensitivity to the flawed objects also responded with greater concern and distress to the mishaps, and the same association was apparent more weakly for boys. These findings led Kochanska and her colleagues to conclude that these responses reflect an emerging system of internal standards leading to a sense of right and wrong.

Thus young children's sense of obligation to normative behavioral standards may be part of a broader sensitivity to normative standards with respect to the integrity of common objects. The same tendency may also be apparent, furthermore, in self-recognition: children at 18 or 19 months respond with embarrassment to a spot of rouge on their noses whereas younger children do not, reflecting an internal standard for their normative physical appearance (Lewis, 2000; Lewis & Brooks-Gunn, 1979). Further research is needed, however, to confirm whether the sensitivity to standards identified by Kagan reflects a truly moral sense, or instead the application of normative standards that are not necessarily moral in nature. Although it is apparent that young children are interested and concerned with objects that have been damaged (especially when a comparable, intact object is presented alongside), no researchers have yet examined young children's evaluative responses to other objects that are different from the norm but are not damaged. To do so, it would be important to compare children's responses to intact and damaged objects with their reactions to objects that are deviant but not damaged (e.g., comparing whole and broken cups to a cup with a finished hole at the bottom; comparing intact and torn blankets with a blanket that is octagonal rather than square). Children as young as 2 years are highly sensitive to these differences in functional design (Kemler Nelson, Herron, & Morris, 2002; Kemler Nelson, Holt, & Chang Egen, 2003), although their emotional and evaluative responses have not yet been assessed. If 2-year-olds respond with "yukky" and emotional concern to objects that are not damaged but simply atypical, then it is possible that their early sensitivity to standards reflects their preoccupation with what is normative in the objects with which they are familiar. This may not become a distinctly moral sensitivity until later in the preschool years, as suggested by the findings of Kochanska and colleagues (1995).

Summary

In their search for predictable constancies in a world of changing experience (a search that Piaget argued characterizes much of early cognitive growth), young children learn about behavioral expectations from attachment figures. As soon as young children are locomotor, these expectations become conveyed through physical interventions, emotional expressions, and words that are incorporated into daily experience and are likely to be incorporated into children's prototypical event representations. If the contemporary account of young children's deontic reasoning (Wellman & Miller, 2003) and the traditional portrayal of the preschooler's moral absolutism (Piaget, 1965) are correct, young children begin to view these expectations and standards as normative obligations. In much the same way that young children respond emotionally to violations of personal appearance (rouge on the nose) and expectations concerning the integrity and intactness of objects, they view behavioral standards as describing normative reality and thus being compelling and obligatory, and violations are sources of concern. This is especially so for moral obligations, which young children early distinguish from social–conventional norms. Even so, young children are conceptually challenged by deontic obligations because of the difficulties of conceiving behavior in future as well as present context (i.e., later consequences as well as present outcomes), and understanding the desires that motivate multiple actors in moral conflicts.

Another challenge is that nascent deontic understanding does not readily translate into moral compliance. The young intuitive moralist daily confronts the reality that obligation is not necessarily accompanied by compliance, despite the child's strong effort to understand the behavioral expectations of those who matter and (at times) their desire to cooperate. And the consequences of failure are significant, including disapproval from attachment figures that may threaten self-esteem. Because these emotional dimensions of moral compliance are significant incentives to acquiring and complying with parents' values, therefore, we turn next to considering the affective influences on conscience development.

CONSCIENCE AND EMOTION

Although there has been considerable interest in the development of moral judgment in older children, researchers recognize that conscience development is more than just conceptual understanding (e.g., Barrett, 1998; Kochanska, 2002a; Laible & Thompson, 2002; Stipek, 1995). Morality involves self-understanding, and the incentives for cooperation and compliance that arise from how a developing child perceives herself or himself and wants to be seen by others. Moral compliance also enlists powerful moral emotions like pride, guilt, shame, and empathy that motivate cooperation, sometimes to avoid the affects that arise from parental disapproval. And temperamental individuality is an important mediator of children's susceptibility to these emotional influences on conscience development.

Developing Self-Understanding and Self-Regulation

Young children cannot act morally until they understand the self as a causal agent and can view the self as an object of evaluation. Moreover, moral development advances in concert with the child's developing self-regulatory capacities and desire to be viewed as acceptable in the eyes of others. Indeed, Kochanska (2002a) has proposed that a developing moral self guides moral conduct in early childhood. In this manner, the growth of conscience is closely associated with the development of self-understanding and self-regulation.

Even infants can experience themselves as causal agents, but the advances in self-understanding most relevant to morality occur during the second and third years. Late in the second year and early in the third, for example, toddlers exhibit many indications of emergent self-representation, such as in their verbal self-referential behavior ("Me big!") (Bates, 1990; Stern, 1985), efforts to assert competence and responsibility as independent agents by refusing assistance (Bullock & Lutkenhaus, 1990; Heckhausen, 1988), identifying simple emotions in themselves (Bretherton, Fritz, Zahn-Waxler, & Ridgeway, 1986), describing the self by gender and in other ways (Ruble & Martin, 1998), and growing interest in how their behavior is regarded by others (Emde & Buchsbaum, 1990; Stipek, Recchia, & McClintic, 1992). Young children are beginning, in other words, to regard themselves in more multidimensional and evaluative ways, and are developing an interest in understanding how others regard them as objects of evaluation (William James's self-as-object) as they are striving to be perceived as competent and responsible. These emergent features of self-representation cause young children to be sensitive to the evaluations of others and to the feelings (such as pride and guilt) deriving from such evaluations, and contributes to their motivation to act in ways that others approve of.

Somewhat later, in the fourth and fifth years, young children begin to perceive themselves in more explicitly characterological terms. To be sure, young children often rely on concrete, observable features and action tendencies in their spontaneous self-descriptions (e.g., "I am big, I can run fast") (Harter, 1999), but they can also use psychological trait terms appropriately as personality self-descriptions (e.g., "I am naughty sometimes, but good with adults") (Eder, 1989, 1990). This suggests that, contrary to earlier portrayals of young children's self-regard, preschoolers think of themselves in personological ways by which they compare themselves with others and from which self-understanding arises. Although it is reasonable to assume that young children's self-descriptions derive, at least in part, from how they are perceived and described by their parents, more study of the nature and influences on preschool children's psychological self-attributions is needed (see Eder & Mangelsdorf, 1997). This is especially important in relation to conscience development because how children perceive themselves as naughty or nice is likely to be motivationally important in morally relevant behavior, and linked in significant ways to the parent–child relationship and the parent's evaluation of the child (Kochanska, 2002a).

These advances in self-understanding not only contribute to the development of the child as a moral being, but also provide a foundation for the growth of self-control and self-regulation (Kopp, 1982, 1987; Kopp & Wyer, 1994). As Kopp has noted, the development of self-regulation is a painstaking process in the early years. *Self-regulation* entails the development of capacities for remembering and generalizing behavioral standards learned from caregivers; the growth of self-awareness as an autonomous, agentic individual; developing a capacity for self-initiated modifications in behavior resulting from remembered parental guidelines; and the growing ability to continuously monitor one's behavior according to these guidelines in diverse circumstances. These are complex achievements and, consistent with the foregoing review, the capacity for competent self-control is, according to Kopp, an achievement of the third year, with self-regulatory capacities emerging somewhat later. This view is consistent with considerable research on behavioral, emotional, and attentional self-regulation, together with allied literatures in developmental neuroscience, suggesting that foundational capacities for self-regulation emerge during the preschool years concurrent with maturational advances in frontal areas of the brain (Shonkoff & Phillips, 2000). Although many achievements in self-management have yet to develop, a 5-year-old is considerably more capable of focusing attention, controlling impulses, and enlisting strategies for managing emotion than is a 2-year-old. This means, of course, that a young child's capacities to comply with external or internalized standards of conduct also develops significantly in early childhood, at the same time that the preschooler's motivation to cooperate and to please people who matter is also growing.

Development of Morally Relevant Emotions

One of the strong motivators for morally compliant behavior is the salient emotion that arises from cooperative and uncooperative conduct. During the second and third years of life, concurrent with other advances in self-representation described, young children also begin to exhibit psychologically self-referential emotions: pride, shame, guilt, and embarrassment (Barrett, 1998; Barrett, Zahn-Waxler, & Cole, 1993; Lewis, 2000). Guilt has been studied most extensively. In an important study, Kochanska and associates (2002) observed children's affective and behavioral responses at 22, 33, and 45 months to experimental situations involving rigged mishaps in which children believed they had damaged the experimenter's special toy. Children exhibited concern and distress at each age, and individual differences in these responses were stable over time and were modestly predictive (especially at 45 months) of a battery of assessments of conscience at 56 months that included compliance with rules, moral themes in story-completion responses, and the child's self-reported moral behavior (Kochanska's moral self). Moreover, children who displayed more guilt at each age were found to be temperamentally more fearful, and their mothers used less power assertion in discipline encounters. These developmental findings are consistent with maternal reports concerning the development of guilt in offspring, which also report significant growth in the affective and behavioral manifestations of guilt over this period (Kochanska, DeVet, Goldman, Murray, & Putnam, 1994; Stipek, Gralinski, & Kopp, 1990; Zahn-Waxler & Robinson, 1995).

Just as the simple joy of success becomes accompanied by looking and smiling to an adult and calling attention to the feat (pride), therefore, so also a toddler's upset at an adult's disapproval grows developmentally into efforts to avoid the caregiver's approbation (shame) or make amends (guilt). As these examples illustrate, these morally relevant emotions are socially evoked in the early years and, as Stipek (1995; Stipek et al., 1992) has noted, the reactions of parents to the child's behavior are crucial. In their responses to the successes and failures of their offspring to comply with behavioral expectations, parents not only provide salient expressions of approval or disapproval but also cognitively structure the young child's interpretation of the event. They do so by explicitly linking their response to the standards that the parent has previously conveyed ("You know better than to hit your sister!"), invoke salient attributions of responsibility ("Why did you hit her?"), and often directly induce the self-referent evaluation and affect ("Bad boy!"). This is important because the causal associations between a child's behavior, consequences to other people, the parent's response, and the experience of moral affect are psychologically complex and are thus not always conceptually clear to young children. By inducing salient feelings of pride, shame, and guilt (and other emotions) and providing a verbal response that makes these causal associations explicit, considerable moral and emotional socialization occurs in parent–child discourse during the early years.

The parent's cognitive structure is important because the parent may provide an interpretation of the event that is different from the child's own. A 4-year-old's struggle with a sibling over a valued toy is a dispute over whose desire will prevail, and to each child the violation of personal rights is salient. But when the parent sanctions the conduct of one or both children the dispute assumes broader moral dimensions, and the parent's construal of the event is likely to be significantly different from the child's own. Although the heightened emotions that accompany discipline encounters like these may undermine either child's depth of processing and understanding of the parent's message, the difference between the child's experience of the event and the adult's communicated interpretation of it is likely to be conceptually provocative to young children. In figuring out what happened (sometimes in the context of subsequent conversation with the parent), young children not only confront inconsistent mental representations of the same event, but also acquire greater insight into the attributions and evaluations that underlie the adult's moral judgments. As we shall see, the manner in which parents discuss misbehavior with young offspring—long after the event has occurred—is associated with the growth of conscience and emotion understanding in young children (see Thompson et al., 2003). In these conversations, furthermore, parents are enlisting their young offspring into a system of cultural as well as moral interpretations of behavior because of how they represent events to which they have responded with approval or disapproval. According to Peggy Miller and her colleagues, for example, Chinese and American mothers describe their children's misbehavior much differently in the presence of the child. American mothers tend to attribute child misconduct to spunk or mischievousness, but Chinese and Chinese-American mothers emphasize much more the shame inherent in misbehavior, each consistent with their cultural values (Miller, Fung, & Mintz, 1996; Miller, Potts, Fung, Hoogstra, & Mintz, 1990).

Although the emergence of moral emotions like guilt, shame, and pride is contingent on the growth of representational self-awareness in young children, therefore, the social contexts in which these emotions are evoked shape the growth of self-understanding (Barrett, 1995; Dunn, 1987). In particular, powerful parental messages of responsibility and the consequences of behavior, together with the salient self-referential emotions with which they are associated, are significant and memorable experiences for young children. As these experiences become incorporated into the child's autobiographical memory and self-referent beliefs, moral evaluations are likely to become part of how children view themselves, and conceive how to relate to others and their relationships with people who matter.

Empathy is another emotional resource for moral conduct that also emerges in early childhood. Consistent with other advances in intersubjective understanding, an empathic capacity emerges during the second year and continues to unfold with growth in emotion understanding in early childhood (Thompson, 1998b; Zahn-Waxler, 2000; Zahn-Waxler & Radke-Yarrow, 1990; Zahn-Waxler & Robinson, 1995). But the sight and sound of another person's distress, fear, or anger is a motivationally complex event for young children. It may lead to sympathetic feelings and prosocial initiatives, but young children may also ignore, laugh at, or aggress toward another in distress, or seek comfort for themselves because of threats to their own emotional security as well as limited social understanding (see Cummings & Davies, 1994; Davies & Cummings, 1994). Consequently, when adults can provide a cognitive structure to assist the child's understanding of the emotions they are witnessing in another, especially by clarifying causality and responsibility, raw empathic arousal can become enlisted into prosocial initiatives toward another person, and into guilt when the child is the perpetrator of another's distress (Zahn-Waxler, 2000; Zahn-Waxler & Radke-Yarrow, 1990; Zahn-Waxler, Radke-Yarrow, Wagner, & Chapman, 1992). Viewed in this light, empathy in itself may not reliably elicit moral responding in young children. But experiences of empathic arousal in the context of the adult's communicated construction of causality and responsibility can be an elicitor of the young child's moral affect and prosocial responding.

Temperamental Individuality

Temperament has a potentially significant developmental influence on conscience that illustrates the different motivational avenues underlying early moral compliance. The realization that young children with different temperamental profiles develop internalized behavioral controls suggests, in other words, that the incentives and sanctions contributing to conscience development may vary for different children in ways that illustrate the multidimensionality of early moral socialization.

This view has been most strongly expressed in the work of Kochanska (1993), who proposed in a theoretical review that conscience development may assume two developmental pathways: first, through the motivation to avoid the affective discomfort and anxiety associated with wrongdoing, and second, through the motivation to maintain good relations with caregivers by exercising behavioral self-control. A child's temperamental profile is influential in shaping which developmental pathway predominantly contributes to the growth of conscience. This view was subsequently elaborated in two studies that showed that for temperamentally fearful young children, measures of conscience were predicted by maternal control strategies that deemphasized power and instead enlisted nonassertive guidance and "gentle discipline." These children are naturally likely to feel upset and anxious after wrongdoing and to become concerned about its negative consequences, Kochanska reasoned, and thus parental practices that enlist the child's preexisting worry without creating overwhelming distress are likely to contribute best to moral internalization. By contrast, for children who were temperamentally relatively fearless, conscience was not predicted by maternal discipline techniques but rather by the security of attachment and maternal warm responsiveness. For these children, the relational incentives of the mother–child relationship motivated cooperation and compliance (Kochanska, 1991, 1995). These associations were partially replicated in a longitudinal follow-up study in which maternal socialization and children's temperament were assessed at age 2 to 3 years, and measures of conscience (assessed via resistance to temptation tasks and responses to semiprojective stories) were obtained at ages 4 to 5 (Kochanska, 1997a). These findings were not replicated, however, in an independent study by Kochanska and associates (2002), nor in a study with much younger girls by van der Mark, Bakermans-Kranenburg, and van IJzendoorn (2002). Taken together, however, the balance of the empirical evidence suggests that temperament may mediate the influence of early parental practices on the development of conscience in young children, although further study is warranted to clarify whether this model is applicable to conscience development beyond early childhood.

Another developmental pathway in conscience development proposed by Kochanska (1993) is also temperamentally mediated. Young children who are high on effortful (or inhibitory) control are capable of exercising self-restraint to resist a forbidden impulse, and it is reasonable to expect that such children would also be more morally compliant. She has confirmed this association in studies showing both contemporaneous and longitudinal associations between early inhibitory control and later measures of conscience in early childhood and school age (Kochanska, Murray, & Coy, 1997; Kochanska, Murray, Jacques, Koenig, & Vandegeest, 1996; see also Kochanska & Knaack [2003], and Kochanska et al. [1994]). In this view, temperament has a direct influence on conscience development, making some young children more capable of exercising self-control with respect to behavioral expectations.

A third portrayal of the role of temperament and conscience development derives from studies that examine individual differences in children's negative reactivity. Children who are temperamentally high in negative emotion, irritability, and difficulty may be more prone to noncompliance, although they may also be more susceptible to guilt because of their sensitivity to disapproval and criticism. Thus predictions concerning the influence of temperamental reactivity on conscience development are somewhat mixed. In one study, Kochanska and colleagues (1994) reported that preschool girls who were high in temperamental reactivity obtained higher scores on a maternal-report dimension of conscience called "affective discomfort," which encompasses guilt, remorse, and efforts to restore good relations with the parent after wrongdoing. Kagan (in press) has reported somewhat similar findings (see also Lehman, Steier, Guidash, & Wanna, 2002).

Another study, however, offers a very different portrayal of the influence of negative reactivity on conscience development. Children's uncooperative behavior during laboratory tasks at 30 months was predicted by the interaction of temperamental reactivity with the child's self-regulatory capabilities (Stifter, Spinrad, & Braungart-Rieker, 1999) and maternal control strategies (Braungart-Rieker, Garwood, & Stifter, 1997). Children high on negative reactivity were more likely to be uncooperative, although this was mediated by the exercise of maternal control or the child's own self-regulatory capabilities. These findings are consistent with Eisenberg's (2000) view that the effects of temperamental reactivity must be viewed in the context of regulatory processes that may enlist this reactivity in constructive or unconstructive directions. The manner to which temperamental negative reactivity influences conscience development—either by heightening children's proneness to misbehavior or their sensitivity to the affective discomforts of noncompliance—clearly requires further exploration.

Taken together, these findings profile multiple developmental pathways to early conscience development, and also highlight the adaptive and maladaptive motivational foundations of moral behavior. As these studies suggest, different young children may be morally compliant for somewhat different reasons. For some, cooperation springs predominantly from the broader capacities for self-control and self-management that are likely to be exhibited in many situations (such as in learning and self-care). For others, maintaining good relations with caregivers—and the threat to relational harmony that accompanies misconduct—is the primary motivator of cooperative behavior. Other children are dispositionally prone to fearful and anxious affect, especially in circumstances associated with prior parental disapproval, and thus moral compliance derives from efforts to avoid these aversive feelings. Research on temperament and conscience shows that the most effective parental strategies to socialize moral compliance in young children depend, in part, on the child's temperamental profile. This is another example of the importance of nonshared environmental influences on early socialization, and is complicated, of course, by the realization that parenting practices are themselves affected by the young child's temperamental profile (Clark, Kochanska, & Ready, 2000).

Furthermore, this research suggests that each temperamentally associated motivational orientation has its strengths and weaknesses. Temperamentally fearless children who comply to maintain good relations with the parent may, for example, be prone to misbehave when they can escape detection. Temperamentally fearful children who readily experience anxious fear when misbehaving may become guilt prone and morally inflexible as a result. The realization that alternative pathways to conscience development arise, in part, from temperamental individuality suggests that these pathways may have far-reaching influences on moral development, an issue that requires further research exploration with children of older ages.

Summary

Young children fail to act consistently with expectations they regard as obligatory because self-control is limited, self-regulation is nascent, and immediate desire often outweighs future consequences in their representation of moral dilemmas. Even so, the consequences of failure are significant: disapproval from attachment figures is accompanied by verbal explanations that clarify responsibility and causality, and the arousal of salient self-referential moral emotions. Temperament mediates these social and emotional processes, but primarily by defining the constellation of intrinsic vulnerabilities and resources that become enlisted into conscience development. One must feel sympathy with young children who are so conceptually attuned to deontic obligations but vulnerable to the emotional consequences of their inability to consistently comply.

Fortunately, young children are assisted by caregivers who convey and enforce behavioral standards and contribute to early moral development through proactive as well as reactive strategies, and support the young child's conceptual foundations for moral understanding. Because young children do not navigate the world of morality by themselves, we turn now to consider the relational influences on conscience development.

RELATIONAL INFLUENCES ON CONSCIENCE DEVELOPMENT

Parents are central figures in the moral world of the young child. They articulate and explain behavioral standards, provide salient attributions of causality and responsibility for misbehavior, elicit moral emotions like empathy and guilt, disapprove and sanction misconduct, and provide some of the most important incentives to compliance. Their influence occurs via at least two avenues: through the broader quality of the parent–child relationship that embeds behavioral compliance within the network of good relations that they share, and through specific proactive efforts and reactive practices by which parents respond to misbehavior and compliance.

Relational Quality

Although moral socialization is often discussed in relation to specific parenting practices (e.g., discipline techniques), the temperament research profiled above suggests that these practices are influential because of the broader relationship context in which they are exercised. Young children are motivated to cooperate with the expectations of parents, for example, to maintain the positive affectionate relationship that they enjoy. Viewed in this light, the parent–child relationship in early childhood can be conceived of as the young child's introduction into a relational system of reciprocity that supports moral conduct by sensitizing the child to the mutual obligations of close relationships. Although the mutual obligations of parents and offspring are certainly not equal in early childhood, the young child is nevertheless motivated by the parent's affectionate care to respond constructively to parental initiatives, appropriate parental values, and maintain and value a positive relationship. Such a mutually responsive parent–child relationship orients children to the human dimensions of moral conduct (e.g., consequences for another) and, more generally, makes the child more receptive to the parent's socialization initiatives, and provides experience with the kinds of "communal" relationships that children may also share with other partners in the years that follow (Kochanska, 2002b; Maccoby, 1984, 1999; Waters, Kondo-Ikemura, Posada, & Richters, 1991).

To Kochanska (2002b), a mutually responsive orientation between parent and child encompasses two features: mutual responsiveness and shared positive affect. In several studies in which these relational qualities were assessed in multiple lengthy home observations of parents with young children, assessments of their mutually responsive orientation were found to predict measures of the child's conscience development both contemporaneously and longitudinally (Kochanska, 1997b; Kochanska & Aksan, 1995; Kochanska, Forman, & Coy, 1999; Kochanska & Murray, 2000). In these studies, for example, children in relationships characterized by high mutual responsivity acted with *committed compliance* (cooperation without reminders) to the parent's requests at 26 to 41 months, and greater *internalization of rules* (compliance when alone or with a peer) in toddlerhood, preschool, and school-age assessments. Similar findings have been reported by Laible and Thompson (2000).

The warmth and responsiveness of the parent–child relationship is thus an important relational incentive for young children's moral compliance, as Kochanska (2002b) has argued. But these studies also reveal additional reasons why a mutually responsive orientation is associated with early conscience development. Mothers in mutually responsive relationships use less power assertion in their interactions with offspring, for example, which may reflect their use of gentler, less coercive influence techniques (Kochanska, 1997b; Kochanska et al., 1999). Children in mutually responsive relationships also show greater empathic responsiveness to simulations of distress enacted by their mothers, and mothers themselves are also more empathic, which may reflect a deeper emotional engagement in their relationship (Kochanska, 1997b; Kochanska et al., 1999). In a behavioral genetic study, Deater-Deckard and O'Connor (2000) concluded that the child's genotypical characteristics help to account for dyadic mutually responsive orientation, and this is an example of evocative gene–environment correlation. A mutually responsive orientation is thus likely to be associated with several other features of the parent–child relationship, which, as Kochanska's other research on the influences of child temperament and gentle discipline suggests, also have important influences on early conscience development. It remains for future research to elucidate these correlates and their developmental consequences.

Kochanska's measures of mutually responsive orientation have been found to be consistent across different situations and stable over several years, suggesting that they capture a rather robust feature of early parent–child relationships. Another index of early relational quality that may also be related to early conscience development is the security of attachment. Like mutually responsive orientation, attachment security is also founded on a positive parent–child relationship based on the parent's sensitive responsiveness to the child's signals and needs (Thompson, 1998a). Attachment theorists have argued that a secure attachment in early childhood creates a more supportive, harmonious parent–child relationship that makes a young child more compliant, cooperative, and responsive to the parent's socialization initiatives (Waters et al., 1991). There is some evidence for this. Londerville and Main (1981) found that infants who were deemed securely attached at 12 months were more cooperative and compliant and less disobedient (but more "troublesome") in play sessions at 21 months, and their mothers were warmer and gentler in their interactions with the toddler. Other studies have also found that securely attached infants were more compliant and positive, and their mothers more supportive and helpful in problem-solving tasks (Bates, Maslin, & Frankel, 1985; Matas, Arend, & Sroufe, 1978). As noted, Kochanska (1995) found that security of attachment was associated with measures of conscience for temperamentally fearless young children, and Laible and Thompson (2000) also noted that the security of attachment predicted measures of early conscience development. These findings are consistent with broader conclusions in the attachment literature that a secure attachment inaugurates a more positive, harmonious relationship to which mother and child mutually contribute (Thompson, 1999). Interestingly, however, neither Laible and Thompson (2000) nor Kochanska have found a significant association between measures of the security of attachment and mutually responsive orientation between parent and child, despite their apparent conceptual overlap.

Attachment theory takes the additional step of proposing that based on experiences of sensitive care, securely attached young children create mental representations of relational experience ("internal working models") that influence their understandings of themselves, relational partners, and how to engage in other close relationships. In this respect, the concept of internal working models provides a conceptual bridge from the processes of behavioral compliance that are motivated by a positive parent–child relationship to the processes of behavioral internalization that provide a foundation for the growth of conscience. In relational experience with the parent, young children create mental representations of many social and psychological processes relevant to conscience: understandings of emotional experiences and their causes and consequences; representations of rules and standards and the reasons they exist; conceptions of the self and its moral dimensions; and understandings of relationships and of relational processes (such as reciprocity, kindness, and fairness) that relate to moral behavior. These representations change considerably with increasing age, of course, and it is likely that the conceptions derived from insecure relationships are somewhat different from those of secure relationships.

There has been little systematic, empirical exploration of the quality of the internal working models of early childhood derived from relational experience that are conscience related, however, partly because defining and assessing *internal working models* is difficult (Thompson, in press; Thompson & Raikes, 2003). Developmental scientists have found that securely attached preschoolers have a more sophisticated understanding of emotion—particularly negative emotions—than do insecurely attached young children (Laible & Thompson, 1998), and secure children also regard themselves more positively than do insecure children (Cassidy, 1988; Verschueren, Marcoen, & Schoefs, 1996). In light of the fact that attachment security predicts individual differences in early conscience development, a better understanding of the relevance of these and other potential features of the internal working models generated by secure and insecure relationships is needed. One approach to addressing this issue is based on the quality of open discourse about emotion and morality fostered by secure parent–child relationships discussed next (see Thompson et al., 2003). Other approaches to elucidating the associations between attachment security, parent–child interaction, children's working models from close relationships, and conscience development also merit exploration.

Relational Processes

The general quality of the parent–child relationship is an important contributor to early conscience development but, as we have seen, it is necessary to conceptually unpack relational quality to understand the specific influences by which relational experience shapes conscience development. Besides parental warmth and responsiveness, two other kinds of relational processes have been studied most extensively: parental discipline practices and proactive strategies, and conversational discourse.

Discipline Practices and Proactive Strategies. The influence on moral development of the parent's disciplinary approach has been extensively studied. Research findings with toddlers and preschoolers are consistent with those of older children in concluding that interventions that are power assertive and coercive elicit children's situational compliance, but also the child's frustration and occasionally defiance. However, discipline that emphasizes reasoning and provides justification is more likely to foster internalized values in young children, even though children may also assert their autonomy through negotiation (Crockenberg & Litman, 1990; Kuczynski & Kochanska, 1990; Kuczynski, Kochanska, Radke-Yarrow, & Girnius-Brown, 1987; Power & Chapieski, 1986). These findings are consistent with the studies reported earlier in this chapter, and underscore the importance of parents' interventions for clarifying issues of causality, responsibility, and obligation that may be unclear in the minds of young children as they are caught up in conflicts involving salient emotions and desires. Young children who witness another's distress, for example, respond more helpfully and prosocially when their mothers also provide emotionally powerful explanations concerning the causes of the person's distress

(Zahn-Waxler, Radke-Yarrow, & King, 1979; Zahn-Waxler et al., 1992). Even with young children, therefore, verbal explanations of the causes and consequences of wrongdoing contribute significantly to moral understanding and the growth of conscience. Not surprisingly, therefore, parents increasingly rely on verbal strategies over physical interventions for eliciting children's compliance beginning in the second year (Dunn & Munn, 1987; Kuczynski et al., 1987).

This straightforward account of the effects of discipline on moral internalization is complicated in several ways, however (Grusec et al., 2000; Kuczynski, Marshall, & Schell, 1997). First, child compliance and moral internalization are not always the central goals in parents' socialization efforts, and thus parents' disciplinary efforts and their impact on the child vary in different domains and circumstances (Grusec & Goodnow, 1994; Holden & Miller, 1999). Encouraging self-assertion, fostering choice, and enhancing parent–child communication and understanding are goals that may compete with values transmission in many everyday conflicts over misbehavior, especially when conflicts concern social–conventional and personal issues rather than moral dilemmas (Dawber & Kuczynski, 1999; Hastings & Grusec, 1998; Nucci, 1996; Nucci & Weber, 1995). This means that discipline encounters are not consistently forums for the internalization of values, and the relation between alternative parental goals, disciplinary interventions, and the development of conscience in these circumstances remains to be better understood. In particular, how can a more acute appreciation of parents' goals in disciplinary encounters clarify the strategies that parents use and, in turn, their influence on the child's developing conscience?

Second, children are themselves influential, not only in the discipline encounter, but also in the construction of values that they appropriate from discipline events (Kuczynski et al., 1997; Lollis & Kuczynski, 1997). Holden, Thompson, Zambarano, and Marshall (1997) reported, for example, that maternal attitudes and discipline practices varied as a function of the child's reaction to her practices, and outcome expectancies are significant influences on parents' use of most child rearing practices, especially spanking (Holden & Miller, 1999; Holden et al., 1999). The reasons for child misbehavior are also an important influence on the child's reactions to parent discipline efforts and their effects, particularly whether children perceive the adult as acting fairly and appropriately in these circumstances. Moreover, how children evaluate and interpret parents' communication of values and standards, which is influenced by their social–cognitive capabilities and preexisting working models, significantly influences the values and rules that the child appropriates from discipline encounters (Grusec & Goodnow, 1994; Kuczynski et al., 1997).

Third, specific parental practices interact with general relationship quality in shaping early conscience, as we describe later concerning parent–child conversations. In other words, children in warm, secure relationships may be more responsive to parental disciplinary practices than children in insecure or harsh relationships. Evidence for this hypothesis has recently been reported by Kochanska, Aksan, Knaack, and Rhines (2004), who assessed attachment security at 14 months, parental discipline practices at 14 to 45 months, and conscience at 56 months. For securely attached children, there was a significant positive longitudinal association between gentle discipline/responsiveness and later conscience; for insecure children, there was no association. Further exploration of the interaction between general relationship quality and specific parenting practices in early conscience development is clearly warranted.

Finally, it is important to note that children appropriate values also when parents act proactively to avert potential misbehavior before it occurs. With younger children, proactive strategies consist largely of attention distraction, providing alternative activities, and other diversionary tactics (Holden, 1983; Holden & West, 1989). But as children mature, parents increasingly enlist conceptually proactive strategies by providing children with an understanding of parental values to prepare them for encounters with conflicting values that may occur outside the home (Grusec et al., 2000; Padilla-Walker & Thompson, in press). Although proactive efforts of this kind become more important when children are exposed to peers, media, community, and other extrafamilial influences (e.g., violent or sexual content on the Internet; peer enticements to underage smoking or drinking), parents are also likely to conceptually prearm younger children against comparable values challenges, such as advertising on children's television or family rules in the homes of peers. Research with immigrant and minority families has shown how significant parental proactive strategies are for maintaining ethnic and cultural identity in the face of the strong contrary values of the dominant culture (e.g., Nanji, 1993; Thornton, Chatters, Taylor, & Allen, 1990), but there has been little inquiry into such conceptually proactive strategies for values socialization in children from the majority culture (see, however, Padilla-Walker & Thompson, in press, for an exception). It is likely that as such proactive conversations occur with greater frequency in early and middle childhood, they provide significant forums for children's developing understanding of values and appropriation of them.

Parent–Child Conversational Discourse. Conversations about values outside of the discipline context may, indeed, be important for several reasons. In the heated emotions of the discipline encounter, which occur whenever a parent confronts a child, however gently, in a conflict of wills about the child's behavior, young children may hear the parent's message but not analyze or understand it deeply (Thompson, 1998a). Depth of processing is not likely to be consistent with a child's disagreement with parental authority, especially if the young child is mobilizing cognitive resources for negotiation or bargaining (Crockenberg & Litman, 1990; Kuczynski et al., 1987). Instead, values are more likely to be discussed and understood outside of the discipline encounter, in conversations when the adult seeks to proactively prearm children against challenges to parental values from extrafamilial sources (as discussed earlier), or in discussions about past events when misbehavior occurred. In these contexts, the child's cognitive resources can be more focused on understanding the parent's message with less competing emotional arousal. Even when parents are not explicitly intending these conversations to be a means of transmitting moral values, the inferences, assumptions, judgments, and other interpretations that parents incorporate into their narrative rendition of past events makes such conversations potent forums for early moral understanding and conscience development.

There is increasing evidence that the content and style of parental discourse during conversations about past events significantly influences conscience development in young children (see Thompson et al., [2003] for a review). Laible and Thompson (2000) focused on parent–child conversations about past events in which the child either misbehaved or behaved appropriately. In these conversations, mothers who more frequently referred to people's feelings had children who were more advanced in conscience development. Even though maternal references to rules and their consequences were also coded in these conversations, it was only maternal references to emotions that predicted conscience development. These findings were replicated in a prospective longitudinal study in which maternal references to feelings (but not references to rules and moral evaluations) during conflict with the child at 30 months predicted the child's conscience development 6 months later (Laible & Thompson, 2002). Similarly, in another study, 2- to 3-year-old children whose mothers used reasoning and humanistic concerns in resolving conflict with them were more advanced in measures of moral understanding in assessments in kindergarten and first grade (Dunn, Brown, & Maguire, 1995). These findings suggest that one of the most important features of parent–child conversations about moral behavior is how they sensitize young children to the human dimensions of misbehavior and good behavior, and help young children to comprehend the effects of their actions on how people feel. Young children are early acquiring behavioral standards with consideration of the humanistic dimensions of wrongdoing.

Other features of parent–child conversational discourse concerning misbehavior are also important. When they are in conflict with their young offspring, mothers who take the initiative to resolve conflict, using justifications to explain and clarify their expectations, and who manage to avoid aggravating and exacerbating tension (such as through threats or teasing) have young children who are more advanced in later assessments of conscience development (Laible, 2004a; Laible & Thompson, 2002). By contrast, mothers who are conversationally "power assertive" when recounting the child's misbehavior in the recent past—conveying a critical or negative attitude, feelings of disappointment or anger, or involving reproach or punishment—had preschool children who obtained lower scores on measures of moral cognition that assessed children's story-completion responses to moral dilemmas (Kochanska, Aksan, & Nichols, 2003). Taken together, these characteristics of maternal conflict-relevant discourse suggest that early conscience development is fostered when mothers provide young children with a richer understanding of the causes and consequences of interpersonal conflict without unduly arousing the child's feelings of defensiveness or threat. Maternal justifications offer many lessons in psychological understanding, of course, as mothers constructively explain their expectations, convey their feelings, and clarify their perceptions of the situation (which usually differ from the child's own). These conclusions are consistent, of course, with the well-documented effects of inductive discipline practices on moral internalization with older children. But these conclusions indicate that these influences are important for younger children also, and are apparent in situations independent of the discipline encounter, such as during their shared recounting of past misbehavior and in family conflict situations when mothers often convey their behavioral expectations before offspring have misbehaved.

More generally, researchers have also found that mothers who use a more elaborative style of discourse, characterized by rich embellishment of the narrative structure of shared recall, have offspring who are more advanced in conscience development than the children of mothers with a more sparse, pragmatic discourse style (Laible, 2004b; Laible & Thompson, 2000). It is likely that the elaborative detail and background information provided by these mothers contributes additional psychological depth to maternal explanations of behavioral standards and reasons for the child's cooperation. Equally important, these elements of maternal discourse—particularly specific references to feelings—interact with the warmth and security of the parent–child relationship in their association with conscience development (Laible & Thompson, 2000; Thompson et al., 2003). Thus broader relational quality interacts with specific features of parent–child discourse to shape young children's earliest understandings of morality and themselves as moral beings.

These conclusions concerning the importance of parent–child conversational discourse in the context of a warm, secure relationship are important not only for understanding conscience development, but also for conceptualizing the developmental influence of the working models inspired by secure or insecure parent–child attachments (Thompson, 2000). Mothers in secure attachments with offspring tend to use a more elaborative style (Reese, 2002), which is consistent with the expectations from attachment theory of the more open, candid communicative style shared by parents and offspring in secure relationships (Bretherton & Munholland, 1999). In relationships of trust and confidence, attachment theorists predict, children can talk openly about feelings, conflicts, and problems with the expectation of an accepting, helpful response. The research reviewed in this section suggests that an elaborative discourse style is one feature of the open communicative style described by attachment theorists and that, in shared communication with such a parent, young children develop mental representations (or working models) of the psychological world that are richer as a result of the adult's discussion of psychological themes. These representations foster the development of a conscience that embeds issues of moral compliance in humanistic respect for others' feelings and well-being, using the example of a parent who takes the initiative in resolving conflict through reasoned explanations, and for whom the motivation for moral behavior is the maintenance of a positive relationship of trust with the parent.

There is much more to be learned about the influence of conversational discourse on conscience development in early childhood. The manner in which discourse references and style are embedded in a rich vocabulary of nonverbal behavior—facial expressions, vocal tone, affective gestures, postural cues—that provide added social and emotional meaning to the adult's words remains to be explored. So also does the style of other conversational forums for parents with young children, especially conversations about future events in which the anticipation of potential misbehavior, and efforts to avert it, may influence the adult's discourse. We are especially interested in another form of moral socialization that may also be conveyed in parent–child conversations: obligatory morality. How do young children learn, in other words, about the moral obligations that are incumbent on them as people, by contrast with the moral prohibitions that so often constitute the corpus of early moral socialization? Do everyday parent–child conversations incorporate values about the obligation to help others in need, to be concerned for distressed individuals, and to contribute to the well-being of others?

Another important field for further research inquiry concerns parents who provide negative or mixed moral messages to their young children. It should be clear from this research review how parents whose conversations with offspring incorporate negative, denigrating, or otherwise unsympathetic portrayals of others' needs or motives, or who emphasize the importance of moral compliance for authoritarian reasons, or who scare or threaten offspring, or who convey self-interested moral orientations, or who seek to justify lying, cheating, or treating others unkindly are likely to instill similar values and dispositions in young children. Moreover, in parent–child relationships of distrust or insecurity, young children are likely to be inclined toward moral dispositions that are more self-protective and perhaps less other oriented than those inspired by caregiving relationships of security and warmth. These negative or mixed moral messages are likely to be apparent in parent–child relationships characterized also by harsh or punitive parental discipline practices and may, in fact, help to account for the more external, punishment-oriented moral values adopted by the offspring of such parents. In short, there is much to be learned by conceptually and empirically exploring the multidimensionality of parent–child relationships in the development of conscience: we can learn about the growth of humanistic, relational values in young children, and about the emergence of self-interested, exploitative moral orientations.

Summary

Relationships are important to conscience development because of the broad and specific features of parent–child interaction that shape young children's comprehension of moral values. The parent–child relationship itself gives credence to these influences. Young children learn about the importance of others' feelings in their conversations with the adult, and they also witness these emotions directly during conflict with siblings or parents, and then talk about the feelings they observed in later conversation. Children learn to care about how others feel because their own feelings are respected, even during conflict with a parent. There is considerably more to understand about relational influences on conscience development as researchers conceptually "unpack" broad differences in security or mutual responsivity to elucidate the constituent processes by which young children become engaged in a system of reciprocity that sensitizes them to the feelings of others, the associations between their actions and others' well-being, and moral conduct.

CONSCIENCE AND MORAL DEVELOPMENT THEORY AND RESEARCH

The portrayal of conscience development emerging from these research literatures is far richer and more interesting than the traditional view of early morality from learning theorists and Piagetian and Kohlbergian approaches. Rather than being self-interested opportunists with a punishment-and-obedience orientation to moral compliance, conscience is rooted in the efforts of young children to understand the normative consistencies in their world and the desires and interests of other people. The incentives for moral cooperation arise not only from the sanctions of parents and other authorities, but also the mutual good will that arises from close relationships of trust that develop between parents and young children (or the insecurity that arises from more conflicted parent–child relationships). Children learn about values from how parents talk about rules and the consequences of violating them, but they learn even more when parents talk about people's feelings and how those feelings are affected by the child's conduct. Young children also learn about conscience from the example of how their parents seek to resolve conflict with them. There are multiple pathways of early conscience development, influenced by temperament, but each involves a warmly responsive parent–child relationship and the parent's use of developmentally appropriate sanctions. Young children acquire values not only in the discipline encounter, however, but in many other forums of everyday family life. These may consist of conversations with the parent about past events (which are likely to include instances of past misbehavior as well as good conduct), or the shared recall of earlier family conflict, or the adult's efforts to proactively equip children with the conceptual skills for confronting challenges to parental values arising from outside the family. Conscience development is closely tied to emotional growth, of course, and to the arousal of self-referential emotions like guilt and shame and other-oriented emotions like empathy that are powerful catalysts for moral understanding as well as self-understanding. In all, conscience development is closely tied to young children's experiences in close relationships, their developing psychological understanding, and their emerging self-awareness as morally responsible individuals.

The time has arrived, therefore, for an updated view of the place of early childhood in moral development theory. Rather than regarding conscience in the toddler and preschool years as distinct from the more reflective, humanistic, relational morality of middle childhood and adolescence, there is value in considering how early childhood provides the basis for the morality of later years. As the work of Kochanska and other scholars has shown, in their developing conceptual skills, relational experiences of security or insecurity, emergence of the moral self, conversations with parents, and other experiences, young children are developing moral orientations that are simpler, but fundamentally similar, to those of older children and adolescents. Understanding how forms of moral judgment, affect, and behavior that are observed in middle childhood and adolescence are rooted in early childhood influences thus constitutes one of many important research tasks for the future.

Another contribution of the study of early conscience to moral development research is its conceptual and methodological breadth. Researchers have been creative in their efforts to capture the relational, conceptual, emotional, temperamental, and other constituents of early conscience. They have also been innovative in exploring the intersection of these developmental influences, whether it concerns the interaction of temperament and parenting practices for defining multiple pathways for conscience development, or understanding how parent–child conversational discourse interacts with broader relational quality in shaping young children's moral understanding. This breadth of approach is critical for the study of a phenomenon as multifaceted as moral behavior, and research on early conscience constitutes a model for the work of scientists concerned with moral development at other ages.

Perhaps most valuable is the view emerging from this research that young children are intuitive moralists who begin to understand values in the context of relationships of significance to them. Young children are neither autonomous moral theorists nor lumps of clay to be shaped by others. They are instead moral apprentices, striving hard to understand, creating their own intuitive morality but also aided by the sensitive guidance of adult mentors in the home who provide lessons about morality in everyday experiences. Such a portrayal of young children enlivens inquiry into the beginnings of conscience.

ACKNOWLEDGMENT

We are very grateful for helpful comments on an earlier version of this manuscript by Grazyna Kochanska, as well as by the editors of the volume.

REFERENCES

Arsenio, W. F., & Kramer, R. (1992). Victimizers and their victims: Children's conceptions of the mixed emotional consequences of victimization. *Child Development, 63,* 915–927.

Arsenio, W. F., & Lover, A. (1999). Children's conceptions of sociomoral affect: Happy victimizers, mixed emotions, and other expectancies. In M. Killen & D. Hart (Eds.), *Morality in everyday life: Developmental perspectives* (pp. 87–128). New York: Cambridge.

Baldwin, D. S., & Moses, L. J. (1996). The ontogeny of social information-processing. *Child Development, 67,* 1915–1939.

Barrett, K. C. (1995). A functionalist approach to shame and guilt. In J. P. Tangney & K. W. Fischer (Eds.), *Self-conscious emotions* (pp. 25–63). New York: Guilford.

Barrett, K. C. (1998). The origins of guilt in early childhood. In J. Bybee (Ed.), *Guilt and children* (pp. 75–90). San Diego: Academic Press.

Barrett, K. C., Zahn-Waxler, C., & Cole, P. M. (1993). Avoiders vs. amenders: Implications for the investigation of guilt and shame during toddlerhood? *Cognition and Emotion, 7,* 481–505.

Bates, E. (1990). Language about me and you: Pronominal reference and the emerging concept of self. In D. Cicchetti & M. Beeghly (Eds.), *The self in transition: Infancy to childhood* (pp. 165–182). Chicago: University of Chicago Press.

Bates, J. E., Maslin, C. A., & Frankel, K. A. (1985). Attachment security, mother-child interaction, and temperament as predictors of behavior-problem ratings at age three years. In I. Bretherton & E. Waters (Eds.), *Growing points in attachment theory and research.*

Monographs of the Society for Research in Child Development, 50 (1–2, Serial no. 209), 167–193.

Biringen, Z., Emde, R. N., Campos, J. J., & Appelbaum, M. I. (1995). Affective reorganization in the infant, the mother, and the dyad: The role of upright locomotion and its timing. *Child Development, 66,* 499–519.

Braungart-Rieker, J., Garwood, M. M., & Stifter, C. A. (1997). Compliance and noncompliance: The roles of maternal control and child temperament. *Journal of Applied Developmental Psychology, 18,* 411–428.

Bretherton, I., Fritz, J., Zahn-Waxler, C., & Ridgeway, D. (1986). Learning to talk about emotions: A functionalist perspective. *Child Development, 57,* 529–548.

Bretherton, I., & Munholland, K. A. (1999). Internal working models in attachment relationships: A construct revisited. In J. Cassidy & P. R. Shaver (Eds.), *Handbook of attachment* (pp. 89–111). New York: Guilford.

Bullock, M., & Lutkenhaus, P. (1988). The development of volitional behavior in the toddler years. *Child Development, 59,* 664–674.

Campos, J., Anderson, D., Barbu-Roth, M., Hubbard, E., Hertenstein, M., & Witherington, D. (1999). Travel broadens the mind. *Infancy, 1,* 149–219.

Campos, J. J., Kermoian, R., & Zumbahlen, M. R. (1992). Socioemotional transformations in the family system following infant crawling onset. In N. Eisenberg & R. A. Fabes (Eds.), *Emotion and its regulation in early development* (pp. 35–40). San Francisco: Jossey-Bass.

Cassidy, J. (1988). Child-mother attachment and the self in six-year-olds. *Child Development, 59,* 121–134.

Clark, L. A., Kochanska, G., & Ready, R. (2000). Mothers' personality and its interaction with child temperament as predictors of parenting behavior. *Journal of Personality and Social Psychology, 79,* 274–285.

Crockenberg, S., & Litman, C. (1990). Autonomy as competence in 2-year-olds: Maternal correlates of child defiance, compliance, and self-assertion. *Developmental Psychology, 26,* 961–971.

Cummings, E. M., & Davies, P. (1994). *Children and marital conflict.* New York: Guilford.

Davies, P. T., & Cummings, E. M. (1994). Marital conflict and child adjustment: An emotional security hypothesis. *Psychological Bulletin, 116,* 387–411.

Dawber, T., & Kuczynski, L. (1999). The question of ownness: Influence of relationship context on parental socialization strategies. *Journal of Social and Personal Relationships, 16,* 475–493.

Deater-Decker, K., & O'Connor, T. G. (2000). Parent-child mutuality in early childhood: Two behavioral genetic studies. *Developmental Psychology, 36,* 561–570.

Dunn, J. (1987). The beginnings of moral understanding: Development in the second year. In J. Kagan & S. Lamb (Eds.), *The emergence of morality in young children* (pp. 91–112). Chicago: University of Chicago Press.

Dunn, J., Brown, J. R., & Maguire, M. (1995). The development of children's moral sensibility: Individual differences and emotion understanding. *Developmental Psychology, 31,* 649–659.

Dunn, J., & Munn, P. (1987). The development of justifications in disputes. *Developmental Psychology, 23,* 781–798.

Eder, R. A. (1989). The emergent personologist: The structure and content of $3\frac{1}{2}$-, $5\frac{1}{2}$-, and $7\frac{1}{2}$-year-olds' concepts of themselves and other persons. *Child Development, 60,* 1218–1228.

Eder, R. A. (1990). Uncovering children's psychological selves: Individual and developmental differences. *Child Development, 61,* 849–863.

Eder, R. A., & Mangelsdorf, S. C. (1997). The emotional basis of early personality development: Implications for the emergent self-concept. In R. Hogan & S. Briggs (Eds.), *Handbook of personality psychology* (pp. 209–240). Orlando, FL: Academic Press.

Eisenberg, N. (2000). Emotion, regulation, and moral development. *Annual Review of Psychology, 51,* 665–697.

Emde, R. N., Biringen, Z., Clyman, R. B., & Oppenheim, D. (1991). The moral self of infancy: Affective core and procedural knowledge. *Developmental Review, 11,* 251–270.

Emde, R. N., & Buchsbaum, H. (1990). "Didn't you hear my Mommy?" Autonomy with connectedness in moral self-emergence. In D. Cicchetti & M. Beeghly (Eds.), *The self in transition: Infancy to childhood* (pp. 35–60). Chicago: University of Chicago Press.

Feinman, S., Roberts, D., Hsieh, K.-F., Sawyer, D., & Swanson, D. (1992). A critical review of social referencing in infancy. In S. Feinman (Ed.), *Social referencing and the social construction of reality in infancy* (pp. 15–54). New York: Plenum.

Flavell, J. H., Miller, P. H., & Miller, S. A. (2002). *Cognitive development* (4th ed.). Upper Saddle River, NJ: Prentice-Hall.

Gralinski, J. H., & Kopp, C. B. (1993). Everyday rules for behavior: Mothers' requests to young children. *Developmental Psychology, 29,* 573–584.

Grusec, J. E., & Goodnow, J. J. (1994). Impact of parental discipline methods on the child's internalization of values: A reconceptualization of current points of view. *Developmental Psychology, 30,* 4–19.

Grusec, J. E., Goodnow, J. J., & Kuczynski, L. (2000). New directions in analyses of parenting contributions to children's internalization of values. *Child Development, 71,* 205–211.

Harris, P. L., & Nunez, M. (1996). Understanding of permission rules by preschool children. *Child Development, 67,* 1572–1591.

Harter, S. (1999). *Developmental approaches to self processes.* New York: Guilford.

Hastings, P. D., & Grusec, J. E. (1998). Parenting goals as organizers of responses to parent-child disagreement. *Developmental Psychology, 34,* 465–479.

Heckhausen, J. (1988). Becoming aware of one's competence in the second year: Developmental progression within the mother-child dyad. *International Journal of Behavioral Development, 11,* 305–326.

Holden, G. W. (1983). Avoiding conflict: Mothers as tacticians in the supermarket. *Child Development, 54,* 233–240.

Holden, G. W., & Miller, P. C. (1999). Enduring and different: A meta-analysis of the similarity in parents' child rearing. *Psychological Bulletin, 125,* 233–254.

Holden, G. W., Miller, P. C., & Harris, S. D. (1999). The instrumental side of corporal punishment: Parents' reported practices and outcome expectancies. *Journal of Marriage and the Family, 61,* 908–919.

Holden, G. W., Thompson, E. E., Zambarano, R. J., & Marshall, L. A. (1997). Child effects as a source of change in maternal attitudes toward corporal punishment. *Journal of Social and Personal Relationships, 14,* 481–490.

Holden, G. W., & West, M. J. (1989). Proximate regulation by mothers: A demonstration of how differing styles affect young children's behavior. *Child Development, 60,* 64–69.

Hudson, J. A. (1993). Understanding events: The development of script knowledge. In M. Bennett (Ed.), *The child as psychologist: An introduction to the development of social cognition* (pp. 142–167). New York: Harvester Wheatsheaf.

Kagan, J. (1981). *The second year: The emergence of self-awareness.* Cambridge, MA: Harvard University Press.

Kagan, J. (in press). Human morality and temperament. In G. Carlo & C. Pope-Edwards (Eds.), *Moral motivation through the lifespan. Nebraska Symposium on Motivation* (Vol. 51). Lincoln: University of Nebraska Press.

Kemler Nelson, D. G., Herron, L., & Morris, C. (2002). How children and adults name broken objects: Inferences and reasoning about design intentions in the categorization of artifacts. *Journal of Cognition and Development, 3,* 301–332.

Kemler Nelson, D. G., Holt, M. G., & Chang Egan, L. (2003). *Two- and three-year-olds infer and reason about design intentions in order to categorize broken objects.* Manuscript submitted for publication, Swarthmore College.

Killen, M., Pisacane, K., Lee-Kim, J., & Ardila-Rey, A. (2001). Fairness or stereotypes? Young children's priorities when evaluating group exclusion or inclusion. *Developmental Psychology, 37,* 587–596.

Kochanska, G. (1991). Socialization and temperament in the development of guilt and conscience. *Child Development, 62,* 1379–1392.

Kochanska, G. (1993). Toward a synthesis of parental socialization and child temperament in early development of conscience. *Child Development, 64,* 325–347.

Kochanska, G. (1995). Children's temperament, mother's discipline, and security of attachment: Multiple pathways to emerging internalization. *Child Development, 66,* 597–615.

Kochanska, G. (1997a). Multiple pathways to conscience for children with different temperaments: From toddlerhood to age 5. *Developmental Psychology, 33,* 228–240.

Kochanska, G. (1997b). Mutually responsive orientation between mothers and their young children: Implications for early socialization. *Child Development, 68,* 94–112.

Kochanska, G. (2002a). Committed compliance, moral self, and internalization: A mediated model. *Developmental Psychology, 38,* 339–351.

Kochanska, G. (2002b). Mutually responsive orientation between mothers and their young children: A context for the early development of conscience. *Current Directions in Psychological Science, 11,* 191–195.

Kochanska, G., Aksan, N., & Nichols, K. E. (2003). Maternal power assertion in discipline and moral discourse contexts: Commonalities, differences, and implications for children's moral conduct and cognition. *Developmental Psychology, 39,* 949–963.

Kochanska, G., & Aksan, N. (1995). Mother-child mutually positive affect, the quality of child compliance to requests and prohibitions, and maternal control as correlates of early internalization. *Child Development, 66,* 236–254.

Kochanska, G., Aksan, N., Knaack, A., & Rhines, H. M. (2004). Maternal parenting and children's conscience: Early security as a moderator. *Child Development, 75,* 1229–1242.

Kochanska, G., Casey, R. J., & Fukumoto, A. (1995). Toddlers' sensitivity to standard violations. *Child Development, 66,* 643–656.

Kochanska, G., DeVet, K., Goldman, M., Murray, K., & Putnam, S. P. (1994). Maternal reports of conscience development and temperament in young children. *Child Development, 65,* 852–868.

Kochanska, G., Forman, D. R., & Coy, K. C. (1999). Implications of the mother-child relationship in infancy for socialization in the second year of life. *Infant Behavior & Development, 22,* 249–265.

Kochanska, G., Gross, J. N., Lin, M.-H., & Nichols, K. E. (2002). Guilt in young children: Development, determinants, and relations with a broader system of standards. *Child Development, 73,* 461–482.

Kochanska, G., & Knaack, A. (2003). Effortful control as a personality characteristic of young children: Antecedents, correlates, and consequences. *Journal of Personality, 71,* 1087–1112.

Kochanska, G., & Murray, K. T. (2000). Mother-child mutually responsive orientation and conscience development: From toddler to early school age. *Child Development, 71,* 417–431.

Kochanska, G., Murray, K. T., & Coy, K. C. (1997). Inhibitory control as a contributor to conscience in childhood: From toddler to early school age. *Child Development, 68,* 263–277.

Kochanska, G., Murray, K., Jacques, T. Y., Koenig, A. L., & Vandegeest, K. (1996). Inhibitory control of young children and its role in emerging internalization. *Child Development, 67,* 490–507.

Kochanska, G., & Thompson, R. A. (1997). The emergence and development of conscience in toddlerhood and early childhood. In J. E. Grusec & L. Kuczynski (Eds.), *Parenting and children's internalization of values* (pp. 53–77). New York: Wiley.

Kopp, C. B. (1982). Antecedents of self-regulation: A developmental view. *Developmental Psychology, 18,* 199–214.

Kopp, C. B. (1987). The growth of self-regulation: Caregivers and children. In N. Eisenberg (Ed.), *Contemporary topics in developmental psychology* (pp. 34–55). New York: Wiley.

Kopp, C. B., & Wyer, N. (1994). Self-regulation in normal and atypical development. In D. Cicchetti & S. L. Toth (Eds.), *Disorders and dysfunctions of the self. Rochester Symposium on Developmental Psychopathology* (vol. 5, pp. 31–56). Rochester, NY: University of Rochester Press.

Kuczynski, L., & Kochanska, G. (1990). Development of children's noncompliance strategies from toddlerhood to age 5. *Developmental Psychology, 26,* 398–408.

Kuczynski, L., Kochanska, G., Radke-Yarrow, M., & Girnius-Brown, O. (1987). A developmental interpretation of young children's noncompliance. *Developmental Psychology, 23,* 799–806.

Kuczynski, L., Marshall, S., & Schell, K. (1997). Value socialization in a bidirectional context. In J. E. Grusec & L. Kuczynski (Eds.), *Parenting and children's internalization of values* (pp. 23–50). New York: Wiley.

Lagattuta, K. (in press). When you shouldn't do what you want to do: Young children's understanding of desires, rules, and emotions. *Child Development* in press.

Laible, D. J. (2004a). Mother-child discourse about a child's past behavior at 30-months and early socioemotional development at age 3. *Merrill Palmer Quarterly, 50,* 159–180.

Laible, D. J. (2004b). Mother-child discourse in two contexts: Links with child temperament, attachment security, and socioemotional competence. *Developmental Psychology, 40,* 979–992.

Laible, D. J., & Thompson, R. A. (1998). Attachment and emotional understanding in preschool children. *Developmental Psychology, 34,* 1038–1045.

Laible, D. J., & Thompson, R. A. (2000). Mother-child discourse, attachment security, shared positive affect, and early conscience development. *Child Development, 71,* 1424–1440.

Laible, D. J., & Thompson, R. A. (2002). Mother-child conflict in the toddler years: Lessons in emotion, morality, and relationships. *Child Development, 73,* 1187–1203.

Lamb, S. (1993). First moral sense: An examination of the appearance of morally related behaviours in the second year of life. *Journal of Moral Education, 22,* 97–109.

Lehman, E. B., Steier, A. J., Guidash, K. M., & Wanna, S. Y. (2002). Predictors of compliance in toddlers: Child temperament, maternal personality, and emotional availability. *Early Child Development and Care, 172,* 301–310.

Lewis, M. (2000). Self-conscious emotions: Embarrassment, pride, shame, and guilt. In M. Lewis & J. M. Haviland-Jones (Eds.), *Handbook of emotions* (pp. 563–573). New York: Guilford.

Lewis, M., & Brooks-Gunn, J. (1979). *Social cognition and the acquisition of self.* New York: Plenum.

Lollis, S., & Kuczynski, L. (1997). Beyond one hand clapping: Seeing bidirectionality in parent-child relations. *Journal of Social and Personal Relationships, 14,* 441–461.

Londerville, S., & Main, M. (1981). Security of attachment, compliance, and maternal training methods in the second year of life. *Developmental Psychology, 17,* 289–299.

Maccoby, E. E. (1984). Socialization and developmental change. *Child Development, 55,* 317–328.

Maccoby, E. E. (1999). The uniqueness of the parent-child relationship. In W. A. Collins & B. Laursen (Eds.), *Relationships as developmental contexts. Minnesota Symposia on Child Psychology* (vol. 30, pp. 157–175). Hillsdale, NJ: Lawrence Erlbaum Associates.

Matas, L., Arend, R. A., & Sroufe, L. A. (1978). Continuity of adaptation in the second year: The relationship between quality of attachment and later competence. *Child Development, 49,* 547–556.

Miller, P. J., Fung, H., & Mintz, J. (1996). Self-construction through narrative practices: A Chinese and American comparison of early socialization. *Ethos, 24,* 237–280.

Miller, P. J., Potts, R., Fung, H., Hoogstra, L., & Mintz, J. (1990). Narrative practices and the social construction of self in childhood. A*american Ethnologist, 17,* 292–311.

Nanji, A. A. (1993). The Muslim family in North America: Continuity and change. In H. P. McAdoo (Ed.), *Family ethnicity: Strength in diversity* (pp. 229–244). Newbury Park, CA: Sage.

Nelson, K. (Ed.). (1978). *Event knowledge: Structure and function in development.* Hillsdale, NJ: Lawrence Erlbaum Associates.

Nucci, L. (1996). Morality and the personal sphere of actions. In E. S. Reed, E. Turiel, & T. Brown (Eds.), *Values and knowledge* (pp. 41–60). Mahwah, NJ: Lawrence Erlbaum Associates.

Nucci, L. P., & Weber, E. K. (1995). Social interactions in the home and the development of young children's conceptions of the personal. *Child Development, 66,* 1438–1452.

Padilla-Walker, L., & Thompson, R. A. (in press). Combating conflicting messages of values: A closer look at parental strategies. *Social Development.*

Piaget, J. (1965). *The moral judgment of the child.* New York: Harcourt, Brace.

Power, T. G., & Chapieski, M. L. (1986). Childrearing and impulse control in toddlers: A naturalistic investigation. *Developmental Psychology, 22,* 271–275.

Repacholi, B. M., & Gopnik, A. (1997). Early reasoning about desires: Evidence from 14- and 18-month olds. *Developmental Psychology, 33,* 12–21.

Reese, E. (2002). Social factors in the development of autobiographical memory: The state of the art. *Social Development, 11,* 124–142.

Ruble, D. N., & Martin, D. L. (1998). Gender development. In W. Damon (Ed.). & N. Eisenberg (Vol. Ed.), *Handbook of child psychology Vol. 3: Social, emotional and personality development* (5th ed., pp. 933–1016). New York: Wiley.

Shonkoff, J. P., & Phillips, D. A. (Eds.). (2000). *From neurons to neighborhoods: The science of early childhood development.* Report of the Committee on Integrating the Science of Early Childhood Development, National Research Council and Institute of Medicine. Washington, DC: National Academy Press

Smetana, J. G. (1981). Preschool children's conceptions of moral and social rules. *Child Development, 52,* 1333–1336.

Smetana, J. G. (1985). Preschool children's conceptions of transgressions: The effects of varying moral and conventional domain-related attributes. *Developmental Psychology, 21,* 18–29.

Smetana, J. G. (1989). Toddlers' social interactions in the context of moral and conventional transgressions in the home. *Developmental Psychology, 25,* 499–508.

Smetana, J. G. (1997). Parenting and the develoment of social knowledge reconceptualized: A social domain analysis. In J. E. Grusec & L. Kuczynski (Eds.), *Parenting and children's internalization of values* (pp. 162–192). New York: Wiley.

Smetana, J. G., & Braeges, J. L. (1990). The development of toddler's moral and conventional judgments. *Merrill-Palmer Quarterly, 36,* 329–346.

Smetana, J. G., Kochanska, G., & Chuang, S. (2000). Mothers' conceptions of everyday rules for young toddlers: A longitudinal investigation. *Merrill-Palmer Quarterly, 46,* 391–416.

Stern, D. N. (1985). *The interpersonal world of the infant.* New York: Basic.

Stifter, C. A., Spinrad, T. L., & Braungart-Rieker, J. M. (1999). Toward a developmental model of child compliance: The role of emotion regulation in infancy. *Child Development, 70,* 21–32.

Stipek, D. (1995). The development of pride and shame in toddlers. In J. P. Tangney & K. W. Fischer (Eds.), *Self-conscious emotions* (pp. 237–252). New York: Guilford.

Stipek, D. J., Gralinski, J. H., & Kopp, C. B. (1990). Self-concept development in the toddler years. *Developmental Psychology, 26,* 972–977.

Stipek, D., Recchia, S., & McClintic, S. (1992). Self-evaluation in young children. *Monographs of the Society for Research in Child Development, 57* (Serial No. 226).

Theimer, C. E., Killen, M., & Stangor, C. (2001). Preschool children's evaluations of exclusion in gender-stereotypic contexts. *Developmental Psychology, 37,* 18–27.

Thompson, R. A. (1998a). Early sociopersonality development. In W. Damon (Ed.). & N. Eisenberg, (Vol. Ed.), *Handbook of child psychology. Vol. 3: Social, emotional, and personality development* (5th ed., pp. 25–104). New York: Wiley.

Thompson, R. A. (1998b). Empathy and its origins in early development. In S. Braten (Ed.), *Intersubjective communication and emotion in early ontogeny* (pp. 144–157). Cambridge, UK: Cambridge University Press.

Thompson, R. A. (1999). Early attachment and later development. In J. Cassidy & P. R. Shaver (Eds.), *Handbook of attachment: Theory, research, and clinical applications* (pp. 265–286). New York: Guilford.

Thompson, R. A. (2000). The legacy of early attachments. *Child Development, 71,* 145–152.

Thompson, R. A. (in press). The development of the person: Social understanding, relationships, self, conscience. In W. Damon & R. M. Lerner (Eds.), *Handbook of child psychology* (6th Ed.), Vol. 3. *Social, emotional, and personality development* (N. Eisenberg, Vol. Ed.). New York: Wiley.

Thompson, R. A., Laible, D. J., & Ontai, L. L. (2003). Early understanding of emotion, morality, and the self: Developing a working model. In R.V. Kail (Ed.), *Advances in Child Development and Behavior* (vol. 31, pp. 137–171). San Diego: Academic.

Thompson, R. A., & Raikes, H. A. (2003). Toward the next quarter-century: Conceptual and methodological challenges for attachment theory. *Development and Psychopathology, 15,* 691–718.

Thornton, M. C., Chatters, L. M., Taylor, R. J., & Allen, W. R. (1990). Sociodemographic and environmental correlates of racial socialization by black parents. *Child Development, 61,* 401–409.

Tomasello, M. (1999). *The cultural origins of human cognition.* Cambridge, MA: Harvard University Press.

Tomasello, M., & Rakoczy, H. (2003). What makes human cognition unique? From individual to collective to shared intentionality. *Mind & Language, 18,* 121–147.

van der Mark, I. L., Bakermans-Kranenburg, M. J., & van IJzendoorn, M. H. (2002). The role of parenting, attachment, and temperamental fearfulness in the prediction of compliance in toddler girls. *British Journal of Developmental Psychology, 20,* 361–378.

Verschueren, K., Marcoen, A., & Schoefs, V. (1996). The internal working model of the self, attachment, and competence in five-year-olds. *Child Development, 67,* 2493–2511.

Waters, E., Kondo-Ikemura, K., Posada, G., & Richters, J. E. (1991). Learning to love: Mechanisms and milestones. In M. R. Gunnar & L. A. Sroufe (Eds.), *Self processes and development. Minnesota Symposia on Child Psychology* (vol. 23, pp. 217–255). Hillsdale, NJ: Lawrence Erlbaum Associates.

Wellman, H. M. (2002). Understanding the psychological world: Developing a theory of mind. In U. Goswami (Ed.), *Handbook of childhood cognitive development* (pp. 167–187). Oxford: Blackwell.

Wellman, H. M., Cross, D., & Watson, J. (2001). Meta-analysis of theory of mind development: The truth about false belief. *Child Development, 72,* 655–684.

Wellman, H. M., & Miller, J. G. (in press). Including deontic reasoning as fundamental to theory of mind. *Psychological Review.*

Wellman, H. M., & Miller, J. G. (2003). *Integrating deontic reasoning and theory of mind.* Unpublished manuscript, University of Michigan (submitted for publication).

Woodward, A. (1998). Infants selectively encode the goal object of an actor's reach. *Cognition, 69,* 1–34.

Zahn-Waxler, C. (2000). The development of empathy, guilt, and internalization of distress: Implications for gender differences in internalizing and externalizing problems. In R. J. Davidson (Ed.), *Anxiety, depression, and emotion* (pp. 222–265). New York: Oxford University Press.

Zahn-Waxler, C., & Radke-Yarrow, M. (1990). The origins of empathic concern. *Motivation and Emotion, 14,* 107–130.

Zahn-Waxler, C., Radke-Yarrow, M., & King, R. A. (1979). Child rearing and children's prosocial initiations toward victims of distress. *Child Development, 50,* 319–330.

Zahn-Waxler, C., Radke-Yarrow, M., Wagner, E., & Chapman, M. (1992). Development of concern for others. *Developmental Psychology, 28,* 126–136.

Zahn-Waxler, C., & Robinson, J. (1995). Empathy and guilt: Early origins of feelings of responsibility. In J. P. Tangney & K. W. Fischer (Eds.), *Self-conscious emotions* (pp. 143–173). New York: Guilford.

11

SOURCES OF INNOVATION AND CHANGE IN SOCIALIZATION, INTERNALIZATION AND ACCULTURATION

LEON KUCZYNSKI
GEOFFREY S. NAVARA
UNIVERSITY OF GUELPH

Contemporary research on socialization in the family is taking place in the context of radically changed assumptions about the process and products of internalization. *Internalization* is the process by which values assumed to be initially external to an individual become incorporated into the individual's thoughts and actions (Grusec & Goodnow, 1994). Prior to the 1980s, research on internalization was guided by a unidirectional and deterministic conception of socialization (Maccoby, 1992). In the traditional view of socialization, internalization was conceived as a process of intergenerational transmission by which children's acquisition and acceptance of values was accomplished through the direct action and practices of socializing agents. The products of internalization were considered in terms of two interconnected problems: the transmission of cultural content such as standards, values, knowledge, attitudes, motives, roles, and practices from the older generation to the younger generation and the fostering of behavioral conformity to the demands and expectations of family and societal authorities (Dubin & Dubin, 1963). An implicit goal of socialization theory was to understand the continuity of values from parents to children and, more generally, the process by which society and culture become reproduced in each succeeding generation (Corsaro, 1997; Valsiner, 1988).

The unidirectional conception of socialization and of internalization has been much critiqued for its limited perspective on the processes and outcomes of socialization at both the macro level of individual and society and the micro level of parent–child relations. Sociologists and anthropologists have critiqued structural–functionalist conceptions of socialization that emphasize such ideas as conformity to social norms and roles and stable transmission of values between generations (Corsaro, 1997; Ferree, 1990; Sapir, 1934; Strauss, 1992; Wrong, 1961). Wrong (1961), for instance, suggested that such ideas assumed that society is much more integrated than it really is and that human nature is much more conforming than it really is. More recently, Valsiner (1988) drew attention to the inability of traditional accounts to account for intergenerational innovation as a product of the internalization process.

Discoveries since the 1970s regarding the active role of children in parent–child interactions and relationships also undermined micro process assumptions of early socialization theory (Hartup, 1978; Kuczynski, 2003). Sources of these changes include ideas that children are from birth prepared to influence parents in a mutual process of influence (Maccoby & Martin, 1983; Rheingold, 1969), the idea that children are inherently active in the process of knowledge construction and in their own moral development (Kohlberg, 1969; Piaget, 1965), and bidirectional causal models that promoted a new understanding of children's contributions to parent–child social interactions (Bell, 1968; Sameroff, 1975) and parent–child relationships (Hinde, 1979; Lollis & Kuczynski, 1997). Empirical reviews of the literature on socialization also increasingly raised concerns about the small size of direct parental effects on children's socialization outcomes (Collins, Maccoby, Steinberg, Hetherington, & Bornstein, 2000; Maccoby & Martin, 1983). Regarding value internalization, evidence for the transmission of similarity between parents and children is modest and tends to concern "mainly political orientations, religious beliefs, and "life styles," not values as such or even general orientations to social reality" (Kohn, 1983, p. 1).

During the past decade, efforts have been underway to integrate accumulated insights concerning parent–child relations into a revitalized conception of socialization in the family (Grusec, Goodnow, & Kuczynski, 2000). In a major updating of socialization theory, Grusec and Goodnow (1994) proposed that the activity of both the parents and of the children need to be addressed in accounts of how parents promote value internalization. Grusec and Goodnow's model of internalization emphasizes the active nature of the child in interpreting, evaluating, and accepting or rejecting the parent's message and also the appropriateness with which it was communicated. In their view optimal socialization practices require that parents make numerous choices in juggling socialization goals for children and that they tailor their messages in a way that acknowledges their children's capacities to interpret parental messages. In our own research we have been exploring the implications of an enhanced focus on human agency and bidirectional causality for the nature of internalized ideas (Kuczynski, Marshall, & Schell, 1997) and the nature of conformity (Kuczynski & Hildebrandt, 1997). An additional challenge for the field is to link new conceptions of socialization processes within the family with wider social systems and culture (Bugental & Goodnow, 1998; Parke & Buriel, 1998; Trommsdorff & Kornadt, 2003).

The purpose of this chapter is to review classic problems with the construct of internalization and new efforts to address them in contemporary socialization theory. We argue that current assumptions regarding the nature of parent–child relations provide numerous directions for considering socialization and internalization as dynamic processes that produce intergenerational change as well as intergenerational similarity. The first part of the chapter considers the new developments in socialization theory. We compare traditional assumptions of the unilateral model of internalization regarding the nature of values, the process of internalization and the products of internalization with the assumptions of the bilateral model of internalization (Table 11.1). Family and other social contexts are assumed to include heterogeneous ideas regarding the values, beliefs, and outlooks that are adaptive for success in a culture. Human agency and bidirectional causality are cornerstones of a

TABLE 11.1

Assumptions of Unilateral and Bilateral Models of Internalization

	Unilateral Internalization	*Bilateral Internalization*
Values	Uncontested, uniform	Contested, diverse
Context	Isolated individuals	Interdependent relationships
	Homogeneous, stable	Heterogeneous, changing
	Constrains	Constrains and enables
Process		
Causality	Unidirectional	Bidirectional–dialectical
Agency	Unequal, passive	Equal, active
Power	Static asymmetry	Interdependent asymmetry
Products		
Content	Similarity	Novel synthesis
Conformity	Compliance/noncompliance	Accommodation/negotiation

dynamic perspective on internalization. Considering parents and children more fully as agents adds processes of choice, resistance, and innovation to accounts of parent–child socialization in addition to its traditional focus on conformity and transmission of similarity. In the second part we propose that a dialectical perspective on bidirectional processes within the family facilitates considering change and transformation as inherent aspects of internalization. The last part of the chapter attempts to link micro processes in the family with macro processes of social change and culture. There we focus on the process of acculturation to illustrate the implications of a dialectical view of internalization for changes within the parent-child intergenerational system and the parent–child intercultural system.

CONTEMPORARY ASSUMPTIONS ABOUT PARENTING AND INTERNALIZATION

Values

Values are desirable, abstract, trans-situational goals that serve as guiding principles in people's lives and as criteria they use to select, justify, and evaluate actions, people, and events (Schwartz, 1992). Broadly speaking, "Values are present whenever people judge some ways of acting, thinking or feeling to be more desirable, more worthwhile, or more important than others" (Goodnow, 1997, p. 341). Research on the socialization of children has approached moral development as a special case of value internalization. Early research on value development was guided by psychoanalytic and social learning theories of the mid 20th century and did not distinguish among types of values. This content-free approach to values implicitly assumed that the development of any values could be understood by very general learning or identification processes (Grusec, 1997; Maccoby, 1992). In recent decades, however, it has been asserted that values differ in their importance as socialization goals for parents within specific cultures (Grusec & Kuczynski, 1980), and it is thought that developmental, regulatory, and socialization processes differ depending on the content of a value (Kuczynski & Hildebrandt, 1997). There have been various proposals for distinguishing among types of values. Distinctions have been made between standards that elicit goals for short-term (immediate compliance) versus long-term (compliance in parent's absence) conformity (Kuczynski, 1984). The social domain perspective has distinguished values in the moral domain from personal, conventional, and prudential domains of interaction (Killen, Lee-Kim, McGlothlin, & Stangor, 2002; Smetana, 1997; Turiel, 2002). Other distinctions have been drawn between individualistic and collectivistic values (Grolnick, Deci, & Ryan, 1997), and it has been argued that alternative moralities might exist based on natural law, justice, community, and divinity (Shweder, Mahapatra, & Miller, 1990; Shweder, Much, Mahaptra, & Park, 1997). Recent cross-cultural research has focused on a system of 10 values: stimulation, self-direction, universalism, benevolence, conformity, tradition, security, power, achievement, and hedonism that are held and socialized to various degrees within a culture (Schwartz, 1992).

In this chapter, it is assumed that it is important to distinguish certain modes of behaving or thinking as "moral" because they are defined, justified, and evaluated as such and are singled out for special training by socializing agents. However, individuals interacting in specific social and historical contexts construct all values, including moral values. Although it is important to identify values that invoke moral forms of justification having to do with harm, equal treatment and fairness (Smetana, 1997), the particular practices to which these forms of reasoning have been applied (e.g., treatment of women and children, race, slavery) have differed over time and within and across cultures. Other behaviors such as those governing religious practices and beliefs, including what one may eat, whom may associate with or exclude, how one may dress, sexual practices, and other forms of social regulation have at different times and in different cultures been treated by socializing agents as having a moral-like status and elicit goals for rigid behavioral conformity or cognitive acceptance. Moreover, individuals use complex forms of reasoning and are inconsistent in their application giving considerable scope for interpretation and conflict (Killen et al., 2002). In this chapter, the discussion of morality with other values is merged because the focus is on a feature of values that have received little attention, namely, the possibility of intergenerational change.

Context of Value Heterogeneity. The social interactions between parents and children that contribute to the process of value internalization do not occur in isolation. Individuals draw on a variety of sources of ideas, which they may incorporate as part of their own process of internalization. Berry, Poortinga, Segall, and Dasen (2002) describe three methods of cultural transmission which vary according to the source of cultural knowledge: (a) *vertical transmission* (parent to child and child to parent), *oblique transmission,* (b) where other adults such as the parents' peers and supporting cultural institutions are socialization agents, and (c) *horizontal transmission,* where peers act as socialization agents. These various sources constitute an "ecology of working models" of sometimes competing ideas that must be integrated, managed, or rejected as ideas for each person's internalization (Kuczynski et al., 1997).

Cultural and social contexts are not static but constantly change as a source of values and other ideas that may be internalized. A historical examination of values suggests that social values change from one generation to another. Social change comes about by immigration, war, economic changes, new technology, and the introduction of new ideas by individuals and groups. There have been continual generational changes in values regarding authority, the environment, gender equality, civil rights, children's rights, norms for sexual behavior, and acceptance of diversity during recent generations. In developing cultures undergoing rapid social change, there have been decreases of collectivistic values and norm-guided asymmetrical relationships and corresponding increases of individual value orientations, even while preferences for interdependence are retained (Kâgitçibâsi, 1996). The nonstable nature of social values means that the values that prevailed during parents' generation may well have changed by the time they reared their own children (Kohn, 1983). Parents experiencing the different circumstances of their children's environments may want to raise their children differently from the way they had been reared themselves to prepare their children for the social circumstances in which they will live their adult lives (Inkeles, 1955).

Social contexts are also heterogeneous with respect to their composition of values and offer diverse perspectives with regard to their interpretation (Goodnow, 1997). Early definitions of culture emphasized the integrated nature of meanings, practices, and values held by groups of people in a given time and place (Strauss, 1992). Concepts such as collectivism versus individualism assume that cultural groups have a shared understanding of the desirable ways of behaving, thinking, or feeling. Yet researchers now argue that there is more diversity of values within cultural groups (Bukowski & Sippola, 1998; Matsumoto, 2001) than what was once believed. Recent research is beginning to emphasize the contradictions, ambiguity, and injustices embedded in cultural practices (Turiel, 2002; Turiel & Wainryb, 2000). Particularly open to challenge are values that privilege the entitlements of the more powerful over the less powerful. "Even in cultures that might publicly or ideologically stress connectedness, interdependence, and duties, autonomy for some groups may be embedded in the structure of society and the makeup of norms and social practices" (Turiel & Wainryb, 2000, p. 252). With regard to interdependence and autonomy, it seems to be the case that girls and women in such societies are expected to be interdependent whereas boys and men have few constraints on their autonomy.

Traditional conceptions of the family also assumed a consistent parental alliance with regard to values. More recent perspectives suggest that experiences, values, and perceptions within the family are much less shared than was once assumed. A mother's values do not always correspond to the father's values (Kohn, 1983). Moreover, as a result of increases in divorce rates during recent decades the specific adults who are engaged in the role of parent and socializing agent for many children are not the same ones who occupied these roles earlier in their development (Tesson, 1987).

The heterogeneity of ideas available to the parent and the child in the cultural and family environments is an important source of change in each person's internalization. The traditional idea of parents communicating some of their greater knowledge to children is, of course, an important aspect of socialization, especially early in children's development. However, as children develop and gain access to popular media, schools, and peer cultures, parental influence becomes progressively less exclusive. Children learn that there are many opinions about which values are appropriate and that provide a basis for successful functioning. These alternative views may provide the basis for children's questioning and reorganization of what they have learned from their parents, and to the extent to which these ideas are communicated during parent–child interactions may contribute to parent–child conflict and the further development of the ideas of not only children but also of parents.

Process

Early research was constrained by a web of assumptions about the nature of parent–child relations that reinforced the idea of internalization as a process by which children were molded by parental actions (Kuczynski, 2003; Kuczynski, Harach, & Bernardini, 1999). Causality was assumed to be unidirectional from parent to child. Agency was attributed to parents who had the goals and capacities to determine the meanings that children acquire during socialization and the power to constrain their behavior. Children were considered to either be passive recipients or reactors to parental practices whose role was limited to complying with and internalizing parental messages. Also implicit in unilateral treatments of process were assumptions concerning context and power. Parents and children were considered to be interacting as separate isolated individuals in a static relationship of unequal power (Hoffman, 1975) where causality and agency was attributed to the more powerful parent.

Contemporary theorizing about socialization processes in the family is guided by a bilateral framework of assumptions (Kuczynski, 2003; Kuczynski et al., 1999). Foremost is the proposition that causality in parent–child relations is bidirectional (Maccoby & Martin, 1983). The singular idea that a child-to-parent direction of influence must be added to a parent-to-child direction of influence has long been fruitful in adding a number of dynamics into internalization processes. The best-researched generalization is that children influence the course of their own socialization by influencing parental choice of discipline and socialization strategies (Grusec & Goodnow, 1994). A second generalization is that children influence many aspects of parental lives such as their level of stress, marital satisfaction, mental health, employment, and the place and nature of the home environment by virtue of being part of the parent's proximal environment (Ambert, 1992). Moreover, in the process of being involved in childrearing, parents experience many challenges, emotional experiences, and opportunities for problem solving. In this way children indirectly cause changes in parental personality, maturity, attitudes, and values (Frankel, 1991; Palkovitz et al., 2003). Last, children may directly act as agents of their parent's continuing socialization during adulthood (Kuczynski et al., 1997). During middle childhood and early adolescence children increasingly bring into the home information and perspectives that contradict or compete with parental viewpoints. Children initiate direct challenges regarding the standards and habits, attitudes, values, and beliefs that parents have developed and may cause parents to examine or change these behaviors (Baranowski, 1978; Peters, 1985; Ta, Kuczynski, Bernardini, & Harach, 1999).

In the current era of theorizing, bidirectional causality is understood to be a part of a larger set of bilateral assumptions about the nature of parent–child relations including human agency, context, and power inequality in the parent–child relationship (Kuczynski, 2003). Agency is ascribed equally to parents and children, who are assumed to have inherent capacities for initiating action, making sense of their interactions with their environments and each other, and resisting threats to autonomy. Parents and children are assumed to interact not as isolated individuals but as participants in an interdependent relationship context that facilitates bidirectional influence. The unequal power between parents and children is conceived as an interdependent asymmetry in which the child derives power from a variety of resources including a close relationship context that makes parents and children receptive and vulnerable to each other's influence.

The significance of this shift from unilateral to bilateral assumptions about family processes is that, where the unilateral assumptions supported thinking about internalization as a unidirectional and static process of transmission, the bilateral assumptions support a conception of internalization as a dynamic process of change throughout the life course. In the next section, we explore four aspects of a bilateral perspective on parent–child relations that have implications for a dynamic conception of internalization: context, human agency, bidirectional processes, and the products of internalization.

The Relationship Context of Internalization

Traditional views of context in the social sciences generally emphasize how the environment constrains human agency by canalizing meaning and placing limits on individual choices (Fine, 1992). Approaching context from the perspective of human agency brings a balanced interest in the enabling effects of context. Social and cultural contexts have been constructed by collective and personal action to support agency, not just to constrain it (Brandtstädter, 1997; Giddens, 1990).

Similar statements can be made about the parent–child relationship as a proximal context of children's development. Kuczynski and Grusec (1997) argue that parents are well placed to constrain and channel children's internalization processes. The parent's privileged position in a long-term relationship and society's legitimization of the parent's power and responsibility over early socialization give parents more resources and also opportunity to influence the child than any other adults or peers. However, the relationship context also incorporates enabling elements that offer children considerable scope to exercise their agency or to negotiate the nature of the constraints placed upon them (Kuczynski, 2003). The parent–child relationship is distinctive from generic adult–child relations because of its long history of interactions (Hinde, 1979; Lollis & Kuczynski, 1997), its long future course, its complex combination of vertical (attachment, authority) and horizontal (intimacy, companionship) power arrangements (Harach & Kuczynski, 1999) and the greater interdependence of the participants during everyday life. These features of the relationship influence parents to be both receptive and vulnerable to their children's influence.

Leeway for the expression of agency is an inherent part of the parent–child relationship context. For example, parents may be willing to tolerate resistance to their requests because they seek to maintain a positive parent–child relationship or wish to foster autonomy, independence, and assertiveness in their children (Hastings & Grusec, 1998). Parents communicate a variety of positions with regard to their acceptance of child's behaviors ranging from what is ideal to what is acceptable, tolerable, or "out of the question" (Goodnow, 1994). Children, in turn, discover how much value stretch the parents' position affords and how much leeway there is for their own creative interpretation or resistance (Goodnow, 1997).

Human Agency

Recent theorizing in parent–child relations has incorporated a much-expanded interest in human agency in the effort to understand processes involved in bidirectional interactions between parents and children (Cummings & Schermerhorn, 2003; Kuczynski et al., 1999). Kuczynski (2003) proposed a conception of agency that decoupled agency from power. Parents and children are proposed to be equal agents even though they are unequal in power. A focus on human agency means a concern with intentional, self-initiated actions and the constructive, interpretive activities of both parents and children in their interactions with each other. The exercise of agency is reflected in their self-initiated efforts to understand and affect interactions with each other and to overcome obstacles to their goals. An enhanced perspective on parents and children as agents is a an important one because it consolidates several decades of findings concerning the active role of children in their socialization experiences in the family (Grusec & Goodnow, 1994; Hartup, 1978; Maccoby & Martin, 1983) and provides a way of integrating key insights into human agency from cognitive psychology and sociology. Two aspects of human agency—the capacity for construction and the expression of autonomy—are particularly important in understanding how the exercise of agency contributes to societal and generational change in the products of internalization.

Agency as Construction.   *Construction* refers to the capacity of parents and children to make sense of their experiences and to create new meanings from their interactions with each other. During the 1990s, many socialization researchers began to abandon transmission models of internalization in favor of a view of children as actively interpreting their socialization experiences (Grusec & Goodnow, 1994; Kuczynski et al., 1997; Lawrence & Valsiner, 1993; Smetana, 1997).

Essential to these theories is that the child actively constructs ideas in the process of internalization. All products of internalization, even that of intergenerational similarity, must be constructed by the child from the ideas and reactions presented by his or her social context. Parents are active in packaging the message so that children can accurately interpret the parent's perspective (Grusec & Goodnow, 1994). However, the constructive capacities of the child places limits on the kinds of ideas a parent might attempt to communicate and how accurately the child interprets the message.

Sociogenetic interpretations of the construction process take the potential for innovation a step further by considering the process by which children apply their newly received knowledge. According to Vygotsky (1978), children make use of information available in the culture in the attempt to solve everyday problems. This process of using cultural knowledge is not passive because children must interpret that information in terms of their own current understanding and they must adapt that knowledge to fit the immediate tasks at hand. Corsaro (1997) argues that internalization involves a process of appropriation, reinvention, and reproduction. Children creatively use information from adult culture for their own purposes and needs. Their interpretation and adaptation of cultural information in everyday life creates new meanings and possibilities for action that they introduce back into the culture.

Lawrence and Valsiner (1993, 2003) consider internalization in conjunction with the parallel and simultaneous process of externalization. In their view, *internalization* refers to the cognitive processing that takes place as children evaluate and attempt to understand the social environment in terms of their personal experiences, needs, and ways of knowing. *Externalization* refers to the further processing that takes place as children manifest or act on what they know. Through the child's interpretation of social input, personal sense is given to the ideas, messages, roles, and relationships that pertain to the person's culture (Lawrence & Heinze, 1997). Thus, innovative construction occurs at two levels. Messages, values, and other information emanating from parents or the culture at large undergo one process of interpretation and transformation as they are internalized and another process of interpretation and transformation as they are externalized.

Cognitive–developmental research has particularly focused on children's constructive activity in value internalization. Social domain perspectives assume that children make their own personal sense of their social interactions from the messages that they receive, the reactions evoked by their behavior, and their own experiences as victims and observers of social transgressions (Smetana, 1997). From this material they construct distinctions between various domains of values including those that are moral (avoiding harm, justice, equal treatment fairness), conventional (situation specific standards of appropriate behavior), prudential (safety and well-being), and personal (autonomous choices) from those that are implicit in their environment. They also develop different modes of reasoning to work through the conflicts and dilemmas that confront them and use these rationales to defend their positions on future occasions.

The idea that children's constructive activity may lead to differences in values between parents and children is also compatible with social domain theory. To the extent that parents provide domain-appropriate information and use domain-appropriate socialization strategies they may promote their children's moral development. However, "In the domain view, parents' communications are aspects of children's social experiences that are used in the construction of social knowledge; these constructions are not direct copies of parents' messages, rules, standards, and values, but are new constructions" (Smetana, 1997, p. 176). Research indicates that conflict and negotiation, and, therefore, dissimilarity in parents and children's views, is most likely in the personal domain (Nucci & Weber, 1995). Although children tend to accept their parent's views on moral and conventional issues, this is a matter of degree. Research indicates that children are likely to disagree with parents' right to prescribe excluding individuals on the basis of race or ethnicity (Killen et al., 2002) or to prescribe actions judged to be immoral, unjust, or unfair (Turiel, 1998). In such cases children may develop values different from those of their parents.

Agency as Autonomy.   Autonomy is a motive for individuals to achieve personal control in interactions with the environment and to resist excessive determination by others. When individuals experience threats to behavioral freedoms or perceive personal injustice they attempt to restore their ability to choose or symbolically assert their autonomy through overt and covert resistance. Children's resistance to adult pressures for conformity has been investigated as early as the second year of life in Western societies (Crockenberg & Littman, 1990; Dunn & Munn, 1985; Kuczynski & Kochanska, 1990; Wenar, 1982). Children's resistance to authority has been reported in various cultures including South Africa (Reynolds, 1991), rural Bolivia (Punch, 2002), and among Muslims (Mayall, 2001) and Indian Asians (Talbani & Hasanali, 2000) undergoing acculturation in Western societies. In adulthood the phenomenon has been investigated under various frameworks including psychological reactance (Brehm, 1981), clinical resistance (Davidson, 1973), and secondary adjustment (Goffman, 1961). The motive to resist threats to autonomy has been documented in contexts of extreme repression such as slavery or authoritarian societies. In such contexts where it is not safe to resist overtly, individuals express resistance in indirect, covert, and creative ways in their everyday lives (Scott, 1990). In traditional hierarchical cultures that stress harmony, cultural practices limiting personal freedoms, most notably affecting women, give rise to cognitive and behavioral forms of resistance (Turiel, 2002), which may contain the seeds for social change.

Recent work in the social domain perspective suggests that children's resistance may stem from their social reasoning. Children may resist the points of view and standards of authorities if they contravene their self-constructed understanding of social situations (Smetana, 2005). Turiel (2002) suggests three ways that conceptions of issues can lead to conflict resistance and opposition. One is when people judge their unequal treatment or restrictions on their activity in moral terms such as justice (Killen et al., 2002). A second way occurs when individuals differ in their acceptance of social conventions. For example, there may be differences between the parental generation and the child's generation with regard to dress, manners, and sexual practices. A third way occurs when children oppose the legitimacy of parental authority over children's choices in the personal domain when children believe that such issues should be left to themselves (Nucci & Weber, 1995). Conflicts during adolescence also occur when there are disagreements over the definition of specific restrictions that have elements of both social convention and personal issues (Smetana, 1997, 2005).

Children's resistance as an expression of agency has several implications for a dynamic model of internalization. First, as indicated in attribution theories of internalization, it may lead to a disjunction between children's public compliance to parental pressures and their private acceptance of the parents' messages (Lepper, 1983). Their children's resistance and protest can lead parents to modify parental childrearing practices. In a study of mothers of 3-year-olds, mothers who changed their attitude toward corporal punishment often reported that they did so because of their children's negative reactions to spanking (Holden, Thompson, Zambarano, & Marshall, 1997). Children's expressions of protest in some cases may lead parents to reflect on their moral positions and lead them to refine their arguments (Pontecorvo, Fasulo, & Sterponi, 2001) or change their attitudes and beliefs (Ta et al., 1999).

Parent and Child Agency in Socialization and Internalization

Regarding parents and children equally as agents highlights a variety of processes that have not received much attention from the perspective of unilateral models of socialization and internalization. These are offered as directions for future research. In the unilateral models of socialization, parents were implicitly considered to be unquestioning conduits in the transmission process who passed on the fixed products of their own childhood internalization without change, to their children (Kuczynski et al., 1997). Regarding parents more fully as agents focuses attention on parents' interpretive and constructive activities with regard to their own internalized products. In the process of externalization parents may actively confront and evaluate the adequacy of the attitudes, beliefs, and values and social definitions that they developed during their own socialization history (Kuczynski et al., 1997).

There may be two consequences of such deliberative processes. First, parents may respond to the conflicting ideas and values prevailing in the surrounding culture and reevaluate, reject, or reconstruct their own ideas so as to make them more adaptive for their own success in a changing society. Second, parents may evaluate and adapt their values in their childrearing decisions for the future success and well-being of their children. Parents may decide to promote values similar to those that they had internalized during childhood. However, sometimes the decision may be to promote values different from their own original acquisitions. Parents do not care equally about all values (Grusec et al., 2000). Intergenerational change may result from choices that parents make regarding which values they hold on to and which they allow to be dropped. Parents select from a range of competing childrearing goals and concerns and strive to accommodate them with regard to the competing goals of their children (Dix & Branca, 2003). Holden and Hawk (2003) describe a number of processes including anticipation, assessment, problem solving, and reflection, that parents engage in as agents promoting their goals with children. Grusec and Goodnow (1994) argue that when parents do wish to transmit a particular value or message, they are most effective when they intervene in a way that enables their children, as agents, to accurately interpret their messages and voluntarily accept them.

A bilateral model of parent–child relations asserts as a working principle that children's agency and the child-to-parent direction of influence should be systematically explored in parallel to the parent's agency and influence. Children, like parents, make sense of messages communicated by the older generation in terms of what they know and their developmentally constrained ways of understanding. Children must also reconcile those views with alternate viewpoints offered by peers, media, schools, and their own self-reflection. Children's own views are challenged by the parent's demands and assertions in everyday interactions. As part of their own externalization processes children must decide whether to accept, manage, or creatively interpret their parent's definitions of situations.

A DIALECTICAL MODEL OF INTERNALIZATION PROCESSES

Kuczynski and Grusec (1997) noted that theoretical treatments of internalization processes in the family are beginning to coalesce around particular conceptions of bidirectional causality. These include transactional (Patterson, 1997), systemic (Garborino, Kostelny,

& Barry, 1997; Parke & Buriel, 1998), and dialectical models of bidirectional causality (Lawrence & Valsiner, 1993; Valsiner, Branco, & Dantas, 1997). We believe that advances can be made by an in-depth exploration of particular models of bidirectionality. In the following section we, therefore, argue the merits of dialectical causality for the study of internalization processes in the family.

Dialectical causality emphasizes the inherent contradictions that exist within and between individuals and their various contexts and the qualitative syntheses that result as these elements actively interact with each other. Contextual models of dialectics suggest that the resolutions of contradictions are always temporary because each synthesis becomes the basis of a new contradiction that can lead toward either positive or negative trajectories (Kuczynski, 2003). The essence of a dialectical view of causality is that individuals interacting with their environments are engaged in a continuous process of change in a changing context and that novel forms emerge constantly in development.

Dialectical causality was a feature of the transactional model originally proposed by Sameroff (1975). However, the element of dialectics was subsequently neglected when behavioral interpretations of transaction as a reciprocal exchange of parent and child stimuli and responses became popular. Dialectics has been explicitly embraced by theoreticians who conceptualize interactions between parents and children as interactions between agents (Hinde, 1997; Lawrence & Valsiner, 1993). Other approaches that consider the meanings that parents and children create from their experiences of conflict with each other may also be compatible with dialectical causality (Grusec & Goodnow, 1994; Kuczynski et al., 1997; Smetana, 1997).

We propose that a dialectical perspective on bidirectional causality offers advantages for analyses of dynamic processes in socialization and internalization. Parent–child socialization considered from the perspective of interacting agents constantly offers up contradictions that feed into the dialectical process. Interactions where parents make demands of their children often pit the parent's needs with the child's needs, the parent's will with the child's will, the parent's understanding of values with the child's understanding, the parent's definitions of a behavior with the child's definitions, and the parent's influence strategies against the child's influence strategies. Within the parent there are contradictions in the parental role, which balances diverse functions such as authority, caretaker, attachment figure, and companion (Harach & Kuczynski, 1999). In addition, parents and children continually come up against a larger ecological context of values and understandings including those of peers, television, the Internet, and school that offer up contradictions and opportunities for further change. In a dialectical perspective, adaptation to change rather than stability is an essential element of successful parenting (Holden & Ritchie, 1988).

The Products of Internalization as Novel Syntheses

An important value of a dialectical conception of process is that it points to a way of reconceptualizing the nature of the products of socialization/internalization/externalization processes. Traditional socialization theory conceptions of the principal products of socialization, the transmission of value content and behavioral conformity, tended to be deterministic such that a desirable outcome was an exact match between the ideas and expectations of the older generation and the responses of the younger generation. The direct transmission of ideas across several generations was viewed as mechanism for intergenerational continuity and the reproduction of society and culture (Corsaro, 1997; Valsiner, 1988). Behavioral conformity to the expectations of parents and institutional authorities was similarly conceived as exact compliance (Kuczynski & Hildebrandt, 1997). Theories differed with regard to external control (Patterson, 1997) or internal control (e.g., Hoffman, 1970; Lepper, 1982) as standards for children's motivations for compliance with parental demands. However, unidirectional socialization theories did not imagine that the final form of the child's conformity would differ from the parent's wishes.

The dialectical idea that outcomes of interaction are temporary syntheses provides a way of reformulating content internalization and behavioral conformity in a dynamic way. In a dialectical view, the content of an individual's internalization and the individual's conformity to socialization pressures are not endpoints of development. Rather they are punctuations in an ongoing process and contain the elements that set the stage for further change.

Content Internalization as Working Models. Kuczynski, Marshall, and Schell (1997) proposed a conception of content internalization, a process by which parents and children construct personal working models of the beliefs, attitudes, and values of their family and cultural contexts. The working model metaphor highlights an important difference from the unilateral conception of internalization as a static product. As described by Lawrence and Valsiner, "The person's intra-mental reconstruction of the world is a highly dynamic structure. It is never finished, but continues as a sufficient support for the person's new encounters with the world" (1993, p. 152). Incorporated in working models, therefore, is the idea that each person's beliefs, values, skills, attitudes, and motives are continuously under development and open to challenge and reconstruction throughout life.

As a result of different life experiences and transactions with each other and other working models available in their ecological contexts, mothers, fathers, and each child in the family develop somewhat different personal working models as a product of their internalization processes. Specific illustrations of the utility of the working model conception for linking processes within the family with macro processes of intergenerational and cultural change are explored in the final section of this chapter.

Conformity as Negotiation and Accommodation. Children's conformity to parental standards can also be conceptualized as a dialectical synthesis. Accumulating research on parent–child conflict has found phenomena that are inconsistent with the traditional deterministic view of compliance as an exact match between the parents' commands and children's responses. Children appear to be less controlled and parents are much less controlling than the traditional perspectives suggests (Eisenberg, 1992; Vuchinich, 1987). Moreover, conflict appears to be a normative, mutually tolerated feature of parent–child relationships (Dunn & Munn, 1985). Such findings have given rise to a relational view of conformity that examines the form and function that conformity and resistance takes in close relationships (Kuczynski & Hildebrandt, 1997). Parental commands and children's responses to them occur in an interdependent relationship context that supports children's expression of agency. Socially competent children are assumed to display a cooperative, coregulated but nonexact form of conformity and resistance that is consistent with the idea of accommodation and negotiation (Kuczynski & Hildebrandt, 1997). *Accommodation,* seen as an expression of autonomy within the boundaries of a relationship, conveys both an expectation of a cooperative response, and also that the form of the cooperative response be chosen by the recipient rather than by the sender of a request. Thus, an accommodating response by children who are inclined to cooperate with a parent's request or accept the premise of the parent's intentions may acknowledge that the parent has been heard, that children attempt to coordinate their own plans with the parent's wishes or that children are willing to positively negotiate an alternative course of action. Similarly, the construct of negotiation conveys the distinctive standards of noncompliance within relationships where children learn to express their resistance within the constraints of an interdependent relationship.

Examination of the form of preschool children's conformity suggests that children express their agency even while complying with a parent's requests. Among children's cooperative responses, distinctions have been made between committed compliance, situational or unwilling compliance, and accommodation. *Committed compliance* is cooperation where agency is apparent in the child's voluntary or enthusiastic cooperation with parental requests (Kochanska & Aksan, 1995). *Situational compliance* corresponds to the traditional idea of compliance to external pressures (Maccoby & Martin, 1983). A similar category is *unwilling compliance,* where children show their agency by complying in a minimal way or complying under protest (Lollis, Kuczynski, Navara, & Koguchi, 2003). *Accommodation,* a newly described category of agency within compliance, is a form of cooperation where the child's attitude is cooperative but the child interjects or suggests creative interpretations and alternatives regarding the form of their compliance. Children's uncooperative responses also take a number of forms including *negotiation, passive noncompliance, simple refusal,* and *defiance* (Crockenberg & Litman, 1990; Kuczynski & Kochanska, 1990; Lollis et al., 2003). Although all forms of noncompliance can be considered as signs of agency, the different categories are considered to differ in terms of the child's assertiveness and social skill.

Considered as a product of internalization processes, the implication is that many of children's responses to parental control do not correspond to the traditional deterministic definition of compliance. The majority of children's responses indicate that transformations occur between the "input" of the parent's commands and the "output" of the child's response. It is important to note that we have thus far only considered children's immediate responses to parental requests. What is missing and poorly understood in research on compliance is the form of compliance in the parent's absence.

Traditionally, out-of-sight conformity was assumed to be controlled by parental monitoring, or parents' continued surveillance of children's behavior outside the home. However, recent perspectives that focus on children's agency suggest that traditional views of parents' ability to control children's out-of-sight behavior have been somewhat optimistic. Corsaro (1997) argues that children collaborate with peers and siblings in a peer culture that operates alongside the adult culture of their parents and other authorities. Moreover, in the peer culture, children collaborate in the process of reworking adult knowledge and find creative ways to evade, judge, or challenge adult rules and collectively gain a measure of control over their own lives (Corsaro, 1997). Parental monitoring of such activities may be illusory because the success of monitoring in part depends on children's voluntary disclosure of their covert activities (Kerr & Stattin, 2000). We suggest, therefore, that children's conformity is best understood as a novel dialectical synthesis that reflects the agency of not only parents but also their children.

In summary, a dialectical perspective on bidirectional influence between parents and children may be advantageous for understanding dynamic processes in socialization and internalization. Dialectical causality is well suited for understanding interactions between parents and children considered as agents with their own goals, perspectives, and sources of information. The perspective guides researchers to accept that the outcomes of socialization and internalization processes are novel syntheses reflecting the agency of parents and children interacting in the context of their mutual relationship rather than linear reflections of parental wishes.

Acculturation: Linking Family Processes to Social Change

In recent decades, sociological and political science research have focused on value change in society without considering micro processes in the family, whereas research on socialization in the family has disregarded macro processes of societal change (Boehnke, Ittel, & Baier, 2002). An important challenge for current theories of socialization is to link these two levels of analysis. In this final section, we explore the possibilities of such a linkage within new bilateral conceptions of socialization using the ideas of working models of internalization, bidirectionality, and parents and children considered equally as agents. To illustrate the possibilities of such a linkage, we focus on the burgeoning literature on acculturation of immigrant families into the values and practices of a new host country.

Recent conceptions of cultural transmission are compatible with the bilateral conceptual framework discussed previously. Influence processes between individual and culture are increasingly understood to be bidirectional and consider the role of individuals as agents in the construction of culture (Berry et al., 2002; Valsiner, 1988). Rather than being a static external entity, culture is shaped and reshaped by the interactions between persons, groups, and their environment (Phalet & Schonpflug, 2001). Similarly, although research on acculturation generally focuses on the cultural adjustments of immigrants to the norms of the culture of settlement, acculturation also is a mechanism for social change, because both cultures undergo changes due to direct or indirect contact with one another (Berry et al., 2002).

Working Models of Generation and Culture

Traditionally, successful socialization was believed to have occurred when the child accepts the cultural values of their parents and complies with their parents' rules and standards. The idea of cultural continuity (Cavalli-Sforza & Fledman, 1981) is appealing, and in some respect desirable, as a mechanism of societal cohesion and continuity between generations (Nauck, 2001; Schonpflug, 2001). However, the idea of working models of internalization presented in this chapter raises the question of whether this continuity can ever be a faithful one.

Earlier, we discussed both similarity and change as being carried forward symbolically in the personal working models of values, attitudes, knowledge, and beliefs that parents and children construct in the process of internalization. In Fig. 11.1 we extend this concept by considering working models of internalization as a mediator of similarity and change at the societal level. The principal elaboration is that as part of their working model processes, parents and children both carry forward and modify the values and practices of their generation and of their culture.

The concept of *generation* has been long proposed as a source of value conflict and as a carrier of social change in values. The study of generation is "centrally concerned with continuity and change how the past feeds into the present and on into the future through the agency of people born and learning at certain periods of time" (Mayall, 2002, p. 37). According to Mannhiem (1928/1952), young people form a generation by being exposed to specific social, historical, and political events and ideas of a particular time period; developing shared ways of interpreting and evaluating situations; and, in some cases, form generation units characterized by face-to-face interactions among its members where they react to issues in similar ways.

Sociologists have recently argued that the process of forming a generation begins in early childhood as children form solidarity groups with peers (Mayall, 2002) a process

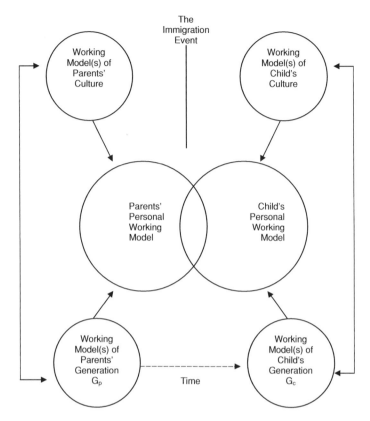

FIG. 11.1   The influence of cultural and generation working models on parents' and child's personal working models in an immigration context.

that Corsaro and Eder (1990) describe as the formation of peer cultures. *Peer culture* is a stable set of activities of routines, artifacts, values, and concerns that children produce and share in interaction with peers (Corsaro & Eder, 1990). For their part, parents also have continuing support and input from their own generational peers including association with cultural organizations, religious groups, and schools as support for existing working models and as input for social change (Berry et al., 2002).

The relationship of generation to the concept of working models is depicted in the bottom portion of Fig. 11.1. Parents, in part, form their working models by internalizing ideas prevalent in the collective working models of their generation. Parents manifest their past generational working models by carrying forward in time certain values, ideas, and outlooks that were formed in the past and may continue to be supported through associations with the parent's generation in the present. These values and ideas of parents may differ from those of their children who are forming a generation of their own through interactions with their own peers. Some continuity in the working models of parents and children is established as parents foster ideas from their generation. Children also have access to the collective working models of their own generation. Changes in working models of parents may occur during individual development as ideas from the child's generation feed back to parents in parent–child social interactions. However, there is evidence that changes due to collective individual development is only one route for effecting social change in values. A second route is generational replacement.

The most systematic study of values bearing on generational change concerns the childrearing values of obedience and independence. Alwin (1988, 1996) documented decreases in the value of strict conformity, manners, patriotism, and religious observance and increases in the value of independence and tolerance in the United States and several European and Asian countries throughout the 20th century. For this particular set of values, the weight of the evidence is that social change was attributable to generational replacement rather than developmental transformation across the lifespan of the individual (Alwin, 1996). That is, change at the societal level is consolidated as the parental generation dies out or loses influence and is replaced by the child's generation.

The contribution of working models of culture in the context of acculturation is also depicted in Fig. 11.1. The idea of culture as a working model builds on constructionist views of culture as a system of meanings (Bruner, 1996) or personal models of conceptual structures, constructed by individuals in the process of social interaction (Valsiner, 2001). Each individual in a cultural setting constructs and acts on a somewhat unique interpretation of that culture.

Research on immigrant populations illustrates the utility of considering culture as a system of ideas constructed and retained as a working model. For immigrant parents, acculturation adds to the problems of generation in increasing distance between parent and child values (Knafo & Schwartz, 2001). Generation may produce differences in working models between parents and children due to social change over time, whereas immigration produces differences in their working models due to changes in place. Parents' working models of culture are formed in the culture of origin but feedback from that culture is disrupted through the event of immigration. This separation has consequences for the working models of both the immigrant parents and of their children. Children's working models of culture are rapidly formed through interactions with working models of the adopted culture. Separated from the supporting context of the culture of their parents, children's construction of continuity with the parents' culture relies almost exclusively on the strategies and efforts of their parents.

As with working models of generation, working models of culture contribute to both cultural stability and change. Several studies suggest that those who attempt to preserve their culture in a host country, but are disconnected from social forces within their country of origin, preserve a working model of culture that eventually becomes outdated. Farver, Bhadha, and Naramj (2002) found that South Asian immigrant parents become more Indian than those left behind as they attempt to transplant and maintain traditional values and beliefs in their new environment. For these immigrant parents, cultural norms and values remained relatively static over the years after immigration—a sort of cultural "snapshot" that sometimes bore little resemblance to the norms or values currently accepted in their culture of origin. Navara and James (2003) found a similar phenomenon in Portuguese immigrants living in Canada. Portuguese immigrant parents maintained traditional values and cultural beliefs while living in Canada over an extended period of time, but after returning to Portugal for a visit often saw great differences between the ideas of culture that they preserved in their own working models of Portuguese culture and the ideas and practices that were currently prevalent in Portugal.

There is little question that children of immigrants develop working models of culture that are different from those of their parents. In fact, it has been argued, "youth whose primary socialization has taken place within the cross-currents of differing cultural fields ... *self-consciously* selected, syncretized and elaborated from more than one heritage" (Vertovec & Cohen, 1999, p. 10). Several studies indicate that the values of children of immigrants are more similar to those of their nonimmigrant peers than they are to those of their parents (Cashmore & Goodnow, 1985; Knafo & Schwartz, 2001; Phinney, Ong, & Madden, 2000). Parke and Buriel (1998) discuss assimilation and biculturalism as the trajectories followed by most children within a few generations following immigration into the United States. Most European immigrants develop assimilated working models in part because they already shared some of the ideas of the previous generations of Europeans who formed the host culture. Some continuity of traditional culture is maintained within the assimilated cultural groups in the form of vestigial "symbolic ethnicity" (Alba, 1990) that imposes little cost on everyday life. Immigrants of non-European cultures of origin including American Indians, Latinos, African Americans, and Asian Americans tended to retain aspects of their traditional cultures and beliefs within a positive dual frame of reference. However, the nature of the ethnic identity continues to undergo transformations the longer the group lives alongside the majority culture. Thus, in the case of Mexican immigrants in the United States, the first generation may identify themselves as "Mexican," whereas their children may prefer either a "Mexican-American" or "Chicano" identity (Buriel & Cardoza, 1993).

Parents as Agents in the Acculturation Process

Acculturation provides a natural field experiment for socialization and internalization in a larger social context. For insiders of a culture, cultural values and practices are often taken for granted. Goodnow (1997) proposes that a great deal of enculturation is accomplished more through the doing of cultural practices rather than thinking through and consciously transmitting them. Moreover, parents who are insiders of a culture benefit from group processes such as living in communities that share similar values and practices that support the transmission of parental values independently of parents' individual efforts (Harris, 1995).

However, the idea of constructing working models of culture is more salient in the process of acculturation where immigrants may attempt to preserve and transmit their culture without the supports that would have been taken for granted in their country of origin. Acculturation brings cultural transmission out of the realm of the unconsidered to the realm of conscious choices made by immigrant parents and children in reconstructing a working model of culture in a new host country.

Immigrants face many contradictions between their imported cultural values and the values prevalent in their adopted society (Fuligni, 1998; Phalet & Schonpflug, 2001; Phinney et al., 2000). Working models developed in the culture of origin may contain elements that are unsupported, denigrated by a hostile host culture, or maladaptive for success in the new environment. Not all traditional values that immigrants bring with them are positive or moral from the standpoint of the adopted culture. Cultural transmission has a "dark side" that was received little attention. Among the transmitted products of most cultures are values of intolerance and inequality formed during centuries of religious and political strife: racial, ethnic, national, religious, tribal, as well as those based on class, caste, and gender. These may have been supported in the relative homogeneity of the culture of origin but are problematic in many host cultures that have become multiculturally constituted and tend to value diversity and tolerance. Parents from traditional patriarchal cultures also may also find themselves challenged by new norms for parent–child relationships that are more democratic than their traditional norms (Trommsdorff & Kornadt, 2003) and unsupportive of traditional authoritarian childrearing practices that they may attempt to transplant into the new environment. In terms of our conceptual framework, parents are abruptly faced with integrating new belief systems, values, and practices of their host countries within their working models. They must decide what aspects of their previous working models must be adapted in order that they themselves can succeed in the new culture and what aspects of their previous culture to preserve or to let go in the socialization of their own children.

Earlier in the chapter, we suggested that not only children but also parents need to be regarded as agents in their own internalization. Specifically, parents may actively confront and evaluate their own attitudes and values and reinterpret, adapt, or reject values and beliefs acquired during their own childhood. This process is more salient when parents experience a cross-cultural relocation and are exposed to societal values that differ from their traditional or socialized beliefs. For example, parental ethnotheories might well change due to contact with another culture. *Parental ethnotheories* are the values, beliefs, and practices that guide the parent in rearing their child (Harkness & Super, 1995). However, the concept of parental ethnotheories explicitly links the traditional literature on childrearing practices with the importance of the cultural context of the parent. Berry and co-workers (2002) noted that the peers of parents may well challenge parental ethnotheories, in essence causing a process by which adaptation or rejection of traditional values can occur.

Berry (1997) proposed that immigrant parents and children might respond to competing cultural beliefs and values in several ways. These include *integration* (maintaining traditional cultural integrity, while moving toward and adopting some cultural values of the dominant society); *separation* (a strong maintenance of traditional cultural values and a resistance to the dominant culture); *assimilation* (where the traditional values are forgone in favor of the dominant culture's values); and *marginalization* (a loss of traditional values and a lack of identification with the dominant culture's beliefs). Marginalization may arise as a response to the dominant culture's stereotypes and prejudices, disillusionment with traditional values, and the possible prejudices and stereotypes of the immigrant themselves. We suggest that these responses may impact different goals and orientations of immigrant parents toward preserving or reworking their original working models of culture and, therefore, different goals and strategies in promoting values in their children to prepare them in the new cultural context.

Of interest here are separation and integration, which both have as goals the fostering of traditional values of the county of origin to a greater or lesser degree. Nagel (1994) uses a shopping cart analogy—parents select elements from their ethnic culture (such as religion, norms, values, symbols, myths, customs, art, music, and dress) to foster in their children. Parents can foster such ideas through direct or purposeful instruction, and by providing opportunities for children to participate in traditional events (Parke, Ornstein, Rieser, & Zahn-Waxler, 1994). Buriel (1985) found that Mexican-American parents attempt to reinforce ethnic behaviors by modeling them or by directly teaching their children about their traditions, beliefs, and values.

Goodnow (1997) described two defensive strategies, pre-arming and cocooning, which parents use to protect cultural and religious values from external influences in the dominant culture. Parents may *pre-arm* their children by denigrating individuals who may attack or threaten them for their practices or ethnicity. Alternatively, they may teach their children in various proactive tactics to avoid or ward off competing messages and influences. Parents may also attempt to maintain certain cultural or religious beliefs by strategically shielding or *cocooning* their children from competing values until desired values are established (Goodnow, 1997).

Parents may cocoon themselves and their children within the adopted culture and preserve their working models of the culture of origin by choosing to live in ethnic neighborhoods, and enrolling children in ethnic schools, developing exclusive ties to ethnic organizations and religious institutions, and establishing associations with other immigrants of their own generation. Knafo (2003) studied religious and nonreligious Israelis who used the cocooning strategy of selecting schools that reflected their own beliefs and values. Knafo found that there were fewer parent–child discussions of values when children attended such high-fit institutions, indicating that the strategy of cocooning may obviate the need for direct parental instruction. Living in ethnic communities also provides children with the opportunities to form associations with peers and other adult role models from the same ethnic group who may support values promoted in their homes, with a certain degree of insulation from the rest of society (Coleman & Hoffer, 1987).

Immigrant parents may also choose to abandon selected traditional values. Families who relocate often have the goal to improve the quality of life for themselves and their children. Chopra and Satinder (2003) found that immigrant parents from East India living in Canada have high educational and occupational expectations of their children and that the children should adopt cultural norms that ensure success. Maintaining traditional beliefs that are incongruent with success in the adopted culture could be perceived as maladaptive to this goal.

Available research indicates that parents who use separation strategies to preserve their cultural heritage may nevertheless adapt their childrearing strategies to prepare their children for success in the society in which they would eventually work and live their adult lives. Zivkovic (reported in Youniss, 1994) compared two groups of Croatian parents who had immigrated to North America. One group that came from a rural area of Croatia relocated in a closed ethnic community in urban northern New Jersey and reported that they wanted their children to retain the Croatian identity, language, dietary customs, and other ethnic traditions. The other group, a sample of highly educated professionals immigrated to the United States after 1950, had largely assimilated balancing their Croatian background with an American identity and showed less interest in having their children retain a Croatian identity. Despite these differences in orientation toward the host culture, both groups adapted their childrearing strategies promoting self-directedness over compliance and valued schooling to prepare their children for success in the host country (Youniss, 1994).

Acculturation Processes of Children

As with parents, children of immigrants construct their own working models of culture and must interpret, select, resist, or manage the competing messages emanating from their family, peers, and culture. Children, particularly if they are born in the host culture or immigrate when they are quite young, approach the problem of acculturation from a different standpoint than their parents because they usually acculturate and learn the language more quickly than their parents, and tend to adopt prevailing host cultural values more thoroughly (Feather, 1975; Georgas, Berry, Shaw, Christakopoulou, & Milonas, 1996; Schumann, 1978, 1986; Tong, 1996). Fitting in with the expectations, practices, and values of the host culture is a matter of practical concern because it there that they live their lives and eventually, work, marry, and raise children of their own. Children, therefore, may face the problem of integrating or managing the sometimes ill-fitting values of their parents within their already acculturated working models of the host culture.

The different rates of transformation of the working models of immigrant parents and their children have repercussions for parent–child relations. Rumbaut and Portes (2001) describe three different modes of acculturation as they relate to children and their parents. *Dissonant acculturation,* which is accompanied by increased parent–child conflict, occurs when there is an acculturation gap between parents and children. When children perceive that parental values conflict with their desire to fit in and succeed within the host culture they might feel embarrassed rather than proud of parents and traditional cultural beliefs and values. *Consonant acculturation,* which is associated with increased family cohesion, occurs where there is little or no acculturation gap between parents and children. *Selective acculturation* occurs when co-ethnic communities buffer the acculturation process by slowing cultural shift and promote partial retention of traditional parental values and beliefs.

Researchers have found that immigrant children often had to cope with dual expectations, negotiating between traditional values and beliefs endorsed at home by their parents and those espoused by their culturally diverse peers at school (e.g., Farver et al., 2002). Parents and children might also maintain different expectations regarding the autonomy of the child in regard to dating preferences (Hyman, Vu, & Beiser, 2000; Talbani & Hasanali, 2000), academic achievement (Hyman, Vu, & Beiser, 2000), values of conformity, collectivism (Goodnow, 1988), and personal rights and familial obligations (Sam & Virta, 2003). These discrepancies often lead to internal conflict and overt and covert resistance (Hyman, Vu, & Beiser, 2002). Researchers have also found that adolescents express resentment at the cultural constraints placed on them and found the idea of maintaining the status quo unappealing. This dissent with traditional cultural values was often expressed in subversive actions, such as wearing North American–style clothing outside of the home, lessened participation in traditional community activities, and going out without parents' knowledge (Talbani & Hasanali, 2000).

Children's agency and the child-to-parent direction of influence are just beginning to be explored in research on acculturation. Recent research on children as cultural brokers reviewed by Parke and his colleagues (Parke & Buriel, 1998; Parke et al., 2003) suggests that children may play a significant role in forming and managing their parents' working models of culture. Immigrant children are often placed in the position of being the public face of the family in a variety of situations such as relating with financial institutions, doctors, and government officials (Buriel & De Ment, 1997). Because of their greater expertise in the host culture, children may become translators of the new language and interpreters of the culture for their parents and thereby play a role in the resocialization of their parents in the norms of the new culture. Studies of Mexican-American and Chinese-American families suggest that brokering is often carried out by female children and may begin in elementary school when children are preadolescents (Buriel & De Ment, 1997; Chao, 2001). "In brokering situations, children act as adults in interactions with their parents, which often gives rise to role reversals involving the transmission of information. That is, child cultural brokers must sometimes 'teach' parents things about the new culture while still maintaining deference and respect consistent with their status as children" (Parke et al., 2003, p. 261). Ambert (1992) speculated that, under these conditions, children are uniquely placed to have either a negative or a positive impact on the parents' adaptation to the new culture. In some cases, successful adaptation may consist in parents learning new ways of living and changing some of their previous attitudes and values by being receptive to the lessons that their children have to offer values that they have adopted from the new society.

There are also other possibilities for children's actions with regard to the working models of their parents that are in need of research. Children's brokering role may cocoon parental working models by obviating the need for parents to directly interact with the dominant culture. This may be accomplished by older children by handling family finances or brokering certain interactions with outside groups such as medical doctors and lawyers.

Little is known about cultural clashes between parents and children in the moral domain, but it is likely that in multicultural nations children and immigrant parents may have different moral standpoints, particularly on issues having to do with interethnic and interracial relations. Killen and associates (2002) asked children what they would do if their parents condoned excluding a person on the basis of race. Elementary school children were conflicted between parental authority and their own moral judgment, whereas adolescents were more likely to judge racial exclusion as wrong and question their parents' moral position. One Asian adolescent talked at length concerning her parents' traditional racism and the need to educate parents about racial equality. Personal experience of the first author of interactions with peers among a first generation of children of Eastern European immigrants after World War II into Canada also suggests that children may be faced with managing negative aspects of cultural transmission. The parents of this generation of assimilated and bicultural children were raised in Eastern Europe during the 1920s and 1930s. Both groups shared a culture that contained among its values elements of religious and ethnic enmity. From the point of view of their children who formed their own working models in the educational institutions and peer groups in North America, various ideas of their parents came to be evaluated as "intolerant," "superstitious," or "irrelevant" in the context of the ethnic and religious diversity of North American culture. Such issues sometimes formed the basis of parent–child conflict and parental change in values. However, in the interest of harmonious long-term family relationships, children also adopted the strategy of "encapsulating" the working models of their parents. That is, children humored parents in their beliefs or cordoned off certain topics within "demilitarized zones" (Hagestad, 1979, reported in Greene & Boxer, 1986) so that conflict between the different generational and cultural working models of parents and children could be avoided.

CONCLUSION

This chapter outlined changes in theory on socialization and internalization processes in the family that are emerging from changed assumptions about the nature of parent–child relations. Bidirectional causality is a given in recent formulations of internalization (Kuczynski & Grusec, 1997). It has long been understood that children influence parenting practices as they impact on children's development, however, the idea that children may have more comprehensive impact that includes input into the parents internalization and development and input into the ideas of their own developing generation is just beginning to be explored. A more comprehensive view of family processes that includes an emphasis on parents and children as agents in the context of their relationships opens additional avenues of research. Cognitive developmental research has led the way in exploring children's constructive processes in internalization. However, this has not been matched with a balanced interest in the parent's constructive processes in their own continuing adult development of values. For instance, how do parents think about their socialization experiences and how do they select which values to pass on, abandon, or modify when they come to socialize their own children? Research is also required on children's perspectives on their parent's socialization efforts. How do children interpret, resist, and negotiate parental messages?

Another expansion in the idea of socialization comes from considering the products of internalization as continuing process both at the level of lifespan individual development and as a contributor to social and generational change. Parents struggle with the products of their own internalization even as they attempt to foster their children's socialization. Both parents and their children must recurrently update their working models of internalization in the light of their transactions with each other and with their changing contexts.

REFERENCES

Alba, R. D. (1990). *Ethnic identity: The transformation of white America.* New Haven, CT: Yale University Press.

Alwin, D. (1988). From obedience to autonomy: Changes in traits desired in children, 1924–1978. *Public Opinion Quarterly, 52,* 33–52.

Alwin, D. F. (1996). Parental socialization in historical perspective. In C. D. Ryff & M. M. Seltzer (Eds.), *The parental experience in midlife* (pp. 105–167). Chicago: University of Chicago Press.

Ambert, A. M. (1992). *The effect of children on parents. Haworth marriage & the family.* New York: Haworth.

Baranowski, M. D. (1978). Adolescent's attempted influence on parental behaviors. *Adolescence, 13,* 585–604.

Bell, R. Q. (1968). A reinterpretation of the direction of effects in studies of socialization. *Psychological Review, 75,* 81–95.

Bernard, J. (1972). *The future of marriage.* New York: World Publishing.

Berry, J. W. (1997). Immigration, acculturation, and adaptation. *Applied Psychology: An International Review, 46*(1), 5–34.

Berry, J. W., Poortinga, Y. H., Segall, M. H., & Dasen, P. R. (Eds.). (2002). *Cross-cultural psychology: Research and applications* (2nd ed.). New York: Cambridge University Press.

Boehnke, K., Itell, A., & Baier, D. (2002). Value transmission and 'Zeitgeist': An under-researched relationship. *Sociale Wetenschappen, 45,* 28–43.

Brandstädter, J. (1997). Action perspectives on human development. In W. Damon & R. M. Lerner (Eds.), *Handbook on child psychology* (5th ed., vol. 1., pp. 807–829). New York: John Wiley & Sons Inc.

Brehm, S. S. (1981). Oppositional behavior in children: A reactance theory approach. In S. S. Brehm, S. M. Kassin, & F. K. Gibbons (Eds.), *Developmental social psychology: Theory and research.* New York: Oxford University Press, 96–121.

Bruner, J. S. (1996). *Acts of meaning.* Cambridge, MA: Harvard University Press.

Bugental, D. B., & Goodnow, J. G. (1998). Socialization processes. In N. Eisenberg (Vol. Ed.), *Handbook of child psychology, Vol. 3: Social, emotional, and personality development.* New York: John Wiley & Sons.

Bukowski, W. M., & Sippola, L. K. (1998). Diversity and the social mind: Social goals, social constructs, and social development. *Developmental Psychology, 34,* 742–746.

Buriel, R. (1985). Locus of control orientations of Anglo- and Mexican-American children. *Psychological Reports, 57*(3, Pt 2), 1121–1122.

Buriel, R., & Cardoza, D. (1993). Mexican American ethnic labeling: An intrafamilial and intergenerational analysis. In M. E. Bernal & G. P. Knight (Eds.), *Ethnic identity: Formation and transmission among Hispanics and other minorities. SUNY series, United States Hispanic studies* (pp. 197–210). Albany: State University of New York Press.

Buriel, R., & De Ment, T. (1997). Immigration and sociocultural change in Mexican, Chinese, and Vietnamese-American families. In A. Booth, A. C. Crouter, et al. (Eds.), *Immigration and the family: Research and policy on U.S. immigrants* (pp. 165–200). Hillsdale, NJ: Lawrence Erlbaum Associates.

Cashmore, J. A., & Goodnow, J. J. (1985). Agreement between generations: A two-process approach. *Child Development, 56,* 493–501.

Cavalli-Sforza, L. L., & Feldman, M. W. (1981). *Cultural transmission and evolution: A quantitative approach.* Princeton University Press.

Chao, R. K. (2001). Extending research on the consequences of parenting style for Chinese Americans and European Americans. *Child Development, 72*(6), 1832–1843.

Chopra, R., & Satinder, K. P. (2003) *Parent and child attitudes toward educational and occupational achievement as a function of acculturation.* Paper presented at the Canadian Psychological Association annual conference, Hamilton, Ontario, Canada.

Coleman, J. S., & Hoffer, T. (Eds.). (1987). *Public and private high schools: The impact of communities.* New York: Basic Books.

Collins, W. A., Maccoby, E. E., Steinberg, L., Hetherington, E. M., & Bornstein, M. H. (2000). Contemporary research on parenting: the case for nature and nurture. *American Psychologist, 55,* 218–232.

Corsaro, W. A. (1997). *The sociology of childhood.* Thousand Oaks, CA: Pine Forge Press.

Corsaro, W. A., & Eder, D. (1990). Children's peer cultures. *Annual Review of Sociology, 16,* 197–220.

Crockenberg, S., & Litman, C. (1990). Autonomy as competence in 2-year-olds: Maternal correlates of child defiance, compliance, and self-assertion. *Developmental Psychology, 26,* 961–971.

Cummings, E. M., & Schermerhorn, A. C. (2003). A developmental perspective on children as agents in the family. In L. Kuczynski (Ed.), *Handbook of dynamics in parent-child relations* (pp. 91–108). Thousand Oaks, CA: Sage.

Davidson, G. C. (1973). Counter-control in behavior modification. In L. A. Hamerlynck, L. Handy, & E. J. Mash (Eds.), *Behavior change: Methodology and practice* (pp. 153–167). Champaign, IL: Research Press.

Dix, T., & Branca, S. H. (2003). Parenting as a goal-regulation process. In L. Kuczynski (Ed.), *Handbook of dynamics in parent-child relations* (pp. 167–188). Thousand Oaks, CA: Sage.

Dubin, E. R., & Dubin, R. (1963). The authority inception period in socialization. *Child Development, 34*(4), 885–898.

Dunn, J. F., & Munn, P. (1985). Becoming a family member: Family conflict and the development of social understanding in the second year. *Child Development: Special Issue: Family Development, 56*(2), 480–492.

Eisenberg, A. R. (1992). Conflicts between mothers and their young children. *Merrill-Palmer Quarterly, 38,* 21–44.

Farver, J. A., Bhadha, B. R., & Naramj, S. K. (2002). Acculturation and psychological functioning in Asian Indian adolescents. *Social Development, 11*(1), 11–29.

Feather, N. T. (1975). *Values in education and society.* New York: Free Press.

Ferree, M. M. (1990). Beyond separate spheres: Feminism and family research. *Journal of Marriage and the Family, 52,* 866–884.

Fine, G. A. (1992). Agency, structure, and comparative contexts: Toward a synthetic interactionism. *Symbolic Interaction, 15*(1), 87–107.

Frankel, J. (1991). On being reared by your children: State of art as reflected in the literature. *Free Inquiry in Creative Sociology, 19,* 193–200.

Fuligni, A. J. (1998). Authority, autonomy, and parent-adolescent conflict and cohesion: A study of adolescents from Mexican, Chinese, Filipino, and European backgrounds. *Developmental Psychology, 34*(4), 782–792.

Garbarino, J., Kostelny, K., & Barry, F. (1997). Value transmission in an ecological context: The high-risk neighborhood. In J. Grusec & L. Kuczynski (Eds.), *Parenting and children's internalization of values: A handbook of contemporary theory* (pp. 307–332). New York: John Wiley & Sons.

Georgas, J., Berry, J. W., Shaw, A., Christakopoulou, S., & Milonas, K. (1996). Acculturation of Greek family values. *Journal of Cross-Cultural Psychology, 27*(3), 329–338.

Giddens, A. (1990). Structuration theory and sociological analysis. In J. P. Clark, C. Modgil, & S. Modgil (Eds.), *Anthony Giddens: Consensus and controversy* (pp. 297–315). London: The Falmer Press.

Goffman, E. (1961). *Asylums.* New York: Anchor Books.

Goodnow, J. J. (1988). Children, families, and communities: Ways of viewing their relationships to each other. In N. Bolger, A. Caspi, G. Downey, & M. Moorehouse (Eds.), *Persons in context: Developmental processes. Human development in cultural and historical contexts* (pp. 51–76). New York: Cambridge University Press.

Goodnow, J. J. (1994). Acceptable disagreement across generations. *New Directions for Child Development, 66,* 51–63.

Goodnow, J. J. (1997). Parenting and the transmission and internalization of values: From social-cultural perspectives to within-family analyses. In J. E. Grusec & L. Kuczynski (Eds.), *Parenting and children's internalization of values: A handbook of contemporary theory* (pp. 333–361). New York: Wiley.

Greene, A. L., & Boxer, A. M. (1986). Daughters and sons as young adults: Restructuring the ties that bind. In N. Datan, A. L. Greene, & H. W. Reese (Eds.), *Life-span developmental psychology: Intergenerational relations* (pp. 125–149). Hillsdale, NJ: Lawrence Erlbaum Associates.

Grolnick, W. S., Deci, E. L., & Ryan, R. M. (1997). Internationalization within the family: The self-determination theory perspective. In J. E. Grusec & L. Kuczynski (Eds.), *Parenting and children's internalization of values: A handbook of contemporary theory* (pp. 135–161). New York: Wiley.

Grusec, J. E. (1997). A history of research on parenting strategies and children's internalization of values. In J. E. Grusec, & L. Kuczynski (Eds.), *Parenting and children's internalization of values: A handbook of contemporary theory* (pp. 3–22). New York: Wiley.

Grusec, J. E., & Goodnow, J. J. (1994). Impact of parental discipline methods on the child's internalization of values: A reconceptualization of current points of view. *Developmental Psychology, 30,* 4–19.

Grusec, J. E., Goodnow, J. J., & Kuczynski, L. (2000). New directions in analyses of parenting contributions to children's acquisition of values. *Child Development, 71,* 205–211.

Grusec, J. E., & Kuczynski, L. (1980). Direction of effect in socialization: A comparison of parent vs. child's behavior as determinants of disciplinary technique. *Developmental Psychology, 16,* 1–9.

Harach, L., & Kuczynski, L. (1999, April). *Defining and constructing relationships from the perspective of parents.* Paper presented at the Society for Research in Child Development, Albuquerque, New Mexico.

Harkness, S., & Super, C. M. (1995). Culture and parenting. In M. H. Bornstein (Ed.), *Handbook of parenting, vol 2: Biology and ecology of parenting* (pp. 211–234). Hillside, NJ: Lawrence Erlbaum Associates.

Harris, J. R. (1995). Where is the child's environment? A group socialization theory of development. *Psychological Review, 102,* 458–489.

Hartup, W. W. (1978). Perspectives on child and family interaction: Past, present and future. In R. M. Lerner & G. B. Spanier (Eds.), *Child influences on marital and family interaction: A life-span perspective* (pp. 23–45). New York: Academic Press.

Hastings, P. D., & Grusec, J. E. (1998). Parenting goals as organizers of responses to parent-child disagreement. *Developmental Psychology, 34*(3), 465–479.

Hinde, R. A. (1979). *Toward understanding relationships.* London: Academic Press.

Hinde, R. A. (1997). *Relationships: A dialectical perspective.* Hove, UK: Psychology Press.

Hoffman, M. L. (1970). Moral development. In P. H. Mussen (Ed.), *Carmichael's manual of child psychology, 2,* (pp. 261–360). New York: Wiley.

Hoffman, M. L. (1975). Moral internalization, parental power, and the nature of parent-child interaction. *Developmental Psychology, 11,* 228–239.

Holden, G. W., & Hawk, K. H. (2003). Meta-parenting in the journey of child rearing: a cognitive mechanism for change. In L. Kuczynski (Ed.), *Handbook of dynamics in parent-child relations* (pp.189–210). Thousand Oaks, CA: Sage.

Holden, G. W., & Ritchie, K. L. (1988). Child rearing and the dialectics of parental intelligence. In J. Valsiner (Ed.), *Child development within culturally structured environments. Parental cognition and adult-child interaction* (pp. 30–59). Norwood, NY: Ablex.

Holden, G. W., Thompson, E. E., Zambarano, R. J., & Marshall, L. A. (1997). Child effects as a source of change in maternal attitudes toward corporal punishment. *Journal of Social and Personal Relationships, 14,* 481–490.

Hyman, I., Vu, N., & Beiser, M. (2000). Post-migration stresses among Southeast Asian refugee youth in Canada: A research note. *Journal of Comparative Family Studies, 31*(2), 281–293.

Inkeles, A. (1955). Social change and social character: The role of parental mediation. *Journal of Social Issues, 11,* 12–23.

Kâgitçibâsi, C. (1996). *Family and human development across cultures: A view from the other side.* Hillsdale, NJ: Lawrence Erlbaum Associates.

Kerr, M., & Stattin, H. (2000). What parents know, how they know it, and several forms of adolescent adjustment: Further support for a reinterpretation of monitoring. *Developmental Psychology, 36,* 366–380.

Killen, M., Lee-Kim, J., McGlothlin, H., & Stangor, C. (2002). How children and adolescents evaluate gender and racial exclusion. *Monographs of the Society for Research and Child Development, 67*(4), 1–29.

Knafo, A. (2003). Contexts, relationship quality, and family value socialization: The case of parent-school ideological fit in Israel. *Personal Relationships, 10,* 373–390.

Knafo, A., & Schwartz, S. H. (2001). Value socialization in families of Israeli-born and Soviet-born adolescents in Israel. *Journal of Cross-Cultural Psychology, 32* (2), 213–228.

Kochanska, G., & Aksan, N. (1995). Mother-child mutually positive affect, the quality of child compliance to requests and prohibitions, and maternal control as correlates of early internalization. *Child Development, 66*(1), 236–254.

Kohlberg, L. (1969). Stage and sequence: The cognitive-developmental approach to socialization. In D. A. Goslin (Ed.), *Handbook of socialization theory and research* (pp. 347–480). Chicago: Rand McNally.

Kohn, M. L. (1983). On the transmission of values in the family: A preliminary reformulation. *Research in Sociology of Education and Socialization, 4,* 1–12.

Kuczynski, L. (1984). Socialization goals and mother-child interaction: Strategies for long-term and short-term compliance. *Developmental Psychology, 20,* 1061–1073.

Kuczynski, L. (2003). Beyond bidirectionality: Bilateral conceptual frameworks for understanding dynamics in parent-child relations. In L. Kuczynski (Ed.), *Handbook of dynamics in parent-child relations* (pp. 1–24). Thousand Oaks, CA: Sage.

Kuczynski, L., & Grusec, J. E. (1997). Future directions for a theory of parental socialization. In J. E. Grusec, & L. Kuczynski (Eds.), *Parenting and the internalization of values: A handbook of contemporary theory* (pp. 398–413). New York: Wiley.

Kuczynski, L., Harach, L., & Bernardini, S. C. (1999). Psychology's child meets sociology's child: Agency, power and influence in parent-child relations. In C. Shehan (Ed.), *Through the eyes of the child: Revisioning children as active agents of family life* (pp. 21–52). Stamford, CT: JAI Press.

Kuczynski, L., & Hildebrandt, N. (1997). Models of conformity and resistance in socialization theory. In J. E. Grusec, & L. Kuczynski (eds.), *Parenting and the internalization of values: A handbook of contemporary theory* (pp. 227–256). New York: Wiley.

Kuczynski, L., & Kochanska, G. (1990). The development of children's noncompliance strategies from toddlerhood to age 5. *Developmental Psychology, 26,* 398–408.

Kuczynski, L., Marshall, S., & Schell, K. (1997). Value socialization in a bidirectional context. In J. E. Grusec, & L. Kuczynski (Eds.), *Parenting and the internalization of values: A handbook of contemporary theory* (pp. 23–50). New York: Wiley.

Lawrence, J., & Heinze, V. (1997). Everyone does it. But who's to blame: Adolescent constructions and reconstructions of shoplifting. In B. D. Cox & C. Lightfoot (Eds.), *Sociogenetic perspectives on internalization* (pp. 45–71). Mahwah, NJ: Lawrence Erlbaum Associates.

Lawrence, J. A., & Valsiner, J. (1993). Conceptual roots of internalization: From transmission to transformation. *Human Development, 36*(3), 150–167.

Lawrence, J. A., & Valsiner, J. (2003). Making personal sense. An account of basic internalization and externalization processes. *Theory and Psychology, 13*(6), 723–752.

Lepper, M. (1983). Social control processes, attributions of motivation, and the internalisation of social values. In E. T. Higgins, D. N. Ruble, & W. W. Hartup (Eds.), *Social cognition and social development: A sociological perspective* (pp. 294–330). Cambridge, UK: Cambridge University Press.

Lollis, S., & Kuczynski, L. (1997). Beyond one hand clapping: Seeing bidirectionality in parent-child relations. *Journal of Social and Personal Relationships, 14,* 441–461.

Lollis, S., Kuczynski, L., Navara, G. S., & Koguchi, Y. (2003) *Children's agency within compliance and non-compliance.* Poster presented at Society for Research in Child Development biennial meeting, Tampa, Florid.

Maccoby, E. E. (1992). The role of parents in the socialization of children: An historical overview. *Developmental Psychology, 28,* 1006–1017.

Maccoby, E. E., & Martin, J. A. (1983). Socialization in the context of the family: Parent–child interaction. In P. H. Mussen (Ed.) & E. M. Hetherington (Vol. Ed.), *Handbook of child psychology: Vol. 4. Socialization, personality, and social development* (4th ed., pp. 1–101). New York: Wiley.

Mannhiem, K. (1928/1932). *The problem of generations, Essays in the sociology of knowledge,* London: Routledge and Kegan Paul.

Matsumoto, D. (2001). Culture and emotion. In D. Matsumoto (Ed.), *The handbook of culture & psychology* (pp. 171–194). New York: Oxford University Press.

Mayall, B. (2001). Understanding childhoods: A London study. In L. Alanen & B. Mayall (Eds.), *Conceptualizing child-adult relations* (pp. 114–1280). London: Routledge/Farmer.

Mayall, B. (2002). *Towards a sociology for childhood: Thinking from children's lives.* Buckingham: Open University Press.

Nagel, J. (1994). Constructing ethnicity: Creating and recreating ethnic identity and culture. *Social Problems, 41,* 152–176.

Nauck, B. (2001). Social capital, intergenerational transmission and intercultural contact in immigrant families. *Journal of Comparative Family Studies. Special Issue: Immigrant and Ethnic Minority Families, 32*(4), 465–488.

Navara, G. S., & James, S. (2003). *Community and professional healers' perceptions and treatment of illness and culture bound disorders.* Paper presented at the Critical Multicultural Counseling conference in Toronto (OISE), Ontario, Canada.

Nucci, L., & Weber, E. K. (1995). Social interactions in the home and the development of young children's conceptions of the personal. *Child Development, 66,* 1438–1452.

Palkovitz, R., Marks, L. D., Appleby, D. W., & Holmes, E. K. (2003). Processes and products of intergenerational relationships. In L. Kuczynski (Ed.), *Handbook of dynamics in parent-child relations* (pp. 307–324) Thousand Oaks, CA: Sage.

Parke, R. D., & Buriel, R. (1998). Socialization in the family: Ethnic and ecological perspectives. In W. Damon (Series Ed.) & N. Eisenberg (Vol. Ed.), *Handbook of child psychology: Vol. 3. Social, emotional, and personality development* (5th ed., pp. 463–552). New York: Wiley.

Parke, R. D., Killian, C. M., Dennis, J., Flyr, M. L., McDowell, D. J., Simpkins, S., Kim, M., & Wild, M. (2003). Managing the external environment: the parent and child as active agents in the system. In L. Kuczynski (Ed.), *Handbook of dynamics in parent-child relations.* (pp. 247–270). Thousand Oaks, CA: Sage.

Parke, R. D., Ornstein, P. A., Rieser, J. J., & Zahn-Waxler, C. (1994). *A century of developmental psychology,* Washington, DC: American Psychological Association.

Patterson, G. R. (1997). Performance models for parenting: A social interactional perspective. In J. E. Grusec & L. Kuczynski (Eds.), *Parenting and the internalization of values: A handbook of contemporary theory* (pp. 193–226). New York: Wiley.

Peters, J. (1985). Adolescents as socialization agents to parents. *Adolescence, 20,* 921–931.

Phalet, K., & Schoenpflug, U. (2001). Intergenerational transmission of collectivism and achievement values in two acculturation contexts: The case of Turkish families in Germany and Turkish and Moroccan families in the Netherlands. *Journal of Cross-Cultural Psychology. Special Issue: Perspectives on Cultural Transmission, 32*(2), 186–201.

Phalet, K., & Schoenpflug, U. (2001). Intergenerational transmission in Turkish immigrant families: Parental collectivism, achievement values and gender differences. *Journal of Comparative Family Studies. Special Issue: Immigrant and Ethnic Minority Families, 32*(4), 489–504.

Phinney, J. S., Ong, A., & Madden, T. (2000). Cultural values and intergenerational value discrepancies in immigrant and non-immigrant families. *Child Development, 71*(2), 528–539.

Piaget, J. (1965). *The moral judgement of the child.* (Trans. M. Gabain.) New York: Free Press.

Pontecorvo, C., Fasulo, A., & Sterponi, L. (2001). Mutual apprentices: The making of parenthood and childhood in family dinner conversations. *Human Development, 44,* 340–361.

Punch, S. (2002). Research with children: The same or different from research with adults? *Childhood: A Global Journal of Child Research, 9*(3), 321–341.

Rheingold, H. L. (1969). The social and socializing infant. In D. A. Goslin (Ed.), *Handbook of socialization theory and research.* Chicago: Rand McNally.

Rumbaut, R. G., & Portes, A. (Eds.). (2001). *Ethnicities: Children of immigrants in America.* New York: Andrew W. Mellon Foundation.

Reynolds, P. (1991). *Dance civet cat: Child labour in the Zambezi Valley.* Athens: Ohio University Press.

Sam, D. L., & Virta, E. (2003). Intergenerational value discrepancies in immigrant and host-national families and their impact on psychological adaptation. *Journal of Adolescence, 26*(2), 213–231.

Sameroff, A. (1975). Transactional models in early social relations. *Human Development, 18*(1–2), 65–79.

Sapir, E. (1934). The emergence of the concept of personality in a study of cultures. *Journal of Social Psychology, 5,* 408–415.

Schonpflug, U. (2001). Decision-making influence in the family: A comparison of Turkish families in Germany and in Turkey. *Journal of Comparative Family Studies, 32*(2), 219–230.

Schumann, J. H. (1978). *The pidginisation process: A model for second language acquisition.* Rowley, MA: Newbury Press.

Schumann, J. H. (1986). Research on the acculturation model for second language acquisition. *Journal of Multilingual and Multicultural Development,7*(5), 379–392.

Schwartz, S. H. (1992). Universals in the content and structure of values: Theoretical advances and empirical tests in 20 countries. In M. P. Zanna (Ed.), *Advances in experimental social psychology* (Vol. 25, pp. 1–64). San Diego, CA: Academic Press.

Scott, J. C. (1990). *Domination and the arts of resistance.* New Haven, CT: Yale University Press.

Shweder, R. A., Mahapatra, M., & Miller, J. G. (1990). Culture and moral development. In J. W. Stigler, R. A. Shweder, & G. S. Herdt (Eds.), (1990). *Cultural psychology: Essays on comparative human development* (pp. 130–204). New York: Cambridge University Press.

Shweder, R. A., Much, N. C., Mahapatra, M., & Park, L. (1997). The "big three" of morality (autonomy, community, divinity) and the "big three" explanations of suffering. In H. M. Brandt & P. Rozin (Eds.), (1997). *Morality and health* (pp. 119–169). Florence, KY: Taylor & Frances/Routledge.

Smetana, J. (1997). Parenting and the development of social knowledge reconceptualized: A social domain analysis. In J. E. Grusec & L. Kuczynski (Eds.), *Parenting and the internalization of values: A handbook of contemporary theory* (pp. 162–192). New York: Wiley.

Smetana, J. (2005). Adolescent-parent conflict: resistance and subversion as developmental process. *Contrarian elements in moral development and moral education* (pp. 69–91). Mahwah, NJ: Lawrence Erlbaum Associates.

Strauss, C. (1992). Models and motives. In R. G. D'Andrade & C. Strauss (Eds.), *Human motives and cultural models* (pp. 1–20). New York: Cambridge University Press.

Ta, L., Kuczynski, L., Bernardini, S. C., & Harach, L. (1999, April). *Parents' perceptions of children's influence in the context of the parent-child relationship.* Paper presented at the Society for Research in Child Development, Albuquerque, New Mexico.

Talbani, A., & Hasanali, P. (2000). Adolescent females between tradition and modernity: Gender role socialization in south Asian immigrant culture. *Journal of Adolescence, 23*(5), 615–627.

Tesson, G. (1987). Socialization and parenting. In K. L. Anderson (Ed.), *Family matters* (pp. 87–111). Agincourt, Ontario: Methuen Publications.

Tong, V. M. (1996). Home language literacy and the acculturation of recent Chinese immigrant students. *The Bilingual Research Journal, 20*(3), 523–543.

Trommsdorff, G., & Kornadt, H. (2003). Parent-child relations in cross-cultural perspective. In L. Kuczynski (Ed.), *Handbook of dynamics in parent-child relations* (pp. 271–306). Thousand Oaks, CA: Sage.

Turiel, E. (1998). Moral development. In W. Damon (Ed.) & N. Eisenberg (Vol. Ed.), *Handbook of child psychology: Vol. 3, Social, emotional, and personality development* (5th ed., pp. 863–932). New York: Wiley.

Turiel, E. (2002). *The culture of morality.* Cambridge: Cambridge University Press.

Turiel, E., & Wainryb, C. (2000). Social life in cultures: Judgments, conflict, and subversion. *Child Development, 71,* 250–256.

Valsiner, J. (1988). Ontogeny of co-construction of culture within socially organized environmental settings. In J. Valsiner (Ed.), *Child development within culturally structured environments: Vol. 2, Social co-construction and environmental guidance in development* (pp. 283–297). Norwood, NJ: Ablex.

Valsiner, J. (2001). *Comparative study of human cultural development*. Madrid, Spain: Fundación Infancia y Aprendiaje.

Valsiner, J., Branco, A. U., & Dantas, C. M. (1997). Co-construction of human development: Heterogeneity within parental belief orientations. In J. E. Grusec & L. Kuczynski (Eds.), *Parenting and the internalization of values: A Handbook of contemporary theory* (pp. 227–256). New York: Wiley.

Vertovec, S., & Cohen, R. (1999). Introduction. In *Migration, diasporas and transnationalism* [The international Library of the Studies of Migration, Vol. 9]. Cheltenham, UK: Edward Elgar.

Vuchinich, S. (1987). Starting and stopping spontaneous family conflicts. *Journal of Marriage in the Family, 49,* 591–601.

Vygotsky, L. S. (1978). *Mind in society*. Cambridge, MA: Harvard University Press.

Wenar, C. (1982). On negativism. *Human Development, 25,* 1–23.

Wrong, D. H. (1961). The oversocialized conception of man in modern sociology. *American Sociological Review, 26,* 183–193.

Youniss, J. (1994). Rearing children for society. In J. G. Smetana (Ed.), *Beliefs about parenting: Origins and developmental implications* (pp. 37–50). San Francisco: Jossey-Bass.

V

SOCIAL INTERACTIONAL, SOCIOCULTURAL, AND COMPARATIVE APPROACHES

This section demonstrates the pervasiveness of morality in all aspects of social life, from early family interactions, to discourse, cultural exchanges, ideologies, and across primate species. The expansiveness of morality, and the ways in which research has delved into complex areas of social life is impressive and extensive. Judy Dunn, in Chapter 12, begins this section with a detailed analysis of the ways in which focusing on young children's interactions in their families provides a window into moral understanding. She draws on her well-known longitudinal studies of families in Pennsylvania, Cambridge, and London which includes extensive videotaped observations of naturalistic family interactions. Dunn's focus is on acquisition of, as well as on individual differences in, moral development. She describes the complex forms of family interactions that contribute to the acquisition of moral concepts. In Chapter 13, Mark Tappan makes an argument for examining moral discourse and integrating moral theory with a sociocultural perspective. He draws on his theoretical model to demonstrate the ways in which moral discourse reveals aspects of individual moral identity. He uses findings from Carol Gilligan and James Wertsch to illustrate what moral identity means to individuals from different perspectives and outlines a sociocultural viewpoint on morality and moral development.

Joan Miller moves the focus of this section to the level of culture, and in Chapter 14 reviews findings to demonstrate that morality is both universal and culturally specific. Her goal is to highlight the variability in moral outlooks, which she believes can and should be accommodated in a view of moral universalism. Her concern is that recognizing the cultural specificity of morality is often ignored in the moral relativism versus universalism debate, and in making her arguments, she draws on her work in India and the United States. Miller carefully compares and synthesizes two broad approaches—cultural psychology and cognitive–developmental approaches to morality—to demonstrate how each view contributes to a pluralistic view of morality and culture.

In Chapter 15, Douglas Fry, an anthropologist, describes research on reciprocity, which he views as the foundation of morality. Drawing on Darwin's theory of the reciprocity principle, Fry reports on the reciprocity of both good (justice) and bad (revenge) deeds carried out by individuals in a wide range of cultures. He describes anthropological work on the justice principle and conflict resolution. His fascinating and detailed observations of customs and rituals in a wide range of cultures provide numerous insights into how morality and reciprocity are intertwined in many aspects of social life. In Chapter 16, Peter Verbeek uses an evolutionary framework to describe comparative research on sociality. He draws on his work with Frans de Waal, and adopting Alan Fiske's theory of four essential aspects of social life (communal sharing, authority ranking, equality matching, and market pricing), along with Jonathan Haidt's social intuitionist model, Verbeek presents evidence for the origins of morality. His interdisciplinary model, using concepts from social psychology, developmental psychology, and primate biology, provides a rich data base for his case for a comparative approach to morality. Finally, in Chapter 17, Peter Kahn expands the parameters of moral interactions to include nature and the environment. His research has examined how individuals conceptualize their relationships with animals, plants, bodies of water, landscapes, and the earth. Kahn's novel research program includes findings with children and adults regarding their views about pollution, recycling, and living with nature and what it means from a moral viewpoint. Kahn's work extends morality to all aspects of social life. Thus, this section forcefully expands the realm of morality to include conceptualizations about interactions between and within families, cultures, and nonhuman primates, and between human and the natural world.

12

MORAL DEVELOPMENT IN EARLY CHILDHOOD AND SOCIAL INTERACTION IN THE FAMILY

JUDY DUNN

INSTITUTE OF PSYCHIATRY

Children face moral issues within their families from very early in their lives. The tensions between a child's own desires and needs, and issues of control, discipline, reciprocity, justice and rights, obligation, and the welfare of others are daily experienced and negotiated with other family members. Young children's parents and siblings talk every day to children and to each other about why people behave and feel the way they do; about what is allowed and what is not; about moral matters pertaining to welfare, fairness, and property rights; and about social rules that reflect the conventional precepts of the particular social system within which the child is growing up. And from their second year, children participate in (and indeed initiate) such conversations with increasing frequency (Bartsch & Wellman, 1995; Dunn, 1988; Tizard & Hughes, 2002). Some of these family discussions focus on relatively minor social rules, some are urgent matters of other people's welfare and rights; some are culture-wide, and some more local issues of practices within the family. Children even in their early years have views on the permissibility of actions, and provide justifications for their views, and they distinguish between different domains of morality and convention (Much & Shweder, 1978; Slomkowski & Killen, 1992; Smetana, 1989; Turiel, 2002).

There are powerful arguments for seeing the family as the medium through which children gradually understand and appreciate wider aspects of the culture, moral judgements, and moral sensibility (Hinde, 2002). There is also evidence that family experiences are related to the notable individual differences between children in their moral sensitivity and behavior. In this chapter, we consider family interaction and children's early moral development within the framework of two broad questions. First, does a focus on young children's interactions within their families provide a useful window on the nature of children's moral understanding and sensibility, and its normative development? Second, how are individual differences in children's family experiences related to differences in children's moral development? Before addressing these two broad questions, a comment on the various theoretical approaches to the relations between moral development and children's experiences within their families is in order.

Perspectives on Family Interaction and Children's Moral Development

In many different theoretical approaches to children's moral development, aspects of family interaction are viewed as important contributors to the developmental story. Although there are shared assumptions about the importance of family experiences, particularly in relation to the development of individual differences in moral development, there are also different emphases in the various accounts. Which features of family experience are emphasized depends on the theoretical perspective of the scholar, and especially on the aspect of moral development being investigated. Thus, some writers emphasize a sociocognitive perspective and view the development of social and emotional understanding as a key part of the development of moral reasoning and judgement, (e.g., Arsenio, chap. 21, this volume; Dunn, Brown, & Maguire, 1995; Killen & Nucci, 1995; Smetana & Braeges, 1990; Turiel, 2002). For these approaches, it is the evidence for social interaction in the family as an influence on the development of social understanding that is relevant—for instance, the research on how family discourse relates to the development of social and emotional understanding (e.g., Dunn, Brown, Slomkowski, et al., 1991; Laible & Thompson, 2002).

Other authors argue for the centrality of the development of the self, and the growth of conscience in moral development (e.g., Hinde, 2002; Kochanska, 1994); many of those concerned with the development of conscience have focused on family discipline and children's response to parent–child conflict as relevant aspects of family experiences. In contrast with this emphasis on parental disciplinary practices, it is the significance of parent–child relationships—rather than parenting—that others emphasize (e.g., Dunn, Hinde, Kochanska). Within this relationship framework, the significance of reciprocity within relationships has been emphasized, as well as the motivating power of relationships for the development of social understanding more broadly considered (e.g., Dunn, 1988). Other researchers whose chief focus is on prosocial development (e.g., Eisenberg & Fabes, 1998) focus on family experiences linked to children's caring behavior, which can include parenting practices, relationship quality, and family influences on understanding feelings.

The broad issue of how emotion and cognition are implicated in moral development has been a key theme in various theoretical accounts. Although much of the classical writing on moral development (especially moral reasoning) has emphasized cognitive processes (following Kohlberg [1984]), it is now recognized by many that emotional relationships with family members are central to the development of moral actions and understanding (e.g., Hinde, 2002; Hoffman, 2000; Kagan, 1984). Theorists have differed in the extent of their emphasis on emotions, and on the particular emotions seen as significant. Those who study prosocial development have stressed empathy, whereas Kagan and Hoffman have both also emphasized anxiety about disapproval or punishment, shame, and guilt; Kagan has also noted the self-satisfaction that comes from doing the right thing. Among the points of convergence between these various theoretical approaches to moral development, arguments for the significance of emotional as well as cognitive processes now stand out. Both the shared perspectives and the differences in theoretical approaches are considered in more detail in this chapter.

We begin with the first general issue: how a focus on children's family interactions can illuminate our understanding of children's moral development.

THE NATURE OF CHILDREN'S MORAL DEVELOPMENT: LESSONS FROM THE STUDY OF FAMILY INTERACTIONS

Key lessons concerning the nature of young children's moral understanding and the social processes implicated in its development have been learned from studies of children's interactions within their families. Some of these key principles are summarized next; we begin with the very early stages of moral sensibility.

Awareness of Other People's Feelings and the Idea of Harm to Others

The first point is that research on children within their familiar social worlds has documented the interest and growing understanding that children show in relation to other people's emotions during their infancy and toddlerhood (Bretherton, Fritz, Zahn-Waxler, & Ridgeway, 1986; Harris, 1994; Thompson, 1998). Understanding the feelings of others, it can be argued, forms a central core of moral sensitivity—the caring dimensions of moral development. Among the aspects of children's family interactions that reveal their growing understanding of others' psychological states and feelings, the following stand out. First, observations of empathic and prosocial behavior (see Carlo, chap. 20, this volume; Hastings & Zahn-Waxler, chap. 18, this volume; Thompson and Meyer, chap. 10, this volume) become increasingly frequent from early in the second year. Children attempt to alleviate the distress of others, and they show concern about other people being frightened or worried, well before they are able to articulate their understanding verbally (Dunn, 1988; Eisenberg & Fabes, 1998; Radke-Yarrow, Zahn-Waxler, & Chapman, 1983). Second, they attempt to alter others' psychological states, showing their grasp of how actions can affect others' emotional states, not only by comforting, but by teasing (deliberate attempts to annoy, disturb or amuse others), and exacerbating their distress, and by deception (Reddy, 1991). Third, as they become verbally articulate they discuss feeling states and other psychological states of both self and other with other family members, the causes of these inner states, and the connections between inner states and actions, with increasing frequency during the third year (Bartsch & Wellman, 1995; Harris, 1994).

Observations of children within their families, then, make clear not only that children are concerned about the welfare of others who are distressed, and show the beginnings of empathic responsiveness to another distress, but that they understand people can cause pain to others (Eisenberg & Fabes, 1998; Hoffman, 2000). It is not, in the second and third year, a wide or differentiated understanding of the notion of harm to others, but although limited, it is an essential foundation for sensitivity to moral issues that are related to the idea of harm to others, and others' welfare (Dunn, 1988).

Awareness of Adult Standards and Social Rules: The Idea of Responsibility

Observations of children within their families also highlight that they show increasing awareness of adult standards, and social rules—what is acceptable and unacceptable behavior—through the second and third year (Dunn, 1988). They both draw the attention of parents to forbidden acts (their own and those of others), and they make attempts to evade adult attention or to deceive adults increasingly during the second and third years. This interest in what is approved and what is not permitted within the family is one theme in a broader concern that children show in behavior or objects that deviate from normal or accepted standards—as Kagan (1981) demonstrated in his book *The Second Year*. Within the family, such deviations are a source of interest and amusement and frequently discussed with parent or sibling. The children's participation in these exchanges demonstrates not only their understanding of the contravention of the ordered relations that are acceptable (Douglas, 1966), their grasp of the shared nature of these standards, but also their understanding of how this knowledge of standards can be used in relationships—used, that is, as a source of shared humor, and as a useful strategy in conflict with other family members. Within the family, children are also beginning to understand the idea of responsibility, that individuals are accountable to others for their prohibited actions, such as causing harm to others or breaches of acceptable behavior. Their growing understanding of accountability during the third year is illustrated by their blaming of others (frequently siblings) and the denial of their own culpability (Dunn, 1988).

What the observations of children within their families show is that the bases of their excuses, justifications—and their jokes—include not only the idiosyncratic practices of a particular family, but some of the key principles of the wide culture outside the family—principles of possession, positive justice, excuses on grounds of incapacity or lack of intention. It appears that some of these principles are understood not in a highly context-specific way, but much more broadly. Children also differentiate between transgressions falling into moral and social conventional domains in the preschool years, an issue that we address in considering the emotions involved in family interaction over cultural breaches, although the early stages of this differentiation are not well documented: we do not know whether such differentiation begins during the second year, for instance.

Patterns of Moral Development

A third key lesson from research on children within their families is that moral development does not necessarily proceed smoothly, and that the same child can within one family relationship demonstrate empathetic behavior, understanding of moral transgressions, and efforts at reparation—and not show this sensibility in the context of another relationship. Moreover, the same child can offer different justifications for the permissibility of transgressions in the context of interactions with different family members. That is, whether children show moral sensibility in action, and how they attempt to justify breaches of cultural rules, depends on the particular relationship within which he or she is interacting, a point made by Hart and Killen (1995). This raises questions about what influences moral actions, moral reasoning, and views on permissibility, which need to be considered separately. In a study in London, we separately assessed the views of 4-year-olds on the permissibility of various social transgressions (name calling, taking a toy from a friend, and excluding a friend from play), and their justifications for their views (Dunn, Cutting, & Demetriou, 2000). The children's opinions on the permissibility of these actions toward their friends were not linked to their justifications in terms of their reflections on the welfare, feelings, or relationships of the victim or violator, and these two features of moral understanding had quite different correlates, as we consider in the section on individual differences. We argued that views on the permissibility of transgressions reflected responses to learned rules, and that justifications reflected the children's sensitivity to the feelings and relationships involved, and were linked to their understanding of feelings more broadly. In considering the development of these different aspects of moral sensitivity, studies of children within their close relationships with family members and friends highlight the central significance of emotion in the developmental accounts.

Emotion and Moral Development

Children's capacities for internalizing and acting morally depend on many basic aspects of cognitive and emotional development, including the use of language, the development of empathy (Hoffman, 2000) and sympathy, the growth of emotion regulation (Eisenberg et al., 1995), the development of understanding of mind together with the understanding that another person's mental and emotional state may differ from one's own (Astington, 1993), and comprehension of cause–effect relations (Dunn & Brown, 1993). Each of these abilities has its own developmental course, and each is important for a range of aspects of development as well as for the growth of moral understanding and behavior. Although most research into moral development has focused on the cognitive underpinnings of these capacities, research on moral development within the family has highlighted the part the role of emotional relationships and emotion understanding in these developments, especially in the early years. (To emphasize the role of emotional relationships in these broad developments is not to suggest that arguments for sociocognitive theories of moral development, in which inferences and abstractions provide the core basis of moral understanding, are inappropriate. Rather, it is to stress that such emotional relationships—at least in early childhood—play a key role in the development of the social understanding that is viewed as core in the sociocognitive theories of moral development).

Three points should be noted here. First, the feelings expressed by children, their mothers, and siblings during conflict over transgressions or matters of moral breaches, for instance, are often marked, and research indicates that children reason and justify their actions more frequently in those disputes in which earlier they had shown most distress and anger (Brown & Dunn, 1996; Dunn, 1988). Distress, anger, and amusement (the latter shown by children in many family disputes about transgressions) highlight the salience of disputes and transgression of rules for children, and these emotions may contribute to the learning that takes place in such confrontations. There may be special potential in the emotionally urgent interactions within the family. As we see in considering individual differences in moral development, family discussion of emotion in conflict is related to early conscience development and prosocial conceptions of relationships (Laible & Thompson, 2000).

The second point is that in some models of early moral development, such as those articulated by Hoffman (1983) and Kagan (1984, 1998), it is the emotions of guilt and fear experienced by children when they fail to live up to the standards set by their parents that are seen as key to their moral development. According to this view, children's understanding of what is moral behavior comes primarily from parental socialization techniques, and the internalization of these norms leads children to experience their moral behavior as self-produced. The children's emotions of guilt, fear, and anxiety during disciplinary encounters are viewed as central in motivating subsequent moral behavior. The emphasis on the connection between emotion, self-awareness, and standards in these models is illuminating. Family observations, however, suggest that a wider range of emotions beyond guilt and fear are important. The significance of positive experiences within parent–child relationships for moral development has recently been stressed (Hinde, 2002; Laible & Thompson, 2000; 2002).

In addition, observations within the family reveal the pleasure and excitement children experience in transgressing rules, in cooperating with siblings in such transgressions, in confronting and teasing—that is, in exerting power within the family. The affective dynamics of family relationships provide powerful motivation for children to understand moral issues and conventional rules—to get their way, to share amusement, or to get out of trouble. The tension between the self-interest that is so powerful a force in children's early years and their family relationships contributes to children's growing understanding of what is acceptable or unacceptable behavior (see for instance Dunn's [1988] emphasis on social relationships as the crucial context for growing understanding). The argument that children are motivated to understand the moral and social rules of their cultural world in part because they need to get things done in their close relationships parallels Bruner's (1983) argument that the motivation to use language is the need to get on with the demands of the culture. In contrast with the models of moral development articulated by Hoffman and Kagan, in this social relationships model the dynamics of children's relationships are central to the growth of children's social understanding, including their moral understanding.

The third point on emotion concerns the important distinction between the moral and conventional domains of cultural practices. It is now well established that children even in the preschool years distinguish between on the one hand moral issues (the welfare of others, fairness, positive justice) and on the other, breaches of conventional rules (see Smetana, chap. 5, this volume; Turiel, chap. 1, this volume). They judge the two types of cultural breach differently, viewing moral issues as not dependent on authority or determined by commonly accepted norms or agreements (Turiel, 2002); conventions are judged to be contingent on rules, authority and agreed-upon norms. Research also indicates that different emotions are associated with moral and conventional events (Arsenio, Gold, & Adams, chap. 21, this volume; Arsenio & Fleiss, 1996). In Arsenio's studies, for instance, when children were asked to consider scenarios involving conventional transgressions, they attributed neutral or somewhat negative emotions to the participants. But in breaches involving harm to others, children attributed very negative emotions to recipients of the transgression and observers (although some positive emotions to the perpetrators—the "happy victimizers").

However, observations within the family indicate that the neat distinction between these two domains may often be blurred during family interactions. Thus, incidents that involve breaches of conventional behavior (poor table manners or jumping with muddy boots on a settee, for instance) are frequently treated by parents as emotionally upsetting, acts that distress them personally. A breach of social convention can be, in the context of family life, treated as a breach of personal welfare. However, it should be noted that Smetana (1989) addressed this issue specifically and did not find evidence that this happened in her toddler sample. How parents treat breaches of acceptable behavior has a profound effect on the development of individual differences in moral sensibility and judgement, and moral behavior.

Self, Self-Interest, and Moral Development

Research on moral development within the family has also highlighted how the drive to understand others and the social world is closely linked to the nature of children's close relationships in the early years. The driving self-concern in the face of powerful others within the family characterizes many of children's interactions with their parents and siblings in the early years, as they develop a more elaborate sense of themselves and an increased capacity to plan. This self-interest invests the understanding of other people and of the social rules of the family world with especial salience. In their family relationships children are discovering how to get others' cooperation, how to understand others' feelings, how to provide comfort, and how to manage disputes. Their self-interest is an important motivating factor in their developing understanding. In addition, a sense of self-efficacy (quite separate from self-interest) can come in considerable part from solving these social problems.

This sense of self-efficacy does not necessarily imply opposition to the interests of others. Blum (1987) for instance argues for a notion of self and of identity formation in which concern for others, or for a community with which one closely identifies, is to reach out to someone or something that shares a part of one's own self. Self-interest should be distinguished here from being selfish and from lack of concern for others. Sympathetic concern for another family member does not conflict with an account of developing social understanding in which concern for self plays a major role. Part of being effective in the social world of the family entails monitoring the response of others to oneself, their approval or disapproval, pleasure, amusement, or displeasure. The interest and delight children show in this realm of what is allowed or prohibited is evident in their pretend play, their stories and jokes, and their questions within the family. Although young children cannot yet see themselves as others see them, and do not stand back as observers of self until middle childhood, they begin to show shame, embarrassment, and guilt during the second and third year, and must at some level be monitoring the response of other people to them.

And the pleasure and excitement that children show in transgressing rules, in teasing and confronting family members, must be acknowledged. Exerting power within their family world is a source of pleasure to them, as is cooperation and shared amusement. The general point is that children take an active part in the interactions within the family, and this participation plays a central part in their moral development and their sense of self. As Hinde notes: "Children don't just assimilate what they are told, they actively construct their moral code on the basis of their experience. And children are motivated by a desire for self-esteem as well as fear of punishment" (2002, p. 52). Disciplinary encounters are one important context in which messages about the proper way to live are given, but only one context among many. And as Hinde emphasized, acquiring morality "is not merely a matter of picking up a series of do's and don'ts: it is part of the development of the self in a particular cultural context" (Hinde, 2002, p. 48). Hinde views moral development as intrinsic to the development of self and identity, and stresses that morality develops as part of, or in parallel with the self-system (see Blasi, 1993).

Children as Family Members

The great majority of empirical studies of family socialization and moral development have focused on mother and child; although theories refer to *parents*, in practice the research on early moral development has been research on mothers (see, for instance, the studies referenced in the review by Thompson [1998]). However, children grow up as members of a family world, and from the first year onward, they show interest in what is happening between other family members. Surprisingly early, children begin to interupt the conversation between other family members, and develop the capacity to turn the topic of such conversation to their own interests (Dunn & Shatz, 1989). Conflict between parents has a major impact on children (Cummings & Davies, 1994; Grych & Fincham, 2001), and disputes between parent and sibling are also usually of much interest (Dunn & Munn, 1985). What is it that catches the attention of young children, and can an investigation of their responses to others' conflict add to our understanding of their moral awareness?

Consider the response of children as young as 18 and 24 months to conflict incidents between their mothers and older siblings. In research in Cambridge, we conducted unstructured naturalistic observations of families, in which family conversations were audiotaped, and a narrative record of interactions between children, their older siblings, and their mothers was kept. The focus was on how the target toddlers behaved when their mothers and older siblings interacted, recording their responses to conflict, jokes, and conversations between the other family members (Dunn, 1988; Dunn & Munn, 1985). When their mothers and siblings were in conflict, first, the topic of the dispute was important to the children: disputes about social rules and about aggression were rarely ignored (only 16% and 17% of incidents, respectively), whereas disputes about power between mother and sibling were ignored in 37% of cases. (These included conflicts in which the sibling repeatedly refused the mother's request; repeatedly, arbitrarily prohibited the mother's action; or persisted in requesting something the mother had refused). When the sibling behaved aggressively to the mother, the children were significantly more likely to censure or punish the sibling than when the dispute was over some conventional rule transgression (here, the children usually laughed or imitated the sibling).

The salience of the disputes to the children differed dramatically by topic; the emotion of the antagonists was also important. In incidents in which the sibling or the mother was angry or upset, children were most likely to watch or to attempt to support one or other antagonist, and relatively unlikely to ignore the interaction between mother and sibling. The children rarely laughed in such incidents. In contrast, in conflict incidents in which their older sibling laughed, the children also laughed or imitated the sibling's action. When the antagonists were emotionally neutral, the children were much more likely to ignore or simply watch. Thus, children of these ages were responsive both to the emotion and the topic of dispute between other family members; in fact, these were likely to be linked. What the children witnessed in such incidents were events in which two important features were combined: a transgression of a rule was explicitly discussed, and a display of emotion was given by people with whom the children had close and complex relationships. Their responses illustrate how already in their second year they were active participants in the daily family dramas.

FAMILY PROCESSES AND INDIVIDUAL DIFFERENCES IN MORAL DEVELOPMENT

Parent–Child Relationships

As noted, in theoretical accounts of the internalization of conscience, parental socialization has been given major prominence. Parental strategies of psychologically oriented discipline coupled with parental warmth and open expression of emotions have been thought to foster the development of children's internalized guilt feelings, and harsh and punitive disciplinary methods interfere with these developments (Grusec & Goodnow, 1994a, 1994b). Until relatively recently, much of the evidence on parental socialization and moral development upon which these ideas were based was retrospective, as noted by Kochanska (1991) in one of the first prospective studies. Since her pioneering study, much recent research has explored the significance of parent–child relationships for later moral development, and this has highlighted a number of issues that deserve mention.

Reciprocal Relationships. The first of these concerns the importance of recognizing the reciprocal nature of parent–child relationships, rather than viewing parental socialization as a one-way, direct influence on children's moral development, as in early work on child-rearing (e.g., Sears, Maccoby, & Levin, 1957). Children interpret, evaluate, and internalize aspects of their parents' behavior, and in turn they influence parental behavior (Grusec, chap. 9, this volume; Grusec & Goodnow, 1994a, 1994b; Kuczynski & Navara, chap. 11, this volume). And the quality of the relationship between child and parent affects both the extent and the direction of influence (Hinde, 2002; Laible & Thompson, 2000). Children tend to emulate and comply with those whom they care about.

Individual Characteristics of Children. The individual characteristics of children (e.g., temperamental characteristics, understanding of emotions and mental states, verbal ability, ability to regulate emotions) contribute to the quality of the parent–child relation-ships, and play a key role in the significance of parent–child relations for moral devel-opment. This is clearly demonstrated in Kochanska's prospective studies of mother–child relationships and later moral development (Clark, Kochanska, & Ready, 2000; Kochanska, 1991; Kochanska, Gross, Lin, & Nichols, 2002; Kochanska & Murray, 2000; Kochanska, Tjebes, & Forman, 1998; and see Thompson and Meyer, chap. 10, this volume), and in recent studies of the links between children's social understanding and their later moral understanding.

Thus, Kochanska showed that maternal socialization techniques for obtaining compli-ance during the preschool period that deemphasized the use of power were associated with the development of children's internalized conscience as 8-year-olds (Kochanska, 1991). However, this was only true for those children who were relatively anxious in terms of temperament. In a later study, the findings highlighted the importance of mutually respon-sive orientation between mother and child at toddler and preschool ages for conscience development at school age, with moral development assessed in terms of observations of moral behavior alone and in peer contexts and moral cognitions (Kochanska & Murray, 2000). Notably, the mutually responsive mother–child interaction—shared cooperation and shared positive affect—at the toddler stage predicted children's future conscience, even after controlling for the developmental continuity of the conscience measure, con-firming the value of the relationship approach to long-term moral outcome.

The idea that children's emerging view of self, in terms of moral dimensions, plays a key role in moral development, which is stressed in various theoretical models (e.g., Hinde, 2002; Kagan, 1984), also receives support in this program of research. In a longitudinal study of compliance and opposition in children from 14 to 56 months, Kochanska (2002) pursued the idea that children's committed compliance with their mothers promoted moral internalization, whereas their opposition interfered with such developments in the moral self, which in turn affected moral conduct. Moral self was assessed by a technique in which children were engaged in conversation with two large puppets, who described themselves in terms of items reflecting nine moral dimensions (confession, apology, reparation, sen-sitivity to violation of standards, internalized conduct, empathy, concern about others' wrong-doing, guilt, and concern about good feeling with parents). For each item, one puppet described itself as being at the low end of the scale, and the other puppet described itself as at the high end. The child was asked to point to the puppet that was "more like me." Internalization was assessed in terms of the child's behavior when left alone with prohibited toys.

Some support was found for this mediational model for boys (following Baron & Kenny's [1986] model). It was also reported that children who were less fearful in tem-perament, and whose mothers relied on more power-assertive discipline, displayed less guilt, whereas guilt related positively to the development of moral self at 56 months, and to less violation of conduct rules. The argument was that fearful temperament led to guilt proneness, and via this guilt to fewer violations of rules.

Management of Conflict in Parent–Child Relationships. Other research has provided further evidence that how mothers deal with control and disputes with their children as toddlers and 2-year-olds is related to children's responses to moral transgressions at school age. In a longitudinal study in Pennsylvania, children were observed at home with their mothers and siblings with hour-long naturalistic observations (Dunn, Brown, & Maguire, 1995) and then their moral orientation and emotion understanding assessed as kindergartners and first graders (Dunn, 1995). The children whose mothers had dealt with conflict, when the children were 33 months, by reasoned argument that took account of the children's position, at kindergarten and first grade responded differently to hypothetical moral transgressions than children whose mothers had not used such reasoned argument. Specifically, the children whose mothers had employed reasoned argument showed more mature moral orientation and more concern with matters of reparation to the victim of transgressions than the other children.

Parallel findings were reported by Laible and Thompson (2002), who showed that constructive maternal behavior in conflict with children at 30 months predicted sociomoral competence and socioemotional understanding at age 3. The strategies that mothers used in conflict and resolution of conflict were the strongest predictors of the children's moral development. For instance, in conflict situations within the laboratory that tended to focus on moral issues, mothers who more frequently discussed emotion had children who scored higher on behavioral internalization in a resistance to temptation task. (For this task, the children were left alone in a laboratory room, having been told by their mothers not to touch some attractive toys; their behavior when alone was videotaped, and coded in terms of behaviors related to touching and playing with the forbidden toys, or self-correcting). The authors concluded that emotion-laden discourse during conflict may have consequences for children's early conscience development because it fosters the development of moral emotions such as empathy and guilt. Although the links between children's sociomoral development and mothers' reasoning and explanation in disciplinary encounters has been reported previously (e.g., Hart, Ladd, & Burleson, 1990; Zahn-Waxler, Radke-Yarrow, & King, 1979), Laible and Thompson (2000, 2002) emphasize that their research suggests that the benefits of maternal explanations to children in the course of disputes transcend disciplinary conflicts, to include the very wide range of issues over which parents and children argue—from factual issues, explanations of people's behavior, social rules, to serious matters of aggression and personal harm (see also Tizard & Hughes [2002] for evidence on the range of issues that 4-year-olds discuss with their mothers).

Discourse About Emotions

Evidence has accumulated from a range of studies that children's participation in family conversations about emotions plays a central in the development of individual differences in emotional understanding (Brown & Dunn, 1996; Denham & Auerbach, 1995; Dunn, Brown, & Beardsall, 1991; Dunn, Brown, Slomkowski, Tesla, & Youngblade, 1991; Howe, 1991; Laible & Thompson, 1998, 2000; Meins et al., 2002; Thompson, 1998). The notion that such emotional understanding is in turn linked to the development of empathy and early conscience development is supported by, for example, Laible and Thompson's (2000) study of 4-year-olds, in which mothers and children conversed about real-life incidents of good and bad behavior, and children's conscience development was assessed with a resistance to temptation situation, and with maternal questionnaires. The mothers who made frequent references to feelings and moral evaluatives had children who showed more behavioral internalization and who were more likely to express guilt after wrong-doing.

Note that here the outcome measure was one of moral behavior and guilt; other research on discourse about feelings has focused on links with moral judgements reflected in response to hypothetical scenarios (e.g., Dunn et al., 1995). It appears from these studies that both moral behavior and moral judgments were linked to maternal discourse measures.

Three important further points were made in Laible and Thompson's (2000) study. First, maternal references to the material consequences of the child's actions, or to social or family rules were unrelated to any dimensions of the children's conscience development, indicating that it was the emotion talk between mother and child that was of key importance for moral development. Second, there was an interaction between the maternal reference to feelings and the child–parent attachment quality, in relation to the development of internalization. For children who were insecurely attached to their mothers or whose mother–child relationships were low in shared positive emotions, higher frequencies of emotion-laden discourse were particularly strongly related to early conscience growth. For those whose relationships with their mothers were moderately secure, and those with average amounts of shared positive feelings, higher levels of maternal references to feelings and moral evaluatives were linked to higher levels of children's internalization. But for the children who were highly secure in their attachments to their mothers, and high in the shared positive feelings, maternal references to feelings and evaluative comments were not associated with higher levels of internalization. It appeared that having a mother who freely discusses feelings and values helped in the early growth of conscience, particularly for those children who because of insecure attachment might otherwise have problems in sharing feelings with her.

Third, the study highlighted the complex nature of early conscience development, which involves the acquisition of different components some of which are related (committed compliance and behavioral internalization) and some of which are not (committed compliance and guilt). It appears that conscience should not be considered a global trait, but a combination of separate skills, with different developmental antecedents. But the general point that a warm, supportive mother–child relationship and early discourse about feelings, values, and behavior foster the early development of conscience appears well established.

Evidence From Research on Disruptive Children

The links between warmth in parent-child relationships, discourse about emotions, children's developing moral awareness and their emotional regulation, and responsiveness have also been explored in research on disruptive children (e.g., Eisenberg et al., 2001; Hughes & Dunn, 2000). Disruptive children have long been thought to show a lack of empathic attitudes to moral dilemmas, but different theoretical accounts attribute the processes underlying this to quite different problems, including general problems in verbal reasoning, specific delays in social understanding, reduced emotional regulation and responsiveness, and negative parental socialization patterns (Hughes & Dunn, 2000).

Hughes and colleagues studied hard-to-manage children's moral behavior, social interactions, and reflective awareness at 4 and then 6 years (with a community rather than a clinic sample), and found that the disruptive children showed early and multifaceted problems in sociomoral reasoning, some general problems in language and social understanding, and associated relative lack of warmth and increased criticism in parent–child relations. Children who showed high levels of anger and distress during observations were less likely to give empathetic justifications in relation to moral transgressions in a story format, and in general the study gave support for the idea that emotional regulation plays a key role in the development of moral behavior. Notably, these restless, inattentive children were especially likely to engage in fantasy play involving pain and violence to others, during videotaped observations of the children playing alone with a friend—whereas other 4-year-olds engaged in pretence involving nurturing, domestic themes—and this measure of their preoccupation with violence made a significant unique contribution to the individual differences in their later moral understanding (Dunn & Hughes, 2001).

Parental Education and Social Background

Maternal education and social background have also been linked to children's early moral development (Dunn, Cutting, & Demetriou, 2000). It was noted earlier that an important distinction needs to be made between children's views on the permissibility of transgressions, and how they justify such views. Although it might be considered mature for a young child to consider the act of taking a toy from another child as a transgression, a child might also say that it is permissible for a friend to take a toy from him because they like each other, and the friend knows that he does not mind. This is a relatively sophisticated rationale for viewing the act as permissible. A judgment that an act is not permissible may in any case be simply a learned convention. As such, children's justifications for their views on transgressions may offer a more illuminating window on children's moral understanding than their accounts of what is permissible, which may simply reflect learned conventions.

The significance of family experiences and backgrounds were found in two studies to be different for children's views on permissibility and for their sophistication in justifying their views. In both studies, children from families with more highly educated parents and those with professional or managerial occupations were more likely to judge transgressions as not permissible (Dunn et al., 2000; Hughes & Dunn, 2000). Such connections could reflect family differences in expectations about and discussion of moral matters, differences in orientation to what is sanctioned or permitted, or in the management of control and discipline. Many of these aspects of family interaction are known to differ with family background (see Hoff-Ginsberg & Tardif [1995] for a review); the proximal processes implicated in links with differences in moral understanding are at present a matter for speculation (see Vinden, 1997).

It was, however, differences in children's understanding of inner states, rather than their social/educational background, that was correlated with the moral orientation reflected in their justifications. The children who offered justifications for their views on transgressions in terms of the welfare or interpersonal relations of the people involved were those who had shown more understanding of emotions and inner states. Temperamental makeup was also important, although in this study, not the dimension of anxiety highlighted in Kochanska's research: rather, those who were rated high on negative emotionality (easily angered or distressed) were less likely to offer interpersonal reasons for their moral views than the other children, whereas highly sociable children were more likely to do so.

Sibling Relationships and Social Processes in Moral Understanding

The attention of researchers to family influence on moral development has been almost exclusively on mothers—their disciplinary strategies, their handling of conflict, their socialization practices, and their discourse about emotions. Yet other family members—fathers, siblings, grandparents, cousins—may well contribute to the experiences affecting children's moral development. (For findings on fathers' discourse about emotions see Fivush, Brotman, Bucknev, & Goodman, 2000; Jenkins, Turrell, Kogushi, Lollis, & Ross, 2003; for findings on fathers' warmth and children's empathy-related responding, see Zhou et al.,

2002). The links between moral behavior and sibling relationships are of particular interest, as they provide support for Piaget's (1932/1965) original argument that children's cooperative experiences and disputes with other children have particular significance for the development of moral reasoning, in which relations of equality were seen as needed for children to construct concepts of fairness.

Links between the quality of sibling relationships and children's moral development have been demonstrated in research in the U.S. Canada, and the U.K. In a longitudinal study in Pennsylvania, for example, children were observed at home with their siblings as preschoolers, and then their moral orientation and emotion understanding as kindergartners and first graders was assessed (Dunn et al., 1995). The findings showed that for children of around 6 years, a wider range of earlier social processes and individual characteristics than maternal discipline and socialization practices were implicated in their moral conceptions, as assessed on their responses to stories about transgressions. Important was not only their mothers' manner of dealing with control and disputes when they were 2 years of age, but the children's understanding of emotions as 40-month-olds, their experiences of positive relationships with their older siblings, and their verbal ability. Those whose siblings had been particularly friendly with them during the observations when the children were 2-years-old were more likely to describe the transgressors in the scenarios as guilty or bad, and to show more mature moral orientation than children whose siblings had not been so friendly. The sibling relationship variables contributed to the moral understanding independently of the other variables.

With such correlational data, causal inferences about the links between the children's experiences with their mothers and siblings, and their later moral sensibility, or about the direction of effects, cannot be drawn. The issue of what processes underlie the connections over time needs further study. But because the children were not yet 3 years of age when the family observations were conducted, it appears unlikely that differences in the children's moral orientation at that age elicited differences in the behavior of other family members. Yet it is quite likely that other differences in the children's social and emotional behavior contributed both to their siblings' friendly behavior and their mothers' control strategies. A 2-year-old who is relatively mature in emotional understanding is likely to be a more rewarding and satisfying companion in play for an older sibling, who is in turn especially friendly and supportive during the early childhood years—and this friendliness itself may contribute to the child's propensity to be sensitive to a victim. Other social processes may well be implicated, and merit study: Are the older siblings who are especially friendly also modeling sensitive moral actions? Or are children who are close and affectionate with their siblings motivated to understand their feelings, and develop a more other-oriented perspective than children whose sibling relationship is more hostile or rivalrous? The general point here is that the children's own behavior and sensitivity may well contribute to both their mothers' and their siblings' behavior.

The possible significance for moral development of another social process key to positive relationships between siblings—namely, shared imaginative play—is suggested by research on close friendships in early childhood. Three longitudinal studies of young friends (one in the U.S., two in the U.K.) showed that children with particularly close, intimate friendships were more likely to give interpersonally oriented justifications concerning moral issues (Dunn et al., 1995; Dunn et al., 2000; Hughes & Dunn, 2000). Specifically, the U.K. studies highlighted the links between the children's shared imaginative play in the preschool years and their moral orientation years later. Again, the direction of effects was not clear. It could be that the quality of the friends' interactions contributed to the development of moral sensibility, or that the friendship deepened in intimacy if the children were sensitive to the moral concerns of their friends. What is notable is that shared pretend play that characterizes both close friendships and close sibling relationships (Brown, Donelan-McCall, & Dunn, 1996; Dunn, 1999; Dunn & Cutting, 1999; Gottman, 1983, 1986; Howes, 1996), and that such shared pretend has been highlighted as significant in the development of mindreading in a number of different studies (Astington & Jenkins, 1995; Howe, Rinaldi, Jennings, & Petrakos, 2002; Youngblade & Dunn, 1995).

What are the proximal processes implicated in the significance of such shared pretend for moral development? Among the processes that might be key are the children's exploration of possible social worlds, and possible transgressions and their sequelae, the coconstruction of dramatic narratives involving moral issues, the exploration of feelings that takes place within joint pretend play, or the discourse about inner states, notably high during joint pretend play (Brown et al., 1996; Hughes & Dunn, 1997), or indeed all of these processes. Discourse about inner states is relatively frequent between siblings—more frequent than between child and parent (Brown et al., 1996)—and has consistently been found to relate to later social understanding. Moreover, 4-year-old children with an older sibling have been reported to be exposed to and to use more mental state talk than those without older siblings (Jenkins et al., 2003).

Cultural Differences

The overwhelming majority of studies of family interaction and young children's moral development have been conducted within Europe or North America. But family interactions, moral codes, and parental practices differ widely between cultures (see Miller, chap. 14, this volume; Turiel, chap. 1, this volume; Wainryb, chap. 8, this volume, for detailed consideration). Such detailed discussion of cultural differences is beyond the scope of this chapter. As just one example, consider the differences in family values revealed in a comparison of Hindu families in India and in U.S. families (Miller & Bersoff, 1995). In the Indian families, there was a stress on the importance of personal desires channeled toward the good of the family as a whole, whereas the U.S. families gave a high priority to communicating about feelings and to personal freedom. The Indian families tended to treat interpersonal issues as socially enforceable moral duties; in contrast, for the families in the U.S. sample, close relationships between people were considered less as moral matters.

In terms of the early development of children considered here, two points deserve emphasis. First, the general point that children show curiosity and interest in the rules and practices of their particular culture very early is supported by studies of children in widely differing cultures; this is not particular to one culture. The Samoan children studied by Ochs (1987) displayed skills of appropriately switching the speech register in which they addressed familiar and less familiar others, before they were $2\frac{1}{2}$ years old. Mongolian children understand by their second year that they must sit only in certain sections of the family tent (Humphrey, personal communication). By 20 months, a Solomon Islander greets unfamiliar visitors with the gestures of hospitality and courtesy that are so important in his culture (Watson-Gegeo & Gegeo, 1987); young Solomon Islanders know that sibling caregivers can be disobeyed and exploited in some circumstances but not in others. The particulars vary, but common to all children in families is the importance of knowing what is allowed or disapproved, and how others will respond to their actions.

The second point is that the different cultural messages to children are likely to be mediated within the family by those aspects of family interaction described here for children in Europe and North America—by talk, emotional messages, the examples of interaction between other family members, as well as direct instruction (see for instance the comparison of moral messages reaching 3-year-olds in American and English families; Dunn & Brown, 1991). Theories that focus on details of moral reasoning predict cultural differences, but given the similarity in children's emotional interests in families everywhere, common features in children's concern for the feelings, goals, and responses of those who share their family world are to be expected (Dunn, 1988).

Genetics

Studies of links between family relationships and experiences and children's moral development rarely are conducted within a genetically sensitive framework. This is a serious limitation: If a style of parental behavior is associated with later individual differences in children's moral development, the possibility that this reflects a genetic link cannot be examined. Yet several lines of evidence suggest that this is important to pursue. First, the early appearance and ubiquity of prosocial propensities is, as Hinde (2002) points out, in harmony with the view that they are in part derived from the child's biological heritage. (See de Waal [1996] for evidence of chimpanzee sharing, sympathy, and third-party intervention in conflicts, and behavior conducive to reconciliation after conflicts. As Hinde [2002] notes, chimpanzees are related to our evolutionary ancestors, and the capacity to show such behaviour may have provided some of the building blocks for human moral behavior, but this is not in itself evidence that chimpanzees have anything comparable to a human moral sense).

Second, more direct evidence of the contribution of genetics to individual differences in moral development comes from twin studies (in which monozygotic twins who are identical genetically are compared with dizygotic twins who are 50% similar genetically, as are full siblings). These studies indicate that a considerable proportion of the variance in prosocial behavior and in empathy is accounted for by genetic factors, with monozygotic twins being more similar in their moral development than dizygotic twins (Eisenberg & Fabes, 1998; Zahn-Waxler, Robinson, & Emde, 1992). There is also evidence from twin research for a genetic contribution to individual differences in children's mindreading and emotional capacities (Ronald, Happé, Hughes, & Plomin, submitted). Parallel evidence for genetic contributions to the variance in psychopathic behavior is also accumulating (Viding, Blair, Moffitt, & Plomin, in press). These findings should be borne in mind when we attempt to understand the mechanisms underlying associations between family relationships and moral understanding. The evidence for genetics does not, of course, imply that family experiences are unimportant, but it demonstrates that heritability is part of the family story that should be included in research if we are to make progress in understanding moral development. Readers interested in this huge and rapidly growing field are referred to Plomin and McGuffin (2003).

SUMMARY AND FUTURE DIRECTIONS

The study of children in their families illuminates the early development of children's awareness of others' emotions, their empathy and concern, their growing understanding of the nature of harm to others, and their increasing grasp of standards and social rules. Children understand in their preschool years how knowledge of moral and conventional issues, of accountability and responsibility, can be used in relationships as a source of shared humor and of conflict strategies. The significance of close relationships both in the normative development of moral understanding and behavior, and in the growth of individual differences is clear. Relationships with others, and particularly parents, play a key role in both normative and individual differences in moral understanding. Both cognitive and affective processes are implicated in these developments. And in everyday life, reasoning and judgment about moral issues are tailored to particular relationships, and may well differ across relationship contexts (Hart & Killen, 1995).

In this chapter, we have considered the links between family relationships and moral development in early childhood. The question of what the role of the family in moral development later in childhood and adolescence may be is an intriguing one. Of the themes discussed in this chapter in relation to early childhood, the possibility that emotion and emotional relationships lessen in importance for moral development after early childhood has been raised (Hinde, 2002); this is just one of several themes on which we lack developmental studies that span early to later childhood. Parental authority on issues of both moral and conventional issues is evident in middle childhood, and it has been argued that in adolescence, questioning and conflict between adolescent and parent is more likely to be over conventional than moral issues.

The issue of which social processes are implicated in the links between family experiences/relationships and moral development needs more research attention: the significance of participation in discourse about moral and conventional issues is clear, but we need more investigation of the role of affective experiences.

In terms of the development of individual differences in moral development, the focus on mothers needs to be broadened to include systematic information on fathers and siblings, key members of children's family worlds.

The significance of moral awareness for children growing up at risk for disruptive behavior also deserves further attention; more generally, the relation of assessments of moral understanding to children's actions when faced with the moral dilemmas of their daily lives merits systematic attention especially within a longitudinal, developmental framework.

Finally, cross-cultural research that moves beyond moral reasoning to document children's moral actions and interactions within their everyday lives with family and friends is needed, as is research within a genetically sensitive framework.

REFERENCES

Arsenio, W., & Fleiss, K. (1996). Typical and behaviourally disruptive children's understanding of the emotional consequences of socio-moral events. *British Journal of Developmental Psychology, 14,* 173–186.

Arsenio, W. F. (1988). Children's conceptions of the situational affective consequences of sociomoral events. *Child Development, 59,* 1611–1622.

Astington, J. W. (1993). *The child's discovery of the mind.* Cambridge, MA: Harvard University Press.

Astington, J. W., & Jenkins, J. M. (1995). Theory of mind development and social understanding. *Cognition and Emotion, 9,* 151–165.

Baron, R. M., & Kenny, D. A. (1986). The moderator-mediator variable distinction in social psychological research: Conceptual, strategic, and statistical considerations. *Journal of Personality and social Psychology, 51,* 1173–1182.

Bartsch, K., & Wellman, H. M. (1995). *Children talk about the mind.* Oxford: Oxford University Press.

Blum, L. (1987). Particularity and responsiveness. In J. Kagan & S. Lamb (Eds.), *The emergence of morality in young children* (pp. 306–337). Chicago: University of Chicago Press.

Blasi, A. (1993). The development of identity: Some implications for moral functioning. In G. G. Noam & T. E. Wren (Eds.), *The moral self* (pp. 99–122). Cambridge, MA: MIT Press.

Bretherton, I., Fritz, J., Zahn-Waxler, C., & Ridgeway, D. (1986). Learning to talk about emotions: A functionalist perspective. *Child Development, 57,* 529–548.

Brown, J. R., Donelan-McCall, N., & Dunn, J. (1996). Why talk about mental states? The significance of children's conversations with friends, siblings, and mothers. *Child Development, 67,* 836–849.

Brown, J. R., & Dunn, J. (1996). Continuities in emotion understanding from 3-6 yrs. *Child Development, 67,* 789–802.

Bruner, J. (1983). *Child's talk.* Oxford: Oxford University Press.

Clark, L. A., Kochanska, G., & Ready, R. (2000). Mothers' personality and its interaction with child temperament as predictors of parenting behavior. *Journal of Personality and Social Psychology, 79,* 274–285.

Cummings, E. M., & Davies, P. (1994). *Children and marital conflict: The impact of family dispute and resolution.* New York: Guilford Press.

de Waal, F. (1996). *Goodnatured.* Cambridge, MA: Harvard University Press.

Denham, S., & Auerbach, S. (1995). Mother-child dialogue about emotions and preschoolers' emotional competence. *Genetic, Social and General Psychology Monographs, 121,* 313–337.

Douglas, M. (1966). *Purity and danger: An analysis of the concepts of taboo.* New York: Praeger.

Dunn, J. (1988). *The beginnings of social understanding.* Cambridge, MA: Harvard University Press.

Dunn, J. (1995). Children as psychologists: The later correlates of individual difference in understanding of emotions and other minds. *Cognition and Emotion, 9,* 187–201.

Dunn, J. (1999). Siblings, friends, and the development of social understanding. In W. A. Collins & B. Laursen (Eds.), *Relationships as developmental contexts: The Minnesota Symposia on Child Psychology* (Vol. 30, pp. 263–279). Mahwah, NJ: Lawrence Erlbaum Associates.

Dunn, J., & Brown, J. (1991). Becoming American or English? Talking about the social world in England and the United States. In M. Bornstein (Ed.), *Cross-cultural approaches to parenting* (pp. 155–172). Hillsdale, NJ: Lawrence Erlbaum Associates.

Dunn, J., Brown, J., & Beardsall, L. (1991). Family talk about feeling states and children's later understanding of others' emotions. *Developmental Psychology, 27,* 448–455.

Dunn, J., Brown, J., Slomkowski, C., Tesla, C., & Youngblade, L. (1991). Young children's understanding of other people's feelings and beliefs: Individual differences and their antecedents. *Child Development, 62,* 1352–1366.

Dunn, J., & Brown, J. R. (1993). Early conversations about causality: Content, pragmatics and developmental change. *British Journal of Developmental Psychology, 11,* 107–123.

Dunn, J., Brown, J. R., & Maguire, M. (1995). The development of children's moral sensibility: Individual differences and emotion understanding. *Developmental Psychology, 31,* 649–659.

Dunn, J., & Cutting, A. (1999). Understanding others, and individual differences in friendship interactions in young children. *Social Development, 8,* 201–219.

Dunn, J., Cutting, A., & Demetriou, H. (2000). Moral sensibility, understanding other, and children's friendship interactions in the preschool period. *British Journal of Developmental Psychology, 18,* 159–178.

Dunn, J., & Hughes, C. (2001). "I got some swords and you're dead!": Violent fantasy, antisocial behavior, friendship and moral sensibility in young children. *Child Development, 72,* 491–505.

Dunn, J., & Munn, P. (1985). Becoming a family member: Family conflict and the development of social understanding in the second year. *Child Development, 56,* 764–774.

Dunn, J., & Shatz, M. (1989). Becoming a conversationalist despite (or because of) having an older sibling. *Child Development, 60,* 399–410.

Eisenberg, N., & Fabes, R. (1998). Prosocial development. In W. Damon (Ed.), *Handbook of child psychology* (Vol. 3, pp. 701–778). New York: Wiley.

Eisenberg, N., Fabes, R. A., Murphy, M., Maszk, P., Smith, M., & Karbon, M. (1995). The role of emotionality and regulation in children's social functioning: A longitudinal study. *Child Development, 66,* 1239–1261.

Eisenberg, N., Loyosa, S., Fabes, R. A., Guthrie, I. K., Reiser, M., Murphy, B. C., Shepard, S., Poulin, R., & Padgett, S. J. (2001). Parental socialization of children's dysregulated expression of emotion and externalizing problems. *Journal of Family Psychology, 15,* 183–205.

Fivush, R., Brotman, M. A., Bucknev, J. P., & Goodman, S. H. (2000). Gender differences in parent-child emotion narratives. *Sex Roles, 42,* 233–253.

Gottman, J. M. (1983). How children become friends. *Monographs of the Society for Research in Child Development, 48,* Serial no. 201.

Gottman, J. M. (1986). The world of coordinated play: same- and cross-sex friendship in young children. In J. M. Gottman & J. G. Parker (Eds.), *Conversations among friends* (pp. 139–191). Cambridge: Cambridge University Press.

Grusec, J., & Goodnow, J. (1994a). Impact of parental discipline methods on the child's internalization of values: A reconceptualization of current points of view. *Developmental Psychology, 30,* 4–19.

Grusec, J. E., & Goodnow, J. J. (1994b). Summing up and looking to the future. *Developmental Psychology, 30,* 29–31.

Grych, J. H., & Fincham, F. D. (Eds.). (2001). *Child development and inter-parental conflict.* Cambridge, UK: Cambridge University Press.

Harris, P. (1994). The child's understanding of emotion: Developmental change and the family environment. *Journal of Child Psychology & Psychiatry, 35,* 3–28.

Hart, C. H., Ladd, G. W., & Burleson, B. R. (1990). Children's expectations of the outcomes of social strategies; relations with sociometric status and maternal disciplinary styles. *Child Development, 61,* 127–37.

Hart, D., & Killen, M. (1995). Perspectives on morality in everyday life. In M. Killen & D. Hart (Eds.), *Morality in everyday life* (pp. 1–20). Cambridge, UK: Cambridge University Press.

Hinde, R. A. (2002). *Why good is good: The sources of morality.* London/New York: Wiley.

Hoff-Ginsberg, E., & Tardif, T. (1995). Socioeconomic status and parenting. In M. H. Bornstein (Ed.), *Handbook of parenting* (Vol. 2, pp. 161–188). Mahwah, NJ: Lawrence Erlbaum Associates.

Hoffman, M. J. (1983). Affective and cognitive processes in moral internalization. In E. T. Higgins, D. Ruble, & W. W. Hartup (Eds.), *Social cognition and social development: A sociocultural perspective* (pp. 236–274). Cambridge, UK: Cambridge University Press.

Hoffman, M. L. (2000). *Empathy and moral development: Implications for caring and justice.* Cambridge, UK: Cambridge University Press.

Howe, N. (1991). Sibling directed internal state language, perspective-taking, and the sibling relationship. *Child Development, 62,* 1503–1512.

Howe, N., Rinaldi, C. M., Jennings, M., & Petrakos, H. (2002). "No! the lambs can stay out because they got cozies": Constructive and destructive sibling conflict, pretend play, and social understanding. *Child Development, 73,* 1460–2473.

Howes, C. (1996). The earliest friendships. In W. M. Bukowski, A. F. Newcomb, & W. W. Hartup (Eds.), *The company they keep: Friendship in childhood and adolescence* (pp. 66–86). Cambridge, UK: Cambridge University Press.

Hughes, C., & Dunn, J. (1997). "Pretend you didn't know": Preschoolers' talk about mental states in pretend play. *Cognitive Development, 12,* 477–499.

Hughes, C., & Dunn, J. (2000). Hedonism or empathy?: Hard-to-manage children's moral awareness, and links with cognitive and maternal characteristics. *British Journal of Developmental Psychology, 18,* 227–245.

Jenkins, J., Turrell, S. L., Kogushi, Y., Lollis, S., & Ross, H. S. (2003). A longitudinal investigation of the dynamics of mental state talk in families. *Child Development, 74,* 905–920.

Kagan, J. (1981). *The second year.* Cambridge, MA: Harvard University Press.

Kagan, J. (1984). *The nature of the child.* New York: Basic Books.

Kagan, J. (1998). *Three seductive ideas.* Cambridge, MA: Harvard University Press.

Killen, M., & Nucci, L. P. (1995). Morality, autonomy, and social conflict. In M. Killen and D. Hart (Eds.), *Morality in everyday life: Developmental perspectives* (pp. 52–86). Cambridge, UK: Cambridge University Press.

Kochanska, G. (1991). Socialization and temperament in the development of guilt and conscience. *Child Development, 62,* 1379–1392.

Kochanska, G. (1994). Beyond cognition: Expanding the search for the ealry roots of internalization and conscience. *Developmental Psychology, 30,* 20–22.

Kochanska, G. (2002). Committed compliance, moral self, and internalization: A mediational model. *Developmental Psychology, 38,* 339–351.

Kochanska, G., Gross, J. N., Lin, M. H., & Nichols, K. E. (2002). Guilt in young children: development, determinants, and relations with a broader system of standards. *Child Development, 73,* 461–82.

Kochanska, G., & Murray, K. T. (2000). Mother-child mutually responsive orientation and conscience development: From toddler to early school age. *Child Development, 71,* 417–431.

Kochanska, G., Tjebes, T. L., & Forman, D. R. (1998). Children's emerging regulation of conduct: restraint, compliance and internalization from infancy to the second year. *Child Development, 69,* 1378–1389.

Kohlberg, L. (1984). *Essays on moral development: 2. the psychology of moral development.* San Francisco: Harper and Row.

Laible, D. J., & Thompson, R. (1998). Attachment and emotional understanding in preschool children. *Developmental Psychology, 34,* 1038–1045.

Laible, D. J., & Thompson, R. A. (2000). Mother-child discourse, attachment security, shared positive affect, and early conscience development. *Child Development, 71,* 1424–1440.

Laible, D. J., & Thompson, R. A. (2002). Mother-child conflict in the toddler years: Lessons in emotion, morality, and relationships. *Child Development, 73,* 1187–1203.

Meins, E., Fernyhough, C., Wainwright, R., Das Gupta, M., Fradley, E., & Tuckey, M. (2002). Maternal mind-mindedness and attachment security as predictors of theory of mind understanding. *Child Development, 73,* 1715–1726.

Miller, J. G., & Bersoff, D. M. (1995). Development in the context of everyday family relationships: culture, interpersonal morality and adaptation. In M. Killen & D. Hart (Eds.), *Morality in everyday life* (pp. 259–282). Cambridge, UK: Cambridge University Press.

Much, N., & Shweder, R. (1978). Speaking of rules: The analysis of culture in the breach. In W. Damon (Ed.), *New directions in child development* (Vol. 2, pp. 19–39). San Francisco: Jossey-Bass.

Ochs, E. (1987). *Culture and language acquisition: Acquiring communicative competence in a Samoan village.* Cambridge, UK: Cambridge University Press.

Piaget, J. (1932). *The moral judgment of the child.* New York: Free Press, 1965.

Plomin, R., & McGuffin, P. (2003). Psychopathology in the postgenomic era. *Annual Review of Psychology, 54,* 205–228.

Radke-Yarrow, M., Zahn-Waxler, C., & Chapman, M. (1983). Children's prosocial dispositions and behavior. In P. H. Mussen (Ed.), *Handbook of child Development, Vol. 4: Socialization, personality, and social development* (pp. 469–546). New York: Wiley.

Reddy, V. (1991). Playing with others' expectations: Teasing and mucking about in the first year. In A. Whiten (Ed.), *Natural theories of mind.* Oxford: Blackwell.

Ronald, A., Happé, F., Hughes, C., & Plomin, R. (in press). The nature and nurture of nice and nasty theory of mind. *Developmental Science.* Manuscript submitted for publication.

Sears, R. R., Maccoby, E. E., & Levin, H. (1957). *Patterns of child rearing.* Evanston, IL: Row, Peterson.

Slomkowski, C. L., & Killen, M. (1992). Young children's conceptions of transgressions with friends and nonfriends. *International Journal of Behavioral Development, 15,* 247–258.

Smetana, J. (1989). Toddlers' social interactions in the context of moral and conventional transgressions in the home. *Developmental Psychology, 25,* 499–508.

Smetana, J. G., & Braeges, J. L. (1990). The development of toddlers' moral and conventional judgments. *Merrill-Palmer Quarterly, 36,* 329–346.

Thompson, R. A. (1998). Early sociopersonality development. In W. Damon (Ed.), *Handbook of child psychology. Vol. 3: Social, emotional and personality development* (pp. 25–104). New York: Wiley.

Tizard, B., & Hughes, M. (2002). *Young children learning.* Oxford: Blackwell.

Turiel, E. (2002). *The culture of morality.* Cambridge, UK: Cambridge University Press.

Viding, E., Blair, R. J. R., Moffitt, T. E., & Plomin, R. (in press). Psychopathic personality indexes strong genetic risk for antisocial behaviour in 7-year-old children. *Journal of Child Psychology and Psychiatry.*

Vinden, P. G. (1997, April). *Parenting and theory of mind.* Paper presented at the Biennial Meeting of the Society for Research in Child Development, Washington, DC.

Watson-Gegeo, K. A., & Gegeo, D. (1987). The social world of Kwara'ae children: Acquisition of language and values. *Manuscript submitted for publication.*

Youngblade, L. M., & Dunn, J. (1995). Individual differences in young children's pretend play with mother and sibling: Links to relationships and understanding of other people's feelings and beliefs. *Child Development, 66,* 1472–1492.

Zahn Waxler, C., Radke-Yarrow, M., & King, R. A. (1979). Child-rearing and children's prosocial initiations towards victims of distress. *Child Development, 50,* 319–330.

Zahn-Waxler, C., Robinson, J. L., & Emde, R. N. (1992). The development of empathy in twins. *Developmental Psychology, 28,* 1038–1047.

Zhou, Q., Eisenberg, N., Loyosa, S. H., Fabes, R., Reiser, M., Guthrie, I. K., Murphy, B. C., Cumberland, A. J., & Shepard, S. A. (2002). The relations of parental warmth and positive expressiveness to children's empathy-related responding and social functioning: A longitudinal study. *Child Development, 73,* 893–915.

13

MEDIATED MORALITIES: SOCIOCULTURAL APPROACHES TO MORAL DEVELOPMENT

MARK B. TAPPAN
COLBY COLLEGE

The purpose of this chapter is to present a sociocultural perspective on the study of moral development, and to review theoretical and empirical work on moral development that has been conducted under the rubric of this perspective. This perspective has emerged over the course of the last decade or so, in response to a variety of challenges to prevailing theories of moral development—in particular, challenges to Kohlberg's (1963, 1969, 1976, 1981, 1984) stage theory of the development of justice reasoning. There is no doubt that researchers and practitioners interested in understanding the vicissitudes of human moral experience owe a singular debt to Kohlberg for bringing the study of moral development into the mainstream of developmental and educational psychology, and his theory is arguably still the best-known theory of moral development. Yet the past 25 years have witnessed a growing awareness of the metatheoretical, theoretical, and methodological limitations of Kohlberg's cognitive–developmental attempt to formally reconstruct the ontogenesis of competence in moral judgment making, via a sequence of six structurally defined, cross-culturally universal stages of justice reasoning.

Among the many and varied critiques of, and challenges to, Kohlberg's project (see, for example, Coles, 1986; Cortese, 1990; Flanagan, 1991; Packer, 1985, 1992; Shweder, 1982; Sullivan, 1977; Turiel, 1983, 2002), the most significant have come from those who have argued that Kohlberg's approach does not sufficiently acknowledge the multidimensional and multivocal nature of the moral domain. In this regard Gilligan's (1977, 1982) critique that classical theories of moral development—Freud's (1923/1960), Piaget's (1932/1965), and, most importantly, Kohlberg's—are flawed because they systematically excluded girls' and women's experience from foundational theory-building research studies is most widely known. Gilligan claimed that, for some people, an orientation other than the "justice voice" charted by Kohlberg, based on his all-male longitudinal research sample, provided the primary focus for moral reasoning and moral action. Specifically, she identified what she and her colleagues called a "care voice," articulated most often by girls and women, and most evident when researchers turned away from an interview protocol employing hypothetical moral dilemmas laden with Kohlbergian justice assumptions, to an open-ended format that emphasized careful tracking of persons on their own terms, in the context of exploring stories told about real-life situations of moral conflict and choice (see Gilligan & Attanucci, 1988; Gilligan, Ward, & Taylor, 1988; Gilligan & Wiggins, 1987).

Although Gilligan's argument about gender differences in moral development has generated the most discussion and debate, as well as conflicting empirical findings (see Baumrind, 1986; Brabeck, 1983; Gilligan & Attanucci, 1988; Gilligan & Wiggins, 1987; Pratt, Golding, & Hunter, 1984; Walker, 1984, 1986), it is her central insight that everyday moral language (not "deep structures" of moral cognition) holds the key to understanding moral experience and moral development that is, in the end, most provocative. For it is this insight that opened the way to the sociocultural exploration of the centrality of words, language, and forms of discourse—particularly narrative (story telling)—in human moral life. This perspective assumes, therefore, that moral thoughts, feelings, and actions are semiotically mediated, and thus socioculturally situated. As such, it necessarily entails an explicitly dialogical conception of the moral self—a conception of the moral self, that is, generated by a move away from a paradigm of cognitive representations and internally held principles, wherein the self is assumed to be a disembodied, transcendental, epistemic subject (see Kohlberg, 1984), toward a paradigm of social construction and intersubjectively possible forms of discourse, wherein the self is assumed to be a shared and/or distributed product of social relations and communicative practices (see Day & Tappan, 1996).

This perspective, as it has been gradually articulated over the past decade, draws centrally from primary scholarship in the "sociocultural" tradition—particularly the work of Vygotsky (1934/1987, 1978, 1981a, 1981b).[1] In recent years a number of scholars, inspired by Vygotsky's insights, have focused sustained attention on the ways in which "mediational means" both physical tools and "psychological" or "semiotic" tools (primarily language), appropriated from the social world, necessarily shape human mental functioning (see Wertsch, 1985, 1991, 1998; also see Bruner, 1986; Cole, 1996; Rogoff, 1990). From this starting point, a sociocultural perspective has been applied to a number of specific issues and problems in human development and education (see Berk & Winsler, 1995; Diaz & Berk, 1992; Forman, Minick, & Stone, 1993; Martin, Nelson, & Tobach, 1995; Moll, 1990; Rogoff & Wertsch, 1984; Tharp & Gallimore, 1988; Wertsch, 1986). Part of this effort has been to move beyond theories that assume the processes, dynamics, and endpoints of human development are universal—transcultural and ahistorical—toward an explicit consideration of the role that the social–cultural–historical–institutional context plays in giving rise to human action and interaction (see Bruner, 1986, 1990; Cole, 1988, 1996; Jahoda, 1992; Packer & Tappan, 2001; Rogoff, 1990; Rogoff & Chavajay, 1995; Rogoff & Lave, 1984; Shweder, 1991; Stigler, Shweder, & Herdt, 1990; Turiel, 2002; Valsiner, 1998; Wertsch, del Rio, & Alvarez, 1995; Winegar & Valsiner, 1992).

Similarly, scholars from a wide range of disciplines have turned to the work of Bakhtin (1981, 1984, 1986, 1990) to illuminate the dialogic character of all words, language, and

---

[1]The term *sociocultural* is used in this chapter to describe these approaches, following Wertsch (1985, 1989, 1991, 1998; Wertsch et al., 1995), mindful, in so doing, that there are other terms currently in use to describe the same approach: "cultural-historical activity theory" (see Cole, 1996), "cultural-historical theory" (see van der Veer & Valsiner, 1991), "sociohistorical theory" (see Cole, 1988; Rogoff, 1990), and "neo-Vygotskian" theory (see Tharp & Gallimore, 1988), among others.

forms of discourse; and hence the fundamentally dialogical nature of the self (see Clark & Holquist, 1984; Emerson, 1986; Hermans & Kempen, 1993; Hermans, Kempen, & van Loon, 1992; Holquist, 1990; Morson & Emerson, 1990; Sampson, 1993a; Wertsch, 1991; Wortham, 2001). Bakhtin was a contemporary of Vygotsky, and although it is doubtful that they ever met, their work shares many fundamental similarities (see Wertsch, 1991). Moreover, as Taylor (1991) argues, Bakhtin's insights are critical to a conception of the self that accurately captures the dialogical realities of everyday life:

> Children plainly need recognition, confirmation, love to grow and be inducted into adult life, at the limit even to survive. But this can be conceived as a monological need, a comfort that they have to receive from others, as they depend on others for food, but that can only contingently come through conversation. Or it can be seen as a need that is essentially fulfilled in a certain form of conversation itself. This latter understanding places dialogue at the very center of our understanding of human life, an indispensable key to its comprehension, and requires a transformed understanding of language. In order to follow up this line of thinking, we need not Mead and his like, but rather Bakhtin. Human beings are constituted in conversation; and hence what gets internalized in the mature subject is not the reaction of others, but the whole conversation, with the interanimation of its voices. Only a theory of this kind can do justice to the dialogical nature of the self. (pp. 313–314)

A sociocultural/dialogical perspective also resonates with, and reflects, the so-called discursive turn in the social sciences, in general, and the field of psychology, in particular, that has been underway for some time now (see, for example, Billig, 1987; Bruner, 1986, 1990; Edwards & Potter, 1992; Gergen, 1982, 1985, 1991, 1994; Harre, 1984; Parker, 1992; Sampson, 1993a, 1993b; Shotter, 1990; Shotter & Gergen, 1989). Defining *discourse* as anything that humans do in their everyday lives that involves speaking (Parker, 1992), and focusing on the central role that speaking, talking, and conversing play in human life, discourse theorists (also called "social constructionists" [see Gergen, 1985, 1994]) "maintain that talk is constitutive of the realities in which we live, rather than expressive of an earlier, discourse-independent reality" (Sampson, 1993b, p. 1221). Moreover, on this view, both language and communication are necessarily shared practices that give rise to the various realities one encounters in everyday life. Because discourse is not the possession of a single individual, but must always be the product of a social and communicative relationship wherein both parties agree on the meaning of the words that pass between them, it follows that "it is not the mind of the single individual that provides whatever certitude we possess [about the world in which we live], but relationships of interdependency" (Gergen, 1994, p. viii).

Mindful of this rich and ever-changing scholarly and intellectual context, the purpose of this chapter, again, is to summarize the central elements of a sociocultural/dialogical perspective on the study of moral development, and to review a variety of theoretical and empirical approaches that have emerged under its relatively broad purview over the course of the past decade or so. It is also fitting that these approaches be considered in a volume such as this one, marking the field of moral development's move into a new millennium.

A sociocultural/dialogical perspective on moral development begins with three claims that capture the fundamental assumptions of Vygotsky's sociocultural psychology:

1. The claim that higher mental functions (mental functions, like decision making, problem solving, deliberate memory, that are not biologically or instinctually motivated) can only be understood when one analyzes and interprets them genetically or developmentally;

2. The claim that higher mental functioning is mediated by words, language, and forms of discourse, which function as "psychological tools" that both facilitate and transform mental action; and

3. The claim that forms of higher mental functioning have their origins in social relations, as "intermental" processes between persons are internalized to become "intramental" processes within persons (Wertsch, 1985, pp. 14–16; see also Berk & Winsler, 1995; Kozulin, 1990; van der Veer & Valsiner, 1991).

When these claims are extended and elaborated, four principles or assumptions emerge that characterize various sociocultural/dialogical approaches to the study of moral development—assumptions that build on and extend central aspects of the theoretical and empirical work of both Vygotsky and Bakhtin:

1. Moral functioning (like all "higher psychological functioning") is necessarily mediated by words, language, and forms of discourse;

2. Such mediation occurs primarily in private or inner speech, in the form of inner moral dialogue;

3. Processes of social communication and social relations necessarily give rise to moral functioning; and

4. Moral development is always shaped by the particular social, cultural, and historical context in which it occurs (see Tappan, 1997).

This chapter is organized around each of these four principles or assumptions. Each one is summarized, and relevant theoretical and empirical work is reviewed, in turn. The chapter then concludes with a number of questions for further inquiry and investigation, both theoretical and empirical.

THE SEMIOTIC MEDIATION OF MORAL FUNCTIONING

Perhaps the central idea in Vygotsky's (1934/1987, 1978) theoretical perspective is the notion that, to understand the mind, we must understand the "tools" that mediate and shape its functioning (see Wertsch, 1985). Although physical ("technical") tools are certainly important in this process, Vygotsky was most interested in the role that "psychological tools," or "signs," play in human mental life. Ultimately, Vygotsky focused his attention on language as the most important psychological tool. Psychological tools, like language, do not simply facilitate the operation of existing mental tasks, argued Vygotsky. Instead, the introduction of new psychological tools (e.g., when new words are learned) fundamentally transforms and reorganizes mental functioning.

This transformation is particularly critical in early childhood, of course, when, with the advent of egocentric speech (as an intermediate step toward inner speech), language begins to be used as an "instrument of thought" in its own right, a "tool" that helps the child plan activities and solve problems:

> The most significant moment in the course of intellectual development, which gives birth to the purely human forms of practical and abstract intelligence, occurs when speech and practical activity, two previously independent lines of development, converge. (Vygotsky, 1978, p. 24)

Thus, Vygotsky's conception of semiotic mediation also shapes his view of the developmental process: he does not envision ontogenesis as a series of incremental quantitative changes, but rather as a series of fundamental qualitative transformations or "revolutions" associated with changes in the psychological tools to which the person has access (Wertsch, 1985).

The assumption that moral functioning (like all "higher psychological functioning") is necessarily mediated by words, language, and forms of discourse is central to a sociocultural perspective on the process of moral development. Moral functioning is the higher psychological process (in Vygotsky's terms) that a person invokes to respond to and resolve a specific problem, conflict, or dilemma that requires a moral decision and a moral action—that is, when one is faced with the question "What is the 'right' or 'moral' thing to do in this situation?"

The concept of mediation is critical here, because for an action to be considered "moral," either by an actor or by an observer, a particular meaning must be associated with that action. This holds whether that action is as "instinctive" as rushing out into busy traffic to rescue a wayward child, or as "deliberative" as weighing the pros and cons of having an abortion. In either case, and in many others, because the designation "moral" is an interpretation of the action in question, generated from the shared assumptions and understandings that constitute culture, moral functioning can never be unmediated. Rather, it is always accomplished with the use of what Vygotsky called "psychological tools" (most importantly, words, language, and forms of moral discourse) that enable the person to think, feel, and act in a particular way—that is, in a way that, in her particular sociocultural context, is understood to be "moral," "right," "good," and so on.

The crucial element here, from a sociocultural perspective, is the link between morality and language—language, that is, used not merely to express moral meaning, but used, primarily, to create moral meaning in the first place. This is a link that is made explicitly by the philosopher Oakeshott (1975; see also Bellah, Madsen, Sullivan, Swindler, & Tipton, 1985; MacIntyre, 1981; Stout, 1988). Oakeshott argues that morality is fundamentally a "practice" or a form of "conduct" that facilitates human interaction: "The conditions which compose a moral practice are not theorems or precepts about human conduct, nor do they constitute anything so specific as a 'shared system of values'; they compose a *vernacular language of colloquial intercourse*" (1975, p. 63; my emphasis). This language, claims Oakeshott, is thus fundamentally pragmatic; it is a tool

> like any other language, it is an instrument of self-disclosure used by agents in diagnosing their situations and in choosing their responses; and it is a language of self-enactment which permits those who can use it to understand themselves and one another, to disclose to one another their complex individualities, and to explore relationships far more varied and interesting than those it has a name for or those which a commonplace acceptance of so-called 'moral values' would allow (1975, p. 63).

From Oakeshott's (1975) perspective, therefore, morality itself is a cultural tool that enables those who use it to accomplish certain things:

> A morality, then, is neither a system of general principles nor a code of rules, but a vernacular language. General principles and even rules may be elicited from it, but (like other languages) it is not the creation of grammarians; it is made by speakers. What has to be learned in a moral education [therefore] is not a theorem such as that good conduct is acting fairly or being charitable, nor is it a rule such as 'always tell the truth,' but how speak the language intelligently. (pp. 78–79)

Duncan (2001) has outlined a conception of moral development based on Vygotsky's (1934/1987) theory of concept formation that echoes many of these assumptions about the nature of morality. His primary argument is that Vygotsky's theory of concept formation, in which the child moves from using "syncretic heaps," to thinking in "complexes," to the use of "potential concepts," can be used as a model for understanding the development of moral ability. On Duncan's view, however, moral ability is not understood as "rule-following behavior." Rather, he defines moral ability, like concept formation, as a "present-centered aptitude for creating meaning" (p. 113). As such, he argues, both conceptual thinking, on Vygotsky's view, and moral ability, are activities that "use the tools of individual intelligence and interpersonal discourse (thought and language) to create something that is not determined by these tools" (p. 118).

Although not embarked on a socioculturally inspired research program, per se, Gilligan (1982, 1983) and her colleagues have presented very compelling evidence regarding the ways in which moral languages and forms of moral discourse mediate and shape persons' responses to moral problems, conflicts, and dilemmas in their lives. In identifying the two different moral voices of "justice" and "care," Gilligan and her colleagues have shown how these two voices represent different ways of speaking about the world of human relationships, different ways of describing and understanding moral problems, and differ-ent approaches to and strategies for resolving such problems (see Gilligan, 1982, 1983; Gilligan, Ward, & Taylor, 1988; Gilligan & Wiggins, 1987).

Gilligan and her colleagues have also developed a method for identifying these voices in persons' narratives of real-life moral conflict and choice—the "Listening Guide" (see Brown, Debold, Tappan, & Gilligan, 1992; Brown & Gilligan, 1991; Brown, Tappan, Gilligan, Miller, & Argyris, 1989). In addition, Gilligan and Attanucci (1988) report that when asked to describe a moral problem or conflict they had recently faced, more than two-thirds of a group of 80 educationally advantaged adolescents and adults living in the U.S. represented the voices of both justice and care in their interview narratives. This finding, and others reported by Gilligan and Attanucci, suggests that (a) justice and care represent two fundamentally different moral languages or forms of moral discourse; (b) persons can speak in the language of both justice and care; and (c) persons therefore can and do use both voices to mediate the process of moral functioning, and thus to help them respond to moral problems and conflicts in their lives.

Tappan (2003) has extended the work of Wertsch (1998) to argue that moral func-tioning, in its cognitive, affective, and active dimensions, should be understood to be, fundamentally and irreducibly, mediated action. Mediated action, according to Wertsch (1998), entails two central elements: an "agent" (the person who is doing the acting), and specific "cultural tools" or "mediational means" (the tools, means, or instruments [both physical and psychological], appropriated from the social world, and then used by the agent to accomplish the action in question). Moral functioning considered as a form of mediated action thus entails focusing on *both* the agent and the cultural tools/mediational means she or he employs in responding to the moral problem, conflict, or dilemma at hand.

In addition, Tappan (1999, 2000, 2005) has drawn on the work of Penuel and Wertsch (1995), who extended the concept of mediated action to the realm of identity development, and Bakhtin (1981), who described identity development as a process of "ideological becoming," to articulate a sociocultural/dialogical conception of moral identity. According to Tappan, moral identity must be seen not as primarily a psychological understanding of oneself as a moral person that comes from access to or reflection on one's "true" or "essential" self (see Blasi, 1984; Damon & Hart, 1988), but rather as a sociocultural process that takes the form of "mediated moral action"—action that is shaped by specific cultural tools and resources. Chief among these tools and resources are moral orientations or ideologies that are carried and transmitted via words, language, and forms of discourse. One finds one's moral identity, therefore, in the ideologically mediated moral action in which one engages, not in the process of reflection on one's inner moral self. And the development of moral identity, on this view, entails a process of "ideological becoming," whereby one selectively appropriates the words, language, and forms of discourse of others with whom one is in dialogue, and in so doing struggles to strike a healthy balance between "authoritative" and "internally persuasive" forms of discourse (see Bakhtin, 1981).

Lightfoot (1997, 2002a, 2002b, 2003) has also used Bakhtin's (1981) distinction between authoritative and internally persuasive discourse to analyze the phenomenon of adolescent risk taking, particularly its moral dimensions. Lightfoot (1997) argues, specifically, that adolescent risk taking must be seen as a form of text construction through which different moral discourses and perspectives come into dialogical contact. As such, engagement with another's discourse contributes directly to the further development and articulation of one's social identity, as well as the awareness that one has a social identity of moral consequence. Lightfoot suggests, therefore, that adolescent risk taking often represents a struggle between various forms of authoritative discourse as they seek to differentiate themselves from their parents, and to forge a separate, distinct, and "autonomous" moral identity. As a result, this struggle between various forms of authoritative discourse, moreover, often leads to the formation of a more internally persuasive form of "ideological consciousness" (i.e., identity):

> Although adolescents' risk-taking can be construed in terms of a struggle with the authoritative discourse of another, it is also a mechanism for creating a discourse of their own, the internally persuasive one that Bakhtin wrote of. By these lights, the reflective awareness that is engendered, the coming into ideological consciousness that follows in the wake of such struggle, is coupled alectically to processes of sociocultural identification. Untanglings and entanglements; engagement with another's point of view is the fountainhead of mindedness. (pp. 113–114)

If moral functioning and activity (like all "higher psychological functioning") is indeed mediated by words, language, and forms of discourse, then inner speech, and inner dialogue, must play a primary role in that process. This issue has been addressed by a variety of sociocultural/dialogical approaches to moral development.

SEMIOTIC MEDIATION IN INNER MORAL DIALOGUE

Vygotsky (1934/1987, 1978) explored a variety of means by which mental life is semiotically mediated. In the end, as indicated, he focused primary attention on the ways in which language, particularly in the form of inner speech, functions as a psychological tool. Just, therefore, as children learn to count first by using fingers, blocks, or other objects before being able to count in their heads, they learn to speak first to others before learning to speak to themselves, in private, inner speech. Once this is accomplished, however, verbal thought becomes possible, the nature of development changes from being biologically determined to being socioculturally shaped, and there is a radical shift in the richness and complexity of consciousness (Vygotsky, 1934/1987; see also Diaz & Berk, 1992; Kohlberg, Yaeger, & Hjertholm, 1968; Zivin, 1979).

Although it is unclear whether Vygotsky viewed monologue or dialogue as the fundamental characteristic of inner speech, the work of Bakhtin (1981) and his colleague

Volosinov (1929/1986) can be used to extend Vygotsky's insights, by focusing, explicitly, on the dialogic nature of inner speech (see also Emerson, 1986; Morson & Emerson, 1990). For Bakhtin and Volosinov, inner speech never consists of pure monologue, in which a person simply talks in a single, solitary "voice." Rather, there is always a dialogue between at least two voices—a dialogue that mediates and shapes human mental functioning in profound ways.

Bakhtin (1981) focuses on the fundamentally dialogic character of all speech:

> In the makeup of almost every utterance spoken by a social person—from a brief response in a casual dialogue to major verbal-ideological works (literary, scholarly and others)—a significant number of words can be identified that are implicitly or explicitly admitted as someone else's, and that are transmitted by a variety of different means. Within the arena of almost every utterance an intense interaction between one's own and another's word is being waged, a process in which they oppose or dialogically interanimate each other. (pp. 354–355)

Volosinov (1929/1986) focuses explicitly on the dialogic character of inner speech:

> Close analysis would show that the units of which inner speech is constituted resemble the *alternating lines of a dialogue*. There was good reason [therefore] why thinkers in ancient times should have conceived of inner speech as *inner dialogue*. (p. 38; emphasis in original)

Tappan (1997) has extended Vygotsky's (1934/1987) general view of the relationship between inner speech and thinking to the realm of moral development, by arguing that when a person (child, adolescent, or adult) is faced with a moral problem, conflict, or dilemma, she or he responds to it by means of inner speech as inner moral dialogue—by talking through the solution to her- or himself—just as she or he responds to any other problem or task with which she or he is faced. Moreover, following Vygotsky, Tappan predicts that such inner moral dialogue should exhibit the same "peculiar" syntactic and semantic characteristics of inner speech. Thus, inner moral dialogue should consist primarily of predicates and other such abbreviated sentence structures. These characteristics, moreover, should contribute to the formation of an idiomatic moral language that constitutes the primary medium for inner moral speech, and thus the means by which inner moral dialogues are conducted–similar, as such, to Oakeshott's (1975) conception of morality as a vernacular or colloquial language.

In addition, Gilligan and Attannucci's (1988) finding that most persons represent both the moral voice of justice and the moral voice of care in their narratives of moral conflict and choice illuminates well the fundamentally dialogical relationship that appears to exist between these two vernacular moral voices. Moreover, many persons describe their own participation, literally, in an ongoing inner dialogue between these two voices—the justice voice speaking the language of fairness and equality, advocating one solution, and the care voice speaking the language of relationship and responsibility, advocating another. After a time, and depending on how the dialogue has proceeded, the person makes a decision, and responds to the moral problem at hand. This suggests that persons are not only polyphonic or multivocal in their moral utterances at any one time (Bakhtin, 1981), but also that they can, and frequently do, oscillate from one voice to another when responding to and resolving moral problems, conflicts, and dilemmas in their lives (see also Brown et al., 1992; Brown & Gilligan, 1991; Brown et al., 1989).

Day (1991) provides additional empirical evidence in support of the view that multiple voices, multiple forms of reasoning, characterize the moral life, both within persons and across the communities they compose. Arguing that moral life is not only storied, but also distinctly theatrical, he explores the phenomenon of the "moral audience"—the ways in which children, adolescents, and adults, in the course of telling stories about their lived moral experience, identify others (real and imagined, alive and dead) that compose an "internalized" audience before whom they act, and by whom they are judged. For the persons in Day's study, moral action always occurs in relationship to other persons; hence actions are always performed and interpreted in terms of these persons as audience. Consistency of moral action thus has much to do with the consistency of the audience to which such actions are played. Moral principles are developed and sustained, or changed, in relation to the parties who compose the audience, and moral actions are mentally rehearsed before them. Moral actions are then retrospectively analyzed and evaluated in terms of the same audience. Day argues, therefore, that we can understand both moral judgment and moral action only when we can grasp the nature of the actor's relationship to the audience(s) before whom she or her most centrally acts. He also suggests that moral development must be understood in terms of the formation and transformation of moral audiences in the experience of moral actors across the lifespan.

The work of Gilligan and her colleagues, Day, and others also highlights the critical importance of narrative in the self-reports of interviewees representing their inner moral dialogues in response to real-life moral conflicts and dilemmas. A number of researchers have explored the variety of ways persons rely on narrative and story telling to chart, carry out, evaluate, and justify the actions they take when confronted with such dilemmas (Attanucci, 1991; Day & Tappan, 1996; Johnston, 1991; Lyons, 1983; Tappan, 1991a, 1991b; Tappan & Brown, 1989; Tappan & Packer, 1991; Ward, 1991; Witherell & Edwards, 1991; Witherell & Noddings, 1991). There is, in fact, a growing consensus that because moral experience, like all lived experience, always occurs in time and in relationship (the fundamental dimensions of narrative [see Gilligan, Brown, & Rogers, 1990]), whenever a person has to report "what really happened," the natural impulse is to tell a story, to compose a narrative that recounts the actions and events of interest in some kind of temporal sequence (see also Bruner, 1986; Mischler, 1986; Polkinghorne, 1988; Sarbin, 1986, 1990).

A recent and very promising empirical exploration and elaboration of these dialogical and narrative insights has been undertaken by Mkhize (2003). Studying indigenous South African *isiZulu* speakers' conception of morality, Mkhize interviewed 52 participants (both women and men) living in urban, suburban, and rural areas of KwaZulu-Natal. Participants were asked to tell a story about a moral conflict or dilemma in their lives, and the narratives were analyzed using a modification of the Listening Guide developed by Gilligan and her colleagues (see Brown & Gilligan, 1991). Mkhize found that conceptions of morality were related to participants' understanding of the self. The view that morality is characterized by connection was associated mainly with what Mkhize calls a "communal" or "familial" self, which was the most common conception of self in the *isuZulu* cultural context. But Mkhize also identified tensions between competing conceptions of the self within persons—tensions, that is, between the communal self and the independent self. These dialogical tensions, moreover, complicated participants' responses to moral conflicts and dilemmas in their lives.

These various approaches illustrate well the ways in which moral functioning is mediated primarily through inner speech as inner moral dialogue, and represented in narrative. Yet they also raise questions regarding the ways in which processes of social communication and social relations give rise, via the medium of language, to moral functioning in the first place.

THE SOCIAL ORIGINS OF MORAL FUNCTIONING

The notion that all higher mental functions have their origin in communicative processes and social relations is another key element of Vygotsky's theoretical framework (Wertsch, 1985). Vygotsky's view here is captured most succinctly in what Wertsch (1985) calls his "general genetic law of cultural development":

> Any function in the child's cultural development appears twice, or on two planes. First it appears on the social plane, and then on the psychological plane. First it appears between people as an interpsychological [intermental] category, and then within the child as an intrapsychological [intramental] category. This is equally true with regard to voluntary attention, logical memory, the formation of concepts, and the development of volition. We may consider this position as a law in the full sense of the word, but it goes without saying that internalization transforms the process itself and changes its structure and functions. Social relations or relations among people genetically underlie all higher functions and their relationships. (Vygotsky, 1981a, p. 163)

Key to this process is the phenomenon of *internalization,* in which "an operation that initially represents an external activity is reconstructed and begins to appear internally" (Vygotsky, 1978, pp. 56–57). As such, Vygotsky's approach provides a developmental perspective not only on the ways in which such higher mental functions as thinking, reasoning, remembering, and willing are mediated by language and other semiotic mechanisms, but also on how such functions necessarily have their origins in the interpersonal relationships that constitute human social life.

From a sociocultural perspective, moral development must entail the internalization of semiotically and linguistically mediated social relations, as external speech becomes inner speech—that is, as overt, external dialogue becomes silent, inner dialogue. This process has been illustrated elegantly by Bhatia (2000) in his exploration of the critical role that language-based socialization strategies and patterns employed by caregivers play in children's construction of what he calls "sociomoral meanings." Bhatia studied Hindi-speaking Indian caregivers interacting with their children; he focuses particular attention on the ways in which children's participation in dialogical and narrative practices enable them to begin to understand cultural conceptions of morality. Declarative, directive, and interrogative communicative patterns and forms of discourse all play central roles in this process, according to Bhatia:

> Hindi-speaking care-givers use social acts to foreground certain aspects of their socio-moral order. Care-givers, through directives such as "behave properly" or "recite the poem to aunty" and declaratives such as "this is bad language" are . . . indexing what Ochs (1996) has referred to as epistemic stances about one's culture. These "epistemic stances: carry important contextual information related to roles, status, social obligations and duty, and provide material from which the construction of socio-moral meanings occurs. (p. 164)

Finally, Bhatia (2000) concludes with these reflections on the relationship between language, human development, and morality that forms the core of a sociocultural perspective on moral development:

[L]anguage as a symbolic form allows human beings to articulate their experiences in a meaningful way. At one level, one may conceive of these forms in terms of "symbols and referents," but at a deeper level, everyday cultural discourse provides a novel language: a language of morals and ethics through which children come to understand what it means to be human. (164)

Similarly, Dunn's (1987) work suggests that children begin to learn from parents, grandparents, caregivers, and even older siblings about social rules, standards of behavior, and the effect of their actions on others' feelings in the second year of life. Moreover, this learning occurs primarily in the context of conversation, as adults and children begin to talk with each other about "right" and "wrong," "good" and "bad," "should" and "shouldn't" (Snow, 1987). Dunn (1987) also reports high correlations between the frequency of maternal talk about feelings to 18-month-olds and subsequent talk about inner states by these children at 24 months.

From a sociocultural perspective, therefore, what is initially communication for and with others regarding rules, standards, and the consequences of their transgression gradually, as a result of communicative interactions over the course of a number of years, becomes communication with oneself regarding what one should and should not do in a given situation: "in inner speech culturally prescribed forms of language and reasoning find their individualized realization. . . . [as] culturally sanctioned symbolic systems are remodeled into individualized verbal thought" (Kozulin, 1986, p. xxxvi). Children, therefore, as Vygotsky predicted, do not simply make internal what was once external, but also both create and transform their own internal plane of moral thinking, feeling, and acting, based on their experiences in the social world.

Another clear description of this process at work in the preschool context has been provided by Buzzelli and Johnston (Buzzelli, 1993; Buzzelli & Johnston, 2001, 2002; Johnston & Buzzelli, 2002). Buzzelli and Johnston study the ways in which children internalize moral norms, and then use these norms to guide their own behavior. In so doing, Buzzelli and Johnston employ an explicitly sociocultural framework to illuminate how interpersonal dialogue between children and teachers is transformed into inner dialogue that children use for "self-regulation":

An important part of children's moral understanding is formed through dialogue with adults who interpret and frame events and rules within a moral context that reflects their own unique perspective. . . . [T]his process is a social one influenced by the words adults use in their dialogue with children. . . . For example, the teacher might ask the child "Is that toy yours?" "Who does it belong to?" "Did you take it?" "What is the rule about taking things that belong to others?" Another teacher may approach the situation differently by asking "Where did you get that toy?" "Did you find it?" "Does it belong to another child?" "What does it mean to take a toy that belongs to someone else?" "How do you think the other child feels?" In the second example each question asked is based upon the child's response to the previous question. The two examples represent different types of questioning within adult–child dialogue. It is through such interactions, by questioning and responding, that adult and child create a shared meaning of the behavior which serves as the basis for the child's moral norm concerning the behavior. (Buzzelli, 1993, p. 383)

Buzzelli also argues, following Bakhtin (1981), that encouraging children to "retell" moral rules in their own words (using internally persuasive discourse) provides the basis for a more positive type of moral self-regulation than simply asking children to "recite" the rules by heart (using the authoritative words of adults—parents or teachers) (see also Tappan, 1991a).

These sociocultural perspectives on moral development suggest that processes of social communication and social relations necessarily give rise to moral functioning. Social interaction, however, always takes place in the context of culture. Thus, moral development is necessarily shaped by the particular social, cultural, and historical context in which it occurs.

THE SOCIOCULTURAL CONTEXT OF MORAL DEVELOPMENT

There is a fundamental connection between human mental functioning and the social, cultural, and historical contexts in which it occurs. This assumption follows directly from the central tenets of Vygotsky's theoretical framework (Wertsch, 1985, 1991). Consider, for example, Vygotsky's (1934/1987) claim that "thought development is determined by language, i.e., by the linguistic tools of thought and by the sociocultural experience of the child" (p. 94). In addition, Vygotsky argues that with the onset of inner speech and verbal thought in early childhood comes a dramatic shift in the nature of development, "from biological to sociohistorical . . . [because] [v]erbal thought is not an innate, natural form of behavior, but is determined by a historical-cultural process and has specific properties and laws that cannot be found in the natural forms of thought and speech" (p. 94).

Despite the importance of these assumptions, claims, and arguments to his research program, Vygotsky never directly addressed many of the critical issues to which they give rise. Specifically, because Vygotsky's own analyses did not move beyond the level of intermental processes, "he did little to spell out how specific historical, cultural, and institutional settings are tied to various forms of mediated action" (Wertsch, 1991, p. 46). Nevertheless, a genuinely "sociocultural approach to mind" can be developed quite easily on the basis of Vygotsky's theoretical insights:

> In order to formulate a more comprehensive sociocultural approach to mental functioning one should identify historically, culturally, and institutionally situated forms of mediated [intermental] action and specify how their mastery leads to particular forms of mediated action on the intramental plane. This amounts to extending Vygotsky's ideas to bring the sociocultural situatedness of mediated action on the intermental plan to the fore. It is the sociocultural situatedness of mediated action that provides the essential link between the cultural, historical, and institutional setting on the one hand and the mental functioning of the individual on the other. (Wertsch, 1991, p. 49)

The development of moral functioning, therefore, like the development of all forms of higher mental functioning, is necessarily and inescapably socioculturally situated. As such, moral development is shaped by social, cultural, historical, and institutional forces, because the various forms of intermental functioning that give rise to intramental processes of moral functioning are mediated by words, language, and forms of discourse that are similarly shaped and contextualized. As the studies reviewed in the previous section illustrate well, the words that a young child uses to help her understand that her actions are "right" or "wrong," "good" or "bad," come out of a specific social, cultural, and linguistic milieu. Moreover, the types of conversations and interactions in which parents and children engage around standards and their transgression are always culturally and historically determined (see Bhatia, 2000; Dunn, 1987; Snow, 1987).

Bellah and associates (1985), whose work focuses on exploring the ways in which Americans talk about moral issues and moral concerns, in both the public and private spheres of their lives, provide additional evidence supporting the claim that moral development is socioculturally situated (as well as semiotically mediated). Key to their analysis is a notion of language that is similar to that used by other sociocultural theorists:

> We use the term [language] to refer to modes of moral discourse that include distinct vocabularies and characteristic patterns of moral reasoning. We use *first language* to refer to the individualistic mode that is the dominant American form of discourse about moral, social, and political matters. We use the term *second languages* to refer to other forms, primarily biblical and republican, that provide at least part of the moral discourse of most Americans. (p. 334)

It is useful, in this context, to link the work of Bellah and co-workers (1985) to that of Gilligan (1982) and her colleagues. In so doing, it becomes clear that the moral voices of justice and care represent two prominent social/moral languages in American culture, at this time in our history. The discourse of justice, fairness, and individual rights has been, and continues to be, the predominant moral language in the U.S.—our "first language." It is the language in which our most important historical moral documents are written (e.g., the Declaration of Independence, the Constitution, and the Bill of Rights), and it is the language that constitutes our modern-day legal system. As such, it is the language that frames the bulk of our public discussions about morality and moral decision making— from discussions about abortion (is a mother's "right" to free choice more important than a fetus' "right" to life?) to discussions about euthanasia (is a patient's "right" to die more important than a doctor's "obligation" to sustain life?).

The discourse of care, compassion, and responsibility in relationships, in contrast, has been, and continues to be, one of our "second languages." Historically it has not occupied a predominant place in our public moral discourse; and when it has entered into the public sphere it has often been denigrated and devalued (see, for example, Kohlberg & Kramer, 1969). But the language of care has always occupied a predominant place in the private lives and relationships of Americans—particularly through the language of caregivers and caregiving as it has been spoken by mothers and others responsible for childcare, nurses, social workers, among others. One of the consequences of the work of Gilligan and her colleagues, however, has been not only to identify the care voice as a moral language typically associated with women and women's experience, but also to legitimize it as a language that has an important role to play in transforming public moral, political, and legal discourse (see also Blum, 1980; Noddings, 1984; Ruddick, 1989).

This view suggests, therefore, that the moral voices of justice and care are certainly not universal, but are rather socioculturally situated—that they are social/moral languages that have emerged out of the American culture of the last 20 years (the culture in which both Gilligan and her colleagues and the children, adolescents, and adults whom they have interviewed have lived). Moreover, because these moral languages have emerged in a specific sociocultural context, a similar effort in another social, cultural, and historical context might well have identified very different moral voices, moral languages, and types of moral discourse.

Similar questions about the degree to which Kohlberg's (1981, 1984) sequence of six structurally defined stages of reasoning about justice and fairness is cross-culturally universal (rather than culturally specific), and thus whether observed cultural differences in moral judgment represent differences in content (allowed by Kohlberg) or structure (assumed, by Kohlberg, to be universal), have been raised numerous times over the past several decades (see Blasi, 1987; Boyes & Walker, 1988; Dien, 1982; Shweder, Maha-patra, & Miller, 1987; Shweder & Much, 1987; Snarey, 1985; Turiel, 1983). Exempli-fying these criticisms is Dien's (1982) argument that Kohlberg's theory cannot be used to understand native Chinese moral experience, because Kohlberg's theory and method both instantiate "the prevailing Western conception of man [sic] as an autonomous be-ing, free to make choices and determine his destiny" (p. 339). As such, claims Dien, Kohlberg's approach adequately captures neither "the Confucian view of man as an in-tegral part of an orderly universe with an innate moral sense to maintain harmony," nor the preferred mode of conflict resolution in China, which focuses on "reconciliation and collective decision making rather than individual choice, commitment, and responsibility" (p. 331).

It is important to clarify here that Dien's criticism is leveled specifically at Kohlberg's theory and research method. There are many other researchers, many of whom also align themselves with the broader cognitive–developmental paradigm, who have conducted cross-cultural research that is much more sensitive to local cultural meanings, messages, interactions, and traditions than is Kohlberg's approach. Much of this work is represented herein (see Helwig, chap. 7; Killen, Margic, & Sinno, chap. 6; Nucci, chap. 24; Smetana, chap. 5; Turiel, chap. 1; and Wainryb, chap. 8, this volume for example).

Of particular relevance, in this regard, is research conducted by Huebner and Garrod (1991, 1993). Huebner and Garrod studied the moral reasoning of adolescent and young adult Tibetan Buddhist monks living in a Tibetan Buddhist monastery in Nepal. They interviewed twenty monks using a "culturally adapted" form of Kohlberg's hypothetical Moral Judgment Interview (Colby & Kohlberg, 1987). After transcribing, translating, and analyzing these interviews, Huebner and Garrod (1993) were able to chart a standard age-related developmental progression in moral judgment among the monks they interviewed (movement from a mean stage of 2 or 3 for the young adolescent group to a mean stage of 3 or 4 for the young adults, based on Kohlberg's developmental sequence). They found, however, that it was very difficult to interpret the monks' moral reasoning using scoring categories provided by Kohlberg's scheme, largely because the notion of *karma*, which was so central to the Buddhist philosophy and to the worldview of the monks with whom they talked, was understandably absent in the Standard Issue Scoring Manual (Colby & Kohlberg, 1987). As a result, Huebner and Garrod (1991) argue, quite forcefully, for the importance of sociocultural sensitivity in the study of moral development:

> In order to map the moral domain of a culture, we must first understand that culture . . . through [its] own history, philosophy, and language. Indeed, the importance of language has been sorely neglected by moral reasoning researchers. More is needed than simply a researcher's ability to collect data in subjects' native language, or even the understanding of "foreign" concepts (such as *karma*) that can be brought into our system by the addition of a single new word to our lexicon. We must strive, too, to understand concepts . . . that cannot be captured in direct word-for-word translation. (p. 350)

More recently, Garrod and his colleagues have undertaken a cross-cultural exploration of the existence of the two moral voices of justice and care (Gilligan, 1982), and the association of political violence and ethnic conflict with these voices, among children living in Bosnia and Herzegovina (Garrod et al., 2003). The children (age 6 to 12) whom Garrod and his colleagues interviewed were more likely to offer solutions to dilemmas involving both animal characters (see Johnston, 1988) and human characters framed in the care perspective than in the justice perspective. Although these voice-related patterns resemble, for the most part, those from studies of children living in North America (see Garrod, Beal, & Shin, 1990), the content of Bosnian children's responses to both types of moral dilemmas reflected their experience with political displacement and their concerns about the role of power, physical force, and violence in conflict resolution. Here is a brief example:

CHILD: The cow couldn't enter the house because the dog was barking. Because the cow can't do any harm. I don't know what should be done.

INTERVIEWER: You can't think of any solution?

C: Maybe if the cow had strong legs, she could kick him. . . .

I: Would that be good?

C: Yes, because it is her house and she can use force.

I: Can you think of another way to solve the problem?

C: The cow could explain to the dog that it's the cow's house and the dog should just leave. I think the dog should leave because people can expel each other from their houses (Garrod, et al., 2003, p. 143)

Given these findings, Garrod and his colleagues conclude with the following caveat, one that applies not only to their research, but also more broadly: "It is important to focus not only on the particular moral orientation—justice or care—represented in the solution that is offered, but also on the content of the children's responses and the motivation for their solution, drawn at least in part from the children's experiences with violence and the struggle of formerly warring groups to live together" (p. 146).

From a sociocultural perspective, both the concept of karma from the Buddhist tradition, and the Bosnian children's experience with violence and political displacement ("expulsion") are socioculturally significant not only because they represent external symbols that have specific religious, moral, or political meaning, but also because they function as semiotic resources that mediate and shape moral thinking, feeling, and acting (see Tappan, 2003). They are, moreover, part of a vernacular moral language whose meaning is shared by those who share the same cultural activities. Thus, the research of Garrod and his colleagues illuminates quite clearly how morality is shaped by culture, on the one hand, and how moral language and forms of moral discourse are shared dialogically, on the other.

In the end, therefore, sociocultural assumptions about mediation, inner moral dialogue, the social origins of moral functioning, and the sociocultural context of moral development come together. If morality is not a naturally occurring universal concept, but is dependent, instead, on words, language, and forms of discourse, as well as on forms and patterns of social interaction, all of which are socioculturally specific, then moral development can not be understood as the result of a constructive process undertaken by transcendental epistemic subjects (Kohlberg's view). Rather, moral development must be seen as the outcome of dialogue, social communication, and social interaction between real, live, speaking persons (not occupants of imaginary "positions," "original" or otherwise [see Rawls, 1970; Kohlberg, 1981, 1984])—dialogue, communication, and interaction, moreover, that occur in specific social, cultural, and historical contexts and settings.

CONCLUSION

This chapter has outlined common characteristics shared explicitly sociocultural/dialogical approaches to the study of moral development. Grounded in Vygotsky's (1934/1987, 1978) empirical and theoretical work on the development of higher mental functioning, and informed by Bakhtin's (1981) conception of the dialogic nature of all discourse, these approaches extend Vygotsky's insights about the semiotic mediation of the mental functioning via inner speech (and inner dialogue), the social origins of higher psychological functioning, and the sociocultural situatedness of human development into the realm of moral development. As such, this perspective not only points toward a new account of the process and dynamics of moral development, but also gives rise to a number of important questions.

Questions about differences in moral development—gender differences, racial differences, social class differences, cultural differences—lie at the heart of many of the current debates in the field of moral development. Thus perhaps it would be useful to focus on such questions, briefly, and to indicate some of the ways in which a sociocultural/dialogical perspective addresses them.

Vygotsky clearly considered differences between persons—for example, differences in reasoning or problem-solving ability—not to be indicators of developmental successes or failures, measured against a universal standard, but rather to be manifestations of the particular, and necessarily differential, effects of sociocultural setting on mental functioning (Wertsch, 1991). From a sociocultural/dialogical perspective, therefore, moral development does not occur in the same way, following the same sequence, for all persons around the globe, but rather it is specific to unique social, cultural, and historical contexts. Moreover, these unique sociocultural settings may well occur within the confines of a larger society, settings defined by those who share similar experiences, values, or social, political, or economic assumptions (see Bellah et al., 1985; Cortese, 1990; Walker, 2000). Thus, from this perspective, gender, racial, cultural, or socioeconomic differences in moral development, and in the forms of moral functioning, exhibited by members of different social groups, are not problems, indicators of developmental deficit, or the function of variables that have to be "controlled." Rather, they are to be expected, and they must be treated as differences, not deviations, by researchers and practitioners alike.

A sociocultural/dialogical perspective on the study of moral development also gives rise to a number of other important questions. One set of empirical questions concerns the degree of correspondence between person's inner moral dialogues and the external interactions and conversations from which they arise, on the one hand, and the moral narratives to which they give rise, on the other. Another set of more educational or applied questions concerns whether or not Vygotsky's (1978) conception of the "Zone of Proximal Development" (ZPD) might provide a helpful model for moral education efforts. On this view, certain activities of adults and more competent peers might encourage children and youth to move through the ZPD, from their actual level of moral functioning to their potential level (see Tappan, 1998a, 1998b; also Moll, 1990; Rogoff & Wertsch, 1984; Tharp & Gallimore, 1988). This last set of questions, needless to say, clearly calls for more work, both theoretical and empirical, regarding how to assess developmental levels of moral functioning in a way that avoids the universal standards that have traditionally been employed to chart developmental progress, and yet provides some means by which distinctions can be drawn between different types/forms/manifestations of moral functioning (while still honoring differences between social groups, as described).

This raises, of course, the question of moral relativism—always a hot button issue in any discussion of moral development. Although this issue cannot be explored in detail here, a sociocultural/dialogical perspective seeks to remain open to all types/forms/manifestations of moral functioning, and thus does not assume, unlike Kohlberg (1981, 1984), that normative moral judgments must be embedded in a theory of moral development. Judgments about developmental adequacy, on the other hand, using differentiation and hierarchical integration, for example, as evidence of ontogenetic progress (see Werner & Kaplan, 1956), are certainly an appropriate, and necessary part of theoretical, empirical, and applied efforts.

Finally, and perhaps most importantly, by linking Vygotskian insights about semiotic mediation and the social origins of mind to a Bakhtinian conception of the dialogic moral self (see Day & Tappan, 1996), a sociocultural/dialogical approach offers a distributed or shared vision of moral development (in contrast to the individualistic/psychological view that has dominated the field for the past century or so). This vision, among other things, sets the stage for a new and powerful understanding of moral community: Communities that promote moral development are not composed of discrete, self-contained, isolated individuals. Rather, successful moral communities consist of dialogical selves engaged in an ongoing process of interpretation, and committed, necessarily, to dialogue, discussion, and mutual exchange across differences (see Burbules, 1993; Oakeshott, 1975; Sandel, 1982; Walzer, 1987). In addition, such a perspective on moral community provides the key to answering critical questions about both "morality" and "development" that must be addressed as the field of moral development enters the 21st century. On this view *morality* must be understood as a discursively mediated practice or activity that facilitates human interaction in community. And *development* must be understood not as an individual achievement, but as a process that, at its core, entails relational, communal, political, and even cultural transformation.

REFERENCES

Attanucci, J. (1991). Changing subjects: Growing up and growing older. *Journal of Moral Education, 20,* 317–328.

Bakhtin, M. (1981). *The dialogic imagination*, ed. M. Holquist, & trans. C. Emerson & M. Holquist. Austin: University of Texas Press.

Bakhtin, M. (1984). *Problems of Dostoevsky's poetics,* ed. & trans. C. Emerson. Minneapolis: University of Minnesota Press.

Bakhtin, M. (1986). *Speech genres and other late essays,* ed. C. Emerson & M. Holquist, & trans. V. McGee. Austin: University of Texas Press.

Bakhtin, M. (1990). *Art and answerability,* ed. M. Holquist & V. Liapunov, & trans. V. Liapunov. Austin: University of Texas Press.

Baumrind, D. (1986). Sex differences in moral reasoning: Response to Walker's (1984) conclusion that there are none. *Child Development, 57,* 511–521.

Bellah, R., Madsen, R., Sullivan, W., Swindler, A., & Tipton, S. (1985). *Habits of the heart: Individualism and commitment in American life.* Berkeley: University of California Press.

Berk, L., & Winsler, A. (1995). *Scaffolding children's learning: Vygotsky and early childhood education.* Washington, DC: NAEYC Press.

Bhatia, S. (2000). Language socialization and the construction of socio-moral meanings. *Journal of Moral Education, 29,* 149–166.

Billig, M. (1987). *Arguing and thinking: A rhetorical approach to social psychology.* Cambridge, UK: Cambridge University Press.

Blasi, A. (1984). Moral identity: Its role in moral functioning. In W. Kurtines & J. Gewirtz (Eds.), *Morality, moral behavior, and moral development* (pp. 128–139). New York: Wiley.

Blasi, A. (1987). The psychological definitions of morality. In J. Kagan & S. Lamb (Eds.), *The emergence of morality in young children* (pp. 83–90). Chicago: University of Chicago Press.

Blum, L. (1980). *Friendship, altruism, and morality*. Boston: Routledge & Kegan Paul.

Boyes, M., & Walker, L. (1988). Implications of cultural diversity for the universality claims of Kohlberg's theory of moral reasoning. *Human Development, 31,* 44–59.

Brabeck, M. (1983). Moral judgment: Theory and research on differences between males and females. *Developmental Review, 3,* 274–291.

Brown, L., Debold, E., Tappan, M., & Gilligan, C. (1992). Reading narratives of conflict and choice for self and moral voice: A relational method. In W. Kurtines & J. Gewirtz (Eds.), *Handbook of moral behavior and development, Vol. 2: Research* (pp. 25–61). Hillsdale, NJ: Lawrence Erlbaum Associates.

Brown, L., & Gilligan, C. (1991). Listening for voice in narratives of relationship. In M. Tappan & M. Packer (Eds.), *Narrative and storytelling: Implications for understanding moral development* (pp. 43–62). San Francisco: Jossey-Bass.

Brown, L., Tappan, M., Gilligan, C., Miller, B., & Argyris, D. (1989). Reading for self and moral voice: A method for interpreting narratives of real-life moral conflict and choice. In M. Packer & R. Addison (Eds.), *Entering the circle: Hermeneutic investigation in psychology* (pp. 141–164). Albany: State University of New York Press.

Bruner, J. (1986). *Actual minds, possible worlds*. Cambridge, MA: Harvard University Press.

Bruner, J. (1990). *Acts of meaning*. Cambridge, MA: Harvard University Press.

Burbules, N. (1993). *Dialogue in teaching: Theory and practice*. New York: Teachers College Press.

Buzzelli, C. (1993). Morality in context: A sociocultural approach to enhancing young children's moral development. *Child and Youth Care Forum, 22,* 375–386.

Buzzelli, C. A., & Johnston, B. (2001). Authority, power, and morality in classroom discourse. *Teaching and Teacher Education, 17,* 873–884.

Buzzelli, C. A., & Johnston, B. (2002).*The moral dimensions of teaching: Language, power and culture in classroom interactions.* New York: Routledge/Falmer Press.

Clark, K., & Holquist, M. (1984). *Mikhail Bakhtin*. Cambridge, MA: Harvard University Press.

Colby, A., & Kohlberg, L. (1987). *The measurement of moral judgment* (vols. 1 & 2). New York: Cambridge University Press.

Cole, M. (1988). Cross-cultural research in the sociohistorical tradition. *Human Development, 31,* 137–152.

Cole, M. (1996). *Cultural psychology: A once and future discipline*. Cambridge, MA: Harvard University Press.

Coles, R. (1986). *The moral life of children*. Boston: Houghton-Mifflin.

Cortese, A. (1990). *Ethnic ethics: The restructuring of moral theory*. Albany: State University of New York Press.

Damon, W., & Hart, D. (1988). *Self-understanding in childhood and adolescence*. New York: Cambridge University Press.

Day, J. (1991). The moral audience: On the narrative mediation of moral 'judgment' and moral 'action'. In M. Tappan & M. Packer (Eds.), *Narrative and storytelling: Implications for understanding moral development* (pp. 27–42). San Francisco: Jossey-Bass.

Day, J., & Tappan, M. (1996). The narrative approach to moral development: From the epistemic subject to dialogical selves. *Human Development, 39,* 67–82.

Diaz, R., & Berk, L. (Eds.). (1992). *Private speech: From social interaction to self-regulation.* Hillsdale, NJ: Lawrence Erlbaum Associates.

Dien, D. (1982). A Chinese perspective on Kohlberg's theory of moral development. *Developmental Review, 2,* 331–141.

Duncan, P. (2001). Educating for moral ability: Reflections on moral development based on Vygotsky's theory of concept formation. *Journal of Moral Education, 30,* 113–129.

Dunn, J. (1987). The beginnings of moral understanding: Development in the second year. In J. Kagan & S. Lamb (Eds.), *The emergence of morality in young children* (pp. 91–112). Chicago: University of Chicago Press.

Edwards, D., & Potter, J. (1992). *Discursive psychology.* London: Sage.

Emerson, C. (1986). The outer word and inner speech: Bakhtin, Vygotsky, and the internalization of language. In G. Morson (Ed.), *Bakhtin: Essays and dialogues on his work* (pp. 21–40). Chicago: The University of Chicago Press.

Flanagan, O. (1991). *Varieties of moral personality: Ethics and psychological realism.* Cambridge, MA: Harvard University Press.

Forman, E., Minick, N., & Stone. C. A. (Eds.). (1993). *Contexts for learning: Sociocultural dynamics in children's development.* New York: Oxford University Press.

Freud, S. (1923/1960). *The ego and the id.* New York: W. W. Norton.

Garrod, A., Beal, C., Jaeger, W., Thomas, J., Davis, J., Leiser, N., & Hodzic, A. (2003). Culture, ethnic conflict, and moral orientation in Bosnian children. *Journal of Moral Education, 32,* 131–150.

Garrod, A., Beal, C., & Shin, P. (1990). The development of moral orientation in elementary school children. *Sex Roles, 22,* 13–27.

Gergen, K. (1982). *Toward transformation in social knowledge.* New York: Springer-Verlag.

Gergen, K. (1985). The social constructionist movement in modern psychology. *American Psychologist, 40,* 266–275.

Gergen, K. (1991). *The saturated self: Dilemmas of identity in contemporary life.* New York: Basic Books.

Gergen, K. (1994). *Realities and relationships: Soundings in social construction.* Cambridge, MA: Harvard University Press.

Gilligan, C. (1977). In a different voice: Women's conceptions of self and morality. *Harvard Educational Review, 47,* 481–517.

Gilligan, C. (1982). *In a different voice: Psychological theory and women's development.* Cambridge, MA: Harvard University Press.

Gilligan, C. (1983). Do the social sciences have an adequate theory of moral development? In N. Haan, R. Bellah, P. Rabinow, & W. Sullivan (Eds.), *Social science as moral inquiry.* New York: Columbia University Press.

Gilligan, C., & Attanucci, J. (1988). Two moral orientations: Gender differences and similarities. *Merrill-Palmer Quarterly, 34,* 223–237.

Gilligan, C., Brown, L., & Rogers, A. (1990). Psyche embedded: A place for body, relationships, and culture in personality theory. In A. I. Rabin, R. Zucker, R. Emmons, & S. Frank (Eds.), *Studying persons and lives.* New York: Springer.

Gilligan, C., Ward, J., & Taylor, J. (Eds.). (1988). *Mapping the moral domain: A contribution of women's thinking to psychological theory and education.* Cambridge, MA: Harvard University Press.

Gilligan, C., & Wiggins, G. (1987). The origins of morality in early childhood relationships. In J. Kagan & S. Lamb (Eds.), *The emergence of morality in young children* (pp. 277–305). Chicago: University of Chicago Press.

Harre, R. (1984). *Personal being: A theory for individual psychology.* Cambridge, MA: Harvard University Press.

Hermans, H., & Kempen, H. (1993). *The dialogical self: Meaning as movement*. New York: Academic Press.

Hermans, H., Kempen, H., & van Loon, R. (1992). The dialogical self: Beyond individualism and rationalism. *American Psychologist, 47,* 23–33.

Holquist, M. (1990). *Dialogism: Bakhtin and his world*. London: Routledge.

Huebner, A., & Garrod, A. (1991). Moral reasoning in a karmic world. *Human Development, 34,* 341–352.

Huebner, A., & Garrod, A. (1993). Moral reasoning among Tibetan monks: A study of Buddhist adolescents and young adults in Nepal. *Journal of Cross-Cultural Psychology, 24,* 167–185.

Jahoda, G. (1992). *Crossroads between culture and mind*. New York: Harvester Wheatshaft.

Johnston, B., & Buzzelli, C. A. (2002). Expressive morality in a collaborative learning activity: A case study in the creation of moral meaning. *Language and Education, 16,* 37–47.

Johnston, D. K. (1988). Adolescents' solutions to dilemmas in fables: Two moral orientations—two problem-solving strategies. In C. Gilligan, J. Ward, J. Taylor, & B. Bardige (Eds.), *Mapping the moral domain* (pp. 49–71). Cambridge, MA: Harvard University Press.

Johnston, D. K. (1991). Cheating: Reflections on a moral dilemma. *Journal of Moral Education, 20,* 283–292.

Kohlberg, L. (1963). The development of children's orientation toward a moral order: Sequence in the development of moral thought. *Vita Humana, 6,* 11–33.

Kohlberg, L. (1969). Stage and sequence: The cognitive-developmental approach to socialization. In D. Goslin (Ed.), *Handbook of socialization theory and research* (pp. 347–480). Chicago: Rand McNally.

Kohlberg, L. (1976). Moral stages and moralization: The cognitive-developmental approach. In T. Lickona (Ed.), *Moral development and behavior* (pp. 31–53). New York: Holt, Rinehart & Winston.

Kohlberg, L. (1981). *Essays on moral development, Vol. I: The philosophy of moral development*. San Francisco: Harper & Row.

Kohlberg, L. (1984). *Essays on moral development, Vol. II: The psychology of moral development*. San Francisco: Harper & Row.

Kohlberg, L., & Kramer, R. (1969). Continuities and discontinuities in childhood and adult moral development. *Human Development, 12,* 93–120.

Kohlberg, L., Yaeger, J., & Hjertholm, E. (1968). Private speech: Four studies and a review of theories. *Child Development, 39,* 691–736.

Kozulin, A. (1986). Vygotsky in context. In L. Vygotsky & A. Kozulin, Ed. & Trans. *Thought and language* (pp. xi–lvi). Cambridge, MA: The MIT Press.

Kozulin, A. (1990). *Vygotsky's psychology: A biography of ideas*. Cambridge, MA: Harvard University Press.

Lightfoot, C. (1997). *The culture of adolescent risk taking*. New York: Guilford Press.

Lightfoot, C. (2002a, October). *Adolescent risk-taking as moral dialogue*. Paper presented at the Second International Conference on the Dialogical Self, Ghent, Belgium.

Lightfoot, C. (2002b, November). *Adolescent risk-taking as moral discourse*. Paper presented at 28th Annual Conference of the Association for Moral Education, Chicago, IL.

Lightfoot, C. (2003). Fantastic self: A study of adolescents' fictional narratives, and aesthetic activity as identity work. In C. Daiute & C. Lightfoot (Eds.), *Narrative analysis: Studying the development of individuals in society*. Thousand Oaks, CA: Sage.

Lyons, N. (1983). Two perspectives: On self, relationships, and morality. *Harvard Educational Review, 53,* 125–145.

MacIntyre, A. (1981). *After virtue: A study in moral theory*. Notre Dame, IN: University of Notre Dame Press.

Martin, L., Nelson, K., & Tobach, E. (Eds.). (1995). *Sociocultural psychology: Theory and practice of doing and knowing*. New York: Cambridge University Press.

Mischler, E. (1986). *Research interviewing: Context and narrative*. Cambridge, MA: Harvard University Press.

Mkhize, N. (2003). *Culture and the self in moral and ethical decision-making: A dialogical approach*. Unpublished doctoral dissertation, University of Natal, Pietermaritzburg, South Africa.

Moll, L. (Ed.). (1990). *Vygotsky and education: Instructional implications and applications of sociohistorical psychology*. Cambridge, UK: Cambridge University Press.

Morson, G., & Emerson, C. (1990). *Mikhail Bakhtin: Creation of a prosaics*. Stanford, CA: Stanford University Press.

Noddings, N. (1984). *Caring: A feminine approach to moral education*. Berkeley: The University of California Press.

Oakeshott, M. (1975). *On human conduct*. Oxford: Clarendon Press.

Ochs, E. (1996). Linguistic resources for socializing humanity. In J. Gumperz & S. Levinson (Eds.), *Rethinking linguistic relativity* (pp. 407–437). London: Cambridge University Press.

Packer, M. (1985). *The structure of moral action: A hermeneutic study of moral conflict*. Basel: S. Karger.

Packer, M. (1992). Toward a postmodern psychology of moral action and moral development. In W. Kurtines, M. Azmitia, & J. Gewirtz (Eds.), *The role of values in psychology and human development* (pp. 30–62). New York: John Wiley.

Packer, M., & Tappan, M. (Eds.). (2001). *Cultural and critical perspectives on human development*. Albany: State University of New York Press.

Parker, I. (1992). *Discourse dynamics*. London: Routledge.

Penuel, W., & Wertsch, J. (1995). Vygotsky and identity formation: A sociocultural approach. *Educational Psychologist, 30*, 83–92.

Piaget, J. (1932/1965). *The moral judgment of the child*. New York: The Free Press.

Polkinghorne, D. (1988). *Narrative knowing and the human sciences*. Albany: SUNY Press.

Pratt, M., Golding, G., & Hunter, W. (1984). Does morality have a gender? Sex, sex role, and moral judgment relationships across the adult lifespan. *Merrill-Palmer Quarterly, 30*, 321–340.

Rawls, J. (1970). *A theory of justice*. Cambridge, MA: Harvard University Press.

Rogoff, B. (1990). *Apprenticeship in thinking: Cognitive development in social context*. New York: Oxford University Press.

Rogoff, B., & Chavajay, P. (1995). What's become of research on the cultural basis of cognitive development? *American Psychologist, 50*, 859–877.

Rogoff, B., & Lave, J. (Eds.). (1984). *Everyday cognition: Its development in social contexts*. Cambridge, MA: Harvard University Press.

Rogoff, B., & Wertsch, J. (Eds.). (1984). *Children's learning in the zone of proximal development* (New directions for child development, No. 23). San Francisco: Jossey-Bass.

Ruddick, S. (1989). *Maternal thinking: Toward a politics of peace*. Boston: Beacon Press.

Sampson, E. (1993a). *Celebrating the other: A dialogical account of human nature*. Boulder, CO: Westview Press.

Sampson, E. (1993b). Identity politics: Challenges to psychology's understanding. *American Psychologist, 48*, 1219–1230.

Sandel, M. (1982). *Liberalism and the limits of justice*. Cambridge, MA: Cambridge University Press.

Sarbin, T. (1986). The narrative as a root metaphor for psychology. In T. Sarbin (Ed.), *Narrative psychology: The storied nature of human conduct*. New York: Praeger.

Sarbin, T. (1990). The narrative quality of action. *Theoretical and Philosophical Psychology, 10*, 49–65.

Shotter, J. (1990). *Knowing of the third kind*. Utrecht: University of Utrecht Press.

Shotter, J., & Gergen, K. (Eds.). (1989). *Texts of identity*. London: Sage.

Shweder, R. (1982). Liberalism as destiny. *Contemporary Psychology, 27*, 421–424.

Shweder, R. (1991). *Thinking through cultures: Expeditions in cultural psychology*. Cambridge, MA: Harvard University Press.

Shweder, R., Mahapatra, M., & Miller, J. (1987). Culture and moral development. In J. Kagan & S. Lamb (Eds.), *The emergence of morality in young children* (pp. 1–82). Chicago: University of Chicago Press.

Shweder, R., & Much, N. (1987). Determinations of meaning: Discourse and moral socialization. In W. Kurtines & J. Gewirtz (Eds.), *Moral development through social interaction* (pp. 197–244). New York: John Wiley.

Snarey, J. (1985). Cross-cultural universality of social-moral development: A critical review of Kohlbergian research. *Psychological Bulletin, 97*, 202–232.

Snow, C. (1987). Language and the beginnings of moral understanding. In J. Kagan & S. Lamb (Eds.). *The emergence of morality in young children* (pp. 112–122). Chicago: University of Chicago Press.

Stigler, J., Shweder, R., & Herdt, G. (1990). *Cultural psychology: Essays on comparative human development*. Cambridge: Cambridge University Press.

Stout, J. (1988). *Ethics after babel: The languages of morals and their discontents*. Boston: Beacon Press.

Sullivan, E. (1977). A study of Kohlberg's structural theory of moral development: A critique of liberal social science ideology. *Human Development, 20*, 352–376.

Tappan, M. (1991a). Narrative, authorship, and the development of moral authority. In M. Tappan & M. Packer (Eds.), *Narrative and storytelling: Implications for understanding moral development* (New directions for child development, No. 54, pp. 5–25). San Francisco: Jossey-Bass.

Tappan, M. (1991b). Narrative, language, and moral experience. *Journal of Moral Education, 20*, 243–256.

Tappan, M. (1997). Language, culture, and moral development: A Vygotskian perspective. *Developmental Review, 17*, 78–100.

Tappan, M. (1998a). Moral education in the zone of proximal development. *Journal of Moral Education, 27*, 125–145.

Tappan, M. (1998b). Sociocultural psychology and caring pedagogy: Exploring Vygotsky's "hidden curriculum." *Educational Psychologist, 33*, 23–33.

Tappan, M. (1999). Authoring a moral self: A dialogical perspective. *Journal of Constructivist Psychology, 12*, 117–131.

Tappan, M. (2000). Autobiography, mediated action, and the development of moral identity. *Narrative Inquiry, 10*, 1–36.

Tappan, M. (2003). *Moral functioning as mediated action*. Manuscript submitted for publication.

Tappan, M. (2005). Domination, subordination, and the dialogical self: Identity development and the politics of "ideological becoming." *Culture and Psychology, 11*, 17–75.

Tappan, M., & Brown, L. (1989). Stories told and lessons learned: Toward a narrative approach to moral development and moral education. *Harvard Educational Review, 59*, 182–205.

Tappan, M., & Packer, M. (Eds.). (1991). *Narrative and storytelling: Implications for understanding moral development* (New directions for child development, No. 54). San Francisco: Jossey-Bass.

Taylor, C. (1991). The dialogical self. In D. Hiley, J. Bohman, & R. Shusterman (Eds.), *The interpretive turn: Philosophy, science, culture* (pp. 304–314). Ithaca, NY: Cornell University Press.

Tharp, R., & Gallimore, R. (1988). *Rousing minds to life: Teaching, learning, and schooling in social context.* Cambridge, UK: Cambridge University Press.

Turiel, E. (1983). *The development of social knowledge: Morality and convention.* Cambridge, UK: Cambridge University Press.

Turiel, E. (2002). *The culture of morality: Social development, context, and conflict.* New York: Cambridge University Press.

Valsiner, J. (1998). *The guided mind.* Cambridge, MA: Harvard University Press.

Van der Veer, R., & Valsiner, J. (1991). *Understanding Vygotsky: A quest for synthesis.* Cambridge, MA: Blackwell.

Volosinov, V. (1929/1986). *Marxism and the philosophy of language* (L. Matejka & I. R. Titunik, Trans.). Cambridge, MA: Harvard University Press.

Vygotsky, L. (1934/1987). Thinking and speech. In L. S. Vygotsky, R. Rieber & A. Carton, Eds., N. Minick, Trans. *The collected works of L.S. Vygotsky, Vol. 1: Problems of general psychology* (pp. 37–285). New York: Plenum Press.

Vygotsky, L. (1978). *Mind in society: The development of higher psychological processes.* Ed. M. Cole, V. John-Steiner, S. Scribner, & E. Souberman. Cambridge, MA: Harvard University Press.

Vygotsky, L. (1981a). The genesis of higher mental functions. In J. Wertsch (Ed.), *The concept of activity in Soviet psychology.* Armonk, NY: M. E. Sharpe.

Vygotsky, L. (1981b). The instrumental method in psychology. In J. Wertsch (Ed.), *The concept of activity in Soviet psychology.* Armonk, NY: M. E. Sharpe.

Walker, J. (2000). Choosing biases, using power and practicing resistance: Moral development in a world without certainty. *Human Development, 43,* 135–156.

Walker, L. (1984). Sex differences in the development of moral reasoning: A critical review. *Child Development, 55,* 677–691.

Walker, L. (1986). Sex differences in the development of moral reasoning: A rejoinder to Baumrind. *Child Development, 57,* 522–526.

Walzer, M. (1987). *Interpretation and social criticism.* Cambridge, MA: Harvard University Press.

Ward, J. (1991). "Eyes in the back of your head": Moral themes in African-American narratives of racial conflict. *Journal of Moral Education, 20,* 267–282.

Werner, H., & Kaplan, B. (1956). The developmental approach to cognition: Its relevance to the psychological interpretation of anthropological and ethnolinguistic data. *American Anthropologist, 58,* 866–880.

Wertsch, J. (1985). *Vygotsky and the social formation of mind.* Cambridge, MA: Harvard University Press.

Wertsch, J. (Ed.). (1986). *Culture, communication, and cognition: Vygotskian perspectives.* New York: Cambridge University Press.

Wertsch, J. (1989). A sociocultural approach to mind. In W. Damon (Ed.), *Child development today and tomorrow.* San Francisco: Jossey-Bass.

Wertsch, J. (1991). *Voices of the mind: A sociocultural approach to mediated action.* Cambridge, MA: Harvard University Press.

Wertsch, J. (1998). *Mind as action.* New York: Oxford University Press.

Wertsch, J., del Rio, P., & Alvarez, A. (Eds.). (1995). *Sociocultural studies of mind*. New York: Cambridge University Press.

Winegar, L. T., & Valsiner, J. (Eds.). (1992). *Children's development within social contexts: Metatheoretical, theoretical, and methodological issues*. Hillsdale, NJ: Lawrence Erlbaum Associates.

Witherell, C., & Edwards, C. P. (1991). Moral versus social-conventional reasoning: A narrative and cultural critique. *Journal of Moral Education, 20*, 293–304.

Witherell, C., & Noddings, N. (Eds.). (1991). *Stories lives tell: Narrative and dialogue in education*. New York: Teachers College Press.

Wortham, S. (2001). *Narratives in action: A strategy for research and analysis*. New York: Teachers College Press.

Zivin, G. (Ed.). (1979). *The development of self-regulation through private speech*. New York: Wiley.

14

INSIGHTS INTO MORAL DEVELOPMENT FROM CULTURAL PSYCHOLOGY

JOAN G. MILLER

NEW SCHOOL FOR SOCIAL RESEARCH

A strong assumption of universalism characterizes psychological theories of moral development within the social constructivist tradition of cognitive developmental theory (e.g., Piaget, 1932; Kohlberg, 1969, 1971) and the distinct domain perspective (e.g., Turiel, 1983, 1988a). It is assumed that stances that treat morality in culturally variable terms give rise to an extreme moral relativism and embody a passive view of the individual, as merely conforming to social expectations. This charge was initially directed by social constructivist theorists (e.g., Kohlberg, 1971; Turiel, 1983) at social learning approaches (e.g., Berkowitz, 1964; Eysenck, 1961), perspectives that draw no distinction between morality and social convention. However, more recently, the same criticism (e.g., Turiel, 2002) has been directed at approaches to moral development within cultural psychology (e.g., Miller, 1994; Shweder, Mahapatra, & Miller, 1987), a perspective that, in contrast to social learning approaches, treats morality as based on a perceived natural law rather than on compliance with societal standards or personal preferences. Cultural psychological approaches to moral development are further criticized (e.g., Turiel & Wainryb, 2000) as being informed by stereotypical views of culture and embodying an insensitivity to contextual considerations.

This chapter begins with an overview of the assumptions of cultural psychology, focusing on theoretical claims that pertain to work on the development of moral outlooks. This is followed by a discussion of cross-cultural findings that not only establish certain universals in moral judgment but that highlight variability in moral outlook that is not presently well accommodated in the existing universalistic psychological models within the social constructivist tradition. In turn, the third section identifies challenges for future theory and research. The argument is made that approaches to moral development within cultural psychology embody a view of individual agency and of the contextual dependence of psychological phenomena and give rise to pragmatic rather than extreme forms of moral relativism. It is argued that to enhance the cultural sensitivity of psychological theories of morality, it is critical to bridge work on moral development in the social constructivist tradition with approaches to moral development within cultural psychology (e.g., Miller, 2001; Shweder, Much, Mahapatra, & Park, 1997).

THEORETICAL ASSUMPTIONS OF CULTURAL PSYCHOLOGY

> Cultural, institutional, and historical forces are 'imported' into individuals' actions by virtue of using cultural tools, on the one hand, and sociocultural settings are created and recreated through individuals' use of mediational means, on the other. The resulting picture is one in which, because of the role cultural tools play in mediated action, it is virtually impossible for us to act in a way that is not sociocultural situated ... Nearly all human action is mediated action, the only exceptions being found perhaps at very early stages of ontogenesis and in natural responses such as reacting involuntarily to an unexpected noise. (Wertsch, 1995, p. 97)

Approaches within cultural psychology are not defined on the basis of their methodology, such as whether they employ comparative or noncomparative research designs, or by their findings, such as whether or not they identify cultural differences. Rather, they are defined conceptually on the basis of their view of psychological processes as dependent on cultural processes that may qualitatively affect their form (Bruner, 1990; Cole, 1990, 1996; Fiske, Kitayama, Markus, & Nisbett, 1998; Markus & Kitayama, 1991; Martin, Nelson, & Tobach, 1995; Miller, 1994, 1997, 1999; Shweder, 1990; Shweder & Sullivan, 1990, 1993). Cultural psychological outlooks assume that psychological functioning always occurs in specific sociocultural contexts and that psychological theories must and, in fact, invariably do, reflect, in part, this sociocultural grounding.

The present discussion focuses on widely shared theoretical assumptions of cultural psychology that bear on understanding the constitutive role of cultural meanings and practices in moral outlooks. Given the heterogeneity of contemporary approaches identified with cultural psychology, the present discussion emphasizes the most central assumptions and claims within this emerging set of perspectives, with a particular focus on cultural theorists working in the area of moral reasoning.

Symbolic Views of Culture

Within the perspective of cultural psychology, *culture* is understood in symbolic terms as meanings and practices and not merely in ecological terms as objective adaptive affordances and constraints (D'Andrade, 1984; LeVine, 1984; Strauss & Quinn, 1997). Developmental psychology has long given attention to ecological aspects of the context (e.g., Bronfenbrenner, 1979; Eccles et al., 1993). This type of approach recognizes that families, schools, and larger communities present individuals with different resources and experiences that serve to enhance or impede particular developmental outcomes.

An ecological perspective on culture is essential to take into account in approaches to understanding moral development and in highlighting the adaptive significance of objective characteristics of the setting. The ecology, for example, may affect the usefulness of particular types of moral outlooks, an observation made by Edwards (1975, 1994) in noting the lesser relevance of the "systems" perspective reflected in stage 4 of Kohlbergian moral reasoning for individuals living in isolated peasant or tribal communities than for individuals living in societies characterized by occupational specialization or formal bureaucratic institutions (Edwards, 1975, 1994). Equally, ecological conditions may provide experiences that are differentially conducive to moral development, a phenomena uncovered by Hart and Atkins (Atkins & Hart, 2003; Hart & Atkins, 2002) in their finding that it is more difficult for poor urban youth to develop a sense of moral identity than it is for suburban youth whose ecology provides them with more frequent opportunities for civic participation. However, it is important to view culture not merely in functional ecological terms, but also to recognize its symbolic properties. From this latter perspective, cultural meanings and practices are understood as bearing an open relationship to adaptive constraints rather than as merely functionally based (LeVine, 1984; Shwederb, 1984; Tobin, Wu, & Davidson, 1989). To give an example, research indicates that Japanese educators tend to consider the preschool practice of having many children assigned to a given teacher as functional in providing children with experience in and promoting their knowing how to be a good member of a group (Tobin et al., 1989). This symbolic value tends to be less central in U.S. contexts, where preschool educators tend to consider it beneficial to have fewer children assigned to a given teacher, so the children may be accorded more individual attention and have more opportunities to exercise individual decision making. Thus, whereas both of these types of preschool classroom practices may be considered adaptive, the basis of their functionality cannot be understood merely by reference to objective constraints, such as teacher resources, but requires also taking into account nonfunctional values, such as pedagogical viewpoints, related to goals for the child's development.

Within a symbolic view, culture is seen in representational, directive, and constitutive terms (D'Andrade, 1984). It is well known that, in terms of their representational functions, cultural meaning systems encompass knowledge structures that provide information about the nature of reality whereas, in terms of their directive functions, they encompass social rules. However, it is less widely appreciated that, in terms of their constitutive functions, cultural meanings function to create social realities that serve to define the shared meanings accorded to particular entities or experiences (Searle, 1969; Shweder, 1984). Thus, for example, the culturally constituted category of a "bride" only has meaning against the backdrop of the agreement within a community to associate particular meanings and institutional practices with this social role. The present considerations imply that appraisals of harm, such as the judgment that abortion constitutes murder, are not based merely on biological facts. Rather, such appraisals depend as well on culturally variable definitions of the meanings to be accorded objective entities and events, such as the definition of the point during a pregnancy when a fetus is to be treated as a person entitled to protection from harm.

As applied to evaluating cross-cultural differences in moral judgment, the present assumptions imply that the relative adequacy of the knowledge assumptions that are brought to bear in moral reasoning (e.g., Turiel, Killen, & Helwig, 1987; Wainryb, 1991) cannot be fully comparatively evaluated in terms of objective criteria, such as the magnitude of harm involved. Rather, such knowledge assumptions reflect, in part, culturally based values that are contributed to experience. To give an example, helping a friend who is experiencing minor need (such as a need for directions to a store) tends to be categorized as a moral obligation by Indian populations and as a matter of personal choice by U.S. populations (Miller, Bersoff, & Harwood, 1990). This cross-cultural difference, however, arises from the greater value placed by U.S. than by Indian respondents on balancing personal freedom of choice with interpersonal commitments rather than from a difference related to individuals' knowledge of the nature of the welfare concerns involved (Miller et al., 1990). Thus, such cross-cultural differences in moral appraisal were observed to remain even when controlling for differences in respondents' assessments of the magnitude of need under consideration and the perceived desirability of helping.

Integrating Concerns With Power and With Meaning in Understanding Culture

The need to recognize the role of power dynamics in patterning cultural forms represents an insight that not only has been prominent within recent postmodern anthropological work (e.g., Abu-Lughod, 1993; Appadurai, 1988) but that is also strongly emphasized by theorists within the distinct domain tradition (Turiel, 1998b; Wainryb & Turiel, 1994). From these perspectives, it is recognized that individuals assume contrasting positions of power within societies and that cultural meanings and practices serve, in part, to perpetuate social relations based on inequality. Thus, for example, a cultural concern with hierarchy is seen as associated with social institutions in which women are given fewer opportunities than men, and in which, in cases, they suffer exploitation and abuse.

While acknowledging the critical importance of recognizing the role of power in structuring social institutions, the caution is raised from a cultural psychology perspective that culture not be viewed only in terms of such considerations. It is argued rather that effort be made to integrate a concern with power dynamics with a concern with symbolic aspects of culture. This type of insight may be illustrated in a recent comparative study examining conceptions of everyday family roles and of feminism among samples of middle age women from Japan and the U.S. (Schaberg, 2002). Although the Japanese women expressed dissent with the gender role practices of their society, their concerns did not map directly onto the issues of seeking greater freedom of choice raised by the U.S. respondents. Valuing patterns of reciprocal interdependence in family relations, the Japanese women called for greater flexibility and accommodation in gender role expectations but rejected the egalitarian model of marital relations emphasized by the U.S. respondents. Equally, the Japanese women embraced a form of feminism that embodies a concern with contributing to the larger social whole and rejected features of what they appraised to be the more individualistic feminist perspective emphasized within the U.S. In sum, it must be recognized that while individuals maintain an active perspective on their cultural practices, dissent tends to be formulated in ways that in most cases does not call for a total abandonment of fundamental cultural commitments and thus that do not simply converge cross-culturally.

Dynamic Views of Culture and Psychology.   As reflected in the discussion by Shweder and LeVine (1984), which more than the highly influential review article on culture and the self by Markus and Kitayama (1991) may be considered one of the earliest and most powerful statements of the agenda of cultural psychology, theorists within cultural psychology have long recognized the importance of treating culture in dynamic terms, as nonuniform and changing. However, in contrast to work from a postmodern perspective and to various claims from a distinct domain framework, work within cultural psychology assumes that some thematic consistencies in cultural outlooks may be observed, thus making it possible to draw certain distinctions between cultural viewpoints (see also Shweder, 1979a, 1979b; Miller, 1997).

A stance that overstates the thematic nature of culture may be criticized as glossing over the heterogeneity and overlap in meanings between and within cultural communities and thus as giving rise to stereotypical claims. This type of stance notably not only may be seen in such classic works in culture and personality as Benedict's *Chrysthanemum and the Sword* (1946), but also characterizes some recent positions in cultural social psychology that have embraced the individualism/collectivism paradigm. Thus, for example, efforts to base global claims about East–West differences in analytic versus holistic thought based on data collected from primarily East Asian cultural populations (e.g., Nisbett, 2003; Nisbett,

Peng, Choi, & Norenzayan, 2001) may be criticized as glossing over important between and within group differences. In fact, it may be noted, that although some recent work that is identified with cultural psychology has been framed within the individualism/collectivism paradigm, this type of framing has been challenged by other cultural psychologists for its inattention to variation between and within cultural groups and cannot be considered a constitutive premise of cultural psychology (Miller, 2002, 2004; Strauss, 2000).

Although there is agreement between cultural psychologists and both distinct domain and postmodern theorists about the need to recognize the multifaceted, dynamic, and frequently conflicting nature of cultural meanings and practices, approaches within cultural psychology take exception with positions that interpret this concern to imply that it is impossible to identify any group differences in cultural outlook and that culture represents merely a contextual effect (Miller, 1997). This conclusion that the blending of cultural forms makes it impossible to distinguish between cultures is drawn, for example, by the postmodern theorist Gergen as he describes the interpenetration of cultural outlooks:

> We are not speaking here of the blending of all, the emergence of monoculture, but rapid and continuous transformations in cultural forms, as they are subject to multiple influences and in their altered state become the impetus for change in other locales . . . if there is a continuous blending, appropriation, dissolution, and the like, how are we to draw distinctions among cultural processes? (Gulerce, 1995, p. 149–150)

In a related view, the conclusion that culture can be considered merely a contextual effect has been forwarded by Turiel and his colleagues (Turiel, 1998b; Turiel & Neff, 2000). In a recent handbook chapter on moral development, Turiel, in fact, titles one of the chapter sub headings "Culture as Context or Context as Context" to communicate his view that culture represents merely a situational influence on behavior (Turiel, 1998a).

In contrast to drawing the conclusion that the hetereogeneity of cultural forms implies that no distinctions can be drawn between cultures or that culture is merely a contextual influence on behavior, cultural psychologists note that it is possible to identify at least some thematic consistencies in cultural views. As discussed more fully in the next section, cultural psychologists also note that whereas psychological processes are contextually dependent, cultural influences on psychological processes cannot be merely reduced to a contextual influence on behavior but rather represent a mediator of contextual influences and thus a consideration that must be taken into account in addition to rather than in lieu of contextual processes. As Geertz (as quoted in Shweder, 1984a) comments in regard to the issue of thematic consistency, for example:

> It's possible to overthematize, and it's possible to underthematize . . . the elements of culture are not like a pile of sand and not like a spider's web. It's more like an octopus, a rather badly integrated creature—what passes for a brain keeps it together, more or less, in one ungainly whole (Shweder, 1984a, p. 19).

In drawing distinctions between cultural views, the stance adopted within cultural psychology may be seen to be similar in kind to that which is adopted in drawing other types of subgroup distinctions in developmental psychology. Thus, for example, in work on theory of mind, the claim is made that 5-year-old children tend to maintain an understanding of false belief whereas 3-year-olds tend to lack such an understanding (e.g., Wellman, 1990). This claim is informative in identifying a developmental difference, although it glosses over the heterogeneity and overlap that distinguish the outlooks of different groups of

3- and of 5-year-old children and thus arguably might be subject to the same types of criticisms as directed at similar types of group generalizations forwarded within cultural psychology. It is recognized in cultural psychology, as it is in other areas of psychology, that although subtleties are lost at less fine grained levels of analysis, for certain purposes it is meaningful to make claims about group differences in behavior. In fact, drawing distinctions between cultural perspectives is considered critical in efforts to give voice to viewpoints that otherwise could not be distinguished from what is the default mainstream outlook in psychological theory (Graham, 1992). As Butler asserts in arguing that the post-modern stance of failing to draw any distinctions between cultural viewpoints ironically gives rise to a position in which it is impossible to give voice to feminist concerns:

> If it is not a female subject who provides the normative model for a feminist politics, then what does? . . . What constitutes the "who," the subject, for whom feminism seeks emancipation? If there is no subject, who is left to emancipate? (1990, p. 327).

The position of theorists within cultural psychology then is to be sensitive not only to the need to avoid stereotypy, but also to the need to avoid stances that overlook the meaningful consistencies that can be located in cultural beliefs and practices. This type of stance is regarded as critical in making it possible to give weight to cultural outlooks that are currently downplayed or overlooked in the formation of basic psychological theory and is seen as no different in kind from the type of stance adopted more generally in developmental psychology in making claims about age-related trends.

Context Dependent Nature of Cultural Influences

Whereas some work from an individualism/collectivism perspective has portrayed cultural influences on behavior as non–contextually dependent (e.g., Oyserman, Coon, & Kemmelmeier, 2002), this does not represent the claims and research findings from a cultural psychology perspective. Rather, work from a cultural psychology perspective takes into account that psychological phenomena are contextually dependent and thus that cultural influences on psychological phenomena are contextually dependent as well.

Confusion regarding this point may exist because of some arguable misinterpretation by theorists regarding the nature of claims made within work in cultural psychology. For example, Turiel and Neff (2000) characterize some of the assertions of cultural theorists as bearing on non–contextually dependent cross-cultural differences—claims that, when formulated in this way, can be easily refuted:

> Members of collectivistic societies are said to subordinate personal goals to those of the group, to make duty-based moral judgments, and to have a sociocentric and interdependent view of the self. Members of individualistic societies are said to make personal goals primary, to make rights-based moral judgments, and to have an egocentric and independent view of self. However . . . it is not so clear that the moral reasoning of individual Americans can be characterized as predominately individualistic. . . . Americans have multiple ways of thinking about the social world that includes concerns with the personal and the collective, and the application of these principles varies between situational contexts (Turiel & Neff, 2000, p. 287).

This type of conclusion may be criticized as a "straw man" position that overlooks the fact that work from a cultural psychology perspective routinely builds in contextual/context variation and is not making claims about non–contextually dependent group differences. It also fails to recognize that the use of labels by cultural psychologists represents a means of expanding psychological constructs and of contributing to basic psychological theory rather than an effort to make claims about the existence of decontextualized group differences in behavior. To give an example, in arguing for a "morality of caring," Gilligan (1977, 1982) was not asserting that girls and women always reason in terms of caring and never give weight to justice issues. Rather, her point was to identify a qualitatively distinct approach to moral reasoning that, she correctly noted, was not then presently represented in psychological theory, with its exclusive focus on the "morality of justice." Likewise, in using the summary label of an "individually oriented morality of caring" versus a "duty-based morality of caring" to refer to some of the consistent differences that I observed across studies in views of interpersonal morality emphasized by Hindu Indian as compared with European-American populations (Miller, 1994), my focus was also to expand theoretical understandings of morality and not to stereotype cultural differences. To give another example, in recently arguing for a developmental model focused on "symbiotic harmony" rather than on "individuation-separation," cultural psychologists Rothbaum, Pott, Azuma, Miyake, and Weisz (2000) sought conceptually to expand present visions of the endpoints of psychological development. No claim was being made that U.S. adolescents always emphasize autonomy, or in all cases are more autonomous than Japanese adolescents, or that Japanese adolescents only form symbiotic ties with others.

In acknowledging that psychological effects are always contextually dependent and in stipulating that culture cannot be reduced to a mere contextual factor, work from a cultural psychology underscores the importance of attending both to culture and context in psychological explanation as well as underscores their mutually constitutive nature. It is not considered enough to attend to the ecological context but rather attention must be given as well to its symbolic significance, just as an attention to symbolic aspects of culture alone is insufficient without consideration of ecological dimensions of the context. For example, comparative research on attachment conducted among middle class and working class Puerto Rican and European-American mothers revealed that the outlook of the mothers was influenced not only by the symbolic meaning systems of their respective cultural communities or by the ecological contextual factor of socioeconomic status but that these two types of considerations interacted (Harwood, Miller, & Irizarry, 1995). Thus, for example, the tendency to emphasize more controling childrearing values was associated with lower socioeconomic status only among the European-American mothers and not linked to lower socioeconomic status among the Puerto Rican mothers. In another example, experimental research on the self descriptions of U.S. and Japanese adult populations both predicted and observed culturally dependent patterns of cross-cultural differences (Cousins, 1989). U.S. respondents employed more abstract self-descriptions on a decontextualized rather than contextualized self-description procedure, whereas Japanese respondents displayed the reverse contextual effect. This interaction of culture and context was interpreted as reflecting the differential meaning of the contextual manipulation in each culture, with Japanese respondents experiencing it as unnatural to describe the self in the condition that supplied no information about the context and U.S. respondents experiencing the decontextualized task as the most meaningful (Cousins, 1989). In sum, within cultural psychology, explanation attends not only to the situational factors typically considered in all psychological explanation, but also to cultural meanings that impact on how contexts are understood and on their impact on psychological responses.

Pragmatic Relativism

A key theoretical premise of cultural psychology is the adoption of pragmatic relativism as a stance that forms a middle ground between the poles of either absolute universalism or extreme relativism. In adopting this position, work within cultural psychology embraces a position that is consonant with the thrust of work on moral reasoning from distinct domain and Kohlbergian perspectives.

Theorists from these various perspectives agree on the need for cultural sensitivity and for gaining familiarity with and understanding the culturally specific knowledge systems and values that affect the meanings that behaviors are given in different cultural settings. Thus, there is agreement that a universalistic stance that accords no weight to cultural meanings in moral appraisal is ethnocentric and morally objectionable. Equally, all of the various perspectives eschew an extreme relativism that requires evaluating practices in terms of purely local criteria. This kind of thrust is articulated forcefully, for example, in recent work by Turiel and his colleagues that has explored the moral outlooks of persons who are in subordinate positions within social hierarchies and whose outlooks may tend to differ from those in dominant social positions (Turiel, 1998a, 1998b; Turiel & Wainryb, 1994, 2000). Notably, in terms of cultural psychology, this kind of sensibility may be seen in the argument made by Bruner regarding the need to precede with as complete an understanding of local cultural viewpoints as possible in appraising social practices:

> Constructivism's basic claim is simply that knowledge is "right" or "wrong" in light of the perspective we have chosen to assume. Rights and wrongs of this kind—however well we can test them—do not sum to absolute truths and falsities. The best we can hope for is that we be aware of our own perspective and those of others when we make our claims of "rightness" and "wrongness." (1990, p. 25)

Likewise, Shweder links cultural psychology with culturally grounded forms of comparative moral appraisal rather than with extreme relativism:

> . . . my version of cultural psychology fully acknowledges that there is no way to avoid making critical judgments about good and bad, right and wrong, true and false, efficient and inefficient. . . . any culture deserving of respect, must be defensible in the face of criticism from "outside." Indeed, in my view one of the distinctive features of cultural psychology is that it is willing to try to make that defense, representing the "inside" point of view in such a way that it can be understood, perhaps appreciated, or at the very least tolerated from an "outside" point of view. (2000, p. 216)

Reflecting this type of position, in their recent edited volume examining issues of culture conflict involving immigrant populations in the U.S., Shweder, Minow, and Markus (2002) explore the difficult decisions and weightings of moral sensibilities that must occur in cases in which the native practices of immigrant populations are illegal to achieve public policy that is both culturally sensitive and ethically sound. If theorists such as Shweder and the other contributors to the volume subscribed to an extreme moral relativism, there would be no need for such an exploration, because in all cases, local practices within a family would be privileged.

It is then important to recognize that this search for morally defensible yet culturally sensitive grounds for understanding cultural practices informs both work in cultural psychology and work from distinct domain and Kohlbergian perspectives, with the differences between the viewpoints more a matter of degree rather than of fundamental agenda. Researchers within cultural psychology are open to acknowledging the role of social meanings in affecting what is considered harm or rights violations. However, the stance that they adopt does not represent an extreme relativism but a recognition that the meanings accorded to practices affect their implications and may influence their moral status. Thus, for example, whereas from the perspective of a culture such as Sweden, the common practice of U.S. parents employing spanking as a means of disciplining their children tends to be judged as objectionable, within a sizeable number of U.S. families, such practices are accorded positive meanings and may even be associated with positive adaptive outcomes (Baumrind, 1996). This suggests that a broad range of cultural practices may be acceptable in achieving culturally valued goals and that, to avoid ethnocentrism, moral appraisals must take this variability into account, even while applying standards that are not purely culturally relative. In sum, whereas appraisals of cultural practices tend to be more relativistic within cultural psychology than in the distinct domain or cognitive developmental approaches to morality, this difference is not reflective of the endorsement of extreme moral relativism or of a culturally blind ethnocentrism within any of the approaches.

CULTURAL INFLUENCES ON MORAL OUTLOOKS

A major contribution of work in cultural psychology to understanding moral development is to identify dimensions of moral reasoning that are presently not fully taken into account in existing psychological theories. Work from a cultural psychology perspective empirically supports the universality of concerns with justice and welfare in moral outlooks as well as of distinctions between issues of morality, social convention, and personal choice. However, as discussed next, it also highlights cultural influences on perception of harm and injustice, qualitative differences in moralities of caring, as well as cultural variability in the role of spiritual concerns in moral outlooks.

Culture and Justice Reasoning

The universality of at least some moral concern with justice issues has been established on both content and formal levels in cross-cultural Kohlbergian research (e.g., Edwards, 1986; Snarey, 1985) as well as in cultural psychological research utilizing the short answer methodology developed by Turiel and his colleagues (e.g., Miller & Bersoff, 1992; Shweder et al., 1987). On a content level, this universality is seen in findings of some concern with harm or injustice in all known cultural groups and of substantial, although not complete, overlap in the types of issues regarded as instances of harm or injustice (e.g., Bersoff & Miller, 1993; Miller & Bersoff, 1992; Snarey, 1985). On a formal level, certain formal distinctions are also made universally. Thus, as Shweder (1982) suggests, both the abstract concept of avoiding harm as well as the abstract principle of justice or of equality of treatment of like cases are found in all moral codes. However, even with this cross-cultural commonality, marked cultural variation exists in the identification of acts of harm and injustice as well as in the priority given to justice considerations relative to competing moral and nonmoral concerns.

Cultural Constructions of Harm and Rights Violations. Cultural meaning systems may be seen to impact on the perception of acts as involving harm or rights violations. This occurs because to instantiate the abstract concepts of harm and injustice in particular cases consideration must be given to conceptions of personhood as well as to the boundaries of the self, conceptions defined in culturally variable ways and based on culturally variable knowledge presuppositions. For example, one must have some criteria for recognizing which entities in the environment qualify as persons and how expansively to define boundaries of the self, such as whether the right to protection from harm extends to nonhuman entities and whether it extends to beliefs and values (Shweder, 1982; Shweder et al., 1997). Equally, to determine that a particular action is discriminatory or unjust requires the application of a content standard for deciding that a case is sufficiently similar or different to another case to be treated as alike or different (e.g., content based criteria on which to decide that a 15-year-old should be treated differently from a middle-aged adult and not be granted a drivers license whereas an 80-year-old should be treated the same and granted one).

In holding contrasting definitions of personhood, views of territories of the self as well as definitions of what constitutes harm, individuals from different cultural backgrounds have been found to vary widely in their concrete moral judgments about issues involving potential justice concerns. Vasudev and Hummel (1987), for example, illustrate how Brahmin respondents in India react to Kohlbergian moral dilemmas with a more encompassing conception of human life than shown typically by U.S. respondents or than assumed by Kohlberg (1971). Rather than limit protection from harm to humans, protection from harm is extended to all forms of life, resulting in a stance that treats vegetarianism as a moral matter. As the following Indian respondent argued when asked in response to the Heinz dilemma whether Heinz should steal to save the life of his pet animal:

> One makes choices between many forms of life, but the overall guiding or spiritual principle should be that all forms of life are of value. In the spiritual tradition, for example, carelessly or needlessly breaking a leaf on a flower is also construed as an act of violence. . . . We in India are vegetarians; the principle of vegetarianism is that life should not be destroyed. (Vasudev & Hummel, 1987, p. 115)

Research also points to cases in which the views of harm and rights that are maintained in the U.S. and in certain other Western populations are more encompassing than those emphasized in certain non-Western communities. Thus, in an investigation that contrasted a secular U.S. adult population to an orthodox religious population in India, it was observed that Indians were more prone than U.S. respondents to treat practices involving gender inequality as morally desirable rather than morally objectionable (e.g., unequal inheritance of men and women) (Shweder et al., 1987). Equally, in an example involving individual differences, the tendency of U.S. adolescents to consider abortion to be immoral as compared with being a matter for personal decision making has been observed to reflect contrasting definitions of personhood and associated assessments of whether or not abortion constitutes an act of harm (Smetana, 1981).

The argument is made by theorists from a distinct domain perspective that these types of cultural differences arise from contrasting real-world knowledge assumptions that are brought to bear in determining whether a particular behavior entails harm rather than from fundamental variation in moral codes (Turiel et al., 1987; Wainryb, 1991). From this perspective, the tendency of Indian respondents to consider it immoral for an eldest son to have a haircut and eat chicken the day after his father's death (Shweder et al., 1987) is seen as reflecting respondents' "unearthly belief-mediated" understandings that such behavior would bring harm to the father through causing his soul not to receive salvation (Turiel et al., 1987). From the perspective of this type of interpretation then, whereas culture is seen as providing knowledge assumptions that impact on individuals' interpretations of the nature of reality, it is not viewed as giving rise to fundamental differences in the tendency to view acts of harm and injustice as immoral. Furthermore, it is assumed that differences in moral outlooks may be resolved through rational analysis that assesses the relative adequacy of contrasting epistemological assumptions.

Although theorists from a cultural psychology perspective concur with this argument from a distinct domain perspective about the need to take culturally based knowledge assumptions into account in interpreting cultural differences in moral outlook (Wainryb, 1991), they differ with the assumption that it is possible to fully adjudicate differences in moral outlook on a rational basis and question the informative nature of the analytic stance that assumes that cultural knowledge may be fully held constant in this way while appraising moral reasoning. As discussed, cultural meaning systems encompass not only representational knowledge but also constitutive presuppositions that are not fully rationally or functionally based. This implies then that categorization of experience (e.g., deciding that a fetus qualifies to be treated as a person) reflects, in part, values that may not be empirically adjudicated by obtaining more facts about a situation. Equally, the analytic stance of attempting to appraise cultural differences in moral outlook while holding constant cultural differences in beliefs and knowledge systems is seen as a position that, in effect, attempts to assess cultural influences on moral outlook while at the same time analytically holding such differences constant. Whereas it is considered valuable to identify the contrasting culturally based meanings that contribute to cultural variation in moral outlook, it is seen as ultimately reductive and untrue to everyday phenomenal experience to partition out those influences to tap a measure of "pure" moral outlook.

In sum, culture plays an important role in everyday justice reasoning through affecting the interpretation of harm and injustice. Justice reasoning, the present considerations imply, cannot be simply self-constructed based on inductively assessing the degree to which actions involve harm or rights violations but reflects, in part, culturally variable epistemological and constitutive presuppositions about the nature of social reality.

Cultural Variation in Priority Given to Justice Considerations. Cultural work also indicates that, even in cases in which individuals' culturally based knowledge assumptions are comparable and they agree about the moral status of the issues of justice and harm involved, cultural variation may exist in the priority that individuals give to justice as compared to competing moral concerns. In these cases, the source of cultural variation lies in certain cultural groups giving relatively greater weight to issues other than justice or individual rights in their moral judgments.

Indirect evidence for this type of effect may be found in the marked cross-cultural differences observed in research on Kohlbergian measures of moral judgment. As Snarey (1985) reported in a survey of Kohlbergian research conducted in over 45 culturally diverse samples, most populations do not reason in postconventional terms but rather tend to emphasize Stage 3 conventional reasoning. Thus, only approximately 6% of responses observed in this cross-cultural Kohlbergian research reflected a mixture of postconventional and conventional concerns (Stage 4 and 5), with only 2% purely postconventional in nature. In emphasizing Stage 3 reasoning, respondents were giving priority in the Kohlbergian dilemmas not to the issues of justice and individual rights but to matters involving role obligations. This sensitivity to the justice issues but prioritizing of the competing interpersonal themes is illustrated, for example, in the following response given by a Kenyan respondent to the Kohlbergian "Joe Dilemma," involving the issue of whether a son should refuse to grant his father's apparently unfair request:

(If a father breaks his word), it will cause hatred because the son will be angry, saying, "I wanted to follow my own intentions, but my father cheated: he permitted me and then refused me" . . . So it is bad . . . (However) the one for the son is worse. Imagine a child disobeying my own words, is he really normal? (Edwards, 1986, p. 425)

The respondent is aware of justice concerns, as seen in his reference to the father having cheated, but accords these concerns lesser priority as compared with the obligation of the son to obey his father's wishes. Although this type of response would have been scored by Kohlberg as merely conventional in nature, it gives evidence of a respondent giving more importance to communitarian than to justice issues (Snarey & Keljo, 1991).

Further evidence that cultural differences exist in the priority given to justice issues relative to competing moral concerns may be seen in experimental research among U.S. and Indian adult and child populations that tapped reasoning about hypothetical conflict situations, in which fulfillment of a justice issue conflicts with fulfilling a competing interpersonal responsibility (Miller & Bersoff, 1992). An idiographic procedure was employed in constructing these conflict situations to insure that individuals viewed the individual justice and interpersonal breaches involved as equivalent in their seriousness. Consonant with the patterns observed in Kohlbergian research, the Indian respondents tended more frequently to give priority to the competing interpersonal obligations than did the U.S. respondents in non–life-threatening situations. Thus, for example, whereas virtually all of the U.S. respondents judged that it was morally wrong to steal a train ticket even if this was the only way to fulfill the interpersonal responsibility of attending a best friend's wedding, a majority of the Indian respondents judged that it was morally required to take part in the wedding, even if this meant having to engage in the justice breach of stealing the ticket.

In sum, cultural variation exists in the moral priority given to justice issues compared with competing moral concerns. Even when cultural groups agree on the moral status of justice issues in a particular case, their judgments may differ as a functioning of competing moral commitments that they hold.

Cultural Variation in Responsibility Judgments.   Although research on judgments of responsibility has tended to proceed independently of work on moral judgment, judgments of responsibility are implicated theoretically in moral judgment and constitute a significant source of cultural variability in everyday moral reasoning. The domain of rule-governed behavior involves voluntary action, in which the agent is judged to have sufficient control over his or her behavior that he or she can at least potentially be held responsible for performing it. An agent tends to be judged less responsible for a given behavior to the extent that the behavior is unintended, the agent lacks the capabilities to understand the consequences of his or her action or to control its execution, or the behavior is influenced by situational pressures (Darley & Zanna, 1982; Fincham & Jaspars, 1980; Heider, 1958).

Evidence that responsibility judgments may be a source of cultural variability in moral judgment may be seen in a cross-cultural study that tapped both U.S. and Indian adults' and children's moral appraisals of justice violations committed under potentially extenuating circumstances (Bersoff & Miller, 1993; see also Miller & Luthar, 1989). It was observed that more Indian than U.S. respondents absolved agents of accountability for justice breaches that had been undertaken in response to situationally induced emotional duress or under circumstances that involved agent immaturity. In turn, not only did U.S. respondents take these types of potentially extenuating circumstances into account less frequently, but they took them into account in differing ways. Thus, strikingly, for U.S. respondents their domain categorization of justice breaches shifted from viewing the breaches as moral violations when the breaches were presented in the abstract to viewing such actions as matters of personal choice when they were presented in the context of potentially extenuating contextual circumstances (e.g., arguing that it was a moral violation to break into a locked house in the case when no extenuating circumstances are present but that it is the agent's own personal decision whether to do this under circumstances in which the agent has been frightened by an unexpected noise). These observed cross-cultural differences result from contrasting culturally based knowledge presuppositions and values, including assumptions regarding the degree agents of different ages and under different situational pressures are regarded as vulnerable to situational influences.

In sum, work on moral accountability judgments provides further evidence that differences in moral categorization of justice breaches may occur even in cases in which there is cross-cultural agreement on the moral status of the justice issues involved. Given that everyday justice reasoning does not occur in relation to abstract cases but always involves contextual circumstances, the present considerations highlight ways that culturally variable background assumptions can give rise to marked concrete differences in everyday moral reasoning.

Culture and Moralities of Caring

Responsiveness to the needs of others has traditionally been viewed as having a moral status that is subordinate to that of justice. It is argued that, in contrast to the negative injunctions of the morality of justice, positive obligations to help others in close relationships are too unbounded in scope to be fully realizable and thus cannot be considered as moral duties (Kohlberg, 1981; Nunner-Winkler, 1984). From this perspective, caring for a friend is regarded as morally desirable but ultimately a matter for personal decision making. Thus, in both the Kohlbergian framework and in the distinct domain perspective, obligations to be responsive to the needs of others in close relationships are considered superogatory expectations that are discretionary in nature rather than matters of duty (Kahn, 1992; Kohlberg, Levine, & Hewer, 1983). Culturally based research challenges these assumptions in highlighting the need to expand the moral domain to include issues of caring and friendship as well as in highlighting the existence of multiple culturally grounded moralities of caring.

In a cultural challenge to the Kohlbergian framework, Gilligan (1977, 1982) argued for the existence of a morality of caring that treats responsiveness to meet the needs of others in close relationships as fully moral. Gilligan maintained that through processes of gender-based socialization, boys develop an autonomous sense of self that gives rise to a morality of justice and that is compatible with the individualism of the larger culture (Gilligan & Wiggins, 1988). In contrast, girls develop a connected view of self that gives rise to a morality of caring, but that is culturally devalued. Although later research challenged the assertion that moralities of caring and of justice are gender related (Walker, 1984), it has supported the existence of a morality of caring and the claim that theories of justice morality need to be broadened to encompass interpersonal responsibilities.

Cultural critiques have extended the work of Gilligan in making the further claim that the morality of caring framework of Gilligan itself is culturally bound. Thus, it has been argued that the view of socialization emphasized in Gilligan's model gives little weight to cultural processes (Miller, 1994). In Gilligan's approach, the morality of caring is portrayed as developing outside of the larger individualistic values of the culture and only the morality of justice is seen as culturally based. However, it must be assumed that socialization of the morality of caring always occurs within a cultural context and thus that the form of this morality is culturally influenced.

In a program of cross-cultural research that we conducted, we demonstrated that the approach to the morality of caring identified by Gilligan is culturally specific and that a qualitatively distinct approach to the morality of caring is found among Hindu Indian populations. In a series of studies, it has been shown that Indian respondents, as compared with U.S. respondents, show a greater tendency to view meeting the needs of others in close relationships as a matter of moral duty rather than of personal choice (Miller & Bersoff, 1995; Miller et al., 1992; Miller & Luthar, 1989), take contextual factors more fully into account in their moral reasoning (Bersoff & Miller, 1992; Miller & Luthar, 1989), give greater weight to interpersonal responsibilities over competing justice obligations (Miller & Bersoff, 1992), treat interpersonal reciprocity in moral rather than personal choice terms (Miller & Bersoff, 1994), and regard moral responsiveness to family and friends as non-contingent on personal affinity and liking (Miller & Bersoff, 1998). Importantly, in each of these investigations, individuals' responses varied depending on the contextual factors being manipulated, with cross-cultural commonalities observed in addition to cross-cultural differences. To give some examples, although Indians showed a greater tendency than U.S. respondents to categorize helping others in moral rather than personal choice terms, even U.S. respondents considered helping as obligatory in cases involving extreme need (e.g., Miller et al., 1990; Miller & Bersoff, 1992). Also, although U.S. respondents tended to emphasize personal choice considerations more than did Indian respondents, even Indians categorized helping in personal choice terms in certain cases that did not involve welfare concerns or in-group bonds (e.g., Miller et al., 1990; Miller & Bersoff, 1994).

The voluntaristic approach to interpersonal commitments observed among U.S. respondents in the studies discussed is congruent with the claims of the morality of caring framework of Gilligan; however, the pattern of results observed among Indians does not conform to the predictions of the morality of caring framework. It was for this reason that new adjectives were introduced to refer to each of these two broad types of perspectives, with the pattern of results observed among U.S. respondents described as reflecting an "individually oriented" morality of caring and that observed among Indian respondents described as a "duty-based" morality of caring (Miller, 1994). In making this claim, the only point was to adopt theoretical language to signal that the pattern of results observed in India are not well captured by Gilligan's morality of caring framework and that there are multiple forms rather than only one form that the "morality of caring" takes. Notwithstanding the charges forwarded by theorists from a distinct domain perspective (e.g., Neff, 2001; Turiel, 2002), the intent of such a label was to contribute to making basic psychological theory more culturally inclusive and not to make the claim that response modes are uniform within each cultural group. As noted, all of the studies documented overlap in responses between cultures and contextual variation within cultures. In fact, even in the paper in which the distinction was first introduced, it was noted (Miller, 1994) that the labels were not intended to map directly onto the individualism/collectivism dichotomy and that more subtle analyses would be expected to reveal other qualitatively distinct approaches to interpersonal morality.

Research conducted in other non-Western cultures has, in fact, identified other approaches to interpersonal morality that differ in important ways from those captured either by the individually oriented approach of Gilligan's morality of caring framework or the duty-based approach identified in India. Thus, for example, research in Japan has documented the existence of approaches to the morality of caring based on senses of *omoiyari* or empathy within one's ingroup (Shimizu, 2001). Within such an approach, emphasis tends to be placed on maintaining good interpersonal relations. Also, in another example, work with various Chinese cultural populations points to the contrasting premises that underlie moral outlooks grounded in Confucian and Taoist thought (Dien, 1982; Ma, 1988, 1989, 1992, 1997). Central to these outlooks is the concept of *jen*, an affectively grounded concept that encompasses such ideas as love, benevolence, and filial piety. In still another example, concerns with social harmony have been observed among Polish populations (Niemczynski, Czyzowska, Pourkos, & Mirsk, 1988) as well among Black Caribs of British Hondura (Gorsuch & Barnes, 1973) and Nigerian Igbo populations (Okonkwo, 1997). In fact, in a review of cross-cultural Kohlbergian research, Snarey and Keljo (1991) make the case for the existence of a *Gemeinschaft* voice of community that they argue was erroneously scored at the conventional level in cross-cultural Kohlbergian research and that represent qualitatively distinctive and culturally diverse forms of the morality of caring.

In sum, the critique of Kohlbergian theory offered by Gilligan pointed to the need to broaden work on morality to include interpersonal responsiveness to family and friends as fully moral concerns rather than to limit morality to justice considerations. What cross-cultural research has added to this insight is to highlight that Gilligan's morality of caring framework constitutes only one culturally specific version of interpersonal morality, with alternative culturally variable moralities of caring found in different sociocultural settings.

Culture and Moralities of Divinity. Finally, a major thrust of cultural research has been to recognize that moral codes encompass not only issues of harm, justice, welfare, friendship, and family ties but entail in many cases spiritual concerns. It was this insight that led Shweder and his colleagues to argue for the existence of a tripartite approach to morality that encompasses concerns with "divinity" in addition to concerns with "autonomy" or justice and concerns with "community" or caring (Shweder et al., 1997).

Some of the earliest evidence for the importance of spiritual considerations in moral reasoning appeared in cross-cultural Kohlbergian responses that revealed religious concerns as informing individual outlooks. It was observed, for example, that Igbo Nigerians base their responses to Kohlbergian moral dilemmas on what they consider to be the revealed truth of a divine being rather than on a secular outlook (Okonkwo, 1997) and that the moral judgments of Algerian respondents are premised on a belief in God as the creator and supreme authority of the universe (Bouhmama, 1984). Research has also demonstrated that orthodox Hindu Indian respondents justify their responses to the Heinz dilemma on the basis of the negative consequences of suffering and spiritual degradation that they believe would ensue from different courses of action (Shweder & Much, 1987) as well as that spiritual concerns underlie the concerns with *karma* and *dharma* in the outlook of samples of Buddhist monks (Huebner & Garrod, 1991).

Notably, a concern with spiritual considerations has also been documented in work with U.S. populations. Haidt, Koller, and Dias (1993), for example, demonstrated that lower class Brazilian children, as well as lower class African-American children, tend to treat certain actions they regard as disgusting or disrespectful in moral terms, such as eating one's dog, even while considering such actions to be harmless. Likewise, Jensen (1997) observed that concerns with sanctity and spirituality inform the outlook of orthodox Baptist adults from the U.S. South. As may be seen in the sample response reproduced below, a practice such as divorce tends to be regarded within this community as a moral affront or sacrilege, in constituting a violation of God's will:

> Divorce to me means (that) you slap God in the face. In other words, you bring reproach upon God. . . . we could lose salvation . . . and that's why I think divorce is shameful. (Jensen, 1997, p. 342)

Even in populations that are secular or at least non-orthodox in their religious outlooks, spiritual considerations have been observed to inform moral viewpoints. In a study of the moral conceptions of Canadian adolescents and adults, Walker, Pitts, Hennig, and Matsuba (1995) noted the salience of concerns with religion, faith, and spirituality in individuals' moral reasoning, concluding that "(f)or many people, their moral framework and understanding is to some extent, if not entirely, embedded in their religion and faith" (p. 403). In another example, a qualitative study of humanitarians and social activists documented that these individuals maintain deep spiritual commitments that underlie their moral codes and that, in part, inspire their involvement in social and political action (Colby & Damon, 1992).

In interpreting the implications of the emphasis on spiritual considerations in moral outlooks, the claim has been made that religious concerns are conventional rather than moral in character (Nucci & Turiel, 1993; Turiel & Neff, 2000), an interpretation favored as well by Kohlberg (1981). In support of this interpretation, Nucci and Turiel (1993) demonstrated that in asking populations of Amish-Mennonite, Dutch Reform Calvinist, and Jewish children whether particular behaviors that involve either religious issues (e.g., premarital sex) or harm (e.g., hitting) would be alright to engage in if there is nothing in the Bible about the act and God had not said anything about it, children treated the religious issues as contingent on God's Word and the matters of harm as noncontingent. This type of methodology, however, poses counterfactuals that arguably may not fully succeed in tapping the perceived moral status of religious injunctions. In contrast to acts with overt harmful consequences, such as hitting, acts that involve spiritual violations, such as premarital sex, have a moral status that is not based on harm and that may be known only through reliance on such authorities as Scripture or the Word of God. Thus, whereas children can observe that the harm of hitting remains, even if God has not said anything about such behavior, they may interpret God's act of not saying anything about premarital sex as implying that there is nothing wrong with such activity. In this case, children would be regarding God not as a conventional authority with the arbitrary power to determine right or wrong, a stance that would reflect a conventional orientation, but rather would be viewing God as an all-knowing source of enlightenment through whom what is morally right or wrong can be known, a moral stance.

In sum, existing research suggests that spiritual issues impact on moral reasoning either indirectly through affecting individuals' real-world knowledge presuppositions or directly through forming an alternative type of moral concern. Spiritual concerns appear to constitute both a source of knowledge about morality, through the vehicle of faith, as well as a type of moral concern based on considerations such as purity and sanctity rather than on considerations of harm or welfare.

FUTURE DIRECTIONS AND CONCLUSION

Culturally based research on morality has increased in recent years, with such work being conducted not only by researchers associated with cultural psychology but by researchers associated with social constructivist perspectives (e.g., Nucci, Saxe, & Turiel, 2000; Turiel, 2002). To build on this growing base of cross-cultural theory and research findings, it is important to approach research questions taking into account the valuable insights that the various perspectives have to offer.

One valuable area of future interchange between these various approaches to moral development is to build conceptual models that integrate a concern with culture with a concern with development. A critique that may be offered of approaches to moral development within cultural psychology is the failure to date to offer a well-developed developmental model. Although culturally based research has been undertaken that examines the socialization of morality in everyday interaction (e.g., Edwards, 1985; Fung, 1999), no systematic, culturally based theories have been offered that capture the developmental changes occurring in children's moral outlooks. Theorists within cultural psychology do not consider enculturation to represent a passive process in which the child merely absorbs the understandings of his or her culture but rather an active one in which meanings are transformed, created, and transformed, even as they influence an individual. However, to date there has been limited exploration of this process by cultural researchers. In turn, it may be argued that whereas researchers in the distinct domain and Kohlbergian traditions have offered developmental theories of morality, their approaches give little weight to cultural influences on the course, direction, and endpoints of child development. It requires then taking into account the insights of both of these traditions to succeed in formulating models of morality that are simultaneously cultural and developmental in nature (Schwartz, 1981).

The area of dissent and cultural change represents another example of a domain in which greater integration is needed between these various approaches to moral development. Although theorists from a distinct domain perspective have conducted important work focusing on questions of dissent, to date this work has tended to give limited attention to respects in which dissent is expressed in culturally variable ways. In this work, there has been a concern with uncovering the contrasting outlooks of individuals in nondominant positions within societies and in documenting that the privileges that certain individuals of higher status are given may entail the oppression of individuals of subordinate rank. However, a limitation of this work has been its tendency to frame research questions in ways that have limited cultural sensitivity. Thus, for example, research conclusions that portray family life in cultures such as India as reflecting arrangements in which men have most of the rights and women most of the duties (Neff, 2001) must be interpreted with caution, given the failure in such research to include probes that ask directly about the responsibilities of men within families (responsibilities that notably are not identical to those of women) and the framing of questions in terms of concepts that tend not to be applied spontaneously by the respondents themselves in everyday interaction (such as use of the concept of rights to refer to the privileges associated with different role relationships in Indian families). In turn, concern with the cultural meanings informing dissent is more prominent in research within cultural psychology. To give an example, in a qualitative study of family interaction, Much (1997) examined the motives of a Hindu Indian adolescent who, against the wishes of both his parents and the cultural beliefs of his community, stopped wearing the Sacred Thread, a holy Hindu Indian religious symbol, because he considered it only a relatively unimportant social convention that merely served to identify him to others as a member of the Brahmin caste. As Much noted, although this action constituted a serious challenge to the authority of both his parents and the larger community, it was framed in a way that did not challenge deeper premises of the culture, such as the fundamental principles of hierarchy and the importance of Brahmin identity. Although researchers in cultural psychology thus tend to give weight to local meanings in their analyses, to date they have paid only relatively limited attention to the perspective of individuals in subordinate social positions. It requires then integrating the attention to subordinate social status that has been privileged in the distinct domain tradition with the attention to local meanings that has been privileged in cultural psychology to attain a fuller appreciation of both the universal and culturally specific aspects of dissent.

More generally, the present considerations underscore the need for greater interchange between researchers in cultural psychology and researchers representing other contemporary traditions in moral development. To realize this goal, it is critical for researchers to appreciate the subtlety of contrasting perspectives and to avoid the tendency to stereotype or to dismiss the claims being made in different traditions. Thus, for example, although it is valid for researchers within the distinct domain perspective to criticize limitations of some work in cultural psychology that is explicitly framed in terms of the individualism/collectivism dichotomy, it becomes a stereotype when this type of criticism is applied in a wholesale way to dismiss all work in cultural psychology (e.g., Turiel, 2002). Likewise, evidence uncovered by cultural psychologists of life satisfaction in traditional gender roles within particular hierarchically structured societies (e.g., Menon & Shweder, 1998) cannot be taken to imply that there is no validity to the claims made by distinct domain theorists about perceived female oppression in such communities.

In conclusion, research on moral development within cultural psychology shares many of its major assumptions, goals, and agenda with work in other more universalistic traditions of research on moral development. This overlap implies that work in cultural psychology should be understood as complementing these alternative approaches, rather than as antithetical to them. It must be recognized that a major challenge for work on moral development is to take into account both culture and context as it explores common as well as culturally variable dimensions of moral outlooks.

REFERENCES

Abu-Lughod, L. (1993). *Writing women's worlds: Bedouin stories*. Berkeley: University of California Press.

Atkins, R., & Hart, D. (2003). Neighborhoods, adults, and the development of civic identity in urban youth. *Applied Developmental Science, 7*(3), 155–164.

Appadurai, A. (1988). Putting hierarchy in its place. *Cultural Anthropology, 3,* 36–49.

Baumrind, D. (1996). The discipline controversy revisited. *Family Relations: Journal of Applied Family and Child Studies, 45*(4), 405–414.

Benedict, R. (1946). *The chrysanthemum and the sword: Patterns of Japanese culture*. Boston: Houghton Mifflin.

Berkowitz, L. (1964). *Development of motives and values in a child*. New York: Basic Books.

Bersoff, D. M., & Miller, J. G. (1993). Culture, context, and the development of moral accountability judgments. *Developmental Psychology, 29*(4), 664–676.

Bouhmama, D. (1984). Assessment of Kohlberg's stages of moral development in two cultures. *Journal of Moral Education, 13,* 124–132.

Bronfenbrenner, U. (1979). *The ecology of human development: Experiments by nature and design*. Cambridge, MA: Harvard University Press.

Bruner, J. (1990). *Acts of meaning*. Cambridge, MA: Harvard University Press.

Butler, J. (1990). Gender trouble, feminist theory and psychoanalytic discourse. In L. Nicholson (Ed.), *Feminism/postmodernism* (pp. 324–340). London: Routledge & Kegan Paul.

Colby, A., & Damon, W. (1992). *Some do care: Contemporary lives of moral commitment*. New York: Free Press.

Cole, M. (1990). Cultural psychology: A once and future discipline? In J. J. Berman (Ed.), *Nebraska Symposium on Motivation, Vol. 38: Cross-cultural perspectives* (pp. 279–335). Lincoln: University of Nebraska Press.

Cole, M. (1996). *Cultural psychology: A once and future discipline*. Cambridge, MA: Harvard University Press.

Cousins, S. D. (1989). Culture and self-perception in Japan and the United States. *Journal of Personality and Social Psychology, 56,* 124–131.

D'Andrade, R. G. (1984). Cultural meaning systems. In R. A. Shweder & R. A. LeVine (Eds.), *Culture theory: Essays on mind, self, and emotion* (pp. 88–119). New York: Cambridge University Press.

Darley, J., & Zanna, M. (1982). Making moral judgments. *American Scientist, 70,* 515–521.

Dien, D. S.-F. (1982). A Chinese perspective on Kohlberg's theory of moral development. *Developmental Review, 2,* 331–341.

Eccles, J. S., Midgley, C., Buchanan, C. M., Wigfield, A., Reuman, D., & MacIver, D. (1993). Development during adolescence: The impact of stage/environment fit. *American Psychologist, 48,* 90–101.

Edwards, C. P. (1975). Societal complexity and moral development: A Kenyan study. *Ethos, 3*(4), 505–527.

Edwards, C. P. (1985). Another style of competence: The caregiving child. In A. D. Vogel & G. F. Melson (Eds.), *The origins of nurturance* (pp. 95–121). Hillsdate, NJ: Lawrence Erlbaum Associates.

Edwards, C. (1986). Cross-cultural research on Kohlberg's stages: The basis for consensus. In S. Modgil & C. Modgil (Eds.), *Kohlberg: Consensus and controversy* (pp. 419–430). Philadelphia: Falmer Press.

Edwards, C. P. (1994). Cross-cultural research on Kohlberg's stages: The basis for consensus. In *New research in moral development* (pp. 373–384). New York: Garland.

Eysenck, H. J. (1961). *Handbook of abnormal psychology: An experimental approach.* New York: Basic Books.

Fincham, F., & Jaspars, J. (1980). Attribution of responsibility: From man the scientst to man as lawyer. In L. Berkowitz (Ed.), *Advances in experiemental social psychology* (Vol. 13, pp. 82–138). San Diego: Academic Press.

Fiske, A. P., Kitayama, S., Markus, H. R., & Nisbett, R. E. (1998). The cultural matrix of social psychology. In *The handbook of social psychology* (Vol. 2, 4th ed., pp. 915–981). New York: McGraw-Hill.

Fung, H. (1999). Becoming a moral child: The socialization of shame among young Chinese children. *Ethos, 27*(2), 180–209.

Geertz, C. (1973). *The interpretation of cultures.* New York: Basic Press.

Gilligan, C. (1977). In a different voice: Women's conceptions of self and of morality. *Harvard Educational Review, 47*(4), 481–517.

Gilligan, C. (1982). *In a different voice: Psychological theory and women's development.* Cambridge, MA: Harvard University Press.

Gilligan, C., & Wiggins, G. (1988). The origins of morality in early childhood relationships. In C. Gilligan, J. Ward, & J. Taylor (Eds.), *Mapping the moral domain: A contribution of women's thinking to psychological theory and education* (pp. 111–138). Cambridge, MA: Harvard University Press.

Gorsuch, R. L., & Barnes, M. L. (1973). Stages of ethical reasoning and moral norms of Carib youths. *Journal of Cross-Cultural Psychology, 4,* 283–301.

Graham, S. (1992). "Most of the subjects were White and middle class": Trends in published research on African Americans in selected APA journals, 1970–1989. *American Psychologist, 47*(5), 629–639.

Gulerce, A. (1995). Culture and self in postmodern psychology: Dialogu in trouble? (An interview with K. J. Gergen). *Culture and Psychology, 1,* 147–159.

Haidt, J., Koller, S. H., & Dias, M. G. (1993). Affect, culture, and morality, or is it wrong to eat your dog? *Journal of Personality and Social Psychology, 65*(4), 613–628.

Hart, D., & Atkins, R. (2002). Civic competence in urban youth. *Applied Developmental Science, 6*(4), 227–236.

Harwood, R. L., Miller, J. G., & Irizarry, N. L. (1995). *Culture and attachment: Perceptions of the child in context.* New York: Guilford Press.

Heider, F. (1958). *The psychology of interpersonal relations.* New York: Wiley.

Huebner, A., & Garrod, A. (1991). Moral reasoning in a Karmic world. *Human Development, 34,* 341–352.

Jensen, L. A. (1997). Different worldviews, different morals: America's culture war divide. *Human Development, 40*(6), 325–344.

Kahn, P. H. (1992). Children's obligatory and discretionary moral judgments. *Child Development, 63,* 416–430.

Kohlberg, L. (1969). Stage and sequence: The cognitive-developmental approach to socialization. In D. A. Goslin (Ed.), *Handbook of socialization theory* (pp. 347–380). Chicago: Rand McNally.

Kohlberg, L. (1971). From is to ought: How to commit the naturalistic fallacy and get away with it in the study of moral development. In T. Mischel (Ed.), *Cognitive development and epistemology* (pp. 151–236). New York: Academic.

Kohlberg, L. (1981). *The philosophy of moral development: Moral stages and the idea of justice* (Vol. 1). New York: Harper & Row.

Kohlberg, L., Levine, C., & Hewer, A. (1983). Moral stages: A current formulation and a response to critics. In J. A. Meacham (Ed.), *Contributions to human development* (Vol. 10, pp. 1–177). Basel, Switzerland: Karger.

LeVine, R. A. (1984). Properties of culture: An ethnographic view. In R. A. Shweder & R. A. LeVine (Eds.), *Culture theory: Essays on mind, self, and emotion* (pp. 67–87). New York: Cambridge University Press.

Ma, H. K. (1988). The Chinese perspective on moral judgment development. *International Journal of Psychology, 23,* 201–227.

Ma, H. K. (1989). Moral orientation and moral judgment in adolescents in Hong Kong, Mainland China, and England. *Journal of Cross-Cultural Psychology, 20,* 152–177.

Ma, H. K. (1992). The moral judgment development of the Chinese people: A theoretical model. *Philosophica, 49,* 55–82.

Ma, H. K. (1997). The affective and cognitive aspects of moral development: A Chinese perspective. In H. Kao & D. Sinha (Eds.), *Asian perspectives on psychology* (pp. 93–109). Thousand Oaks, CA: Sage.

Markus, H. R., & Kitayama, S. (1991). Culture and the self: Implications for cognition, emotion, and motivation. *Psychological Review, 98*(2), 224–253.

Martin, L. M. W., Nelson, K., & Tobach, E. (Eds.). (1995). *Sociocultural psychology: Theory and practice of doing and knowings.* New York: Cambridge University Press.

Menon, U., & Shweder, R. A. (1998). The return of the "white man's burden": The moral discourse of anthropology and the domestic life of Hindu women. In R. A. Shweder (Ed.), *Welcome to middle age!: (And other cultural fictions)* (pp. 139–188). Chicago: University of Chicago Press.

Miller, J. G. (1994). Cultural diversity in the morality of caring: Individually oriented versus duty-based interpersonal moral codes. *Cross-Cultural Research: The Journal of Comparative Social Science, 28*(1), 3–39.

Miller, J. G. (1997). Theoretical issues in cultural psychology. In J. W. Berry, Y. H. Poortinga, & J. Pandey (Eds.), *Handbook of cross-cultural psychology, Vol. 1: Theory and method* (2nd ed., pp. 85–128). Boston: Allyn & Bacon.

Miller, J. G. (1999). Cultural psychology: Implications for basic psychological theory. *Psychological Science, 10*(2), 85–91.

Miller, J. G. (2001). Culture and moral development. In D. Matsumoto (Ed.), *The handbook of culture and psychology* (pp. 151–169). New York: Oxford University Press.

Miller, J. G. (2002). Bringing culture to basic psychological theory: Beyond individualism and collectivism: Comment on Oyserman et al. (2002). *Psychological Bulletin, 128*(1), 97–109.

Miller, J. G. (2004). The cultural deep structure of psychological theories of social development. In R. J. Sternberg & E. L. Grigorenko (Eds.), *Culture and competence: Contexts of life success* (pp. 11–138). Washington, DC: American Psychological Association.

Miller, J. G., & Bersoff, D. M. (1992). Culture and moral judgment: How are conflicts between justice and interpersonal responsibilities resolved? *Journal of Personality & Social Psychology, 62*(4), 541–554.

Miller, J. G., & Bersoff, D. M. (1994). Cultural influences on the moral status of reciprocity and the discounting of endogenous motivation. *Personality and Social Psychology Bulletin: Special Issue: The self and the collective, 20*(5), 592–602.

Miller, J. G., & Bersoff, D. M. (1995). Development in the context of everyday family relationships: Culture, interpersonal morality, and adaptation. In M. Killen & D. Hart (Eds.), *Morality in everyday life: Developmental perspectives* (pp. 259–282). New York: Cambridge University Press.

Miller, J. G., & Bersoff, D. M. (1998). The role of liking in perceptions of the moral responsibility to help: A cultural perspective. *Journal of Experimental Social Psychology, 34*(5), 443–469.

Miller, J. G., Bersoff, D. M., & Harwood, R. L. (1990). Perceptions of social responsibilities in India and in the United States: Moral imperatives or personal decisions? *Journal of Personality and Social Psychology, 58*(1), 33–47.

Miller, J. G., & Luthar, S. (1989). Issues of interpersonal responsibility and accountability: A comparison of Indians' and Americans' moral judgments. *Social Cognition, 7*(3), 237–261.

Much, N. C. (1997). A semiotic view of socialisation, lifespan development and cultural psychology: With vignettes from the moral culture of traditional Hindu households. *Psychology & Developing Societies: Special Issue: Cultural constructions and social cognition: Emerging themes, 9*(1), 65–106.

Neff, K. D. (2001). Judgments of personal autonomy and interpersonal responsibility in the context of Indian spousal relationships: An examination of young people's reasoning in Mysore, India. *British Journal of Developmental Psychology, 19,* 233–257.

Niemczynski, A., Czyzowska, D., Pourkos, M., & Mirski, A. (1988). The Cracow study with Kohlberg's moral judgment interview: Data pertaining to the assumption of cross-cultural validity. *Polish Psychological Bulletin, 19*(1), 43–53.

Nisbett, R. E. (2003). *The geography of thought: How Asians and westerners think differently—and why.* New York: Free Press.

Nisbett, R. E., Peng, K., Choi, I., & Norenzayan, A. (2001). Culture and systems of thought: Holistic versus analytic cognition. *Psychology Review, 108*(2), 291–310.

Nucci, L. P., Saxe, G. B., & Turiel, E. (Eds.). (2000). *Culture, thought, and development.* Mahwah, NJ: Lawrence Erlbaum Associates.

Nucci, L., & Turiel, E. (1993). God's word, religious rules, and their relation to Christian and Jewish children's concepts of morality. *Child Development, 64*(5), 1475–1491.

Nunner-Winkler, G. (1984). Two moralities? A critical discussion of an ethic of care and responsibility versus an ethic of rights and justice. In W. M. Kurtines & J. L. Gewirtz (Eds.), *Morality, moral behavior and moral development* (pp. 348–361). New York: John Wiley.

Okonkwo, R. (1997). Moral development and culture in Kohlberg's theory: A Nigerian (Igbo) evidence. *IFE Psychologia: An International Journal, 5*(2), 117–128.

Oyserman, D., Coon, H., & Kemmelmeier, M. (2002). Rethinking individualism and collectivism: Evaluation of theoretical assumptions and meta-analyses. *Psychological Bulletin, 128*(1), 3–72.

Piaget, J. (1932). *The moral judgment of the child.* London: Routledge & Kegan Paul.

Rothbaum, F., Pott, M., Azuma, H., Miyake, K., & Weisz, J. (2000). The development of close relationships in Japan and the United States: Paths of symbiotic harmony and generative tension. *Child Development, 71*(5), 1121–1142.

Searle, J. R. (1969). *Speech acts: An essay in the philosophy of language.* Cambridge, MA: Cambridge University Press.

Schaberg, L. (2002). *Toward a cultural broadening of feminist theory; A comparison of everyday outlooks on social roles, dissent, and feminism among United States and Japanese adults.* Unpublished doctoral dissertation, University of Michigan, Ann Arbor.

Schwartz, T. (1981). The acquisition of culture. *Ethos, 9,* 4–17.

Shimizu, H. (2001). Japanese adolescent boys' senses of empathy (*omoiyari*) and Carol Gilligan's perspectives on the morality of care: A phenomenological approach. *Culture and Psychology, 7*(4), 453–475.

Shweder, R. A. (1979a). Rethinking culture and personality theory part I: A critical examination of two classical postulates. *Ethos, 7*(3), 255–278.

Shweder, R. A. (1979b). Rethinking culture and personality theory part II: A critical examination of two more classical postulates. *Ethos, 7*(3), 255–278.

Shweder, R. A. (1982). Beyond self-constructed knowledge: The study of culture and morality. *Merrill-Palmer Quarterly, 28*(1), 41–69.

Shweder, R. A. (1984a). Preview: A co covy of culture theorists. In R. A. Shweder & R. F. Levine (Eds.), *Culture theory: Essays on mind, self, and emotion* (pp. 1–24). Cambridge, UK: Cambridge University Press.

Shweder, R. A. (1984b). Anthropology's romantic rebellion against the enlightenment, or there's more to thinking than reason and evidence. In R. A. Shweder & R. A. LeVine (Eds.), *Culture theory: Essays on mind, self, and emotion* (pp. 27–66). Cambridge, UK: Cambridge University Press.

Shweder, R. A. (1990). Cultural psychology—What is it? In J. W. Stigler, R. A. Shweder, & G. Herdt (Eds.), *Cultural psychology: Essays on comparative human development* (pp. 27–66). New York: Cambridge University Press.

Shweder, R. A. (2000). The psychology of practice and the practice of the three psychologies. *Asian Journal of Social Psychology, 3,* 207–222.

Shweder, R. A., & LeVine, R. A. (1984). *Culture theory: Essays on mind, self, and emotion.* Cambridge, UK: Cambridge University Press.

Shweder, R. A., Mahapatra, M., & Miller, J. G. (1987). *Culture and moral development: The emergence of morality in young children* (pp. 1–83). Chicago: University of Chicago Press.

Shweder, R. A., Minow, M., & Markus, H. (Eds.). (2002). *Engaging cultural differences: The multicultural challenge in liberal democracies.* New York: Russell Sage Foundation.

Shweder, R. A., & Much, N. C. (1987). Determinants of meaning: Discourse and moral socialization. In W. M. Kurtines & J. L. Gewirtz (Eds.), *Moral development through social interaction* (pp. 197–244). New York: John Wiley & Sons.

Shweder, R. A., Much, N. C., Mahapatra, M., & Park, L. (1997). The "big three" of morality (autonomy, community, divinity) and the "big three" explanations of suffering. In A. M. Brandt (Ed.), M*orality and health* (pp. 119–169). New York: Routledge.

Shweder, R. A., & Sullivan, M. A. (1990). The semiotic subject of cultural psychology. In *Handbook of personality: Theory and research* (pp. 399–416). New York: The Guilford Press.

Shweder, R. A., & Sullivan, M. A. (1993). Cultural psychology: Who needs it? *Annual Review of Psychology, 44,* 497–527.

Smetana, J. (1981). Reasoning in the personal and moral domains: Adolescent and young adult women's decision-making regarding abortion. *Journal of Applied Developmental Psychology, 2*(3), 211–226.

Snarey, J. R. (1985). Cross-cultural universality of social-moral development: A critical review of Kohlbergian research. *Psychological Bulletin, 97*(2), 202–232.

Snarey, J., & Keljo, K. (1991). In a Gemeinschaft voice: The cross-cultural expansion of moral development theory, *Handbook of moral behavior and development, Vol. 1: Theory* (pp. 395–424). Hillsdale, NJ: Lawrence Erlbaum Associates.

Strauss, C. (2000). The culture concept and the individualism-collectivism debate: Dominant and alternative attributions for class in the United States. In L. Nucci & G. E. Saxe (Eds.), *Culture, thought, and development* (pp. 85–114). Mahwah, NJ: Lawrence Erlbaum Associates.

Strauss, C., & Quinn, N. (1997). *A cognitive theory of cultural meaning.* New York: Cambridge University Press.

Tobin, J. J., Wu, D. Y. H., & Davidson, D. H. (1989). *Preschool in three cultures: Japan, China, and the United States.* New Haven, CT: Yale University Press.

Turiel, E. (1983). *The development of social knowledge: Morality and convention.* Cambridge, UK: Cambridge University Press.

Turiel, E. (1997). Beyond particular and universal ways: Contexts for morality. In H. D. Saltzstein (Ed.), *Culture as a context for moral development: New perspectives on the particular and the universal* (Vol. 76, pp. 87–105). San Francisco: Jossey-Bass.

Turiel, E. (1998a). The development of morality. In N. Eisenberg (Ed.), *Handbook of child psychology: Social, emotional, and personality development* (Vol. 3, pp. 863–892). New York: Wiley.

Turiel, E. (1998b). Notes from the underground: Culture, conflict, and subversion. In J. Langer & M. Killen (Eds.), *Piaget, evolution, and development* (pp. 271–296). Mahwah, NJ: Lawrence Erlbaum Associates.

Turiel, E. (2002). *The culture of morality: Social development, context, and conflict.* New York: Cambridge University Press.

Turiel, E., Killen, M., & Helwig, C. C. (1987). Morality: Its structure, functions, and vagaries. In J. Kagan & S. Lamb (Eds.), *The emergence of morality in young children* (pp. 155–243). Chicago: University of Chicago Press.

Turiel, E., & Neff, K. (2000). Religion, culture, and beliefs about reality in moral reasoning. In K. S. Rosengren, C. N. Johnson, & P. L. Harris (Eds.), *Imagining the impossible: Magical, scientific, and religious thinking in children* (pp. 269–304). New York: Cambridge University Press.

Turiel, E., & Wainryb, C. (1994). Social reasoning and the varieties of social experiences in cultural contexts. In H. W. Reese (Ed.), *Advances in child development and behavior* (Vol. 25, pp. 289–326). San Diego, CA: Academic Press.

Turiel, E., & Wainryb, C. (2000). Social life in cultures: Judgments, conflict, and subversion. *Child Development, 71*(1), 250–256.

Vasudev, J., & Hummel, R. C. (1987). Moral stage sequence and principled reasoning in an Indian sample. *Human Development, 30*(2), 105–118.

Wainryb, C. (1991). Understanding differences in moral judgments: The role of informational assumptions. *Child Development, 62*(4), 840–851.

Wainryb, C., & Turiel, E. (1994). Dominance, subordination, and concepts of personal entitlements in cultural contexts. *Child Development, 65*(6), 1701–1722.

Walker, L. J. (1984). Sex differences in the development of moral reasoning: A critical review. *Child Development, 55*(3), 677–691.

Walker, L. J., Pitts, R. C., Hennig, K. H., & Matsuba, M. K. (1995). Reasoning about morality and real-life moral problems. In M. Killen & D. Hart (Eds.), *Morality in everyday life: Developmental perspectives* (pp. 371–407). New York: Cambridge University Press.

Wellman, H. (1990). *The child's theory of mind.* Cambridge, MA: MIT Press.

Wertsch, J. V. (1995). Sociocultural research in the copyright age. *Culture and Psychology, 1*(1), 81–102.

CHAPTER

15

RECIPROCITY: THE FOUNDATION STONE OF MORALITY

DOUGLAS P. FRY

ÅBO AKADEMI UNIVERSITY AND UNIVERSITY OF ARIZONA

In *The Descent of Man,* originally published in 1871, Charles Darwin (1871/1998, p. 131) arrived at the conclusion that *reciprocity* was the foundation stone of morality, writing that "...the social instincts—the prime principle of man's moral constitution—with the aid of active intellectual powers and the effect of habit, naturally lead to the golden rule, 'As ye would that men should do to you, do ye to them likewise;' and this lies at the foundation of morality." In citing a Christian tenet, was Darwin simply being ethnocentric? Was the belief system of his own culture unduly influencing his thinking? Or, conversely, does this Christian sentiment actually reflect, as Darwin asserted, a true underpinning of morality? This chapter suggests that anthropological data across many cultures correspond with Darwin's supposition that reciprocity constitutes a central feature of morality. This idea is referred to as the *reciprocity principle.*

Building on Darwin's observations, Westermarck (1906/1924) developed a model of moral emotions that is congruent with the theory of natural selection (Arnhart, 1998; de Waal, 2001, pp. 350–353; Ginsberg, 1982, p. 6; Takala & Wolf, in press). Like Darwin, Westermarck gave reciprocity a central position in his theorizing. Westermarck (1906/1924) used the term *retributive emotions* to refer to feelings associated with "paying back in kind," either *retributive kindly emotions* related to reciprocating good deeds, or *resentment* for bad deeds. Additionally, Westermarck's model proposed two subcategories for each type of emotion depending on the presence or absence of *moral approval* or *disapproval.* Arnhart points out that "Moral disapproval is a form of resentment, and moral approval is a form of retributive kindly emotion. But in contrast to the non-moral emotions [for example, those that involve a particular individual's self-interested desire for revenge or feelings of personal gratitude], the moral emotions show *disinterestedness* and apparent *impartiality*" (1998, p. 4, emphasis mine).

In the time since Darwin highlighted the Golden Rule as the foundation of morality and Westermarck developed his model of retributive emotions, the corpus of ethnographic data amassed on societies from around the world substantiate the universality of reciprocity in human affairs. Brown (1991, p. 139), for example, in compiling a list of human universals, points out that across cultural settings, reciprocity is a key aspect of morality. Likewise, Killen and de Waal (2000) note, in correspondence with Westermarck's model, that reciprocity can involve positive exchanges as in trade or negative exchanges as in revenge. Thus, an underlying moral principle is basically that one good turn deserves another, and likewise, one bad deed deserves another.

A great deal of data on moral systems exists within anthropology, but this material is rarely nested within explicit considerations of morality. Anthropologists may wax long on exchange relationships, reciprocal obligations, or the importance of sharing without using the words *moral, morality,* or *moral code.* Likewise, ethnographic accounts describe traditions, legal systems, religion, formal and informal social control, the punishment of wrongdoers, and the practices of self-redress and compensation—all topics with moral elements—but usually offer no explicit connection to morality. For unknown reasons, the direct linking of such topics to morality seems to be an anthropological taboo. This situation leads to the necessity of borrowing models and concepts from other fields when discussing anthropological data relevant to morality. Another unfortunate implication of this anthropological neglect of morality is that explicit considerations of moral development are few and far between.

Several types of anthropological information are used in this chapter, roughly categorized as ethnographic examples, generalizations based on comparative ethnographic surveys, and cross-cultural studies. Unless otherwise noted, the ethnographic examples are based on first-hand fieldwork by professional anthropologists, with the fieldwork usually having been conducted in the twentieth century. Although methods vary somewhat from one fieldworker to the next, the overall approach is to engage in participant observation within a culture, record observations and interviews in fieldnotes, and cross-check the validity of information across several different sources. Of course, some degree of intracultural variation generally exists among individuals and among communities of the same society. The possibility of intracultural variability means that findings from one field location may not be applicable to another (e.g., see Fry, 1999a, p. 727).

Another type of anthropological material used in this chapter stems from comparative surveys of the ethnographic literature. For instance, scholars such as Boehm (1999, 2000), Brown (1991), Hoebel (1967), Reyna (1994), Sahlins (1965), and Service (1971b) derive generalizations about cross-cultural trends and patterns from extensively surveying ethnographic data on many cultures. Finally, this chapter draws on systematic cross-cultural studies (e.g., Ericksen & Horton, 1992; Leavitt, 1977; Otterbein & Otterbein, 1965) that sample cultures from the ethnographic population, code the ethnographic data for certain variables, and usually employ statistical analyses for hypothesis testing.

Topically, this chapter explores the reciprocity principle in relation to cross-cultural material. This exploration entails a consideration of both the reciprocity of good deeds and the reciprocity of bad deeds (revenge)—two sides of the reciprocity principle. Several broad conclusions are offered: First, the manner in which the reciprocity principle "plays out" relates to both social distance and social organization. Second, combining a consideration of social organization with the reciprocity principle yields insights about the most serious form of revenge seeking, lethal revenge. Third, seeking lethal revenge is not a human universal. Whereas a concept of justice may be linked to the reciprocity principle across human societies, specific paths to justice are extremely variable from one culture to the next. Consequently, attaining justice does not always involve bloodshed. The major topics to be considered include social distance related to empathy, sympathy and antipathy, moral aspects of social rules and obligations, social control, the justice of revenge seeking—including lethal revenge—and conflict resolution.

KINSHIP: THE ORIGINAL BASIS FOR EMPATHY AND SYMPATHY?

Hamilton (1964) hypothesized that the degree of biological relatedness between individuals affects the ways that they treat each other. The more closely individuals are related, the more helping, sharing, and caring should be expected, while harmful behaviors such as serious aggression, should be minimized in accordance with the closeness of the genetic relationship. To apply Westermarck's (1906/1924) terms, retributive kindly emotions and associated good deeds would be expected to be most frequently and most strongly manifested among close relatives. Hamilton reasoned that because relatives share a certain percentage of alleles in common, helping relatives is an indirect way to enhance one's own genetic fitness. Hamilton called this idea *inclusive fitness,* proposing that "the social behaviour of a species evolves in such a way that in each behaviour-evoking situation the individual will seem to value his neighbours' fitness against his own according to the coefficients of relationship appropriate to that situation" (1964, p. 19). Hamilton was not suggesting that individuals consciously calculate how much they are related before behaving kindly, benignly, or harmfully toward others. Rather, natural selection performs this evolutionary "cost–benefit" analysis over many generations.

The concept of inclusive fitness, also sometimes called *kin selection,* provides one answer to an evolutionary problem, mentioned long ago by Darwin (1871/1998, p. 135), regarding how altruistic acts such as defending others in the group from danger could have evolved by natural section if such deeds are detrimental to the fitness of the actor. Hamilton's (1964) answer to this problem conceptually extends an individual's fitness to encompass also the fitnesses of biological relatives, because kin share certain alleles. Thus when an individual protects and cares for close relatives, the caregiver is thus enhancing his or her own inclusive fitness. This concept provides a model for the origin of sympathy, empathy, and other emotions conducive to caring and sharing. Such emotions and the good deeds they foster may well have initially evolved within groups of relatives. Among humans, they are often extended to some degree by moral prescription to distant relatives and nonrelatives.

Helping close relatives is considered to be so normal and natural that it is generally taken for granted. Sahlins (1965) calls attention to nineteenth century anthropologist Edward Tyler's dictum that, as a primary principle of social life, *kindness* goes with *kindred,* an observation that is reflected in the common derivation of these two words. A comment by Sather on the Sama Dilaut sea people of Malaysia reflects this typical cross-cultural feature: ". . . a person has the right to expect aid from a kinsman" (2004, p. 142).

Sahlins proposes that reciprocity comes in three forms: generalized, balanced, and negative. In his scheme, these kinds of so-called reciprocity form a continuum from "assistance freely given" in generalized reciprocity to "self-interested seizure, appropriation by chicanery or force" in negative reciprocity (Sahlins, 1965, p. 144). Sahlins (1965) uses copious cross-cultural illustrations to demonstrate that the three types of reciprocity relate to kinship distance: generalized reciprocity is typical among close kin whereas negative reciprocity is most likely among nonkin.

Generalized reciprocity "refers to transactions that are putatively altruistic, transactions on the line of assistance given and, if possible and necessary, assistance returned. . . . 'sharing,' 'hospitality,' 'free gift,' 'help,' and 'generosity'" (1965, p. 147).

Sahlins points out that generalized reciprocity—for example, the nursing of a child by its mother—lacks any expectation of direct repayment. The fact that generalized reciprocity is natural among close kin is illustrated by Marshall's (1961, p. 231) observation about the !Kung (nowadays called the Ju/'hoansi) of the African Kalahari that altruism, generosity, kindness, and sympathy are most likely among relatives.

Balanced reciprocity entails direct and equal exchanges, as seen in trade. The Ju/'hoansi, for example, engage in the back-and-forth giving of non-equivalent gifts, that "balance out in the long run" (Lee, 1993, p. 103). Among the Sama Dilaut, ". . . gifts of food, exchanged between kin and cluster allies, are regularly received with a verbal pledge of return; thus reciprocity is expressed simultaneously in words as well as in material transaction" (Sather, 2004, p. 133).

Sahlins' *negative reciprocity* involves an attempt to get something for nothing through haggling, theft, seizure, deceit, and so on. It can involve aggression, and again, the cross-cultural data indicate that negative reciprocity tends to occur at the greatest social distances. Sahlins' (1965, p. 149) comment that, "it is a long way from suckling a child to a Plains Indians' horse-raid," reflects the arrangement of altruistic-to-harmful behaviors along the social distance continuum.

As a cross-cultural pattern, Sahlins' types of reciprocity vary with social distance in correspondence with Hamilton's (1964) inclusive fitness concept (see Alexander, 1979, p. 57). This pattern shows that relatives are less likely to harm one another than are nonrelatives, and furthermore, that relatives are prone to feel empathy and sympathy toward each other and regularly engage in acts of kindness and compassion for one another. Pertaining to both helping and harming, a study by Dunbar, Clark, and Hurst (1995) suggests that behavioral decisions do in fact relate to inclusive fitness considerations. These researchers analyzed historical data on Viking populations and found that kinship was involved in decisions regarding both alliance formation and revenge murder. Viking alliances were more likely among relatives than among unrelated families, and the kin-based alliances also proved to be longer in duration and involved fewer preconditions than alliances among nonrelatives. Furthermore, Dunbar and associates (1995) conclude that homicides reflect both inclusive fitness theory and cost–benefit ratios. Nonrelatives were murdered at times for no economic gain—such as during drunken brawls—whereas relatives were infrequently killed to begin with, but when a relative was killed, there always existed some substantial benefit for the killer.

A final point of possible confusion deserves explicit mention. By Sahlins' definitions, only balanced reciprocity actually involves a two-way exchange, whereas the other types of so-called reciprocity are unidirectional. Of course, an act of negative reciprocity, such as theft, can lead to a reprisal, thus creating a two-way negative exchange. Sahlins' original definition of negative reciprocity, however, only deals with the initial act intended to get something for nothing, not possible countermeasures. Under the reciprocity principle, the main point is that one bad deed leads to another—to revenge—or a good act results in a reciprocal positive deed. Sahlins' negative reciprocity leaves out the revenge, just has his generalized reciprocity leaves out a positive payback. Neither category actually involves reciprocity at all.

Another concept, *reciprocal altruism,* has relevance for understanding the origin and development of morality. Reciprocal altruism basically corresponds with what Sahlins calls *balanced reciprocity,* or direct and equal exchange, but emphasizes that repayments may not be instantaneous. The originator of the reciprocal altruism concept, biologist Robert Trivers (1985, p. 361; see Trivers, 1971), explains the concept as "the trading of altruistic acts in which benefit is larger than cost so that over a period of time both enjoy a net gain." Again, the Ju/'hoansi provide an example in that "the person who receives a gift of meat must give a reciprocal gift some time in the future" (Marshall, 1961, p. 239). In a world without refrigerators, hoarding a large kill simply results in a lot of spoiled meat; sharing the kill with others, by contrast, leads to return gifts of meat in the future. Marshall (1961, p. 236) highlights the *reciprocal obligations* inherent in such a system: "the person one shares with will share in turn when he gets meat and people are sustained by a web of mutual obligation." The anthropological literature is overflowing with examples of reciprocal exchange and the networks of mutual obligations created by such reciprocity (e.g., Berndt, 1972; Dentan, 1968, p. 49; Sather, 2004; Tonkinson, 2004).

The term *mutual social obligations* refers to expectations that favors, gifts, and services will be repaid. Obligations are reinforced by custom and the nature of particular kinship relations. For example, among the Zapotec of Mexico, *compadres* (godparents) are obligated to perform certain ritual activities and give particular gifts to their godchildren. And more generally, a Zapotec when invited to a ceremony or wedding is socially obligated to attend, bringing certain gifts in repayment of previous debts. Obligations can pass from one generation to the next. Although the specifics differ, social obligations and reciprocal exchange exist in every culture.

As Trivers notes, inclusive fitness and reciprocal altruism are compatible concepts. Both mechanisms may have been involved in the evolutionary development of emotions such as sympathy and empathy and the compassionate, helpful, and at times truly altruistic deeds that can flow from such sentiments. Darwin (1871/1998) saw both *intellect* and *habit* as contributing to people's widespread adherence to the Golden Rule. Clearly people intellectually grasp the benefits that result from engaging in balanced exchange— reciprocal altruism. Across the ethnographic spectrum, as will soon be considered, social rules encourage the expression of generosity and kindness beyond a person's immediate kin. Children are socialized to share and to fulfill social obligations. Unwilling persons are pressured to do so. Thus most people develop the prosocial habits, as noted by Darwin, that help to extend acts of kindness beyond kinship.

RULES AND OBLIGATIONS: MAINTAINING THE MORAL COMMUNITY

Westermarck's (1906/1924) moral emotions were not in and of themselves *moral*. Fletcher explains that in Westermarck's scheme, certain retributive emotions "... *became* moral when—after society had come gradually to recognize and sanction the modes of behavior to which they referred—they acquired the qualities of generality, disinterestedness, and impartiality" (1982, p. 204). According to Westermarck, retributive emotions initially evolved due to the survival value they conferred on the individuals expressing them. Subsequently, certain moral emotions, those sentiments that expressed approval or disapproval of certain acts became sanctioned by society and, correspondingly, punishments for misdeeds were impartially and generally applied. In other words, moral approval and disapproval no longer reflected simply the self-centered interests of particular individuals, but instead were widely felt and shared by disinterested members of the community. Mackie suggests that "from cooperation in resentment to moral disapproval or indignation is a further step, but not an enormous one. It requires that certain *kinds* of behavior should be cooperatively resented and opposed and seen as generally harmful" (1982, p. 154).

Everywhere people have rules of proper conduct and norms related to fulfilling social obligations. Everywhere people punish violators of these rules and shirkers of obligations (see Brown, 1991). Boehm (1999, 2000) has recently given considerable thought to the evolution of morality in humans. He argues convincingly that simple nomadic foragers provide the best proxies for ancestral human groups and conceptualizes morality primarily in political terms. A central feature is egalitarianism. Members of nomadic forager bands, with great consistency, "head off attempts of individuals to exert domination or control" (Boehm, 2000, p. 81). Boehm (1999, 2000) points out that like current nomadic foragers, the nomadic hunter-gatherers of the evolutionary past also must have lived in egalitarian moral communities. An extensive survey of the ethnographic literature led Boehm (1999, p. 72) to the conclusion that members of moral communities are expected to be generous, cooperative, unbossy, and unarrogant. Furthermore, nomadic bands, with remarkable consistency are cooperative and moralistically sanction deviants. "In effect, the band keeps a dossier on every individual, noting positive and negative points" (Boehm, 1999, p. 73). A prominent moral feature of nomadic hunter-gatherer society is "an ethic of sharing that selectively extends to the entire group the cooperation and altruism found within the family" (Boehm, 1999, p. 67).

The ubiquity of reciprocal meat sharing in nomadic hunter-gatherer society is unambiguous (Boehm, 1999, p. 183; Ingold, 1999; Knauft, 1991, pp. 393–394; Lee & Daly, 1999, p. 4; Lee & DeVore, 1968, p. 12; for examples see Clastres, 1972; Honigmann, 1954, p. 89; Leacock, 1954, pp. 7, 33; Lee, 1993; Marshall, 1961; Service, 1971a, p. 75; Woodburn, 1982). The Guayaki of South America have a rule for sharing manifested as a food taboo: A hunter should never eat the meat of the animals he has killed. This taboo reinforces the fact that people are interdependent and must share with each other; each hunter gives his game to others and in return receives meat from other hunters (Clastres, 1972, p. 169).

Among the Paliyan of India, hunting groups generally consist of five to ten persons. As in social relations generally, no one dominates the decision making; the members of the hunting group operate via discussion and consensus (Gardner, 1972, p. 415). At the end of the hunt, the game is meticulously apportioned into equivalent piles. Not only are the shares of meat equal, but also each contains identical types of meat. "When all have agreed that the piles are of equal size, each hunter takes one, whatever his role in the hunt" (Gardner, 1972, pp. 415–416).

The Netsilik Inuit of the Canadian Arctic strongly believed that every man should hunt and had clear rules for sharing meat. Balikci (1970, pp. 176–177) explains how lazy men were disliked, criticized, and sometimes even ostracized by the others in the group. By contrast, if illness or accident temporarily incapacitated a productive hunter who regularly shared with others, he and his family were aided with gifts of food (Balikci, 1970, pp. 176–177).

These examples not only reflect the reciprocity principle of morality, but also illustrate some of the specific social rules for sharing and for meeting other types of social obligations within moral communities. Growing up in these communities, children have numerous opportunities to learn socially correct moral behavior, through observation as well as through receiving socializing rewards and punishments from their elders (see Dentan, 1968, pp. 59–61; Fry, 1999a, pp. 724–727).

SOCIAL CONTROL: MORAL APPROVAL AND DISAPPROVAL

Primeval man, at a very remote period, was influenced by the praise and blame of his fellows. It is obvious, that the members of the same tribe would approve of conduct which appeared to them to be for the general good, and would reprobate that which appeared evil .... It is, therefore, hardly possible to exaggerate the importance ... of the love of praise and the dread of blame. (Darwin, 1871/1998, p. 136)

Universally, humans express moral disapproval and apply sanctions against those who violate the social rules (Black, 1993; Brown, 1991, p. 138). Disapproval ranges from nasty looks and malicious gossip through ridicule, sarcasm, and harangues to the infliction of injury, ostracism, and even execution (Boehm, 1999, 2000; Fry, 2006). A society need not have a central authority or strong leadership positions to apply such sanctions; group members individually and in concert effectively express moral disapproval and apply social control measures.

Among the nomadic Montagnais-Naskapi foragers of Canada, social control was maintained by rewarding and encouraging positive behavior—that is, by showing moral approval—and also by applying ridicule and scorn that reflected negative public opinion—moral disapproval (see Reid, 1991, p. 245; Speck, 1935, p. 44). Such behavior is typical in nomadic hunter-gatherer societies (see Boehm, 1999). In response to the most serious transgressions, such as committing incest, constant trouble making, or murder (if the killer was not killed by the victim's kin), the guilty party faced ostracism from the band. "In Naskapi society, expulsion is equal to a death sentence," writes Lips (1947, p. 469), and he recounts how a man was banished from his band in about 1870 due to repeatedly hunting within the hunting grounds of others. He and his family attempted to join neighboring groups, but other bands did not accept him. Apparently his reputation was known. Eventually, he and his family starved to death. This punishment brings to mind how the missionary Le Jeune had observed in the 1630s not only the generous and cooperative side of native life, but also the importance they placed on "getting even" with serious wrongdoers. He wrote, "So enraged are they against every one who does them an injury, that they eat the lice and other vermin that they find upon themselves—not because they like them, but only, they say, to avenge themselves and to eat those that eat them" (Leacock, 1981, p. 194). Thus the reciprocity principle is being applied even to lice!

Turnbull (1961) provides another ethnographic illustration of the social control measures used to uphold rules and obligations, this time in African Mbuti society, as he describes the crime of Cephu. Cephu ignored the rules of cooperative hunting and meat sharing and attempted to cheat the others in the band. The band members responded with moral disapproval. They ridiculed, insulted, criticized, lectured, and laughed at Cephu before finally suggesting that he and his family could leave the band, a punishment that would have been disastrous for Cephu and his kin, because such a small group could not have hunted effectively. When faced with criticism, ridicule, and the threat of ostracism, Cephu apologized profusely and delivered all of the ill-acquired meat to the band.

Events like this serve as lessons in moral development for the young. The ever-present children are privy to the nature of the moral transgressions by persons like Cephu and see and hear, firsthand, the powerful social control exercised by the group.

Universally, morally approved actions—good behaviors—are valued and rewarded. Among nomadic hunter-gatherers, as in most societies, good behaviors typically include generosity, sharing, fulfilling obligations, and getting along with others without excessive violence or repeated trouble making. Social rules tend to promote desired acts of generosity and respect for others. Among the Ju/'hoansi, for example, the ideal son-in-law "should be a good hunter, he should *not* have a reputation as a fighter, and he should come from a congenial family of people who like to do *hxaro,* the Ju/'hoan form of traditional exchange" (Lee, 1993, p. 81, italics in original). The moral ideals of the Sama Dilaut include sensitivity to duty, compassion, concern for the needs of others, and generosity (Sather, 2004, p. 135). Tonkinson writes that the ideal Australian Mardu adult is "agreeable, unassuming, self-effacing, unselfish, and ever ready to share with kin and fulfill ritual and kinship obligations without complaint rather than being egotistical or boastful to excess" (2004, p. 94). Social ideals and their corresponding social rules can be seen as prescriptions for extending the kindness associated with Sahlins' (1965) generalized reciprocity beyond the immediate family. As mentioned, for instance, rules for sharing meat with nonrelatives are typical in nomadic forager societies.

At the same time, rules against morally disapproved actions—bad behavior—develop that outlaw the types of conduct that Sahlins classifies as negative reciprocity, acts that exploit other individuals or the group as a whole as in Cephu's greedy behavior. Across human societies, disapproved behaviors typically include theft, stinginess, rape, assault, and murder (see Boehm, 1999, 2000; Brown, 1991, p. 138).

THE RECIPROCITY OF REVENGE: ONE PATH TO JUSTICE

Seeking vengeance, extracting revenge, demanding satisfaction, getting even, paying back, evening the score, retaliating: There are many ways to express the balancing notion implied by the revenge-seeking side of the reciprocity principle. Basically, one bad turn deserves another. Among the horticultural tribes of the Upper Xingu River basin in Amazonia, the reciprocity principle is apparent in the *Yawari* contest:

> The Yawari is a ritual in which members of opposed tribes pair off as kinsmen, but then hurl insults and subsequently wax-tipped spears at one another.... The spear must be tipped with wax and it must be thrown well below the waist. The rules of the event are such that aggressors and their targets change roles. *If a villager inflicts too much harm he may find himself equally injured moments later.* (Gregor, 1994, pp. 250, 253, italics added)

The nonviolent people of Ifaluk Atoll in Micronesia have a word, *paluwen,* for a payback. "Ilefagomar was not invited to the birth hut of another woman when she ought to have been. She later 'paid back' this woman by not calling her to her own labor and birth celebration several months later" (Lutz, 1988, p. 175).

The third example stems from a story by a conflict resolution specialist about a man at an airline check-in counter in the U.S. The man was exceptionally rude and insulting to the check-in clerk. After the obnoxious passenger went on his way, the observer expressed empathy to the clerk about the difficulties of his job. The clerk, who had kept his cool while assisting the offensive traveler, confided that whereas the man was bound for New York, his checked luggage was on its way to Los Angeles.

As these examples illustrate, bad behavior can evoke paybacks. The last example is interesting for the airline clerk's clever, indirect means of implementing his revenge within the constraints of a work environment (see Björkqvist, Österman, & Kaukiainen, 1992). In these examples, individuals take the initiative to balance an injustice. In other words, people redress a perceived personal wrong. However, in punishing the bad behavior of another, the retaliators also could be viewed as acting morally to the extent that they are helping to uphold the social rules of their community that reflect the general and impartial moral disapproval of certain behaviors. In such situations, the retaliators would be expected to experience what Westermarck (1906/1924) referred to as moral emotions. Additionally, their punishing actions may fit what Trivers (1971) called *moralistic aggression*—responses that punish wrongdoers for their immoral actions.

In the following example, the Mardu punish a man for violating a social rule against incest (Tonkinson, 2004). Aside from showing moral disapproval, the application of a sanction helps to preserve good relations with a neighboring band. An unmarried man in his late twenties, named Djadu, repeatedly ignored warnings to cease having sexual liaisons with two young women from a neighboring band. These particular women were related to Djadu in such a way as to be inappropriate sexual partners. Thus Djadu's behavior was immoral. The members of the two groups met several times to discuss the problem. At the meetings Djadu attempted to justify his behavior. Finally, three of his older brothers ordered him to stand and accept his punishment. As Djadu stood in the open, five of his classificatory elder brothers threw spears at him, mostly one at a time so he could have a chance to dodge, attempting to wound Djadu in his thigh. The aim was to punish him, not kill him. Djadu parried several spears, but in the end received two thigh wounds. The punishers delivered several severe club blows for good measure.

In terms of moral development among the young, children are present and witness such scenes. They pick up from observation which behaviors are morally approved and which behaviors are morally disapproved. Tonkinson explains:

> Before it can walk or talk, a small child should learn about sharing with others. . . . Through entreaty, ridicule, threat, withdrawal of support, peer-group pressure, and so on, the child will learn to conform. From the models that surround it in the immediate family and band, it will learn about sex roles and the division of labor. But the keys to self-regulation lie in child's development of a strong sense of compassion (*nyaru*), which will impel it to be generous and to look after others; in shame and embarrassment (*gurnda*), which will inhibit it from many antisocial or immoral behaviors; and in a yearning for family and home estate (*gudjil*), which will act to draw the wanderer back throughout his or her lifetime. (1978, pp. 120–121)

Descriptions that reflect the reciprocity principle are so pervasive in the anthropological literature that this foundation stone of morality in all likelihood applies to humans across social circumstances. In fact, the reciprocity principle may also apply to some nonhuman primates and other species as well (e.g., see de Waal, 2001, chap. 11; Flack & de Waal, 2000). As part of the balance, the payback deed should be more or less equivalent to the original deed (Daly & Wilson, 1988). Little favors likely bring little favors in return; a serious misdeed tends to elicit a greater payback than a minor breach of rules or social obligations.

Lethal Aggression and the Reciprocity Principle

It bears emphasis that most conflicts in human communities are nonlethal, and most people deal with perceived bad deeds without any violence whatsoever, whether or not they engage in a payback. Taking a life in exchange for a life is arguably the most severe manifestation retaliatory justice, an idea reflected in the following quote by Westermarck:

> The most sacred duty which we owe our fellow-creatures is to respect their lives. I venture to believe that this holds good not only among civilized nations, but among the lower races as well; and that, if a savage recognizes that he has any moral obligations at all to his neighbours, he considers the taking of their lives to be a greater wrong than any other kind of injury inflicted upon them. (1906/1924, p. 328)

Daly and Wilson (1988) have argued that the desire for blood revenge is a human universal. "The inclination to blood revenge is experienced by people in all cultures, and that the act is therefore unlikely to be altogether 'absent' anywhere" (Daly & Wilson, 1988, p. 227). However, a careful review of the cross-cultural data suggests that their argument can benefit from refinement. In short, their assertion goes beyond what the ethnographic data can support. The discussion that follows raises several complexities not considered by Daly and Wilson (1988). First, it is useful to distinguish among *individual self-redress, feud,* and *war*. Second, a more nuanced understanding of how lethal aggression relates to the reciprocity principle can be gained by adding *social organization* to the analysis. Third, a substantial percentage of societies have moral codes that do not allow lethal revenge (Ericksen & Horton, 1992), such as those with nonviolent belief systems (see Fry, 1999a, 2004, 2006). Therefore, rather than simply evoking the reciprocity principle as the *only* relevant moral precept, other aspects of a society's moral code and worldview also must be considered to attain an understanding of a given society's moral response to lethal aggression.

Types of Lethal Aggression

Across the cultural spectrum of societies, blood revenge, when it does occur, fits certain patterns called *individual lethal self-redress, feud,* and *war*. *Individual lethal self-redress* is when a relative of a homicide victim retaliates against the perpetrator. The actual killer is the preferred target of revenge. A variation of individual self-redress is when a close biological relative of the perpetrator, such as a brother, but not any member of a larger kin group, is targeted in place of the actual killer (see Boehm, 1999, p. 80).

Boehm (1987) succinctly catches the elements of feud, the second type of lethal revenge. *Feud* is "deliberately limited and carefully counted killings in revenge for a previous homicide, which takes place between two groups on the basis of specific rules for killing, pacification, and compensation" (p. 194).

Prosterman's (1972) definition of war corresponds with the common usage of the word and differentiates warfare from homicides, individual self-redress killings, and feuding between corporate groups. *War* is

> a group activity, carried on by members of one community against members of another community, in which it is the primary purpose to inflict serious injury or death on multiple nonspecified members of that other community, or in which the primary purpose makes it highly likely that serious injury or death will be inflicted on multiple nonspecified members of that community in the accomplishment of that primary purpose. (Prosterman, 1972, p. 140)

Prosterman's (1972) definition highlights that war is a group activity, occurs between communities, is not focused against a particular individual, as in lethal self-redress, or against a person's corporate group—such as a kin group, as occurs in feuding—but rather is focused against nonspecified members of another community. Revenge, of course, is only one variable that may be related to warfare.

Types of Social Organization

Types of lethal aggression vary in relation to social organization. Service (1971b; see also Reyna, 1994) proposes four basic categories of human social organization: bands, tribes, chiefdoms, and states. Boehm (1999) makes finer distinctions: nomadic hunter-gatherers (corresponding to Service's bands), acephalous tribes and big-man societies (together roughly corresponding to Service's tribes), sedentary foragers and chiefdoms (called chiefdoms by Service), and primitive kingdoms, ancient civilizations, and modern states (all variants of states, in Service's system).

For the most part, Service's (1971b) four-part scheme is adequate for considering the reciprocity of lethal aggression. *Bands* are small in size, variably consisting of about twenty-five persons at any given time, are politically egalitarian, lack clear leadership, are nomadic or seminomadic, and engage in hunting and gathering as a subsistence strategy. Individuals shift readily among different bands. Consequently, anthropologists refer to band composition as being flexible and in flux. Additionally, band society lacks ranked social classes and tends not to be rigidly subdivided into corporate subgroups on the basis of kinship or other distinctions. This last point, although often ignored, is of critical importance in understanding patterns of lethal aggression in bands. In contrast to tribes, chiefdoms, and states, nomadic, egalitarian hunter-gatherer band society is the oldest and simplest form of human social organization, extending back at least a million years into humanity's evolutionary past.

Compared to nomadic hunter-gatherer bands, *tribes* represent a recent form of social organization, emerging with the agricultural revolution some 10,000 years ago. Tribes tend to be sedentary and typically engage in horticulture, although some practice herding. Tribal settlements may contain 100 or more persons. In tribal society, leadership is weak, hence Boehm's (1999) use of the term *acephalous* in connection to tribes, although headmen, "big men," and other leadership roles may emerge in tribes. Tribal leaders attempt to exert their will through the art of persuasion and by leading through example, because they lack, for the most part, other forms of coercive power. The presence of only weak authority positions really means that tribal social organization remains largely egalitarian. Unlike bands, however, tribes tend to be segmented politically into *lineages*—societal subgroups with membership based on descent from a common ancestor—clans, or other kinship distinctions.

Chiefdoms exhibit considerable variability, although the existence of a social hierarchy is a distinguishing feature. Some chiefdoms vest minor authority in the chiefs, whereas in other cases, chiefs have considerable authority. Chiefs are entitled to special privileges. Commoners pay tribute to chiefs, some of which the chiefs then redistribute back to their subjects. The economies of chiefdoms tend to be based on farming, fishing, or both. Boehm's (1999) scheme makes special mention of sedentary foragers, or to use an alternative name, complex hunter-gatherers (Kelly, 1995). In considering lethal aggression and the reciprocity principle, it is absolutely critical not to intermingle nomadic hunter-gatherer bands with complex hunter-gatherer chiefdoms, as periodically occurs (e.g., Daly & Wilson, 1988; Ember, 1978; Gat, 2000). Complex sedentary hunter-gatherers are socially ranked societies with rulers and commoners, and sometimes slaves as well. Population densities tend to be higher than in nomadic hunter-gatherer societies. Complex hunter-gatherers exploit rich natural resources such as salmon runs. Ethnographically, this type of society is very rare, limited to such groups as the Ainu of Japan and some societies on the Northwest Coast of North America (Kelly, 1995, p. 302).

As recently as 5,000 to 6,000 years ago some early chiefdoms under went further organizational transformations, and the world's first *states* were born. The economy of states rests on agriculture. Rulers of states wield considerably more power than do the rulers of chiefdoms. Economic specialization, social class distinctions, centralized political and military organization, the use of writing and mathematics, urbanization, large-scale irrigation of crops, and the development of bureaucracy characterize states, ancient and modern (Boehm, 1999, p. 146; Service, 1971b, pp. 166–169).

In summary, in uncentralized bands and tribes, leadership and political power are weak and dispersed. In chiefdoms and especially in states, political power is centralized at the top of a social hierarchy (Reyna, 1994). Social relations in bands and tribes are relatively egalitarian compared to those of chiefdoms and states (Boehm, 1999, 2000).

Social Organization, Lethal Aggression, and Justice Seeking

Reyna (1994) presents an overview of the typical reasons for fighting at different levels of social organization. He proposes that when aggression occurs in band society, it is relatively harmless. People sometimes fight, but grudges are personal affairs. In bands, most fighting is between individuals and nonlethal, although killings can occur. As Malinowski notes: "Under conditions where portable wealth does not exist; where food is too perishable and too clumsy to be accumulated and transported; where slavery is of no value because every individual consumes exactly as much as he produces—force is a useless implement for the transfer of wealth" (1941, p. 538).

Turning to tribes, Reyna (1994) points out that aggression still stems from personal grudges, but now can involve kin militia. Groups of fighters tend to be related, because tribal communities are organized on the basis of kin groups. The term *kin militia* is appropriate at the tribal *level* because fighting groups can be temporarily assembled on the basis of kinship ties. In tribal societies, there are no professional standing armies and no hierarchical military structures. Fighting most often involves brawls, raids, and ambushes between kin groups.

Within chiefdoms, chiefly militias come into play (Reyna, 1994). The leaders and military specialists have authority to command obedience from the ranks, as illustrated in large chiefdoms such as Tahiti, Tonga, Fiji, and Hawaii (Hickson, 1986, p. 284; Reyna, 1994, p. 44; Service, 1978, pp. 268–272). In chiefdoms, battles are more common than within tribal organization. In some large-scale chiefdoms, such as Fiji with six social classes, warfare involved large, bloody battles (Carneiro, 1990, p. 200). Fijian chiefs tried to put as many men into combat as possible. Although standing armies did not exist and there was no formal draft, every man was expected to fight when ordered onto the field by his chief (Carneiro, 1990). Again, complex hunter-gatherers fit the chiefdom pattern. Kelly contrasts complex hunter-gatherers as "non-egalitarian societies, whose elites possess slaves, *fight wars,* and overtly seek prestige" with simple hunter-gatherers that consist of "small, *peaceful,* nomadic bands, men and women with few possession[s] and are equal in wealth, opportunity, and status" (1995, p. 293, italics added; see also Binford, 2001, p. 432).

States tend to have large permanent armies led by military specialists operating within hierarchical command structures (Reyna, 1994). Under such conditions, elaborate military campaigns and protracted wars are possible.

The phrase "taking justice into one's own hands" catches the essence of personal self-redress, whether lethal or not. One problem with self-redress is that the actor's idea of justice may be perceived by the recipient as unjust, as an unwarranted or overzealous attack. Self-redress can lead to spirals of escalating conflict. Brögger (1968, p. 231), who conducted fieldwork in southern Italy, recounts a series of events that began when a man named Domenico cut down several trees to make charcoal. Guiseppe requested some of the charcoal, as partial owner of the trees, but Domenico refused to give him any. As a result of an ensuing argument, Guiseppe became furious and stole some of Domenico's rabbits. Domenico retaliated by cutting down Guiseppe's vineyard late one night. Ultimately Guiseppe became so enraged that he killed Domenico.

Is the use of lethal self-redress related to social organization? Based on a careful examination of systems of justice in 650 societies representing different kinds of social organization, Hobhouse, Wheeler, and Ginsberg (1915) reached a conclusion that has held the tests of time. Lethal self-redress is most common among hunter-gatherer subsistence systems and steadily decreases in use as patterns of subsistence shift toward agriculture or herding. In their large cross-cultural sample, Hobhouse, and associates (1915, p. 71) found self-redress to be present in about 90% of the simplest hunter-gatherer societies but in less than 15% of the most agriculturally reliant societies. These researchers concluded that "... as we mount the [economic/social organizational] scale there is more government and more of the public administration of justice within society ... " (Hobhouse et al., 1915, p. 254).

A half century later, the renowned legal anthropologist E. Adamson Hoebel expressed a similar conclusion about how law and justice are painted across the wide canvass of social organization: "... the tendency is to shift the privilege rights of prosecution and imposition of legal sanctions from the *individual* [as in self-redress] and his *kin-group* [as in feuding] over to clearly defined *public officials* representing the society as such [as in courts of law]" (1967, p. 327, italics mine). The main point is that the key administrators of justice sequentially change as social complexity increases from the individual, to kin-groups, and eventually to public officials.

Using a sample of 186 societies called the Standard Cross-Cultural Sample (SCCS) that represents major cultural provinces in the world, Ericksen and Horton (1992) replicated the fundamental results of Hobhouse and his colleague's (1915) classic study and substantiated the veracity of Hoebel's reading of the general trends. Ericksen and Horton (1992, pp. 73–74) found that lethal individual self-redress is about seven times more likely to occur among hunter-gatherer band societies than in all other types of societies. Additionally, Ericksen and Horton compared the likelihood of self-redress in unstratified or egalitarian societies—that is, the pattern typically found in uncentralized bands and tribes—and in stratified or hierarchical societies—basically, chiefdoms and states—and found over five times the self-redress among the unstratified group. Finally, Ericksen and Horton (1992, p. 74) found adjudication to dominate in the most complex type of political economies. In other words, well-developed chiefdoms and states usurp from individuals and kin groups the right to administer justice after a homicide. Those at the top have the authority to judge and the power to enforce their rulings. In modern states, homicides rarely result in individual acts of self-redress or in feuding between corporate kin groups. Instead, most citizens accept that the administration of justice lies in the hands of the state. Should a citizen take the law into his or her own hands, the state judicial system treats such acts of self-redress as new crimes, not as the legitimate administration of justice. States claim the right to administer justice.

It is important to highlight a recurring pattern among simple nomadic foragers: the targets of revenge tend to be the killers themselves (e.g., Kelly, 2000; Peterson, 1991, p. 375). This point is clearly apparent in Ju/'hoansi homicide data (Lee, 1979, pp. 382–396). Of twenty-two homicides, eleven were initial homicides. Revenge was sought against four of the killers, attempts that ultimately led to eleven more violent deaths, including the four killers themselves, one relative of a killer, and several revenge seekers and bystanders. Much of the bloodshed revolved around repeated attempts to execute two of the original four killers, who were notoriously violent men (Lee, 1979). Ericksen and Horton's cross-cultural study of vengeance also supports the generalization that among simple nomadic foragers, if revenge is sought, individual family members of the victim, not larger kin groups, tend to target the actual killer (1992, Table 2, see case numbers 2, 13, 77, 79, 90, 91, 119, 122, 124–129, 137, 180, 186; see also Fry, 2006).

Whereas Ericksen and Horton's findings demonstrate that individual self-redress is relatively more likely in band societies than in hierarchical societies, feuding that pits kin group against kin group is not common in bands for the simple reason that most band societies lack well-developed cohesive kin organizations (see Knauft, 1991, p. 405).

Band societies rarely have, for instance, matrilineal or patrilineal segments, that is, groups of relatives that reckon their common descent from a shared female or male ancestor, respectively (Fry, 2006). Instead, in a majority of simple nomadic forager societies, each person thinks in terms of his or her own unique set of relatives. Of course, the kin networks of two persons in nomadic bands may overlap, but even two brothers usually have different kin networks after marriage due to each having a different set of in-laws. This is a main reason why a pattern of individual self-redress at the immediate family level—as contrasted with a pattern of protracted feuding between larger kin groups—typifies simple band societies. Band level social organization tends to lack the types of corporate subgroups that are well developed in more complex societies (Kelly, 2000).

Whereas revenge killings in simple nomadic band societies are almost always under-taken by the victim's close relatives who target the particular individual who killed their family member, by contrast, once social segmentation enters the picture, as is typical of tribal societies, a killing is perceived as a loss not only to the victim's immediate family, but more generally to members of the same patrilineage, subclan, clan, and so on. In seeking revenge, the victim's larger kin organization may target anyone belonging to the killer's kin group. Kelly (2000) refers to this phenomenon as *social substitutability*. In segmented societies, such as tribes, retaliatory justice seeking may alternate back and forth between clans or lineages. Each killing prompts a retaliation, which in turn prompts a counter-retaliation and then a counter-counter-retaliation. In other words, social substitutability facilitates feuding. Among states, social substitutability can facilitate war, as one act of violence (for instance, a terrorist attack) provokes retaliation not solely against the actual perpetrators, but against anyone belonging to the same national or religious group as the attackers. The idea of social substitutability has relevance for understanding some types of warfare and other types of intergroup violence in today's world.

Clearly, individual self-redress and feuding relate to social organization. Is the presence or absence of warfare also related to social organization? A number of cross-cultural studies show that sociopolitical complexity and warfare go hand-in-hand (see van der Dennen, 1995, chap. 2; Hobhouse et al., 1915; Johnson & Earle, 1987; Leavitt, 1977; Malinowski, 1941; Reyna, 1994; Simmons, 1937; Wright, 1942, p. 66). As van der Dennen concludes, "one of the most consistent and robust findings is the correlation between 'primitivity' and absence of war or low-level warfare, or in other words, the correlation between war and civilization" (1995, p. 142).

Table 15.1 summarizes the relationships between social organization and the three types of lethal aggression under consideration, namely, individual self-redress, feud, and war. The overall pattern is that individual self-redress is typical of band organization, feuds are typical of tribes, and warfare is most common in chiefdoms and states. Adding social organization to the equation and untangling individual self-redress, feud, and war from one another expands our knowledge beyond the claim that a general desire for blood revenge is a human universal.

The Variability of Lethal Aggression: Balancing Reciprocity and Other Moral Principles

Neither feuding nor warring are human universals (Bonta, 1993; Bonta & Fry, in press; Fry, 1999a; 2001, 2004, 2006). For instance, the Mardu, the Paliyan, and the Batek of Malaysia do not feud or war (Endicott, 1988; Gardner, 2004; Tonkinson, 2004). Additionally, non-violence is a central aspect of the Paliyan (Gardner, 1972, 2004) and Batek moral codes, as illustrated by Endicott: "The Batek abhor interpersonal violence and have generally fled

TABLE 15.1
Patterns of Lethal Aggression in Relation to Social Organization

	Nomadic Hunter-Gatherer Bands	Tribes	Chiefdoms	States
Self-Redress Revenge Homicide	Typical	Variable	Rare	Rare
Feud	Rare	Typical	Variable	Rare
Warfare	Rare	Variable	Typical	Typical

Note: Individual self-redress homicide is typical of simple nomadic hunter-gatherer society. Such societies tend to lack the corporate kin groups (e.g., clans and patrilineages) that typify tribal society. In tribal society, revenge seeking shifts from individuals toward kin groups, and thus feuding becomes possible. Feuding is repressed once central authority develops, as within chiefdoms and, especially, states. A series of cross-cultural studies show that warfare is most common and most fully developed in chiefdoms and states. This table is intended to reflect the broad cross-cultural patterns or central tendencies. See the text for further discussion and relevant references.

from their enemies rather than fighting back. I once asked a Batek man why their ancestors had not shot the Malay slave-raiders, who plagued them until the 1920s ... with poisoned blowpipe darts. His shocked answer: 'Because it would kill them!'" (1988, p. 122).

For a sample of fifty cultures, Otterbein and Otterbein (1965, Table 3) found lethal feuding to be frequent in only eight societies (16 percent), infrequent in 14 (28 percent), and absent in the remaining 28 societies (56 percent). Ericksen and Horton (1992) found what they call the classic blood feud—that is, when both the malefactor and his relatives are considered appropriate targets of vengeance—to exist in 34.5 percent of the 186 societies in the SCCS. Overall, some form of kin group vengeance—basically individual self redress or feud—was considered legitimate in 54 percent of the cross-cultural sample and not legitimate in the remaining 46 percent of the societies.

Even in societies where either individual self-redress or feud were socially permitted, by no means was lethal revenge always carried out. In the societies where kin group vengeance was legitimately allowed, it was considered to be a moral imperative in 42% of the cultures and presumably often occurred in such cases, was viewed as the most appropriate course of action in 16%, was seen as merely one possibility among other options, depending on circumstances in 20%, and was used only as the option of last resort in 22% of the cases. Of the 46% of the overall sample of societies wherein kin group vengeance was not socially legitimate, the vast majority (81%) employed third-party assisted dispute settlement processes of various types (Ericksen & Horton, 1992, pp. 62, 74). Viewing Otterbein and Otterbein's (1965) and Ericksen and Horton's (1992) cross-cultural studies together, between one third and one half of societies allow feuding and the rest do not, and even when socially permitted, other approaches to settling grievances are often adopted in place of lethal revenge seeking. Thus, the anthropological data do not offer much support for the contention that blood revenge is ubiquitous across cultural circumstances.

CONFLICT RESOLUTION: OTHER PATHS TO JUSTICE

Although violence may be the most noticeable way through which people handle conflict, a close examination of cross-cultural data reveals that people usually deal with conflicts without physical aggression. Most conflict management among humans is nonviolent. Humans have a great capacity for getting along with each other peacefully, preventing physical aggression, limiting the scope and spread of violence, and restoring the peace following aggression (Fry, 2000, 2001). Conflict and aggression are not synonymous. *Conflict* can be defined as "a perceived divergence of interests—where interests are broadly conceptualized to include values, needs, goals, and wishes—between two or more parties, often accompanied by feelings of anger or hostility" (Fry, 1999a, p. 719; following Rubin, Pruitt, & Kim, 1994). *Aggression* means the infliction of harm, pain, or injury on other individuals.

Dealing with conflict through aggression may harm relationships in ways that nonviolent approaches do not. Recent research shows that peacemaking and reconciliation are important among various nonhuman primate species (Aureli & de Waal, 2000; Cords & Killen, 1998; de Waal, 1989, 1996). Conflict resolution also occurs in all human societies and often helps to return strained relationships to normalcy—to restore the balance between disputants (Brown, 1991; Fry, 2000, 2004; Nader, 1990; Sather, 2004).

Diversity and Creativity in Conflict Resolution: Examples From Aboriginal Australia

A couple of recurring themes reverberate through the literature on native Australia: First, conflict resolution mechanisms are well developed. Second, the seeking of revenge through violent self-redress is the least favored path to justice. Before considering a specific example that illustrates these points, the diversity of conflict resolution methods used by native Australians to keep violence in check deserves mention. These methods include the following:

1. providing hearings for accusers and defendants alike to make their cases before either the juries of public opinion or to talk about a problem as a group with a possible result that the elders arrive at a lawful course of action to be followed (e.g., Berndt, 1965, pp. 176, 185; Tonkinson, 2004);

2. compensating aggrieved parties for damages (Berndt, 1965, p. 185; Elkin, 1931);

3. engaging in duels, contests, juridical fights, and the like, wherein both the rules adhered to by the participants and, if necessary, the intervention by other persons limit aggression, making serious injuries uncommon (Berndt, 1965, pp. 181, 194–197; Goodale, 1974, pp. 133–134; Hart & Pilling, 1979, pp. 80–87; Wheeler, 1910, pp. 134–135, 140–147);

4. venting of emotions through public insults, harangues, and arguments (e.g., Berndt, 1965, p. 177; see also Williams, 1987, p. 97);

5. punishing wrongdoers, often by administering nonlethal spear wounds to the thigh, as in the previously described example involving a Mardu man (Hart & Pilling, 1979, pp. 79–83; Tonkinson, 1978, pp. 118, 124; 2004; Wheeler, 1910, pp. 135–138); and

6. reconciling antagonists via participation in joint rituals and ceremonies (e.g., Berndt, 1965, pp. 187–190; Berndt & Berndt, 1945, pp. 262–266).

Of course, the specifics of such procedures vary from region to region. In South Australia, among the Lakes area tribes, the payment of a debt (*kopara*) can cancel a grievance so as to prevent bloodshed and preserve friendly relations between groups (Elkin, 1931). In the Aboriginal system of thought, and in accordance with the reciprocity principle, deaths typically are attributed to sorcery and theoretically must be avenged, or balanced, by the death of the sorcerer or by someone close to him. However, to actually kill someone by physical violence is the choice of last resort. There are various preferred options for balancing a death. The Lakes area tribes evoke their *kopara* system of reciprocity to prevent actual bloodshed.

A typical pattern runs like this. A dying person dreams of a particular man or men and tells his relatives of the dream. The person's kin then suspect that a particular individual, or in some cases a clan, has caused their relative's death by sorcery. To be sure, they balance the corpse on the heads of two squatting men. An elder taps two inquest sticks together and asks the deceased whether the person or persons in the dream are responsible. The corpse answers in the affirmative by falling off the two squatting men's heads. Once the inquest has revealed the identity of the guilty party, the relatives of the deceased perceive that they are owed a *kopara* debt related to this death. The relatives may attempt to balance the death, in other words, by collecting the *kopara* debt in various ways.

One intriguing nonviolent option involves the exchange of a life for a life, but in a ceremonial way so that no one is actually killed. To become a man, a youth must be circumcised and initiated into manhood. When this rite of passage occurs, the youth is "killed," symbolically speaking, and replaced by a new adult identity that is more valued in society. The *kopara* debt incurred by the original sorcery killing can be balanced as one of the dead person's relatives assumes the role of circumcising a youth from the accused killer's group, thus symbolically "killing" the youth. Elkin writes: "This is a strange sort of punishment or revenge, but the discipline associated with the period of initiation, together with the increased importance and responsibility felt by the individual is no doubt, in most cases, a very wise course and of great social value. The aborigines certainly prefer it to quarrelling and fighting" (1931, p. 197). This conflict resolution procedure accords well with the reciprocity principle of morality, illustrating the balancing of a perceived wrong in a nonviolent way.

Restoring the Balance Among the Netsilik Inuit

Traditionally, interpersonal conflicts in Netsilik society were handled in many ways (Balikci, 1970). Avoidance was practiced. Quarreling and fighting were prevented or limited due to a set of concerns: people feared aggressive retaliation, loss of beneficial relationships, sorcery by an opponent, and social pressure of various kinds. Moreover, the Netsilik utilized both physical and verbal ritualized contests to settle disputes without bloodshed.

Contests had definite rules. In a stylized physical fight, a man who challenged another had to receive the first blow (Balikci, 1970, pp. 185–186). The two opponents stripped to the waist and stood opposite each other. Back and forth, each struck the other one time in turn, using blows directed at either the forehead or a shoulder. Note the reciprocity at the micro level. This exchange continued until one man gave up. A Netsilik man explained that "After the fight, it is all over; it was as if they had never fought before" (Balikci, 1970, p. 186).

Verbal song duels also were used to settle disputes. Balikci (1970) explains how the community-wide audience eagerly laughed and joked as they listened to the lyrics composed privately by two opponents. Each man's wife sang the song composed by her husband while he accompanied her by beating a drum and dancing for the audience. Scathing lyrics included "accusations of incest, bestiality, murder, avarice, adultery, failure at hunting, being henpecked, lack of manly strength, etc." (Balikci, 1970, p. 186). Under the rules of song dueling, opponents had a free range to blast their antagonists in verse. In some cases, both parties were satisfied to have been able to reciprocally insult and deride their opponents publicly, so a dispute was brought to a close. If anger remained, the disputants might move on to a fighting contest. Balikci (1970, p. 189) reports that the outcome of the physical contest once and for all settled the matter.

CONCLUSION

Everywhere, reciprocity is a key element of human moral thinking. Humans repay good deeds and revenge bad ones. Across the spectrum of human societies, fulfilling obligations is good but shirking them is bad; generosity is good and stinginess bad; kindness is good and gratuitous aggression is bad. An aspect of the reciprocity principle is that paybacks, whether positive or negative, should be roughly equal to the original deeds. Sahlins (1965) picked up on the balance of positive exchange when he used the term *balanced reciprocity*. Correspondingly, "an eye for an eye," "a tooth for a tooth," and "a life for a life" reflect the balance of negative paybacks.

Many forms of conflict resolution in the ethnographic record entail attempts to restore the balance between disputants. In fact, the Sierra Zapotec of Mexico even use the phrase "to make the balance" (Nader, 1990). The payment of compensation for damages is one common way to restore the balance without bloodshed (e.g., Berndt, 1965; Black, 1993; Elkin, 1931; Hoebel, 1967). Another way to restore the balance is to punish someone who clearly has violated the social rules (Black, 1993), as in the nonviolent social control applied of the Mbuti man, Cephu (Turnbull, 1961), and the physical punishment of the Mardu fellow, Djadu (Tonkinson, 2004). The central idea is that persons who commit moral transgressions should pay. The payment currency, however, varies with culture, the price for misdeeds being extracted via physical punishment, social ridicule, withdrawal of support, demand for material compensation, and so on. A balanced payback is seen as just and right. Too little or too much may be perceived by the recipient and others as un-just. Thus, at a fundamental level, the idea of justice in humans is linked to the reciprocity principle, but the specific paths to justice are extremely variable.

Both cultural variation and cross-cultural patterns are apparent in the material considered in this chapter (Fry & Fry, 1997). For instance, the specific rules for meat sharing differ for the Guayaki, Paliyan, Netsilik, and Ju/'hoansi (Balikci, 1970; Clastres, 1972; Gardner, 1972; Lee, 1993; Marshall, 1961), as might be expected of societies from different continents. At the same time, meat sharing across nomadic forager societies invariably reflects moral rules and social obligations that link people in networks of reciprocity.

The reciprocity principle interacts with various features of social life such as kinship distance, social organization, and other moral precepts. The interplay of genetic relationship with helping and harming behavior—the effects of inclusive fitness, in other words—has been noted. The closest relatives are not held accountable for the exact repayment of gifts and acts of kindness—the cross-cultural pattern Sahlins (1965) dubbed *generalized reciprocity*—because "repayment" comes in the currency of inclusive fitness. At the other extreme, close biological relatives only rarely kill one another (see Daly & Wilson, 1988; Dunbar et al., 1995; Lee, 1979), another observation that accords well with the inclusive fitness concept. In exceptional cases, such as a man murdering his own brother, revenge is considered nonsensical by members of the family (Balikci, 1970; Westermarck, 1906/1924); to avenge a death within the same family would be a double loss to the family, not a payback. Again, the inclusive fitness concept makes this intelligible.

Social organization also interacts with the reciprocity principle. In examining types of lethal aggression, an overall pattern emerges wherein individual self-redress is most common of bands, feuds between corporate kin groups typify tribes, and war is typical of chiefdoms and states. Of course, wars among states are usually not waged strictly for revenge (Ferguson, 1984, 1990), but sometimes the revenge motive comes into play, as in the recent U.S. war against Afghanistan, launched in the wake of the 9/11 terrorist attacks. Politicians seem to prefer the word *justice,* with its moral and legal implications, over *revenge,* with possible vindictive connotations, when *justifying* such attacks to their constituents and to the world community (e.g., see Israely, 2003).

The case involving the Italian peasants, Domenico and Guiseppe, illustrates the danger of unilaterally seeking justice through revenge whether by self-redress, feud, or war (Brögger, 1968). One party's act of justice may precipitate a countering act of justice from the other side, leading to a spiral of escalating abuses (Rubin et al., 1994). Conflict resolution, a social art highly developed in humans, offers alternative paths to justice that make unnecessary the violence of personal self-redress, feud, and war. The cross-cultural data demonstrate the wealth of nonviolent approaches that humans regularly employ to make the balance—to attain just solutions to conflicts—without breaking the peace (Fry, 2000, 2001, 2006). The *kopara* debt and the song duel are but two examples that make the balance without the use of violent revenge.

The widespread existence of alternative avenues to justice is one reason why Daly and Wilson's (1988) assertion about the ubiquity of blood revenge is too narrowly formulated. Aside from the effects of social organization, the reciprocity principle also interacts with other moral precepts, such as a universal moral prohibition against murder within human societies (Brown, 1991; Hoebel, 1967). Ericksen and Horton's (1992) cross-cultural research shows that blood revenge is far from ubiquitous. In sum, Daly and Wilson (1988) are following in the footsteps of Darwin (1871/1998) and Westermarck (1924) by emphasizing the reciprocity principle as a centerpiece of human morality, but the ethnographic data do not support as tight a linking of this principle to blood revenge as Daly and Wilson (1988) propose. Human's make the balance in diverse ways, many of which are not lethal.

Darwin observed that "No tribe could hold together if murder, robbery, treachery, etc., were common" (1871/1998, p. 120). Darwin (1871/1998) also observed that with the advent of nation states, the concept of community had broadened dramatically. This development suggested a new possibility:

> As man advances in civilization, and small tribes are united into larger communities, the simplest reason would tell each individual that he ought to extend his social instincts and sympathies to all the other members of the same nation, though personally unknown to him. This point being once reached, there is only an artificial barrier to prevent his sympathies extending to the men of all nations and races. (Darwin, 1871/1998, pp. 126–127)

One way to facilitate the extension of such sympathies to humanity overall is to shift away from seeking justice via revenge at the international level and instead create conflict resolution procedures and international institutions that assure justice for the world's peoples and nations through nonviolent means.

ACKNOWLEDGMENTS

This chapter has benefited from discussions with Heikki Sarmaja and Jukka-Pekka Takala. Additionally, I thank Melanie Killen, Judi Smetana, and Jukka-Pekka Takala for reading and commenting on the chapter. Some of the material in this chapter was gathered during research funded by the United States Institute of Peace (USIP-023-99F) and the National Science Foundation (03-13670).

REFERENCES

Alexander, R. (1979). *Darwinism and human affairs.* Seattle: University of Washington Press.

Arnhart, L. (1998). Westermarck's ethics as Darwinian natural right. Paper presented at the Westermarck Symposium, November 18–21, Helsinki.

Aureli, F., & de Waal, F. B. M. (Eds.). (2000). *Natural conflict resolution.* Berkeley: University of California Press.

Balikci, A. (1970). *The Netsilik Eskimo.* Garden City, NY: The Natural History Press.

Berndt, R. M. (1965). Law and order in Aboriginal Australia. In R. M. Berndt & C. H. Berndt (Eds.), *Aboriginal man in Australia: Essays in honour of Emeritus Professor A. P. Elkin* (pp. 167–206). London: Angus & Robertson.

Berndt, R. M. (1972). The Walmadjeri and Gugadja. In M. G. Bicahieri (Ed.), *Hunters and gatherers today* (pp. 177–216). Prospect Heights, IL: Waveland.

Berndt, R., & Berndt, C. (1945). A preliminary report on field work in the Ooldea region, Western South Australia. *Oceania, 15,* 239–266.

Binford, L. R. (2001). *Constructing frames of reference: An analytical method for archaeological theory building using hunter-gatherer and environmental data sets.* Berkeley: University of California Press.

Björkqvist, K., Österman, K., & Kaukiainen, A. (1992). The development of direct and indirect aggressive strategies in males and females. In K. Björkqvist & P. Niemalä (Eds.), *Of mice and women: Aspects of female aggression* (pp. 51–64). Orlando: Academic Press.

Black, D. (1993). *The social structure of right and wrong.* San Diego: Academic Press.

Boehm, C. (1987). *Blood revenge: The enactment and management of conflict in Montenegro and other tribal societies* (2nd paperback ed.). Philadelphia: University of Pennsylvania Press.

Boehm, C. (1999). *Hierarchy in the forest: The evolution of egalitarian behavior.* Cambridge: Harvard University Press.

Boehm, C. (2000). Conflict and the evolution of social control. In L. D. Katz (Ed.), *Evolutionary origins of morality: Cross-disciplinary perspectives* (pp. 79–101). Bowling Green, OH: Imprint Academic.

Bonta, B. D. (1993). *Peaceful peoples: An annotated bibliography.* Metuchen, NJ: Scarecrow Press.

Bonta, B. D., & Fry, D. P. (in press). Lessons for the rest of us: Learning from peaceful societies. In M. Fitzduff & C. E. Stout (Eds.), *Psychological approaches to dealing with conflict and war.* Westport, CT: Praeger.

Brögger, J. (1968). Conflict resolution and the role of the bandit in peasant society. *Anthropological Quarterly, 41,* 228–240.

Brown, D. E. (1991). *Human universals.* New York: McGraw-Hill.

Carneiro, R. L. (1990). Chiefdom-level warfare as exemplified in Fiji and the Cauca Valley. In J. Haas (Ed.), *The anthropology of war* (pp. 190–211). Cambridge, UK: Cambridge University Press.

Clastres, P. (1972). The Guayaki. In M. G. Bicchieri (Ed.), *Hunters and gatherers today* (pp. 138–174). Prospect Heights, IL: Waveland.

Cords, M., & Killen, M. (1998). Conflict resolution in human and nonhuman primates. In J. Langer & M. Killen (Eds.), *Piaget, evolution, and development* (pp. 193–218). Mahwah, NJ: Lawrence Erlbaum Associates.

Daly, M. & Wilson, M. (1988). *Homicide.* New York: Aldine de Gruyter.

Darwin, C. (1871/1998). *The descent of man.* New York: Prometheus Books.

de Waal, F. B. M. (1989). *Peacemaking among primates*. Cambridge, MA: Harvard University Press.

de Waal, F. B. M. (1996). *Good natured: The origin of right and wrong in humans and other animals*. Cambridge, MA: Harvard University Press.

de Waal, F. B. M. (2001). *The ape and the sushi master: Cultural reflections of a primatologist*. New York: Basic Books.

Dentan, R. K. (1968). *The Semai: A nonviolent people of Malaya*. New York: Holt, Rinehart, & Winston.

Dunbar, R. I. M., Clark, A., & Hurst, N. (1995). Conflict and cooperation among the Vikings: Contingent behavioral decisions. *Ethology and Sociobiology, 16,* 233–246.

Elkin, A. P. (1931). The kopara: The settlement of grievances. *Oceania, 2,* 191–198.

Ember, C. (1978). Myths about hunter-gatherers. *Ethnology, 17,* 439–448.

Endicott, K. (1988). Property, power and conflict among the Batek of Malaysia. In T. Ingold, D. Riches, & J. Woodburn (Eds.), *Hunters and gatherers 2: Property, power, and ideology* (pp. 110–127). Oxford: Berg.

Ericksen, K. P. & Horton, H. (1992). 'Blood feuds': Cross-cultural variations in kin group vengeance. *Behavior Science Research, 26,* 57–85.

Ferguson, R. B. (1984). A reexamination of the causes of Northwest Coast warfare. In R. B. Ferguson (Ed.), *Warfare, culture, and environment* (pp. 267–328). Orlando: Academic Press.

Ferguson, R. B. (1990). Explaining war. In J. Haas (Ed.), *The anthropology of war* (pp. 26–55). Cambridge, UK: Cambridge University Press.

Flack, J. C., & de Waal, F. B. M. (2000). "Any animal whatever": Darwinian building blocks of morality in monkeys and apes. In L. D. Katz (Ed.), *Evolutionary origins of morality: Cross-disciplinary perspectives* (pp. 1–29). Bowling Green, OH: Imprint Academic.

Fletcher, R. (1982). On the contribution of Edward Westermarck. The process of institutionalization: A general theory. In T. Stroup (Ed.), *Edward Westermarck: Essays on his life and works, Acta Philosophica Fennica, 34,* 195–217.

Fry, D. P. (1999a). Peaceful societies. In L. R. Kurtz (Ed.), *Encyclopedia of violence, peace and conflict* (vol. 3, pp. 719–733). San Diego: Academic Press.

Fry, D. P. (1999b). Aggression and altruism. In L. R. Kurtz (Ed.), *Encyclopedia of violence, peace and conflict* (vol. 1, pp. 17–33). San Diego: Academic Press.

Fry, D. P. (2000). Conflict management in cross-cultural perspective. In F. Aureli & F. B. M. de Waal (Eds.), *Natural conflict resolution* (pp. 334–351). Berkeley: University of California Press.

Fry, D. P. (2001). Is violence getting too much attention? Cross-cultural findings on the ways people deal with conflict. In J. M. Ramirez & D. S. Richardson (Eds.), *Cross-cultural approaches to research on aggression and reconciliation* (pp. 123–148). Huntington, NY: Nova Science Publishers.

Fry, D. P. (2004). Conclusion: Learning from peaceful societies. In G. Kemp & D. P. Fry (Eds.), *Keeping the peace: Conflict resolution and peaceful societies around the world* (pp. 185–204). New York: Routledge.

Fry, D. P. (2006). *The human potential for peace: An anthropological challenge to assumptions about war and violence*. New York: Oxford University Press.

Fry, D. P., & Fry, C. B. (1997). Culture and conflict resolution models: Exploring alternatives to violence. In D. P. Fry & K. Björkqvist (Eds.), *Cultural variation in conflict resolution: Alternatives to violence* (pp. 9–23). Mahwah, NJ: Lawrence Erlbaum Associates.

Gardner, P. (1972). The Paliyans. In M. G. Bicchieri (Ed.), *Hunters and gatherers today* (pp. 404-407). Prospect Heights, IL: Waveland.

Gardner, P. (2004). Respect for all: The Paliyans of South India. In G. Kemp & D. P. Fry (Eds.), *Keeping the peace: Conflict resolution and peaceful societies around the world* (pp. 53–71). New York: Routledge.

Gat, A. (2000). The human motivational complex: evolutionary theory and the causes of hunter-gatherer fighting. Part I. Primary somatic and reproductive causes. *Anthropological Quarterly, 73*, 20–34.

Ginsberg, M. (1982). The life and work of Edward Westermarck. In T. Stroup (Ed.), *Edward Westermarck: Essays on his life and works, Acta Philosophica Fennica, Volume 34* (pp. 1–23). Helsinki: The Philosophical Society of Finland.

Goodale, J. C. (1974). *Tiwi wives: A study of the women of Melville Island, North Australia* (1st paperback ed.). Seattle: University of Washington Press.

Gregor, T. (1994). Symbols and rituals of peace in Brazil's Upper Xingu. In L. E. Sponsel & T. Gregor (Eds.), *The anthropology of peace and nonviolence* (pp. 241–257). Boulder, CO: Lynne Rienner.

Hamilton, W. D. (1964). The genetical evolution of social behaviour, II. *Journal of Theoretical Biology, 7*, 17–52.

Hart, C. W. M., & Pilling, A. (1979). *The Tiwi of North Australia* (fieldwork ed.). New York: Holt, Rinehart, & Winston.

Hickson, L. (1986). The social context of apology in dispute settlement: A cross-cultural study. *Ethnology, 25*, 283–294.

Hobhouse, L. T., Wheeler, G. C., & Ginsberg, M. (1915). *The material culture and social institutions of the simpler peoples: An essay in correlation*. London: Chapman & Hall.

Hoebel, E. A. (1967). *The law of primitive man: A study in comparative legal dynamics*. Cambridge, MA: Harvard University Press.

Honigmann, J. J. (1954). *The Kaska Indians: An ethnographic reconstruction*. Publications in Anthropology, number 51. New Haven, CT: Yale University Press.

Ingold, T. (1999). On the social relations of the hunter-gatherer band. In R. B. Lee & R. Daly (Eds.), *The Cambridge encyclopedia of hunters and gatherers* (pp. 399–410). Cambridge, UK: Cambridge University Press.

Israely, J. (2003). A moral justification for war exists. *Time* (European ed.), *161*(8), 57.

Johnson, A. W., & Earle, T. (1987). *The evolution of human societies: From foraging group to agrarian state*. Stanford, CA: Stanford University Press.

Kelly, R. C. (2000). *Warless societies and the origin of war*. Ann Arbor: University of Michigan Press.

Kelly, R. L. (1995). *The foraging spectrum: Diversity in hunter-gatherer lifeways*. Washington, DC: Smithsonian Institution Press.

Killen, M., & de Waal, F. B. M. (2000). The evolution and development of morality. In F. Aureli & F. B. M. de Waal (Eds.), *Natural conflict resolution* (pp. 352–372). Berkeley: University of California Press.

Knauft, B. (1991). Violence and sociality in human evolution. *Current Anthropology, 32*, 391–428.

Leacock, E. (1954). The Montagnais hunting territory and the fur trade. Memoirs of the American Anthropological Association. *American Anthropologist, 56*(2), part 2, memoir number 78.

Leacock, E. (1981). Seventeenth-century Montagnais social relations and values. In W. C. Sturtevant (Gen. Ed.) & J. Helm (Vol. Ed.), *Handbook of North American Indians, Vol. 6: Subarctic* (pp. 190–195). Washington, DC: Smithsonian Institution.

Leavitt, G. C. (1977). The frequency of warfare: An evolutionary perspective. *Sociological Inquiry, 47*, 49–58.

Lee, R. B. (1979). *The !Kung San: Men, women, and work in a foraging community.* Cambridge, UK: Cambridge University Press.

Lee, R. B. (1993). *The Dobe Ju/'hoansi* (2nd ed.). Fort Worth: Harcourt Brace College Publishers.

Lee, R. B., & Daly, R. (1999). Introduction: Foragers and others. In R. B. Lee & R. Daly (Eds.), *The Cambridge encyclopedia of hunters and gatherers* (pp. 1–19). Cambridge, UK: Cambridge University Press.

Lee, R. B., & DeVore, I. (1968). Problems in the study of hunters and gatherers. In R. B. Lee & I. DeVore (Eds.), *Man the hunter* (pp. 3–12). Chicago: Aldine.

Lips, J. (1947). *Naskapi law.* Philadelphia: American Philosophical Society.

Lutz, C. (1988). *Unnatural emotions: Everyday sentiments on a Micronesian Atoll and their challenge to Western theory.* Chicago: University of Chicago Press.

Mackie, J. L. (1982). Morality and the retributive emotions. In T. Stroup (Ed.), *Edward Westermarck: Essays on his life and works, Acta Philosophica Fennica* (Vol. 34, pp. 144–157). Helsinki: The Philosophical Society of Finland.

Malinowski, B. (1941). An anthropological analysis of war. *American Journal of Sociology, 46,* 521–550.

Marshall, L. (1961). Sharing, talking, and giving: Relief of social tensions among !Kung Bushmen. *Africa, 31,* 231–249.

Nader, L. (1990). *Harmony ideology: Justice and control in a Zapotec mountain village.* Stanford, CA: Stanford University Press.

Otterbein, K. F., & Otterbein, C. S. (1965). An eye for an eye, a tooth for a tooth: A cross-cultural study of feuding. *American Anthropologist, 67,* 1470–1482.

Peterson, N. (1991). Warlpiri. In D. Levinson (Ed. in Chief) & T. E. Hays (Vol. Ed.), *Encyclopedia of World Cultures, Vol. II: Oceania* (pp. 373–376). Boston: G. K. Hall.

Prosterman, R. L. (1972). *Surviving to 3000: An introduction to the study of lethal conflict.* Belmont, CA: Duxbury-Wadsworth.

Reid, G. (1991). Montagnais-Naskapi. In D. Levinson (Ed. in Chief) & T. O'Leary & D. Levinson (Vol. Eds.), *Encyclopedia of world cultures, Vol. I: North America* (pp. 243–246). Boston: G. K. Hall.

Reyna, S. P. (1994). A mode of domination approach to organized violence. In S. P. Reyna & R. E. Downs (Eds.), *Studying war: Anthropological perspectives* (pp. 29–65). Amsterdam, The Netherlands: Gordon & Breach.

Rubin, J. Z., Pruitt, D, G., & Kim, S. H. (1994). *Social conflict: Escalation, stalemate, and settlement* (2nd ed.). New York: McGraw-Hill.

Sahlins, M. D. (1965). On the sociology of primitive exchange. In M. Banton (Ed.), *The relevance of models for social anthropology* (pp. 139–236). New York: Tavistock.

Sather, C. (2004). Keeping the peace in an island world: The Sama Dilaut of Southeast Asia. In G. Kemp & D. P. Fry (Eds.), *Keeping the peace: Conflict resolution and peaceful societies around the world* (pp. 123–147). New York: Routledge.

Service, E. R. (1971a). *Profiles in ethnology* (Rev. ed.). New York: Harper & Row.

Service, E. R. (1971b). *Primitive social organization: An evolutionary perspective* (2nd ed.). New York: Random House.

Service, E. R. (1978). *Profiles in ethnology* (3rd ed.) New York: Harper & Row.

Simmons, L. W. (1937). Statistical correlations in the science of society. In G. P. Murdock (Ed.), *Studies in the science of society* (pp. 495–517). New Haven, CT: Yale University Press.

Speck, F. G. (1935). *Naskapi: The savage hunters of the Labrador Peninsula.* Norman: University of Oklahoma Press.

Takala, J.-P., & Wolf, A. P. (Eds.). (in press). *Evolution and the moral emotions*. Stanford, CA: Stanford University Press.

Tonkinson, R. (1978). *The Mardudjara Aborigines: Living the dream in Australia's desert*. New York: Holt, Rinehart, & Winston.

Tonkinson, R. (2004). Resolving conflict within the law: The Mardu Aborigines of Australia. In G. Kemp & D. P. Fry (Eds.), *Keeping the peace: Conflict resolution and peaceful societies around the world* (pp. 89–104). New York: Routledge.

Trivers, R. L. (1971). The evolution of reciprocal altruism. *Quarterly Review of Biology, 46,* 35–57.

Trivers, R. L. (1985). *Social evolution*. Menlo Park, CA: Benjamin/Cummings.

Turnbull, C. M. (1961). *The forest people: A study of the Pygmies of the Congo*. New York: Simon & Schuster.

van der Dennen, J. M. G. (1995). *The origin of war* (2 vols). Groningen, The Netherlands: Origin Press.

Westermarck, E. (1906/1924). *The origin and development of the moral ideas, in two volumes* (2nd ed., rpt.). London: Macmillan.

Wheeler, G. C. (1910). *The tribe, and intertribal relations in Australia*. London: John Murray.

Williams, N. M. (1987). *Two laws: Managing disputes in a contemporary aboriginal community*. Canberra: Australian Institute of Aboriginal Studies.

Woodburn, J. (1982). Egalitarian societies. *Man, 17,* 431–451.

Wright, Q. (1942). *A study of war*. Chicago: University of Chicago Press.

16

Everyone's Monkey: Primate Moral Roots

Peter Verbeek
Miyazaki International College

Elckerlijc is a late 15th century Dutch morality play. It is the counterpart of the English play *Everyman*. *Elckerlijc* is Old Dutch for "everyone." In *Elckerlijc* and subsequent morality plays the main character embarks on a journey of discovery that results in the learning of a moral lesson. *Elckerlijc* makes the point that we cannot take with us from this world anything that we have received. We can only take what we have given.

Sociality defines our species. The need to belong through interpersonal attachments is a fundamental human motivation (Baumeister & Leary, 1995). Fiske (1992) captures the essence of our sociality as he states that "throughout our lives we seek, make, sustain, repair, adjust, judge, construe, and sanction relationships" (p. 689). Although our social relations may take on a myriad of appearances, we do not engage in them in an arbitrary way. Instead, we tend to proceed according to a set of expectations, norms, and standards that help differentiate right from wrong and that are collectively referred to as *morality*. As Walker (1996) succinctly states: "Morality prescribes people's activities, regulates social interactions, and arbitrates conflicts" (p. 174). In turn, the expectations, norms, and standards that prescribe our relations are linked to a small set of elementary relational forms that encompass sociality in all cultures and among all social primates. These elementary relational forms emerge spontaneously and sequentially during development (Fiske, 1992), as children appear universally predisposed to learn about relationships in certain ways (see Laursen & Hartup, 2002).

Our social relations are as much structured by expectations, norms, and standards as they are empowered by emotion. For instance, people tend to care deeply about reciprocity aspects of their social relations. Troublesome exchange relations with close partners can make us feel guilty and depressed (O'Connor, Berry, Weiss, & Gilbert, 2002); cheaters and unequal payoffs in reciprocal relations can anger us (Rozin, Lowery, Imada, & Haidt, 1999). The gratitude of others for the help we gave can encourage us to help again (Mc-Cullough, Emmons, Kilpatrick, & Larson, 2001).

Like the philosopher Adam Smith (*The Moral Sentiments*, 1759/1976) before him, Charles Darwin recognized the integral connection between reciprocity and emotion in morality. Darwin's important insight was that he identified this link as key to uncovering the biological basis of morality. In *The Descent of Man,* he wrote: "But there is another and more powerful stimulus to the development of the social virtues, namely the praise and the blame of our fellow men. The love of approbation and the dread of infamy, as well as the bestowal of praise or blame, are primarily due (. . .) to the instinct of sympathy; and this instinct no doubt was originally acquired, like all the other social instincts, through natural selection" (Darwin, 1871/1981, p. 164). Darwin's insights helped to inspire the recent "biologizing" of morality, much of which focuses on the interplay between emotion and reciprocity (e.g., Alexander, 1987; de Waal, 1996; Frank, 1988; Ridley, 1996; Wilson, 1993).

In its psychological essence morality is the ability to distinguish right from wrong and to behave accordingly. Philosophical and theoretical debates on morality have centered on the question of whether the concepts of right and wrong are relative or axiomatic, and on whether pondering this opposition is futile. As a topic of empirical research morality is a multifold concept that requires multiple levels of analysis using the methods and perspectives of multiple disciplines. The present volume is a case in point. From the perspective of psychobiology, morality is a prime aspect of social behavior and a key focus is the biological origin of it. The questions of how and why morality became an integral component of human sociality tend to stimulate both reasoned and passionate debates. In fact, both in our moral acts and our debates about them, we appear as much coerced and empowered by our passions as guided by reason. This realization can give us clues about the extant nature of morality as well as remind us of the constraints on our ability to uncover the natural history of it. In comparative research we cannot interpret nature from our emotional feelings or philosophies of what constitutes right or wrong, nature is neither, nor is it a combination of both; nature just is.

The principal aim of this chapter is to review primate research for behaviors that can be seen as forerunners of human morality. If morality is rooted in our evolutionary past, it is reasonable to assume that it may have originated in an ancestry that we share with other animals. If so, we should be able to detect behaviors that can be seen as forerunners of morality in the natural behavior of currently living animals, especially those most closely related to us, the nonhuman primates (see de Waal, 1996).

The chapter is structured around five basic assumptions that in turn are derived from two recently introduced theories: (1) the unified theory of social relations (Fiske, 1992), and (2) the social intuitionist model of moral judgment (Haidt, 2001). The first assumption is that human sociality consists of four basic forms: communal sharing, authority ranking, equality matching, and market pricing (Fiske, 1992). The second assumption is that whatever the context and content, and whatever the substance and surface form of the interaction, people's primary frames of reference in social life are the same four elementary relational models (Fiske, 1992). The third assumption is that people make moral judgments and take ideological positions with reference to these basic structures (Fiske, 1992). The fourth assumption is that moral intuitions (including moral emotions) come first and directly cause moral judgements (Haidt, 2001; 2003a, 2003b). Finally, the fifth assumption is that we can use comparative research to uncover forerunners of morality in extant nonhuman primates.

Based on these five basic assumptions evidence is presented in support of two main propositions regarding the primate origins of morality. First, it is proposed that nonhuman primate sociality can be comprehensively described by at least three, and possibly all four, elementary forms that comprise human sociality (see Fiske, 1992; Haidt, 2001; Haslam, 1997). Second, it is proposed that nonhuman primates exhibit emotions that are linked to these elementary forms of sociality. Departing from the listed theory-based assumptions, it is suggested that evidence in support of these propositions constitutes support for a general claim that morality is rooted, in part, in our primate ancestry.

The chapter starts with a brief discussion of the recent history of biological approaches to morality. Next, selected observations from research on brown capuchin monkeys (*Cebus apella*) are presented. These observations are used as a point of departure for subsequent discussions of primate sociality and emotion. The chapter proceeds with a consideration of the evidence, syntheses of the main strands of thought, and suggestions for future comparative research on morality. Theoretical and empirical links to child and adolescent development are attempted throughout the main sections.

Because of the primarily primate view of the chapter work on other animals that has relevance to the natural dimensions of human morality has been left out. As such, this chapter is best seen as a comparative sketch rather than an attempt at a full-fledged comparative investigation. Hopefully the chapter provides food for thought, chiefly by offering suggestions for organizing existing comparative findings and for exploring new research venues in this important area.

SEARCHING FOR MORALITY'S BIOLOGICAL ROOTS: RECONCILING GOODNESS WITH FITNESS

Inclusive Fitness

The systematic study of the biological bases of morality was relatively long in coming, in part because evolutionary scientists could not convincingly reconcile other-oriented sacrifices and apparent good deeds with individual fitness. Darwin had wrestled with this evolutionary enigma to no avail. An early 20th-century Russian treatise on the evolution of mutual aid that did connect reciprocity with fitness (Kropotkin, 1902) was, until fairly recently, largely ignored. Two seminal publications did change the way evolutionary scientists think about altruistic behavior and reciprocity and laid the foundation for the recent upsurge in comparative biological approaches to morality. The first offers a kin-based solution to the natural selection of other oriented deeds. In a 1964 journal article William Hamilton (see also 1963, 1971) argued that an individual could benefit from aiding a close relative, even at a risk to self, because relatives share a certain percentage of alleles (see also Hamilton, 1971). Aiding a relative in a way that contributes to the survival and reproductive success of the relative mediates the passing on of the alleles that the benefactor shares with the recipient of the altruistic act. Hamilton called this evolutionary concept *inclusive fitness*. It is also referred to as *kin selection*.

Reciprocal Altruism

The second publication, by Robert Trivers (1971), offers an explanation for the evolution of *reciprocal altruism*, that is, the notion that aiding a nonrelative at a cost to self can benefit one's own fitness if and when the nonrelative returns the favor in due course. Participants in the reciprocal exchange of other-directed deeds thus experience both the role of benefactor as well as beneficiary and it is a matter of time for benefits to accrue to each participant. Taking his cues from Darwin, Trivers also offered an emotion-based explanation for the psychological mechanism underpinning reciprocal altruism (Trivers, 1971). Triver's notion of reciprocal altruism has inspired both further theorizing, especially through game-theory models (Axelrod & Hamilton, 1981; Boyd, 1992; Lotem, Fishman & Stone, 2003), emotion models, as well as comparative empirical work on animal abilities that can be seen as forerunners of human morality (de Waal, 1996). It is beyond the scope of this chapter to discuss recent work on game-theory models inspired by the notion of reciprocal altruism. This does not imply that the importance of this work should be minimized. For instance, the recent finding from multitype game theory that a mix of opportunistic and unopportunistic individuals within the same population can be an evolutionary stable strategy (Lotem et al., 2003) can have important theoretical consequences for future empirical research.

Other Models

Attachment.   The inclusive fitness and reciprocal altruism models do not exhaust the full spectrum of possible biological bases of morality. For instance, friendship, a potentially beneficial communal relationship between nonrelatives, in which indebtedness may actually harm the relationship, does not fit the reciprocal altruism model very well (Silk, in press). Friendship, at least as it is perceived in the Western world, involves issues of loyalty, trust, commitment, and honesty, which makes it a potential moral phenomenon (Bukowski & Sippola, 1996). The attachment system that is common among mammals, and the emotions associated with it (Bowlby, 1969, 1973), is likely to be one of the potential precursors of friendship, and as such, should feature in any biological approach to morality.

Emotions as Commitment Devices.   Reciprocal altruism does not explain well how (a) altruism starts, (b) individuals handle the calculus of costs and benefits in real life, or (c) dilemmas of short-term gains versus long-term fitness consequences are overcome. Frank (1988) proposes that emotions act as commitment devices that help individuals to resolve such dilemmas. Frank (1990) argues that moral emotions such as anger, shame or guilt, not unlike feelings of hunger, can and do compete with feelings that spring from rational calculations about material payoffs. He reasons that it is exactly for this reason they can help individuals to solve commitment problems. The commitment model's point of departure is that an individual who is believed always to pursue self-interest is excluded from many valuable opportunities. On purely theoretical grounds, Frank's commitment model thus suggests that the moving force behind moral behavior lies not in rational analysis but in the emotions.

Triver's and Frank's ideas about the emotional underpinning of moral reciprocity[1] have recently been extended by new theoretical work on the primacy of emotion in morality (e.g., Fessler & Haley, 2003; Haidt, 2001), which is being validated, in part, by an increasing body of empirical work (e.g., brain imaging research: Moll, de Oliveira-Souza, & Eslinger, 2003). This chapter focuses on comparative research that is directly or indirectly inspired by these basic biological models of morality.

---

[1]Predating Triver's reading of Darwin's original suggestions about the link between emotion and moral reciprocity are Westermarck's (1924) ideas about the evolution of moral emotions. As for Kropotkin's writings on mutual aid (Kropotkin, 1902), Westermarck's model was, until recently, mostly overlooked by comparative workers on morality. See also, Fry, chap. 15, this volume.

EVERYONE'S MONKEY

The following narrative describes an observation of a social conflict and its aftermath in a captive group of brown capuchin monkeys (*Cebus apella*).[2]

> The two male brown capuchin monkeys hang out together a lot. They play, groom, and eat together, and they fight and make up, like close companions do. The youngest of the pair, a juvenile, still spends much time with his mother. The older monkey, a young adult, has no relatives in this captive group. This afternoon a piece of celery that his friend has just grabbed from the afternoon food tray catches the juvenile's eye. With a shriek the juvenile sprints over to his friend and grabs hold of the celery piece, only to be met by fierce opposition from his friend, who appears to have no desire to part with his prized piece of food or share with the youngster. Being unsuccessful in getting what he wants the juvenile throws a temper tantrum that alerts the entire group, including his mother, who rushes over with the dominant female of the group in tow. The young adult male flees from the scene, celery piece in hand, with the two adult females in close pursuit. After several rounds of chase up and down the entire indoor enclosure, the females let up, and the young adult male retreats to a spot as far away as possible from his female assailants. He is still holding his piece of celery. The youngster, who started it all, joins his mother who has sat down to groom the dominant female who previously joined her in chasing her son's friend. The threesome is sitting in the middle of a passage way to the outdoor part of the enclosure. After about a minute or two the young adult male wanders over to the entrance of the passageway, celery stick still firmly in hand. He's met by a few glances from the females, but the grooming continues, and his young male friend shows no interest in his arrival. Apparently sensing that, at least for now, no harm will come to him, the young adult male quickly enters and exits the passageway, and then returns to his previous spot. Left in the entrance of the passageway is his piece of celery which is claimed, only seconds later, by his young friend.

This snapshot of social life in a captive capuchin monkey group can easily be transcribed into a slice of human sociality. Let's imagine for a moment that the protagonist is a high school boy and his young friend a first grader, and that the action takes place on a playground, and we have the ingredients for a human morality play. After failing to share with his friend (a desired behavior in most human cultures), the teenager is chastised by two adults upon which he retreats, reflects, and decides to give his prized food to his friend. Moreover, after having been confronted with a succession of other-condemning moral emotions—the anger of his friend at his refusal to share, and the indignation of his friend's mother at upsetting her son—he has learned the moral lesson that sharing is a good deed that is expected among friends.

The fact that this capuchin observation can be so easily transcribed into a human episode does not justify interpreting this example of animal behavior in an anthropomorphic way. Nor, should we, as Morgan's Canon dictates "interpret an action as the outcome of the exercise of a higher psychical faculty, if it can be interpreted as the outcome of the exercise of one which stands lower in the psychological scale" (Morgan, 1894, p. 53), and explain this sequence of events in a monkey group as a monkey morality play. For one, we cannot conclude that the protagonist intentionally brought the celery stick to his friend. Perhaps he dropped it by accident or merely lost interest in it. What we can detect from this observation,

---

[2]This observation was recorded as part of the research reported in Verbeek and de Waal (1997). For a detailed description of the captive housing also see de Waal and Davis (2003).

however, are aspects of capuchin social emotion and reciprocity that are relevant to the propositions tested in this chapter. Note, for instance, that various relationships can be inferred from the narrative. Reading between the lines we can discern a close affiliative relationship between the two males, an attachment bond between the young male and his mother, and an agonistic aid and grooming relationship between the dominant female of the group and the young male's mother.[3] It also appears that emotions play an important role in the interaction among the monkeys in this group, judging, for instance, by the effect of the youngster's temper tantrum on his mother's behavior. In summary, as limited as it is in scope, the observation provides us with a glimpse of the basic structure and dynamics of sociality among captive brown capuchin monkeys. As such, it serves as a good starting point for the next section of this chapter, which reviews evidence in support of the prediction that nonhuman primate sociality, like our own sociality, can be described by three, and possibly four basic social forms.

ELEMENTARY FORMS OF PRIMATE SOCIALITY

Sociality is one of the most important aspects of the overall evolution of primates (Imanishi, 1960; Itani, 1985). From birth until death, monkeys and apes are preoccupied with kin, nonkin, dominance, and sexual relations, and the intricacies of social exchange and reciprocity in each of these relational domains. Social life offers specific adaptive advantages to primates. For instance, exploring and exploiting what nature affords is facilitated by living in a social group (Wrangham, 1987). Social living also reduces vulnerability to predators (van Schaik & van Hooff, 1983). And, related to this, as individuals tend to differ in temperament, an experience or discovery by one individual can potentially benefit another (Kummer, 1971). Finally, novel ways of acting on what nature affords, for good or ill, can be passed on from individual to individual through social learning.

Although local specifics of social structure vary between and within species (Barrett, Gaynor, & Henzi, 2002; Boesch & Boesch-Ackerman, 2000; Manson, Rose, Perry, & Grose-Louis, 1999; Mori, Belay, & Iwamoto, 2003), it appears that four elementary social forms comprehensively describe sociality as it is found across the primate taxon (Fiske, 1992; Haidt, 2001; Haslam, 1997). Tellingly, these four elementary forms of sociality were not originally proposed to describe the social life of our evolutionary cousins but rather that of our own species. Drawing on classical social theory and contemporary ethnographic as well as experimental evidence, Fiske (1992) identified four elements of sociality that in combination make up human sociality across all cultures: communal sharing, authority ranking, equality matching, and market pricing. What this unified theory of social relations suggests is that irrespective of the context and surface form of the interaction, people's primary frames of reference in social life are the same four elementary relational models. People are thus predisposed to understand relationships in four basic ways and experience moral emotions and make moral judgements in conjunction with this understanding. Where cultures differ, according to Fiske, is in the rules they use to implement the four models.

Another way to look at this to distinguish between the deep structure and surface structure of social relations (Laursen & Hartup, 2002). In the case of friendship, for instance, the developmental stable deep structure consists of basic communal sharing norms, while the surface structure is developmental labile (Laursen & Hartup, 2002; see also Hartup, 1996; Hartup & Stevens, 1997). The deep structures of the four basic forms

---

[3]For systematic data on these relationships see Verbeek (1995).

of sociality are most likely shaped by natural selection, while development and culture mold the surface structures.

An increasing amount of evidence from research on monkeys and apes confirms what Fiske suggested at the end of his treatise, namely that nonhuman primates share at least three and possibly all four of these elementary forms of sociality with us. In the following sections, these four elementary forms of sociality are described and selected examples from the primate literature that correspond to each are cited. To help establish a link to human development, each main section is prefaced by a brief description of the specific elementary social form and ways in which it has been observed to unfold in child and adolescent development. As proposed for our own species, the review below shows that among nonhuman primates these four forms of sociality are not necessarily mutually exclusive and may co-occur, overlap, or transform from one into the other within the same species or community.

Communal Sharing

The *unified theory of social relations* (UTSR; Fiske, 1992) defines communal sharing relations as relations in which members of a group treat each other as the same. Reciprocal exchange in communal sharing relations does not depend on balancing what you get with what you contribute. What matters is to belong to the group and to pitch in according to one's abilities and opportunities. Moral judgment and ideology within the context of communal sharing centers on within-group caring, kindness, altruism, and selfless generosity (Fiske, 1992).

Communal sharing most likely has its roots early in life when, in concert with their emerging perceptive abilities, young infants learn to "pitch in" in the emotional sharing with their primary caregivers in (Trevarthen, 1980). Throughout early childhood, harmonious communal relations with peers increasingly matter to children as cross-cultural observations of peer conflict resolution clearly show (Butovskaya & Kozintsev, 1999; Killen & Sueyoshi, 1995; Verbeek & de Waal, 2001). An increasing body of research also shows that the socioemotional and cognitive framework associated with the deep structure of communal sharing relations further crystallizes during middle childhood. School-age children, for instance, tend to favor behaviors that initiate and sustain communal relations over prosocial behaviors that are less tied to social continuity and integration, such as transitory helping and sharing (Greener & Crick, 1999). Moreover, recent cross-cultural interview studies suggest that, with the exception of aggressive individuals, older children and adolescents tend to generally be more tolerant of differences among peers than they are intolerant (Killen, Crystal, & Watanabe, 2002). As research proceeds in this area we may thus find that inclusion, rather than exclusion, may be the developmental communal sharing norm.

The normative unfolding of deep structures of communal sharing relations can provide a context for the early development and specific enculturation of moral principles concerning justice, fairness, and equality (Killen & de Waal, 2000). The extent and quality of adult scaffolding within specific societal and cultural contexts plays an important role in this developmental process. For instance, in contrast to communal values of justice, fairness, and equality, children may also experience and integrate aggression norms and hatred that are linked to us-versus-them issues, such as racism, group honor, and deindividuation of the members of an opposing group (Varna, 1993; see also Fiske, 1992). In this context, Ishida (1969) concludes from comparing various Western and Asian cultures that the more intense the desire to keep harmony within groups with a strong in-group consciousness, the stronger the tendency to fight any enemy that is perceived to threaten the inner harmony of the group. Culture and ethnicity, as well as kinship, in fact, are important mediators of the extent to which children internalize specific moral rights and wrongs associated with communal sharing relations.

Communal Sharing Relations Among Nonhuman Primates

Kinship. Kin relations, which structure social interactions in a wide variety of primate species (Silk, 2001; Smuts, Cheney, Seyfarth, Wrangham, & Struhsaker, 1987), provide a framework for communal sharing among monkeys and apes. The quintessential kin relationship among primates is the parent–offspring attachment bond. The nature of this early bond may affect social development in various ways, from the young primate's ability to establish and maintain subsequent relationships (Harlow & Harlow, 1965), to the ability to manage the aftermath of social conflicts (Weaver & de Waal, 2000).

Kin Recognition and Conflict Management. Studies show that monkeys and apes recognize their own kin as well as discriminate among the social relations of other group members (Gouzoules & Gouzoules, 1987; Parr & de Waal, 1999). This ability may allow individuals to predict the behavior of others and involve relatives in agonistic or affiliative interactions (Aureli, Cozzolino, Cordischi, & Scucchi, 1992; Aureli, Veenema, van Panthaleon van Eck, & van Hooff, 1993; see Massey, 1977). For instance, aiding others in fights, that is, helping at a risk to self, is prevalent among kin, especially female kin (Chapais, 1983; Cheney, 1983; Silk, 1982).

Conflicts of interest between individuals are a fact of life in all social groups, including communal sharing groups such as kin groups. Group living confers significant benefits to individuals, however, and findings from naturalistic observations as well as experimental studies suggest that natural selection has favored behavioral mechanisms that help restore relations interrupted by conflict to preconflict communal levels. Postconflict behavior among nonhuman primates was not systematically examined until the late 1970s (e.g., de Waal & van Roosmalen, 1979; see also Chance, 1984). Prior to that much of the research focus in primatology was on what happened during competition and aggression (e.g., Popp & DeVore, 1979), not on what happened afterward.

A recent review (Aureli, Cords, & van Schaik, 2002) shows that friendly postconflict reunions—the primate way of making peace (de Waal, 1989)—has now been systematically researched in thirty New and Old World primate species and demonstrated at the group level in twenty-eight species (see also section on postconflict consolation). Friendly postconflict reunions have been observed in the wild (nine species to date) and in captivity (twenty-five species). In two species studied so far (long-tailed macaques, *Macaca fascicularis*: Aureli, 1992; Aureli, van Schaik, & van Hooff, 1989; chimpanzees, *Pan troglodytes*: Arnold & Whiten, 2001; Preuschoft, Wang, Aureli, & de Waal, 2001) postconflict peacemaking was shown in both the wild and in captivity, albeit it in the case of one (chimpanzees) at a significantly lower rate in the wild. The degree of kinship is a significant factor in the occurrence of peaceful postconflict reunions. Especially in species in which matrilineal kin cooperate closely, such as macaques, related opponents are more likely to restore relations to preconflict communal levels than nonkin (Aureli et al., 2002).

Dispersal Patterns and Kin Relations. Dispersal patterns among nonhuman primates accomplish what growing up in the same family ("co-residence," Lieberman, Tooby, &

Cosmides, 2002; Westermarck, 1921; Wolf, 1995) tends to do for people: the avoidance of offspring-producing matings among close kin ("inbreeding"). In fact, research on a wide range of species show that close kin who do stay together in the natal group generally tend to avoid sexual intercourse (de Waal, 2001; but see Mitani, Watts, & Muller, 2002). Long hailed as a moral victory over the beast within (e.g., Lévi-Straus, 1969; Freud, 1918), comparative findings now suggest that incest avoidance is based on evolved behavioral mechanisms that people share, in part, with other primates (see de Waal [2001] for a discussion).

In species in which males disperse from the natal group when they reach maturity, matrilineal kin tend to show prosocial behavior toward each other. In these species, other-directed behaviors such as grooming, alarm calling at the detection of predators, and the handling of each other's infants occur significantly more among female kin than nonkin (Bernstein, 1991; Silk, 2001). In species in which females disperse from the natal group, strong communal ties among male kin are common (Boinski, 1994; Goodall, 1986; Strier, 2000). Chimpanzee males, for instance, spend much time together in activities ranging from grooming to hunting and patroling the borders of their communal habitat on the look out for signs of neighboring groups (Goodall, 1986; Mitani et al., 2002). Males who spend much time together have also been observed to reconcile their conflicts at a higher rate than males who spend less time together (Arnold & Whiten, 2001). Recent field studies and DNA analyses suggest, however, that communal relations among adult male chimpanzees are not exclusively based on kinship (Gagneux, Boesch, & Woodruff, 1999; Goldberg & Wrangham, 1997; Mitani et al., 2002; but see Constable, Ashley, Goodall, & Pusey, 2001). At least in some communities unrelated chimpanzee males appear to share strong bonds as well. Unrelated bonded chimpanzee males have been found to be close in age and rank, and may be attracted to each other because they grew up together and share similar social interests and power throughout their lives (Mitani et al., 2002). Closely bonded wild chimpanzee males have been observed as being "strongly compatible" (Arnold & Whiten, 2001), and, as such, can perhaps best be described as friends.

Friendship. Friendship is a special type of communal relationship that is not ad-dressed in great detail in Fiske's unified theory of social relations. Although the benefits of friendship may seem apparent, the question of why friendship has evolved is more complicated than it appears at first glance. Although relatives can have friendly relations, friendship is by definition a relationship between nonrelatives. Inclusive fitness can thus not be evoked to explain the ultimate cause of friendship. Reciprocal altruism also does not appear to fit friendship very well, because true friendship between adults, at least in the Western understanding of it, does not require that benefits are always reciprocated (Hinde, 2002; Lydon, Jamieson, & Holmes, 1997; Mills & Clark, 1994). As Silk (2002a) suggests, reciprocity in the sense of obligations based on indebtedness and balanced tit-for-tat exchanges may actually jeopardize friendship. The reciprocity among friends is of an emotional nature; we care deeply about and enjoy treating our friends right, and feel bad when we wittingly or (more likely) unwittingly treat them wrong, or are treated wrong by them. As such, friendship has a direct link to the emotional underpinning of morality: it engenders feelings of right and wrong. Friendship most likely has roots in the early attachment bond between offspring and parents that is common among mammals.

Primatologists are skittish about using labels for behavior that appear functional from a human perspective, rather than descriptive from the proverbial perspective of a visiting Martian (see Kummer, Dasser, & Hoyningen-Huene, 1990; de Waal, 1991a, for an ex-change of views on anthropomorphic labels). As Silk (2002a) recounts, for this reason the label *friendship* for close bonds among nonkin was initially avoided before it gradually became an accepted entry in the ethograms of primate researchers. A recent review by Silk (2002a) shows that the term *friendship* has been used to describe primate relationships that are characterized by extraordinary proximity or grooming or both (Cords, 1997); mutual preference (Colvin, 1983); tolerance and attachment (Noë & Sluijter, 1995); and low aggression or a positive ratio of affiliative over aggressive behavior (Goodall, 1986; Noë & Sluijter, 1995; all reviewed in Silk, 2002a). As we saw in the discussion of close bonds among wild chimpanzee males, friendship bonds among monkeys and apes have also been linked to an increased tendency to make peace through friendly postconflict reunions (Aureli et al., 2002).

Food Tolerance. Compared to nonkin, primate kin relations are characterized by greater tolerance around food (Feistner & McGrew, 1989; Yamada, 1963), and a greater likelihood of cooperation in obtaining food (de Waal & Davis, 2003). Whereas active food sharing is rare among primates in the natural habitat (Feistner & McGrew, 1989), wild chimpanzees of various communities have been observed to share meat after collective hunts (Boesch & Boesch-Acherman, 2000; Goodall, 1986; see also Nishida, Hosaka, Nakamura, & Hamai, 1995; Teleki, 1973). Wild white-faced capuchin monkeys (*Cebus capucinus*) have been observed to do the same (Perry & Rose, 1994). Inasmuch such meat sharing is communal and not linked to effort extended during the hunt or subsequent reciprocity, it can be seen as a rudimentary form of communal sharing.

In captivity, brown capuchin monkeys may show remarkable tolerance around food, for instance by allowing others to collect the morsels they drop while eating (de Waal, Luttrell, & Canfield, 1993), even when separated by a mesh partition in an experimental set-up (de Waal, 1997b). In subsequent experiments on members of the same captive group, brown capuchins cooperated to obtain food (Mendres & de Waal, 2000), and shared food rewards following such cooperation (de Waal & Berger, 2000). Kinship plays a role in this experimental form of communal sharing, however, as was shown in the most recent experiment on this group in which kin pairs were more likely to cooperate than nonkin pairs, irrespective of whether the food reward was presented in a clumped or dispersed fashion (de Waal & Davis, 2003).

Intercommunity Aggression. To the human observer, conflict and aggression in the context of communal sharing relations of monkeys and apes can take on a distinct xenophobic quality, not unlike what we can observe in our own species. Goodall (1986) was among the first to report on aggressive encounters between wild chimpanzees of neighboring communities. Among her reports is the account of a fission of an established community, followed by a series of lethal attacks by members of the founder community on the newly established community that ultimately resulted in its annihilation. In addition to Goodall's report a number of observations of violent raids into neighboring communities in which primarily bonded males took part, have been reported (e.g. Nishida, Hiraiwa-Hasegawa, Hasegawa, & Takahata, 1985). Recent accounts include cases of infanticide committed by gangs of adult males from neighboring communities (Kutsukake & Matsusaka, 2002; Watts, Mitani, & Sherrow, 2002). The functional significance of lethal intercommunity aggression remains unclear, but may include improved access to food and incorporation of more females into a community (Wrangham, 1999). Lethal intergroup as well as intragroup coalition attacks by males on other males have also been reported for wild white-faced capuchin monkeys (*Cebus capucinus;* Gros-Louis, Perry, & Manson, 2003).

Authority Ranking

Social Dominance.   According to the UTSR (Fiske, 1992), in authority ranking relations, individuals attend to their position in dominance hierarchies.[4] Higher ranking
people tend to get more and better things, and get them sooner, than their subordinates. At
the individual level social dominance has been linked to survival, reproduction, and other
fitness related issues (Caryl, 1979; Drews, 1993), including adverse effects on mental and
physical health (Houston, Babyak, Chesney, Black, & Ragalnd, 1997).

As Fiske (1992) points out, a certain *noblesse oblige* may play a role in authority
ranking relations. If subordinates have a choice they may follow new leaders if the old
ones failed to offer adequate provisions or protection. For people in many cultures the
authority role in fact implies the moral obligation to look after subordinates. Fiske (1992)
adds that authority ranking relations can also be perceived as aversive or have real victims;
the modern history of many countries is replete with intimidation, imprisonment, torture,
execution, and disappearance of people who contest or refuse to accept the legitimacy of
the authority of leaders.

Piaget (1932/1965; discussed in Turiel, 2002) considered young children's tendency to
defer to parents and other adults and hold them in awe an early recognition of moral obligation, which he referred to as *heteronomy*. Research conducted over the past twenty years,
suggests, however, that morality emerges in a broader context of social development and is
as much linked to children's "horizontal" interactions with peers as it is to their "vertical"
experiences with family members and other adults (Killen & Hart, 1995; Turiel, 2002).
Dominance relations among peers are relatively understudied in child development, but
naturalistic as well as controled observations suggest their prevalence and impact on the
moral contexts and sequels of peer conflict management (reviewed in Verbeek, Hartup, &
Collins, 2000). Once established, for instance, dominance hierarchies tend to be linked to
decreased rates of conflict and aggression in peer groups of young children (Strayer, 1992).
Interestingly, across cultures, even very young children may combine coercive with cooperative strategies in establishing and maintaining dominance status (Charlesworth, 1996).

Authority Ranking Among Nonhuman Primates

Hierarchical relations linked to the tendency of individuals to either dominate or be subordinate to other individuals are basic to social life in many primate species (Smuts et al.,
1987). Several studies suggest that nonhuman primates are able to perceive within-group
dominance hierarchies (Bovet & Washburn, 2003; Datta, 1983; Gouzoules, Gouzoules, &
Marler, 1984). Within-group hierarchical relations are often meshed in with kin and other
affiliative relations (de Waal, 1986), with hierarchies extending within and across close
kin groups (Chapais, 1992; Gouzoules & Gouzoules, 1987). Dominance and the communication of power asymmetries may serve to avoid escalation of intergroup conflicts into
damaging fights (Preuschoft & van Schaik, 2000; see also Lorenz, 1963/1966).

Two main perspectives have guided much of the research on primate dominance. One
treats dominance as a behavioral style characteristic: an individual style in social interaction based on prior attributes (e.g., Drews, 1993; Wilson, 1975). The other view emphasizes

---

[4]*Dominance hierarchies* are complex social structures involving linear or nonlinear rankings among individuals in a group. Dominance relations in a linear hierarchy are transitive; thus, if A dominates B and B
dominates C, then A also dominates C. Nonlinear hierarchies contain one or more intransitive triads: $A > B$,
$B > C$, but $C > A$.

the dynamics of a stable group and sees dominance as an emergent property of social interactions (e.g., Bernstein, 1980; Francis, 1988). Recent research that combines behavioral
with physiological measures bridges these two views. As an example, in a series of studies
on wild baboons (*Papio anubis*), Sapolsky (1990, 1993) showed how adrenocortical function, behavior style, and social context may interact in primate dominance. He found that,
after controlling for rank, socially adept male baboons tended to show low basal glucocorticoid levels indicative of the absence of chronic stress. Sapolsky explains that the socially
savvy male baboons tended to discriminate between threatening (overt threat from a rival)
and neutral interactions (mere presence of a rival), and distinguish between winning and
losing (good and bad outcomes of a fight). These socially advantageous behavioral traits
were observed to be stable over time, and these "low glucocorticoid" males tended to have
longer tenures in the dominant cohort of their group. In contrast, subordinate individuals
in groups with high levels of redirected aggression (commonly targeted at subordinate
individuals) and low levels of friendly postconflict reunions tended to show the enduring
elevated basal glucocorticoid levels that are linked to chronic social stress. Interestingly,
Sapolsky comments that the dominant baboon males without the socially adept behavioral
style described tended to be as hypercortisolemic as subordinates.

It is not necessarily so that across primate species subordinate status constitutes a life
of chronic stress, nor do dominant individuals of other species enjoy the apparent absence
of chronic stress exhibited by the socially adept baboon males studied by Sapolsky. For
instance, a recent study on wild Japanese macaques (*Macaca fuscata*) suggests that during
the breeding season it is the dominant males of this species who exhibit elevated cortisol
levels, rather than the subordinate males (Barrett et al., 2002). In wild chimpanzee males
urinary and fecal measures of cortisol correlate positively and significantly with dominance rank (Mitani et al., 2002). Moreover, a recent informal meta-analysis involving four
Old World and three New Word monkey species showed that elevated cortisol levels in
subordinates were contingent on two conditions. In species where subordinate individuals
showed higher relative cortisol levels, they (1) were subjected to higher rates of stressors, and (2) experienced decreased opportunities for social (including close kin) support
(Abott et al., 2002; see also Goyman & Wingfield, 2004). In sum, what the recent evidence
shows is that dominance rank among nonhuman primates is linked to individual differences in behavioral style and stress reactivity. Moreover, the link between stress reactivity
and dominance style is mediated by the particular communal dynamics within a given
group.

Equality Matching

Direct and Indirect Reciprocity.   The UTSR holds that in equality matching individuals keep track of the imbalances among them. The operating principle is that when people
who relate in equality matching mode receive a favor, they feel obligated to reciprocate by
returning a favor (Fiske, 1992). Equality matching can structure work such as people who
work for others who in turn work for them (e.g., I'll help you with your grant proposal in
return for your help with my chapter). As Fiske (1992) suggests, gratitude or obligation
to reciprocate may transform equality matching relations into authority ranking relations.
If benefactions continue to be unbalanced, recipients may accumulate debts that they may
ultimately have to pay back in respect, loyalty, deference, or submission.

In addition to the direct reciprocity of one-on-one exchanges, equality matching can
also take an indirect form when support is given to individuals who have helped others
(Milinski, Semmann, & Krambeck, 2002). Experimental and game theory studies suggest

that supporting individuals who have helped others can indirectly return benefits through an enhanced reputation of effectiveness and reliability in reciprocity and cooperation (Milinski et al., 2002; Nowak & Sigmund, 1998). As Alexander (1987) puts it: "In complex social systems with much reciprocity, being judged as attractive for reciprocal interactions may become an essential ingredient for success" (p. 100). Social prestige and the corresponding deference of others who acknowledge such prestige has also been linked to this indirect process of helping others who help others (Henrich, & Gil-White, 2001; see also Alexander, 1987). Punishment of cheaters—those who do not reciprocate in kind—has been extensively studied as an evolved mechanism through which a system of indirect reciprocity can be maintained (Clutton-Brock & Parker, 1995; Fehr & Gächter, 2002).

Equality matching relations emerge during early childhood. For instance, observational research shows that preschool children's peer conflicts often center on the insistence on equality, even distribution, tit-for-tat reciprocity and turn taking (Killen & de Waal, 2000; Verbeek et al., 2000). The developmental literature also suggests that an early understanding of equality constitutes the basis for a later understanding of equity (Killen & Hart, 1995).

Equality Matching Among Nonhuman Primates

Equality matching among primates is more difficult to detect than communal sharing or authority ranking relations. Especially in studies on wild populations, reciprocity is hard to measure when it is significantly delayed in time or involves different behaviors or "currencies" (Silk, in press; see also de Waal, 1997a). Equality matching among nonhuman primates can take the form of direct and indirect reciprocity. Primates aid each other, for instance, in hunting (e.g., Boesch & Boesch, 1989), or agonistic interactions, and may reciprocate aid directly to the aid giver, or indirectly to individuals who have supported others (de Waal, 1977; de Waal & Luttrell, 1988; Silk, 1992; Watanabe, 1979). New studies show that wild chimpanzee males may groom and support each other reciprocally (Watts, D. P., 2002). Unrelated male chimpanzees also share meat for coalitionary support (Mitani et al., 2002). Inasmuch cooperating chimpanzee males are not kin (see section on communal sharing) such reciprocity can be seen as equality matching as defined by the UTSR.

Judging from the findings on chimpanzees, grooming seems to be a good candidate to qualify for equality matching relations among nonhuman primates. Grooming is beneficial because ectoparasites, dry skin flakes, and dirt are removed in the process, and wounds are cleaned (Henzi & Barrett, 1999). Moreover, the readily observable relaxation effect of grooming has been confirmed at the physiological level through data on heart rate reduction and the increase of beta-endorphin levels linked to grooming (Aureli & Smucny, 2000). The costs of grooming include time and energy expenditure as well as a potentially risky reduction in vigilance (Cords, 1995). The research to date shows, however, that favors are not as equally matched as far as grooming is concerned. In some primate species, grooming proceeds mostly up the hierarchy, with subordinates grooming higher ranked individuals (e.g., Seyfarth, 1977), while in other species grooming occurs down the hierarchy, in the reverse sense (e.g., Parr, Matheson, Bernstein, & de Waal, 1997). Much of the data on grooming involves female monkeys. Authority ranking relations can describe such interactions. In some instances, grooming has been observed to be temporally reciprocal; with partners switching roles within a grooming bout (baboons [*Papio cynocephalus*] Barrett & Henzi, 2001). This temporally reciprocal form of grooming is referred to as *time matching*. The occurrence of time matching among wild baboons has been observed to be most frequent during periods with low aggression and dominance interactions (Barrett et al., 2002). In a study on captive female rhesus monkeys (*Macaca mulatta*), de Waal (1991c) found that, independent of kinship, females of similar rank were reciprocally attracted to each other and showed this by exchanging grooming duties. These latter findings on time matching and reciprocal grooming among individuals close in rank do seem to match the UTSR definition of equality matching.

Multiple Currency Exchanges.   Primate reciprocity extends across behaviors, for instance in cases where individuals help conspecifics that previously groomed them in fights (Hemelrijk, 1994; see also Perry, 1996; Seyfarth & Cheney, 1984; Silk, 1992). In a similar vein, members of a captive group of chimpanzees were more likely to share clumped food with individuals who groomed them about two hours earlier than with other individuals (de Waal, 1997a).

Following Rules and Making Peace.   Prescriptive rules that individuals have learned to follow because other individual tend to actively reinforce them, may govern, in part, equality matching among chimpanzees (de Waal, 1991b; see also Nishida et al., 1995; de Waal, 1996), but there is little or no systematic evidence for this yet in other apes or monkeys. Finally, as we saw, aggressive conflicts of interests between individuals are likely to be reconciled through friendly postconflict reunions when other, more weighty interests converge (de Waal, 2000a; de Waal & Aureli, 1997). Communal relations such as kin relations and friendship can constitute shared interests among former opponents, but so can equality matching relations such as working relationships. In a demonstration of the latter, Cords and Thurnheer (1993) showed that pairs of captive long-tailed macaques who had previously cooperated to obtain desirable food in an experimental task, reconciled artificially provoked conflicts at a higher rate than before the food task. It thus seemed that the monkey pairs in this experiment had developed a valuable (working) relationship that now motivated them to make peace at an increased rate.

Market Pricing

Emotionally Charged Exchange Expectations.   In market pricing individuals shape relations according to ratio values of goods and services (Fiske, 1992). Although cultural contextual factors have been shown to affect the developmental timing of their emergence (e.g., Jahoda, 1983), the developmental literature suggests that market pricing relations are a universal and integral part of children's social development. Although market pricing relations do not shape nonhuman primate society in any way comparable as they do ours, it is likely that other primates share our ability to aggregate exchanges over time and keep track of ratios of such exchanges. In fact, a recent study on brown capuchin monkeys suggests that this particular New World monkey has a rudimentary sense of market pricing relations (Brosnan & de Waal, 2003). In this experiment female monkeys were trained to exchange a small rock with the experimenters for a food reward, a piece of cucumber or a grape. Earlier work with the monkeys had shown that they much preferred grapes to cucumbers. Once they were trained up to the level of accomplishing a swift trade with the experimenter they were paired off for the actual experiment. During the experiment partners either received the same reward for swapping with the experimenter (a cucumber slice) or the more desired grape, for the same amount of work, or in some cases, for doing no work at all. The monkeys who observed unfair treatment and failed to benefit from it often refused to continue to exchange rocks with the experimenters. Some monkeys even refused the cucumber slices they did receive for their work, or threw it at the experimenters. Brosnan and de Waal conclude that their study shows that some monkeys may have emotionally charged expectations about social exchanges that lead them to dislike inequity (de Waal, 2000b).

SUMMARY PROPOSITION ONE

Following other researchers (Fiske, 1992; Haidt, 2001; Haslam, 1997) it is proposed in this chapter that nonhuman primate sociality can be described by the same four elementary forms that describe our own sociality. The observation of a social conflict among captive brown capuchin monkeys that started the first half of this chapter hinted at basic modes of sociality in this primate species. The observation suggested communal relations based on kinship and preferential affiliation (mother–son; two males, respectively) as well as authority ranking relations (adult females). The review that followed provided evidence for the proposition that capuchin monkeys and other nonhuman primates share at least three elementary forms of sociality with us. The review also suggests that these basic modes of sociality are observed in the wild as well as in captivity. The evidence in support of market pricing relations among nonhuman primates is still thin, but work on theoretical models may yet provide us with testable hypotheses in this domain (e.g., Noë, van Schaik, & van Hooff, 1991).

Extensive research with children and adults has revealed the ways in which expectations, norms, and standards govern human relationships. To a certain degree, the same can be said with regard to nonhuman primate social relations. Speaking about human relations, Fiske (1992) defines social goals that vary among individuals as *motives*. When motives are widely shared they are referred to as *values*. When values are observed from the point of view of their function for the collectivity they are called *norms*. When people insist that they and others must pursue such norms, they are seen as *moral standards*. Finally, when people justify the legitimacy of a social system with reference to such a purpose, it is called an *ideology* (Fiske, 1992).

In evolutionary terms we can speak of values in the context of behaviors shaped by natural selection that enhance the fitness of individuals and that are widely shared within a population. Norms can be seen as arising out of values as emergent properties. In the context of the elementary forms of primate sociality we can detect evolutionary norms of "rights" and "wrongs." It may be the right thing to do for a capuchin monkey, for instance, to make up with a former opponent after a fight to restore relations to postconflict communal levels. Effective communal relations, in which damage caused by aggression is regularly repaired, may ultimately be in the best interest of winners and losers alike, because it has the potential to increase the reproductive success of both. It may also be in the immediate interest of both opponents to make up. Peaceful contact among former opponents reduces stress caused by conflict. For instance, heart rate levels decline to baseline levels following friendly postconflict reunions between former opponents, and they do so much more markedly then following postconflict interactions with third parties (Smucny, Price, & Byrne, 1997). The same holds for self-directed behaviors, another observable sign of stress, such as nervous self-scratching (Aureli & van Schaik, 1991; Castles & Whiten, 1998; Das, Penke, & van Hooff, 1998). Peacemaking after conflict, may thus be the right thing to do, both from an ultimate as well as proximate perspective.

There is no need to postulate anything that approximates human-like cognitive functioning in apes and monkeys to account for such norms. Monkeys do not need to know right from wrong to do what natural selection has selected as the right thing for them to do.

The ability to recognize individuals and read their behavior, coupled with some recollection of previous interactions, suffices. The rewards and pains linked to social inclusion or rejection can provide individual monkeys and apes with the motivation to pursue shared social goals (see Nesse, 1990; see also this chapter's section on primate social emotions). No communication of moral standards or ideology is needed for our evolutionary cousins.

In comparison, in our own species rules about what constitutes right or wrong are formalized through language and internalized. As Alexander (1987) points out, potential conflicts of interest among mutually dependent parties require rules about acceptable versus unacceptable behavior. As Killen and de Waal (2000) suggest, morality arises in the face of tensions between socially cohesive and potentially destructive tendencies: moral systems are designed to promote the first and control the second. Making peace, in this context, is clearly connected to moral development. That is, young children seem to be predisposed to working out conflicts through negotiation and compromise, just as has been observed with nonhuman primates (Verbeek & de Waal, 2001). Children can use these experiential encounters to achieve moral understanding, and that is the qualitative difference between children and nonhuman primates (Killen & de Waal, 2000).

Primatologists Brosnan and de Waal (2002) recently made a case for proximate behavioral research. They offer that increasingly sophisticated modeling techniques can help to explain the reasons for a behavior's existence in a species' repertoire, but no matter how elegant or compelling an evolutionary scenario, it is useless if the animal lacks the capability of behaving as the theory predicts (see Stamps, 1991). For that reason, Brosnan and de Waal argue, we need to study proximate mechanisms, the actual capacities and response patterns that evolved in the animal to fulfil these evolutionary requirements. Darwin pointed toward what we should look at to better understand the proximate causes of morality, namely the interplay between the emotions of social exchange and our ability to sympathize with others. That brings us to the testing of the second proposition of this chapter, the notion that nonhuman primates exhibit emotions that are linked to the four basic modes of sociality that make up their social life.

PRIMATE SOCIAL EMOTIONS

> After an extended fight during which A supported E against N and, in turn, received support from D, A initiates play-wrestle with the victim N. It appeared as if his motivation to affiliate with N overtook his aggression toward her. N sensed the "change in attitude" of A; she did not flee, but instead, albeit wearily, reciprocated A's play advances.

Here we are visiting again with our main protagonist, the young male capuchin monkey ("A" in the above narrative). This time he supports the dominant female of the group ("E") in aggression directed a young adult female ("N"). It so happens that he has a strong bond with the victim; they spend a lot of time together playing, grooming, and sitting in close proximity to each other. For all intent and purposes they are friends. The remarkable aspect of this observation is the speed at which the protagonist switches from an aggressive mode to a play mode. What is equally remarkable is that the victim picks up his honest signal and reciprocates his play advances.[5] What clearly mediated this interaction was emotion at several levels, for instance, as expressed in face and posture by the interactants in this episode.

---

[5]In reference to the primacy of moral emotions and intuitions over moral judgements, Haidt (2001) proposes that affective evaluation of this kind occurs so quickly, automatically, and pervasively that it is generally thought to be an integral part of perception.

This narrative suggests that, as in our own species, emotion is at the heart of capuchin monkey's social life. To paraphrase Walker's (1996) statement about morality: emotion prescribes people's activities, regulates social interactions, and fuels as well as reconciles conflicts. The same may hold true for our closest evolutionary relatives. Once regarded as peripheral process with little relevance to survival, mounting evidence now suggests that emotion plays a central role in the ways individuals perceive, explore, and exploit the physical and social environment (Verbeek & de Waal, 2002; see also Nesse, 1990). The roots of the emotion system date back to early evolutionary history. Many animals, including primates, share basic limbic structures located in the areas of the brain underlying the neocortex that mediate emotion. Two decades ago Zajonc (1980) argued that the emotion system has primacy over the cognitive system in every sense: it came first in phylogeny, it emerges first in ontogeny, and it is more powerful when the two systems are in conflict (cited in Haidt, 2001). Recent developments in affective neuroscience give credence to Zajonc's early insights about the primacy of emotion in many aspects of social life (Panksepp, 1998).

Moral emotions occupy a prominent place in the pantheon of human social emotions. Based on their prominence we can predict that precursors of human moral emotions may be observable in other extant primates. In the observation narrative that started this chapter, emotion stands out as an important component of the various behavioral interactions among the capuchin monkeys. The young adult's male refusal to share triggered a temper tantrum in the juvenile male, and this emotional outburst, in turn, triggered an angry reaction in the youngster's mother. These emotions were linked to the circumstances and consequences of social reciprocity: in this case a refusal to share between close companions. For the purpose of this chapter *moral emotions* are defined as emotions linked to the circumstances and consequences of acts of reciprocity. This does not imply that capuchin monkeys exhibit moral emotions to any degree that people do, but rather that we may be able to observe social emotions in our closest relatives that may be forerunners of the moral emotions that are intimately connected with human morality.

In humans, moral emotions function at various levels to various degrees of intensity. For example, we may feel guilty for not thanking our friends for the travel gift they brought back for us, or feel anger about the stinginess of a sibling. Or we may feel indignation about being cheated out of a chance for promotion by a selfish colleague. As such, moral emotions transcend the self and extend to others. They are as much about give and take and tit for tat as they are about sharing and cooperating. They can be other condemning, such as anger and indignation, other praising, such as gratitude and elevation, or self-conscious, such as shame and guilt (Haidt, 2003b; see also Trivers, 1971). Whichever form they take, they are about the expectations, norms, and standards that prescribe our social exchanges with others.

The idea that passion (emotion) may have primacy over reason (cognition) in some important areas of sociality, in particular moral aspects, is slowly taking hold. Haidt (2001, 2003a), for instance, presents evidence that suggests that moral judgement is caused by moral emotions and quick moral intuitions, and is followed (when needed) by slow, ex post facto moral reasoning. His model is supported, to some extent, by brain imaging studies that illustrate the primacy of emotion in moral behavior and judgment, and that map the corticol–subcorticol loops that organize social emotion, cognition and motivation in moral functioning (Heekeren, Wartenburger, Schmidt, Schwintowski, & Villringer, 2003; Moll et al., 2002, 2003; Sanfey, Rilling, Aronson, Nystrom, & Cohen, 2003; Stone, Cosmides, Tooby, Kroll, & Knight, 2002).

Within areas of psychology that focus on rational deliberation and the development of cognitive abilities in moral development (e.g., Helwig & Turiel, 2002; Turiel & Neff, 2000), Haidt's social intuitionist model of moral judgement is viewed with some suspicion. Criticism centers on the argument that substantial empirical evidence in support of the model is still mostly lacking within key areas of psychology (as an illustration of this debate see Pizarro & Bloom [2003] versus Haidt [2003a]. Although this criticism may be well founded with regard to developmental research, little research exists that approaches moral development from a social intuitionist perspective, research in other areas provides indirect or direct support for Haidt's model.

Social psychologists, for instance, are charting the unconscious nature of our social behavior (Bargh, 1994; Greenwald & Banaji, 1995), and have demonstrated the principal role of emotion in judgment and decision making (Forgas, 1995). Moreover, social psychological research suggests that moral behavior covaries more with moral emotion than with moral judgement (Haidt, 2001). Cognitive scientists are on the same wavelength in stressing the critical role of emotion in moral judgments (Nichols, 2002). Neuroscientists are now mapping in healthy subjects the brain–behavior relationships underlying emotion that intersect with earlier accounts of moral deficiencies observed in neuropsychiatric disorders (Moll et al., 2003; see also Blair, 1995; Kiehl et al., 2001). Developmental psychologists with a focus on social development are pursuing similar links among the regulation and expression of emotions and children's prosocial and antisocial behaviors and moral development (Cohen & Strayer, 1996; Eisenberg, 2000; Roberts & Strayer, 2003). This confluence of research activity in key areas of psychology and neuroscience converges with recent research and theorizing in nonhuman primate research on the role of emotion in social behavior in general (van Hooff & Aureli, 1994), and in conflict resolution following aggression, in particular (e.g., Aureli et al., 2002; Aureli & Whiten, 2003). As Darwin suggested, empathy and sympathy may at the basis of moral emotion, and the following sections explore the specific role of empathy and sympathy as basic primate social emotions in more detail.

From a Sense of Others to Sensing Others

For moral emotions to affect our mood and fill our consciousness (see Russell, 2003) we must first perceive the circumstances and consequences of reciprocity. Our ability to do so may be closely linked to our basic ability to transcend selfishness, namely our ability to vicariously share affective states with others. As Darwin suggested (1971/1981, p. 77), research now shows that many other animals share our ability to match each other other's joy, distress, or anger. As we saw, the young capuchin monkey who was faced with his friend's refusal to share threw a temper tantrum[6] in response. His emotional display not only drew attention from every member of his group, but also aroused and motivated his mother to come over and chase his stingy friend. The arousal of the mother showed through her pilo-erection[7]: the hairs of much of her body stood erect even before she came

---

[6]Trivers (1985) proposed that temper tantrums could benefit young by retaining parental attention. Potegal, Kosorok, and Davidson (1996; cited in Potegal, 2000) found that in children tantrums usually consist of the two partially independent processes of anger and distress. Anger may best describe the young capuchin male's tantrum following his friend's refusal to share.

[7]*Pilo-erection* is one of the observable manifestations of emotion in nonhuman primates; it is normally associated with angry aggression. Other behavioral manifestations of emotion include displacement activities such as self-scratching, self-grooming, and body shake (Maestripieri et al., 1992; Schino et al., 1996).

over to chase her son's friend. It appeared that she vicariously related to the distress of her son, which motivated her to intervene on his behalf. The mother–infant attachment bond surely enhanced the affective state matching between capuchin mother and son, but such affective resonance is not restricted to close kin.

Cells and whole organisms react to other cells or organisms in distinct ways. Biologists call this basic reactive tendency *prototaxis*. Without it life as we know it cannot sustain itself. Related to prototaxis is the innate ability of animals to recognize living things as being distinct from nonliving things. As Lovelock (1991) puts it: "Anything living can mean any matter of life or death to an animal: it can be edible, a helper, a potential mate, or a lethal threat- all questions of prime significance for an animal's survival and reproductive success" (p. 7). The instant and automatic process of perceiving living things thus has comprehensive adaptive value (Lovelock, 1991). Signals aid in broadcasting and perceiving what a living thing affords for good or ill. Whether they consist of displays or songs, smells or touch, communicative signals aid senders and receivers in navigating the environment of living things. Signals are especially important in primate social perception and action, for instance to acknowledge dominance and submission (Preuschoft & van Schaik, 2000). Particularly in social contexts such as dominance interactions, signals may be integral to the outward manifestation of concomitant emotional states such as fear and anger. Signals are also important in the aftermath of social conflict. Following conflict primates may signal to their former opponent their benign intent (see Silk, 2002b). In fact, friendly postconflict reunions can only effectively take place when such signals are honest and understood.

Basic Social Emotions: Empathy and Sympathy

For many social animals emotion is the glue that holds the social fabric together. Basic to this process is *affective resonance* or *emotional contagion*, which is the tendency to automatically mimic and synchronize expressions, vocalizations, postures, and movements with those of another and, as a consequence, to converge emotionally (Hartfield, Cacioppo, & Rapson, 1993). When the matched state is an aversive state we also speak of *distress at another's distress*[8] (Haidt, 2003b). Affective resonance may be the precursor for empathy, and for sympathy as Darwin perceived it, as well as for the moral emotions that he proposed grew out of it.

Opinions about what exactly constitutes an emotion continue to widely differ (Russell, 2003), with existing definitions of emotion ranging from the simple to the complex. Cabanac (2002), for instance, proposes that *emotion* is any mental experience with high intensity (awareness; perceived bodily changes) and high hedonic content (pleasure/displeasure). More complex definitions often emphasize the primary role of cognition in emotion (Lazarus, 1991; see also Lane & Nadel, 2000),[9] or describe emotions as a set of discrete adaptations produced by natural selection linked to costs and benefits of different courses of action (Fessler & Haley, 2003; see also Cosmides & Tooby, 2000).

Perhaps one assumption shared by most workers on emotions is that an emotion involves distinctive physiology, expression (e.g., facial expression), as well as action tendency. As Haidt (2003b) suggests, when matched against this basic template, distress at another's

---

[8]Distress at another's distress is also commonly referred to as *personal distress*. Considering that this term refers to persons, distress at another's distress is the term best suited for this comparative review.

[9]Panksepp and co-workers (2002) point out that it is often overlooked that brain stimulation can induce emotional states, giving evidence for the fact that emotion can exist without a cognitive trigger or content.

distress is not an emotion at all, because other than distress it has no distinctive physiology, expression, or action tendency. However, although distress at another's distress has no specific action tendency linked to it, it can motivate individuals to selfishly seek ways to alleviate their own distress that they "caught" from observing a distressed other. Infant monkeys, for example, may approach, embrace, mount, or even pile on top of a distressed peer, as de Waal (1996) observed in a group of rhesus macaques (*Macaca mulatta*). As de Waal comments, the distress of one infant seems to spread to its peers, which then soothe their own arousal.

Empathy and sympathy are constructs related to distress at another's distress. *Empathy* is thought to arise out of distress at another's distress by adding an other-directed action component to the mix. For instance, from the second year on children actively offer help when distressed by the distress of others. The kind of help offered, however, is often what the bystander child herself finds comforting (Hoffman, 1982). More targeted helping occurs from about the third year, when children become aware that other people's feelings can differ from their own (Hoffman, 1982). *Sympathy*, in turn, involves feelings of sorrow or concern for the predicament of others. Sympathy does not necessarily involve sharing another's distress, but does involve targeted attempts to alleviate the distress in the other (Eisenberg, 2000). Following these definitions, empathy and sympathy can be seen as emotions, whereas distress at another's distress cannot. Following these definitions, *empathy* may be the suggested term to describe the earlier described capuchin mother's vigorous response to her son's temper tantrum, as it observably combined distress at another's distress with an other-directed action.[10]

Research on Affective Resonance and Empathy Among Nonhuman Primates

Similar to research on humans, measuring distress at another's distress or empathy in animals requires measuring physiological processes as well as behavior. To date there is less research on the former than on the latter, and studies that combine physiological with behavioral observations remain few. Nevertheless, the available research suggests that distress at another's distress and empathy occurs in a variety of species. Preston and de Waal (2002) reviewed a number of early studies in this area and a few studies mentioned in their review are briefly cited herein. Mason (1965), for example, is mentioned as being the first to study arousal reduction through body contact in chimpanzees. As pet owners may know from experience, dogs may display reassuring behavior toward a human simulating distress (Zahn-Waxler, Hollenbeck, & Radke-Yarrow, 1984), a behavior that may have its roots in the social attentiveness of their wild ancestor the wolf (*Canis lupus;* see Fox, 1975). Rats and pigeons confronted with a distressed member of their species not only showed distress, but readily engaged in tasks that helped to end the conspecific's distress (Church, 1959; Watanabe & Ono, 1986). And when pressing a bar for food is linked with an electric shock to another monkey, monkeys give up on the food reward by not pressing the bar (Masserman, Wechkin, & Terris, 1964). These early studies suggest that animals may act to alleviate or prevent the distress of members of their species. It remains to be determined, however, what best explains the specific responses to distressed conspecifics in these studies. Perhaps watching a distressed conspecific was aversive to some animals, whereas distress at another's distress or empathy may have been at the basis of the behavior

---

[10]Empathy as a mediator of altruism toward kin is likely to have arisen out of the mother–infant attachment bond which, in and by itself, is seen as a product of natural selection (Harlow & Harlow, 1965; see also Hoffman, 1982; Weaver & de Waal, 2000).

of others (Flack & de Waal, 2000). Irrespective of the ultimate level of explanation, these selected findings do suggest that the animals in these studies transcended selfishness by vicariously sharing affective states with others.

The bulk of observations of empathy-related behaviors come from research on nonhuman primates. Some of the evidence from this work is anecdotal (e.g., de Waal, 1989, 1996, 1997c; Goodall, 1986; Ladygina-Kohts, 1935/2002; O'Connell, 1995; Yerkes, 1925). Other findings come from more systematic research, including postconflict or "reconciliation" research. This research was discussed in previous sections, but one particular area of focus in this field, third-party interactions, merits review in the present section. In this observational research, postconflict interactions between former opponents are compared to matched-control observations of the social behavior of the same individuals not preceded by conflict (de Waal & Yoshihara, 1983; Veenema, Das, & Aureli, 1994). This method allows observers to determine whether former opponents are likely to come together in peaceful reunions shortly after conflict at a rate that exceeds chance. This controlled method of observation also allows observers to determine whether other group members are inclined to offer postconflict comfort to distressed conflict participants through grooming, mere physical contact, or other friendly behaviors. Friendly postconflict contacts between former conflict participants and third parties initiated by the latter is referred to in the primate research literature as *consolation*.

Consolation was first described in captive chimpanzees (de Waal & van Roosmalen, 1979). Since this first finding consolation has been investigated in wild chimpanzees (Arnold & Whiten, 2001), and in a variety of nonhuman primates species, but many of these studies failed to find a systematic occurrence of it (e.g., in macaques: de Waal & Aureli, 1996). Notable exceptions are studies on Guinea baboons (*Papio papio*; Petit & Thierry, 1994), mountain gorillas (*Gorilla gorilla beingei*; Watts, 1995), spectacled langurs (*Trachipithecus obscurus*; Arnold & Barton, 2001), and brown capuchin monkeys (*Cebus apella*; Verbeek & de Waal, 1997). However, in these studies recipients of aggression solicited consolation from bystanders rather than it being offered by other group members, as initially observed in chimpanzees (de Waal & van Roosmalen, 1979). Postconflict consolation remains a rich area to explore differences and similarities in empathy-related behaviors between monkeys and apes (de Waal & Aureli, 1996; Watts, Colmanares, & Arnold, 2000). Perhaps a more systematic emphasis on individual differences and physiological responses to conflict (Aureli & Smucny, 2000) can help to bring into focus whether and how consolation among monkeys and apes can be seen as a behavioral forerunner of a moral concern for victims in our own species.

SUMMARY PROPOSITION TWO

Adam Smith (1759/1976), David Hume (1739/1969), and at a more recent date, Jean Piaget (1932/1965), all saw sympathy as the foundation of morality (all cited in Haidt, 2003b). Charles Darwin (1871/1981) shared this view. Darwin offered the additional, and, for our present purposes crucial, insight, that sympathy evolved (perhaps from a basic sense of others) as the most likely precursor of the specific emotions that sustain our morality. Evidence reviewed in this chapter gives some credence to the proposition that nonhuman primates show specific emotions that are linked to the elementary forms of sociality that they share with us. In particular there's evidence of empathy-like responding in conflict interactions among monkeys as well as apes. More systematic work in this area is needed, however, to better understand the form and function of empathy and sympathy-like responses in nonhuman primate sociality.

Trivers (1971) suggested that evolution shaped specific emotions as proximate mechanisms that cause individuals to engage in reciprocal altruism. For instance, he proposed that gratitude encourages individuals to repay benefactors, just as anger motivates individuals to punish cheaters (Trivers, 1971). Three decades later his ideas have become an integral part of contemporary psychological approaches to morality. In a recent *Psychological Bulletin* article the authors state that gratitude is indeed an important moral emotion, functioning both as a response to moral behavior and as a motivator of moral behavior (McCullough, Emmons, Kilpatricks, & Larson, 2001). Other emotions have been highlighted as lubricants of the moral process, including guilt. Based on its elicitors and action tendencies guilt has been suggested to grow out of communal relationships and the attachment system (Baumeister, Stillwell, & Heatherton, 1994). Guilt motivates people to treat their partners well (Baumeister et al., 1994). Lewis (1993) adds that in guilt situations one appraises one's actions as bad, not one's whole self. In a similar vein, Haidt (2003b) comments that guilt motivates people to apologize and confess, not as a way to debase themselves but as a way to restore or improve their relationships.

Do emotions drive communal and equality matching relations among nonhuman primates as well? Can we detect something akin to moral emotions in nonhuman primates? There are some tantalizing first indications that, provided we use suitable methods, we may be able to do so. Research by Aureli, Das, and Veenema (1997; reviewed in Aureli and Smucny, 2000), for instance, used behavioral indicators, such as self-scratching, to measure the level of stress following social conflict in long-tail macaques. They found an elevation in both aggressors and victims. The elevation was especially high after conflict with a valuable partner, one with whom the subjects often associated or cooperated. The authors conclude that the observed anxiety therefore most likely concerned the state of the relationship (see Aureli & Schaffner, 2002). What is seen as postconflict anxiety among nonhuman primate friends may be a precursor of postconflict guilt in our own species. Similar methods can be used to investigate and map emotions in other areas of nonhuman primate sociality and help to identify how empathy and related processes may provide a basis for context-specific social emotions. Such investigations can help to increase our understanding of to what extent primate social emotions can be seen as forerunners of moral emotions in our own species.

EPILOGUE: EVERYONE'S JOURNEY

> Openness to life grants a lightning-swift insight into the life situation of others. What is necessary?—to wrestle with your problems until its emotional discomfort is clearly conceived in an intellectual form—and then act accordingly (Hammarskjöld, 1983, p. 8).

As the contributions to this volume attest, we are steadily increasing our understanding of how morality unfolds during child and adolescent development. In contrast, we know precious little about the environmental pressures that may have shaped the social behavior of our human ancestors. We are primarily confined to theoretical models for making inferences about the what and the why of the social behaviors that natural selection has favored in our evolutionary history. We do have recourse, however, as far as increasing our empirical understanding of the biological bases of morality is concerned. A rough sketch for a more detailed comparative painting of the biological roots of our morality is already available. A comparative look at the behavior of extant nonhuman primates shows that we share basic patterns of social behavior with apes and monkeys. The evolution of other-directed and altruistic behavior within the context of four basic shared modes of sociality can be explained, in part, by theoretical models, including inclusive fitness (e.g., communal sharing among kin), reciprocal altruism (e.g., equality matching through direct or indirect reciprocity), or attachment theory (communal sharing among nonkin). Other types of social modes that we share with other primates, and that are linked to what we as humans might perceive as right or wrong, such as authority ranking, still defy "easy" ultimate explanations. Social dominance, for instance, can confer benefits to dominant individuals (e.g., privileged access to resources; social bonding) as well as to subordinate individuals (e.g., a "check" on the escalation of intergroup conflicts into damaging fights; social bonding). We also know that authority ranking can be detrimental to fitness for dominants and subordinates alike due to chronic stress associated with status positioning. Proximate investigations have helped to clarify the picture as they suggest that social adeptness may offset stress in dominant primates (Sapolsky, 1990, 1993), and social support can help offset stress in subordinate monkeys and apes (Abott el al., 2002). Further comparative research within this general framework can help to identify more clearly to what degree the expectations, norms, and standards that make up morality today are derived, in part, from the evolutionary norms that constitute the deep structure of primate sociality.

Comparative research convincingly shows that we share with other social animals the ability to transcend selfishness by matching the affective states of others. Comparative research also strongly suggests that the inclination to act on affective resonance, an emotion-action pattern we have come to refer to as *empathy*, is also present in other social animals, in particular nonhuman primates. In mammals, empathy most likely grew out of the attachment system where it has obvious benefits as a mediator of altruism toward kin (Hoffman, 1982) as well as toward closely affiliated nonkin (Batson & Shaw, 1991).

It remains to be shown to what extent sympathy, as presently defined in the developmental literature as feelings of sorrow for the predicament of others combined with targeted attempts to alleviate their distress, is found in nonhuman primates or other social mammals. Alternatively, it may turn out that from an evolutionary perspective the current distinction between empathy and sympathy is a matter of semantics only. The available comparative evidence on animal forms of empathy (e.g., postconflict consolation in some monkeys and apes) may already provide initial support for Darwin's ideas about the evolution of what he called *sympathy*. Alternatively, sympathy can be seen as having grown out of empathy-related responses in conjunction with the emergence of an ability to infer mental states in others.

Casting a Wide Net: Extending the Comparative Approach

An effective comparative approach to morality rests on cross-fertilization of ideas and methods across disciplines. To some degree this is already taking place (Cords & Killen, 1998). For instance, comparative researchers have adapted controlled observation methods that were developed for studying conflict and its aftermath in nonhuman primates for studying the same in young children. Using this method, preschoolers and first graders from different cultural backgrounds have been observed to spontaneously, without adult intervention, resolve peer conflict in a peaceful manner (Butovskaya, Verbeek, Ljungberg, & Lunardini, 2000; Verbeek & de Waal, 2001). They do so, in part, through friendly postconflict reunions. The form and timing of these postconflict events is remarkably similar to that of peaceful postconflict contacts among monkeys and apes (Silk, 2002b). Among Western preschool children the strongest predictor of peacemaking, be it immediately after conflict termination or with some delay through postconflict contacts, is preconflict interaction (Laursen & Hartup, 1989; Verbeek & de Waal, 2001). This suggests that, similar to what has been found for nonhuman primates, restoring communal relations to preconflict levels is important for young children.

Developmental research inspired, in part, by comparative perspectives, shows that empathic responses to peers are important mediators of cooperative behavior in young children (Barnett, 1987; Batson & Oleson, 1991; Eisenberg & Fabes, 1991; Fabes, Eisenberg, Eisenbud, 1993; Fabes et al.,1994; Hoffman, 1982; Roberts & Strayer, 2003; Zahn-Waxler & Smith, 1992; Zahn-Waxler, Radke-Yarrow, Wagner, & Chapman, 1992). Moral understanding seems to grow out of empathic and conciliatory tendencies (Dunn & Slomkowski, 1992; Killen & Nucci, 1995; Killen, Ardila-Rey, Barrakkatz, & Wang, 2000).

A comprehensive comparative approach to morality can also benefit from a closer look at special populations as well as systematic within and between culture comparisons. Abused children, for instance, may be deprived of early opportunities to develop crucial links among empathy, moral emotions, and moral understanding. Early naturalistic observational work suggests that young children who are physically abused by their parents tend to show fear or anger in response to witnessing a distressed peer, compared to the empathic interest or comforting behavior often shown by nonabused peers (George & Main, 1979; Main & George, 1985). There is also initial evidence that is suggestive of a possible link between conduct disorder in adolescence and affective morality (Cimbora & McIntosh, 2003; see also Cohen & Strayer, 1996).

The ways in which empathy is nurtured by parents and teachers may differ significantly from culture to culture. For instance, compared to U.S. parents, Japanese parents are generally more likely to emphasize empathy *(omoiyari)* in socialization (Azuma, 1986, 1994). For Japanese parents and teachers empathy is a principal means toward the child's receptivity *(sunao)* to adult modeling and wishes (Lebra, 1994; Lewis, 1988, 1995): the ideal Japanese child grows up skillful in avoiding conflicts, attending to subtle behavioral cues, and "reading" minds (Rothbaum, Pott, Azuma, Miyake, & Weisz, 2000). Findings obtained with naturalistic observations, as well as ratings by parents and teachers, suggest that Japanese preschoolers are less assertive and show less anger and aggression than their U.S. peers (Kobayashi-Winata & Power, 1989; Zahn-Waxler, Friedman, Cole, Mizuta, & Hiruma, 1996). The possible effect of this early developmental experience on subsequent moral development begs further systematic comparative investigation.[11]

A key issue to address in future comparative research on morality is the proximate link between empathy and sympathy and moral emotions. Comparative research, including work on nonhuman primates, should help us to better understand how an ability to match and perceive the affective state of others converges with moral emotional processes in producing moral judgment as well as behavior.

We have come a long way from Descartes' assertion that animals are mere automata to research that shows that monkeys hooked up to a neural interface can learn to control a robot arm with their thoughts (Carmena et al., 2003). By many measures, nonhuman primates are sophisticated actors, and learning about their sociality is helping us to understand how the stage for morality has been set by natural selection. The stage for morality may be set by nature, but we write the scenes for our human morality plays. In the play *Everyman* the

---

[11]An increasing number of Japanese adolescents and young adults is withdrawing from society by shutting themselves in their rooms for years on end. This acute social withdrawal process has been labeled as a seemingly new psychiatric phenomenon referred to as *hikikomori* (Watts, J., 2002). The systematic study of this phenomenon has only just begun and the relevance to the comparative study of moral development is readily apparent.

protagonist embarks on a journey that ultimately results in learning an important moral lesson. For humanity's sake, we can only hope that for the human primate the journey has only just begun.

REFERENCES

Abott, H. H., Keverne, E. B., Bercovitch, F. B., Shively, C. A., Mendoza, S. P., Saltzman, W., Snowdon, C. T., Ziegler, T. E., Banjecvic, M., Garland, T., Jr., & Sapolsky, R. (2002). Are subordinates always stressed? A comparative analysis of rank differences in cortisol levels among primates. *Hormones and Behavior, 43*(1), 67–82.

Alexander, R. D. (1987). *The biology of moral systems.* New York: Aldine de Gruyter.

Arnold, K., & Barton, R. A. (2001). Post-conflict behaviour of spectaccled leaf monkeys (*Trachipithecus obscurus*). II Contact with third parties. *International Journal of Primatology, 22,* 243–266.

Arnold, K., & Whiten, A. (2001). Post-conflict behaviour of wild chimpanzees (*Pan troglodytes schweinfurthii*) in the Budongo forest, Uganda. *Behaviour, 138,* 649–690.

Aureli, F. (1992). Post-conflict behaviour among wild long-tailed macaques (*Macaca fascicularis*). *Behavioral Ecology and Sociobiology, 31,* 329–337.

Aureli, F. (1997). Post-conflict anxiety in nonhuman primates: The mediating role of emotion in conflict resolution. *Aggressive Behavior, 23,* 315–328.

Aureli, F., Cords, M., & van Schaik, C. P. (2002). Conflict resolution following aggression in gregarious animals: A predictive framework. *Animal Behaviour, 64,* 325–343.

Aureli, F., Cozzolino, R., Cordischi, C., & Scucchi, S. (1992). Kin-directed redirection among Japanese macaques: An expression of a revenge system? *Animal Behaviour, 44,* 283–291.

Aureli, F., Das, M., & Veenema, H. (1997). Differential kinship effect on reconciliation in three species of macaques (*Macaca fascicularis, M. fuscata,* and *M. sylvanus*). *Journal of Comparative Psychology, 111,* 91–99.

Aureli, F., Preston, S. D., & de Waal, F. B. M. (1999). Hear rate responses to social interactions in free-moving rhesus macaques (*Macaca mulatta*): A pilot study. *Journal of Comparative Psychology, 113,* 59–65.

Aureli, F., & Schaffner, C. M. (2002). Relationship assessment through emotional mediation. *Behaviour, 139,* 393–420.

Aureli, F., & Smucny, D. (2000). The role of emotion in conflict and conflict resolution. In F. Aureli & F. B. M. de Waal (Eds.), *Natural conflict resolution.* Berkeley, CA: University of California Press.

Aureli, F., & van Schaik, C. P. (1991). Post conflict behaviour in long-tailed macaques (*Macaca fascicularis*). *American Journal of Primatology, 19,* 39–51.

Aureli, F., van Schaik, C. P., & van Hooff, J. A. R. A. M. (1989). Functional aspects of reconciliation among captive long-tailed macaques (*Macaca fascicularis*). *American Journal of Primatology, 19,* 39–51.

Aureli, F., Veenema, H. C., van Panthaleon van Eck, C. J., & van Hooff, J. A. R. A. M. (1993). Reconciliation, consolation, and redirection in Japanese macaques (*Macaca fuscata*). *Behaviour, 124,* 1–21.

Aureli, F., & Whiten, A. (2003). Emotions and behavioral flexibility. In D. Maestripieri (Ed.), *Primate psychology* (pp. 289–323). Cambridge, MA: Harvard University Press.

Axelrod, R., & Hamilton, W. D. (1981). The evolution of cooperation, *Science, 211,* 1390–1396.

Azuma, H. (1986). Why study child development in Japan? In H. Stevenson, H. Azuma, & K. Hakuta (Eds.), *Child development and education in Japan* (pp. 3–12). New York: Freeman.

Azuma, H. (1994). Two modes of cognitive socialization in Japan and the United States. In P. Greenfield & R. Cocking (Eds.), *Cross-cultural roots of minority child development* (pp. 275–284). Hillsdale, NJ: Lawrence Erlbaum Associates.

Bargh, J. A. (1994). The four horsemen of automaticity: Awareness, intention, and control in social cognition. In R. S. Wyer, Jr. & T. K. Srull (Eds.), *Handbook of social cognition* (Vol. I, pp. 1–40). Hillsdale, NJ: Lawrence Erlbaum Associates.

Barnett, M. A. (1987). Empathy and related responses in children. In N. Eisenberg & J. Strayer (Eds.), *Empathy and its development* (pp. 146–162). Cambridge, UK: Cambridge University Press.

Barrett, L., Gaynor, D. , Henzi, P. (2002). A dynamic interaction between aggression and grooming reciprocity among female chacma baboons. *Animal Behaviour, 663,* 1047–1053.

Barrett, L., & Henzi, S. P. (2001). The utility of grooming in baboon groups. In R. Noë, J. A. R. A. M. van Hooff, & P. Hammerstein (Eds.), *Economics in nature.* (pp. 119–145). Cambridge, UK: Cambridge University Press.

Batson, C. D., & Oleson, K. C. (1991). Current status of the empathy-altruism hypothesis. In M. Clark (Ed), *Review of personality and social psychology: Prosocial behavior* (pp. 62–85). Newbury Park, CA: Sage.

Batson, C. D., & Shaw, L. L. (1991). Evidence for altruism: Toward a pluralism of prosocial motives. *Psychological Inquiry, 2,* 107–122.

Baumeister, R. F., & Leary, M. R. (1995). The need to belong: desire for interpersonal attachments as a fundamental human motivation. *Psychological Bulletin, 117*(3), 497–529.

Baumeister, R. F., Stillwell, A. M., & Heatherton, T. F. (1994). Guilt: An interpersonal approach. *Psychological Bulletin, 115,* 243–2667.

Bernstein, I. S. (1980). Dominance: A theoretical perspective for ethologists. In D. R. Omark, F. F. Strayer, & D. G. Freedman (Eds.), *Dominance relations: An ethological view of human conflict and social interaction.* New York: Garland.

Bernstein, I. S. (1991). The correlation between kinship and behavior in non-human primates. In P. G. Hepper (Ed.), *Kin recognition* (pp. 6–29). Cambridge, UK: Cambridge University Press.

Blair, R. J. R. (1995). A cognitive developmental approach to morality: investigating the psychopath. *Cognition, 57*(1), 1–29.

Boesch, C., & Boesch, H. (1989). Hunting behavior of wild chimpanzees in the Taï National Park. *American Journal of Physical Anthropology, 78,* 547–573.

Boesch, C., & Boesch-Acherman, H. (2000). *The chimpanzees of the Taï forest: Behavioral ecology and evolution.* Oxford: Oxford University Press.

Boinski, S. (1994). Affiliation patterns among male Costa Rican squirrel monkeys. *Behaviour, 130,* 191–209.

Bovet, D., & Washburn, D. A. (2003). Rhesus macaques (*Macaca mulatta*) categorize unknown conspecifics according to their dominance relations. *Journal of Comparative Psychology, 117*(4), 400–405.

Bowlby, J. (1969). *Attachment and loss: Attachment.* New York: Basic Books.

Bowlby, J. (1973). *Attachment and loss: Separation: Anxiety and anger.* New York: Basic Books.

Boyd, R. (1992). The evolution of reciprocity when conditions vary. In A. H. Harcourt & F. B. M. de Waal (Eds.), *Coalitions and alliances in humans and other animals* (pp. 473–489). Oxford: Oxford University Press.

Brosnan, S. F., & de Waal, F. B. M. (2002). A proximate perspective on reciprocal altruism. *Human Nature, 13,* 129–152.

Brosnan, S. F., & de Waal, F. B. M. (2003). Monkeys reject unequal pay. *Nature, 425,* 297–299.

Bukowski, W. M., & Sippola, L. K. (1996). Friendship and morality: (How) are they related? In W. M. Bukowski, A. F. Newcomb, & W. W. Hartup (Eds.), *The company they keep. Friendship in childhood and adolescence* (pp. 238–261). Cambridge, UK: Cambridge University Press.

Butovskaya, M., & Kozintsev, A. G. (1999). Aggression, friendship, and reconciliation in primary school children. *Aggressive Behavior, 25,* 125–139.

Butovskaya, M. L, Verbeek, P., Ljungberg, T., & Lunardini, A. (2000). A multicultural view of peacemaking among young children. In F. Aureli & F. B. M. de Waal (Eds.), *Natural conflict resolution* (pp. 243–260). Berkeley: University of California Press.

Cabanac, M. (2002). What is emotion? *Behavioural Processes, 60,* 69–83.

Carmena, J. M., Lebedev, M. A., Crist, R. E., O'Doherty, J. E., Santucci, D. M., Dimitrov, D. F., Patil, P. G., Henriquez, C. S., & Nicolelis, M. A. L. (2003). Learning to control a brain-machine interface for reaching and grasping by primates. *PloS Biology, 1*(2), 1–16.

Caryl, P. G. (1979). Communication by agonistic displays: What can game theory contribute to ethology? *Behaviour, 68,* 136–169.

Castles, D. L., & Whiten, A. (1998). Post-conflict behaviour of wild olive baboons. II. Stress and self-directed behaviour. *Ethology, 104,* 148–160.

Chapais, B. (1983). Dominance, relatedness, and the structure of female relationships in rhesus monkeys. In R. A. Hinde (Ed.), *Primate social relationships: An integrated approach* (pp. 209–219). Sunderland, MA: Sinauer Associates.

Chapais, B. (1992). The role of alliances in social inheritance of rank among female primates. In A. H. Harcourt & F. B. M. de Waal (Eds.), *Coalitions and alliances in humans and other animals* (pp. 29–59). Oxford: Oxford Science Publications.

Chance, M. R. A. (1984). Biological systems synthesis of mentality and the nature of the two modes of mental operation: Hedonic and agonic. *Man-Environment Systems, 14,* 143–157.

Charlesworth, W. R. (1996). Co-operation and competition: Contributions to an evolutionary and developmental model. *International Journal of Behavioral Development, 19,* 25–39.

Cheney, D. L. (1983). Extrafamilial alliances among vervet monkeys. In R. A. Hinde (Ed.), *Primate social relationships: An integrated approach* (pp. 278–286). Sunderland, MA: Sinauer Associates.

Church, R. M. (1959). Emotional reactions of rats to the pain of others. *Journal of Comparative & Physiological Psychology, 52,* 132–134.

Cimbora, D. M., & McIntosh, D. N. (2003). Emotional responses to antisocial acts in adolescent males with conduct disorder: A link to affective morality. *Journal of Clinical Child and Adolescent Psychology, 23*(2), 296–301.

Clutton-Brock, T. H., & Parker, G. A. (1995). Punishment in animal societies. *Nature, 373,* 209–216.

Cohen, D., & Strayer, J. (1996). Empathy in conduct disordered and comparison youth. *Developmental Psychology, 32,* 988–998.

Colvin, J. (1983). Description of sibling and peer relationships among immature male rhesus monkeys. In *Primate social relationships: An integrated approach* (pp. 20–27). Oxford: Blackwell Scientific.

Constable, J. L., Ashley, M. V., Goodall, J., & Pusey, A. E. (2001). Noninvasive paternity assignment in Gombe chimpanzees. *Molecular Ecology, 10*(5), 1279–1300.

Cords, M. (1995). Predator vigilance costs of allogrooming in wild blue monkeys. *Behaviour, 132,* 559–569.

Cords, M. (1997). Friendship, alliances, reciprocity and repair. In A. Whiten & R. W. Byrne (Eds.), *Machiavellian intelligence II* (pp. 24–49). Cambridge, UK: Cambridge University Press.

Cords, M. (2002). Friendship among adult female blue monkeys. *Behaviour, 139,* 291–314.

Cords, M., & Killen, M. (1998). Conflict resolution in human and nonhuman primates. In J. Langer & M. Killen (Eds.), *Piaget, evolution, and development* (pp. 193–218). Mahwah, NJ: Lawrence Erlbaum Associates.

Cords, M., & Thurnheer, S. (1993). Reconciliation with valuable partners by long-tailed macaques. *Ethology, 93,* 315–325.

Cosmides, L., & Tooby, J. (2000). Evolutionary psychology and the emotions. In M. Lewis & J. M. Haviland-Jones (Eds.), *Handbook of emotions* (2nd ed., pp. 91–3115). New York: Guilford Press.

Darwin, C. (1871/1981). *The descent of man.* Princeton, NJ: Princeton University Press..

Das, M., Penke, Z., & van Hooff, J. A. R. M. (1998). Postconflict affiliation and stress related behavior of long-tailed macaque aggressors. *International Journal of Primatology, 19,* 53–71.

Datta, S. B. (1983). Patterns of agonistic interference. In R. A. Hinde (Ed.), *Primate social relationships* (pp. 289–297). Oxford: Blackwell.

de Waal, F. B. M. (1977). The organization of agonistic relations within two captive groups of Java-monkeys (*Macaca fascicularis*). *Zeitschrift für Tierpsychogologie, 44,* 225–282.

de Waal, F. B. M. (1982/1998). *Chimpanzee politics: Power and sex among apes* Baltimore, MD: The Johns Hopkins University Press.

de Waal, F. B. M. (1986). The integration of dominance and social bonding in primates. *Quarterly Review of Biology, 661,* 459–479.

de Waal, F. B. M. (1989). *Peacemaking among primates.* Cambridge, MA: Harvard University Press.

de Waal, F. B. M. (1991a). Complementary methods and convergent evidence in the study of primate social cognition. *Behaviour, 118,* 297–320.

de Waal, F. B. M. (1991b). The chimpanzee's sense of social regularity and its relation to the human sense of justice. *American Behavioral Scientist, 34,* 335–349.

de Waal, F. B. M. (1991c). Rank distance as a central feature of rhesus monkey social organization: A sociometric analysis. *Animal Behaviour, 41,* 383–395.

de Waal, F. B. M. (1996). *Good natured: The origin of right and wrong in humans and other animals.* Cambridge, MA: Harvard University Press.

de Waal, F. B. M. (1997a). The chimpanzee's service economy: Food for grooming. *Evolution and Human Behavior, 18,* 375–386.

de Waal, F. B. M. (1997b). Food-transfers through mesh in brown capuchins. *Journal of Comparative Psychology, 111,* 370–380.

de Waal, F. B. M. (1997c). *Bonobo: The forgotten ape.* Berkeley, CA, University of California Press.

de Waal, F. B. M. (2000a). Primates-A natural heritage of conflict resolution. *Science, 289,* 586–590.

de Waal, F. B. M. (2000b). Attitudinal reciprocity in food sharing among brown capuchin monkeys. *Animal Behaviour, 60,* 253–361.

de Waal, F. B. M. (2001). *The ape and the sushi master.* New York: Basic Books.

de Waal, F. B. M., & Aureli, F. (1996). Conflict resolution and distress alleviation in monkeys and apes. In C. S. Carter, B. Kirkpatrick, & I. Lenderhendler (Eds.), *The integrative neurobiology of affiliation* (pp. 317–328). New York: Annals of the New York Academy of Sciences.

de Waal, F. B. M., & Aureli, F. (1997). Consolation, reconciliation, and a possible cognitive difference between macaque and chimpanzee. In A. E. Russon, K. A. Bard, & S. T. Parker

(Eds.), *Reaching into thought: The minds of the great apes* (pp. 80–110). Cambridge, UK: Cambridge University Press.

de Waal, F. B. M., & Berger, M. L. (2000). Payment for labor in monkeys. *Nature, 404,* 563.

de Waal, F. B. M., & Davis, J. M. (2003). Capuchin cognitive ecology: cooperation based on projected returns. *Neuropsychologia, 41,* 221–228.

de Waal, F. B. M., & Luttrell, L. M. (1988). Mechanisms of social reciprocity in three primate species: symmetrical relationship characteristics or cognition? *Ethology and Sociobiology, 9,* 101–118.

de Waal, F. B. M., & Luttrell, L. M., & Canfield, M. E. (1993). Preliminary data on voluntary food sharing in brown capuchin monkeys. *American Journal of Primatology, 29,* 73–78.

de Waal, F. B. M., & van Roosmalen, A. (1979). Reconciliation and consolation among chimpanzees. *Behavioral Ecology and Sociobiology, 5,* 55–66.

de Waal, F. B. M., & Yoshihara, D. (1983). Reconciliation and redirected affection in rhesus monkeys. *Behaviour, 85,* 224–241.

Drews, C. (1993). The concept and definition of dominance in animal behaviour. *Behaviour, 125,* 283–313.

Dunn, J., & Slomkowski, C. (1992). Conflict and the development of social understanding. In C. U. Shantz & W. W. Hartup (Eds.), *Conflict in child and adolescent development* (pp. 70–92). Cambridge, UK: Cambridge University Press.

Eisenberg, N. (2000). Emotion, regulation, and moral development. *Annual Review of Psychology, 51,* 665–697.

Eisenberg, N., & Fabes, R. A. (1991). Prosocial behavior and empathy: A multimethod developmental perspective. In P. Clark (Ed.), *Review of personality and social psychology* (Vol. 12, pp. 34–61). Newbury Park, CA: Sage.

Fabes, R. A., Eisenberg, N., & Eisenbud, L. (1993). Behavioral and physiologica correlates of children's reactions to others in distress. *Developmental Psychology, 29,* 655–663.

Fabes, R. A., Eisenberg, N., Karbon, M., Bernzweig, J., Speer, A. L., & Carlo, G. (1994). Socialization of children's vicarious emotional responding and prosocial behavior: Relations with mothers' perceptions of children's emotional reactivity. *Developmental Psychology, 30,* 44–55.

Fehr, E., & Gächter, S. (2002). Altruistic punishment in humans. *Nature, 415,* 137–140.

Feistner, A. T. C., & McGrew, W, C. (1989). Food-sharing in primates: a critical review. In P. Seth & S. Seth (Eds.), *Perspectives in primate biology* (pp. 21–36). New Delhi: Today and Tomorrow' Press.

Fessler, D. T., & Haley, K. J. (2003). The strategy of affect: Emotions in human cooperation. In P. Hammerstein (Ed.), *Genetic and cultural evolution of cooperation.* Cambridge, MA: MIT Press.

Fiske, A. P. (1992). Four elementary forms of sociality: Framework for a unified theory of social relations. *Psychological Review, 99,* 689–723.

Flack, J. C., & de Waal, F. B. M. (2000). Any animal whatever. Darwinian building blocks of morality in monkeys and apes. *Journal of Consciousness Studies, 7*(1–2), 1–29.

Forgas, J. P. (1995). Mood and judgment: The affect infusion model. *Psychological Bulletin, 117,* 39–66.

Fox, M. W. (1975). Evolution of social behavior in canids. In M. W. Fox (Ed.), *The wild canids. Their systematics, behavioral ecology and evolution.* New York: Van Nostrand.

Francis, R. C. (1988). On the relationship between aggression and social dominance. *Ethology, 78,* 223–237.

Frank, R. H. (1988). *Passions with reason: The strategic role of the emotions.* New York: Norton.

Frank, R. H. (1990). A theory of moral sentiments. In J. J. Mansbridge (Ed.), *Beyond self-interest* (pp. 71–96). Chicago: The University of Chicago Press.

Freud, S. (1918). *Totem and taboo*. Trans. A. A. Brill. New York: Moffat, Yard & Co.

Gagneux, P., Boesch, C., & Woodruff, D. (1999). Female reproductive strategies, paternity, and community structure in wild West African chimpanzees. *Animal Behaviour, 57*, 19–32.

George, C., & Main, M. (1979). Social interactions of young abused children: Approach, avoidance, and aggression. *Child Development, 50*, 306–318.

Goldberg, T., & Wrangham, R. W. (1997). Genetic correlates of social behaviour in wild chimpanzees: Evidence from mitochondrial DNA. *Animal Behaviour, 54*, 559–570.

Goodall, J. (1986). *The chimpanzees of Gombe: Patterns of behavior.* Cambridge, MA: Harvard University Press.

Gouzoules, S., & Gouzoules, H. (1987). Kinship. In B. B. Smuts, D. L. Cheney, R. M. Seyfarth, R. W. Wrangham, & T. T. Struhsaker (Eds.), *Primate societies* (pp. 299–305). Chicago: University of Chicago Press.

Gouzoules, S, & Gouzoules, H., & Marler, P. (1984). Rhesus monkey (*Macaca mulatta*) screams: Representational signaling in the recruitment of agonistic aid. *Animal Behaviour, 32*, 182–193.

Goyman, W., & Wingfield, J. C. (2004). Allostatic load, social status and stress hormones: the costs of social status matter. *Animal Behaviour, 67*, 591–602.

Greener, S. H., & Crick, N. R. (1999). Normative beliefs about prosocial behavior in middle childhood: What does it mean to be nice? *Social Development, 8*, 349–363.

Greenwald, A. G., & Banaji, M. R. (1995). Implicit social cognition: Attitudes, self esteem, and stereotypes. *Psychological Review, 102*, 4–27.

Gros-Louis, J., Perry, S., & Manson, J. H. (2003). Violent coalitionary attacks an intraspecific killing in wild white-faced capuchin monkeys (*Cebus capucinus*). *Primates, 44*(4), 341–346.

Haidt, J. (2001). The emotional dog and its rational tail: A social intuitionist approach to moral judgment. *Psychological Review, 108*, 814–834.

Haidt, J. (2003a). The emotional dog does learn new tricks: A reply to Pizarro and Bloom *Psychological Review, 110*(1), 197–198.

Haidt, J. (2003b). The moral emotions. In R. J. Davidson, K. R. Scherer, & H. H. Goldsmith (Eds.), *Handbook of affective sciences* (pp. 852–870). Oxford: Oxford University Press.

Hamilton, W. D. (1963). The evolution of altruistic behavior. *American Naturalist, 96*, 354–356.

Hamilton, W. D. (1964). The genetical evolution of social behaviour, II. *Journal of Theoretical Biology, 7*, 17–52.

Hamilton, W. D. (1971). Selection of selfish and altruistic behavior. In J. F. Eisenberg & W. S. Dillon (Eds.), *Man and beast: Comparative social behavior* (pp. 59–91). Washington, DC: Smithsonian Institution Press.

Hammarskjöld, D. (1983). *Markings*. New York: Ballantine Books.

Harlow, H. F., & Harlow, M. K. (1965). The affectional systems. In A. M. Schier, H. F. Harlow, & F. Stollnitz (Eds.), *Behavior of nonhuman primates* (Vol. 2). London: Academic Press.

Hartup, W. W. (1992). Conflict and friendship relations. In C. U. Shantnz & W. W. Hartup (Eds.), *Conflict in child and adolescent development* (pp. 186–215). Cambridge, UK: Cambridge University Press.

Hartup, W. W. (1996). The company they keep: Friendships and their developmental significance. *Child Development, 67*, 1–13.

Hartup, W. W. & Stevens, N. (1997). Friendships and adaptation in the life course. *Psychological Bulletin, 121*, 355–370.

Haslam, N. (1997). Four grammars for primate social relations. In J. A. Simpson & D. T. Kenrick (Eds.), *Evolutionary social psychology* (pp. 297–316). Mahwah, NJ: Lawrence Erlbaum Associates.

Hatfield, E., Cacioppo, J. T., & Rapson, R. L. (1994). *Emotional contagion.* Cambridge, UK: Cambridge University Press.

Heekeren, H. R., Wartenburger, I., Schmidt, H., Schwintowski, H. P., & Villringer, A. (2003). An fMRI study of simple ethical decision-making. *NeuroReport, 14*(9), 1215–1219.

Helwig, C. C., & Turiel, E. (2002). Children's social and moral reasoning. In C. Hart & P. Smith (Eds.), *Handbook of childhood social development* (pp. 475–490). Malden, MA: Blackwell.

Hemelrijk, C. K. (1994). Support for being groomed in long-tailed macaques, *Macaca fascicularis, Animal Behaviour, 48,* 479–481.

Henrich, J., & Gil-White, F. J. (2001). The evolution of prestige. Freely conferred deference as a mechanism for enhancing the benefits of cultural transmission. *Evolution and Human Behavior, 22,* 165–196.

Henzi, S. P., & Barrett, L. (1999). The value of grooming to female primates. *Primates, 40,* 47–59.

Hinde, R. A. (2002). *Why good is good. The sources of morality.* London: Routledge.

Hoffman, M. L. (1982). Development of prosocial motivation: Empathy and guilt. In N. Eisenberg (Ed.), *The development of prosocial behavior.* New York: Academic Press.

Hume, D. (1739/1969). *A treatise of human nature.* London: Penguin.

Imanishi, K. (1960). Social organization of subhuman primates in their natural habitat. *Current Anthropology, 1,* 393–407.

Ishida, T. (1969). Beyond the traditional concepts of peace in different cultures. *Journal of Peace Research, 6,* 133–145.

Itani, J. (1985). The evolution of primate social structures. *Man, 58,* 593–611.

Jahoda, G. (1983). European "lag" in the development of an economic concept: A study in Zimbabwe. *British Journal of Developmental Psychology, 1,* 113–120.

Kiehl, K. A., Smith, A. M., Hare, R. D., Menderk, A., Forster, B. B., Brink, J., & Liddle, P. F. (2001). Limbic abnormalities in affective processing by criminal psychopaths as revealed by functional magnetic resonance imaging. *Biological Psychiatry, 50*(9), 677–684.

Killen, M., Ardila-Rey, A., Barakkatz, M., & Wang, P-L. (2000). Preschool teachers perceptions about conflict resolution, autonomy, and the group in four countries: United States, Colombia, El Salvador, and Taiwan. *Early Education & Development, 11,* 73–92.

Killen, M., Crystal, D. S., & Watanabe, H. (2002). Japanese and American children's evaluations of peer exclusion, tolerance of differences, and prescriptions for conformity. *Child Development, 73*(6), 1788–1802.

Killen, M., & de Waal, F. B. M. (2000). The evolution and development of morality. In F. Aureli & F. B. M. de Waal (Eds.), *Natural conflict resolution* (pp. 352–372). Berkeley: University of California Press.

Killen, M., & Hart, D. (1995). *Morality in everyday life: Developmental perspectives.* Cambridge, UK: Cambridge University Press.

Killen, M. & Nucci, L. P. (1995). Morality, autonomy, and social conflict. In M. Killen D. Hart (Eds.), *Morality in everyday life: Developmental perspectives* (pp. 52–86). Cambridge, UK: Cambridge University Press.

Killen, M., & Sueyoshi, L. (1995). Conflict resolution in Japanese social interactions. *Early Education and Development, 6,* 317–334.

Kobayashi-Winata, H., & Power, T. G. (1989). Child rearing and compliance: Japanese and American families in Houston. *Journal of Cross-Cultural Psychology, 20,* 333–356.

Kropotkin, P. (1902). *Mutual aid: A factor in evolution.* London: Alan Lane.

Kummer, H. (1971). *Primate societies*. Chicago: Aldine.

Kummer, H., Dasser, V., & Hoyningen-Huene, P. (1990). Exploring primate social cognition: Some critical remarks. *Behaviour, 112*, 84–98.

Kutsukake, N., & Matsusaka, T. (2002). Incident of intense aggression by chimpanzees against an infant from another group in Mahale Mountains National Park, Tanzania. *American Journal of Primatology, 58*(4), 175–180.

Ladygina-Kohts, N. N. (1935/2001). *Infant chimpanzee and human child: A classic 1935 comparative study of ape emotions and intelligence*. Ed. F. B. M. de Waal. New York: Oxford University Press.

Lane, R. D., & Nadel, L. (2000). *Cognitive neuroscience of emotion*. New York: Oxford University Press.

Laursen, B., & Hartup, W. W. (1989). The dynamics of preschool children's conflicts. *Merrill-Palmer Quarterly, 35*, 281–297.

Laursen, B., & Hartup, W. W. (2002). The origins of reciprocity and social exchange in friendships. In B. Laursen & W. G. Graziano (Eds.), *Social exchange in development*. New Directions for Child and Adolescent Development (No 95, pp. 27–40). San Franciso: Jossey-Bass.

Lazarus, R. S. (1991). *Emotion and adaptation*. New York: Oxford University Press.

Lebra, T. S. (1994). Mother and child in Japanese socialization: A Japan-US comparison. In P. Greenfield & R. Cocking (Eds.), *Cross-cultural roots of minority child development* (pp. 259–274). Hillsdale, NJ: Lawrence Erlbaum Associates.

Lévi-Straus, C. (1969). *The elementary structures of kinship, revised edition*. London: Eyre & Spottiswoode.

Lewis, C. C. (1988). Cooperation and control in Japanese nursery schools. In G. Handle (Ed.), *Childhood socialization* (pp. 125–142). New York: Aldine de Gruyter.

Lewis, C. C. (1995). *Educating hearts and minds: Reflections on Japanese preschool and elementary education*. Cambridge, UK: Cambridge University Press.

Lewis, M. (1993). Self-conscious emotions: Embarrassment, pride, shame, and guilt. In M. Lewis & J. Haviland (Eds.), *Handbook of emotions* (pp. 563–573). New York: Guilford Press.

Lieberman, D., Tooby, J., & Cosmides, L. (2002). Does morality have a biological basis? An empirical test of the factors governing moral sentiments relating to incest. *Proceedings of the Royal Society of London, B. Biological Sciences, 270*(1517), 819–826.

Lorenz, K. (1963/1966). *On aggression*. New York: Harvest/Harcourt Brace Jovanovich.

Lotem, A., Fishman, M. A., & Stone, L. (2003). From reciprocity to unconditional altruism through signaling benefits. *Proceedings Royal Society London B: Biological Sciences, 270*, 199–205.

Lovelock, J. (1991). Mother earth: Myth or science? In C. Barlow (Ed.), *From Gaia to selfish genes*. Cambridge, MA: MIT Press.

Lydon, J. E., Jamieson, D. W., & Holmes, J. G. (1997). The meaning of social interactions in the transition from acquaintanceship to friendship. *Journal of Personality and Social Psychology, 73*, 536–548.

Maestripieri, D., Schino, G., Aureli, F., & Troisi, A. (1992). A modest proposal: Displacement activities as indicators of emotions in primates. *Animal Behavior, 44*, 967–979.

Main, M., & George, C. (1985). Responses of abused and disadvantaged toddlers to distress in agemates: A study in the day care setting. *Developmental Psychology, 21*, 407–412.

Manson, J. H., Rose, L. M., Perry, S., & Gros-Louis, J. (1999). Dynamics of female female relationships in wild *Cebus capucinus*: data from two Costa Rican sites. *International Journal of Primatology, 20*, 697–706.

Mason, W. A. (1965). Determinants of social behavior in young chimpanzees. In A. M. Schrier, H. F. Harlow & F. Stollnitz (Eds.), *Behavior of nonhuman primates* (pp. 335–364). New York: Academic Press.

Masserman, J., Wechkin, M. S., & Terris, W. (1964). Altruistic behavior in rhesus monkeys. *American Journal of Psychiatry, 121,* 584–585.

Massey, A. (1977). Agonistic aids and kinship in a group of pigtail macaques. *Behavioral Ecology and Sociobiology, 2,* 31–40.

McCullough, M. E., Emmons, R. A., Kilpatrick, S. D., & Larson, D. B. (2001). Is gratitude a moral affect? *Psychological Bulletin, 127*(2), 249–266.

Mendres, K. A., & de Waal, F. B. M. (2000). Capuchins do cooperate: The advantage of an intuitive task. *Animal Behaviour, 60,* 523–529.

Milinksi, M., Semmann, D., & Krambeck, H. J. (2002). Donors to charity gain in both indirect reciprocity and political reputation. *Proceedings Royal Society London B: Biological Sciences, 269*(1494), 881–883.

Mills. J., & Clark, M. S. (1994). Communal and exchange relationships: Controversies and research. In R. Erber & R. Gilmour (Eds.), *Theoretical frameworks for personal relationships* (pp. 29–42). Hillsdale, NJ: Lawrence Erlbaum Associates.

Mitani, J. C., Watts, D. P., & Muller, M. N. (2002). Recent developments in the study of wild chimpanzee behavior. *Evolutionary Anthropology, 11,* 9–25.

Moll, J., de Oliveira-Souza, R., & Eslinger, P. J. (2003). Morals and the human brain: A working model. *Neuroreport, 14*(3), 299–305.

Moll, J., de Oliveira-Souza, R., Eslinger, P. J., Bramati. I. E., Mourao-Miranda, J., Andreiuolo, P. A., & Pessoa, L. (2002). The neural correlates of moral sensitivity: A functional magnetic resonance imaging investigation of basic and moral emotions. *Journal of Neuroscience, 22*(7), 2730–2736.

Morgan, C. L. (1894). *An introduction to comparative psychology.* London: W. Scott.

Mori, A., Belay G., & Iwamoto, T. (2003). Changes in unit structures and infanticide observed in Arsi geladas. *Primates, 44,* 217–223.

Nesse, R. M. (1990). Evolutionary explanations of emotions. *Human Nature, 1,* 261–289.

Nichols, S. (2002). Norms with feeling: Towards a psychological account of moral judgment. *Cognition, 84*(2), 221–236.

Nishida, T., Hiraiwa-Hasegawa, M., Hasegawa, T., & Takahata, Y. (1985). Group extinction and female transfer in wild chimpanzees in the Mahale Mountains National Park, Tanzania. *Zeitschrift für Tierpsychologie, 67,* 281–301.

Nishida, T., Hasegawa, T., Hayaki, H., Takahata, Y., & Uehara, S. (1992). Meat-sharing as a coalition strategy by an alpha male chimpanzee? In T. Nishida, W. C. McGrew, P. Marler, M. Pickford & F. B. M. de Waal (Eds.), *Topics in primatology, Vol. I: Human origins* (pp. 159–174). Basel: Karger.

Nishida, T., Hosaka, K., Nakamura, M., & Hamai, M. (1995). A within-group gang attack on a young adult male chimpanzee: Ostracism of an ill-mannered member? *Primates, 36,* 207–211.

Noë, R., & Sluijter, A. A. (1995). Which adult male savanna baboons form coalitions? *International Journal of Primatology, 16,* 77–105.

Noë, R., van Schaik, C. P., & van Hooff, J. A. R. A. M. (1991). The market effect: An explanation for pay-off asymmetries among collaborating animals. *Ethology, 87,* 97–118.

Nowak, M. A., & Sigmund, K. (1998). Evolution of indirect reciprocity by image scoring. *Nature, 393,* 573–576.

O'Connell, S. M. (1995). Empathy in chimpanzees: Evidence for theory of mind. *Primates, 36,* 397–410.

O'Connor, L. E., Berry, J. W., Weiss, J., & Gilbert, P. (2002). Guilt, fear, submission, and empathy in depression. *Journal of Affective Disorders, 71,* 19–27.

Panksepp, J. (1998). *Affective neuroscience.* New York: Oxford University Press.

Panksepp, J., Moskal, J. R., Panksepp, J. B., & Kroes R. A. (2002). Comparative approaches in evolutionary psychology: Molecular neuroscience meets the mind. *Neuroendocrinology Letters Special Issue, 23*(Suppl. 4), 105–115.

Parr, L. A. & de Waal, F. B. M. (1999). Visual kin recognition in chimpanzees. *Nature, 399,* 647–648.

Parr, L. A., Matheson, M. D., Bernstein, I. S., & de Waal, F. B. M. (1997). Grooming down the hierarchy: allogrooming in captive brown capuchin monkeys. *Animal Behaviour, 54,* 361–367.

Perry, S. (1996). Female-female social relationships in wild white-faced capuchin monkeys (*Cebus capucinus*). *American Journal of Primatology, 40,* 167–182.

Perry, S. & Rose, L. (1994). Begging and transfer of coati meat by white-faced capuchin monkeys, *Cebus capucinus. Primates, 35,* 409–415.

Petit, O., & Thierry, B. (1994). Reconciliation in a group of Guinea baboons (*Papio papio*). In J. J. Roeder, B. Thierry, J. R. Anderson, & N. Herrenschmidt (Eds.), *Current primatology* (Vol. 2, pp. 137–145). Strasbourg: Université Louis Pasteur.

Piaget, J. (1932/1965). *The moral judgment of the child.* Trans. M. Gabain. New York: Free Press.

Pizarro, D. A., & Bloom, P. (2003). The intelligence of the moral intuitions: Comment on Haidt (2001). *Psychological Review, 110*(1), 193–196.

Popp, J. L., & DeVore, I. (1979). Aggressive competition and social dominance theory: Synopsis. In D. Hamburg & E. McCown (Eds.), *The great apes* (pp. 317–338). Menlo Park, CA: Benjamin/Cummings.

Potegal, M. (2000). Post-tantrum affiliation with parents. The ontogeny of reconciliation. In F. Aureli & F. B. M. de Waal (2000). *Natural conflict resolution* (pp. 253–255). Berkeley: University of California Press.

Potegal, M., Kosorok, M. R., & Davidson, R. J. (1996). The time course of angry behavior in the temper tantrums of young children. *Annals of the New York Academy of Sciences, 749,* 31–45.

Preston, S. D., & de Waal, F. B. M. (2002). Empathy: Its ultimate and proximate bases. *Behavioral and Brain Sciences, 25*(1), 1–20.

Preuschoft, S., & van Schaik, C. P. (2000). Dominance and communication. Conflict management in various social settings. In F. Aureli & F. B. M. de Waal (Eds.), *Natural conflict resolution.* Berkeley: University of California Press.

Preuschoft, S., Wang, X., Aureli, F., & de Waal, F. B. M. (2001). Reconciliation in captive chimpanzees: a re-evaluation with controlled methods. *International Journal of Primatology, 23,* 29–50.

Ridley, M. (1996). *The origins of virtue.* New York: Penguin Books.

Roberts, W., & Strayer, J. (2003, April). Towards, away, and against: Emotions and prosocial behavior. In K. Kokko & S. Côté (Chairs), *Prosocial and aggressive behaviors over the life course.* Symposium conducted at the meeting of the Society for Research in Child Development, Tampa, FL.

Rothbaum, F., Pott, M., Azuma, H., Miyake, K., & Weisz, J. (2000). The development of close relationships in Japan and the United States: Paths of symbiotic harmony and generative tension. *Child Development, 71,* 1121–1142.

Rozin, P., Lowery, L., Imada, S., & Haidt, J. (1999). The CAD triad hypothesis: A mapping between three moral emotions (contempt, anger, disgust) and three moral codes (community, autonomy, divinity*). Journal of Personality and Social Psychology, 76,* 574–586.

Russell, J. A. (2003). Core affect and the psychological construction of emotion. *Psychological Review, 110*(1), 145–172.

Sanfey, A. G., Rilling, J. K., Aronson, J. A., Nystrom, L. E., & Cohen, J. D. (2003). The neural basis of economic decision-making in the ultimatum game. *Science, 300,* 1755–1758.

Sapolsky, R. M. (1990). Adrenocortical function, social rank, and personality among wild baboons. *Biological Psychiatry, 28,* 862–878.

Sapolsky, R. M. (1993). Endocrinology alfresco: Psychoendocrine studies of wild baboons. *Recent Progress in Hormone Research, 48,* 437–468.

Schino, G., Perretta, G., Taglioni, A. M., Monaco, V., & Troisi, A. (1996). Primate displacement activities as an ethopharmacological model of anxiety. *Anxiety, 2,* 186–191.

Seyfarth, R. M. (1977). The model of social grooming among adult female monkeys. *Journal of Theoretical Biology, 65,* 671–698.

Seyfarth, R. M., & Cheney, D. L. (1984). Grooming, alliances, and reciprocal altruism in vervet monkeys. *Nature, 308,* 541–543.

Silk, J. B. (1982). Altruism among female *Macaca radiata*: Explanations and analysis of patterns of grooming and coalition formation. *Behaviour, 79,* 162–168.

Silk, J. B. (1992). The patterning of intervention among male bonnet macaques: Reciprocity, revenge, and loyalty. *Current Anthropology, 33,* 318–325.

Silk, J. B. (2001). Ties that bond: The role of kinship in primate societies. In L. Stone (Ed.), *New directions in anthropological kinship* (pp. 71–92). Boulder, CO: Rowman and Littlefield.

Silk, J. B. (2002a). Using the "f" word in primatology. *Behaviour, 139,* 421–446.

Silk, J. B. (2002b). The form and function of reconciliation in primates. *Annual Review of Anthropology, 31,* 21–44.

Silk, J. B. (in press). The evolution of cooperation in primate groups. In H. Gintis, S. Bowles, R. Boyd & E. Fehr (Eds.), *Moral sentiments and material interests: On the foundations of cooperation in economic life*. Cambridge, MA: MIT Press.

Smith, A. (1759/1976). *The theory of moral sentiments*. Ed. A. M. Kelley, D. D. Raphaek & A. L. Macfie. Oxford: Clarendon Press.

Smucny, D. A., Price, C. S., & Byrne, E. A. (1997). Post-conflict affiliation and stress reduction in captive rhesus macaques. *Advances in Ethology, 32,* 157.

Smuts, B. B., Cheney, D. L., Seyfarth, R. M., Wrangham, R. W., & Struhsaker, T. T. (1987). *Primate societies*. Chicago: University of Chicago Press.

Stamps, J. A. (1991). Why evolutionary issues are reviving an interest in proximate behavioral mechanisms. *American Zoologist, 31,* 338–348.

Stamps, J. (2003). Behavioural processes affecting development: Tinbergen's fourth question comes of age. *Animal Behaviour, 66,* 1–13.

Stone, V. E., Cosmides, L., Tooby, J., Kroll, N., & Knight, T. (2002). Selective impairment of reasoning about social exchange in a patient with bilateral limbic system damage. *Proceedings National Academy of Science, 99*(17), 11531–11536.

Strayer, F. F. (1992). The development of agonistic and affiliative structures in preschool play groups. In J. Silverberg & P. Gray (Eds.), *Aggression and peacefulness in humans and other primates* (pp. 150–172). Oxford: Oxford University Press.

Strier, K. B. (2000). From binding brotherhoods to short-term sovereignty: The dilemma of male Cebida. In P. M. Kappeler (Ed.), *Primate males* (pp. 72–83). Cambridge, UK: Cambridge University Press.

Teleki, G. (1973). *The predatory behavior of wild chimpanzees*. Lewisburg: Bucknell University Press.

Trevarthen, C. (1980). The foundations of intersubjectivity: Development of Interpersonal and cooperative understanding in infants. In D. Olson (Ed.), *The social foundations of language and thought*. New York: W. W. Norton.

Turiel, E. (2002). *The culture of morality*. Cambridge, UK: Cambridge University Press.

Turiel, E., & Neff, K. (2000). Religion, culture, and beliefs about reality in moral reasoning. In K. S. Rosengren, C. N. Johnson, & P. L. Harris (Eds.), *Imagining the impossible: Magical, scientific, and religious thinking in children* (pp. 269–304). New York: Cambridge University Press.

Trivers, R. L. (1971). The evolution of reciprocal altruism. *Quarterly Review of Biology, 46,* 35–57.

Trivers, R. L. (1985). *Social evolution*. Menlo Park, CA: Benjamin/Cummings.

van Hooff, J. A. R. A. M., & Aureli, F. (1994). *Social homeostasis and the regulation of emotion*. In S. H. M. van Goozen, N. E. van de Poll, & J. A. Sergeant (Eds.), *Emotions: Essays on emotion theory*. Hillsdale, NJ: Lawrence Erlbaum Associates.

van Schaik, C. P., & van Hooff, J. A. R. A. M. (1983). On the ultimate causes of primate social systems. *Behaviour, 85,* 91–117.

Varna, V. (1993). *How and why children hate*. London: Kingsley.

Veenema, H. C., Das, M., & Aureli, F. (1994). Methodological improvements for the study of reconciliation.*Behavioural Processes, 31,* 29–38.

Verbeek, P. (1995). *Agonism and its aftermath in a captive group of* Cebus apella. Master's Thesis, Emory University.

Verbeek, P., Hartup, W. W., & Collins, W. A. (2000). Conflict management in children and adolescents. In F. Aureli & F. B. M. de Waal (Eds.), *Natural conflict resolution* (pp. 34–53). Berkeley: University of California Press.

Verbeek, P., & de Waal, F. B. M. (1997). Postconflict behavior of captive brown capuchins in the presence and absence of attractive food. *International Journal of Primatology, 18*(5), 703–725.

Verbeek, P., & de Waal, F. B. M. (2001). Peacemaking among preschool children. *Peace and Conflict. Journal of Peace Psychology, 7,* 5–28.

Verbeek, P., & de Waal, F. B. M. (2002). The primate relationship with nature: Biophilia as a general pattern. In P. H. Kahn & S. R. Kellert (Eds.), *Children and nature: Psychological, sociocultural and evolutionary investigations*. Cambridge, MA: MIT Press.

Walker, L. J. (1996) Is one sex morally superior? In M. R. Merrens & G. G. Brannigan (Eds.), *The developmental psychologists. Research adventures across the life span* (pp. 173–188). New York: McGraw-Hill.

Watanabe, K. (1979). Alliance formation in a free-ranging troop of Japanese macaques. *Primates, 20,* 459–474.

Watanabe, S., & Ono, K. (1986). An experimental analysis of "empathic" response: Effects of pain reactions of pigeon upon other pigeon's operant behavior. *Behavioural Processes, 13,* 269–277.

Watts, D. P. (1995). Post-conflict social events in wild mountain gorillas. II. Redirection, side directions and consolation. *Ethology, 100,* 158–174.

Watts, D. P. (2002). Reciprocity and interchange in the social relationships of wild male chimpanzees. *Behaviour, 139,* 343–370.

Watts, D. P., Colmenares, F., & Arnold, K. (2000). Redirection, consolation, and male policing: how targets of aggression interact with bystanders. In F. Aureli & F. B. M. de Waal (Eds.), *Natural conflict resolution* (pp. 281–301). Berkeley: University of California Press.

Watts, D. P., Mitani, J. C., & Sherrow, H. M. (2002). New cases of inter-community infanticide by male chimpanzees at Ngogo, Kibale National Park, Uganda. *Primates, 43*(4), 263–270.

Watts, J. (2002). Tokyo public health experts concerned about "hikikomori." *The Lancet, 359*(9312), 1131.

Weaver, A.C., & de Waal, F. B. M. (2000). The development of reconciliation in brown capuchin monkeys. In F. Aureli & F. B. M. de Waal (Eds.), *Natural conflict resolution* (pp. 216–218). Berkeley: University of California Press.

Westermarck, E. (1921). *The history of human marriage* 5th ed. *Edition*. London: Macmillan.

Westermarck, E. (1906/1924). *The origin and development of the moral ideas, in two volumes* (2nd ed.). London: Macmillan.

Wilson, E. O. (1975). *Sociobiology: The new synthesis.* Cambridge, MA: Belknap Press, Harvard University Press.

Wilson, J. Q. (1993). *The moral sense.* New York: Free Press.

Wolf, A. P. (1995). *Sexual attraction and childhood association: A Chinese brief for Edward Westermarck.* Stanford, CA: Stanford University Press.

Wrangham, R. (1987). Evolution of social structure. In B. B. Smuts, D. L. Cheney, R. M. Seyfarth, R. W. Wrangham & T. T. Struhsaker (Eds.), *Primate societies* (pp. 282–297). Chicago: Chicago University Press.

Wrangham, R. (1999). Evolution of coalitionary killing. *Yearbook Physical Anthropology, 42,* 1–30.

Yamada, M. (1963). A study of blood-relationship in the natural society of the Japanese macaque-an analysis of co-feeding, grooming, and playmate relationships in Minoo-B troop. *Primates, 4,* 43–65.

Yerkes, R. M. (1925). *Almost human.* New York: Century.

Zahn-Waxler, C., Hollenbeck, B., & Radke-Yarrow, M. (1984). The origins of empathy and altruism. In: M. W. Fox & L. D. Mickley (Eds.), *Advances in animal welfare science,* (pp. 21–39). Washington, DC: Humane Society of the United States.

Zahn-Waxler, C., & Smith, K. D. (1992). The development of prosocial behavior. In V. B. Van Hasselt & M. Hersen (Eds.), *Handbook of social development* (pp. 229–256). New York: Plenum Press.

Zahn-Waxler, Radke-Yarrow, Wagner, E., & Chapman, M. (1992). Development of Concern for others. *Developmental Psychology, 28,* 126–136.

Zahn-Waxler, C., Friedman, R., Cole, P., Mizuta, I., & Hiruma, N. (1996). Japanese and United States preschool children's responses to conflict and distress. *Child Development, 67,* 2462–2477.

Zajonc, R. B. (1980). Feeling and thinking: Preferences need no inferences. *American Psychologist, 35,* 151–175.

NATURE AND MORAL DEVELOPMENT

PETER H. KAHN, JR.
UNIVERSITY OF WASHINGTON

Whatever disagreements exist about morality, and there are many, people understand that morality deals with people's relationships with other people. Yet is it also possible that people have moral relationships with nature? With animals? Plants? Bodies of water? Landscapes? The earth? In this chapter, I discuss empirical and conceptual literature across diverse fields that answers yes to these question. Moreover, I believe this literature supports the proposition that nature plays an important and perhaps irreplaceable role in moral development and the moral life.

In providing this account, I build on a broad framing of the moral domain. Morality includes the traditional moral–developmental view, as circumscribed by Piaget (1932/1969) and Kohlberg (1984), that focuses on justice, rights, and obligations. Morality also includes a broader set of considerations focused on long-term character traits, virtue, human flourishing, and a teleology asking what it means to be fully human and to live meaningfully, and seeking moral endpoints for human lives. This broader view of morality dates back to Aristotle's delineation in *Nichomachean Ethics* of the ethical virtues (e.g., courage, temperance, friendship, wisdom, and justice), and has been drawn on by both modern moral philosophers (Foot, 1978; MacIntyre, 1984; Williams, 1985) and developmental psychologists (Campbell & Christopher, 1996; Lourenço, 2000).

The course of this chapter is as follows. The first section reviews literature on children's interactions with animals, the role of animals as moral facilitators in children's residential treatment centers, the development of environmental moral reasoning, and adolescents' moral environmental activism. Section 2 focuses on the field of conservation behavior. Section 3 brings together diverse literatures that suggest that connection to nature enhances people's physical and psychological well-being. Section 4 extends this last idea and suggests that humans, in ancestral times, came of age not only with nature, but with wild nature, and that this connection to wildness remains an essential human need. Section 5 seeks an answer to the question, if humans need connection with nature, let alone wild nature, then why are humans destroying nature so readily? Finally, Section 6 suggests that moral relationships with nature do not develop independently of human–human moral relationships, but dialectically inform one another in ontogenesis.

THE DEVELOPMENT OF CHILDREN'S MORAL RELATIONSHIPS WITH NATURE

If it is difficult for the reader to think of nature as having moral standing, or of a child being in a moral relationship with a nonhuman moral other, think of animals. Think of a dog. Kick one, and by most accounts it feels pain. Kick a boulder, and by most accounts only your foot hurts. It would appear, then, that the dog's sentiency—its capability to feel pain— establishes some form of human obligation such that, for example, one cannot with moral impunity bash open the skulls of domestic animals for personal enjoyment. Indeed, such sentiency grounds various philosophical theories of animal rights. For example, Regan (1986) argues that "[p]ain is pain wheresoever it occurs. If your neighbor's causing you pain is wrong because of the pain that is caused, we cannot rationally ignore or dismiss the moral relevance of the pain your dog feels" (p. 33).

Yet how is it that children even come to care about the sentiency of animals? In a year-long study in a preschool setting, Myers (1998) focused on 3- to 6-year-old-children's relationships with a wide variety animals, including a dog, turtles, a guinea pig, goldfish, doves, ferrets, pythons, a spider monkey, bugs, and squirrels. Based on his observations, field notes, interviews, and videotaped sessions, Myers proposes that young children begin to understand that animals display four properties that remain constant across many different interactions: *agency* (a dog decides to eat and acts accordingly), *affectivity* (a dog appears to enjoy playing with the child), *coherence* (a dog is able to coordinate its movements in response to the child's actions), and *continuity* (the dog's repeated interactions become regularized into a relationship with the child). Such understandings make it possible for children to recognize that animals have their own subjective states and can have interests in interacting with the child ("my dog wants to play with me"). In Myers' (1998) view, "animals appear to be optimally discrepant social others by the time of early childhood, offering just the right amount of similarity to and difference from the human pattern and other animal patterns to engage the child. Crucially, animals are social others . . . because they display the hallmarks of being truly subjective others" (p. 10).

Because children come to understand an animal as a social other, animals can become a source of companionship and support. For example, Covert, Whirren, Keith, and Nelson (1985) found that 75% of the children in their study between ages 10 and 14 said that they turned to their pets when they were upset. More generally, Melson (2001) writes in her account of animals in the lives of children that one "of the most important yet unrecognized functions of pets—from dogs to goldfish—for children may be their *thereness*. . . . This constant availability may be a major reason why many children bestow the honorific 'my best friend' on their pets. . . . Their animate, responsive proximity makes children feel less alone in a way that toys and games, television or video, even interactive media, cannot" (p. 59).

Children's understanding an animal as a social other also appears to lead at least some children to accord moral standing to animals. One 4-year-old girl in Myers (1998) study, for example, said that it is wrong to squish a spider "because it has to have its freedom" (p. 147). Myers also found that preschool children frequently expressed moral sensitivity to harms to animals. For example, in one field note entry, Myers recorded the language two children used in attributing animal emotion and desire as the reason for why a turtle put its head back in its shell after a child touched its tail: "Maybe . . . Cause he's scared. . . . [Another child then says]: Maybe he doesn't want us to do that" (p. 90).

In other literature, Kahn and Friedman (1995) interviewed 72 economically impoverished African-American urban children in first, third, and fifth grades about their environmental views and values. Results showed that 84% of the children said that animals were an important part of their lives. In their reasons, 11% of these children's justifications emphasized biocentric considerations, including that animals have intrinsic values or rights. For example, one fifth-grade child said that it is wrong to throw garbage in a local waterway because "Fishes, they want to live freely, just like we live freely. . . . They have to live in freedom, because they don't like living in an environment where there is so much pollution that they die every day" (p. 1412). Thus not only does this child accord fish desires ("they want to live freely") but embeds such desires within a judgment for humans to respect such desires (not to pollute the waterway) because it would cause harm to the fish ("there is so much pollution that they die every day").

Moral dimensions of children's relationships with animals have emerged as well in the therapeutic literature. For example, Katcher and Wilkins (1993, 1998, 2000) have engaged in over a decade of work with children diagnosed with autism, developmental disorder, attention-deficit hyperactivity disorder, conduct disorder, and oppositional-defiant disorder, structuring interventions around children's interactions with animals. Katcher and Wilkins found that such children persisted in learning the skills and information necessary for them to handle the animals. Moreover, through such interactions with animals, these children also demonstrated an increase in attention span, a decrease in hostile and aggressive behavior, and an increase in cooperative behavior. Indeed, the skill and care these children displayed in handling and caring for the animals led visitors frequently to ask, "Why are these children in residential treatment?" One part of an explanation may be that animals, in the words of Myers (1998), "pose less potential [than humans] for deceit, competition, manipulation, betrayal, and rejection" (p. 115). Katcher (2002), for example, reports that when children were bitten by small rodents (as they frequently were) they "explained the biting as defensive: 'He was frightened,' 'I held him too tightly,' 'I reached in the cage too quickly'" (p. 182). According the Katcher (2002), these children also "accepted the authority of the zoo instructors as legitimate and not imposed by force or institutional control" (p. 185).

Children's moral relationships with nature may begin with animals, but it does not end there. Rather, at a minimum, it appears that children sometimes bring moral obligatory reasoning to bear on their relationship with nonsentient nature as well. For example, in a series of studies, Kahn and his colleagues (Howe, Kahn, & Friedman, 1996; Kahn, 1997, 1999; Kahn & Friedman, 1995; Kahn & Lourenço, 2002) examined children's environmental moral reasoning by drawing on the social domain literature of Turiel (1983, 1998), Nucci (1981, 1996), Smetana (1983, 1995), and others where a moral obligation is assessed, in part, based on the criterion judgments of prescriptivity (the act under consideration is judged not all right to perform), rule contingency (the act is not all right to perform even if the law or a rule says it is all right), and generalizability (the act is not all right for people in another country to perform, even if people in that country perform the act). Based on these criterion judgments, and in consort with children's moral justifications, results showed across diverse populations that the majority of the children believed it was morally obligatory not to throw garbage in a local waterway. Oftentimes children's reasons focused on the harm such actions would bring to human beings or animals living in the water or depending upon the water source. But sometimes children also showed concern for the intrinsic value of nonsentient nature itself. For example, one fifth-grade African-American child from the inner city of Houston Texas said that it is not all right to throw trash in their local bayou, "Because water is what nature made; nature didn't make water to be purple and stuff like that, just one color. When you're dealing with what nature made, you need not destroy it" (Kahn, 1999, p. 162). Similarly, a fifth-grade Brazilian child living in a remote village near the headwaters of the Amazon River said that it is not all right to throw trash in their river (the Rio Negro), "Because the river was not made to have trash thrown in it, because the river belongs to nature" (p. 162). In both cases, a child offers a moral conception (in terms of a teleology) of the proper endpoint of nature, and that the good arises with nature reaching that end and being complete.

This literature—although only emerging in recent years—suggests that children develop moral relationships with (and engage in moral reasoning about) both sentient and nonsentient nature. It is also the case that nature provides a powerful content area by which to structure moral education. As a case in point, consider Thomashow's (2002) teaching of high school students in New Hampshire. Instead of lecturing to them about environmental issues, she found means to engage them in actual environmental decision making. Specifically, abutting a little-known 287-acre river park was a 2.3-acre parcel of land that the city was trying to decide how best to manage. Thomashow worked with the city government and citizen groups such that they agreed that a group of adolescent students would be given control for what happened to this piece of land. Following this agreement, the adolescents worked long hours garnering, sorting, and synthesizing relevant data (including much time spent on the land and surrounding areas). They developed alternative environmental managements plans, and agreed on one in particular: that people would be able to circumnavigate the 2.3-acre area but not go into the interior, so as to protect its fauna and flora. However, at a subsequent City Council meeting, the city's planning board said that they had received a grant to build a boardwalk into the interior of the 2.3 acre area. At the point, heated controversy ensued, because the adolescents believed the city was reneging on their agreement. Toward the end of the meeting, the student spokesperson stood up and said:

> This is not about the boardwalk. . . . This is about including us as citizens in this decision and keeping your promise. We didn't take this responsibility lightly. We have done our best to research and make the best possible decision for the good of the land and the people of Keene. You simply have to believe in us and honor your commitment. This is about whether you really think we are a part of this city, whether we deserve to make a decision that affects the place where we live. Your decision to involve us, or not, will determine our future commitment to this town and to public decision-making. (pp. 269–270)

This student's statement helped to sway the council, and to put into place a long-term program whereby students were asked to manage seven other pieces of public land. Thus, in this case, the protection of nature was embedded within a moral educational framework not unlike that of Kohlberg's just community (Kohlberg, 1980; Power, 1988). Adolescents were given real power to effect change and correlative duties to do so responsibly, worked cooperatively, sought to understand the views and values of other stakeholders, and sought to build community on a social and political level.

CONSERVATION BEHAVIOR

In human–human relationships, acts often come under moral purview even if the magnitude of harm is small. For example, if I steal your BIC pen, most people would consider my act as wrong from a moral perspective. In contrast, in human–nature relationships, the magnitude of harm itself often plays a critical role in establishing whether the act comes under moral purview. For example, if I pick up some fallen branches in the woods for firewood, most people would say "that's fine." Yet if the same act is conducted by thousands of people in the same location, the cumulative action can (and in many places does) lead to deforestation and the ecological collapse of the area. In this new context, most people would consider the same initial act (of a single individual picking up fallen branches for firewood) as wrong from a moral perspective. The point here is that we live in a world of increasing population and decreasing natural resources. Accordingly, conservation behavior has become a moral activity, and warrants our consideration.

The classic studies in the area of conservation behavior have focused on recycling behavior. For example, De Young (1989) investigated the views of thirty-two recyclers and fifty-nine nonrecyclers. He found that both groups were similar in their prorecycling attitudes, extrinsic motivation, and the degree to which they viewed recycling as important. However, the groups differed in terms of the degree to which they required additional information about recycling. Nonrecyclers said that they lacked information about how to recycle (e.g., how much space and time to allot to the activity, what can be recycled, how material must be prepared, and where to go for assistance). De Young proposed that, in shaping people's recycling behaviors, attitudes may often matter less than correct information. Other studies have focused on changing people's recycling behavior by controlling the reward structures (Diamond & Loewy, 1991) and the force of communication about the importance of the activity (Burn & Oskamp, 1986). Elsewhere in the literature, studies have focused on water and energy conservation. For example, Moore, Murphy, and Watson (1994) found over a 3-year period that water conservation was increased by the influence of media interventions and water costs. They also found that reported conserving behavior was better predicted by stated intentions than by knowledge. Along similar lines, Brandon and Lewis (1999) found that income and demographic features did not predict increased energy conservation, but that environmental attitudes (coupled with informational feedback) did.

Many factors have been examined that might underlay and predict conservation behavior. These factors include environmental concern (Dunlap, Vanliere, Mertig, & Jones, 2000), stated intentions (Moore et al., 1994), lifestyle choices (Leonard-Barton, 1981), informational techniques (De Young, 1989; Vining & Ebreo, 1990), positive motivational techniques (De Young & Kaplan, 1985/1986), environmental attitudes (Guagnano, Dietz, & Stern, 1995; Kaiser, Wölfing, & Fuhrer, 1999; Werner et al., 1995), values (Schultz & Zelezny, 1999; Schwarz, 1994; Vining & Ebreo, 1992), and intrinsic satisfactions (De Young, 1985/1986; Lee & De Young, 1994). However, perhaps the most overarching finding from this body of research is that all such factors are only weakly related to pro-environmental behaviors (Vining & Ebreo, 2002).

Given the comparatively large amount of research conducted in this area, why has it not led to more generalized and important results? One answer is that it has been poorly served by its emphasis on behavior, prediction, and simple causal linkages, as if there are direct external factors (such as economic costs, framed as contingencies of reinforcement) or internal factors (such as a value) that explain conservation behavior. But as social domain theorists have cogently argued (Killen, 1989, 1990; Smetana, Bridgemen, & Turiel, 1983; Turiel, 1983, 1998, 2002; Turiel & Davidson, 1986), social behaviors are often related to diverse forms of reasoning within a domain (vertical organization) and to the coordination of reasoning across domains (horizontal organization). For example, in his reanalysis of the Milgram experiment, Turiel (1983) showed that subjects' decision of whether or not to continue shocking an experimental confederate drew substantively on not only subjects' moral considerations (e.g., of harm to others) but social conventional considerations (e.g., of expectations not to disrupt a scientific study sanctioned by a prestigious university). Thus, conservation behavior needs not so much to be linked to specific judgments but situated within the structural organizations of social knowledge.

Another answer is that the field of conservation behavior has not been grounded within a developmental framework. For example, in Vining and Ebreo's (2002) review of the literature on theoretical and methodological perspectives on conservation behavior, the words *child* or *children* do not appear even once. There are at least two reasons that this absence seems problematic. The first is that to effect change societally, we need to influence children and engage them substantively in the issues of import so that they are positioned to become responsible citizens if not leaders. This point seems obvious: Educate children. And conduct research with children to help support the educational process. The second reason addresses a critique that has been leveled at the field of conservation behavior, that it has offered little in the way of new or powerful theorizing (Vining & Ebreo, 2002). What I would suggest, following Piaget's (1971a, 1971b) account of genetic epistemology, is that psychological theories gain validity when foundational constructs are shaped by a dialectic between philosophical categories of knowledge and their psychological genesis. For example, in the moral domain it is not enough to say that an "is" does not lead to an "ought" (the naturalistic fallacy), and then engage in merely speculative philosophical theorizing about what morality requires. Rather, it is increasingly recognized that an "ought" also implies a "can"—that a valid moral philosophical theory needs to build on an accurate account of moral development and moral capabilities (Scheffler, 1986, 1992; Williams, 1985). What this means for the field of conservation behavior is that it needs to pay greater attention to its foundational constructs (e.g., is "behavior" even the best way to frame the issues of interest?) and developmental origins.

CONNECTION TO NATURE FOR PHYSICAL AND PSYCHOLOGICAL WELL-BEING

Virtually all moral theories take seriously human physical and psychological well-being. Consequentialist theories, for example, do so perhaps most directly by framing a theory in terms of what produces the best state of human affairs overall (as judged from an impersonal standpoint giving equal weight to the interest of everyone), where "best" is usually closely aligned with what is physically and psychologically best for humans (Scheffler, 1988; Smart & Williams, 1973). Similarly, deontological theories to a large degree are concerned about justice and rights because such matters impact people's physical and psychological well-being (Beehler, 1978). In other words, an account of what promotes human physical and psychological well-being is necessary for moral theory, and for that matter for most anyone who seeks to help others and society at large.

The proposition I would like to advance, then, is that connection to nature fosters physical and psychological well-being; and this connection is too often overlooked in psychological accounts of human development. As a starting point to support this proposition, consider a study conducted by Ulrich (1984), who examined the potential differences in the recovery of patients after gallbladder surgery depending on whether the patients were assigned to a room with a view of a natural setting (a small stand of deciduous trees) or a view of a brown brick wall. Patients were paired on relevant variables that might effect recovery (e.g., age, sex, weight, tobacco use, and previous hospitalization). The results showed that "patients with the natural window view had shorter postoperative hospital stays, and far fewer negative comments in nurses' notes ('patient is upset,' 'needs much encouragement') and tended to have lower scores for minor postsurgical complications such as persistent headache or nausea requiring medication. Moreover, the wall-view patients required many more injections of potent painkillers, whereas the tree-view patients more frequently received weak oral analgesics such as acetaminophen" (Ulrich, 1993, p. 107).

Other studies have supported the restorative effects of nature, whether it is viewed directly or as a visual representation. For example, Moore (1982, cited in Ulrich, 1993) found that prison inmates whose cells looked out onto nearby farmlands and forests needed less health care services than inmates whose cells looked out onto the prison yard. In a dental clinic, Heerwagen (1990) presented patients with either a large mural depicting a spatially open natural landscape or no mural at all. Patient data included heart rate measurements and affective self-ratings. Results suggest that patients felt less stressed on days when the mural was present. In another study, Ulrich and colleagues (1991) exposed 120 participants to a stressful movie, and then to videotapes of various natural and urban settings. They collected data on stress recovery through subjects' self-ratings of affective states, as well as heart rate, muscle tension, skin conductance, and pulse transit time. Taken together, their results showed that stress "recovery was faster and more complete when subjects were exposed to natural rather than urban environments" (p. 201).

Although nature has been shown to be restorative, nature is not a homogenous construct, and certain forms of nature have been shown to be more restorative than others. For example, Ulrich and Lunden (1990) randomly assigned 166 patients undergoing open-heart surgery with visual stimulation of two different types of nature pictures (either an open view with water or a moderately enclosed forest scene), an abstract picture, or a control condition consisting of either a white panel or no picture at all. Their results showed that the patients exposed during surgery to the picture of an open nature view with water experienced much less postoperative anxiety than the control groups and the groups exposed to the other types of pictures.

Kaplan and Kaplan have approached this topic from a different direction with similar results. Namely, they have conducted extensive research on individuals' preferences for different sorts of landscapes (Kaplan & Kaplan, 1989; see also, e.g., R. Kaplan, 1973, 1977, 1985; and S. Kaplan, 1983, 1987, 1992). They found, for example, that low-action waterscapes were "a highly prized element in the landscape" (p. 9). So were landscapes that were open, yet defined, with "relatively smooth ground texture and trees that help define the depth of the scene" (p. 48). According to Kaplan and Kaplan, such landscapes "can be called parklike or woodlawn or savanna" (p. 48). In contrast, they found that people consistently reported low preferences for settings that were blocked, such as a dense tangle of understory vegetation dominating the foreground of a scene. Such findings did not appear to be directly attributable to a wide variety of competing explanations, such as knowledge about an environment, urban versus rural upbringing, or race.

Why do people's preferences for nature fall out in this pattern? Early research by Wohlhill (1968) provided tentative evidence that middle levels of complexity—the richness or number of different objects in the scene—largely explained environmental preferences. Kaplan and Kaplan found partial support for this hypothesis insofar as people did not prefer scenes that lacked complexity. Yet high degrees of complexity did not by itself increase preference. Thus, it "is now quite clear that there is more to experimental aesthetics than optimal complexity" (S. Kaplan, 1992, p. 595). Kaplan and Kaplan (1989) found, for example, that in judging landscapes people appear "to be heavily influenced by the potential for functioning in the setting. Thus indications of the possibility of entering the setting, of acquiring information, and of maintaining one's orientation emerge as consistently vital attributes" (p. 38). In particular, two important landscape characteristics emerged in their research. One characteristic they call *legibility*—that one could find one's way back if one ventured further into the scene depicted. Such scenes offer visual access, but with distinct and varied objects to provide notable landmarks. A second characteristic they call *mystery*—that one could acquire more information by venturing deeper into the scene and changing one's vantage point. Such scenes include winding paths, meandering streams, and brightly lit areas partially obscured by some foliage.

As with healthy landscapes, human contact with animals can also promote physiological health and psychological well-being. Consider, for example, the common aquariums that—at least in years past—inhabit waiting rooms in many dental offices. Does the conspicuous placement of these aquariums reflect but an arbitrary cultural convention? In a simple experiment, Katcher, Friedmann, Beck, and Lynch (1983) found that watching an aquarium resulted in significant decreases in blood pressure below the resting level in both hypertensive and normal subjects. In a more detailed experiment, Katcher, Segal, and Beck (1984) examined the influence of aquarium contemplation on patients about to undergo oral surgery. After the surgery, the oral surgeon (who was unaware of the nature of the pretreatment) made assessments of the patients' comfort level during surgery, as did an observer, and the patient. Results showed that aquarium contemplation was as effective as hypnosis in relaxing patients and in increasing their comfort level during surgery. In another study (Beck & Katcher, 1996, chap. 1) researchers examined the influence of pets on the course of heart disease. Tracking ninety-two patients, and accounting for social variables known to be associated with mortality from heart disease, it was found that the mortality rate among people with pets was about one-third of patients without pets. Contact with animals also positively affects people who have organic or functional mental disorders (see Katcher & Wilkins, 1993, for a review). For example, hundreds of clinical reports show that when animals enter the lives of aged patients with chronic brain syndrome (which follows from either Alzheimer's disease or arteriosclerosis) that the patients smile and laugh more, and become less hostile to their caretakers and more socially communicative. A number of studies also show that through interactions with animals (such as a dog, cat, bird, dolphin, or even small turtle) autistic children have more focused attention, social interaction, positive emotion, and speech.

In Kaplan and Kaplan's (1989) reading of hundreds of studies, they conclude that the "immediate outcomes of contacts with nearby nature include enjoyment, relaxation, and lowered stress levels. In addition, the research results indicate that physical well-being is affected by such contacts. People with access to nearby-natural settings have been found to be healthier than other individuals. The longer-term, indirect impacts also include increased levels of satisfaction with one's home, one's job, and with life in general" (p. 173). "Viewed as an amenity," Kaplan and Kaplan (1989) write, "nature may be readily replaced by some greater technological achievement. Viewed as an essential bond between humans and other living things, the natural environment has no substitutes" (p. 203).

WILDNESS AND HUMAN FLOURISHING

Some scholars have not only focused on the physical and psychological benefits of connection to nature, but emphasized that humans came of age in the company of wildness—wild animals, wild landscapes—and that this connection to wildness still comprises a fundamental human need.

Shepard (1978, 1995, 1996, 1998) has been one of the strongest proponents of this view. For example, Shepard (1998) writes that the transformation of societies from hunter-gatherer to agrarian took place over the past twelve thousand years, which is insignificant "in terms of human history that began with the appearance of *Homo sapiens* some four hundred thousand years ago, our genus, *Homo*, at two million years, and our family, *Hominidae*, six million years ago" (p. 81). Wild animals, Shepard (1996) says, were among the first objects of classificatory thinking, and that "the human species emerged enacting, dreaming, and thinking [wild] animals and cannot be fully itself without them" (p. 4). Although Shepard acknowledges the research discussed previously that shows the physical and psychological benefits of interacting with companion animals (such as dogs and cats), it is a grudging acceptance. For in Shepard's (1996) view, domestic animals are "biological slaves who cringe and fawn or perform" as we wish, and "are not a glorious bonus on life; rather they are compensations for something desperately missing," "vestiges and fragments from a time of deep human respect for animals, whose abundance dazzled us in their many renditions of life" (p. 151).

Turner (1996), like Shepard, offers passion and on occasion biting words for the loss of wildness and our acceptance of poor substitutes:

> We visit the zoo or Sea World to see wild animals, but they have been tamed, rendered dependent, obedient. We learn nothing of their essential life in nature. We do not see them hunt or gather food. We do not see them mate. We do not see them interact with other species. We do not see them interact with their habitat. Their numbers and their movements are determined by human artifice. We see them controlled. We see them trained. In most cases they are as docile, apathetic, and bored as the people watching them. If we visit wild animals in sanctuaries, we are protected by buses and Land Rovers and observation towers. We are separated from any direct experience of the wild animals we came to visit. (p. 29)

Turner (1996) also emphasizes wild lands, and defines a place as *wild* "when its order is created according to its own principles of organization—when it is self-willed land. Native people usually (though definitely not always) 'fit' that order, influencing it but not controlling it" (p. 112). Moreover, Turner argues that such wild places have "autonomy," which does not involve a radical separation from others, but "interconnectedness, elaborate iteration, and feedback" (p. 113), which create the possibility of change and thereby freedom. Thus for Tuner—not unlike for Piaget (1932/1969) and Kohlberg (1984)—autonomy does not involve an "anything goes" mentality, but self-organization and self-regulation. Autonomy is impeded when adults are coercive—in Turner's case, when adults control land and animals; in Piaget's and Kohlberg's case, when adults coerce children. As Turner says, the "important point is that whatever kind of autonomy is in question—human freedom, self-willed land, self-ordering systems . . . all are incompatible with external control" (p. 113). For this reason, Turner argues against most of the activities carried out by environmental organizations, be they by wildlife managers or conservation biologists. Rather, he says:

> We need big wilderness, big natural habitat, not more technological information about big wilderness. Why not work to set aside vast areas where we limit all forms of human influence: no conservation strategies, no designer wilderness, no roads, no trails, no satellite surveillance, no over-flights with helicopters, no radio collars, no measuring devices, no photographs, no GPS data . . . no typographical maps. Let whatever habitat we can preserve go back to its own self-order as much as possible. Let wilderness again become a blank on our maps. (p. 120)

Against this backdrop of "self-willed land" it becomes clearer how fear of the natural plays an important role in the human experience of the wild. Fear may help us to recognize that we are not completely in control, but part of interconnected systems. "To come upon a grizzly track," Turner (1996) writes, "is to experience the wild in a most intimate, carnal way, an experience that is marked by gross alterations in attention, perception, body language, body chemistry, and emotion. Which is to say you feel yourself as part of the biological order known as the food chain, perhaps even as part of a meal" (p. 85). Fear, of course, is only one aspect of the human experience of wildness, but it is worth emphasizing because of the seeming paradox that although people seek to minimize fearful interactions in their lives so as to prosper, in so doing they may impede their own well-being. One partial explanation of this paradox may be that fear of the natural is experienced differently than fear of humans or of the human-built environment.

Physiological data bear on this proposition. In a series of studies, Öhman and his colleagues (Öhman, 1979; Öhman, Dimberg, & Öst, 1985; Öhman, Erixon, & Löfberg, 1975) created a version of a Pavlovian conditioning experiment wherein they first conditioned aversive responses by showing subjects either fear-relevant natural stimuli (such as snakes and spiders) or neutral stimuli (such as geometric figures) and paired each slide presentation with a mild electric shock. The researchers then presented the same slides ten to forty additional times without the electric shock. Based on measures of subjects' skin conductance and heart rate, they thereby assessed the extinction rate of the fear response acquired earlier. Results showed that natural fear-related stimuli were much more resistant to extinction (forgetting) than the neutral stimuli. Similar findings appeared when contrasting snakes and spiders to dangerous human artifacts such as handguns and frayed electrical wires (Cook, Hodes, & Lang, 1986; Hugdahl & Karker, 1981). Similar findings also appeared when subjects were presented with subliminal stimuli. For example, Öhman (1986; Öhman & Soares, 1993) modified the conditioning experiments such that after the learning phase (with the electric shock), subjects were presented with the same slides for 15 to 30 milliseconds (such that the slides could not be consciously recognized) and then immediately "masked" by a slide of another stimulus. Results showed that the natural fear-related stimuli (snakes and spiders), but not the other stimuli, could elicit strong aversive physiological responses (see Ulrich [1993] for a review of this body of research).

The proposition that (a) humans distinguish between fear of the natural and human, and (b) that experiencing fear of the natural, within limits, forms part of healthy psychological functioning helped to structure a study by Kahn, Saunders, and Myers (2001) conducted at Brookfield Zoo (outside of Chicago, Illinois) on children's conceptions of bats. One of the exhibits at the zoo is the "Australia House," a darkened, cave-like enclosure, about 80 feet long, that people enter and walk through. The exhibit houses Rodrigues fruit bats. One of the most notable features of this exhibit is that there is no barrier between the exhibit animals and the public. Thus, as people walk through the exhibit, they not only look at and hear the bats, but experience their immediate proximity. Indeed, as the bats fly around the mostly darkened enclosure, they at times swoop within inches of the people in the exhibit. In this context, Kahn and colleagues conducted semistructured interviews with 120 children across four age groups (6 to 7, 9 to 10, 12 to 13, and 15 to 16 years old) after the children finished the exhibit. In one set of findings, results showed that the majority of children felt a sort of fear with bats. For example, children said directly that they were afraid of bats, or believed that the bats could hurt them, or would prefer not to sleep in a place where bats could fly around freely. At the same time, children often seemed to appreciate such fear in their lives. For example, they preferred that the Australia House remain as it is (and for the zoo not to construct a wire mesh barrier between the bats and humans), or said they felt more alert in the Australia House, or rejected the analogy that their feeling around bats is anything like the feeling they get when walking down a dark city street at night. Although, from Turner's perspective, the zoo environment offers an impoverished connection to wildness, it does offer some connection, and to that extent a venue for research on this topic.

ENVIRONMENTAL GENERATIONAL AMNESIA

If the human experience of wildness—that involves living in the presence of other self-regulating systems—is still a central human need for human flourishing, it is not a need that is well recognized by modern people. Why not? One explanation is that we, as children, have come of age in an existing environment that is already degraded, and we use these conditions as the baseline to construct our knowledge of what constitutes a normal and reasonably healthy environment. The crux here is with each ensuing generation, the amount of environmental degradation increases; but each generation in its youth takes that degraded condition as the nondegraded condition, as the normal experience. Kahn (1997, 1999, 2002) has called this psychological phenomenon environmental generational amnesia.

Developmental precursors to environmental generation amnesia emerged in Kahn and Friedman's (1995) research on the environmental views and values of economically poor African-American children living in Houston, Texas. Houston is one of the more environmentally polluted cities in the United States. Local oil refineries contribute not only to the city's air pollution, but also to distinct oil smells during many of the days. Local rivers can be thought of as sewage transportation channels more than fresh waterways. Garbage is commonly found alongside the local rivers. In this context, while interviewing seventy-two children in first, third, and fifth grades, Kahn and Friedman found that although the children understood in general about the idea of air pollution, water pollution, and garbage, statistically fewer children believed that Houston had any of these problems itself. Such findings support the proposition that children are constructing an environmental baseline of normality in the context of an unhealthy environment.

On many occasions while lecturing in public, Pyle (2002) asks his audience whether they can remember a particular place in nature from their childhood, a place "they went repeatedly to play, explore, sulk, or think; a small, particular corner of the landscape where they went to make forts, catch creatures, and mess about with water and plants" (p. 306). Most people can. Then he asks his audience how many of them could return to their special places and find them substantially intact. Very few can. Most find such a realization distressing. According the Pyle, humans need not only the large wild places, but local untrammeled areas, even a vacant lot, by which to connect to nature. Such areas, according to Pyle, protect us from what he calls the extinction of experience whereby lack of interaction with rich ecosystems leads to lack of concern for their protection, which leads to further lacks of interactions. Thus the extinction of experience is a cycle whereby environmental impoverishment begets greater environmental impoverishment.

Fredston (2001) also points to the problem of environmental generational amnesia from her decades of experience rowing more than twenty thousand miles of some of the wildest coast lines in the arctic waters. On one of her trips to Norway, she mentions that much of Norway's built environment has an aesthetic that most towns in Alaska (where she lives) lack. But she adds:

> Still, even the undeniably beautiful portions of the Norwegian coast that send visitors from more developed, congested parts of Europe into raptures seemed sterile to us. . . . That experience frightened us to the marrow. It made us realize that, like the perpetually grazing sheep [in Norway], centuries of human habitation have nibbled away not only at the earth but at our perception of what constitutes nature. When we do not miss what is absent because we have never known it to be there, we will have lost our baseline for recognizing what is truly wild. In its domestication, nature will have become just another human fabrication. (p. 217)

Fredston then recognizes that the " 'Norwegianification' of Alaska is occurring, one project at a time, with each road, each bridge, each new house built where none has been before" (p. 219).

The problem of environmental generational amnesia offers an important area for future systematic research. One line of investigation could continue to focus on what children know about environmental problems, and to distinguish experiential knowledge from what DeVries (1997) calls "school varnish"— such as rote memorization of environmental problems. A second line of investigation could focus on historical events and records. For example, Hand (1997) documents that while many centuries ago the forests in the Highlands of Scotland were as "grand as any on earth" (p. 12), today they are one of the most deforested lands in the world. Yet, according to Hand, the Scots of today have virtually no conception of a forest, of its ecological vastness or beauty. Hand presents these ideas in an essay titled "The Forest of Forgetting." It is a forgetting that crosses generations. A third line of investigation could focus cross-culturally. If, as proposed, environmental generational amnesia is tied to a constructivist account of knowledge formation, then it should appear universally.

THE MORAL DIALECTIC CROSS-SPECIES

A subfield within developmental psychology—sometimes referred to as *naïve biology* (Inagaki & Hatano, 2002) or *folkbiology* (Coley, 1995; Medin & Atran, 1999)—focuses on children's conceptions of the biological world (Carey, 1985; Gelman, 2003; Gelman, Spelke, & Meck, 1983). One of the findings is that young children engage in a good deal of *personification,* which refers to "their attempts to predict and explain behaviors and properties of animals and plants by using their relatively rich knowledge about humans" (Inagaki & Hatano, 2002, p. 1). For example, a 5 year-old boy in a study by Inagaki and Hatano (2002) said: "We can't keep it (a rabbit) forever the same size. Because, like me, if I were a rabbit, I would be 5 years old and become bigger and bigger" (p. 51). Here the child applies his knowledge about human growth to an animal.

However, one could imagine a developmental account that is less unidirectional, as well as applying in the moral domain. Imagine, for example, a 4-year-old boy, John, whose home environment includes a gentle Chesapeake Bay Retriever and a 7-year-old brother. As part of exploring the world around him, imagine that one day John pulls on the ears and nose of his Retriever. Kids do these sort of things. In response, the dog gently nips John and then moves away. John then tries pulling on the ears and nose of his older brother, and the brother responds largely in kind, swatting John's hand and moving away. We can use this event, a single snapshot in time, as a place holder for the kind of events by which John constructs similarity relationships between two sentient creatures: dog and human. Next imagine that John tries sitting on the back of his dog, and again the dog gently nips and moves away; but when he tries the same activity with his older brother, he finds he gets a piggyback ride—sometimes. This event is a placeholder for John's construction of differences between dog and human, again as just a snapshot in time. The proposition is that such explorations and interactions happen daily, and on a microgenetic level lead humans to a bidirectional cross-species construction of knowledge. As Shepard (1996) suggests: "Of each species we can say, 'I am not that—and yet, just in this one respect, it is like a part of me,' and so on, as though with every 'I am not that one' we keep some bit of them. We take in the animal, disgorge part of it, discover who we are and are not" (p. 72). And, it could be added, we discover what the nonhuman world is, and is not.

Evidence for the construction of moral similarities and differences across species emerged in Kahn's (1999) research on environmental moral reasoning, and particularly his characterization of two forms of biocentric reasoning. One form occurred through establishing isomorphic relationships. Here children compared natural entities (usually animals) directly with humans. For example, one child said: "Fishes, they want to live freely, just like we live freely.... They have to live in freedom, because they don't like living in an environment were there is much pollution that they die every day" (Kahn, 1999, p. 101). Thus an animal's desire ("to live freely") is viewed to be equivalent to that of a human's desire, and because of this direct equivalency children reasoned that animals merit the same moral consideration as do humans. Such isomorphic reasoning should not be confused with *personification,* where an animal or plant is likened to a human or human quality; rather here a moral feature (such as freedom) is deemed important to both nature and humans, and on that basis a moral principle (such as to protect freedom) is applied equally to both nature and humans ("Fishes, they want to live freely, just like we live freely").

A second form of biocentric reasoning occurred through establishing transmorphic relationships. For example, a fifth-grade child said:

> Fish need the same respect as we need.... Fishes don't have the same things we have. But they do the same things. They don't have noses, but they have scales to breathe, and they have mouths like we have mouths. And they have eyes like we have eyes. And they have the same co-ordinates we have.... A co-ordinate is something like, if you have something different, then I'm going to have something, but it's going to be the same. Just going to be different. (Kahn, 1999, p. 101, 104)

This child appears to draw on a word, *co-ordinate,* he encountered in some other context to help him explain that although fish are in some respects not the same as people (they do not have noses like people do) that in important functions (such as breathing and seeing) they are the same. Thus, he moves beyond a reciprocity based on directly perceivable and salient characteristics to be able to establish moral equivalences based on functional properties. Said differently, through transmorphic reasoning the child is able now to coordinate similarities with differences cross species: a developmental achievement.

The cross-species dialectic can and often does play out not only by affirming the moral but the immoral. The literature shows, for example, close linkages between child abuse, domestic violence, and animal abuse (Ascione & Arkow, 1999). In one study, for example, Quinlisk (1999) found that of the homes that had reported domestic violence, 72% also indicated that there was animal abuse. Some of the written qualitative comments included "He killed the ferret just to scare us" (p. 170). Or "Because I was late getting home he put my cat in the microwave. The cat died later that night" (p. 170). Ascione and Arkow (1999) suggest that violence "directed against animals is often a coercion device and an early indicator of violence that may escalate in range and severity against other victims" (p. xvii). Other literature suggests that particularly aggressive acts against animals are an early indicator in children of future psychopathology (Arkow, 1999; Kellert & Felthous 1985), and that exposure to animal abuse can desensitize children to violence between humans (Ascione, 1993).

These cases highlight the (im)moral dialectic on the level of the individual. The dialectic also occurs societally when certain groups of people are likened to animals and equally mistreated. Most notably, Spiegel (1988) documents in the United States similarities between the treatment of African Americans and animals. Both have been enslaved, branded, hunted, transported, sterilized, and used without consent in painful and sometimes deadly medical experiments. The justifications often coincide, as well. Consider some of Spiegel's (1988) juxtapositions from others' published writings:

1a. "(The horse) is by Nature a very lazy animal."

1b. "The Negro if left to himself will not work, he will lie down and bask in the sun." (p. 41)

2a. "They said that the cries they [the dogs] emitted when struck, were only the noise of a little string that had been touched, but that the whole body was without feeling."

2b. "Negroes . . . are void of sensibility to a surprising degree." (p. 61)

3a. "A trained dog is a joy and pride."

3b. "A state of bondage, so far from doing violence to the law of nature, develops and perfects it; and that, in that state (the Negro) enjoys the greatest amount of happiness, and arrives at the greatest degree of perfection, of which his nature is capable." (p. 39)

4a. "Unless one is initially prepared to adopt a rather rampant anthropomorphism in respect to animals, they can have no rights."

4b. "Negroes have no rights which the white man is bound to respect." (pp. 88–89)

Some of these statements were made by distinguished people. For example, it was Justice Taney, a member of the United States Supreme Court who heard the Dred Scott case, who said that "Negroes have no rights which the white man is bound to respect."

Future research on the cross-species moral dialectic seems wide open. As shown, it could focus on early ontogeny, and basic developmental mechanisms by which children construct concepts of similarities and differences between humans and nature. It could focus on how such constructions are then implicated in moral judgments. And it could focus on mistreatments of animals and humans, in interpersonal settings (such as the family context) and as codified by a society. Throughout such investigations I would expect not only direct correspondences (e.g., an abusive father might beat his son and his dog) but complicated interplays that might be hard to predict at the onset of any investigation, particularly at the societal level.

To illustrate this point, consider Sax's (2000) booklength exposition of animals in the Third Reich. As is well known, "Nazis herded human beings, branded them with numbers, neutered them, and slaughtered them industrially, as people had traditionally done with animals" (p. 22). The Nazis also operated, according to Sax, on a fundamental paradigm based on predator and prey. Nazi ideology extolled animals like the wolf and eagle, and espoused not so much maliciousness as indifference to those it would kill. Indeed, the Nazis passed strict laws protecting animals from abuse, and proscribing in minute detail how they must be provided for, transported, bred, and slaughtered. As Himmler said, speaking to leaders of the SS in October 1943:

> Whether nations live in prosperity or starve to death interests me only in so far as we need them as slaves for our culture. . . . We shall never be rough or heartless when it is not necessary; that is clear. We Germans, who are the only people in the world who have a decent attitude toward animals, will also assume a decent attitude toward these human animals. But it is a crime against our own blood to worry about them . . . . (Fest, 1970, quoted in Sax, 2000, p. 115)

According to Sax, an "unarticulated purpose of the Nazi animal protection laws was to accustom people to think of euthanasia as a positive thing. By desensitizing people, the killing of animals helped open the way for the mass murder of human beings" (p. 169).

Of course, Nazis could treat animals brutally, as well. For example," ... some members of the SS were required to rear a German shepherd for twelve weeks, then strangle the dog under the supervision of an officer" (p. 169). But, again, such brutality often seemed to serve the larger goal of desensitizing Germans to the suffering of non-Aryan sentient life.

CONCLUSION

A good deal of research and scholarship lies at the intersection of nature and moral development. This work draws from various literatures, including developmental psychology, environmental psychology, psychophysiology, sociobiology, conservation behavior, conservation psychology, ecopsychology, human ecology, and environmental education. Taken together, the literature points in a reasonably clear direction.

As *Homo sapiens,* we came of age in close contact with a rich and varied natural environment, and to a large degree unrecognized by modern people we still depend on nature for our physical and psychological well-being. As Dubos (1968) writes: "It is questionable that man can retain his physical and mental health if he loses contact with the natural forces that have shaped his biological and mental nature" (quoted in Shepard, 1998, p. 147). Along similar lines, Kalpan and Kalpan (1989) write that as "phychologists we have heard but little about gardens, about foliage, about forest and farmland.... Perhaps this resource for enchancing health, happiness, and wholeness has been neglected long enough" (p. 198). Moreover, the importance of nature extends even further. As other literature suggest, through interactions with animals, children develop empathy and construct concepts of reciprocity and otherness that are hallmarks of human morality. Children at times reason about their relationships with nature from a moral perspective. This perspective has features that are morally obligatory (based on criterion judgments of prescriptivity, rule contingency, and generalizability) and can be based on both anthropocentric moral considerations (such as human welfare) and biocentric moral considerations (such as that nature has intrinsic value, rights, or a teleology that needs to be respected). Children's connection to wild aspects of nature, be they large tracts of undeveloped "self-willed" land or even fearful encounters with animals, allows for the development of moral understandings about autonomy, self-organization, and freedom. Finally, the literature suggests that children's moral development through interaction with nature furthers human–human morality; and vice versa, both on a microgenetic and macrogenetic level in ontogenesis.

REFERENCES

Arkow, P. (1999). The evolution of animal welfare as a human welfare concern. In F. R. Ascione and P. Arkow (Eds.), *Child abuse, domestic violence, and animal abuse: Linking the circles of compassion for prevention and intervention* (pp. 19–37). West Lafayette, IN: Purdue University Press.

Ascione, F. R. (1993). Children who are cruel to animals: A review of research and implications for developmental psychopathology. *Anthrozoös, 6*(4), 226–247.

Ascione, F. R., & Arkow, P. (Eds.). (1999). *Child abuse, domestic violence, and animal abuse: Linking the circles of compassion for prevention and intervention.* West Lafayette, IN: Purdue University Press.

Beck, A., & Katcher, A. (1996). *Between pets and people.* West Lafayette, IN: Purdue University Press.

Beehler, R. (1978). *Moral life.* New Jersey: Rowman & Littlefield.

Brandon, G., & Lewis, A. (1999). Reducing household energy consumption: A qualitative and quantitative field study. *Journal of Environmental Psychology, 19,* 75–85.

Burn, S. M. & Oskamp, S. (1986). Increasing community recycling with persuasive communication and public commitment. *Journal of Applied Social Psychology, 16,* 29–41.

Campbell, R. L., & Christopher, J. C. (1996). Moral development theory: A critique of its Kantian presuppositions. *Developmental Review, 16,* 1–47.

Carey, S. (1985). *Conceptual change in childhood.* Cambridge, MA: MIT Press.

Coley, J. D. (1995). Emerging differentiation of folkbiology and folkpsychology: Attributions of biological and psychological properties to living things. *Child Development, 66,* 1856–1874.

Cook, E. W., Hodes, R. L., & Lang, P. J. (1986). Preparedness and phobia: Effects of stimulus content on human visceral conditioning. *Journal of Abnormal Psychology, 98,* 448–459.

Covert, A. M., Whirren, A. P., Keith, J., & Nelson, C. (1985). Pets, early adolescents, and families. *Marriage and Family Review, 8,* 95–108.

DeVries, R. (1997). Piaget's social theory. *Educational Researcher, 26*(2), 4–17.

De Young, R. (1985/1986). Encouraging environmentally appropriate behavior: The role of intrinsic motivation. *Journal of Environmental Systems, 15,* 281–292.

De Young, R. (1989). Exploring the difference between recyclers and non-recyclers: The role of information. *Journal of Environmental Systems, 18,* 341–351.

De Young, R., & Kaplan, S. (1985/1986). Conservation behavior and the structure of satisfactions. *Journal of Environmental Systems, 15,* 233–242.

Diamond, W. D & Loewy, B. Z. (1991). Effects of probabilistic rewards on recycling attitudes and behavior. *Journal of Applied Social Psychology, 21,* 1590–1607.

Dubos, R. (1968). Environmental determinants of human life. In David C. Glass (Ed.), *Environmental influences* (pp. 149–150). New York: Rockefeller University Press.

Dunlap, R. E., VanLiere, K. D., Mertig, A. G., & Jones, R. E. (2000). Measuring endorsement of the New Ecological Paradigm: A revised NEP scale. *Journal of Social Issues, 56,* 425–442.

Fest, J. (1970). *The face of the Third Reich: Portraits of the Nazi leadership.* Trans. Michael Bullock. New York: Pantheon.

Foot, P. (1978). *Virtues and vices.* Berkeley and Los Angeles: University of California Press.

Fredston, J. (2001). *Rowing to latitude: Journeys along the Arctic's edge.* New York: North Point Press.

Gelman, R., Spelke, E., & Meck, E. (1983). What preschoolers know about animate and inanimate objects. In D. Rogers & J. A. Sloboda (Eds.), *The acquisitions of symbolic skills* (pp. 297–326). New York: Plenum.

Gelman, S. (2003). *The essential child: Origins of essentialism in everyday thought.* New York: Oxford University Press.

Guagnano, G. A., Stern, P. C., & Dietz, T. (1995). Influences on attitude-behavior relationships: A natural experiment with curbside recycling. *Environment and Behavior, 27,* 699–718.

Hand, G. (1997). The forest of forgetting. *Northern Lights, 13*(1), 11–13.

Heerwagen, J. (1990). The psychological aspects of windows and window design. In K. H. Anthony, J. Choi, & B. Orland (Eds.), *Proceedings of the 21st Annual Conference of the Environmental Design Research Association.* Oklahoma City: EDRA.

Howe, D., Kahn, P. H., Jr., & Friedman, B. (1996). Along the Rio Negro: Brazilian children's environmental views and values. *Developmental Psychology, 32,* 979–987.

Hugdahl, K., & Karker, A. C. (1981). Biological vs. experiential factors in phobic conditioning. *Behavior Research and Therapy, 19,* 109–115.

Inagaki, K., & Hatano, G. (2002). *Young children's naïve thinking about the biological world.* New York: Psychology Press.

Kahn, P. H., Jr. (1997). Children's moral and ecological reasoning about the Prince William Sound oil spill. *Developmental Psychology, 33,* 1091–1096.

Kahn, P. H., Jr. (1999). *The human relationship with nature: Development and culture.* Cambridge, MA: MIT Press.

Kahn, P. H., Jr. (2002). Children's affiliations with nature: Structure, development, and the problem of environmental generational amnesia. In P. H. Kahn, Jr., & S. R. Kellert (Eds.), *Children and nature: Psychological, sociocultural, and evolutionary investigations* (pp. 93–116). Cambridge, MA: MIT Press.

Kahn, P. H., Jr., & Friedman, B. (1995). Environmental views and values of children in an inner-city Black community. *Child Development, 66,* 1403–1417.

Kahn, P. H., Jr., & Lourenço, O. (2002). Water, air, fire, and earth— A developmental study in Portugal of environmental moral reasoning. *Environment and Behavior, 34,* 405–430.

Kahn, P. H., Jr., Saunders, C. D., & Myers, G. (2001, April). *Children's conceptions of bats: Toward a biophilic account of fear caring.* Paper presented at the biennial meeting of the Society for Research in Child Development, Minneapolis, MN.

Kaiser, F. G., Wölfing, S., & Fuhrer, U. (1999). Environmental attitude and ecological behaviour. *Journal of Environmental Psychology, 19,* 1–19.

Kaplan, R. (1973). Some psychological benefits of gardening. *Environment and Behavior, 5,* 145–152.

Kaplan, R. (1977). Patterns of environmental preference. *Environment and Behavior, 9,* 195–216.

Kaplan, R. (1985). Nature at the doorstep: Residential satisfaction and the nearby environment. *Journal of Architectural and Planning Research, 2,* 115–127.

Kaplan, R., & Kaplan, S. (1989). *The experience of nature: A psychological perspective.* New York: Cambridge University Press.

Kaplan, S. (1983). A model of person-environment compatibility. *Environment and Behavior, 15,* 311–332.

Kaplan, S. (1987). Aesthetics, affect, and cognition: Environmental preferences from an evolutionary perspective. *Environment and Behavior, 19,* 3–32.

Kaplan, S. (1992). Environmental preference in a knowledge-seeking, knowledge-using organism. In J. H. Barkow, L. Cosmides, & J. Tooby (Eds.), *The adapted mind: Evolutionary psychology and the generation of culture* (pp. 581–598). New York: Oxford University Press.

Katcher, A. (2002). Animals in therapeutic education: Guides into the liminal state. In P. H. Kahn, Jr., & S. R. Kellert (Eds.), *Children and nature: Psychological, sociocultural, and evolutionary investigations* (pp. 179–198). Cambridge, MA: MIT Press.

Katcher, A., Friedmann, E., Beck, A., & Lynch, J. (1983). Looking, talking, and blood pressure: The physiological consequences of interaction with the living environment. In A. Katcher & A. Beck (Eds.), *New perspectives on our lives with companion animals.* Philadelphia: University of Pennsylvania Press.

Katcher, A., Segal, H., & Beck, A. (1984). Comparison of contemplation and hypnosis for the reduction of anxiety and discomfort during dental surgery. *American Journal of Clinical Hypnosis, 27,* 14–21.

Katcher, A., & Wilkins, G. (1993). Dialogue with animals: Its nature and culture. In S. R. Kellert & E. O. Wilson (Eds.), *The biophilia hypothesis* (pp. 173–197). Washington, DC: Island Press.

Katcher, A., & Wilkins, G. (1998). Animal-assisted therapy in the treatment of disruptive behavior disorders. In A. Lundberg (Ed.), *The environment and mental health* (pp. 193–204). Mahwah, NJ: Lawrence Erlbaum Associates.

Katcher, A., & Wilkins, G. (2000). The Centaur's lessons: Therapeutic education through care of animals and nature study. In A. Fine (Ed.), *The handbook on animal assisted therapy: Theoretical foundations and guidelines for practice* (pp. 153–178). New York: Academic Press.

Kellert, S. R., & Felthous, A. R. (1985). Childhood cruelty toward animals among criminals and noncriminals. *Human Relations, 38,* 1113–1129.

Killen, M. (1989). Context, conflict, and coordination in social development. In L. T. Winegar (Ed.), *Social interaction and the development of children's understanding* (pp. 119–146). Norwood, NJ: Ablex.

Killen, M. (1990). Children's evaluations of morality in the context of peer, teacher-child and familial relations. *Journal of Genetic Psychology, 151,* 395–410.

Kohlberg, L. (1980). High school democracy and educating for a just society. In R. L. Mosher (Ed.), *Moral education: A first generation of research* (pp. 20–57). New York: Praeger.

Kohlberg, L. (1984). *Essays on moral development: The psychology of moral development* (vol. 2.). San Francisco: Harper & Row.

Lee, Y., & De Young, R. (1994). Intrinsic satisfaction derived from office recycling behavior: A case study in Taiwan. *Social Indicators Research, 31,* 63–76.

Leonard-Barton, D. (1981). Voluntary simplicity lifestyles and energy conservation. *Journal of Consumer Research, 8,* 243–252.

Lourenço, O. (2000). The aretaic domain and its relation to the deontic domain in moral reasoning. In M. Laupa (Ed.) & W. Damon (Ser. Ed.). *Rights and wrongs: How children and young adults evaluate the world. New directions for child development* (pp. 47–61). San Francisco, CA: Jossey-Bass.

MacIntyre, A. (1984). *After virtue*. Nortre Dame, IN: University of Nortre Dame Press.

Medin, D. L, & Atran, S. (Ed.). (1999). *Folkbiology*. Cambridge, MA: MIT Press.

Melson, G. F. (2001). *Why the wild things are: Animals in the lives of children*. Cambridge, MA: Harvard University Press.

Moore, E. O. (1982). A prison environments' effect on health care service demands. *Journal of Environmental Systems, 11,* 17–34.

Moore, S., Murphy, M., & Watson, R. (1994). A longitudinal study of domestic water conservation behavior. *Population & Environment, 16,* 175–189.

Myers, G. (1998). *Children and animals: Social development and our connections to other species*. Boulder, CO: Westview.

Öhman, A. (1979). Fear relevance, autonomic conditioning, and phobias: A laboratory model. In P. O. Sjödén, S. Bates, & W. S. Dockens (Eds.), *Trends in behavior therapy*. New York: Academic Press.

Öhman, A. (1986). Face the beast and fear the face: Animal and social fears as prototypes for evolutionary analyses of emotion. *Psychophysiology, 23,* 123–145.

Öhman, A., Dimberg, U., & Öst, G. (1985). Animal and social phobias: biological constraints on learned fear responses. In S. Reiss & R. R. Bootzin (Eds.), *Theoretical issues in behavior*. New York: Academic Press.

Öhman, A., Erixon, G., and Löfberg, I. (1975). Phobias and preparedness: Phobic versus neutral pictures as conditioned stimuli for human autonomic responses. *Journal of Abnormal Psychology, 84,* 41–45.

Öhman, A., & J. J. F. Soares (1993). On the automaticity of phobic fear: Conditioned responses to masked phobic stimuli. *Journal of Abnormal Psychology, 102,* 121–132.

Piaget, J. (1932/1969). *The moral judgment of the child*. Glencoe, IL: Free Press.

Piaget, J. (1971a). *Genetic epistemology*. New York: Norton.

Piaget, J. (1971b). *Psychology and epistemology*. New York: Viking.

Power, C. (1988). The just community approach to moral education. *Journal of Moral Education, 17,* 195–208.

Pyle, R. M. (2002). Eden in a vacant lot: Special places, species, and kids in the neighborhood of life. In P. H. Kahn, Jr. & S. R. Kellert (Eds.), *Children and nature: Psychological, sociocultural, and evolutionary investigations* (pp. 305–327). Cambridge, MA: MIT Press.

Quinlisk, J. A. (1999). Animal abuse and family violence. In F. R. Ascione & P. Arkow (Eds.), *Child abuse, domestic violence, and animal abuse: Linking the circles of compassion for prevention and intervention* (pp. 168–175). West Lafayette, IN: Purdue University Press.

Regan, T. (1986). The case for animal rights. In D. VanDeVeer and C. Pierce (Eds.), P*eople, penguins, and plastic trees* (pp. 32–39). Belmont, CA: Wadsworth.

Sax, B. (2000). *Animals in the Third Reich: Pets, scapegoats, and the Holocaust.* New York: Continuum.

Scheffler, S. (1986). Morality's demands and their limits. *The Journal of Philosophy, 10,* 531–537.

Scheffler, S. (Ed.). (1988). *Consequentialism and its critics.* New York. Oxford University Press.

Scheffler, S. (1992). *Human morality.* New York: Oxford University Press.

Schultz, P. W., & Zelezny, L. (1999). Values as predictors of environmental attitudes: Evidence for consistency across 14 countries. *Journal of Environmental Psychology, 19,* 255–265.

Schwartz, S. H. (1994). Are there universal aspects in the structure and content of human values?*Journal of Social Issues, 50,* 19–45.

Shepard, P. (1978). *Thinking animals.* New York: Viking.

Shepard, P. (1995). Virtually hunting reality in the forests of simulacra. In M. E. Soulé & G. Lease (Eds.), *Reinventing nature?: Responses to postmodern deconstruction* (pp. 17–29). Washington, DC: Island Press.

Shepard, P. (1996). *The others: How animals made us human.* Washington, DC: Island Press.

Shepard, P. (1998) *Coming home to the Pleistocene.* Washington, DC: Island Press.

Smart, J. J. C., & Williams, B. (1973). *Utilitarianism for and against.* Cambridge, UK: Cambridge University Press.

Smetana, J. G. (1983). Social-cognitive development: Domain distinctions and coordinations. *Developmental Review, 3,* 131–147.

Smetana, J. G. (1995). Morality in context: Abstractions, ambiguities and applications. In R. Vasta (Ed.), *Annals of Child Development, 10,* 83–130.

Smetana, J. G., Bridgeman, D. L., & Turiel, E. (1983). Differentiation of domains and prosocial behavior. In D. L. Bridgeman (Ed.), *The nature of prosocial development* (pp. 163–183). New York: Academic Press.

Spiegel, M. (1988). *The dreaded comparison: Human and animal slavery.* New York: Mirror Books.

Thomashow, C. (2002). Adolescents and ecological identity: Attending to wild nature. In P. H. Kahn, Jr. & S. R. Kellert (Eds.), *Children and nature: Psychological, sociocultural, and evolutionary investigations* (pp. 259–278). Cambridge, MA: MIT Press.

Turiel, E. (1983). *The development of social knowledge.* Cambridge, UK: Cambridge University Press.

Turiel, E. (1998). Moral development. In W. Damon (Ed.), *Handbook of child psychology,* N. Eisenberg (Ed.), *Vol. 3: Social, emotional, and personality development* (pp. 863–932). New York: Wiley.

Turiel, E. (2002). *The culture of morality: Social development and social opposition.* Cambridge, UK: Cambridge University Press.

Turiel, E. & Davidson, P. (1986). Heterogeneity, inconsistency, and asynchrony in the development of cognitive structures. In I. Levin (Ed.), *Stage and Structure: Reopening the debate* (pp. 106–143). Norwood, NJ: Ablex.

Turner, J. (1996). *The abstract wild.* Tucson: The University of Arizona Press.

Ulrich, R. S. (1984). View through a window may influence recovery from surgery. *Science, 224,* 420–421.

Ulrich, R. S. (1993). Biophilia, biophobia, and natural landscapes. In S. R. Kellert & E. O. Wilson (Eds.), *The biophilia hypothesis* (pp. 73–137). Washington, DC: Island Press.

Ulrich, R. S., & Lunden, O. (1990, June). *Effects of nature and abstract pictures on patients recovering from open heart surgery.* Paper presented at the International Congress of Behavioral Medicine, Uppsala, Sweden.

Ulrich, R. S., Simons, R. F., Losito, B. D., Fiorito, E., Miles, M. A., & Zelson, M. (1991). Stress recovery during exposure to natural and urban environments. *Journal of Environmental Psychology, 11,* 201–230.

Vining, J., & Ebreo, A. (1990). What makes a recycler?: A comparison of recyclers and non-recyclers. *Environment and Behavior, 22,* 55–73.

Vining, J., & Ebreo, A. (1992). Predicting recycling behavior from global and specific environmental attitudes and changes in recycling opportunities. *Journal of Applied Social Psychology, 22,* 1580–1607.

Vining, J., & Ebreo, A. (2002). Emerging theoretical and methodological perspectives on conservation behavior. In R. B. Bechtel & A. Churchman (Eds.), *Handbook of Environmental Psychology* (pp. 541–558). Hoboken, NJ: John Wiley.

Werner, C. M., Turner, J., Shipman, K., Twitchell, F. S., Dickson, B. R., Bruschke, G. V., & Von Bismarck, W.B. (1995). Commitment, behavior, and attitude change: An analysis of voluntary recycling. *Journal of Environmental Psychology, 15,* 197–208.

Williams, B. (1985). *Ethics and the limits of philosophy.* Cambridge, MA: Harvard University Press.

Wohlwill, J. F. (1968). Amount of stimulus exploration and preference as differential functions of stimulus complexity. *Perception and Psychophysics, 4,* 307–312.

VI

EMPATHY, EMOTIONS, AND AGGRESSION

The chapters in this section describe research on moral emotions, empathy, sympathy, altruism, and aggression. These dimensions of morality have often been described as in opposition with moral reasoning and reflection. That is, theorists have pitted "cold, hard, logical reasoning" against "hot, intuitive emotions." The authors in this section go beyond this dichotomized and often stereotyped portrayal of emotions versus moral cognition and instead provide integrative and dynamic theories about the relative contributions of emotions, empathy, and rationality in the development of morality. Furthermore, the authors describe ways in which interpretations of aggressive acts depend on the meaning given to these acts by the participants. The researchers describe a wealth of research and theories on how empathy, altruism, and emotions are part of individuals' interpretations of social events and their judgments and moral reasoning. In Chapter 18 by Paul Hastings, Carolyn Zahn-Waxler, and Kelly McShane, the authors draw on biological, social, and psychophysiological evidence to describe the multiple levels that are necessary to understand the role of empathy in humans and animals. Empathic responses are part of our biological heritage, and the authors provide numerous examples of how empathy has been studied from different research traditions. Their chapter also describes new findings in the area of morality and neuroscience, an exciting new field of research that has drawn together experts in social science and biology.

Chapter 19, by Nancy Eisenberg, Tracy Spinrad, and Adrienne Sadovsky, provides further differentiation between empathy and sympathy, two central moral constructs. The authors describe the philosophical origins of these constructs and the extensive and well-documented evidence for how empathy and sympathy play different roles in children's and adults' social interactions and interpretations of moral situations. Describing their extensive empirical work in the area of empathy and sympathy, the authors successfully argue for the differentiated and integrative ways in which these constructs serve as the basis for the acquisition of morality in development.

Gustavo Carlo's Chapter 20 extends the discussion of empathy and care to altruism. Carlo posits that the multilevel complexity of prosocial behaviors helps to understand the interplay among individual (including biological), interpersonal, and broader social contextual mechanisms associated with these behaviors. Like the other authors, he argues against a view of human nature as solely "selfish" or "moral." An in-depth examination of how empathetic and care responses are manifested and acted on in daily social interactions is essential. Carlo provides detailed evidence of prosocial behaviors from cross-cultural and cross-ethnic research, which has greatly expanded the demographic database of knowledge about prosocial development.

In Chapter 21, Marie Tisak identifies how social–cognitive and social information processing models help to elucidate an understanding of aggressive behavior in delinquent youth. She demonstrates the necessity for understanding how individuals encode the intentions of others and make social and moral judgments and how this encoding influences aggressive behavior. Again, Tisak cautions against labeling individuals as "aggressive" or "selfish." She provides a comprehensive and creative integration of diverse theoretical models to explain juvenile delinquency. Investigating how moral emotions and moral cognition bear on the understanding of aggression in children and youth is a complex process, but her chapter demonstrates that ultimately this is a necessary step if we are to move the field away from dichotomized portrayals of human nature, and advance the scientific understanding of prosocial development.

18

WE ARE, BY NATURE, MORAL CREATURES: BIOLOGICAL BASES OF CONCERN FOR OTHERS

PAUL D. HASTINGS
CONCORDIA UNIVERSITY

CAROLYN ZAHN-WAXLER
UNIVERSITY OF WISCONSIN, MADISON

KELLY MCSHANE
CONCORDIA UNIVERSITY

In recent decades there has been a heightened interest in the origins and development of caring behaviors, and on factors that contribute to individual differences in these patterns. There has been an emphasis, as well, on both normative and non-normative expressions of concern for others, as empathy may be appropriate, muted, or excessive. Both biological and environmental processes have been implicated in the emergence of these different patterns. Although multiple factors in the environment influence biological processes, this chapter focuses on a review of theories and research emphasizing the associations between biological factors and the development of empathy, sympathy, altruism, and prosocial behavior.

Over two centuries ago in his "Theory of Moral Sentiments," Adam Smith (1790) described *empathy* as the ability to understand another's perspective and to have a visceral or emotional reaction. In just the last few decades, this conception of empathy has become reflected in research approaches. Operational definitions now focus on these components in terms of (a) *affective expression* (an emotional joining in), (b) *cognition* (apprehending or understanding the other's experience), and (c) *physiology* (autonomic nervous system activity, and more recently hormonal and neural substrates). From the work of Hoffman (1982), Eisenberg and Fabes (1998), Zahn-Waxler and Robinson (1995), and others (e.g., Grusec, 1991), *empathy* is defined here as the recognition and sharing of another's emotional state. Closely related to empathy are *sympathy* and *compassion,* which reflect orientation toward another's distress or pain, and feelings of sadness or concern on behalf of that person. *Prosocial behavior* constitutes actions taken to benefit another's well-being, including actions to alleviate their distress. Thus, the broad behavioral category of prosocial behavior can encompass *altruism,* which promotes another's needs at some cost to oneself. These constructs are not interchangeable, and each conveys a range of meanings and motives. However, they all reflect, to some degree, expressions of concern for the welfare of others, and hence are part of the broad area of interest. In prior work (Hastings, Zahn-Waxler, Usher, Robinson, & Bridges, 2000), these related affective, cognitive and behavioral reactions have been grouped under the rubric *concern for others* (p. 531).

The chapter begins with a review of theories supporting the proposition that empathy (and related constructs) should be predictably linked to biological processes. This review includes consideration of psychoevolutionary theory, ethology and sociobiology, functional theories of emotion, and developmental perspectives. Then, empirical evidence illustrating links between concern for others and biological functioning is reviewed. This includes consideration of genetics, neuroanatomy and neurophysiology, neuroendocrine (hormone) systems, autonomic nervous system (ANS) processes, and temperament. Research on concern for others in humans, primates, and other species is considered, as well as a developmental perspective. Future avenues of research are suggested for each of the five aspects of biological functioning considered. Given the scope of this chapter, this review focuses on representative studies to best provide a comprehensive analysis.

BIOLOGICAL EXPLANATIONS AND THEORIES OF EMPATHY AND ALTRUISM

Kin Selection

Current theories regarding genetic and neurohormonal substrates of empathy and prosocial behavior owe much to E. O. Wilson's (1975, 1978) sociobiological speculations about the evolution of altruistic behavior. A key question for Wilson was how natural selection could support the evolution of altruism, which by definition compromises personal fitness. *Kin selection* is used to explain the presence of altruism found in various animal species. According to Wilson, a network of individuals linked by kinship within a population cooperate and engage in altruistic acts with one another and thereby increase the average genetic fitness of the network as a whole, even if such behavior reduces the individual fitness of certain members of the group. The percentage of shared or common genes is hypothesized to be an important determinant of altruism displayed among species members, such that more altruism is directed toward more closely related kin than toward distant kin or unrelated conspecifics.

The existence of altruistic behavior has posed a central dilemma for evolution theorists. It raises the question of how such a behavior could evolve when it appears to decrease the Darwinian fitness of the individual engaging in it. Early theories attempted to resolve the issue by reducing all caring behaviors to self-serving or self-destructive actions (Zahn-Waxler & Radke-Yarrow, 1990). Thus, altruism is redefined from being other-oriented to being selfish. However, not all theories that pose underlying biological bases take this approach. Observations, theoretical propositions, and complex mathematical models all converge on rational models for humans' experiences of concern for the welfare of others, as an adaptive and evolutionarily successful aspect of human functioning.

Reciprocal Altruism and the Evolution of Cooperation

Several sociobiologists have suggested that altruism could evolve through reciprocity (Trivers, 1971, 1983). Trivers' model was intended to explain how certain altruistic behaviors could be selected for in cases where the recipient is not biologically related, which rules out kin selection. Under certain conditions, natural selection favors altruistic behaviors because these actions eventually benefit the altruistic organism at a later time. Performing an altruistic act elicits a reciprocal altruistic act by the beneficiary, and these histories of benefit build over time. Thus, the expectation of future reciprocal altruism supports the current altruistic behavior, despite the delay in actual reinforcement of the behavior.

Cooperation and helping behavior are observed in species other than humans, including several types of nonhuman primates, birds, hunting dogs, dolphins, and whales. Individuals benefit when the group cooperates to defend itself from predators. In Trivers' view, reciprocal altruism among humans takes place in a number of contexts and in all cultures. Often these behaviors occur at small cost to the altruist and provide significant benefit to the recipient. Like E. O. Wilson, Trivers does not consider helping behavior between parent and offspring to be "true" altruistic acts. Rather, it merely contributes to the survival of a parent's genes invested in their offspring.

Other sociobiologists (e.g., Rachlin, 2002; Tooby & Cosmides, 1996) have argued that altruism among nongenetically related members of a species increases the odds of reproduction and species survival. Sober and Wilson (1998) examined research on social species and constructed mathematical models demonstrating that the probability of group survival is higher if some members of the group are altruistic, even to the point of self-sacrifice. For example, by drawing predators away from the other group members, the altruist can ensure that the majority of group members survive a threat even if the altruist itself was lost. Conversely, in a group consisting exclusively of nonaltruists, each selfishly self-preserving member could lead predators toward the group in an effort to offer alternative targets, thereby increasing both the likelihood of individual survival and the likelihood of multiple group members being injured or killed. Within the former social group, the altruistic characteristic could be preserved across generations if it was encoded on a recessive gene, such that the loss of a homozygous altruist from the group would not decrease the probability of altruists being born to surviving heterozygous group members. Over multiple generations, the social group with the recessive gene for altruism would grow more rapidly and be more likely to thrive than the group lacking such a characteristic.

EVOLUTION OF FAMILY-RELATED BEHAVIORS: RESPONSIBILITY, AFFILIATION, AND CONCERN FOR OTHERS

Evolution of Mammals and Extended Caregiving

The evolution of concern for others is most evident—and has been most often studied—within mammalian family relationships. MacLean (1985) has argued that evolutionary changes in the brain are associated with the development of family-related behaviors, such as affiliation and responsibility for others. He proposed that the capacity for empathy emerged in connection with the evolution of mammals 180 million years ago in late Triassic times. Mammals are warm-blooded creatures that nurture, nourish, and protect their young, as opposed to reptilian, cold-blooded creatures who abandon their offspring. When mammals developed "a family way of life" the stage was set for increased exposure (and responsiveness) to pain, separation, and suffering in others: the stimuli for empathy.

MacLean's analysis of the mammalian triune brain (1990) focused on interconnections of the limbic system with the prefrontal cortex. Whereas one part of the limbic system is involved with feelings, emotions, and behaviors that protect self-preservation, another part appears to be concerned with expressive and feeling states conducive to sociability and preservation of the species. The later evolutionary development of the human neo-cortex, including expansion of the underlying prefrontal cortex enabled such functions as anticipation and planning, as well as feelings of responsibility for others. The newer brain structures coupled with the acquisition of connective neural circuits made it possible for affect (associated with family-related, caregiving functions) to be experienced in combination with cognitive insight into others. In this view, the capacity for empathy evolved from natural selection pressure for long-term parental care of offspring, especially among mammals. Some sociobiological theories of human development also emphasize the role of attachment and long-term parenting in the development of empathy (MacDonald, 1984).

Brain Circuits for Emotions and Attachments

Current models of the neurophysiology of affective processes draw on both evolutionary and functional theories of emotion, which hold that emotions evolved and have been preserved because they promote adaptive responses to salient events (Johnson-Laird & Oatley, 1992; Lazurus, 1991). Emotions are the neural representations of the relations between the self and evoking stimuli, as manifested through automatic and stereotypic changes in arousal states and connections of brain systems, and their impact on autonomic and somatic activity (Damasio, 2000). Thus, all emotions contribute to the regulation of behavior.

Circuits for several distinct emotions, including anger-rage, anxiety-fear, and separation-panic, appear to be wired into the brain by the genetic heritage of mammals (albeit the behavioral competence of this heritage is refined by experience; LeDoux, 1996; Panksepp, 1981, 1982, 1986). Applying this reasoning to empathy, Preston and de Waal (2002) argued that perceiving another individual activates within the perceiver a representation of the other, its state, and its situation. The activation of this representation primes the perceiver, through the generation of neurological and somatic responses, to act upon its awareness of the other's state and situation (the Perception-Action Model). Thus, empathy, sympathy and prosocial behavior arise from the evolution of basic emotion processes within the salient mammalian niches of extended parental care for offspring, and repeated interactions with familiar members of the social group.

Notions of kin-related altruism and reciprocal altruism in gene-based evolutionary theory may be explained by the brain processes that mediate the formation of social attachments (Panksepp, 1986). In this view, social sensitivities, which arise from social bonding and yield friendly and helpful behaviors toward kin, are mediated partially by inhibitory processes driven by multiple subcortical and cortical regions. During social interactions, animals may become better attuned to the emotions of their conspecifics, and thereby more able to alleviate others' distress. Indeed, in human research, resemblance in a variety of physical, demographic, and psychological attributes that connote familiarity or familial bonds— including appearance, religious affiliation, socioeconomic status, abilities, attitudes, and personality—has long been considered an important factor in the likelihood to engage in altruism (Radke-Yarrow, Zahn-Waxler, & Chapman, 1983; Rushton, 1989). However, this preferential direction of prosocial behaviors toward more familiar others does not, in itself, support exclusively egoistic motive. Indeed, Batson (1991) has persuasively argued that multiple motivations may underlie or contribute to altruism, including empathic awareness of and sympathy for others.

Correspondingly, MacLean emphasized the role of systems in the prefrontal cortex as well as the limbic system, with neural interconnections that may enable an individual to "feel one's way into another person in the sense of empathy" (1973, p. 42). In other words, later-evolving neural systems allow empathy to be regulated in a "top-down" fashion, and not exclusively as an automatic response below the threshold of conscious control (Preston & de Waal, 2002). Hoffman (1977) extended this line of reasoning to early human development, suggesting that these brain connections integrate primitive emotional responses with higher order cognitive awareness. This produces empathic arousal that predisposes individuals toward actively prosocial engagement.

Development of Empathy and Altruism in Humans

In humans, complex facial motor patterns are present at a very early age that allow infants to match facial emotion expressions of others (e.g., Field, Woodson, Greenberg, & Cohen, 1982; Haviland & Lelwica, 1987; Meltzoff & Moore, 1977). Newborns cry in response to other infants' cries (Sagi & Hoffman, 1976; Simner, 1971). Thus, precursors for empathy are present at birth, and then elaborated on by neurological and cognitive maturation, and the accrual of social experiences within and outside the family (Brothers, 1989).

Hoffman (1975, 1982) has provided the most comprehensive developmental account of the (ontogenetic) evolution of empathy and caring behaviors in humans. Early moral development is a joint function of cognitive, affective, and social processes. Hoffman defined empathy as a "vicarious affective response that is more appropriate to someone else's situation than to one's own situation" (p. 93). *Global empathy* is the first of four hypothesized developmental levels of empathy. The reflexive crying of infants in response to the crying of other infants is viewed as a primitive, biological precursor of empathic arousal (Sagi & Hoffman, 1976). It is an innate, hard-wired response connecting humans as social beings to the emotional plights of others. It is seen first in infants, before the development of a sense of others as physical entities distinct from the self. Hence, distress cues from the other become confounded with unpleasant feeling aroused in the self, making it difficult to distinguish the separate sources of distress.

The second level of empathy, referred to as *egocentric empathy*, is believed to begin with the emergence of object permanence and self–other differentiation during the second year of life. Here, children become aware that another person (rather than the self) is in distress. Consequently, self-distress begins to diminish. However, children still cannot fully distinguish between their own and the other person's internal states. *Egocentric empathy* entails comforting the victim in ways that would ameliorate one's own distress. With the onset of role-taking capabilities, during the third year of life, children become aware that other people's needs and feelings may differ from one's own. This marks the third stage of empathic development, *empathy for another's feelings*. Children become able to empathize with a wider range of emotions and develop increasingly elaborated prosocial repertoires in their developing capacity to help and comfort others in distress. The fourth level, *empathy for another's life condition*, extends beyond immediate situations to more distant circumstances for which abstraction is required. This level of empathic development is thought to emerge by late childhood. As children begin to construct social concepts, feelings of empathic distress may be applied toward an entire group or class of people (e.g., the homeless, poor, or oppressed).

Research has provided general support for Hoffman's proposals about the early development of empathy and prosocial behaviors (Zahn-Waxler & Radke-Yarrow, 1982; Zahn-Waxler, Radke-Yarrow, Chapman, & Wagner, 1992). In two longitudinal studies of one to $2\frac{1}{2}$-year-old children, children's responses to distress in others were assessed, using both naturalistic observations and standardized distress probes. Reactions to distresses that children witnessed as bystanders, as well as those that they caused in others, were studied. During the second year of life, self-distress waned and a constellation of caring patterns emerged and increased with age. The first prosocial responses emerged around 1 year of age. Often they took the form of providing physical comfort (hugs, kisses, gentle pats). These patterns sometimes appeared to comfort the helper as well, likely representing a mix of egocentric and other-oriented concern. Egocentric empathy was evident in such responses as the child seeking out the caregiver and bringing her to the distressed victim, and offering a toy to an upset or tired parent.

But prosocial responses that were more clearly victim-oriented also began to emerge around this time. Empathy for another's feelings could be seen in young children's facial expressions and soothing vocalizations. Over the course of the second year, they showed increasingly more attuned expressions of help and comfort, for example, bringing a bottle or pacifier to a crying infant, trying to get a bandage for someone who had been cut, or sharing a prized possession desired by another child. Some children would try more than one way of helping if the victim's problems persisted. By 2 years of age, most children showed the (a) cognitive capacity to interpret, in simple ways, physical and psychological states of others; (b) emotional capacity to experience, affectively, the states of others; and (c) behavioral repertoire that permits attempts to alleviate discomfort in others. This general developmental progression was also demonstrated using standardized distress probes with a large sample of monozygotic and dizygotic twins who were studied from 1 to 3 years of age (Zahn-Waxler, Robinson, & Emde, 1992; Zahn-Waxler, Schiro, Robinson, Emde, & Schmitz, 2001). Stable individual differences in children's concern for others over time also were seen in the three longitudinal studies.

RESEARCH ON THE BIOLOGICAL BASES OF EMPATHY

Clearly, a variety of theoretical perspectives put the roots of human empathy in our biology. Researchers have used a similarly diverse range of methods to demonstrate, or evaluate, the hypothesized links. The plethora of conceptions, operational definitions, and measurements of empathy and related constructs, and also of biological processes, complicates the task of integrating the results of empirical research. Throughout our review, therefore, we try to distinguish whether biological correlates are specific to one of the multiple components of concern for others, or share relations across empathy, sympathy, prosocial behavior, and some related constructs including affect recognition and affect matching.

Genetics

Fundamental to the support of gene-based evolutionary explanations for concern for others is evidence that empathy and related constructs are, indeed, heritable. Behavior genetics research is conducted to determine whether, and to what degree, characteristics can be attributed to genetic inheritance. Twin studies and adoption studies are the traditional methodologies, and far more investigations of the heritability of concern for others have utilized the former. As they are conceived from a single fertilized ovum, monozygotic (identical) twins share 100% of their genes; conversely, as they are conceived from separate ova fertilized by separate spermatozoa, dizygotic (fraternal) twins share on average

50% of their genes—the same amount of genetic material as shared by nontwin siblings. Therefore, for any given characteristic, the amount of variability across individuals that can be attributed to heritable, genetic factors can be derived from the extent to which the siblings of monozygotic twins are more similar on that characteristic than are the siblings of dizygotic twins. Were monozygotic twins found to be perfectly (100%) concordant, and dizygotic twins concordant half the time (50%), it would suggest the characteristic in question is completely genetically determined. This is rarely the case with complex psychological variables, however, and variability in a characteristic that cannot be attributed to genetic inheritance is presumed to result from environmental influences. (It should be noted that twin studies are subject to many limitations, and that the logic of relative genetic and environmental contributions is not without its critics; see Collins, Maccoby, Steinberg, Hetherington, & Bornstein [2000] for a recent review.)

Studies of adult monozygotic and dizygotic twins have compared their self-reported empathy and prosocial behavior (Davis, Luce, & Kraus, 1994; Loehlin & Nichols, 1976; Matthews, Batson, Horn, & Rosenman, 1981; Rushton, Fulker, Neale, Blizard, & Eysenck, 1984; Rushton, Fulker, Neale, Nias, & Eysenck, 1986). Typically these studies have shown a strong heritable component, with between 40% and 70% of the variability in self-reported empathy, altruism, nurturance, or kindness attributed to genetic factors. Davis and colleagues (1994) examined the heritability of three facets of concern for others: empathic concern, personal distress, and perspective taking. There were significant heritability estimates for the two affective dimensions, empathic concern and personal distress, but not for the cognitive construct of perspective taking. This pattern is consistent with the view that evolutionary forces have preserved the emotional basis of concerned and caring interpersonal responsiveness.

Studies that rely on self-report questionnaires have potential methodological confounds, including social desirability and biased response tendencies (e.g., preferences for more or less extreme ratings). These tendencies may themselves be heritable, thereby conflating estimates of genetic contributions to empathy and altruism. More objective means of assessing concern for others should provide more valid evidence of genetic influence. In programmatic research by Zahn-Waxler and colleagues (Zahn-Waxler et al., 1992; Zahn-Waxler et al., 2001), the empathic and prosocial responses of young children have been directly observed, to minimize problems associated with questionnaires and to examine genetic influence prior to long socialization histories.

Three forms of other-oriented concern (affective, cognitive, and behavioral), as well as self-concern and lack of concern, were examined, based on children's observed responses to expressions of distress by others. The key other-oriented reactions included (a) facial and vocal expressions of empathic concern (e.g., sad look, sympathetic or consoling tone); (b) hypothesis testing (effort to explore or understand the distress); and (c) prosocial behavior (e.g., help, share, comfort victim). Self-distress consisted of upset expressions (e.g., cry, fuss, whimper). Lack of concern was noted in displays of active indifference to another's distress (i.e., callous, aggressive, laughing at another's distress or injury). Children were seen at 14, 20, 24, and 36 months. In the initial heritability analyses (Zahn-Waxler et al., 1992), genetic influence was present at 14 months for all components of caring, self-distress, and for indifference, with between 23% and 35% of the variability in these reactions attributable to genetics. By 20 months, genetic influence remained only for empathic concern (28%) and indifference (29%). In subsequent analyses with the full sample (hence greater statistical power) and inclusion of two later time points (Zahn-Waxler et al., 2001), genetic influence was present at all time points for most of the measures of concern for others. The magnitude of genetic influence on observed measures of concern, however, remained modest. Self-concern and lack of concern did not show clear, consistent patterns of heritability.

Across samples, methodologies, and developmental periods, therefore, there is consistent evidence that multiple aspects of concern for others are, in part, genetically based. The exact amount of the contribution to variability in empathy and prosocial behavior that is made by heritable, genetic factors remains to be determined. Obtaining exact, replicable, and valid heritability indices may be important for future efforts to model the prevalence and dominance/recessiveness of "empathy traits" within the population. Having reasonable confidence that evolution has preserved these traits or qualities within the human species, however, it behooves researchers to begin identifying where empathy is encoded in human genotypes. This is not to suggest that genes code for empathy directly, or that there is a single gene associated with empathy. Genes code for enzymes, structural proteins, and regulatory factors that, in the context of the environment, influence patterns of brain chemistry and neurohormonal systems. As with most, if not all, complex psychological phenomena, polygenic influences on empathy are presumed.

With the rapid rate of progress in techniques for isolating and identifying genes, and the recent mapping of the entire human genome, molecular genetics may help to identify evolutionary contributions to complex psychological characteristics. There is, however, little research on the genes associated with empathy, sympathy, altruism, and prosocial behavior. One investigation targeted the dopamine D2 receptor gene (DRD2), given the role of dopaminergic neurons in human impulsivity, aggression, and appetitive behaviors (Comings, MacMurray, Johnson, Dietz, & Muhleman, 1995). However, men with varying haplotypes (number of repeated sequences of base pairs) for the gene were not found to differ on self-reported altruism. Given the frequent links between genes associated with the serotonergic systems and various affective processes (Hariri & Weinberger, 2003), these would seem to be reasonable candidates to target. In one recent study that combined genetic and neuroimaging techniques, variations in the serotonin transporter gene were found to predict differences in amygdala response during mimicry of pictures of faces expressing emotion (Hariri, et al., 2002) (the amygdala being intricately involved in emotional processes).

Future research would benefit from studies of connections between genotypic variation; physiological activation at the neurological, hormonal, and autonomic levels; and experiences and manifestations of empathy and prosocial behaviors. In addition, cross-sectional or longitudinal examinations of the timing and effects of gene activity in early childhood, and moderating effects of the environment on gene expression through socialization and life experiences, could make important contributions to developmental models of empathy. Recent research on genetic polymorphisms, life stress, and symptoms of depression by Caspi and colleagues (2003) exemplifies an integrative approach that could be applied more broadly, in this instance to sociomoral development as reflected in concern for others.

Neuroanatomy and Neurophysiology

Concurrent with the recent advances in molecular genetics, striking progress in neuroscience and brain imaging techniques has occurred over the past two decades. These have advanced the understanding of the neurophysiology of emotional processes, and increased the neuroscientific perspective on empathy (Eslinger, 1998; Harris, 2003). This field of research builds on the neuroanatomical and evolutionary research and theorizing on emotion and empathy by several neuroscientists, including Brothers (1989), Buck (1985), Gray (1987), MacLean (1973), and Tomkins (1982). As described, the evolution of the brain from reptilian to mammalian structure appears to support affective processes that are integral to effective familial bonds and integrated social networks (Buck, 1999; MacLean, 1970). Research on animal neurophysiology and parental care, clinical examinations of humans who have experienced lesions or other brain injuries, and examinations of intact brains using electroencephalographic (EEG), structural and functional magnetic resonance imaging (fMRI), and positron emission tomography (PET) imaging techniques have all contributed to insights into the neural structures and systems that are involved in concern for others and related constructs.

MacLean (1985) proposed that the thalamocingulate division of the limbic system is integrally involved in aspects of nurturing and affiliative behavior. Studies of maternal care-giving supported this, as lesions of rats' thalamocingulate curtailed maternal care of pups (Peredery, Persinger, Blomme, & Parker, 1992). Recent fMRI studies showed that similar regions are active in human mothers who chose to breastfeed their young infants (Lorber-baum et al., 2002), and that orbitofrontal activation is predictive of mothers' self-reported positive affect when viewing pictures of their own infants (Nitschke et al., 2004). Other studies have focused on brain regions involved in nonparental manifestations of concern for others. Eslinger and his colleagues (1989, 1994, 1996) conducted studies on empathy in adult brain injury patients with a variety of cerebral lesions (for an integrative review, see Eslinger, 1998). Both patients with frontal lesions and those with posterior lesions scored much lower than nonlesioned adults on self-rated and family-reported empathy, with more than 50% of frontal lesion patients scoring more than two standard deviations below population means. Conversely, in a more recent study, Shamay-Tsoory, Tomer, Yaniv, and Aharon-Peretz (2002) found that patients with unilateral prefrontal (dorsolateral and or-bitofrontal) cortex lesions scored lower than both nonlesioned control adults and patients with unilateral posterior (parietal) cortex lesions on self-reported empathy in recorded conversations, whereas patients with posterior lesions did not differ from controls.

In their interpretations of their data, Eslinger and his colleagues (1996, 1998) have also principally concentrated on the effects of frontal lesions (rather than posterior lesions) on empathy. They found that the deficits of lesioned patients were similar for measures thought to tap into the more cognitive (Hogan empathy scale) and more emotional (Mehrabian & Epstein empathy scale) components of empathy, but the sites of lesions predicted some specificity in the nature of the deficits. Dorsolateral prefrontal lesions, particularly in the left hemisphere, were linked to limited perception and understanding of others' emotional states. Patients with orbitofrontal lesions were able to accurately perceive and understand others' emotions, but they did not use this awareness to guide or regulate their social behavior; these patients were rated as lowest on empathy and described as the most socially impaired. Eslinger (1996, 1998) has suggested the dorsolateral frontal system is more associated with cognitive aspects of empathy, whereas the orbitofrontal system may support emotional aspects of empathy.

Recent studies have used fMRI and EEG to examine the links between empathy-related emotional processing and neural functioning in healthy, nonpatient adults. In a test of per-spective taking and social-cognitive reasoning, Farrow and colleagues (2001) tested the differences in neural activity when making "empathic and forgivability judgments," and social judgments that did not involve inferences about mental states or appropriate behav-ior, in response to a series of realistic, open-ended social scenarios. Empathic judgments involved inferring the most probable state of mind of the character in the situation. For-givability judgments required participants to choose which of two bad or criminal actions was more forgivable for the character to make. Compared to baseline social reasoning, making both empathic and forgivability judgments activated the left superior frontal gyrus, orbitofrontal gyrus, and precuneus. Empathic judgments were uniquely linked to activity in the left anterior middle temporal and left inferior frontal gyri, whereas forgivability judgments activated the posterior cingulate. Thus, although the conceptually related processes of cognitive empathy (consciously trying to understand another's state or motivation) and forgiving shared some neural systems, there was also evidence of neurophysiological specificity that distinguished between these aspects of concern for others. In a study of hemispheric activation using EEG procedures, Harmon-Jones, Vaugh-Scott, Mohr, Sigelman, and Harmon-Jones (2004) showed that the effect of increased left frontal cortical activity following insult could be eliminated when high levels of sympathy were induced.

Other studies have utilized participants' recognition and mimicry of pictures of facial expressions of emotions to infer links about empathy-related processes and neural activity. These methods are presumed by researchers to tap into cognitive empathy (recognizing and understanding another's emotion) and possibly emotional contagion (shared experience of another's emotional state). Several of these studies have implicated a role for the amygdala in empathic processes. Although the amygdala is often linked most strongly to fear-related processes (LeDoux, 1996), a number of studies have implicated amygdala function in the processing of a range of emotion stimuli (e.g., Davis & Whalen, 2001). Hariri and colleagues (2000, 2002) found that the amygdala was activated when participants were asked to imitate images portraying emotional expressions, suggesting that the amygdala is involved in emotion recognition and/or emotional contagion. Moreover, both stable personality characteristics (Canli, Sivers, Whitfield, Gotlib, & Gabrieli, 2002) and functional polymorphisms of the serotonin transporter gene (5HTTLPR) (Hariri et al., 2002) have been found to predict variations in amygdala response to emotion stimuli. Thus, neuroscience is beginning to offer insights into individual differences in the physiological activation that may support concern for others.

One exciting new direction in the neuroscience of empathy (Preston and de Waal, 2002) is the explication of the functions of mirror neurons (di Pelligrino, Fadiga, Fogassi, Gallese, & Rizzolatti, 1992). First identified in the frontal systems of monkeys, mirror neurons are activated both by watching other monkeys or humans engage in goal-directed actions, and also by engaging in that action oneself, such that mirror neurons are implicated in the understanding and imitation of others (Gallese, Fadiga, Fogassi, & Rizzolatti, 1996; Rizzolatti & Arbib, 1998). More recently, fMRI studies have identified the activity of mirror neurons in analogous prefrontal cortex circuitry in humans (Iacoboni et al., 1999, 2001). Adolphs (2002) has suggested that mirror neurons might react to emotions as well as actions, facilitating one's recognition of another's display of emotion by constructing an on-line somatosensory reproduction of the emotional expression. Similarly, Wolf, Gales, Shane, and Shane (2001) proposed that mirror neurons could be involved in the development of empathy from perception and joint attention.

The association of mirror neuron activity with perception of actions does not necessarily implicate their activity in emotional processes. Iacoboni and Lenzi (2002) responded to the hypothesized link between mirror neurons and empathy by pointing out that, in humans, mirror neurons have been located in the frontoparietal circuit, which is principally associated with somatosensory functions. However, the frontoparietal circuit is also linked to the more emotional limbic system via the insular cortex. Iacoboni and Lenzi then presented new evidence from an fMRI study showing that the insula is activated when participants are asked to imitate facial expressions presented on slides (Iacoboni, in press, as reported in Iacoboni & Lenzi, 2002). Activation of the insula has also emerged in other imaging studies of emotional processing (Phillips, Drevets, Rauch, & Lane, 2003). Thus, there appears to be a functional link between visual representation systems and emotion systems that could support, at least, an awareness of others' emotional experiences that would facilitate empathy.

Decety and Chaminade (2003) recently reported evidence for the roles of these neural systems in sympathy. They conducted PET scans of adult participants while they watched videos of actors describing brief scenarios with sad or neutral content, while expressing sad, neutral, or happy affect. Thus, there were both matched (e.g., sad content–sad expression) and mismatched (e.g., sad content–happy expression) emotional stimuli. After each scenario, participants rated the actor's mood, and the extent to which they liked the actor (used as an index of sympathy). Listening to the actors expressing sadness activated the left dorsal prefrontal cortex and left inferior frontal gyrus, and the lateral orbital gyrus and temporal pole. In addition, the matched sad–sad condition was associated with activation of the left precuneus, left middle occipital gyrus, and right mediodorsal thalamic nucleus; this condition also elicited the highest ratings of liking the actor. The authors interpreted these patterns of activation as constituting a network of emotion processing that simulates the affective experiences of others within the observer (see also Ruby & Decety, 2001).

There is also evidence for the salience of neurodevelopmental processes in the associations between activity in brain regions, and empathy and prosocial behavior. Specifically, the timing of lesions seems to be important: lesions that occur early in development have more profound impacts on empathic processes. Malkova, Mishkin, Suomi, and Bachevalier (1997) reported that bilateral lesions of the amygdala and hippocampus in infant monkeys produced strong socioemotional deficits that worsened with age, whereas the same lesions in adult monkeys produced milder deficits. Eslinger (1998) described two case studies of early occurring (3 years, 7 years), localized prefrontal lesions in pediatric patients followed into adulthood. Both manifested later empathic deficits and difficulties with cooperative interpersonal relationships as adults. However, given the substantial plasticity of the brain in early development and the probability that early injuries may produce substantial reorganizations of neural systems, comparisons of the effects of lesions across ages are not straightforward. Additional work on the neurophysiological systems active during healthy children's empathic processing is needed.

Overall, efforts to illuminate the neurological underpinnings of empathy and concern for others have made substantial progress in the past 5 years, but this research also underscores the inherent complexity of these affective interpersonal processes. Creative methods have been developed for measuring empathy within the physical constraints of neuroimaging laboratories, but to date the work has focused less on empathy per se, and more on related processes of emotion perception and recognition. These have included having participants look at facial expressions of emotions, identify the emotions, or mimic the emotions. Conversely, studies that presented affective stimuli in contexts that added meaning to the target's situations and experiences (e.g., Decety & Chaminade, 2003; Farrow et al., 2001) begin to approach the more ecologically meaningful manipulations and measures that are increasingly being used in social and developmental research (see Carlo, chap. 20, this volume). However, the substantial physical constraints on conducting imaging studies also place corresponding limitations on studying the neural processes associated with concern for others. This is particularly true for research involving children; thus far, imaging studies have not provided new insights into the changes in neural functions that accompany the development of concern for others.

The wide variations in methods of assessing and eliciting individual differences in empathy and related processes have increased the challenge of identifying consistent results. Across the studies reviewed here, at least fifteen distinct brain sites have been implicated in empathy. Although empathy and other features of concern for others may well be widely distributed processes relying on the functional connectivity between neural systems, some of the sites identified may reflect specific methodological features of a given study. For example, affective information may be processed very differently when it is presented in visual (e.g., Davis & Whalen, 2001) versus auditory (e.g., Farrow et al., 2001) or mixed modalities (e.g., Decety & Chaminade, 2003). Research has shown that the primate amygdala is more active when processing visual than auditory stimuli (Amaral, Price, Pitkanen, & Carmichael, 1992; Bradley, 2000). Across studies, methods and research teams, there was only clear evidence of replicated associations between empathy and neural activation for five sites: the amygdala, the insula, the precuneus, the dorsolateral cortex, and the orbitofrontal cortex.

By extending from Preston and de Waal's (2002) observations, it would appear that this consistent pattern of empathy-related neural activation might both support and extend MacLean's (1990) theory of the mammalian triune brain and Hoffman's (1982) theory of the early development of empathy. The insula connects the cortical sensory areas to the limbic system, and particularly the amygdala (Bradley, 2000). The amygdala is rich in connections to diverse brain regions, and may act to converge and coordinate multiple systems for adaptive affective responses (Tranel & Damasio, 2000). Notably, the amygdala projects to several prefrontal and frontal systems, providing the potential for functional connectivity with the orbitofrontal cortex directly, and the dorsolateral cortex indirectly. In turn, developmental studies of infant cognition in primates and humans (Diamond & Goldman-Rakic, 1989) have confirmed that the dorsolateral cortex is involved in such executive self-regulatory functions as inhibitory control, which may be necessary for decreasing personal distress and coordinating other-oriented prosocial behaviors. This frontal development begins in the latter half of the first year of life, and continues through the toddler and preschool years (Fox, Schmidt, & Henderson, 2000). Thus, in its early stages it appears to immediately precede children's diminution of self-distress and their increased capacity for concern for the welfare of others. Of course, these suggested pathways and processes are speculative. Neuroscientists should make efforts to verify the involvement of these regions, and the networks of communications between them, using multiple and convergent indices of empathic processes.

Similarly, efforts to introduce greater complementarity and convergence across lesion studies and neuroimaging studies would be helpful. Both approaches have their limitations. On the one hand, fMRI and PET studies may point out systems involved in empathic processes, but that may not be necessary for them. On the other hand, with examinations of lesioned patients, it may be difficult to determine whether a lesion interferes with empathy or with the ability to express or act on empathy. Researchers could overcome these limitations, however, by utilizing the unique strengths of imaging and lesion studies to converge on firm conclusions about the neural underpinnings of empathy.

A final consideration is that neuroscience has yet to reveal how patterns of activation across neural systems contribute or give rise to the emotional experience of empathy. A completely reductionist argument would be that empathy simply is a specific pattern of brain activity, but this seems to be an incomplete answer that disregards subjective experience and self-awareness. This issue is not specific to the neuroscience of empathy, of course. Understanding the translation of the physiological to the experiential is a vexing but essential challenge for neurology, psychology, and philosophy.

Neuroendocrinology

The vast majority of research on the relations between hormonal functions and concern for others has focused on the areas of parental (and more specifically, maternal) care for offspring, and interactions between mates or other kin. Although much of this research has been conducted using rats, primates, or other animals, there have been an increasing number of hormone studies on humans. Thus, a great deal is known about the hormones that facilitate feeding, retrieval, protecting, grooming, defending, and otherwise nurturing those with whom mammals share genes. Little is known about the role of hormones in empathy and prosocial behaviors directed toward nonrelatives (e.g., peers, acquaintances, or strangers), especially in humans. Some researchers have used hormones to assess the possible benefits of being the recipient of prosocial behaviors.

The reproductive and stress hormone systems have been well studied in animals and humans. There are several documented associations between quality of parental care and reproductive hormones (i.e., estradiol, progesterone, and testosterone). For example, Fleming, Ruble, Krieger, and Wong (1997) reported that increases in the ratio of estradiol to progesterone over the course of pregnancy predicted maternal responsiveness to newborn infants. The links between testosterone levels and paternal behavior appear to be quite variable across mammalian species (e.g., Dixson & George, 1982; Reburn & Wynne-Edwards, 1999; Trainor & Marler, 2001). Yet most studies of humans show inverse relations between testosterone and fathers' nurturance of infants (Nunes, Fite, & French, 2000; Storey, Walsh, Quinton, & Wynne-Edwards, 2000). Fathers have lower circulating levels of testosterone than men without children, and testosterone levels are negatively correlated with reported sympathy toward recorded cries of unrelated infants in both fathers and men without children (Fleming, Corter, Stallings, & Steiner, 2002). In a study of associations between sex hormones and concern for others outside the realm of parental care, Harris, Rushton, Hampson, and Jackson (1996) found that salivary testosterone levels of both men and women were negatively correlated with their self-reported empathy, altruism, and prosocial behavior. Therefore, in male and female humans, female sex hormones appear to support concern and care (for infants, at least), whereas the male sex hormone acts against positive, other-oriented affective and behavioral responses to others.

With regard to the stress hormones, a few studies document relations between glucocorticoids (cortisol, corticosterone) and quality of parental care. Interestingly, although circulating cortisol levels typically are used to index the level of arousal of the hypothalamic–pituitary–adrenal (HPA) axis system in reaction to stress, Fleming and colleagues (1987, 1997; Stallings, Fleming, Corker, Wortham, & Steiner, 2001) have found positive relations between salivary cortisol levels and mothers' sympathy toward the cries of unrelated infants, and mothers' positive responsiveness toward their own infants. Their interpretation of these data is consistent with evolutionary and functional models of empathy, in that perceiving the needs of an infant evokes moderate physiological arousal in a mother, such that she is motivated to address the infant's needs. Conversely, very low or very high levels of cortisol could reflect HPA under- or overarousal, respectively, which would either fail to motivate care giving or overwhelm the mother's capacity to coordinate an effective prosocial response. It is not clear, however, that the same processes of HPA arousal and empathic responsiveness are effective in men (Fleming et al., 2002). Studies of the associations between cortisol and empathy or prosocial behavior outside the area of parental care are notably lacking.

Research on cortisol reactivity has provided more consistent evidence of the benefits of being the recipient of prosocial behavior from others (see DeVries, Glasper, & Detillon, 2003, for a review). Sapolsky and Ray (1989) reported that basal cortisol levels of high-ranking male baboons were inversely associated with the amount of time spent in positive social interactions with females and infants. Several laboratory studies with humans have also shown that receiving social support from an interaction partner predicts decreased cortisol reactions to stressors (e.g., Kirschbuam, Klauer, Filipp, & Hellhammer, 1995), a relation that held across twenty-two studies in a recent meta-analysis (Thorsteinsson & James, 1999). DeVries (2002; Devries et al., 2003) and others (Insel, Gingrich, & Young, 2001) have suggested that the calming or homeostatic effect of receiving prosocial, supportive behaviors on the HPA system may be mediated by the regulatory functions of a peptide hormone called oxytocin.

Peptide hormones associated with reproductive processes have also been implicated in parental care and affiliation. Levels of circulating prolactin are positively associated with the quality of both maternal and paternal responsiveness to the needs of offspring in humans (e.g., Corter & Fleming, 1995; Storey et al., 2000) and other mammals (e.g., Bridges, DiBiase, Loundes, & Doherty, 1985; Roberts, Jenkins, Lawler, Wegner, & Newman, 2001). Oxytocin is also emerging as one of the new targets of neuroendocrine research on prosocial behavior in humans. Its role in mammalian reproduction, childbirth, and lactation is well documented (Carter, 2003). A substantial body of animal research has supported the role of oxytocin in parental care, mate attachment, and affiliative behaviors by both males and females (Carter, 2003; Insel, 2002), but thus far there is less evidence that it serves the same social-emotional functions in humans.

Taylor and colleagues (2000) have proposed that oxytocin supports the alternative, and more typically female, stress response of "tend or befriend" when threatened, as a different evolutionarily supported reaction to danger or challenge than "fight or flight." *Tending* refers to protection of the self and offspring to promote safety, and *befriending* refers to the creation of supportive social networks, which also confer greater protection, through prosocial and affiliative actions. Interestingly, both prolactin and oxytocin have been implicated in the modulation of the stress axis (Neumann, 2003). In addition to reducing HPA reactivity (Carter, 1998), one of oxytocin's other regulatory properties is the stimulation of the parasympathetic branch of the autonomic nervous system, resulting in reductions of respiratory and cardiac arousal (Porges, 2001; Uvnas-Moberg, 1998). These calming effects may reduce the experience of personal distress and the likelihood of freezing or fleeing when others are perceived as being injured, endangered, or upset, such that prosocial actions can occur. Research on the hypothesized relations between oxytocin's functions and concern for others in humans has potential for further clarifying the hormonal regulation of prosocial behavior.

A final consideration is the influence of development on the relations between hormones and concern for others. Although there is an extensive literature on cortisol and other hormones in relation to children's adaptive and maladaptive behaviors, this research has not yet been extended to include empathy and prosocial behavior. It seems unlikely that the reproductive hormones are strong contributors to empathic responsiveness in the toddler and early childhood years, as their concentrations and interindividual variability are simply too low prior to the preadolescent years. For example, despite well-documented associations between testosterone and aggression in adults, the links between testosterone and aggressive behavior in children and youth are less consistent (Booth, Johnson, Granger, Crouter, & McHale, 2003; Constantino et al., 1993). The glucocorticoids have traditionally been characterized as the "slow road" to arousal (Snowdon & Zeigler, 2000), taking many seconds to many minutes to influence autonomic processes. However, children's empathy-related autonomic reactions to evocative stimuli are very rapid. Early emerging patterns of emotion and behavior that comprise concern for others initially may be supported by other physiological systems, and then incorporate hormonal systems as these mature. Future research in developmental psychophysiology needs to address the possibility of ontological changes in the roles played by hormones in the development of empathy and prosocial behavior.

Autonomic Processes

Although activation of brain regions may contribute to the cognitive and affective aspects of empathy and sympathy, and circulating hormones may convey signals from the brain, actually engaging in altruistic or prosocial behavior requires recruitment of the ANS and bodily processes. There has been substantially more research on the relations between humans' concern for others and such autonomic measures as heart rate, blood pressure, skin conductance, and respiration than on neurophysiological or neuroendocrinological processes. This prevalence may be due to the more proximal connection of autonomic processes to behavior; to the less intensive, demanding or invasive assessment procedures available; to the lower cost of autonomic research; and to the earlier development of technologies for measuring autonomic activity.

Since Darwin (1872/1998) and James (1884) proposed that distinct patterns of autonomic activity probably corresponded to discernibly distinct emotions like anger, fear, disgust, sadness, and joy, emotion researchers have been testing and debating the validity of the "autonomic specificity" proposal. There are many logical reasons for this proposal (Ekman, 1999; Levenson, 2003). Subjectively, we experience different autonomic states when we feel different emotions. Functionally, the adaptive motor action patterns thought to be motivated by the experience of discrete emotions call on the differential utilization of autonomic processes. Socially, the communication of individual state and intent to conspecifics in the social group requires that postural, olfactory (apocrine sweat glands), and facial cues be reliable for distinguishing between emotions. Conversely, critics of the meaningfulness and replicability of research purporting to support the autonomic specificity proposal (e.g., Caccioppo, Klein, Berntson, & Hatfield, 1993; Mandler, 1980; Zajonc & McIntosh, 1992) have argued that a generalized state of autonomic arousal can support a wide range of motor responses. Thus, whether one feels excited, scared, or angry, one may experience an elevated heart rate, higher blood pressure, and faster respiration rate to prepare for action.

What is not disputed is that emotional processes do involve changes in autonomic functions. Therefore, when the perception of distress or need in another evokes feelings of empathy or sympathy, changes in heart rate, skin conductance, or other somatic systems should be expected. These autonomic changes are elicited by a variety of underlying processes, including the sympathetic and parasympathetic branches of the ANS (Brownley, Hurwitz, & Schneiderman, 2000). For example, heart rate accelerates when the relative influence of the excitatory (arousing, or upregulating) sympathetic branch is greater than that of the inhibitory (calming, or downregulating) parasympathetic branch of the ANS. Mathematical algorithms applied to recorded patterns of cardiac activity can distinguish the relative parasympathetic (e.g., respiratory sinus arrhythmia, or vagal tone, from variability of interbeat intervals; Porges, 1991, 1995) and sympathetic (e.g., preejection period [PEP] from impedance cardiography; Sherwood, 1993) influences on heart functions. Conversely, secretion by the eccrine sweat glands, which determine electrodermal conductivity (skin conductance levels), is exclusively controlled by the sympathetic branch (Dawson, Schell, & Filion, 2000). Thus, the measurement and analyses of autonomic recordings also provide some insights into the probable neurological contributors to states of somatic activity.

Early studies on autonomic correlates of empathy were conducted by clinical researchers who were interested in understanding how competent therapists were able to accurately perceive the states and needs of their clients (e.g., Bowman & Gieson, 1982). One supposition was that empathy would lead to autonomic synchrony between the therapist and client, such that the two participants would have more concordant patterns of heart rate activity during more effective therapy sessions. Greenblatt (1972) monitored the heart rates of a therapist and a client across several sessions, and found that the sessions for which the therapist reported feeling more attentive to and aware of the client's feelings were also the sessions in which the dyad manifested the greatest concordance of heart rates. Similarly, Robinson, Herman, and Kaplan (1982) reported that clients described therapists as more empathic when therapists and clients had more highly correlated skin temperatures and skin conductance during therapy sessions. Levenson and Ruef (1992) measured an array of autonomic measures, including heart rate, skin conductance, and pulse amplitude, while couples engaged in conversation: Participants made more accurate ratings of their partners' negative affect when the two had experienced more similar physiological profiles. However, a similar pattern was not found for self-reported empathy on a standard questionnaire.

In early work by Craig (1968; Craig & Wood, 1969) heart rate of participants was measured as they watched other people submerge their hands into very cold ice water, and as participants immersed their own hands. In the former condition, thought to assess vicarious and empathic sharing of the stressful experience, the heart rates of participants slowed. Conversely, heart rates accelerated when participants experienced the stress and discomfort directly. Heart rate deceleration (HRD) has been linked with both the outward direction of attention to take in information (e.g., Cacioppo & Sandman, 1978), and the experience of sadness (Ekman, Levenson, & Friesen, 1983), whereas heart rate acceleration (HRA) is more prototypical of withdrawal and fear (Ekman et al., 1983). HRD is likely to result from relatively increased parasympathetic and decreased sympathetic activity, which has also been associated with outward-directed orientation (Porges, 1991). Thus, HRD is as a good candidate for being an autonomic correlate of other-oriented, empathic responses, whereas HRA seems to reflect personal distress and a focus on one's own discomfort (see Batson & Oleson, 1991).

Subsequent attempts to replicate Craig's findings have met with mixed results. Mehrabian, Young, and Sato (1988) differentiated between more empathic and less empathic participants using a standardized questionnaire, and measured their heart rates and skin conductance while they watched a videotape of a crying infant. Similar to Craig's reports, more empathic participants experienced HRD while watching the video, whereas those with less empathy experienced an initial slight HRD followed by HRA. However, more empathic participants also had greater skin conductance levels than less empathic individuals, suggesting that they were experiencing sympathetic activation or personal distress. Similarly, in work with young children, some with behavior problems (Zahn-Waxler, Cole, Welsh, & Fox, 1995), HRD in response to a videotaped depiction of a sad child predicted more empathic and prosocial responses toward injured adults, but higher heart rate (all children) and skin conductance (girls only) also were associated with being more prosocial. Wisenfeld, Whitman, and Malatesta (1984) showed a film of crying infants to more empathic and less empathic women, and found that the more empathic women experienced greater HRA, greater skin conductance, and stronger reported desire to pick up the infants, compared to the less empathic women. Thus, across several studies, there is some inconsistency regarding whether empathic responsiveness is more closely associated with autonomic activation and arousal, or autonomic inhibition and regulation.

The greatest corpus of work on the relations between heart rate, HRD and HRA, and aspects of concern for others is contained in the developmental studies conducted by Eisenberg, Fabes, and their colleagues (e.g., Eisenberg, Fabes, Bustamante, et al., 1988a; Eisenberg, Fabes, Miller, et al., 1989; Eisenberg, Schaller, Fabes, et al., 1988b) over the past 15 years. Across several studies, these researchers have utilized a variety of ways to measure changes in heart rate, including the arithmetic difference between heart rate during emotionally evocative and affectively neutral events (e.g., Eisenberg et al., 1989; Eisenberg et al., 1998), the difference between heart rate before and after evocative events (e.g., Eisenberg et al., 1988a), and the linear slope of heart rate change over the course of presenting an evocative stimulus (e.g., Eisenberg et al., 1992; Eisenberg et al., 1998). Like the work of Wisenfeld and Mehrabian, these studies typically used videotaped scenarios of someone in distress or difficulty (e.g., a girl with spina bifida going through difficult physical therapy) to evoke vicarious physiological reactivity. Sympathy and prosocial behavior, and personal distress and lack of helpfulness, have been measured through coding of observed affect and behavior; verbal reports of reactions to the stimuli; and self, mother, teacher, and peer reports of empathy and prosocial behavior on standard questionnaires. Across these investigations, Eisenberg, Fabes, and their colleagues have put extensive effort into decomposing the meaning of cardiovascular reactivity and concern for others.

When significant associations between heart rate and concern for others have been found, heart rate most often has been negatively correlated with measures of prosocial responding, or positively correlated with signs of distress (e.g., Eisenberg et al., 1989; Eisenberg et al., 1996b; Eisenberg, Fabes, Schaller, Carlo, & Miller, 1991a). Across the majority of studies conducted by Eisenberg and Fabes, HRD usually has been associated with some measures of sympathy and prosocial behavior, and HRA typically has not (Eisenberg et al., 1990; Fabes, Eisenberg, & Miller, 1990). However, the relations have been low to moderate in magnitude, and sometimes inconsistent. For example, within one study, HRD was associated with observations of helping behavior in the laboratory, but not with observations of prosocial behavior with peers in the classroom (Eisenberg et al., 1990). Similarly, HRD has been associated with concern for others in one age group but not in a second group (e.g., younger but not older school-age children; Eisenberg et al., 1989), or for one gender but not the other (e.g., boys but not girls; Eisenberg, Fabes, Schaller, et al., 1991b). Finally, some studies have failed to find any association between HRD and indices of concern for others (e.g., Eisenberg et al., 1992), or the reverse pattern of findings has emerged, with HRA predicting sympathy or prosocial behavior (e.g., Holmgren, Eisenberg, & Fabes, 1998). Overall, although a noteworthy number of associations between HRD and concern for others have been found in this set of studies, qualified results call into question the universality of a sharp dichotomy between autonomic indices of sympathy versus personal distress (HRD versus HRA).

Eisenberg, Fabes, and their colleagues have examined other indices of autonomic arousal, specifically skin conductance and respiratory sinus arrhythmia (vagal tone), in a smaller number of their studies of sympathy and personal distress. In five studies that included measures of skin conductance responses to filmed stimuli (Eisenberg et al., 1996b; Eisenberg et al., 1991a; Eisenberg et al., 1991b; Fabes, Eisenberg, & Eisenbud, 1993; Holmgren et al., 1998), higher skin conductance was negatively associated with one or more measures of concern for others, or positively associated with one or more measures of personal distress and avoidance behaviors (e.g., gaze aversion). In one of these studies, however, higher skin conductance levels in young girls predicted more prosocial behavior according to teacher reports (Holmgren et al., 1998), akin to the results reported in Zahn-Waxler and colleagues (1995); in another study, higher skin conductance levels in boys predicting teachers' reports of less negative emotionality and emotional intensity (Eisenberg et al., 1996b). There is, then, modestly consistent empirical evidence indicating that higher levels of skin conductance reflect anxious overarousal that can sometimes interfere with sympathetic and prosocial responses to others experiencing distress (e.g., Eisenberg et al., 1991a).

Eisenberg, Fabes, and their colleagues also have examined associations between parasympathetic influence and concern for others, assessing cardiac measures in terms of heart rate variability or vagal tone in neutral rather than emotion evoking states. In one study (Fabes, Eisenberg, Karbon, Troyer, & Switzer, 1994), greater heart rate variability was associated with comforting behavior in boys but not girls. In a second (Fabes et al., 1993), heart rate variability was positively correlated with girls' self-reported sympathy, but not with their helpfulness. Eisenberg and colleagues (1996b) reported that vagal tone was not associated with teachers' reports of sympathy in either boys or girls. Finally, Eisenberg and colleagues (1996a) found that vagal tone was negatively correlated with peers' reports of girls' prosocial behavior and not associated with any measures of boys' concern for others. Again, this latter result matched that of research by Zahn-Waxler and colleagues (1995), showing that preschool-aged children's vagal tone was negatively correlated with their empathic concern toward adults' simulations of injuries.

There is, then, relatively little consistency across studies in the relations between vagal tone and children's concern for others. Because vagal tone can be an index of both self-regulatory skills and threshold for arousal (e.g., Porges & Byrne, 1992), perhaps this inconsistency should not be unexpected. If children with high vagal tone have a high threshold for arousal, they may not react to mild or moderate distress in others, and therefore appear to lack sympathy or the willingness to help. However, when evocative stimuli are strong enough to trigger arousal, children's self-regulatory skills may help to calm personal distress, evoke empathy, and coordinate effective, prosocial responses.

Overall, some studies indicate that high arousal interferes with empathy and prosocial behavior, whereas other studies do not find this pattern of interference. It may be that under certain living conditions and with certain child characteristics, self-distress and empathic distress may coexist, and high arousal might not necessarily diminish prosocial actions. Such a pattern is suggested in research on preschool aged children with behavior problems (Zahn-Waxler et al., 1995). Heightened anxiety also may be associated with more prosocial behavior in children of depressed and distressed parents (Zahn-Waxler, 2000). Such associations may not prevail in the long term, as these children are also likely to develop impoverished peer relations, have difficulty sharing, and be generally less prosocial with friends (Denham, Zahn-Waxler, Cummings, & Iannotti, 1991; Zahn-Waxler, Cummings, McKnew, & Radke-Yarrow, 1984).

There is very little information on the longitudinal connections between autonomic physiology and the development of concern for others. Without multiple time-point studies, it is impossible to discern whether measures of physiological arousal merely reflect an individual's current state of functioning, or whether they reveal some underlying dispositional characteristic that is likely to be stable and contribute to subsequent development. To our knowledge, there is only one prospective study that attempted to predict later empathy and prosocial behavior from earlier measures of cardiac function (Hastings et al., 2000). Children who had higher heart rates and lower vagal tone while watching an empathy-inducing video stimulus were described by their teachers, 2 years later, as more prosocial than children who did not show these autonomic patterns. However, these cardiac measures did not predict later observed behavior, self-reported empathy, or mother-reported empathy and prosocial behavior. Thus, there was little to suggest that these indices of autonomic reactivity were stable, influential contributors to the development of concern for others. Incorporating follow-up assessments and examining the stability of the inter-relations between physiology and empathy is an important step for future research.

Another consideration from this literature pertains to methods used to elicit empathy-related autonomic responses. The technique of choice has been to show participants filmed stimuli depicting others in distress. Although this does increase experimental control and standardization across participants, it leaves the field open to the criticism that whatever pattern of consistent results we can distill may be a function of our method. Autonomic arousal while passively watching videotaped materials may only be a pale reflection of the kinds of cardiovascular and electrodermal reactions that occur when someone actually interacts with another person who is sad, distressed, or in need of help. Researchers would do well to develop alternative means of triggering autonomic physiological processes, to better identify patterns of heart rate change or skin conductance that are the most accurate indices of empathy.

Temperament

The final approach to understanding individual differences in patterns of concern for others that we consider here is to identify how empathy and related constructs are associated with other stable traits that might reflect dispositional characteristics. Support for the argument that such traits are rooted in biological factors includes growing evidence for the heritability (Campos, Barrett, Lamb, Goldsmith, & Stenberg, 1983; Matheny & Dolan, 1980; Plomin, 1986) and stability over time (Goldsmith, 1983) of various aspects of temperament. *Temperament* is individual differences in reactivity and self-regulation presumed to be constitutionally (genetically and biologically) based, but also influenced over time by maturation and experience (Hinde, 1989; Rothbart & Derryberry, 1981; Thomas, Chess, Birch, Hertzig, & Korn, 1963). Aspects of childhood temperament are thought to provide an origin or substrate for the development of adult personality traits. Although there are not one-to-one links between temperament and personality, there are significant communalities (Ahadi, Rothbart, & Ye, 1992; Digman, 1990). Thus, although temperament is at best an indirect measure of biopsychology, examinations of the links between temperament and concern for others may reveal how underlying biological processes are coordinating observable patterns of behavior.

Considerable effort has gone into identifying the best ways to conceptualize and measure temperament. Currently, investigators either tend to employ quantitative measures along multiple continuous dimensions of temperament (e.g., Rothbart, Ahadi, & Hershey, 1994), such that a child might have a profile of temperament scores, or to make distinctions between groups of individuals manifesting distinct temperaments (e.g., Kagan, Reznick, & Snidman, 1987), such that a child conforms to a specific temperament type. Researchers who prefer the former approach often combine multiple temperament dimensions into a smaller number of higher order factors, which typically conform to the three groups most often distinguished by researchers in the latter camp: Inhibited/Slow-to-warm, Sociable/Easy-going, and Difficult/Negatively-reactive (for a review, see Putnam, Sanson, & Rothbart, 2002). *Inhibited/slow-to-warm* refers to consistent patterns of anxiety, distress, shyness, withdrawal, and avoidance when encountering unfamiliar people, objects, or situations, and not being easily calmed when aroused. *Sociable/easy-going* describes a pattern of being composed and not easily aroused, soothable when aroused, attentive and focused, and interested in and positive toward others. *Difficult/negatively-reactive* encompasses negative emotional reactivity, including a low threshold for frustration, strong expressions of anger when aroused, high motor activity, and low soothability. Despite several decades of research on temperament and on concern for others, it is only relatively recently that researchers have attempted to merge these literatures by examining whether temperamental traits are associated with individual differences in concern for others.

Inhibited/Slow-to-Warm.   Children characterized as temperamentally inhibited are seen as experiencing ineffective self-regulation of emotional reactivity when encountering novelty or challenges, such that normally adaptive orienting and arousal become exaggerated and interfere with the coordination of appropriate coping responses (Calkins & Fox, 2002). Given that inhibited children tend to withdraw from social partners, the active component of their concern for others may be blocked such that they would be less likely to provide effective comfort or assistance. A number of researchers have documented negative correlations between temperamental inhibition or shyness and various indices of children's concern. Stanhope, Bell, and Parker-Cohen (1987) found that preschoolers described as shy by their mothers were less prosocial toward unfamiliar adults in a laboratory than less shy children, although mothers' reports of their helpful behaviors at home did not differ. Toddlers' observed withdrawal from familiar playmates has been found to predict less prosocial behavior with peers at age 9 (although not at preschool age; Howes & Phillepsen, 1998); shyness and prosocial behavior also were inversely correlated at 9 years. Kindergarten-aged children described by their mothers as more shy responded to simulations of distress with fewer demonstrations of sympathy (Kienbaum, Volland, & Ulich. 2001). Eisenberg and colleagues also found that higher parent and teacher ratings of "negative emotionality" (an index of fear, distress, and anger) were associated with less sympathy expressed while viewing a filmed depiction of distress (Guthrie et al., 1997) and fewer peer nominations of prosocial behavior (Eisenberg et al., 1996b) in school-aged children. Thus, across a small set of studies with diverse methodologies, temperamental inhibition has been consistently and inversely associated with children's sympathy and prosocial behavior toward peers and strangers.

Two longitudinal studies of the links between children's inhibition and their concern for others have been conducted (Hastings, Rubin, & Mielcarek, in press; Young, Fox, & Zahn-Waxler, 1999). In the analyses of Young and colleagues (1999), the patterns of high reactivity and arousability that characterize inhibition at 4 months of age did not predict toddlers' empathy and prosocial behaviors toward mothers and experimenters who simulated injuring themselves. In concurrent analyses, behaviorally inhibited toddlers were less empathic and prosocial toward an experimenter than less inhibited children; however, more and less inhibited children reacted similarly to mothers' distress simulations. In the analyses of Hastings and colleagues, toddlers' inhibition did not predict prosocial responses 2 years later directly, but childrearing experiences were found to moderate the associations between earlier inhibition and later prosocial behavior by girls. For example, when mothers were highly protective (warm but intrusively controlling) of inhibited female toddlers, their daughters directed more prosocial behavior toward mothers 2 years later, suggesting that particularly close parent–child relationships were fostered.

These studies suggest that the anxiety induced by unfamiliar others can overwhelm the self-regulatory abilities of temperamentally inhibited children and interfere with their capacity to engage in effective, other-oriented helping behaviors. When familiar figures like parents are present to confer a sense of safety, this external source of emotion regulation allows inhibited children to act on their empathic awareness of others' distress in sympathetic and prosocial ways. That the relations appear to be stronger concurrently than over time is somewhat perplexing, given that temperament is generally viewed as a stable disposition. However, as indicated in the research by Hastings and colleagues, other factors, such as parental socialization, may moderate the longitudinal relations between temperament and concern for others.

This possibility is also support in the research by Kochanska (1991, 1997), in which early inhibition tends not to predict conscience assessed 2 or more years later (see also Kochanska, DeVet, Goldman, Murray, & Putnam, 1994). Rather, maternal childrearing practices often moderate the link between earlier inhibition and later conscience. In this work, *conscience* has been conceptualized as internalization of appropriate standards of conduct, an important milestone in moral development (Dienstbier, 1984; Grusec & Kuczynski, 1997). Although conscience cannot be directly equated to concern for others, there are important parallels in the constructs (Zahn-Waxler, 2000), and evidence for conscience can be seen in tendencies to behave in concerned and nonaggressive ways toward others. Kochanska has found that more highly inhibited toddlers are more likely to develop conscience when their mothers use gentle discipline practices, rather than more punitive and fear-inducing techniques. Conversely, conscience appears to be fostered in less inhibited toddlers through the quality of the mother–child attachment relationship. Hastings and colleagues (in press) also found evidence of maternal childrearing moderating the link between inhibition in toddler-age girls and their later prosocial behavior. Future studies should continue this effort to identify moderating and mediating processes in the development of concern for others, to clarify the ways in which temperament contributes to children's moral emotions and behaviors.

Sociable/Easy-Going.   In many ways, sociability is the opposite of inhibition. The research on inhibited/slow-to-warm children typically compares more inhibited children to less inhibited children who, presumably, are also more sociable. Because sociability is an aspect of temperament that reflects interest in and orientation toward others, more sociable children would be expected to engage in more prosocial behavior. There is some support for this hypothesis. Preschool-aged children who engage in more social interactions also show more helping behaviors (Eisenberg & Hand, 1979; Eisenberg, Pasternack, Cameron, & Tryon, 1984). Similar findings have been reported in subsequent studies (e.g., Farver & Branstetter, 1994; Kochanska et al., 1994). Miller and Jansen op de Haar (1997) interviewed mothers of children nominated by their teachers as highly empathic, and found that these mothers characterized their children as highly sociable and expressive of positive affect. Specific dimensions of temperament often subsumed by the broader construct of sociable/easy-going, such as attentional control and regulation, also are associated with indices of concern for others in school-aged children (e.g., Eisenberg et al., 1995; Eisenberg et al., 1998). Thus, children who are temperamentally more sociable/easy-going are more likely to demonstrate concern for others.

Difficult/Negative-Emotionality.   Fewer studies have examined how being temperamentally intolerant of frustrations and prone to angry outbursts is associated with concern for others. As mentioned, negative emotionality, which taps into difficult temperament, was inversely associated with sympathy and prosocial behavior (Eisenberg et al., 1996b; Guthrie et al., 1997). Denham (1986) found that more angry children evidenced greater difficulty engaging in caring behaviors and understanding others' emotions. Farver and Branstetter (1994) reported that difficult children were less prosocial toward their peers than were easy children. Kochanska and colleagues (1994) found that mothers reported less internalization of moral standards for preschool-aged boys who showed more impulsive/sensation-seeking tendencies. Finally, Young and colleagues (1999) found that a pattern of reactivity linked to difficult temperament in 4-month-old infants predicted less empathic responses to adults' simulations of injuries at 2 years. Thus, across half a dozen studies involving a range of childhood periods and a variety of measures, more difficult temperament has been associated with less empathy and prosocial behavior in children.

Although there have been relatively few direct studies of difficult temperament and concern for others, inferences can be drawn through the relations of both constructs with a third aspect of behavior: aggression. There is ample research that children with more difficult temperaments also are more aggressive (Bates, Bayles, Bennet, Ridge, & Brown, 1991; Rubin, Hastings, Stewart, Chen, & Nicholson, 1998). In turn, there is a sizable literature showing that more aggressive children and adults feel less empathy and show less sympathy and prosocial behavior (Hastings et al., 2000; Miller & Eisenberg, 1988). Therefore, the chain of relations between difficult temperament, aggression, and concern would suggest that dispositions toward anger may both cause the use of aggression to accomplish goals and interfere with the ability to engage in actions that benefit the well-being of others. Future research is necessary to verify this inference.

CONCLUSION

Given the relative youth of empirical efforts to identify the biological bases of empathy and prosocial behavior, the scope of investigations and the implications of results are quite impressive. Across studies of genetic, neuroanatomical, neurophysiological, neuroendocrine, autonomic, and temperamental aspects of functioning, logical and predictable relations between concern for others and biopsychological processes have been identified. This can be taken as indirect support for evolutionary and sociobiological theories on empathy: The evidence for the biological underpinnings of empathy is compatible with arguments that nature has selected for and preserved this affective capacity. To the extent that empathy is a necessary prerequisite for altruism and compassion, therefore, the roots of human morality can be traced through our biology to the evolution of our species. We are, by nature, moral creatures. The task of charting the biology of concern for others is by no means near completion. We have offered several specific suggestions for new directions of research. We conclude with suggestions of five potentially informative directions for future research that cut across aspects of biology and physiology.

Measuring Concern for Others

Investigations of the biological correlates of empathy and prosocial behavior can only be truly informative if the measures of empathy and prosocial behavior are reliable and valid. If evolutionary and functional theories of emotion are valid, empathy has been preserved over the course of human evolution because it has improved humans' adaptations to salient and meaningful events in the natural environment. Researchers' attempts to elicit their participants' empathy have often been limited by the physical and practical constraints of their laboratory paradigms. Are viewing a film or looking at faces evolutionarily meaningful and ecologically valid ways to tap into empathic processes? Even if such techniques are effective for eliciting empathy, is it necessarily the case that these artificial laboratory procedures activate the identical physiological systems that support empathy and prosocial behavior in the real world? Until researchers can manage to get equivalent accuracy for both their physiological and their behavioral measures, confidence in the reported associations between biology and empathy must remain tempered.

Multiple Levels of Analysis

Although some researchers have begun to look at the interrelations of different physiological systems (e.g., Hariri et al., 2002), the vast majority of studies on the biology of concern for others have concentrated on a single level of biological functioning. Of course, genes, brain activity, hormones, autonomic processes, and temperament do not function independently of one another; nor do they only make independent contributions to affective and behavioral responses. We know very little about how the temporal and interactive relations between these multiple levels of physiological activity contribute to psychological phenomena, including concern for others. Advancing our research efforts to address this gap in our understanding requires expanding and improving the technological, methodological, and statistical components of research.

Biology–Environment Interactions

The call for attention to multiple levels of analysis is not limited to examining what goes on inside the body. As a discipline, psychology has moved away from the old nature versus nurture argument, and it is now widely accepted that both biology and experience contribute to complex psychological characteristics, in interactive, bidirectional ways. Temperament researchers have been examining the contributions made to children's behavior by the interactions between dispositional traits and parenting practices for several years (e.g., Kochanska, 1991), and recently researchers have begun to look at gene–environment interactions as well (e.g., Caspi et al., 2003). However, much more empirical attention needs to be given to the issue of the joint contributions made by biological and environmental factors to concern for others. Such investigations could include examining which aspects of the social and physical environment foster and suppress individual differences in the biological processes that support empathy, what kinds of life experiences produce changes in the physiological systems that are necessary for empathy, whether some components of the biology of empathy are more amenable to environmental influences than others, and other complex and exciting questions.

From Correlation to Causation?

Due primarily to ethical and practical constraints, the vast majority of studies conducted on the aspects of human physiological functioning that are associated with concern for others have been correlational. It would be wonderful to be able to conduct a controlled experimental manipulation that would reliably evoke the same level and quality of empathy in all participants in one treatment condition, but no empathy in the participants in a second group, and to measure the physiological differences between the groups. This might never happen. Humans carry with them their genetically encoded and experientially shaped individual propensities to experience empathy more or less easily, with greater or lesser intensity, and in response to a range of stimuli. Similarly, researchers may be a long way from being able to manipulate humans' biological states and reliably measure differences in the levels of empathy that are induced. Without clear and irrefutable experimental procedures, however, we will have to be satisfied with saying "These are the biological events that occur when one feels empathy," instead of saying "When these biological events occur, one feels empathy."

Developmental Considerations

Does the biology of concern for others change with age? Do toddlers, adolescents, and elders experience the same kinds of neural activation, hormone secretion, and autonomic arousal when they feel empathy? Are there maturational events that trigger the on-set or off-set of gene activities that affect prosocial behavior? Are individual differences in the physiological processes associated with empathy developmentally stable? These are the kinds of questions that need to be addressed by developmental psychologists with interest in the biological bases of concern for others. Currently, the literature is not sufficient to provide answers. Different aspects of physiology tend to be examined with different age groups. For example, there are many studies of temperament and autonomic processes in relation to empathy in children, but almost no studies of the links between children's empathy and their hormonal or neurophysiological functioning. In addition, the vast majority of studies on the biology of concern for others are single time-point investigations that are not effective for illuminating developmental processes. Although they are costly and difficult, and require patience and perseverance, more longitudinal investigations need to be undertaken to advance our understanding of the developmental psychophysiology of concern for others.

ACKNOWLEDGMENTS

The authors thank Drs. Jack Nitschke, Virginia Penhune, Natalie Phillips, and Barbara Woodside for their helpful comments on sections of this chapter.

REFERENCES

Adolphs, R. (2002). Recognizing emotion from facial expressions: Psychological and neuro-logical mechanisms. *Behavioral and Cognitive Neuroscience Reviews, 1,* 21–62.

Ahadi, S. A., & Rothbart, M. K. (1994). Temperament, development, and the Big Five. In C. F. Halverson Jr., G. A. Kohnstamm, & R. P. Martin (Eds.), *The developing structure of temperament and personality from infancy to adulthood* (pp. 189–207). Hillsdale, NJ: Lawrence Erlbaum Associates.

Ahadi, S. A., Rothbart, M. K., & Ye, R. (1993). Children's temperament in the US and China: Similarities and differences. *European Journal of Personality, 7,* 359–377.

Amaral, D. G., Price, J. L., Pitkanen, A., & Carmichael, S. T. (1992). Anatomical organization of the primate amygdaloid complex. In J. P. Aggleton (Ed.), *The amygdala: Neurobiological aspects of emotion, memory, and mental dysfunction* (pp. 1–66). New York: Wiley-Liss.

Bates, J. E., Bayles, K., Bennett, D. S., Ridge, B., & Brown, M. M. (1991). Origins of ex-ternalizing behavior problems at eight years of age. In D. J. Pepler & K. H. Rubin. *The development and treatment of childhood aggression* (pp. 93–120). Hillsdale, NJ: Lawrence Erlbaum Associates.

Batson, C. (1991). *The altruism question: Towards a social-psychological answer.* Hillsdale, NJ: Lawrence Erlbaum Associates.

Batson, C. D., & Oleson, K. C. (1991). Current status of the empathy-altruism hypothesis. In M. S. Clark (Ed.), *Prosocial behavior. Review of personality and social psychology* (Vol. 12, pp. 62–85). Thousand Oaks, CA: Sage.

Booth, A., Johnson, D. R., Granger, D. A., Crouter, A. C., & McHale, S. (2003). Testosterone and child and adolescent adjustment: The moderating role of parent-child relationships. *Developmental Psychology, 39,* 85–98.

Bowman, J. T., & Giesen, J. M. (1982). Predicting ratings of counselor trainee empathy with self-report anxiety measures and skin conductance. *Counselor Education and Supervision, December,* 154–161.

Bradley, M. M. (2000). Emotion and motivation. In J. T. Cacioppo, L. G. Tassinary, & G. G. Berntson (Eds.), *Handbook of psychophysiology* (2nd ed., pp. 602–642). Cambridge, UK: Cambridge University Press.

Bridges, R. S., DiBiase, R., Loundes, D. D., & Doherty, P. C. (1985). Prolactin stimulation of maternal behavior in female rats. *Science, 227,* 782–784.

Brothers, L. (1989). A biological perspective on empathy. *American Journal of Psychiatry, 146,* 10–19.

Brownley, K. A., Hurwitz, B. E., & Schneiderman, N. (2000). Cardiovascular psychophysiology. In J. T. Cacioppo, L. G. Tassinary, & J. T. Capioppo (Eds.), *Handbook of psychophysiology* (2nd ed., pp. 224–264). New York: Cambridge University Press.

Buck, R. (1985). Prime theory: An integrated view of motivation and emotion. *Psychological Review, 92,* 389–413.

Buck, R. (1999). The biological affects: A typology. *Psychological Review, 106,* 301–336.

Cacioppo, J. T., Klein, D. J., Berntson, G. G., & Hatfield, E. (1993). The psychophysiology of emotion. In Lewis, M. & Haviland, J. M. (Eds.), *Handbook of emotions* (pp.119–142). New York: Guilford.

Cacioppo, J. T., & Sandman, C. A. (1978). Physiological differentiation of sensory and cognitive tasks as a function of warning, processing demands, and reported unpleasantness. *Biological Psychology, 6,* 181–192.

Calkins, S. D., & Fox, N. A. (2002). Self-regulatory processes in early personality development: A multilevel approach to the study of childhood social withdrawal and aggression. *Development and Psychopathology, 14,* 477–498.

Campos J. J., Barrett K., Lamb M. E., Goldsmith H. H., & Stenberg C. (1983). Socioemotional development. In M. M. Haith & J. J. Campos (Eds.), *Handbook of child psychology, Vol. 2: Infancy and psychobiology* (pp. 783–915). New York: Wiley.

Canli, T., Sivers, H., Whitfield, S. L., Gotlib, I. H., & Gabrieli, J. D. E. (2002). Amygdala response to happy faces as a function of extraversion. *Science, 296,* 2191.

Carter, C. S. (1998). Neuroendocrine perspectives on social attachment and love. *Psychoneuroendocrinology, 23,* 779–818.

Carter, C. S. (2003). Developmental consequences of oxytocin. *Physiology and Behavior, 79,* 83–397.

Caspi, A., Sugden, K., Moffitt, T. E., Taylor, A., Craig, I. W., Harrington, H., et al. (2003). Influence of life stress on depression: Moderation by a polymorphism in the 5-HTT gene. *Science, 301,* 386–389.

Collins, W. A., Maccoby, E. E., Steinberg, L., Hetherington, E. M., & Bornstein, M. H. (2000). Contemporary research on parenting: The case for nature and nurture. *American Psychologist, 55,* 218–232.

Comings, D. E., MacMurray, J., Johnson, P., Dietz, G., & Muhleman, D. (1995). Dopamine DR receptor gene (DRD2) haplotypes and the defense style questionnaire in substance abuse, Tourette syndrome, and controls. *Biological Psychiatry, 37,* 798–805.

Constantino, J. N., Grosz, D., Saenger, P., Chandler, D. W., Nandi, R., & Earls, R. J. (1993). Testosterone and aggression in children. *Journal of the American Academy of Child and Adolescent Psychiatry, 32,* 1217–1222.

Corter, C. M., & Fleming, A. S. (1995). Psychobiology of maternal behavior in human beings. In M. H. Bornstein, *Handbook of parenting, Vol. 2: Biology and ecology of parenting* (pp. 87–116). Hillsdale, NJ: Lawrence Erlbaum Associates.

Craig, K. D. (1968). Physiological arousal as a function of imagined, vicarious, and direct stress experiences. *Journal of Abnormal Psychology, 73,* 513–520.

Craig, K. D., & Wood, K. (1969). Physiological differentiation of direct and vicarious affective arousal. *Canadian Journal of Behavioural Sciences, 1,* 98–105.

Damasio, A. R. (2000). A second chance for emotion. In R. D. Lane & L. Nadel, Lynn (Eds.), *Cognitive neuroscience of emotion: Series in affective science* (pp. 12–23). London, Oxford University Press.

Darwin, C. (1872/1998). *The expression of the emotions in man and animals*. New York: Oxford University Press.

Davis, M., & Whalen, P. J. (2001). The amygdala: Vigilance and emotion. *Molecular Psychiatry, 6,* 13–34.

Davis, M. H., Luce, C., & Kraus, S. J. (1994). The heritability of characteristics associated with dispositional empathy. *Journal of Personality, 62,* 369–391.

Dawson, M. E., Schell, A. M., & Filion, D. L. (2000). The electrodermal system. In J. T. Cacioppo, L. G. Tassinary, & J. T. Cacioppo (Eds), *Handbook of psychophysiology* (2nd ed., pp. 200–223). New York: Cambridge University Press.

Decety, J., & Chaminade, T. (2003). Neural correlates of feeling sympathy. *Neuropsychologia, 41,* 127–138.

Denham, S. A. (1986). Social cognition, prosocial behavior, and emotion in preschoolers: Contextual validation. *Child Development, 57,* 194–201.

Denham, S. A., Zahn-Waxler, C. Cummings, E. M., & Iannotti, R. J. (1991). Social competence in young children's peer relations: Patterns of development and change. *Child Psychiatry and Human Development, 22,* 29–44.

DeVries, A. C. (2002). Interaction among social environment, the hypothalamic-pituitary adrenal axis, and behavior. *Hormones and Behavior, 41,* 405–413.

DeVries, A. C., Glasper, E. R., & Detillion, C. E. (2003). Social modulation of stress responses. *Physiology and Behavior, 79,* 399–407.

di Pelligrino, G., Fadiga, L., Fogassi, L., Gallese, V., & Rizzolatti, G. (1992). Understanding motor events: A neurophysiological study. *Experimental Brain Research, 91,* 176–180.

Diamond, A., & Goldman-Rakic, P. S. (1989). Comparison of human infants and rhesus monkeys on Piaget's AB task: Evidence for dependence on dorsolateral prefrontal cortex. *Experimental Brain Research, 74,* 24–40.

Dienstbier, R. A. (1984). The role of emotion in moral socialization. In C. Izard, J. Kagan, & R. B. Zajonc (Eds.), *Emotions, cognitions, and behaviours* (pp. 484–513). New York: Cambridge University Press.

Digman, J. M. (1990). Personality structure: Emergence of the five-factor model. *Annual Review of Psychology, 41,* 417–440.

Dixson, A. F., & George, L. (1982). Prolactin and parental behaviour in a male new world primate. *Nature, 299,* 551–553.

Eisenberg, N., & Fabes, R. A. (1998). Prosocial Development. In W. Damon (Series Ed.) & N. Eisenberg (Vol. Ed.), *Handbook of child psychology: Social emotional and personality development* (5th ed., Vol. 3, pp. 701–778). New York: John Wiley & Sons.

Eisenberg, N., Fabes, R. A., Bustamante, D., Mathy, R. M., Miller, P. A., & Lindholm, E. (1988a). Differentiation of vicariously induced emotional reactions in children. *Developmental Psychology, 24,* 237–246.

Eisenberg, N., Schaller, M., Fabes, R. A., Bustamante, D., Mathy, R. M., Shell, R., & Rhodes K. (1988b). Differentiation of personal distress and sympathy in children and adults. *Developmental Psychology, 24,* 766–775.

Eisenberg, N., Fabes, R. A., Carlo, G., Troyer, D., Speer, A. L., Karbon, M., & Switzer, G. (1992). The relations of maternal practices and characteristics to children's vicarious emotional responsiveness. *Child Development, 63,* 583–602.

Eisenberg, N., Fabes, R. A., Karbon, M., Murphy, B. C., Wosinski, M., Polazzi, L., Carlo, G., & Juhnke, C. (1996a). The relations of children's dispositional prosocial behaviour to emotionality, regulation, and social functioning. *Child Development, 67,* 974–992.

Eisenberg, N., Fabes, R. A., Murphy, B., Karbon, M., Smith, M., & Maszk, P. (1996b). The relations of children's dispositional empathy-related responding to their emotionality, regulation, and social functioning. *Developmental Psychology, 32,* 195–209.

Eisenberg, N., Fabes, R. A., Miller, P. A., Fultz, J., Shell, R., Mathy, R. M., & Reno, R. (1989). Relation of sympathy and personal distress to prosocial behavior: A multimethod study. *Journal of Personality and Social Psychology, 57,* 55–66.

Eisenberg, N., Fabes, R. A., Murphy, B., Smith, M., Maszk, P., & Karbon, M. (1995). The role of emotionality and regulation in children's social functioning: A longitudinal study. *Child Development, 66,* 1360–1384.

Eisenberg, N., Fabes, R. A., Schaller, M., Carlo, G., & Miller, P. A. (1991a). The relations of parental characteristics and practices to children's vicarious emotional responding. *Child Development, 62,* 1393–1408.

Eisenberg, N., Fabes, R. A., Schaller, M., Miller, P., Carlo, G., Poulin, R., Shea, C., & Shell, R. (1991b). Personality and socialization correlates of vicarious emotional responding. *Journal of Personality and Social Psychology, 61,* 459–470.

Eisenberg, N., Fabes, R. A., Shepard, S. A., Murphy, B. C., Jones, S., & Guthrie, I. K. (1998). Contemporaneous and longitudinal prediction of children's sympathy from dispositional regulation and emotionality. *Developmental Psychology, 34,* 910–924.

Eisenberg, N., Fabes, R., Miller, P., Shell, R., Shea, C., & May-Plumlee, T. (1990). Preschoolers' vicarious emotional responding and their situation and dispositional prosocial behaviour. *Merrill-Palmer Quarterly, 36,* 507–529.

Eisenberg, N., & Hand, M. (1979). The relationship of preschoolers' reasoning about prosocial moral conflicts to prosocial behavior. *Child Development, 50,* 356–363.

Eisenberg, N., Pasternack, J. F., Cameron, E., & Tryon, K. (1984). The relation of quantity and mode of prosocial behavior to moral cognitions and social style. *Child Development, 55,* 1479–1485.

Ekman, P. (1999). Basic emotions. In T. Dalgleish & M. J. Power (Eds.), *Handbook of cognition and emotion* (pp. 45–60). New York: John Wiley & Sons.

Ekman, P., Levenson, R. W., & Friesen, W. V. (1983). Autonomic nervous system activity distinguishes among emotions. *Science, 221,* 1208–1210.

Eslinger, P. J. (1996). Conceptualizing, describing, and measuring components of executive function: A summary. In G. R. Lyon & N. A. Krasnegor (Eds.), *Attention, memory, and executive function* (pp. 367–395). Baltimore, MD: Paul H. Brookes Publishing.

Eslinger, P. J. (1998). Neurological and neuropsychological bases of empathy. *European Neurology, 39,* 193–199.

Eslinger, P. J., Easton, A., Grattan, L. M., & Van Hoesen, G. W. (1996). Distinctive forms of partial retrograde amnesia after asymmetric temporal lobe lesions: Possible role of the occipitotemporal gyri in memory. *Cerebral Cortex, 6,* 530–539.

Fabes, R. A., Eisenberg, N., & Miller, P. A. (1990). Maternal correlates of children's vicarious emotional responsiveness. *Developmental Psychology, 26,* 639–648.

Fabes, R. A., Eisenberg, N., Karbon, M., Troyer, D., & Switzer, G. (1994). The relations of children's emotion regulation to their vicarious emotional responses and comforting behaviours. *Child Development, 65,* 1678–1693.

Fabes, R., Eisenberg, N., & Eisenbud, L. (1993). Behavioral and physiological correlates of children's reactions to others in distress. *Developmental Psychology, 29,* 655–663.

Farrow, T. F. D., Zheng, Y., Wilkinson, I. D., Spence, S. A., Deakin, J. F. W., Tarrier, N., Griffths, P. D., & Woodruff, P. W. R. (2001). Investigating the functional anatomy of empathy and forgiveness. *Neuroreport, 12,* 2433–2438.

Farver, J. A. M., & Branstetter, W. H. (1994). Preschoolers' prosocial responses to their peers' distress. *Developmental Psychology, 30,* 334–341.

Field, T. M., Woodson, R., Greenberg, R., & Cohen, D. (1982). Discrimination and imitation of facial expressions by neonates. *Science, 218,* 179–181.

Fleming, A. S., Corter, C., Stallings, J., & Steiner, M. (2002). Testosterone and prolactin are associated with emotional responses to infant cries in new fathers. *Hormones and Behavior, 42,* 399–413.

Fleming, A. S., Ruble, D., Krieger, H., & Wong, P. Y. (1997). Hormonal and experiential correlates of maternal responsiveness during the pregnancy and the puerperium in human mothers. *Hormones and Behavior, 31,* 145–158.

Fleming, A. S., Steiner, M., & Anderson, V. (1987). Hormonal and attitudinal correlates of maternal behaviour during the early postpartum period in first-time mothers. *Journal of Reproductive and Infant Psychology, 5,* 193–205.

Fox, N. A., Schmidt, L. A., & Henderson, H. A. (2000). Developmental psychophysiology: Conceptual and methodological perspectives. In J. T. Cacioppo, L. G. Tassinary, & G. G. Berntson (Eds.), *Handbook of psychophysiology* (2nd ed., pp. 665–686). Cambridge, UK: Cambridge University Press.

Gallese V., Fadiga L., Fogassi L., & Rizzolatti G. (1996). Action recognition in the premotor cortex. *Brain, 119,* 593–609.

Goldsmith, H. H. (1983). Genetic influences on personality from infancy to adulthood. *Child Development, 54,* 331–355.

Grattan, L. M., Bloomer, R. H., Archambault, F. X., & Eslinger, P. J. (1994). Cognitive flexibility and empathy after frontal lobe lesion. *Neuropsychiatry, Neuropsychology, and Behavioral Neurology, 7,* 251–259.

Grattan, L. M., & Eslinger, P. J. (1989). Higher cognition and social behavior: Changes in cognitive flexibility and empathy after cerebral lesions. *Neuropsychology, 3,* 175–185.

Gray, J. A. (1987). The psychology of fear and stress (2nd ed.). New York: Cambridge University Press.

Greenblatt, M. (1972). Two hearts in three-quarter time: psychosomatic issues in a stuffy of the psychophysiology of the psychotherapeutic interview. *Psychiatric Annals, 2,* 6–11.

Grusec, J. E. (1991). The socialization of altruism. In M. S. Clark (Ed.), *Prosocial behavior. Review of personality and social psychology* (Vol. 12, pp. 9–33). Thousand Oaks, CA: Sage Publications.

Grusec, J. E., & Kuczynski, L. (1997). *Parenting and children's internalization of values.* New York: John Wiley & Sons.

Guthrie, I. K., Eisenberg, N., Fabes, R. A., Murphy, B. C., Holmgren, R., Mazsk, P., & Suh, K. (1997). The relations of regulation and emotionality to children's situational empathy related responding. *Motivation and Emotion, 21,* 87–108.

Harmon-Jones, E., Vaughn-Scott, K., Mohr, S., Sigelman, J., & Harmon-Jones, C. (2004). The effect of manipulated sympathy and anger on left and right frontal cortical activity. *Emotion, 4*(1), 95–101.

Hariri, A. R., Bookheimer, S. Y., Mazziotta, J. C. (2000). Modulating emotional responses: Effects of a neocortical network on the limbic system. *Neuroreport, 11,* 43–48.

Hariri, A. R., Mattav, V. S., Tessitore, A., Kolachana, B., Fera, F., Goldman, D., et al. (2002). Serotonin transporter genetic variation and the response of the human amygdala. *Science, 297,* 400–403.

Hariri, A. R., & Weinberger, D. R. (2003). Imaging genomics. *British Medical Bulletin, 65,* 259–270.

Harris, J. A., Rushton, J. P., Hampson, E., & Jackson, D. N. (1996). Salivary testosterone and self-report aggressive and pro-social personality characteristics in men and women. *Aggressive Behavior, 22,* 321–331.

Harris, J. C. (2003). Social neuroscience, empathy, brain integration, and neurodevelopmental disorders. *Physiology & Behavior, 79,* 525–531.

Hastings, P. D., Rubin, K. H., & Mielcarek, L. (in press). Helping anxious boys and girls to be good: The links between inhibition, parental socialization, and the development of prosocial behavior. *Merrill-Palmer Quarterly.*

Hastings, P. D., Zahn-Waxler, C., Robinson, J., Usher, B., & Bridges, D. (2000). The development of concern for others in children with behavior problems. *Developmental Psychology, 36,* 531–546.

Haviland, J. M., & Lelwica, M. (1987). The induced affect response: 10-week-old infants' responses to three emotion expressions. *Developmental Psychology, 23,* 97–104.

Hinde, R. A. (1989). Temperament as an intervening variable. In G. A. Kohnstamm, J. E. Bates, & M. Rothbart (Eds.), *Temperament in childhood* (pp. 27–33). Oxford, UK: John Wiley & Sons.

Hoffman, M. L. (1975). Developmental synthesis of affect and cognition and its implications for altruistic motivation. *Developmental Psychology, 11,* 607–622.

Hoffman, M. L. (1977). Empathy, its development and prosocial implications. In H. E. Howe (Series Ed.) & C. B. Keasy (Vol. Ed.), *Nebraska symposium on motivation: Social Cognitive development* (pp. 169–217). Lincoln, NB: University of Nebraska Press.

Hoffman, M. L. (1982). Affect and moral development. *New Directions for Child Development, 16,* 83–103.

Holmgren, R. A., Eisenberg, N., & Fabes, R. A. (1998). The relations of children's situational sympathy-related emotions to dispositional prosocial behaviour. *International Journal of Behavioural Development, 22,* 169–293.

Howes, C., & Phillipsen, L. (1998). Continuity in children's relations with peers. *Social Development, 7,* 340–349.

Iacoboni, M., Koski, L., Brass, M., Bekkering, H., Woods, R. P., Dubeau, M.-C., Mazziotta, J. C., & Rizzolatti, G. (2001). Reafferent copies of imitated actions in the right superior temporal cortex. *Proceedings of the National Academy of Sciences of the United States of America, 98,* 13995–13999.

Iacoboni, M., & Lenzi, G. L. (2002). Mirror neurons, the insula, and empathy. *Behavioral and Brain Sciences, 25,* 39–40.

Iacoboni, M., Woods, R. P., Brass, M., Bekkering, H., Mazziotta, J. C., & Rizzolatti, G. (1999). Cortical mechanisms of human imitation. *Science, 286,* 2526–2528.

Insel, T. R. (2002). Implications for the neurobiology of love. In S. G. Post, L. G. Underwood, J. Schloss, & W. B. Hurlbut (Eds.), *Altruism & altruistic love: Science, philosophy, and religion in dialogue* (pp. 254–263). London: Oxford University Press.

Insel, T. R., Gingrich, B. S., & Young, L. J. (2001). Oxytocin: who needs it? *Progress in Brain Research, 133,* 59–66.

James, W. (1884). What is an Emotion? *Mind, 9,* 188–205.

Johnson-Laird, P.-N., & Oatley, K. (1992). Basic emotions, rationality, and folk theory. *Cognition and Emotion, 6,* 201–223.

Kagan, J., Reznick, J. S., Snidman, N. (1987). The physiology and psychology of behavioral inhibition in children. *Child Development, 58,* 1459–1473.

Kienbaum, J., Volland, C., & Ulich, D. (2001). Sympathy in the context of mother-child and teacher-child relationships. *International Journal of Behavioral Development, 25,* 302–309.

Kirschbaum, C., Klauer, T., Filipp, S. H., & Hellhammer, D. H. (1995). Sex-specific effects of social support on cortisol and subjective responses to acute psychological stress. *Psychosomatic Medicine, 57,* 23–31.

Kochanska, G. (1991). Socialization and temperament in the development of guilt and conscience. *Child Development, 62,* 1379–1392.

Kochanska, G. (1997). Multiple pathways to conscience for children with different temperaments: From toddlerhood to age 5. *Developmental Psychology, 33,* 228–240.

Kochanska, G., DeVet, K., Goldman, M., Murray, K., & Putnam. S. P. (1994). Maternal reports of conscience development and temperament in young children. *Child Development, 65,* 852–868.

Lazurus, R. S. (1991). *Emotion and adaptation.* New York: Oxford University Press.

LeDoux, J. E. (1996). The emotional brain: The mysterious underpinnings of emotional life. New York: Simon & Schuster.

Levenson, R. W. (2003). Blood, sweat, and fears: The autonomic architecture of emotion. *Annals of the New York Academy of Sciences, 1000,* 348–366.

Levenson, R. W., & Ruef, A. M. (1992). Empathy: A physiological substrate. *Journal of Personality and Social Psychology, 63,* 234–246.

Loehlin, J. C., & Nichols, R. C. (1976). *Heredity, environment, and personality: A study of 850 sets of twins.* Austin: University of Texas Press.

Lorberbaum, J. P., Newman, J. D., Horwitz, A. R., Dubno, J. R., Lydiard, R. B., Hamner, M. B., et al. (2002). A potential role for thalamocingulate circuitry in human maternal behavior. *Biological Psychiatry, 51,* 431–445.

MacDonald, K. (1984). An ethological-social learning theory of the development of altruism: Implications for human sociobiology. *Ethology and Sociobiology, 5,* 97–109.

MacLean, P. D. (1970). The triune brain, emotion and scientific basis. In F. O. Schmitt (Ed.), *The neurosciences: Second study program* (pp. 336–349). New York: Rockefeller University Press.

MacLean, P. D. (1973). *A triune concept of the brain and behaviour: Hincks memorial lectures.* Oxford, UK: University of Toronto Press.

MacLean, P. D. (1985). Brain evolution relating to family, play, and the separation call. *Archives of General Psychiatry, 42,* 405–417.

MacLean, P. D. (1990). A reinterpretation of memorative functions of the limbic system. In E. Goldberg (Ed.), *Contemporary neuropsychology and the legacy of Luria. Institute for research in behavioral neuroscience* (pp. 127–154). Hillsdale, NJ: Lawrence Erlbaum Associates.

Malkova, L., Mishkin, M., Suomi, S. J., & Bachevalier, J. (1997). Socioemotional behavior in adult rhesus monkeys after early versus late lesions of the medial temporal lobe. *Annals of the New York Academy of Science, 807,* 538–540.

Mandler, G. (1984). *Mind and body: The psychology of emotion and stress.* New York: Norton.

Matheny, A. P., & Dolan, A. B. (1980). A twin study of personality and temperament during middle childhood. *Journal of Research in Personality, 14,* 224–234.

Matthews, K. A., Batson, C. D., Horn, J., & Rosenman, R. H. (1981). "Principles in his nature which interest him in the fortune of others . . .": The heritability of empathic concern for others. *Journal of Personality, 49,* 237–247.

Mehrabian, A., Young, A. L., & Sato, S. (1988). Emotional empathy and associated individual differences. *Current Psychology: Research and Reviews, 7,* 221–240.

Meltzoff , A. N., & Moore, M. K. (1977). Imitation of facial and manual gestures by human neonates. *Science, 198,* 75–78.

Miller, P. A., & Jansen op de Haar, M. A. (1997). Emotional, cognitive, behavioral, and temperament characteristics of high-empathy children. *Motivation and Emotion, 21,* 109–125.

Miller, P. A., & Eisenberg, N. (1988). The relation of empathy to aggressive and externalizing/antisocial behavior. *Psychological Bulletin, 103,* 324–344.

Neumann, I. D. (2003). Brain mechanisms underlying emotional alterations in the peripartum period in rats. *Depression and Anxiety, 17,* 111–121.

Nitschke, J. B., Nelson, E. E., Rusch, B. D., Fox, A. S., Oakes, T. R., & Davidson, R. J. (2004). Orbitofrontal cortex tracks positive mood in mothers viewing pictures of their newborn infants. *Neuroimage, 21,* 583–592.

Nunes, S., Fite, J. E., & French, J. A. (2000). Variation in steroid hormones associated with infant-care behavior and experience in male marmosets (*Callithrix kuhlii*). *Animal Behavior, 60,* 857–865.

Panksepp, J. (1981). The ontogeny of play in rats. *Developmental Psychobiology, 14,* 327–332.

Panksepp, J. (1982). Toward a general psychobiological theory of emotions. *Behavioral and Brain Sciences, 5,* 407–467.

Panksepp, J. (1986). The neurochemistry of behavior. *Annual Review of Psychology, 37,* 77–107.

Peredery, O., Persinger, M. A., Blomme, C., & Parker, G. (1992). Absence of maternal behavior in rats with lithium/pilocarpine seizure-induced brain damage: Support of MacLean's triune brain theory. *Physiology and Behavior, 52,* 665–671.

Phillips, M. L., Drevets, W. C., Rauch, S. L., & Lane, R. (2003). Neurobiology of emotion perception I: The neural basis of normal emotion perception. *Biological Psychiatry, 54,* 504–514.

Plomin, R. (1986). Behavioral genetic methods. *Journal of Personality, 54,* 226–261.

Porges, S. W. (1991). Vagal tone: An autonomic mediator of affect. In J. Garber & K. A. Dodge (Eds.), *The development of emotion regulation and dysregulation* (pp. 111–128). New York: Cambridge University Press.

Porges, S. W. (1995). Cardiac vagal tone: A physiological index of stress. *Neuroscience and Biobehavioral Reviews, 19,* 225–233.

Porges, S. W. (2001). The polyvagal theory: Phylogenetic substrates of a social nervous system. *International Journal of Psychophysiology, 42,* 123–146.

Porges, S. W., & Byrne, E. A. (1992). Research methods for measurement of heart rate and respiration. *Biological Psychology, 34,* 93–130.

Preston, S. D., & de Waal, F. B. M. (2002). Empathy: Its ultimate and proximate bases. *Behavioral and Brain Sciences, 25,* 1–72.

Putnam, S. P., Sanson, A. V., & Rothbart, M. K. (2002). Child temperament and parenting. In M. Bornstein (Ed.), *Handbook of parenting, Vol. 1: Children and parenting* (2nd ed., pp. 255–277). Mahwah, NJ: Lawrence Erlbaum Associates.

Rachlin, H. (2002). Altruism and selfishness. *Behavioral and Brain Sciences, 25,* 239–296.

Radke-Yarrow, M., Zahn-Waxler, C., & Chapman, M. (1983). Children's prosocial dispositions and behaviours. In P. H. Mussen and E. M. Hetherington (Eds.), *Handbook of child psychology, Vol. IV: Socialization, personality, and social development* (pp. 469–545). New York: John Wiley and Sons.

Reburn, C. J., & Wynne-Edwards, K. E. (1999). Hormonal changes in males of a naturally biparental and a uniparental mammal. *Hormones and Behavior, 35,* 163–176.

Rizzolatti, G., & Arbib, M. A. (1998). Language within our grasp. *Trends in Neurosciences, 21,* 188–194.

Roberts, R. L., Jenkins, K. T., Lawler Jr, T., Wegner, F. H., & Newman, J. D. (2001). Bromocrip-
tine administration lowers serum prolactin and disrupts parental responsiveness in common
marmosets (*Callithrix j. jacchus*). *Hormones and Behavior, 39*, 106–112.

Robinson, J. W., Herman, A., & Kaplan, B. J. (1982). Autonomic responses correlated with
counselor-client empathy. *Journal of Counselling Psychology, 29*, 195–198.

Rothbart, M. K., Ahadi, S. A., & Hershey, K. L. (1994). Temperament and social behavior in
childhood. *Merrill-Palmer Quarterly, 40*, 21–39.

Rothbart, M. K. & Derryberry, D. (1981). Development of individual differences in temperament. In M. E. Lamb & A. L. Brown (Eds.), *Advances in developmental psychology*
(pp. 37–86). Hillsdale, NJ: Lawrence Erlbaum Associates.

Rubin, K. H., Hastings, P., Chen, X., Stewart, S., & McNichol, K. (1998). Intrapersonal and
maternal correlates of aggression, conflict, and externalizing problems in toddlers. *Child
Development, 69*, 1614–1629.

Ruby, P., & Decety, J. (2001). Effect of subjective perspective talking during simulation of
action: A PET investigation of agency. *Nature Neursocience, 4*, 546–550.

Rushton, J. P. (1989). Genetic similarity in male friendships. *Ethology and Sociobiology, 10*,
361–373.

Rushton, J. P., Fulker, D., Neale, M. C., Blizard, R. A., & Eysenck, H. J. (1984). Altruism and
genetics. *Acta Geneticae Medicae et Gemellologiae Roma, 33*, 265–271.

Rushton, J. P., Fulker, D. W., Neale, M. C., Nias, D. K. B., & Eysenck, H. J. (1986). Altruism
and aggression: The heritability of individual differences. *Journal of Personality and Social
Psychology, 50*, 1192–1198.

Sagi, A., & Hoffman, M. L. (1976). Empathic distress in the newborn. *Developmental Psychology, 12*, 175–176.

Sapolsky, R. M., & Ray, J. C. (1989). Styles of dominance and their endocrine correlates among
wild olive baboons (*Papio anubis*). *American Journal of Primatology, 18*, 1–13.

Shamay-Tsoory, S. G., Tomer, R., Yaniv, S., & Aharon-Peretz, J. (2002). Empathy deficits in
Asperger syndrome: A cognitive profile. *Neurocase, 8*, 245–252.

Sherwood, A. (1993). Use of impedance cardiography in cardiovascular reactivity research.
In J. J. Blascovich & E. S. Katkin (Eds.), *Cardiovascular reactivity to psychological
stress & disease* (pp. 157–199). Washington, DC: American Psychological Association.

Simner, M. L. (1971). Newborn's response to the cry of another infant. *Developmental Psychology, 5*, 136–150.

Smith, A. (1790). *The theory of moral sentiments*. London: A. Millar.

Snowdon, C. T., & Ziegler, T. E. (2000). Reproductive hormones. In J. T. Cacioppo, L. G.
Tassinary, & J. T. Capioppo (Eds.), *Handbook of psychophysiology* (2nd ed., pp. 368–396).
New York: Cambridge University Press.

Sober, E., & Wilson, D. S. (1998). *Unto others: The evolution and psychology of unselfish
behavior*. Cambridge, MA: Harvard University Press.

Stallings, J., Fleming, A. S., Corter, C., Worthman, C., & Steiner, M. (2001). The effects of
infant cries and odors on sympathy, cortisol, and autonomic responses in new mothers and
nonpostpartum women. *Parenting: Science and Practice, 1*, 71–100.

Stanhope, P., Bell, R. Q., & Parker-Cohen, N. Y. (1987). Temperament and helping behavior
in preschool children. *Developmental Psychology, 23*, 347–353.

Storey, A. E., Walsh, C. J., Quinton, R. L., & Wynne-Edwards, K. E. (2000). Hormonal
correlates of paternal responsiveness in new and expectant fathers. *Evolution and Human
Behavior, 21*, 79–95.

Taylor, S. E., Klein, L. C., Lewis, B. P., Gruenewald, T. L., Gurung, R. A. R., & Updegraff, J. A. (2000). Biobehavioral responses to stress in females: Tend-and-befriend, not fight-or-flight. *Psychological Review, 107,* 411–429.

Thomas, A., Chess, S., Birch, H. G., Hertzig, M. E., & Korn, S. (1963). *Behavioral individuality in early childhood.* Oxford, UK: New York University Press.

Thorsteinsson, E. B., & James, J. E. (1999). A meta-analysis of the effects of experimental manipulations of social support during laboratory stress. *Psychology and Health, 14,* 869–886.

Tomkins, S. (1982). Personology is a complex, lifelong, never-ending enterprise. *Personality and Social Psychology Bulletin, 8,* 608–611.

Tooby, J., & Cosmides, L. (1996). Friendship and the banker's paradox: Other pathways to the evolution of adaptations for altruism. In W. G. Runciman, & J. M. Smith (Eds.). (1996). *Evolution of social behaviour patterns in primates and man. Proceedings of the British Academy, Vol. 88* (pp. 119–143). London: Oxford University Press.

Trainor, B. C., & Marler, C. A. (2001). Testosterone, paternal behavior, and aggression in the California mouse, *Peromyscus californicus. Hormones and Behavior, 40,* 32–42.

Tranel, D., & Damasio, A. R. (2000). Neuropsychology and behavioral neurology. In J. T. Cacioppo, L. G. Tassinary, & G. G. Berntson (Eds.), *Handbook of psychophysiology* (2nd ed., pp. 119–141). Cambridge, UK: Cambridge University Press.

Trivers, R. L. (1971). The evolution of reciprocal altruism. *The Quarterly Review of Biology, 46,* 35–37.

Trivers, R. L. (1983). The evolution of sex. *Quarterly Review of Biology, 58,* 62–67.

Uvnas-Moberg, K. 1998. Oxytocin may mediate the benefits of positive social interaction and emotions. *Psychoneuroendocrinology, 23,* 819–835.

Wiesenfeld, A. R., Whitman, P. B., & Malatesta, C. Z. (1984). Individual differences among adult women in sensitivity to infants: Evidence in support of an empathy concept. *Journal of Personality and Social Psychology, 46,* 118–124.

Wilson, E. O. (1975). *Sociobiology: The new synthesis.* Cambridge, MA: Harvard University Press.

Wilson, E. O. (1978). *On human nature.* Cambridge, MA: Harvard University Press.

Wolf, N. S., Gales, M. E., Shane, E., & Shane, M. (2001). The developmental trajectory from amodal perception to empathy and communication: The role of mirror neurons in this process. *Psychoanalytic Inquiry, 21,* 94–112.

Young, S. K., Fox, N. A., & Zahn-Waxler, C. (1999). The relations between temperament and empathy in 2-year-olds. *Developmental Psychology, 35,* 1189–1197.

Zahn-Waxler, C. (2000). The development of empathy, guilt, and internalized distress: Implications for gender differences in internalizing and externalizing problems. In R. J. Davidson (Ed.), *Anxiety, depression, and emotion* (pp. 223–265). New York: Oxford University Press.

Zahn-Waxler, C., Cole, P. M., Welsh, J. D., & Fox, N. A. (1995). Psychophysiological correlates of empathy and prosocial behaviors in preschool children with behavior problems. *Development and Psychopathology, 7,* 27–48.

Zahn-Waxler, C., Cummings, E. M., McKnew, D. H., & Radke-Yarrow, M. (1984). Altruism, aggression, and social interactions in young children with a manic-depressive parent. *Child Development, 55,* 112–122.

Zahn-Waxler, C., & Radke-Yarrow, M. (1982). The development of altruism: Alternative research strategies. In N. Eisenberg (Ed.), *The development of prosocial behavior* (pp. 109–137). New York: Academic Press.

Zahn-Waxler, C., & Radke-Yarrow, M. (1990). The origins of empathic concern. *Motivation and Emotion, 14,* 107–130.

Zahn-Waxler, C., Radke-Yarrow, M., Wagner, E., Chapman, M. (1992). Development of concern for others. *Developmental Psychology, 28,* 126–136.

Zahn-Waxler, C., & Robinson, J. (1995). Empathy and guilt: Early origins of feelings of responsibility. In J. P. Tangney & K. W. Fischer (Eds.), *Self-conscious emotions: The psychology of shame, guilt, embarrassment, and pride* (pp. 143–173). New York: Guilford Press.

Zahn-Waxler, C., Robinson, J. L., & Emde, R. N. (1992). The development of empathy in twins. *Developmental Psychology, 28,* 1038–1047.

Zahn-Waxler, C., Schiro, K., Robinson, J. L., Emde, R. N., & Schmitz, S. (2001). Empathy and prosocial patterns in young MZ and DZ twins: Development and genetic and environmental influences. In R. Emde, R. Plomin, & J. K. Hewitt (Eds.), *The transition from infancy to early childhood* (pp. 141–162). Oxford: Oxford University Press.

Zajonc, R. B., & McIntosh, D. N. (1992). Emotions research: Some promising questions and some questionable promises. *Psychological Science, 3,* 70–74.

19

EMPATHY-RELATED RESPONDING IN CHILDREN

NANCY EISENBERG
TRACY L. SPINRAD
ADRIENNE SADOVSKY
ARIZONA STATE UNIVERSITY

The constructs of empathy and sympathy have been discussed by philosophers interested in morality for many years (e.g., Blum, 1980; Hume, 1748/1975). In addition, for decades, numerous psychologists have assigned empathy and sympathy a central role in moral development, especially as a factor that motivates prosocial behavior (e.g., helping and sharing) and inhibits aggression toward others (Batson, 1991; Feshbach, 1975; Hoffman, 1982; Miller & Eisenberg, 1988; Staub, 1979). People who experience others' emotion and feel concern for them are expected to be motivated to help and not hurt other people. In addition, sympathy is viewed by some theorists as contributing to the development and elicitation of higher level moral reasoning (e.g., Eisenberg, 1986; Eisenberg, Zhou, & Koller, 2001; Hoffman, 2000). Empathy and sympathy can direct attention to others' needs; empathy may engender feelings of concern for others in pain, need, or distress; and empathy and sympathy may reorganize ways of thinking about others' needs and the effects of one's behavior on others (Hoffman, 2000; Zahn-Walxer, Radke-Yarrow, & King, 1979). Thus, empathy and sympathy are believed to contribute to an orientation towards others' feelings and needs, which is incorporated in moral reasoning and reflected in social behavior (Batson, 1991; Eisenberg, 1986; Hoffman, 2000). Moreover, sympathy can be viewed in its own right as a moral emotion that is a part of moral values, reasoning, and behavior.

Because of important differences between various phenomena labeled empathy, it is useful to try to differentiate between empathy and related reactions (i.e., sympathy and personal distress), reactions that often, but probably not always, stem from the initial emotional reaction to another. Thus, *empathy* is an affective response that stems from the apprehension or comprehension of another's emotional state or condition and is similar to what the other person is feeling or would be expected to feel in the given situation. For example, when a person views someone else who is sad and consequently feels sad himself or herself, that person is experiencing empathy. In the view adopted here, empathy must involve at least a modicum of self–other differentiation (Hoffman, 2000; Lewis, 2002), such that the individual is aware at some level that the emotion or emotion-eliciting context is associated with the other person, not the self. Thus, empathy involves both some cognition (the degree to which this is true can vary considerably across situations) and emotion. Sometimes empathy is the outcome of direct exposure to another's emotion; at other times it is based on information regarding another's situation. For instance, if a person views another individual in a situation likely to elicit an emotion (e.g., at the funeral of a loved one or the wedding of one's only child), then the viewer might experience an empathic response even if the person being observed does not overtly exhibit emotion. In this case, it is likely that the empathic response was due to the observer accessing stored information about the effects of being in the given situation (e.g., experiencing the death of a loved one), or mentally putting oneself in the other's situation. Thus, an empathic response may be either fairly automatic (although it must involve at least some self–other differentiation) or based on the cognitive process of accessing information relevant to another's emotional state (see Eisenberg, Shea, Carlo, & Knight, 1991).

In most situations, especially after infancy, empathy is likely to lead to sympathy, personal distress, or perhaps both of these emotional reactions (probably experienced sequentially). *Sympathy* is an emotional response stemming from the apprehension of another's emotional state or condition, that is not the same as the other's state or condition but consists of feelings of sorrow or concern for the other. Thus, if a girl sees a sad boy and feels concern for him, then she is experiencing sympathy. Such a sympathetic response often is based on empathic sadness (or, in some situations, empathy with a different emotion). However, it is probable that sympathy can also be generated from cognitive perspective taking or accessing information from memory that is relevant to the other's experience (in addition to, or instead of, empathy).

Further, empathy also can lead to personal distress. *Personal distress* is a self-focused, aversive affective reaction to the apprehension of another's emotion (e.g., discomfort, anxiety; Batson, 1991). Personal distress often may stem from *empathic overarousal*—that is, high levels of vicariously induced aversive emotion (see Hoffman's, 2000, discussion of empathic overarousal). However, it is possible that personal distress sometimes stems from other emotion-related processes (e.g., shame), from accessing relevant information in mental storage, or through cognitively trying to take the perspective of others (which creates an aversive emotional state). Thus, empathy, sympathy, and personal distress are expected to involve somewhat different emotional experiences (Eisenberg, Shea, et al., 1991).

Based on these definitions of empathy-related responding, empathy is viewed as value neutral, sympathy as an emotional aspect of morality (because it is an important source of moral motivation), and personal distress as a reaction that may often lead to an egoistic orientation rather than an other-oriented, moral orientation. However, given that empathy often may produce sympathy, it may be a precursor to sympathy and moral behavior in some contexts. According to this perspective, whether a behavior is moral or not depends on its motivation; thus, behaviors based on sympathy generally are moral whereas those based on personal distress or other self-related motives are not.

Other investigators do not make as many distinctions in empathy-related responding as those just discussed. Consider the following definitions:

> ... an affective response more appropriate to another's situation than one's own. (Hoffman, 2000, p. 4)

> ... an other-oriented emotional reaction to seeing another suffer. (Batson, 1991, p. 58)

For example, Hoffman's (2000) definition subsumes empathy and sympathy, although he also notes that empathic distress often is at least partly transformed into sympathetic distress, which would be something akin to Batson's (1991) definition of empathy. Despite these differences, many investigators examining empathy and sympathy are interested in emotional responses to others' needs that serve as a motive for behavior toward others.

Major issues in theory and research concerning empathy and sympathy include definitional issues, the early development of empathy and sympathy, measurement issues, and the correlates (especially moral behavior) and origins of individual differences in empathy and sympathy (including factors related to individual differences in empathy and sympathy). Definitional issues have already been reviewed; measurement issues are discussed primarily as they relate to other topics. In the remainder of this chapter, topics covered include the development of empathy and sympathy, their relation to moral behavior, adjustment, and social competence; the potential role of emotion-related regulation in individual differences in empathy; gender differences in empathy; and the socialization of empathy and sympathy.

THE EARLY DEVELOPMENT OF EMPATHY-RELATED RESPONDING

In both theory and empirical findings, empathy emerges early in life. Moreover, from an early age, it is related to prosocial behavior. *Prosocial behavior* is voluntary behavior intended to benefit another (e.g., Mussen & Eisenberg-Berg, 1977; Staub, 1979). Prosocial behaviors may be moral or nonmoral, depending on the motive underlying the behavior. First the emergence of empathy and sympathy and its developmental links to prosocial behavior are examined; in later sections, the relations of empathy-related responding to prosocial behavior and other aspects of socioemotional functioning are discussed in greater detail.

Hoffman's Theory

True empathy likely emerges in the second year of life. Hoffman (1982, 2000) proposed a theoretical model that delineates the role of infants' self-awareness and self–other differentiation in its emergence, as well as empathy's relation to prosocial behavior (Hoffman, 1982, 2000). Hoffman outlines the developmental shift over time from self-concern in response to others' distress to empathic concern for others that results in other-oriented prosocial behavior.

In Hoffman's first stage, newborns and infants display rudimentary empathic responses that are manifested as "global empathy." This stage is defined by a period in which the young infant does not differentiate between the self and other (at least in regard to emotional states), and infants experience self-distress in response to others' distress. The newborn's reactive or contagious crying in response to the sound of another's cry is viewed as a simple form, or precursor of, global empathy. Later during the first year of life, infants are thought to seek comfort for their own distress when exposed to others' distress or to merely exhibit interest (if any response at all; e.g., Hay, Nash, & Pedersen, 1981).

Around the second year of life, the period of "egocentric empathy" emerges. The toddler is now capable of differentiating one's own and others' emotional responses and shows evidence of a rudimentary understanding of others' emotions. Thus, toddlers can experience empathic concern for another, rather than solely seek comfort for themselves. Although many researchers believe infants begin to differentiate the self from others during the first year of life (Harter, 1998), toddlers probably do not distinguish well between their own and another's internal states (see Hoffman, 2000; Radke-Yarrow & Zahn-Waxler, 1984, for descriptions of such behavior). Thus, toddlers can try to comfort another person, but such prosocial behavior is likely to involve toddlers' giving the other person what they themselves find comforting. Empathy at this stage differs from the previous stage because toddlers are more likely to respond with appropriate empathic affect.

The period of "empathy for another's feelings" emerges with the rudimentary development of role-taking abilities as early as 2 to 3 years of age. According to Hoffman (1982), this stage marks the period in which children are increasingly aware of other people's feelings and that other people's perspectives may differ from their own. Thus, prosocial actions reflect an awareness of the other person's needs (versus the egocentric empathy of the previous stage). Moreover, with the development of language, children begin to empathize and sympathize with a wider range of emotions than previously.

Following the progression of global empathy to empathy for another's feelings, Hoffman (1982) suggested that children begin to exhibit the ability to experience empathic responses even when the other person is not physically present (e.g., if they hear or read about someone in distress). By late childhood, with the emergence of greater cognitive maturity, children can empathize with another person's general condition or plight. Further, children eventually understand the plight of an entire group or class of people and may respond empathically.

Thus, Hoffman (1982) proposed that with increasing cognitive maturation, children are better able to respond with concern to others' distress. There is some empirical support for Hoffman's theory. As suggested by Hoffman, there is evidence of global empathy in newborns and young infants. Newborns have been found to cry in response to the cries of other infants (Hay et al., 1981; Sagi & Hoffman, 1976; Simner, 1971) and show more distress in response to another infant's crying than their own (Dondi, Simion, & Caltran, 1999), suggesting that infants are biologically predisposed to experience a rudimentary form of empathy. However, some researchers have questioned the interpretation of these findings (Eisenberg & Lennon, 1983; Thompson, 1987); for example, infants may simply find a novel cry to be more aversive than their own cry.

Regardless, it is clear that infants are responsive to others' emotional signals. For instance, in a study in which mothers expressed sadness in view of their 9-month-old infants, the infants displayed more negative emotional expressions and tended to avert their gaze away from their mothers. On the other hand, the infants expressed more joy during a condition in which mothers' expressions of joy were induced (Termine & Izard, 1988).

Research on social referencing provides evidence that infants not only are responsive to others' emotional signals but also make use of others' emotional displays to guide their own behavior. In these procedures, infants are confronted with an ambiguous situation and, upon looking at their caregivers' expressions, determine how to react. For example, 1-year-olds avoid crossing an apparent drop-off on a visual cliff or an unusual toy when their mothers display overt negative affect toward the event and are more willing to engage in these situations when their mothers exhibit positive emotion (Gunnar & Stone, 1984; Klinnert, 1984; Sorce, Emde, Campos, & Klinnert, 1985).

As proposed by Hoffman (1982), prosocial behaviors also have been associated with indices of cognitive maturation. Toddlers who display evidence of self-recognition (indicating a self–other distinction) tend to be relatively empathic and are likely to display prosocial behaviors (Bischof-Kohler, 1991; Johnson, 1982; Zahn-Waxler, Radke-Yarrow, Wagner, & Chapman, 1992; Zahn-Waxler, Schiro, Robinson, Emde, & Schmitz, 2001). Further, children's hypothesis testing (e.g., attempts to label or understand the injury, either verbally or in visual search patterns, such as looking repeatedly from the person's injured foot to the chair that the person stumbled on) at ages 2 and 4 to 5 in response to witnessed distress (another indication of perspective taking) has been related to children's prosocial behaviors (Zahn-Waxler, Cole, Welsh, & Fox, 1995; Zahn-Waxler, Robinson, & Emde, 1992). Moreover, preschool children's emotion knowledge has been positively related to prosocial behavior toward adults who express negative emotion (Denham & Couchoud, 1991).

Empirically Documented Age-Related Changes in Empathy-Related Responding

Empirical data generally support the view that the capacity for empathy or sympathy, as well as the tendency to experience these emotional reactions, continues to increase with age from the early years into adolescence. This developmental trend is probably due to age-related advances in children's understanding of others' feelings and thoughts (see Eisenberg, Murphy, & Shepard, 1997), based partly on advances in perspective taking (e.g., Selman, 1980; Shantz, 1975) during this period and because children continually are exposed to emotion-evoking interpersonal experiences and to adults' attempts to socialize their responses to such experiences.

Much of the research indicating that empathy and sympathy increase with age has been conducted with toddlers and young children. Consistent with Hoffman's (2000) theory, between 12 and 18 months of age, toddlers clearly react to others' negative emotions (often with orienting and distress reactions) and sometimes exhibit concern and prosocial behavior (including positive contact and verbal reassurance) in response to another's distress. Moreover, during this age span, there appears to be a decrease in self-oriented distress reactions (Zahn-Waxler & Radke-Yarrow, 1982; Zahn-Waxler et al., 1992; see also Kaneko & Hamazaki, 1987).

Changes in empathy-related reactions continue into the second and third year of life. Zahn-Waxler and colleagues (Robinson, Zahn-Waxler, & Emde, 2001; Zahn-Waxler et al., 2001) studied toddlers' empathy-related responding to an experimenter and their mother feigning injuries at 14, 20, 24, and 36 months of age. They found an increase with age in facial, vocal, and gestural/postural expressions of concern when children viewed either their mother or an experimenter fake injuries. (i.e., in the second year of life for reactions toward mother and into the third year of life for reactions to the stranger; Robinson et al., 2001). Self-distress in these contrived situations declined with age, particularly from 14 to 24 months (Zahn-Waxler et al., 2001; also see Kochanska, DeVet, Goldman, Murray, & Putnam, 1994). Indifference decreased from 14 to 20 months of age and then increased between 24 and 36 months (Zahn-Waxler et al., 2001). van der Mark, Ijzendoorn, and Bakermans-Kranenburg (2002) also found an increase in empathy/prosocial responding (combined) from 16 to 22 months when toddlers' mothers were distressed. However, unlike Robinson and co-workers (2001), they noted an age-related decline in reactions to strangers' distress. Moreover, observations of young children's responses to their siblings' distress indicate that they recognize others' distress and are capable of responding with attempts to comfort (Dunn, 1988). Thus, empathy and sympathy seem to increase with age in the early years. Such findings suggest that young children are increasingly capable of moral behavior with age.

With increasing age, preschoolers are more likely to respond to others' distress with empathy and prosocial behaviors (Eisenberg & Fabes, 1998; Lennon & Eisenberg, 1987). Phinney, Feshbach, and Farver (1986), for example, found preschoolers' empathic reactions to crying peers to be relatively infrequent, yet older preschoolers responded empathically more often than did younger preschoolers. Moreover, consistent with a cognitive-developmental perspective, empathic responses continue to involve more sophisticated perspective-taking skills with age in the elementary school years (e.g., Strayer & Roberts, 1997). In an early review, Lennon and Eisenberg (1987) noted an age-related increase in self-report measures of empathy in the late preschool and elementary school years; it was not clear if the age trend continued into adolescence. In a meta-analysis of studies since 1983, Eisenberg and Fabes (1998) found an age-related increase in empathy and sympathy across childhood and adolescence, at least for observational and self-report indices (but not for solely facial or physiological indices). However, they did not examine when in childhood the age-related changes were most evident. Nonetheless, it is fairly clear that there are increases in self-reported empathy in the elementary school years (Lennon & Eisenberg, 1987), although not necessarily in sympathy across only a couple years of age (Eisenberg, Fabes, Murphy, et al., 1996).

Findings are mixed in regard to age-related changes in empathy-related reactions in adolescence. Using the same or similar measures, some investigators have found increases in sympathy (Davis & Franzoi, 1991; Olweus & Endresen, 1998) and a decline in personal distress during adolescence (Davis & Franzoi, 1991; Eisenberg, Cumberland, Guthrie, Murphy, & Shepard, 2003); others have not (Karniol, Gabay, Ochion, & Harari, 1998) or have found a mixed pattern of results (especially for empathic distress) varying by gender (Olweus & Endresen, 1998). Findings of change were more evident in longitudinal rather than cross-sectional studies, especially those with larger sample sizes (see Davis & Franzoi, 1991; Eisenberg et al., 2003).

Unfortunately, nearly all of the existing relevant data with older children and adolescents are self-reported, so it is not clear if other measures of empathy-related responding change with age. Moreover, in the studies involving adolescence, usually dispositional empathy-related responding was assessed, so little is known about differences in the context that might affect changes with age in such responding. Nonetheless, the fact that empathy and sympathy frequently have been found to increase with age suggests that with development, children increasingly have the capacity for behavior that is sensitive to the welfare of others.

The Relation of Empathy-Related Responding to Prosocial Tendencies

Numerous theorists have argued that individuals who are prone to empathy and sympathy are more likely than people who are less empathic or sympathetic to act in prosocial ways (e.g., Batson, 1991; Hoffman, 2000; Mussen & Eisenberg-Berg, 1977; Staub, 1979). As discussed, prosocial behaviors can be performed for a host of reasons, including egoistic concerns, and sympathy is believed to be especially likely to motivate *altruistic behaviors* (often defined as prosocial behaviors motivated by other-oriented or moral concerns/emotion rather than egoistic or pragmatic concerns; Eisenberg, 1986).

Generally, only prosocial behaviors based on altruistic motives (e.g., sympathy or moral values) are considered to be moral. Batson (1991, 1998) argued that sympathy is associated with the desire to reduce another person's distress or need and therefore is likely to motivate altruistic behavior. In contrast, Batson proposed that personal distress, because it is experienced as aversive, is associated with the motivation to reduce one's own distress. Thus, people who experience personal distress are expected to escape from contact with the needy or distressed other, if possible, and to assist only when doing so is the easiest way to alleviate their own distress.

Although early studies of the relation between empathy and prosocial behavior often did not obtain significant associations (see Underwood & Moore, 1982), recent research involving more evocative stimuli and different measures generally has found an association. Most of the early studies on children's empathy involved the use of picture story measures of empathy, in which children were told a number of very short stories about emotional events (e.g., a child who lost his or her dog or is at a birthday party), and were asked how they felt after hearing each story. There is reason to believe that these picture story measures tapped children's inclination to provide the desired or socially appropriate response more than children's actual empathic emotion (Eisenberg & Lennon, 1983; Eisenberg-Berg & Lennon, 1980; Lennon, Eisenberg, & Carroll, 1983; Miller, 1979). In fact, in a meta-analytic investigation in which picture story measures were examined separately from other indices of empathy, such measures were unrelated to children's prosocial behavior (measured in a variety of ways; Eisenberg & Miller, 1987). Moreover, younger children's self-reported empathy (or sympathy) toward others in experimental settings (e.g., after viewing a videotape of distressed or needy others) often (but not always) has been weakly related or unrelated to their helping and sharing with others in need or distress (Eisenberg & Fabes, 1990), probably because young children have difficulty assessing or reporting their emotional reactions.

In contrast, when investigators have used most other types of measures (e.g., facial indices used with children, physiological indexes, self-report questionnaires used with older children and adults, and experimental manipulations), they tend to find a significant positive association between empathy or sympathy and a variety of measures of prosocial behavior (see Eisenberg & Miller, 1987; Eisenberg & Fabes, 1990, 1998). For example, Zahn-Waxler and her colleagues have found that observed sympathetic concern and prosocial behavior (often measured in response to another in pain or distress) co-occur even in the second year of life (Young, Fox, & Zahn-Waxler, 1999; Zahn-Waxler, Robinson, & Emde, 1992; also Spinrad & Stifter, 2002), as well as in early childhood (e.g., Zahn-Waxler et al., 1995; also see Miller, Eisenberg, Fabes, & Shell, 1996). This finding does not mean, however, that prosocial behavior based on empathy or sympathy is the norm in young children; children often do not seem to experience concern for others in distress (e.g., as assessed by their facial/gestural reactions or, occasionally, prosocial actions; Howes & Farver, 1987; Lamb & Zakhireh, 1997).

Consistent with Eisenberg and Fabes' (1998; Eisenberg, Fabes, & Spinrad, in press) review, in recent years investigators have found associations of empathy and sympathy with prosocial behavior in studies involving child-reported measures of sympathy or empathy and observed or adult-reported prosocial behavior (e.g., Eisenberg et al., 1999; Krevans & Gibbs, 1996; Strayer & Chang, 1997), observed facial sympathy and physiological markers of sympathy and adults' reports of prosocial behavior (e.g., Holmgren, Eisenberg, & Fabes, 1998), observed indices of both empathy and sympathy and prosocial responding (Denham, Mitchell-Copeland, Strandberg, Auerbach, & Blair, 1997; Trommsdorff & Friedlmeier, 1999), and primarily self reports of both constructs (e.g., Carlo, Roesch, & Melby, 1998; Litvack-Miller, McDougall, & Romney, 1997). As might be expected if sympathy fosters altruism, Carlo, Hausmann, Christiansen, and Randall (2003) found that adolescents' self-reported sympathy was more strongly related to reported need-related or altruistic prosocial behaviors than to high levels of prosocial behaviors performed in the view of others. Nonetheless, findings often have been modest in strength, and significant relations often have not been obtained with all measures (e.g., Holmgren et al., 1998; Roberts & Strayer, 1996; Strayer & Chang, 1997).

It is possible that some of the inconsistency in findings is due not only to the type of measure of empathy, but to the fact that empathy, rather than sympathy, likely was assessed in some studies. There doubtlessly is variation across studies in the degree to which sympathy is elicited (due to differences in the contextual factors such as the degree of need and the familiarity of the target of sympathy), which might account for variation in findings across studies. Moreover, although not examined systematically, it is likely that the context in which prosocial behavior is assessed also affects the degree of relation between sympathy (or empathy) and prosocial behavior. One would expect a stronger relation between sympathy and prosocial behavior if the prosocial behavior is in a situation in which it is likely to be performed for moral rather than egoistic or pragmatic reasons. For example, prosocial behaviors elicited in the absence of an adult (who might reward, approve, or scold the child) or by a person who appears to be in distress are more likely to be performed for altruistic reasons than prosocial behaviors performed when the target of aid has little need or there is a socializer observing the child. The importance of context is consistent with a social learning perspective, although the focus on motivation is reminiscent of cognitive developmentalists' emphasis on the importance of reasoning and motives in morality.

In contrast to relations with empathy or sympathy, personal distress reactions appear to be unrelated, or negatively related, to children's prosocial behaviors (e.g., Carlo et al., 2003; Eisenberg et al., 1999; Holmgren et al., 1998; Litvack-Miller et al., 1997; Trommsdorff & Friedlmeier, 1999; Zahn-Waxler, Radke-Yarrow, et al., 1992; see Eisenberg & Fabes, 1998). Moreover, fearfulness in toddlers—which would be expected to heighten children's tendencies to experience personal distress—has been negatively related with toddlers' empathic concern for an experimenter (but not for their mother; van der Mark et al., 2002), perhaps because fearful children are likely to be inhibited when dealing with strangers.

Because of the possible role of social desirability in self-reports of empathy, sympathy, and prosocial behavior, perhaps the strongest support for an association between the two constructs comes from research involving physiological, facial, or behavioral measures. Research with young children is an example of such work (Zahn-Waxler, Radke-Yarrow, et al., 1992; Zahn-Waxler et al., 2001). In addition, Eisenberg, Fabes, and their colleagues have conducted a series of studies in which they used self-report, facial, and physiological measures of empathy-related responding when children viewed videotapes of others in distress or need. In a first series of studies, they validated that children and adults tended to exhibit facial concerned attention or empathic sadness in sympathy-inducing contexts and, to a lesser degree, facial distress in situations believed to elicit personal distress. Moreover, older children's and adults' self-reports of their sympathy and personal distress were somewhat consistent with the emotional context (especially for sympathy; Eisenberg, Fabes, et al., 1988; Eisenberg, Fabes, Schaller, Miller, et al., 1991; Eisenberg, Schaller, et al., 1988; see Eisenberg & Fabes, 1990). Young school-aged children's self-reports of sympathy and personal distress were less differentiated and contextually appropriate than those of older children and adults, although their reports of emotional responses in the evocative situations generally were not random. Moreover, as predicted, study participants exhibited higher heart rate and skin conductance, both of which have been viewed as measures of emotional arousal (Lazarus, 1974; MacDowell & Mandler, 1989;

Winton, Putnam, & Krauss, 1984) in the distressing situations. Heart rate deceleration often appears to reflect interest in, and processing of information coming from, external stimuli, in this case, the sympathy-inducing stimulus person (Cacioppo & Sandman, 1978). Thus, when heart rate deceleration co-occurs with the processing of important information about another's emotional state or situation, it may tap a process that contributes to the experience of sympathy (see the Hastings, Zahn-Waxler, & McShane, chap. this volume).

In a second set of studies, Eisenberg, Fabes, and colleagues examined relations of individual differences in multiple markers of sympathy or personal distress (i.e., physiological, facial, and self-reported) with individual differences in a variety of measures of prosocial behavior. They exposed children and sometimes adults to empathy-inducing film clips, assessed their self-reported, facial, and physiological reactions to these clips, and then examined relations of individual differences in these reactions with children's and adults' helping or sharing with needy/distressed individuals (or others like them) when it was easy to avoid contact with the needy other. Across multiple studies, Eisenberg and colleagues found associations between empathy-related responding and prosocial behavior. By mid-elementary school or later, children's reports of positive mood to an empathy-inducing film tend to be negatively related with their prosocial behavior, whereas reports of negative mood often have been positively related (helping or donating; e.g., Eisenberg & Fabes, 1990; Eisenberg et al., 1989; Fabes, Eisenberg, & Eisenbud, 1993; Fabes, Eisenberg, & Miller, 1990). Even among preschoolers, reports of sad reactions (e.g., by pointing to pictures of facial expressions) to an empathy-inducing film have been positively related to subsequent helping of distressed children in a film whereas reports of happiness have been negatively related with helping (Miller et al., 1996). However, young children's reports of empathy and sympathy often have not been related with their prosocial behavior (Eisenberg & Fabes, 1990; Eisenberg & Miller, 1987).

Findings for physiological markers of sympathy and personal distress are somewhat more consistent than those for self-reported empathy-related responding. Generally, heart rate deceleration versus acceleration during the critical, evocative portion of an empathy-inducing film has been related to higher levels of prosocial behavior (Eisenberg & Fabes, 1990; Eisenberg et al., 1989; Eisenberg et al., 1990; also see Zahn-Waxler et al., 1995). Similarly, Fabes, Eisenberg, Karbon, Troyer, and Switzer (1994) found that heart rate acceleration (versus deceleration) was negatively related to young elementary school children's quality (but not quantity) of comforting behavior (see contrast with Eisenberg et al., 1993). In contrast, heart rate acceleration assessed while children view an entire empathy-inducing film (rather than an evocative short segment) has been positively related with prosocial behavior (Hastings, Zahn-Waxler, Robinson, Usher, & Bridges, 2000), perhaps because heart rate deceleration in response to viewing an especially evocative event lasts only a brief period of time. Moreover, when the empathy-evoking stimuli are not highly evocative, higher levels of heart rate (or skin conductance) may reflect a mild empathic response rather than no response at all (and not personal distress; see Liew, Eisenberg, Losoya, Guthrie, & Murphy, 2003).

In addition, higher levels of skin conductance during exposure to evocative empathy stimuli have been correlated with lower levels of prosocial behavior. Such skin conductance responding is believed to be a marker of personal distress (Fabes et al., 1993; Holmgren et al., 1998; compare with Zahn-Waxler et al., 1995). For example, skin conductance reactivity accounted for a significant amount of the variance in helping behavior, above and beyond all other predictors (i.e., facial reactions), in a study of elementary school children (Fabes, Eisenberg, Karbon, Bernzweig, et al., 1994). However, there are few studies involving skin conductance.

Consistent with Zahn-Waxler, Radke-Yarrow, and colleagues' (1992) findings with young children, Eisenberg and colleagues have found that facial concerned attention (or sadness) when children view empathy-inducing films, an injured adult, or hear a crying infant tends to be positively related to prosocial behavior whereas facial distress or happiness in these circumstances tends to be negatively related, although this pattern of findings is more consistent for boys than for girls (Eisenberg & Fabes, 1990; Eisenberg et al., 1990; Eisenberg et al., 1993; Fabes et al., 1990; Fabes, Eisenberg, Karbon, Bernzweig, et al., 1994; Miller et al., 1996; contrast with Fabes, Eisenberg, Karbon, Troyer, et al., 1994; also see Roberts & Strayer, 1996). Thus, facial reactions in a specific situation tend to predict subsequent prosocial responding toward the same or similar victims.

Sometimes investigators have found that the relations between empathy/sympathy and prosocial behavior are moderated by other variables. For example, Knight, Johnson, Carlo, and Eisenberg (1994) found the effects of sympathy were moderated by dispositional perspective taking, whereas Miller and co-workers (1996) found that they were moderated by moral reasoning (prosocial children were those high in sympathy *and* perspective taking or moral reasoning, respectively).

In summary, consistent with Hoffman's (2000) theory, there is considerable evidence for an association between empathy-related responding and children's prosocial behavior. There are few conceptual reasons not to expect such a relation, although in cognitive–developmental theory, emotion traditionally has not been viewed as being very relevant to morality (Kohlberg,1969). The aforementioned relation appears to emerge at an early age, tends to be consistent across childhood, and still evident in adolescence (e.g., Eisenberg, Carlo, Murphy, & Van Court, 1995; Eisenberg et al., 1999; Eisenberg, Miller, Shell, McNalley, & Shea, 1991; Estrada, 1995). Moreover, sympathy in childhood predicts prosocial tendencies in early adulthood (Eisenberg et al., 2002). It is likely that sympathy is a stronger correlate than empathy of prosocial behavior—especially that which is altruistically related—although this issue has not been adequately tested.

The Relation of Empathy-Related Responding With Social Competence and Adjustment

The process of empathizing with another would be expected to increase the likelihood of a child understanding another person's feelings and responding in a sensitive manner. Similarly, if children experience sympathetic concern, then they are likely to be motivated to behave in an appropriate and sensitive, as well as prosocial, manner. Thus, there is a natural conceptual link between empathy or sympathy and social competence. Conversely, children who tend to become highly aroused (with negative emotion) when exposed to others' emotions would be expected to become self-focused or dysregulated in their social behavior (Batson, 1991); consequently, personal distress would be expected to relate to low social competence.

Consistent with these arguments, Eisenberg and Miller (1987) found a positive, albeit weak, association between measures of empathy-related responding and diverse measures of social competence in a meta-analysis. However, at that time, relevant data were limited, and many of the studies used the problematic picture story measure of empathy. In more recent studies, children's dispositional or situational empathy and sympathy have been linked with a variety of measures of social competence, including peer sociometric status, adults' reports of children's socially appropriate behaviors, self-reported agreeableness, and children's enacted responses (with puppets) to various hypothetical social conflicts with peers, concurrently and 2 years prior (Adams, 1983; Eisenberg & Fabes, 1995; Eisenberg,

Fabes, Murphy et al., 1996; Sneed, 2002; Zhou et al., 2002). In addition, empathy or sympathy has been associated with children's perspective taking (e.g., Eisenberg & Fabes, 1998; Roberts & Strayer, 1996; compare with Denham, Renwick-DeBardi, & Hewes, 1994), which would be expected to foster social competence. In a longitudinal study, with social competence relations often held over 2 to 6 years (Murphy, Shepard, Eisenberg, Fabes, & Guthrie, 1999). Similar concurrent relations between adult-reported dispositional sympathy and peer- and adult-reported social competence and popularity have been found for Indonesian third graders (Eisenberg, Liew, et al., 2001).

Shyness and inhibition appear to be linked with empathy, at least in some situations, whereas sociability may be less related. Young and associates (1999) found 2-year-old children's inhibition toward an unfamiliar stranger (but not toward their mother) was negatively related with their global empathy (but not concerned expressions) when the stranger feigned injury. Shyness was negatively associated with girls', but not boys', sympathy in a study of young school children (Eisenberg, Fabes, Karbon, et al., 1996), whereas preschoolers' shyness was negatively related with concerned reactions only for boys (and shyness was positively related to concern for girls with warm teachers; Kienbaum, Volland, & Ulich, 2001). In the Eisenberg et al. (1996) study, boys' shyness was not related with sympathy, although younger boys who were shy appeared to prone to distress while viewing an empathy-inducing film. In research with adolescents, social anxiety was associated with high dispositional personal distress (but not sympathy) in one study (Davis & Franzoi, 1991), whereas sociability was unrelated with a similar measure of sympathy in another study (Carlo et al., 1998).

Children's aggressive tendencies also have been negatively correlated with situational measures of empathy-related responding, but not until about 6 years of age. Gill and Calkins (2003) found that 2-year-olds' concerned or empathic responding to an experimenter feigning an injury and to a tape of a crying infant was higher for children with externalizing problems. In addition, they found that aggressive children were physiologically less regulated (on an index of vagal tone). Gill and Calkins suggested that the aggressive children were more prone to empathic overarousal (overly high levels of empathy that are likely to be dysregulating) and that regulated children might distract themselves or otherwise regulate their empathic arousal when the needy people were strangers. Moreover, in a study of 5-year-olds, empathic/prosocial reactions were positively related to aggression (Kienbaum, 2001), whereas in another study, empathy was linked to lower levels of problem behaviors at ages 6 to 7 but not 4 to 5 (Hastings et al., 2000; also see Zahn-Waxler et al., 1995). In young children, aggressiveness also is sometimes positively related with prosocial behavior (Yarrow et al., 1976; see Eisenberg & Fabes, 1998). It is possible that aggressive children are more assertive and are thus more likely to approach others and attend to their needs. Because most studies of empathy with young children have assessed attention to and responses to someone who is hurt, interpersonal style (e.g., inhibition) likely influences many of the findings (e.g., Young et al., 1999).

In contrast to findings with young children, aggression and related externalizing problems tend to be negatively related to empathy/sympathy in children about 6 years and older. For example, low empathy as reported by youth or adults has been correlated with aggression (Strayer & Roberts, 2004), psychoticism (Saklofske & Eysenck, 1983), competitiveness (Barnett, Matthews, & Howard, 1979), delinquency (Cohen & Strayer, 1996), and bullying (Warden & Mackinnon, 2003). Hastings and colleagues (2000) found that 4- to 5-year-olds with behavior problems (including externalizing) declined in their levels of observed concern and adult- or child-reported concern/empathy by age 6 to 7 years. In addition, greater concern for others at 4 to 5 years of age predicted a decrease in the stability and severity of problem behaviors (including externalizing problems) 2 years later, and concern at 6 to 7 years of age predicted decreases in the stability of problem behaviors at 9 to 10 years old. Further, Fabes, Eisenberg, Karbon, Troyer, and their colleagues (1994) found that mothers' reports of kindergartners' and third graders' aggressive coping were positively associated with markers of boys' (but not girls') personal distress (heart rate acceleration and facial stress) when the children heard a crying infant. Zhou and associates (2002) found that school children's situational facial and reported empathy was correlated with both relatively high social competence and low levels of children's externalizing problems; this relation seemed to be somewhat stronger with age. By grades 4 to 7, children's empathy when viewing slides depicting others experiencing negative emotion or in negative situations had stronger unique relations with children's contemporaneous social skills and low levels of externalizing problems than did empathy with positive slides. This relation between empathy with negative slides and low problem behaviors held even when controlling for level of empathy 2 years before. Thus, the relation between empathy/sympathy and aggression may vary depending on whether empathy is in response to others' positive or negative emotions or situations.

Low levels of empathy also appear to contribute to the development of psychopathic tendencies. Psychopaths or people with psychopathic traits are less physiologically responsive to emotion-inducing stimuli (often mildly evocative slides) and to cues of others' distress than are nonpsychopaths (Blair, 1999; Blair, Jones, Clark, & Smith, 1997; Levenston, Patrick, Bradley, & Lang, 2000; Sutton, Vitale, & Newman, 2002; also see Hastings et al., 2000). Thus, children who are not reactive to mild empathy-inducing stimuli may be at risk for externalizing problems. In fact, Liew and co-workers (2003) found that boys (but not girls) who exhibited higher physiological responsivity when viewing slides depicting mild negative events or facial expressions were better regulated and had fewer externalizing problem behaviors than did their less responsive peers. Because the stimuli were very mild, physiological arousal probably did not indicate personal distress (as it likely does in studies involving more evocative stimuli; also see Hastings et al., 2000). Thus, the lack of empathy, as well as empathic overarousal (i.e., personal distress), may contribute to problems in socioemotional development.

Empathy-Related Responding and Emotion Regulation

Eisenberg and colleagues (e.g., Eisenberg & Fabes, 1992; Eisenberg et al., 1994) have suggested that both the experience of various empathy-related responses and individual differences in predispositions to such responding are linked to regulation. As noted, personal distress is believed to frequently stem from empathic overarousal—feelings of empathy that are so arousing that they are experienced as aversive. In contrast, individuals who experience sympathy appear to be affectively aroused, but not to so distressing a level that one becomes self-focused. Thus, whether children and adults can manage their empathic reactions in specific contexts may affect their tendency to experience sympathy or personal distress (and, consequently, their moral behavior). Moreover, individuals who are better regulated in general would be predicted to be prone to sympathy, whereas those who are low in regulation would be expected to be predisposed to experience personal distress.

Researchers seldom have assessed individuals' regulation of emotion in a given setting and their empathy-related responding in the same setting. However, psychophysiological data support the prediction that people in situations likely to elicit a reaction akin to personal distress are more aroused than when they are exposed to sympathy inducing situations (via videotapes or recall of real-life events; Eisenberg & Fabes, 1990; Eisenberg, Fabes, Schaller, Carlo, et al., 1991; Eisenberg, Fabes, et al., 1988; Eisenberg, Fabes, Schaller, Miller, et al., 1991; Eisenberg, Schaller, et al., 1988). The fact that arousal differs in the two situations does not necessarily indicate that regulation also differs; however, it suggests that personal distress involves a higher level of arousal than sympathy that is probably somewhat less modulated by regulatory activities.

There is considerably more research pertaining to the relation of dispositional regulation (i.e., relatively stable individual differences in regulation) with individual differences in empathy-related responding (either in specific situations or dispositional sympathy), at least past the first few years of life (such a relation may not hold at a young age; see Gill & Calkins, 2003). In regard to children's expression of sympathy and personal distress in response to specific stimuli, there appears to be a very modest positive relation between markers of sympathetic responding and dispositional regulation. For example, Eisenberg and Fabes (1995) found that children who displayed concerned facial reactions to a sympathy-inducing film were high in attentional control (an aspect of regulation) and low in unregulated coping behaviors. Similarly, Guthrie and colleagues (1997) found modest positive relations between teachers' and parents' reports of children's attentional regulation and children's facial sadness, self-reported sadness or sympathy, and heart rate deceleration versus acceleration (a marker of other-directedness of attention and, hence, sympathy) in response to an empathy-inducing film. Further, children's, parents', and teachers' reports of children's dispositional sympathy have been associated with adults' (parents' or teachers') reports of children's abilities to regulate their attention or emotion-induced behavior (e.g., Eisenberg, Fabes, Murphy, et al., 1996; Eisenberg, Fabes, Shepard, et al., 1998; Eisenberg, Liew, & Pidada, 2001; Murphy et al., 1999). Similarly, parents' reports (Rothbart, Ahadi, & Hershey, 1994) and self-reports (Sneed, 2002) of children's empathy have been positively related to children's regulation (Rothbart et al., 1994). Dispositional regulation also has been associated with sympathy in adulthood, although sometimes only when individual differences in negative emotionality have been controlled in the analyses (Eisenberg et al., 1994; Eisenberg & Okun, 1996; Okun, Shepard, & Eisenberg, 2000). The positive association between sympathy and regulation is consistent with data indicating a negative relation between sympathy and the predisposition to anger or intense negative emotions (Carlo et al., 1998; Eisenberg, Fabes, Murphy, et al., 1996; Murphy et al., 1999; Roberts & Strayer, 1996) although empathy/sympathy may be positively related with expressivity or intensity of emotions more generally (Eisenberg et al., 1994; Roberts & Strayer, 1996; see Eisenberg, Wentzel, & Harris, 1998). It is also consistent with the finding that elementary school boys with attention deficit hyperactivity disorder (ADHD)—who clearly have problems with regulation (Nigg, 2001)—are lower on empathy than non-ADHD boys (Braaten & Rosen, 2000).

There are few data on the relation of individual differences in personal distress to regulation. Ungerer and associates (1990) found that 12-month-olds' distressed responses to viewing a tape of a peer fretting (i.e., sucking on oneself, one's clothing, or an object) and crying—presumably indices of personal distress—were associated with lower levels of optimal regulatory strategies at approximately 20 weeks of age when presented with a distressing stimulus (i.e., the mother maintaining a still, noninteractive face). In addition, Guthrie and co-workers (1997) found that children who exhibited heart rate acceleration (versus deceleration) in response to an empathy-inducing film were viewed by adults as relatively unregulated. Furthermore, Eisenberg, Fabes, Murphy, et al. (1996) found that heart rate acceleration in response to a distressing film clip was related to self-reports and teachers' reports of low dispositional sympathy for boys (but not girls). When dispositional personal distress has been assessed with questionnaire measures in adulthood, researchers have found consistent and moderately strong negative relations between personal distress and dispositional regulation (Eisenberg et al., 1994; Eisenberg & Okun, 1996; Okun et al., 2000).

Thus, overall, there is some evidence that regulatory processes are involved in whether individuals experience sympathy or personal distress. However, because most of the evidence is correlational, causal relations cannot be ascertained with certainty. However, there also is preliminary evidence that participation in an experimental intervention program designed to promote regulation (e.g., by teaching children about emotions and how to inhibit their behavior when upset) was linked with increases in empathy (Greenberg & Kusche, 1997), a finding that provides some initial tentative support for a causal relation between regulation and empathy. The fact that regulation is linked to empathy-related responding suggests that empathy, sympathy, and personal distress involve biologically based temperamental predispositions (because many aspects of regulation appear to be temperamentally based; Rothbart & Bates, 1998) and that adults' attempts to promote children's regulatory abilities are likely to have a positive effect on empathy-related responding. Indeed, there is some initial evidence that regulation mediates the negative relation between adults' expression of negative emotion in the home and children's sympathy (Eisenberg, Liew, et al., 2001).

Gender Differences in Empathy-Related Responding

A commonly held gender stereotype is that girls and women are significantly more empathic and sympathetic than boys and men (e.g., Martin, 1987). Yet, the strength of empirical evidence to bolster this belief about children is mixed.

Eisenberg and Lennon (1983, 1987) and Eisenberg and Fabes (1998) drew attention to the discrepancy between public perception and empirical data on gender differences in children's sympathy and empathy through meta-analyses of extant work. Corresponding effect sizes were inconsistent across studies; empirical support for such gender differences ranged from small to overwhelmingly large. Eisenberg and colleagues speculated the range of effect sizes might be due to the specific method used to assess children's sympathy and empathy and the meta-analytic results support this supposition.

The largest gender divergences and effect sizes have been found for self-report measures of empathy and sympathy, which are one of the most popular means of assessment. Self-report research involving questionnaires either not previously reviewed or published since the Eisenberg and Fabes (1998) review bolsters the argument that girls have greater empathy and sympathy than do boys (see Eisenberg, Zhou, & Koller, 2001; Karniol, Gabay, & Ochion, 1998; Litvack-Miller et al., 1997; Olweus & Endresen, 1998; Van Tilburg, Unterberg, & Vingerhoets, 1992), although not all findings support this conclusion (see Humphries, Parker, & Jagers, 2000; Sneed, 2002). Eisenberg and Lennon (1983) suggested the use of self-reports might invoke demand characteristics because children may be aware of what is being assessed (sympathy or empathy) and attempt to provide responses in line with prevailing gender stereotypes.

In contrast to findings for self-reports on questionnaire measures, the pattern of data is less consistent for children's self-reported reactions to empathy-inducing stimuli in a specific situation (rather than a questionnaire about general levels of empathy and sympathy). Eisenberg and Lennon (1983) reported an overall very small effect size, favoring girls, associated with these works. Most of the early studies used Feshbach and Roe's (1968) measure of empathy, which involved exposing children to short vignettes (accompanied by slides) about a child in an emotion-arousing situation and then asking children how they feel. Such measures have not been widely used recently and tend not to elicit gender differences (Kasari, Feeman, & Bass, 2003).

In recent studies, investigators have tended to tap empathy and sympathy through the use of more evocative films, slides, or puppet shows. These procedures have found some gender differences favoring girls (Kienbaum et al., 2001; Strayer & Roberts, 1997; Zahn-Waxler, Robinson, & Emde, 1992; Zhou et al., 2002). Similarly, investigators who rely on others (e.g., parents and teachers) to rate children's levels of empathy and sympathy typically find raters attribute higher levels to girls than to boys (Eisenberg, Fabes, Shepard, et al., 1998; Hastings et al., 2000; Holmgren et al., 1998; Murphy et al., 1999; see Eisenberg & Fabes, 1998; Eisenberg & Lennon, 1983; Lennon & Eisenberg, 1987, for reviews).

Conversely, modest, if any, sex differences in empathy and sympathy have been found with measures over which participants have less conscious control. For example, non-verbal measures, such as those that rely on children's facial expressions in response to sympathy- and empathy-inducing situations, typically fail to differ across males and females (Eisenberg, Fabes, Schaller, & Miller, 1989; Eisenberg & Lennon, 1983; Eisenberg & Fabes, 1998). Facial measures entail researchers coding children's emotional reactions, such as facial distress or concern (intense interests, eyebrows furrowing) in response to sympathy-inducing stimuli (such as a film involving a distressed victim). Nonetheless, recently a few investigators, albeit certainly not all (Holmgren et al., 1998), have reported sex differences in facial responses. For example, Strayer and Roberts (1997) found 5- to 13-year-old girls exhibited significantly greater facial empathy than did boys in response to videotapes designed to elicit emotional response. Similarly, Hastings and colleagues (2000) noted that 4- to 7-year-old girls displayed significantly greater facial concern to simulated episodes in which someone was hurt than did male peers; Zahn-Waxler and associates (2001) obtained the same finding in a longitudinal study of toddlers. In addition, Zhou and co-workers (2002) reported that young elementary school girls exhibited more positive emotion when viewing slides depicting others in positive situations than did boys (although girls and boys did not differ on such responding 2 years later or in negative facial reactions to negative slides). Thus, support for gender differences in children's facial sympathetic and empathic responses is weak but growing. Moreover, Eisenberg and Fabes (1998), in their meta-analysis, found a gender difference favoring girls for observational measures of empathy and sympathy, which typically included facial and behavioral and gestural indices of empathy. It is possible more contemporary research is finding such differences because both data collection and coding procedures for facial responses are more differentiated than in the past.

Another common nonverbal, unobtrusive measure of children's emotional reactions is their physiological responses to sympathy- and empathy-provoking situations. Little empirical work supports gender differences in physiological responses to sympathy- and empathy-inducing scenarios (Eisenberg & Fabes, 1998; Guthrie et al., 1997; see also Zahn-Waxler et al., 1995), perhaps because physiological responses can reflect a variety of underlying reactions well beyond sympathy and empathy. In addition, the meaning of the physiological response may vary with the evocativeness of the empathy-inducing stimulus (Liew et al., 2003).

In summary, the degree of sex differences in children's empathy and sympathy fluctuates considerably across studies, likely due to the use of different methods. The pattern is strongest for self-report (especially questionnaire) indices, over which individuals have the greatest conscious control. When such control is less feasible—as with facial or behavioral responses—girls still are more empathic and sympathetic, but the effects are much less pronounced.

Interestingly, gender differences in self-reports of empathy and sympathy become more marked as children age (Eisenberg & Fabes, 1998). This pattern runs parallel to the reported greater adherence to traditional gender roles as children age (Ruble & Martin, 1998). Conceivably, there is a strong link between the two developmental patterns; older children, who are savvier than younger children in regard to gender stereotypes, may strive to ensure their behaviors match those embedded within their respective gender schema (e.g., see Karniol et al., 1998; Eisenberg, Zhou, & Koller, 2001, for relations between self-reported sympathy and femininity).

Taken together, data published in recent years suggest that the public perception of gender differences in empathy and sympathy is possibly exaggerated. Certainly, some degree of gender difference is likely to exist, given that all effect sizes favor females over males. However, it is possible that part of the gender difference in measures of empathy and sympathy is due to children's desire to adhere to gender-stereotypic conceptions, perhaps to bolster their image with other people as well as their own self-image.

SOCIALIZATION OF EMPATHY-RELATED RESPONDING

As hypothesized by Hoffman (1981) decades ago, there is little doubt that empathy has a hereditary basis. Indeed, monozygotic (identical) twins have been found to be more similar in empathy-related responding across the lifespan than have fraternal twins (Emde et al., 1992; Loehlin & Nichols, 1976; Matthews, Batson, Horn, & Rosenman, 1981; Rushton, Fulker, Neale, Nias, & Eysenck, 1986; Zahn-Waxler, Robinson, & Emde, 1992; Zahn-Waxler et al., 2001). It is likely that part of the hereditary influence on empathy-related responding is genetically transmitted through biologically based individual differences in children's dispositional regulation and proneness to experience emotion (see Eisenberg & Fabes, 1998; Eisenberg, Wentzel, et al., 1998).

Nonetheless, it is likely that environmental factors, including interactions with care-givers, can either promote or inhibit the development of sympathy and personal distress. Thus, environmental influences may vary from child to child (see Plomin et al., 1993), even in the same family, due to many factors (e.g., differences in birth order, parental age, family composition, and resources when children are different ages, as well as different interactions between parental behaviors and child characteristics due to both hereditary and environmental factors). Parents' socialization practices often may partly reflect parents' genetic makeup, which is passed on to offspring and may affect children's capacity for empathy. However, even if socialization practices have some biological basis, children's experience when exposed to these parental behaviors can be viewed as at least partly an aspect of their social environment, and children's observation of, and interactions with, socializers also likely contribute to individual differences in empathy-related reactions above and beyond any contribution due to heredity.

Similarities in Parents' and Children's Empathy-Related Responding

Although the reasons for this association are not clear, there seems to be a relation between parents' (especially mothers') reports of their own dispositional sympathy and that of same-gender children in the elementary school years. Mothers' sympathy (or perspective taking combined with sympathy) has been positively related with their early to mid-elementary school-age daughters' sympathy (Eisenberg et al., 1992; Eisenberg & McNally, 1993;

Fabes et al., 1990) and negatively related with daughters' personal distress (Eisenberg, Fabes, Schaller, Carlo, et al., 1991). Conversely, mothers' personal distress sometimes has been related with either daughters' low empathic responding or sons' and daughters' inappropriate positive emotion in response to distressed or needy others (Eisenberg et al., 1992; Fabes et al., 1990). Mothers' sympathy usually has not been related with sons' sympathy (although a positive relation was found by Eisenberg et al., 1992), whereas fathers' sympathy has been linked with sons' sympathy (Eisenberg, Fabes, Schaller, Carlo, et al., 1991). It is possible that individual differences in parents' sympathy caused differences in same-sex children's sympathy, but it is also plausible that genetic factors were partly responsible for the similarity in sympathy. However, the fact that the association is within sex seems to argue against a genetic explanation, unless genes related to empathy are carried on the sex chromosomes.

In contrast, the relation between parents' and children's empathy (rather than sympathy and personal distress) is less consistent, with some investigators finding a relation (Trommsdorff, 1991) and others finding either little association (Kalliopuska, 1984; Strayer & Roberts, 1989), or a complex pattern of relations (Barnett, King, Howard, & Dino, 1980). In one study in which mothers and children watched an empathy-inducing film together, mothers who exhibited high facial distress and heart rate acceleration during a distressing film had children who also did so (Eisenberg et al., 1992). Thus, it is unclear if parents and children are similar in their empathic arousal.

Interestingly, Tucker, Updegraff, McHale, and Crouter (1999) found that early adolescents' (boys and girls ages 10 to 12) empathy was positively related with their younger sisters' (2 to 3 years younger) empathy, whereas older brothers' (but not sisters') empathy was related with younger brothers' empathy. The authors posited that younger siblings might model or identify with older siblings.

Quality of the Parent–Child Relationship and Children's Empathy-Related Responding

In general, sympathy (and sometimes empathy) has been linked to a high quality relationship with the caregiving parent and with supportive parenting. For example, although the findings have not been entirely consistent (e.g., Pastor, 1981) or sometimes have involved complex, moderated relations (e.g., Radke-Yarrow, Zahn-Waxler, Richardson, Susman, & Martinez, 1994), children who are securely attached tend to display more empathic concern toward an injured stranger (but not mother) at 22 (but not 16) months (van der Mark et al., 2002), and are relatively sympathetic and prosocial (often these variables were not differentiated) at age 3 to 4 (Kestenbaum, Farber, & Sroufe, 1989; Waters, Wippman, & Sroufe, 1979). Children with secure attachments may attend to and want to please their parents more than other children (Waters, Hay, & Richters, 1986), which may facilitate parental attempts to foster empathy and sympathy. Moreover, the quality of early attachments is important to the development of a sense of connection to others and positive valuing of other people, characteristics likely to foster sympathetic responding (Staub, 1992).

Consistent with attachment theory, maternal responsiveness (i.e., contingent responding) in infancy also has been found to predict later empathic responding. For example, Kochanska, Forman, and Coy (1999) found that maternal responsivity at 9 months predicted higher levels of toddlers' empathy and prosocial responsiveness at 22 months. Moreover, maternal sensitivity at 10 months has been positively related with toddlers' concerned attention to adults' feigned distress at 18 months of age (Spinrad, 1999).

Similarly, some investigators have found a positive relation between children's or adolescents' empathy or sympathy and warm, empathic parenting (Robinson, Zahn-Waxler, & Emde, 1994; Trommsdorff, 1991; Zahn-Waxler, Radke-Yarrow, & King, 1979), parental affection, or nurturance (Barnett et al., 1980; Eisenberg-Berg & Mussen, 1978; Krevans & Gibbs, 1996), whereas others have not (e.g., Eisenberg, Fabes, Schaller, Carlo, et al., 1991; Iannotti, Cummings, Pierrehumbert, Milano, & Zahn-Waxler, 1992; Janssens & Gerris, 1992; Kienbaum et al., 2001; also see van der Mark et al., 2002). In other cases, findings were mixed. Carlo and associates (1998) found an association between adolescents' self-reported sympathy and paternal (but not maternal) support only for adolescents who were low in both anger and sociability. Zhou and co-workers (2002) found weak relations between parental warmth and children's facial or self-reported empathy to positive, but not negative, evocative slides. Although Bryant (1987) found no relation between general parental support and empathy for 7- and 10-year-olds, maternal report of expressions of support during times of stress predicted children's empathy. Maternal support when children are under stress may foster empathy more than overall level of maternal warmth.

Consistent with the notion that warm, supportive parenting is positively related with empathy and sympathy, Crockenberg (1985) reported that parents who display intense or frequent anger tend to have toddlers who are low in other-oriented concern and high in self-concern (also see Denham & Grout, 1992; Denham et al., 1994; compare with Denham & Grout, 1993). Similarly, Hastings and colleagues (2002) found that parental report of their own negative affect (anger, disappointment, and conflict) in interactions with their children was negatively related with children's empathy (but not concern) at 7 years of age (but no significant relations were obtained at age 5). Moreover, there appears to be a relatively consistent relation between parental abusive behavior and low levels of empathy in children (George & Main, 1979; Howes & Eldredge, 1985; Main & George, 1985; see Miller & Eisenberg, 1988).

Warm rather than hostile relationships with other family members and adults also may contribute to children's empathy and sympathy. Bryant (1987) found that children who had significant relationships with grandparents and other older people tended to be higher in empathy (Bryant, 1987). In addition, Tucker and colleagues (1999) found that boys who had positive relations with older siblings were more empathic than boys with less positive sibling relationships. Kienbaum and associates (2001) found a weak, positive relation between teachers' warmth and children's concerned reactions to puppets' enacted distress. Similarly, Donohue, Perry, and Weinstein (2003) found that children whose teachers used learner-centered practices that were supportive and took the children's abilities and needs into account were more empathic.

Relations of Parental General Disciplinary Practices to Children's Empathy-Related Responding

Findings regarding links between disciplinary practices and empathy are somewhat inconsistent, perhaps in part because sympathy and personal distress seldom have been differentiated in this research (e.g., Barnett et al., 1980). Nonetheless, some investigators have found a positive association between inductive practices (e.g., parental use of reasoning) and children's empathy and sympathy (e.g., Janssens & Gerris, 1992; Krevans & Gibbs, 1996; Miller, Eisenberg, Fabes, Shell, & Gular, 1989; Zahn-Waxler et al., 1979; also see Denham et al., 1994). Hoffman (1983, 2000) has argued that inductions orient children to the needs of others in a manner that is not so threatening or arousing that children become self-concerned or fail to process the information well. Somewhat consistent with this view, Miller and co-workers (1989) found that maternal inductions were positively related with children's facial sadness and negatively related with facial distress in response to empathy-inducing film clips; however, the negative relation for distress held only when mothers' reported reactions were not high in intensity.

Relations between empathy-related responding and parental control likely are complex, although in general, harsh control seems to be negatively related to sympathy or positively related to personal distress. In one study of preschoolers' sympathy and empathy and personal distress, mothers' infrequent use of negative control (i.e., nonphysical power assertion or negative appraisals of the child) was related with children's self-reported concern in response to viewing distressed children in a film. However, physical control (physical punishment or physically guiding the child's actions) was positively associated with the preschoolers' facial sadness (when mothers expressed high levels of maternal affect) and negatively related with their facial distress (Miller et al., 1989). In studies of empathy, parents' use of power assertion has been negatively related (Janssens & Gerris, 1992; Krevans & Gibbs, 1996) or unrelated (Bryant, 1987; Feshbach, 1975) with children's empathy. Moreover, parental demandingness (i.e., expectations of mature behavior) and limit setting have been positively related with children's empathy (Bryant, 1987; Janssens & Gerris, 1992; also see Krevans & Gibbs, 1996), whereas paternal (but not maternal) indulgence has predicted low levels of empathy for boys (findings were mixed for girls; Bryant, 1987). Consistent with a number of these findings, Hastings and colleagues (2000) found that a composite score of authoritarian parenting (including mothers' discouragement of expressivity, issues of prohibitions and reprimands, control by anxiety inductions, strict supervision, and corporal punishment) minus authoritative parenting (the use of reasoning and guidance, encouragement of independence, support for open expression of emotion) was negatively related with children's concern for others and empathy and positively related to disregard for others at age 7. However, when the children were 5 years old, this index of parenting related only with low empathy (and not concern).

In summary, although the data are not highly consistent, the general pattern of findings suggests that parents who use reasoning for discipline, set high standards for their children, and are not overly derogatory or punitive are relatively likely to rear empathic (or perhaps sympathetic) children. However, the relevant data are limited in quantity, especially in regard to the disciplinary correlates of children's sympathy. Nonetheless, it is likely that parents play a role in helping children deal with interpersonal situations in regulated and productive ways (which would be expected to foster the development of sympathy rather than personal distress) and in teaching children to attend to and value the welfare of others.

Parental Emotion-Related Disciplinary Practices

Recently investigators have increasingly examined parental reactions to children's emotional displays and emotion-related behavior, and such reactions appear to be associated with children's sympathy and personal distress. In general, parental practices that promote children's ability to deal constructively with their own negative emotion seem to foster sympathy rather than personal distress. This may be because children who cannot adequately cope with their emotions tend to become overaroused (experience high levels of vicarious negative emotion) and, thus, experience a self-focused reaction (personal distress) to others' distress or need.

Parents who are strict with regard to children's expression of emotion may deny them opportunities for learning about feelings and their regulation (Gottman, Katz, & Hooven, 1997). Eisenberg, Fabes, Schaller, Carlo, and Miller et al. (1991) found that parents' reports of restrictiveness in response to children's expression of anxiety and sadness in a variety of contexts were positively correlated with facial and physiological markers of boys' (but not girls') distress when viewing a sympathy-inducing film, accompanied by self-reports of low distress in reaction to the film. Thus, sons of restrictive parents seemed prone to experience distress when confronted with others' distress, but either denied or did not acknowledge to themselves what they were feeling.

However, it is important to note that the effect of parental restrictiveness may vary with both the situation in which the emotion is expressed and the age of the child. Parents who discouraged their same-sex elementary school children from expressing emotions that would be hurtful to others had children high in self-reported sympathy (Eisenberg, Fabes, Schaller, Carlo, et al., 1991). Parents who try to discourage children's hurtful emotional displays likely focus their children's attention on the effects their emotions have on others. However, restrictiveness in regard to the display of hurtful emotions was associated with high levels of personal distress in younger (kindergarten) girls (but not boys). Mothers of these girls appeared less supportive in general; thus, for younger girls, this sort of maternal restrictiveness may have reflected age-inappropriate restrictiveness or low levels of support (Eisenberg et al., 1992).

Parents also teach children ways to deal with their negative emotions. A mode of coping with emotional stress that often appears to be constructive is acting directly upon the problem, that is, trying to change factors in the environment that have caused the distress (Lazarus & Folkman, 1984; Sandler, Tein, Mehta, Wolchik, & Ayers, 2000; Sandler, Tein, & West, 1994). Eisenberg, Fabes, Schaller, Carlo, and Miller (1991) found that boys (but not girls) whose parents encouraged them to deal instrumentally with situations causing their own sadness or anxiety were more likely to exhibit markers of sympathy rather than personal distress in empathy-inducing contexts. Boys who are able to modulate their negative emotions in this way may be better able than other boys to regulate their empathic arousal and, consequently, more likely to experience sympathy. However, Eisenberg and colleagues (1993) did not find that mothers' reports of using problem solving when their children were distressed or anxious were related with their children's facial distress and heart rate response to a crying baby (although they did relate to greater helping).

Maternal behaviors in ongoing evocative situations (that do not involve discipline) that direct children's attention to another's situation or help children to feel the other's distress also have been associated with sympathy (Fabes, Eisenberg, Karbon, et al., 1994). For example, mothers' references to their own sympathy and sadness and their attempts to induce perspective taking or highlight another's feelings or situation have been associated with boys' reports of sympathy and sadness (Eisenberg et al., 1992). In contrast, there may be fewer relations of such maternal practices to children's empathy (Eisenberg, Losoya, et al., 2001; Iannotti et al., 1992). Parental attempts to promote perspective taking are also often part of parental inductive discipline (Hoffman, 2000), and as discussed, this sort of induction has been specifically associated with empathy (Krevans & Gibbs, 1996).

Findings are mixed in regard to whether the mere labeling or discussion of emotions fosters empathic or sympathetic tendencies (e.g., Barnett, Howard, King, & Dino, 1980; Barnett, King, Howard, & Dino, 1980) Belden, Kuelbli, Pauley, and Kindleberger (2003) found that mothers' questions about their children's emotional reactions, states of mind, or interpretations about the motivation for a good deed performed by their child in the past were positively correlated with children's self-reported empathy. Eisenberg and co-workers (1993) found no relation between mothers' reported discussion of emotion when their children were distressed or anxious and children's distressed reactions to a crying infant. Fabes, Eisenberg, Karbon, et al. (1994) found no relation between mothers' actual use of emotion terms when viewing evocative films and children's sympathy; however, the degree to which mothers were warm and directed their children's attention to the emotional content of the film was positively related with markers of children's sympathy, and negatively related with markers of personal distress, in second graders but not kindergartners. Further, Eisenberg, Losoya, et al. (2001) found that parental labeling of emotions or talking about emotions when viewing slides depicting emotion was unrelated with children's facial reactivity to empathy-inducing slides. Parental discussion of emotion may be associated with children's sympathy primarily when such discussion fosters perspective taking and an understanding of emotion (see Dunn, Brown, & Beardsall, 1991; Dunn, Brown, Slomkowski, Tesla, & Youngblade, 1991), and when such discussion occurs in everyday interactions that are not characterized by either conflict or a high degree of parental anger in response to children's behavior (see Denham et al., 1994; Dunn & Brown, 1994). Thus, parental warmth combined with the tendency to focus children's attention on what is happening to others in their social world may promote children's feelings of sympathy more than simply labeling or discussing emotion (Fabes, Eisenberg, Karbon, et al., 1994). Moreover, parental discussion of emotion appears to be linked with children's regulation (Gottman et al., 1997), which may indirectly promote sympathy.

Frequent parental expression of emotions that are neither hurtful nor hostile in view of children (albeit not necessarily directed at them) also may encourage children to experience others' emotions (Eisenberg, Fabes, Schaller, Miller, et al., 1991). For example, the expression of soft, nonassertive negative emotions in the home has been positively associated with girls' (especially younger girls') sympathy. In contrast, both boys and girls from homes in which hostile negative emotions frequently are expressed seem to be prone to personal distress (Eisenberg et al., 1992). Denham and associates (1994) found that mothers who, when asked to simulate emotions, tended to exhibit intense negative emotions (that sometimes were disturbing to the child) had children who expressed relatively less concern in response to peers' emotions. It is likely that degree and quality of family expressiveness not only reflects the quality of family interactions, but also teaches children what emotions, and how much emotion, they are expected to display and experience and how to regulate their emotions (Gottman et al., 1997; see Halberstadt, Crisp, & Eaton, 1999).

Even parental expression of more assertive or hostile parental negative emotion has been linked to higher sympathy in children if it is moderate in quantity. Moreover, the relation of parental assertive negative expressivity to children's empathy-related responding appears to be moderated by children's level of dispositional negative regulation. For example, Valiente and colleagues (2004) found a negative relation between children's situational sympathy and parents' negative expressivity, but only for children low in regulation. In addition, for children moderate or low in regulation, personal distress was relatively high regardless of the level of parental expression of negative emotion, whereas for well-regulated children, personal distress was low when parents expressed little negative emotion but increased with the levels of parental expression of negative emotion.

Of course, cultures differ in the degree to which they value the direct expression of emotion and encourage children to express their emotions (e.g., Zahn-Waxler, Friedman, Cole, Mizuta, & Hiruma, 1996). Thus, relations between parental expressivity and children's empathy and sympathy may vary across cultures. For example, Eisenberg and co-workers (2001) found that parents' (primarily mothers') reported expression of positive emotions was positively related to American, but not Indonesian, children's sympathy. In contrast, parent-reported expression of negative emotions was more consistently negatively related with adults' reports of Indonesian children's sympathy. In Indonesia, the experience or overt expression of intense emotions—positive or negative—tends to be discouraged because it is believed to undermine social relationships and to cause illnesses (e.g., Geertz, 1976; Mulder, 1996; Wellenkamp, 1995). The devaluing of emotionality in Java might account for the different pattern of relations in the two cultures.

The findings already reviewed generally support the view that children's tendencies to respond with sympathy versus personal distress are in part learned, although many factors may moderate the effectiveness of socialization and genetic factors often may be involved in the process. Moreover, the socialization process likely is bi-directional. For example, Fabes, Eisenberg, Karbon, Bernzweig, and co-workers (1994) found that mothers' perceptions of how distressed their children became when exposed to others' distress were greater for younger (kindergarten) than older (second grade) children. These mothers were warmer and displayed more positive and less negative emotion when telling stories about another in distress to younger than older children; it appeared mothers were trying to buffer younger children's reactions to the stories. Indeed, if mothers viewed their kindergartner as emotionally vulnerable, then they were especially likely to display positive rather than negative emotion when telling the stories.

CONCLUSIONS

Knowledge of the development and correlates of children's empathy and sympathy has grown considerably in the past three decades. Clearly, empathy and sympathy are linked to important domains of children's functioning, such as their prosocial behavior and adjustment. In addition, it seems likely that socialization, as well as heredity, contribute to individual and gender differences in empathy-related responding. Moreover, although not discussed in detail in this chapter, sympathy has been linked with higher level moral reasoning (Eisenberg, 1986; Eisenberg, Zhou, & Koller, 2001). However, in much of the research, measures of empathy, sympathy, and even prosocial behavior are not clearly differentiated (or are combined), especially in studies of young children. This lack of differentiation likely contributes to the inconsistencies across findings. Moreover, observational measures of constructs have often been used to study empathy-related responding in young children, whereas self- or other-reports have been used to assess empathy and sympathy in older children and adolescents. Thus, differences in findings, as well as some of the findings in regard to age trends, could be partly due to methodological variations across age groups. Furthermore, there are few longitudinal or genetically informed studies of empathy and sympathy, so it is especially difficult to draw causal conclusions about the role of socialization in its development.

In future research, it is important to differentiate between empathy, sympathy, and personal distress so their differential relations to socioemotional functioning and socialization can be documented. In addition, it would be useful to delineate in greater detail the causal relations and processes that mediate and moderate the relations observed in the literature. For example, information on how children's affective and cognitive processing in socialization encounters mediates the relations of parental socialization practices to empathy-related responding is needed. Further, the ways in which children's temperament moderates the effectiveness of parental practices that appear to foster empathy or sympathy merit greater attention. Finally, more attention to context is needed. Relatively little is known about situational variables that stimulate or evoke empathy and sympathy and the conditions under which children are likely to experience personal distress. Nor is there much research on cultural differences in the origins and correlates of empathy-related responding. Empathy and sympathy likely are less valued in some cultures than others, and socialization practices that promote empathy-related responding likely differ depending on how much it and emotionality more generally are valued. Finally, the role of empathy and sympathy in other aspects of morality besides prosocial or aggressive behavior (e.g., conscience, moral reasoning) is an issue for future research.

ACKNOWLEDGMENT

Work on this chapter was funded by a grant from the National Institutes of Mental Health (2 R01 MH60838).

REFERENCES

Adams, G. R. (1983). Social competence during adolescence: Social sensitivity, locus of control, empathy, and peer popularity. *Journal of Youth and Adolescence, 12,* 203–211.

Barnett, M. A., Howard, J. A., King, L. M., & Dino, G. A. (1980). Antecedents of empathy: Retrospective accounts of early socialization. *Personality and Social Psychology Bulletin, 6,* 361–365.

Barnett, M. A., King, L. M., Howard, J. A., & Dino, G. A. (1980). Empathy in young children: Relation to parents' empathy, affection, and emphasis on the feelings of others. *Developmental Psychology, 16,* 243–244.

Barnett, M. A., Matthews, K. A., & Howard, J. A. (1979). Relationship between competitiveness and empathy in 6- and 7-year-olds. *Developmental Psychology, 15,* 221–222.

Batson, C. D. (1991). *The altruism question: Toward a social-psychological answer.* Hillsdale, NJ: Lawrence Erlbaum Associates.

Batson, C. D. (1998). Altruism and prosocial behavior. In D.T. Gilbert, S.T. Fiske, & G. Lindzey (Eds.), *The handbook of social psychology* (Vol. 2, pp. 282–316). Boston: McGraw-Hill.

Belden, A., Kuebli, J., Pauley, D., & Kindleberger, L. (2003, April). Predicting children's empathy from family talk about past good deeds. Paper presented at the biennial meeting of the Society for Research in Child Development, Tampa, FL.

Bischof-Kohler, D. (1991). The development of empathy in infants. In M.E. Lamb & H. Keller (Eds.), *Infant development: Perspectives from German-Speaking countries* (pp. 245–273). Hillsdale, NJ: Lawrence Erlbaum Associates.

Blair, R. J. R. (1999). Responsiveness to distress cues in the child with psychopathic tendencies. *Personality and Individual Differences, 27,* 135–145.

Blair, R. J. R., Jones, L., Clark, F., & Smith, M. (1997). The psychopathic individual: A lack of responsiveness to distress cues? *Psychophysiology, 34,* 192–198.

Blum, L. A. (1980). *Friendship, altruism and morality.* London: Routledge and Kegan Paul.

Braaten, E. B., & Rosen, L. A. (2000). Self-regulation of affect in attention deficit-hyperactivity disorder (ADHD) and non-ADHD boys: Differences in empathic responding. *Journal of Consulting and Clinical Psychology, 68,* 313–321.

Bryant, B. K. (1987). Mental health, temperament, family, and friends: Perspectives on children's empathy and social perspective taking. In N. Eisenberg & J. Strayer (Eds.), *Empathy and its development* (pp. 245–270). Cambridge, UK: Cambridge University Press.

Cacioppo, J. T., & Sandman, C. A. (1978). Physiological differentiation of sensory and cognitive tasks as a function of warning processing demands and reported unpleasantness. *Biological Psychology, 6,* 181–192.

Carlo, G., Hausmann, A., Christiansen, S., & Randall, B. A. (2003). Sociocognitive and behavioral correlates of a measure of prosocial tendencies for adolescents. *Journal of Early Adolescence, 23,* 107–134.

Carlo, G., Roesch, S. C., & Melby, J. (1998). The multiplicative relations of parenting and temperament to prosocial and antisocial behaviors in adolescence. *Journal of Early. Adolescence, 18,* 266–290.

Cohen, D., & Strayer, J. (1996). Empathy in conduct-disordered and comparison youth. *Developmental Psychology, 32,* 988–998.

Crockenberg, S. (1985). Toddlers' reactions to maternal anger. *Merrill-Palmer Quarterly, 31,* 361–373.

Davis, M. H., & Franzoi, S. (1991). Stability and change in adolescent self-consciousness and empathy. *Journal of Research in Personality, 25,* 70–87.

Denham, S. A., & Couchoud, E. A. (1991). Social-emotional predictors of preschoolers' responses to adult negative emotion. *Journal of Child Psychology and Psychiatry, 32,* 595–608.

Denham, S. A., & Grout, L. (1992). Mothers' emotional expressiveness and coping: Relations with preschoolers' social-emotional competence. *Genetic, Social, and General Psychology Monographs, 118,* 75–101.

Denham, S. A., & Grout, L. (1993). Socialization of emotion: Pathway to preschoolers' emotional and social competence. *Journal of Nonverbal Behavior, 17,* 205–227.

Denham, S. A., Mitchell-Copeland, J., Strandberg, K., Auerbach, S., & Blair, K. (1997). Parental contributions to preschoolers' emotional competence: Direct and indirect effects. *Motivation and Emotion, 21,* 65–86.

Denham, S. A., Renwick-DeBardi, S., & Hewes, S. (1994). Emotional communication between mothers and preschoolers: Relations with emotional competence. *Merrill-Palmer Quarterly, 40,* 488–508.

Dondi, M., Simion, F., & Caltran, G. (1999). Can newborns discriminate between their own cry and the cry of another newborn? *Developmental Psychology, 35,* 418–426.

Donohue, K. M., Perry, K. E., & Weinstein, R. S. (2003). Teachers' classroom practices and children's rejection by their peers. *Applied Developmental Psychology, 24,* 91–118.

Dunn, J. (1988). *The beginnings of social understanding*. Oxford: Blackwell.

Dunn, J., & Brown, J. (1994). Affect expression in the family, children's understanding of emotions, and their interactions with others. *Merrill-Palmer Quarterly, 40,* 120–137.

Dunn, J., Brown, J., & Beardsall, L. (1991). Family talk about feeling states and children's later understanding of others' emotions. *Developmental Psychology, 27,* 448–455.

Dunn, J., Brown, J., Slomkowski, C., Tesla, C., & Youngblade, L. (1991). Young children's understanding of other people's feelings and beliefs: Individual differences and their antecedents. *Child Development, 62,* 1352–1366.

Eisenberg, N. (1986). *Altruistic emotion, cognition, and behavior*. Hillsdale, NJ: Lawrence Erlbaum Associates.

Eisenberg, N., Carlo, G., Murphy, B., & Van Court, P. (1995). Prosocial development in late adolescence: A longitudinal study. *Child Development, 66,* 911–936.

Eisenberg, N., Cumberland, A. Guthrie, I. K., Murphy, B. C., & Shepard, S. A. (2003). *Age changes in prosocial responding and moral reasoning in adolescence and early adulthood*. Arizona State University. Manuscript under editorial review.

Eisenberg, N., & Fabes, R. A. (1990). Empathy: Conceptualization, assessment, and relation to prosocial behavior. *Motivation and Emotion, 14,* 131–149.

Eisenberg, N., & Fabes, R. A. (1992). Emotion, regulation, and the development of social competence. In M. S. Clark (Ed.), *Review of Personality and Social Psychology, Vol: 14: Emotion and social behavior* (pp. 119–150). Newbury Park, CA: Sage.

Eisenberg, N., & Fabes, R. A. (1995). The relation of young children's vicarious emotional responding to social competence, regulation, and emotionality. *Cognition and Emotion, 9,* 203–229.

Eisenberg, N., & Fabes, R. A. (1998). Prosocial development. In W. Damon (Series Ed.) & N. Eisenberg (Vol. Ed), *Handbook of child psychology, Vol. 3: Social, emotional, and personality development* (5th ed., pp. 701–778). New York: Wiley.

Eisenberg, N., Fabes, R. A., Bustamante, D., Mathy, R. M., Miller, P., & Lindholm, E. (1988). Differentiation of vicariously-induced emotional reactions in children. *Developmental Psychology, 24,* 237–246.

Eisenberg, N., Fabes, R. A., Carlo, G., Speer, A. L., Switzer, G., Karbon, M., & Troyer, D. (1993). The relations of empathy-related emotions and maternal practices to children's comforting behavior. *Journal of Experimental Child Psychology, 55,* 131–150.

Eisenberg, N., Fabes, R. A., Carlo, G., Troyer, D., Speer, A. L., Karbon, M., & Switzer, G. (1992). The relations of maternal practices and characteristics to children's vicarious emotional responsiveness. *Child Development, 63,* 583–602.

Eisenberg, N., Fabes, R. A., Karbon, M., Murphy, B. C., Carlo, G., & Wosinski, M. (1996). Relations of school children's comforting behavior to empathy-related reactions and shyness. *Social Development, 5,* 330–351.

Eisenberg, N., Fabes, R. A., Miller, P. A., Fultz, J., Mathy, R. M., Shell, R., & Reno, R. R. (1989). The relations of sympathy and personal distress to prosocial behavior: A multimethod study. *Journal of Personality and Social Psychology, 57,* 55–66.

Eisenberg, N., Fabes, R. A., Miller, P. A., Shell, C., Shea, R., & May-Plumlee, T. (1990). Preschoolers' vicarious emotional responding and their situational and dispositional prosocial behavior. *Merrill-Palmer Quarterly, 36,* 507–529.

Eisenberg, N., Fabes, R. A., Murphy, B., Karbon, M., Maszk, P., Smith, M., et al. (1994). The relations of emotionality and regulation to dispositional and situational empathy-related responding. *Journal of Personality and Social Psychology, 66,* 776–797.

Eisenberg, N., Fabes, R. A., Murphy, B., Karbon, M., Smith, M., & Maszk, P. (1996). The relations of children's dispositional empathy-related responding to their emotionality, regulation, and social functioning. *Developmental Psychology, 32,* 195–209.

Eisenberg, N., Fabes, R. A., Schaller, M., Carlo, G., & Miller, P. A. (1991). The relations of parental characteristics and practices to children's vicarious emotional responding. *Child Development, 62,* 1393–1408.

Eisenberg, N., Fabes, R. A., Schaller, M., & Miller, P. A. (1989). Sympathy and personal distress: Development, gender differences, and interrelations of indexes. *New Directions in Child Development, 44,* 107–126.

Eisenberg, N., Fabes, R. A., Schaller, M., Miller, P. A., Carlo, G., Poulin, R., et al. (1991). Personality and socialization correlates of vicarious emotional responding. *Journal of Personality and Social Psychology, 61,* 459–471.

Eisenberg, N., Fabes, R. A., Shepard, S. A., Murphy, B. C., Jones, S., & Guthrie I. K. (1998). Contemporaneous and longitudinal prediction of children's sympathy from dispositional regulation and emotionality. *Developmental Psychology, 34,* 910–924.

Eisenberg, N., Fabes, R. A., & Spinrad, T. L. (in press). Procoial development. In W. Damon & R. M. Lerner (Series Eds.) & N. Eisenberg (Vol. Ed.), *Handbook of child psychology, Vol. 3: Social, emotional, and personality development* (6th ed.). New York: Wiley.

Eisenberg, N., Guthrie, I., Cumberland, A., Murphy, B. C., Shepard, S. A., Zhou, Q., & Carlo, G. (2002). Prosocial development in early adulthood: A longitudinal study. *Journal of Personality and Social Psychology, 82,* 993–1006.

Eisenberg, N., Guthrie, I. K., Murphy, B. C., Shepard, S. A., Cumberland, A., & Carlo, G. (1999). Consistency and development of prosocial dispositions: A longitudinal study. *Child Development, 70,* 1360–1372.

Eisenberg, N. & Lennon, R. (1983). Gender differences in empathy and related capacities. *Psychological Bulletin, 94,* 100–131.

Eisenberg, N., Liew, J., & Pidada, S. (2001). The relations of parental emotional expressivity with the quality of Indonesian children's social functioning. *Emotion, 1,* 107–115.

Eisenberg, N., Losoya, S., Fabes, R. A., Guthrie, I. K., Reiser, M., Murphy, B. C., et al., (2001). Parental socialization of children's dysregulated expression of emotion and externalizing problems. *Journal of Family Psychology, 15,* 183–205.

Eisenberg, N., & McNally, S. (1993). Socialization and mothers' and adolescents' empathy-related characteristics. *Journal of Research on Adolescence, 3,* 171–191.

Eisenberg, N., & Miller, P. (1987). The relation of empathy to prosocial and related behaviors. *Psychological Bulletin, 101,* 91–119.

Eisenberg, N., Miller, P. A., Shell, R., McNalley, S., & Shea, C. (1991). Prosocial development in adolescence: A longitudinal study. *Developmental Psychology, 27,* 849–857.

Eisenberg, N., Murphy, B., & Shepard, S. (1997). The development of empathic accuracy. In W. Ickes (Eds.), *Empathic accuracy* (pp. 73–116). New York: Guilford Press.

Eisenberg, N., & Okun, M. A. (1996). The relations of dispositional regulation and emotionality to elders' empathy-related responding and affect while volunteering. *Journal of Personality, 64,* 157–183.

Eisenberg, N., Schaller, M., Fabes, R. A., Bustamante, D., Mathy, R., Shell, R., & Rhodes, K. (1988). The differentiation of personal distress and sympathy in children and adults. *Developmental Psychology, 24,* 766–775.

Eisenberg, N., Shea, C. L., Carlo, G. & Knight, G. (1991). Empathy-related responding and cognition: A "chicken and the egg" dilemma. In W. Kurtines & J. Gewirtz (Eds.), *Handbook of moral behavior and development, Vol. 2: Research* (pp. 63–88). Hillsdale, NJ: Lawrence Erlbaum Associates.

Eisenberg, N., Wentzel, M., & Harris, J. D. (1998). The role of emotionality and regulation in empathy-related responding. *School Psychology Review, 27,* 506–521.

Eisenberg, N., Zhou, Q., & Koller, S. (2001). Brazilian adolescents' prosocial moral judgment and behavior: Relations to sympathy, perspective taking, gender-role orientation, and demographic characteristics. *Child Development, 72,* 518–534.

Eisenberg-Berg, N., & Lennon, R. (1980). Altruism and the assessment of empathy in the preschool years. *Child Development, 51,* 552–557.

Eisenberg-Berg, N., & Mussen P. (1978). Empathy and moral development in adolescence. *Developmental Psychology, 14,* 185–186.

Emde, R. N., Plomin, R., Robinson, J., Corley, R., DeFries, J., Fulker, D. W., et al. (1992). Temperament, emotion, and cognition at fourteen months: The MacArthur Longitudinal Twin Study. *Child Development, 63,* 1437–1455.

Estrada, P. (1995). Adolescents' self-reports of prosocial responses to friends and acquaintances: The role of sympathy-related cognitive, affective, and motivational processes. *Journal of Research on Adolescence, 5,* 173–200.

Fabes, R. A. & Eisenberg, N. (1996). *An examination of age and sex differences in prosocial behavior and empathy.* Unpublished data, Arizona State University.

Fabes, R. A., Eisenberg, N., & Eisenbud, L. (1993). Behavioral and physiological correlates of children's reactions to others' distress. *Developmental Psychology, 29,* 655–663.

Fabes, R. A., Eisenberg, N., Karbon, M., Bernzweig, J., Speer, A. L., & Carlo, G. (1994). Socialization of children's vicarious emotional responding and prosocial behavior: Relations with mothers' perceptions of children's emotional reactivity. *Developmental Psychology, 30,* 44–55.

Fabes, R. A., Eisenberg, N., Karbon, M., Troyer, D, & Switzer, G. (1994). The relations of children's emotion regulation to their vicarious emotional responses and comforting behavior. *Child Development, 65,* 1678–1693.

Fabes, R. A., Eisenberg, N., & Miller, P. (1990). Maternal correlates of children's vicarious emotional responsiveness. *Developmental Psychology, 26,* 639–648.

Feshbach, N. D. (1975). The relationship of child-rearing factors to children's aggression, empathy, and related positive and negative behaviors. In J. DeWit & W. W. Hartup (Eds.), *Determinants and origins of aggressive behavior* (pp. 426–436). The Hague, Netherlands: Mouton.

Feshbach, N. D., & Roe, K. (1968). Empathy in six- and seven-year-olds. *Child Development, 39,* 133–145.

Geertz, C. (1976). *The religion of Java.* Chicago: University of Chicago Press.

George, C., & Main, M. (1979). Social interactions of young abused children: Approach, avoidance, and aggression. *Child Development, 50,* 306–318.

Gill, K. L., & Calkins, S. D. (2003). Do aggressive/destructive toddlers lack concern for others? Behavioral and physiological indicators of empathic responding in 2-year-old children. *Development and Psychopathology, 15,* 85–91.

Gottman, J. M., Katz, L. F., & Hooven, C. (1997). *Meta-emotion: How families communicate emotionally.* Mahwah, NJ: Lawrence Erlbaum Associates.

Greenberg, M. T., & Kusche, C. A. (1997, April). *Improving children's emotion regulation and social competence: The effects of the PATHS curriculum.* Paper presented at the biennial meeting of the Society for Research in Child Development, Washington D.C.

Gunnar, M. R., & Stone, C. (1984). The effects of positive maternal affect on infant responses to pleasant, ambiguous, and fear-provoking toys. *Child Development, 55,* 1231–1236.

Guthrie, I. K., Eisenberg, N., Fabes, R. A., Murphy, B. C., Holmgren, R. T., & Suh, K. (1997). The relations of regulation and emotionality to children's situational empathy-related responding. *Motivation and Emotion, 21,* 87–108.

Halberstadt, A. G., Crisp, V. W., & Eaton, K. L. (1999). Family expressiveness: A retrospective and new directions for research. In P. Philippot, R. S. Feldman, & E. Coats (Eds.), *The social context of nonverbal behavior* (pp. 109–155). New York: Cambridge University Press.

Harter, S. (1998). The development of self-representations. In W. Damon (Ed.) & N. Eisenberg (Series Ed.), *Handbook of child psychology. Social, emotional and personality development* (pp. 553–617). New York: Wiley.

Hastings, P. D., Zahn-Waxler, C., Robinson, J., Usher, B., & Bridges, D. (2000). The development of concern for others in children with behavior problems. *Developmental Psychology, 36,* 531–546.

Hay, D. F., Nash, A., & Pedersen, J. (1981). Responses of six-month-olds to the distress of their peers. *Child Development, 52,* 1071–1075.

Hoffman, M. L. (1981). Is altruism part of human nature? *Journal of Personality and Social Psychology, 40,* 121–137.

Hoffman, M. L. (1982). Development of prosocial motivation: Empathy and guilt. In N. Eisenberg (Ed.), *The development of prosocial behavior* (pp. 281–313). New York: Academic Press.

Hoffman, M. L. (1983). Affective and cognitive processes in moral internalization. In E. T. Higgins, D. N. Ruble, & W. W. Hartup (Eds.), *Social cognition and social development: A sociocultural perspective* (pp. 236–274). Cambridge, MA: Cambridge University Press.

Hoffman, M. L. (2000). *Empathy and moral development: Implications for caring and justice.* Cambridge, UK: Cambridge University Press.

Holmgren, R. A., Eisenberg, N., & Fabes, R. (1998). The relations of children's situational empathy-related emotions to dispositional prosocial behavior. *International Journal of Behavioral Development, 22,* 169–193.

Howes, C., & Eldredge, R. (1985). Responses of abused, neglected, and non-maltreated children to the behaviors of their peers. *Journal of Applied Developmental Psychology, 6,* 261–270.

Howes, C., & Farver, J. (1987). Toddlers' responses to the distress of their peers. *Journal of Applied Developmental Psychology, 8,* 441–452.

Hume, D. (1748/1975). *Enquiry into the human understanding.* Ed. P. Nidditch. Oxford: Clarendon Press.

Humphries, M. L., Parker, B. L., & Jagers, R. J. (2000). Predictors of moral reasoning among African American children: A preliminary study. *Journal of Black Psychology, 26,* 51–64.

Iannotti, R. J., Cummings, E. M., Pierrehumbert, B., Milano, M. J., & Zahn-Waxler, C. (1992). Parental influences on prosocial behavior and empathy in early childhood. In J. M. A. M. Janssens & J. R. M. Gerris (Eds.), *Child rearing: Influence on prosocial and moral development* (pp. 77–100). Amsterdam: Swets & Zeitlinger.

Janssens, J. M. A. M., & Gerris, J. R. M. (1992). Child rearing, empathy and prosocial development. In J. M. A. M. Janssens & J. R. M. Gerris (Eds.), *Child rearing: Influence on prosocial and moral development* (pp. 57–75). Amsterdam: Swets & Zeitlinger.

Johnson, D. B. (1982). Altruistic behavior and the development of self in infants. *Merrill-Palmer Quarterly, 28,* 379–388.

Kalliopuska, M. (1984). Relation between children's and parents' empathy. *Psychological Reports, 54,* 295–299.

Kaneko, R. & Hamazaki. T. (1987). Prosocial behavior manifestations of young children in an orphanage. *Psychologia, 30,* 235–242.

Karniol, R., Gabay, R., & Ochion, Y. (1998). Is gender or gender-role orientation a better predictor of empathy in adolescence? *Sex Roles, 3,* 45–59.

Karniol, R., Gabay, R., Ochion, Y., & Harari, Y. (1998). Is gender or gender-role orientation a better predictor of empathy in adolescence? *Sex Roles, 39,* 45–59.

Kasari, C., Freeman, S. F. N., & Bass, W. (2003). Empathy and response to distress in children with Down syndrome. *Journal of Child Psychology and Psychiatry, 44,* 424–431.

Kestenbaum, R., Farber, E.A., & Sroufe, L.A. (1989). Individual differences in empathy among preschoolers: Relation to attachment history. In N. Eisenberg (Ed.), *New directions for child development, Vol. 44: Empathy and related emotional responses* (pp. 51–64). San Francisco: Jossey-Bass.

Kienbaum, J. (2001). The socialization of compassionate behavior by child care teachers. *Early Education & Development, 12,* 138–153.

Kienbaum, J., Volland, C., & Ulich, D. (2001). Sympathy in the context of mother-child and teacher-child relationships. *International Journal of Behavioral Development, 25,* 302–309.

Klinnert, M. D. (1984). The regulation of infant behavior by maternal facial expression. *Infant Behavior and Development, 7,* 447–465.

Knight, G. P., Johnson, L. G., Carlo, G., & Eisenberg, N. (1994). A multiplicative model of the dispositional antecedents of a prosocial behavior: Predicting more of the people more of the time. *Journal of Personality and Social Psychology, 66,* 178–183.

Kochanska, G., DeVet, K., Goldman, M., Murray, K., & Putnam, S. P. (1994). Maternal reports of conscience development and temperament of young children. *Child Development, 65,* 852–868.

Kochanska, G., Forman, D. R., & Coy, K. C. (1999). Implications of the mother-child relationship in infancy for socialization in the second year of life. *Infant Behavior and Development, 22,* 249–265.

Kohlberg, L. (1969). Stage and sequence: The cognitive-developmental approach to socialization. In D. A. Goslin (Ed.), *Handbook of socialization theory and research* (pp. 347–480). Chicago: Rand McNally.

Krevans, J., & Gibbs, J. C. (1996). Parents' use of inductive discipline: Relations to children's empathy and prosocial behavior. *Child Development, 67,* 3263–3277.

Lamb, S., & Zakhireh, B. (1997). Toddlers' attention to the distress of peers in a daycare setting. *Early Education & Development, 8,* 105–118.

Lazarus, R. S. (1974). A cognitively oriented psychologist looks at biofeedback. *American Psychologist, 30,* 553–561.

Lazarus, R. S., & Folkman, S. (1984). *Stress, appraisal, and coping* (pp. 282–325). New York: Springer.

Lennon, R. & Eisenberg, N. (1987). Gender and age differences in empathy and sympathy. In N. Eisenberg & J. Strayer (Eds.), *Empathy and its development* (pp. 195–217). New York: Cambridge University Press.

Lennon, R., Eisenberg, N., & Carroll, J. (1983). The assessment of empathy in early childhood. *Journal of Applied Developmental Psychology, 4,* 295–302.

Levenston, G. K., Patrick, C. J., Bradley, M. M., & Lang, P. J. (2000). The psychopath as observer: Emotion and attention in picture processing. *Journal of Abnormal Psychology, 109,* 373–385.

Lewis, M. (2002). Empathy requires the development of the self. *Behavioral and Brain Sciences, 25,* 41–42.

Liew, J., Eisenberg, N., Losoya, S. H., Guthrie, I. K., & Murphy, B. C. (2003). Maternal expressivity as a moderator of the relations of children's vicarious emotional responses to their regulation, emotionality, and social functioning. *Journal of Family Psychology, 17,* 584–597.

Litvack-Miller, W, McDougall, D., & Romney, D. M. (1997). The structure of empathy during middle childhood and its relationship to prosocial behavior. *Genetic, Social & General Psychology Monographs, 123,* 303–324.

Loehlin, J. C., & Nichols, R. C. (1976). *Heredity, environment, and personality.* Austin: University. Texas Press.

Main, M., & George, C. (1985). Responses of abused and disadvantaged toddlers to distress in agemates: A study in the day care setting. *Developmental Psychology, 21,* 407–412.

MacDowell, K. A., & Mandler, G. (1989). Constructions of emotion: Discrepancy, arousal, and mood. *Motivation and Emotion, 13,* 105–124.

Martin, C. L. (1987). A ratio measure of sex stereotyping. *Journal of Personality and Social Psychology, 52,* 489–499.

Matthews, K. A., Batson, C. D., Horn, J., & Rosenman, R. H. (1981). Principles in his nature which interest him in the fortune of others: The heritability of empathic concern for others. *Journal of Personality, 49,* 237–247.

Miller, P., & Eisenberg, N. (1988). The relation of empathy to aggression and externalizing/antisocial behavior. *Psychological Bulletin, 103,* 324–344.

Miller, P. A., Eisenberg, N., Fabes, R. A., & Shell, R. (1996). Relations of moral reasoning and vicarious emotion to young children's prosocial behavior toward peers and adults. *Developmental Psychology, 32,* 210–219.

Miller, P. A., Eisenberg, N., Fabes, R. A., Shell, R., & Gular, S. (1989). Mothers' emotional arousal as a moderator in the socialization of children's empathy. In N. Eisenberg (Ed.), *The development of empathy and related vicarious responses. New directions in child development* (pp. 65–83). San Francisco: Jossey-Bass.

Miller, S. M. (1979). Interrelationships among dependency, empathy, and sharing. *Motivation and Emotion, 3,* 183–199.

Mulder, N. (1996). *Inside Indonesian society: Cultural change in Indonesia.* Amsterdam: The Pepin Press.

Murphy, B. C., Shepard, S. A., Eisenberg, N., Fabes, R. A., & Guthrie, I. K. (1999). Contemporaneous and longitudinal relations of dispositional sympathy to emotionality, regulation, and social functioning. *Journal of Early Adolescence, 19,* 66–97.

Mussen, P., & Eisenberg-Berg, N. (1977). *Roots of caring, sharing, and helping: The development of prosocial behavior in children.* San Francisco: Freeman.

Nigg, J. T. (2001). Is ADHD a disinhibitory disorder? *Psychological Bulletin, 127,* 571–598.

Okun, M. A., Shepard, S. A., & Eisenberg, N. (2000). The relations of emotionality and regulation to dispositional empathy-related responding among volunteers-in-training. *Personality and Individual Differences, 28,* 367–382.

Olweus, D., & Endresen, I. M. (1998). The importance of sex-of-stimulus object: Age trends and sex differences in empathic responsiveness. *Social Development, 7,* 370–388.

Pastor, D. L. (1981). The quality of mother-infant attachment and its relationship to toddlers' initial sociability with peers. *Developmental Psychology, 17,* 326–335.

Phinney, J., Feshbach, N., & Farver, J. (1986). Preschool children's responses to peer crying. *Early Childhood Research Quarterly, 1,* 207–219.

Plomin, R., Emde, R. N., Braungart, J. M., Campos, J., Corley, R., Fulkner, D. W., et al. (1993). Genetic change and continuity from fourteen to twenty months: The MacArthur Longitudinal Twin Study. *Child Development, 64,* 1354–1376.

Radke-Yarrow, M., & Zahn-Waxler, C. (1984). Roots, motives, and patterns in children's prosocial behavior. In E. Staub, D. Bar-Tal, J. Karylowski, & J. Reykowski (Eds.), *Development and maintainance of prosocial behavior: International perspectives on positive behavior* (pp. 81–99). New York: Plenum.

Radke-Yarrow, M., Zahn-Waxler, C., Richardson, D. T., Susman, A., & Martinez, P. (1994). Caring behavior in children of clinically depressed and well mothers. *Child Development, 65,* 1405–1414.

Roberts, W., & Strayer, J. (1996). Empathy, emotional expressiveness, and prosocial behavior. *Child Development, 67,* 449–470.

Robinson, J. L., Zahn-Waxler, C., & Emde, R. N. (1994). Patterns of development in early empathic behavior: Environmental and child constitutional influences. *Social Development, 3,* 125–145.

Robinson, J. L., Zahn-Waxler, C., & Emde, R. N. (2001). Relationships context as a moderator of sources of individual differences in empathic development. In R. N. Emde & J. K. Hewitt (Eds.), *Infancy to early childhood: Genetic and environmental influences on developmental change* (pp. 257–268). Oxford: Oxford University Press.

Rothbart, M. K., Ahadi, S. A., & Hershey, K. L. (1994). Temperament and social behavior in childhood. *Merrill-Palmer Quarterly, 40,* 21–39.

Rothbart, M. K., & Bates, J. E. (1998). Temperament. In W. Damon (Series Ed.) & N. Eisenberg (Vol. Ed.), *Handbook of child psychology, Vol. 3: Social, emotional, personality development* (pp. 105–176). New York: Wiley.

Ruble, D. N., & Martin, C. L. (1998). Gender development. In W. Damon (Ed.), *Handbook of child psychology* (pp. 933–1016). New York: Wiley.

Rushton, J. P., Fulker, D. W., Neal, M. C., Nias, D. K. B., & Eysenck, H. J. (1986). Altruism and aggression: The heritability of individual differences. *Journal of Personality and Social Psychology, 50,* 1192–1198.

Sagi, A., & Hoffman, M. L. (1976). Empathic distress in the newborn. *Developmental Psychology, 12,* 175–176.

Saklofske, D. H., & Eysenck, S. B. G. (1983). Impulsiveness and venturesomeness in Canadian children. *Psychological Reports, 52,* 147–152.

Sandler, I. Tein, J., Mehta, P. Wolchik, S., & Ayers, T. (2000). Coping efficacy and psychological problem of children of divorce. *Child Development, 71,* 1099–1118.

Sandler, I. N., Tein, J., & West, S. G. (1994). Coping, stress and the psychological symptoms of children of divorce: A cross-sectional and longitudinal study. *Child Development, 65,* 1744–1763.

Selman, R. L. (1980). *The growth of interpersonal understanding: Developmental and clinical analysis.* New York: Academic Press.

Shantz, C. U. (1975). The development of social cognition. In E. M Hetherington (Ed.), *Review of child development research* (Vol. 5, pp. 257–323). Chicago: University of Chicago Press.

Simner, M. L. (1971). Newborn's responses to the cry of another infant. *Developmental Psychology, 5,* 136–150.

Sneed, C. D. (2002). Correlates and implications for agreeableness in children. *Journal of Psychology, 136,* 59–67.

Sorce, J. F., Emde, R. N., Campos, J. J., & Klinnert, M. D. (1985). Maternal emotional signaling: Its effect on the visual cliff behavior of 1-year-olds. *Developmental Psychology, 21,* 195–200.

Spinrad, T. L. (1999, April). *Toddlers' vicarious emotional responses and prosocial behaviors: The role of infant temperament and maternal behavior.* Paper presented at the Society for Research in Child Development, Albuquerque, NM.

Spinrad, T. L., & Stifter, C. A. (2002, April). *Toddlers' vicarious emotional responses and prosocial behaviors: Links with toddlers' compliance and noncompliance.* Poster presented at the International Conference for Infant Studies, Toronto, Canada.

Staub, E. (1979). *Positive social behavior and morality, Vol 2: Socialization and development.* New York: Academic Press.

Staub, E. (1992). The origins of caring, helping, and nonaggression: Parental socialization, the family system, schools, land cultural influence. In P. M. Oliner, L. Baron, L. A. Blum, D. L. Krebs, & M. Z. Smolenska, (Eds.), *Embracing the other: Philosophical, psychological, and historical perspectives on altruism* (pp. 390–412). New York: New York University Press.

Strayer, J., & Chang, A. (1997, April). *Children's emotional and helping responses as a function of empathy and affective cues.* Paper presented that biennial meeting of the Society for Research in Child Development, Washington, D.C.

Strayer, J., & Roberts, W. (1989). Children's empathy and role taking: Child and parental factors, and relations to prosocial behavior. *Journal of Applied Developmental Psychology, 10,* 227–239.

Strayer, J., & Roberts, W. (1997). Facial and verbal measures of children's emotions and empathy. *International Journal of Behavioral Development, 20,* 627–649.

Strayer, J., & Roberts, W. (2004). Empathy and observed anger and aggression in five-year-olds. *Social Development, 13,* 1–13.

Sutton, S. K., Vitale, J. E., & Newman, J. P. (2002). Emotion among women with psychopathy during picture perception. *Journal of Abnormal Psychology, 111,* 610–619.

Thompson, R. A. (1987). Empathy and emotional understanding: The early development of empathy. In N. Eisenberg & J. Strayer (Eds.), *Empathy and its development* (pp. 119–143). New York: Cambridge University Press.

Termine, N. T., & Izard, C. E. (1988). Infants' responses to their mothers' expressions of joy and sadness. *Developmental Psychology, 24,* 223–229.

Trommsdorff, G. (1991). Child-rearing and children's empathy. *Perceptual Motor Skills, 72,* 387–390.

Trommsdorff, G., & Friedlmeier, W. (1999). Motivational conflict and prosocial behaviour of kindergarten children. *International Journal of Behavioral Development, 23,* 413–429.

Tucker, C. J., Updegraff, K. A., McHale, S., & Crouter, A. C. (1999). Older siblings as socializers of younger siblings' empathy. *Journal of Early Adolescence, 19,* 176–198.

Underwood, B., & Moore, B. (1982). Perspective-taking and altruism. *Psychological Bulletin, 91,* 143–173.

Ungerer, J. A., Dolby, R., Waters, B., Barnett, B., Kelk, N., & Lewin, V. (1990). The early development of empathy: Self-regulation and individual differences in the first year. *Motivation and Emotion, 14,* 93–106.

Valiente, C., Eisenberg, N., Fabes, R. A., Shepard, S. A., Cumberland, A., & Losoya, S. H. (2004). Prediction of children's empathy-related responding from their effortful control and parents' expressivity. *Developmental Psychology, 40,* 911–926.

van der Mark, I. L., van Ijzendoorn, M. H., & Bakermans-Kranenburg, M. J. (2002). Development of empathy in girls during the second year of life: Associations with parenting, attachment, and temperament. *Social Development, 11,* 451–468.

Van Tilburg, M. A. L., Unterberg, M. L., & Vingerhoets, A. J. J. M. (1992). Crying during adolescence: The role of gender, menarche, and empathy. *British Journal of Developmental Psychology, 20,* 77–87.

Warden, D., & Mackinnon, S. (2003). Prosocial bullies, bullies, and victims: An investigation of their sociometric status, empathy, and social problem-solving strategies. *British Journal of Developmental Psychology, 21,* 367–385.

Waters, E., Hay, D., & Richters, J. (1986). Infant-parent attachment and the origins of prosocial and antisocial behavior. In D. Olweus, J. Block, & M. Radke-Yarrow (Eds.), *Development of antisocial and prosocial behavior: Research, theories, and issues* (pp. 97–125). Orlando, FL: Academic Press.

Waters, E., Wippman, J., & Sroufe, L. A. (1979). Attachment, positive affect, and competence in the peer group: Two studies in construct validation. *Child Development, 50,* 821–829.

Wellencamp, J. C. (1995). Cultural similarities and differences regarding emotional disclosure: Some examples from Indonesia and the Pacific. In J. W. Pennebaker (Ed.), *Emotion disclosure, and health* (pp. 293–311). Washington, D.C.: American Psychological Association.

Winton, W. M., Putnam, L. E., & Krauss, R. M. (1984). Facial and autonomic manifestations of the dimensional structure of emotion. *Journal of Experimental Social Psychology, 20,* 195–216.

Yarrow, M. R., Waxler, C. Z., Barrett, D., Darby, J., King, R., Pickett, M., & Smith, J. (1976). Dimensions and correlates of prosocial behavior in young children. *Child Development, 47,* 118–125.

Young, S. K., Fox, N. A., & Zahn-Waxler, C. (1999). The relations between temperament and empathy in 2-year-olds. *Developmental Psychology, 35,* 1189–1197.

Zahn-Waxler, C., Cole, P. M., Welsh, J. D., & Fox, N. A. (1995). Psychophysiological correlates of empathy and prosocial behaviors in preschool children with problem behaviors. *Development and Psychopathology, 7,* 27–48.

Zahn-Waxler, C., Friedman, R. J., Cole, P. M., Mizuta, I., & Hiruma, N. (1996). Japanese and United States preschool children's responses to conflict and distress. *Child Development, 67,* 2462–2477.

Zahn-Waxler, C. & Radke-Yarrow, M. (1982). The development of altruism: Alternative research strategies. In N. Eisenberg (Ed.), *The development of prosocial behavior* (pp. 109–137). New York: Academic Press.

Zahn-Waxler, C., Radke-Yarrow, M., & King, R. A. (1979). Child rearing and children's prosocial initiations toward victims of distress. *Child Development, 50,* 319–330.

Zahn-Waxler, C. Radke-Yarrow, M., Wagner, E., & Chapman, M. (1992). Development of concern for others. *Developmental Psychology, 28,* 126–136.

Zahn-Waxler, C., Robinson, J. L., & Emde, R. N. (1992). The development of empathy in twins. *Developmental Psychology, 28,* 1038–1047.

Zahn-Waxler, C., Schiro, K., Robinson, J. L., Emde, R. N., & Schmitz, S. (2001). Empathy and prosocial patterns in young MZ and DZ twins: Development and genetic and environmental influences. In R. N. Emde & J. K. Hewitt (Eds.), *Infancy to early childhood: Genetic and environmental influences on developmental change* (pp. 141–162). Oxford: Oxford University Press.

Zhou, Q., Eisenberg, N., Losoya, S. H., Fabes, R. A., Reiser, M., Guthrie, I. K., et al. (2002). The relations of parental warmth and positive expressiveness to children's empathy-related responding and social functioning: A longitudinal study. *Child Development, 73,* 893–915.

20

CARE-BASED AND ALTRUISTICALLY BASED MORALITY

GUSTAVO CARLO
UNIVERSITY OF NEBRASKA-LINCOLN

> Children are completely egoistic; they feel their needs intensely and strive ruthlessly to satisfy them . . . we do not on that account call the child "bad," we call him "naughty"; he is no more answerable for his evil deeds in our judgement than in the eyes of the law. And it is right that this should be so; for we may expect that before the end of the period which we count as childhood, altruistic impulses and morality will awaken the little egoist . . . (Freud, 1900/1965, p. 284)

There is a long-standing belief held by many parents, educators, and professionals that children are primarily egoistic and selfish. According to some scholars, children are necessarily motivated to focus on meeting their own needs, and these desires often lead to selfish actions. Although there is ample evidence of the selfish tendencies of children, other scholars point to the substantial evidence that children often express care-based, prosocial behaviors (actions intended to benefit others; Eisenberg & Fabes, 1998). To what extent is there evidence for the existence of care-based, prosocial behaviors in children? How do those behaviors emerge and change over time?

The study of prosocial behaviors is relevant and important to understanding moral development. Traditionally, developmental psychologists considered beneficent-centered and justice-centered theories of morality as relatively separate aspects of morality, or these aspects were pitted against each other (see Gibbs & Schnell, 1985). There is, however, increasing recognition that although formal societal laws or rules do not usually regulate the enactment of prosocial behaviors, prosocial acts often engender a duty or obligation that could be judged as morally right or wrong by members of our society. For example, a community leader who aids homeless families might be viewed as a highly moral person. Conversely, a husband who fails to assist his sickly wife might be viewed as less moral. Contemporary scholars have acknowledged the importance of integrating beneficent-centered and justice-centered approaches to develop more ecologically valid, comprehensive models of moral development (Gibbs & Schnell, 1985; Hoffman, 2000; Lapsley, 1996). This chapter summarizes what is known regarding the development and correlates of prosocial behaviors, including altruism. In doing so, we present a scholarly perspective on the role of prosocial behaviors in the broader context of morality.

Understanding the development and correlates of behaviors that benefit society should be of interest to all. The study of prosocial behaviors has far-reaching implications for understanding group and individual level processes associated with morality, aggression, interpersonal relationships, mental health and well-being, and mental pathology (see Carlo & Randall, 2001; Eisenberg & Fabes, 1998; Staub, 1978). The study of prosocial behaviors provides an opportunity to examine psychological and social psychological processes from a positive framework, which helps to provide a more balanced understanding of human behavior (see Seligman & Csikszentmihalyi, 2000). Moreover, the multilevel complexity of prosocial behaviors challenges social and behavioral scientists to understand the interplay among individual (including biological), interpersonal, and broader social contextual mechanisms associated with these behaviors. Thus, the study of prosocial behaviors presents many potential benefits to improving society and to furthering our understanding of human behavior.

In the first section, we present a brief discussion of the foundation of the concept of beneficence to place the study of prosocial behaviors in its historical context. The second section discusses a core issues of debate in this area of study—namely, the definition of prosocial behaviors. We also discuss the various types of prosocial behaviors, including prosocial behaviors motivated by altruism. The third section focuses on developmental and gender differences and on the correlates of prosocial behaviors, including discussions of biological, age, gender, sociocognitive, and socialization correlates of those behaviors. The fourth section shifts the emphasis to the broader social context and discusses cross-cultural and cross-ethnic research on prosocial behaviors. Finally, suggestions for future directions for theory and research are noted. Although page limitations and the breadth of knowledge in this area preclude a comprehensive review of the existing literature, other recent reviews of the literature are available (see Batson, 1998; Bierhoff, 2002; Carlo, Fabes, Laible, & Kupanoff, 1999; Carlo & Randall, 2001; Eisenberg & Fabes, 1998; Fabes, Carlo, Kupanoff, & Laible, 1999; Hoffman, 2000). We begin the review with a brief discussion on the philosophical foundations of prosocial behaviors.

PHILOSOPHICAL AND THEOLOGICAL FOUNDATIONS

The philosophical roots of care- and beneficence-based behaviors are evident in the early writings of Western and Eastern philosophers and religious scholars. In Christianity, Judaism, and Islam, God and Allah are endowed with traits of forgiveness and generosity. Buddhism and Hinduism, similarly, espouse strong convictions regarding respect, consideration of others, and altruism. The Christian parable of the Good Samaritan reflects the strong endorsement of selflessly motivated behaviors for the benefit of others. In addition, many of the primary figures in religious and early philosophical writings (e.g., Jesus, Confucius, Muhammad) were personified with traits and actions that strongly reflected the virtues of generosity, helpfulness, forgiveness, and altruism.

Among the early Greek philosophers (e.g., Aristotle, Plato), the virtues of acquiring a strong moral character were emphasized through rationality and practice. Descartes

(1622/1972) noted that emotions and prosocial tendencies emanate from physiological processes (spirits) that flow through "pores of the brain." As he wrote, "...liberality, generosity, and love depend upon an abundance of spirits, and form in us that humor which renders us complaisant and benevolent to everyone" (p. 73). Other philosophers, such as Hobbes (1651/1962), Hume (1751/1957), Kant (1785/1993), and Rousseau (1773/1962), elaborated on the moral nature of humans. For example, Hume (1751/1957) noted that humans have inherent virtuous tendencies such as sympathy that motivate action in times of need. Although sympathy and compassion were not deemed to be the only sources of moral action, Hume promoted those emotional processes as providing the meaning for moral action. In contrast to Hume, Kant (1785/1993) promoted the primacy of reason and rationality. As he stated, "It is clear...that all moral concepts have their seat and origin completely a priori in reason, and indeed in the most ordinary human reason just as much as in the most highly speculative" (pp. 22–23).

Blum (1980), a philosopher influenced by Hume's writings on morality, rebuked the emphasis on rationality and cognitions proposed by Kant and other moral philosophers as the primary determinants of morality. Blum (1980) advocated the central role of compassion and sympathy in moral action rather than moral principles. Blum (1980) summarized, "...I argue that action motivated by altruistic emotions is morally good because it involves 'direct altruism'—a direct concern for and responsiveness to the weal and woe of others. This view contrasts with the Kantian view, according to which moral action must be grounded in universal moral principles morally binding on the agent; the latter view, I argue, cannot encompass more than a small range of morally good beneficent action" (p. 5).

In summary, religious scholars and philosophers have long debated the moral nature of humans and the underlying cognitive or affective motives for moral actions. Psychological researchers and scholars have added their scientific methods and analytical perspectives to those questions in recent years. Although much has been achieved in furthering our understanding of prosocial and moral development, there are still many gaps in our understanding. We now turn to one of the most debated and controversial aspect of the study of prosocial behaviors: the definitions of prosocial behaviors and altruism.

DEFINITIONAL ISSUES

At the crux of discussion and debate in the study of prosocial behavior are definitional issues. In his comprehensive volumes on prosocial behaviors, Staub (1978, 1979) defined *prosocial behaviors* as actions intended to benefit other people (see also Carlo & Randall, 2001; Eisenberg & Fabes, 1998). Such behaviors often include sharing, comforting others, instrumental helping, money or goods donations, volunteerism, or cooperative behaviors. It is important to distinguish prosocial behaviors from other positive social skills or characteristics, which might be related but distinct. For example, there are many investigations on different sources of support or attachment (e.g., social, peer, parenting) that primarily tap into the network of supportive relationships or into perceptions of warmth, admiration, or respect. Other researchers examine social competence, which is a broad construct and often includes social interaction and communication skills. Moreover, there are studies of other constructs (e.g., moral reasoning, perspective taking, social responsibility) that are distinct but theoretically pertinent to explaining prosocial behaviors.

Once we ponder the definition of prosocial behaviors, we begin to appreciate the varieties of prosocial behaviors and the challenges and complexities of studying these phenomena. For example, are there qualitative differences among different types of prosocial behaviors? Should we emphasize the underlying intentions or the consequences of such behaviors? Can we accurately assess the underlying motives for those behaviors? What about behaviors that result in benefits for both the helper and the recipient of helping? And should the short- and long-term consequences of such behaviors be considered?

The difficulty of answering those questions is probably best exemplified by the debate surrounding the notion of altruism, a subset of prosocial behaviors. Several definitions of altruism have been proposed, but for purposes of this chapter, *altruism* is defined as behaviors intrinsically motivated by the primary desire to benefit others (Carlo & Randall, 2001; Eisenberg & Fabes, 1998). Altruism is often engaged in the absence of obvious external rewards and it usually incurs a cost to the self. This definition is challenging because it requires an assessment of the intention or motive behind the act, namely, discerning whether the behavior was primarily intended to benefit others. Thus, no matter what the consequences (to the self or others), one key is to determine whether the primary intent was to help others. An additional important consideration is that altruism is defined in part by intrinsic processes such as compassion for others, internalized values or principles, or a strong prosocial self-identity (see Staub, in press). This contrasts to other types of prosocial behaviors that might be motivated by extrinsic processes or concerns (e.g., social approval, money, social power) or by the avoidance of punishment. Two of the strengths of this definition lie in its ability to avoid the pitfalls of distinguishing between long- and short-term consequences of prosocial behaviors and that actions that could benefit both the helper and the recipient are not excluded. In addition, the definition circumvents the often asked question about whether there are qualitative differences between material (e.g., goods, resources) and nonmaterial (e.g., approval, self-esteem enhancement) benefits. By definition, all benefits to others of such actions are considered relatively equal.

Investigators of altruism have often focused on examining the underlying motives for these behaviors and much of this research has been conducted by social psychologists with college students (see Batson, 1998; Latané & Darley, 1970) or case histories (e.g., rescuers of Jews during the Holocaust; Oliner & Oliner, 1988). In much of the research, serious questions have been posed on whether altruism is truly selflessly or selfishly motivated. Batson (1998), in his research, noted that empathy is the primary motivator of altruism and has presented systematic research to support this hypothesis. In contrast, Cialdini and his colleagues argue that apparent altruistic behaviors are egoistically (selfishly) motivated behaviors (Cialdini, Brown, Lewis, Luce, & Neuberg, 1997). There are still other scholars who posited that there are individuals who exhibit altruistic tendencies early in life and whose behaviors remain relatively stable over time and across situations (Carlo & Randall, 2001; Eisenberg & Fabes, 1998; Staub, 1978). It is also likely that there are prosocial behavioral situations where conflicting selfish and selfless motives exist (Batson, 1998; Carlo, Allen, & Buhman, 1999). Although the debate continues on the existence of altruism, there is consensus on the importance of distinguishing the underlying motives for prosocial behaviors.

As noted, one of the challenges to the study of altruism is that it is difficult to assess its underlying motivation, and this is particularly challenging in studies with children. Because of this difficulty, most researchers of children's prosocial behaviors have not distinguished altruism from other forms of prosocial behaviors. In addition, although scholars have identified empathy (and sympathy) and internalized norms, values and principles as motives for altruistic behaviors, the link between altruism and internalized norms, values, and principles is less studied in children than the link between altruism and empathy (see Eisenberg, chap. 19, this volume, for a review of the empathy–altruism link). Thus, we augment the limited research on altruism in children with prior theory and research conducted with adults whenever it is necessary.

Classification of Prosocial Behaviors

The discussion of the definitional issues associated with studying prosocial behaviors implies that there is a need for careful distinctions between the various types of prosocial behaviors. One of the first large, systematic studies of moral character in children was conducted by Hartshorne and his colleagues during the late 1920s. One of the central objectives of their studies was to examine the interrelations among different indices of moral conduct. The researchers included many different indices of moral behaviors, including markers of prosocial behavior such as sharing resources with people less fortunate, cooperation, honesty, and good citizenship. Hartshorne, May, and Shuttlesworth (1930) found that the interrelations among the different indices of moral behaviors were weak or modest suggesting that there are distinct dimensions of moral character. Based on their findings, these researchers posited a theory that implied that the study of morality needs to be behavior specific.

Interestingly, Hartshorne and associates (1930) observations were somewhat ignored or overlooked by most prosocial behavior scholars. With a few notable exceptions, most researchers have treated all prosocial behaviors as equal. However, there are several reasons to examine different types of prosocial behaviors. First, prior researchers have pointed out the importance of distinguishing between selflessly and selfishly motivated prosocial behaviors. Second, some prosocial behaviors are evident early in childhood; others are not frequently observed until later childhood or adolescence (see Eisenberg & Fabes, 1998). This suggests different developmental trajectories and correlates of those behaviors. And third, there is growing empirical evidence on task-specific cognitive and emotional correlates of specific forms of prosocial behaviors (e.g., Carlo, Kinght, Eisenberg, & Rotenberg, 1991). The differentiation of prosocial behaviors is needed to better account for those findings and to better explain prior inconsistent empirical relations between prosocial behaviors and theoretically relevant correlates.

Although there are many possible ways for classifying prosocial behaviors, Carlo and Randall (2001) relied on prior theory and research (Batson, 1998; Eisenberg & Fabes, 1998; Latane & Darley, 1970; Staub, 1978) to identify six common categories of prosocial tendencies—altruism, dire, emotional, public, anonymous, and compliant (see Carlo, Hausmann, Christiansen, & Randall, 2003; Carlo & Randall, 2001, 2002). The prosocial tendency categories were chosen to be broad enough to include several specific forms of prosocial behaviors within each category and yet allow researchers to develop relatively specific predictions. *Altruism* was operationally defined as actions intended primarily to benefit others, with an explicit cost to the self. *Dire* tendencies refer to actions that benefit others during emergency situations. *Emotional* tendencies are prosocial behaviors that result from a response to affectively laden situations. *Public* tendencies are defined as beneficial actions conducted in front of others. Actions that are conducted without other people's knowledge are referred to as *anonymous* tendencies. *Compliant* tendencies refer to requested or asked for prosocial behaviors. Using this classification scheme, a measure of prosocial tendencies (PTM) was developed to use with adolescents (Carlo et al., 2003; Carlo & Randall, 2002).

The research using the PTM is still in its infancy but the evidence thus far has produced some interesting findings. For example, in one study (Carlo et al., 2003), middle adolescents reported more anonymous and altruistic helping than did early adolescents. This latter finding was consistent with the notion that anonymous and altruistic helping might require relatively more sophisticated perspective taking (e.g., perspective taking that requires abstraction, forethought, and hypothetical deductive reasoning) than other types of helping. Moreover, in another study among late adolescents, altruistically inclined adolescents reported higher levels of internalized, principled prosocial moral reasoning, perspective taking, sympathy, ascription of responsibility, and lower levels of hedonistic and approval-oriented prosocial moral reasoning (Carlo & Randall, 2002). In contrast, late adolescents who reported more helping in public contexts were more likely to be concerned with their own needs, were more concerned with gaining others' approval, were less sensitive to others' needs, engaged in less sophisticated forms of reasoning and perspective taking, and were more likely to ascribe responsibility to others. The findings using the PTM thus far suggest that different forms of prosocial behaviors are related distinctly to different theoretically relevant correlates.

The PTM might not capture the wide range of existing prosocial behaviors. Indeed, there is research on other types of prosocial behaviors. For example, Eberly identified two dimensions of prosocial behaviors in the family environment: affective/supportive (nurturance and caring) and helpfulness (helping with household chores Eberly & Motemayor, 1998, 1999). Furthermore, there are a number of studies on volunteerism and service learning (see Stukas & Dunlap, 2002 and Yates & Youniss, 1999), especially among adolescents, and there are studies of cooperative behaviors in children (e.g., Knight & Chao, 1991). Future research is needed to examine the links among the different types of prosocial behaviors. Nonetheless, the notion of classifying prosocial behaviors into distinct types could lead to new promising ways of understanding prosocial development. Scholars who study aggression have shown the many benefits of differentiating between different types of aggressive behaviors. A more fine grained analysis of different types of prosocial behaviors might help to reconcile a number of inconsistencies in prior empirical studies. Furthermore, the need to distinguish between different types of prosocial behaviors might provide an impetus for newer conceptual models and new methodological approaches (e.g., new measures, the use of multiple methods). Perhaps more importantly, more efficient prevention and intervention programs designed to foster specific types of prosocial behaviors might be feasible.

Biological and Evolutionary Mechanisms

Animal Research. Ethologists have long noted the evolutionary basis for altruism (Sober & Wilson, 1998; Wilson, 1978). One of the suggested paradoxes of altruism is that when altruism involves risk to one's self, it is difficult to understand the evolutionary adaptive function of this behavior. However, there are several ethological theories surrounding the evolutionary adaptive function of altruism. Genetic similarity and kin selection hypotheses both suggest that children engage in prosocial behaviors to increase reproductive success and fitness. The *reciprocal altruism hypothesis* refers to the expected frequent interactions with siblings and friends and the belief that continued relationships might result in behaviors between children that benefit each other (Sober & Wilson, 1998). Those hypotheses imply that prosocial behaviors and altruism ought to be more frequently directed at relatives and individuals with common personal characteristics (e.g., close friends) than strangers and acquaintances. Thus, the adaptive function of altruism for reproduction of the gene pool, not necessarily the individual's survival, appears to be the key (de Waal, 1996).

Careful observations of social interactions among animals have assisted scholars in uncovering the evolutionary basis for altruism and prosocial behaviors (e.g., cooperation). Perhaps more important, comparative psychology has helped to identify cross-species similarities in altruism and related prosocial behavioral responses. Although altruistic behaviors have been documented in many animal species, much of the focus has been on altruism in higher species such as the great apes and chimpanzees (see de Waal, 1996, for excellent examples) Animal researchers have shown that great apes and chimpanzees exhibit a range of prosocial behaviors including cooperation, nurturance, and altruistic-like behaviors (de Waal, 1996).

Another avenue of animal research that can inform scholars in prosocial development is research in neurophysiology. Researchers studying neurophysiological functioning in animals can help identify the neurological and physiological mechanisms that facilitate prosocial responding such as nurturance, cooperation, and sociability. For example, scholars have suggested that physiological reactivity (e.g., arousal) and self-regulation are related to prosocial responding (see Eisenberg & Fabes, 1998; Rothbart, Ahadi, & Hershey, 1994). Research on neurophysiological processes such as hypothalamic–pituitary–adrenal axis and frontal cortical functioning, which are associated with arousability and self-regulation, could provide insights on internal mechanisms associated with prosocial responding. Indeed, research on rodents suggests that early maternal care experiences impact later sensitivity to distress (e.g., Liu et al., 1997). Furthermore, researchers have noted the importance of central neuropeptides such as oxytocin and vasopressin in affiliative behaviors during mother–infant bonding and other positive social behaviors (see Carter, 1998; Gimpl & Fahrenholz, 2001). Other potential fruitful avenues for animal research on prosocial responding include examination of early maternal care experiences on self-control (e.g., impulsivity, see Carlo & Bevins, 2002).

The potential for comparative psychology research to inform prosocial behavior scholars has not been fully achieved. Evidence for cross-species similarities (or differences) serves to augment the evolutionary importance of prosocial behaviors. Moreover, research on the development of prosocial behaviors in other animal species (such as great apes and chimpanzees) can help to elucidate the antecedents of these behaviors. In addition, neurophysiological research could isolate specific microlevel, neural, and physiological mechanisms associated with prosocial responding. Combined with the findings from research on humans, those areas of research can provide a powerful approach to understanding prosocial development.

Human Research. What about research with humans? Several studies with humans suggest a genetic and biological basis for altruism and prosocial behaviors. First, studies of twins yield evidence that empathy have a strong heritable component (Emde et al., 1992; Matthews, Batson, Horn, & Rosenman, 1981; Zahn-Waxler, Robinson, & Emde, 1992). Second, empathy and prosocial behaviors have been linked theoretically and empirically to biological mechanisms such as temperament (Kagan, in press; Rothbart et al., 1994). Third, empathy-like responding is present early in life and across many animal species (Carlo & Randall, 2001; Hoffman, 2000). And fourth, there is accumulating evidence on the temporal stability of prosocial behaviors across the lifespan (Eisenberg et al., 1999). Although much more research is needed to directly examine the biological basis for prosocial behaviors, the overall evidence and existing theory suggests strongly that there is a biological basis for these behaviors.

In recent years, there has been an increased interest in the links between temperament and prosocial behaviors. Kagan (in press), for example, points out that individual differences in behavioral inhibition might partially account for individual differences in early conscience development. Similarly, Eisenberg and Fabes (1992) suggest that children who exhibit high levels of prosocial behaviors are likely to exhibit optimal levels of emotionality through a combination of emotion regulation and affective reactivity proneness.

Research has accumulated that supports these hypotheses. Rothbart and co-workers (1994) found that individual differences in negative affectivity (sadness and fear) in infancy were predictive of prosocial traits in early childhood. In a series of studies, Eisenberg and her colleagues have demonstrated that socially competent and prosocial children tend to have a combination of good emotion regulation skills and express moderate levels of affectivity (see Eisenberg, in press; Eisenberg & Fabes, 1998).

In summary, theory and research on the biological basis of prosocial behaviors in humans is just beginning but shows much promise, especially in accounting for individual differences in early moral development. Furthermore, temperament and other biological approaches (e.g., cognitive neuroscience) to research on prosocial behaviors provide innovative methodological approaches to understanding the biological basis of these behaviors. Evolutionary theories provide possible insights into the adaptive function of altruism and might help us to understand the far-reaching implications of those behaviors.

Developmental and Gender Differences

Early in life children express tendencies such as sadness, sorrow, and concern for others, which are linked to prosocial behaviors (see Eisenberg & Fabes, 1998). However, there are substantial, age-related changes in the frequency of expressed prosocial behaviors over time. As noted by Eisenberg and Fabes (1998) in their meta-analytic review of the literature, prosocial behaviors increase with age from childhood to adolescence. The greatest age increases are evident from preschool to adolescence and the smallest age increases are evident from infancy to preschool, from childhood to adolescence, and during adolescence. However, the magnitude of the age increases varies by the specific characteristics of the studies (e.g., type of prosocial behavior, year of publication, study design).

Gender differences in prosocial behaviors have also been of interest to researchers in this area. Gilligan (1982) posited that existing psychological theories, especially moral development theories, did not adequately reflect the female perspective. Of particular relevance to moral development was her notion that girls and women are socialized and oriented toward issues of care and interpersonal relationships. Those issues, according to Gilligan (1982), were not adequately reflected in early theories of moral development, such as Kohlberg's justice-oriented stage theory (Kohlberg, 1969). The identification of care and benevolence as an important domain of morality helped to redress the overemphasis on justice issues and, more importantly, spurred interest in gender differences in prosocial behaviors.

According to gender socialization theorists (Gilligan, 1982; Maccoby & Jacklin, 1974; Whiting & Edwards, 1988), girls, more than boys, are encouraged to exhibit nurturance and care behaviors. The process begins early in life through gender-specific practices by parents, other family members, peers, other adults (e.g., teachers), and through institutional policies (e.g., gender segregation). For example, girls might be praised or encouraged to show nurturance and express sadness whereas boys might be punished or teased for expressing nurturance or for expressing sadness. The impact of those gender-specific experiences on prosocial behaviors accumulates and intensifies over time (Fabes et al., 1999).

Although several studies show that there is little or weak evidence for gender differences in justice-oriented moral reasoning (Walker, 1984, 1991), scholars have noted that gender differences in moral reasoning might be present in specific contexts. That is, because gender is a proxy variable that reflects gender-specific biological and socialization mechanisms, specific contexts might pull for gender-specific socialization tendencies such as gender-role stereotyped behaviors (Carlo, Koller, Eisenberg, Dasilva, & Frohlich, 1996).

Furthermore, it is important to note that gender might play an important moderator role in the relations between theoretically relevant predictors and prosocial behaviors. This possibility might have significant implications for the development of gender-specific prevention and intervention programs. Supportive evidence for the importance of context stems from research on prosocial moral reasoning. Several researchers have noted modest but consistent gender differences in prosocial behavioral contexts using measures of prosocial moral reasoning (see Eisenberg & Fabes, 1998). Perhaps more importantly, in a recent meta-analytic review, investigators concluded that girls and women scored higher than boys and men on care-oriented (prosocial) moral reasoning, whereas men and boys scored higher on justice-oriented moral reasoning (Jaffe & Hyde, 2000).

What about gender differences in prosocial behaviors? Several reviews of the literature yield evidence for modest, yet consistent, gender differences in prosocial behaviors particularly in adolescence. In a meta-analytic review of gender differences in prosocial behaviors, Fabes and colleagues (1999) showed that gender differences in prosocial behaviors were greatest between childhood and early adolescence. Similarly, Eisenberg and Fabes (1998) found strong gender differences in prosocial behaviors increased with age. However, gender differences in prosocial behaviors appear to vary as a function of the qualities of the studies. Indeed, gender differences in prosocial behaviors among children and adolescents disappeared once other study qualities were statistically controlled. In those reviews, girls consistently exhibited greater levels of prosocial behaviors than boys. Interestingly, in a review of gender differences in prosocial behaviors with college students and adults, Eagly and Crowley (1986) found that men were more likely to engage in instrumental (risky/chivalrous) types of prosocial behaviors than women; women were more likely to engage in nurturant types of prosocial behaviors than men. In summary, although gender differences in prosocial behaviors are present and relatively consistent across studies, scholars acknowledge that the magnitude of the differences varies as a function of the study context, measurement and study qualities (e.g., self-report versus observational measures, nurturing versus volunteerism behaviors).

Parenting, Sibling, Peer, and Media Correlates

Research on social contextual influences of prosocial behaviors has centered mostly on studying the impact of family members, parents, peers, and the media on prosocial behaviors. Although those socializing agents and their influence are important, it is important to acknowledge the reciprocal and bidirectional impact of prosocial behaviors (Carlo & Randall, 2001). An important determinant of prosocial behaviors is that children and adolescents have the opportunities to practice prosocial behaviors as well as to receive the rewards of engaging in, and benefiting from, prosocial behaviors directed at them. Thus, prosocial behavior opportunities can become the training grounds for exhibiting those behaviors and benefiting from their consequences.

Parents and siblings have been identified as key socializing agents of prosocial development during childhood (Chase-Lansdale, Wakschlag, & Brooks-Gunn, 1995; Dunn & Munn, 1986; Eisenberg & Murphy, 1995; Whiting & Edwards, 1988). By adolescence, however, scholars note that peers become increasingly important socializing agents of prosocial development (see Carlo, Fabes, Laible, & Kupanoff, 1999). It is also likely that the media plays an increasingly important role, although research on this possibility is relatively sparse. Unfortunately, there has also been relatively less research on the impact of other socializing agents such as teachers, extended family members, and other important adults or peers.

Parents.   Theoretically, parents can influence children's prosocial development in several ways. Warm and supportive relationships with those social agents are expected to foster and promote prosocial tendencies (see Barnett, 1987; Carlo, Fabes et al., 1999; Eisenberg & Murphy, 1995). Parents might coach and guide their children's prosocial behaviors by providing direct verbal messages (e.g., beliefs, attitudes) about desirable behaviors. Furthermore, children might be encouraged or directed toward behaving in specific ways when presented with prosocial moral decision-making situations. Children are also apt to learn about prosocial behaviors by directly observing their parents' (and perhaps other adults') prosocial behaviors. Moreover, parents and caregivers are likely to create affective family environments that facilitate or discourage prosocial tendencies (Carlo, Roesch, & Melby, 1998).

Indeed, many researchers have examined the relations between parental support and attachment and children's and moral development, although most of the research has focused on empathy and sympathy rather than prosocial behaviors. In general, the findings show modest (but inconsistent) positive relations between parental support and attachment and prosocial development (Dekovic & Janssens, 1992; Eberly & Montemayor, 1998; see Eisenberg & Murphy, 1995). In addition, children who exhibit higher levels of prosocial and moral development generally have authoritative parents (high support, high demanding) rather than authoritarian parents (low support, high demanding) or neglectful parents (low support, low demanding; Baumrind, 1991; see Maccoby & Martin, 1983).

Based on prior conceptualizations of parenting and moral development, Grusec and Goodnow (1994) outlined a number of variables that impact children's internalization of moral values. Although the model focused on values internalization, the model might also be useful in summarizing parent and child variables associated with prosocial behaviors. These theorists noted that there are two main components necessary for value internalization: acceptance and understanding. Children's willingness to accept moral messages from their parents is hypothesized to be contingent on a number of variables including judgments of the appropriateness of the parents' reactions, the type of misdeed, the type of discipline, the clarity and consistency of the message, the perceived significance, the perceived threat to children's autonomy, and the individual characteristics (e.g., temperament) of the parents and children (Grusec & Goodnow, 1994). Although the model provides a rich framework for research on the socializing influence of parenting on moral development, relatively little research has actually been conducted to test specific aspects of the model.

One aspect of moral socialization that has been examined empirically is the impact of parental disciplining techniques on children's moral development (Hoffman & Salzstein, 1967; Krevins & Gibbs, 1996; see Hoffman, 1983, 2000). Parents' use of inductions and explanations (a technique that has been linked to authoritative parenting) has been linked to prosocial behaviors. Theorists suggest that this technique might be effective in fostering prosocial behaviors because it often transmits direct moral messages (e.g., parental values) in a well emotionally regulated manner. Furthermore, often parents who use inductions induce empathy and perspective taking in their children by pointing out the beneficial or harmful consequences of their moral actions. In contrast, parents who use power assertive (and to a lesser extent, love withdrawal) disciplining techniques (often used by authoritarian parents) have children who exhibit lower levels of prosocial and moral development. These techniques are often exhibited in an emotionally overarousing manner, which compromises the moral message (Hoffman, 2000). Worse, if the parent enforces this technique with physical punishment, the parent serves to model aggressive behaviors. Over time, the frequent use of power assertion is likely to distance the parent or caregiver from the child, which might lead to fear and distrust.

Although most scholars emphasize transgressive behavioral contexts as powerful opportunities for moral socialization, considerably less attention has been devoted to the strong socialization influence of prosocial behavior contexts on moral development (Grusec, 1991). However, prosocial behavior contexts can be powerful socialization venues for prosocial moral development. Children have strong desires to gain their parents and other people's approval and positive affection and this motive can serve as a powerful means to foster desirable moral behaviors and to mitigate antisocial behaviors. Children might be rewarded for appropriate displays of prosocial behaviors or children's prosocial behaviors might be neglected, minimized, or even punished. It is important to note that the feedback that children receive in these prosocial behavior contexts might result from socialization agents other than parents (e.g., peers). In addition, parents can transmit direct and subtle messages to children regarding the appropriateness and expected behaviors through their reactions to children's prosocial behaviors (or their failure to exhibit prosocial behaviors). Over time, the cumulative experiences in prosocial behavior contexts might result in changes to children's cognitive and emotional scripts regarding prosocial behaviors, which in turn, might affect their moral self-concept and future prosocial behaviors (Dix & Grusec, 1983; Padilla-Walker & Carlo, 2004; see Carlo & Randall, 2001). Consistent with this notion, there is evidence that positive feedback (e.g., praise) can increase the likelihood of future prosocial behaviors, especially if the feedback is provided in a manner that could enhancement a dispositional attribution or promote a prosocial self-concept (Dix & Grusec, 1983; Grusec & Redler, 1980). Furthermore, there is some preliminary evidence that adolescents' expected parental reactions to prosocial behaviors are more consistently associated with social behaviors than adolescents' expected reactions to antisocial behaviors (Wyatt & Carlo, 2002). Clearly, more research is needed to further examine the potential impact of prosocial behavior contexts on children's moral development.

Siblings. Although conflict among siblings is relatively common, prosocial behaviors among siblings have also been commonly observed (Dunn & Munn, 1986). By toddlerhood, young children are capable of simple perspective taking and exhibit empathic responding. Those skills, along with a developing self-understanding and language skills, undoubtedly contribute to an increase in prosocial behaviors in early childhood. Older siblings can serve as models for prosocial (and antisocial) behaviors and offer opportunities for younger siblings to practice prosocial behaviors (Tucker, Updegraff, McHale, & Crouter, 1999). Furthermore, younger siblings might learn about the consequences of exhibiting prosocial behaviors or failing to exhibit prosocial behaviors by observing their older siblings. However, the extent of sibling influence on prosocial behaviors is probably contingent on the sibling's own social-cognitive abilities, emotional responsiveness, and emotion regulation skills (Garner, Jones, & Palmer, 1994). Dunn (1988) emphasizes that most siblings show some understanding of the consequences of their behaviors on others by anticipating the reactions of adults. She stresses that children who develop this understanding might develop a positive sense of self and a connectedness that enables future prosocial actions.

Unfortunately, research on the influence of siblings on prosocial behaviors is sparse. In a naturalistic study of siblings, Dunn (1988) found strong longitudinal evidence that toddlers exhibited cooperative and coordinated, reciprocal behaviors directed toward mutual prosocial goals. The findings are concordant with the notion that prosocial behaviors among siblings might foster closer sibling relationships. In addition, the researchers found that many of the prosocial behaviors were exhibited during play interactions, suggesting that play contexts are important training fields for the expression of prosocial behaviors

(Dunn, 1988). Consistent with sociobiological perspectives, other researchers found that cooperative behaviors were more frequent among siblings and friends than among acquaintances (Knight & Chao, 1991).

Peers.   The significance of peer relationships has long been recognized as a venue for moral socialization by developmental scholars. Peer interactions offer opportunities for applying and receiving prosocial behaviors from socialization agents who are socially similar in power and status. Piaget was one of the first to recognize the importance of peer relationships for children's understanding of fairness and justice (Piaget, 1932/1965). Youniss (1994) noted that children learn principles of reciprocity and open communication through their interactions with peers. In addition to acquiring an understanding of reciprocity and fairness, children gain a deeper understanding of their moral self through social comparisons, by exposure to differing perspectives on moral issues, and they can observe and practice new modes of providing instrumental help (Berndt, 1989; Furman & Buhrmester, 1985). Furthermore, peers offer additional sources of support and warmth (Belle, Burr, & Cooney, 1987), which are important elements of prosocial behaviors. Finally, peers are important sources of feedback to children (Youniss, 1980). They can provide reinforcement or punishers that can foster or diminish prosocial behaviors in children (Carlo, Fabes et al., 1999). As children display prosocial behaviors toward peers, they are likely to benefit from reciprocal displays of prosocial behaviors (Bukowski & Sippola, 1996). Over time, those reciprocal prosocial displays can result in greater intimacy and trust, which can form the basis for positive moral development.

There is considerable evidence on the impact of peer relationships on prosocial development, although much of the work has focused on the rewarding or punishing impact of peers (see Eisenberg & Fabes, 1998). Other researchers have shown that children who exhibit high levels of prosocial behaviors tend to have higher ratings of peer acceptance and status (Schonert-Reichl, 1999; Wentzel & McNamara, 1999). Although peers can increasingly become influential as socializing agents as children enter adolescence, there is still considerable evidence that parents continue to exert their influence on prosocial development into adolescence (Carlo, Roesch et al., 1998; Laible & Carlo, 2004; Laible, Carlo, & Raffaelli, 2000; Wyatt & Carlo, 2002). Thus, the evidence to date is consistent with the importance of peers on children's prosocial development; however, further research is needed to examine the mechanisms by which peers exert their influence and on the reciprocal, bidirectional effects of peer interactions and prosocial behaviors.

Media.   In the 1970s, there were a number of studies that showed the influence of positive television and film models on prosocial behaviors (Huston & Wright, 1998; see Staub, 1979). In those studies, researchers showed that children who observe a prosocial model could generate future prosocial behaviors, especially when the communication of values and the need was clear and when the model was perceived as physically, socially, or psychologically similar to the observer. Hearold (1986), in a meta-analysis, found a very strong effect size (.83) of watching prosocial behavior television programs on children's altruism (helping and giving) across thirty-six studies. Furthermore, the overall effect size for watching prosocial television was over twice as strong as the overall effect size for watching antisocial television programs! Thus, not only is there strong evidence for the influence of exposure to television programs on prosocial behaviors, but the findings suggest that watching prosocial television can have relative more impact than watching antisocial television programs. Unfortunately, few studies have been conducted examining the influence of film on children's prosocial behaviors since those early studies. However, it should be noted that studies designed to examine children's (and adults') reactions to films that depict children in need or distress have also been shown to be effective in inducing sympathy reactions, which in turn, facilitate prosocial behaviors (e.g., Eisenberg et al., 1989). In summary, there is convincing evidence that exposure to films that contain prosocial content or depict needy others can influence children's prosocial tendencies.

Despite the widely held belief that children can be influenced by the media, scholars have noted that the impact of media other than television or film needs to be investigated. Films and television shows might be a weak form of influence on children's prosocial behaviors. New forms of media that are more interactive such as Internet-based media and video games might be more powerful influences than noninteractive media such as books, magazines, and television (Brown & Witherspoon, 2002). On the other hand, at least among adolescents in the U.S., magazines and novels have become an extremely popular medium of entertainment. Publishers have become more adept at targeting children and adolescents and the market of magazines for adolescent boys (usually centered on sports and activities) and girls (usually centered around fashions, beauty, celebrities, and relationships) has boomed. The tremendous amount of investment in those targeted advertising campaigns and the parallel reported sales figures reflects entrepreneurs' perceptions of the effectiveness of media on children's consumerism behaviors. However, research is lacking on whether the content of magazines and novels impacts prosocial development. The potential for understanding how different types of media can affect children's prosocial behaviors has not been adequately explored.

General Summary. At this point, the research on the impact of socializing agents on children's prosocial behavior is heavily skewed toward examining the influence of parenting. Despite existing gaps in the research (e.g., studies of paternal influence, multivariate studies, longitudinal studies), in general, there is ample evidence for the importance of parents on children's prosocial behaviors. However, research on other socializing agents such as siblings, peers, and the media suggest the importance for the need for further studies examining the multilevel system influences of children's prosocial behaviors. Moreover, an understanding of the reciprocal, bi-directional influences of prosocial behaviors between socializing agents and children is needed.

Sociocognitive Correlates

A set of correlates of prosocial behaviors that has received much attention from theorists and researchers is social cognitive skills. Much of the early work in this area stemmed from cognitive–developmental theorists who posited that age-related advances in cognitive development might help to explain age-related changes in prosocial behaviors. Two of the sociocognitive skills identified as important predictors of prosocial behavior were perspective taking and moral reasoning (research on the links between prosocial behaviors and empathy and sympathy is reviewed by Eisenberg, chap. 19, this volume).

Perspective Taking. Although Mead (1934) has been credited with the term *role taking* (i.e., perspective taking), it was Piaget's seminal work (e.g., Piaget, 1926/1959) that spurred research on the development of perspective taking skills (see Flavell, Botkin, Fry, Wright, & Jarvis, 1968). *Perspective taking* refers to understanding another's situation and implies the ability over time to differentiate between others and self (Shantz, 1983). Closely related to perspective taking are the notions of "decentration" and "egocentrism" (see Looft, 1972;

Piaget, 1926/1959). *Decentration* refers to the ability to shift attention to more than one aspect of an event and *egocentrism* refers to a lack of differentiation of subject and objects in social interactions.

Operationally, several different types of perspective taking have been identified. Most of these types of perspective taking have been classified (Eisenberg & Fabes, 1998; Ford, 1979; Kurdek, 1978; Shantz, 1983; Underwood & Moore, 1982) into at least three distinct, yet theoretically related, categories. First, *social* (or *cognitive*) *perspective taking* refers to the increasing understanding of another's thoughts, intentions, and situation. Second, *affective perspective taking* is defined as the ability to understand the emotional state of another. And third, *perceptual* (or *spatial*) *perspective taking* is the ability to understand the literal visual point of view of another. Although perspective taking is considered an important sociocognitive skill that may be associated with the development of several social behaviors, much of the research on perspective taking has been focused on the relations between perspective taking and prosocial behaviors.

The notion that the increased awareness of another's situation often leads to prosocial behaviors has had considerable discussion in both social and developmental psychology. Several theorists (Batson, 1998; Eisenberg, Shea, Carlo, & Knight, 1991; Hoffman, 2000) have argued that understanding another's thoughts and feelings facilitates other-oriented processes and behaviors such as sympathy, comforting, sharing, or volunteering, and that these processes may also lead to reduction of aggressive and antisocial forms of behaviors (although not always; see Feshbach, 1987). This process may occur in several ways. One view (e.g., Batson, 1998; Davis, Hull, Young, & Warren, 1987) is that perspective taking often leads to sympathy for the plight of others, which in turn facilitates behaviors aimed at reducing the other's distress. According to some of these authors, individuals who are adept at perspective taking may be primed for sympathetic responses, which might induce values or principles (Hoffman, 2000) or prime moral cognitions (Eisenberg, 1986) consonant with helping others in need. A second view is that perspective taking may lead to a state of disequilibrium (e.g., Krebs & Russell, 1981) as a result of awareness of distress in the individual's environment. This awareness, in turn, may result in behavior patterns (i.e., helping or some other prosocial behavior) to attempt to reduce the disequilibrium. Several lines of indirect evidence are consistent with these causal inferences; in particular training studies (e.g., Chalmers & Townsend, 1990; Iannotti, 1978) aimed at promoting perspective-taking skills and reducing maladjustment.

The empirical evidence on the relations between perspective taking and prosocial behavior is mixed. Several studies have shown that perspective taking is associated positively with prosocial behaviors, whereas some others have shown no significant relations. Underwood and Moore (1982), in a meta-analytic review of the literature, noted that "even where reliable associations between altruism and perspective taking measures have been identified, the relationships are not dramatically large" (p. 169). However, those investigators concluded that there is "an extraordinarily reliable—if only moderately large— relationship [between perspective taking and altruism]" (words in brackets added, p. 169). For example, the overall correlation between social perspective taking and prosocial behaviors was .28 (Underwood & Moore, 1982). Furthermore, they argued for a need to delineate the circumstances under which the relation between perspective taking and prosocial behavior might be unusually strong or weak. Other reviewers of the literature concurred with these conclusions (see Eisenberg & Miller, 1987; Krebs & Russell, 1981; Kurdek, 1978).

In an attempt to explain the reasons for the inconsistencies in prior findings, Carlo and associates (1991) showed that more consistent relations between perspective taking and prosocial behavior could be obtained when the task characteristics of the perspective taking measure and the prosocial behavior measure match. Moreover, in a follow-up study, Knight, Johnson, Carlo, and Eisenberg (1994) presented evidence that prosocial behaviors could be better predicted if the joint influence of perspective taking, sympathy, and a task-relevant cognitive skill (i.e., understanding the value and units of money for a money donation task) was examined. Those studies suggest that task specific competencies are important predictors of prosocial behavior (see also Knight, Bohlmeyer, Schneider, & Harris, 1993; Midlarsky & Hannah, 1985; Peterson, 1983) and that perspective taking ought not to be viewed as sufficient, or even relevant, to predicting all types of prosocial behaviors.

In recent years, there has been a shift toward investigating social cognition in very young children. This work has been dominated by theory of mind researchers (see Flavell & Miller, 1998). The focus in this recent work has been on examining understanding of beliefs, desires, intentions, perceptions, thinking, and emotions in early childhood (although some work has focused on older children; see Bosacki & Astington, 1999). Investigators attempt to understand the child's thinking about their mental states and its relations to their social world. Although the early research findings are promising, research on the links between theory of mind and prosocial behaviors is just beginning (Cassidy, Werner, Rourke, Zubernis, & Balaraman, 2003; Ginsburg et al., 2003; Moore, Barresi, & Thompson, 1998).

Moral Reasoning. A second important area of research on the links between social cognition and prosocial behaviors concerns the role of moral reasoning. *Moral reasoning* refers to thinking in dilemma situations where issues of justice, fairness, or caring are prevalent. Often, an individual's style of moral reasoning reflects an orientation to the needs of others or their own. Furthermore, individuals' preference for some types of moral reasoning might be linked to values or emotions (e.g., sympathy, guilt) that facilitate responding to others' needs. Two types of moral reasoning have been the focus of much attention in the moral development research: justice-oriented (Kohlberg, 1969; Rest, 1983; Turiel, 1998) and care-oriented, prosocial (Eisenberg, 1986) moral reasoning. Of the two, care-oriented, prosocial moral reasoning has been most strongly conceptually linked to prosocial behaviors.

Prosocial moral reasoning is thinking about dilemma situations in which one's needs are in conflict with the needs of others in the relative absence of formal laws or rules (Carlo, Eisenberg, & Knight, 1992; Eisenberg, 1986). Prosocial moral reasoning is theorized to increase in sophistication with age due to increases in cognitive development skills such as perspective taking, hypothetical deductive reasoning, abstract thinking, and forethought skills (Eisenberg, 1986).

In 1979, Nancy Eisenberg published the first of a series of papers that reported the findings of the first longitudinal study devoted exclusively to examining prosocial development across the lifespan (Eisenberg-Berg, 1979). To date, the ongoing study spans from preschool to young adulthood (see Eisenberg et al., 2002). Although the study examines several theoretically relevant variables associated with prosocial behaviors, the focus of the study has been prosocial moral reasoning. Eisenberg has found that children and adolescents endorse specific types of reasons for helping others including hedonistic, approval oriented, needs oriented, stereotypic, and empathic and internalized norms or principle reasons. Table 20.1 presents a summary of the levels of prosocial moral reasoning.

A number of investigators have found that other-oriented and higher levels of prosocial moral reasoning are associated with higher levels of prosocial behaviors (see Eisenberg &

TABLE 20.1
Eisenberg's Levels of Prosocial Moral Reasoning

Prosocial Moral Reasoning Level	Approximate Grade School Period of Frequent Occurrence	Description
Hedonistic, pragmatic orientation	Preschool, early elementary school	Behavior satisfies own needs, gains for self
Needs of others orientation	Preschool, elementary school	Concern for physical, material, and psychologicaal needs of others in simple terms
Stereotyped, approval-focused orientation	Elementary school and secondary school	Stereotyped images of good and bad people and concern for gaining others' approval
Empathic orientation	Late elementary school and secondary school	Reasoning reflects an emphasis on perspective taking and empathic feeling for others
Internalized values orientation	Minority of secondary school students and high school students and beyond; no elementary school students	Focus on internalized values, norms; desire to maintain contractual obligation; belief in dignity, rights, and equality

Adapted from Eisenberg (1982).

Fabes, 1998). For example, Eisenberg and Shell (1986) found other-oriented and higher level types of prosocial moral reasoning to be associated with high cost but not low cost helping behaviors (see also Eisenberg, Carlo, Murphy, & Van Court, 1995; Eisenberg et al., 2002; Eisenberg, Miller, Shell, McNalley, & Shea, 1991). Carlo and his colleagues also found those types of prosocial moral reasoning to predict prosocial behaviors (Carlo et al., 1996; Carlo et al., 2003; Wyatt & Carlo, 2002). In a recent study, researchers presented evidence that prosocial moral reasoning mediated the relations between both sympathy and perspective taking and prosocial behaviors (Eisenberg, Zhou, & Koller, 2001). A meta-analytic review concurred that there is an overall positive relation between prosocial moral reasoning and prosocial behaviors (Underwood & Moore, 1982). Overall, then, there is substantial support for an association between prosocial moral reasoning and prosocial behaviors.

Other Social Cognitions.   Other recent work on social cognitions has focused on the association between attributions and prosocial behaviors. For example, Nelson and Crick (1999) showed that adolescents who made benign attributions (as opposed to hostile attributions) in ambiguous situations were more likely to be rated by peers as highly prosocial. This research suggests that children who exhibit high levels of prosocial behaviors are more prone to interpret ambiguous events in ways that promote positive social interactions. Wyatt and Carlo (2002) found that adolescents who expect their parents to react appropriately to prosocial and antisocial behaviors are more likely to exhibit more prosocial behaviors and less antisocial behaviors. Interestingly, the findings suggest that expected parental reactions to prosocial behavior situations were consistently more associated with adolescents' social behaviors than expected parental reactions to antisocial behaviors. Taken together, these studies yield promising evidence on the role of children's attributions and expectancies on their prosocial behaviors (see also Eisenberg & Fabes, 1998).

FUTURE DIRECTIONS IN PROSOCIAL DEVELOPMENT RESEARCH

Much has been learned about the antecedents and correlates of prosocial behaviors in children and adolescents. However, there are still many questions and issues that need further study. This section discusses some of those issues. First, there is great need to further integrate prosocial behaviors within the broader context of moral development theory and research. Second, there is a need to establish more connections between prosocial behaviors and other areas of psychological research (e.g., well-being and pathology) that can further our understanding of human functioning. And third, studies of prosocial behaviors across diverse contexts including cross-cultural studies are necessary to provide ecological validity to existing theories of prosocial development.

Prosocial Behaviors in the Broader Context of Moral Development

In the last few decades, cognitive–developmental theories have provided a rich understanding of cognitive-based mechanisms relevant to understanding moral development. However, many scholars have noted the limitations of theories of morality that do not adequately account for associated affective processes (Eisenberg, 1986; Hoffman, 2000; Lapsley, 1996). Newer conceptions of moral development are beginning to delineate the interrelations between moral cognitions and emotions (Eisenberg, 1986; Gibbs, 2003; Hoffman, 2000). Furthermore, researchers have begun to acknowledge the role of emotion regulation mechanisms on moral functioning and prosocial behaviors (see Eisenberg, in press; Kochanska, 1993).

Of equal importance is the need to integrate beneficent- and prohibition-oriented moralities (Gibbs, 1991). Much of the prior moral development research emphasized morality in prohibition-oriented and transgressive contexts (Eisenberg, 1982). That is, much of the prior research focused on moral development processes in contexts where established rules, laws, and other formal societal proscriptions exist and help to guide moral decision making and behaviors or in contexts where children misbehave and break those socially proscribed rules or laws. However, as noted, moral decisions and behaviors sometimes occur in contexts where proscriptions are relatively absent (e.g., prosocial behavior contexts) or they might occur in contexts where beneficence and prohibition issues conflict. Indeed, some of the most difficult and challenging moral dilemmas are those in which beneficence and prohibition concerns conflict.

Consider the classic Heinz dilemma used to assess prohibition-oriented moral reasoning. In this vignette, individuals are asked to decide whether Heinz should steal a drug from a pharmacy that could save his wife's life. One of the aspects of the vignette that enhances the evocative nature of the dilemma is the fact that it is Heinz's wife, rather than a stranger, whose life is at stake. In addition to the justice, propriety rights, and human life concerns involved in this dilemma, it is also important to acknowledge the implicit, relationship-based duty or obligation that Heinz has toward his wife. The dilemma is challenging because there is conflict between Heinz's obligations to his wife (care-based moral considerations) and his obligations to societal laws and prohibitions (justice-based considerations).

Prior studies that have examined individuals' responses to prohibition-oriented and prosocial-oriented moral reasoning dilemma stories have been mixed. In some studies, researchers found that individuals' reasoning across the two contexts was associated moderately (Eisenberg, Lennon & Roth, 1983; Krebs, Denton, Vermeulen, & Carpendale, 1991), whereas other researchers found no significant associations (Eisenberg et al., 1983;

Kurdek, 1981). The findings appeared to vary as a function of how the interview responses were scored (see Eisenberg et al., 1983). In an unpublished study using objective measures of justice-based moral reasoning and prosocial moral reasoning (using standardized scoring and administration procedures), investigators reported a nonsignificant relation ($r = .13$) between overall composites indices of the Defining Issues Test (the DIT) and the Prosocial Reasoning Objective Measure (the PROM) in a sample of college students (Carlo, 2001). Thus, the findings to date suggest that individuals can distinguish between prosocial-based and justice-based moral contexts.

Both prosocial- and justice-oriented contexts are important and relevant aspects of morality. As Gibbs (2003) and others (e.g., Lapsley, 1996) have noted, the integration of beneficent-centered and justice-centered approaches can provide a rich framework for understanding moral development. The challenge is how to accomplish a successful integration. Although cognitive–developmental theories are useful to explain moral decision-making processes, many scholars have noted the limitations of those theories explaining moral behaviors (Blasi, 1980; Lapsley, 1996). Of course, it is important to note that understanding moral decision making is worthwhile in and of itself because such decisions (e.g., distributing resources, decision involving freedom of expression) can have profound impact on society (Rest, 1979). However, there is great demand for social scientists to provide answers to understanding moral development beyond decision making. To accomplish a more comprehensive account of moral development, it is necessary to adopt broader theoretical perspectives that account for moral behaviors, as well as cognitions and emotions.

One possibility is to adopt broader theoretical frameworks such as social cognitive theories that allows for the integration of individual and social contextual influences on moral development (e.g., Bandura, 1991; Carlo & Randall, 2001; Eisenberg, 1986; Staub, 1978, 1979). For example, Bandura's (1991) social cognitive theory is flexible enough to allow for the study of moral development accounting for the influence of cognitions, emotions, motivation, and context. Because social–cognitive theories acknowledge the multiple influences of moral conduct, much of the existing research on moral development is compatible with those theories. Another possible framework that could integrate the multiple influences of moral development is the work on moral identity. There are many different conceptions of moral identity but common to most frameworks is the notion that moral identity involves the extent to which individuals develop an integrated sense of ethical self regarding cognitions, emotions, and behaviors (Blasi, 1983; Colby & Damon, 1988; Hart & Fegley, 1995; Lapsley, 1996). Hart and his colleagues' (Hart, in press; Hart & Fegley, 1995) work on care exemplars is particularly noteworthy because it focuses on understanding the person and environment characteristics of individuals who are recognized by peers as personifying a strong sense of moral commitment through their care-based actions. Although these approaches have somewhat different foci and methodologies, each approach has much to offer to inform scholars about the broad field of moral development.

Prosocial Behaviors and Well-Being and Pathology

Children and adolescents who exhibit high levels of prosocial behaviors might benefit from a number of mental health outcomes. For example, because prosocial behaviors require good emotion regulation and social–cognitive skills (see Eisenberg & Fabes, 1998), one might expect that children with those characteristics would be less prone to conduct and mood disorders. Furthermore, prosocial behaviors are important to building and maintaining positive and supportive social relationships, which might enhance social support and social adjustment. In turn, social support and good social skills might buffer or protect children and adolescents who are at high risk for maladjustment. Moreover, researchers have shown that individuals who assist others are most likely to assist others when they are in a positive mood (Carlson & Miller, 1987) and positive mood has been shown to be associated with positive health outcomes (Salovey, Rothman, Detweiler, & Steward, 2000).

Unfortunately, research is quite limited on the potential links between prosocial behaviors and mental health. However, there is suggestive evidence on the positive health and social outcomes of individuals who frequently engage in prosocial behaviors (but see Hay & Pawlby, 2003). For example, with regard to positive social adjustment, children and adolescents who exhibit high levels of prosocial behaviors are often socially skilled and popular, deemed more trustworthy, high academic performers, report less loneliness, and are socially responsible (Capara, Barbaranelli, Pastorelli, Bandura, Zimbardo, & Chen, 2000; Rotenberg et al., in press; Wentzel, 1991; see Eisenberg & Fabes, 1998). A recent study showed that prosocial behavior was related positively to self-esteem in adolescents (Laible, Carlo, & Roesch, 2004). Researchers have also shown that those children and adolescents are characteristically empathic and sympathetic, which has been linked negatively to aggression, delinquency, and externalizing behaviors (Miller & Eisenberg, 1988). Moreover, investigators have shown moderate negative relations between aggression and prosocial behaviors (Carlo & Randall, 2002; Carlo et al., 2003; Crick & Gropeter, 1995; Wyatt & Carlo, 2002). Of perhaps equal importance is the need for more research on children and adolescents from high-risk environments who exhibit high levels of prosocial behaviors (see for example, Hart & Fegley, 1995). This latter type of research not only helps us to understand children who succeed against the odds, but the research also provides a more balanced perspective on the characteristics of children from high risk environments.

Prosocial Behaviors Across and Within Ethnic and Cultural Groups

For years, cultural psychologists have noted socialization practice differences by people from different societies that promote children's prosocial behaviors (Whiting & Whiting, 1975). For example, in some societies, young children are assigned household duties and responsibilities that foster social responsibility and prosocial behaviors. In other societies, prosocial behaviors are encouraged through formal curriculum requirements in early education programs. Even across early education programs, there are differences in the aspects of morality that are emphasized; some might focus on empathy and respect and others might focus on reasoning and problem solving. The impact of these and other wide-ranging socialization practices and experiences on prosocial development in different societies is little understood.

Unfortunately, the range of prosocial behaviors in cross-cultural investigations has been somewhat limited. In their classic study of six cultures, the Whitings and their colleagues found cultural variations in levels of exhibited prosocial behaviors (Whiting & Whiting, 1975; see also Whiting & Edwards, 1988). For example, cultures that exhibited higher levels tended to have larger families, placed greater importance on women, had less specialized careers, and had less centralized governments. In addition, gender differences in prosocial behaviors were more pronounced in those cultures. The gender differences favoring girls and women were attributed to greater responsibility for the welfare of the family (e.g., younger siblings) and to the assignment of responsible, household chores early in life. Recent investigators of cooperative behaviors also found greater gender differences among children from Brazil than among children from the U.S. (Carlo, Roesch, Knight, & Koller, 2001).

Other early psychological research of cultural variations in prosocial behaviors was concerned with cross-national studies of cooperative and competitive behaviors. Research on cooperative, prosocial, and moral behaviors has yielded important nationality differences. For example, Mexicans and Mexican Americans prefer cooperative social behaviors to a greater extent than do European Americans (see Knight, Bernal, & Carlo, 1995). Stevenson (1991) noted that Chinese and Japanese families espouse helping around the house, helping classroom peers, and doing good for their society. In one study with older adolescents (Ma, 1989), Chinese adolescents reportedly were more willing to risk their lives to save another, more oriented toward human sentiments, and more oriented toward abiding the laws than were adolescents from England. Ma (1989) proposed that these findings were consistent with the familial emphases of human sentiment, collectivism, group solidarity, and obedience (authoritarian style) of Chinese children and adolescents.

Several studies of prosocial and care-based moral reasoning and motives also suggest wide cultural variations. For example, investigators reported Brazilian children and adolescents less preferred empathic and internalized modes of prosocial moral reasoning than did European American children and adolescents (Carlo et al., 1996). In late adolescence, European Americans more preferred approval-oriented prosocial moral reasoning than Brazilians (Carlo, Roesch, & Koller, 1999). Skoe and her colleagues (1999) reported nationality differences in care-oriented moral reasoning between Canadians and Norwegian adolescents. Boehnke, Silbereisen, Eisenberg, Reykowski, and Palmonari (1989) found that Italian and German adolescents reported different motives for prosocial behaviors. In a study of children and adults from Papua New Guinea, Tietjen (1986) found few differences in prosocial moral reasoning between those children and children from Western cultures; however, adults' prosocial moral reasoning differed from that of adults in Western cultures.

Of particular interest to psychologists is whether models of prosocial and moral behavior are cross-culturally equivalent. Consistent with prior research conducted with European Americans, research conducted with Brazilian adolescents indicated that higher levels of prosocial moral reasoning were associated positively with prosocial behaviors (Carlo et al., 1996; Eisenberg et al., 2002). Furthermore, as has been found in samples from the U.S., institutionalized Brazilian adolescents (delinquents and orphans) scored lower on prosocial moral reasoning than low socioeconomic status, noninstitutionalized Brazilian adolescents (Carlo, Koller, & Eisenberg, 1998). Similar to age-related differences in prosocial moral reasoning with samples from the U.S. and Brazil, researchers in Israel found that motives for money donations increased in sophistication with age such that younger children were more likely to be concerned with compliance and external issues and older children more likely reported internal or intrinsic motives (Bar-Tal, Raviv, & Leiser, 1980; Raviv, Bar-Tal, & Lewis-Levin, 1980). Consistent with prior research in the U.S., other studies showed that higher levels of prosocial behaviors were associated with more social acceptance (in Finland) and higher levels of academic achievement (in China; Chen, Liu, Rubin, Cen, Gao, & Li, 2002; Pakaslahti, Karjalainen, & Keltikangas-Jarvinen, 2002). Further research is needed to examine the cross-cultural validity of theoretical models of prosocial development in other cultures.

Studies of prosocial and moral behaviors in ethnic minority groups from the U.S. have been few. Ramirez and Castaneda (1974) and Steward and Steward (1973) pointed out that parents of Mexican descent attempt to instill a sense of collectivism and cooperation in their children. Williams (1991) found that high-income Mexican-American families valued more what others did to help them than did high-income European-American families. Consistent with these findings, a number of researchers have shown that

Mexican-American children and adolescents more prefer cooperative to competitive behaviors than European-American children and adolescents (see Eisenberg & Fabes, 1998; also Knight et al., 1995). However, studies of other types of prosocial behaviors and with other minority groups are lacking.

In summary, cross-cultural and cross-ethnic studies of prosocial behaviors can provide insights into the developmental mechanisms, and the varieties, of prosocial behaviors. Questions about the universality of prosocial behaviors can be addressed through cross-cultural methodologies, which might provide a better understanding of the development of those behaviors. Furthermore, cross-cultural studies allow researchers to test the parameters of the applicability of our knowledge concerning prosocial behaviors. However, progress in this area of research depends on the examination of prosocial behaviors in a wider array of cultures, with more sophisticated research designs (e.g., longitudinal studies and multivariate approaches), and the development of culturally valid measures of prosocial behaviors. Moreover, some scholars have suggested prosocial development might be better understood through methodologies that simultaneously examine both within- and between-culture variables (Carlo et al., 2001). This latter approach provides us insights on the limits of existing within-culture models, acknowledges the complex, multilevel influences of prosocial development, and facilitates the development of ecologically grounded models of prosocial development.

ACKNOWLEDGMENTS

The author greatly appreciated the assistance of Maria de Guzman, Sam Hardy, Laura Padilla, and Stacy Steil. The author also appreciates the helpful feedback of Melanie Killen and Judi Smetana. Funding support for writing this chapter was provided by the John Templeton Foundation, the American Psychological Association, and a grant (NSF 0132302) from the National Science Foundation.

REFERENCES

Bandura, A. (1991). Social cognitive theory of moral thought and action. In W. M. Kurtines & J. L. Gewirtz (Eds.), *Handbook of moral behavior and development, Vol. 1: Theory* (pp. 45–103). Hillsdale, NJ: Lawrence Erlbaum Associates.

Bar-Tal, D., Raviv, A., & Leiser, T. (1980). The development of altruistic behavior: Empirical evidence. *Developmental Psychology, 16,* 516–524.

Barnett, M. A. (1987). Empathy and related responses in children. In N. Eisenberg & J. Strayer (Eds.), *Empathy and its development* (pp. 146–162). Cambridge, UK: Cambridge University Press.

Batson, C. D. (1998). Altruism and prosocial behavior. In D. T. Gilbert, S. T. Fiske, & G. Lindzey (Eds.), *The handbook of social psychology, Vol. 2* (4th ed., pp. 282–316). Boston: McGraw-Hill Companies.

Baumrind, D. (1991). The influence of parenting style on adolescent competence and substance use. *Journal of Early Adolescence, 11,* 56–95.

Belle, D., Burr, R., & Cooney, J. (1987). Boys and girls as social support theorists. *Sex Roles, 17,* 657–665.

Berndt, T. J. (1989). Obtaining support from friends during childhood and adolescence. In D. Belle (Ed.), *Children's social networks and social supports* (pp. 308–331). New York: John Wiley & Sons.

Bierhoff, H. (2002). *Prosocial behaviour.* New York: Psychology Press.

Blasi, A. (1980). Bridging moral cognition and moral action: A critical review of the literature. *Psychological Bulletin, 88,* 1–45.

Blasi, A. (1983). Moral cognition and moral action: A theoretical perspective. *Developmental Review, 3,* 178–210.

Blum, L. A. (1980). *Friendship, altruism, and morality.* London: Routledge & Kegan Paul.

Boehnke, K., Silbereisen, R. K., Eisenberg, N., Reykowski, J., & Palmonari, A. (1989). Developmental pattern of prosocial motivation: A cross-national study. *Journal of Cross-Cultural Psychology, 20,* 219–243.

Bosacki, S., & Astington, J. W. (1999). Theory of mind in preadolescence: Relations between social understanding and social competence. *Social development, 8,* 237–255.

Brown, J. D., & Witherspoon, E. M. (2002). The mass media and American adolescents' health. *Journal of Adolescent Health, 31,* 153–170.

Bukowski, W. M., & Sippola, L. K. (1996). Friendship and morality. In W. M. Bukowski & A. F. Newcomb (Eds.), *The company they keep: Friendship in childhood and adolescence* (pp. 238–261). Cambridge, UK: Cambridge University Press.

Capara, G. V., Barbaranelli, C., Pastorelli, C., Bandura, A., & Zimbardo, P. G. (2000). Prosocial foundations of children's academic achievement. *Psychological Science, 11,* 302–306.

Carlo, G. (2001, April). The cost of following in Kant's footsteps: Moral development embedded in context (title changed). In D. Lapsley (Chair), *Moral Development at the Crossroads: Integrative Approaches.* Symposium at the Society for Research on Child Development, Minneapolis, MN.

Carlo, G., Allen, J. B., & Buhman, D. C. (1999). Facilitating and disinhibiting prosocial behaviors: The nonlinear interaction of trait perspective taking and trait personal distress on volunteering. *Basic and Applied Social Psychology, 21,* 189–197.

Carlo, G., & Bevins, R. A. (2002). The need for proximal mechanisms to understand individual differences in altruism. *Behavioral and Brain Sciences (Commentary), 25,* 255–256.

Carlo, G., Eisenberg, N., & Knight, G. P. (1992). An objective measure of adolescents' prosocial moral reasoning. *Journal of Research on Adolescence, 2,* 331–349.

Carlo, G., Fabes, R. A., Laible, D. J., & Kupanoff, K. (1999). Early adolescence and prosocial/moral behavior II: The role of social and contextual influences. *Journal of Early Adolescence, 19,* 133–147.

Carlo, G., Hausmann, A., Christiansen, S., & Randall, B. A. (2003). Sociocognitive and behavioral correlates of a measure of prosocial tendencies for adolescents. *Journal of Early Adolescence, 23,* 107–134.

Carlo, G., Knight, G. P., Eisenberg, N., & Rotenberg, K. J. (1991). Cognitive processes and prosocial behavior among children: The role of affective attributions and reconciliations. *Developmental Psychology, 27,* 456–461.

Carlo, G., Koller, S., & Eisenberg, N. (1998). Prosocial moral reasoning in institutionalized delinquent, orphaned, and noninstitutionalized Brazilian adolescents. *Journal of Adolescent Research, 13,* 363–376.

Carlo, G., Koller, S. H., Eisenberg, N., DaSilva, M., & Frohlich, C. (1996). A cross-national study on the relations among prosocial moral reasoning, gender role orientations, and prosocial behaviors. *Developmental Psychology, 32,* 231–240.

Carlo, G., & Randall, B. (2001). Are all prosocial behaviors equal? A socioecological developmental conception of prosocial behavior. In F. Columbus (Ed.), *Advances in psychology research* (Vol. II, pp. 151–170). Huntington, NY: Nova Science Publishers.

Carlo, G., & Randall, B. A. (2002). The development of a measure of prosocial behaviors for late adolescents. *Journal of Youth and Adolescence, 31,* 31–44.

Carlo, G., Roesch, S. C., Knight, G. P., & Koller, S. H. (2001). Between or within-culture variation? Culture group as a moderator of the relations between individual differences and resource allocation preferences. *Journal of Applied Developmental Psychology, 22,* 559–579.

Carlo, G., Roesch, S. C. & Koller, S. H. (1999). Cross-national and gender similarities and differences in prosocial moral reasoning between Brazilian and European-American college students. *Interamerican Journal of Psychology, 33,* 151–172.

Carlo, G., Roesch, S. C., & Melby, J. (1998). The multiplicative relations of parenting and temperament to prosocial and antisocial behaviors in adolescence. *Journal of Early Adolescence, 18,* 266–290.

Carlson, M., & Miller, N. (1987). Explanation of the relation between negative mood and helping. *Psychological Bulletin, 102,* 91–108.

Carter, C. S. (1998). Neuroendrocrine perspectives on social attachment and love. *Psychoneuroendocrinology, 23,* 779–818.

Cassidy, K. W., Werner, R. S., Rourke, M., Zubernis, L. S., & Balaraman, G. (2003). The relationship between psychological understanding and positive social behaviors. *Social Development, 12,* 198–221.

Chalmers, J. B., & Townsend, M. A. R. (1990). The effects of training in social perspective taking on socially maladjusted girls. *Child Development, 61,* 178–190.

Chase-Lansdale, P. L., Wakschlag, L. S., & Brooks-Gunn, J. (1995). A psychological perspective on the development of caring in children and youth: The role of the family. *Journal of Adolescence, 18,* 515–556.

Chen, X., Liu, M., Rubin, K. H., Cen, G., Gao, X., & Li, D. (2002). Sociability and prosocial orientation as predictors of youth adjustment: A seven-year longitudinal study in a Chinese sample. *International Journal of Behavioral Development, 26,* 128–136.

Cialdini, R. B., Brown, S. L., Lewis, B. P., Luce, C., & Neuberg, S. L. (1997). Reinterpreting the empathy-altruism relationship: When one into one equals oneness. *Journal of Personality and Social Psychology, 73,* 481–494.

Colby, A., & Damon, W. (1992). *Some do care: Contemporary lives of moral commitment.* Toronto: Free Press.

Crick, N. R., & Gropeter, J. K. (1995). Relational aggression, gender, and social-psychological adjustment. *Child Development, 66,* 710–722.

Davis, M. H., Hull, J. G., Young, R. D., & Warren, W. G. (1987). Emotional reactions to dramatic film stimuli: The influence of cognitive and emotional empathy. *Journal of Personality and Social Psychology, 52,* 126–133.

Dekovic, M., & Janssens, J. M. A. M. (1992). Parents' child-rearing style and children's sociometric status. *Developmental Psychology, 28,* 925–932.

Descartes, R. (1622/1972). *Treatise of man.* Cambridge, MA: Harvard University Press.

De Waal, F. (1996). *Good natured: The origins of right and wrong in humans and other animals.* Cambridge, MA: Harvard University Press.

Dix, T., & Grusec, J. E. (1983). Parental influence techniques: An attributional analysis. *Child Development, 54,* 645–652.

Dunn, J. (1988). *The beginnings of social understanding.* Cambridge, MA: Harvard University Press.

Dunn, J., & Munn, P. (1986). Siblings and the development of prosocial behaviour. *International Journal of Behavioral Development, 9,* 265–294.

Eagly, A. H., & Crowley, M. (1986). Gender and helping behavior: A meta-analytic review of the social psychological literature. *Psychological Bulletin, 100,* 283–308.

Eberly, M. B., & Montemayor, R. (1998). Doing good deeds: An examination of adolescent prosocial behavior in the context of parent/adolescent relationships. *Journal of Adolescent Research, 13,* 403–432.

Eberly, M. B., & Montemayor, R. (1999). Adolescent affection and helpfulness toward parents: A 2-year follow-up. *Journal of Early Adolescence, 19,* 226–248.

Eisenberg, N. (1982). The development of reasoning regarding prosocial behavior. In N. Eisenberg (Eds.), *The development of prosocial behavior* (pp. 219–249). New York: Academic Press.

Eisenberg, N. (1986). *Altruistic emotion, cognition and behavior.* Hillsdale, NJ: Lawrence Erlbaum Associates.

Eisenberg, N. (in press). The development of empathy-related responding. In G. Carlo & C. P. Edwards (Eds.), *The 51ˢᵗ Annual Symposium on Motivation: Moral motivation.* Lincoln: University of Nebraska Press.

Eisenberg, N., Carlo, G., Murphy, B., & Van Court, P. (1995). Prosocial development in late adolescence: A longitudinal study. *Child Development, 66,* 1179–1197.

Eisenberg, N., & Fabes, R. A. (1992). Emotion, regulation, and the development of social competence. In M. S. Clark (Ed.), *Review of personality and social psychology: Emotion and social behavior* (Vol. 14, pp. 119–150). Newbury Park: Sage.

Eisenberg, N., & Fabes, R. A. (1998). Prosocial development. In W. Damon (Series Ed.) & N. Eisenberg (Vol. Ed.), *Handbook of child psychology, Vol. 3: Social, emotional, and personality development* (5th ed., pp. 701–778). New York: John Wiley.

Eisenberg, N., Fabes, R. A., Miller, P. A., Fultz, J., Mathy, R. M., Shell, R., & Reno, R. R. (1989). The relations of sympathy and personal distress to prosocial behavior: A multimethod study. *Journal of Personality and Social Psychology, 57,* 55–66.

Eisenberg, N., Guthrie, I. K., Cumberland, A., Murphy, B. C., Shepard, S. A., Zhou, Q., & Carlo, G. (2002). Prosocial development in early adulthood: A longitudinal study. *Journal of Personality and Social Psychology, 82,* 993–1006.

Eisenberg, N., Guthrie, I. K., Murphy, B. C., Shepard, S. A., Cumberland, A., & Carlo, G. (1999). Consistency and development of prosocial dispositions: A longitudinal study. *Child Development, 70,* 1360–1372.

Eisenberg, N., Lennon, R. & Roth, K. (1983). Prosocial development: A longitudinal study. *Developmental Psychology, 19,* 846–855.

Eisenberg, N., & Miller, P. A. (1987). The relation of empathy to prosocial and related behaviors. *Psychological Bulletin, 101,* 91–119.

Eisenberg, N., Miller, P. A., Shell, R., McNalley, S., & Shea, C. (1991). Prosocial development in adolescence: A longitudinal study. *Developmental Psychology, 27,* 849–857.

Eisenberg, N., & Murphy, B. (1995). Parenting and children's moral development. In M. H. Bornstein (Ed.), *Handbook of parenting* (Vol. 4, pp. 227–257). Mahwah, NJ: Lawrence Erlbaum Associates.

Eisenberg, N., Shea, C. L., Carlo, G., & Knight, G. P. (1991). Empathy-related responding and cognition: A "chicken and the egg" dilemma. In W. M. Kurtines & J. L. Gewirtz (Eds.), *Handbook of moral behavior and development Vol. 2: Research* (pp. 63–88). Hillsdale, NJ: Lawrence Erlbaum Associates.

Eisenberg, N., & Shell, R. (1986). Prosocial moral judgment and behavior in children: The mediating role of cost. *Personality and Social Psychology Bulletin, 12,* 426–433.

Eisenberg, N., Zhou, Q., & Koller, S. (2001). Brazilian adolescents' prosocial moral judgment and behavior: Relations to sympathy, perspective taking, gender-role orientation, and demographic characteristics. *Child Development, 72,* 518–534.

Eisenberg-Berg, N. (1979). Development of children's prosocial moral judgment. *Developmental Psychology, 15,* 128–137.

Emde, R. N., Plomin, R., Robinson, J., Corley, R., DeFries, J., Fulker, D. W., et al. (1992). Temperament, emotion, and cognition at fourteen months: The MacArthur Longitudinal Twin Study. *Child Development, 63,* 1437–1455.

Fabes, R. A., Carlo, G., Kupanoff, K., & Laible, D. (1999). Early adolescence and prosocial/moral behavior I: The role of individual processes. *Journal of Early Adolescence, 19,* 5–16.

Feshbach, N. D. (1987). Parental empathy and child adjustment/maladjustment. In N. Eisenberg and J. Strayer (Eds.), *Empathy and its development* (pp. 271–291). New York: Cambridge University Press.

Flavell, J. H., Botkin, P., Fry, C., Wright, J., & Jarvis, P. (1968). *The development of role-taking and communication skills in children.* New York: John Wiley.

Flavell, J. H., & Miller, P. H. (1998). Social cognition. In W. Damon (Series Ed.), & D. Kuhn & R. S. Siegler (Vol. Ed.), *Handbook of child psychology, Vol. 2: Cognition, perception, and language* (5th ed., pp. 851–898). New York: John Wiley.

Ford, M. (1979). The construct validity of egocentrism. *Psychological Bulletin, 86,* 1169–1188.

Freud, S. (1900/1965). *The interpretation of dreams.* New York: Avon Books.

Furman, W., & Buhrmester, D. (1985). Children's perceptions of the personal relationships in their social networks. *Developmental Psychology, 21,* 1016–1024.

Garner, P. W., Jones, D. C., & Palmer, D. J. (1994). Social cognitive correlates of preschool children's sibling caregiving behavior. *Developmental Psychology, 30,* 905–911.

Gibbs, J. C. (1991). Toward an integration of Kohlberg's and Hoffman's theories of morality. In W. M. Kurtines & J. L. Gewirtz (Eds.), *Handbook of moral behavior and development Vol. 1: Theory* (pp. 183–222). Hillsdale, NJ: Lawrence Erlbaum Associates.

Gibbs, J. C. (2003). *Moral development & reality: Beyond the theories of Kohlberg and Hoffman.* Thousand Oaks, CA: Sage.

Gibbs, J. C., & Schnell, S. V. (1985). Moral development "versus" socialization: A critique. *American Psychologist, 40,* 1071–1080.

Gilligan, C. (1982). *In a different voice: Psychological theory and women's development.* Cambridge, MA: Harvard University Press.

Gimpl, G., & Farenholz, F. (2001). The oxytocin receptor system: Structure, function, and regulation. *Physiological Reviews, 81,* 629–683.

Ginsburg, H. J., Ogletree, S. M., Silakowski, T. D., Bartels, R. D., Burk, S. L., & Turner, G. M. (2003). Young children's theories of mind about empathic and selfish motives. *Social Behavior and Personality Development, 31,* 237–244.

Grusec, J. (1991). Socializing concern for others in the home. *Developmental Psychology, 27,* 338–342.

Grusec, J. E., & Goodnow, J. J. (1994). Impact of parental discipline methods on the child's internalization of values: A reconceptualization of current points of view. *Developmental Psychology, 30,* 4–19.

Grusec, J. E., & Redler, E. (1980). Attribution, reinforcement, and altruism: A developmental analysis. *Developmental Psychology, 16,* 525–534.

Hart, D. (in press). The development of moral identity. In G. Carlo & C. P. Edwards (Eds.), *The 51st Annual Symposium on Motivation: Moral motivation.* Lincoln: University of Nebraska Press.

Hart, D., & Fegley, S. (1995). Altruism and caring in adolescence: Relations to self-understanding and social judgment. *Child Development, 66,* 1346–1359.

Hartshorne, H., May, M. A., & Shuttleworth, F. K. (1930). *Studies in the nature of character*. New York: MacMillan.

Hay, D. F., & Pawlby, S. (2003). Prosocial development in relation to children's and mothers' psychological problems. *Child Development, 74,* 1314–1327.

Hearold, S. (1986). A synthesis of 1043 effects of television on social behavior. In G. Comstock (Ed.), *Public communication and behavior* (Vol. 1, pp. 65–130). Orlando, FL: Academic Press.

Hobbes, T. (1651/1962). *Leviathan*. Ed. M. Oakeshotte. New York: Dutton.

Hoffman, M. L. (1983). Affective and cognitive processes in moral internalization. In E. T. Higgins, D. N. Ruble, & W. W. Hartup (Eds.), *Social cognition and development: A sociocultural perspective* (pp. 236–274). Cambridge, UK: Cambridge University Press.

Hoffman, M. L. (2000). *Empathy and moral development: Implications for caring and justice*. Cambridge, UK: Cambridge University Press.

Hoffman, M. L., & Saltzstein, H. D. (1967). Parent discipline and the child's moral development. *Journal of Personality and Social Psychology, 5,* 45–57.

Hume, D. (1751/1957). *An inquiry concerning the principles of morals*. Indianapolis, IN: The Bobbs-Merrill Co.

Huston, A. C., & Wright, J. C. (1998). Mass media and children's development. In W. Damon (Series Ed.) & I. E. Sigel & K. A. Renninger (Vol. Eds.), *Handbook of child psychology, Vol. 4: Child psychology in practice* (5th ed., pp. 999–1058). New York: John Wiley.

Iannotti, R. J. (1978). Effect of role-taking experiences on role taking, empathy, altruism, and aggression. *Developmental Psychology, 14,* 119–124.

Jaffee, S., & Hyde, J. S. (2000). Gender differences in moral orientation: A meta-analysis. *Psychological Bulletin, 126,* 703–726.

Kagan, J. (in press). Human morality and temperament. In G. Carlo & C. P. Edwards (Eds.), *The 51st Annual Symposium on Motivation: Moral motivation*. Lincoln: University of Nebraska Press.

Kant, I. (1785/1993). *Grounding for the metaphysics of morals*. Indianapolis, IN: Hackett Publishing Co.

Knight, G. P., Bohlmeyer, E. M., Schnieder, H., & Harris, J. D. (1993). Age differences in temporal monitoring and equal sharing in a fixed-duration sharing task. *British Journal of Developmental Psychology, 11,* 143–158.

Knight, G. P., & Chao, C. (1991). Cooperative, competitive, and individualistic social values among 8- to 12-year old siblings, friends, and acquaintances. *Personality and Social Psychology Bulletin, 17,* 201–211.

Knight, G. P., Johnson, L. G., Carlo, G., & Eisenberg, N. (1994). A multiplicative model of the dispositional antecedents of a prosocial behavior: Predicting more of the people more of the time. *Journal of Personality and Social Psychology, 66,* 178–183.

Knight, G., Bernal, M., & Carlo, G. (1995). Socialization and the development of cooperative, competitive, and individualistic behaviors among Mexican American children. In E. E. Garcia & B. M. McLaughlin (Eds.), *Meeting the challenge of linguistic and cultural diversity in early childhood education, Vol. 6: Yearbook in early childhood education* (pp. 85–102). New York: Teachers College Press.

Kochanska, G. (1993). Toward a synthesis of parental socialization and childtemeprament in early development of conscience. *Child Development, 64,* 325–347.

Kohlberg, L. (1969). Stage and sequence: The cognitive-developmental approach to socialization. In D. Goslin (Ed.), *Handbook of socialization theory and research*. Stokie, IL: Rand McNally.

Krebs, D. L., Denton, D. L., Vermeulen, S. C., & Carpendale, J. I. (1991). Structured flexibility of moral judgement. *Journal of Personality and Social Psychology, 61,* 1012–1023.

Krebs, D., & Russell, C. (1981). Role-taking and altruism. In J. P. Rushton & R. M. Sorrentino (Eds.), *Altruism and helping behavior: Social, personality, and developmental perspectives* (pp. 137–165). Hillsdale, NJ: Lawrence Erlbaum Associates.

Krevins, J., & Gibbs, J. C. (1996). Parents' use of inductive discipline: Relations to children's empathy and prosocial behavior. *Child Development, 67,* 3263–3277.

Kurdek, L. (1978). Perspective taking as the cognitive basis of children's moral development: A review of the literature. *Merrill-Palmer Quarterly, 24,* 3–28.

Kurdek, L. (1981). Young adults' moral reasoning about prohibitive and prosocial dilemmas. *Journal of Youth and Adolescence, 10,* 263–272.

Laible, D. J., & Carlo, G. (2004). The differential relations of maternal and paternal support and control to adolescent social competence, self-worth, and sympathy. *Journal of Adolescent Research, 19,* 759–782.

Laible, D. J., Carlo, G., & Raffaelli, M. (2000). The differential relations of parent and peer support on adolescent adjustment. *Journal of Youth and Adolescence, 29,* 45–59.

Laible, D. J., Carlo, G., & Roesch, S. C. (2004). Pathways to self-esteem: The role of parent and peer attachment, empathy, and social behaviors. *Journal of Adolescence, 27,* 703–716.

Lapsley, D. K. (1996). *Moral psychology.* Boulder, CO: Westview.

Latané, B. & Darley, J. M. (1970). *The unresponsive bystander: Why doesn't he help?* New York: Appleton-Crofts.

Liu, D., Diorio, J., Tannanbaum, B., Caldji, C., Francis, D., Freedman, A., et al. (1997). Maternal care, hippocampal, glucocorticoid receptors, and hypothalamic-pituitary-adrenal responses to stress. *Science, 277,* 1659–1662.

Looft, W. R. (1972). Egocentrism and social interaction across the life span. *Psychological Bulletin, 78,* 73–92.

Ma, H. K. (1989). Moral orientation and moral judgement in adolescents in Hong Kong, mainland China, and England. *Journal of Cross-Cultural Psychology, 20,* 152–177.

Maccoby, E. E., & Jacklin, C. N. (1974). *The psychology of sex differences.* Stanford, CA: Stanford University Press.

Maccoby, E. E., & Martin, J. A. (1983). Socialization in the context of the family: Parent-child interaction. In E. M. Hetherington (Ed.), *Handbook of child psychology: Vol. 4, Socialization, personality, and social development* (pp. 1–101). New York: Wiley.

Matthews, K. A., Batson, C. D., Horn, J., & Rosenman, R. H. (1981). "Principles in his nature which interest him in the fortune of others . . . ": The heritability of empathic concern for others. *Journal of Personality, 49,* 237–247.

Mead, G. H. (1934). *Mind, self, and society.* Chicago: University of Chicago Press.

Midlarsky, E., & Hannah, M. E. (1985). Competence, reticence, and helping by children and adolescents. *Developmental Psychology, 21,* 534–541.

Miller, P. A., & Eisenberg, N. (1988). The relation of empathy to aggression and externalizing/antisocial behavior. *Psychological Bulletin, 103,* 324–344.

Moore, C., Barresi, J., & Thompson, C. (1998). The cognitive basis of future-oriented prosocial behavior. *Social Development, 7,* 198–218.

Nelson, D. A., & Crick, N. R. (1999). Rose-colored glasses: Examining the social information-processing of prosocial young adolescents. *Journal of Early Adolescence, 19,* 17–38.

Oliner, S. P. & Oliner, P. M. (1988). *The altruistic personality: Rescuers of Jews in Nazi Europe.* New York: Free Press.

Padilla-Walker, L. M., & Carlo, G. (2004). "It's not fair!" Adolescents' constructions of appropriateness of parental reactions to antisocial and prosocial situations. *Journal of Youth and Adolescence, 33,* 389–401.

Pakaslahti, L., Karjalainene, A., & Keltikangas-Jarvinen, L. (2002). Relationships between adolescent prosocial problem-solving strategies, prosocial behaviour, and social acceptance. *International Journal of Behavioral Development, 26,* 137–144.

Piaget, J. (1926/1959). *The language and thought of the child.* London: Routledge & Kegan Paul Ltd.

Piaget, J. (1932/1965). *The moral judgment of the child.* Trans. M. Gabain. London: Kegan Paul.

Peterson, L. (1983). Role of donor competence, donor age, and peer presence on helping in an emergency. *Developmental Psychology, 19,* 873–880.

Ramirez, M., & Castaneda, A. (1974). *Cultural democracy, biocognitive development, and education.* New York: Academic Press.

Raviv, A., Bar-Tal, D., & Lewis-Levin, T. (1980). Motivations for donation behavior by boys of three different ages. *Child Development, 51,* 610–613.

Rest, J. R. (1979). *Development in judging moral issues.* Minneapolis: University of Minnesota Press.

Rest, J. (1983). Morality. In P. Mussen (Series Ed.) and J. H. Flavell & E. Markman (Vol. Eds.), *Handbook of child psychology: Vol. 3. Cognitive development* (pp. 556–629). New York: John Wiley.

Rotenberg, K. J., Fox, C., Green, S., Ruderman, L., Slater, K., Stevens, K., & Carlo, G. (in press). Construction and validation of a children's interpersonal trust belief scale. *British Journal of Developmental Psychology.*

Rothbart, M. K., Ahadi, S. A., & Hershey, K. L. (1994). Temperament and social behavior in childhood. *Merrill-Palmer Quarterly, 40,* 21–39.

Rosseau, J. J. (1773/1962). *Emile.* New York: Columbia University Press.

Salovey, P., Rothman, A. J., Detweiler, J. B., & Steward, W. T. (2000). Emotional states and physical health. *American Psychologist, 55,* 110–121.

Schonert-Reichl, K. A. (1999). Relations of peer acceptance, friendship adjustment, and social behavior to moral reasoning during early adolescence. *Journal of Early Adolescence, 19,* 249–279.

Seligman, M. E. P., & Csikszentmihalyi, M. (2000). Positive psychology: An introduction. *American Psychologist, 55,* 5–14.

Shantz, C. U. (1983). Social cognition. In P. H. Mussen (Series Ed.) & J. H. Flavell & E. M. Markman (Eds.), *Handbook of child psychology: Vol. 3. Cognitive development.* New York: Wiley.

Skoe, E. E. A., Hansen, K. L., Willy-Tore, M., Bakke, I., Hoffmann, T., Larsen, B., & Aasheim, M. (1999). Care-based moral reasoning in Norwegian and Canadian early adolescents: A cross-national comparison. *Journal of Early Adolescence, 19,* 280–291.

Sober, E., & Wilson, D. S. (1998). *Unto others: The evolution and psychology of unselfish behavior.* Cambridge, MA: Harvard University Press.

Staub, E. (1978). *Positive social behavior and morality: Social and personal influences* (Vol. 1). New York: Academic.

Staub, E. (1979). *Positive social behavior and morality: Socialization and development* (Vol. 2). New York: Academic.

Staub, E. (in press). The roots of goodness: The fulfillment of basic human needs and the development of inclusive caring, helping and nonagression, moral courage, active bystandership, and altruism born of suffering. In G. Carlo & C. P. Edwards (Eds.), *The 51st Annual Symposium on Motivation: Moral motivation*. Lincoln: University of Nebraska Press.

Stevenson, H. W. (1991). The development of prosocial behavior in large-scale collective societies: China and Japan. In R. A. Hinde & J. Grovel (Eds.), *Cooperation and prosocial behaviour* (pp. 89–105). Cambridge, UK: Cambridge University Press.

Steward, M., & Steward, D. (1973). The observation of Anglo-, Mexican-, and Chinese-American mothers teaching their young sons. *Child Development, 4,* 329–337.

Stuckas, A. A., & Dunlap, M. R. (2002). Community involvement: Theoretical approaches and educational initiatives (Special Issue). *Journal of Social Issues, 58 (3).*

Tietjen, A. (1986). Prosocial moral reasoning among children and adults in a Papau New Guinea society. *Developmental Psychology, 22,* 861–868.

Tucker, C. J., Updegraff, K. A., Mc Hale, S. M., & Crouter, A. C. (1999). Older siblings as socializers of younger siblings' empathy. *Journal of Early Adolescence, 19,* 176–198.

Turiel, E. (1998). The development of morality. In W. Damon (Series Ed.) & N. Eisenberg (Vol. Ed.), *Handbook of child psychology, Vol. 3: Social, emotional, and personality development* (5th ed., pp. 863–932). New York: John Wiley.

Underwood, B., & Moore, B. (1982). Perspective-taking and altruism. *Psychological Bulletin, 91,* 143–173.

Walker, L. (1984). Sex differences in the development of moral reasoning: A critical review. *Child Development, 55,* 677–691.

Walker, L. J. (1991). Sex differences in moral reasoning. In W. M. Kurtines & J. L. Gewirtz (Eds.), *Handbook of moral behavior and development, Vol. 2: Research* (pp. 333–364). Hillsdale, NJ: Lawrence Erlbaum Associates.

Wentzel, K. R. (1991). Relations between social competence and academic achievement in early adolescence. *Child Development, 62,* 1066–1078.

Wentzel, K. R., & McNamara, C. C. (1999). Interpersonal relationships, emotional distress, and prosocial behavior in middle school. *Journal of Early Adolescence, 19,* 114–125.

Whiting, B. B., & Whiting, J. W. M. (1975). *Children of six cultures: A psychocultural analysis.* Cambridge, MA: Harvard University Press.

Whiting, B. B., & Edwards, C. P. (1988). *Children of different worlds.* Cambridge, MA: Harvard University Press.

Williams, F. L. (1991). Interfamily economic exchange: A function of culture and economics. *Lifestyles: Family and Economic Issues, 12,* 235–252.

Wilson, E. O. (1978). *On human nature.* Cambridge, MA: Harvard University Press.

Wyatt, J. M., & Carlo, G. (2002). What will my parents think? Relations among adolescents' expected parental reactions, prosocial moral reasoning, and prosocial and antisocial behaviors. *Journal of Adolescent Research, 17,* 646–666.

Yates, M., & Youniss, J. (Eds.). (1999). *Roots of civic identity: International perspectives on community service and activism in youth.* Cambridge, UK: Cambridge University Press.

Youniss, J. (1980). *Parents and peers in social development: A Sullivan-Piaget perspective.* Chicago: University of Chicago Press.

Youniss, J. (1994). Children's friendship and peer culture: Implications for theories of networks and support. In F. Nestmann & K. Hurrelmann (Eds.), *Social networks and social support in childhood and adolescence* (pp. 75–88). Berlin: Walter de Gruyter.

Zahn-Waxler, C., Robinson, J. L., & Emde, R. N. (1992). The development of empathy in twins. *Developmental Psychology, 28,* 1038–1047.

21

Children's Conceptions and Displays of Moral Emotions

William F. Arsenio
Jason Gold
Erin Adams
Yeshiva University

Is children's morality mostly the result of early emotional processes involving fear, guilt, love, and empathy, with few direct connections to reasoning? Or, alternatively, is children's morality mostly the result of cognitive principles that act to overcome irrational and sometimes immoral affective impulses? Almost 20 years have passed since Gibbs and Schnell's (1985) important effort to recognize and reconcile the tension between these historical affective and cognitive views of moral development. Yet, despite notable progress in understanding the origins of children's moral development since then (see Nucci, 2001; Turiel, 1998, for reviews), attempts to bridge the affective/cognitive divide are still relatively rare. Our goal is to summarize two related literatures, which, we believe, illustrate one important way in which children's cognitions and emotions about moral events can converge in a larger, coherent model of moral development.

Much of this review stems from two basic questions: what emotions do children expect various moral acts to produce, and how do these emotional expectancies influence children's moral behavior? This focus on children's conceptions of the emotional consequences of victimization and harm is part of a much larger literature on the connections between children's understanding of emotions and emotional processes and their social competence (see Denham, 1998; Saarni, 1999, for reviews). Numerous studies, for example, have shown that variations in children's conceptions of the links between social events and emotional outcomes (affect-event links) are connected with differences in their socially competent behaviors as well as their risk for psychopathology (e.g., Garner, Jones, & Miner, 1994; Schultz, Izard, & Ackerman, 2000). By contrast, less is known about how children view the emotional consequences of affectively charged moral transgressions involving deliberate harm and victimization, in particular, and whether these moral affect–event links have a meaningful influence on their related behavior.

The following review reveals that many of the relevant studies in this area focus on three more specific questions: (a) why do young children and even some adolescents expect moral victimizers to feel positive emotions (e.g., happiness) after victimizing others?; (b) do children actually display positive emotions in these contexts?; and (c) are individual differences in children's conceptions and displays of "happy victimization" predictive of behavioral differences? At first this shift from a general interest in moral affect–event links to a narrower focus on what has sometimes been called the "happy victimizer" expectancy may seem surprising. Once the empirical findings and their potential significance are elaborated, however, we believe that reasons for this focus on "happy victimization" will become evident. Studies are reviewed indicating that many young children expect moral victimizers to feel happy following successful acts of victimization (conceptions of moral emotions), and results from several observational studies reveal that young children's tendency to display positive emotions (displays of moral emotions) are related to their aggression as well as to more general aspects of their social competence.

These issues are addressed in several major sections beginning with an introductory conceptual overview of the importance and psychological role of affect-event links, both in general and as they apply to children's and adolescents' moral development. This overview is followed by several sections describing research on normative age-related changes and emerging individual differences in children's happy victimizer expectancy, including a description of their potential theoretical meaning and significance. A subsequent section summarizes research suggesting that children's happy victimizer expectancy may be a product of certain cognitive constraints (e.g., involving Theory of Mind), or the methodological limitations of earlier studies in this area. These summaries of work on children's conceptions of moral emotions are followed by a review of research on the actual emotions young children display during aggressive and conflictual interactions with peers. Finally, this chapter concludes with a description of a recent study which shows the potential diagnostic strength of happy victimizer conceptions for differentiating behaviorally disruptive and nondisruptive adolescents.

CONCEPTIONS OF SOCIOMORAL EMOTIONS: A THEORETICAL FRAMEWORK

> A child's readiness to go to school, to brave the dentist, to seek out a new friend, or to run away from punishment is based on an appraisal of how he or she will feel when facing those situations. (Harris, 1985, p. 162)

Harris's quote captures some of the basic ideas underlying this chapter; that is, we often remember the emotional antecedents and consequences of social events, and we can then use those affect-event links for anticipating the potential emotional outcomes of different courses of action. Moreover, we would argue, these emotion outcome expectancies are likely to be especially useful when it comes to the sorts of affectively intense experiences that children (and adults) have in the context of moral transgressions in which one person deliberately harms another in the pursuit of various material and psychological gains.

There is a growing body of research on the importance of these affect–event links or situational affect, not only in relation to children's moral development (to be discussed), but also in connection with broad patterns of children's internalizing and externalizing behaviors (see, e.g., Izard, Fine, Mostow, Trentacosta, & Campbell, 2002, for a related review). Yet, the conceptual model of how these affect–event links form and why they are predictive of long-term behavior is often quite vague. The next few paragraphs provide a brief summary of a model that both highlights the importance of these affect–event links and that also begins to address some of the broader questions about how affect and cognition interact. This general model of situational affect is then followed by a more specific description of the development of moral affect–event links.

Situational Affect

A Brief General Model. Damasio (1994, 2003) and his colleagues have developed a biologically based account of how emotions and cognition interact to influence behavior. One key issue is how to address the complexity of certain forms of decision making in the context of real-world time constraints; that is, how do we reduce potentially unlimited courses of action in any situation to a manageable number? As Brown (1996, p. 154) put it, "rigorously logical decisions are impossible in most of the situations adapting organisms face . . . affectivity provides a method for inventing provisional or 'good enough' knowledge structures" (1996, p. 154).

Damasio (1994, 2003) has argued that "somatic markers" are one way in which emotions may provide such "good enough" knowledge structures. Over time, as specific behaviors and cognitions become associated with positive or negative outcomes, a form of somatic marker or gut feeling is formed "which protects you against future losses, . . . and then allows you *to choose from fewer alternatives*" (Damasio, 1994, p. 173). In other words, once the field of possible options has been narrowed, a person can use higher level cognitive processes much more efficiently.

Despite the significant role it accords to cognitive processes, the somatic marker model seems to emphasize affective primacy in the broadest sense (similar to moral intuitionist accounts by Wilson [1993] and Haidt [2001]). Damasio, however, makes a critical additional distinction between primary and secondary emotions. As described by functionalist theories (e.g., Izard, 1991), certain broad categories of events (e.g., attaining a goal, or having a goal thwarted by someone) elicit primary or discrete emotions, which include specific motivational tendencies, facial expressions, and physiological consequences. Overall, these core emotions (e.g., happiness, sadness, anger, and fear) are largely seen as innate and preorganized. In addition to these highly adaptive primary emotions, however, the next step in an evolutionary sense was "the *feeling of the emotion* in connection to the object that excited it" (Damasio, 1994, p. 132).

This human ability to become aware of the connections between object "X" and its typical emotional consequences plays a pivotal role in adaptive human functioning (Damasio, 2003). It is easy to imagine, for example, the functional role that being afraid plays when a large "mean" peer is approaching. Decision making becomes tightly focused (should I run? hide?) and physiological responses become mobilized for action. But by becoming aware of the connections between specific objects or events and emotions, entirely new options become available. For example, becoming aware of the connection between that "bully" and the intense fear he or she elicits makes it possible to plan ahead ("where does he hang out and how can I avoid him?") and also to make more subtle discriminations ("but wait, he never bothers little kids like me"). This ability to become aware of our emotions, the shift from "emotion" to "feeling," helps us unpack more automatic event–emotion connections in a way that provides a profoundly new level of behavioral flexibility. And a key feature of this transition is our developing understanding and memory of environmentally important affect–event links.

The Sociomoral Context.   What influence does this general ability to understand the connections between situations and emotions have on children's moral development? In previous work (Arsenio & Lover, 1995) we outlined a four-step model of how sociomoral affect links (including moral events as well as other events involving more or less prescriptive interpersonal limits) are formed and act to guide children's sociomoral reasoning and behavior. Briefly, the first two steps emphasize the claim that different types of sociomoral events (e.g., victimization versus low-cost helping) are likely to have systematically different emotional outcomes, and, consequently, that children's conceptions of these affect–event links reflect these distinctions. The third step involves the understanding and application of these affect–event links to different situations, that is, the conscious awareness described by Damasio that allows such links to be more fully understood and flexibly deployed. Finally, the fourth step is an initial attempt to describe how this affectively charged knowledge could underlie the formation of more general moral principles. So, for example, children might coordinate their own negative emotional experiences resulting from being unfairly victimized with their observations that others usually feel similarly in the same situation, and in doing so lay a foundation for emerging principles of reciprocity and fairness.

Although children's moral development is certainly more complex than simply "summing" across similar affect–event links, certain core aspects of this approach appear to be implicitly shared by different sociomoral theorists. Turiel (1983), for example, recognized that the cognitive–developmental focus on moral prescriptions as emerging "from the perceptions of the consequences to the victims" (p. 35) is compatible with socialization accounts of children's sociomoral development in which parental inductions involve "reasoning with the child, and in the process, highlighting the effects of the child's action to himself or herself and to others" (p. 176). Yet, some of the specific findings from the literature on children's conceptions of moral emotions (e.g., most preschoolers' expectation that moral transgressors are happy) are, at least initially, difficult to integrate with existing sociomoral theories.

"Happy Victimization"—A Conceptual Overview

There have been several studies on the broader aspects of children's conceptions of sociomoral affect–event links (e.g., Arsenio, 1988; Arsenio & Fleiss, 1996) including transgressions of moral (involving harm and unfairness), conventional (involving the smooth coordination of interpersonal behaviors), and personal (involving issues primarily affecting oneself) limits (see Turiel, 1998 and Nucci, 2001 on these domains). Much of the literature on sociomoral affect–event links, however, has come to focus on one especially surprising finding—the "happy victimizer" expectancy; that is, many children's apparent belief that victimizers feel happy following successful acts of victimization. We have argued elsewhere (Arsenio & Lover, 1995) that age-related changes from younger children's strongly positive view of the emotional consequences of victimization to older children's more negative or mixed emotion expectations may reflect a major transition in children's moral sensibilities. At the center of this transition, or *moral attributional shift*, is the claim that young children initially view victimization as involving two relatively separate sets of emotional reactions—victimizers who are happy because of their gains and victims who feel quite negatively because of their losses and the unfairness of such acts. By contrast, older children integrate these reactions, so that the pain and negative emotions of their victims act to reduce and finally replace any happiness that victimizers might feel.

The theoretical and practical reasons for this interest in the happy victimizer expectancy are not hard to understand. At a theoretical level, the pervasiveness of young children's happy victimizer expectancy seems difficult to reconcile with existing sociomoral theories (e.g., Hoffman, 2000; Turiel, 1998), which converge on the belief that "an awareness of victim harm, a sense of empathic distress, and a fear of external sanctions should all lead children to expect that victimizers well feel negative emotions, for example, sadness, fear, and guilt" (Arsenio & Kramer, 1992, p. 916). Although even young children are aware of the harm produced by victimization, it does not seem to influence how they expect victimizers to feel. At a related pragmatic level, if expectancies have even a modest effect on behavior, then such an expectancy could act to promote ongoing patterns of victimization in young children.

At the same time, there are many reasons to question the psychological meaning of this happy victimizer expectancy. There is, for example, extensive research showing that preschool age children consider acts of victimization as morally wrong, even in the absence of specific rules or adult sanctions (see Turiel, 1998, for a review). Other research suggests that early aspects of conscience and guilt formation have a clear influence on young children's behaviors in ways that seem inconsistent with a simple positive view of victimization (e.g., Kochanska, Padavich, & Koenig, 1996). Collectively, young children's empathic abilities, their understanding of moral rules, and their strong emotional ties to others make it seem implausible that they would simply expect victimizers to feel happy as a result of the gains produced by victimization. Yet, that is exactly what much of the research in this area suggests.

Some researchers have begun to examine the role that potential methodological and child cognitive factors might play in producing this expectancy. We share their view that the meaning of this expectancy is not as straightforward as initially claimed (e.g., Arsenio & Kramer, 1992; Nunner-Winkler & Sodian, 1988). We also believe, however, that a closer examination of this literature will reveal some of the complexities that underlie both normative moral development as well as the emergence of individual differences in moral trajectories that lead to aggression and conduct disorders in some children.

RESEARCH ON CHILDREN'S CONCEPTIONS OF MORAL EMOTIONS

Initial Research—Conceptions of Happy Victimization

The first evidence of a happy victimizer expectancy emerged in studies designed to examine children's conceptions of a wide variety of affect–event links. In one influential early study (Barden, Zelko, Duncan, & Masters, 1980), kindergartners, third graders, and sixth graders were presented with a variety of social events and asked how they would feel if these events actually happened to them. According to Barden et al. (1980), the most notable age-related change involved acts of undetected dishonesty in which a child steals something desirable and is not caught. Unlike third and sixth graders, who expected negative emotional outcomes, nearly half of the kindergartners expected to feel happy, presumably because of the gains resulting from the theft. In another study, these researchers (Zelko, Duncan, Barden, Garber, & Masters, 1986) assessed adults' expectations regarding children's situational affect for the same group of events. Although adults were generally accurate in their judgments, their expectation for kindergartners' views of undetected dishonesty differed markedly from the children's own view. Adults primarily expected that young children would say they would feel scared or angry, and almost never mentioned the happiness actually selected by almost half of kindergartners. This discrepancy, the authors noted, could have important implications for adults' moral socialization of young children because it suggested that adults do not have a very accurate sense of how young children view these acts of victimization.

The first study explicitly designed to study this happy victimizer conception in detail was conducted by Nunner-Winkler and Sodian (1988). These authors began with the idea that moral events are likely to produce intense but conflicting emotions given that "a person who violates a moral rule may, for instance, experience joy at the success of his or her forbidden behaviors and or guilt, shame, or remorse at his or her immoral behavior" (p. 1323). They also argued that children's expectation that they would feel unpleasant emotions following victimization is an important component of their moral motivation (a view shared by researchers who address empathic processes in moral development).

In their three-part study they assessed 4-, 6-, and 8-year-olds' conceptions of moral emotions following acts of victimization. In the first part, about 75% of the 4-year-olds and 50% of the 6-year-olds, but only 10% of the 8-year-olds, expected that successfully stealing someone's candy would make the victimizer happy. And despite a number of manipulations to increase the salience of the costs of such acts for the victims, similar results were obtained for young children in subsequent study manipulations. Consequently, Nunner-Winkler and Sodian argued that these results reflected a moral attributional shift from younger children's largely outcome orientation, "victimizers are happy if they get what they want," to older children's more fundamentally moral orientation, "victimizers feel bad because they see what they did to the victims (and they might also get in deserved trouble)."

One way of explaining this transition involves young children's nonmoral cognitive limitations. So, for example, young children might expect victimizers to feel both positive and negative emotions, but the "outcome salience" of these stories ("he wanted the swing, so he pushed the other kid off and got the swing") might make the positive emotions more available. Young children's cognitive difficulties acknowledging mixed emotions in any situation (e.g., Harter & Buddin, 1987) might then preclude children's reporting of any additional negative emotions, even if their complete representations of these events included these negative emotions. Nunner-Winkler and Sodian, however, rejected this explanation because the most dramatic of their salience manipulations still failed to alter young children's attribution of positive emotions to victimizers.

Our own earlier findings (Arsenio, 1988; Arsenio & Ford, 1985) led us to question Nunner-Winkler and Sodian's description of a near complete age-related reversal in 4- to 8-year-old children's moral attributions (we found more positive emotions in older children). At the same time, it seemed that Nunner-Winkler and Sodian were too quick to reject their original view that victimization is likely to produce quite mixed emotions in the victimizer. On the one hand, victimization often is the quickest and easiest way to obtain desirable gains, whether it is a 2-year-old grabbing another child's toy, or a nation seizing another nation's assets. On the other hand, basic human commonalties in our affective reactions to being victimized and our active cognitive understanding of these reactions should make it difficult for most people to maintain predominantly positive views of victimization. With these ideas in mind, we took a closer look at young children's moral attributions, with a particular focus on whether certain methodological constraints were obscuring young children's more mixed view of the emotional consequences of victimization.

In our two-part study, 4-, 6-, 8-year-olds were asked to judge the likely emotional consequences of acts of victimization and to provide rationales for those judgments for both victims and victimizers. Based on results from the first part, we asked children to assess the emotional reactions of victims first, followed by the reactions of the victimizers in the second part. (Victimizing acts were stealing someone's dessert and getting a turn on the swing by pushing another child off.) In addition, in one condition the story characters were described as being good friends, and in the other condition the participant was placed in the role of the victim and the victimizer was described as the victim's closest friend. Yet, despite these attempts to increase the salience of the victims' losses, nearly all of the 4- and 6-year-olds expected the victimizer to feel happy, as did about half of the 8-year-olds. Surprisingly, the friendship manipulation (being harmed by your best friend) had no influence on children's attributions.

This pattern changed, however, when children were probed about their emotion attributions. Based on our expectation that cognitive limitations might affect children's reporting of all of their emotion expectancies for victimizers, participants were also asked a series of probe questions to assess other potential attributions beyond their initial judgments. The three increasingly direct probe questions began with the simple "could he or she [the victimizer] be feeling anything else?" If the child said no, another probe was asked, "could he or she be feeling [an opposite valence emotion from the one originally selected]?", and, if needed, a final probe that specifically directed the participant's attention to the victim. These results revealed that nearly all of the 8-year-olds and three quarters of the 6-year-olds responded to the least direct probe ("anything else?"), whereas two thirds of the 4-year-olds insisted that victimizers could only be feeling happy, even after being explicitly directed to the loss and suffering experienced by the victim on the final probe. Moreover, a separate manipulation check using essentially the same probe sequence for victims' emotions indicated that almost none of the children altered their exclusively negative emotion attributions. Consequently, it seemed unlikely that the observed probe changes for victimizers were the result of the probe methodology itself.

The results for the 4-year-olds in this study were unexpected given our salience manipulations, but they were quite consistent with Nunner-Winkler and Sodian's findings. Because we also assessed children's conceptions of victims' emotions (which is rarely done in these studies), we concluded that 4-year-olds seem to view victims and victimizers as having two non-interacting sets of emotional expectancies to this single event. The findings for 6- and 8-year-olds, however, supported the notion of an age-related moral attributional shift, although one far less dramatic and complete than previously found. Even though nearly all 6-year-olds and most 8-year-olds initially expected victimizers to feel happy, they also provided negative emotion expectancies when asked the least directive probe question. Finally, all of these findings emerged even though the victims and victimizer were clearly described as close friends, which weakens the frequent claim that the happy victimizer expectancy simply reflects children's views about how bullies (who might be prone to such acts) would feel.

We interpreted this subtler shift, from 4-year-olds expectations that victimizers are simply happy to 8-year-olds' mixed emotional expectancies, as reflecting a changing awareness of a basic moral conflict: to victimize is to gain desirable outcomes and feel happy, but to be victimized is to lose what is yours and feel sad, angry, and other clearly negative emotions. In a larger sense, we argued, children's understanding of reciprocity and fairness depend on the ability and spontaneous tendency both to understand and feel that the victim's pain and loss will moderate one's own happiness regarding the gains produced by victimization. But even if these descriptions are correct, the critical questions of how and why this transition takes place remain.

Happy Victimizers—Other Cultures and Contexts

Several subsequent studies provided additional evidence of a happy victimizer expectancy in other cultures and contexts, even as they also raised questions about the timing and nature of any age-related moral attributional shift. For example, two studies by Murgatroyd and Robinson (1993, 1997) extended the age range of participants into adulthood while also examining the potential influence of onlookers' presence on moral emotion judgments.

In their first study, Murgatroyd and Robinson (1993) focused on two major issues: (a) is the decline in happy victimizer attributions complete by age 8 (as Nunner-Winkler & Sodian, 1988, argued); and (b) is that decline primarily the result of moral considerations or a fear of external sanctions? In the first three parts of their study, they found that happy victimizer attributions remained high in 6- to 8-year-olds (about 50%), but, unsurprisingly, children altered their attributions when they thought an adult authority had witnessed the victimization. In this onlooker context, 4- to 5-year-olds expected victimizers would feel sad, whereas 7- to 10-year-olds expected victimizers to feel scared, a result seen as supporting the importance of external sanctions in children moral attributions. Although this claim can be questioned, given the obvious methodological emphasis on being caught in the act, it does raise interesting issues about how emotion conceptions of detected and undetected victimization are integrated. Perhaps more importantly, in part four of this study, about one third of college-age participants expected adult victimizers to feel happy after physically intimidating someone to obtain a desirable residence. The authors concluded that "the results of all these studies strongly support the suggestion that some children and adults do judge a wrongdoer to feel happy" (1993, p. 108).

In a follow-up study, Murgatroyd and Robinson (1997) found additional evidence that the presence of onlookers (mothers and teachers) influences participants' moral emotion attributions. This time some of the onlookers were described as misunderstanding the circumstances of the victimizing act in ways that led them to approve these behaviors. This "approval" led more children and adolescents to expect that victimizers would feel happy. Emotion attributions from another part of the study, however, suggested that when participants did attribute negative emotion to victimizers, these attributions were based more on moral considerations than on the potential fear of external sanctions from the onlookers.

A study by Lourenco (1997) at about the same time also suggested that the age-related moral attributional shift is far from complete in school children. Lourenco conducted his study in Portugal because he believed that the predominantly Catholic population, with its strong emphasis on the immorality of harming others for gain, would provide a stringent cross-cultural test of the validity of the happy victimizer expectancy. Ninety children, evenly divided between 4-, 6-, and 8-year-olds, were asked about the emotional consequences of successful acts of victimization (stealing candy and seizing someone's swing). Children were first asked about whether the victimizer was a good or bad boy and why, followed by questions about the emotional reaction of victimizers, probes about those emotions (similar to those used by Arsenio & Kramer, 1992), and a final question about victims' emotions.

Results revealed that more than 90% of the 4- and 6-year-olds and 66% of the 8-year-olds expected victimizers to feel happy, even though all children judged the victimizers to be "bad" because of what they had done. When children were probed about these attributions about half of the 8-year-olds altered their initially positive views of victimization for the first probe (versus nearly 90% in Arsenio & Kramer, 1992). Moreover, the majority of even 8-year-olds justified victimizers' emotions by referring to the positive outcomes produced by victimization, even though all children attributed negative emotions to the victimizer.

Lourenco concluded that the happy victimizer expectancy is "a genuine, robust or 'first-order phenomenon . . . (a fact not an artifact)" (1997, p. 434). These findings were also seen as more supportive of a developmentally late, subtle moral attributional shift (i.e., more like the findings of Arsenio & Kramer, 1992, and Murgatroyd & Robinson, 1993, than of Nunner-Winkler & Sodian, 1988). Even though Portuguese 8-year-olds held somewhat less positive views of victimizers than their younger peers, a clear majority of 8-year-olds still expected victimizers to feel happy. In fact, these 8-year-olds were even less likely to alter their positive views of victimization when probed or asked to provide mixed emotion attributions than had been previously found.

In his discussion, Lourenco argued that at least some of these findings are consistent with Turiel's (1983) view regarding the emergence of children's moral understanding. Specifically, even the youngest children understood that victimization is immoral (or at least "bad") and would make victims feel negative emotions. And when children's emotion rationales did not focus on the outcomes of victimization, these explanations involved genuinely moral issues such as fairness and harm, rather than references to external sanctions. At the same time, Lourenco acknowledged that children's seeming moral concern for victims made the happy victimizer expectancy even harder to understand, and he emphasized the need for observational studies to begin to address some of these issues.

Individual Differences

Whereas most studies have focused on normative age-related changes in children's moral emotion judgments, other investigators began to examine how individual differences in these conceptions related to other aspects of children's psychological functioning. For example, as part of a longitudinal study of children's moral sensibility, Dunn, Brown, and Maguire (1995) included an assessment in which children (both as kindergartners and one year later in first grade) judged how they would feel after victimizing a friend or a sibling. Although participants expected to be happy in less than half of their judgments, there was a significant level of 1-year stability in children's happy victimizer attribution, and there was no overall decline in happy victimizer attributions from kindergarten to first grade. Interestingly, "those whose siblings had been particularly friendly with them as 2-year-olds were [subsequently] more likely to describe the transgressors' feeling as guilty or bad" (Dunn et al., 1995, p. 657).

Another area where happy victimizer expectancies and moral emotions, in general, have been shown to be important is in research on maltreated children. In one study (Smetana et al., 1999a, 1999b), for example, the moral judgments and emotion attributions of two groups of maltreated preschoolers (physically abused versus neglected) were compared with those of nonmaltreated peers. Children judged whether transgressions were permissible or not, whether this depended on the presence of a teacher, and whether the act would be acceptable if the underlying rule was changed, as well as being asked about the emotional responses of both victimizers and victims. In addition, children were asked these questions about both hypothetical transgressions as well as actual transgressions in which they either victimized someone or were victimized.

Overall, it was found that maltreated and nonmaltreated children did not differ in their (nonemotional) moral judgments, in that children from both groups evaluated moral transgressions as quite serious, punishable, and wrong even if there were no rule. Although the hypothetical versus actual context and the nature of the transgression (e.g., physical versus verbal) had systematic effects on children's judgments, their maltreatment status did not. By contrast, children's emotion attributions did differ as a function of their maltreatment status, although in somewhat complex ways. Another relevant finding is that children with a stronger happy victimizer expectancy (across events) judged moral transgressions as "less serious and less generalizably wrong and were less likely to be victims of moral transgressions" (Smetana et al., 1999b, p. 279). Perhaps these children were seen as potentially "happier" victimizers by their peers, and, consequently, other children avoided initiating conflict with them. More generally, Smetana et al., found that both maltreated and nonmaltreated children were more likely to attribute positive emotions to hypothetical victimizers than to victims.

Cognitive Constraints and Other Issues

Despite this accumulating body of research on normative and individual differences in children's happy victimizer expectancy, there has been a strong sense that, at least in part, this expectancy is the result of a combination of methodological limitations and cognitive constraints that have little do with moral concerns. In particular, questions have been raised about two issues: (a) the finding that preschoolers seem unaffected by even the most overt attempts to influence their happy victimizer attributions (e.g., "what if he saw his friend was on the ground crying"; Arsenio & Kramer, 1992); and (b) the age and extent to which children's conceptions of victimizers emotions undergo a moral attributional shift (e.g., from positive to mixed/negative). This section describes the results of several studies designed to address these issues.

One explanation for young children's seeming "moral obtuseness" (point a) begins with research indicating that young children have difficulty acknowledging mixed emotional reactions to any event (e.g., Harris, 1983; Harter & Buddin, 1987). Consequently, it may be cognitively impossible for young children to acknowledge the victimizers' emotional conflict (i.e., happiness from their gain, but also negative emotions resulting from their immoral behavior). We examined this claim as part of the Arsenio and Kramer study described (1992, but reported in Arsenio & Kramer, 1991). In addition to the moral emotion attribution task, children were presented with nonmoral stories that were developed to assess a more general understanding of mixed emotions (Harris, 1983). A very strong relation was found between children's tendency to acknowledge mixed emotions in nonmoral situations and their response to the first moral probe, that is, "could he/she [the victimizer] be feeling anything else?" For all but two children (out of forty-eight), the ability to attribute mixed emotions to actors in *nonmoral* stories was a prerequisite for acknowledging that *moral* victimizers could feel both happy and additional negative emotions. This finding, however, still does not explain why young children overwhelmingly attribute simple (unmixed) positive emotions to victimizers rather than unmixed negative emotions, no matter how salient the victims' losses are made.

Another attempt to examine the potential role of cognitive constraints on the happy victimizer expectancy began with a focus on children's Theory of Mind–related abilities involving desire/intention, outcomes, and moral concerns. In this multi-experiment study (Yuill, Perner, Pearson, Peerbhoy, & van den Ende, 1996) 3- to 10-year-old children were presented with a number of stories in which a child intended to do something but where the moral nature of the motive (i.e., intentionally harmful versus morally neutral) and the outcome (successful versus not successful) were varied. So, for example, stories involved a victimizer either intending to harm another child (deliberately throwing a ball at a disliked child's head) and succeeding or not succeeding, or an actor attempting a morally neutral act (throwing a ball to another child) and succeeding or not.

Evidence was found for a shift from happy victimizer attributions (labeled "wicked desires") in a clear majority of 5- to 7-year-olds to a more mixed view of the affective reactions of victimizers by age 10. In addition, however, an earlier stage was found in which 3-year-olds were more likely to attribute negative emotions to victimizers than 5- to 7-year-olds. This earlier stage, Yuill et al. argued, stemmed from an "objective" orientation, which had little to do with the moral intentions of the actor because "Objectivist children never... recognized the possibility of being pleased at achieving something bad and thus seemed unable to grant the actor freedom to feel anything but bad" (p. 466). In contrast, 5- to 7-year-olds' emotion judgments reflected the strong influence of intention–outcome matches, that is, "if you get what you want you feel happy." Finally, 10-year-olds were clearly affected by the moral nature of the act, as seen in their focus on harm and unfairness in their rationales for victimizers.

This study highlights the potential cognitive constraints that seem to be affecting 3- to 7-year-olds moral emotion judgments. For 5- to 7-year-olds, in particular, the moral issues were less salient than the match between desires and outcomes, unless those moral concerns were explicitly highlighted. For example, in one experiment, 3- and 5-year-olds were either asked, "Was that a good thing for the boy/girl to do?" (moral salience) or "Was that what the boy/girl wanted to happen?" (personal salience) prior to judging moral victimizers' emotional responses. Although 3-year-olds were not influenced by these conditions, 5-year-olds attributed more intensely positive emotions to the successful victimizer in the personal salience than in the moral salience condition.

Yuill et al. argue that, collectively, their findings clarify why Nunner-Winkler and Sodian (1988) found a marked drop in 8-year-olds' happy victimizer attributions as opposed to the more subtle shift to mixed emotion attributions by 10-year-olds in this study. Two issues are involved: first, Nunner-Winkler and Sodian specifically asked children whether the moral act was good or bad prior to assessing children's emotion attribution; and second, all of the stories involved victimization. In other words, Nunner-Winkler and Sodian's (1988) methodology acted to eliminate one very important step in children's judgments about moral emotions, that is, the judgment about whether a particular match between a desire and a goal (getting what you wanted) even has a moral element. Killen and Nucci (1995) have argued that many, perhaps most, personal goals do not involve moral conflicts between the self and others. If this is true, children may first need to recognize that a particular behavior has a moral component before attempting to apply those moral principles.

Although this moral "recognition" issue is clearly important, it does not address the fact that even after simplifying young children's decision making (e.g., by presenting just moral events) they still routinely attribute positive emotions to victimizers whose victimization produces clear material and psychological gains. Keller, Lourenco, Malti, and Saalbach (2003) recognized this problem, and they set out to assess several alternative explanations of the psychological meaning of happy victimizer attributions. One goal was to examine whether it is important to distinguish between children's expectations about how they themselves would feel in the role of the victimizer versus children's attributions regarding hypothetical victimizers. If children attributed more positive emotions to victimizers than themselves, Keller et al. reasoned, this might suggest that happy victimizer expectancies were just implicit judgments about "bad actors" (the kinds of children who would commit such transgressions in the first place [but see Arsenio & Kramer, 1992; Barden et al., 1980]).

Another goal was to address the distinction between a "deontic" or moral point of view ("what is the {morally} right feeling after the violation?" Keller et al., 2003, p. 4) and a "cognitive-predictive" orientation ("How *does* the protagonist feel after *getting* what he or she desired?" p. 4), that is, the distinction between "ought" and "is." Young children, the authors argued, may be answering an "is" judgment in their moral attributions for victimizers. Given that the victimizer set out to do X and succeeded then, of course, he or she feels happy. If, however, young children are asked about how such a person "ought" to behave, their emotion judgments and rationales might reveal that they actually reject such behavior as unacceptable. In other words, young children construe questions about victimizers' emotions as intended to assess children's understanding of the match between intention/desire and outcomes (as in Yuill et al., 1996), although they do not morally approve of these behaviors. In contrast, older participants may initially view the question as intended to focus on the moral issue. As a result older children may either attribute negative emotions to the victimizer or assume that victimizer is a "bad actor" (not like them or most people) and consequently will feel happy.

Over 120 children, including about half of 5- to 6-year-olds and half of 8- to 9-year-olds, were interviewed regarding acts of victimization (one involved stealing and the other a broken promise). About half of the children were from Portugal and half from Germany. Children were asked a series of questions about the transgression beginning with, "Is this right what X did?" Participants were then asked about how the victimizer would feel and how they (the participants) would feel as the victimizer (with the two questions counterbalanced). Finally, two additional questions were asked, including whether it was right or wrong for the victimizer to feel the way he or she did and why, and whether the victimizer was a good or bad person and why.

Children did, in fact, make a clear distinction between the emotions they attributed to themselves as victimizers versus those attributed to hypothetical victimizers (see also Van Zee, Lemerise, Arsenio, Gregory, & Sepcaru, 2000; as well as Keller, Schuster, Fang, Tang, & Edelstein, 1996, for comparable findings from a Chinese sample). About 67% of the younger children versus about 40% of the older children attributed positive emotions to the hypothetical victimizers, whereas about 50% of the younger children, but only 10% of the older children, expected to feel happy. As hypothesized, these findings for children's "cognitive–predictive" emotion judgments ("how would X feel?") were qualified in important ways by children's deontic judgments ("was it right to feel X?"), although this was complicated by some cultural differences. In the older age group, nearly all children from both countries either judged that victimizers would feel negative emotions, and that this was the right way to feel, or that victimizers would feel positive emotions, but this was the wrong way to feel. Almost 90% of the younger German children also provided this moral profile (i.e., unhappy and the right thing or happy but the wrong thing). By contrast, nearly 40% of the younger Portuguese children expected that victimizers would feel happy and this was the right way to feel. A subsequent analysis, however, indicated that Portuguese children were not as unaware of the moral implications of victimization as they first appeared to be. All of these Portuguese children also evaluated these happy victimizers as being "bad people," suggesting that young Portuguese children also distinguish between descriptive and prescriptive judgments of moral emotions.

The authors concluded that "contrary to what has been postulated so far (Lourenco, 1997; Nunner-Winkler & Sodian, 1988), children's attributions of positive emotions do not necessarily indicate children's emotional and moral immaturity or their moral motivation" (p. 14). Despite a few differences in the judgments of Portuguese and German children, both younger and older children expected that when they were in the role of the victimizer they would feel less happy than would a hypothetical victimizer. Perhaps more important, even when children did attribute positive emotions to victimizers (presumably because of their focus on the salience of desire/outcome matches), they ultimately rejected those positive responses as not right or as coming from a bad person. In terms of developmental findings, younger children were more likely to take a cognitive–predictive stance ("how does the victimizer feel after *getting* what she desired," Keller et al., 2003, p. 15), and the older children more frequently take a moral stance ("How should the protagonist feel after *stealing* the desired good?," p. 15). Yet, regardless of their initial emotion attributions, both age groups rejected victimization when it was viewed from a moral stance.

One other study needs to be described before discussing all of this research on cognitive and methodological explanations of the happy victimization expectancy. In this study we (Arsenio, Ramos-Marcuse, & Hoffman, 2005; Ramos-Marcuse & Arsenio, 2001) examined the moral reasoning of a group of developmentally at-risk 4- and 5-year-old African-American and Latino young children from mostly single-parent, lower socioeconomic status families. About 50% of this group had been referred to a university-based clinic because of early behavioral problems, and the other half of the children came from preschools in the same community served by the clinic.

Our primary goal was to examine young children's moral emotion attributions and other aspects of their moral reasoning using an interactive methodology in which children could enact their response using toys and other props. The specific instrument we used (i.e., Kochanska et al.s', 1996 "moral" version of the MacArthur Story Stem Battery) is a part of a growing number of assessments specifically constructed to elicit the attention and participation of young children by allowing them to use puppets and other interactive materials to enact their responses in age-appropriate "play" contexts (Buchsbaum, Toth, Clyman, Cicchetti, & Emde, 1992; Oppenheim, Emde, & Warren, 1997; and see, also, Denham, 1998). Our basic interest was in whether preschool age children would still attribute only unqualified positive emotions to victimizers (as in Arsenio & Kramer, 1992) or whether this different methodology might reveal other more "mixed" views of victimization.

Children were presented with four stories involving potential acts of victimization. For example, in one story the participants were asked to imagine they wanted a turn on another child's bike, and that when the child refused they pushed him or her off the bike and took a turn. Children used play figures and props to enact their responses. In addition to responding to a sequence of prompts (such as "what happens next?"), children were directly asked how they would feel and why following their acts of victimization. Children's expectations of how they would feel immediately following their acts of victimization were scored separately from their subsequent narrative responses. So, for example, if a child initially said, "I was happy I pushed him off the bike cause now I got a turn", this was scored separately from responses to subsequent probes ("What happened next?"). Children's narrative response were coded into several different categories including: (a) ill gains (a focus on material gain produced by victimization); (b) rule focus (would not break a rule); (c) adult assistance (asking an adult for help); (d) taking responsibility (admitting blame, apologizing, or making reparations), (e) aggression (verbal or physical intentional harm); and (f) death/killing (mention of killing or dying).

Children were also given an assessment of their expressive language ability (Gardner, 1990), and parents and other professionals working with the children completed appropriate versions of the Child Behavior Checklist (Achenbach, 1997) to assess broad patterns of internalizing and externalizing behaviors in children. (Other aspects of the study not reported here focused on child attachment patterns and parents' social support and parenting styles.)

Preliminary analyses revealed that the clinic and nonclinic children did not differ in terms of gender, race/ethnicity, or their expressive language abilities, but that as expected clinic children were rated as having significantly higher externalizing but not internalizing behaviors than the comparison children. Contrary to expectations, however, the two groups did not differ in terms of their initial emotion attributions or their rationales for those emotions. Nearly 80% of the time children said that they expected to be happy following their acts of victimization (clinic $M = 3.15$, comparison $M = 3.21$ out of four stories), and children nearly always justified their emotions by referring to the concrete gains produced by victimization. So even after attempting to present these victimization stories using contextualized, age-appropriate materials, and placing participants in the role of the victimizers, the usual happy victimizer expectancy emerged, and it was explained by desirable gains produced by these acts.

Other revealing group differences emerged, however, in the subsequent narratives that children provided for follow-up probes (e.g., "What happened next?"). Although clinic and nonclinic children did not differ in their mention of low-level aggressive responses, ("He would take his bike and hit me"), rule references, or mention of ill gains, they did differ in their other narrative responses. Perhaps most importantly, nonclinic children mentioned attempts to be positively responsive to their victims, including offering apologies, making reparations, or admitting blame (e.g., "But I would give him his bike back.") nearly twice as often as clinic children (21% versus 11% of all narrative responses). Another significant group difference involved a less common but revealing response. Nearly half of the clinic children versus 17% of the nonclinic group mentioned death or killing at least once in their narratives for the four stories (e.g., "I'd kill him if he tried to get his bike back.").

The lack of group differences in happy victimizer expectancies was unexpected and inconsistent with some findings for older children (Lemerise, Scott, Diehl, & Bacher, 2000) and adolescents. Yet, overall, these findings provide support for Keller et al.s' (2003) and some of our own previous claims (Arsenio & Lover, 1995) that young children's happy victimizer expectancy is not simply the result of "wicked desires" or another form of gross moral immaturity. The two groups' tendencies to provide clearly different rationales following their initial happy victimizer attribution and the nature of these different rationales argues against viewing young children as simply being "morally obtuse." Instead, as we discuss next, it may be that young children have initial cognitive, and sometimes behavioral, difficulties shifting their focus from the salient material and emotional gains produced by victimization to the losses experienced by victims.

Collectively, the studies described in this section offer somewhat different explanations for why most young children (below age 5) expect victimizers to feel happy, whereas older children's attributions seem to differ markedly from study to study. Keller and colleagues (1996, 2003) explain these issues in two ways. One is that the previous happy victimizer findings are mostly artifactual in that children either believe they are describing how "bullies" or "bad actors" who would commit such a transgression are feeling (i.e., the self–other perspective questions). In addition, they argue, there are age-related cognitive changes that lead young children to view interviewers' questions as being about desire/intention matches, whereas older children frame these judgments in moral terms from the beginning. These apparent age-related changes are, however, less important than a broad agreement across ages that victimizers' positive emotions are unacceptable. Implicitly, then, this view suggests that happy victimization plays a very small role in children's actual moral development.

One response to these claims is that the clear demand characteristics of Keller et al. studies act to undermine these broad claims. Prior to making any emotion judgments, children in this study were always asked to judge whether the transgression was the "right thing to do" and nearly all children said it was not. Subsequent questions then focused on the rightness or wrongness of the victimizers' response and finally on whether the victimizer was good or bad. Given the clear salience of moral concerns for the experimenter, it is not surprising that most children eventually renounced the positive emotions of the victimizer.

Yet the study by Yuill et al. (1996) suggests that Keller et al. have touched on something more important than just children's understanding of what is considered "socially desirable." Another way of seeing the happy victimizer expectancy is in terms of how salient moral concerns must become before children realize they take precedence over achieving desire–outcome matches that require harming others. So, when Yuill et el. systematically highlighted either the moral or personal salience of potential desire–outcome matches, they found that young children (5-year-olds) altered their views of how the victimizer would feel accordingly. Similarly, as Keller et al. (2003) increased the salience of moral issues in their methodology, more and more children seemed to become aware of the moral aspects of victimization (see also Arsenio & Kramer, 1992). Seen in this light, the question raised by the happy victimizer expectancy is not whether young children have any moral understanding—they clearly do—but what it takes for them to routinely and spontaneously apply that understanding when it comes into potential conflict with their own competing desires.

Based on these studies, it would be a mistake to conclude that the happy victimizer expectancy is simply a methodological artifact. Yet, the larger psychological meaning and significance of this conception is still unclear. In the next few sections we describe two types of research that may help to clarify these issues. The first section summarizes observational work on the actual emotions children display when victimizing others, and the second section focuses on whether individual differences in adolescents' tendencies to attribute positive emotions to victimizers are associated with their behavioral status. Both types of research are especially relevant for Keller et al.s' (2003) observation that "in some applied contexts in which the happy victimizer phenomenon is important, such as the cognitive and emotional representation of bullying, it seems necessary to explore fully the emotional sensitivity of children" (p. 16).

OBSERVATIONAL STUDIES OF VICTIMIZATION-RELATED EMOTIONS

As Lourenco (1997) and others have noted, a fair amount is known about children's conceptions of moral emotions, but almost nothing is known about the actual emotions children display in these contexts. At the most general normative level, it is unclear how often children actually display positive emotions after victimizing others. It seems highly unlikely that young children, in particular, are happy as often following victimization as their pervasive happy victimizer conceptions would seem to suggest. Still, do they display a "meaningful" level of positive emotions following their actual acts of victimization, and how should *meaningful* be defined?

Before the available observational research on this topic can be described, two significant limitations of these studies must acknowledged. First, this work focuses on just preschoolers. Despite the emergence of some new technologies for studying older children's naturalistic acts of victimization (see Coie & Dodge, 1998), to date, pragmatic and developmental factors (e.g., preschoolers conceal neither their aggression nor emotion displays) have limited this research to younger children. A second limitation is that none of these studies assess victimization per se. Instead they focus on conflict or aggression, both of which are relevant but not necessarily identical to studying victimization.

Several studies have been explicitly designed to assess children's anger during conflicts and provocative situations. For example, Fabes and Eisenberg (1992) examined how the different ways in which preschoolers responded to anger-eliciting situations (e.g., by venting versus active but nonaggressive resistance) are related to assessments of social competence. Hubbard and her colleagues (e.g., Hubbard et al., 2002) have also observationally assessed young school-age children's anger and how it relates to particular forms of aggressive behaviors. Yet, even though this exclusive focus on anger is interesting in its own right, it is not directly relevant for assessing the broader range of emotions that might be linked with victimization (Lemerise & Dodge, 2000). Several other studies, however, do begin to clarify the role of other victimization-related emotions in children's behavior.

In an initial study, Arsenio and Killen (1996) examined 4- to 5-year-old preschoolers during their semistructured table play with peers. Specifically, twenty-seven children were brought together in groups of three (for four sessions each) and videotaped while playing with a small number of toys at a table. Coding addressed several aspects of children's conflicts, as well as the emotions they displayed for a period of 15 seconds before and after conflicts, and during the entire conflict episode (using the AFFEX system; Izard, Dougherty, & Hembree, 1983).

More then 250 conflicts were observed, with the majority involving object disputes in which the conflict initiator gained control of the object. As expected, participants' emotions did not differ prior to conflicts, but during conflicts initiators were more likely to be happy, whereas recipients expressed more sadness, anger, and surprise. Moreover, conflict initiators displayed very few negative emotions, but all of these were angry displays. Additional analyses revealed connections between individual differences in children's emotions and the frequency with which they were involved in conflicts. (Analyses were based on the percentage of time children displayed particular emotions, rather than total time, because children who were involved in more conflicts would also have more available time to display emotions. A related approach is used in all of the studies reported in this section; that is, emotion results are based on the percentage of emotions that were of a certain type for each child. This approach controls for different levels of child expressivity and has been found to more strongly predictive of children's behavior than using the simple frequency of their emotion displays.)

Among several results, it was found that children who initiated more conflicts showed a somewhat higher percentage of happiness during these conflicts ($r = .28$), whereas children who were targeted for conflicts more frequently displayed a higher percentage of all negative emotions, but especially anger ($r = .57$). Although interesting, these findings raised additional questions. One concern was with the particular observational context chosen. Preschoolers' table play is a common event, but in this particular task children were presented with materials that did not belong to anyone (no child had selected the materials). It is unclear, then, whether this task really assessed victimization-related emotions as opposed to emotions resulting from conflicts or disagreements not involving deliberate harm. Another issue was whether the observed connections between children's conflict emotions and their rates of conflictual behaviors were primarily related to children's conflict emotions per se, or to a more general emotional dispositional pattern. For example, some children may be more prone to anger in all situations, and this global hostile predisposition may produce both more hostile conflict emotions, as well as a greater number of conflicts.

With these issues in mind, we conducted a second study (Arsenio & Lover, 1997) to address the connections between both children's conflict- and nonconflict-related emotions and their behavior in a more naturalistic setting (i.e., during unstructured freeplay). Thirty-seven preschoolers were observed over the course of a 6-week summer day camp program. Children's "happy," "sad," and "angry" emotion displays were assessed both during and outside of conflicts using Denham's (1986; Denham, McKinley, Couchoud, & Holt, 1990) live-action coding system; children's aggressive and nonaggressive conflicts were also recorded.

A total of seventy-six conflicts were observed, including twenty-nine aggressive conflicts and forty-four nonaggressive conflicts, but more than 1,000 emotion displays were observed. In terms of the connections between children's emotions and their conflictual behaviors, children who displayed a higher percentage of either anger or happiness during their aggressive conflicts were more likely to initiate aggression, and those who displayed higher percentages of baseline anger (i.e., outside of aggression and nonaggressive conflicts) were also somewhat more likely to initiate aggression. By contrast, few connections were observed between children's emotions and their nonaggressive conflicts. Given the small number of aggressive acts, however, these findings had to be interpreted with some caution.

Despite their limitations, these two studies underscore the importance of assessing positive conflict-related emotions in addition to the more traditional focus on conflict anger. These studies also begin to suggest that positive conflict emotions may play an especially important role in predicting individual differences in preschoolers' aggressive and conflictual behaviors. It was clear that another more extensive study was needed to assess whether victimization-related happiness, as such, has an important role to play in children's behavior.

This third study (Arsenio, Cooperman, & Lover, 2000) included an ethnically diverse group of fifty-one preschoolers (twenty-seven girls and twenty-four boys) between the ages of 4 and $5\frac{1}{2}$ who were observed over a 1-year period. Emotions were coded with the same system used in the Arsenio and Lover study (1997), and multiple aspects of preschoolers' aggression were also recorded. *Aggression* was defined as including either physical or verbal harm and it was distinguished from nonaggressive conflicts (e.g., simple disagreements) and from rough-and-tumble play. In addition to these observations, children were administered (a) an assessment of emotion-related knowledge (adapted from Denham, 1986) in which children were asked to label and recognize several basic emotions and to judge the emotion outcomes of several types of familiar events; and (b) a standard preschool picture sociometric assessment, which was used to derive ratings of children's acceptance by their peers.

Overall, a total of 168 aggressive interactions were observed. Most children initiated at least one act of aggression ($M = 3.29$) and were targeted at least once ($M = 3.29$), although, as is often found (Coie & Dodge, 1998), about 20% of the children initiated nearly half of all aggression. The emotions children displayed differed strongly depending on the context. Outside of their aggressive conflicts (the "baseline" context) children were quite happy (91% of their total baseline displays), but during their aggressive interactions this dropped to just 25% (of their total aggression-related displays). However, children's aggression-related emotions were quite different depending on their role in that aggression. Recipients of aggression were mostly angry (more than 50% of their displays), sad, or had neutral expressions. By contrast, aggressors' emotions displays were relatively evenly divided between anger and happiness (about 40% for each). Interestingly, recipients of aggression were also significantly more likely to be distressed (anger or sadness) when aggressors were happy.

Other analyses indicated that children's emotion dispositions (and emotion knowledge) were related to both their aggressive behavior and peer acceptance. Overall, children who displayed more baseline anger and less baseline happiness (as a percentage of their baseline displays) were more aggressive and less accepted by their peers. By contrast, children who displayed more aggression-related happiness were more aggressive and less liked than their peers. In other words, as in Arsenio and Lover (1997), participants' baseline and aggression-related percentage happiness had opposite connections with their social functioning (and percentage aggression-related and baseline happiness were unrelated to each other).

A mediation analysis provided additional support for the potentially unique role of positive aggression-related emotions. Previous work by Denham (1986; Denham et al., 1990) suggested that some of the connections between children's affective dispositions and whether they were liked or not by peers were indirect; that is, preschoolers' affective tendencies influenced their prosocial behavior and, in turn, prosocial behavior influenced their acceptance by peers. When similar effects were assessed in the present study, it was found that the significant connections between all of the affective correlates of children's peer acceptance (emotion knowledge, aggression-related happiness, baseline anger, and baseline happiness) were mediated by their aggressiveness. In other words, children's emotion-related abilities and tendencies were connected to aggression, and this link with aggression accounted for the influence of these affective variables on peer acceptance. The only exception was aggression-related happiness, which had both the indirect link to peer acceptance (through aggression) as well as somewhat of a direct link. In discussing this finding, we noted that "relatively non-aggressive children may view highly aggressive peers who are often happy during aggression as not taking these typically aversive acts seriously or, even worse, enjoying being mean" (Arsenio et al., 2000, p. 445). What is unknown, however, is whether that happiness stemmed from an actual enjoyment of aggression or the material gains often associated with preschoolers' aggression (e.g., getting the desired toy or turn without waiting).

Research by a different research group lends some support to the patterns of findings reported in these three observational studies. Miller and Olson (2000) were also interested in whether the affective qualities of preschoolers' conflicts (aggressive and nonaggressive) were related to teacher and peer ratings of children's social competence. A group of sixty 4- to 5-year-olds who attended Head Start preschool classrooms participated, with nearly all of the children from low-income European-American families.

Children were videotaped in groups of five as they played with a variety of age-appropriate toys. Most of the approximately 15-minute sessions involved free play, but there was also a brief structured activity. Children were videotaped once early in the year and again 9 months later. In addition, at both times, teachers rated children's disruptive behaviors and children assessed their peers' negative social status (a combination of disruptiveness and being disliked) using a sociometric procedure. Subsequently, the videotapes were used to record the frequency that children initiated conflicts, and their emotional responses during those conflicts (typically a single predominant emotional response [see also Arsenio et al., 2000]). Children's emotional responses were coded as either anger, mild positive, mild negative, and a category called *gleeful taunting*, "high intensity inappropriate positive affect" (p. 344), which occurred during acts of victimization (e.g., teasing and destroying others' property).

Although there were changes in the mean levels of some of the emotions that children displayed over time, the most interesting findings involved the connections between children's initially assessed emotions and a composite measure of children's negative behavior (from a combination of the teacher and peer assessments) at the later assessment. Children's initial anger and mild positive emotions (as a proportion of their displays) were not related to the composite measure of their negative behavior. By contrast, children's gleeful taunting, mild negative emotions, and neutral affect at the beginning of the year were predictive of more negative behavioral ratings 9 months later. Analyses of the unique contributions of these variables, however, indicated that gleeful taunting predicted more than six times the variance in the behavior composite than either mild negative emotions or neutral affect.

Although gleeful taunting was most predictive of children's initiation of conflict, children's anger or mild negative affect (as conflicts targets) was most predictive of their being targeted for conflicts. In other words, "gleeful taunting may function to instigate conflict among preschool children (e.g., by taking toys and laughing, or teasing and other forms of relational aggression), whereas anger and mild negative affect may appear primarily as emotional reactions to another child's actions" (Miller & Olson, 2000, p. 348).

In their subsequent discussion of these finding, Miller and Olson noted that their findings for gleeful taunting are quite consistent with the role of victimizer happiness in Arsenio and colleagues' observational studies. Based on their own short-term longitudinal findings, they argued that gleeful taunting may have damaging consequences not only during preschool, but possibly for children's long-term adjustment. And, as we report in a subsequent section, there are some emerging data on adolescents' conceptions of moral emotions that are consistent with this last claim. In terms of children's anger, Miller and Olson's failure to find a connection between anger proneness (when initiating conflicts) and rates of conflict initiation are consistent with the more extensive Arsenio et al. study (2000) than with the Arsenio and Lover (1997) study.

A full discussion of the role of anger in children's aggressive and nonaggressive conflicts is beyond the scope and focus of the present chapter (but see Lemerise & Dodge, 2000). The observational studies described in this section, however, do raise questions about the pervasive focus on anger (and only anger) in many theoretical and clinical approaches to aggression. One topic for future research is the distinction between anger that occurs outside the context of conflicts versus anger during conflicts. In the two observational studies that assessed anger both during and outside of aggression (Arsenio & Lover, 1997; Arsenio et al., 2000), nonaggression-related anger was clearly related to children's initiation of aggression. Although more research is needed to clarify the nature of this nonaggressive anger, it may contribute to the strongly held view that anger is very closely linked with aggression.

For the present purposes, several things are clear. Contrary to some studies suggesting that preschoolers' almost always expect victimizers to feel happy (e.g., Arsenio & Kramer, 1992; Lourenco, 1997; Nunner-Winkler & Sodian, 1992), preschoolers' seem to display happiness during about half or so of their actual aggressive acts of victimization (roughly comparable to self-as-victimizer attributions in some studies, e.g., Barden et al., 1980; Keller et al., 2003). Second, there are marked individual differences underlying children's tendencies to be happy victimizers. Finally, preschoolers' displays of positive emotions during their aggressive and nonaggressive conflicts are much more problematic for children's social competence and psychological adjustments than has been previously understood. In terms of children's moral development, these findings provide support for the importance of positive emotions in the context of victimization. Although young children's actual happy victimization is less extensive than their conceptions of happy victimization, observed happy victimization is both relatively common and it is connected with important individual differences in moral behavior.

ADOLESCENTS' CONCEPTIONS OF THE EMOTIONAL CONSEQUENCES OF DIFFERENT FORMS OF AGGRESSION

In this last section we describe a study that addresses the different roles of anger and happiness (as well as other emotions) in connection with adolescents' conceptions of various forms of aggression and victimization. Several unresolved issues underlie this work.

First of all, most research on children's conceptions of moral emotions has focused on age-related normative changes in younger children (age 4 to 10); little is known about adolescents' conceptions and whether individual differences in these conceptions are related to behavior. Another less obvious issue is that most of the work on children's conceptions of moral emotions has examined the consequences of clearly unprovoked aggression. By contrast, little is known about children's affect–event links involving the sorts of provoked aggression often studied by researchers explicitly interested in aggression (see Arsenio & Lemerise, 2004, for a more general discussion of the provoked and unprovoked distinction).

Dodge, Crick, and their colleagues have argued for the importance of distinguishing between reactive aggression in which (mis)perceived threats and frustrations are resisted with aggression, and proactive aggression in which desirable material or psychological outcomes are obtained by victimizing others (e.g., Dodge & Coie, 1987). Research indicates that teachers' ratings of children's reactive aggression (e.g., "blames others in a fight" and "overreacts angrily to accidents"; Dodge & Coie, 1987, p. 1149) are linked with children's tendency to attribute hostile intentions to others in ambiguous situations, that is, a "hostile attribution bias" (see Coie & Dodge, 1998, for a review). By contrast, proactive aggression (e.g., "threatens and bullies others" and "uses physical force to dominate") is not associated with misperceptions of others' intention, but rather with children's judgments that they are effective at being aggressive and that aggression produces desirable outcomes, or "it's easy and it works."

Although reactive aggression is often described as "hot-headed" and proactive aggression as "cold-blooded," research on the emotional correlates of these two forms of aggression has really only begun. To date, Hubbard and colleagues (e.g., Hubbard et al., 2002) have found some important connections between ratings of children's reactive aggression and their behaviors during a "rigged" board game. For example, "(R)eactive aggression, but not proactive aggression, was positively related to skin conductance reactivity and angry nonverbal behaviors" (p. 1101). For proactive aggression, only a single emotional correlate has been examined, but it is one with special relevance for this chapter. Children have sometimes rated how they would expect to feel on a 5-point scale (from "very bad" to "very good") after responding aggressively to a peer's nonaggressive provocation. In one study (Dodge, Lochman, Harnish, Bates, & Pettit, 1997), proactive aggressive children expected to feel more positively following proactive aggression than either reactive aggressive or nonaggressive children. Moreover, this was the only measure of children's social information processing (out of seven) that was uniquely associated with a particular subtype of aggression.

In a recent study, we (Arsenio, Grossman, & Gold, 2003, 2004) sought to extend the Dodge et al. (1997) research by examining adolescents' conceptions of the emotional outcomes of different forms of aggression. Our goals were both to obtain a normative picture of these expected emotional consequences and to examine whether adolescents with behavior problems would view the consequences of such events differently from their peers. Another focus was on examining whether adolescents with reactive and proactive aggressive tendencies would differ in their emotion expectancies for specific types of aggression.

A total of 100 adolescents (about two-thirds boys) participated, and nearly all were from low socioeconomic status, single parent families living in an economically disadvantaged urban environment. About two thirds of the adolescents were African American and most of the remaining participants were Latino. Of the 100 participants, half had been formally diagnosed as meeting DSM-IV (American Psychiatric Association, 1994) criteria for either conduct disorder or oppositional defiant disorder. These adolescents attended special classes for behaviorally disruptive adolescents, and their nondisruptive peers came from the same public school system.

Adolescents were individually administered a multipart interview, which included an assessment of their verbal abilities (the Peabody Picture Vocabulary Test, 3rd ed.; Dunn & Dunn, 2001), as well as assessments of their reasoning regarding three different types of aggression, including reactive aggression, proactive aggression, and a third category we called *unprovoked proactive aggression*. Unlike the stories typically used to depict proactive aggression, unprovoked proactive aggression involved acts of victimization (e.g., stealing and physical harm to obtain material goods) that involved no prior provocation. This last category was added because it corresponds to the types of victimization used in nearly all of happy victimizer studies described.

Participants were asked to judge the likely emotional outcomes of stories describing each of these three types of aggression by dividing up ten chips as desired between five emotion categories (happy, sad, mad, scared, and neutral affect) for each story. For proactive and unprovoked aggression, adolescents were asked to imagine themselves in the role of the person who initiated the aggression, whereas for reactive aggression they were placed in the role of the target of the ambiguously caused outcome. In addition to these emotion attributions, participants made judgments about other defining features of each form of aggression. So for example, for reactive aggression participants made judgments about the intentions of the "provocateurs" responsible for the negative but ambiguously caused outcomes. Finally, the adolescents' teachers completed assessments of the participants' reactive and proactive aggressive tendencies (Dodge & Coie, 1987) as well as their overall externalizing patterns (Achenbach, 1991).

Preliminary analyses indicated that the two groups of adolescents did not differ in terms of their age, gender, racial/ethnic composition, or socioeconomic status. (Behaviorally disruptive adolescents did, however, have lower verbal abilities than their peers, and this was controlled for whenever possible in subsequent analyses.) Overall, adolescents expected to feel quite differently in response to these three forms of aggression. Adolescents expected that ambiguously caused provocative ("reactive") events would mostly make them feel angry ($M = 5.82$ out 10 possible) and, to a lesser extent, just neutral affect ($M = 3.27$). Additional analyses indicated that this choice of anger or neutral affect was linked to judgments about the presumed intention of the provocateur: if participants attributed more hostile intentions (across four stories) to provocateurs then they expected to be angrier, whereas if they saw the provocations as less intentional they expected to feel more neutral. By contrast, for provoked proactive aggression adolescents mostly expected to feel neutral affect ($M = 5.07$), with a mix of other emotions (means for happy $= 1.12$, sad $= 1.29$, mad $= 2.20$, and scared $= 0.24$), whereas for unprovoked proactive aggression (moral victimization) they selected a range of emotions including sadness ($M = 3.38$), happiness ($M = 2.35$), and neutral affect ($M = 2.19$).

Other analyses, however, revealed that behaviorally disruptive adolescents differed from their peers in some of these emotion attributions. Although the two groups did not differ in their emotion chip judgments for reactive or provoked proactive aggression, behaviorally disruptive adolescents did rate themselves as feeling happier on a 5-point scale ($1 =$ very bad to $5 =$ very good, $M = 3.14$ versus comparison $M = 2.77$) following acts of provoked aggression. Behaviorally disruptive adolescents also expected to feel significantly happier than their peers following their unprovoked acts of victimization (emotion chip $M = 3.28$ for behaviorally disruptive adolescents and 1.42 for comparison group). This last difference was significant after controlling for multiple emotion comparisons, and neither finding was influenced by group differences in verbal abilities.

In addition to using the emotion chips, adolescents made a number of other emotion-related judgments regarding unprovoked aggression. Specifically, they produced their own emotion terms for how they would feel (discrete emotion judgment) and why (rationale) first for themselves as victimizers and then for their victims. Although both groups attributed negative emotions to themselves as victimizers nearly half the time, behaviorally disruptive adolescents were more than twice as likely than their peers to expect to feel happy (27% versus 12%) and only half as likely to expect to feel mixed emotions (both positive and negative emotions; 16% versus 29%). Perhaps even more striking, comparison adolescents were three times more likely to refer to moral issues ("it's wrong," "it wasn't fair") than to outcomes ("I got the ticket I wanted") in justifying their emotions (61% moral rationales versus 20% outcomes rationales). By contrast, behaviorally disruptive adolescents were more likely to justify their emotions by referring to the desirable outcomes of victimization than to potential moral concerns (28% moral rationales versus 42% outcome rationales).

The two groups did not, however, differ in their views of how their victims would respond to these events. Both groups overwhelmingly expected their victims to feel exclusively angry (56% for behaviorally disruptive versus 49% for comparison youth) or a mixture of anger and sadness (28% versus 27%, respectively). And their rationales for victims' emotions were generally quite similar, mostly focusing on moral concerns raised by this victimization (47% versus 57% for behaviorally disruptive and comparison youth, respectively).

Taken together, these findings indicate that adolescents distinguish between the emotional consequences of these three forms of aggression, including the two forms of proactive aggression that have not been previously compared. Moreover, the results for reactive aggression confirm the importance of adolescents' inferences regarding the intentions of others in ambiguous situations. When adolescents believed that ambiguous provocations were intentional, they were more likely to be angry, whereas if they believed the provocation was unintentional, they were more likely to say they would be neutral about the event.

Not only were adolescents' conceptions of the emotional consequences of these forms of aggression highly differentiated, but there were also some important group differences in their emotion expectancies. Compared to their peers, behaviorally disruptive adolescents expected to feel happier following their acts of both provoked and unprovoked aggression (although only for the 5-point scale for provoked aggression). These group differences are especially striking for two related reasons: they were the only aggression-related emotion differences; and, in absolute terms, neither group expected to feel especially happy following these acts. For unprovoked aggression, behaviorally disruptive adolescents assigned slightly more than three out of ten chips to the happy category and for unprovoked assigned they expected to feel only slightly more than neutral. In other words, happy victimizer–like attributions were not especially pervasive for adolescents, but they were still highly predictive of their behavioral status.

Two other findings stand out. Analyses revealed very few connections between adolescents' reactive and proactive aggressive tendencies (as rated by teachers) and their emotion attributions, with one exception. Adolescents who were rated as more proactively aggressive expected to feel significantly more emotionally positive following acts of unprovoked aggression, and this finding was not moderated by adolescents' behavioral status. In other words, adolescents who were seen as more likely to threaten and bully others (but not to overreact to others' ambiguous provocations) expected to feel happier than their peers following acts of victimization (see also Dodge et al., 1997). The other noteworthy finding is that despite differences in the two groups' expectations for happy victimization, there was little disagreement that the victim would feel very negatively as a result of the unfairness and harm from being victimized.

Collectively, these findings suggest that (a) although the overall prevalence of happy victimizer conceptions decline from early childhood to adolescence, these conceptions do not disappear completely with age (see also, Murgatroyd & Robinson, 1993, 1997); and (b) individual differences in happy victimizer expectancies are more closely related to behavioral differences in older than in younger children. These findings also underscore an important unresolved question (Arsenio & Lemerise, 2001), namely, how are some aggressive children able to understand the victims' emotional plight without having that knowledge affect their own emotional responses as victimizers (see Cohen & Strayer, 1996; Hoffman, 2000).

CONCLUSION

This chapter started out with two sets of question, a more general set—what emotions do children expect sociomoral acts to produce, and how do these expectancies influence behavior?—and the following more specific questions: (a) why do young children and even some adolescents expect moral victimizers to feel positive emotions (e.g., happiness) after victimizing others?; (b) do children actually display positive emotions in these contexts?; and (c) are individual differences in children's conceptions and displays of happy victimization predictive of behavioral differences?

The present analysis of the literature suggests that working answers can be given to the last two questions, but that the answer to the first question is more tentative and complex. First, it appears that preschoolers, at least, often do display positive emotions while victimizing others. Although the available studies focused on aggressive victimization only (and not on the acts of undetected theft often used in happy victimizer studies) a consistent picture emerged in which preschool victimizers appear to be happy even though they know they are being observed or videotaped by adults. At the same time it is important to note that the absolute frequency of these positive displays are less than would be expected from some studies of preschoolers' conceptions of happy victimization (e.g., Arsenio & Kramer, 1992; Lourenco, 1997; Nunner-Winkler & Sodian, 1988). Yet, interestingly, the displays rates are roughly consistent with some studies in which preschoolers were asked to about their own likely responses as victimizers (e.g., Barden et al., 1980; Keller et al., 2003; but see also Ramos-Marcuse & Arsenio, 2001).

This normative picture of preschoolers' happy victimizer displays, however, is less revealing than the major individual differences in those displays. In answer to the last specific question ("are differences in children's conception and displays of happy victimization predictive of behavioral differences?"), variations in preschoolers' displays of positive victimizer emotions appear to be clearly related to individual differences in their aggressive behaviors. Moreover, positive victimization is associated not only with higher levels of aggression, but also with active rejection by preschool peers (Arsenio et al., 2000; Miller & Olson, 2000). Miller and Olson's findings are especially striking in that gleeful taunting predicted negative peer and teacher ratings 9 months later and gleeful taunting predicted more than six times the variance in negative peer and teacher ratings than any other affective variable (including anger). Although the findings for adolescents' conceptions are somewhat less dramatic, they also suggest that differences in how children view the emotional consequences of victimization are predictive of important behavioral differences.

These answers to the last two specific questions also provide a partial answer to the first question, "why do young children and some adolescents expect moral victimizers to feel happy after victimizing others?" In part, it is because at least some children and adolescents expect victimization to produce desirable outcomes that, in turn, make them happy. But this applies to only a minority of the more aggressive and behaviorally disruptive children. What about the rest of the children, especially the majority of preschoolers—are their happy victimizer conceptions just the result of underlying cognitive constraints or methodological limitations? Unless young children are repeatedly reminded of the immoral nature of victimizing others (e.g., Keller et al., 2003) they seem resistant to changing their nearly exclusive positive views of victimization (especially when it produces material gains), despite strong attempts to highlight the victim's pain and losses. Yet the idea that young children are fundamentally and willfully immoral seems highly implausible.

One way of addressing this issue begins with Dunn (1988) and her colleagues' seminal observational research, in which they looked at very young children's ($1\frac{1}{2}$- to 3 year-olds) behavior with mothers, peers, and siblings in the context of the home. When children were 24 months old it was noted that "The association between incidents in which the child was reprimanded for hurting another—the most clearly moral issue—and the child's hilarity is particularly striking" (p. 40). Furthermore, "The feeling expressed by parent, by sibling, or by child is often highly marked, and the children we studied were in their third year more likely to reason in those disputes that had earlier caused them most distress and anger. They also showed much delight and amusement over transgressions" (p. 180).

Dunn's observations highlight that young children's moral development is very much a work in progress. Some of young children's desires, from wanting their sibling's toy to pushing a friend off a swing, lead them to violate the rights of others and cause suffering even as these acts "deliver the goods" for the victimizer. For most young children, early parent–child interactions may combine with children's empathic tendencies in a way that makes the transition from children's gleeful victimization to a more moral and emotionally mixed view of victimization appear almost seamless. Yet we still argue that age-related changes in young children's strongly positive views of victimization to older children's more mixed expectations reflect a major transition in children's moral development, a transition not negotiated with equal success by all children.

In conclusion, we offer several very brief suggestions for future research. Oddly, despite the interest in both children's conceptions and displays of victimization-related emotions, there is no research on potential connections between these conceptions and emotion displays. For example, are individual differences in children's conceptions of moral emotions associated with their actual emotions displays in these contexts? Although it may be very difficult to assess children's emotion beyond the preschool years, Dunn's (1988) observations (see also Kochanska et al., 1996 for a brief review) suggest that it may be especially useful to examine children in the earliest stages of their moral development, that is, between $1\frac{1}{2}$ to 3 years of age. Longitudinal studies during this age range, as well as later, are also needed to examine whether early differences in children's displays and conceptions of moral emotions are predictive of long-term behavioral outcomes.

Another issue involves the connections between children's moral emotion attributions and their moral judgments. Some of us have argued elsewhere (Arsenio & Lover, 1995) that children's understanding of affect–event links may provide important "raw material" in the construction of related moral principles. For example, knowing that nearly all people feel similar negative emotions about being victimized could help to inform moral principles of fairness and reciprocity. To date, however, support for the expected connections between children's moral evaluations and related emotion attributions (e.g., Smetana et al., 1999b;

Smetana, Campione-Barr, & Yell, 2003) has been mixed, at best. More research is needed to address this critical issue.

Finally, the psychological meaning of preschoolers' pervasive happy victimizer conceptions remains unclear. Although the weight of the available observational research and studies on older children's conceptions of moral emotion indicate the happy victimizer conception is not just a methodological artifact, the lack of variation in preschoolers' conceptions is still puzzling.

Despite the focus of most of this review (and much of our own work) we conclude by suggesting that research on children's conceptions of moral emotion needs to be expanded beyond the happy victimizer issue. There is a growing literature on more general aspects of children's situational affect (often included along with emotion recognition tasks as part of composite emotion knowledge tasks), and this work has shown that variations in children's beliefs about emotional outcomes are predictive of a variety of internalizing and externalizing behaviors (e.g., Fine, Izard, Mostow, Trentacosta, & Ackerman, 2003; Schultz et al., 2000). Similarly, initial efforts to expand research on children's conceptions of sociomoral emotions (e.g., Arsenio & Fleiss, 1996; Hughes & Dunn, 2000) suggest that this broadened focus is important for a more complete understanding of children's sociomoral behavior.

REFERENCES

Achenbach, T. (1991). *Manual for the child behavior checklist/4-18 and 1991 profile*. Burlington: University of Vermont, Department of Psychiatry.

Achenbach, T. (1997). *Guide for the caregiver-teacher report form for ages 2-5*. Burlington: University of Vermont, Department of Psychiatry.

American Psychiatric Association. (1994). *Diagnostic and statistical manual of mental disorders* (4th ed.). Washington, DC: Author.

Arsenio, W. (1988). Children's conceptions of the situational affective consequences of sociomoral events. *Child Development, 59,* 1611–1622.

Arsenio, W., Cooperman, S., & Lover, A. (2000). Affective predictors of preschoolers' aggression and peer acceptance: Direct and indirect effects. *Developmental Psychology, 36,* 438–448.

Arsenio, W., & Fleiss, K. (1996). Typical and behaviourally disruptive children's understanding of the emotional consequences of sociomoral events. *British Journal of Developmental Psychology, 14,* 173–186.

Arsenio, W., & Ford, M. (1985). The role of affective information in social-cognitive development: Children's differentiation of moral and conventional events. *Merrill-Palmer Quarterly, 31,* 1–18.

Arsenio, W., Gold, J., & Adams, E. (2004). Adolescents' emotion expectancies regarding aggressive and nonaggressive events: Connections with behavior problems. *Journal of Experimental Child Psychology, 89,* 338–355.

Arsenio, W., Grossman, E., & Gold, J. (2003, April). Adolescents' conceptions of aggression and nonaggression emotion-related outcomes: Connections with externalizing behaviors. In E. Lemerise (Chair), *Contributions of Emotion Processes to Social Competence and Adjustment*. Symposium conducted at the biennial meeting of the Society for Research in Child Development, Tampa, FL.

Arsenio, W., & Killen, M. (1996). Preschoolers' conflict-related emotions during peer disputes. *Early Education & Development, 7,* 43–57.

Arsenio, W., & Kramer, R. (1991, April). Happy victimizers and their victims: Children's understanding of moral affect and mixed emotions. Poster presented at the biennial meeting of the Society for Research in Child Development, Seattle, WA.

Arsenio, W., & Kramer, R. (1992). Victimizers and their victims: Children's conceptions of the mixed emotional consequences of victimization. *Child Development, 63,* 915–927.

Arsenio, W., & Lemerise, E. (2001). Varieties of childhood bullying: Values, emotion processes, and social competence. *Social Development, 10,* 59–73.

Arsenio, W., & Lemerise, E. (2004). Aggression and moral development: Integrating the social information processing and moral domain models. *Child Development, 74,* 987–1002.

Arsenio, W., & Lover, A. (1997). Emotions, conflicts, and aggression during preschoolers' freeplay. *British Journal of Developmental Psychology, 15,* 531–546.

Arsenio, W., & Lover, A. (1995). Children's conceptions of sociomoral affect: Happy victimizers, mixed emotions and other expectancies. In M. Killen & D. Hart (Ed.), *Morality in everyday life: Developmental perspectives* (pp. 87–128). Cambridge, UK: Cambridge University Press.

Arsenio, W., Ramos-Marcuse, F., & Hoffman, R. (2005). Young at risk children's emotionally-charged moral narratives: Relations with behavior problems, parental social support, and family disciplinary techniques. Manuscript in preparation.

Barden, C., Zelko, F., Duncan. S., & Master, J. (1980). Children's consensual knowledge about the experiential determinants of emotion. *Journal of Personality and Social Psychology, 39,* 968–976.

Brown, T. (1996). Values, knowledge, & Piaget. In E. Reed, E. Turiel., & T. Brown (Eds.), *Values and knowledge* (pp. 137–170). Mahwah, NJ: Lawrence Erlbaum Associates.

Buchsbaum, H., Toth, S., Clyman, R., Cicchetti, D., & Emde, R. (1992). The use of a narrative story-stem technique with maltreated children: Implications for theory and practice. *Development and Psychopathology, 4,* 603–625.

Cohen, D., & Strayer, J. (1996). Empathy in conduct disordered and comparison youth. *Developmental Psychology, 32,* 988–998.

Coie, J. D., & Dodge, K. A. (1998). Aggression and antisocial behavior. In W. Damon (Series Ed.) & N. Eisenberg (Vol. Ed.), *Handbook of child psychology, Vol. 3: Social, emotional, and personality development* (pp. 779–862). New York: Wiley.

Damasio, A. (1994). *Descartes' error: Emotion, reason, and the human brain.* New York: Avon.

Damasio, A. (2003). *Looking for Spinoza: Joy, sorrow, and the feeling brain.* New York: Harcourt.

Denham, S. (1986). Social cognition, prosocial behavior, and emotion in preschoolers: Contextual validation. *Child Development, 61,* 1145–1152.

Denham, S. (1998). *Emotional development in young children.* New York: Guilford Press.

Denham, S., McKinley, M., Couchoud, E., & Holt, R. (1990). Emotional and behavioral predictors of preschool peer ratings. *Child Development, 61,* 1145–1152.

Dodge, K. A., & Coie, J. D. (1987). Social-information-processing factors in reactive and proactive aggression in children's peer groups. *Journal of Personality and Social Psychology, 53,* 1146–1158.

Dodge, K. A., Lochman, J. E., Harnish, J. D., Bates, J. E., & Pettit, G. S. (1997). Reactive and proactive aggression in school children and psychiatrically impaired chronically assaultive youth. *Journal of Abnormal Psychology, 106,* 37–51.

Dunn, J. (1988). *The beginnings of social understanding.* Cambridge MA: Harvard University Press.

Dunn, J., Brown, J., & Maguire, M. (1995). The development of children's moral sensibility: Individual differences and emotion understanding. *Developmental Psychology, 31,* 649–659.

Dunn, L., & Dunn, L. (2001). *Peabody Picture Vocabulary Test* (3rd ed.). Circle Pines, MN: AGS.

Fabes, R., & Eisenberg, N. (1992). Young children's coping with interpersonal anger. *Child Development, 63,* 116–128.

Fine, S., Izard, C., Mostow, A., Trentacosta, C., & Ackerman, B. (2003). First grade emotion knowledge as a predictor of fifth grade self-reported internalizing behaviors in children from economically disadvantaged families. *Development and Psychopathology, 15,* 331–342.

Gardner, M. (1990). *Expressive one-word picture vocabulary test* (Rev. ed.). Los Angeles: Western Psychological Services.

Garner, P., Jones, D., & Miner, J. (1994). Social competence among low-income preschoolers: Emotion socialization practices and social cognitive correlates. *Child Development, 65,* 622–637.

Gibbs, J., & Schnell, S. (1985). Moral development "versus" socialization: A critique. *American Psychologist, 40,* 1071–1080.

Haidt, J. (2001). The emotional dog and its rational tail: A social intuitionist approach to moral development. *Psychological Review, 108,* 814–834.

Harris, P. (1983). Children's understanding of the link between situation and emotion. *Journal of Experimental Child Psychology, 36,* 490–509.

Harris, P. (1985). What children know about the situations that provoke emotions. In M. Lewis & C. Saarni (Ed.), *The socialization of emotion* (pp. 161–186). New York: Plenum.

Harter, S., & Buddin, N. (1987). Children's understanding of the simultaneity of two emotions: A five-stage developmental acquisition sequence. *Developmental Psychology, 23,* 388–399.

Hoffman, M. (2000). *Empathy and moral development: Implications for caring and justice.* Cambridge, UK: Cambridge University Press.

Hubbard, J., Smithmyer, C., Ramsden, S., Parker, E., Flanagan, K., Dearing, K., et al. (2002). Observational, physiological, and self-report measures of children's anger: Relations to reactive vs. proactive aggression. *Child Development, 73,* 1101–1118.

Hughes, C., & Dunn, J. (2000). Hedonism or empathy?: Hard-to-manage children's moral awareness and links with cognitive and maternal characteristics. *British Journal of Development Psychology, 18,* 227–245.

Izard, C. (1991). *The psychology of emotions.* New York: Plenum.

Izard, C., Dougherty, L., & Hembree, E. (1983). *A system for affect expression identification by holistic judgments (Affex).* Newark: University of Delaware, Instructional Resources Center.

Izard, C., Fine, S., Mostow, A., Trentacosta, C., & Campbell, J. (2002). Emotion processes in normal and abnormal development preventive intervention. *Development and Psychopathology, 14,* 761–787.

Keller, M., Schuster, P., Fang, F., Tong, H., & Edelstein, W. (1996, November). *Cognition and motivation in the development of moral feelings in early childhood.* Paper presented at Conference of the Association for Moral Education, Ottawa.

Keller, M., Lourenco, O., Malti, T., & Saalbach, H. (2003). The multifaceted phenomenon of "happy victimizers": A cross-cultural comparison of moral emotions. *British Journal of Developmental Psychology, 21,* 1–18.

Killen, M., & Nucci, L. (1995). Morality, autonomy, and social conflict. In M. Killen & D. Hart (Eds.), *Morality in everyday life: Developmental perspectives* (pp. 52–86). Cambridge, UK: Cambridge University Press.

Kochanska, G., Padavich, D., & Koenig, A. (1996). Children's narratives about hypothetical moral dilemmas and objective measures of their conscience: Mutual relations and socialization antecedents. *Child Development, 67,* 1420–1436.

Lemerise, E., & Dodge, K., (2000). The development of anger and hostile interactions. In M. Lewis & J. Haviland (Eds.), *Handbook of emotions* (2nd ed., pp. 594–606). New York: Guilford Press.

Lemerise, E., Scott, M., Diehl, D., & Bacher, B. (2000). *Understanding the emotions of victims and victimizers: Developmental, peer acceptance, and aggression-level effects.* Unpublished manuscript.

Lourenco, O. (1997). Children's attributions of moral emotions to victimizers: Some data, doubts, and suggestions. *British Journal of Developmental Psychology, 15,* 425–438.

Miller, A., & Olson, S. (2000). Emotional expressiveness during peer conflicts: A predictor of social maladjustment among high-risk preschoolers. *Journal of Abnormal Child Psychology, 28,* 339–352.

Murgatroyd, S., & Robinson, E. (1993). Children's judgments of emotion following moral transgressions. *International Journal of Behavioral Development, 16,* 93–111.

Murgatroyd, S., & Robinson, E. (1997). Children's and adults' attributions of emotion to a wrongdoer: The influence of the onlookers' reaction. *Cognition and Emotion, 11*(1), 83–101.

Nucci, L. (2001). *Education in the moral domain.* Cambridge, UK: Cambridge University Press.

Nunner-Winkler, G., & Sodian, B. (1988). Children's understanding of moral emotions. *Child Development, 59,* 1323–1338.

Oppenheim, D., Emde, R., & Warren, S. (1997). Children's narrative representations of mothers: Their development and associations with child and mother adaptation. *Child Development, 68,* 127–138.

Ramos-Marcuse, F., & Arsenio, W. (2001). Young children's emotionally-charged moral narratives: Relations with attachment and behavior problems and competencies. *Early Education & Development, 12,* 165–184.

Saarni, C. (1999). *The development of emotional competence.* New York: Guilford.

Schultz, D., Izard, C., & Ackerman, B. (2000). Children's anger attribution bias: Relations to family environment and social adjustment. *Social Development, 9,* 284–301.

Smetana, J., Campione-Barr, N., & Yell, N. (2003). Children's moral and affective judgments regarding provocation and relataliation. *Merrill-Palmer Quarterly, 49,* 209–236.

Smetana, J., Daddis, C., Toth, S., Cicchetti, D., Bruce, J., & Kane, P. (1999a). Effects of provocation on preschoolers' understanding of moral transgressions. *Social Development, 8,* 335–348.

Smetana, J., Toth, S., Cicchetti, D., Bruce, J., Kane, P., & Daddis, C. (1999b). Maltreated and nonmaltreated preschoolers' conceptions of hypothetical and actual moral transgressions. *Developmental Psychology, 35,* 269–281.

Turiel, E. (1983). *The development of social knowledge: Morality and convention.* Cambridge, UK: Cambridge University Press.

Turiel, E. (1998). The development of morality. In W. Damon (series Ed.) & N. Eisenberg (Vol. Ed.), *Handbook of child psychology, Vol. 3: Social, emotional, and personality development* (5th ed., pp. 863–932). New York: Wiley.

Van Zee, K., Lemerise, E., Arsenio, W., Gregory, D., & Sepcaru, S. (2000, April). *Developmental and contextual influences on "happy victimizer" expectancies.* Paper presented at the annual Conference on Human Development, Memphis.

Wilson, J. (1993). *The moral sense*. New York: Free Press.

Yuill, N., Perner, J., Pearson, A., Peerbhoy, D., & van den Ende, J. (1996). Children's changing understanding of wicked desires: From objective to subjective and moral. *British Journal of Developmental Psychology, 14,* 457–475.

Zelko, F., Duncan S., Barden, R., Garber, J., & Masters, J. (1986). Adults' expectancies about children's emotional responsiveness: Implication for the development of implicit theories of affect. *Developmental Psychology, 22,* 109–114.

22

AGGRESSION, DELINQUENCY, AND MORALITY: A SOCIAL–COGNITIVE PERSPECTIVE

MARIE S. TISAK
JOHN TISAK
BOWLING GREEN STATE UNIVERSITY

SARA E. GOLDSTEIN
UNIVERSITY OF NEW ORLEANS

This chapter focuses on aggression and delinquency in the context of relating social thinking with social behavior, specifically interrelations among aggression, delinquency, and morality. In the last 25 years, a tremendous amount of research via cognitive–developmental models has investigated the connection between social thinking and social behavior. However, with some exceptions (e.g., Harvey, Fletcher, & French, 2001), there has not been a discussion of the relationship among the different social–cognitive models as they relate to aggression, delinquency, and morality. Therefore, we describe the major theoretical social–cognitive paradigms that focus on these constructs including the social-domain model (Turiel, 1978, 1983), social–cognitive theory (Bandura, 1986), social information-processing theory (Crick & Dodge, 1994; Dodge & Crick, 1990), and the social cognitive information-processing model (Huesmann, 1988, 1998). Within this context, we discuss the manner in which these theories, in parallel and collectively, contribute to our understanding of the association between social–cognitive development and aggression.

THE CONNECTION BETWEEN AGGRESSION AND MORALITY

Various definitions have been utilized in studying morality (e.g., Kohlberg, 1969; Piaget, 1932/1965; Turiel, 1983), but generally *morality* consists of two dimensions. One dimension concerns positive actions and behaviors that benefit others, including sharing, helping, and comforting, which are usually referred to as prosocial behaviors (see Eisenberg, Spinrad, & Sadovsky, chap. 19, this volume, and Carlo, chap. 20, this volume).

The second dimension concerns negative actions and behaviors that could result in negative consequences to others and is referred to as *inhibitory* or *negative morality* (Tisak, 1986). The negative component includes actions pertaining to violations of the rights and welfare of individuals (Turiel, 1978, 1983), such as hitting someone, and violation of fairness (e.g., stepping in front of someone in line).

Aggression is part of the negative component of morality. There has been extensive debate on the various definitions of aggression (see reviews by Coie & Dodge, 1998; Parke & Slaby, 1983) but in this chapter, *aggression* refers to "any form of behavior that is intended to injure someone physically or psychologically," (Berkowitz, 1993, p. 3). Berkowitz's (1993) definition is also consistent with other descriptions, such as "behavior that is aimed at harming or injuring another person or persons" (Parke & Slaby, 1983, p. 550), as well as the definition of aggression expressed by Eron (1987), which is "an act that injures or irritates another person" (p. 435).

These definitions of aggression allow for the consideration of different forms of aggressive behavior, including property loss (e.g., theft, damage), direct physical acts (e.g., hitting, pushing), direct verbal attacks (e.g., threats, name calling), and more circuitously, relationally oriented behavior (e.g., spreading rumors, social exclusion with the intent to harm relationships). It is important to note that although relationally oriented aggression has been referred to as indirect (Björkqvist, Österman, & Kaukiainen, 1992; Lagerspetz, Bjökqvist, & Peltonen, 1988), relational (Crick, 1995), and social (Cairns, Cairns, Neckerman, Ferguson, & Gariepy, 1989; Galen & Underwood, 1997) aggression, in general these three constructs refer to a similar set of socially manipulative behaviors (see Underwood, Galen, & Paquette [2001a, 2001b] for further discussion.). These characterizations of aggression and the definition of the negative component of morality are interconnected due to the concern for the aggressor's violations of the rights and welfare of individuals (Tisak, 1995; Turiel, 1987).

DISTINCTIONS AMONG MORAL AND AGGRESSIVE BEHAVIORS

Although morality and aggression are interrelated, it is important to emphasize that not all negative moral violations involve aggression. A number of researchers have investigated moral violations that are distinct from aggression. For example, researchers have studied children's beliefs about lying to others (e.g., Bussey, 1992; Taylor, Lussier, & Maring, 2003), youths' beliefs about the fairness of laws (Helwig & Jasiobedzka, 2001) and the fairness of resource allocation (Sigelman & Waitzman, 1991). Helwig, Zelazo, and Wilson (2001) studied children's beliefs about scaring or embarrassing somebody. Others have investigated the development of prejudice beliefs in children (e.g., Augoustinos & Rosewarne, 2001; Killen, Lee-Kim, McGlothlin, & Stangor, 2002; Kowalski, 2003) and stereotyping (Horn, Killen, & Stangor, 1999). Although all these are moral infractions, they are not, by definition, aggression, even though they all entail infractions of others' rights and welfare.

CONGRUENCE AND DISTINCTIONS BETWEEN AGGRESSION AND DELINQUENCY

Although aggression can be a form of delinquency, all delinquent acts are not aggressive behaviors. It is also important to define delinquency. Specifically, *delinquency* is a legal term; delinquent acts are considered criminal offenses (committed by youth under the age of 18 years), which are determined either by federal, state (Anderson, 2003; Kowalski & Wilke, 2001), or municipal ordinance (*Anderson's*, 2003). However, as reported by Kowalski and Wilke (2001), some states lower the age to 17 (ten states) and even 16 years (three states), which has several implications. For example, if persons are no longer considered juveniles (as determined by the state), they could be prosecuted as adults, resulting in different criminal procedures and consequences. Regardless of the source, it is estimated that over two million arrests of youth under the age of 18 years have occurred in 2000 (National Center for Juvenile Justice [NCJJ], 2001) and 2001 (Federal Bureau of Investigation [FBI], 2002). These statistics strongly suggest that juvenile offenders must be included in the assessment of social thinking about issues pertaining to aggression.

Categories of delinquent criminal acts have been defined by federal agencies (e.g., FBI, 1994; NCJJ, 1989). The major categories include (a) crimes against persons, such as assault, (b) crimes against property, such as burglary, (c) drug law violations, such as drug use, (d) crimes against public order, such as disorderly conduct, (e) status offenses, such as truancy, and (f) motor vehicle violations, such as driving under suspension. Further discussion of these categories is reported in Tisak and Jankowski (1996) and Tisak, Tisak, and Goldstein (2004).

Additionally, as noted by Black (1968) and Wiebush (1993), criminal offenses may vary in severity, intent, and type of punishment within a particular crime category, which define the offense as either a felony or a misdemeanor. As an illustration, crimes such as robbery, homicide, and aggravated assault are crimes against persons and are usually classified as felony crimes. However, even though simple assault is included within the category of crimes against persons, this type of assault is considered a misdemeanor. Correspondingly, criminal acts within the category of crimes against property can be classified as either a misdemeanor, such as trespassing, or as a felony, such as burglary (Tisak & Jankowski, 1996).

It is important to recognize that aggression may or may not be considered a delinquent act. That is, depending on the severity of the aggression, the form of the aggression, as well as whether the aggressive behavior is designated as a crime by an existing ordinance, the act may or may not be classified as delinquency. As an illustration, aggressive behavior that involves harming others through relationships (which is central to the way that indirect, relational, and social aggression have been defined and operationalized) is typically not a delinquent act. In addition, consider two incidences of verbal aggression: name calling involving insults to a peer's appearance versus threatening to seriously injure a peer or a member of a peer's family, especially with a use of a weapon. The former is not considered a delinquent act, whereas the latter is. Nonetheless, numerous aggressive behaviors indeed fall within the realm of delinquency, including crimes against persons as well as crimes against property.

Correspondingly, not all delinquent acts are aggressive. For example, certain drug violations would not be considered aggressive (e.g., marijuana use) nor would several types of status offenses (e.g., truancy). It is also important to note, however, that a predominance of research in developmental psychology has focused on nondelinquent aggressive actions, which occur in the school setting, such as a child pushing a peer down or stealing a peer's lunch. One explanation may be that most of the research focuses on early and middle childhood and behaviors that typically occur in a school setting.

Theories of Social–Cognitive Development and Relationship to Social Behavior

Nonaggressive, aggressive, and delinquent youths' evaluations of social issues and their relationship to aggressive behavior have been explained from many different theoretical models, too many to review here. This chapter focuses on social–cognitive models that are most germane to aggression and delinquency. Given the tremendous number of studies that have explored the relationship between social thinking and aggression, it is important that these models be examined. Furthermore, for each model, we have selectively considered the research most relevant to the intersection of morality, aggression, and delinquency.

Domain Model of Social Cognition

One important model in understanding the relationship between social–cognitive development and aggression is the domain model of social cognition poised by Turiel (1978, 1983). The basis of the social domain model is the premise that concepts are organized within different social knowledge domains, which are constructed out of the individual's interaction with the environment (Turiel, 1978, 1983). Specifically, three distinct social domains have been identified. The *moral domain* (as described) pertains to the rights and welfare of others. Examples of behavior that fall within the moral domain are hitting and stealing because they involve the violation of individual's rights and welfare. The *conventional domain* pertains to arbitrary rules of conduct, which facilitate the social organization of individuals. An example of a behavior falling within the conventional domain is social address, such as calling a teacher by his or her formal name instead of the first name (Turiel, 1983). The *personal domain*, which has been described by Nucci (1981; Nucci & Turiel, 2000), concerns actions that primarily affect the individual, such as choice of friends.

With regard to the moral domain, Turiel (1983) illustrates that there are three ways in which a child gains information regarding moral transgressions. The child may be a victim and therefore has direct experiences of the consequences of the acts, such as being hurt or losing an object. A child may be the instigator and receives information from the victim (his or her response, such as crying or protesting), as well as the response from others, including teachers, parents, and peers. A third way in which a child learns about the ramifications of negative moral actions is by being a witness; consequently he or she sees the impact on the victim as well as the response to the instigator on the part of others.

The majority of research using the social domain theoretical approach during the last 25 years has focused on children's evaluations of moral rules in comparison to conventional violations (for past reviews see Helwig, Tisak, & Turiel, 1990; Smetana, 1995; Tisak, 1995; and for current reviews see Harvey et al., 2001; Smetana, chap. 5; Turiel, chap. 1, this volume). Typically the stories pertaining to negative morality, using the social domain model consists of physical or direct transgressions such as stealing a toy, stealing someone's lunch, hitting, or pushing a child.

Morality and Conventions: Nonaggressive Populations.   With some exceptions to be described, most of the research within the social domain model has concentrated on nonaggressive children and adolescents. Moreover, the predominant methodology has been individual semistructured interviews. The results have been consistent in demonstrating that children from as young as 3 years of age consider it wrong to negate rules pertaining to morality, including aggressive acts. Furthermore, moral violations are still considered wrong even if there are no rules regulating the behaviors. In addition, negative moral violations are considered wrong across contexts, such as schools or towns (see reviews in Helwig et al., 1990; Smetana, 1995; Tisak, 1995). In contrast, conventional rules are considered arbitrary. They can be negated and the violations of conventions are only wrong if there is an explicit rule, and the rules do not generalize from one context to another.

Additionally, rules regulating morality are considered more important and violations more wrong than conventional violations.

Interestingly, the reasons or justifications children and adolescents provide in supporting their evaluations of negative moral behaviors pertain to individual's rights, welfare, and justice. For example, justifications for physical and psychological harm focus on welfare, whereas acts such as stealing, concern both welfare and the issue of fairness. The justifications that relate to the negative effects on others lend credence to the definitions of aggression described (Coie & Dodge, 1998; Eron, 1987; Parke & Slaby, 1983; Turiel, 1987). In contrast to the justifications provided for the moral behaviors, the reasons supporting conventional judgments pertained to sanctions, custom, order and authority (Turiel, 1983).

Morality and Personal/Prudence: Nonaggressive Populations. Another area of research based on the domain model of social reasoning has been the assessment of children's thinking about personal acts, in comparison to conventions and negative moral behaviors. As noted, behaviors characterized within the personal domain are those that primarily affect the individual, and usually do not involve health or harm (Nucci, 1981; Nucci & Turiel, 2000), such as the choice of friends or recreational activity. When asked to rank moral transgressions, conventional violations, as well as personal violations, children rank moral transgressions as the most wrong, whereas the personal violations are considered the least wrong. The overall findings reveal that children from a young age consider actions, such as choice of friends, to be under personal jurisdiction and outside societal regulations and moral concerns (see reviews in Helwig et al., 1990; Smetana, 1995; Tisak, 1995).

Nonetheless, there are personal behaviors that may involve harm to oneself, which are referred to as *prudential behaviors* (Tisak & Turiel, 1984). Thus, moral and prudential behaviors are similar in that the consequences of both actions can result in harm or injury. However, the major distinction between negative moral behaviors and prudential acts is that the former involves social interactions between people (one child hitting another child), and the prudential acts concern only the individual (putting oneself in harm's way). Research has shown that children as young as preschool age (Tisak, 1993) consider moral transgression more wrong than prudential violations. Furthermore, although preschoolers consider it wrong for mothers to permit either moral or prudential acts, they consider the moral violations, but not prudential violations, wrong, when mothers permit the acts to occur.

Morality, Conventions, and Personal: Diverse Populations. The domain model of social cognition also has assessed relationships between social thinking and social behavior. For example, in an earlier study, Smetana (1981) reported that women who viewed abortion as a personal issue (primarily affecting the mother) rather than a moral issue (pertaining to the welfare of the fetus) were more likely to state that abortion was acceptable and were more likely to seek an abortion. In a later study Smetana (1984) found that children who were abused considered psychological distress to be more universally wrong than did neglected children. However, neglected children considered the unfair distribution of resources to be more universally wrong than did abused children.

Other research with aggressive and delinquent children and adolescents has demonstrated that the type of act being evaluated is instrumental in influencing social evaluations by early school-aged aggressive children (Dodge & Price, 1994), aggressive and nonaggressive adolescents (Crane-Ross et al., 1998), and adolescent offenders (Tisak & Jankowski, 1996; Tisak, Lewis, & Jankowski, 1997; Tisak et al., 2004). Nucci and Herman (1982), for example, examined school-aged children categorized as normally behaved with those labeled as behaviorally disordered. The criteria for categorizing children as behaviorally disordered were based on a range of behaviors, such as fidgetiness, fighting, clowning, depression, and hallucination. The researchers found that both groups of children rated moral transgressions as more wrong than conventional violations; violations of rules concerning personal issues were rated as least wrong. Nonetheless, Nucci and Herman (1982) reported that normal children were more likely to view moral transgressions as wrong in the absence of explicit rules than did behaviorally disordered children. In addition, normal children were more likely to view personal items as within personal jurisdiction than did the behaviorally disordered children.

Another interesting finding reported by Nucci and Herman (1982) was that when considering moral transgressions, children with behavioral disorders were inclined to focus on conventional components of these acts (e.g., the acts could lead to punishment or the acts were forbidden) instead of the negative implications that the behaviors had for the victim. In a related study, Astor (1994) found that violent and nonviolent children considered unprovoked aggressive situations to be wrong and justified their responses using moral justifications (e.g., welfare issues). In contrast, only the violent children considered it acceptable to use aggression in a provoked situation (e.g., in response to name calling) and also justified their responses by referring to moral justifications (e.g., reciprocal justice).

Other research with older populations has also noted a relationship between social thinking and aggression. Specifically, Crane-Ross and colleagues (1998) found that adolescents' belief that aggression is acceptable predicted aggressive behavior, and the belief that conventional violations (i.e., arbitrary rules of conduct, such as forms of address) are legitimate, predicted convention-violating behavior.

Research has also used the domain model to investigate youth offenders' evaluations of moral, conventional, and personal rules (Tisak & Jankowski, 1996). Consistent with past research, youth offenders (felons and misdemeanants) considered moral rules more important and the transgressions more wrong than conventional rules and violations. Additionally, the youth offenders judged the moral (aggressive) transgressions to be less acceptable when permitted by authority and more deserving of punishment as compared to conventional violations. Again congruent with prior research, personal rules were ranked less important than both moral and conventional transgressions.

At the same time, however, there were differences in judgments due to offender status and the domain of the rule, in particular the conventional and personal rules. In particular, the felons, in contrast to the misdemeanants, rated the personal rules to be more important and the violators of conventional rules to be more deserving of punishment. In comparison to the misdemeanants, the felons may have had greater experiences with punishments for various criminal offenses, and therefore became more sensitive to punishment issues. The felons had a higher rate of arrests (mean = 6.9 for the felons; 2.16 for the misdemeanants) for a greater diversity of criminal offenses (Tisak & Jankowski, 1996).

Tisak and Jankowski (1996) reported that the reasons provided by the youth offenders for the conventional and moral (aggressive) acts were not consistent with prior research findings. That is, in response to the moral and the conventional transgressions, the youth offenders referred to both moral and conventional reasons to support their judgments. Although the moral reasons concerned the welfare of the victim, they also utilized a variety of conventional reasons, such as the existence of law, punishment, and the need for explicit laws to prevent the behaviors from occurring.

As further discussed by Harvey and colleagues (2001), it may be that youth who are frequently aggressive are viewing aggressive behavior more similarly to the way that their less aggressive peers view other types of social behaviors. In other words, aggressive youth may be viewing aggressive behavior as social conventions (see Tisak & Jankowski, 1996) or as matters typically within the personal domain (Harvey et al., 2001).

Assessment of Dimensions of Criminal Activity: Delinquent Populations. Based on the theoretical premise of the domain model, it would be expected that youth who are involved in the criminal justice system (youth offenders) would not evaluate various delinquent behaviors, including those that encompass aggression, in the same manner. In a recent study (Tisak et al., 2004), adolescent offenders were asked to assess a series of behaviors with regard to whether it would be legitimate for the government to make laws prohibiting the criminal acts. The criminal behaviors evaluated were designed to represent the different delinquent dimensions identified by the criminal justice system (e.g., FBI, 1994, 2001).

Therefore in support of this premise, confirmatory factor analyses demonstrated that items representing different dimensions of criminality (i.e., severe physical harm, sexual offenses, weapon offenses, theft, motor vehicle, property damage, drugs, status offenses, and public order) formed a unidimenional scale (one factor for each dimension). Additionally, the authors (Tisak et al., 2004) calculated the percentages of youth offenders who did not think it was acceptable to have laws regulating these illegal behaviors. The results revealed that 16.1% (severe physical harm) to 60% (status offenses) of the youth offenders did not think it was acceptable to have laws prohibiting these behaviors. The findings suggest that not only are there different dimensions of delinquent activity, but that youth offenders' thinking about the legitimacy of the government to make laws regulating these acts depended on the dimension, with more offenders' stating that nonaggressive acts should not be within the realm of the legal system.

Social–Cognitive Model

Bandura's (1986, 1991) social–cognitive theory also has examined how aggressive and nonaggressive children differ in their thinking about their social world. Whereas the domain model of social cognition is based on Piagetian constructivism (Turiel, 1983), Bandura's social–cognitive theory is based on learning theory. Specifically, Bandura's theory focuses on both the development of behavior and competencies (e.g., how do children learn to behave aggressively?), and the regulation of behavior (e.g., what type of cognitions might deter a child from hitting another child?). Social–cognitive theory includes a broad range of behaviors, not just aggression, but the models discussed in the following sections represent specific outgrowths of social cognitive theory that focus on aggression. However, Bandura's social cognitive theory (1986, 1991) is discussed first, because it provides a useful framework to consider the relations between social and moral thought and social behavior.

According to social–cognitive theory (Bandura, 1986, 1991), several processes are involved in the development and learning of social behavior. One critical factor is *observational learning,* whereby a child watches an adult or another child engage in a particular behavior and learns how to also engage in the behavior. Exploratory activities (e.g., exploratory play) and verbal instruction (e.g., direct teaching on the part of a parent or a teacher) are also important learning opportunities. Once a behavior has been learned, a child then integrates this new behavior into his or her preexisting behavioral repertoire. In the process of integration and cognitive synthesis, rules and strategies for contextualized action (i.e., when and where particular behaviors should be and can be emitted) are established. At first, engaging in a novel behavior in a particular context is challenging and requires a good deal of cognitive effort. However, over time and with practice the behavior becomes routine and a high degree of cognitive effort is no longer needed.

Once a behavior has become routine in a specific context, *perceived self-efficacy*, or an individual's beliefs about her or his "capabilities to organize and execute the courses of action required to produce given attainments" (Bandura, 1997, p. 3), become important. Social–cognitive theory posits that beliefs about one's abilities in one situation often generalize to beliefs about abilities in other situations. That is, perceived self-efficacy with regard to one activity is related to perceived self-efficacy with regard to another activity.

Moral thinking comes into play with regard to people's beliefs about what happens when they engage in action (their outcome expectancies), and whether they want those results to occur. Social cognitive theory contends that several types of outcome expectancies are important, including (a) beliefs about what happens externally (e.g., "if I hit the kid, will I get his toy?"), (b) beliefs about what happens to others (e.g., " if I hit the kid, will it hurt him?"), and (c) beliefs about what I think of myself (e.g., "if I hit the kid, will I think that I am a mean, nasty boy?"). Thus, if individuals exercise forethought, they can anticipate the way that they will feel about engaging in various types of behavior, and this forethought might either encourage or discourage the particular behavior.

Bandura and colleagues (Bandura, 1999; Bandura, Caprara, Barbaranelli, Pastorelli, & Regalia, 2001) have proposed two aspects of this process, referred to as *moral agency*— inhibitive agency and proactive agency. *Inhibitive agency* refers to the ability to refrain from acting in a negative manner toward others, and *proactive agency* is the ability to behave prosocially or humanely. Once people have engaged in an action, they react negatively or positively. If they act in a negative manner toward others, it is likely that they will engage in negative self-evaluations (e.g., "that was so mean, I really hurt that kid when I hit him"), which acts to deter future, similar behavior. Similarly, positive self-evaluations encourage future, similar behavior.

However, according to social–cognitive theory, negative self-reactions or self-sanctions for aggressive or other types of transgressive behavior need to be activated to discourage such behavior. There are several different mechanisms by which self-sanctions might not be activated (Bandura, 1991, 1999), which would then make aggressive or transgressive behavior more likely. Individuals can engage in moral justification, whereby they make aggression or other transgressive behaviors acceptable by justifying it as worthy or moral (e.g., killing during war combat). People can also use their language to make a transgressive act seem less negative (e.g., using time-out as a form of discipline rather than hitting a child). Additionally, people can compare a negative act to one of greater magnitude to make the act seem relatively benign (e.g., name calling may not seem that bad compared to threatening someone with a knife).

People can also distance themselves from causing the harmful outcomes, which they contribute to, for example, by diffusing responsibility (e.g., a group of boys beat up a classmate, and they all feel like their individual role was not as important) or by minimizing the harm that their action caused (e.g., a girl hits a classmate but thinks to herself, "at least I didn't draw any blood"). Social–cognitive theory also points out that dehumanizing the victim can also help justify harmful conduct (e.g., a girl thinks it is okay to tease an overweight classmate because she is not popular, rather than another child with real feelings), as can blaming the victim (e.g., the boy who left his wallet on the lunch table deserved to have it stolen). Thus, when individuals engage in a line of thinking that allows them to justify or minimize the effects of their interpersonally harmful behavior, social–cognitive theory posits that harmful behavior is more likely.

The social–cognitive theoretical model (Bandura, 1991) has stimulated a number of studies focusing on aggressive and nonaggressive children's thinking about their values and beliefs regarding aggressive actions (Arsenio, 1988; Bear, 1989; Boldizar, Perry, & Perry, 1989; Dodge, Lochman, Harnish, Bates, & Pettit, 1997; Guerra, Nucci, & Huesmann, 1994; Hudley, 1992; Huesmann & Guerra, 1997; Perry, Perry, & Rasmussen, 1986). As an illustration, Archer and Haigh (1997) reported that higher instrumental scores (having control over others) predicted higher levels of reported acts of physical aggression. Furthermore, other researchers have shown that aggression is related to children's belief that aggression is acceptable (Guerra & Slaby, 1990; Perry & Bussey, 1977; Slaby & Guerra, 1988). Moreover, aggressive children are more confident that their aggression will result in tangible rewards (e.g., get what they wanted), in contrast to nonaggressive children (Crane-Ross et al., 1998; Perry et al., 1986).

In a classic study based on the social cognitive theory, Boldizar and associates (1989) asked aggressive and nonaggressive children to indicate how badly they would feel when particular consequences resulted from their aggressive acts. Aggressive and nonaggressive children differed in the values they placed on the outcome of aggression. Compared to nonaggressive children, the aggressive individuals valued control over the victim and were less concerned about the suffering of the victim, about retaliatory action on the part of the victim, and about the possibility of peer rejection due to their aggressive behavior.

With regard to relational aggression, Delveaux and Daniels (2000) found positive associations between ratings of relationally aggressive conflict resolution strategies and the social goals of the desire to maintain relationships among the peer group and the desire to avoid trouble. Consistent with these findings, Goldstein and Tisak (2004) reported that relationally aggressive adolescents had relatively positive outcome expectancies for their relationally aggressive behavior. Finally, there is also evidence suggesting that youth who are relatively approving of responding to peer provocation with indirect aggression are more likely to use indirect aggression themselves (Musher-Eizenman et al., 2004).

Social Information-Processing Model

A third paradigm investigating the association between thinking about aggression and aggressive behavior is based on Dodge's (Dodge & Crick, 1990) social information-processing model. This model was derived from cognitive, social psychological, as well as social learning theories, to elucidate the relationship between children's thinking and their social behavior. According to the social information-processing model, a child's response to a problematic behavioral situation (e.g., being hit) is a function of following a sequence of steps in the processing of social information. The revised model includes a series of six interactive steps (Crick & Dodge, 1994). The first step includes the encoding of both external and internal cues based on the situational information (e.g., noting that the instigator looked surprised at what happened). An interpretation of the cues (e.g., judging it was an accident because the person has not done this in the past) defines the second step in the process. In the third step, children choose a desired outcome or goal (e.g., retaliating or walking away).

In the fourth step, Crick and Dodge (1994) indicate that children access from memory possible responses (e.g., how they responded in the past). However, for a new situation, they may have to generate a unique behavioral response. Step five is referred to as *response decision*. There are several important components to the decision process, such as the child's evaluation of the quality of the social behavior, which usually is based on "moral rules or values (e.g., a belief that hitting people is a bad thing to do)" (p. 89). The other aspects of the response decision include *outcome expectancies,* that is, what could be the result of the behavior; *self-efficacy evaluations,* referring to how successful a child believes that he or she would be in performing the behavior; and *response selection,* or searching for the most positive response to enact (pp. 90–91).

Finally, based on their evaluation, children proceed to the final step, in which they behaviorally enact to the situation. In summary, as described by Crick and Dodge (1994), children undergo a decision-making process prior to enacting a behavioral response to a social cue that includes evaluation, outcome expectation analysis, self-efficacy evaluation, as well as the response selection, and enactment.

Huesmann (1988) also proposed an information-processing framework. However, Huesmann's model was designed to explain the cognitive mechanisms that contribute to the development and maintenance of aggressive behavior. In a more recent paper, however, Huesmann (1998) describes a model that integrated the Crick and Dodge (1994) and his earlier (1988) models. In this revised model, Huesmann emphasizes four steps. Step one involves attending to and interpreting situational cues (e.g., a child noticing that a peer is looking her or his way, and interprets the look as a mean glare). Thus, Crick and Dodge's (1994) steps one and two appear to be included in step one of Huesmann's (1988) model. Step two of Huesmann's (1998) unified model pertains to script search and retrieval, with a *script* being a mental representation of how an event typically transpires and the types of behaviors and responses that typically occur within the context of a particular event (e.g., a child's ideas about what typically happens when two peers get into an argument). This process is similar to step four of Crick and Dodge's model.

Step three of Huesmann's (1988) model involves script evaluation, which pertains to individual's evaluations of whether a script is acceptable for a particular situation. Evaluating whether the script is acceptable entails deciding whether the script is appropriate (e.g., a child believes that it is okay to hit a peer if involved in a conflict), whether the script will lead to a desired outcome (e.g., a child believes that hitting a peer will result in obtaining a toy that the peer is playing with), and whether the child is able to enact the particular behavior spelled out by the script (e.g., a child considers whether he or she is able to hit a peer). Step three has overlapping dimensions of step five of Crick and Dodge's (1994) model. Finally, step four of Huesmann's (1998) model involves a behavioral response as well as an evaluation of the consequences of the behavioral response. For example, a child hits another child who had been playing with a desired toy, obtains the desired toy for him- or herself, and gets reprimanded by a teacher who witnessed the incident. Additionally, the child evaluates the environment's responses to the incident (e.g., perhaps the child was pleased by the extra attention from the teacher).

Consistent with both the Crick and Dodge (1994) and the Huesmann (1998) models, research demonstrates that aggressive children often process information about social situations in a way that differs from their nonaggressive peers. That is, research has shown that aggressive children, in contrast to their nonaggressive peers, perceive, interpret, and evaluate their social behavior in a way that enhances the likelihood of aggressive behavior (Boxer & Dubow, 2002; Crick & Dodge, 1994; Dodge & Crick, 1990; Huesmann, 1988, 1998). Therefore, aggressive youth are considered to be less competent in their processing of social information than their nonaggressive peers, and the manner in which they process social information contributes to a likelihood of behaving aggressively in the future.

To illustrate, consider how aggressive children search their environment for social cues (steps one and two in Crick and Dodge [1994] and step one in Huesmann [1998]). Research demonstrates that aggressive children, in contrast to their nonaggressive peers, search their environment for fewer cues and are less attentive to socially relevant cues.

Moreover, aggressive youth typically remember hostile cues more often than other types of cues (Dodge & Newman, 1981). Finally, Crick (1995) found that relationally aggressive children, as compared to their nonrelationally aggressive peers, perceived greater hostility in relational provocation situations.

To further illustrate the distinction between aggressive and nonaggressive children's thinking abut aggression, consider research demonstrating differing efficacy beliefs about responding to social situations (step three of Huesmann's model, step five of Crick and Dodge's model; Perry et al., 1986), differing goals for social situations (step three of Huesmann's model, step three of Crick and Dodge's model; e.g., Delveaux & Daniels, 2000; Erdley & Asher, 1996; Lochman, Wayland, & White, 1993), or the research pertaining to outcome expectancies for aggression (step three of Huesmann's model, step five of Crick and Dodge's model; e.g., Cuddy & Frame, 1991; Goldstein & Tisak, 2004; Hall, Herzberger, & Skowronski, 1998).

Social Processing Theory: Peers' Responses as a Victim of Aggression.

Although the majority of research has focused on what an aggressive child versus a nonaggressive child would do in an aggressive or ambiguous situation, another important component is the investigation of how children think peers respond as a victim of aggression. In earlier research it was shown that children consider retaliation to be a normative response for a victim of peer aggression (Piaget, 1932/1965; Rogers & Tisak, 1996; Youniss, 1980). Dodge (1980) also reported that when an aggressive act was perceived to be intentional, aggressive as well as nonaggressive boys responded in kind with aggression. A series of observational studies (Nucci & Nucci, 1982; Nucci & Turiel, 1978; Smetana, 1984; Tisak, Nucci, & Jankowski, 1996) found that aggression occurs quite frequently in the preschool environment and that retaliation is one of the most common forms of response to aggression by peers. These data support other research showing that retaliation is considered legitimate in response to an unprovoked act of aggression (Ferguson & Rule, 1988; Rogers & Tisak, 1996).

There are several factors that appear to influence children's thinking about peers' response as a victim of aggression. One factor is that children must be able to produce solutions that are viable, and they must be competent to evaluate the effectiveness of the solution (Crick & Dodge, 1994). For example, it has been reported that aggressive children often respond with aggression in situations where it is not warranted, or in ambiguous situations (Dodge, 1980; Dodge & Somberg, 1987). Furthermore, in the Richard and Dodge (1982) study, aggressive boys were asked to generate and evaluate solutions to interpersonal conflicts. The aggressive boys were only able to generate one effective response and the other solutions were mainly hostile in content.

When evaluating children's thinking about peers' responses to aggression it is also critical to consider that children and adolescents recognize what peers would do may be different from what peers should do (Sobesky, 1983; Tisak & Turiel, 1988). In fact, a number of studies (Rogers & Tisak, 1996; Tisak & Tisak, 1996a, 1996b) reveal that children and adolescents make a distinction between peers' expected (would) and peers' prescribed (should) behavior. For example, Rogers and Tisak (1996) reported that as a victim of physical harm and property loss, fourth and sixth graders indicated that peers should report the incident to an authority such as a teacher because of the concern for the peer's well being. However, they recognized that the victim was more likely to retaliate against the instigator as a way of "pay back." The younger children (second graders) responded that a victim would most likely tell an authority and judged that is what the victim should do. As the researchers explain, older children were more likely to state that peers would retaliate because of the need for independence. These findings lend further support to the claim that a number of variables may be influencing children's evaluations of peers' responses to aggression.

A third variable that appears to influence children's thinking about peer responses to aggression is the relationship of the individuals involved in the dispute (Dodge & Coie, 1987; Perry, Perry, & Kennedy, 1992; Rogers & Tisak, 1996; Tisak, Maynard, & Tisak, 2002; Tisak & Tisak, 1990, 1996a, 1996b; Tisak et al., 1997). Both aggressive and nonaggressive children consider the past behavior of the peer whose behavior is in question when making intent attributions (Dodge, 1980; Dodge & Frame, 1982). As discussed, the way in which a child thinks about the causes of a particular negative social situation (e.g., being bumped in the hallway) is critical for determining whether or not a child reacts aggressively in a particular social situation. Hostile intent is more likely to be assumed if the provocateur's past behavior has been physically aggressive (Boxer & Tisak, 2005; Dodge, 1980; Dodge & Frame, 1982).

As an example, Boxer and Tisak (2005) reported that elementary school-aged children view aggression as a trait in that aggression is perceived to continue across time and across contexts. Furthermore, these children did not believe that peers who are thought to be aggressive could be changed. Other research (Goldstein, Tisak, Persson, & Boxer, 2004) suggests that this may also the case with regard to peers who are seen as relationally aggressive. Specifically, Goldstein and associates (2004) reported that elementary school aged children were more likely to attribute hostile intent to peers known to be relationally aggressive, as compared to peers known to be prosocial.

Likewise, a series of studies have demonstrated that variables, such as the status of the victim to the perpetrator (being a good friend or an acquaintance), are important in children's thinking about peers' response to aggression (Tisak et al., 2002; Tisak & Tisak, 1996a, 1996b). Also important is the form of the aggression. For example, Tisak and Tisak (1996b) found that when the aggressive act involves physical harm, young adolescents (sixth and eighth graders) indicated that the victim would retaliate against both a good friend and an acquaintance. In response to whether retaliating was the right thing to do after an incident of physical harm, these adolescents indicated that when the aggressor was a good friend, the victim should either talk it over with the aggressor or walk away to avoid an escalation of aggression. However, in response to an acquaintance, adolescents indicated that the right thing to do would be to walk away.

In contrast, when the aggression involved stealing by a friend, young adolescents stated that peers would and should confront the perpetrator to demand restitution. When the instigator was an acquaintance, however, the adolescents indicated that peers would be expected and should involve an authority, namely, a teacher (Tisak & Tisak, 1996b). These data further support the assertion that in considering responses to aggression, individuals take into consideration several social–contextual variables, such as the relationship of the aggressor to the victim, the type of aggressive acts, beliefs about what peers would do and should do in such a situation, and the ramifications of response choices.

Social Processing Skills: The Delinquent Population. Overall the literature reviewed suggests that, in comparison to nonaggressive children, aggressive youth think about information in different ways, which may account for their aggressive behavior. In the majority of the studies, participants have been young school-aged children. Therefore, most of these aggressive children had not committed criminal offenses. However, as noted over two million arrests of youth under the age of 18 years occurred in 2001 (FBI, 2002), suggesting that youth offenders are a critical population to include in assessing their social processing skill (e.g., with regard to their views about aggression and their thinking about peers' responses as victims of aggression). Indeed, past research has shown that nonaggressive adolescents' social thinking differs from those who have engaged in criminal offenses (Chandler, 1973; Hains, 1984; Hoffman, Wolf, & Addad, 1997; Slaby & Guerra, 1988; Tisak & Jankowski, 1996; Tisak et al., 1997). For example, Chandler (1973) compared the role-taking skills of delinquent (those with multiple police contacts) and nondelinquent, 11- and 13-year-olds. In comparison to the nondelinquent children, delinquent children were deficient in their ability to separate their point of view from that of others.

In a relevant and classic study, Slaby and Guerra (1988) compared three groups of adolescents (15 to 18 years of age) on their beliefs about aggression. One group consisted of adolescents incarcerated for serious criminal acts including robbery, rape, and murder. They were compared to high school students rated by teachers as being either high or low on aggression. The authors reported that "low-aggressive, high-aggressive, and antisocial-aggressive [incarcerated] groups represent increasing levels of aggression that were consistently related to both a decreasingly extensive display of social problem-solving skills and an increased endorsement of nonnormative beliefs concerning aggression" (Slaby & Guerra, 1988, p. 586). For example, in comparison to the low- and high-aggressive adolescents, the incarcerated group believed that aggression was legitimate, that aggression helped them to avoid negative images of themselves, and that victims do not suffer. Furthermore, the incarcerated adolescents were the most likely to solve problems by interpreting the situation as hostile, choosing hostile solutions, and not seeking additional facts to assess the problem.

Other researchers have also shown that youth offenders' solutions to problems are not very adept. Tisak and colleagues (1997) investigated adolescent offenders' thinking about the role of a bystander when either a friend or an acquaintance of the bystander was the victim of an aggressive act. There were several interesting findings. First, these youth judged that peers would respond when a friend was a victim of either hitting or stealing, but not when the victim was an acquaintance. In research with nonaggressive populations, adolescents indicated that peers would respond regardless of the relationship of the witness to the victim (Tisak & Tisak, 1996b). Second, when the aggression involved hitting, the majority either could not generate a response or generated a hostile response (e.g., fight the aggressor). They rarely suggested negotiation or mediation strategies as nonaggressive adolescents do (Tisak, 1986; Tisak & Tisak, 1996a, 1996b). One interpretation is that the youth offenders did not consider the parties involved capable of resolving the aggressive encounter. This assessment might demonstrate one area in which the youth offenders exhibited a deficiency in the processing of social information (Tisak et al., 1997).

Additionally, another important finding pertained to when youth offenders were asked whether the bystander's response was appropriate. Even when they indicated the behavior of the bystander was not appropriate (e.g., to fight or to take the money him- or herself) they, nonetheless, were unable to generate a viable solution.

Finally, other research has shown that delinquent youth, in comparison to their nondelinquent peers, have a distortion in their processing of social information. For example, Liau, Barriga, and Gibbs (1998) assessed whether there was a difference between delinquent and nondelinquent adolescents on the association between self-serving cognitive distortions (e.g., being self-centered, blaming others) and overt antisocial behaviors (i.e., confrontational, such as fighting) versus covert antisocial behaviors (i.e., concealed acts, such as stealing). The authors reported a stronger relationship between "self-serving cognitive distortion" and antisocial behavior for the delinquent versus the nondelinquent population. Furthermore, participants' agreement with overt antisocial behavior (e.g., "people need to be roughed up once in a while"; p. 336) was associated with overt antisocial behavior. Conversely, agreeing with the covert antisocial behavior (e.g., "if someone is careless enough to lose a wallet, they deserve to have it stolen"; p. 336) was associated with covert antisocial behavior. Interestingly, there was no relationship between agreeing with covert antisocial behavior and overt antisocial behavior and vice versus.

CONCLUSIONS AND FUTURE DIRECTIONS

In this chapter we reviewed several social–cognitive paradigms in discussing the interconnection between aggression, delinquency, and morality. Although these theoretical models are utilized in parallel, they illustrate the importance of investigating the connection between social–cognitive development and aggression. Specifically, the social–cognitive theories described postulate that aggressive and delinquent individuals perceive, interpret, and evaluate their social world in a manner that is consistent with behaving aggressively and being involved in delinquent behaviors.

This discussion leads to new research focusing on the integration of the social–cognitive models to further our understanding of aggressive and delinquent behaviors as they pertain to morality. For example, continued investigations about values and beliefs that are associated with different forms of aggression and delinquency are warranted. Additionally, the inclusion of justification data to understand the child's thinking about aggression will also facilitate our understanding of their perceptions, interpretations and evaluations of issues pertaining to aggression and delinquency.

As a final point it is important to note that the integration of these models can be usefully in understanding other developmental processes. For example, Lemerise and Arsenio (2000) have integrated the social information-processing model (Crick & Dodge, 1994) and Turiel's (1983) domain model in understanding emotional processes in development. Therefore, in addition to exploring the relationship among the social–cognitive models to aggression and delinquency, these models are also important in assessing other developmental processes as other researchers (e.g., Harvey et al., 2001; Lemerise & Arsenio, 2002) have demonstrated.

ACKNOWLEDGMENT

We thank Paul Boxer and David Mullins for their assistance, suggestions, and comments.

REFERENCES

Anderson's Ohio family law handbook (14th ed., 2003). Cincinnati, OH: Anderson Publishing Co.

Archer, J., & Haigh, A. M. (1997). Do beliefs about aggressive feelings and actions predict reported levels of aggression? *British Journal of Social Psychology, 36,* 83–105.

Arsenio, W. F. (1988). Children's conceptions of situational affective consequences of sociomoral events. *Child Development, 59,* 1611–1622.

Astor, R. A. (1994). Children's moral reasoning about family and peer violence: The role of provocation and retribution. *Child Development, 65,* 1054–1067.

Augoustinos, M., & Rosewarne, D. L. (2001). Stereotype knowledge and prejudice in children. *British Journal of Developmental Psychology, 19,* 143–156.

Bandura, A. (1986). *Social foundations of thought and action.* Englewood Cliffs, NJ: Prentice-Hall.

Bandura, A. (1991). Social cognitive theory of moral thought and action. In W. M. Kurtines & J. L. Gewitz (Eds.), *Moral behavior and development: Advances in theory, research, and applications* (Vol 1., pp. 45–103). Hillsdale, NJ: Lawrence Erlbaum Associates.

Bandura, A. (1997). *Self-efficacy: The exercise of control.* W. H. Freeman and Company: New York.

Bandura, A. (1999). Moral disengagement in the perpetration of inhumanities. *Personality and Social Psychology Review, 3,* 193–209.

Bandura, A., Caprara, G. V., Barbaranelli, C., Pastorelli, C. & Regalia, C. (2001). Sociocognitive self-regulatory mechanisms governing transgressive behavior. *Journal of Personality and Social Psychology, 80,* 125–135.

Bear, G. G. (1989). Sociomoral reasoning and antisocial behaviors among normal sixth graders. *Merrill-Palmer Quarterly, 35,* 181–196.

Berkowitz, L. (1993). *Aggression: Its causes, consequences, and control.* Philadelphia: Temple University Press.

Björkqvist, K., Österman, K., & Kaukiainen, A. (1992). The development of direct and indirect aggressive strategies in males and females. In K. Björkqvist & P. Niemeliä (Eds.), *Of mice and women: Aspects of female aggression* (pp. 51–64). San Diego, CA: Academic Press.

Black, H. C. (1968). *Black law dictionary.* St. Paul, MN: West Publishing Company.

Boldizar, J. P., Perry, D. G., & Perry, L. C. (1989). Outcome values and aggression. *Child Development, 60,* 571–579.

Boxer, P., & Dubow, E. F. (2002). A social cognitive information processing model for school-based aggression reduction and prevention programs: Issues for research and practice. *Applied and Preventive Psychology, 10,* 177–192.

Boxer, P., & Tisak, M. S. (2005). Children's beliefs about the continuity of aggression. *Aggressive Behavior, 31,* 172–188.

Bussey, K. (1992). Lying and truthfulness: Children's definitions, standards, and evaluative reactions. *Child Development, 63,* 129–137.

Cairns, R. B., Cairns, B. D., Neckerman, H. J., Ferguson, L. L., & Gariepy, J. (1989). Growth and aggression: 1. Childhood to early adolescence. *Developmental Psychology, 25,* 320–330.

Chandler, M. J. (1973). Egocentrism and antisocial behavior: The assessment and training of social perspective-taking skills. *Developmental Psychology, 9,* 326–337.

Coie, J. D., & Dodge, K. A. (1998). Aggression and Antisocial Behavior. In W. Damon (Series Ed.) & N. Eisenberg (Vol. Ed.), *Handbook of child psychology: Vol. 3, Social, emotional, and personality development* (5th ed., pp. 779–862). New York: Wiley.

Crane-Ross, D. A., Tisak, M. S., & Tisak, J. (1998). Aggression and conventional rule violation among adolescents: Social-reasoning predictors of social behavior. *Aggressive Behavior, 24,* 347–365.

Crick, N. R. (1995). Relational aggression: The role of intent attributions, feelings of distress, and provocation type. *Development and Psychopathology, 7,* 313–322.

Crick, N. R., & Dodge, K. A. (1994). A review and reformulation of social Information-processing mechanisms in children's social adjustment. *Psychological Bulletin, 115,* 74–101.

Cuddy, M. E., & Frame, C. (1991). Comparisons of aggressive boys' self- efficacy and outcome expectancy beliefs. *Child Study Journal, 21,* 135–152.

Delveaux, K. D., & Daniels, T. (2000). Children's social cognitions: Physically and relationally aggressive strategies and children's goals in peer conflict situations. *Merrill-Palmer Quarterly, 46,* 672–692.

Dodge, K. A. (1980). Social cognition and children's aggressive behavior. *Child Development, 51,* 162–170.

Dodge, K. A., & Coie, J. D. (1987). Social-information processing factors in reactive and proactive aggression in children's peer groups. *Journal of Personality and Social Psychology, 53,* 1146–1158.

Dodge, K. A., & Crick, N. R. (1990). Social information-processing bases of aggressive behavior in children. *Personality and Social Psychological Bulletin, 16,* 8–22.

Dodge, K. A., & Frame, C. L. (1982). Social cognitive biases and deficits in aggressive boys. *Child Development, 53,* 620–635.

Dodge, K. A., Lochman, J. E., Harnish, J. D., Bates, J. E., & Pettit, G. S. (1997). Reactive and proactive aggression in school children and psychiatrically impared chronically assaultive youth. *Journal of Abnormal Psychology, 106,* 37–51.

Dodge, K. A., & Newman, J. P. (1981). Biased decision-making processes in aggressive boys. *Journal of Abnormal Psychology, 90,* 375–379.

Dodge, K. A., & Price, J. M. (1994). On the relation between social information processing and socially competent behavior in early school-aged children. *Child Development, 65,* 1385–1397.

Dodge, K. A., & Somberg, D. A. (1987). Hostile attributional biases among aggressive boys are exacerbated under conditions of threats to self. *Child Development, 1,* 213–224.

Erdley, C. A., & Asher, S. R. (1996). Children's social goals and self efficacy perceptions as influences on their responses to ambiguous provocation. *Child Development, 67,* 1329–1344.

Eron, L. D. (1987). The development of aggressive behavior from the perspective of a developing behaviorism. *American Psychologist, 42,* 435–442.

Federal Bureau of Investigation (FBI). (1994). *Uniform crime report for the United States.* Washington, D.C.: U.S. Department of Justice.

FBI. (2002). *Uniform Crime Report for the United States.* Washington, D.C.: U.S. Department of Justice.

Ferguson, T. J., & Rule, B. G. (1988). Children's evaluations of retaliatory aggression. *Child Development, 59,* 961–968.

Galen, B. R., & Underwood, M. K. (1997). A developmental investigation of social aggression among children. *Developmental Psychology, 33,* 589–600.

Goldstein, S. E., & Tisak, M. S. (2004). Adolescents' outcome expectancies about relational aggression within acquaintanceships, friendships, and dating relationships. *Journal of Adolescence, 27,* 283–302.

Goldstein, S. E., Tisak, M. S., Persson, A. P., & Boxer, P. (2004*). Children's attributions for and reactions to the ambiguous provacation of relationally aggressive, overtly aggressive, and prosocial peers.* Manuscript submitted for publication.

Guerra, N. G., Nucci, L., & Huesmann, L. R. (1994). Moral cognition and childhood aggression. In. L. R. Huesmann (Ed.), *Aggressive behavior: Current perspectives* (pp. 13–33). New York: Plenum Press.

Guerra, N. G., & Slaby, R. G. (1990). Cognitive mediators of aggression in adolescent offenders: 2: Intervention. *Developmental Psychology, 26,* 269–277.

Hains, A. A. (1984). Variables in social cognitive development: Moral judgment, role-taking, cognitive processes, and self-concept in delinquents and nondelinquents. *Journal of Early Adolescence, 4,* 65–74.

Hall, J. A., Herzberger, S. D., & Skowronski, K. J. (1998). Outcome expectancies and outcome values as predictors of children's aggression. *Aggressive Behavior, 24,* 439–454.

Harvey, R. J., Fletcher, J., & French, D. J. (2001). Social reasoning: A source of influence on aggression. *Clinical Psychology Review, 21,* 447–469.

Helwig, C. C., & Jasiobedzka, U. (2001). The relation between law and morality: Children's reasoning abut socially beneficial and unjust laws. *Child Development, 72,* 1382–1393.

Helwig, C. C., Tisak, M. S., & Turiel, E. (1990). Children's social reasoning in context. *Child Development, 61,* 2068–2078.

Helwig, C. C., Zelazo, P. D., & Wilson, M. (2001). Children's judgments of psychological harm in normal and noncanonical situations. *Child Development, 72,* 66–81.

Hoffman, H., Wolf, Y., & Addad, M. (1997). Moral judgment by criminals and conformists as a tool for examination of sociological predictions. *International Journal of Offender Therapy and Comparative Criminology, 41,* 180–198.

Horn, S. S., Killen, M., & Stangor, C. (1999). The influence of stereotypes on adolescent moral reasoning. *Journal of Early Adolescence, 19,* 98–113.

Hudley, C. A. (1992). Attributions for pride, anger, and guilt among incarcerated adolescents. *Criminal Justice & Behavior, 19,* 189–205.

Huesmann, L. R. (1988). An information processing model for the development of aggression. *Aggressive Behavior, 14,* 13–24.

Huesmann, L. R. (1998). The role of social information processing and cognitive schema in the acquisition and maintenance of habitual aggressive behavior. In R. G. Geen & E. Donnerstein (Eds.), *Human aggression: Theories, research, and implications for social policy* (pp. 73–109). San Diego, CA: Academic Press.

Huesmann, L. R., & Guerra, N. G. (1997). Children's normative beliefs about aggression and aggressive behavior. *Journal of Personality and Social Psychology, 72,* 408–419.

Killen, M., Lee-Kim, J., McGlothlin, H., & Stangor, C. (2002). How children and adolescents evaluate gender and racial exclusion. *Monographs of the Society for Research in Child Development, 67*(4, Serial No. 271).

Kohlberg, L. (1969). Stage and sequence: The cognitive-developmental approach to socialization. In Gosling, D. (Ed.), *Handbook of socialization theory and research* (pp. 347–480). Chicago: Rand McNally.

Kowalski, G. S., & Wilke, A. S. (2001). Juvenile delinquency prediction. In C. D. Bryant (Ed.), D. Luckenbill & D. Peck (Vol. Eds.), *Encyclopedia of criminology and deviant behavior, Vol 11: Crime and juvenile delinquency* (pp. 352–358). Philadelphia: Runner-Routledge.

Kowalski, K. (2003). The emergence of ethnic and racial attitudes in preschool-aged children. *Journal of Social Psychology, 143,* 677–690.

Lagerspetz, K. M., Björkqvist, K., & Peltonen, T. (1988). Is indirect aggression typical of females? Gender differences in aggressiveness in 11- to 12-year-old children. *Aggressive Behavior, 14,* 403–414.

Lemerise, E. A., & Arsenio, W. F. (2000). An integraded model of emotion processes and cognition in social information processing. *Child Development, 71,* 107–118.

Liau, A. K., Barriga, A. Q., & Gibbs, J. C. (1998). Relations between self-serving cognitive distortions and overt vs. covert antisocial behavior in adolescents. *Aggressive Behavior, 24,* 335–346.

Lochman, J. E., Wayland, K. K., & White, K. J. (1993). Social goals: Relationship to adolescent adjustment to social problem solving. *Journal of Abnormal Child Psychology, 21,* 135–151.

Musher-Eizenman, D. R., Boxer, P., Danner, S., Dubow, E. F., Goldstein, S. E., & Heretick, D. (2004). The relation between self-regulatory and environmental factors and aggressive behavior: Social-cognitive information-processing mediators. *Aggressive Behavior, 30,* 389–408.

National Center for Juvenile Justice (NCJJ). (1989). *Juvenile court statistics.* Washington, D.C.: Government Printing Office.

NCJJ. (2001). *Crime in the United States 2000.* Washington, D.C.: Government Printing Office.

Nucci, L. P. (1981). The development of personal concepts: A domain distinct from moral or societal concepts. *Child Development, 52,* 114–121.

Nucci, L. P., & Herman, S. (1982). Behavioral disordered children's conceptions of moral, conventional, and personal issues. *Journal of Abnormal Child Psychology, 10,* 411–426.

Nucci, L. P., & Nucci, M. (1982). Children's social interactions in the context of moral and conventional transgressions. *Child Development, 53,* 403–412.

Nucci, L. P., & Turiel, E. (1978). Social interactions and the development of social concepts in preschool children. *Child Development, 49,* 400–407.

Nucci, L. P., & Turiel, E. (2000). The moral and the personal: Sources of conflicts. In L. Nucci, G. Saxe, & E. Turiel (Eds), *Culture, thought, and development* (pp. 115–140). Mahwah, NJ: Lawrence Erlbaum Associates.

Parke, R. D., & Slaby, R. G. (1983). The development of aggression. In E. M. Hetherington (Ed.) & P. H. Mussen (Series Ed.), *Handbook of child Psychology, Vol 4: Socialization, personality, and social development.* (pp. 567–641). New York: Wiley.

Perry, D. G., & Bussey, K. (1977). Self-reinforcement in high- and low-aggressive boys following acts of aggression. *Child Development, 48,* 653–657.

Perry, D. G., Perry, C., & Kennedy, E. (1992). Conflict and the development of antisocial behavior. In C. U. Shantz & W. W. Hartup (Eds.), *Conflict in child and adolescent development* (pp. 301–329). New York: Cambridge University Press.

Perry, D. G., Perry, L. C., & Rasmussen, P. (1986). Cognitive social learning meadiators of aggression. *Child Development, 57,* 700–711.

Piaget, J. (1932/1965). *The moral judgment of the child.* New York: Free Press.

Richard, B. A., & Dodge, K. A. (1982). Social maladjustment and problem solving in school-aged children. *Journal of Consulting and Clinical Psychology, 50,* 226–233.

Rogers, M. J., & Tisak, M. S. (1996). Children's reasoning abut responses to peer aggression: Victim's and witness's expected and prescribed behaviors. *Aggressive Behavior, 22,* 259–269.

Sigelman, C. K., & Waitzman, K. A. (1991). The development of distribute justice orientations. Contextual influences on children's resource allocations. *Child Development, 62,* 1367–1378.

Slaby, R. G., & Guerra, N. G. (1988). Cognitive mediators of aggression in adolescent offenders I. Assessment. *Developmental Psychology, 24,* 580–588.

Smetana, J. G. (1981). Reasoning in the personal and moral domains: Adolescent and young adult women's decision-making regarding abortion. *Journal of Applied Developmental Psychology, 2,* 211–226.

Smetana, J. G. (1984). Toddlers' social interactions regarding moral and conventional transgressions. *Child Development, 55,* 1767–1776.

Smetana, J. G. (1995). Morality in context: Abstractions, ambiguities, and applications. In R. Vasta (Ed.), *Annals of child development* (Vol 10, pp. 83–130). London: Jessica Kingsley.

Sobesky, W. E. (1983). The effects of situational factors on moral judgments. *Child Development, 54,* 575–584.

Taylor, M., Lussier, G. L., & Maring, B. L. (2003). The distinction between lying and pretending. *Journal of Cognition and Development, 4,* 299–323.

Tisak, J., Maynard, A. M., & Tisak, M. S. (2002). AIRA: Measurement of adolescents' judgments regarding intentions to respond to physical and verbal aggression. *Aggressive Behavior, 28,* 207–223.

Tisak, M. S. (1986). Children's conceptions of parental authority. *Child Development, 57,* 166–176.

Tisak, M. S. (1993). Preschool children's judgments of moral and personal events involving physical harm and property damage. *Merrill-Palmer Quarterly, 39,* 375–390.

Tisak, M. S. (1995). Domains of social reasoning and beyond. In R. Vasta (Ed.), *Annals of child development* (Vol. 11, pp. 95–130). London: Jessica Kingsley.

Tisak, M. S., & Jankowski, A. M. (1996). Societal rule evaluations: Adolescent offenders' reasoning about moral, conventional, and personal rules. *Aggressive Behavior, 22,* 195–207.

Tisak, M. S., Lewis, T., & Jankowski, A. M. (1997). Expectations and prescriptions for responding to peer aggression: The adolescent offenders' perspective. *Aggressive Behavior, 23,* 149–160.

Tisak, M. S., Nucci, L., & Jankowski, A. M. (1996). Preschool children's social interactions involving moral and prudential transgressions: An observational study. *Early Education and Development, 6,* 169–180.

Tisak, M. S., & Tisak, J. (1990). Children's conceptions of parental authority, friendship, and sibling relations. *Merrill-Palmer Quarterly, 36,* 347–367.

Tisak, M. S., & Tisak, J. (1996a). My sibling's but not my friend's keeper: Reasoning about responses to aggressive acts. *Journal of Early Adolescence, 16,* 324–339.

Tisak, M. S., & Tisak, J. (1996b). Expectations and judgments regarding bystanders' and victims' responses to peer aggression among early adolescents. *Journal of Adolescence, 19,* 383–392.

Tisak, M. S., Tisak, J., & Goldstein, S. E. (2004). *Laws governing juvenile criminal activity: Assessing the perspective of the youth offender.* Manuscript submitted for publication.

Tisak, M. S., & Turiel, E. (1984). Children's conceptions of moral and prudential rules. *Child Development, 55,* 1030–1039.

Tisak, M. S., & Turiel, E. (1988). Variation of seriousness of transgressions and children's moral and conventional concepts. *Developmental Psychology, 24,* 352–357.

Turiel, E. (1978). Social regulations and domains of social concepts. In W. Damon (Ed.), *New directions for child development, Vol. 1: Social cognition.* San Francisco, CA: Jossey-Bass.

Turiel, E. (1983). *The development of social knowledge: Morality and convention.* Cambridge, MA: Cambridge University Press.

Turiel, E. (1987). Potential relations between the development of social reasoning and childhood aggression. In D. Crowell, I. Evans, & C. R. O'Donnell (Eds.), *Childhood aggression and violence: Sources of influence, prevention and control* (pp. 95–114). New York: Plenum.

Underwood, M. K., Galen, B. R., & Paquette, J. A. (2001a). Hopes rather than fears, admirations rather than hostilities: A response to Archer and Björkqvist. *Social Development, 10,* 275–280.

Underwood, M. K., Galen, B. R., & Paquette, J. A. (2001b). Top ten challenges for understanding gender and aggression in children: Why can't we all just get along? *Social Development, 10,* 248–266.

Weibush, R. G. (1993). Juvenile intensive supervision. The impact on felony offenders diverted from institutional placement. *Crime and Delinquency, 39,* 68–89.

Youniss, J. (1980). *Parents and peers in social development: A Sullivan-Piaget Perspective.* Chicago: University of Chicago Press.

VII

Moral Education, Character Development, and Community Service

The chapters in this section focus on applications of moral development theories and research to community service and educational programs. Chapter 23, by Daniel Hart, Robert Atkins, and Thomas Donnelly, addresses the role of community service in moral development. As Hart, Atkins, and Donnelly note, scholars have tracked and used community service as an index of the "moral health" of American adolescents; community service can be seen as a measure of committed moral action. Furthermore, community service can serve as a powerful tool for facilitating moral development, particularly in adolescence. The authors demonstrate how opportunities for community service address fundamental moral questions, which include what is the right thing to do and what are the qualities that make for a good person. The authors draw on their extensive research on moral identity formation, personality influences, and criteria for morally exemplary action to situate community service in a broader conceptual and developmental framework, one that examines antecedents and outcomes of community service in adolescent development.

The next three chapters are written by moral education theorists who have developed, evaluated, and measured the effectiveness of moral and character education programs. The two dominant approaches to moral education can be characterized in terms of traditional character education and approaches that focus on stimulating reflective reasoning, or what Darcia Narvaez refers to in Chapter 26 as *rational moral education*. These two approaches stem from different philosophical positions; following from Aristotle, *traditional character education* is designed to inculcate virtuous traits of character. Following from Kant, *reflective reasoning* approaches aim to encourage children to "know the good," usually defined in terms of universalist Kolhlbergian stage 6 concepts of justice. There has been considerable debate over the years about the virtues of these two approaches, but recently, and as reflected in two of the chapters in this section, there also have been attempts to reach a détente through a synthesis of the two positions.

In Chapter 24, Larry Nucci critiques the character education agenda and discusses the developmental aims of moral education from the perspective of social–cognitive domain theory. He elaborates on the implications of this theoretical perspective for moral education and classroom practices, including the social–emotional climate of the classroom, classroom management, conflict resolution, and attempts to engage students in service learning. Nucci outlines the requirements of a developmental approach to moral education, including a correspondence between the domain of the focal issues of the curricula and the content of the school assignments, and engagement in cognitive reflection. Chapter 25, by Marvin Berkowitz, Stephen Sherblom, Melinda Bier, and Victor Battistich, attempts to bridge the great divide between character education and reflective reasoning approaches by focusing on the broader construct of positive youth development. With the aim of identifying the characteristics that lead to healthy psychosocial development, they analyze components and identify common characteristics of several different conceptual approaches to youth development, including prevention science, social–emotional learning, and character education, and then evaluate the components of school-based implementation programs that appear to be effective in stimulating positive youth development. Chapter 26, by Darcia Narvaez, offers a different vision of a hybrid approach. Her approach, which she calls *Integrative Ethical Education,* builds on the strengths of moral and character education approaches, while also including insights from recent research in cognitive science. After reviewing other approaches, she elaborates on her model, which is grounded on the notion of expertise development, and she carefully and thoroughly elucidates a detailed model of moral education. The four chapters in this section are informed by different theoretical traditions and have very different visions, but they indicate that the theories and issues discussed by scholars in this handbook are very much at the heart of current debates about how best to apply moral development theories to classrooms, schools, parenting, and the various other contexts that youth inhabit.

23

COMMUNITY SERVICE AND MORAL DEVELOPMENT

DANIEL HART
RUTGERS UNIVERSITY

ROBERT ATKINS
RUTGERS UNIVERSITY

THOMAS M. DONNELLY
RUTGERS UNIVERSITY

Almost every activity in which children and adolescents participate has moral dimensions, and consequently almost every activity that individuals engage in can be explored from a moral perspective. During the history of investigation on moral development, these investigations have included the relation of moral development to sexual behavior, drug use, cheating in school, and delinquency, to name a few (for reviews of literature at different points in time, see Blasi, 1980; Hartshorne & May, 1928; Turiel, 1998). A century of research cannot be accurately condensed in a sentence, but the evidence suggests that the relation of moral development to daily activities is complicated and often difficult to discern.

Against the backdrop of one hundred years of research on the relation of a wide range of youthful activities to moral development, it might be asked why an entire chapter in a handbook on moral development is devoted to community service. There are two reasons that make a review of the relation of community service to moral development especially important and consequently deserving of the extended consideration provided in this chapter. The first is that community service has often been used to assess the moral health of generations of American adolescents. For example, Putnam (2000), in his enormously influential review of the well-being of democratic life in the United States, judged that high levels of voluntary community service in recent cohorts of youth may be the only promising sign of civic vitality in younger Americans. Similarly, year-to-year changes in voluntary community service are used to track change in adolescents' prosocial behavior (e.g., Child Trends, 2002). Because community service is one of the most prominent public indicators of moral virtue in American youth, it warrants careful exploration. As we explain in later sections, community service does not always reflect prosocial motivation—adolescents may volunteer to improve their prospects for admission to college, for example—and consequently we do not endorse reliance on rates of community service participation as an unambiguous marker of moral health. Nonetheless, because community service frequently both contributes to public welfare and reflects moral sensibilities, we do judge it to be an important indicator of ethical life.

Second, community service is not only viewed as a sign of moral character, but also as an exceptionally powerful means for facilitating moral development. In its report extolling the virtues of community service, the National Commission on Service-Learning concluded that community service "helps students increase their knowledge of community needs, become committed to an ethic of service, and develop a more sophisticated understanding of politics and morality" (2001, p. 26). Youniss and Yates (1997) suggested that youth participation in community service contributes to moral development by generating interest in addressing community problems and increasing confidence in one's ability to be an effective force for change.

The broad interest in community service combined with the recent emergence of substantial research on the topic make the time ripe for a thorough examination of community service and moral development. In the sections that follow, we develop a conceptual framework within which community service and moral development can be examined, identify the developmental pathways that lead children and adolescents into community service, and assess the influence of community service on moral development in youth.

CONCEPTUAL FRAMEWORK

Community Service

Community service refers to voluntary activity that benefits the community. Researchers who study community service and its relation to development make five distinctions. First, many researchers believe that motivations for community service vary substantially (e.g., Omoto & Snyder, 1995). For example, although many people performing community service do so to contribute to the welfare of their fellow citizens, others become involved in community service for instrumental purposes such as adding an activity to a college application in the hopes of improving the odds of admission. The same behavior—community service—can therefore have strikingly different motivational underpinnings.

Second, some researchers believe that the duration of community service is an important characteristic. Community service performed over a long period of time is viewed as a better marker of moral character than is occasional community service (e.g., Hart & Fegley, 1995). Similarly, duration may be important for understanding the influence of community service on development. It is certainly reasonable to assume that there is a dosage–effect relation, with frequent community service over an extended period of time having a greater effect on development than infrequent community service.

Third, the type of community service activity may be very important. McClellan and Youniss (2003) suggested that the developmental effects of participation in cleaning up a neighborhood park or filing papers at a neighborhood center may be very different from those resulting from working in a soup kitchen. Killen and Horn (2000) noted that community service participation may reflect moral concerns, social–conventional concerns, or personal issues and they emphasized that the influence of these factors on moral development is not uniform.

Fourth, the extent to which community service is genuinely voluntary is likely to be of consequence (e.g., Stukas, Snyder, & Clary, 1999). At the extremes, the benefits derived from community service that is performed as an alternative to incarceration probably are different than those that idealistic adolescents receive from their volunteer efforts in Amnesty International. Within these extremes, there is a great deal of interest in the question of whether adolescents benefit from community service mandated by their schools (e.g., McClellan & Youniss, 2003).

Finally, many advocates for community service believe that structured reflection and discussion are necessary for community service to foster psychological development (e.g., Leming, 2001). This is because the implications of the community service activities may not be fully evident. For example, serving food to homeless adults in an urban soup kitchen can be an opportunity to explore issues such as mental illness, poverty, and social justice; explorations of these topics can benefit from introspection and guided discussion.

Two points should be made about these five qualities of community service. First, the empirical basis for the importance of the five distinctions concerning community service is thin. Consequently, it is impossible to estimate precisely the empirical consequences of ignoring these distinctions, as most research does. Second, there are no studies in which all five qualities have been assessed. It is certainly possible that if such research were conducted, the findings would suggest that some combinations of qualities are tightly linked to moral development and that other combinations are not. This would be an advance over the current state of knowledge, in which the relations of community service to moral development are relatively weak and diffuse. Although there is not as yet compelling evidence demonstrating that the distinctions are important and that some combinations of distinctions are relevant and others are not, the distinctions do have sufficient face validity to conclude that community service is a multifaceted construct.

The Moral Domain

Advocates for community service sometimes see it as the cure to whatever moral ills afflict youth in the United States. For example, The National Commission on Service-Learning suggested that community service can prepare "students for citizenship through involvement in citizen action," reduce "violence and sexual activity," and increase the "sense of responsibility" (2001, p. 4). As we noted in the previous section, community service connotes a range of activities of varying durations, and at least some of these are associated with the assortment of morally related outcomes noted by the National Commission on Service-Learning. However, the National Commission's report, and the views of many advocates reflected in the report, seems to suggest that the benefits of community service can be found across all aspects of moral functioning. Such a perspective seems to minimize the distinctive qualities of both community service and of the moral domain. We believe that advances in understanding are most likely if community service is considered in relation to a differentiated view of the moral domain and moral psychology. In our view community service is more closely aligned with some aspects of morality than with others.

Three Moral Questions.   Williams (1995, p. 551) has suggested that the moral domain traditionally considered by philosophers is constituted of attempts to answer three broad questions: (1) What is the right thing to do?; (2) How is the best possible state of affairs achieved?; and (3) What qualities make for a good person? The first of these questions, focusing on the right thing to do, stakes out the traditional territory of deontic theories like Kant's (1964), which seek to promote human autonomy and individual rights. The second question, concerned with public welfare, has occupied utilitarian and political philosophers. Finally, virtue ethicists from Aristotle through the present time have sought to identify the characteristics essential to being a moral person. Williams argues that although the three questions overlap to a large degree—and consequently most philosophical theories seek to answer all three—each provides a slightly different orientation to moral life.

Community service is potentially related to all three questions. Certainly advocates of community service believe that adolescents' deontic reasoning, their views of a good society, and their character can be improved through community service. To preface the conclusion to this chapter, our review of the research literature suggests that the best evidence for a relation between moral life and community service is within the facet of morality concerned with the best possible state of affairs. In other words, entry into community service seems to be motivated by individuals' efforts to bring about the best possible state of affairs rather than to seek justice or to pursue virtue (for a review of motives associated with volunteering, see Clary et al., 1998).

Psychological Underpinnings. Moral action, of which community service is presumed to be one form and to be one source, has roots in cognition, emotion, and behavior (for a discussion, see Hart, Burock, London, & Miraglia, 2003). Cognition is involved in relatively automatic inferences about the feelings and thoughts of others, social norms (e.g., Haidt, 2001), and in the deliberative judgments that precede some actions and structure automatic inferences (Hart & Killen, 1995). Emotion and affect, particularly sympathy and distress, are profoundly important in the motivation of prosocial behavior (Eisenberg & Fabes, 1998). Finally, a host of processes govern the initiation and termination of behaviors that together constitute moral action. Typically, advocates of the importance of community service as marker and source of moral life have overlooked the complicated psychological machinery involved in moral action. As we proceed through the review, we examine the links of community service to the different components of moral psychology.

Overview

We proceed in two directions. The next section reviews research in which community service is an outcome. Most of this research presumes that community service is an important marker of moral action, and consequently the goal is to understand the precursors to community service. We integrate this research by adapting a conceptual model developed in our previous research (Hart, Atkins, & Ford, 1998, 1999). This section is followed by a review of research which views community service as a source for moral development; we again use our conceptual model to integrate the research, but in this section seek to identify how community service might influence, rather than follow from, the elements of the conceptual model. In the final section, we offer concluding and integrative comments.

PATHWAYS TO COMMUNITY SERVICE

Why do some people invest their personal resources (time, energy, safety, financial capital) into actions that benefit others? A full answer to this question is likely to require an *organismic* explanation, according to which a multitude of individual and contextual

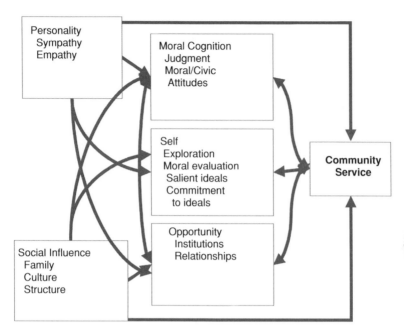

FIG. 23.1   Developmental pathways to entry into community service.

factors interact over time to produce volunteer community service. In this section, we discuss many of these factors, using a conceptual model for organization.

Conceptual Model

In this chapter, we adapt our model of moral identity formation (Hart, Atkins, & Ford, 1998, 1999) and focus it specifically on community service. This model is depicted in Figure 23.1. On the left edge of the model are *personality* and *social influences,* characteristics presumed to be enduring influences on individuals' behavior. *Personality* can be defined as the "distinctive and unique pattern of thinking, feeling, and behaving that determines how we respond to different situations" (Caspi, 1998, p. 318). To foreshadow the results of the review, research suggests that persons who are better able to regulate their emotions, interact well with others, and are characterized by generally positive moods are more likely to participate in community service than are others without these characteristics.

The model also posits that enduring social influences contribute to entry into community service. For example, research demonstrates that parental relationships and familial social class are linked directly to community service and to related factors.

In the center column of the model are the mediating factors proposed to influence, and to be influenced by, community service: moral judgment/attitudes, self and identity, and opportunities. The available evidence suggests that these variables develop and change more than the constructs at the left edge of the model, and consequently we posit that intervention is best directed here, rather than targeted at personality and social influences (Hart, Atkins, & Ford, 1998).

Moral judgments and moral attitudes include the constellation of cognitions that are associated with moral action. Developmental psychologists in the tradition of Piaget (1965) and Kohlberg (1963/1984) have accrued some evidence to indicate that moral judgment development is related to community service (Comunian & Gielen, 1995). Social psychologists have more frequently studied attitudes and values, which are also largely cognitive, and these too have relations to community service (Wilson & Musick, 1997).

Self-conceptions and ideals also are associated with entry into community service. Moral action may require the adoption of idealized self-images that secure commitment to challenging prosocial undertakings. In turn, particularly stressful moral actions may contribute to self-images capable of sustaining commitment (Hart, Yates, Fegley, & Wilson, 1995).

Finally, participation in community service is much more likely when individuals are members of social networks and institutions that provide opportunities to participate in moral action. Of course, individual and social influences affect one's relationship with these social networks and institutions. For example, many participants in community service report that they were recruited by their friends and family (Independent Sector, 1999).

Penner (2002) has proposed a model similar to ours to account for sustained volunteering in adulthood, and Eisenberg (see Eisenberg & Fabes, 1998) has related many of the components in our model to the development of prosocial behavior. Penner's model is organized temporally and suggests that an array of demographic factors, personality traits, and personal values motivate and sustain volunteering. *Volunteering* and *community service* are largely synonymous, and therefore the overlap between Penner's model and ours is unsurprising. Similarly, community service can be seen as one form of prosocial behavior (e.g., Omoto & Snyder, 1995), and consequently the vast literature on prosocial behavior can be drawn upon to flesh out our account of the factors associated with community service.

Personality and Prosocial Behavior

Empathy. *Empathy*, the awareness and affective reaction to another's emotional experience, is an important constituent to the prosocial personality. Empathy has two dimensions. The first dimension of empathy, *perspective taking*, is a cognitive process that improves as a child becomes less egocentric and develops the ability to see the world from the point of view of others (Lapsley, 1996). Spontaneous helping is more likely if the individual is able to infer the perspective of others who are in need of assistance (Unger & Thumuluri, 1997).

The second dimension of empathy, *empathic concern* or *sympathy*, refers to the observer's affective response of concern and compassion for someone in need (Davis et al., 1999). The propensity for sympathy is correlated with volunteering (Davis et al., 1999; Eisenberg et al., 1989; Eisenberg & Okun, 1996); those who understand another's perspective and experience compassion for others in need are more likely to enter community service than are those who do not. For example, Penner, Fritzsche, Craiger, and Freifeld (1995) describe their measure of the prosocial personality, which has scales for *other-oriented empathy,* or sympathy, and *helpfulness,* the propensity to aid others. They report that both scales predicted volunteering. Similarly, in a large sample drawn from readers of Sunday newspapers, Penner (2002) found that persons high in other-oriented empathy are more likely to volunteer, and to persist longer in volunteer roles, than are others. The same pattern is true of individuals high in helpfulness (Penner & Finkelstein, 1998; Penner & Fritzsche, 1993).

Emotional Regulation and Emotionality.   The tendency to experience sympathy when witnessing others in need appears to be associated with emotional regulation and emotional tone. *Emotional regulation* refers to the capability for appropriate modulation of affect and impulse. Low emotional regulation may result in prolonged, exaggerated mood states that interfere with effective adaptation. Depression, for example, is a consequence of an inability to temper profoundly negative emotions. Similarly, frequent outbursts of angry aggression signal an inability to regulate affect arising in conflicts with others. When low emotional regulation is paired with chronically negative moods or emotional tone, personal distress is likely to result when an individual is exposed to the needs of others; conversely, individuals who tend toward positive emotionality and higher levels of emotional regulation are more likely to experience sympathy when confronted with the others in need (Eisenberg, 2000; Eisenberg & Fabes, 1998).

There is evidence to suggest that childhood emotional regulation and positive emotionality predict prosocial behavior into adulthood. For example, a longitudinal study conducted by Newman, Caspi, Moffit, and Silva (1997) with a sample of children from New Zealand provides additional evidence that childhood disposition predicts prosocial behavior. Newman and his colleagues (1997) found that in comparison to other children, children who were poor in emotional regulation and prone to negative emotions were less likely to behave prosocially in adulthood. Hart, Atkins, and Ford (1998) used data from the National Longitudinal Survey of Youth to examine the relationship of emotion regulation (as indexed by internalization and externalization) to volunteering in adolescence. Internalizing and externalizing tendencies in youth, assessed through maternal reports, were inversely related to entry into community service 2 years later.

Social Functioning. Prosocial children are more outgoing and socially competent (Eisenberg & Okun, 1996; Eisenberg & Fabes, 1998) than children low in prosocial tendencies. Moreover, empathetic and prosocial children are likely to enjoy positive social interactions with their peers (Farver & Branstetter, 1994). Finally, as compared to their peers who are less empathetic, children categorized as prosocial also tend to be lower in aggression and other types of externalizing behaviors (Eisenberg, 2003). Consequently, we infer that children and adolescents likely to become involved in community service are unlikely to be extremely aggressive.

Personality Traits. In two studies of volunteers in different Big Brothers/Big Sisters agencies, researchers using the Sixteen Personality Factor Questionnaire (16PF) found significant differences in personality traits between the volunteers who were judged to be a good fit with the program and those who were not (Herman & Usita, 1994; Spitz & MacKinnon, 1993). Similar to children categorized as prosocial, successful volunteers had scores on the 16PF that suggested that they were more extraverted and socially competent than unsuccessful volunteers (Herman & Usita, 1994; Spitz & MacKinnon, 1993). Moreover, volunteers who were judged to be a poor fit for the Big Brothers/Big Sisters program tended to have scores on the 16PF suggestive of rigidity, social inhibition, and anxiety (Herman & Usita, 1994; Spitz & MacKinnon, 1993). In our review of the literature, we found no evidence suggesting that particular personality profiles were more likely to benefit from community service than others.

Krueger, Hicks, and McGue (2001) reached similar conclusions based on their study of a sample of adults. Their study used the Multidimensional Personality Questionnaire (MPQ) and several questionnaires that measured antisocial and prosocial behavior. Krueger and his colleagues found that altruistic and antisocial behaviors were associated with different underlying personality profiles. Adults with high scores on the altruism measures had high scores on the MPQ scale for positive emotionality. Adults with high scores on the antisocial scales were characterized by high levels of negative emotionality and low levels of emotional regulation (Krueger et al., 2001).

In summary, the research on personality traits and prosocial behavior suggests that individuals who are typically positive in mood, able to regulate emotion, frequently experience sympathy, and are effective in interactions with others are more likely to become involved in community service. We hasten to note that this profile is neither specific nor necessary. Positive moods, effective social interactions, and emotional regulation can characterize many constellations of specific personality traits. Moreover, our review suggests that personality characteristics facilitate, but are not necessary for, entry into community service.

Social Influences

A large body of evidence has established the importance of social influences like the home environment, neighborhoods, and schools in child development (Shonkoff & Phillips, 2000). Thus it should not be surprising that research on prosocial behavior and specifically volunteering suggests that enduring social influences affect entry into community service.

Family Characteristics. A variety of family characteristics influence prosocial behavior. Studies that have focused specifically on volunteering suggest that familial resources of adolescents influence the likelihood that adolescents will participate in community service (Hart, Atkins, & Ford, 1998; Nolin, Chaney, & Chapman, 1997). Youth from affluent, well-educated families are more likely to volunteer than are adolescents from other families. As Musick, Wilson, and Bynum (2000) suggested, in comparison to lower status parents, affluent parents "have more social contacts, are aware of a broader range of social issues, and feel more efficacious" (p. 1540). Consequently, affluent parents may be more likely to model prosocial behaviors, such as community service, than their less affluent counterparts (Wilson, 2000).

Parental Practices. A large body of research suggests that, beginning at birth, the nature and quality of the child–parent relationship plays a major role in socializing children to become empathetic and prosocial individuals. Socialization for prosocial action seems to occur most successfully in family environments in which parents are emotionally sensitive and responsive to the concerns of their children (Koestner, Franz, & Weinberger, 1990). For example, results from a study conducted by Clary and Miller (1986) of volunteers at a crisis counseling center indicated that the individuals who maintained their volunteer commitment were more likely to report that their parents were nurturing. Many studies have found that moral and prosocial development of children is enhanced when parents explain their reasons for rules and listen carefully to their children's views (e.g., Krevan & Gibbs, 1996). This disciplinary practice, known as *parental induction*, is particularly valuable in stimulating prosocial responding when the parent is able to focus the child's attention on how their behavior affects others. The use of power assertive techniques such as physical punishment to modify behavior hinders prosocial development (Eisenberg & Fabes, 1998).

Parents as Prosocial Role Models. In addition to structuring home environments that contribute to the emotional regulation and positive emotionality leading to prosocial behavior, parents serve as models for their children. Nolin, Chaney, and Chapman (1997) found that youth participation in community service is increased by the presence in the home of a parent who volunteers. Not only do parents serve as role models for community service, but for activism as well. For example, Rosenhan (1970) found that young adults involved in the civil rights movement of the 1960s were likely to have had parents who were involved in "altruistic cause[s] during some extended period of the respondents' formative years" (Rosenhan, 1970, p. 262).

Moral Reasoning and Attitudes

Adults and adolescents often offer moral goals and motivations to explain their entry into community service. For example, Omoto and Snyder (2002) found that AIDS volunteers referred frequently to humanitarian obligations in their accounts of the origins of their work, a finding that emerges in studies of adult volunteers as well (Hodgkinson & Weitzman, 1992; Wilson & Musick, 1997). Our ongoing research using the National Educational Longitudinal Survey (NELS:1988)[1] suggests that moral attitudes are very important in motivating volunteering in youth. Participants in the NELS:1988 judged the self-descriptiveness of the item "I feel it is important to help others in the community." Those who judged this characteristic to be very descriptive of the self in the tenth grade were more likely to perform community service in twelfth grade than peers with lower levels of civic obligation. This relation held even after extensive controls for other variables. The association is depicted in Figure 23.2. Evident in this figure is that those with a sense of obligation to others in their community are substantially more likely to engage in community service 2 years later than are those who do not value contributing to the public good. Flanagan, Bowes, Jonsson, Csapo, & Shlebanova (1998) and Yates and Younis (1999) report similar findings from their survey of 5,654 adolescents from seven countries. They found that volunteers, compared to nonvolunteers, attached greater importance to helping the less fortunate, helping one's society/country, and improving one's community, a pattern evident in all seven countries.[2]

Another line of research has studied the association between the developmental sophistication of moral reasoning and volunteering. Most frequently, developmental sophistication of moral reasoning has been assessed using Colby and Kohlberg's scheme (1987). According to Kohlberg (1963/1984), moral judgment develops through a sequence of six stages with the earlier stages (stages 1 and 2) found only in children and the last stages found only among the most sophisticated adults (Stages 5 and 6). An individual's stage

---

[1] The analyses presented here use the National Educational Longitudinal Study of 1988 (NELS:88) database (see Curtin, Ingels, Wu, & Hoyer, 2002 for details). The original sample of approximately 25,000 students is a representative sample of eighth graders in the U.S. in 1988. There were a total of five data collections between 1988 and 2000. The data were collected when the typical student was in eighth, tenth, & twelfth grade, and 2 and 8 years out of high school (note that some students were not in the typical grade or may have dropped out of school). At tenth and twelfth grade, new students were added to make each grade a national representative sample. The analyses presented are based on those people surveyed in 2000 that had no missing data for the relevant variables (7,889 or 8,339 out of 12,144 surveyed in 2000, for the two analyses, respectively). Using logistic regression, we separately regressed (a) frequent community service in twelfth grade (see Figure 23.2) and (b) level of civic obligation in twelfth grade (see Figure 23.3) on frequent community service and level of civic obligation in tenth grade, controlling for tenth grade race, gender, religion, parent's socioeconomic status, and their parents' marital status in eighth grade. For the first logistic regression, the -2 log likelihood was 8543.339, with Cox and Snell r^2 of .125 for the model. For the second, the -2 log likelihood was 9727.455, with Cox and Snell r^2 of .108 for the model.

[2] Using the original authors' table, we calculated difference scores (volunteers minus nonvolunteers scores) for each country, and then took a mean of the difference score across the seven countries for each index.

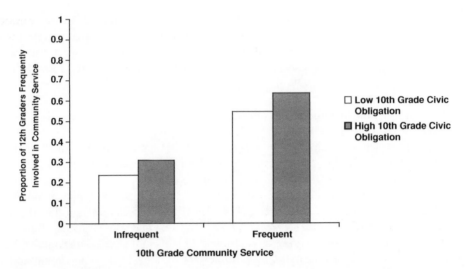

FIG. 23.2 Proportion of twelfth graders frequently involved in community service by level of community service in tenth grade and tenth-grade level of civic commitment.

of moral development is typically assessed by coding responses to questions concerning the proper course of action in a hypothetical dilemma (e.g., "Should the character in the story break into the store and steal the drug necessary to save his wife's life?") and justifications for important moral values (e.g., "Why should you keep a promise?"). Because of its focus on rights and appropriate action, Kohlberg's measure is usually perceived as an assessment of deontic reasoning. There are now thousands of studies in this tradition, and the evidence is compelling for both development in childhood and adolescence and for an association of developmental sophistication and behavior (for a discussion, see Hart, Burock, & London, 2003).

Although there are few studies that have examined community service explicitly, the available research suggests that those with sophisticated moral judgment are more likely to volunteer than are those whose moral reasoning is relatively immature. For example, Comunian and Gielen (1995) assessed the moral reasoning of adolescents who were volunteers and those who were not, and found that the former were more sophisticated in moral reasoning than were the latter.

Self and Identity

As depicted in the model, the self plays a role in supporting participation in community service. Few empirical studies have directly explored the role that the self plays in supporting moral action such as community service. However, it seems reasonable to suspect that individuals who have self-concepts that prioritize helping others are more likely to value activities, such as community service, that benefit others than those who place less priority on helping others in their self-concepts. In fact, several studies have found that adults' commitment to volunteer (Lyndon & Zanna, 1990; Reich, 2000), and voluntary actions (Callero & Pillavin, 1983) are predicted by the degree to which the commitment is related to the self-identity.

In one of the few studies of self and identity in adolescents involved in community service, Hart and Fegley (1995) assessed multiple facets of the sense of self in urban youth who had demonstrated long-term commitments to community-based organizations. They found that adolescents deeply involved in community service perceived their actual selves (their selves in daily life) to be closer to their ideal selves, to their images of their parents, and to their selves of the past and the future, than did youth in a comparison group. Hart and Fegley interpreted these findings to suggest that enduring commitment to community service in adolescence is facilitated by salient personal ideals and parental models, and by a sense of personal identity over time—that what one does in the present is a reflection of the self in the past and the foundation for what one shall become in the future. Although the findings are suggestive, the cross-sectional design of the study makes it difficult to determine whether these qualities of self and identity preceded community service or were created by it.

Opportunities

Neighborhoods. Most of the research on the effect of neighborhoods on moral development has considered the role that neighborhood conditions such as high levels of poverty, low levels of education, and high rates of unemployment play in facilitating the transmission of antisocial behaviors (see Jencks & Mayer, 1990 for a review). Although more study is needed on how neighborhoods affect prosocial behavior such as volunteering, most of the reviewed research suggested that as neighborhood resources decline so does volunteering (Wuthnow, 1998). For example, Hart et al. (1998) found that children growing up in neighborhoods with more neighborhood resources in the form of clubs and teams are more likely to perform community service. Atkins and Hart (2003) found that youth in urban neighborhoods with high levels of poverty were less likely than their counterparts in less impoverished and suburban neighborhoods to perform community service.

Recent work suggests that, besides the role adults have in structuring opportunities within neighborhoods for youth to participate in community service, the effect of neighborhoods on youth participation in community service is also influenced by other youth. Using two nationally representative data sets, Hart and colleagues (2004) found that youth living in neighborhoods with high percentages of other children, or *youth bulges,* were more likely to volunteer than their counterparts in less child-saturated communities. It should be noted that the youth bulge effect on volunteering did not operate in neighborhoods where the rates of poverty were extreme (greater than 40%). In these neighborhoods the combination of extreme poverty and high concentrations of children may have overwhelmed the neighborhood's capacity to structure opportunities for youth to participate in community service (Hart, Atkins, Markey, & Younniss, 2004).

Schools. Schools can, and often do, require adolescents to participate in community service as a condition of graduation, or more typically, of membership in clubs and organizations. Service is usually required because school officials believe that it contributes to the academic and social development of youth. As mentioned in the introduction, the evidence concerning the educational benefits of mandated service is quite sparse, although there are indications that it may produce some of the same benefits as voluntary service (Donnelly, Hart, & Atkins, in preparation). It is interesting to note that Killen and Horn (2000) found that students who used moral reasoning to describe their school-mandated community service experiences were more likely to benefit from the experience.

In this section, we discuss only the research concerning the link of school qualities to genuinely voluntary entry into community service. There is evidence to suggest that school attachment predicts youth volunteering (Flanagan, Bowes, Jonsson, Csapo, & Shlebanova, 1998). These studies provide modest support for the assertion that school environment influences volunteering. However, more research is required in this area to gain a fuller understanding of the school's influence in facilitating prosocial behaviors such as volunteering.

Despite our limited understanding of the contribution schools make to volunteering, we do know that in industrialized countries, virtually all youth spend a significant portion of their childhood and adolescents in some form of school. Furthermore, youth develop prosocially when they spend significant amounts of time in environments that emphasize helping others with peer and adult role models who are kind and nurturing (Rosenthal, Feiring, & Lewis, 1998). These two facts suggest that schools have the potential to affect prosocial behavior. In fact, some researchers of moral development have suggested that the schools' role in providing youth with lessons to develop moral identities concerned with justice, fairness, and perspective taking may be just as important as improving numerical and literacy skills (Lapsley, 1996; Moller & Reich, 1999).

Summary

Consistent with the model depicted in Figure 23.1, the reviewed findings suggest that a complex range of psychoemotional processes and institutional factors influence community service participation. Factors likely to promote community service include personality attributes such as positive emotionality, sophisticated moral judgment, and social supports that facilitate community service participation.

INFLUENCE OF COMMUNITY SERVICE ON MORAL DEVELOPMENT

According to the model depicted in Figure 23.1, enduring personality and social characteristics, moral judgments and attitudes, the sense of self, and opportunities for moral action all influence participation in community service, as previously discussed. In this section we examine the evidence of the extent to which community service influences one's (a) moral reasoning and attitudes, (b) development of the self, (c) opportunity for action, (d) personality, and (e) social characteristics.

Moral Reasoning and Attitudes

Participation in community service provides a real-world context in which participants can explore moral questions, engage in moral discourse, perform moral actions, and reflect on complicated moral issues. It is for these reasons that community service has been extolled as a context for moral development (e.g., National Commission on Service-Learning, 2001). Although the potential for community service to facilitate moral development is clear, the research evidence is quite thin. We review research on the relation of volunteering and community service first to moral judgment sophistication, and then to moral values and attitudes.

Moral Reasoning. Several studies have assessed the influence of community service on moral judgment development. As noted in the previous section, moral judgment maturity is often assessed within Kohlberg's (1963/1984) theoretical framework, according to which development proceeds through a sequence of increasingly sophisticated stages. Evaluation studies therefore compare the average stage of participants in the community service activity to the average stage of those without the community service experience.

Conrad and Hedin (1982) evaluated twenty-seven experience-based education programs, six of which had matched control groups. These experiential programs were of four types: volunteer community service, career internship, community study/political action, and adventure education. The programs evaluated were chosen because they were deemed excellent. The effect of service learning on moral reasoning was evaluated for two experiential programs and one comparison group. Participants were in either in one of the two service learning programs or in social studies classes aimed at increasing social and personal responsibility (a matched control group). All participants were tested before and after the programs with the Defining Issues Test (DIT), based on Kohlberg's (1963/1984) theory. Participants in the service learning programs had significant DIT gains, whereas those in the control groups did not. This pattern suggests that service learning with active reflection (in well-run programs) promotes moral reasoning development.

Batchelder and Root (1994) examined the effects of service learning on a small (forty-eight service learning, forty-eight controls) group of college undergraduates. Students participating in service learning also kept journals about their experiences. Social problem solving (involving thinking about social problems in terms of the complexity of the problem, ways of coping, and information-gathering plans), prosocial decision making (involving interpretations of needs, ability to assist, motivations, and intensions), and levels of prosocial reasoning (based on Eisenberg and Fabes' [1998] model, which has many similarities to Kohberg's model) were assessed in both groups. Batchelder and Root (1994) found that service learning students had higher levels of some aspects of social problem solving than the nonservice students. They also found that journal entries for the service students in the last week of class were higher on prosocial reasoning compared to their first journal entry. Together, the findings suggest a facilitative influence of service on the development of moral judgment.

Boss (1994) studied change in moral reasoning ability in students in two ethics classes with identical curricula and the same instructor, differing only in that students in one class were required to perform 20 hours of community service and keep a journal of their experience. Moral reasoning ability was measured with the DIT. Boss found that the community service group had a significantly higher mean DIT gain of 8.61 (12.39 standard deviation) compared to the control group's 1.74 (10.04 standard deviation) gain. Boss (1994) claimed that her results indicate that community service and ethical discourse are both necessary for facilitating moral judgment development.

Political activism may be considered an extreme form of community service, in that it is the involvement of one's free time for the sake of a political or social cause. There is some evidence that young adulthood political activism leads to increased adult moral reasoning and behavior. Nassi (1981) surveyed activists in the free speech movement at Berkeley in 1964 and 1965, along with students in student government and a cross-section of students in the same year at Berkeley as comparison groups 15 years later. Using a measure based on Kohlberg's scale, Nassi found that those who were activists as undergraduates had higher levels of moral reasoning 15 years later. Of course, it is possible that the individual differences in moral judgment detected 15 years following college preceded, rather than followed from, the protest activities.

Franz and McClelland (1994) used survey archive data collected from thirty-one adults who had participated in the 1960s social movement and forty-seven adults of the same age who had not been active in social movements. They found that activists scored higher in moral reasoning than did nonparticipants. This is another example of political activists having higher levels of moral reasoning ability later in life compared to nonactivists.

Moral Attitudes. Not only can participation in community service increase one's moral reasoning ability, but also it can positively change one's moral attitudes. Boss (1994) found some striking statements made by students in their conclusions on their experience with volunteering. Some students indicated that their attitudes toward others, particularly those different from them, had changed for the better. For example, one student changed her negative stereotype of senior citizens from "crotchety and boring" to "nice." Another student went from feeling that people that went to the soup kitchen were "either crazy or retarded" to believing that they were "quite normal."

Conrad and Hedin's (1982) evaluation, described in an earlier section, found that community service may affect moral attitudes as well as facilitating moral judgment development. They created the Social and Personal Responsibility Scale (SPRS) to measure the students' sense of personal duty, concern for others' welfare, efficacy, and compacity to act responsibly. Conrad and Hedin found that participation in community service was associated with an increase on the SPRS. Specifically, they found that twenty-three of the twenty-seven community service groups increased on the SPRS, with no increases or declines in the six control groups. This is particularly surprising, because the control groups were constituted from students in social studies course aimed at improving moral attitudes. Conrad and Hedin (1982) inferred that moral attitude change may be effected more easily by changing behavior (encouraging students to participate in community service) than through direct tuition.

Hamilton and Fenzel (1988) examined the differential effects of community service on adolescents' moral attitudes. Data for forty-four participants were available. They also used the SPRS to measure moral attitude changes. Subscales were created from the SPRS, one corresponding to Social Responsibility and the other to Personal Responsibility. Community service participants had small but significant increases on the Social Responsibility subscale.

In a well-designed study, Leming (2001) examined the effect of high school seniors' participation in school-monitored community service combined with structured ethical reasoning reflection on moral sensitivity. Participants in the program were compared to seniors participating in service but with few opportunities for ethical reflection and to seniors with neither community service experience nor ethical reflection opportunities. Students were assessed using paper and pencil tests and questionnaires. Responses to three "right versus right" dilemmas were coded on three dimensions: ethical awareness, acceptance of responsibility, and framing issues with proper use of language/structure (as taught by the Building Decision Skills curriculum). In seven out of nine instances (three dilemmas by three dimensions), the structured ethical reasoning group had significantly higher scores than the limited reflection group. In one out of nine, the limited reflection group had a significantly higher score than the no service group. Based on this study, it seems that the structured ethical reasoning reflection increased students' moral reasoning abilities, compared to students that were not given such training, but that performing community service alone does not increase moral reasoning abilities. It is not clear whether it was the ethical reasoning training alone or its combination with performing community service that lead to this increase in moral reasoning ability, because there was no group that was given only structured ethical reasoning with no community service.

Jennings (2002) analyzed data from a national sample of protestors and nonprotestors from the high school class of 1965, with follow-up surveys from 316 four-wave college

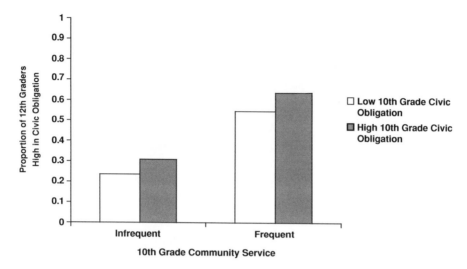

FIG. 23.3 Proportion of twelfth graders highly committed to their communities by level of community service in tenth grade and tenth-grade level of civic commitment.

graduate respondents in 1973, 1982, and 1997 (when they were approximately 50 years old), 30% of whom were protestors. He found several indications of moral attitude differences between the two groups over time. For example, protestors had higher levels of opposition to prayers in school at all time points, but that the difference appeared to increase substantially as a result of the protest experience (percent opposed to prayers in school for protestor minus nonprotestor: 1965, 7%; 1973, 22%; 1982, 30%; and 1997, 26%). Also, protestors had higher levels of civic tolerance at all time periods (percent of people with a high level of civic tolerance for protestors minus nonprotestors: 1965, 3%; 1973, 19%; 1982, 24%; and 1997, 14%), but once again the difference increased following protest activity. This study suggests that community involvement may amplify minor differences in moral attitudes that preceded the protest activities.

Our own research with the NELS:88, discussed earlier, suggests that community service can change moral attitudes. Specifically, we predicted that community service experience would deepen adolescents' judgment of responsibility to the community ("It is important to help others in my community").[3] Adolescents were categorized as either highly committed or weakly committed. As Figure 23.3 illustrates, those who participate frequently in community service in tenth grade are more likely to become highly committed in twelfth grade than are those who are not active in community service, even after controlling for tenth-grade civic commitment.

Development of the Self

Youniss and Yates (1997) suggest that adolescents' sense of self and identity can develop through linking the self to the prevailing sociohistoric context and through the construction of transcendent personal meaning. This process of connecting the self to a context and identifying transcendent meaning occurs in social relationships and social groups. Youniss

---

[3]We estimated this difference (based on tables presented in the original article) by taking the mean of student government and cross-sectional nonactivists separately for men and women, getting a difference score between these and men and woman activists, and averaging these difference scores.

and Yates (1997) argue that community service activity often occurs within a network of particularly potent social relationships and social groups, and for this reason community service can be a powerful contributor to identity development.

Youniss and Yates (1997) studied what they called *transcendence*, a quality of identity that can be identified in the written and spoken comments of adolescents concerning their community service experiences. Adolescents who describe their community service experiences in serving others in need as involving individuals who are fully responsible for their own predicaments, and consequently as individuals with little in common with the self, are characterized as evidencing no transcendence. Those adolescents whose reflections indicate that others in need are individual humans who are trapped by a confluence of factors are considered to reflect a degree of transcendence. Finally, adolescents for whom experience with those in need results in the joining of personal responsibility to the perception of the injustice are viewed as achieving a high degree of transcendence.

Youniss and Yates (1997) studied transcendence development in a group of high school students participating in community service. They found that the experience of community service seemed to promote the development of transcendence in students over the course of a year.

In a study inspired by the work of Youniss and Yates (1997), Hofer (1999) studied thirty-eight members of Youth Fire Police and Youth Red Cross and thirty-eight adolescents in a matched comparison group from a small German city to examine the effects of service on transcendence and identity. Participants responded to questions about two fictitious situations, with responses coded using the three-level transcendence category system developed by Yates and Youniss (1999). Hofer (1999) found that volunteers had higher scores than the comparison group (1.45 versus 1.02). Hofer also assessed participants' identity statuses, using Marcia's (1980) scheme. According to Marcia (1966), the four identity statuses are: diffusion (one does not commit to an ideology, and has no identity crisis), foreclosure (one simply adopts one's parents' or society's ideology), moratorium (one delays commitment to an ideology while actively struggling for one's identity), and achievement (after consideration and struggle, one attains a sense of identity). Diffusion reflects poor adjustment, whereas identity achievement is associated with the best developmental outcomes. Hofer found that volunteers were more likely than those in the comparison group to be characterized as identity achievers, and those in the comparison group were more likely than volunteers to be assigned to the diffusion status.

Opportunity for Action

Participating in community service appears to effect enduring changes in individuals' social networks that in turn heighten the probability of future involvement in community service. For example, Wilson and Musick (1997) analyzed data from the American's Changing Lives panel survey (House, 1995) which surveyed people 25 years and older in the U.S. in 1986 with a follow-up survey in 1989 ($n = 2,846$). They examined the relationship of factors that were related to a formal volunteering index (sum of types of volunteer work in the past year) and an informal helping index (summing the types of helping in the past year). Of particular interest is the relation of formal volunteering and informal helping in 1986 and to the same variables measured 3 years later. Wilson and Musick (1997) used structural equation modeling to examine the relations among these variables, and found evidence that formal volunteering in 1986 apparently led to increases in informal helping 2 years later.

Service learning, in which social science–type classes are combined with hands-on service, does have some positive short- and long-term effects on future community service. A recent evaluation of the National Learn and Serve America School and Community Based Program suggests that community service increases the likelihood of future participation in volunteering (Melchior et al., 1999). Impacts on the participants and the community were assessed by examining seven middle schools and ten high schools and approximately 1,000 Learn and Serve participants and controls. The typical participant engaged in 70 hours of direct service, and 76% of participants had direct contact with service recipients. Also, 67% of participants discussed their community service in class and 44% kept a journal. Of the respondents, 80% felt they made a difference in their service.

Postprogram evaluations were based on twenty measures, such as education performance and attitudes, civic and social attitudes, volunteering, and involvement in risky behaviors. Analyses of program participants' outcomes in relation to comparison groups were performed with regression analyses, controlling for differences in baseline scores and characteristics. Of relevance here, a 1-year follow-up study found that the high school students involved in the program provided twice the number of volunteer hours as those that were not in the service-learning program, although there was no difference between participants and controls in middle school. This is another example of community service leading to an increase in future community service.

McAdam (1988) surveyed individuals who volunteered and those whose applications were accepted but never showed up for the Freedom Summer 1964 registration of black voters and operation of Freedom Schools where public schools had been closed in Mississippi. Participation in this social movement may be considered an extreme version of community service. He found that 46% of volunteers and 33% of no shows (applied to and accepted for volunteering, but did not show up) were presently active in at least one sociopolitical movement. Also, 70% of volunteers and 50% of no shows were members of political associations.

Personality

It is also possible that participation in community service can influence one's personality. If personality is construed broadly so as to include self, identity, and morality, then as we have seen participation in community service can change personality. However, in this review the domain of personality is limited to enduring traits and traitlike behaviors. In a previous section, we suggested research demonstrated that persons high in sympathy, positive moods, emotional regulation, and social prowess were most likely to become involved in community service. To the best of our knowledge, there are no studies that assess the effects of community service on change in personality traits. Possibly the lack of research on this topic reflects the enormous difficulty of studying change in personality, a problem resulting from the substantial stability in personality (for a review, see Roberts & DelVecchio, 2000) and the difficulty in isolating specific factors which produce change in it (Hart, Atkins, & Fegley, 2003). Although these obstacles are real, we believe that future research is warranted on the relation of community service to change in personality. Researchers who have studied the lives of those deeply involved in community service regularly report that activists are profoundly affected by their experiences (e.g., McAdam, 1989; Nassi, 1981), and consequently it is reasonable to hypothesize that small amounts of personality change might occur in those with more modest commitments to community service.

Social Characteristics

Participation in community service may influence one's location in the matrix of family and class. Fendrich (1993) studied black alumni of Florida A&M University who protested against race segregation, an activity with obvious relations to community service, and a comparison group composed of alumni who had been active in student government. Fendrich found that those who protested sought more advanced degrees and were more likely to enter the helping professions than those who were members only of student government. Nassi's (1981) research was similar in design, as it involved a survey of former Berkeley free-speech movement activists and controls. She found that activists made approximately $9,400 less than nonactivists, measured 15 years after the protest experience. However, most other social characteristics, such as church attendance, marital status, and occupational commitments, were similar for activists and nonactivists. In a similar study, Franz and McClelland (1994) found that sixties activists had more education than nonactivists (16.1 versus 14.6 years, respectively). Activists had fewer children than nonactivists (means of 0.8 and 1.6 children at ages 31 and 41 for participants versus 1.2 and 2.1 at ages 31 and 41 for nonparticipants, respectively). Thus, there is some evidence to suggest that community service may influence enduring social relationships, family structure, and social class.

CONCLUSION

Because community service participation is easily measured and its virtues for moral education are readily grasped, public discussion of youth morality will continue to invoke volunteering, service-learning, and community service. Community service for the foreseeable future will remain a prominent marker of the civic health and moral well-being of young cohorts of Americans, and will continue to be the solution that many offer to the problem of youthful immorality.

These views receive some support from our review of the literature. We found considerable evidence to indicate that many of the qualities associated with community service in childhood, adolescence, and adulthood are those that are linked to moral development. People high in sympathy, prosocial attitudes, moral judgment sophistication, and identity integration, qualities which most would agree are important to moral character, are associated with participation in community service. Consequently, participation in community service indirectly indexes these facets of moral character.

Our review also found, however, that nonmoral factors are important influences on entry into community service. For example, emotional regulation, social class, educational achievement, and the opportunities afforded by neighborhoods, schools, and social institutions all influence entry into community service. Moreover, the current state of the research base does not permit an estimation of the relative importance for entry into community service of this set of nonmoral factors. Finally, it is worth noting that the relative importance of moral and nonmoral factors for entry into community service may vary from generation to generation. It is certainly possible, for instance, that the steady increase in youth volunteering that has occurred over the past several decades is fueled as much by a desire to gain an experience valued by colleges and universities in the admissions process as it is by a change in fundamentally moral qualities. Care is warranted, then, in using volunteering as the index of the moral well-being of a cohort of adolescents.

Our review also suggested that community service has beneficial effects on moral development. The evidence is clearest for a positive influence of community service on moral judgment and attitudes, and on the likelihood for participation in community service in the future. In terms of the conceptual model in Figure 23.1, the research evidence is weaker for the influence of community service on self and identity, on personality, and on enduring social context. These components of the model map roughly onto the traditional domains of moral philosophy mentioned in the introduction. For example, the contributions of community service to development seem to be focused largely on deepening an appreciation for right (deontic) action, as evidenced largely in change on measures of moral judgment reflecting Kohlberg's theory, and on the utilitarian concern with creating the best of all possible worlds. There is little research evidence to indicate that community service deepens virtue, or effects systematic change in individuals to produce more ethical character. These patterns in the literature may reflect as much the preferences of researchers for favored constructs, however, as they do the particular effects of community service on broad moral domains. It is certainly possible that future research could demonstrate that community service influences the developmental of moral character.

In terms of moral psychology, the effects of community service are clearest for cognition and action. As noted, there is a reasonably substantial body of research to suggest that community service both facilitates the development of deontic reasoning, at least as it is measured by Kohlberg's measure, and deepens the sense of commitment to the public good. Moreover, research consistently demonstrates that those who become involved in community service are more likely than those who are not to volunteer in the future. We did not find any evidence, however, to indicate that community service influences sympathy, perspective taking, or personality traits. Again, this conclusion rests as much on what has been studied as much as it does on patterns of findings; future research could demonstrate that community service does influence moral emotions.

There is an enormous need for additional research. Throughout our review, we relied on studies with very small samples, studies with convenience samples, and studies that trace development over very short periods of time. Very few of the studies feature the rigor and scale that engender confidence in the generalization of findings to the population. Similarly, none of the studies reviewed in this chapter is decisive support for community service as a powerful form of moral development intervention.

In our view, rigorous research is desperately needed that addresses the five qualities of community service reviewed in the introduction: voluntary versus mandated service, duration of community service, type of service, motivation for service, and the importance of reflection. A few studies have touched on one or more of these qualities, but often the studies did not focus specifically on moral qualities, had small samples, or led to conflicting results. For example, consider the issue of whether required community service can facilitate moral development. Metz and Youniss (2003) compared a cohort of adolescents who were not required to participate in community service with a later cohort from the same high school required to do service, and found that the benefits of community service for civic development were apparently not diminished by the requirement to participate in it. Other researchers are skeptical (e.g., Stukas, et al., 1999), and whether similar effects would be found for moral qualities are unknown. Similarly, although it is plausible that the benefits of voluntary community service on moral development vary directly as a function of the amount of time engaged in it and the type of service performed, there has been too little research to estimate accurately the mediating influence of these factors on the value of community service for youth development.

Our review found more research on the last of these issues, the importance of reflection and discussion as a necessary accompaniment to community service. Several researchers report that community service without reflection and discussion has only limited value (e.g., Leming, 2001). Indeed, substantial change can seem to occur in youth participating in programs in which time spent in reflection and discussion is much greater than that actually spent in community service (e.g., the youth studied by Youniss & Yates, 1997). Even in programs in which participants spend more time in discussion and reflection than in service, the service activity appears to be crucially important. Little moral judgment development seems to occur in participants who only reflect and discuss moral issues (Boss, 1994), and attitudes change little in civics classes without a service component (Conrad & Hedin, 1982). Consequently, like other reviewers, we conclude that reflection and discussion are important components in programs that use community service to facilitate moral development.

Although a great deal remains to be learned about community service and youth development, the current state of the research supports optimism about its value for children and adolescents. We found no research that suggested that volunteering and community service harm youth, and as our review suggests, many studies find that community service can facilitate development. Surely there is no single route to facilitating moral development in children and adolescents; however, our review suggests that involving youth in activities that benefit their communities can be synthesized into a broad-based effort to promote ethical development.

REFERENCES

Atkins, R., & Hart, D. (2003). Neighborhoods, adults and the development of civic identity in urban youth. *Applied Developmental Science, 7,* 156–165.

Atkins, R., & Hart, D. (2004). Moral identity development and school attachment. In D. Lapsley & D. Narvaez (Eds.), *Morality development: The self and identity* (pp. 65–82). Mahwah, NJ: Lawrence Associates Erlbaum.

Batchelder, T. H., & Root, S. (1994). Effects of an undergraduate program to integrate academic learning and service: Cognitive, prosocial cognitive, and identity outcomes. *Journal of Adolescence, 17,* 341–355.

Blasi, A. (1980). Bridging moral cognition and moral action: A critical review of the literature. *Psychological Bulletin, 88,* 593–637.

Boss, J. A. (1994). The effect of community service work on the moral development of college ethics students. *Journal of Moral Education, 23,* 183–190.

Callero, P. L., & Pillavin, J. A. (1983). Developing a commitment to blood donation: The impact of one's first experience. *Journal of Applied Social Psychology, 13,* 1–16.

Caspi, A. (1998). Personality development across the life-course. In N. Eisenberg (Vol. Ed.), *Handbook of child psychology, Vol. 3: Social, emotional, and personality development* (pp. 311–388). New York: Wiley.

Child Trends. (2002). Volunteering. Retrieved June 24, 2003, from http://www. childtrendsdatabank.org/socemo/prosocial/20Volunteering.htm0

Clary, E. G., & Miller, J. (1986). Socialization and situational influences on sustained altruism. *Child Development, 57,* 1358–1369.

Clary, E. G., Snyder, M., Ridge, R. D., Copeland, J., Stukas, A. A., Haugen, J., & Miene, P. (1998). Understanding and assessing the motivations of volunteers: A functional approach. *Journal of Personality and Social Psychology, 74,* 1516–1530.

Comunian, A., & Gielen, U. (1995). Moral reasoning and prosocial action in Italian culture. *The Journal of Social Psychology, 135,* 699–706.

Conrad, D., & Hedin, D. (1982). The impact of experiential education on adolescent development. In D. Conrad & D. Hedin, (Eds.), *Child and Youth Services*, special issue *Youth participation and experiential education, 4,* 57–76.

Curtin, T. R., Ingels, S. J., Wu, S., & Heuer, R. (2002). *National Education Longitudinal Study of 1988: Base-Year to Fourth Follow-up Data File User's Manual (NCES 2000–323).* Washington, D.C.: U.S. Department of Education, National Center for Education Statistic. Retrieved Jan 23, 2005, from http://nces.ed.gov/pubs2002/2002323.pdf

Davis, M., Mitchell, K., Hall, J., Lothert, J., Snapp, T., & Meyer, M. (1999). Empathy, expectations, and situational preferences: personality influences on the decision to participate in volunteer helping behaviors. *Journal of Personality, 67,* 469–503.

Donnelly, T. M., Hart, D., Youniss, J., & Atkins, R. (in prep.). *High school predictors of adult civic engagement: The roles of volunteering, civic knowledge, extracurricular activities, and attitudes.*

Eisenberg, N. (2000). Emotion, regulation, and moral development. *Annual Review of Psychology, 51,* 665–697.

Eisenberg, N. (2003). Prosocial behavior, empathy, and sympathy. In M. Bornstein & L. Davidson (Eds.), *Well-being: Positive development across the life course. Crosscurrents in contemporary psychology* (pp. 253–265). Mahwah, NJ: Lawrence Erlbaum Associates.

Eisenberg, N., & Fabes, R. (1998). Prosocial development. In N. Eisenberg (Vol. Ed.), *Handbook of child psychology, Vol. 3: Social, emotional, and personality development* (pp. 701–778). New York: Wiley.

Eisenberg, N., Miller, P., Schaller, M., Fabes, R., Fultz, J., Shell, R., & Shea, C. (1989). The role of sympathy and altruistic personality traits in helping: A reexamination. *Journal of Personality, 57,* 41–67.

Eisenberg, N., & Okun, M. (1996). The relations of dispositional regulation and emotionality to elders' empathy-related responding and affect while volunteering. *Journal of Personality, 64,* 157–183.

Farver, J. M., & Branstetter, W. H. (1994) Preschoolers' prosocial responses to the peers' distress. *Developmental Psychology, 30,* 334–341.

Fendrich, J. M. (1993). *Ideal citizens: The legacy of the Civil Rights movement.* Albany: State University of New York Press.

Flanagan, C., Bowes, J., Jonsson, B., Csapo, B., & Shlebanova, E. (1998). Ties that bind: correlates of adolescents' civic commitments in seven countries. *Journal of Social Issues, 54,* 457–477.

Franz, C. F., & McClelland, D. C. (1994). Lives of women and men active in the social protests of the 1960s: A longitudinal study. *Journal of Personality and Social Psychology, 66,* 196–205.

Haidt, J. (2001). The emotional dog and its rational tail: A social intuitionist approach to moral judgment. *Psychological Review, 108,* 814–834.

Hamilton, S. F., & Fenzel, L. M. (1988). The impact of volunteer experience on adolescent social development: Evidence of program effects. *Journal of Adolescent Research, 3,* 65–80.

Hart, D. (2005). The development of moral identity. In G. Carlo & C. P. Edwards (Eds.), *Nebraska symposium on motivation: Moral motivation through the lifespan: Theory, research, & application, 51.* Lincoln: University of Nebraska Press.

Hart, D., Atkins, R., & Fegley, S. (2003). Personality and development in childhood: A person-centered approach. *Monographs of the Society for Research in Child Development, 68* (1, Serial No. 272).

Hart, D., Atkins, R., & Ford, D. (1998). Urban America as a context for the development of moral identity in adolescence. *Journal of Social Issues, 54,* 513–530.

Hart, D., Atkins, R., & Ford, D. (1999). Family influences on the formation of moral identity in adolescence: Longitudinal analyses. *Journal of Moral Education, 28,* 375–386.

Hart, D., Atkins, R., Markey, P., & Youniss, J. (2004). Youth bulges in communities: The effect of age structure on adolescent civic knowledge and civic participation. *Psychological Science, 15,* 591–597.

Hart, D., Burock, D., & London, B. (2003). Prosocial tendencies, antisocial behavior, and moral development in childhood. In A. Slater & G. Bremner (Eds.), *Introduction to Developmental Psychology* (pp. 334–356). Oxford: Blackwell.

Hart, D., Burock, D., London, B., & Miraglia, A. (2003). Moral development in childhood. In M. Bornstein, L. Davidson, C. Keyes, K. Moore (Eds.), *Well-being: positive development across the life course* (pp. 355–371). Mahwah, NJ: Lawrence Erlbaum Associates.

Hart, D., & Fegley, S. (1995). Prosocial behavior and caring in adolescence: Relations to self-understanding and social judgment. *Child Development, 66,* 1346–1359.

Hart, D., & Killen, M. (1995). Introduction: Perspectives on morality in everyday life. In M. Killen & D. Hart (Eds.), *Morality in everyday life: Developmental perspectives* (pp. 1–20). New York: Cambridge University Press.

Hart, D., Yates, M., Fegley, S., & Wilson, G. (1995). Moral commitment among inner-city adolescents. In M. Killen & D. Hart (Eds.), *Morality in everyday life: Developmental perspectives* (pp. 317–341). New York: Cambridge University Press.

Hartshorne, H., & May, M. A. (1928). *Studies in deceit.* New York: McMillan.

Herman, K. C., & Usita, P. M. (1994). Predictive validity of the 16 PF in screening volunteers for Big Brothers/Big Sisters. *Psychological Reports, 74,* 249–250.

Hodgkinson, V., & Weitzman, M. (1992). *Giving and volunteering in the United States.* Washington, D.C.: Independent Sector.

Hofer, M. (1999). Community service and social cognitive development in German adolescents. In M. Yates & J. Youniss (Eds.), *Roots of civic identity: International perspectives on community service and activism in youth.* (pp. 114–134). New York: Cambridge University Press.

House, J. S. (1995). *Americans' changing lives: Waves I and II, 1986 and 1989.* Ann Arbor, MI: Inter-university Consortium for Political and Social Research.

Independent Sector. (1999). *Giving and volunteering in the United States: Findings from a national survey.* Retrieved September 11, 2003, from http://www.independentsector.org/GandV/default.htm

Jencks, C., & Mayer, S. (1990). The social consequences of growing up in a poor neighborhood. In L. E. Lynn & M. McGeary (Eds.), *Inner city poverty in the United States* (pp. 11–186). Washington, D.C.: National Academy Press.

Jennings, M. K. (2002). Generation units and the student protest movement in the United States: An intra- and intergenerational analysis. *Political Psychology, 23*(2), 303–323.

Kant, I. (1964). *The metaphysical principal of morals.* Indianapolis: Bobbs-Merrill Co.

Killen, M., & Horn, S. (2000). Facilitating children's development of morality, community, and autonomy: A case for service-learning experiences. In W. van Haaften, T. Wren, & A. Tellings (Eds.), *Moral sensibilities and education II: The schoolchild* (pp. 89–113). Bemmel, The Netherlands: Concorde Publishing House.

Koestner, R., Franz, C., & Weinberger, J. 1990. The family origins of empathic concern: A 26-year longitudinal study. *Journal of Personality and Social Psychology, 58,* 709–717.

Kohlberg, L. (1963/1984). *The psychology of moral development: The nature and validity of moral stages.* San Francisco: Harper & Row.

Krevan, J., & Gibbs, J. C. (1996). Parents' use of inductive discipline: Relations to children's empathy and prosocial behavior. *Child Development, 67,* 3263–3277.

Krueger, R. F., Hicks, B. M., & McGue, M. (2001). Altruistic and antisocial behavior: In-dependent tendencies, unique personality characteristics, distinct etiologies. *Psychological Science, 12*, 397–402.

Leming, J. S. (2001). Integrating a structured ethical reflection curriculum into high school community service experiences: Impact on students' sociomoral development. *Adolescence, 36*, 33–45.

Latané, B., Liu, J. H., Nowak, A., Benevento, M., & Zheng, L. (1995). Distance matters: Physical space and social impact. *Personality and Social Psychology Bulletin, 21*, 795–805.

Lapsley, D. K. (1996). *Moral psychology.* Boulder: Westview Press.

Lydon, J. E., & Zanna, M. P. (1990). Commitment in the face of adversity: A value-affirmation approach. *Journal of Personality and Social Psychology, 58*, 1040–1047.

Marcia, J. E. (1966). Development and validation of ego-identity status. *Journal of personality and Social Psychology, 3*, 551–558.

McAdam, D. (1988). *Freedom summer.* New York: Oxford University Press.

McAdam, D. (1989). The biographical consequences of activism. *American Sociological Review, 54*, 744–760.

McClellan, J., & Youniss, J. (2003). Two systems of youth service: Determinants of volun-tary and required youth community service. *Journal of Youth and Adolescence, 32*, 47–58.

Melchior, A., Frees, J., LaCava, L., Kingsley, C., Nahas, J., Power, J., et al. (1999). *Summary report: National evaluation of Learn and Serve America school and community based programs.* Waltham, MA: The Center for Human Resources: Brandeis University.

Metz, E., & Youniss, J. (2003). September 11 and service: A longitudinal study of high school students' views and responses. *Applied Developmental Science, 7*, 148–155.

Moller, S., & Reich, R. (1999). Families and schools as compensating agents in moral devel-opment for a multicultural society. *The Journal of Moral Education, 28*, 283–298.

Musick, M. A., Wilson, J., & Bynum, W. B. (2000). Race and formal volunteering: The differential effects of class and religion. *Social Forces, 78*, 1539–1571.

Nassi, A. (1981). Survivors of the sixties: Comparative psychosocial and political development of former Berkeley student activists. *American Psychologist, 36*, 753–761.

National Commission on Service-Learning. (2001). *Learning in deed: The power of service-learning for American schools.* Retrieved June 24, 2003, from http://servicelearningcommission.org/slcommission/report.html

Newman, D., Caspi, A., Moffitt, T., & Silva, P. (1997). Antecedents of adult interpersonal func-tioning: Effects of individual differences in age 3 temperament. *Developmental Psychology, 33*, 206–217.

Nolin, M. J., Chaney, B., & Chapman, C. (1997). *Student participation in community service activity.* Washington, D.C.: U.S. Department of Education, National Center for Educational Statistics.

Omoto, A. M., & Snyder, M. (1995). Sustained helping without obligation: Motivation, longevity of service, and perceived attitude change among AIDS volunteers. *Journal of Personality and Social Psychology, 68*, 671–686.

Omoto, A. M., & Snyder, M. (2002). Considerations of community: The context and process of volunteerism. *American Behavioral Scientist, 45*, 846–867.

Penner, L. (2002). Dispositional and organizational influences on sustained volunteerism: An interactionist perspective. *Journal of Social Issues, 58*, 447–467.

Penner, L. A., & Finkelstein, M. (1998). Dispositional and structural determinants of volun-teerism. *Journal of Personality and Social Psychology, 74*, 525–537.

Penner, L. A., & Fritzsche, B. A. (1993). *Measuring the prosocial personality: Four construct validity studies.* Toronto, Canada: American Psychological Association.

Penner, L. A., Fritzsche, B. A., Craiger, J. P., & Freifeld, T. R. (1995). Measuring the prosocial personality. In J. Butcher & C. D. Spielberger (Eds.), *Advances in personality assessment* (vol. 10). Hillsdale, NJ: Lawrence Erlbaum Associates.

Piaget, J. (1965). *The moral judgment of the child.* New York: Norton.

Putnam, R. (2000). *Bowling Alone in America: The Collapse and Revival of American Community.* New York, NY: Simon and Schuster.

Reich, W. (2000). Identity structure, narrative accounts, and commitment to a volunteer role. *Journal of Psychology, 134,* 422–432.

Roberts, B. W., & Delvecchio, W. F. (2000). The rank-order consistency of personality traits from childhood to old age: A quantitative review of longitudinal studies. *Psychological Bulletin, 126,* 3–25.

Rosenhan, D. L. 1970. The natural socialization of altruistic autonomy. J. Macaulay & L. Berkowitz (Eds.). *Altruism and helping behavior* (pp. 251–268). New York: Academic Press.

Rosenthal, S., Feiring, C., & Lewis, M. (1998). Political volunteering from late adolescence to young adulthood: patterns and predictors. *Journal of Social Issues, 54,* 477–494.

Shonkoff, J., & Phillips, D. (Eds.). (2000). *From neurons to neighborhoods: The science of early childhood development.* Washington, D.C.: National Research Council.

Spitz, R., & MacKinnon, J. (1993). Predicting success in volunteer community service. *Psychological Reports, 73,* 815–818.

Stukas, A., Snyder, M., & Clary, E. G. (1999). The effects of "mandatory volunteerism" on intentions to volunteer. *Psychological Science, 10,* 59–64.

Turiel, E. (1998). The development of morality. In N. Eisenberg (Ed.), *Handbook of child psychology: Social, emotional, and personality development* (5th ed., pp. 863–932). New York: Wiley.

Unger, L., & Thumuluri, L. (1997). Trait empathy and continuous helping: the case of voluntarism. *Journal of Social Behavior and Personality, 12,* 785–800.

Walker, L., Taylor, J. H. (1991). Family interactions and the development of moral reasoning. *Child Development,62,* 264–283.

Williams, B. (1995). Ethics. In A. C. Grayling (Ed.), *Philosophy: A guide through the subject* (pp. 546–582). New York: Oxford University Press.

Wilson, J. (2000). Volunteering. *Annual Review of Sociology, 26,* 215–240.

Wilson, J., & Musick, M. (1997). Who cares? Toward an integrated theory of volunteer work. *American Sociological Review, 62,* 694–713.

Wuthnow, R. (1998). *Loose connections: Joining together in America's fragmented communities.* Cambridge, MA: Harvard University Press.

Yates, M., & Youniss, J. (1999). *Roots of civic identity: International prespectives on community service and activism in youth.* New York: Cambridge University Press.

Youniss, J., & Yates, M. (1997). *Community Service and Social Responsibility in Youth.* Chicago: The University of Chicago Press.

24

Education for Moral Development

Larry Nucci
University of Illinois at Chicago

Most of the applications of developmental research to moral education have roots in the work of Lawrence Kohlberg and his colleagues (Lapsley, chap. 2, this volume; Power, Higgins, & Kohlberg, 1989a). As depicted within Kohlberg's theory, moral development moves from earlier stages, in which morality is intertwined with self-interest and social norms, to later, more mature stages, in which morality as justice is differentiated from and displaces social convention as the basis for moral judgments. During the 1960s and early 1970s a considerable amount of evidence was generated in support of this description of moral development (Kohlberg, 1984). The nonarbitrary directionality and seeming universality of moral growth as described in this research had considerable appeal among educators hoping to avoid the relativism of values clarification (Raths, Harmin, & Simon, 1976), and perceived limitations of traditional approaches to socialization. Whereas traditional values education emphasized the inculcation of students into the norms of society (Ryan, 1989), the emphasis on moral reasoning advocated by Kohlberg liberated teachers from the charge of inculcating children within a particular value system favored by one or another cultural or religious group within society. At the same time, the Kohlberg sequence provided teachers with a clear rationale for challenging the moral positions of their students, thus avoiding the value neutrality of values clarification. By the mid-1970s, enough interest had been generated by the Kohlbergian approach to lead one educator, Fraenkel (1976), to write about what he perceived to be the "Kohlberg bandwagon." By the mid-1980s, however, the interest in the Kohlbergian approach to moral education had begun to wane (Power, Higgins, & Kohlberg, 1989b; Turiel, 1989).

 In part, the movement away from Kohlberg-based moral education can be attributed to limitations in the theory and research base that informed the resulting educational practices. This chapter discusses those issues in the context of examining developmental work that has moved beyond Kohlberg. To a considerable degree, however, and as discussed in the following section, the movement away from Kohlberg during the 1980s was a reflection of the fissures and cracks that had begun to appear more generally in the modernist tradition that had formed the intellectual base for progressive education and political liberalism.

This chapter examines the current state of developmental approaches to moral education post-Kohlberg. Following a brief review of the recent trends that have impacted the field of moral education, the chapter explores the implications of more recent developmental research on the establishment of developmental aims of moral education and generation of classroom practices. With respect to the latter, the chapter first presents a discussion of practices that directly focuses on students' social interactions. This includes establishment of the classroom social–emotional climate, developmentally appropriate forms of classroom management and conflict resolution, as well as recent efforts to engage students in service learning. Each of these practices is thought to contribute to the experiential sources of information children employ to construct their conceptions of morality and social norms, as well as their capacity to engage in moral action. The chapter concludes with an examination of developmental approaches to the use of the regular academic curriculum for moral education. This final section explores recent work that coordinates students' development of concepts of morality and social systems with educational practices that engage students in critical moral reflection upon the larger society.

RECENT TRENDS

Kohlberg's (1984) moral theory was an extension of Piaget's (1932) seminal work on the moral development of young children. As in Piaget's theory, Kohlberg assumed that children constructed their morality, rather than directly acquiring moral values from parents and teachers or other agents of socialization. Kohlberg, like Piaget, also viewed morality as moving through a sequence of developmental stages toward progressively more adequate ways of engaging in moral judgments that direct one's actions. Unlike most psychologists of his era, Kohlberg explicitly acknowledged the philosophical implications of his moral psychology. Thus, Kohlberg (1981) wrote extensively regarding the neo-Kantian basis of his moral psychology, and the arguments, both empirical and philosophical that sustained his claims of having identified a universal sequence of stages of moral growth.

Some of the more important challenges to Kohlberg's theory have come from critics who have viewed his commitment to Kantian universals, and progressive vision of development as rooted in a culturally situated conception of humanity and social history. The Kantian philosophical underpinnings of Kohlberg's moral theory were assaulted by postmodernists such as Richard Rorty (1973, 1979, 1988) who argued for abandonment of what were referred to as the grand narrative theories of the enlightenment. (A more detailed discussion of the Kantian assumptions of Kohlberg's theory is contained in Lapsley, chap. 2, volume). In a similar vein, the cultural anthropologist, Shweder (1982), entitled a review of Kohlberg's (1981) first volume of collected works, *Liberalism as Destiny,* and decried what he saw as the culturally biased imposition of Western enlightenment values through the supposed universal Kohlberg stage sequence. In the context of his review, Shweder (1982) pointed to MacIntyre's (1984) critique of John Rawls' (1971) *A Theory of Justice* as heralding the end of the "enlightenment project" and with it, the universalist motivations that sustained the structuralism of Piaget and Kohlberg in psychology and of Levi Strauss in his own field of anthropology. At roughly this same time, Carol Gilligan (1982) published *In a Different Voice,* which reported on the findings of her studies of the moral judgment of women. Despite the failure of subsequent research to support the bold claims of a basic difference in men's and women's moral orientations (see Turiel

[1998] for a comprehensive review of this research; also, Walker, chap. 4, this volume), Gilligan's work continues to be viewed as forging an opening for pluralist rather than universal accounts of morality.

Of course, not everyone has embraced the pluralist sentiments of postmodernism. Instead, the space opened up by the end of modernity has been largely filled by calls for a return to tradition, and with it the rapid rise of popular interest in character education, so much so, that we are now in the midst of what Ryan (1996) has referred to as the "Character education bandwagon." This new bandwagon is the latest incarnation of what Wynne (1986) has called "The great tradition in education" and is defined by an emphasis on the transmission of broadly shared societal values, and the instilling of "virtue" in children through attachment to the social group and the gradual shaping of habits of prosocial conduct. These calls for character education are generally accompanied by claims of social decay and moral crisis (Bennett, 1992, 1998; Bloom, 1988; Himmelfarb, 1994; Putnam, 2000, 2003). Thus, the return to tradition and traditional forms of socialization are justified as taking us back to a period when things were better. Wynne perhaps best captured this sentiment when he stated that, "By many measures youth conduct was at its best in 1955" (1987, p. 56).

The claims of social decay have been disputed, and the evidence of a moral youth crisis has been put into historical context by writers who point to the cyclical nature of such claims throughout recorded history (Turiel, 2002). They tend to occur during periods of rapid social change such as we are currently experiencing. The shifts in social life in the past 50 years brought about through technology, globalization, and the outcomes of the civil rights and women's movements have had broad consequences. Thus, the calls for attention to our moral moorings have an objective basis and resonate with the anxieties of the general public. Within the American context, periods of social anxiety and rapid social change have been coupled with a rise of interest and influence of Christian evangelism (Fogel, 1999). The first three centuries of the American experience were each marked by periods of religious fervor know as "Great Awakenings." As the late 20th century approached the second Christian millennium, efforts were undertaken by evangelists, such as Jerry Falwell, and Pat Robertson to generate a fourth "Great Awakening" (Fogel, 1999). The effects of the most recent period of religious renewal, which began in the late 1960s, continue to reverberate through American society including the calls for character education. In its most extreme form the advocacy for character education in the public schools assumes a reactionary premodern stance through calls for a return to prayer in schools, the posting of the Ten Commandments on school walls, and opportunities for students to engage in bible study. The current U.S. Secretary of Education, Rod Paige, had the following to say in an interview in Tennessee:

> All things equal, I would prefer to have a child in a school that has a strong appreciation for the values of the Christian community, where a child is taught to have a strong faith.... The reason that Christian schools and Christian universities are growing is a result of a strong value system. In a religious environment the value system is set. That's not the case in a public school where there are so many different kids with different kinds of values. (Brummett, 2003, p. A15)

The views of Secretary Paige reflect one reaction to the challenges of postmodernity. For the most part, however, the responses of school systems to the calls for character education have drawn from the deep well of American pragmatism and have focused essentially on a search for what will "work" to reduce aggression, increase prosocial conduct, and a sense of community among students (Murphy, 1998; Ryan & Bohlin, 1998). In short, mainstream character education is about creating "nice people," emphasizing what Rest, Narvaez, Bebeau, and Thoma (1999) refer to as "interpersonal morality." With this pragmatism, however, moral education loses the progressive moral vision that modernist developmental theories such as Kohlberg's offered. Thus, the broader purpose of moral education as enabling a citizenry to reach a postconventional principled moral orientation (Kohlberg & Mayer, 1972) is at risk of becoming reduced to conformity to the moral status quo. By definition, such a conventional moral orientation ensures that whatever moral shortcomings may exist within the current social consensus are not examined. In effect it is a recipe for guaranteeing moral blindness in the name of moral virtue.

Finally, hybrid efforts have been launched in an attempt to "split the difference" between Kohlberg and traditional character education (Berkowitz, 2002; Lickona, 1991). In the hands of such pragmatists, the Kohlberg approach becomes a placeholder for practices aimed at developing moral judgment (Berkowitz, 2002). (For an excellent overview of these hybrid approaches see Narvaez, chap. 26, this volume.) The effort to coordinate paradigms with such divergent underlying assumptions is always difficult and generally problematic (Overton, 1998). Within the field of moral education, the trend over time is for hybrid approaches to lose their connection to developmental research and to move toward the practices and values that complement the concerns for order and compliance that are at the core of traditional character education, and the conventional values of schools as institutions. For example, in the latest version of one of the most influential of these hybrid approaches, Lickona (2004) outlines "Ten essential virtues" that form the content of character. Along with this new "bag of virtues" that include hard work, humility, gratitude, and fortitude (wisdom is listed as the number one virtue, justice as number two), comes advice with how to target a virtue a week, a month, and even a yearly virtue theme. The latter comes with a developmental proposal for how to sequence attention to these virtues by grade level (e.g., orderliness in kindergarten, effort in first grade, kindness in second grade). It is a sequence without foundation in developmental research or any discernible connection to moral growth.

BEYOND KOHLBERG: FROM GLOBAL STAGES TO DOMAINS

The changes brought about by the end of modernism and the cyclical ascent of political conservatism account for some of the reactionary movement away from Kohlberg and toward traditional character education. In addition to those larger shifts in the intellectual and social landscape are advances in the knowledge base that have unearthed limitations in Kohlberg's description of moral growth (Rest et al., 1999; Turiel, 1998). Among the more salient problems for Kohlberg's theory as they pertain to the present discussion regarding moral education are the inconsistencies in expression of moral stage within individuals across contexts (Carpendale & Krebs, 1992; Teo, Becker, & Edelstein, 1995), the lack of fit between the Kohlberg assessment of moral growth and the moral judgments of persons from non-Western cultures (Dien, 1982; Snarey & Keljo, 1991), and the general lack of correspondence between moral reasoning and behavior when defined in terms of Kohlberg stage (Blasi, 1980; Colby & Damon, 1992).

Although these problems with Kohlberg's (1984) moral psychology have led some to conclude that the entire developmental enterprise is in its "epicycle" phase (Shweder, 1982), both the philosophical (Laden, 2001) and psychological work on moral development has progressed in ways that address the concerns for attention to pluralism and context. This more recent work continues the search for commonalities in human morality from a rational and constructivist orientation that was the centerpiece of Kohlberg's work. However, the depiction of development as moving inexorably toward a universal moral endpoint, where decision making is accounted for by a single cognitive structure of principled moral judgment, has been replaced by a conception of moral and social reasoning that is more heterogeneous and multifaceted (Rest et al., 1999; Sokol & Chandler, 2004; Turiel, 2002). The bulk of this chapter centers around the implications for moral education that stem from this more recent work in what is referred to as *social–cognitive domain theory* (Smetana, chap. 5, this volume; Turiel, 1983, 1998; Turiel & Davidson, 1986). This view of social development holds that children construct social concepts within discrete developmental frameworks that are generated out of qualitatively differing aspects of their social interactions. As has been described in other chapters in this volume, domain theory differentiates between moral concepts of the nonarbitrary and therefore universal features of social relations pertaining to matters of human welfare and fairness, and concepts about social conventions that are the contextually dependent and agreed upon social rules of a given social system (Turiel, 1983). The domains of morality and convention are further differentiated from conceptions of personal matters of privacy and individual discretion (Nucci, 1996). In contrast with the Kohlbergian view of development, in which morality is gradually differentiated from and eventually displaces convention as a basis for making moral judgments, domain theory maintains that conceptions of morality and convention coexist as separate conceptual frameworks throughout the developmental process. These domains correspond to what Piaget (1985) referred to as partial systems with respect to the mind as a totality. Each partial system forms an internally equilibrated structure that may operate on its own as in the case of moral judgments about unprovoked harm, or may interact with other systems requiring interdomain coordination as in the case of judgments regarding the right or wrong of social conventions privileging men over women within traditional societies (Neff, 2001; Turiel & Wainryb, 2000; Wainryb & Turiel, 1994). Thus, domain theory anticipates in ways that Kohlberg's stage theory does not that the weight given to moral and nonmoral considerations in rendering a moral judgment may shift from context to context and from one cultural setting to another (Turiel, Hildebrandt, & Wainryb, 1991).[1]

REDEFINING THE DEVELOPMENTAL AIMS OF MORAL EDUCATION

This more complex account of moral and social development has led to corresponding modifications in statements of the developmental aims of moral education (Nucci, 1997, 2001; Turiel, 1989). In contrast to the straightforward goal of stimulating movement through a single developmental sequence of moral reasoning (Kohlberg & Mayer, 1972), more current views acknowledge the heterogeneity at work in children's social reasoning. The core focus of moral education from a developmental perspective continues to be on students' conceptions of fairness, human welfare and rights, and the application of

---

[1] The view of contextualized moral decision making that emerges from domain theory has much in common with recent moral philosophy building from John Rawls later works (Rawls, 1993, 2001). In these more recent formulations, the rational and universal moral core of justice as fairness is coordinated with the pluralist claims of feminism and identity politics (Laden, 2001). Rather than viewing such local claims as antithetical to a universal ethics, justice as fairness is seen as central to the arguments for pluralist rather than hegemonic definitions of social values. Enlightenment concerns for a rational and nonarbitrary basis for arriving at moral positions did not end with the demise of modernity. Instead the application of moral reasoning has been recast in these newer philosophical treatments as guiding the search for reasonable moral solutions concordant with respect for local tradition and custom along with a willingness to critically examine the status quo (Laden, 2001).

those moral understandings to issues of everyday life (Nucci, 1997). This includes the construction of understandings of morality in interpersonal relations (Damon, 1988), as well as the development of concepts of the fairness of social practices (Thorkildsen, 2000).

In addition to attention to development in the moral domain, however, moral education is also seen as including a focus on the development of conceptions within other domains of social knowledge (i.e., societal convention, the personal) that would bear on the capacity of students to coordinate the moral and nonmoral components of contextualized social values and actions (Nucci, 2001; Turiel, 1989). For example, in contrast with the classical Kohlbergian treatment of convention as an inferior basis for arriving at moral decisions, concepts of convention are recognized as integral to students' appreciation for communal societal norms as well as the capacity for critical moral reflection on the existing social system. In acknowledging the importance of convention in structuring everyday social interaction, this approach to children's social development addresses some of the basic concerns of traditional education that schooling contribute to students' appreciation of such commonly shared social norms. Conventions include the norms of dress, forms of address, and social "manners" that often constitute the points of conflict between children and parents (Smetana, 2002), and students and teachers (Smetana, 2005). Although most children have acquired the content of their society's conventions by early elementary school, the purpose of such rules is not easily understood. It is not until middle to late adolescence that children develop a coordinated understanding of conventions as constituent elements of social systems (Nucci, Becker & Horn, 2004; Turiel, 1983). In addition, the course of development in the construction of concepts of convention involves phases during which children and adolescents question the importance and even the need for such consensually determined social standards (see Lapsley, chap. 2, this volume). It is little wonder, then, that traditional efforts to directly instill such values without attention to development and the construction of such broader underlying conceptions of conventions seem to fall flat.

Evidence that children at all points in development are capable of evaluating actions and social norms in moral terms means that educators may engage students in critical moral reflection at all grade levels. The goals of moral education are not limited to the stimulation of progressively higher levels of social and moral reasoning (Kohlberg & Mayer, 1972), but are extended to the more complex task of increasing the ability and tendencies of students to evaluate and coordinate the moral and nonmoral elements of multifaceted social issues (Nucci, 2001; Turiel, 1989). This becomes particularly important in contexts where the norms of peer culture or society at large overlap with morality. For example, issues of social exclusion and school bullying engage students' concepts about convention and personal choice as well as concerns for fairness and harm (Horn, 2003; Killen, Stangor, Price, Horn, & Sechrist, 2004). In such cases, teachers have both a responsibility and the capacity to influence the degree to which their students attend to the moral aspects of cultural practices. This stated goal of moral education is uncontroversial when applied to issues such as school bullying where there is considerable adult consensus about the moral status of the actions. Matters become more complex for educators, however, once the goal of engaging students in critical moral reflection becomes extended to the broad matrix of societal norms and customs touched on by the school curriculum. Such attention to the morality of extant social practices inevitably results in the generation of controversy, and may place the educator in the position of supporting students' questioning of prevailing community standards on moral grounds. It is precisely at such junctures, however, that moral education moves beyond the shared goal of creating "nice people" toward the ethical imperative of empowering students to engage in genuinely moral lives (Schubert, 1997).

THE PRACTICE OF MORAL EDUCATION

The remaining sections of this chapter focus on approaches to educational practices. As stated, the framework for this chapter is the recent work on social cognitive domain theory. All developmental approaches, however, share a common view that moral growth comes about through the child's progressive construction of ways of understanding the world, and not just an accommodation to the positions and practices of adults and society. For this reason, many of the specific practices that have emerged from educational research conducted within the classical Piagetian and Kohlberg paradigms (e.g., Berkowitz & Gibbs, 1983; DeVries & Zan, 1994; Lind, 2003; Power et al., 1989a, 1989b) remain relevant and are incorporated within this review. The discussion also incorporates relevant practices that have emerged from applications of other developmental perspectives (e.g., Noddings, 2002; Watson, 2003) germane to moral education. The discussion of educational practices is divided into two major sections. The first explores the ways in which schools may contribute to students' moral and social growth through direct social experience. This section examines issues pertaining to the emotional climate of schools and classrooms, developmental approaches to classroom management and discipline, and the provision of service learning. The second section explores moral education through the use of the academic curriculum.

School-Based Social Interactions and Moral Growth

A basic premise of structural–developmental psychology, which has guided social–cognitive domain theory (and Kohlberg's theory), is that a child's knowledge is constructed out of actions (Inhelder & Piaget, 1969; Piaget, 1965). Observational studies of children and adults in school, home, and free-play settings have provided a consistent body of evidence that the forms of social interaction associated with morality are qualitatively different from the social interactions children employ to construct their basic understandings of societal convention, and matters of personal prerogative (see Nucci, 2003a for a comprehensive review). Interactions having to do with morality tend to focus on the effects those actions have on the welfare of others. In the case of moral events, children experience such interactions as victims, perpetrators, or third-person observers. Interactions around societal conventions, in contrast, tend to focus on the norms or rules that apply, along with feedback regarding the social organizational function of the norm (e.g., to maintain classroom order). To be discussed in greater detail, these domain-related patterns of social interaction are also associated with differing forms of emotional experience and emotional expression (Arsenio & Lover, 1995). Throughout development, then, the emotional climate of the school, and the pattern of peer and student–teacher interactions form a basic context within which schools either unwittingly or self-consciously contribute to students' social and moral development (Hansen, 1995). The sections that follow first examine the ways in which emotion is integrated within the child's construction of moral knowledge and how that process is affected by the establishment of a moral climate of trust. The process of establishing trust in the classroom is then further elaborated in a discussion of developmental discipline and its role in contributing to students' moral and social growth. Issues related to school rules lead to a discussion of the special case of adolescent resistance and the implications of such normative resistance for classroom practices. Finally, this portion of the chapter explores recent efforts to impact students' moral and social growth through direct social experiences associated with service learning.

Establishing a Moral Climate of Trust.   There has been a great deal of attention paid in recent years to the topic of moral emotion, accompanied by suggestions for ways in which school practices might foster the emotional component of moral functioning. Unfortunately, much of what has been written has served to further the misconception that cognition and affect operate independently. For example, latter day emotivists have made claims that peoples' responses to moral events are directed by a set of inborn affective triggers, and that moral reasoning occurs after the fact as a means to explain our own reactions to ourselves (Green & Haidt, 2002; Haidt, 2001; Izard, 1986). Such models are built from research indicating that humans possess a number of inborn capacities to display and to recognize in others basic emotions such as anger, sadness, and joy (Ekman, 1993), and that human infants appear to be primed to respond empathically to the distress of others (Emde, Hewitt, & Kagan, 2001; Ludemann, 1991; Sternberg, Campos, & Emde, 1983). From an evolutionary/adapative view of intelligence one may argue that such basic emotional schemata provide a "quick and dirty" response to social problems that may be a part of our evolutionary heritage. Unmediated raw emotion, however, is hardly adaptive in the social world. Critics have argued that such emotivist models fail to adequately account for the ways in which cognitions constructed over a person's lifetime alter or enter into the regulation of affect, and final appraisal of a social situation (Pizarro & Bloom, 2003). Moreover, such emotivist theories misrepresent the ways in which affect and cognition are intertwined, even in the case of such inborn affective response systems (Damasio, 1996).

An alternative and arguably more comprehensive theory of the role of affect as it relates to children's moral and social development has been provided by Arsenio and his colleagues (Arsenio & Lover, 1995). Arsenio's work demonstrates that children associate different feelings with different domains of social events. Issues of social conventions generally elicit "cool" or neutral affect on the part of children. This holds for acts of compliance as well as transgressions (Arsenio, 1988). To the extent that children experience "hot" emotions, it is on the part of adults who occasionally respond with anger to children's conventional transgressions (Shweder, Mahapatra, & Miller, 1987). Issues of morality, however, are viewed by children as filled with "hot" emotions of anger, fear, and sadness among victims of transgressions, and happiness among all parties in the cases where moral situations turn out fairly (Arsenio, 1988).

Emotions are routinely stored as part of the construction of social–cognitive representations (Arsenio & Lover, 1995). Repeated experience with events having similar emotional outcomes allow children to form generalized social scripts (Karniol, 2003). These scripts constitute substrates for the procedural knowledge described within information theory accounts of moral action (see Narvaez, chap. 26, this volume for an account of an information processing view of moral development and education) and in the view of some researchers, the beginnings of our moral character (Kochanska, 1993). As children coordinate these affect-laden social scripts, they extract commonalities in their experiences to generate moral concepts of fairness or victimization. Seemingly automatic reactions to familiar moral events result from the affective triggering of the procedural knowledge or scripts associated with these broader conceptual frameworks of moral judgment and reasoning. Thus, affect serves as a heuristic in the rapid selection of actions in familiar contexts (Gilovich, Grifffin, & Kahneman, 2002). The cross-cultural commonalities that we observe in the meaning of moral acts may be accounted for in part because of the basic similarities in meanings that people attribute to the emotions that accompany moral events.

The role of affect in such social constructions also means that individual variations in the affective experiences of children are reflected in their moral orientations. For example, variations in the early construction of moral schemata, such as differences in the child's temperament (Kochanska, 1993), the degree of anger displayed by adults in reactions to children's transgressions, or the warmth in reaction to children's prosocial conduct (Cumberland-Li, Eisenberg, Champion, Gershoff, & Fabes, 2003; Emde, Birigen, Clyman, & Oppenheim, 1991) appear to impact the way in which children construct their basic concepts of the social world and how to react within interpersonal situations. The core of morality is the capacity to engage in moral reciprocity. For the child growing up in an affectively supportive environment, the construction of moral reversibility (fairness) is supported by the experience of "goodwill" that comes from acts of fair reciprocity (Aresnio & Lover, 1995). This goodwill complements the positive feelings and happiness that children experience when they engage in acts of prosocial conduct (Eisenberg, 1986). In contrast, children with long-term patterns of victimization and peer rejection tend to establish a pattern of "ill will," distorting the construction of moral reciprocity in support of aggressive actions toward others (Arsenio & Lover, 1995). From the perspective of the classroom teacher, this effect of early emotional experience helps to explain the variations they observe in children's tendencies to respond to peers in fair and caring or aggressive ways. It also implies that an important element of a teacher's approach to children's moral and social growth is the establishment of a classroom climate and teacher practice that maximizes the likelihood that students experience goodwill during their time at school.

The importance of an emotionally supportive environment for the construction of morality has not been lost on proponents of moral education. For some educators the establishment of a caring environment and an overall "ethic of care" is the most essential component of moral education (Noddings, 2002). Critical to the establishment of a caring orientation is the capacity to accept care from others. This requires a school and classroom climate in which students can afford to be emotionally vulnerable, and in which that vulnerability extends to the student's willingness to risk engagement in acts of kindness and concern for others (Noddings, 2002). This notion of an ethic of care is related to a more general conceptualization of the school and classroom environment around the establishment of relationships based on trust (Watson, 2003). Trust carries with it the affective connections of care, regulated by moral reciprocity, and continuity. Thus trust corresponds essentially to what Arsenio and Lover describe as an "orientation of goodwill." Trust is basic to the construction of an overall sense of school or classroom community that in turn is one of the primary predictors of prosocial conduct in schools (Battistich, Solomon, Watson, & Schaps, 1997). Trust has been accorded a central role not only in the effective management of classrooms, but also in the overall success of efforts at school reform more generally (Bryk & Schneider, 2002).

Developmental Discipline.   Establishing trust within classrooms has been the focus of Watson's work within what she describes as *developmental discipline* (Watson, 2003). The basic goal of developmental discipline is to enlist children's intrinsic motivations for autonomy and social connection to help students engage in moral conduct for their own reasons (Deci, 1995). Although Watson (2003) grounds her approach to developmental discipline in attachment theory, it has much in common at a practical level with the classroom management practices that DeVries and Zan (1994) advocate for preschool settings based on their reading of Piaget and Kohlberg. Both developmental approaches integrate affective warmth from a caring adult with an emphasis on the uses of moral discourse and reflection as a tool for behavioral change and moral growth. In these approaches there is an appreciation that moral development requires student's construction of their own understandings of fairness and not simply the appropriation of adult norms and values.

Teachers employing developmental discipline minimize their use of power assertion, and focus instead on efforts to engage students in reflection on their own motivations and feelings as well as the effects that their actions have had on others. Thus, the teacher's responses are designed to encourage students to integrate the emotional and consequential information generated around moral actions in the children's construction of moral understandings. Conflicts are resolved by mediating discourse between or among students with encouragement to find their own solutions, rather than resorting to teacher-imposed resolutions. This approach is consistent with evidence that preschool and elementary school age children prefer to resolve their own moral disputes rather than have an adult-imposed solution (Killen, Breton, Ferguson, & Handler, 1994). Transgressors are encouraged to find ways to make reparations for the harm or injustice they have caused, rather than having the teacher administer an expiative punishment.

DeVries and Zan (1994), as well as Watson, advocate the involvement of students in the construction or modification of the rules governing school conduct. For Watson (2003), engagement of students in the process of establishing classroom customs is an aspect of community building that contributes to the overall atmosphere of trust. Following Piaget (1932), DeVries and Zan (1994) advocate children's evaluation and modification of school rules to encourage the construction of young children's autonomous morality and movement away from their heteronomous conception of rules and norms as the eternal and inviolable constructions of adults. More recently, however, they have accommodated their Piagetian stance to differentiate between moral norms that they describe as relating to fair treatment of people and animals and the fair distribution of goods, from discretionary norms that refer to classroom procedures and conventions (DeVries & Zan, 2003).

The more recent positions taken by these developmental educators (DeVries, Hildebrandt, & Zan, 2000) are consistent with research indicating that attention to the domain of social norms is an important variable in the effectiveness of classroom practices. Observational studies conducted of the relative frequency of rule violations in first- through eighth-grade classrooms have consistently indicated that the vast majority of misconduct is with respect to violations of conventions rather than in the form of moral transgressions (Blumenfeld, Pintrich, & Hamilton, 1987; Nucci & Nucci, 1982). This indicates that the assimilation of all classroom management issues to morality runs the risk of diminishing the force of moral argumentation by directing it around issues that are primarily matters of convention, and limit the extent to which classroom interactions can be employed as a way to engage students' thinking about convention. Interview studies conducted with preschool (Killen et al., 1994) and elementary school children grades two through seven (Nucci, 1984) indicate that students evaluate teacher responses to transgressions in terms of their concordance with the domain defining features of the actions. Domain-concordant responses to violations of school or classroom conventions such as being out of line or not raising one's hand before speaking consist of teacher statements referring to the governing rules or by statements engaging students to consider the disruptions to classroom organization or social functioning that result from the transgression. Directing students to consider the consequences of such actions on the welfare of others, on the other hand, are responses concordant with moral transgressions. Students across grade levels were found to rate domain-concordant responses higher than they rated domain-discordant ones (e.g., providing a moral response to a conventional transgression; Killen et al., 1994; Nucci, 1984). Fifth graders and above extended their evaluations of responses to transgression to include their evaluation of the teachers such that teachers who consistently responded to transgressions in a domain-concordant manner were rated more knowledgeable and effective than teachers who consistently provided domain-discordant responses (Nucci, 1984).

Research conducted on the effectiveness of developmental discipline on students' prosocial behavior has been largely supportive (Battistich et al., 1997). However, recent decisions by the Developmental Studies Center to eliminate developmental discipline from their teacher training options raises some important questions regarding the viability of such student centered approaches to classroom management. Up until 2002, Watson's approach to classroom management and discipline had been an integral component of the work of the Child Development Project (Watson, Solomon, Battistich, Schaps, & Solomon, 1989), perhaps the most successful of the hybrid efforts to integrate traditional and developmental approaches to education. (An overview of this program is contained in Narvaez, chap. 26, this volume.) The decision reached by the Developmental Studies Center (not endorsed by Watson) was based on the conclusion that the amount of effort to train teachers to effectively engage in developmental discipline was beyond what was considered practical for their teacher in-service offerings (Watson, personal communication November, 2003). This set of events mirrors a general pattern of abandonment of developmental approaches to education by proponents of hybrid programs, and raises more general questions about the practicality of efforts to prepare teachers to engage in moral education solely through the mechanism of in-service seminars and retreats. These issues of teacher preparation are taken up again in the discussion about uses of the academic curriculum.

School Rules, Resistance, and the Special Case of Adolescents.

Most of the research conducted on classroom interactions and moral growth has been done in elementary school settings. Adolescence, however, particularly during the middle school and high school freshman years, poses a set of challenges and opportunities that need to be addressed separately. Among the developmental changes that typify these years are two broad shifts in reasoning about social convention and the personal domain. With respect to social convention, young adolescents enter a phase in which they question the basis upon which they upheld conventions during middle childhood (Nucci et al., 2004; Turiel, 1983). The support for conventions as reflecting the norms of authority established in support of the goal of maintaining basic order (e.g., to keep kids from running in the hallways) evaporates as young people reconsider the arbitrariness of conventional regulations, and conclude that they are "simply the arbitrary dictates of authority" (Turiel, 1983). In many cases, students at this level of development continue to adhere to conventions to maintain smooth relations with teachers or avoid sanctions. However, students at this level are unable to produce a conceptual rationale for the conventions themselves (Nucci et al., 2004). Thus, there is greater tendency for students at this point in development to engage in the violation of school conventions (Geiger & Turiel, 1983; Nucci & Nucci, 1982). By middle adolescence, about age 15 or the sophomore year of high school, most American adolescents have moved to the next level of reasoning about social convention (Nucci et al., 2004). At this level conventions are viewed as constituent elements of the social system structuring hierarchical relations, and coordinating interactions among members of a society or societal institution such as the school (Turiel, 1983).

Coincident with these developmental shifts in concepts of convention are basic changes in the ways in which adolescents draw the boundaries between convention and what they consider to be matters of personal prerogative and privacy (Smetana, 2002). Areas where the conventions and norms of the family and school touch on personal expression (dress, hairstyle), personal associations (friendships), personal communication (phone, e-mail), access to information (Internet), and personal safety (substance use, sexuality) become zones of dispute wherein adolescents lay increasing claims to autonomy and control. Family disputes across cultures are largely around such issues as adolescents begin to appropriate greater areas of personal jurisdiction from what had been areas of parental influence or control (Smetana, 2002). Within school settings, students also lay claim to zones of personal privacy and prerogative (Smetana & Bitz, 1996). They are also somewhat more willing, however, to accept conventions regulating conduct within the school setting such as public displays of affection (kissing in public) that would be considered personal in nonschool contexts (Smetana & Bitz, 1996). Nevertheless, the combined developmental phase of negation of convention with the extension of what is considered personal renders the period of early adolescence a difficult transition as students struggle with the norms of schools as institutions.

In discussing the educational implications of this period of early adolescent transition, Smetana (2005) refers to the work of Eccles and her colleagues as providing a window into the mismatch that currently exists between schools and young adolescents around these normative issues. These researchers (Eccles et al., 1993; Eccles, Wigfield, & Schiefele, 1998) have provided evidence that, despite the increased maturity of adolescents, middle schools and junior high schools emphasize greater teacher control and discipline and offer fewer opportunities for student involvement in decision making, choice, and self-management than do elementary school classrooms. Accordingly, Eccles and her colleagues (1998) have reported that the mismatch between adolescents' efforts to attain greater autonomy and the schools' increased efforts at control resulted in declines in junior high students' intrinsic motivation and interest in school.

From a developmental perspective, the responses of schools to this period of transition amount to a defensive maneuver to maintain order through institutional power while waiting out a passing developmental storm. An alternative approach recommended by Eccles (Eccles et al., 1993, 1998) is that schools include more opportunities for students to have input into the norms governing classroom practices. More specifically, Smetana's (Smetana & Bitz, 1996) research and the observational studies of student transgressions (Geiger & Turiel, 1983; Nucci & Nucci, 1982) indicate that the focus of such student input and discourse should be around matters of social convention and personal prerogative. Other work exploring the impact of developmental discourse around issues of convention has demonstrated that such discussion can effectively contribute to students' levels of understanding about the social functions of such norms (Nucci & Weber, 1991). Thus, schools and classroom teachers would be able to come out of their foxholes to engage students in discourse that would contribute to their social development as well as the smooth functioning of schools as educational institutions.

Although the majority of adolescent misconduct is around issues of convention, some of the efforts to establish autonomy and identity entail engagement in risk taking and moral transgressions (Lightfoot, 1997). The Swiss developmentalist, Oser (2005; Oser & Veugelers, 2003) has argued that educators should view such moral misconduct as an essential component for moral growth, and seize on moral transgressions as an opportunity for what he refers to as "realistic discourse." Oser's (in press) position is that "negative morality" like mistakes in math class comprises the basis from which a genuine moral epistemology and moral orientation arise. His approach to moral misconduct in adolescence is to make it the subject of moral discourse in which students must confront one another's actual misdeeds and interpretations of their motives and the consequences of their actions (Oser & Veugelers, 2003). Oser's approach builds from prior work done in the Kohlberg tradition on what is referred to as the "just community" (Power et al., 1989a, 1989b). Teachers leading these discussion sessions encourage participants to engage in what are referred to as transactive forms of discourse found in prior research to lead to moral development (Berkowitz & Gibbs, 1983; Oser, 1991). Teachers support forms of discourse that entail efforts by each speaker to extend the logic of the prior speaker's argument, refute the assumptions of the argument, or provide a point of commonality between competing positions. The processes advocated by Oser have been employed with considerable success by others working within the Kohlberg tradition (Blakeney & Blakeney, 1991) to alter the misconduct and recidivism among behaviorally disordered children and adolescents.

Many of the moral conflicts of adolescence are not straightforward matters confined to the moral domain. Issues of peer exclusion and harassment call on students' conceptions of peer conventions of dress and behavior, personal domain construals of the selection of personal associations and friendships, and moral concepts of harm and fairness (Horn, 2003; Killen, Lee-Kim, McGlothlin, & Stangor, 2002). The uses of moral discourse around such issues in the absence of attention to the ways in which students are focusing on the nonmoral aspects of a given situation of peer exclusion are ineffective. For example, peer systems of social status and hierarchy employ conventions of dress and behavior as markers of group membership (Horn, 2003). Middle adolescents, having just constructed an understanding of conventions as constituent elements of social systems, tend also to be more likely than younger or older adolescents to justify exclusion of peers whose clothing or behavior does not conform to peer conventions (Horn, 2003). Focusing only on the fairness or harm involved does not address the motivations and justifications for exclusion maintained by a young person whose focus is on the importance of peer conventions in defining group membership and identity status. An effective discourse around such a multifaceted social issue starts with an examination of the presumptive importance of the conventions as modes for defining group membership, social status, and personal identity (Horn, 2005). Only after students have had an opportunity to fully explore the meaning and ramifications of their use of conventions to define group membership is a discussion of the moral implications of such peer exclusion fruitful.

Service Learning: Connecting Social Experiences With the Community. An emerging trend in approaches to moral education has been the extension of school-based social experiences to include community service activities. Efforts to promote youth engagement in community service are not new, and in the U.S. can be traced back to William James who regarded service to the broader community and nation as the "Moral Equivalent to War" (Killen & Horn, 2000). When community service is linked to the school curriculum in the form of mandated requirements it is given the label "service learning." Programs for service learning are diverse and include a range of activities from tutoring or coaching youth sports to working in a community soup kitchen. For this reason the impact of service learning has been somewhat difficult to evaluate. Nonetheless, some conclusions have begun to emerge indicating that well-run service-learning programs lead to an increased level of civic engagement (Andersen, 1998; Youniss, McLellan, & Mazer, 2001; Youniss & Yates, 1997), and are associated with an increase in positive moral action and a decrease in rates of delinquent conduct (Hart, Atkins & Ford, 1998).

At least two factors appear to be important for service learning to positively impact students' social growth. The first is that some degree of choice as to the nature of the particular activity a student takes part in seems to be important for the activity to have positive benefit (Andersen, 1998; Barker & Eccles, 1997; Leming, 1999). The importance of choice is linked to student motivation as well as identity formation. In this regard, Leming (1999) reported that when programs force students into so-called voluntary service activities, they result in alienation among adolescents who see through what they perceive to be blatant attempts by schools to make them into particular sorts of people.

The second critical factor is that the service-learning activity be linked to a period of reflection (Andersen, 1998; Youniss et al., 2001; Youniss & Yates, 1998. The degree of reflection varies from program to program from such minimal activities as writing a one-page reaction paper to keeping a daily journal (Killen & Horn, 2000). The importance of reflection rests in the opportunities it affords for students to share feelings and experiences, and to connect those experiences to their own social values and sense of self (Andersen, 1998). Killen and Horn (2000) suggest that such reflection engages students in considering issues of fairness and social inequality that foster moral growth, and may also touch upon consideration of the ways in which conventional stereotypes constrain outgroups such as the poor and disabled. Opportunities for reflection on service activities may also engage students in discovering one's connections to others and concomitant sense of responsibility and efficacy (Killen & Horn, 2000). Finally, it has been proposed that the effectiveness of service learning to foster the connection between moral actions and personal identity stems from the student's own reflection upon the ideological assumptions of service agencies, and the moral impact of service activities in relation to the values maintained by the individual student (Youniss et al., 2001; Youniss & Yates, 1997).

Moral Education Through the Curriculum

Up to this point the focus of discussion has been the contributions schools make to students' moral and social growth through direct social experience such as classroom management strategies, the social and emotional climate and structure of schools, and provision of service-learning opportunities. These efforts to impact moral and social values through reflection on lived experience contribute to the development of interpersonal morality essential to the establishment of moral character. The moral and social understandings constructed through direct social experience can also be generated through reflection on moral and social events presented through academic curriculum. Within the traditional approaches to character education, the curriculum has been used to present instances of moral virtue, or as opportunities for students to extract the moral lessons presented in historical and literary events or personages. For example, Bennett (1996) provided a popular compendium of stories from the Bible and other literary sources as well as descriptions of the lives of American historical figures such as Booker T. Washington intended to embody the virtues of responsibility, courage, compassion, loyalty, honesty, friendship, persistence, hard work, discipline, and faith. Leaving aside questions about the particular collection of virtues focused on by Bennett (1996), research exploring the impact of this approach to the use of curricula has demonstrated that merely presenting moral stories does not result in the intended effects on children's moral development (Narvaez, 2002). The moral arguments presented in such texts are understood differently by children within a given classroom as a function of the variations in their conceptions of morality. Children do not generally extract moral story themes as intended by the writer or assumed by the instructor (Narvaez, 2002). Thus, the simple exposure of students to presumably moral content does not result in moral development.

Effective use of the curriculum for the promotion of moral growth involves selection of a moral or social values issue contained within a particular lesson or assignment, and the generation of a reflective discussion around the focal issue (Lockwood & Harris, 1985; Simon, 2001). The lesson may also make use of role playing, simulation, and written work to further engage students in active learning. Effective use of the curriculum also requires a correspondence between the content of moral and social values lessons and the academic goals of the teacher (Higgins, 1991). Elements critical to the effective use of curricula to stimulate moral and social development are (a) correspondence between the domain of the focal issue(s) of the lesson and the content of the discourse or written assignments (Nucci, 2001), and (b) employment of tasks requiring the student to engage in cognitive reflection (Lind, 2003; Oser, 1991). With respect to the latter, critical reflection may be stimulated by the forms of transactive discourse described above (Oser, 1991) and in other sources (Cazden, 2003), or through written assignments. In both cases, stimuli for the students' reflection come in the form of teacher questions requiring students to generate their own answers and to integrate divergent perspectives (Lind, 2003; Rest, 1986).

A developmental approach to use of the curriculum for moral growth also recognizes the unique role of curricular sources of moral content for the broader goals of moral education. Challenging students' broader conceptions of the morality of social systems, particularly the cultural assumptions and values of the system they inherit, requires going beyond direct personal experience. Through the academic curriculum, schools introduce students to the storehouse of knowledge about the factual assumptions of the natural world, the history of peoples and civilizations, and the reflections and interpretations people have given to their lived experiences in literature and the arts. As such, the academic curriculum presents the primary medium through which schools may extend moral education beyond the goal of fostering basic interpersonal morality toward a broader capacity for critical moral reflection on the social system and practices that frame day-to-day social interactions (Schubert, 1997). This latter goal was originally conceived within the context of Kohlbergian theory as moving students toward postconventional, principled stages of moral judgment (Kohlberg & Mayer, 1972). Work indicating that morality and convention constitute distinct conceptual and developmental frameworks (Turiel, 1998), however, has led to proposals that students may be encouraged to employ their moral understandings to evaluate social practices at all points in development (Nucci, 2001).

Generating correspondence between the domain of the focal issue and the questions or assignments intended to generate critical reflection requires that teachers engage in an analysis of the domain-related features of the lesson (Nucci, 2001). Illustrative examples of the application of domain concordant values education are provided in Nucci (2001). An example used to illustrate discussion around social convention is a unit drawn from American history in which George Washington refused to accept a letter from King George II of England because it was addressed to Mr. George Washington rather than President George Washington (pp. 180–181). Students in the history unit were directed to consider why Washington returned the letter, and what significance his action had for establishing formal recognition of the United States as a country by the English government. The domain-concordant lesson focused on the function that conventions establishing formal titles serve in differentiating among members within a social system in terms of social position and social hierarchy. None of the discourse in this case centers on moral issues of fairness or human welfare.

In contrast with this example of convention, a history unit exploring the events surrounding John Brown's raid into Kansas formed the basis of a moral lesson focusing on issues of justice and revenge (Nucci, 2001, pp. 184–185). The actions of John Brown and his sons in their efforts to incite a slave rebellion formed the basis of questions directing students to consider whether the effort to free slaves justified the killing that John Brown and his sons committed. In this case, none of the discourse explored governing rules or conventions, but instead focused on the moral elements of fairness and welfare.

A study exploring the impact of domain-concordant moral and social values education on eighth-grade students found that engaging students in classroom discussion and subsequent written assignments about moral issues that focused on considerations of fairness and human welfare was effective in raising students' moral reasoning (Nucci & Weber, 1991). On the other hand, treating a moral issue as a matter of convention by directing the discourse and subsequent written assignments to the rules and norms surrounding actions and the impact on the social system that would result from changes in the governing rules had no impact on students' levels of moral reasoning. Conversely, moralizing social conventions by attempting to get students to consider their impact on human welfare, rights, and fairness did not affect their reasoning about convention, whereas focusing discussion around these same conventional issues on the social organizational functions of the governing rules and norms did lead to development in students' concepts about societal conventions and social systems (Nucci & Weber, 1991). Perhaps most important, instruction that was domain concordant led to a greater frequency in students' tendencies to spontaneously coordinate the moral and conventional elements of social issues, such as women's suffrage, entailing matters of overlap between morality and convention (Nucci & Weber, 1991). This ability to engage in cross-domain coordination is central to the capacity for students to engage in critical moral evaluation of social practices. Recent work on children's conceptions of political systems has indicated that even elementary age school children can engage in meaningful consideration of the morality of various forms of government (Helwig, 1998). Moreover, children tend to spontaneously favor democratic systems that afford individual rights and opportunities for citizens to participate in national governance (Helwig, 1998). Thus, educational efforts to engage students in critical moral reflection afforded by domain-concordant moral pedagogy are concordant with the broader purposes of civics education for students within pluralist democracies.

An issue not generally incorporated as a formal component of moral education is the role of informational assumptions in coloring our view of the morality of actions (Wainryb, 2000). For example, parents who believe that corporal punishment is an effective way to educate children about correct behavior tend to override their awareness that such punishment is painful to the child, and view the act of corporal punishment as morally acceptable (Wainryb, 1991). When such parents are presented with credible information from social science that corporal punishment is no more effective than other forms of discipline, these same parents alter their positions and evaluate corporal punishment as wrong because of the pain and harm that it causes to the child (Wainryb, 1991). In sum, the moral status of corporal punishment shifts as a function of the assumptions people make about the effects of the act. Awareness of the informational assumptions maintained by members of other cultures is also critical to the tendency of children and adolescents to exhibit tolerance of cultural practices maintained by members of other cultures (Wainryb, Shaw, & Maianu, 1998; Wainryb, Shaw, Langley, Cottam, & Lewis, 2004). For example, moral evaluations of groups that engage in the cultural practice of genital cutting of women and girls are substantially affected by whether or not one believes that members of other cultures interpret such cutting as producing long-term harmful effects (Nussbaum, 1999; Shweder, 2003). Children and adolescents are quite capable of differentiating between their own evaluation of the morality of an action and their moral evaluation of members of another culture once differences in informational assumptions are made explicit (Wainryb et al., 1998).

Education for critical moral reflection entails not only an analysis of the social–cognitive domains at issue in a given curricular assignment, but also an exploration by the teacher of whether or not disagreements about the morality of the focal issue is a function of differences in the informational beliefs maintained by students and members of the broader society. For example, in our efforts to generate discourse around the death penalty (Nucci & Multack, 2003), an issue made highly salient for our students by the suspension of capital punishment ordered by the Governor of Illinois in 2002, we discovered that the moral aspects of this issue were obscured by the disagreements students had over such factual matters as whether capital punishment is less expensive than lifetime incarceration, whether it is a deterrent to major crime, whether it is disproportionately imposed on minorities, and whether substantial numbers of errors are made in the conviction of individuals for capital crimes, the reason Governor Ryan gave in for his suspension of the practice in Illinois (Ryan, 2003). To engage in a discussion of the morality of the death penalty it was first necessary to direct the students in teams to seek information from the library and Internet to reach some consensus around these underlying factual disagreements.

At this point the application of the domain-based curricular approach to moral education has been limited to demonstration projects within districts that have requested its implementation (Nucci, 2000). Although these projects have been deemed a success by the researchers, teachers, administrators, and district parents (Nucci, 2003b), widespread implementation or adoption of this curricular approach is likely to face obstacles. The primary challenge facing domain-based social and moral education is shared by all current efforts to apply developmental research to moral education, namely, teacher preparedness to carry out the practices associated with moral and social growth. As described with respect to the current fate of developmental discipline (Watson, 2003), developmentally based teaching requires a skill set that is not generally provided through current preservice teacher education. A recent study of teachers' perceptions of their own efficacy with respect to character education indicated that most teachers feel ill-prepared to engage in even the most basic practices associated with traditional character education, let alone the more demanding practices of a developmental approach to moral and social education (Milson, 2003). In the case of domain-based moral education, this skill set includes an ability to identify issues within the curriculum that correspond to moral, conventional, and personal issues, as well as an ability to help students coordinate domain components of heterogeneous issues. At the present time an effort is underway to assess the efficacy of introducing these skills for use of the academic curriculum through the preservice undergraduate elementary teacher certification program at the University of Illinois at Chicago (Nucci, Drill, Larson & Brown, 2005). It will take several years, however, to determine whether this effort at teacher preparation proves effective.

CONCLUSIONS

Research on children's moral development has progressed considerably since Kohlberg's (Power et al., 1989a, 1989b) initial attempts to apply developmental theory to moral education. This research has demonstrated that one can maintain Kohlberg's progressive vision of moral education (Kohlberg & Mayer, 1972) while also attending to the diversity and heterogeneity of lived moral systems (Laden, 2001). Educational research includes work relevant to the integration of affective climate and classroom social interactions that foster interpersonal morality, and basic human decency (DeVries & Zan, 1994; Noddings, 2002; Watson, 2003) along with an appreciation for the conventions and norms that structure smooth social discourse and the organization of social systems (Nucci, 2001). A basic premise of this chapter, however, is that the construction of interpersonal morality (Rest et al., 1999) in and of itself stops short of the ethical requirement that educational practices prepare students to employ moral understandings to question the morality of the normative system that they inherit. Thus, moral education needs to include opportunities for students to question the status quo. Such opportunities may arise in the context of student challenges to the norms structuring the school and classroom. It was also argued, however, that the academic curriculum affords an excellent opportunity to engage students in consideration of the importance and function of convention in structuring social systems, along with opportunities to explore the moral contradictions of various social systems including their own.

The research reviewed in this chapter did not directly touch on the engagement of teaching to foster a particular kind of person or moral character. Moral agency, however, and the construction of the moral aspects of self are imbedded within each of the practices reviewed. Much has been written about the moral self, and a comprehensive treatment of the issues surrounding this construct is contained within Lapsley and Narvaez (2004). It is questionable, however, that one can separate out the construction of one's morality from the construction of self (Nucci, 2004). As the philosopher Frankena (1978) argues, the morality that we construct in the form of our moral principles, and the morality "of doing and being" (p. 53) are complementary aspects of the same morality such that for every principle there is a corresponding disposition or tendency to act in accordance with it. As we engage children in meaningful reflection on the nature of their own actions and relations with others as is done through "developmental discipline," as well as the moral reflections and constructions that occur through a developmental use of the curriculum, we engage in the process of challenging students' conceptions of the very values and ways of reasoning about the social world that comprise their personal makeup. What we have learned in the past three decades about children's moral and social development permits a variegated approach to preparing students to handle moral controversy, complexity, and heterogeneity. This is not the sort of thing likely to warm the heart of political figures such as the current Secretary of Education and his desire for value simplicity and consistency. However, it comes far closer to the reality of moral functioning and the requisites for a genuinely democratic citizenry (Helwig, 1998).

REFERENCES

Andersen, S. M. (1998). *Service learning: A national strategy for youth development.* Position Paper issued by the Task Force on Education Policy. Washington, D.C.: Institute for Communitarian Policy Studies, George Washington University.

Arsenio, W. (1988). Children's conceptions of the situational affective consequences of sociomoral events. *Child Development, 59,* 1611–1622.

Arsenio, W., & Lover, A. (1995). Children's conceptions of socio-moral affect: Happy victimizers, mixed emotions, and other expectancies. In M. Killen and D. Hart (Eds.). *Morality in everyday life* (pp. 87–130). New York: Cambridge University Press.

Barker, B., & Eccles, J. (1997, April). *Student council volunteering, basketball, or marching band: What kind of extracurricular involvement matters?* Symposium: Adolescent involvement in community. Biennial meeting of the Society for Research in Child Development. Washington, D.C.

Battistich, V., Solomon, D., Watson, M., & Schaps, E. (1997). Caring school communities. *Educational Psychologist, 32,* 137–151.

Bennett, W. (1992). *The de-valuing of America: The fight for our culture and our children.* New York: Simon & Schuster.

Bennett, W. (1996). *The book of virtues for young people: A treasury of great moral stories.* Carmichael, CA: Touchstone Books.

Bennett, W. (1998). *The death of outrage: Bill Clinton and the assault on American ideals.* New York: Simon & Schuster.

Berkowitz, M. W. (2002). The science of character education. In W. Damon (Ed.), *Bringing in a new era in character education.* Stanford, CA: Hoover Institution Press.

Berkowitz, M., & Gibbs, J. (1983). Measuring the developmental features of moral discourse. *Merrill-Palmer Quarterly, 24,* 399–410.

Blakeney, C., & Blakeney, R. (1991) Understanding and reforming moral misbehavior among behaviorally disorder children. *Journal of Behavioral Disorders, 16,* 135–143.

Blasi, G. (1980). Bridging moral cognition and moral action: A critical review of the literature. *Psychological Bulletin, 88,* 1–45.

Bloom, A. (1988). *The closing of the American mind.* New York: Simon & Schuster.

Blumenfeld, P. C., Pintrich, P. R., & Hamilton, V. L. (1987). Teacher talk and students' reasoning about morals, conventions, and achievement. *Child Development, 58,* 1389–1401.

Brummett, J. (2003, April 13). United Christian States of America [column]. *Las Vegas Review-Journal,* A15.

Bryk, A. S., & Schneider, B. (2002). *Trust in schools.* New York: Russell Sage Foundation.

Carpendale, J., & Krebs, D. (1992). Situational variation in moral judgment: In a stage, or on a stage? *Journal of Youth and Adolescence, 21,* 203–224.

Cazden, C. (2003). *Classroom discourse: The language of teaching and learning* (2nd ed.). Portsmouth, NH: Heinemann Press.

Colby, A., & Damon, W. (1992). *Some do care: Contemporary lives of moral commitment.* New York: Free Press.

Cumberland-Li, A., Eisenberg, N., Champion, C., Gershoff, E., & Fabes, R. A. (2003). The relation of parental emotionality and related dispositional traits to parental expression of emotion and children's social functioning. *Motivation and Emotion, 27,* 27–56.

Damasio, A. (1996). *Descartes' error: Emotion, reason and the human brain.* New York: Avon.

Damon, W. (1988). *The moral child.* New York: The Free Press.

Deci, E. (1995). *Why we do what we do: The dynamics of personal autonomy.* New York: G. P. Putnam.

DeVries, R., Hildebrandt, C., & Zan, B. (2000). Constructivist early education for moral development. *Early Education & Development, 11,* 9–35.

DeVries, R., & Zan, B. (1994). *Moral classrooms, moral children: Creating a constructivist atmosphere for early education.* New York: Teachers College Press.

DeVries, R., & Zan, B. (2003). When children make rules. *Educational Leadership, 61,* 64–67.

Dien, D. S. (1982). A Chinese perspective on Kohlberg's theory of moral development. *Developmental Review, 2,* 331–341.

Eccles, J. S., Midgley, C., Wigfield, A., Buchanan, C. M., Reuman, D., Flanagan, C., & Mac Iver, D. (1993). Development during adolescence: The impact of stage-environment fit on adolescents' experiences in schools and families. *American Psychologist, 48,* 90–101.

Eccles, J. S., Wigfield, A., & Schiefele, U. (1998). Motivation to succeed. In W. Damon (Ed.), & N. Eisenberg (Vol. Ed.), *Handbook of child psychology, Vol. 3: Social, emotional, and personality development* (5th ed., pp. 1017–1095). New York: Wiley.

Eisenberg, N. (1986). *Altruistic emotion, cognition and behavior.* Hillsdale, NJ: Lawrence Erlbaum Associates.

Ekman, P. (1993). Facial expressions and emotion. *American Psychologist, 48,* 384–392.

Emde, R., Birigen, Z., Clyman, R., & Oppenheim, D. (1991). The moral self of infancy: Affective core and procedural knowledge. *Developmental Review, 11,* 251–270.

Emde, R., Hewitt, J. K., & Kagan, J. (2001). *Infancy to early childhood: Genetic and environmental influences on developmental change.* Oxford, UK: Oxford University Press.

Fogel, R. W. (1999). *The fourth great awakening and the future of egalitarianism.* Chicago: University of Chicago Press.

Fraenkel, J. R. (1976). The Kohlberg bandwagon: Some reservations. *Social Education, 40,* 216–222.

Frankena, W. K. (1978). *Ethics.* Englewood Cliffs, NJ: Prentice-Hall.

Geiger, K., & Turiel, E. (1983). Disruptive school behavior and concepts of social convention in early adolsecence. *Journal of Educational Psychology, 75,* 677–685.

Gilligan, C. (1982). *In a different voice: Psychological theory and women's development.* Cambridge, MA: Harvard University Press.

Gilovich, T., Grifffin, D., & Kahneman, D. (2002). *Heuristics and biases: The psychology of intuitive judgment.* New York: Cambridge University Press.

Greene, J., & Haidt, J. (2002). How (and where) does moral judgment work? *Trends in Cognitive Sciences, 6*(12), 517–523.

Haidt, J. (2001). The emotional dog and its rational tail: A social intuitionist approach to moral judgment. *Psychological Review, 108,* 814–834.

Hansen, D. T. (1995). Teaching and the moral life of classrooms. *Journal for a Just & Caring Education, 2,* 59–74.

Hart, D., Atkins, R., & Ford, D. (1998). Urban America as a context for the development of moral identity in adolescence. *Journal of Social Issues, 54,* 513–530.

Helwig, C. (1998). Children's conceptions of fair government and freedom of speech. *Child Development, 69,* 518–531.

Higgins, A. (1991). The just community approach. In W. M. Kurtines, & J. L. Gewirtz (Eds.). *Handbook of moral behavior and devlopment, Vol. 3: Applications* (pp. 111–142). Hillsdale, NJ: Lawrence Erlbaum Associates.

Himmelfarb, G. (1994). *One nation, two cultures.* New York: Knopf.

Horn, S. S. (2003). Adolescents' reasoning about exclusion from social groups. *Developmental Psychology, 39,* 71–84.

Horn, S. (2005). Adolescents' peer interactions: Conflict and coordination between personal expression, social norms, and moral reasoning. In L. Nucci (Ed.), *Conflict, contradiction, and contrarian elements in moral development and education* (pp. 113–127), Mahwah, NJ: Lawrence Erlbaum Associates.

Inhelder, B., & Piaget, J. (1969). The early growth of logic in the child. New York: W. W. Norton.

Izard, C. (1986). Approaches to developmental research on emotion-cognition relationships. In D. Bearison, & H. Zimiles (Eds.). *Thought and emotion: Developmental perspectives* (pp. 21–38). Hillsdale, NJ: Lawrence Erlbaum Associates.

Karniol, R. (2003). Egocentricism versus protocentrism: The status of self in social prediction. *Psychological Review, 110*(3), 564–580.

Killen, M., Breton, S., Ferguson, H., & Handler, K. (1994). Preschoolers evaluations of teacher methods of intervention in social transgressions. *Merrill-Palmer Quarterly, 40,* 399–415.

Killen, M., & Horn, S. (2000). Facilitating children's development about morality, community and autonomy: A case for service-learning experiences. In W. van Haaften, T. Wren, & A. Tellings (Eds.). *Moral sensibilities and education II: The schoolchild* (pp. 89–115). Bemmel, The Netherlands: Concorde Publishing.

Killen, M., Lee-Kim, J., McGlothlin, H., & Stangor, C. (2002). How children and adolescents evaluate gender and racial exclusion. *Monograph of the Society for Research in Child Development, 67*(4, Serial No. 271).

Killen, N., Stangor C., Price, B. S., Horn, S., & Sechrist, G. B. (2004). Social reasoning about racial exclusion in intimate and non-intimate relationships. *Youth and Society, 35*, 293–322.

Kochanska, K. (1993). Toward a synthesis of parental socialization and child temperment in early development of conscience. *Child Development, 64*, 325–347.

Kohlberg, L. (1981). *Essays on moral development, Vol. 1: The philosophy of moral development*. San Francisco: Harper and Row.

Kohlberg, L. (1984). *Essays on moral development, Vol 2: The psychology of moral development*. San Francisco: Harper and Row.

Kohlberg, L., & Mayer, R. (1972). Development as the aim of education. *Harvard Educational Review, 42*, 449–496.

Laden. A. S. (2001). *Reasonably radical: Deliberative liberalism and the politics of identity*. Ithica, NY: Cornell University Press.

Lapsley, D. K., & Narvaez, D. (Eds.). (2004). *Moral development, self, and identity*. Mahwah, NJ: Lawrence Erlbaum Associates.

Leming, J. (1999). *The impact of integrating a structured ethical reflection program into high school service-learning experiences of students' sociomoral development*. Unpublished manuscript, Southern Illinois University, Carbondale, Il.

Lickona, T. (1991). *Educating for character: How our schools can teach respect and responsibility*. New York: Bantam Books.

Lickona, T. (2004). *Character matters: How to help our children development good judgment, integrity, and other essential virtues*. Carmichael, CA: Touchstone Books.

Lightfoot, C. (1997). *The culture of adolescent risk-taking*. New York: Guilford.

Lind, G. (2003). *Moral ist lehrbar. Handbuch zur theorie und praxis moralischer und demokratischer bildung*. [Morality can be taught. Handbook on theory and practice of moral and democratic education]. Munich, Germany: Oldenbourg-Verlag.

Lockwood, A. L., & Harris, D. E. (1985). *Reasoning and democratic values: Ethical problems in United States history*. New York: Teachers College Press.

Ludemann, P. (1991). Generalized discrimination of positive facial expressions by 7-month old infants. *Child Development, 62*, 55–67.

MacIntyre, A. (1984). *After virtue* (2nd ed.). Notre Dame, IN: University of Notre Dame Press.

Milson, A. J. (2003). Teachers' sense of efficacy for the formation of students' character. *Journal of Research in Character Education, 1*(2) 89–106.

Murphy, M. M. (1998). *Character education in America's blue ribbon schools: Best practices for meeting the challenge*. Lancaster, PA: Technomic Publishing.

Narvaez, D. (2002). Does reading moral stories build moral character? *Educational Psychology Review, 14*, 155–171.

Neff, K. D. (2001). Judgements of personal autonomy and interpersonal responsibility in the context of Indian spousal relationships: An examination of young people's reasoning in Mysore, India. *British Journal of Developmental Psychology, 19*, 233–257.

Noddings, N. (2002). *Educating moral people: A caring alternative to character*. New York: Teachers College Press.

Nucci, L. (1984). Evaluating teachers as social agents: Students' ratings of domain appropriate and domain-inappropriate teacher responses to transgressions. *American Educational Research Journal, 21*, 367–378.

Nucci, L. (1996). Morality and the personal sphere of actions. In E. Reed, E. Turiel, & T. Brown (Eds.), *Values and knowledge* (pp. 41–60). Hillsdale, NJ.: Lawrence Erlbaum.

Nucci, L. (1997). Moral development and character formation. In H. J. Walberg & G. D. Haertel (Eds.). *Psychology and educational practice* (pp. 127–157). Berkeley, CA: McCutchan.

Nucci, L. (2000, May). *Discovering ethical leadership*. Invited plenary address, Fifth annual Wallace Research Symposium on Talent Development. Iowa City: The University of Iowa.

Nucci, L. (2001). *Education in the moral domain*. Cambridge, UK: Cambridge University Press.

Nucci, L. (2003a). Social interaction and the construction of moral and social knowledge. In J. I. M. Carpendale & U. Muller (Eds.). *Social interaction and knowledge*. Mahwah, NJ: Lawrence Erlbaum Associates.

Nucci, L. (2003b). *Discovering ethical leadership program evaluation: Year 4*. Unpublished technical report, University of Illinois at Chicago.

Nucci, L. (2004). Reflections on the moral self construct. In D. K. Lapsley, & D. Narvaez (Eds.). *Moral development, self, and identity* (111–132). Mahwah, NJ: Lawrence Erlbaum Associates.

Nucci, L., Becker, K., & Horn, S. (2004, June). *Assessing the development of adolescent concepts of social convention*. Paper presented at the annual meeting of the Jean Piaget Society, Toronto, CA.

Nucci, L., Drill, K., Larson, C., & Browne, C. (2005). Integrating character education into the preparation of urban teachers: Implementation and evaluation. Unpublished manuscript, University of Illinois at Chicago.

Nucci, L., & Multack, N. V. (2003). *Middle-school moral and social values lessons: Park Ridge, IL District 64*. Unpublished document, University of Illinois at Chicago.

Nucci, L. & Nucci M. S. (1982). Children's social interactions in the context of moral and conventional transgressions. *Child Development, 53,* 403–412.

Nucci, L., & Weber, E. (1991). Research on classroom applications of the domain approach to values education. In W. Kurtines & J. Gewirtz (Eds.), *Handbook of moral behavior and development: Vol. 3, Applications* (pp. 251–266). Hillsdale, NJ: Lawrence Erlbaum Associates.

Nussbaum, M. (1999). *Sex and social justice*. Oxford, UK: Oxford University Press.

Oser, F. K. (1991). Professional morality: A discourse approach. In W. Kurtines & J. Gewirtz (Eds.). *Handbook of moral development, Vol. 2: Research* (pp. 191–228). Hillsdale, NJ: Lawrence Erlbaum Associates.

Oser, F. (2005). Negative morality and the goals of education. In L. Nucci (Ed.) *Conflict, contradiction, and contrarian elements in moral development and education* (pp. 129–153). Mahwah, NJ: Lawrence Erlbaum Associates.

Oser, F. K., & Veugelers, W. (2003). *Teaching in moral and democratic education*. Bern: Peter Lang Verlag.

Overton, W. F. (1998). Developmental psychology: Philosophy, concepts, and methodology. In R. M. Lerner (Ed.). *Theoretical models of human development, Vol 1: Handbook of child psychology* (5th ed. pp. 107–188). New York: Wiley.

Piaget, J. (1932). *The moral judgment of the child*. New York: Free Press.

Piaget, J. (1965). *The child's conception of number*. New York: W.W. Norton.

Piaget, J. (1985). *The equilibration of cognitive structures*. Chicago: University of Chicago Press.

Pizzaro, D. A., & Bloom, P. (2003). The intelligence of moral intuitions: Comment on Haidt (2001). *Psychological Review, 110,* 193–196.

Power, C., Higgins, A., & Kohlberg, L. (1989a). *Lawrence Kohlberg's approach to moral education*. New York: Columbia University Press.

Power, C., Higgins, A., & Kohlberg, L. (1989b). The habit of the common life: Building character through democratic community schools. In L. Nucci. (Ed.). *Moral development and character education: A dialogue* (pp. 125–144). Berkeley, CA: McCutchan.

Putnam, H. D. (2003). *Better together: Restoring the American community.* New York: Simon & Schuster.

Putnam, R. D. (2000). *Bowling alone: The collapse and revival of American community.* New York: Simon & Schuster.

Raths, L., Harmin, M. & Simon, S. (1976). Selection from *Values and teaching.* In D. Purpel & K. Ryan (Eds.). *Moral education . . . it comes with the territory* (pp. 75–115). Berkeley, CA: McCutchan.

Rawls, J. (1971). *A theory of justice.* Cambridge, MA: Harvard University Press.

Rawls, J. (1993). *Political liberalism.* New York: Columbia University Press.

Rawls, J. (2001). *Justice as fairness: A restatement.* Cambridge, MA: Harvard University Press.

Rest, J., Narvaez, D., Bebeau, M., & Thoma, S. (1999). *Postconventional moral thinking: A neo-Kohlbergian approach.* Mahwah, NJ: Lawrence Erlbaum Associates.

Rest, J. R. (1986). *Moral development: Advances in research and theory.* New York: Praeger.

Rorty, R. (1973). Criteria and necessity. *Nous, 7,* 313–379.

Rorty, R. (1979). *Philosophy and the mirror of nature.* Princeton, NJ: Princeton University Press.

Rorty, R. (1988). *Contingency, irony, and solidarity.* Cambridge, UK: Cambridge University Press.

Ryan, G. (2003, January 11). *I will not stand for it.* Invited address to the Northwestern University College of Law, Evanston, IL.

Ryan, K. (1989). In defense of character education. In L. Nucci. (Ed.). *Moral development and character education: A dialogue* (pp. 3–17). Berkeley, CA: McCutchan.

Ryan, K. (1996). Character education in the United States: A status report. *Journal For a Just and Caring Education, 2,* 75–84.

Ryan, K., & Bohlin, K. E. (1998). *Building moral character in schools.* San Francisco: Jossey-Bass.

Schubert, W. (1997). *Curriculum, perspective, paradigm, and possibility.* Upper Saddle River, NJ: Prentice-Hall.

Shweder, R. (1982). Liberalism as destiny: Review of Lawrence Kohlberg's *Essays on moral development, Vol. I: The philosophy of moral development. Contemporary Psychology, 27,* 421–424.

Shweder, R. (2003). What about female genital mutilation? And why understanding culture matters. In R. Shweder (Ed.). *Why do men barbeque?* (pp. 168–216). Cambridge, MA: Harvard University Press.

Shweder, R., Mahapatra, M., & Miller, J. (1987). Culture and moral development. In J. Kagan & S. Lamb (Eds.). *The emergence of morality in young children.* Chicago: University of Chicago Press.

Simon, K. (2001). *Moral questions in the classroom.* New Haven, CT: Yale University Press.

Smetana, J. G. (2002). Culture, autonomy, and personal jurisdiction in adolescent-parent relationships. In H. W. Reese and R. Kail (Eds.). *Advances in child development and behavior* (Vol. 29, pp. 51–87). New York: Academic Press.

Smetana, J. G. (2005). Adolescent-parent conflict: Resistance and subversion as developmental process. In L. Nucci (Ed.), *Conflict, contradiction, and contrarian elements in moral development and education* (pp. 69–91). Mahwah, NJ: Lawrence Erlbaum Associates.

Smetana, J., & Bitz, B. (1996). Adolescents' conceptions of teachers' authority and their relations to rule violations in school. *Child Development, 67,* 1153–1172.

Snarey, J., & Keljo, K. (1991). In a Gemeinschaft voice: The cross-cultural expansion of moral development theory. In W. M. Kurtines & J. L. Gewirtz (Eds.), *Handbook of moral behavior and development* (Vol. 2, pp. 395–424). Hillsdale, NJ: Lawrence Erlbaum Associates.

Sokol, B., & Chandler, M. (2004). A bridge too far: On the relations between moral and secular reasoning. In Carpendale, J., & Muller, U. (Eds.). *Social interaction and the development of* knowledge (pp. 155–174). Mahwah, NJ: Lawrence Erlbaum Associates.

Sternberg, C., Campos, J., & Emde, R. (1983). The facial expression of anger in seven month old infants. *Child Development, 54,* 178–184.

Teo, T., Becker, G., & Edelstein, W. (1995). Variability in structured wholeness: Context factors in L. Kohlberg's data on the development of moral judgment. *Merrill-Palmer Quarterly, 41,* 381–393.

Thorkildsen, T. A. (2000). Children's coordination of procedural and commutative justice in school. In W. van Haaften, T. Wren, & A. Tellings (Eds.). *Moral sensibilities and education II: The school age child* (pp. 61–88). Bemmel, Netherlands: Concorde Publishing House.

Turiel, E. (1983). *The development of social knowledge: Morality and convention.* Cambridge, UK: Cambridge University Press.

Turiel, E. (1989). Multifaceted social reasoning and educating for character, culture, and development. In L. Nucci (Ed.). *Moral development and character education: A dialogue* (pp. 161–182). Berkeley, CA: McCutchan.

Turiel, E. (1998). The development of morality. In W. Damon (Ed.) & N. Eisenberg (Vol. Ed.). *Handbook of child psychology, Vol. 3: Social, emotional, and personality development* (5th ed., pp. 863–932). New York: Academic Press.

Turiel, E. (2002). *The culture of morality: Social development, context, and conflict.* Cambridge: UK: Cambridge University Press.

Turiel, E., & Davidson, P. (1986). Heterogeneity, inconsistency, and asynchrony in the development of cognitive structures. In Iris Levin, (ed.), *Stage and structure: Reopening the debate.* New Jersey: Ablex.

Turiel, E., Hildebrandt, C., & Wainryb, C. (1991). Judging social issues: Difficulties, inconsistencies and consistencies. *Monographs for the Society for Research in Child Development, 56*(Serial No. 224).

Turiel, E., & Wainryb, C. (2000). Social life in cultures: Judgments, conflicts, and subversion. *Child Development, 71,* 250–256.

Wainryb, C. (1991). Understanding differences in moral judgments: The role of informational assumptions. *Child Development, 62,* 840–851.

Wainryb, C. (2000). Values and truths: The making and judging of moral decisions. In M. Laupa (Ed.). *New directions for child development: Rights and wrongs: How children evaluate the world* (pp. 33–46). San Francisco: Jossey-Bass.

Wainryb, C., Shaw, L. A., Langley, M., Cottam, K., Lewis, R., (2004). Children's thinking about diversity of belief in the early school years: Judgments of relativism, tolerance, and disagreeing persons. *Child Development, 75,* 687–703.

Wainryb, C., Shaw, L. A., & Maianu, C. (1998). Tolerance and intolerance: Children's and adolescents' judgments of dissenting beliefs, speech, persons, and conduct. *Child Development, 69,* 1541–1555.

Wainryb, C., & Turiel, E. (1994). Dominance, subordination, and concepts of personal entitlements in cultural contexts. *Child Development, 65,* 1701–1722.

Watson, M. (2003). *Learning to trust: transforming difficult elementary classrooms through developmental discipline.* San Francisco, CA: Jossey-Bass.

Watson, M., Solomon, D., Battistich, V., Schaps, E., & Solomon, J. (1989). The child development project: Combining traditional and developmental approaches to values education. In L. Nucci. (Ed.). *Moral development and character education: A dialogue* (pp. 51–92). Berkeley, CA: McCutchan.

Wynne, E. (1986). The great tradition in education: Transmitting moral values. *Educational Leadership, 43,* 4–9.

Wynne, E. (1987). Students and schools. In K. Ryan & G. F. McLean (Eds.), *Character development in schools and beyond* (pp. 97–118). New York: Praeger.

Youniss, J., McLellan, J. A., Mazer, B. (2001). Voluntary service, peer group orientation, and civic engagement. *Journal of Adolescence Research, 16,* 456–468.

Youniss, J. & Yates, M. (1997). *Community service and social responsibility in youth.* Chicago: University of Chicago Press.

25

Educating for Positive Youth Development

Marvin W. Berkowitz
Stephen A. Sherblom
Melinda C. Bier
Victor Battistich
University of Missouri-St. Louis

Throughout history, cultures have wrestled with questions of how best to raise children so that they might live well and become admirable people. The continuance of our society, our way of life, and the health of our nation depend on the healthy development of all our children. Social science, in its various forms, has much to offer on the question of how best to support positive youth development. Growing discourse among disciplines, and between theorists and practitioners, has helped to transcend some of the traditional boundaries and limitations of the various approaches concerned with development. The growing discourse provides an opportunity to bring people and programs into conversation regarding common objectives, differences in language and terminology, and the compatibility of conceptual frameworks. This chapter informs that discussion with a conceptual overview of disciplines addressing the positive side of youth development and a discussion of their educational implications.

Several fields of inquiry and intervention in the social sciences concerned with children's growth and welfare have developed similar perspectives regarding children's healthy development. There is a growing articulation of what youth need for positive development and an initial consensus on how to conceptualize it. These areas of inquiry include (but are not limited to) character education (Berkowitz & Bier 2004; Lickona, 1991), social and emotional learning (Collaborative for Academic, Social, and Emotional Learning [CASEL], 2002; Weissberg & O'Brien 2004), and prevention science (Catalano, Berglund,

Ryan, Lonczak, & Hawkins, 2002; Greenberg, Domitrovich, & Bumbarger, 2001). Each discipline has come to advocate a holistic approach to positive development because they see that whichever parts of youth development they support depend on the success of other parts, and ultimately, on the success of the whole child. In addition to these education-related areas of inquiry and intervention, multiple areas of psychological research exist and are being developed that provide empirical support regarding youth development. These include positive psychology (Aspinwall & Staudinger, 2003; Seligman & Csikszentmihalyi, 2000), applied developmental psychology (Lerner, Wertlieb, Jacobs, & 2003), and the cataloguing of psychosocial developmental assets (Scales & Leffert, 1999). Each of these approaches to positive youth development is reviewed, and educational implications are discussed.

There are two ways to conceptualize the intellectual relationships among these seemingly disparate lines of inquiry. One is to identify the overlaps, commonalities, and shared purposes among the different disciplines and focus on that common core (Reese, 2000). An example of this kind of synthesis is the *Civic Character Initiative* (Character Education Partnership, 2003). The Character Education Partnership and the Freedom Forum initiated this effort to bring a group of leaders from "service learning," "social and emotional learning," "character education," and "civic education" together to articulate their common goals. Collectively, this group of scholars and practitioners generated a list of the qualities a child needs to develop to have a productive sense of civic character. These qualities include honesty, respect, social and emotional competencies, empathy and compassion, leadership for social justice, and critical thinking. *Civic Character's* model of development does not include everything of importance that each of these fields has identified over their years of study. Rather, the commonality highlighted by the model can be seen as a construct of development on which they can all agree. This construct represents the development of personal characteristics relevant to promoting responsible and caring citizens who act to build safe, just, and free societies locally, nationally, and internationally.

In contrast to this approach, the authors of this chapter propose that it would be useful for a model of development to be more flexible and far reaching. It should encompass the skills and concerns highlighted by all relevant approaches, and not merely reflect their points of overlap. All of the movements we review here are ultimately concerned with the positive development of children, although each approach has its own language and emphasis. Those concerned with prevention science focus on children's ability and tendency to choose healthy actions and lifestyles. Those interested in social–emotional learning are most centrally interested in the development of children's social and emotional competencies. Character educators focus on the development of the multiple aspects of children's moral personality and behavior. Positive psychology categorizes the psychological strengths youth need to develop, and applied developmental science integrates a number of theoretical perspectives within developmental psychology useful to understanding children's development. All are necessary to create a well-rounded understanding of positive youth development.

There are certainly shortcomings to the selection of positive youth development as a rubric for this comprehensive vision. First, it has been used, and is currently being used, by others for a variety of purposes (Blum, 2003; Moore & Halle, 2000; Roth, Brooks-Gunn, Murray, & Foster, 1998; Wertlieb, Jacobs, & Lerner, 2003), including as a name for a particular curriculum (Caplan et al., 1992). Second, the descriptor *positive* is open to a wide variety of interpretations, and this ambiguity may generate confusion. However, the up side of this vagueness is that it is not difficult to find agreement that children's development should be positive rather than negative. We can all agree that children should be somewhat compassionate and have some ability to put the interest of others before their own interest, but the discussion of specifically how much compassion they should feel, or how generous and selfless they should be to be psychologically healthy people of good character is another matter entirely. There are serious philosophical and ideological questions concerning how each virtue is to be integrated into "optimal development." That discussion, however, is beyond the scope of this chapter, and requires going beyond what has been addressed in each of these fields. For the purpose of this chapter *positive youth development* is the unifying term for the cumulative ideals of the several approaches described here, and its exact meaning remains open to further discussion.

APPROACHES TO CHARACTERIZING POSITIVE YOUTH DEVELOPMENT

There are several traditions that can lay claim to describing how children might best develop to be psychologically healthy. Prevention science, social–emotional learning, and character education all have created theory, conducted research, and crafted interventions to support youth development. The basic conceptions of each approach are addressed.

Prevention Science

Much of the research in the various fields of prevention is driven by the goal of preventing specific problem behavior such as delinquency, early substance use and abuse, conduct disorders, teen pregnancy, school failure, and dropout (Albee & Gullotta, 1997). Research funding has tended to be problem driven and hence does not encourage a more holistic assessment or intervention into the child's well-being (Maggs & Schulenberg, 2001). This has begun to change.

In September 1996, the Social Development Research Group at the University of Washington School of Social Work began examining existing evaluations of youth development programs and summarizing the state of the field (Catalano et al., 2002). Specifically, they documented and described the shift toward highlighting characteristics of positive youth development, and the commonality between risk and protective factors linked to problem behaviors in youth. They researched both theoretical and empirical definitions of positive youth development, identified evaluations of interventions, and outlined elements contributing to success or failure in these programs and evaluations.

They evaluated seventy-five programs concerned with positive youth development and designated twenty-five of these programs "effective." The twenty-five effective programs were found across community, school, and family settings, with eight of them taking place in only one environment, and seventeen combining strategies in either two or all three settings. Effective programs showed positive changes in youth behavior in a number of areas, namely, interpersonal skills, quality of peer and adult relationships, self-control, problem solving, cognitive competencies, self-efficacy, commitment to schooling, and academic achievement. Although a range of strategies were used to produce these changes, the themes common to successful programs included methods to strengthen social and emotional competencies, increasing healthy bonding, providing opportunities and recognition for those youth who do engage in positive behavior, and helping family and community communicate a unified message to youth regarding expectations and standards. The study documented that positive youth development programs engage the family through parent skills training, through involving parents in program implementation, and through involving parents in the actual program design.

As that review highlights, the field has been moving in the direction of promoting a preventive strategy more encompassing than the past piece-meal approach (Catalano et al., 2002; MacDonald & Valdivieso, 2000). This literature has come to use the term *positive youth development* (PYD) for processes and outcomes deemed necessary for healthy prosocial and personally successful development. These include (a) social cognitions about morality, normative behavior, justice, and peer relations; (b) assessments of the effective use of leisure time; (c) social skills and communicative abilities related to friendships and emotion regulation in close relationships; (d) vocational, educational, and social identity; and (e) active involvement in activities related to citizenship and community improvement (Bumbarger & Greenberg, 2002). The shift in strategy is intended to move the field from a "deficit model" of risk reduction to a competence-enhancement model that centrally emphasizes health promotion. Health promotion highlights enhancing competence, self-esteem, and well-being generally, and encourages a more holistic, developmental, and ecological approach to development. Bumbarger and Greenberg (2002) point out that religious youth groups, scouts, clubs, youth sports teams, volunteer opportunities, and other community-based supports for youth were not traditionally set up to address problems or deal primarily with "problem children." Rather, they were seen as making "good" citizens better, and helping good kids stay good. Drawing on this tradition, the field of prevention science can be said to be evolving toward promotion of health and competence (Albee & Gullotta, 1997).

Battistich (2001) argues that interventions that are effective typically support core competencies: "inclinations and abilities that are relevant to success in a wide range of situations, such as understanding of self and others, communication and social interaction skills, and abilities to think critically and resolve interpersonal problems" (p. 3). Interventions that enhance these core competencies are likely to strengthen capacities to deal with a variety of life stressors. Greenberg and colleagues (2001) reviewed primary prevention programs to determine which interventions had been found effective in reducing symptoms of psychopathology in school age children. Their summary of "best practices" gives a clear indication of the direction of this part of the prevention field. They emphasized longer term over shorter term intervention, developmentally earlier rather than later intervention, programs directed at risk and protective factors rather than focusing on problem behaviors, and those aimed at changing institutions and environments and not just individuals. They also recommended packages of coordinated strategies over individual programs and recognized the strength of integrated models of intervention across school, home, and community.

School-based crime prevention is another area of prevention science in which there are similar changes. The federal government has been increasingly involved in supporting safe and drug-free schools through violence reduction programs, removing handguns, promoting conflict resolution, and curbing the use of drugs and alcohol. The 1986 Drug-Free Schools and Communities Act legislation provided funds to states to develop and operate school-based drug prevention programs and in 1994 this legislation was expanded to authorize expenditures on school-based violence prevention programs.

Gottfredson's (2001) review of effective delinquency prevention programs cites similar trends in school-based crime prevention toward involving whole schools rather than focusing on individual students, achieving consistency and clarity in communicating norms about acceptable behavior, and favoring comprehensive instructional programs that focus on a range of social competency skills. These include developing self-control and learning stress management, responsible decision making, thinking, social problem solving, and communication skills. Programs tend toward sustained engagement rather than single-shot interventions.

In summary, like much social science, prevention science has become more holistic and situates youth development ecologically in the surrounding social environments. The focus of intervention is moving from targeted behavior problems in the individual to larger community health issues, and from a deficit model focused on prevention to a positive model promoting the development of self-esteem, self-control, intra- and interpersonal skills, connection to friends and institutions, a prosocial orientation, and a positive identity.

Emotional Intelligence and Social and Emotional Learning

Emotional Intelligence is an interdisciplinary and multifaceted field (Bar-On & Parker, 2000), which became popularized with the advent of Daniel Goleman's best selling book *Emotional Intelligence* (1995). However, as a psychological concept, emotional intelligence has a large body of theoretical and empirical literature to support current efforts (Bar-On & Parker, 2000; Cohen, 1999). Emotional intelligence has historically been thought to be part of *social intelligence,* sometimes called *social competence,* and is rooted in a long tradition in psychology including Thornedike (1905), Kelly (1955), Rogers (1961), and Rotter (1966). *Social competence* is defined as "the possession and use of the ability to integrate thinking, feeling, and behavior to achieve social tasks and outcomes valued in the host context and culture" (Topping, Bremner, & Holmes, 2000, p.3). By this definition emotional intelligence or competence is seen as one dynamic in what is currently being conceived as social–emotional learning.

The rich literature of emotional competence has much to contribute to understanding the emotional side of social–emotional learning. Saarni (1999) reviewed the development of emotional competence, which is conceived as having three primary contributors: one's self or ego identity; one's moral sense or character; and one's developmental history. The overlap with character education is clear here; a moral sense is posited as a source of emotional growth. The components of emotional competence are those skills needed to be self-efficacious, particularly in emotion-eliciting relationships—the ability to manage emotions, enhance self-esteem, and become resilient and adaptive.

Lazarus' (1991) theory that each emotion is associated with a core relational theme provides substance to conceptualizing what children should be taught regarding emotions (Saarni, 1999). For example, anger, when seen in relational terms comes about through a perceived offense against me and mine. Anxiety comes about through perceiving an uncertain threat, or the uncertainty of the challenge of a known threat. Emotions such as fright, guilt, shame, sadness, envy, jealousy, disgust, happiness, pride, relief, hope, and love all are best understood in the relational context in which they arise. The emotional part of social–emotional learning, then, should educate children to understand the role emotions play in their lives, their relationships, and in the constitution of their selves. Emotional competence in the areas of empathy (feeling with someone), sympathy (feeling for someone), and guilt (accepting responsibility when you have done something bad or wrong) directly impacts moral perception and the likelihood that you will respond to other people when they are in need (Eisenberg, 1982; Eisenberg & Miller, 1987; Hoffman, 1978, 1982; Saarni, 1999). This overlap and complementarity with character education in the development of emotional competence carries over to social–emotional learning more broadly conceived.

Cohen (2001) defines *social and emotional education* as referring to "learning skills, understandings, and values that enhance our ability to read others and ourselves and then, to use this information to become flexible problem solvers and creative learners" (p. xiii). This is done through learning to process, manage, and express the social and emotional aspects of our experience and our lives. This is claimed to provide the platform for learning generally, with obvious academic side effects, and for moral development through learning to be self-reflective, responsible, caring, cooperative, and an effective social problem solver. Children's social and emotional capacities powerfully affect their ability to listen and communicate, concentrate, recognize, understand, and problem solve in the social world, moderate their own emotional states so they are not controlled by them, and resolve conflicts adaptively (Cohen, 2001, pp. 3–4).

CASEL was founded in 1994 to provide leadership to educators, researchers, and policy makers regarding social and emotional learning and its place in school curriculum and practice (CASEL, 2002). They define social and emotional learning as "the process of developing the ability to recognize and manage emotions, develop caring and concern for others, make responsible decisions, establish positive relationships, and handle challenging situations effectively" (2002, p. 3). These positive outcomes are supported by the development of five core social and emotional competencies:

1. *Self-awareness:* being aware of your own feelings in each situation and having a realistic assessment of your own abilities.

2. *Social awareness:* being aware of what other people are feeling and being able to take the perspectives of others. Cultural awareness that enables ease of mixing in diverse groups is part of this social awareness.

3. *Self-management:* self-control, delay of gratification, and handling one's emotions all help people persevere in the face of challenge or defeat.

4. *Relationship skills:* establishing healthy and meaningful relationships; being cooperative; engaging in conflict negotiation; and demonstrating general "people skills." Additionally, being able to maintain one's autonomy in the face of social pressure, such as "peer pressure," is a relational skill.

5. *Responsible decision making:* the ability to assess risks and consider relevant facts and likely consequences in making an informed decision. This correlates with respecting others (in taking their perspective into consideration) and taking responsibility for one's own choices and actions.

CASEL (2002) emphasizes the need for safe, caring, supportive learning environments. The academic benefits accompanying these kinds of environments include stronger student attachment to school and greater motivation to learn. They acknowledge the overlap between social–emotional learning and character education, suggesting "the best evidence-based programs of each have much in common" (2002, p. 11). It is argued that character education programs that incorporate a social–emotional learning component are more effective than programs without a social–emotional learning component.

Character Education

Like all of the approaches reviewed here, character education is interested in promoting the development of certain traits in young people. Unlike the others, character education explicitly begins from a moral perspective and straightforwardly promotes moral competencies. Although most of the approaches discussed in this chapter develop strengths related to moral competencies in one way or another, their impact is largely secondary to their primary goal of preventing risky behavior, promoting emotional competencies, or supporting social and emotional learning.

Character education has been a vital part of the school curricula throughout the history of the U.S. Stanhope (1992) reported that in 1901, the National Education Association endorsed character training in the schools, stating that "the fundamental consideration in any system of schools is the development of . . . moral character" (p. 110). Character education was initially developed in religiously based teaching before being adopted in schools and later being researched by academics. Its nature and scope have continued to change. Academic work in character education in the U.S. can be traced to the 1920s and 1930s, when it had a period of popularity before fading into the background (Dewey & Tufts, 1932; Hartshorne & May, 1928; Kilpatrick, 1925; Maher, 1933). Most character education currently being discussed is part of a reemergence that gained popularity in the 1980s and 1990s (Berkowitz & Bier, 2003; Lickona, 1991).

As in the other fields of inquiry, character education means many things to many people. The Maryland Value Education Commission created a list of ten character objectives for students' development that is fairly representative of common goals (Stanhope, 1992). Students should develop:

1. Personal integrity and honesty rooted in respect for the truth, intellectual curiosity, and love of learning;

2. A sense of duty to self, family, school, and community;

3. Self-esteem rooted in the recognition of one's potential;

4. Respect for the rights of all persons regardless of their race, religion, gender, age, physical condition, or mental state;

5. A recognition of the right of others to hold and express differing views, combined with the capacity to make discriminating judgments among competing opinions;

6. A sense of justice, rectitude, and fair play, and a commitment to them;

7. A disposition of understanding, sympathy, concern, and compassion for others;

8. A sense of discipline and pride in one's work and respect for the achievements of others;

9. Respect for one's property and the property of others, including public property; and

10. Courage to express one's convictions.

Other virtues put forward by character educators include good citizenship, the productive use of time and talent, fairness, trustworthiness, respect for law, thoughtfulness, fidelity, responsibility, self-control, humility, fortitude, wisdom, positive attitude, caring, and sociomoral reasoning competency (Bennett, 1991; Benninga, 1991; Berkowitz, 1997; Goble & Brooks, 1983; Josephson, 2004; Lickona, 1991, 2004; Noddings, 2002). Although character educators have various conceptual frames by which they believe children develop their particular list of virtues, describing their differences is beyond the scope of this chapter. We do, however, describe one endeavor to articulate a broader and more psychological description of character, Berkowitz's (1997) "moral anatomy."

The Moral Anatomy.   The moral development and character education fields also have been moving in the direction of outlining what is needed for positive youth development. It has been argued elsewhere (Berkowitz, 1997) that we first need to define the moral person as the goal or outcome of such an enterprise. Moral psychology, particularly the study of cognitive–developmental capacities relating to moral reasoning (e.g., Damon, 1988; Kohlberg, 1976, 1984; Narvaez, 1999; Nucci, 2001; Piaget, 1932/1965; Turiel, 2002), has been the main force in bringing issues of moral functioning to the fore of the social sciences. This perspective is rooted in the theoretical work of John Dewey (1908/1960) and closely aligned with the progressivist approach to education that argued that moral development is impacted greatly by the social culture of the institutions in which children are raised and educated, especially schools. One should not attempt to educate for positive youth development without understanding what development entails and without having some description of the person it is designed to develop. Kohlberg, for example, argued that identifying the nature, path, processes, and end point of moral reasoning was essential to attempting to foster development of moral reasoning (Kohlberg & Mayer, 1972).

The "moral anatomy" is another response to this conceptual need. The idea behind this framework is that we oversimplify moral psychology when we consider it a relatively homogenous construct. In fact, moral psychology is a complex set of diverse constructs that comprise the totality of moral personhood. The moral anatomy is an attempt to tease apart the constituent parts of moral personhood. An optimally developed person must have a broad set of psychological skills and characteristics that impact moral functioning, including:

- Responsible personal and prosocial behavior. This refers to individual choices that qualify as moral (behavior, action).

- Habits of prosocial interaction and character. This refers to enduring tendencies to engage in moral interaction and to exhibit virtues (personality, habit).

- *Emotional competency:* understanding self and others as a basis for successful social interaction, appropriate emotional responses to sociomoral situations, capacities for appropriate mature emotional control (emotional competence; affective self-control).

- *Prosocial values and attitudes*: commitment to values and virtues associated with "character." This refers to affectively charged cognitions about moral issues (values, attitudes).

- *Sociomoral reasoning competency*: age-appropriate cognitive capacities to perceive, wrestle with, and logically resolve the complexities of the moral aspects of life and real-life moral contexts (cognition; reasoning).

- *Possessing a mature, integrated self-system*: including a central role for moral identities (e.g. "ethical or moral person"; "loving parent"; "religiously or spiritually devote person"). This includes self-reflection leading to both a commitment to a moral self and a perceived sense of oneself as a moral being (self-concept; moral identity).

- Foundational skills that support prosocial, responsible, and caring functioning that are not intrinsically moral concepts (e.g. perspective taking, empathy, perseverance, courage, loyalty).

These constructs provide the foundation for moral agency.

This model suggests that positive character and positive development are complex multifaceted phenomena, akin to Gardner's (1983) notion of multiple intelligences. Just as Gardner argues that intelligence is not a unitary construct but rather an array of multiple intelligences with each individual having a profile of such competencies, the moral anatomy suggests that positive youth development entails a parallel set of psychological competencies and that each individual has a unique profile.

It further suggests that educating for (or parenting for) positive youth development requires a complex, multifaceted set of educational strategies. No one strategy or limited set of strategies is likely to impact all the diverse psychological categories that comprise the optimally developed person. For example, to promote the development of sociomoral reasoning requires at least providing the opportunity to discuss social and moral problems with peers in a structured, guided fashion. Sociomoral reasoning develops through a process of interactive construction of ways of knowing, and this results from the interpenetration of meaning making between oneself and others. So peer interaction around moral issues is a theoretically justified and empirically grounded means of promoting such development (Berkowitz, 1985). This may have no impact on personality, however, or little impact on emotional competency, which are theoretically different psychological constructs that develop through different mechanisms. Direct skill training may be necessary for aspects of social and interpersonal competency, for example, conflict resolution or anger management. Likewise certain types of behavior, such as democratic participation, require direct experience, and didactic strategies will surely prove inadequate. On the other hand, didactic strategies may be adequate for transferring social or moral knowledge about topics such as manners and social norms, but be inadequate to encourage behavior based on those facts. In the early days of Kohlberg's attempt to apply his moral psychological theory to education (Kohlberg & Mayer, 1972), Kohlberg argued against such didactic approaches. However, later on he embraced a more inclusive, multifaceted approach and recognized the power of social advocacy and modeling for value development (Power, Higgins, & Kohlberg, 1989).

It is central to this model that different, even seemingly opposing, theories need to be integrated to account for the complexity and diversity of moral psychological functioning. Much akin to the Indian parable of the Blind Men and the Elephant (Berkowitz, 1997), we are often blind to the big picture of positive development when we start from a single theoretical framework or a single psychological construct. Although expediency may call for a narrowly crafted educational strategy, ultimately no school would be satisfied with partially developed students as their product (graduates). Would educators feel satisfied with altruistic, caring graduates who lie and cheat? Or with honest students who sadistically bully others? So, at least ideally, educating for positive youth development needs to be comprehensive, multifaceted, and methodologically diverse. A number of approaches to conceptualizing positive development have been put forward in the field of psychology, especially in the field of child development.

Positive Psychology and Applied Developmental Science

Positive psychology is a movement within psychology to refocus intellectual energy to the study of positive aspects of human development and experience, and away from the traditional bias of clinical psychology toward the study of dysfunction. Picking up on an argument made earlier by humanist psychologists (Allport, 1960; Maslow, 1962; Rogers, 1961) and various other developmental (Greenberger & Sorenson, 1974) and prevention-oriented psychologists (Jahoda, 1958), positive psychologists hope to refocus our professional attention from problematic development to the requirements and promise of healthy development (Seligman, 1999). The hope is that a better understanding of these aspects of human life will allow us to prevent the pathologies that come about as a result of problematic development. Research suggests that certain human strengths, such as wisdom, courage, future mindedness, optimism, spirituality, hope, and interpersonal skills, can act as buffers against psychological problems (Peterson & Seligman, 2004; Seligman, 2002).

The Positive Psychology Network (Seligman & Csikszentmihalyi, 2000) is a coordinated research effort to address these underresearched areas of psychology. Positive psychology is categorized into three areas: subjective well-being, positive character, and positive institutions (Cameron, Dutton, & Quinn, 2003). *Subjective well-being* includes the study of life satisfaction, fulfillment, and positive emotions such as happiness, joy, and admiration. *Positive character* includes the personality traits and interpersonal skills needed for optimal development and has much in common with the aims and models of character education. *Positive institutions* focuses on ways in which organizations and institutions can support positive psychology by encouraging civic engagement and giving voice to members. Positive institutions support individual responsibility, nurturance, altruism, and work ethic (Gilham & Seligman, 1999).

Generating a catalogue of what needs to be developed is one of the key projects of the positive psychology movement. Building on a review of the world's literature on virtue and character development, Peterson and Seligman (2003) have identified six core sets of positive psychological characteristics, traditionally called *virtues:* wisdom and knowledge; courage; love; justice; temperance; and transcendence. Each virtue has several character strengths that contribute to its development.

1. *Wisdom and knowledge*: Positive traits that entail the acquisition and use of knowledge; with the corollaries of creativity, curiosity, open mindedness, and perspective taking.

2. *Courage*: Positive traits that involve the exercise of will to accomplish goals in the face of opposition, both external and internal, with its corollaries of bravery, persistence, and integrity.

3. *Love and humanity*: Positive traits with an explicitly interpersonal focus—love, kindness, and social intelligence.

4. *Justice*: Positive traits with an explicitly civic focus—citizenship, fairness, and leadership.

5. *Temperance*: Positive traits that protect us against emotional excesses—forgiveness and mercy, humility and modesty, prudence, moderation, and self-regulation.

6. *Transcendence*: Positive traits that connect us to the larger universe—appreciation of beauty, gratitude, hope, humor, and spirituality (Peterson & Seligman, 2003).

Through this endeavor to categorize the character strengths and virtues, positive psychology facilitates dialogue in the research community and contributes to the consensus we are outlining.

Another strand in psychology that supports the positive developmental approach is called *applied developmental science* (Lerner, Wertlieb, & Jacobs, 2003). Applied developmental science is described as an integration of a number of theoretical perspectives within developmental psychology: a dynamic (or systems) approach to organism–context relations; a lifespan view of human development; and the ecological view of development first put forth by Bronfenbrenner (Bronfenbrenner, 1979; Lerner, Fisher, & Weinberg, 2000). Applied developmental science seeks to link research on child development with a rich understanding of the context in which children develop, and to utilize both literatures to formulate public policy meant to address that context, whether in ameliorating problems or supporting positive development (Roth & Brooks-Gunn, 2003). "In this view, then, policy and program endeavors do not constitute secondary work, or derivative applications, conducted after basic research evidence has been compiled. Quite to the contrary, policy development and implementation, and program design and delivery, become integral components of the research" (Lerner, Fisher, & Weinberg, 2000,

p. 12). The efforts of applied developmental scientists are sometimes referred to as promoting positive youth development. Like prevention science, applied developmental science shifts the focus from the prevention of specific problems (drug abuse, risky sexual behavior, etc.) to identifying "the features of and the factors accounting for positive development" (Lerner, 2001, p. 254). This meshes well with the "assets model" of resilience promotion that outlines the social and psychological assets that typically underpin healthy development (Scales, Benson, Leffert, & Blyth, 2000).

The Search Institute's *Developmental Assets*

The Search Institute published a synthesis of scientific research on the resources needed by adolescents to support their healthy development (Scales & Leffert, 1999). Titled *Developmental Assets,* this work pulls together research from a broad range of developmental and social sciences into a set of four external assets and four internal assets found to contribute to resiliency and "immunity" to social ills. The first external asset is having supportive, positive, and fulfilling relationships with adults in one's family, community, and school. The second asset is called *empowerment,* and entails having adolescents feel that they are perceived positively as contributors to society and community. The third external asset involves knowing clearly what your family and community expect of you. This continuity between family and community provides youth with the necessary guidance to make good choices and regulate their own behavior. The final external asset is having a community with a rich array of activities and opportunities for engagement, allowing youth a safe exposure to a variety of experiences and responsibilities.

As an internal asset youth must become committed to learning, and this value must be strongly supported by family, community, and school personnel. This asset encompasses developing children's achievement motivation, supporting their engagement in school, demanding they consistently accomplish homework requirements, and encouraging their becoming bonded to school. To embody a second asset, children must come to hold a set of positive values to serve as a basis for their choices and actions. This includes valuing caring and equality, social justice, integrity, honesty, and personal responsibility. The third internal asset requires adolescents to develop social competencies that allow them to confront new situations and interact effectively with others. Interpersonal competence includes becoming empathic and sensitive, thereby supporting positive friendships and becoming culturally competent in one's subculture. Conflict resolution also is a form of social competence. The fourth and last internal asset involves developing a positive self-concept and accompanying beliefs that allow them an integrated view of themselves. This contributes to a sense of personal power, self-esteem, sense of purpose, and positive view of their personal future. Independently and collectively, these assets support positive youth development. The educational implications involved in this growing consensus are discussed in the following section.

EDUCATING FOR POSITIVE YOUTH DEVELOPMENT

Having reviewed several perspectives on what needs to develop in youth and how those areas of development can be supported, we now address the role of educators in this process. It is important to identify core characteristics of effective practice in educating for positive youth development. There are two sets of evidence on which to draw: (a) research on the effects of parenting on positive youth development, and (b) research on

various educational movements that fall under the educating for positive youth development umbrella. Each is discussed in turn.

Parenting for Positive Youth Development

There is much more known empirically about the impact of parental behavior on child
outcomes than about the impact of schools on child outcomes. Fortunately, the analogy
between parenting and educating is clear and justifiable. Teachers are, at least in part,
surrogate parents to students, and parents are children's earliest teachers. Like parents,
teachers are adults with supervisory, caretaker responsibility for children and provide an
opportunity for emotional attachment. Additionally, parents and teachers both provide
children with feedback regarding their competence, likeability, and worth, and sometimes
dramatically influence children's self-esteem. They strongly impact the broad developmental outcomes of children not only through what they teach explicitly and what they
model, but also through their relationship itself. Hence it is fair to hypothesize that many of
the practices of parents that have been found to positively impact child development may
also apply to the behavior of teachers (Damon, 1988). There is empirical evidence of such
a parallel. Wentzel (2002) has demonstrated that middle school teachers who manifest
behaviors parallel to effective parenting have students who are more behaviorally ordered
and who achieve better academic outcomes. Specifically, such teachers model motivation
toward schoolwork, use more nurturing and less negative messages to students, set fewer
restrictions and rules, and expect more from students.

In a review of the parenting literature that focused on eight positive youth outcomes
(altruism, social orientation, self-control, compliance, self-esteem, moral reasoning, conscience, and empathy), Berkowitz and Grych (1998) were able to identify five core parental
behaviors that most clearly promoted those outcomes:

1. *Induction:* the process by which parents explain their disciplinary behavior, outlining for the
   child the consequences of the child's choices and actions. This assists the child in developing
   empathy, altruism, and moral reasoning while helping to establish social understanding.

2. *Nurturance:* a characteristic of parenting involving warmth and affection, attentiveness,
   and openness to the child's experience. This supports children's self-esteem and sense of
   belonging.

3. *Demandingness:* the process of holding high but realistic standards for the child, providing
   the support necessary to achieve at a high level and monitoring their progress. This requires
   involvement with the child at a deep level for a sustained period.

4. *Modeling:* a process of teaching by example, of being the exemplar you want your child
   to witness. Children often copy adult behaviors, words, and even unspoken attitudes and
   body posture.

5. *Democratic family processes:* including children in family decision making empowers
   them to begin to make decisions for themselves, involves them in negotiations in which
   they are required to listen and take other's perspectives, and gives them a stake in upholding
   decisions and standards to which they were a willing party.

Each of these can readily be applied to teacher behavior (Berkowitz & Grych, 2000;
Wentzel, 2002). Baumrind (1971, 1991) defined two of these—demandingness (high expectations) and nurturance (love, affirmation)—as the two characteristics most identified
with authoritative parenting. Authoritative parenting, in turn, has been demonstrated to

produce an array of positive developmental outcomes in an extensive body of literature and has been directly tied to positive youth development (Berkowitz & Grych, 1998; Damon, 1988). Wentzel (2002) has reported that the strongest predictors of middle school students' prosocial behavior, prosocial attitudes, and academic achievement are high expectations (demandingness) and low number of negative messages (nurturance). These findings suggest that authoritative teacher–student relationships promote positive youth development and academic success. Furthermore, Watson (2003) has relied on the parent–child attachment literature to design a model for teacher behavior around discipline issues that promotes positive child development.

Clearly schools can learn much from the parenting literature about how to educate for positive youth development (Berkowitz & Grych, 2000). It makes sense to create teacher training modules that focus on such behaviors as inductive discipline and praise, democratic school and classroom management, the promotion of positive social bonding, and expecting and effectively supporting high levels of performance. Furthermore, emphasizing and nurturing educators' understanding of the power of their own lives, deeds, and words as catalysts for children's positive development is a critical feature of effective teacher preparation (Sizer & Sizer, 1999).

What Works in Character Education

Another source of understanding the characteristics of effective education for positive youth development comes from research in character education. A recent survey of the empirical research on character education has drawn conclusions about "what works" in character education and has identified areas where research is needed to help set a research agenda for the field. Character education was defined broadly in this project (Berkowitz & Bier, 2003). In fact, it essentially parallels what has been referred to here as educating for positive youth development. Hence the preliminary conclusions of the project are presented here as a window on a comprehensive approach to how schools can effectively promote the broad development of good character in students.

The literature review included 111 empirical studies of school-based programs designed to promote the positive development of students. Most centrally these programs were defined as character education, risk reduction, social–emotional learning, or service learning initiatives. Criteria for scientific rigor were applied to each study (Berkowitz & Bier, 2003), resulting in a set of sixty-six studies representing thirty-three programs that fall under the rubric of educating for positive youth development and that have evidence of being effective. From this set of studies, conclusions were drawn about the common practices and implementation strategies of the programs and the developmental outcomes reported.

Common Practices of Effective Programs

The thirty-three educating for positive youth development programs identified as having empirical evidence of effectiveness shared many implementation strategies. However, conclusions about these strategies can only be stated in terms of frequency of usage and not in terms of causality of developmental outcomes. The thirty-three programs averaged more than eight implementation strategies each. In other words, as suggested in the discussion of the moral anatomy, they were multifaceted educational approaches to fostering positive youth development. None of the studies tested for the independent effects of single strategies; rather, all of the research was designed to assess the cumulative impact of the set of strategies that comprised the particular educational program. Hence, no conclusions can be drawn that any particular strategy is an effective cause of the observed student developmental outcomes. We can only state that a particular implementation strategy occurs frequently as a component in programs that have been shown to be effective at promoting youth development. Nonetheless, this is sufficient to suggest that we can effectively promote the desired outcomes.

The most commonly shared implementation strategies, in descending order of frequency, are professional development for those implementing the initiative; student-centered peer discussions; interactive strategies such as class meetings, student governance, and peer tutoring that contribute to perspective-taking experiences; problem-solving and decision-making training; direct training of social, emotional, and personal management skills (such as conflict resolution or anger management); cooperative learning; self-management skills training and awareness; parent training and involvement; shared reading/story telling; and games/puppets.

Additionally, initiatives should be integrated throughout the academic curriculum both in terms of the content of the curriculum (e.g., focus on responsible relationships in literature, identification and reflection on ethical issues in social studies and science) and the pedagogy employed to deliver that curriculum (e.g., cooperative learning, guided class discussions, constructivism). Initiatives should include a wide array of such strategies woven together under a common unifying vision for school and student development.

The most frequently found outcomes for programs utilizing these strategies, in descending order of frequency, were improved sociomoral cognition; prosocial behavior and attitudes; development of problem-solving skills; reduction of violence and aggression; decrease in substance use; development of emotional competency; moderation of risk attitudes; improved school behavior; increased academic achievement and academic goal setting; and improved self-expectations and motivation. These findings can be supplemented with suggestions from other research and program reviews (e.g., Blum, 2003; CASEL, 2002; Nation et al., 2003; Park & Peterson, 2003; Solomon, Watson, & Battistich, 2001). Optimal education for positive youth development should also incorporate (a) An articulated philosophy statement that includes the desired character goals of the school and the shared vision of the school's purpose; (b) A committed staff that has been adequately trained (and who are adequately supported in an on-going manner) to implement the program fully and faithfully; (c) Student empowerment strategies such as peer conflict resolution, student governance, and collaborative problem solving; (d) Opportunities for service to others, such as service learning, community service, and school-based responsibilities; (e) Developmental discipline; that is, discipline strategies focused on the long-term improvement of student character and skills rather than using punitive behaviors to bring about the immediate cessation of the undesirable behavior; (f) Ongoing evaluation and feedback of data to ensure that desired student outcomes are being achieved and to continuously improve the implementation process; (g) Leadership commitment to sufficient and sustained implementation at both the school and district level; (h) Practices that strengthen student-teacher relationships and increase students' perception of school as a caring community to which they belong.

CONCLUSION

There is already some overlap between the various fields of inquiry discussed here. These fields are generally converging on a vision of positive youth development and working toward a more comprehensive model of understanding human growth and change. Each of these social sciences is moving toward rendering a fuller picture of the youth being discussed to make more useful their own primary research and interventions. As complementary as these approaches appear, much conceptual work needs to be done to synthesize their various terminology, insights, and practices.

However, a continued dialogue between these approaches promises a far richer and more complete understanding of how to educate for positive youth development. The research we have cited indicates that when parents, educators, and schools have the ability to support these aspects of youth development, children thrive, and the school's themselves flourish.

REFERENCES

Albee, G. W., & Gullotta, T. P. (1997). Primary prevention's evolution. In G. W. Albee & T. P. Gullotta (Eds.), *Primary prevention works* (pp. 3–32). New York: Sage.

Allport, G. (1960). *Personality and social encounter*. Boston: Beacon.

Aspinwall, L. G., & Staudinger, U. M. (2003). *A psychology of human strengths: fundamental questions and future directions for a positive psychology*. Washington D.C.: American Psychological Association.

Bar-On, R., & Parker, J. D. (2000). *The handbook of emotional intelligence*. San Francisco: Jossey-Bass.

Battistich, V. (2001). Commentary on "Preventing mental disorders in school-aged children." *Prevention & Treatment, 4,* Article 3, posted March 30, 2001.

Baumrind, D. (1971). Current patterns of parental authority, *Developmental Psychology Monographs, 4.*

Baumrind, D (1991). The influence of parenting style on adolescent competence and substance use. *Journal of Early Adolescence, 11,* 56–95.

Bennett, W. (1991). Moral literacy and the formation of character. In J. S. Benninga (Ed.), *Moral character and civic education in the elementary school.* (pp. 131–138). New York: Teacher's College.

Benninga, J. S. (1991). *Moral character and civic education in the elementary school*. New York: Teacher's College.

Berkowitz, M. W. (1985). The role of discussion in moral education. In M. W. Berkowitz & F. Oser (Eds.), *Moral education: theory and application* (pp. 197–218). Hillsdale, NJ: Lawrence Erlbaum Associates.

Berkowitz, M. W. (1997). The complete moral person: anatomy and formation. In J. M. Dubois (Ed.), *Moral issues in psychology: personalist contributions to selected problems* (pp. 11–41). Lanham, MD: University Press of America.

Berkowitz, M. W., & Bier, M. C. (2003). *What works in character education*. Presentation at the Character Education Partnership National Forum 2003, Washington, D.C.

Berkowitz, M. W., & Bier, M. C. (2004). Research-based character education. *Annals of the American Academy of Political and Social Science, 591,* 72–85.

Berkowitz, M. W., & Grych, J. H. (1998). Fostering goodness: Teaching parents to facilitate children's moral development. *Journal of Moral Education, 27,* 371–391.

Berkowitz, M. W., & Grych, J. H. (2000). Early character development and education. *Early Education and Development, 11,* 55–72.

Blum, R. W. (2003). Positive youth development: a strategy for improving adolescent health. In F. Jacobs, D. Wertlieb, & R. Lerner (Eds.), *Handbook of applied developmental science, Vol. 2: Enhancing the life chances of youth and families* (pp. 237–252). Thousand Oaks, CA: Sage.

Bronfenbrenner, U. (1979). *The ecology of human development*. Cambridge, MA: Harvard University Press.

Bumbarger, B., & Greenberg, M. T. (2002). Next steps in advancing research on positive youth development. [Electronic version]. *Prevention & Treatment, 5,* article 16. Retrieved June 24, 2002, from http://journals.apa.org/prevention/volume5/pre0050015a.html

Cameron, K. S., Dutton, J. E., & Quinn, R. E. (2003). Foundations of positive organizational scholarship. In K. S. Cameron, J. E. Dutton, & R. E. Quinn (Eds.), *Positive organizational scholarship: Foundations of a new discipline* (pp. 33–47). San Francisco: Berrett-Koehler.

Caplan, M., Weisberg, R. P., Grober, J. H., Silvo, P. J., Grady, K., & Jacoby, C. (1992). Social competence promotion with inner city and suburban young adolescents. *Journal of Consulting and Clinical Psychology, 60,* 56–63.

Catalano, R., Berglund, L. M., Ryan, J., Lonczak, H., & Hawkins, D. (2002). Positive youth development in the United States: Research findings on evaluations of positive development programs [Electronic version]. *Prevention & Treatment, 5,* Article 15. Retrieved Aug. 1, 2003 from http://journals.apa.org/prevention/volume5/pre0050015a.html

Character Education Partnership. (2003). *Pathways to civic character: A shared vision for America's schools.* Unpublished manuscript, Washington D.C.: Character Education Partnership.

Cohen, J. (1999). Social and emotional learning past and present: A psycho-educational dialogue. In J. Cohen (Ed.), *Educating hearts and minds: Social emotional learning and the passage into adolescence* (pp. 3–23). New York: Teachers College Press.

Cohen, J. (Ed.). (2001). *Caring classrooms/intelligent schools: The social emotional education of young children.* New York: Teacher's College Press.

Collaborative for Academic, Social, and Emotional Learning (CASEL). (2002). *Safe and sound: An educational leader's guide to evidence-based social and emotional learning programs.* Chicago: CASEL.

Damon, W. (1988). *The moral child: Nurturing children's natural moral growth.* New York: Free Press.

Dewey, J. (1908/1960) *Theory of the moral life.* New York: Holt, Reinhart, and Winston.

Dewey, J., & Tufts, J. A. (1932). *Ethics* (rev. ed.). New York: Henry Holt.

Eisenberg, N. (Ed.). (1982). *The development of prosocial behavior.* New York: Academic Press.

Eisenberg, N., & Miller, P. A. (1987). The relation of empathy to prosocial and related behaviors. *Psychological Bulletin, 101,* 91–119.

Gardner, H. (1983). *Frames of mind: The theory of multiple intelligences.* New York: Basic Books.

Gilliham, J. E., & Seligman M. E. P. (1999). Footsteps on the road to positive psychology. *Behavior Research and Therapy, 37,* 163–173.

Goble, F., & Brooks, B. D. (1983). *The case for character education.* Ottawa, IN: Green Hills Publishing.

Goleman, D. (1995). *Emotional intelligence.* New York: Bantam.

Gottfredson, D. G. (2001). *Schools and delinquency.* Cambridge, UK: Cambridge University.

Greenberg, M. T., Domitrovich, C., & Bumbarger, B. (2001). The prevention of mental disorders in school-aged children: Current state of the field. *Prevention & Treatment, 4,* article 1.

Greenberger, E., & Sorenson, A. B. (1974). Toward a concept of psychosocial maturity. *Journal of Youth and Adolescence, 3,* 329–358.

Hartshorne, H., & May, M. A. (1928). *Studies in deceit.* New York: Macmillan.

Hoffman, M. L. (1978). Toward a theory of empathic arousal and development. In M. Lewis & L. Rosenblum (Eds.), *The development of affect* (pp. 227–256). New York: Plenum.

Hoffman, M. L. (1982). Development of prosocial motivation: empathy and guilt. In N. Eisenberg (Ed.), *Development of prosocial behavior* (pp. 281–313). New York: Academic Press.

Jahoda, M. (1958). *Current concepts of positive mental health.* New York: Basic Books.

Josephson, M. (2004). The hidden costs of unethical behavior. Retrieved June, 2004 from http://www.josephsoninstitute.org/

Kelly, G. A. (1955). *A theory of personality: The psychology of personal constructs.* New York: Norton.

Kilpatrick, W. H. (1925). *Foundations of method.* New York: Macmillan.

Kohlberg, L., & Mayer, R. (1972). Development as the aim of education. *Harvard Educational Review, 42,* 449–496.

Kohlberg, L. (1976). Moral stages and moralization. In T. Lickona (Ed.), *Moral development and behavior* (pp. 31–53). New York: Holt, Reinhart and Winston.

Kohlberg, L. (1984). *The Psychology of Moral Development.* San Francisco: Harper & Row.

Lazarus, R. S. (1991). *Emotion and adaptation.* New York: Oxford University Press.

Lerner, R. (2001). Promoting promotion in the development of prevention science. *Applied Developmental Science, 5,* 254–257.

Lerner, R., Fisher, C. B., & Weinberg, R. A. (2000). Toward a science for and of the people: Promoting civil society through the application of developmental science. *Child Development, 71,* 11–20.

Lerner, R. M., Wertlieb, D., & Jacobs, F. (2003). Historical and theoretical bases of applied developmental science. In R. M. Lerner, D. Wertlieb, & F. Jacobs, (Eds.), *Handbook of applied developmental science* (vol. 1, pp. 1–30). Thousand Oaks, CA: Sage Publications.

Lickona, T. (1991). *Educating for character: How our schools can teach respect and responsibility.* New York: Bantam.

Lickona, T. (2004). *Character matters: How to help our children develop good judgment, integrity, and other essential virtues.* New York: Simon & Schuster.

MacDonald, G. B., & Valdivieso, R. (2000). Measuring deficits and assets: how we track youth development now, and how we should track it. In *Youth development: Issues and challenges.* Philadelphia: Public/Private Ventures.

Maggs J. L., & Schulenberg, J. (2001). Editors' introduction: prevention as altering the course of development and the complementary purposes of developmental and prevention sciences. *Applied Developmental Science, 5,* 196–200.

Maslow, A. H. (1962). *Toward a psychology of being.* Princeton, NJ: Van Nostrand Co.

Maher, M. (1933). *Psychology.* New York: Longmans, Green, & Co.

Moore K. A., & Halle, T. G. (2000). *Preventing problems vs. promoting the positive: What do we want for our children?* Washington, D.C.: Child Trends.

Narvaez, D. (1999). Using discourse processing methods to study moral thinking. *Educational Psychology Review, 11*(4), 377–393.

Nation, M., Crusto, C., Wandersman, A., Kumpfer, K., Seybolt, D., Morrissey-Kane, E., & Davino, K., (2003). What works in prevention: Principles of effective programs. *American Psychologist, 58,* 449–456.

Noddings, N. (2002). *Educating moral people: A caring alternative to character education.* New York: Teacher's College Press.

Nucci, L. P. (2001). Education in the moral domain. Cambridge, UK: Cambridge University Press.

Park, N., & Peterson, C. (2003). Virtues and organizations. In Cameron, K. S., Dutton, J. E., & Quinn, R. E. (Eds.), *Positive organizational scholarship* (pp. 33–47). San Francisco: Berrett-Koehler.

Peterson, C., & Seligman, M. E. P. (2003). *The values in action classification of strengths and virtues*. Washington, D.C.: American Psychological Association.

Peterson, C., & Seligman, M. E. P. (2004). The positive psychology of youth development. Paper presented at Annenberg/Sunnyland Positive Youth Development Conference. March, 2004, Annenberg Foundation Trust at Sunnyland.

Piaget, J. (1932/1965). *The moral judgment of the child*. New York: Free Press.

Power, F. C., Higgins, A., & Kohlberg, L. (1989). *Lawrence Kohlberg's approach to moral education*. New York: Columbia University Press.

Reese, W. J. (2000). Public schools and the elusive search for the common good. In L. Cuban & D. Shipps (Eds.), *Reconstructing the common good in education* (pp. 13–31). Stanford CA: Stanford University Press.

Rogers, C. (1961). *On becoming a person*. New York: Houghton Mifflin.

Roth, J. L., & Brooks-Gunn, J. (2003). What is a youth development program? identification of defining principles. In F. Jacobs, D. Wertlieb, & R. Lerner, (Eds.), *Handbook of applied developmental science* (vol. 2, pp. 197–224). Thousand Oaks, CA: Sage.

Roth, J., Brooks-Gunn, J., Murray, L., & Foster, W. (1998). Promoting healthy adolescents: synthesis of youth development program evaluations. *Journal of Research on Adolescence, 8*, 423–459.

Rotter, J. B. (1966). Generalized expectancies for internal versus external control of reinforcement. *Psychological Monographs, 80*, 1–28.

Saarni, C. (1999). *The development of emotional competence*. New York: Guilford.

Scales, P. C., Benson, P. L., Leffert, N., & Blyth, D. A. (2000). Contribution of developmental assets to the prediction of thriving among adolescents. *Applied Developmental Science, 4*(1), 27–46.

Scales, P. C., & Leffert, N. (1999). *Developmental assets: A synthesis of the scientific research on adolescent development*. Minneapolis: Search Institute.

Seligman M. E. P. (1999). Teaching positive psychology. *APA Monitor Online, 30*(7). Retrieved October 1, 2003 from www.apa.org/monitor/julaug99/speaking.html

Seligman, M. E. P. (2002). Positive psychology, positive prevention, and positive therapy. In C. Snyder & S. Lopez (Eds.), *Handbook of positive psychology* (pp. 3–9). New York:Oxford University Press.

Seligman, M. E. P., & Csikszentmihalyi, M. (2000). Positive psychology: An introduction. *American Psychologist, 55*, 5–14.

Sizer, T., & Sizer, N. F. (1999). *The students are watching: Schools and the moral contract*. Boston: Beacon Press.

Solomon, D., Watson, M. S., & Battistich, V. A. (2001). Teaching and schooling effects of moral/prosocial development. In V. Richardson, (Ed.), *Handbook of research on teaching*, (4th ed., pp. 566–603). Washington, D.C.: American Educational Research Association.

Stanhope, R. (1992). *Character education: a compilation of literature in the field from 1929 to 1991*. Unpublished Dissertation, University of Pittsburgh.

Thorndike, E. L. (1905). *The elements of psychology*. New York: A. G. Seiler.

Topping, K., Bremner, W., & Holmes, E. A. (2000). Social competence: The social construction of the concept. In R. Bar-On & J. D. Parker (Eds.), *The handbook of emotional intelligence* (pp. 28–39). San Francisco: Jossey-Bass.

Turiel, E. (2002). *The culture of morality: Social development, context, and conflict*. New York: Cambridge University Press.

Watson, M. (2003). *Learning to trust.* San Francisco: Jossey-Bass.

Weissberg, R. P., & O'Brien, M. U. (2004). What works in school-based social and emotional learning programs for positive youth development. *Annals of the American Academy of Political and Social Science, 591,* 86–87.

Wertlieb D., Jacobs F., & Lerner R. M. (Eds.). (2003). *Handbook of applied developmental science, Vol. 3: Promoting positive youth and family development: Community systems, citizen, and civil society.* Thousand Oaks, CA: Sage Publications.

Wentzel, K. R. (2002). Are effective teachers like good parents? Teaching styles and student adjustment in early adolescence. *Child Development, 73,* 287–301.

CHAPTER

26

INTEGRATIVE ETHICAL EDUCATION

DARCIA NARVAEZ
UNIVERSITY OF NOTRE DAME

Much of the debate over moral education in recent decades has centered around the advantages and disadvantages of two dominant educational approaches to the moral formation of children, referred to as *traditional character education* and *rational moral education.* Traditional character education focuses on the inculcation of virtuous traits of character as the proper aim of education. In contrast, rational moral education seeks to facilitate the development of autonomous moral judgment and the ability to resolve disputes and reach consensus according to canons of fairness. The first approach, then, is concerned with the educational requirements that contribute to the formation of character. The second is concerned with the development of reasoning and autonomy. Unfortunately, the debate has often taken on an either/or quality that has obscured common ground and integrative possibilities. In this chapter a third way, called *integrative ethical education,* is introduced. It offers a holistic approach to ethical education that, on the one hand, acknowledges the goal of cultivating reflective reasoning and a commitment to justice, required for the development of democratic communities and, on the other hand, acknowledges that the demands of citizenship in a pluralistic democracy and the ability to engage in deliberative democratic procedures depend on having a character of a certain kind.

In this chapter, the main themes of the two dominant approaches to moral and character education are reviewed. These prototypes align tolerably well with philosophical positions associated with Aristotle and Kant, respectively. The relation of these prototypes to specific educational strategies employed in moral and character education are discussed, including how recent models have attempted to reconcile them. Integrative ethical education is introduced as a view that is built on the best from these two traditions but also incorporates knowledge from cognitive science, best practice instruction, and the ancient Greek notions of *techne* and *eudaimonia.*

These debates are better understood once they are placed in historical context. In the first section, the stage is set by identifying the terms of reference for the debate between traditional character education and rational moral education (the cognitive–developmental approach).

MORAL EDUCATION IN A PLURALISTIC DEMOCRACY

Gutman (1987) points out the universal agreement that the family has preeminent responsibility for the moral and character formation of children. Nevertheless, democratic polities have a profound interest in the moral formation of its citizens. Although families have first priority in educating their children, the state has its own interest because democracies require skilled and active citizens. Indeed, according to Gutmann (1987): "Moral[1] education in a democracy is best viewed as a shared trust of the family and the polity, mutually beneficial to everyone who appreciates the values of both family life and democratic citizenship" (p. 54).

The state's interest in moral formation is manifested primarily through the common, or public, school where representatives of the state, the teachers, cultivate citizenship and civic engagement in their young charges. Nevertheless, the moral agenda of schools has proven to be contentious in the history of U.S. education, particularly as societal diversity increased. As the country became more culturally heterogeneous over the course of its history, the values that seemed obvious for public schools to teach became increasingly obscured by fundamental debates about the nature of a pluralistic democratic society and the purpose of schooling. Families became less willing to cede the proper role of character education to schools. In fact, some argued that parents should be the ones to teach values, not teachers. As Lickona (1991b) put it:

> Should the schools teach values? Just a few years ago, if you put that question to a group of people, it was sure to start an argument. If anyone said yes, schools should teach children values, somebody else would immediately retort, *whose* values? (p. 3)

Prior to the 20th century, character development was one of the primary goals of education. Schools were considered places for conveying factual information, including facts about the moral life. Over the course of the 20th century the purpose of school narrowed to teaching "the basics" (i.e., reading, writing, arithmetic), and educators tried to stay out of the battles over religious and moral values. As if to fill the vacuum, new approaches to moral character formation arose. In the 1960s, more liberal, less directive approaches to values education were tried such as values clarification (e.g., Raths, Harmin, & Simon, 1976), which supports the values the child brings to the classroom, and moral dilemma discussion (e.g., Power, Higgins, & Kohlberg, 1989), which promotes critical thinking about fairness and the development of moral reasoning. These approaches were strongly criticized. Advocates of traditional character education attacked them for allowing students to have a say in decisions that the traditionalists consider adult prerogatives, and for avoiding the strong prohibitions and rewards that traditionalists think are better suited to fostering good character (e.g., Wynne, 1991). In fact, since the 1950s, traditional moralists have blamed youth behavior (e.g., crime, cheating, drug use, pregnancy) not only on the media, materialism, privatism, and divorce, but also on liberal programs in schools that convey value neutrality (e.g., Ryan & McLean, 1987) and "de-value America" (Bennett,

---

[1]Note that *moral* and *ethical* are used interchangeably.

1992). As a means to stop the cultural decline, traditionalists rallied around directive character education (see Nash, 1997). Subsequently, they persuaded politicians, presidents, and legislatures to take up the call for character education. At the beginning of the 21st century, the number of schools adopting character education programs was on the rise; forty-seven states received federal funding for character education and fourteen states had mandated it (*Los Angeles Times,* 2003).

Irrespective of whether or not moral education is an explicit and intentional part of the curriculum, values education is embedded in the fabric of classrooms and instructional practice. For example, moral considerations are evident in how teachers treat students (DeVries, Hildebrandt, & Zan, 2000), in the policies and procedures teachers put in place and in the instructional strategies they use (Solomon, Watson, & Battistich, 2002), in how teachers set and uphold standards, decide on grades, and respect cultural differences (Kessler, 2001). In other words, moral considerations infuse the "hidden curriculum" (Jackson, 1968; Jackson, Boostrom, & Hansen, 1998). Values are inextricably linked to school and classroom life. Teachers, as representatives of the community and the primary liaison between the child and the society, must be given the authority to help children develop character skills that promote active and positive citizenship because the community, like the family, is responsible for raising good citizens (Gutmann, 1987).

Educators themselves bring up a pragmatic issue. How can they teach values when they are struggling to deliver on academics—basic knowledge in science, literacy, critical thinking? Of course, the same quick answer applies: schools are already teaching values, whether they want to or not, intentionally or not. There is no need to add a new course. The solution advocated here is well expressed by Starratt (1994):

> Rather than add on new courses in ethics, teachers can make use of an abundance of ethically pregnant material already in the curriculum that has not been attended to. It is not a question of working longer hours; it is a question of working smarter, of improving the quality of all the human interactions now taking place in the normal school day. (pp. 11–12)

If citizens can agree that moral education necessarily is part of schooling and that educators teach values as much as they grade papers, can we agree on what should be taught and how; in other words, what moral education should look like in action? Not necessarily. This is contentious, too. In fact, this is the heart of the matter. We examine the foundations of the debate in the next section. The two contending approaches to the character formation of children are outlined in terms of their philosophical assumptions about character development.

TWO COMPETING PARADIGMS

Moral education debates can be characterized as a perceived clash between two philosophical perspectives (O'Neill, 1995), one representing particularist claims regarding virtue, or character ethics (MacIntyre, 1981; Noddings,[2] 2002), and the other representing universalist claims regarding justice and reasoning (Frankena, 1973; Kant, 1949), or rule ethics. The two types of theories are not mutually exclusive but differ in emphasis and in how they circumscribe morality (O'Neill, 1995). These disparate foci lead to different premises, conclusions, and applications.

---

[2]The caring perspective denoted by Noddings is a variant of particularism that emphasizes relation rather than agent-centered virtues, and emphasizes setting up the conditions for good relations.

Rule Ethics

A rule ethics approach focuses on what is the right thing to do in a particular moral situation (e.g., Frankena, 1973; Hare, 1963; Rawls, 1971). Rule ethics circumscribes morality to obligatory action and is driven by reasoning about such action. For Kant, famously, this means acting according to respect for persons (Kant, 1949). Moral conduct is that which accords with applicable principles for a particular situation; principles in conformance with universalizable obligatory action are necessary for anyone who finds himself or herself in a similar situation (e.g., Kant's categorical imperative).

In comparison to classical character ethics to be described, rule ethics is a minimalist theory in two senses (Norton, 1991). First, morality is simplified and few demands are made on individuals. Rule ethics attends to deontic judgments about obligation in narrow slices of human life, leaving free from moral evaluation huge stretches of life. It narrows the range of morality, excluding such things as one's choice of friends, vocation, and leisure activities from the auspices of the moral life (which fall under the guidance of prudence, which Kant considered separate from morality). Second, it is minimal not only because it shields from moral evaluation vast segments of human experience, but also because it reduces moral obligation to that which can be formulated with respect to universal moral principles. Morality becomes what is universally applicable.

> Modern morality is minimalist by virtue of its understanding of rules as applicable uniformly to everyone under the requirements of "universalizability" and "impartiality." If what is right for anyone must be right for everyone in relevantly similar circumstances, then what is right must be such as can be recognized and acted upon by persons who possess very little in the way of developed moral character. (Norton, 1991, p. xi)

Thus, this lowest common denominator becomes what is demanded of everyone. Rule ethics attends to the development of character only when necessary for rule-abiding behavior. In contrast, conduct expected from virtuous individuals in character ethics—living a good life (e.g., cultivating courage and prudence)—becomes supererogatory, not required of the moral agent.

Character Ethics

The focal concerns for character ethics are the nature of a good life and the attributes necessary to live a good life (e.g., Anscombe, 1958; Hursthouse, 1999; McDowell, 1997). The central questions are "What sort of person should I be?" and "How should I live my life?" Hence the focus is on the agent. These concerns lead directly to the problem of character development because the attributes of moral character are not present at birth. Virtues or excellences must be deliberately nurtured. Although classical theory does not ignore the need for rules for those who do not have the requisite moral character to guide their behavior, rules are subordinated to character development and viewed instrumentally for that end.

In contrast to the rule–ethics perspective, character ethics maintains that nothing in a life is devoid of moral meaning. All human conduct has moral relevance. The choices one makes in all realms of life influence and reflect one's character development. Moreover, continuous moral growth is demanded of individuals, with no upper limit. Individuals are held responsible for their own self-actualization and for maintaining good character. There are two areas in which rule ethics and character ethics are paradigmatically far apart, the nature of moral personhood and the importance of community.

The Nature of Personhood

The two philosophical paradigms are distinguishable in how they view moral personhood, "thinly" or "thickly" (Williams, 1985). Rule ethics focuses on action, defining the individual as a bearer of rights that others must respect through right action (O'Neill, 1995). Here, the moral person is defined thinly, as one who takes just action but whose required universalizable rules for actions denote negative duties (i.e., to do no harm) and are exclusive of positive duties such as benevolence and the responsibility for self-development. Character ethics, on the other hand, emphasizes the quality of agents, rather than action per se, and the inherently moral, social, and political aspects of individuality. In this view, personhood is defined thickly, as essentially moral, founded in virtues, values, and responsibilities (Hursthouse, 1999). The individual is responsible for discovering what virtues and values are inherent in the self, and for cultivating them. Moral action is derivative of moral character. Clearly then, whereas rule ethics requires only a thin notion of personhood to make it work, virtue ethics requires a fuller specification of personhood, a thick notion that says something about how virtues contribute to living well the life that is good for one to live (Cunningham, in press).

The Need for Community

Unlike rule ethics, character ethics emphasizes the support of the community in developing moral personhood. The individual is embedded in a community that offers support and encouragement in the process of self-actualization. "The conception of the polis, then, is that of an institutionalized social organization designed to afford maximum realization of values by individuals, as well as optimal utilization of the values realized" (Norton, 1991, p. 14). This is the essence of *eudaimonia* (flourishing). In this Aristotelian view, every individual actualizes virtues in self with the support necessary from friends, associates, and society as a whole. Thus, character ethics considers community vital for human virtue and human thriving. In contrast, the communal life of the Kantian agent is not assumed and may not be required (Norton, 1991). Although an abstracted community is used in determining principles and actions, rule ethics almost seems to view the concrete community as an obstacle to individual flourishing. Biological and psychological evidence suggest that the former perspective, that of character ethics, is the correct view. Individuals cannot flourish alone.

The next section discusses how the two dominant paradigms in ethics are instantiated in approaches to moral and character education. The moral rational education approach, associated with Kohlberg and the cognitive–developmental tradition, is better aligned with Kantian rule ethics, whereas traditional character education is better aligned with character ethics. In addition, several integrative educational approaches that seek to blend aspects of each philosophical paradigm are described.

APPROACHES TO MORAL AND CHARACTER EDUCATION

How are these two philosophical perspectives, rule ethics and character ethics, instantiated in approaches to moral and character education? Here, classic educational approaches influenced by each philosophical perspective are illustrated, followed by brief descriptions of several integrative approaches.

The Cognitive–Developmental Approach of Kohlberg

Those who advocated a universalist, rule-ethics perspective (e.g., Kohlberg, 1981; Power et al., 1989) contend that the educator should facilitate the development of reflective reasoning about justice and fairness. This perspective is influenced not only by rule ethics, which emphasizes reason and intent, but by Piagetian stage theories of moral development, where the emphasis is on how children construct moral perspectives, think through competing options, resolve dilemmas, and justify conclusions (Kohlberg, 1981, 1984). A common instructional method of the rational moral education approach, also known as the "cognitive–developmental" approach, is moral dilemma discussion. The purpose of discussion is to help children advance to higher stages of moral reasoning. There is an internal standard of adequacy, that moral reasoning framed from the perspective of higher stages is better in that it can solve more complex social problems. Robust discussion of moral perspectives provides the disequilibrating experiences that motivate development to higher levels of moral reasoning.

In the rational moral education approach, the adult acts as a facilitator of student development, through the design of activities that include peer discussion of moral dilemmas and other perspective-taking opportunities. Foremost is learning to take an impartial moral point of view in which one considers the welfare of everyone alike, sets aside egoism, acts on principle, and is willing to universalize one's principles (Frankena, 1973, p. 114). The goal of the cognitive–development approach is to move children to higher levels of understanding through the provision of role-taking opportunities and other practical sociomoral experiences that arise in the natural life of classrooms (Oser, 1991). Development occurs in a bottom-up fashion, among students: interaction with peers compels perspective taking and induces cognitive disequilibrium (Piaget, 1932/1965), pressing students to build new understandings that propel them forward to increasingly adequate and more complex reasoning and perspective taking.

Reflective reasoning is believed to bring about the appropriate attitudes and behaviors that are conducive to ethical behavior and citizenship (Oser, 1991) by nurturing autonomous moral agents who are able to function as rational actors committed to the higher demands of justice. In fact, interventions that use moral dilemma discussion positively influence moral judgment scores (Blatt & Kohlberg, 1975; Rest, 1986), and moral judgment consistently contributes to predicting moral action (Thoma, 1994), although both effects are small.

The rational moral education approach is sometimes described as an indirect approach to moral development (e.g., Solomon, Watson, Battistich, Schaps, & Delucchi, 1992) because children are not directly instructed on what to believe and how to act but are rather encouraged to test their perspectives and examine their adequacy against the viewpoints of arguments made from the perspective of higher stage complexity. The teacher's role is to facilitate the discussion, pitch arguments at higher stages, and make sure that multiple perspectives are aired. The aim is to change structure, not beliefs, by emphasizing the processes of thinking, not its content. Students develop in the processes of reasoning morally, taking the perspectives of others, making good decisions, and creating more complex conceptual understandings. By emphasizing the processes of reasoning about justice, the question about whose values are being taught is moot (Kohlberg, 1981).

Originally, Kohlberg focused on pure dilemma discussion to promote moral reasoning; little emphasis was given to anything else, including the school climate. But in the second generation of Kohlberg's school interventions, the implementation of "just communities" demanded explicit attention to how everyone was getting along. Students were immersed in an environment where they learned to "understand and to feel justice" by being treated justly and being expected to act justly (Power et al., 1989, p. 25). By adding the dimension of moral culture (Durkheim, 1925/1973), the just-community approach supported specific moral norms with corresponding behavioral content (e.g., be on time; do not fight; Power, 2004). Just-community schools were intended to "embody principles of justice in a moral atmosphere" that would "promote moral development" (Reed, 1997, p. 194). Dilemma discussion became a necessary tool that community members used to create a just and democratic community.

Kohlberg's approaches have been described as child centered and have been criticized for disregarding successful traditional educational methods, such as direct teaching of good and bad behavior (Benninga, 1991). Rational moral education has been denounced for its lack of explicit content and for giving too much power to children by allowing them to make decisions about rules that should be non-negotiable and adult prerogatives, such as punishments for rule violations (Wynne, 1991). For example, Wynne and Ryan (1993) decry "making schools and classrooms more" democratic, "which means more authority for pupils and less for teachers" (p. 16) and lament "the hostility towards the unapologetic use of appropriate punishment as a tool to maintain order" (p. 21).

Two additional criticisms bear mentioning. One of the deepest criticisms of Kohlberg's theory is the empirical gap between moral judgment and action (Blasi, 1980): individuals often do not act in accord with their reasoning. In other words, moral judgment alone is insufficient for moral action. Kohlberg eventually admitted there were factors other than justice reasoning that play a role in moral behavior (Kohlberg, Levine, & Hewer, 1983). Second, not surprisingly given its roots, Kohlberg's approach neglects the personological dimensions of action, embracing a thin notion of character, and emphasizing reasoning over all other aspects of morality. Noted some time ago (Blasi, 1980), Kohlberg's theory neglects the broader emphasis on moral personhood (e.g., identity) that character ethics provides and is described in the next section.

What is particularly valuable about the rational moral education approach is the awareness that knowledge is constructed through stimulating cognitive experience (Piaget, 1932/1965), that adult coaching and student development go hand in hand (DeVries & Zan, 1999), and that deliberative reasoning skills are necessary for civic engagement (Gutmann, 1987; Gutmann & Thompson, 1996). Kohlberg's approach is commendable for its emphasis on right action and its avoidance of relativism in pressing for justice. Nucci (chap. 24, this volume; 2001) describes an offspring of Kohlberg's original cognitive–developmental approach, supplying various ideas on how to apply a domains approach to support a moral classroom climate, for example, through the discussion of dilemmas about conventions and morality.

A Traditional Character-Ethics Approach

There is no one dominant methodological approach to traditional character education as there has been in rational moral education. Instead, there are diverse perspectives on what good character education looks like. That said, it is possible to identify points of view that are widely shared and for which there is some consensus. The universal starting point is an assumption that there are universal core values that should be taught. (For additional insightful discussion of the state of the world according to traditionalists, see Nucci, chap. 24, this volume.)

In most traditional character education programs, tradition, authority, and obedience are emphasized over reasoning, autonomy, and social justice. Wynne is illustrative of a more traditional approach whose followers believe that an educator should stress the development of habits and dispositions consonant with community traditions (Wynne, 1991; Wynne & Ryan, 1993). Rooted in rote methods and conventional content, the traditional character education perspective is less concerned about how children reason or solve social problems and more concerned about making sure children learn virtuous behavior and display traits of moral character (e.g., Wynne & Ryan, 1993). Here the results of character education are paramount. The content of morality is emphasized rather than the processes of moral reasoning in contradiction to the cognitive–development approach. The ultimate goal is to socialize individuals to behave properly. It is assumed that virtuous individuals living a good life by nature make for a strong community.

Wynne and Ryan (1993) recommend that, to "reclaim our schools," the school as a whole must convey consistent messages to students about moral character, and the community must reward the proper attitudes and behaviors expected of students. A school that builds character emphasizes "core values" in all that it does (e.g., Ryan & Bohlin, 1999). The adults are clearly in charge and have the knowledge that children must learn. Instruction and knowledge flows top-down from adult to child, unlike in rational moral education where there is co-construction of moral practice. Instead, adults primarily guide and mentor children away from prohibited behaviors and toward appropriate personal attitudes, dispositions, and behaviors. As Wynne (1991) says, adults are expected "to shape and determine the immediate behavior of the young, to form their character" (p. 143).

Wynne (1997) names policies, people, and environments "for-character" if they help form good character. He says that for-character methods have been around for a long time and have been found in preliterate cultures. In his examples of instruction, Wynne is explicit in supporting a "sophisticated behaviorism" (1997, p. 65) because he contends that "a learner's internal state is largely shaped by directing his behavior" (p. 65). Wynne's (1997) greatest emphasis is on designing environments that support good character. For-character educators need to "recognize how environments help or hurt character formation" (p. 64). They analyze their school and classroom environments in terms of how supportive they are of good character formation and redesign the environments, if necessary, with the help of parents, colleagues, pupils, and community members. In his view, environmental factors such as teacher grading and instructional policies are as critical as focusing on content that increases patriotism. There is a clear awareness that everything a teacher does conveys values.

Wynne (1991) has suggested that for-character schools have a number of characteristics. For example, in these schools adults model good character and help to maintain a common sense of purpose in the school through ceremonies that stress school values. School documents describe the school's policies clearly and with justification. Good behavior and swift discipline are emphasized. Although academics are primary and are emphasized with frequent testing and awards, there are also times for fun. Students have opportunities to engage in many kinds of service to others in and outside the school. If necessary, parents are confronted when their behaviors are harmful to their children. According to Wynne (1991, p. 146), an unpublished study found "favorable statistical relations between a pro-character focus and academic emphasis in some schools" (Wynne & Iverson, 1989).

Often called a teacher-centered and direct teaching approach (Benninga, 1991; Solomon et al., 2002), the traditional character education approach is rued by its critics for its superficiality, for its inability to adapt to the progressive transformation of educational practice, and for trying to solve the wrong problems (Kohn, 1997a, 1997b; Nash, 1997). For example, Kohn criticizes traditionalists for trying to solve social, political, and economic problems by changing the characters of individuals, a "fix-the-kids" approach, that ignores the well-documented influence of social context on behavior (e.g., Harman, 1999; Mischel, 1990). Second, Kohn scoffs at their use of ineffective, outdated teaching methods such as exhortation, memorization, and punishment, methods that make incorrect assumptions about how people learn (Anderson, 1989). Third, Kohn berates traditionalists for an implicit negative view of human nature that is evident in the emphasis on self-control, as if humans were inherently self-centered and aggressive, rather than on positive human characteristics like empathy (Hoffman, 2000). For these reasons, developmental psychologists have pointed to multiple limitations of the traditional approach, one of which is its lack of lasting effectiveness in promoting prosocial behavior (Leming, 1997). The approach might work for immediate compliance to moral exhortation, but the empirical evidence indicates most often that it has no lasting effects on moral motivation or moral reasoning (Solomon et al., 2002).

Kohlberg (1981) excoriates the traditionalists in several ways. He criticizes their use of indoctrination and the practice of rewarding and punishing compliance with an adult set of rules. He berates their interpretation of community as submission to authority. Foremost, he challenges the "bag of virtues" approach for two reasons. First, although individuals may agree on a set of labels for desirable virtues, they can in fact hold disparate understandings of what the labels refer to. Second, one can emphasize a set of virtues that rest on or lead to injustice, as in the case of the ancient Greeks whose *eudaimonia* was reserved for perhaps 10% of the population. Most fundamentally, Kohlberg was concerned about promoting ethical relativism, and the dangers of claiming that any set of core or "positive values" could be foundational (Kohlberg, 1984). One might also criticize the traditionalists for not fully embracing the teleological perspective of Aristotelian theory in which "virtue is the right action as the rationally determined mean between two extremes within the capabilities and conditions of a particular person" (G. Zecha, personal communication, August 14, 2004) and which accords with *eudaimonia* or human flourishing.

Two of the emphases of the traditional character education approach deserve a closer look. First, the importance of content. Progressive traditions have often deemphasized the content of learning and stressed the processes of learning (e.g., Dewey, 1913), focusing, for example, on critical thinking rather than on the memorization of facts. However, cognitive scientists have realized more recently that expert knowledge is a combination of content, having more and better organized knowledge, and strategic or process knowledge, knowing how and when to apply the knowledge (Hogarth, 2001). Experts not only think better, they have more to think about (Alexander, 1992). Of course, the content experts learn is not just any content, it is content critical to performance in the domain and it is learned in a developmentally appropriate manner.

Second, traditional character educators emphasize the importance of the environment in shaping behavior. Although the behaviorist paradigm reflected in this view has long been discredited, developmental psychology has since realized the power of ecological systems and the dynamic interactions between the person and context in shaping persons and their outcomes (e.g., Bronfenbrenner, 1979). Human development occurs best in environments that match the needs of the child.

As noted, both the rational moral education and the traditional character education approaches have their strengths and weaknesses. Whereas rational moral education adopts constructivism and adult coaching, fosters reasoning for civic engagement, and avoids relativism, it can be criticized for a narrow emphasis on moral reasoning, whether in dilemma discussion or a just community, which is insufficient for moral action and misses the centrality of moral identity in moral behavior. Traditional character education rightly emphasizes the importance of content and demonstrated some insight into the impact of environments. However, it can be faulted for a changing set of core virtues open to the charge of relativism, for downplaying the importance of autonomy, and for a problematic pedagogy. Consequently, several research psychologists have attempted to build unifying models. To those we turn next.

Integrative Approaches

Discussion about the conflict between the rational moral education approach and traditional character education often becomes polarized. Indeed, on one level, the two camps use terms of reference that, in reflecting theoretical or ideological commitments, appear incommensurate or evoke different frames of understanding. For example, Kohlberg (1981) was averse to indoctrination whereas traditionalists (Ryan & Bohlin, 1999; Wynne, 1985/1986) argued that indoctrination is good. Several researchers have advocated bridging the divide (e.g., Benninga, 1991; Berkowitz, 2002; Lickona, 1991). Three integrative frameworks are described briefly.

Moral Anatomy. Berkowitz (1997; chap. 25, this volume) proposed a multidimensional integrative model of the moral person and a comprehensive approach to moral education that is informed by various psychological literatures. More than anyone else, Berkowitz integrates moral identity and personality into a character education model. He proposes a moral anatomy, which comprises the seven necessary components of a moral person. (In his essays, he names the parts but does not necessarily define them.)

Berkowitz starts with the component that is the goal and outcome of all the other components, moral behavior. A person cannot be described as moral unless they behave morally. Second, a moral person must have a moral character, the dispositional and personological aspects of behavior, the "internalized tendencies that produce right behavior" (1997, p. 16) that result from habitual but reflective action. The third critical component is moral values, which are "affectively laden beliefs concerning the rightness and wrongness of behaviors or end states which are intrinsically potentially harmful and are universal and unalterable in their prescriptivity" (1997, p. 18). Fourth, moral reasoning adds moral authority, the ability to determine what is right and wrong. Fifth, moral emotion is the power supply for action, integrating values and reason, and occurs in two forms. One form may be described as affective responses to others. These prosocial emotions include empathy, sympathy, and compassion. The other form is composed of self-critical emotions such as shame, guilt, and regret. Sixth, moral identity is an aspect only recently studied that appears to be necessary for moral exemplarity. Finally, the moral person also enlists metamoral characteristics for effective moral functioning. These elements include such things as self-discipline and perseverance.

How does Berkowitz apply the moral anatomy to moral education? Moral education must be driven by an explicit school mission and be embedded in the context of total school reform (Berkowitz & Bier, in press). Educators must be committed to be role models and embrace a democratic governance structure. Educators should attempt to positively influence peer norms. Berkowitz advocates cultivating character through peer moral dilemma discussion, community meetings, and opportunities for moral action. Berkowitz, Sherblom, Bier, and Battistich (chap. 25, this volume) go further and integrate the moral anatomy with cross-disciplinary approaches to positive youth development.

Berkowitz supports an approach that steers between rational moral education and traditional character education. He splits the moral person into separate pieces such as emotions, behavior, and reasoning without clear empirical evidence for doing so. He gives few details about each element in the anatomy, not describing any aspect precisely. Moreover, he speaks in generalities about instruction. As a result, content and process, what should be taught and how are largely unspecified. His view seems to resemble Lickona's, which is discussed next.

Educating for Character. Lickona (1991a, 1991b) proposed an integrative model that incorporates right thinking, based in Platonic thought, and right behavior, based in Aristotelian thought. He agrees that the goal of character education is to build qualities of good character, called virtues. Virtues have three parts: moral knowledge, moral feeling, and moral behavior. It is not enough to behave well, one must know what justice is and what it means when relating to others; one must care about justice and react to injustice; and one must act justly. Character education is about knowledge, appreciation, and practice, or head, heart, and hand. Lickona blends cognitive development with traditional character education practices. For example, Lickona (2004, p. xxv) lists ten essential virtues to teach (wisdom, justice, fortitude, self-control, love, a positive attitude, hard work, integrity, gratitude, and humility) and he spells out how to lead a discussion about moral dilemmas (1991b, chaps. 13 and 14).

Lickona's (1997) comprehensive approach to character education advocates cultivating the virtues through "the total moral life of the school" (p. 46). Lickona describes twelve mutually supportive strategies for a comprehensive strategy toward character education. The first nine focus on the classroom and the last three, the school. First, the teacher is a caregiver, moral model, and moral mentor in relationships with the students. The teacher treats students with respect and discusses morally significant events occurring in the world around them. The teacher mentors students with direct moral instruction through story telling and discussion, providing corrective feedback when they are hurtful to others. Second, the teacher creates a caring classroom community by shaping a positive peer community through high expectations, discussion of positive virtues, and coaching on living them.

Third, teachers use moral discipline. This means that discipline is a tool for character development, used to help students develop respect, reasoning, and self-control. Rules are based on values (e.g., caring) and the needs of others. When violated, consequences reinforce obligations toward others and the benefits of the rule for self and others. Fourth, teachers create a democratic classroom community in which students are involved in shared decision making about classroom issues. The primary means for creating a democratic community is having class meetings in which students are able to voice their concerns and solve problems of getting along.

Fifth, teachers nurture values through the curriculum by "mining the school curriculum for its moral potential" (p. 53) and making use of published character education materials. Sixth, teachers use cooperative learning to help students learn to get along with each other and deepen a sense of community. Seventh, teachers develop a "conscience of craft" (Green, 1999) by combining high expectations with high support. Eighth, teachers cultivate ethical reflection, helping students to reflect on the perspectives of others, consider the concrete requirements of the virtues and their practice, make thoughtful decisions, and critique themselves. Ninth, teachers help students to resolve conflicts peacefully with conflict resolution skills.

Strategies for character formation are applied at the school level as well. First, the school creates a positive moral culture by explicitly adopting practices that foster respect among all constituencies and that support the development of virtue. Second, the school develops opportunities for students to show care in the community through service learning and other face-to-face learning experiences. Third, the school recruits parents and community members as partners in character education efforts through mutual support. Schools should educate parents and community members on how character is formed and the importance of all adults in these efforts. Schools can provide school-based and home-based family activities that support the school's character education curricula. Lickona's Center for the Fourth and Fifth Rs offers workshops on these principles to hundreds of teachers annually.

Given that Lickona selects several core values to emphasize, he seems to fall into a "bag of virtues" approach, yet he offsets this with an emphasis on moral reasoning development. In addition, he tries to be more systematic by delineating the elements of moral functioning (moral knowing, feeling, and doing), although this splitting of functions is not grounded in psychological science. He takes a middle of the road approach to instruction, viewing teachers as both role models and facilitators of children's development. He does not provide a systematic pedagogy, unlike the Child Development Project, which is discussed next.

Child Development Project.   The Developmental Studies Center offers perhaps the premier approach to character education in the country, perhaps in the world. Although it began in the early 1980s with school reform efforts aimed at increasing social and ethical development in what was called the Child Development Project (Solomon et al., 1988), Developmental Studies Center programs quickly expanded to include academic development, particularly literacy. From its inception, the Developmental Studies Center has developed research-based interventions strongly rooted in developmental psychology and motivation theory. Taking a clearly progressive approach to character education, Schaps, Battistich, and Solomon (1997) make evident their view of human nature:

> Our basic assumption is that when children's needs are met through membership in a school community, they are likely to become affectively bonded with and committed to the school, and therefore inclined to identify with and behave in accordance with its expressed goals and values. (p. 127)

The Developmental Studies Center group agrees with Deci and Ryan (1985) that individuals have three basic needs—autonomy, belongingness and competence—that influence the level of individual engagement with school based on the degree to which the needs are met. According to the center (e.g., Battistich, Solomon, Watson, & Schaps, 1997), these needs are best met in a group setting which provides "a focus for identification and commitment" (p. 138) and in which students can "participate actively in a cohesive, caring group with a shared purpose; that is, a community" (p. 138). A *caring community* is one where members feel cared about and care about others, influence group activities, share in decisions relevant to the group, have common values, norms, and goals, and feel a sense of belonging to and identification with the group. The Developmental Studies Center builds a sense of community through activities such as collaborating on common academic goals; providing and receiving help from others; practicing social competencies; and exercising autonomy by making decisions about classroom life. Students are provided with multiple opportunities to discuss the experiences of others, which aids in building empathy and perspective taking skills. Students are guided in reflecting on their own behaviors in light of prosocial values such as fairness, respect, and social responsibility.

Developmental Studies Center programs are designed to broadly influence the intellectual, social, and ethical development of children through direct and indirect methods called "guided autonomy" (Solomon et al., 2002). This integrative methodology is apparent in the fact that teachers coach students as they construct understandings and make decisions in three realms, the social, the ethical, and the intellectual. Adults directly guide the students as they build autonomy and help students to become caring, principled, and self-disciplined. Indirect methods are reflected in the two "essential conditions" required for long-term learning and growth in intellectual, social, and moral domains namely, participation in a caring community of learners and challenging engaging learning experiences. Activities promote social awareness and skill development. The approach immerses the child in a coherent caring community that includes not only the classroom and the school, but after-school activities and parental involvement. Developmental Studies Center programs are implemented only within schools who demonstrate a commitment to its complete implementation, including teacher training and professional development.

Research studies of Child Development Project implementations indicate that in comparison to control schools, students make positive gains in targeted areas. Using classroom observations, individual interviews, and student questionnaires, program students exhibited more prosocial behavior in the classroom (Solomon, Watson, Delucchi, Schaps, & Battistich, 1988), more democratic values and interpersonal understanding (Solomon, Watson, Schaps, Battistich, & Solomon, 1990), and social problem-solving and conflict resolution skills (Battistich, Solomon, Watson, Solomon, & Schaps, 1989). Students in Child Development Project schools were more likely to view their classroom as communities that led them to adhere to salient classroom values and respond to hypothetical prosocial dilemmas with more autonomous, other-oriented moral reasoning (Solomon et al., 1992).

The most important variable positively influenced by participation in Child Development Project programs is students' sense of community. This variable is positively related to multiple positive outcomes including an increase in self-reported concern for others, conflict resolution skills, altruistic behavior, intrinsic prosocial motivation, trust in and respect for teachers, enjoyment of helping others learn as well as academic engagement (Battistich, Solomon, Watson, & Schaps, 1996; Watson, Battistich, & Solomon, 1997).

The Child Development Project approach is the most comprehensive and systematic of those outlined here. It is rooted in motivation theory which highlights the importance of community. The project promotes the best of direct and indirect teaching in its use of guided autonomy. However, it delineates only a small set of concrete skills for students to learn constructively.

The integrative approaches of Lickona, Berkowitz, and the Developmental Studies Center are multidimensional, aligned with the best insights of important literatures, and bridge the divide between the traditional character education and rational moral education in interesting ways. A new approach, Integrative Ethical Education, has some of these same features. It extends these approaches by providing systematic views of both character and pedagogy. Moreover, IEE endeavors to integrate the ancient Greek notion of *techne,* expertise, as well as *eudaimonia,* human flourishing in community, an emphasis taken up by the positive psychology movement in recent years (Seligman & Csikszentmihalyi, 2000; Snyder & Lopez, 2002). These efforts are made possible only now given advances in behavioral science.

INTEGRATIVE ETHICAL EDUCATION

In recent years, an alternative approach to character education has been proposed in an attempt to reconcile the insights of traditional character education and rational moral education with current research (Anderson, Narvaez, Bock, Endicott, & Lies, 2003; Narvaez, 2005; Narvaez, Bock, & Endicott, 2003; Narvaez, Endicott, Bock, & Lies, 2005). The theoretical model is called *Integrative Ethical Education,* and it brings together the considerations discussed in previous sections. Three foundational ideas of the model are discussed, each followed by two implications for practice. The first idea, the notion of moral expertise, provides a specific content for what to teach. The second idea, moral education as transformation, focuses on the necessary changes in instruction and environment that must accompany the transformation of the child. The third idea, human nature as cooperative and self-actualizing, addresses the specific contexts for moral growth.

Foundational Idea 1: Moral Development Is Developing Expertise

The Integrative Ethical Education model is built on the notion of expertise development. *Expertise* refers to a refined, deep understanding that is evident in practice and action. It does not refer to a technical competence (Hansen, 2001) nor to mere intellectual ability. Expertise harnesses the full capacities of the individual, "flowing" in a synchrony of all systems working together in a goal-directed fashion to express virtue in action. First, expertise is described in a general way and then in the domain of morality.

Experts and novices differ from one another in three basic ways. First, experts in a particular domain have more and better organized knowledge than novices (Chi, Glaser, & Farr, 1988; Sternberg, 1998). Expert knowledge is of several kinds that interact in performance, for example, declarative (what), procedural (how), conditional (when and how much). Second, experts perceive and react to the world differently, noticing details and opportunities that novices miss. Third, experts behave differently. Whereas novices use conscious, effortful methods to solve problems, expert skills are highly automatic and effortless. Expertise requires a great deal of practice that is beyond the usual everyday amount of exposure to a domain; therefore, it must be deliberately cultivated (Ericsson & Charness, 1994).

Moral experts demonstrate holistic orientations in one or more of the four processes. Experts in ethical sensitivity are better at quickly and accurately reading a moral situation and determining what role they might play. They role take and control personal bias in an effort to be morally responsive to others. Experts in ethical judgment have many tools for solving complex moral problems. They reason about duty and consequences, responsibility, and ethical codes. Experts in ethical focus cultivate ethical self-regulation that leads them to prioritize ethical goals. They foster an ethical identity that leads them to revere life and deepen commitment. Experts in ethical action know how to keep their "eye on the prize," enabling them to stay on task and take the necessary steps to get the ethical job done. They are able to intervene courageously and take initiative for others. Experts in a particular excellence have more and better organized knowledge about it, have highly tuned perceptual skills for it, have deep moral desire for it, and have highly automatized, effortless responses. In short, they have more content knowledge and more process knowledge. (It should be noted that Ryan & Lickona [1987] also pointed to the importance of both content and process knowledge for moral agency).

Implication 1: Educators Should Teach the Processes and Skills of Moral Behavior.
Moral behavior requires all four processes for successful completion: ethical sensitivity,

ethical judgment, ethical focus, and ethical action (based on Rest, 1983). Those who complete a moral behavior have applied skills in each of these areas. They noticed a moral need, imagined and reasoned about what action to take, focused themselves on taking the action, and followed through to its completion. Each process includes a set of skills. The notion of "skills" here is not equivalent to traits in the everyday sense, in which a trait is available for one to exhibit wherever one goes, like a badge or a birth mark. Such a notion is empirically unsupported (Mischel, 1990). Instead, skills align with the empirical finding that behavior is consistent in circumstances that correspond to a consonant set of person–environment features, including social–contextual expectations (Cervone & Shoda, 1999). That is, an individual acts the same way in similar situations. Skills form an embodied cognition (Varela, Thompson, & Roach, 1991), a holistic and contextualized understanding that engages the entire brain–mind–body system and is evident in action.

The sampling of skills listed in Table 26.1 represent the type of expertise each process entails (elsewhere, three subskills are suggested for each skill). The twenty-eight skills were sampled from those considered to be moral exemplars (e.g., Martin Luther King, Jr.),

TABLE 26.1
Integrative Ethical Education: Ethical Skills

Ethical sensitivity
    Understand emotional expression
    Take the perspective of others
    Connecting to others
    Responding to diversity
    Controlling social bias
    Interpreting situations
    Communicate effectively

Ethical judgment
    Understanding ethical problems
    Using codes and identifying judgment criteria
    Reasoning generally
    Reasoning ethically
    Understand consequences
    Reflect on the process and outcome
    Coping and resiliency

Ethical focus
    Respecting others
    Cultivate conscience
    Act responsibly
    Help others
    Finding meaning in life
    Valuing traditions and institutions
    Developing ethical identity and integrity

Ethical action
    Resolving conflicts and problems
    Assert respectfully
    Taking initiative as a leader
    Implementing decisions
    Cultivate courage
    Persevering
    Work hard

from classic virtues (e.g., prudence, courage) and modern virtues (e.g., assertiveness, resilience), as well as from a review of scholarship in morality, development, citizenship, and positive psychology. Skills include those that promote justice and the flourishing of self and others, individual and community. A minimal level of competence in these skills is required of adult citizens for a pluralistic democracy to flourish.

Implication 2: Educators Should Teach Both Moral Virtue and Moral Reasoning. Moral expertise involves reasoning, virtue, autonomy, and excellence. Reason guides the individual in determining action according to the mean between two extremes, the mean appropriate in the circumstances and for the individual (G. Zecha, personal communication, August 14, 2004). Yet the common understandings of reasoning and virtue are inadequate in light of psychological science. Reasoning and virtue are described and reformulated, each in turn.

Deliberate moral reasoning and decision making are vital for mature moral judgment. Deliberative reasoning is able to provide objective rationale that can be challenged and revised, reputed, or accepted (Gutmann & Thompson, 1996). Mature reasoning about justice has often compelled changes in longstanding cultural practices and brought about key reforms such as the abolition of slavery and the promotion of human rights (Rawls, 2001). As Kohlberg championed (1981, 1984), programs that cultivate morality must nurture mature moral judgment.

However, the longstanding perspective in the social sciences, that conscious deliberative reasoning is primary and unconscious thought is secondary, is undergoing a paradigm shift, reversing this view (Lakoff & Johnson, 1999; Varela, 1999). The conscious mind appears to be a secondary apparatus to a multiplicity of nonconscious, decision-making systems (Damasio, 1996, 1999; Hogarth, 2001; Reber, 1993; Varela et al., 1991). The common view of the human as rational agent is being challenged. Recent psychological research demonstrates that humans are not rational agents in the classical sense (e.g., Bargh & Ferguson, 2000). Instead of being driven by the principles of a conscious rational mind, humans have a "bounded rationality" that uses subconscious, "good enough" heuristics to make decisions (Gigerenzer & Selten, 2001; Kahneman, 2003). Heuristics are intuitions built from repeated experience that are retained in implicit memory systems and which may or may not be verbally expressible (Hasher & Zacks, 1984; Keil & Wilson, 1999). Many decisions are made without reasoning at all but based on pattern recognition, as with experts when their skills are automatized (Bargh & Ferguson, 2000). In fact, perception and behavior are closely intertwined (Hurley, 2002), so much so that biochemical–physiological changes and "somatic markers" built from perceptual experience often drive decisions and subsequent action (Damasio, 1999).

If most human behavior is not consciously controlled but automatic (Bargh & Chartrand, 1999; Bargh & Ferguson, 2000), there are implications for the description and study of human morality (see Lapsley & Narvaez, 2004, 2005; Narvaez & Lapsley, 2005). Moral decisions are made both by the conscious system and by systems outside of conscious awareness. Each system contributes to moral decisions and actions. Varela (1999) describes the interconnection of these systems in expert moral agency:

> A wise (or virtuous) person is *one who knows what is good and spontaneously does it.* It is this immediacy of perception and action which we want to examine critically. This approach stands in stark contrast to the usual way of investigating ethical behavior, which begins by analyzing the intentional content of an act and ends by evaluating the rationality of particular moral judgments. (p. 4)

Varela's definition of virtue is reminiscent of Ryan and Lickona's (1987, pp. 26–27) real-life example of a 14-year-old boy's response to a middle-aged woman who boarded a city bus in the middle of a Minnesota winter. She had a thin coat, no shoes, and worn socks. The boy walked to the front of the bus as she was placing her coins in the meter and handed her his shoes, saying that she needed them more than he. The integration of moral perception and behavior, of conscious and intuitive judgment, is apparent in this case of lightning quick response to human need in one's community, an expression of virtue in action.

What is virtue? Often the predominant interpretation of virtues appears to be that they are habits or patterns of behavior that are gained by repeating the desired behavior over and over. This, of course, is overly simplistic and represents only one of the ways that Aristotle (1988) understood the nature of virtues and how they are acquired. The less dominant interpretation of Aristotle's view is that virtues/excellences are patterns of behavior developed with practice, effort, and guidance from parents, teachers, and mentors, until external guidance is unnecessary (Urmson, 1988). In other words, virtue development requires apprenticeship under the guidance of others. In this view, virtues are not cultivated in isolation but with the help of the community. Moreover, virtues are not cultivated through blind obedience or rote memorization, but with guided reflection.

The outcome or goal of virtue cultivation is expressed by Plato's *techne* in the broadest sense, a type of know-how demonstrated by the successful artisan, politician, or just person (Plato, in *The Republic*). This know-how or expertise is more than procedural knowledge; it includes the whole of one's being (Hursthouse, 2003). For example, an expert desires excellence in the domain. Similarly, the virtuous person desires excellence in virtue, so much so that the desire is reflected not only in behavior but in preferences and choices; it is what the person likes to do (Urmson, 1988). Thus, cultivating virtue requires shaping not only behavior but also perceptions and desires in developmentally appropriate ways. Initial guidance from parents and teachers involves coaxing desires and motivation (perception and sensibilities) as well as reactions and responsive behaviors (habitual responses). Gradually, the individual takes on the shaping of these responses in the self. Character development becomes autopoetic or self-organizing (Maturana & Varela, 1980).

Foundational Idea 2: Education Is Transformative and Interactive

Education is transformative and interactive in at least two ways. First, children transform themselves in response to and by acting on the environment (Varela et al., 1991). It is now commonly understood that humans construct knowledge and understanding from active experience (Anderson, 1989; Piaget, 1952). From experience, individuals construct schemas (generalized knowledge structures composed of emotion–cognition–behavior concepts) that form and change with further experience (Piaget, 1952, 1970). These schemas facilitate information processing, direct attention, drive anticipatory sets and expectations, and orchestrate the understanding of events and goals (Taylor & Crocker, 1981). Schemas filter stimuli based on what the person has learned to value and expect based on meaningful experience (Higgins, 1996; Kirsch, 1999). Schemas are built from incidental experience (influencing the intuitive mind) as well as coached experience (influencing also the deliberative mind). For example, a child whose attention is repeatedly drawn to his or her effect on the welfare of others develops a set of schemas that differ from those of a child whose attention is drawn to looking attractive.

The notion of constructivism has been further refined by a greater understanding of how cognition is "situated" or contextualized (Derry & Lesgold, 1996), how cognition forms a dynamic system of interaction between actor and environment (Thelen & Smith, 1994), how cognition is ultimately embodied in multiple physiochemical systems (Damasio, 1999), and how mind is inextricably linked with body and environment (Lakoff & Johnson, 1999). Intelligence is embodied in action, including moral intelligence (Varela, 1999) and it can be cultivated in the community, including the classroom community.

Education is transformative and interactive in a second way. Children flourish and are highly motivated when the social environment meets their needs for belonging, competence, and autonomy (Deci & Ryan, 1985; Eccles, 2004). Consequently, to cultivate student expertise (in any area) adults should transform environments and instruction based on the needs of the students at their levels of development generally and within the domain.

Implication 1: Educators Should Set Up Well-Structured Environments That Foster Appropriate Ethical Intuitions.   Human understanding can be split into two forms, that of the *adaptive unconscious,* which learns automatically without effort (Hasher & Zacks, 1984; Wilson, 2002), and that of the *deliberative mind,* which learns through effortful processing (Hogarth, 2001). The former is discussed in this section. Most of what humans know resides in the adaptive unconscious, not the explicit mind. Environments automatically educate our intuitions about how to act and react (Hogarth, 2001). The mind learns from the structural regularities among people and objects in the environment (Frensch, 1998). Recurrent patterns are noticed and recorded effortlessly by more primitive parts of the brain (at least three forms of automatic information processing have been identified: basic, primitive, and sophisticated; see Hogarth, 2001). Perceptions are fine tuned from repeated attentive interaction with the environment. Most of what we know resides in tacit knowledge, including intuitions about how things work (Sternberg & Torff, 2001). Thus, for example, from repeated social interaction with members of their cultural group, children learn how close to stand to someone, how to share gaze with someone, how to treat different parts of the body, and so on (Hall, 1981). Many of these cultural behaviors are learned without explicit instruction and become automatized without effort.

Because much of our behavior is based on our tacit knowledge or intuitions (Hogarth, 2001; Sternberg, 2001), adults must create environments that tune up the right intuitions in children. The environment includes the climate or atmosphere, which refers to the culture of the social environment in both a broad and a specific sense. In the broad sense the climate includes the structures of the environment, the overt and hidden systems of rewards and punishment, the goals and aspirations of the environment, and the general discourse about goals. In the specific sense, climate has to do with how people treat one another, how they work together, how they make decisions together, what feelings are encouraged, and what expectations are nurtured. A positive climate meets the needs of the child and fosters a sense of belonging to the larger group (Baumeister & Leary, 1995).

Prosocial behavior is nurtured in climates that foster flourishing and the "developmental assets" that support resiliency (Benson, Leffert, Scales, & Blyth, 1998; Wang, Haertel, & Walberg, 1998). In fact, caring schools and classrooms have specific characteristics that are associated with multiple positive outcomes for students. According to Solomon and associates (2002), caring school and classroom communities have the following characteristics: (a) student autonomy, self-direction, and influence; (b) student interaction, collaboration, and participation in open discussion; (c) teacher warmth, acceptance, support, and modeling; (d) training in social skills; and (e) opportunities for helping others. A well-structured environment for teaching character has these characteristics.

Implication 2: Educators Should Design Instruction to Move Students From Naïveté to Competence in Ethical Know-How. Moral expertise can be built systematically using a holistic immersion approach that enlists both the deliberative mind and the intuitive mind. Based on Marshall (1995), Integrative Ethical Education presents four levels of knowledge in a fully developed conceptual network or schema. Through explicit instruction (to develop the deliberative mind) and immersion (to develop the intuitive mind) in the domain or skill, students learn to solve domain problems. First they build *identification knowledge,* learning to see the big picture of the domain through exposure to a myriad of examples. For example, in learning how to stop bullying, student attention is focused on multiple examples of bullying (e.g., what it looks like in different contexts, with different people and tasks). Once students have a sense of the big picture, they build *elaboration knowledge.* Their attention is drawn to key facts and specific detail in the domain to elaborate on their initial intuitions about the domain. For example, students are coached to practice responses to say to bullies in particular situations. Third, students learn specific sets of procedures to apply and practice, building *procedural knowledge* in the domain. For example, students can learn to avoid bullying others by becoming more aware of the precursors to bullying (e.g., frustration). They learn techniques for expressing feelings in respectful ways. Last, students construct *execution knowledge,* by fine-tuning declarative, procedural, and conditional knowledge as they solve problems of different kinds in varied contexts. For example, students can practice and coach one another in appropriate responses outside the classroom. As students cycle through these levels of schema building, theory is integrated in concert with the intuitions that form from immersion in a well-structured climate and environment. Children are apprentices to moral virtue, building expertise from situated experience filtered with explicit guidance and theory.

To develop sophisticated knowledge about something, one must be coached and practice extensively in a focused way (Ericsson & Charness, 1994; Ericsson & Smith, 1991). A good coach works within Vygotsky's (1935) "zone of proximal development" using Bruner's (1983) "scaffolding," providing only as much guidance as the student needs to solve the problem and "fading" as skills develop. With guidance, children build moral responses across a variety of contexts, accumulating a repertoire of schemas and responses to apply throughout their lives. Children cultivate their contextualized intelligence or embodied cognition, in the context in which it is to be applied (e.g., Rogoff, 1990; Rogoff & Lave, 1984). For example, children who experience coached, focused practice as volunteers continue to volunteer as adults (Youniss & Yates, 1997).

Ethical education should not be an add on but become integrated in all that a school does (Simon, 2001). Rather than teach character opportunistically, teachers should slightly modify their academic instruction to systematically and regularly address ethical skills (Starratt, 1994). The skills are parsed in such a way that an educator can focus on one or several during instruction and assess progress in acquisition.[3] Without encouraging environments and deliberative instruction of these skills in school, many children may otherwise never develop them.

Direct and indirect methods of instruction are used with each skill: directly, with explanation and metacognitive guidance for self-regulation (teaching the deliberative mind), and indirectly, with immersion in environments that promote the skill (teaching the intuitive mind) (Hogarth, 2001). For example, the teacher both models and expects respectful

---

[3]Although some skills overlap or could be placed into multiple categories, we have tried to simplify the picture for the purposes of practicality in the classroom.

behavior (immersion) and also explicitly coaches the student on what it looks like. Learning a skill means changing oneself to be the kind of person who fully embodies the skill, consciously and intuitively. The skill flavors and modifies one's perceptions, attention, desires, and intuitions, as well as semantic, procedural, and conditional knowledge. The skills are simultaneously process focused and content rich and are refined throughout one's life.

Foundational Idea 3: Human Nature Is Cooperative and Self-Actualizing

Humans thrive under particular psychological and social circumstances that vary little with age. For example, children and adolescents flourish when they obtain the right balance of relatedness, competence, and autonomy (Deci & Ryan, 1985; Watson & Eckert, 2003). In short, humans' natural propensity for cooperative behavior is nurtured in communal settings. By its very nature, moral expertise is relational. It develops within a community and is shared in community. Virtue, reasoning, and community are not separable, as contemporary perspectives sometimes seem to imply. To live without one another is to live an incomplete, if not inhuman, life. In fact, evolutionary psychology is uncovering facts about human nature that suggest communal values are embedded in our genetic code and species memory (de Waal, 1996). Humans are by nature cooperative and social creatures (Fiske, 2004; Ridley, 1996). Indeed, Darwin wrote much more about humanity's moral sensibilities than about human selfishness (Loye, 2002). Significantly, Darwin's private notebooks, finally published in 1974, set forth a theory of moral agency as a culmination of his theory of natural selection (Loye, 2002). (Of course, our heritage promotes tribal loyalty at the expense of nontribal members so that control of bias toward outsiders becomes a necessary skill for the ethical person.)

Implication 1: Educators Should Help to Build Community Inside and Outside the School. There are two types of community that greatly influence the lives of children, the school community and the local community. Successful schools and classrooms form caring communities (Bryk & Schneider, 2002). In fact, intrinsic motivation for academic achievement is greatest within environments that nurture a sense of belonging, competence, and autonomy (Deci & Ryan, 1985). When teachers use pedagogical strategies that foster a climate with these three characteristics, they facilitate both academic achievement and moral development (Mullen, Narvaez, & Turner, 2005; Turner, Narvaez, & Mullen, 2005).

The importance of the local community cannot be overstated. Character development requires community in two ways. First, the child's community is the niche for learning character. The community builds the environments and provides the role models and necessary coaching by those with more expertise. Second, the child's community is the canvas for expressing character. It is the place where the skills of character are practiced and embodied. One cannot become virtuous by watching television or reading books. One must learn through interaction with others in the community, in both shaping responses and in applying them. Virtue is action (Aquinas) and it is developed through action in community (Aristotle).[4]

Integrative Ethical Education provides top-down principles for implementation that are to be balanced with a bottom-up adaptation to local community needs. The top-down portion is the set of guidelines for optimal functioning (twenty-eight skills) and the novice-to-expert pedagogy. As noted, the set of guidelines includes fundamental assumptions about the purpose of schooling (to nurture effective global citizens) and a set of skills

---

[4]Of course, the moral individual must be able to function in multiple communities and to step outside the perspective of her tradition as in postconventional thinking.

for individuals to learn in community (for flourishing). The set of guidelines is presented to teachers and community members who in turn represent the bottom-up portion of the model.

The bottom-up aspect of the model is the necessary local adaptation of the framework of skills to the community context. Each community discusses the framework in terms of specific community perspectives, needs, and diversity, adapting them according to its own common understandings of moral being. For example, in the Community Voices and Character Education project, small groups of educators met with community members to develop a local vision for ethical development. They decided how to distribute the teaching of the skills among subject areas, school-wide projects, and homeroom/advisory periods. School leadership teams involving educators and community members created activities that required students to involve community members in student learning (e.g., interviewing elders and parents about what a skill looks like in their culture). When using community-embedding approaches, students bring back information from the community to the classroom that provides the backdrop for conversations not only about the skills but about the diversity in how the skills are applied, showing how groups often have different practices that reflect the same underlying value (Fullenwider, 1996) or how practices may reflect conventional rather than moral differences (Nucci, 2001).

In the Integrative Ethical Education approach, universal principles and skills meet local particularities and are melded together by the community itself. Thus, optimal functioning is grounded in the specific context of the individual and his or her community. This top-down and bottom-up combination allows each community to adapt the guidelines within certain parameters, those of optimal functioning within a pluralistic democracy.

Implication 2: Educators Should Foster Self-Regulation in Students and Community Members. Plato believed that human existence is essentially a problem to the self, in particular it is an identity problem. For Plato, "it is the problem of deciding what to become and endeavoring to become it" (Urmson, 1988, p. 2). In other words, the final responsibility for character development lies with the individual. In their choices and actions, orientations and time allocations, individuals address the question: Who should I be? In an Integrative Ethical Education environment, students are provided with tools for self-regulation in character formation.

Individuals can be coached not only in skills and expertise but in domain-specific self-efficacy and self-regulation (Zimmerman, Bonner, & Kovach, 2002). The most successful students learn to monitor the effectiveness of the strategies they use to solve problems and, when necessary, alter their strategies for success (Anderson, 1989). Coaching self-regulation requires enlisting the deliberative mind to help the intuitive mind. Armed with theoretical knowledge, the deliberative mind, for example, plays a critical role in learning by selecting the environments from which the intuitive mind learns effective behaviors, thereby accelerating implicit learning (Hogarth, 2001) (e.g., different intuitions are developed when reading a good book than when playing violent video games). Moreover, the deliberative mind can actually play a role in modifying brain malfunctioning by overriding harmful or misdirected impulses and replacing them with socially appropriate behaviors (Schwartz & Begley, 2002).

The perception of personal agency is formed from our self-regulatory skills and lies at the heart of the sense of self (Zimmerman, 2000). According to Zimmerman (2000), self-regulation is acquired in stages, which resemble the processes of scaffolding learning in the zone of proximal development. First, through observation the child vicariously induces the skill by watching a model. Second, the child imitates the model with assistance. Third, the child independently displays the skill under structured conditions. Finally, the child is able to use the skill across changing situations and demands. With adult coaching in identifying the path toward self-actualization, each student can monitor ethical skill development and hone a particular set of expert skills. Virtuous individuals must be autonomous enough to monitor their behavior and choices. Once developed, virtues must be maintained through the selection of appropriate friends and environments (Aristotle, 1988).

Truly democratic ethical education empowers all involved—educators, community members, and students—as they form a learning community together, developing ethical skills and self-regulation for both individual and community actualization (Rogoff, Turkanis, & Bartlett, 2001). The purpose of ethical behavior is to live a good life in the community. Together community members work out basic questions such as: How should we get along in our community? How do we build up our community? How do we help one another flourish? Each individual lives within an active ecological context (Bronfenbrenner, 1979) in which, ideally, the entire community builds ethical skills together.

The Community Voices and Character Education Project

As mentioned, the Integrative Ethical Education model is an outgrowth from the work done during the Minnesota Community Voices and Character Education Project.[5] In the final year of the project, the effects on middle school students and teachers were evaluated using self-report questionnaires of perceptions, attitudes, and behaviors. Because the application of the model was locally controlled, each site's implementation was unique and could not be compared with another. Thus, for a particular implementation the numbers tested were small. Nevertheless, for student responses, we compared program schools with a comparision group (from another school not involved in the project) and we compared schools with high and low activity in the project. There were three schools who implemented broadly (curriculum, school-wide projects, advisory/homeroom) and fairly deeply (almost all if not every teacher). We compared students at high implementing schools ($n = 151$) with schools that were low implementers ($n = 183$). Students at high implementation schools showed significantly more gains than students at low implementation schools in several variables such as student connectedness to school and positive perceptions of teacher attitudes and behavior ($p < .01$). Students at high implementation schools also showed significant gains in concern for others whereas students at low implementation schools showed a loss ($p < .01$). Two of the high implementing schools reported that they spent the majority of their time on ethical sensitivity skills. In comparison to the control school, students at these two sites were significantly higher on gain scores in concern for others, a measure of ethical sensitivity. Thus, deep and broad implementation of ethical skill instruction had positive significant effects on students, whereas minimal implementation had little positive effect (Narvaez, Endicott, Bock, & Lies, 2005).

CONCLUSION

> Living well depends upon reweaving our ethical theories into the warp and woof of our scientific heritage, attending to the myriad consequences such a project will have for the way we live our lives and the manner in which we structure our collective moral institutions. Casebeer (2003, p. x)

---

[5]Materials, including activity guides and teacher-designed lesson plans, are available from the Minnesota Department of Education or from the Center of Ethical Education website (http://cee.nd.edu).

The goal of this chapter was to present a model of character education that integrates cognitive science with traditional and progressive approaches to character development. The Integrative Ethical Education framework was introduced, which combines individual and community flourishing, rational moral education, and traditional character education perspectives with a cognitive science view of human learning and cognition. In comparison to other integrative approaches, it provides a more cohesive and systematic framework. Moreover, Integrative Ethical Education views the ancient Greek understanding of ethics as still relevant today: ethics is the practical and moral wisdom learned for community living and under the guidance of the community.

In the realm of character formation there are many questions yet to be researched. First, we need to know more about each area of ethical expertise. Simon (1995) argued that to study a phenomenon we must have a mental representation of the problem area. Ericsson and Smith (1991) suggest that for any expert domain, researchers must capture the nature of superior performance, spelling out the nature of daily expert performance. Peterson and Seligman (2004) have paved the way by identifying a set of twenty-four character strengths and virtues, many of which are moral, using a systematic method of selection. Next, experts demonstrating these strengths need to be studied to determine the nature of their skills and how they were developed.

Second, there are a myriad of issues concerning instruction and acquisition, many of which overlap with issues in subject matter areas. For example, how can we help students develop self-regulation in ethical development? Alexander, Kulikowich, and Schulze (1994) found that development in a domain occurs as a result of the interplay of skill (knowledge) and thrill (interest). Educators need to tap into the natural thrill of morality (Klinger, 1978) to enhance student's long-term and sustained personal investment in ethical skill development. For example, moral dilemma discussion engages student interest in moral judgment. Teachers need to develop methods for engaging the other processes relevant for moral behavior.

Third, larger community issues bear examination as well. A successful approach to character development requires building and sustaining community in schools and neighborhoods (Damon, 1997; Selznick, 1992). How do we encourage sustainable, cohesive, mutually supportive communities in today's society? How do we motivate communities to take on a holistic construction of children's characters from an early age? Further, a well-structured environment for children includes regulating the aspects of culture to which children are exposed. Currently, our society is not conducive to the development of virtues or self-control (Baumeister & Exline, 1999). Instead, the mass media, one of the greatest influences on children in the 21st century, is geared to use children for economic gain (Quart, 2003) and has many negative effects on children (Strasberger & Wilson, 2002). How do we regulate the media to prevent its ill effects on the young (Steyer, 2002), such as promoting excessive consumerism (Kasser, 2002) and violence (Anderson et al., 2003; Huesmann, Moise-Titus, Podolski, & Eron, 2003)?

Finally, to coach children to develop good character, we need adults who cultivate good character in themselves. How do we help teachers develop an orientation to the ongoing challenge of building and maintaining good character in themselves? Campbell (2004) offers valuable insight into the working minds and classroom challenges of teachers and their need for ethical knowledge and coaching. Professional ethics courses for teachers might be designed according to Integrative Ethical Education principles outlined here. Yet teachers are not the only adults who educate children in moral formation. Parents and community members are also character coaches. In a free society, how do we cultivate and support virtuous personhood in parents, community members, and each other in ways that supports individual and community flourishing? These and other questions provide a full agenda for researchers in the years to come.

ACKNOWLEDGMENTS

For helpful comments on earlier drafts, I want to express my appreciation to Dan Lapsley, Gerhard Zecha, Clark Power and my colleagues at the University of Notre Dame's Center for Ethical Education and at the Erasmus Institute during 2003 and 2004, my students, and the volume editors. Thanks to the Erasmus Institute for supporting a year of writing.

REFERENCES

Alexander, P. A. (1992). Domain knowledge: Evolving themes and emerging concerns. *Educational Psychologist, 27,* 33–51.

Alexander, P. A., Kulikowich, J. M., & Schulze, S. K. (1994). How subject-matter knowledge affects recall and interest. *American Educational Research Journal, 31,* 313–337.

Anderson, C., Narvaez, D., Bock, T., Endicott, L., & Lies, J. (2003). *Minnesota Community Voices and Character Education: Final evaluation report.* Roseville: Minnesota Department of Education.

Anderson, C. A., Berkowitz, L., Donnerstein, E., Huesmann, L. R., Johnsons, J. D., Linz, D. et al. (2003). The influence of media violence on youth. *Psychological Science in the Public Interest, 4*(3), 81–110.

Anderson, L. M. (1989). Learners and learning. In M. C. Reynolds (Ed.), *Knowledge base for the beginning teacher* (pp. 85–99). Oxford: Pergamon Press.

Anscombe, G. E. M. (1958). Modern moral philosophy. *Philosophy, 33,* 1–19.

Aristotle. (1988). *Nicomachean ethics.* (Trans. W. D. Ross). London: Oxford.

Bandura, A. (1978). Social learning theory of aggression. *Journal of Communication, 28*(3), 12–29.

Bargh, J. A., & Ferguson, M. J. (2000). Beyond behaviorism: On the automaticity of higher mental processes. *Psychological Bulletin, 126,* 925–945.

Bargh, J. A., & Chartrand, T. (1999). The unbearable automaticity of being. *American Psychologist, 54,* 462–479.

Battistich, V., Solomon, D., Watson, M., & Schaps, E. (1996). *Enhancing students' engagement, participation, and democratic values and attitudes.* Ann Arbor, MI: Society for the Psychological Study of Social Issues.

Battistich, V., Solomon, D., Watson, M., & Schaps, E. (1997). Caring school communities. *Educational Psychologist, 32,* 137–151.

Battistich, V., Solomon, D., Watson, M., Solomon, J., & Schaps, E. (1989). Effects of an elementary school program to enhance prosocial behavior on children's social problem-solving skills and strategies. *Journal of Applied Developmental Psychology, 10,* 147–169.

Baumeister, R., & Leary, M. (1995). The need to belong: Desire for interpersonal attachments as a fundamental human motivation. *Psychological Bulletin, 117,* 497–529.

Baumeister, R. F., & Exline, J. J. (1999). Virtue, personality and social relations: Self-control as the *moral* muscle. *Journal of Personality, 67,* 1165–1194.

Bennett, W. J. (1992). *De-valuing of America: The fight for our culture and our children.* New York: Touchstone.

Benninga, J. S. (1991). *Moral, character, and civic* education. New York: Teachers College Press.

Benson, P., Leffert, N., Scales, P., & Blyth, D. (1998). Beyond the "village" rhetoric: Creating healthy communities for children and adolescents. *Applied Developmental Science, 2*(3), 138–159.

Berkowitz, M. W. (1997). The complete moral person: Anatomy and formation. In J. DuBois (Ed.), *Moral issues in psychology: Personalist contributions to selected problems.* Lanham, MD: University Press of America.

Berkowitz, M. W. (2002). The science of character education. In W. Damon (Ed.), *Bringing in a new era in character education.* Stanford, CA: Hoover Institution Press.

Berkowitz, M., & Bier, M. (in press). The interpersonal roots of character education. In D. K. Lapsley & F. C. Power (Eds.), *Character psychology and character education.* Notre Dame, IN: University of Notre Dame Press.

Berliner, D. C. (1994). Expertise: The wonder of exemplary performances. In J. N. Mangieri & C. C. Block (Eds.), *Creating powerful thinking in teachers and students.* Fort Worth, TX: Harcourt, Brace College.

Blasi, A. (1980). Bridging moral cognition and moral action: A critical review of the literature. *Psychological Bulletin, 88,* 1–45.

Blatt, M., & Kohlberg, L. (1975). The effects of classroom discussion upon children's level of moral judgment. *Journal of Moral Education, 4,* 129–161.

Bronfenbrenner, U. (1979). *The ecology of human development.* Cambridge, MA: Harvard University Press.

Bruner, J. (1983). *Child's talk: Learning to use language.* New York: Norton.

Bryk, A., & Schneider, B. (2002). *Trust in schools: A core resource for improvement.* New York: Russell Sage.

Campbell, E. (2004). *The ethical teacher.* Maidenhead, PA: Open University Press.

Casebeer, W. D. (2003). *Natural ethical facts: Evolution, connectionism, and moral cognition* Cambridge, MA: MIT Press.

Cervone, D., & Shoda, Y. (1999). Social-cognitive theories and the coherence of personality. In D. Cervone & Y. Shoda (Eds.), *The coherence of personality: Social-cognitive bases of consistency, variability and organization* (pp. 3–36). New York: Guilford Press.

Chi, M. T. H., Glaser, R., & Farr, M. J. (1988). *The nature of expertise.* Hillsdale, NJ: Lawrence Erlbaum Associates.

Cunningham, M. (in press). Classical moral theory focuses on what is a good life for a human being to live. In D. K. Lapsley & F. C. Power (Eds.), *Character psychology and character education.* Notre Dame, IN: University of Notre Dame Press.

Damasio, A. (1996). *Descartes' error: Emotion, reason and the human brain.* New York: Avon.

Damasio, A. (1999). *The feeling of what happens.* New York: Harcourt and Brace.

Damon, W. (1997). *The youth charter.* New York: Free Press.

Deci, E., & Ryan, R. (1985). *Intrinsic motivation and self-determination in human behavior.* New York: Academic Press.

Derry, S., & Lesgold, A. (1996). Towards a situated social practice model for instructional design. In D. C. Berliner & R. C. Calfee (Eds.), *Handbook of educational psychology* (pp. 787–806). New York: Simon Schuster MacMillan.

DeVries, R., Hildebrandt, C., & Zan, B. (2000). Constructivist early education for moral development. *Early Education & Development, 11,* 9–35.

DeVries, R., & Zan, B. (1999). *Moral classrooms, moral children: Creating a constructivist atmosphere in early education.* New York: Teachers College Press.

de Waal, F. (1996). *Good natured: The origins of right and wrong in humans and other animals.* Cambridge, MA: Harvard University Press.

Dewey, J. (1913). *The school and society.* Chicago: University of Chicago Press.

Durkheim, E. (1925/1973). *Moral education: A study in the theory and application of the sociology of education.* New York: Free Press.

Eccles, J. S. (2004). Schools, academic motivation, and stage-environment fit. In R. M. Lerner, & L. Steinberg (Eds.), *Handbook of adolescent psychology* (2nd ed.). New York: Wiley.

Ericsson, K. A., & Charness, N. (1994). Expert performance: Its structure and acquisition. *American Psychologist, 49,* 725–747.

Ericsson, K. A., & Smith, J. (1991). *Toward a general theory of expertise.* New York: Cambridge University Press.

Fiske, S. (2003). *Social beings.* New York: Wiley.

Frankena, W. K. (1973). *Ethics.* Englewood Cliffs, NJ: Prentice-Hall.

Frensch, P. A. (1998). One concept, multiple meanings: On how to define the concept of implicit learning. In M. A. Stadler, & P. A. Frensch (Eds.), *Handbook of implicit learning.* Thousand Oaks, CA: Sage.

Fullinwider, R. K. (1996). "Multicultural education: Concepts, policies, and controversies. In R. K. Fullinwider (Ed.), *Public education in a multicultural society* (pp. 4–6, 16). New York: Cambridge University Press.

Gigerenzer, G., & Selten, R. (2001). *Bounded rationality: The adaptive toolbox.* Cambridge, MA: MIT Press.

Green, T. E. (1999). *Voices.* Notre Dame, IN: University of Notre Dame Press.

Gutmann, A. (1987). *Democratic education.* Princeton, NJ: Princeton University Press.

Gutmann, A., & Thompson, D. (1996). *Democracy and disagreement.* Cambridge, MA: Harvard University Press.

Hall, E. T. (1981). *Beyond culture.* New York: Doubleday.

Hansen, D. T. (2001). Teaching as a moral activity. In V. Richardson (Ed.), *Handbook of research on teaching* (4th ed., pp. 826–857). Washington, DC: AERA.

Hare, R. M. (1963). *Freedom and reason.* New York: Oxford University Press.

Harman, G. (1999). Moral philosophy meets social psychology: Virtue ethics and the fundamental attribution error. *Proceedings of the Aristotelian Society New Series, CXIX,* 316–331.

Hasher, L., & Zacks, R. T. (1984). Automatic processing of fundamental information, *American Psychologist, 39,* 1372–1388.

Higgins, E. T. (1996). Knowledge activation: Accessibility, applicability and salience. In E. T. Higgins & A.W. Kruglanski (Eds.), *Social psychology: Handbook of basic principles* (pp. 133–168). New York: Guilford Press.

Hoffman, M. L. (2000). *Empathy and moral development: Implications for caring and justice.* New York: Cambridge University Press.

Hogarth, R. M. (2001). *Educating intuition.* Chicago: University of Chicago Press.

Huesmann, L. R., Moise-Titus, J., Podolski, C., & Eron, L. D. (2003). Longitudinal relations between children's exposure to TV violence and their aggressive and violent behavior in young adulthood: 1977–1992. *Developmental Psychology, 39,* 201–221.

Hurley, S. L. (2002). *Consciousness in action.* Cambridge, MA: Harvard University Press.

Hursthouse, R. (1999). *On virtue ethics.* Oxford: Oxford University Press.

Hursthouse, R. (2003, Fall). Virtue ethics. In E. N. Zalta (Ed.), *The Stanford encyclopedia of philosophy.* Retrieved March 31, 2005 from http://plato.stanford.edu/archives/fall2003/entries/ethics-virtue/

Jackson, P. (1968). *Life in classrooms.* New York: Holt, Rinehart & Winston.

Jackson, P., Boostrom, R. E., & Hansen, D. T. (1998). *The moral life of schools*. San Francisco: Jossey-Bass.

Kahneman, D. (2003). A perspective on judgment and choice: Mapping bounded rationality. *American Psychologist, 58,* 697–720.

Kant, I. (1949). *Fundamental principles of the metaphysics of morals*. New York: Liberal Arts Press.

Kasser, T. (2002). *The high price of materialism*. Cambridge, MA: MIT Press.

Keil, F. C., & Wilson, R. A. (1999). Explaining explanations. In F. C. Keil & R. A. Wilson (Eds.), *Explanation and cognition* (pp. 1–18). Cambridge MA: Bradford MIT Press.

Kessler, R. (2001). Soul of students, soul of teachers: Welcoming the inner life to school. In L. Lantieri (Ed.), *Schools with spirit: Nurturing the inner lives of children and teachers* (pp. 107–131). Boston: Beacon Press.

Kirsch, I. (Ed.). (1999). *How expectances shape experience*. Washington, DC: American Psychological Association.

Klinger, E. (1978). Modes of normal conscious flow. In K. S. Pope & J. L. Singer (Eds.), *The stream of consciousness: Scientific investigations into the flow of human experience* (pp. 225–258). New York: Plenum.

Kohlberg, L. (1981). *The philosophy of moral development: Essays on moral development* (vol. I). New York: Harper & Row.

Kohlberg, L. (1984). *The psychology of moral development: Essays on moral development* (vol. II). New York: Harper & Row.

Kohlberg, L., Levine, C., & Hewer, A. (1983). *Moral stages: A current formulation and a response to critics*. Basel: Karger.

Kohn, A. (1997a). The trouble with character education. In A. Molnar (Ed.), *The construction of children's character* (pp. 154–162). Chicago: University of Chicago Press.

Kohn, A. (1997b). How not to teach values: A critical look at character education. *Phi Delta Kappan, February,* 429–439.

Lakoff, G., & Johnson, M. (1999). *Philosophy in the flesh: The embodied mind and its challenge to Western thought*. New York: Harper Collins Publishers.

Lapsley, D., & Narvaez, D. (2004). A social-cognitive view of moral character. In D. Lapsley & D. Narvaez (Eds.), *Moral development: Self and identity* (pp. 189–212). Mahwah, NJ: Lawrence Erlbaum Associates.

Lapsley, D., & Narvaez, D. (2005). Moral psychology at the crossroads. In D. Lapsley & Power, C. (Eds.), *Character psychology and character education* (pp. 18–35). Notre Dame, IN: University of Notre Dame Press.

Leming, J. (1997). Research and practice in character education: A historical perspective. In A. Molnar (Ed.), *The construction of children's character* (pp. 31–44). Chicago: University of Chicago Press.

Lickona, T. (1991a). An integrated approach to character development in the elementary school classroom. In J. Benninga (Ed.), *Moral, character, and civic education* (pp. 67–83). New York: Teachers College Press.

Lickona, T. (1991b). *Educating for character*. New York: Bantam.

Lickona, T. (1997). Educating for character: A comprehensive approach. In A. Molnar (Ed.), *The construction of children's character* (pp. 45–62). Chicago: University of Chicago Press.

Lickona, T. (2004). *Character matters*. New York: Touchstone.

Loye, D. (2002). The moral brain. *Brain and Mind, 3,* 133–150.

MacIntyre, A. (1981). *After virtue*. London: Duckworth.

Marshall, S. P. (1995). *Schemas in problem solving*. Cambridge, UK: Cambridge University Press.

Maturana, H. R., & Varela, F. J. (1980). *Autopoiesis and cognition.* Dordrecht: Reidel.

McDowell, J. (1997). Virtues and vices. In R. Crisp & M. Slote (Eds.), *Virtue ethics* (pp. 141–162). Oxford, UK: Oxford University Press.

Mischel, W. (1990). Personality dispositions revisited and revised: A view after three decades. In L. A. Pervin (Ed.), *Handbook of personality: Theory and research* (pp. 111–134). New York: Guilford.

More schools make ethics part of curriculum. (2003, Nov. 5). *Los Angeles Times.*

Mullen, G., Narvaez, D., & Turner, J. (2005). *Student perceptions of climate influence character and motivation.* Paper presented at the American Educational Research Association, Montreal.

Narvaez, D. (2005). *Educating moral intuition.* Manuscript in preparation.

Narvaez, D., Bock, T., & Endicott, L. (2003). Who should I become? Citizenship, goodness, human flourishing, and ethical expertise. In W. Veugelers & F. Oser (Eds.), *The positive and negative in moral education* (pp. 43–63). New York: Peter Lang.

Narvaez, D., Endicott, L., & Bock, T., Lies, J. (2005). Minnesota's Community Voices and Character Education Project. *Journal of Research in Character Education.*

Narvaez, D., & Lapsley, D. (2005). The psychological foundations of every day morality and moral expertise. In D. Lapsley & Power, C. (Eds.), *Character psychology and character education* (pp. 140–165). Notre Dame, IN: University of Notre Dame Press.

Nash, R. J. (1997). *Answering the "virtuecrats."* New York: Teachers College Press.

Noddings, N. (2002). *Educating moral people.* New York: Teachers College Press.

Norton, D. (1991). *Democracy and moral development: A politics of virtue.* Berkeley: University of California Press.

Nucci, L. (2001). *Education in the moral domain.* New York: Cambridge University Press.

O'Neill, O. (1995). *Towards justice and virtue: A constructive account of practical reasoning.* Cambridge, UK: Cambridge University Press.

Oser, F. K. (1991). Professional morality: A discourse approach. In W. Kurtines & J. Gewirtz (Eds.), *Handbook of moral development, Vol. 2: Research* (pp. 191–228). Hillsdale, NJ: Lawrence Erlbaum Associates.

Peterson, C., & Seligman, M. E. P. (2004). *Character strengths and virtues.* New York: Oxford University Press.

Piaget, J. (1952). *The origin of intelligence in children.* New York: International University Press.

Piaget, J. (1932/1965). *The moral judgment of the child.* (Trans. M. Gabain). New York: Free Press.

Piaget, J. (1970). *Genetic Epistemology.* (Trans. E. Duckworth). New York: Columbia University Press.

Plato (1974). *The Republic.* (Trans. D. Lee). London: Penguin Books.

Power, C., Higgins, A., & Kohlberg, L. (1989). *Lawrence Kohlberg's approach to moral education.* New York: Columbia University Press.

Quart, A. (2003). *Branded: The buying and selling of teenagers.* New York: Perseus Books.

Raths, L., Harmin, M., & Simon, S. (1976). Selections from *Values and teaching.* In D. Purpel & K. Ryan (Eds.), *Moral education . . . it comes with the territory* (pp. 75–115). Berkeley, CA: McCutchan.

Rawls, J. (1971). *A theory of justice.* Cambridge, MA: Harvard University Press.

Rawls, J. (2001). *Justice as fairness.* Cambridge, MA: Harvard University Press.

Reber, A. S. (1993). *Implicit learning and tacit knowledge: An essay on the cognitive unconscious.* New York: Oxford University Press.

Reed, D. R. C. (1997). *Following Kohlberg: Liberalism and the practice of democratic community.* Notre Dame, IN: University of Notre Dame Press.

Rest, J. (1983). Morality. In J. Flavell & E. Markham (Eds.), *Cognitive development*. From P. Mussen (Ed.), *Manual of child psychology* (vol. 3, pp. 556–629). New York: Wiley.

Rest, J. R. (1986). *Moral development: Advances in research and theory*. New York: Praeger.

Ridley, M. (1996). *The origins of virtue*: *Human instincts and the evolution of cooperation*. New York: Viking Press.

Rogoff, B. (1990). *Apprenticeship in thinking: Cognitive development in social context*. New York: Oxford University Press.

Rogoff, B., & Lave, J. (1984). *Everyday cognition: Its development in social context*. Cambridge, MA: Harvard University Press.

Rogoff, B., Turkanis, C. G., Bartlett, L. (2001). *Learning together: Children and adults in a school community*. New York: Oxford University Press.

Ryan, K., & Bohlin, K. E. (1999). *Building character in schools*. San Francisco: Jossey-Bass.

Ryan, K., & Lickona, T. (1987). Character development: The challenge and the model. In K. Ryan & G. F. MacLean (Eds.), *Character development in schools and beyond* (pp. 3–35). New York: Praeger Press.

Ryan, K., & MacLean, G. F. (1987). (Eds.), *Character development in schools and beyond*. New York: Praeger Press.

Schaps, E., Battistich, V., & Solomon, D. (1997). School as a caring community: A key to character education. In A. Molnar (Ed.), *The construction of children's character* (pp. 127–139). Chicago: University of Chicago Press.

Schwartz, J. M., & Begley, S. (2002). *The mind and the brain: Neuroplasticity and the power of mental force*. New York: Harper Collins.

Seligman, M., & Csikszentmihalyi, M. (2000). Positive psychology: An introduction. *American Psychologist, 55*(1), 5–14.

Selznick, P. (1992). *The moral commonwealth*. Berkeley: University of California Press.

Simon, H. A. (1995). The information-processing theory of mind. *American Psychologist, 50*, 507–508.

Simon, K. G. (2001). *Moral questions in the classroom: How to get kids to think deeply about real life and their schoolwork*. New Haven, CT: Yale University Press.

Snyder, C. R., & Lopez, S. J. (2002). *Handbook of positive psychology*. New York: Oxford University Press.

Solomon, D., Watson, M. S., & Battistich, V. A. (2002). Teaching and school effects on moral/prosocial development. In V. Richardson (Ed.), *Handbook for research on teaching*. Washington, DC: American Educational Research Association.

Solomon, D. Watson, J., Battistich, V., Schaps, E., & Delucchi, K. (1992). Creating a caring community: Educational practices that promote children's prosocial development. In F. K. Oser, A. Dick, & J.-L. Patry (Eds.), *Effective and responsible teaching: The new synthesis* (pp. 383–396). San Francisco: Jossey-Bass.

Solomon, D., Watson, M., Delucchi, K., Schaps, E., & Battistich, V. (1988). Enhancing children's prosocial behavior in the classroom. *American Educational Research Journal, 25*, 527–554.

Solomon, D., Watson, Schapes, E., Battistich, V., & Solomon, J. (1990). Cooperative learning as part of a comprehensive program designed to promote prosocial development. In S. Sharan (Ed.), *Cooperative learning: Theory and research* (pp. 231–260). New York: Praeger.

Starratt, R. J. (1994). *Building an ethical school: A practical response to the moral crisis in schools*. London: The Falmer Press.

Sternberg, R. (1998). Abilities are forms of developing expertise, *Educational Researcher, 3*, 22–35.

Sternberg, R. J. (1999). Intelligence as developing expertise. *Contemporary Educational Psychology, 24*(4), 359–375.

Sternberg, R. J. (2001). Why schools should teach for wisdom: The balance theory of wisdom in educational settings. *Educational Psychologist, 36,* 227–245.

Sternberg, R. J., & Torff, B. (2001). *Understanding and teaching the intuitive mind: Student and teacher learning.* Mahwah, NJ: Lawrence Erlbaum Associates.

Steyer, J. P. (2002). *The other parent.* New York: Atria Books.

Strasburger, V. C., & Wilson, B. J. (2002). *Children, adolescents, and the media.* New York: Sage.

Taylor, S. E. & Crocker, J. (1981). Schematic bases of social information processing. In E. T. Higgins, C. P. Herman, & M. P. Zanna (Eds.), *Social cognition: The Ontario symposium* (vol. 1, pp. 89–134). Hillsdale, NJ: Lawrence Erlbaum Associates.

Turner, J., Narvaez, D., & Mullen, G. (2005). *Student Perceptions of Climate Influence Character and Motivation.* Manuscript in preparation.

Urmson, J. O. (1988). *Aristotle's ethics.* Oxford: Blackwell.

Varela, F. (1999). *Ethical know-how: Action, wisdom, and cognition.* Stanford, CA: Stanford University Press.

Varela, F. J., Thompson, E., & Rosch, E. (1991). *The embodied mind: Cognitive science and human experience.* Cambridge, MA: MIT Press.

Vygotsky, L. S. (1935). *The mental development of children in the process of learning.* Oxford, UK: Uchpedgiz.

Wang, M. C., Haertel, G. D., & Walberg, H. J. (1998). Building educational resilience. *Phi Beta Kappa Fastbacks, 430,* 7–61.

Watson, M., Battistich, V., & Solomon, D. (1997). Enhancing students' social and ethical development in schools: An intervention program and its effects. *International Journal of Educational Research, 27*(7), 571–586.

Watson, M., & Eckert, L. (2003). *Learning to trust.* San Francisco: Jossey-Bass.

Williams, B. (1985). *Ethics and the limits of philosophy.* Cambridge, MA: Harvard University Press.

Wilson, T. D. (2002). *Strangers to ourselves: Discovering the adaptive unconscious.* Cambridge, MA: Harvard University Press.

Wilson, T. D. (2003). *Strangers to ourselves: Discovering the adaptive unconscious.* Cambridge, MA: Belknap Press.

Wynne, E. A. (1985/1986). The great tradition in education: Transmitting values. *Educational Leadership, 6.*

Wynne, E. A. (1991). *Character and academics in the elementary school.* New York: Teachers College Press.

Wynne, E. A. (1997). For-character education. In A. Molnar (Ed.), *The construction of children's character* (pp. 63–76). Chicago: University of Chicago Press.

Wynne, E. A., & Iverson, B. (1989). *Academics in for character schools.* Unpublished manuscript, College of Education, University of Illinois, Chicago.

Wynne, E. A., & Ryan, K. (1993). *Reclaiming our schools.* New York: Merrill.

Youniss, J., & Yates, M. (1997). *Community service and social responsibility in youth.* Chicago: University of Chicago Press.

Zimmerman, B. J. (2000). Attaining self regulation: A social cognitive perspective. In M. Boekaerts, P. Pintrich, & M. Zeidner (Eds.), *Handbook of self-regulation* (pp. 13–39). New York: Academic Press.

Zimmerman, B. J., Bonner, S., & Kovach, R. (2002). *Developing self-regulated learners.* Washington, DC: American Psychological Association.

INDEXES

Author Index

Numbers in *italics* indicate pages with complete bibliographic information.

A

Aasheim, M., 103, *114,* 570, *578*
Abott, H. H., 434, 445, *447*
Aboud, F. E., 162, 163, 164, 165, 166, *176, 178*
Abrahams, B., 126, *149*
Abramovitch, R., 157, 159, *181,* 192, 193, 194, *209,* 216, *237*
Abu-Lughod, L., 12, 29, *31,* 211, 212, 219, 221, *232,* 378, *392*
Achenbach, T., 593, 601, *605*
Ackerman, B., 581, *605, 607, 608*
Adams, E., *605*
Adams, G. R., 526, *539*
Adams, P., 124, 126, *151*
Addad, M., 623, *627*
Adelson, J., 74, 79, *88,* 186, 187, 188, *207*
Adler, J. E., 106, *111*
Adolphs, R., 492, *506*
Ahadi, S. A., 501, *506, 514,* 529, *546,* 557, 558, *578*
Aharon-Peretz, J., 491, *514*
Aksan, N., 268, 269, 282, 285, 287, *293,* 311, *323*
Alba, R. D., 315, *320*
Albee, G. W., 685, 686, *697*
Alexander, P. A., 711, 725, *726*
Alexander, R. D., 402, *418,* 424, 435, 438, *447*
Allen, J. B., 554, *572*
Allen, J. P., 255, *261*
Allen, W. R., 286, *296*
Allport, G. W., 160, 166, 167, *176,* 691, *697*
Alpert, R., 246, *265*
Alvarez, A., 352, *374*
Alwin, D. F., 314, *320*

Amaral, D. G., 494, *506*
Amato, M., 162, 164, 166, *176*
Ambert, A. M., 304, 318, *320*
American Psychiatric Association, 600, *605*
Amnesty International, 227, *233*
Andersen, S. M., 669, 670, *674*
Anderson, C. A., 716, 724, 725, *726, 730*
Anderson, D., 50, *65,* 270, *291*
Anderson, L. M., 711, 719, 723, *726*
Anderson, V., 495, *510*
Anderson's Ohio family law handbook, 613, *624*
Andreiuolo, P. A., 439, *455*
Angle, S. C., 199, 200, *206*
Anscombe, G. E. M., 706, *726*
Anshel, D., 217, *236*
Antill, J. K., 170, *176*
Antipoff, H., 21, *31*
Apospori, E., 165, *177*
Appadurai, A., 378, *392*
Appelbaum, M. I., 270, *291*
Appiah, K. A., 230, 232, *233*
Appleby, D. W., 304, *325*
Appleby, R. S., 79, *89*
Arbib, M. A., 492, *513*
Arbreton, A., 172, *178*
Archambault, F. X., *510*
Archer, J., 619, *624*
Ardila-Rey, A., 170, 173, *179,* 192, *207,* 217, 218, *233, 235,* 273, *293,* 446, *453*
Arend, R. A., 283, *295*
Argyris, D., 356, 358, *368*
Argyris, D. E., 100, *110*
Aristotle, 719, 724, *726*

Subject Index

An environmentally friendly book printed and bound in England by www.printondemand-worldwide.com

PEFC Certified

This product is
from sustainably
managed forests
and controlled
sources

www.pefc.org

PEFC™

PEFC/16-33-415

Mixed Sources
Product group from well-managed
forests, and other controlled sources
www.fsc.org Cert no. TT-COC-002641
© 1996 Forest Stewardship Council

FSC

This book is made entirely of chain-of-custody materials

#0712 - - C0 - 254/178/44 - PB